CW00664117

HELM IDENTIFICATION GUIDES

SHRIKES & BUSH-SHRIKES

HELM IDENTIFICATION GUIDES

SHRIKES & BUSH-SHRIKES

Including wood-shrikes, helmet-shrikes, flycatcher-shrikes, philentomas, batises and wattle-eyes

Tony Harris and Kim Franklin

CHRISTOPHER HELM
A & C Black • London

Distributed in Southern Africa by
Russel Friedman Books CC
PO Box 73
Halfway House
1685
South Africa

Christopher Helm (Publishers) Ltd., a subsidiary of A & C Black (Publishers) Ltd., 35 Bedford Row, London WC1R 4JH

0-7136-3861-3

A CIP catalogue record for this book is available from the British Library

Printed in Singapore

CONTENTS

PREFACE

An unmistakable order rules organic nature, as it also rules the worlds of crystals and stars
(Blasius 1857)

This book deals with 'shrike' diversity. It covers 114 species of 21 genera in the families Laniidae and Malaconotidae. These are a group of spectacular predators, many with brilliant colours, striking displays and sounds. They have diverse foraging and breeding strategies and occupy a wide spectrum of terrestrial habitats, from sparsely vegetated deserts to tropical forests. Their identification provides the basis for understanding the unmistakable order present in their biology, ecology and interrelationships, viewed as a snapshot in time of their dynamic and evolving history.

The primary objective of the book is to serve as a guide, in the broadest sense, to the diversity of shrikes and their close relatives. This is achieved by providing as much information as possible, with a particular emphasis on communication behaviour, for general interest as well as for conservationists and specialists. The approach highlights gaps in the knowledge of the group, and provides a comprehensive reference base for future work.

ACKNOWLEDGEMENTS

Many people have assisted over the past 20 years in my quest to understand the biology and relationships of shrikes. A book of this nature is invariably a team effort, not only between publisher, artist and author, but more particularly because it relies on the generous assistance and contribution of many individuals and organisations.

Foremost is the support and sacrifices made by my family, particularly Judy. Without her understanding and encouragement, and the support of Barry, Emma and Amy, this project would not have survived. Other family members, particularly my mother Rita and Ray and Trish Bradley, are sincerely thanked for their support.

Throughout my research career, I have been especially grateful for the discussions, guidance and influence provided by Alan Kemp, Bob Brain and the late John Dunning.

My editor, Robert Kirk, and artist, Kim Franklin, are thanked for their professionalism, understanding, patience and friendship shown throughout this project.

I appreciate and have been extremely fortunate to have benefited from the expertise, field observations or tape recordings provided by Mark Andrews, Claude Chappuis, Ron Demey, Françoise Dowsett-Lemaire and Bob Dowsett, Jennifer Horne, Warwick Tarboton and Carl Vernon.

Librarians Linda Birch, Ronel Goode and Effie Warr are particularly thanked for their help in locating references.

The following assisted in many different ways, and all are sincerely thanked: Katy Ackermann, Robert Adlard, Jacques Alamargot, David Allan, John Ash, the late Dylan Aspinwall, Neil Baker, Reinhilde Battheu, Gordon Bennett, Pat Benson, Rob Bentley, Aldo Berruti, the late Richard Brooke, André Brosset, Bruno and Heidi Bruderer, John Carlyon, Clide Carter, Rodney and Tamar Cassidy, Cecile Chekubi, Inga and Meike Chinnery, Hugh Chittenden, Patrice Christy, Phillip Clancey, Brian Colahan, Nigel Collar, Jeremy and Marian Cooke, Peter Colston, Alan Cordes, Digby Cyrus, Pat Davey, Richard Dean, Hartwig Dedekind, John Dittami, Pierre du Toit, Will Duckworth, Bill Edwards, Marie Favard, Charles Francis, Martin and Doreen Goetz, Steven Goodman, Dylis Hoets, Otto Hubsch, Kit Hustler, Michael Irwin, Des Jackson, Niels Jacobsen, Sharon Jensen, Brigitte Joerges, David Johnson, Nigel Johnston-Stewart, John Jones, Saskia Kempff, Ron Kettle, Joris Komen, Evgeny Kurochkin, Frank Lambert, Mary LeCroy, Norbert Lefranc, Pauline Leinberger, Michel Louette, Rowland McVicker, Dr M.A. Macdonald, Gordon Maclean, the late Alec Manson, John Mendelsohn, Courtney Meredith, Bob and Bev Mills, Jacob Mokwena, Gérard Morel, Csaba Moskat, Audrey Msimanga, Inez Myburgh, Terry Oatley, Vincent Parker, Don Parry, Eric Pasquet, David Pearson, Tommy Pedersen, Nic Peet, Huw Penry, Dr M.A. Peirce, Annamare Pitt, Derek Pomeroy, Pilai Poonswad, Andrea Priori, Elaine Pryce, Robert Prys-Jones, Richard Ranft, Anne Rasa, Dr J.V. Remsen, Dr G. Rheinwald, Kees Roselaar, Colin Saunders, Clive and Janice Scheepers, Alister Scott, Jo Scott, Ken Scriven, the late William Serle, Lucia Severinghaus, Cathy Sharp, the late Charles Sibley, Charles Siegel, Dot Skelly, Edith Sonnenschein, Peter Steyn, Bob Stjernstedt, Laura Stratten, Barry Taylor, Peter Thompson, Silvia Thompson, Glen and Sheila Trollope, Alan Tye, Don Turner, Alan and Ros Urban, Martin and Jill Urban, Martin van Schoor, Anthony and Danie van Zyl, Jane Walker, Micheal Walters, David Wells, Martin Wilson, Pyong-oh Won, Andre' Yagodovsky, Satoshi Yamagishi, Reuven Yosef and Steven Zack.

My shrike mentor, Eugene Panow, is thanked for his assistance and permission to use diagrams from his book *Die Würger der Paläarktis*, and Barry Harris for reproducing some of these and the sound maps.

The following institutions and staff members (see above) are thanked for access to or supply of material from their collections; American Museum of Natural History, Durban Museum, Library of Natural Sounds (Cornell University), Alexander Library (Edward Grey Institute of Field Ornithology), FitzPatrick Bird Communication Library (Transvaal Museum), Louisiana State University Museum of Zoology, Museum Alexander Koenig, Natural History Museum of Kenya, Natural History Museum of Zimbabwe, National Sound Archive (The British Library), Percy FitzPatrick Institute of African Ornithology, The Natural History Museum (Tring), Transvaal Museum, Yale Peabody Museum.

Breeding data were extracted from the following Nest Record Card schemes: Kenya, South Africa, Zambia and Zimbabwe.

Finally, logistical and financial support, provided mainly by the Transvaal Museum and Swiss Ornithological Institute, is gratefully acknowledged.

Tony Harris
P.O. Box 36844
Menlo Park, 0102
South Africa

e-mail: qman@mailbox.co.za

SPONSORSHIP

SCHWEIZERISCHE VOGELWARTE SEMPACH/SWISS ORNITHOLOGICAL INSTITUTE/STATION ORNITHOLOGIQUE SUISSE

The Swiss Ornithological Institute is a private foundation for ornithological research and conservation. It covers a wide range of topics from bird migration and avian ecology to population monitoring and nature conservation. Cooperation in ecotourism with the travel agency ArcaTour provides some funds to support particularly valuable projects outside Switzerland. This book on the shrikes of the world is considered to be just such a project.

LAYOUT and METHODS

The book is divided into four sections:

1. Introduction. Divided into two parts. (i) The history and characteristic features of shrikes are discussed and a challenge offered to birdwatchers, conservationists and full-time ornithologists to view species from a behavioural perspective. It provides a methodology for defining species and discovering relationships. (ii) The communication behaviour of the 21 genera is summarised and relationships discussed. Some acoustic characters are mapped. The section concludes with a glossary and anatomical drawing.

2. Colour Plates. 41 colour plates of 114 species are arranged primarily according to general similarity, and secondarily according to relationships between genera. Options for listing species include a systematic approach (according to relationships), size, region, habitat or similarity. The similarity approach has been used to assist the reader in identification. Each plate shows differences in sex, age, polymorphism and as much geographical variation as possible, subject to constraints of space. An attempt has been made to scale illustrations and to provide a hint of habitat preference to aid identification.

Each species is supported on the opposite page with a distribution map, showing breeding range (yellow), non-breeding range (blue), or where a species is sedentary and spends all its life in the same area (green). Owing to the small scale of the map, only the general range of each species is outlined, with more information provided in the species texts. Beside each map is a short caption which briefly outlines the species characteristics, main identification features, similar species, habitat and range. Each species is cross-referenced to the main text.

3. Species accounts. These are based on 20 years of personal research, a thorough survey of the scientific literature up to early 1999, and unpublished information from colleagues. The arrangement of species follows the approach used for the colour plates and is not entirely indicative of relationships, for which see Communication Summaries and Relationships. The use of numerous sub- headings is intended to facilitate guiding the reader through the text and in the location of information. Where possible, original sources of information have been cited. The text attempts to summarise current knowledge and to highlight gaps. Where information is available, each account has subheadings in the following order: *Field Identification, Characteristics, Flight, Comparisons, Description, Geographical Variation, Hybrids and Abnormal Plumage, Moult, Range, Habitat and Status, Movements, Social Organisation and General Behaviour, Sounds, Breeding Biology, Measurements and Weights.*

Each species is introduced by its English vernacular name[430, 431, 676] followed by any alternative names in parentheses, its scientific name[116, 206] and plate number. Relative size (total length) is described as very small (<12 cm), small (12–17 cm), medium (18–21 cm), large (22–25 cm) and very large (>25 cm). As an indication, the width of a page here is 15.6 cm and the length 23.4 cm. The formal plumage description documents adult breeding ♂ and ♀, and immature and juvenile stages where known of the nominate race, unless stated otherwise. Where polymorphism occurs each morph is described. Each recognised geographical race is briefly described and its range indicated by country. In Moult, where known, the particular feathers moulting, month and locality are specified. *Range, Habitat and Status* lists breeding and non-breeding range by country. Conservation status categories conform to those used by BirdLife International for Red Data Book species[343]. *Social Organisation and General Behaviour* also documents visual behaviour associated with territorial advertisement and threat, as well as maintenance and roosting behaviour. Food consumed is listed according to order or family, followed by vernacular names of recorded prey items in brackets.

The description of sounds begins with a brief summary of the types of sound produced, such as whistles, harsh calls and mechanically produced 'fripping' made by the wings or bill-snapping. This is followed by a description of sounds used in territorial advertisement, defence and threat. In addition alarm, contact, roosting, courtship and begging calls are described. Extensive use has been made of the collections housed in the FitzPatrick Sound Communication Library (Transvaal Museum), National Sound Archive (British Library) and the Library of Natural Sounds (Cornell University), as well as numerous private collections, particularly those of Claude Chappuis.

Calls are notoriously difficult to convey satisfactorily. Traditionally, transcriptions have been used, more recently sonagrams. Both have obvious limitations, and while the inclusion of sonagrams would have been desirable, they continue to have limited value to the non-specialist. However, sources of sonagrams are listed with references. Published transcriptions have been included in their original language, because many sounds are geographically variable and are graded in pitch, tempo (repetition rate), amplitude (loudness) and length. Due to various internal and external factors, as well as context, there will inevitably be a range of sounds described. Although many published transcriptions have been cited, the general rules applicable to most of these and my own transcriptions are as follows: (i) calls are written in italic (*tcha*); (ii) pitch is denoted by the letters used in the alphabet, generally *i* or *e* for high-pitched sounds, *o, u* or *a* for low-pitched sounds (these are usually combined with qualifiers, such as harsh, soft, high-pitched, etc);

(iii) repetition rate — rapidly repeated notes are joined together (*huhuhu*), separated by a few dashes when slower (*hu-hu-* or *hu--he*), and separated by dots when repeated very slowly (*hu....hu*); (iv) capital letters denote emphasised or loud sounds; (v) exclamation marks indicate short sharp loud sounds; (vi) a sound ending with a dash (*tcha-*) represents only part of a series, and vii) sound length is indicated by the length of the transcription, short (*tch*) or long (*tchaaaaaa).*

The section on *Breeding Biology* deals with season (breeding activity by month, which when unqualified implies unspecified breeding activity). This is followed by the country (in parentheses), displays, nest including height in metres (m), size in millimetres (mm), with outside diameter abbreviated to (OD) and inside diameter to (ID), eggs including size in millimetres (mm), incubation (period), nestling (period) including a description of hatchlings when known, predation, longevity and brood parasites.

The species account ends with *Measurements and Weights.* The range and mean of adult ♂♂ and sometimes ♀♀ or of an unsexed or combined sex sample (♂♀?) are listed. The linear measurements of the nominate race, unless stated otherwise, are in millimetres (mm) and include: wing, tail, bill (specified from bill tip to base of skull where known, and in all my own measurements) and tarsus. My own measurements[500,] follow standard procedures[814.] Weight is given in grams (g).

4. The final section contains *Appendix A* and *B,* which lists taxonomic (species limits) and systematic (relationship) problems, and potential taxonomic characters, with their respective references. A *Bibliography* and *Index* are also provided.

INTRODUCTION

The whole is greater than the sum of its parts

History

The origin of shrikes, like their *c.*400-year-old classification history, is controversial. In the early Cretaceous *c.*120 million years ago on the supercontinent of Gondwanaland in the southern hemisphere, an extraordinarily successful avian radiation began which resulted in the order Passeriformes. Of the *c.*27 orders of living birds (*c.*9,000 species), just over half (*c.*5,200) are passerines. As the supercontinent began to break up, the passerines which were on Laurasia (now North America and Eurasia) apparently gave rise to the oscines (songbirds) as the continent drifted north leaving Africa behind. In the Upper Cretaceous, the Oriental region of Eurasia and the Ethiopian region of Africa had contact via the faunal bridge provided by the Tethys Sea (depression between Laurasia and Gondwanaland). During the Miocene *c.*24 million years ago Eurasia probably had an Ethiopian avifauna or, put another way, Africa today has a relic Eurasian avifauna. Shrikes were part of this radiation[65, 446, 897, 921].

An African shrike origin has been proposed based on plumage characteristics, which suggests that ancestral shrikes were forest species[165, 284]. This suggestion is supported by the hypothesis that Palearctic migration had its origins in Africa[461]. However, recent molecular evidence suggests they probably originated in the Australasian region during the Tertiary period[184, 921]. The earliest shrike-like fossil (*Lanius miocaenus*) is known from the Lower Miocene of Europe[14, 142]. The earliest evidence of shrikes and man appears in Egyptian art from Dynasty XII (1991–1786 B.C.)[233]. However, it was not until the mid-1600 A.D., in the classifications of Francis Willughby (1676) and later those of Carl Linnaeus (1759), John Latham (1781), Hans Gadow (1883)[321], and others, that the first Western written descriptions appeared for the genus *Lanius*, which are the only shrikes that occur in Europe. As a consequence, the die was cast against which all other shrikes were to be judged. Members of this genus became known as 'true shrikes', which later also included *Corvinella* and *Eurocephalus*, forming the family Laniidae. The other 18 genera discussed here are now thought to form the family Malaconotidae or 'bush-shrikes'[291].

Interest in shrikes has flourished since at least the mid-nineteenth century, with major works by Walden (1867)[166], Ogilvie-Grant (1902)[358], Schiebel (1906)[671], Miller (1931)[255], Olivier (1944)[165], Vaurie (1955)[211], Ullrich (1971)[373], Panov (1983, 1996)[284], Harris and Arnott (1988)[205], Lefranc (1993, 1997)[285, 675], and Schön (1994)[536–537, 788–791]. In addition, detailed coverage of a few species is provided in handbooks like Dement'ev and Gladkov (1968)[214], Ali and Ripley (1987)[224], Cramp and Perrins (1993)[257], Glutz von Blotzheim and Bauer (1993)[484], and Urban, Fry and Keith (1997)[676]. The emphasis in all monographs cited, with the exception of one[205], has been on true shrikes, as have two dedicated symposia (1995, 1998)[939, 975]. The most comprehensive recent coverage of true shrikes is given by Lefranc (1997)[675].

While some convergence in providing information on the same group is unavoidable, it is hoped that the behavioural emphasis given here, and the coverage of the malaconotids (Malaconotidae) for the first time, will serve to complement these works.

Characteristics of shrikes

Today, true shrikes are distributed throughout Eurasia, North America and Africa. Most species occupy open areas consisting of a mosaic of short grass, bushes and trees. Some occur in extremely sparsely vegetated desert areas, others in woodland and forest edge, and one species is confined to forest. The genus *Lanius* occurs from within the Arctic Circle to the tropics and south to the tip of Africa. The two other true shrike genera, and all malaconotids, have a mainly African distribution, except for wood-shrikes *Tephrodornis* and philentomas *Philentoma*, which are found in the Oriental region of SE Asia. Malaconotids cover a wide range of habitats, most of which are densely vegetated, varying from arid thorn scrub to montane and tropical forest.

The distribution of the two families is generally well documented. It is interesting to note a number of similar species pairs which are separated within discrete ranges and are therefore allopatric. These patterns suggest they were originally a single conspecific species which subsequently separated, probably due to climatic changes effecting large-scale vegetation changes. This resulted in separate populations which, over time, diverged enough to become reproductively exclusive and hence considered separate species, like the Northern and Southern White-crowned Shrike. At the other extreme, some species have similar widely separated populations that show no divergence, like the Mountain Sooty Boubou. Between these extremes are species which share a common boundary and are therefore sympatric, but differ very little, like Black-fronted and May-coloured Bush-shrikes, or others which are considered a single species, but which show enormous geographical variation, like the Long-tailed Shrike in Asia.

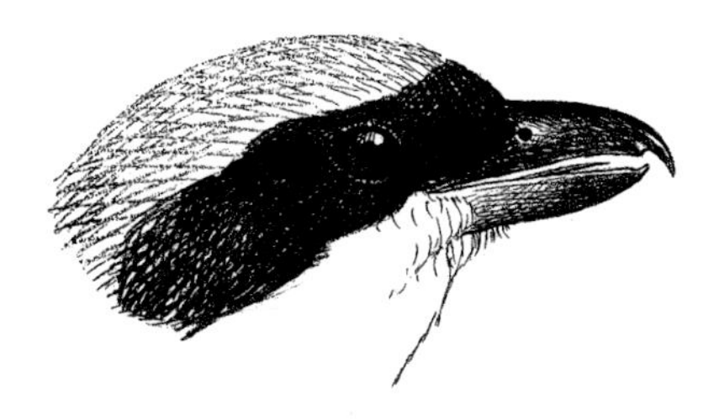

Typical bill shape of Lanius *species*

Externally true shrikes, particularly *Lanius*, have a short, strong, sharp, hooked bill with a small falcon-like 'tooth' on either side of the upper mandible near the tip, and a corresponding notch in the lower mandible. In the early classifications mentioned above, this was one of the reasons shrikes were placed with hawks[684, 790]. This feature, developed to varying degrees in all species discussed here, also occurs in many other birds. Evidence of this is found in some of their original scientific and current vernacular names, such as song-shrike and crow-shrike (family Cracticidae), cuckoo-shrike (Campephagidae), shrike-vireo and pepper-shrike (Vireonidae), swallow-shrike (Artamidae), shrike-thrush and shrike-tit (Pachycephalidae), vanga-shrikes (Vangidae), antshrike (Formicariidae), shrike-babbler (Timaliidae) and shrike-tyrant (Tyrannidae).

Plumage characteristics, including coloration, which in true shrikes is usually a combination of white, grey, black and brown, often reddish-brown in *Lanius*, as well as their dark face-mask and finely barred brown juveniles are not unique, but also occur in some other birds including malaconotids. As a family, malaconotids are more colourful, with bright green, yellow and red evident in some members. They may also exhibit spectacular colour polymorphism (different colour morphs within a single species)[112, 113, 115, 471]. In addition, Grey-headed and Orange-breasted Bush-shrikes, which occur in different genera, show a remarkably close resemblance, even with similar geographical variation. This has led to the suggestion that the smaller species may derive some benefit from mimicking the larger, more aggressive species[528, 613, 625]. Some malaconotids have brilliant yellow or red eyes, others spectacular eye-wattles which fill with blood when the bird is excited and protrude like small horns above the eye. Melanistic morphs occur in both families, and both have similar moult strategies, with an annual single complete post-breeding moult. A few migrant *Lanius* vary from partial suspension of moult while migrating to two complete annual moults[691].

Although the internal anatomy of these families shows many similarities, differences have been noted in certain muscle[897, 918] and bone structures[898-901, 920]. Differences in these and other structures, like sperm shape[902], show similarities with corvids (crows, jays, etc., family Corvidae) and provide an important clue to the ancestry of shrikes[634]. Studies of genetic material (DNA or deoxyribonucleic acid)[184, 886] and behaviour[205, 219] provide additional support for a common corvid ancestor linking the two families.

Behaviourally, most true shrikes are rather raptor-like, being pugnacious and capable of feeding on relatively large prey, including small vertebrates like rodents, lizards and birds. As a result, members of *Lanius* are sometimes used in falconry[395]. Although seasonally variable, insects form the bulk of food consumed, with some species being exclusively insectivorous. Many high-latitude species rely on small mammals and birds in winter when the temperature is too low for insect activity. Interestingly, true shrikes are able to tolerate chemically noxious invertebrate prey[205, 1077]. True shrikes have strong legs and the habit of grasping prey with the foot, and *Lanius* that of impaling or wedging and caching prey (derivation of the Latin generic name is 'butcher'). Surprisingly, these features are not confined to true shrikes but are found in malaconotids as well as other birds[363]. For example, even diminutive batises sometimes impale prey or hold prey with the foot. While some of the larger malaconotids regularly take small vertebrates, all are mostly insectivorous, often feeding on venomous prey like wasps, bees and other members of the insect order Hymenoptera. The removal of the stinging apparatus appears to be innate in both families[417]. Certain other behaviours are typical of most true shrikes, such as their habit of perching out on an exposed site and in an upright stance. In this position, individuals advertise their presence and forage by the sit-and-wait or still-hunting technique, scanning the surrounding ground and flying down to capture prey once detected. Gleaning off foliage and aerial capture is less frequent. Some members hover, others occasionally pirate prey (kleptoparasitism), feed on carrion or rarely even cannibalise their own young. Most malaconotid bush-shrikes typically have a more horizontal posture. They creep and skulk within the canopy or undergrowth, from where they glean prey. Some are largely terrestrial, while others, like the flycatcher-shrikes, philentomas, batises and wattle-eyes, hunt like a flycatcher and snap up prey, mainly from the foliage.

Within the true shrikes, *Lanius* are strong swift flyers, including some long-distance migrants travelling *c.*20,000 km each year[883]. These birds tend to be characterised by more pointed wings, with the 10th primary reduced. Interestingly, these shrikes, unlike other passerines, do not lay down much fat prior to migration, probably because they are able to take advantage, en route, of exhausted passerines as a source of food[841, 842]. Typically, when changing perch they drop down and fly low and close to the ground, with a final swoop up to perch like a small hawk. The other two genera in this group are rather poor flyers, as are most malaconotids, with the exception of the Red-eyed Flycatcher-shrike which is an intra-African migrant. Seasonal altitudinal movements occur in both families.

The breeding behaviour of these families shows many similarities. Most true shrikes and malaconotids are resident and territorial. Those that migrate usually hold small non-breeding territories. Monogamy is the common breeding system, with a few records of polygyny in *Lanius*. In the true shrikes, cooperative breeding (breeding pair with helpers) occurs in all *Corvinella* and *Eurocephalus*, and a few *Lanius*. In malaconotids it only occurs in the helmet-shrikes *Prionops*, with helpers recorded only occasionally in a number of other genera. Details of other features of breeding behaviour, such as courtship-feeding, the role of the sexes in nest-building, incubation and brooding vary with each genus, but show no major distinction between the two families. For example, nests vary considerably. In true shrikes, they are generally large, untidy, usually uncamouflaged structures often incorporating man-made materials. *Eurocephalus* and Souza's Shrike are exceptions, with their nests resembling those of some malaconotids. At one extreme, malaconotid nests may be small, neat, well-camouflaged, moulded structures that incorporate much spider web, but at the other extreme are flimsy, transparent, dove-like structures. Bark strips are a common construction material in many genera, with the most elaborate nests being made by the tiny *Dyaphorophyia* wattle-eyes, which secure a large leaf above the nest as a roof. Egg coloration overlaps between the families, while clutch size varies with latitude from large (7–9 eggs) at high latitudes to small (2–3 eggs) in the tropics.

Breeding behaviour is the consequence of communication, particularly mate recognition. The respective communication systems of Laniidae and Malaconotidae are different. True shrikes use predominantly harsh calls, the feature from which their common name is derived. Harsh calls are combined with whistles in *Corvinella* and some *Lanius*, the latter having a warbling song, usually with mimicry. One species has been shown to lure vulnerable prey species by mimicking their calls[956]. In contrast, malaconotid males use predominantly whistled calls, to which their mates respond in duet, usually with harsh calls. Interestingly, within a number of genera, male calls are similar, while those of females are different. Warbling songs with mimicry are absent. Display-flights are common in both families. In malaconotids they are usually accompanied by rump fluffing, which reaches its most developed form in puffback shrikes *Dryoscopus*. Malaconotids are also characterised by 'fripping' sounds made by the wings and chattering bill-snapping sounds. Interestingly, many of the cooperative breeding species, being gregarious (*Corvinella*, a few *Lanius* and the helmet-shrikes, but not *Eurocephalus*), share many visual and acoustic signals independent of relationships.

Recent study at a molecular level, specifically comparisons of genetic DNA, has shown that the true shrikes, although in the same superfamily, are not as closely related to malaconotids as previously thought. It has also revealed that a number of genera not formerly considered to be shrikes or part of the Malaconotidae (considered as a subfamily Malaconotinae of an enlarged family Corvidae by these authors) are in fact closely related to this family[184]. These findings are supported by studies on communication behaviour[205]. On the strength of this and field experience of all but four genera, the following shrike-like birds are included in this book; true shrikes (*Eurocephalus*, *Corvinella* and *Lanius*), bush-shrikes (*Malaconotus*, *Chlorophoneus*, *Telophorus*, *Rhodophoneus*, *Tchagra*, *Antichromus*, *Laniarius*, *Dryoscopus*, *Nilaus* and *Lanioturdus*), wood-shrikes (*Tephrodornis*), helmet-shrikes (*Prionops*), flycatcher-shrikes (*Bias* and *Megabyas*), philentomas (*Philentoma*), batises (*Batis*) and wattle-eyes (*Platysteira* and *Dyaphorophyia*).

It would have been desirable to broaden the comparison to include other related families, particularly the Madagascan vangas which are undoubtedly closely related to the malaconotids. However, classification of vangas is in flux, complicated by the evolution of extremely diverse body forms on this island. Although I have studied the literature and known vocalisations, my lack of personal field experience and their uncertain relationships combined to exclude them, and Ward's Flycatcher (*Pseudobias wardi*), from this work[208, 226, 227, 232, 243, 283, 288, 679, 741, 770, 903, 904].

The challenge

At the dawn of the new millennium, the combined knowledge of ecology, behaviour, distribution, systematics and genetics of birds is without equal in the animal kingdom. In the early 20th century the field was dominated by a few individuals and progressed slowly. Today the situation is reversed, as the field advances at an ever-increasing rate with many thousands of participants. Birdwatchers comprise by far the largest component, and they have shown that they are at the forefront of many significant advances in the study of birds. The reason for this is simple: they are out in the field searching for and identifying species with a refreshingly critical eye. Not only are they active in ever-increasing numbers, armed with sophisticated equipment, they are also progressively better informed as more and more identification literature is made available. Their observations are constantly being incorporated into the literature. This book is no exception.

Overlapping these positive developments are threatened habitats, declining populations and critical conservation issues. The combined effect has been to focus new attention on the concept of 'species', and particularly on species limits. Traditionally in biology, taxonomists identify and describe species, documenting any geographical variation and in so doing prescribe species limits. Conservationists rely on species to monitor and manage environments. Consequently, since taxonomy must precede conservation (although not necessarily birdwatching), there is increasing pressure at the species level, on a wide range of conservation issues that range from minimum population size to genetic variability[310, 343, 369, 408, 447, 479, 480, 488]. It is also equally apparent that avian taxonomists, for a variety of reasons, are becoming as endangered as some of the species they have described[439].

As a consequence of these developments, this book attempts to provide not only an identification guide but also a new perspective and challenge for birdwatchers, conservationists, students and full-time ornithologists. The perspective involves a shift in how the reader perceives species, and particularly the role of behaviour and its quantification in defining species.

The theory—defining species and discovering relationships

At least since the time of Aristotle (*c*.350 B.C.), man has attempted to understand and order the objects that surround him, by grouping like objects in a system of classification. As already hinted, taxonomy is that branch of biological science that deals with species identification and classification (species is Latin for 'appearance' or 'kind'). Closely allied to it is systematics, the study of relationships between species.

Classifications rely on comparisons of similarities and differences, the unit of comparison being known as a 'character' in biology. Characters include any attribute of the organism, either internal or external features. Some of these have already been mentioned, such as coloration, patterns, shapes and structures (morphology). Others include developmental attributes and parasites. Biochemical characters are also used, including physiological processes, proteins and genetic material (chromosomes, nuclear DNA or mitochondrial DNA). Behaviour is also a character. Some of the potential taxonomic characters found in shrikes are listed with references in Appendix B p.383. Organisms with similar characters are grouped together. However, the use of morphological and biochemical characters alone is usually not enough to predict how an organism will behave.

Natural classifications are based on Darwin's (1859)[10], proposal of a 'tree of life', which represents the principle of a common ancestor with modified descendants in a branching, tree-like pattern of relationships. In natural classifications, only those characters with the same structure and apparent evolutionary origin (homologous characters) should be compared. However, in practice it is often extremely difficult to decide which structures are homologous and which structures are analogous, the result of convergent evolution. For example, the wings of birds and insects are not homologous structures, although they resemble each other superficially and have a similar function, that of flight. The wing in birds has evolved from the forelimb, and in insects from an appendage other than a leg, hence they are analogous structures. Many other similar characters are now known to be the result of convergent evolution, such as plumage patterns and bill shape in birds. Systematists are continually searching for homologous, biologically meaningful characters to help understand the branching patterns of relationships.

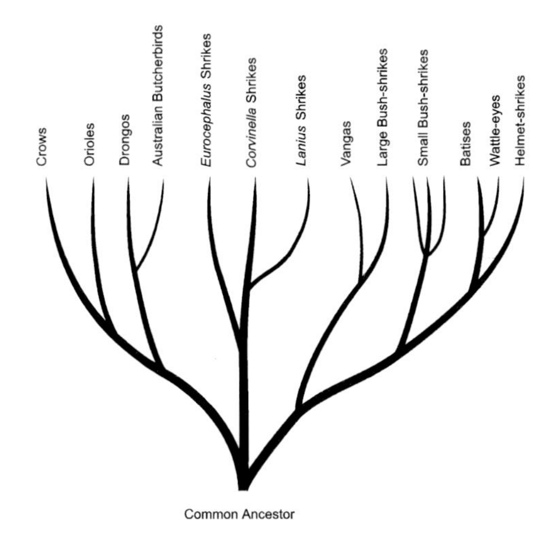

The classic 'tree of life'

Plants and animals are classified according to a hierarchical system devised by the 18th-century Swedish botanist Carl Linnaeus. The fundamental unit in this system is the species. Species are grouped into genera, which are in turn grouped into families—and so on upwards in more inclusive categories. This system is usually indicative of relationships. For any classification to be meaningful it is imperative that the fundamental units of species should be correctly identified, since they form the foundation and building blocks of the system.

The reader may be surprised to learn that there is little consensus among taxonomists as to what constitutes a species, or practically how the members of a species can be recognised. This problem manifests itself in so-called 'lumpers' and 'splitters'. A recent survey revealed at least 30 definitions of this fundamental unit[1078.] Just as species themselves have evolved, so has our understanding of this apparently real biological unit. Are species simply a group of organisms sharing similar characters? In short what is the nature of species and how are they formed? The search for answers to these questions is ongoing. Over time it has resulted in the formulation of various theoretical species concepts, of which the Biological (Isolation) Species Concept[135,] is the most commonly assumed definition. Central to this concept is the process of reproductive isolation. More recently another concept appears to be gaining popularity, known as the Phylogenetic Species Concept[1073, 1078,] which focuses on the historical patterns of character variation. However, no concept has yet been formulated which satisfies all issues in this controversial field. Subjective problems such as the validity of subspecies, incipient or sibling species, superspecies and others, or the very real phenomenon of hybridisation[924,] continue to fuel the debate, for which see[565, 611, 1073, 1074, 1075, 1076, 1078.]

The definition adopted here, which some believe is fundamentally similar to the Biological Species Concept[1076,] is based on processes which ensure that the gametes (eggs and sperm) from the two sexes of the same species come together in fertilisation. Known as the Recognition Concept of species, it applies to all sexually reproducing organisms, and of special interest is the subset of signals and behaviour known as the 'specific-mate recognition system' (SMRS)[132.] This is a co-adapted communication system between the sexes, whose many interactive components include visual, auditory, tactile, chemical, electrical and possibly even other energy signals. These components, which ensure that fertilisation takes place, can be thought of as the cohesion or bond that holds together similar individuals (the population) in time and space (the habitat). The resultant effect is a species, the individuals of which share a common SMRS.

In addition to this, I view a contemporary species as only representing a stage in the life of a lineage, or twig, on the branching tree of life. In essence, each successful lineage has a birth (speciation), a period of change, during which mate recognition, through natural selection, becomes progressively more co-adapted, interdependent and consequently more type-specific, until the system stabilises. Once stabilised it is believed to represent a real biological unit or species until its death (extinction) or transmutation into a new lineage.

This process is subject to evolutionary change at the population level, through natural selection, like all other aspects of an organism. However, the concept predicts that the components forming the SMRS will be stable and show the least variation in time and space. Theoretically, at least, this provides a measure of species similarity.

The practice—studying specific-mate recognition

Fortunately for us, birds use mainly acoustic and visual cues in mate recognition, signals which lie more or less within our own acoustic and visual range. While this has obvious advantages in studying such characters, their description and quantification still pose major challenges. In practice, we have only just begun to measure variation in some acoustic signals of a few common species. Quantification of visual signals and displays remains virtually untouched. Hence, real species identification remains a challenge.

The validity of behaviour as a taxonomic character has been widely questioned. Wilson (1975)[77,] wrote, 'Social behaviour comprises the set of phenotypes (appearance of characters) farthest removed from DNA. As such it is a very labile phenomenon, the one most subject to amplification in the transcription of information from genes to the phenotype of individuals...' However, the congruence in the relationships derived from social behaviour on the one hand and DNA on the other suggests that social behaviour is not as labile as originally believed. Furthermore, knowing the molecular code does not necessarily make it possible to predict behaviour involved in specific-mate recognition. Various studies have demonstrated that behaviour is a valid character in unravelling relationships when subject to the rules of homology[716, 779.] In addition, behaviour also has an important contribution in conservation biology[1072.]

The use of social behaviour in understanding relationships in shrikes was pioneered by Ullrich (1971)[373,] and later more extensively in the landmark studies by Panov (1983)[284,] of Palearctic *Lanius*. Similar characters have been used to assess relationships in some African shrikes, batises and wattle-eyes[205.]

If the true nature of species and their relationships is to be discovered, an holistic approach must be adopted with details of as many characters as possible compared, but with the realisation that at the species level *the whole is greater than the sum of its parts*. Stated another way, individuals which share a common specific-mate recognition form a species; such recognition involves communication behaviour, and communication behaviour involves much more than simple morphological or biochemical characters. Behaviour, particularly the co-adapted visual and acoustic signals used in specific-mate recognition, is believed to provide the ultimate measure of species similarity in birds. Interpreting such signals, in practical terms, remains a challenge.

The underlying theme of this introduction is highlighted by the recent controversial case of the Bulo Burti Boubou[543, 862, 863]. This species was described as new to science, based solely on the DNA of a single specimen. Previously, no bird species had been described on this basis. Unfortunately, since it was not preserved, apart from some blood, feathers, photographs and sound recordings, no other comparative characters can be assessed[542, 680]. To date, no other specimens have been discovered. Its inclusion in the book is based primarily on my goal of portraying shrike diversity, irrespective of species status. Whether it is a distinct species, or simply a hybrid or abnormal individual of an existing species like Red-naped Bush-shrike, remains unanswered with the available information.

The challenge and excitement of discovering species is not new, whether simply identifying a new bird for your list or actually discovering and describing a species new to science. The challenge offered here incorporates both these, but with the added excitement of verifying existing species limits by discovering the unique bond which unites individuals into that real biological unit, known as species. Its discovery will provide a better understanding of the true nature of species, of their conservation and of *the unmistakable order which rules organic nature.*

Shrike communication

Specific-mate recognition is thought to be achieved in a hierarchical manner, beginning with broad generalised messages, such as 'bird', and progressively narrowing down in a cascade of visual and acoustic stimulus-response signals that carry the codes for species, gender, age, status and, ultimately, individuality. In birds, similar signals are used in different situations to convey different messages. For example, signals used in territorial threat against conspecific intruders contain many of the same signals used in courtship. The context in which communication takes place is critical to an understanding of messages.

Both families have relatively small visual and acoustic repertoires, which average fewer than about 15 main visual and a similar number of acoustic signals. However, this lack of variety is compensated by grading within signals. For example, visual signals may vary in duration, repetition rate, amplitude of movement and surface area exposed. Similarly, acoustic signals may vary in duration, repetition rate (tempo), pitch (frequency) and amplitude (loudness).

Geographical variation is known to occur in potential visual signals, and finds expression in the different races. It is a well-known phenomenon in acoustic signals, resulting in dialects. Such variation occurs in many other characters which show graded properties. The specific-mate recognition system is predicted to show little variation.

Superimposed on local variation are other characteristics, of a much broader regional nature, and which are shared in different genera. For example, in West Africa species of a number of widespread genera have calls with a buzzy quality. Similarly, calls tend to be delivered faster and with a larger whistled component in Central and North Africa than they are in southern Africa. Such properties suggest that there is not only subtle variation in the ecology or niche of species from different areas, but possibly also variation in the acoustic niche occupied in different areas. In the same way as the acoustic environment appears to influence signals, so too does a species's social system. For example, a number of gregarious, cooperative breeding species show many similarities in their signalling systems. These similarities are believed to be due to convergence, and do not necessarily indicate a close relationship. The specific-mate recognition system, once teased out from this, is predicted to be distinctive. Interestingly, the communication system of *Eurocephalus* lacks this convergence, in spite of having a similar social system to other co-operative shrikes.

The two families discussed here show a number of similarities, as well as major differences, in their communication behaviour. Both families, with the exception of *Eurocephalus* in Laniidae, use harsh calls and whistles. *Eurocephalus* has nasal bleating calls and does not whistle. In the true shrikes, whistling is usually in the form of rapid frequency-modulated sounds. However, *Corvinella* and a few *Lanius* have long-drawn-out whistles or a short whistled phrase. *Lanius* is unique in both families in being the only genus which has a complex song and which contains mimicry. In true shrikes, generally the repertoire of both sexes is similar. They use harsh calls extensively in territorial advertisement, threat and alarm. Begging calls are generally loud nasal sounds. Malaconotids differ, most using simple repetitive whistles in territorial advertisement, with harsh calls used predominantly in territorial threat and alarm. However, in this family the sexes in most genera use different calls. Males tend to whistle, while females generally give harsh calls, usually in duet. Begging calls are softer and usually higher-pitched sounds. The family is also characterised by rump-fluffing displays, 'fripping' sounds made by the wings, and bill-snapping, which should probably more correctly be described as tongue-clicking. As already mentioned, the calls of males of different species within some genera are remarkably similar, but those of the females are different. This stresses the importance of co-adaptation in specific-mate recognition (i.e. in both sexes). There is also a tendency in some genera, for example in batises, for males of two different species, where their ranges meet, to countersing with similar calls[700]. This, combined with the observation in field playback experiments, that males of two closely related species respond to each other, clearly does not necessarily mean that they are conspecific. It is equally likely that females use different parts of a signal for species recognition. In addition, the recognition of males by females is thought to be more important in specific-mate recognition than male-male recognition[525, 861].

As previously suggested, communication behaviour is believed to have a special significance at the species level. A comparison of homologous signals is predicted to provide the basis for understanding their relationships and evolutionary history or phylogeny.

Many different relationships have been proposed using various characters. However, there can only be one evolutionary history. Most studies of relationships suffer similar deficiencies, namely restricted character coverage and the ubiquitous problem of homology and convergence. In spite of this, the many attempts are considered useful, because they map the distribution of various characters in the different species, and so provide additional pieces of the intriguing jigsaw puzzle. Here, no attempt is made to review every character, but rather to accept the phylogeny constructed on DNA-DNA hybridisation as the most viable hypothesis yet provided. Not because DNA is more real or more basic than morphology or behaviour, but simply because results of a DNA programme reflect more numerous and independent characters to ensure that degrees of simple matching actually measure homology[215].

The relationships achieved with this method indicate that all the species included here form part of the vast superfamily Corvoidea. It includes crows, ravens, jays, magpies, nutcrackers, choughs etc., vireos, shrike-vireos etc., wood-swallows, swallow-shrike, shrike-thrushes, shrike-tit, whistlers etc., cuckoo-shrikes, vangas, old world flycatchers like monarchs, fantails and magpie-larks. It has also shown orioles, drongos, ioras, fairy bluebirds and leafbirds, Australo-Papuan babblers, robins and flycatchers, the Logrunner and Chowchilla, quail-thrushes, rockfowl and rock-jumpers, birds-of-paradise, Australian magpies, currawongs, butcherbirds, the Bornean Bristlehead and others to be part of the same assemblage. The true shrikes (Laniidae) are given family status, while the bush-shrikes are placed as a subfamily Malaconotinae of the family Corvidae[184]. Here I raise this subfamily to family status based primarily on its relative size. In addition, in a few cases, atypical species in more uniform genera have been placed in their own genus. In most cases these revert to proposals made in earlier classifications, and has been done to highlight what are believed to be important differences. The linear arrangement of species in this book is not intended to represent exact relationships. These are better portrayed three dimensionally. Relationships are therefore discussed in the following section.

While the relationships derived from DNA-DNA hybridisation have produced some unexpected results, it is interesting to note that six of the nine families listed in the introduction (other than Laniidae and Malaconotidae), as being shrike-like by early taxonomists[321], are now found to be related on this method. Many of these relationships have been corroborated with other characters, such as muscle and bone, and communication behaviour[205, 897, 899]. It remains to be seen how similar the communication behaviour is of the other members of the superfamily.

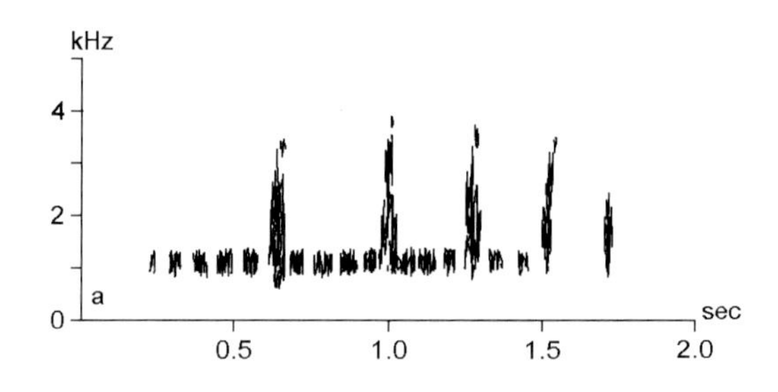

A typical shrike sonagram

Communication summaries and relationships

The following section summarises what are believed to be the main acoustic and visual components of the communication system of genera comprising the families Laniidae and Malaconotidae. Visual signals are enclosed in parentheses. It is presented as a basis on which to compare other families. Where marked variation exists within genera, some of the important differences are mapped and presented diagramatically.

Each summary is followed by a brief overview of relationships within and between genera. Problems of species limits and relationships are highlighted in Appendix A, and potential taxonomic characters are listed in Appendix B.

Eurocephalus (White-crowned shrikes) Plate 1

Species: *anguitimens*, *rueppelli*

Basic structure Complex, loud, with harsh squeaks, squawks and nasal bleating combined with stuttering, chattering and twittering calls, usually given in chorus; frequently calls on take-off (flicks tail on settling; other visual signals described below). **Duetting** Well developed, often in chorus. **Territorial advertisement** Obvious advertising apparently lacking (apparently mainly advertised with visual signals, perch exposed, static marking). **Territorial threat** Apparently initiated by dominant bird with bleating *Kaekaew* to which other group members respond by chorusing with various stuttering *K-K-K-Kaew*, chattering *kek-kek-*, nasal bleating *skwee-kwee-kwee*, *Kaeeer* or *weeyer-* combined with harsh *Chuk-* or *WOK-* sounds (group members perch loosely in exposed positions with much tail-flicking and wing-shuffling). Threat signalled with low growling *Krrrr* sounds (bill open, neck and crest raised). **Alarm** Noisy affair, one bird initiates with loud nasal *Kaeeeer*, others immediately respond with repeated *KeeKeeKee-* calls in chorus (while foraging, some birds act as sentries). **Courtship** Little known. In possible courtship display-flight, birds give repeated *kikek-kikek*, rapid *tchetche-* calls and squeaky notes. Pair-bonds apparently maintained with duets, ♂ *Kaaeer*, ♀ *KaeKae* (possible courtship display-flight involved suspected dominant pair in high, slow flight with exaggerated wingbeats, followed by slow gliding descent with wings held in rigid V; courtship-feeding unknown. **Contact** Bleating *Kaee*, repeated *K-KaeeKe-* and stuttering *Kida-kida-kida-* calls used in greeting display or when approaching fledglings with food. Excited *tchetche-* chitter given when preferred food found. Duetting common between presumed dominant pair. Individuals separated from the group call *K-KaeeK...K-KaeeK-* repeatedly in flight (greeting display between certain individuals involves drooping wings on landing, partly raising them, half-open above the back, followed by weakly fluttering them at side of body). **Roosting** Much calling prior to settling down, then purring growls and soft chortling *ka-ka-ka-kakrrrrr* sound (jostle for positions, huddled together on branch). **Begging** Loud wheezy persistent *skea-skea-skea-* calls by chicks and fledglings in one species; juveniles in another give sharp, piercing *skeet* calls (crouched wing-fluttering).

Relationships

Eurocephalus is usually thought to consist of two separate species, based primarily on differences in plumage and widely separate ranges. However, both species are little known and their vocalisations appear rather similar, with calls of *anguitimens* sounding like a slower version of *rueppelli*[500]. Apparently *rueppelli* reacts strongly to playback of *anguitimens* calls[431, 481]. It has been suggested that this species pair forms a superspecies[180]. Here they are retained as separate species awaiting additional comparative information.

Traditionally the genus was placed with helmet-shrikes *Prionops*, initially on the basis of similar tarsal scutellation (arrangement of plates on the leg), and later on social behaviour (gregarious cooperative breeders), barred juveniles and nest structure[202, 573, 612]. More recently a study of hindlimb musculature, although concluding that it is closely related to the helmet-shrikes, found important similarities with true shrikes[918]. Little other internal anatomy is known except for a few cranial osteological characters, including details of nostril ossification and a double foramen condition of the ectethmoid plate. These are similar to *Corvinella* and *Lanius*, but unlike helmet-shrikes or any other malaconotid[235, 500]. Much of the general behaviour of *Eurocephalus* is dissimilar to helmet-shrikes. For example when foraging, prey may be held in the foot like *Lanius*, *Corvinella* and some malaconotids, but not *Prionops*. *Eurocephalus* will hang upside-down in search of prey like *Corvinella* and some malaconotids, a behaviour not found in *Lanius* or *Prionops*. In addition, like other true shrikes but unlike *Prionops* both members of the genus consume toxic prey, such as millipedes[205, 352, 416]. DNA-DNA hybridisation studies place *Eurocephalus* with the true shrikes[184].

Although its harsh bleating vocalisations, which lack whistles and warbling song, show a closer resemblance to true shrikes than to malaconotids (communication behaviour is totally unlike helmet-shrikes), social behaviour shows little similarity to cooperative *Corvinella* or *Lanius*[205]. However, a shallow wing-up submissive or greeting display does bear a weak resemblance to displays in these genera.

Of all genera considered to form Laniidae, *Eurocephalus* is the least shrike-like. Its anatomical and behavioural characters suggest that it is the most primitive living shrike. Its rather jay-like behaviour, combined with other characters, suggests that it shares a common ancestor with the corvids (Corvidae).

Corvinella (Very long-tailed shrikes) Plate 1

Species: *corvina, melanoleuca*

Basic structure Complex, noisy with a variety of loud sonorous whistles, harsh rasping, buzzing, chattering, chirping and twittering sounds. Often calls in flight (visual signals described below). **Duetting** Well developed, includes chorusing. **Territorial advertisement** Whistle calls (appears to advertise mainly with visual signals, perches exposed, static marking and body movements). **Territorial threat** Initiated by one or two individuals with loud sonorous whistles in one species, or distinctive warbling call in the other. Calls attract group members who join in, in complex chorus with a variety of whistles and harsh calls. Opposing groups use similar calls, like repeated *tlee-teeoooo* or *twee-dl-ooo* whistles and harsh chattering *kzzzrkzzzr-*, scolding *Tchzrrr-* and hoarse *scis-scis*, rattling *brrreeeu-* and other calls which develop into a communal chattering racket. Duet in one species consists of *teelooo* by ♂, with higher-pitched *tleeeu* by ♀ (perch exposed, upright, flicks and jerks tail while calling; group members come together in tree or on ground, face each other and repeatedly bow, head down with wings raised up, body feathers fluffed out exposing flanks, and flick tail while calling). **Alarm** One species gives a harsh grating, scolding *Tchzrrr-Tchzrrr-*, the other a short harsh *twe-kik...wee-ti-kik* phrase or rasping *kzzzz-kzzzz-kzzzz-*. Call attracts other members (probably with body movements). **Courtship** Breeding ♀ whistles repeatedly from nest in one species, but in the other has distinctive harsh repeated call. In at least one species ♂ and ♀ often sing in duet (courtship-feeding present). **Contact** Various harsh *tchzaaa-tchzaaa-* calls and whistles. Sonorous whistles or hard *squee squee* in flight (greeting display similar to territorial display; young have similar display, raise and flutter up-held wings, with head up). **Roosting** In one species warbling call given prior to entering roost. **Begging** By breeding ♀ on nest a repeated *tzzeeew-*, and that of young a loud repeated nasal *tzzeeeer-* (see *Contact*: ♀ adopts crouched posture, wings slightly open, drooped and fluttering).

Relationships

In this genus, because both species have long tails but look very different, they have sometimes been placed either in separate genera, with *melanoleuca* in the genus *Urolestes*[202, 609, 631], or in the same genus based on structure (long tail and lanceolate forehead feathers) and similar social behaviour[3, 206, 207, 481, 918]. The latter view is supported here, particularly since their communication behaviour is similar. Calls of *corvina* differ by being delivered faster and with a buzzy quality. Interestingly, an aberrant *melanoleuca* has been seen with a yellow bill typical of *corvina*[500].

Their superspecies status is controversial[184, 431, 481], but their position in the true shrikes is supported by a close relationship to *Lanius* based on cranial morphology, jaw and hindlimb anatomy and general and communication behaviour, particularly in the cooperative species[184, 205, 431, 897, 918]. Owing to these similarities *Corvinella* has sometimes been placed in *Lanius*[16]. DNA-DNA hybridisation studies suggest it is most closely related to *Lanius*, with both being closely related to *Eurocephalus*. Its relationship to corvids is supported on feather structure, egg coloration, anatomy, ecology and behaviour.

Lanius (True shrikes) Plates 2–12

Species: *sphenocercus, excubitor, meridionalis, ludovicianus, minor, excubitoroides, mackinnoni, cabanisi, dorsalis, somalicus, collaris, newtoni, nubicus, senator, bucephalus, cristatus, isabellinus, tigrinus, souzae, collurio, gubernator, vittatus, collurioides, schach, tephronotus, validirostris*

Basic structure Graded system of predominantly harsh, loud sounds of different pitch, length and repetition rates. A few species have rather quiet calls. Similar calls used in different contexts by both sexes, ♀ generally less vocal. All species have notes which are of a broad and/or narrow band type. In general the broader the band, the harsher the sound. Broad-band notes vary from high-pitched short sharp *tsik* to lower-pitched *chak*, or longer, higher-pitched *tzzeee* and *keerrr* sounds to lower *tschaa* or *tscha* notes. Some notes have a distinctive buzzy quality. Less harsh, narrow-band notes show similar variation. Repetition rate varies from slowly repeated single notes to faster chattering or very fast trills, a characteristic of some species. Similarly, some species combine harsh calls with simple whistles, varying in pitch, form and length, while others have a short whistled phrase. Most species appear to have a warbling song consisting of harsh and rapidly modulated whistles, which usually contain mimicry (most species perch exposed, static marking in upright stance; other visual signals described below). **Duetting** Except in cooperative breeding species, generally poorly developed and only recorded in few species. In at least two cooperative breeding species, duetting and chorusing is well developed. **Territorial advertisement** Repeated loud harsh *kscha*-type notes, often disyllabic and usually given as a repeated 2-note phrase, variously described as *Jerjert, tzert-tzert, check-cherr, dssch-dsch, ko-ick* or *kerr-ick.* One insular species has a continuous, monotonously repeated *juurt-juurt-juurt-* call. A few Holarctic species with mainly grey and white plumage combine harsh calls with short high-pitched fluted whistles. These may vary in pitch, form and length, from single high-pitched *prrii-* or *kwiet* to double *tri-rli* or *tij-tij* notes. A few of these species combine the whistle with a buzzy note: *tzzweet-* or *tchilip-.* A few other species (African with mainly grey and white or grey, black and white plumage) have longer-drawn, lower-pitched *tuuoooooo-* whistles. Still other African species (with mainly grey and white plumage) have a short musical phrase combining whistles and harsh buzzy notes: *tzuptzup-bzzze-bzzze* or *tchechetcher-brr-we-weet* (static marking in exposed upright position, often with tail swinging, wagging or cocking movements, some species reportedly fluttering wings also; a few species perform high 'inspection' flights, while cooperative breeders static-mark and patrol boundaries). **Territorial threat** Rapidly repeated territorial calls. At highest intensity, alarm and even begging calls. Snaps bill in intense aggression. (More erect stance, scapulars raised, tail swinging or fanning. In one species upright head-nodding. At higher intensity, body-bowing and switching from side to side, tail flicking and fanning, wing jerking, flicking or fluttering. At highest intensity, by horizontal posture, fluffed-out body feathers, raised crest and tail fanned. Physical contact not uncommon. When mobbing may adopt upright posture with wings open.) Cooperative-breeding species defend territory with group displays, initiated by breeding bird with buzzy whistles, in one species with metallic-sounding *kyoir-l* call which develops into excited duetting chorus with mate and group members. Calls reminiscent of *Corvinella.* (Group display; members sit close together, lower heads, open bills, rocking back and forwards, waving, swinging and fanning tails and fluttering outstretched or drooped, slightly open wings while calling and changing perch frequently. At higher intensity, duet and dance, alternately jumping up and down about a foot into the air, tail waved up and down on landing.) **Alarm** Two main types: (i) repeated long harsh *keerrr-* sounds given by most grey and white or black and white species; or (ii) rapidly repeated, short harsh notes giving a chattering *cha-cha-cha-* effect, given by most brown-plumage species. A few species appear to combine both types. Confirmation required in the use of whistled calls in this context. Snaps bill in intense aggression (tail flicked sideways, up and down and fanned, head and body feathers raised).

Courtship Contains elements seen in territorial threat in addition to contact notes, trills, excited whistles and warbling song with mimicry. (Wing-fluttering, body-bowing, turning head or facing body away, tail-fanning and, in one species, upright head-nodding and body-bobbing. One species combines movements with feet pattering. Display-flying by ♂ common, usually with tail fanned. In a few species given by both sexes, either together or individually. Flights may be high spiral, circular, descending, gliding or hovering, others low and undulating or a fast, rolling zigzag or switching back and forth. Courtship-feeding present.) ***Pre-copulation*** ♂ contact calls, ♀ begs. Begging call usually given during copulation. (♂ may present food and usually flutters wings, ♀ in crouched wing-fluttering posture; ♂ may fan tail and switch from side-to-side before mounting.) ***Nest-site display*** Excited song with trills and mimicry. (♂ may choose site, hops about in bush or tree, sits in crotch while raising and lowering (nodding) or swaying or twisting head from side-to-side, tail fanned in horizontal or cocked in vertical position, and quivered in some species.) **Contact** Short harsh *tcha*-type notes, and apparently in some species with whistled calls (probably body movements, and some species have group meetings—'parliaments'). **Roosting** Contact-type calls (cooperative-breeding species roost together, other species apart). **Begging** Usually repeated long harsh nasal sounds characterised by numerous harmonics. Buzzy sounds have also been reported for some species. (In appeasement turns bill away, or in one species the head is laid back with bill vertical, at high intensity by upright bill-up posture or open-wing fluttering posture; begging posture typically crouched, wing-fluttering.)

Relationships

The general uniformity of members of *Lanius* has resulted in little consensus as to relationships within the genus. For example, the brown Eurasian shrikes have at times been lumped into a single species, or split into at least three separate species. Hybridisation between the three is known from a number of overlap areas, and hence defining species limits continues to be a problem. Initial attempts to understand relationships were based exclusively on the analysis of external plumage characteristics and resulted in various arrangements, for example Eurasian shrikes and African fiscals[3, 165, 166, 206, 211, 358, 671, 727]. The first comprehensive use of behavioural communication characters to establish relationships was attempted by Panov[284, 600]. The following diagram illustrates his interpretation of relationships in this genus.

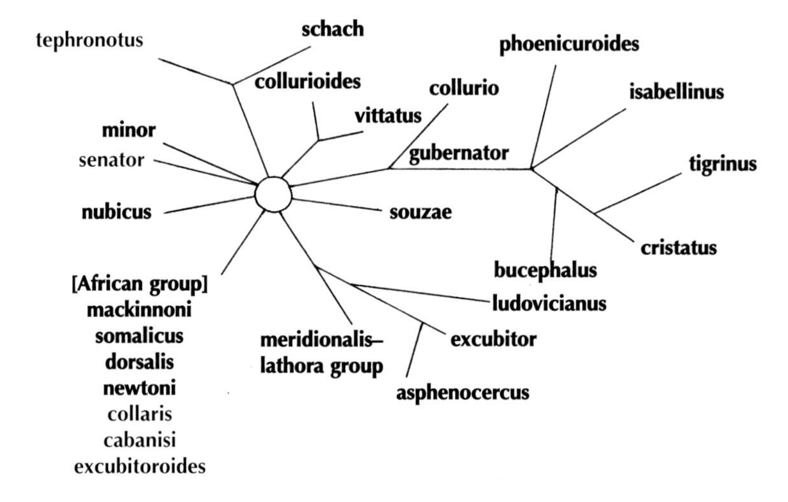

Diagram showing the relationship of members of the genus Lanius *(after Panov)*

The relationship of *Lanius* to other genera has been based on skeletal, muscular and other anatomical characters such as sperm, and biochemical characters such as egg-white protein, serology and DNA[154, 184, 235, 894, 897–902, 918–920]. There is general consensus that the genus is closely related to *Corvinella* and forms part of the true shrikes, which are most closely related to the corvids.

The following analysis of vocalisations combines my study on mainly African species with those of Panov on Eurasian species[284, 600]. The analysis suggests that alarm calls (harsh chatters or *keeer*-type calls), and whistled advertising calls (short, long or a whistled phrase) and others, may be useful in understanding relationships. This approach maps two major divisions: (i) a mainly grey and black group; and (ii) a mainly brown group, with an intermediate group of brown, grey and black species.

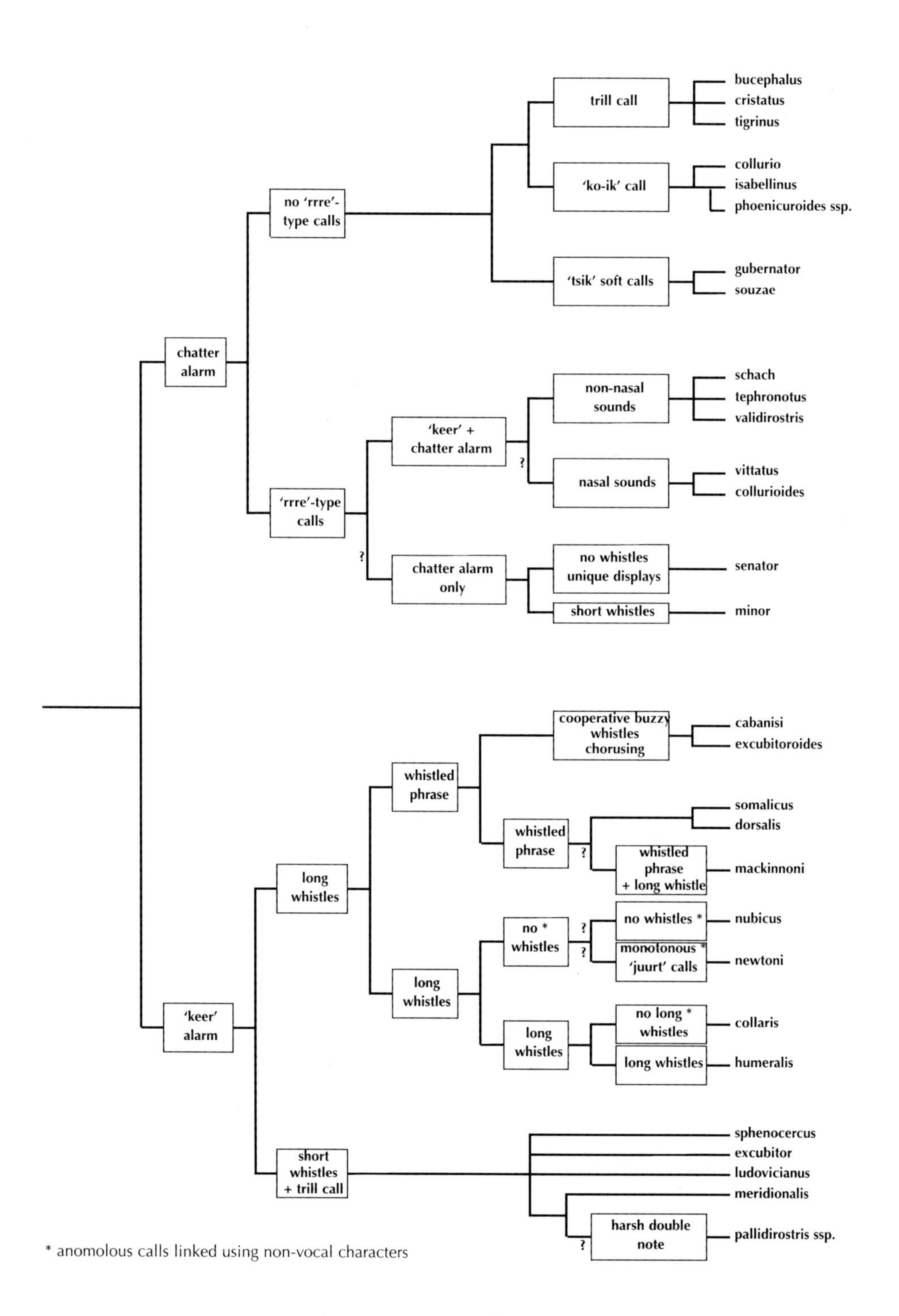

Map of some communication characteristics of Lanius

Malaconotus (Large bush-shrikes) Plates 13–15

Species: *lagdeni, cruentus, blanchoti, monteiri, gladiator, alius*

Basic structure In largest species remarkably uniform; consists of slowly repeated low-pitched, drawn-out, mournful whistles and harsh, raucous tearing sounds accompanied by loud bill-snapping (clicking). In single smaller species (*alius*), vocalisations are different, although known only from a few phrases of various repeated disyllabic whistles (visual signals described below). **Duetting** In large species poorly developed; ♀ gives irregular harsh calls. Unknown in small species. **Territorial advertisement** Large species give slowly repeated, low-pitched, mournful drawn-out whistles of at least two types: (i) low-pitched drawn-out *uuuuuuuh*, which may include a terminal upward inflection; and (ii) a shorter note of similar pitch with more abrupt start and finish: *hoop* or *toot*. Rival ♂♂ may call simultaneously or alternately. In *blanchoti*, ♀ duets irregularly with harsh raucous tearing *Skeeeeer-* sounds. In little-known smaller *alius*, has various disyllabic whistles in repeated short phrases (*blanchoti* signals in an inclined posture, displaying breast with tail hanging vertically down and head bowed downwards with each call; may static-mark in relatively exposed position). **Territorial threat** Larger species give loud bill-snapping combined with short hollow whistles, *Klip!-Klip!-phoou*, sometimes with 'wing-fripping' sounds in flight. At high intensity, produces repeated raucous rasping or tearing sounds and harsh explosive squawks, apparently by both sexes. (Clicks produced as bill raised, whistle given as bill lowered onto breast, nape slightly raised. At higher intensity crouches in hunched posture, back feathers raised, bill held open showing black palate, head swayed from side to side, tail fanned.) **Alarm** Large species give loud *Klip!-* bill-snapping, harsh drawn-out raucous rasping and short harsh explosive *Squok-* sounds, in addition to staccato *KKK-K-K-K* or *ke-ke-ke-* sounds. **Courtship** In large species appears similar to territorial threat, with rapid bill-snapping (rattle) *Klip!-Klip!-* followed by short *phoou-* whistles. May give a short whistle in flight. ♀ duets occasionally with repeated harsh drawn-out calls in response to ♂ whistles. (In *blanchoti* appears similar to territorial threat: ♂ gives fluttering display-flight, tail fanned, interspersed with gliding in which wings held back and slightly elevated. Rump-fluffing unconfirmed. ♂ adopts crouched posture, slowly fluttering wings in half-spread position, breaks off twigs and passes these to presumed ♀. Courtship-feeding present, both give loose wing-fluttering.) **Contact** Soft repeated plaintive mewing *phoee-* whistles in *blanchoti* (when breeding often flutters half-open wings when near ♀). **Roosting** Unknown. **Begging** Adult, nestling and juvenile *blanchoti* give soft repeated buzzing *zzhoreer-* sounds (as for contact).

Relationships

The genus *Malaconotus*, which is here thought to comprise only the very large bush-shrikes, was originally defined on the Grey-headed Bush-shrike *M. blanchoti*[614]. Some authors have retained this arrangement[48, 204, 206, 207, 336-338], others expanded the genus to include all green-backed bush-shrikes, merging *Chlorophoneus* and *Telophorus* in this genus[3, 30, 180, 291, 431, 631]. This arrangement was originally proposed by Mayr and Amadon without reasons[609]. Although little known, the anatomy of the large bush-shrikes, such as the lack of mouth spots, and their general and communication behaviour, as well as DNA-DNA hybridisation, differ markedly from the smaller *Chlorophoneus* bush-shrikes and others. Traditionally the members of the *Malaconotus* as treated here are thought to form a single superspecies, but relationships, distributions and limits within the genus remain unclear and controversial[21, 79, 145, 345, 458, 605, 626, 745]. For example, Fiery-breasted *M. cruentus* and Lagden's Bush-shrike *M. lagdeni* are considered by some authors to form their own superspecies[460, 493]. The Green-breasted Bush-shrike *M. gladiator*, while unlike the other species in coloration, has similar calls and eye colour to Monteiro's Bush-shrike. This has led to suggestions that they represent colour morphs of the same species, or that Green-breasted is a colour morph of Grey-headed Bush-shrike[345, 864]. In addition, some members of this genus, and some of the smaller *Chlorophoneus* canopy bush-shrikes, exhibit an unusual, apparent mimetic coloration. Consequently, some authors believe that the smaller species may derive some benefit from mimicking the more aggressive larger species[528, 625]. Alternatively, they may simply be subjected to the same selection pressures[613]. It has also been suggested that the larger birds may simply represent a single polymorphic species[113, 180, 342]. This gains support in the sporadic occurrence, at widely distant localities, of what is believed to be Monteiro's Bush-shrike *M. monteiri*, race *perspicillatus*[343, 989]. This enigmatic bush-shrike has at times been considered conspecific with Grey-headed Bush-shrike. In addition, an unusual specimen from Kakamega Forest (Kenya) was described, but subsequently lost. Some authors consider it to be Monteiro's, others think it may have been a Fiery-breasted Bush-shrike. The original description suggests an aberrant (perhaps partially albinistic) form of Grey headed Bush-shrike[318, 618, 631]. This evidence supports the not infrequent occurrence of abnormal plumages in this species. However, although most species are little known, and many vocalisations are rather similar, behavioural comparisons, combined with potential signal areas (plumage and eye colour), suggest that most appear to be distinct species, with probable polymorphism occurring only in Fiery-breasted Bush-shrike. Based mainly on these characters, Grey-headed appears to be most closely related to Monteiro's and Green-breasted Bush-shrike. This group is closely related to a vocally distinct group, comprising Lagden's and Fiery-breasted Bush-shrike. The relationship of the smaller Uluguru Bush-shrike *M.? alius* remains obscure. It is virtually unknown, but differs from the larger members in having a reddish-brown eye. Its vocalisations are unlike other members of this genus, and suggest that it may be more closely related to the Madagascan vangas.

The relationship of *Malaconotus* to other genera remains obscure. DNA-DNA hybridisation studies place it as the most primitive bush-shrike group in the Malaconotidae[184]. Some communication behaviour suggests similarities with helmet-shrikes and vangas.

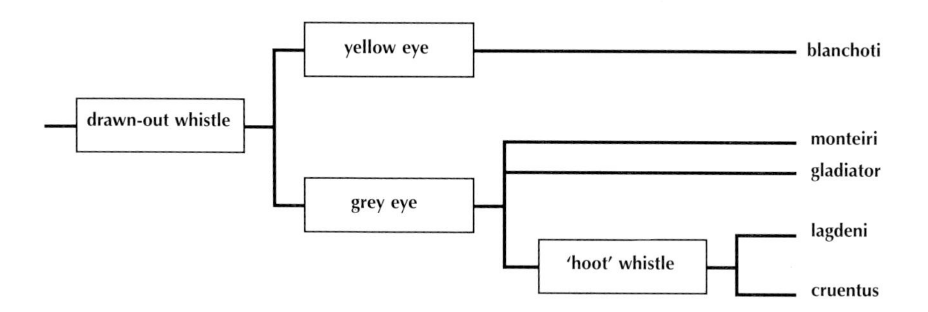

Map of some communication characteristics of Malaconotus

Chlorophoneus (Small bush-shrikes) Plates 15–19

Traditionally combined with other green bush-shrikes, but here restricted to the small forest and woodland canopy and dense undergrowth species

Species: *sulfureopectus*, *bocagei*, *multicolor*, *nigrifrons*, *olivaceus*, *dohertyi* and ***viridis*** (including ***quadricolor***)

Although ***kupeensis*** was originally described as a member of this genus, it is here treated as monotypic because its known communication behaviour fits none of the currently recognised genera

Basic structure Two groups: canopy species give repeated short whistles at different rates and number of notes; undergrowth species give more complex repeated short whistle phrase. Both groups combine whistles with harsh churrs, drawn-out rasping, tearing, and double bill-clashing sounds (visual signals described below). **Duetting** Present, poorly developed. **Territorial advertisement** Some canopy species give long series of repeated short *hwe-hwe-* or *hu-hu-* whistles at various pitches and rates. Others give slowly delivered, lower-pitched hollow single *hooui* or disyllabic *whoop-Weeup* whistles. Undergrowth species usually give disyllabic whistles in a 3–4 note phrase, like *kong-koit-koit* or *kwit-kwit-kwit---work*. In both groups ♀ duets irregularly with single harsh *skizzz* or double drawn-out rasping or tearing *zzweeerrr-zzweeerrr* sounds (upright posture exposing breast, some species bowing forwards, then bending head back with bill inclined while calling; sometimes perch exposed, possibly static-marking). **Territorial threat** Repeated whistles combined with harsh drawn-out tearing calls and double *killlik-killlik* bill-clashing and 'wing-fripping' (body-bowing and more horizontal, sleek posture with bill open displaying black palate). **Alarm** Variety of harsh sounds ranging from short low-pitched *Kruk* and *grrr* churrs to longer, higher-pitched rasping, tearing and bill-clashing sounds. **Courtship** Similar to territorial threat with excited 'wing-fripping' (similar to territorial threat, includes much chasing and bouncing in tandem through vegetation as ♂ follows ♀; both sexes bow and sway the body, rump feathers probably fluffed out; courtship-feeding absent). **Contact** Duetting and low-pitched, barely audible *grrr* churrs (probably with body movements). **Roosting** Unknown. **Begging**: High-pitched *seee-* or *seeeep* (crouched wing-fluttering).

Relationships

Controversial with little consensus on the limits of this genus. *Chlorophoneus* is here considered to include only those mainly green bush-shrikes, with a small body and bill, which occur in dense undergrowth and forest or woodland canopy. Although the genus was originally described on the Olive Bush-shrike *C. olivaceus*, few early authors recognised the genus as here constituted[202]. Some authors only include the canopy species[16, 336-338, 610], with most submerging *Chlorophoneus* in the genus *Telophorus*. This appears to be based mainly on the presence of a black gorget in the undergrowth species, a feature which is prominent in Bokmakierie *Telophorus zeylonus*[168, 180, 204, 206, 207]. Still others prefer to lump both genera in *Malaconotus*[3, 291, 350, 430, 481, 631]. The genus is here defined on morphological, such as presence of mouth spots, and distinctive general, reproductive and communication behavioural characters. These are different to *Malaconotus* and *Telophorus*[116, 205, 331], with the black gorget representing an apparent convergent character.

The genus consists of two superspecies, one made up of forest and woodland canopy species, comprising Black-fronted *C. nigrifrons*, Many-coloured *C. multicolor*, Olive *C. olivaceus*, Orange-breasted *C. sulfureopectus* and Bocage's Bush-shrikes *C. bocagei*. The other is formed by the two dense undergrowth species, namely Doherty's *C. dohertyi* and Gorgeous Bush-shrike *C. viridis*[180]. All three canopy forest species show extensive polymorphism, with an interesting parallel, copycat plumage found in the larger *Malaconotus* bush-shrikes (see Relationships under *Malaconotus*)[112, 113]. Black-fronted and Many-coloured Bush-shrikes are undoubtedly each other's closest relatives, and are sometimes considered conspecific[3, 291, 431]. They are here retained as a separate species for the following reasons: (i) although ♂♂ resemble each other superficially, ♀♀ are distinctive (this characteristic repeats in a number of genera discussed in this book); (ii) the tail is green in both sexes of *nigrifrons*, but mainly black with broad yellowish tips in ♂ *multicolor*, particularly where ranges are close; (iii) *nigrifrons* lacks white on the head and yellowish tips to secondaries and tertials, both of which are characteristic of most *multicolor*; (iv) eye maroon in *nigrifrons*, reddish-mauve to purple in *multicolor*; (v) juveniles distinctly barred below in *nigrifrons*, but indistinct or lacking in *multicolor* (however there is geographical variation, with some individuals showing barring on the head); (vi) *nigrifrons* is smaller with a smaller bill and shows a broader habitat tolerance, which includes montane, lowland and woodland (*multicolor* is larger, with a heavier bill and mainly restricted to lowland forest, except for *graueri* in the E range, where found in montane forest); (vii) calls require greater study, but although both species share a similar basic repertoire[431], differences exist in whistle notes of ♂, and to a greater extent in harsh note of ♀, a feature which repeats itself in other genera discussed in this book. Additional characters are awaited to help resolve this complex situation. Black-fronted is also closely related to Olive Bush-shrike[205]. Based on plumage and vocalisations, Orange-breasted and Bocage's Bush-shrike appear to be each other's closest relative. This is supported by the possible hybrid described between these two species[775, 776].

The other two members of this genus, the lowland Gorgeous Bush-shrike and the montane Doherty's Bush-shrike, are closely related on morphological and behavioural (including communication) characters. In spite of some authors retaining *viridis* and *quadricolor* as separate species[180, 206, 338], they are here considered conspecific on the basis of anatomy and behaviour (particularly communication behaviour), especially similarities in vocalisations[3, 145, 291, 431, 500]. However, the calls of female *viridis* are unknown and may prove decisive.

DNA-DNA hybridisation studies suggest that the canopy forest and woodland species diverged later than the undergrowth species. It also places members of this genus closest to the Bokmakierie[184]. However, as previously mentioned *Telophorus* differs in a number of aspects from *Chlorophoneus*. It is here suggested that *Chlorophoneus* is more closely related to *Rhodophoneus* in the presence of mouth spots, nest structure and egg coloration. In addition, *Rhodophoneus* appears fairly closely related to *Telophorus* on behavioural and morphological characters[16, 205, 633, 918].

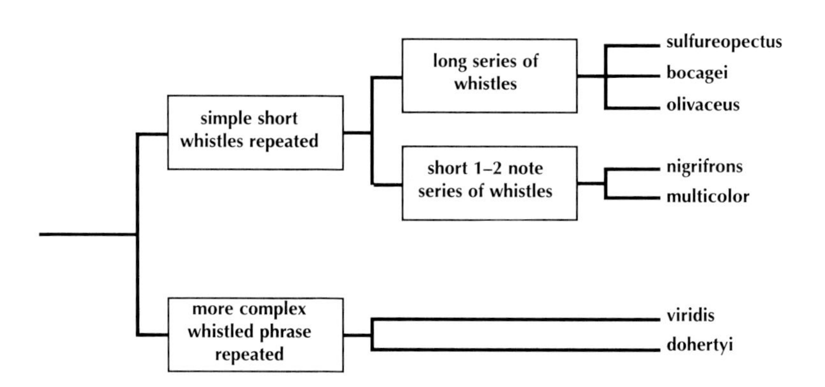

Map of some communication characteristics of Chlorophoneus

Chlorophoneus? (Mount Kupé Bush-shrike) Plate 19

Originally placed in ***Chlorophoneus*** but here thought to be better placed in its own genus, as yet unnamed

Species: *kupeensis*

Basic structure Little known; various repeated whistles, harsh babbler-like calls, insect-like grating and other harsh sounds (visual signals described below). **Duetting** Unknown. **Territorial advertisement** At least three different whistles thought to be used in this context: (i) a single quiet, clear liquid *crooa* whistle, which rises and falls in pitch, also given in a series of 3–4 notes; (ii) rarely heard, trisyllabic series of 3 ascending whistles, with a slight inflection at the end of each note, and repeated up to 6 times, although persistent calling also reported (tone of call more like Many-coloured Bush-shrike *Chlorophoneus multicolor* than the lower notes of Green-breasted Bush-shrike *Malaconotus gladiator*); (iii) a loud rapidly fluctuating nasal whistle, repeated several times (sits in very upright posture). **Territorial threat** Loud, harsh, babbler-like chatter with a few short introductory notes *thec-thec-kh-kh-kh,* followed by 3–4 rapid *tchrraa-tchrraa-tchrraa-* notes repeated at *c.*2–3 notes/sec for up to *c.*30 notes. Length of notes also variable, call often accompanied by loud 'wing-fripping' (body held upright and forward, wings drooped and flicked with tail fanned, neck slightly extended with body bowed more to sides, probably combined with body-swaying). **Alarm** When disturbed, makes harsh scolding *ke-ke-ke-*, often ending with a *churr.* Also produces noisy harsh bill-clattering or snapping (clashing?) (upright posture with tail fanned). **Courtship** Little known. (♀ persistently submissive towards ♂, crouching in probable mating posture, with wings drooped and fluttering, head up and bill open. Suggests courtship-feeding probably takes place.) **Contact** Appears to be signalled with an almost continuous cicada-like grating sound *gr-i-i-i-k...gr-i-i-i-k-* or *grrr-grrr-grrr-,* repeated every 3–5 sec. Sometimes initiated with bill-clashing sounds. **Roosting** Unknown. **Begging** Juvenile believed to beg with harsh sounds (probable crouched wing-fluttering).

Relationships

This species was placed by its discoverer in *Chlorophoneus.* It is traditionally believed to be intermediate between the smaller *Chlorophoneus* and larger *Malaconotus* bush-shrikes. It is nearly as large as members of *Malaconotus* and with a similar underwing pattern, but without the massive bill. It has the green and grey common to both groups, and the black face-mask and breast-band of some *Chlorophoneus.* Not surprisingly it has been placed by various workers in either *Chlorophoneus*[338, 349], or *Telophorus*[16, 206, 207, 605], or else in *Malaconotus,* in which these genera are often submerged[3, 180, 431].

Recently, much new information has become available (see species account). Based on current knowledge about its plumage, soft-part colours (palate orange, not black like other bush-shrikes), and communication behaviour, the species fits none of the genera to which it was formerly assigned. The available characters suggest a closer relationship to *Chlorophoneus* than to *Malaconotus.* It is probably better placed as intermediate between *Chlorophoneus, Platysteira* and *Bias,* although its babbler-like call is reminiscent of a vanga. Whatever its true affinities, it will probably be found better placed in its own genus. It is here reluctantly retained in its original genus awaiting additional characters.

Telophorus (Bokmakierie bush-shrike) Plate 20

Traditionally combined with other green bush-shrikes, but here restricted to its own genus

Species: *zeylonus*

Basic structure Complex, not well understood; ringing whistles and trills, with a wide variety of harsh tearing, stuttering, croaking, slashing, growling and clicking sounds (visual signals described below). **Duetting** Very well developed. **Territorial advertisement** Repeated ringing whistled phrases, sometimes as single drawn-out *houuuu* note, more often in multi-note phrases, very variable like *huu-huhuhu* or wok-wok, pairs having a number of duet combinations. ♀ duets regularly with longer, more rapidly repeated series of high-pitched *teuteuteuteuteu-* whistles or *trrrree* trills and lower *wikwikwikwikwik* phrases (inclined, upright stance, head and bill up, exposing bright throat and breast-band, tail fanned; in flight tail fanned displaying yellow tips). **Territorial threat** Complex duetting climaxing in *trrrrrree* trills, croaking *grrrr,* tearing *zzzzeee,* slashing *zzzz-* and clicking *K-K-K-* and other sounds including 'wing-fripping' (typical upright posture with bowing, side-to-side and tense, jerky body movements, wing-flicking and tail-fanning; neighbouring pairs may chase each other on ground or in a bush, with much posturing and tail-fanning). **Alarm** Low-pitched *Tok-Tok-, krrrr-* and harsh scolding sounds. **Courtship** Appears similar to territorial threat (similar to territorial threat, with much chasing and hopping in tandem through vegetation, rump-fluffing unknown; courtship-feeding absent). **Contact** Duetting, softer whistles, croaking *grrrr* and tearing *skizzzz-* sounds (probably with body movements). **Roosting** Unknown. **Begging** Nestlings have soft, guttural, hissing *gherrr-* sounds, fledglings higher-pitched *zzrrreee-* or *zzrrriii-* sounds (crouched wing-fluttering).

Relationships

The genus was described on the Bokmakierie *T. zeylonus,* but it has traditionally been combined with those members of *Chlorophoneus* which have a similar black gorget or breast-band. Alternatively it is included in *Malaconotus* with all other mainly greenish bush-shrikes. This merger was proposed without reasons[609] (for additional references see Relationships under *Malaconotus*). The Bokmakierie is here placed in its own genus because it is distinct from members of *Chlorophoneus.* It differs by lacking mouth spots and in having a different nest structure, egg coloration, general behaviour and, particularly, communication behaviour[19, 205, 331].

Although the Bokmakierie appears to be the closest relative of *Chlorophoneus,* it shows an even closer relationship, based on morphology and communication behaviour, to the genus *Tchagra.* Based on similar characters, it also shows an apparent close relationship to *Rhodophoneus.* In turn, this latter genus appears closely related to *Chlorophoneus,* but unfortunately few comparative characters are known for *cruentus.*

Rhodophoneus (Rosy-patched Shrike) Plate 20

Species: *cruentus*

Basic structure Not well known; piercing, thin high-pitched, quavering, melodious ringing whistles, repeated monotonously. Also has harsh and rasping sounds (visual signals described below). **Duetting** Well developed, ♀ whistle slightly lower-pitched than ♂. **Territorial advertisement** Single or disyllabic whistles, often in monotonous duets, ♂ gives *Twee-u*, ♀ responds with *tzee-ur* notes. (Sexes often in same bush, may face each other, stretching up with bill pointing upwards on first note, wings drooped at sides, then bow or bob down with second note in their call. Continue this performance monotonously for long periods.) **Territorial threat** Apparently similar to territorial advertisement but with much counter-singing. (♂♂ perched close together, on ground, in a bush or tree, counter-singing with similar whistles and stretch and bowing movements. At high intensity, chase each other about with out-stretched wings and tails fanned, or perch in a bush, bobbing up and down to each other, alternately flashing pink throat and rump while calling.) **Alarm** Harsh grating *krrrr-* or scolding *zwerrrrk-zwerrrrk-* notes. **Courtship** Little known (two ♂♂ counter-singing, stretching and bowing and then following a ♀ probably involved in courtship). **Contact** Duetting over long distances, short distance unknown (probably with body movements). **Roosting** and **Begging** Unknown.

Relationships

The genus was described on the Rosy-patched Shrike *R. cruentus*. Apart from being retained in its own genus[207, 336, 431, 481, 610, 631,] it has also been been placed in *Tchagra*[3, 206,] and *Telophorus*[16, 633.]

Its inclusion in *Tchagra* lacks support, as it differs in the presence of mouth spots, nest structure, egg coloration and communication behaviour[180, 500.] It appears more closely related on these characters to *Chlorophoneus*, but is here thought to show a closer relationship to *Telophorus* on general and communication behaviour[205, 431, 633.]

Laniarius (Boubous and gonoleks) Plate 21–24

Species: *leucorhynchus, poensis, fuelleborni, funebris, atrococcineus, erythrogaster, barbarus, mufumbiri, atroflavus, luehderi, ruficeps, liberatus, ferrugineus, aethiopicus, turatii, bicolor*

Basic structure Medium to low-pitched repeated ringing whistles, some disyllabic, and combined with harsh croaking, tearing, snarling, ratchet-clicking and nasal twanging sounds. Generally pairs tend to have a number of duet types (visual signals described below). **Duetting** Well developed, particularly in crimson boubous, which have incredibly fast response times, resulting in a whiplash quality. Duets may be antiphonal or partially overlapping. **Territorial advertisement** ♂ calls vary from long-drawn-out single *huuuuoo* to shorter *huoo-* or disyllabic *hu-wee* or *whee-oo*, to very fast *quip-quip* whistles. Some species also use croaking or snoring *horrr, Haaw* or *kow* sounds. Most ♀♀ respond in duet with harsh tearing *zzeerrr, Tjerr* or ratchet-like *Ka-Ka-KKKKK* clicking calls, but in at least three species they respond with whistles as well as harsh calls (upright stance, stretches up, bobs head and while calling depresses head and body in shallow bow with tail slightly fanned; in one species, head suddenly raised up, retracted and thrown forward with swelling of throat). **Territorial threat** Rapidly repeated whistles, ratchet, tearing, croaking and harsh calls combined with a nasal swishing, twanging *Tchanananana* sound, often accompanied by excited 'wing-fripping' in display-flight. (Wings drooped, tail fanned and rump fluffed out.) Descending display-flight with twanging call accompanied by slow exaggerated wingbeats with head held up. When perched, bows and sways body from side to side and jerks tail up and down. Horizontal stance with bill open exposing black palate during intense threat.) **Alarm** Low-intensity repeated *Tik-* or *Tuk-* sounds, at higher intensity harsh *ke-ke-ke-* or explosive sounds. **Courtship** Similar to territorial threat. After copulation birds may give noisy harsh *kch-kch-* or churring sounds. (Like territorial threat, but much tandem bouncing through vegetation and short flights, ♂ gliding after ♀. Also observed wing-quivering while presumed mate collected nesting material. After calling, ♂ bends forward, depresses wings and fluffs out rump. Tail raised and fanned. When ♀ responds in duet, she thrusts down and forwards with each note. ♀ crouches and quivers wings prior to copulation. Courtship-feeding absent.) **Contact** Duetting and soft low-pitched churrs at close range (probably with body movements). **Roosting** Similar to low-intensity alarm, repeated *Tik-* notes. **Begging** High-pitched *seeee* or *pseeep* sounds (crouched wing-fluttering).

Relationships

The genus is morphologically rather uniform, but forms at least three groups on ecology and plumage: (i) black mainly forest species; (ii) black and white mainly dense bush and riverine species; and (iii) black and crimson or yellow species occupying thornbush and papyrus swamps. There is little consensus on relationships within the genus. One view considers it to be formed of two superspecies. One of these consists of the black and white boubous, which include Tropical *L. aethiopicus*, Southern *L. ferrugineus*, Swamp *L. bicolor* and Turat's Boubou *L. turatii*, combined with the mainly black and crimson or yellow species, including Crimson-breasted *L. atrococcineus*, Black-headed *L. erythrogaster*, Yellow-crowned *L. barbarus*, Papyrus Gonolek *L. mufumbiri*, Yellow-breasted Boubou *L. atroflavus* and three rather atypical species, Lühder's *L. luehderi* and Red-naped Bush-shrike *L. ruficeps* and Bulo Burti Boubou *L. liberatus*. The other superspecies is formed by the all-black boubous, including Sooty *L. leucorhynchus*, Mountain Sooty *L. poensis*, Fülleborn's Black Boubou *L. fuelleborni* and Slate-coloured Boubou *L. funebris*[180]. Some authors also combine the species into smaller superspecies and species groups[481].

Traditionally *Laniarius* is thought to be most closely related to either *Tchagra*, *Telophorus* (including *Chlorophoneus*) or *Dryoscopus*[3, 16, 206]. Its communication behaviour suggests two distinct groups, one formed by the black and white boubous and all-black boubous, and the other by the single yellow boubou and crimson gonoleks. Both groups are more similar to *Chlorophoneus* and *Telophorus* than they are to *Tchagra* or *Dryoscopus*. Interestingly, DNA-DNA hybridisation studies suggest a closer relationship with *Nilaus* than to any of the other genera, with their sister group being *Chlorophoneus* and *Telophorus*[184].

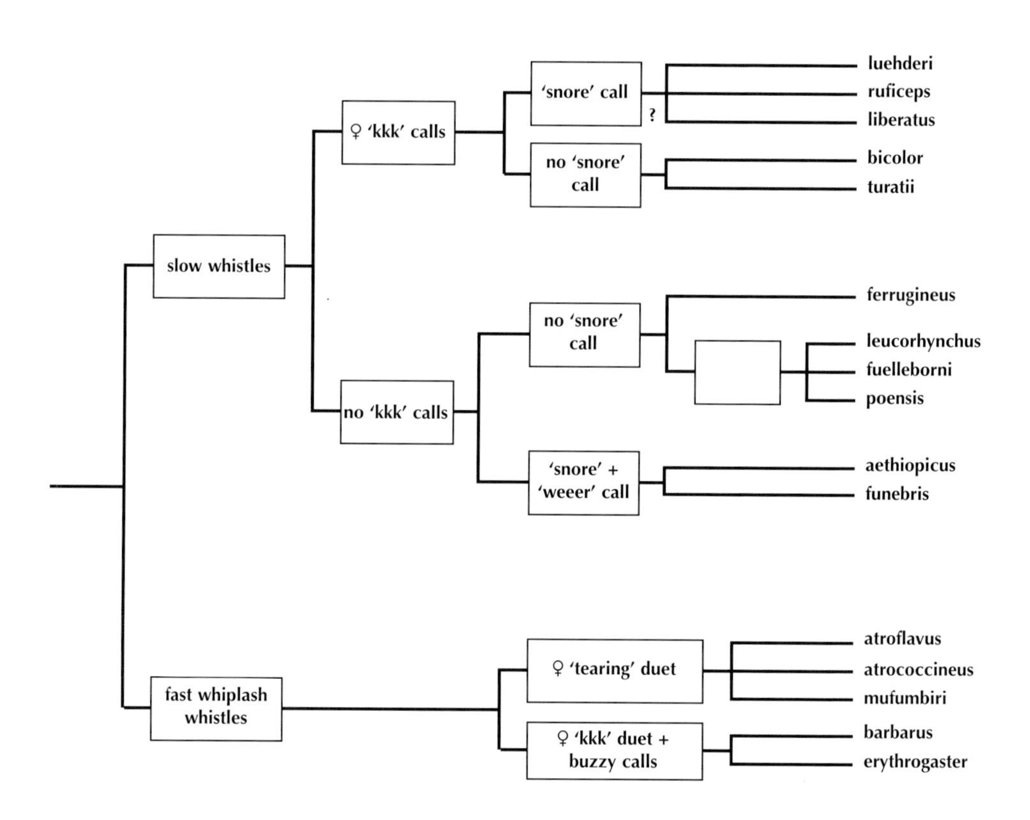

Map of some communication characteristics of Laniarius

Dryoscopus (Puffbacks) Plate 25–26

Species: *senegalensis*, *cubla*, *pringlii*, *gambensis*, *angolensis*, *sabini*

Basic structure Repeated explosive whistles, particularly disyllabic notes, often combined with percussive clicking, harsh rasping and tearing sounds, usually rather nasal in quality (genus characterised by fluffing out back and rump feathers in 'puffback' display; other visual signals described below). **Duetting** Poorly developed, ♀ responding erratically with harsh notes. **Territorial advertisement** Long or short series of repeated explosive disyllabic *Tchew* or *wee-U* whistles, often with loud click to produce *K!-weeU*. One species also has long sequence which descends in pitch and repetition rate. ♀ duets with harsh tearing or rasping *chikerrr-* or *Tzzrrrr* sounds (♂ exposed, upright posture). In display-flight, fans tail, fluffs out lower back and rump to form typical 'puffback' display. On landing, bows body and sways from side to side. **Territorial threat** Rapid whistling, harsh clicking and rasping sounds with ♀ joining in with repeated rasping calls. Noisy 'wing-fripping' (similar to territorial advertisement but with frequent display-flights and excited body movements, sometimes with bill partly open displaying black palate). **Alarm** Harsh rasping *Kzzzrrrr* or *ke-ke-* and loud *K!-K!-K!-* bill-clicking and 'wing-fripping' sounds. **Courtship** Similar to territorial threat. Repeated whistles or click-whistles by ♂; sounds may become slower, more rolling. In one species, ♂ gives repeated penetrating high-pitched *Tzeet* whistles while escorting ♀ during nest building. Display accompanied by much 'wing-fripping'. ♀ duets with harsh *tzzerrr* or *Tzk-tzzerrr* calls. ('Puffback' display includes bowing, drooping and vibrating wings with tail spread. Makes short butterfly flights with rump expanded, and may drop vertically through the air with raised wings. Also chases ♀ about with fast zigzag display-flight. Courtship-feeding present.) **Contact** Short scolding, rasping and churring sounds (probably with body movements). **Roosting** Unknown. **Begging** Repeated penetrating high-pitched *Tzzeeee-* in one widespread species, but described as low chatter in another restricted species (crouched wing-fluttering).

Relationships

Four marginally overlapping species are thought by some authors to form a superspecies comprising Black-backed *D. cubla*, Black-shouldered *D. senegalensis*, Northern *D. gambensis* and Pringle's Puffback *D. pringlii*[180]. Other authors consider their overlap too great for inclusion in a single superspecies[481]. Apparently some hybridisation takes place, which has prompted the suggestion that they are best regarded as allospecies[207]. Two other puffbacks are included in the genus, these being Sabine's *D. sabini* and Pink-footed Puffback *D. angolensis*. They are not included in the above superspecies, because they have allopatric, and discontinuous ranges[180]. Puffbacks have traditionally been placed between *Nilaus* and *Tchagra*[3, 206, 207, 431, 481], between *Laniarius* and *Tchagra*[610], or between *Laniarius* and the flycatcher-shrikes, batises and wattle-eyes[16]. This latter arrangement is supported by reproductive and communication behaviour. DNA-DNA hybridisation studies suggest *Tchagra* is its closest relative[184].

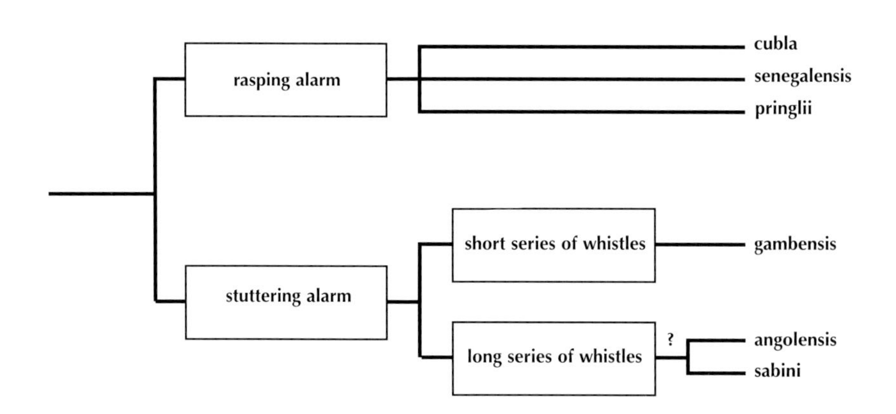

Map of some communication characteristics of Dryoscopus

Antichromus (Blackcap Bush-shrike) Plate 27

Traditionally placed in ***Tchagra***, but here placed in its original genus

Species: *minuta*

Basic structure Short cheery whistled phrase (sounding rather bulbul-like) and harsh tearing, mewing and nasal calls (visual signals described below). **Duetting** Present, reasonably well developed. **Territorial advertisement** ♂ gives cheery *tuwertuwee* whistled phrase. ♀ duets irregularly with nasal *cherrrruu*. Both sexes call while perched or in display-flight, particularly in ♂ whose display is accompanied by initial 'wing-fripping' (static marking in exposed position, and display-flight by both sexes; ♂ display consists of level flight with sudden upward check, at the apex of which raises head and crest and gives whistled phrase, followed by downward glide with tail fanned). **Territorial threat** At high intensity calls of ♂ and ♀ often followed by repeated harsh tearing *tzzerrr-* and *Tzik-* sounds with much 'wing-fripping' (repeated display-flights; or, while perched, moves about excitedly bowing, jerking the body from side to side, flicking wings and cocking tail). **Alarm** Slowly repeated harsh *Tzik-Tzik-*, rattling *Kzrrrr-* and other harsh churring and *chuck* notes. **Courtship** Little known; frequent flight-song display and contact calling (apparently similar to territorial threat, includes fluffing-out of rump feathers in flight; courtship-feeding unknown). **Contact** Soft *tzik-* and *chirp* calls by ♂, answered by ♀ with bleating or mewing nasal *maeeer-* sounds (probably with body movements). **Roosting** Repeated low-pitch harsh *tzrr-tzrr-*. **Begging** Fledgling gives mewing nasal *maeeer-* sound like ♀ contact (probably crouched wing-fluttering).

Relationships

Originally placed in the genus *Telophorus*, then *Bocagia*, which was renamed *Antichromus*. Later placed in *Tchagra* without reason, presumably because of its similar chestnut wing coloration[3, 206, 987, 1069]. Retained in this genus by all subsequent workers[16, 168, 207, 431, 481]. Although little known, the species is here placed back in *Antichromus* for the following reasons: (i) it is sexually dimorphic, unlike members of *Tchagra*; (ii) its plumage is not that similar to *Tchagra*, particularly in its short ungraduated, completely black tail and different eye colour; (iii) its behaviour is different, particularly communication behaviour. In addition, its nest is usually decorated with snake skin, unlike most members of *Tchagra*. Similarities to this genus include some general plumage aspects, particularly chestnut wings. Eggs resemble one of the types of eggs found in Black-crowned Tchagra *Tchagra senegala*[328]. Display-flight has some elements which are similar to *Tchagra* display, including 'wing-fripping', rump-fluffing, raised head and crest and terminal descending glide. However, these are shared by a number of other genera. Display differs in being given by both sexes and takes the form of a more level flight, with a distinct sudden shallow upward check, and short whistled phrase. Vocalisations are different to *Tchagra*[205]. Although this species appears to be distantly related to *Tchagra* on some characters, many other characters suggest a closer relationship to *Laniarius* and *Dryoscopus*.

Tchagra (Tchagras) Plate 27–28

Species: *senegala*, *tchagra*, *australis*, *jamesi*

Basic structure Whistles, either a continuous lilting song or short repeated notes in series, beginning fast and slowing down, notes becoming longer at the end. Pitch may remain the same or descend slightly. These are combined with harsh tearing notes, rattling trills, rolling, bubbling, chucking and nasal sounds (visual signals described below). **Duetting** Well developed, ♀ gives harsh sounds. **Territorial advertisement** Lilting descending whistle or rapidly repeated series of *teu-teu-* whistles at same pitch, slowing down at end. Usually given in display-flight with initial 'wing-fripping'. ♀ duets irregularly with long harsh rattling *trrrrrrrr-* trill or nasal *cheru-* notes. (Calls in inclined upright stance. Display-flight in most species involves a steep climb, at the top of which the head is held up, crest raised, followed by start of call, and jerky gliding descent, tail fanned, rump sometimes fluffed out.) **Territorial threat** Excited, complex duetting, including explosive whistling, trilling *trrreeeee-*, growling, purring, rolling, bubbling, chucking, tearing *zzweet*, rattling, clashing and whooping whistles, some sounds rather nasal, including *pitcheuu-* and *cheru-*, combined with noisy 'wing-fripping'. (Display-flight with rump fluffed out and, while perched, with slow side to side head movements with bill open exposing black palate. When very excited, postures with body, bowing and stretching with bill up, fanning, cocking and flicking tail, also jerky side to side body movements. May move about on ground with head up, tail tensely wagging, raised and lowered, or rotated, sometimes with slight fanning.) **Alarm** Harsh churrs, *Krrrr-*, *tzzerrr-* and *Chuk-Chuk-* notes. **Courtship** Similar to territorial threat with repeated display-flights. In one species, ♂ observed foraging and collecting nesting material on ground while giving warbling song (normally flight-song) and territorial threat calls mixed together (similar to territorial threat; courtship-feeding absent). **Contact** Soft, barely audible throaty sounds like *chuk-*, *twet*, longer *tzzerrr* and nasal *ptchew* (probably with body movements). **Roosting** Unknown. **Begging** Soft guttural hissing *gherrr* or *ghuurr* sounds by nestlings and louder nasal *tzzerrr-* calls by fledglings (crouched wing-fluttering).

Relationships

A remarkably uniform genus comprising two widespread species and two rather restricted species. Black-crowned Tchagra *T. senegala* occurs throughout Africa, including North Africa and on the Arabian Peninsula. Some authors consider the other three species to form a superspecies, consisting of the widespread Brown-headed *T. australis*, Southern Tchagra *T. tchagra* and the diminutive Three-streaked Tchagra *T. jamesi*[180], or alternatively of Brown-headed and Southern Tchagra with Three-streaked tchagra independent, this despite a possible hybrid between Brown and Three-streaked Tchagra[481, 766]. Communication behaviour suggests these three species are closely related, with Black-crowned Tchagra more distant.

The genus appears closely related to *Telophorus*, *Rhodophoneus* and *Antichromus*. This is supported by external morphological characters, including the absence of mouth spots. It is also strongly supported on behavioural characters, particularly communication behaviour. DNA-DNA hybridisation suggests *Dryoscopus* is its closest relative[184].

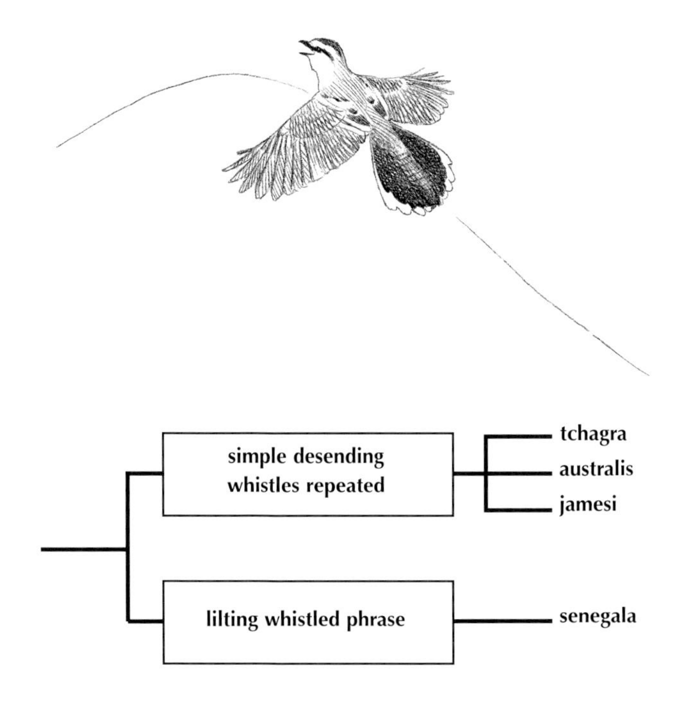

Map of some communication characteristics of Tchagra

Tephrodornis (Wood-shrikes) Plate 28

Species: *gularis*, *pondicerianus*

Basic structure Little known; rapidly repeated short series of ascending, descending or rapidly accelerating loud ringing whistles, varying in repetition rate. Also has repeated disyllabic whistles. One species (*gularis*) keeps up an incessant chorus. Whistles occasionally punctuated with harsh, tearing and other notes with similar quality to helmet-shrikes. The other species apparently has a warbling song of whistles and softer trills (visual signals described below). **Duetting** Unknown, probably present, requires confirmation. **Territorial advertisement** Loud clear series of ringing, rapidly repeated *tutututu*, *pi-pi-i-i-i* or *whi-whi-whi-whee* and disyllabic *witoo*- whistles, sometimes punctuated with harsh, tearing *Tzzurr* or *chaa* notes, probably in duet (postures unknown). **Territorial threat** Unknown. **Alarm** Harsh *cha-cha-* chattering, scolding and swearing notes, some reminiscent of alarm calls in true shrikes. Bill-snapping and 'wing-fripping' unknown (upright stance). **Courtship** Little unknown; brief song heard in breeding season, consists of a longer repeated whistle phrase with softer trills. A description of a shrill warbling song possibly also in this context (signals unknown; courtship-feeding unknown). **Contact** Whistled calls, harsh chattering and scolding notes. At short range, softer short *tik* and *wik* notes probably maintain contact (probably with body movements). **Roosting** and **Begging** Unknown (probably crouched wing-fluttering).

Relationships

Tephrodornis was originally placed with or close to the helmet-shrikes in the family Prionopidae[16, 202]. In spite of similarities in jaw musculature with this family[897], it was later moved to cuckoo-shrikes in the family Campephagidae, apparently based primarily on its soft back feathers[29, 612, 894]. However, recent DNA-DNA hybridisation has confirmed that it is closely related to the helmet-shrikes[184]. Unfortunately breeding and communication behaviour has been little studied, but the characters that are known, such as social and some communication behaviour, nest structure and eggs, suggest helmet-shrikes are its closest relative.

Megabyas (Red-eyed Flycatcher-shrike) Plate 29

Species: *flammulatus*

Basic structure Repeated whistles given in short phrases and harsh churring, rasping and metallic-sounding, possibly bill-snapping sounds (visual signals described below). **Duetting** Probably present and poorly developed, ♀ responding with harsh calls, but requires confirmation. **Territorial advertisement** Song of ♂ a long powerful series of repeated brief phrases, usually 2–3 notes separated by silences, with emphasis on last note of each phrase: *titiwit...titiwit...* Other calls tuneless, repeated upslurred notes, gradually ascending scale and becoming shorter, higher-pitched with metallic-sounding clicks: *chewy-chewy-chewy...chui-chui...teesy-teesy...ticlik...ticlik.* Both sexes also give melodious rapid disyllabic *tuwick* or *chuick-chuick* whistles. ♀ believed to respond (duet?) to ♂ with churring or rasping notes (very upright stance, remains motionless except for characteristic slow swinging of tail from side to side). **Territorial threat** Unknown. **Alarm** While mobbing gives harsh grating screams. **Courtship** Both sexes call on the wing. Known to make insect-like rasping trill *prrrt* at the nest (both sexes give slow display-flight with rapid wingbeats resulting in rhythmic droning ('wing-fripping'?) while calling on the wing. Courtship-feeding unknown). **Contact** Both sexes give repeated thin high-pitched penetrating *tseee-* or *zit-zit-* whistles and harsh nasal *tsit* sounds. Flight call a rolling *tsrrrt* (probably with body movements). **Roosting** and **Begging** Unknown (probably crouched wing-fluttering)

Relationships

The taxonomic history of *Megabyas* is similar to *Bias*, in which it is sometimes submerged[95, 116, 204, 481]. This is supported by the observation that their skulls are similar, except that the bill is hooked and shrike-like and not as flat as in *Bias*[456]. However, the ecology, morphology, social organisation and general behaviour, flight and vocalisations of *flammulatus* are sufficiently different to *musicus* for it to be retained in its own genus[16, 18, 180, 431, 456, 610, 676]. This view is supported here. Its communication behaviour suggests its closest relative is *Bias*. Its relationship to other malaconotids is obscure, primarily because of the lack of comparative characters. It appears to be related to wattle-eyes (*Platysteira* and *Dyaphorophyia*) and batises (*Batis*).

Bias (Crested Flycatcher-shrike) Plate 29

Species: *musicus*

Basic structure Loud percussive whistles and harsh notes (visual signals described below). **Duetting** Probably occurs. **Territorial advertisement** Calls while perched, but more often in flight. Song a repeated, variable sequence of few loud whistles and sharp percussive notes: *wit-ti-tu* or *tiewp-tiewp-*. Also has longer *Hweeet* or descending *cheeeyuw* sounds. May begin or end with harsh rattling *churrr* or *Tchzz* notes and repeated *chi-* sounds. ♀ call a long rasping *kchchew,* possibly in duet. (Display-flight involves shallow, slow wingbeats, exposing white wing-patches, crest erect and rump fluffed out.) **Territorial threat** Phrases longer, speeds up and rises in pitch. Sequence ending often prolonged. At higher intensity, ends song with lower-pitched *tyew-tyiew,* first note sharply downslurred. Both sexes give guttural notes followed by descending grating *zzrrr* call (♂ perches exposed in upright posture, crest erect, neck extended, flicks wings and wags head from side to side while calling; followed by display-flight). When anxious, crouches in hunched posture, sleeks plumage, lowers flattened head and extends neck forward. **Alarm** Harsh swearing call, also gives buzzy bill-clashing like *Chlorophoneus* and bill-snapping (stretches legs and body up, erects crest, jerkily flicks both wings, nervously fans outer tail feathers). **Courtship** Similar to territorial threat. While nest-building calls *che-chick-choo* or *chip, we-chip* repeatedly. (♂ display similar to territorial flight-song, except wingbeats slower in circling, swooping flight around ♀. ♂ displays white underparts and fluffed-out rump. In nest selection, crouches, neck and head horizontal, spreads forward, quivers wings and fluffs out rump. ♂ escorts ♀ back and forth during nest-building, gives display-flights. Only ♀ builds. Courtship-feeding unknown, but predicted to be present. **Contact** Loud calls. (Greeting display includes song and acrobatic display-flights by ♂. ♀ perches exposed, upright, bill up, flicks wing-tips, wags tail, then crouches in horizontal posture, fans and closes outer-tail feathers in jerky manner, bobs head up and down.) **Roosting** Gives song from exposed perch, followed by loud scolding territorial song. (♂ leads, makes steep spiral glides above roost site. Joined by ♀ then young, which roost apart from adults.) **Begging** Long nasal call. Fledglings and immatures give similar ♀ rasping *kchchew* call (probably begs with crouched wing-fluttering).

Relationships

This little-known enigmatic genus, although consistently associated with flycatchers, has variously been placed in the family Muscicapidae[180, 610], Platysteiridae[95, 206], Malaconotidae[205], or subfamilies of these, such as the Monarchinae of Muscicapidae[18]. It is most closely related to *Megabyas,* with which it is sometimes considered conspecific (see *Megabyas*)[95, 116, 204, 481]. Its relationships to other malaconotids remain obscure, primarily because of the lack of comparative characters. It shares general and communication behavioural characters with some other malaconotids, particularly wattle-eyes (*Platysteira* and *Dyaphorophyia*) and batises (*Batis*)[95, 205, 676].

Philentoma (Philentomas) Plate 29

Species: *velatum*, *pyrhopterum*

Basic structure Little known; in one species, loud clear whistles and harsh grating notes with batis and bush-shrike quality, in the other, soft disyllabic whistles (visual signals little known). **Duetting** Unknown. **Territorial advertisement** In one species, long descending series of slowly repeated ringing whistles, varying in pitch and repetition rate, from high-pitch *he---he---he-* to lower *ho---ho---ho-* or disyllabic *hwee-*. In the other, slow soft disyllabic *hweeet---hweeet-* or faster *hwee-hwee-*. Context of harsh metallic sounds unknown (one species (*velatum*) has rather hunched calling posture, the other flicks wings slightly when perched). **Territorial threat** Unknown, except makes 'fripping' sounds in flight, presumably when excited. **Alarm** Harsh calls vary from grating metallic churrs, scraping *Zrrr-* and a loud squirrel-like *chuk-uk* probably given in this context. Bill-snapping unknown. **Courtship**, **Contact** and **Roosting** Unknown (courtship-feeding unknown). **Begging** High-pitched repeated *tzeet-tzeet-* (probably crouched wing-fluttering).

Relationships

The two species in this genus were originally placed in the genus *Drymophila*; however, this name being preoccupied, they were assigned to *Philentoma*. It was long thought to be a member of the flycatcher family Muscicapidae, and later to belong with the monarch flycatchers in the family Monarchidae[116]. Although poorly known anatomically, cranial and long-bone characters are similar to other malaconotids, and like some bush-shrikes it exhibits polymorphism[500]. Recent DNA-DNA hybridisation studies have shown it to be a vangine not a monarchine[184]. This places it in an assemblage with wood-shrikes, vangas, helmet-shrikes, batises and wattle-eyes. The genus is included in this book on this evidence. Both species are little known. Their whistled calls are reminiscent of batises *Batis*, boubous *Laniarius* and small forest canopy bush-shrikes *Chlorophoneus*.

Nilaus (Brubru) Plate 30

Species: *afer*

Basic structure Variably pitched whistled trill, repeated disyllabic whistles, drawn-out squeaky high-pitched call, combined with chattering, harsh rasping and nasal sounds (visual signals described below). **Duetting** Poorly developed, ♀ duets irregularly with higher-pitched call. **Territorial advertisement** ♂ gives monotonously repeated loud whistled trills of varying pitch and repetition rate, from high-pitched *prrrriiii* to lower-pitched, slower *b-r-r-r-u-u-u-u*. ♀ duets with few high-pitched squeaky *eeeu* sounds (posture upright, throat expanded, tail slightly fanned, crest raised slightly and white eyebrow expanded. ♀ fans tail while calling). **Territorial threat** Rapidly repeated short high-pitched trills combined with excited 'wing-fripping' and frequent *eeeu-eeeu* duetting by ♀. Counter-singing common (bowing, tail flicking, rapid side to side body movements, and zigzag display-flights with exaggerated wingbeats, usually accompanied by loud 'wing-fripping'; ♀ responds in duet while flicking tail open and closed and bowing rapidly). **Alarm** Rapidly repeated chattering *chiK-chiK-* and harsh rasping *tzzrr* sounds. **Courtship** ♂ gives repeated trilling whistle and repeated high-pitched disyllabic *tuet-tuet-* and *weep-weep-* whistles with food in the bill. ♂ gives trill before and after copulation (a report of ♂ bowing to ♀ probably given in this context; courtship-feeding unknown, but thought probably to occur). **Contact** Duetting and in non-breeding season also a repeated, penetrating high-pitched *piep-piep-* whistle. At short range gives repeated single *tu* or disyllabic *tu-wit* calls (probably with body movements). **Roosting** Unknown. **Begging** Unknown (probably crouched wing-fluttering).

Relationships

Nilaus is an enigmatic genus with puzzling relationships, as evident in its taxonomic history. It has variously been placed in the Laniidae, Malaconotidae, Prionopidae and Muscicapidae[2, 20, 205, 289, 610, 612, 894]. Its batis-like plumage, helmet-shrike-like tarsal scutellation and nest, and true shrike-like bill, juvenile plumage and behaviour have fuelled the debate.

It is generally rather poorly known, and has received little attention in anatomical studies; however, it shares similar hindlimb musculature, cranial and long-bone characters with other members of the Malaconotidae[500, 901, 918].

Its communication behaviour, although poorly known, conforms to the general malaconotid plan. However, it is unparalleled in the family with its loud rapid trilling whistles. The only other genera which have trilling components, although lower-pitched, are *Telophorus* and *Tchagra*. DNA-DNA hybridisation studies suggest a closer relationship with *Laniarius*[184].

Lanioturdus (White-tailed Shrike) Plate 30

Species: *torquatus*

Basic structure Loud penetrating high-pitched whistles, often as a descending crescendo or with explosive quality. Combined with harsh churring, tearing, nasal and ratchet notes (visual signals described below). **Duetting** Fairly well developed, ♀ responds with harsh notes. **Territorial advertisement** Repeated clear *huuuu, poo-eee* or descending crescendo *heeeU* whistles. ♀ duets irregularly with harsh churring *kirrrrr* or tearing *tchzeeu* sounds (both sexes stretch neck, expose breast and raise bill while calling). **Territorial threat** Rapidly repeated whistles, counter-singing and harsh ratchet *Chuk-K-K-KKK,* nasal *kzzzp-* or *krrank-* sounds by ♂, responded in duet with *ktchzrrr* sounds by ♀ (adopts crouched horizontal posture in threat, glaring at the intruder). **Alarm** At low intensity, repeated *Chuk-* or *Tok-* and stuttering nasal *chiKchiK-*; at high intensity harsh *TzuK-, Cha-* and explosive *Skzeer-* sounds. **Courtship** In display-flight ♂ gives repeated *tchuee-tchuee-* whistles combined with 'wing-fripping'. Pairs indulge in rapid duets (display-flight consists of steep upward climb, followed by descending, jerky glide with rump fluffed out; courtship-feeding apparently absent but ♂ feeds ♀ during breeding. **Contact** Duetting at long range, hollow metallic *chink-* at close range near nest (probably with body movements). **Roosting** Repeated *Tok-Tok-* sounds (roost separately in canopy of larger trees). **Begging** Nestlings give soft high-pitched *seee-seee-*, fledglings *cheerr-* sounds (probably crouched wing-fluttering).

Relationship

Lanioturdus, as its name suggests, is an enigmatic genus with puzzling relationships, as evident in its taxonomic history. Although this strange-looking species, with its disproportionately long legs and short tail was originally believed to be a bush-shrike, it has also been placed with the flycatchers in Muscicapidae, or with the wattle-eyes in the genus *Platysteira.* It shares many similarities with this and the genus *Batis,* including jaw musculature[92, 180, 205, 490, 676, 897]. In addition, its eggs resemble those of helmet-shrikes[590]. Traditionally it has been associated with *Prionops* and/or *Nilaus*[3, 16, 206, 207, 610], or with *Malaconotus* (including *Chlorophoneus*)[168]. Cranial and long-bone characters are similar to other members of the family[490, 500]. General and communication behaviour confirms its inclusion in Malaconotidae[205]. Based on communication behaviour, it appears most closely related to *Laniarius.*

Batis (Batises) Plate 31–34

Species: *capensis, margaritae, mixta, fratrum, pririt, molitor, soror, senegalensis, orientalis, perkeo, minor, minulla, poensis, minima, diops, ituriensis*

Basic structure Series of repeated, short whistled notes by ♂, usually interspersed with harsh notes by ♀. ♂ whistles rather similar, either low-pitched or medium- to high-pitched. Series of two types: long (>*c.*10 notes) and short (<*c.*10 notes), given at the same or descending pitch. Some species capable of interspecific song-matching. Ecologically separable into three groups; mainly eastern forest species (EFS), mainly western and central forest species (WFS) and savanna woodland species (SWS) (visual signals described below). **Duetting** Poorly developed, ♀ responding erratically with harsh notes. **Territorial advertisement** Repeated whistles by ♂. EFS have low-pitched, slowly repeated *hu--hu-* notes, which in WFS are high-pitched *eep--eep-* or faster *hehehehe-* notes, and in SWS variable medium- or high-pitched, short descending *he-ho-hu* series and/or long series at same or descending pitch. ♀ duets with churring and *jirrowirrowirr-* chuntering in EFS and *Wik* in WFS and SWS. (♂ calls from exposed perch, body inclined, head up, throat expanding, tail fanned and flicked.) **Territorial threat** Repeated whistles and flight song. In SWS and probably WFS, includes whistles, croaking frog-like *grrruu-*, rolling *prrreeo* trills, nasal *querk* and buzzy *zzurri* sounds. In EFS, faster whistles and repeated chuntering, churrs and nasal calls often with emphasised *jrreeE* ending. Display in all groups accompanied by bill-snapping and loud 'wing-fripping'. (In flight, head up, flies excitedly in circular or zigzag motion, crown and rump erected. When perched head and/or body swayed from side to side, body bowed, tail fanned, flicked and swung. May stand very upright, bill up, breast and crown plumage fluffed out and wrists exposed. Full threat, crouches, crown ruffled, wrists exposed, back hunched, tail half-spread and bill pointing at opponent.) **Alarm** Harsh chattering *chiKchiK-*, bill-snapping and 'wing-fripping'. **Courtship** Little known; similar to territorial threat. (Excited display flying with rump fluffed out. EFS on landing flash white-spotted rump feathers, raise wings slightly above back, then droop them. Courtship-feeding present.) **Contact** Various short, abrupt *chik* and *tsit* notes and churrs (probably with body movements). **Roosting** Alarm chattering. **Begging** Loud high-pitched buzzing *ksshkissh-* chatter (crouched wing-fluttering).

Relationships

The genus *Batis* is characterised by great uniformity in appearance and behaviour. There is little consensus on its relationships, being traditionally placed in the flycatcher family Muscicapidae[18, 610,] or Platysteiridae[116, 204, 431, 481,] or in various subfamilies. For example in the Monarchinae or Platysteirinae of Muscicapidae[95, 291, 893,] or as the subfamily Malaconotinae of Laniidae[16, 205.] DNA-DNA hybridisation studies also place it in the subfamily Malaconotinae, but of the family Corvidae in an enlarged superfamily Corvoidea. Their subfamily Malaconotinae also includes bush-shrikes, helmet-shrikes, wood-shrikes, philentomas, wattle-eyes and vangas[184.]

There is little consensus on species limits and relationships within this African genus[180, 287, 431, 481.] It can be divided into three groups, based mainly on ecology, plumage, eye colour and communication behaviour: (i) species mainly inhabiting eastern and southern forests (EFS); (ii) species mainly inhabiting western and central forests, forest edge and rich, moderately moist woodlands (WFS); and (iii) mainly savanna woodland species (SWS). The five mainly eastern and southern forest species constitute a well-defined group, which has usually been considered to form a single superspecies, comprising Cape *B. capensis*, Forest *B. mixta*, Woodwards' *B. fratrum*, Margaret's *B. margaritae* and Ruwenzori Batis *B. diops*[180, 676.] The four mainly western and central forest species (WFS) constitute a less well-defined group, but which have white underwing-coverts and yellow eyes. It consists of Gabon *B. minima*, Angola *B. minulla* and Bioko Batis *B. poensis*. These three having a similar communication system. Although the communication system of the Ituri Batis *B. ituriensis* is unknown, its vocalisations are predicted to be the same as the other three members of this group. Some authors consider Gabon and Ituri to form one superspecies, with Angola and Bioko Batis as independent[676;] others consider all four to form a superspecies with the Black-headed Batis *B. minor*[180.] The remaining seven mainly savanna woodland species also have yellow eyes, but have dark underwing-coverts. Their communication behaviour is similar. They comprise Chinspot *B. molitor*, Black-headed *B. minor*, Mozambique *B. soror*, Pririt *B. pririt*, Senegal *B. senegalensis*, Grey-headed *B. orientalis* and Pygmy Batis *B. perkeo*. These have variously been considered as a single superspecies, excluding Black-headed Batis[180,] or as two superspecies (Chinspot/Mozambique and Grey-headed/Senegal) with three independent species (Black-headed, Pririt and Pygmy)[431,] or with Chinspot, Mozambique and probably Pririt forming one superspecies, and Grey-headed forming another with Senegal or Black-headed[481.] Alternatively, Senegal, Grey-headed, Chinspot, Mozambique and Pririt are thought to form a superspecies, with Pygmy and Black-headed independently distinct[676.] A mathematical analysis of plumage characters concluded that Mozambique and Pririt were very close to each other and close to Chinspot, and that Black-headed and Grey-headed are close, but that Pygmy and Senegal are independently distinct[286.] Based on communication behaviour these batises form at least two groups, one formed by Chinspot and Black-headed, the other by Mozambique, Grey-headed, Pririt, Pygmy and Senegal (see Appendix A).

Traditionally batises are thought to be most closely related to wattle-eyes (*Platysteira* and *Dyaphorophyia*) and flycatcher-shrikes (*Bias* and *Megabyas*). This relationship is supported by communication behaviour and DNA-DNA hybridisation results[184, 205.]

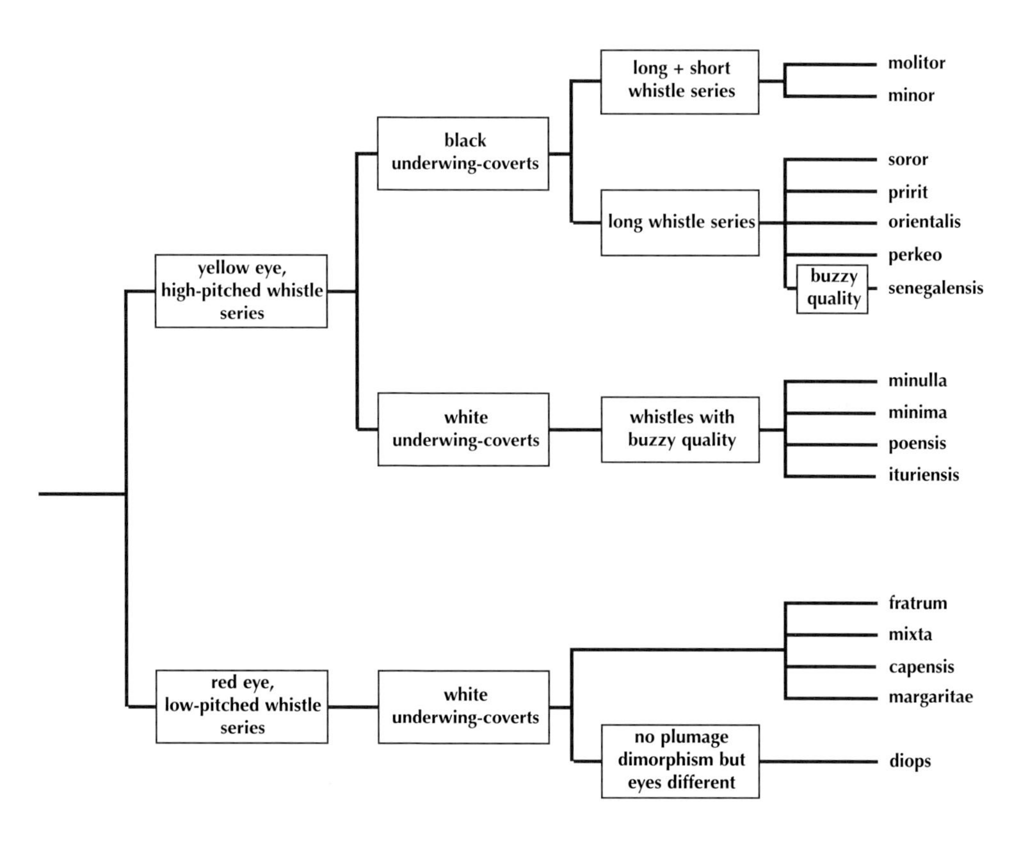

Map of some communication characteristics of Batis

Dyaphorophyia (Small wattles) Plate 36–38

Species: *tonsa*, *castanea*, *blissetti*, *jamesoni*, *chalybea*, *concreta*

Basic structure Not well understood; series of repeated short whistles and variety of wheezing, bleating, grating, grunting, nasal, hollow and frog-like sounds. Some explosive, others with whip-lash quality. Sexes indulge in same-sex countersinging which may develop into a chorus (visual signals described below). **Duetting** Not recorded for certain, requires confirmation. **Territorial advertisement** Usually series of repeated short *hu-* or *he-*, disyllabic *tlet-* or trisyllabic *tututu* and longer series, given at a constant or descending pitch. One species (*castanea*) has tinkerbird-like repeated *tlop-* whistle, another (*jamesoni*) a mechanical-sounding *wippy* note (exposed, crest raised, upright posture, bill up, wattles swollen, also jerky upward movements of head and neck). **Territorial threat** In display-flight, varied; hollow *tok-* notes, grunting or guttural frog-like notes with explosive ending *wuK!* or *gwoK!*, explosive notes, *ptick-kwow*, whiplash *pkwup* or ascending *TuuE!zzglU*, nasal *Gruuk* and others. Combined with loud bill-snapping and whirring 'wing-fripping' (crest erect, upright posture, exposed throat and breast, rump fluffed out and wattles erect, turns head while calling). **Alarm** Rapid series of popping *pop-pop-*, chattering *chichi-* and other harsh rasping sounds, combined with bill-snapping and 'wing-fripping'. **Courtship** Similar to territorial threat, includes repeated piercing *slit-slit-* whistle and nasal *ptooee-* sounds. (Both sexes dart back and forth at great speed, ♂ flies around ♀, also crouches, bows, fluffs out rump, droops wings, expands wattles and swoops down in front of ♀. Display appears similar to *Platysteira*. Courtship-feeding present.) **Contact** Short *pec*, *wop* or *wuk* sounds (pair members remain close together). **Roosting** unknown. **Begging** Harsh, often nasal *naaat-* and *kchay-kchay-* sounds (crouched wing-fluttering).

Relationships

The history of the relationships of *Dyaphorophyia* is similar to *Platysteira* and *Batis* (see Relationships under *Batis*). Some authors unite this genus with *Platysteira*[3, 95, 116, 180, 204, 207, 481], others retain it in its original genus[92, 338, 431, 456, 471, 631]. The latter approach is supported here on the basis of distinct morphology and behaviour. Traditionally these small *Dyaphorophyia* wattle-eyes are thought to be most closely related to the larger *Platysteira* wattle-eyes, batises (*Batis*) and flycatcher-shrikes (*Bias* and *Megabyas*). This relationship is supported by communication behaviour and DNA-DNA hybridisation studies[184]. Like other malaconotids, males of at least one species exhibit polymorphism[471].

Species limits within the genus are controversial, particularly with respect to the little-known Jameson's *D. jamesoni* and Red-cheeked Wattle-eye *D. blissetti*. These are morphologically and behaviourally very similar, but their ranges are separated by the distinctive Black-necked Wattle-eye *D. chalybea*. Although many authors consider these three conspecific[3, 16, 289], others believe they are distinct species[116, 431, 481, 610], or allospecies[207]. Jameson's and Red-cheeked Wattle-eyes are here retained as separate species for convenience, until additional comparative information is available.

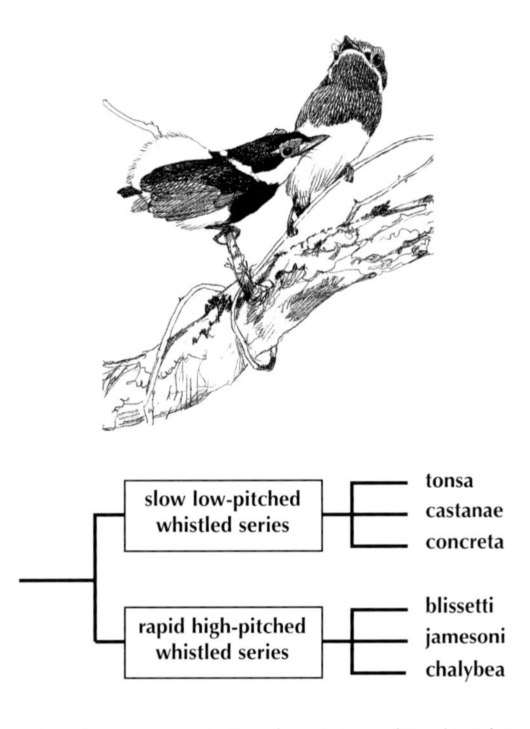

Map of some communication characteristics of Dyaphorophyia

Platysteira (Large wattle-eyes) Plate 36–38

Species: *laticincta*, *peltata*, *cyanea*, *albifrons*

Basic structure Not well understood; repeated series of whistles at same or descending pitch, combined with short harsh or buzzy notes, many indescribable. Phrase begins simply and becomes more complex. Apparently both sexes produce similar calls (visual signals described below). **Duetting** Present and fairly well developed, ♀ response erratic. **Territorial advertisement** Rapid long series of repeated monosyllabic *wich-wich-* and disyllabic *wichy-wichy-* whistles combined with short harsh repeated *zit-*, churring and batis-like chuntering or rasping notes. ♀ duets with similar repeated *weech-* or *zurr-* calls. Some species also have a repeated short descending series of *he-her-her-huu* whistles. (♂ usually calls from exposed perch, body inclined, head up, throat expanding with each call, head swayed slowly from side to side, and tail slightly fanned.) **Territorial threat** Similar to advertisement, but series faster, longer, and higher-pitched. Also includes various difficult-to-describe repeated rasping, nasal, repeated buzzy *jutzy-* sounds, often in duet. Combined with bill-snapping and 'wing-fripping' (bow and oscillate rapidly from side to side, give rapid zigzag display-flights with rump fluffed out; brightly coloured wattles enlarged and crest raised). **Alarm** Rapidly repeated harsh, rasping *chit-chit-* sounds with bill-snapping and 'wing-fripping'. **Courtship** Little known, appears similar to territorial threat. (Similar to territorial threat, includes dipping and hovering flights around ♀. Prior to copulation ♂ fluffs out rump. Courtship-feeding present.) **Contact** Short sharp *juk* or *zuk* (probably body movements). **Roosting** Unknown. **Begging** Repeated *chchchch-* or *tzrray-* chatter (crouched wing-fluttering).

Relationships

The history of relationships in *Platysteira* are similar to *Batis* (see Relationships under *Batis*). Relationships and species limits are not well understood, particularly since two of the four species are little known. The genus is generally believed to comprise a single superspecies, formed of Black-throated *P. peltata*, Banded *P. laticincta*, Brown-throated *P. cyanea* and White-fronted Wattle-eye *P. albifrons*[180]. The specific status of Banded Wattle-eye is controversial: it is believed by some authors to be conspecific with Black-throated Wattle-eye[3, 16, 180, 338, 431, 481, 676], while others retain it as a separate species[116, 610]. It is here tentatively retained as a separate species on the basis of differing calls and external morphology. Traditionally the large *Platysteira* wattle-eyes are thought to be most closely related to the smaller *Dyaphorophyia* wattle-eyes, batises (*Batis*) and flycatcher-shrikes (*Bias* and *Megabyas*). This relationship is supported by communication behaviour and DNA-DNA hybridisation results[184, 205].

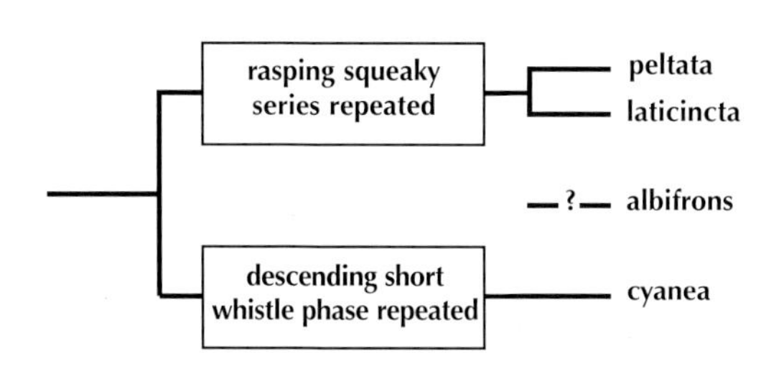

Map of some communication characteristics of Platysteira

Prionops (Helmet-shrikes) Plates 39–41

Species: *plumatus, poliolophus, retzii, gabela, scopifrons, caniceps, alberti*

Basic structure Complex, but generally little known; sounds generally have a nasal quality with phrases combining whistle notes, often disyllabic, with rolling, gobbling, twittering, buzzing, chattering, churring and growling sounds, some rather crow-like. Calls usually given in duet and chorus, often combined with bursts of rapid bill-snapping. Choruses variable, mostly of descending sequences which begin fast, high-pitched and complex, and end slower, lower-pitched and simple, often with a gobbling or rolling quality. This sequence appears reversed in one species. Calling initiated by dominant birds (visual signals described below). **Duetting** Very well developed; includes chorusing. **Territorial advertisement** Uncertain (appear to advertise mainly with visual signals, birds being highly visible when moving). **Territorial threat** Performed by the group in chorus singing. Most species begin with rapid short *tz-tz-* notes followed by rolling *Jor-rrreeeea* and *cherow-* sounds, then buzzy *zrrreeeeu-* and growling *gruu-* or *goo-ria-* notes, finally ending with slower rolling *kloop-* or *chirro-roe* sounds. One species has a repeated shrill and clear *tlu-uk*, possibly given in this context. 'Wing-fripping' recorded in one species (*caniceps*). (Group members bunch together, heads and necks stretched upwards, tail fanned. May fluff out rump and body feathers and raise crest. This accompanied by at least two displays, varying between species. Include either slow, side to side head-swaying, or exaggerated body-bowing, rocking back and forwards, wings held slightly open. May give slow fluttering flights with body feathers fluffed out. At high intensity has upright posture, crest raised and bill opened in threat. Swoop and dive-bomb predators and rival groups.) **Alarm** Rapid bursts of bill-snapping, low growlng sounds, and at higher intensity, sharp *ZeeZee-* screams and squeals. **Courtship** Little known, generally performed in silence, or at most with subdued begging calls (in two species involves slow body posturing, wings held away from body, usually drooped and slowly flapped. Courtship-feeding apparently absent, but confirmation required). **Contact** Includes chorusing and greeting calls like *chairrer-, cherow-* and *Jor-rreeea,* also soft nasal notes, bill-snapping and repeated high-pitched *zit-zit-* sounds in flight. **Roosting** Low growls and chuckling sounds (huddle together on branch). **Begging** Chattering or buzzing *tzzrrree-* (in adults and young, crouched wing-fluttering).

Relationships

The genus was originally split into *Prionops* and *Sigmodus* and placed in its own family Prionopidae, along with 18 other genera. It is interesting to note that originally *Nilaus, Tephrodornis* and *Eurocephalus* were part of this family, apparently on the basis of similar tarsal scutellation[202, 610]. The family was later reduced to include only *Prionops, Sigmodus* and *Eurocephalus*[206, 612]. Originally *Prionops* included only those helmet-shrikes with conspicuous frontal feathers and black bill, such as White *P. plumatus* and Grey-crested Helmet-shrike *P. poliolophus.* Yellow-crested Helmet-shrike *P. alberti* probably also fits here[180]. Members of *Sigmodus* lack prominent frontal feathers and have reddish bills. It was made up of Retz's *P. retzii,* Chestnut-fronted *P. scopifrons* and Chestnut-bellied Helmet-shrike *P. caniceps*[610]. The Gabela Helmet-shrike *P. gabela* probably also fits here[180]. Some authors maintain these as separate genera[16], but most unite them in *Prionops*[3, 206, 207, 431, 481]. Interestingly, there is a difference in jaw musculature between the two genera, specifically between Chestnut-bellied and White Helmet-shrike[897]. In addition Chestnut-bellied Helmet-shrike nestlings have two bare patches of skin on the head which have not been described in other helmet-shrike nestlings[683].

Relationships within the genus remain largely unknown, primarily because of a lack of detailed studies, but also because obvious differences in individual species recognition appear to be masked by a complex convergent communication system based on a cooperative social organisation. Relationships based on external morphology suggest that the genus comprises a species group of White, Grey-crested and Yellow-crested Helmet-shrike, a superspecies of Retz's and Gabela Helmet-shrike, and the two independently distant Chestnut-bellied and Chestnut-fronted Helmet-shrike[180].

Relationships of this genus to other malaconotids are not well understood and opinions show little consensus. It has been placed between the true shrikes and bush-shrikes[205, 206], between the vangas and bush-shrikes[431, 610], between the bulbuls (Pycnonotidae) and bush-shrikes[481], or between the cuckoo-shrikes (Campephagidae) and some bush-shrikes[16]. DNA-DNA hybridisation studies suggest it is closely related to wood-shrikes and vangas, within an assemblage which also includes the philentomas, batises and wattle-eyes[184]. This is supported by anatomical and behavioural, including communication characters[288, 232, 500, 897].

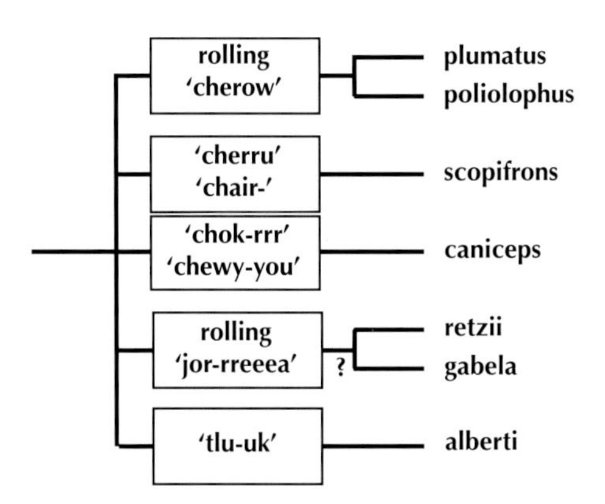

Map of some communication characteristics of Prionops

GLOSSARY[570, 693]

Alar tract: pertaining to the wing.
Albinistic (albinism): lacking pigment.
Allopatric: refers to the geographical distribution of species occurring in different places without overlap.
Allopreening: the preening of one bird by another, usually of the same species. Preening is the arrangement, cleaning, and general maintenance of plumage using the bill.
Altitude migration (movement): seasonal migration or movement from one altitude to another.
Alula: also known as the 'bastard wing'; consists of small feathers attached to the first digit.
Arboreal: living in trees.
Austral: of the southern hemisphere.
Axillaries: feathers in the 'armpit' between the the body and the wing.
Boreal: of the northern hemisphere.
Brood division: the behaviour in a breeding pair whereby each adult cares for specific young in the brood.
Brood parasitism: the laying of eggs of one species in the nest of another species, with subsequent care for the parasite young provided by the host. Usually interspecific, occasionally intraspecific.
Call-up: tape recorded or mimicked sounds used to attract birds.
Carpals: small bones of 'wrist', forming the forward-pointing prominence of the folded wing.
Caudal: pertaining to the tail.
Cline (clinal): a geographic gradient in a certain character.
Congeneric: of the same genus.
Conspecific: of the same species.
Cooperative breeding: the phenomenon of non-breeding birds attending the nest of breeding members of their species and carrying out some or all of the behaviours performed by the adults.
Counter-singing: singing in rivalry with another male.
Density: the number of units (individuals or pairs) per unit area.
Ecotone: a habitat created by the juxtaposition of different habitats.
Endemic: confined to a restricted area.
Endogenous: concerned with internal mechanisms.
Fledging success: either the average number of offspring fledged per family, or the percentage of hatchlings that fledge.
Fledgling: a bird that has recently fledged.
Frontal: forehead (see Topography—frontal band).
Genotype: the total genetic message found in a cell or an individual (see Phenotype).
Hatching success: percentage of eggs that hatch.
Habitat: the particular environment, consisting of fauna, flora, soil and climate, occupied by a particular organism and to which it is adapted.
Holarctic: faunal region of the northern hemisphere north of the tropics, combining the Palearactic and Nearctic regions.
Home range: an area to which an individual restricts most of its activity, and from which intruders are not excluded.
Immature: not adult; term used to describe a variety of plumage stages following Juvenile. Often includes juvenile stage if precise age not known; Sub-adult sometimes used for later stages.
Juvenile: the first feathered plumage after down plumage. Sometimes used to distinguish young, as opposed to adult plumage. In some species it is indistinguishable from Immature plumage.
Kleptoparasitism: the robbing of birds of other species of their prey; piracy.
Loop migration: a migration pattern in which the autumn migration pathway differs from the pathway in spring.
Lores: the area on the sides of the face between the base of the upper mandible and the eye.
Monotypic: a term applied to a taxon that has only one unit in the immediately subordinate category, e.g. a genus with only one species.
Morph: a specific form or colour condition in a polymorphic species.
Nearctic: North American faunal region.
Neossoptiles: term applied to natal down plumage.
Nesting success: survival of eggs or nestlings.
Niche: the environmental condition to which a species is best adapted for survival.
Nominate race: the race that bears the species name when that species is judged to be polytypic, e.g. *Lanius collaris collaris.*
Oriental: faunal region which lies mainly between 68° and 135°E and between 10°S and 32°N. Also known as the Indian region.
Paleractic: faunal region of Europe, North Africa and Asia north of the tropics. Often subdivided into E and W, the division being roughly the Ural Mts.
Phenotype: the way in which the genetic message of an individual is expressed in its morphology, physiology, and behaviour (see Genotype).

Play-back: tape recorded playback of sounds.
Polygyny: general term for mating system in which individual males regularly mate with two or more females in course of a breeding season.
Polymorphism: occurrence of more than one distinct form in a population.
Polytypic: term applied to a taxon that has more than one unit in the immediate subordinate category, e.g. a species with a number of races.
Post-breeding (moult): refers to moult taking place after breeding.
Post-juvenile (moult): refers to the plumage change from juvenile or immature to adult.
Pterylosis: the arrangement of contour feathers on the skin.
Race: subpopulation within a species that is distinguishable by one or more morphological characteristics and, sometimes, by physiological or behavioural characteristics.
Resident: inhabiting a given locality throughout the year.
Sclertotic ring: a cartilaginous ring in the eye.
SD: standard deviation (statistics)
Sedentary: not migratory.
Song-matching: singing the same song as a conspecific rival or members of a closely related species.
Species group: a group of closely related and often sympatric species.
Static marking: the behaviour of perching prominently in an exposed position. Believed to serve an advertising function.
Subadult: the last stage of Immature plumage.
Subspecies: see Race.
Sundas: islands off SE Asia. Divided into Greater Sundas (Borneo, Sumatra, Java and Bali) and Lesser Sundas (islands to the SE, including Lombok, Sumbawa, Sumba, Flores, Timor, Tanimbar and other smaller islands).
Superspecies: a group of two or more closely related species that replace each other geographically.
Sympatric: occurring in the same place (refers to the geographical distribution of species).
Taiga: northern forest belt of Scandinavia and Asia.
Territory: any area defended by one or more individuals against intrusion by others of the same or different species.
Ulna: bone of the forelimb.
Vermiculations: a dense pattern of fine wavy lines.
Wallacea: faunal region comprising the C Indonesian islands of Salawesi, the Moluccas and Lesser Sundas.
Wing formula: mainly a mathematical representation of the shape of the distal part of the wing.
Wing-fripping: mechanically produced sound made by the wings in flight.

TOPOGRAPHY

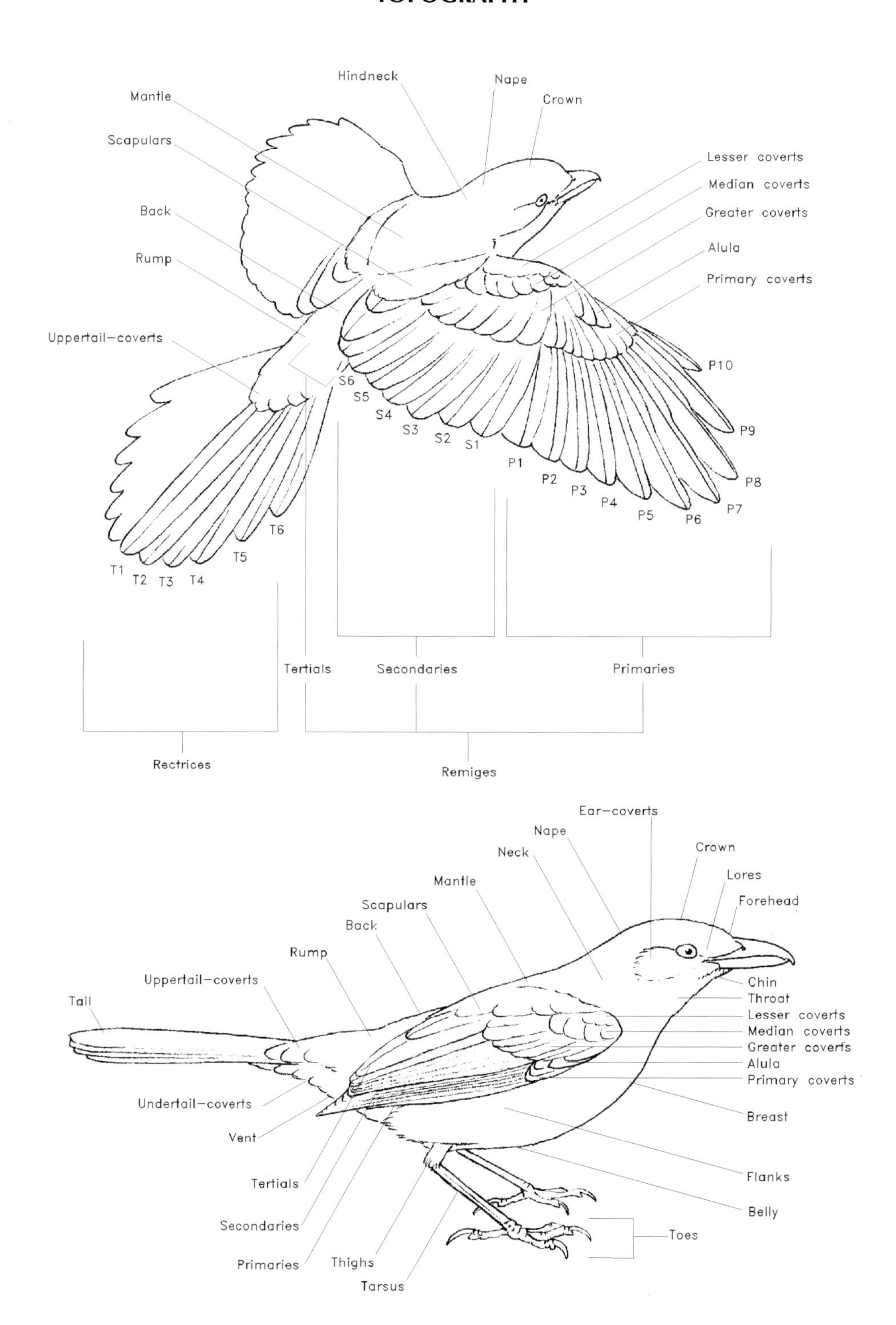

Hindneck
Nape
Mantle
Crown
Scapulars
Lesser coverts
Median coverts
Back
Greater coverts
Alula
Rump
Primary coverts
Uppertail-coverts
P10
S6
S5
S4
P9
S3
S2
S1
P1
P8
P2
P3
P7
P4
P5
P6
T6
T5
T1
T2
T3
T4
Tertials
Secondaries
Primaries
Rectrices
Remiges
Ear-coverts
Nape
Crown
Neck
Lores
Mantle
Forehead
Scapulars
Back
Rump
Uppertail-coverts
Tail
Chin
Throat
Lesser coverts
Median coverts
Greater coverts
Alula
Primary coverts
Undertail-coverts
Breast
Vent
Tertials
Flanks
Belly
Secondaries
Toes
Primaries
Thighs
Tarsus

HEADS AND PATTERNS

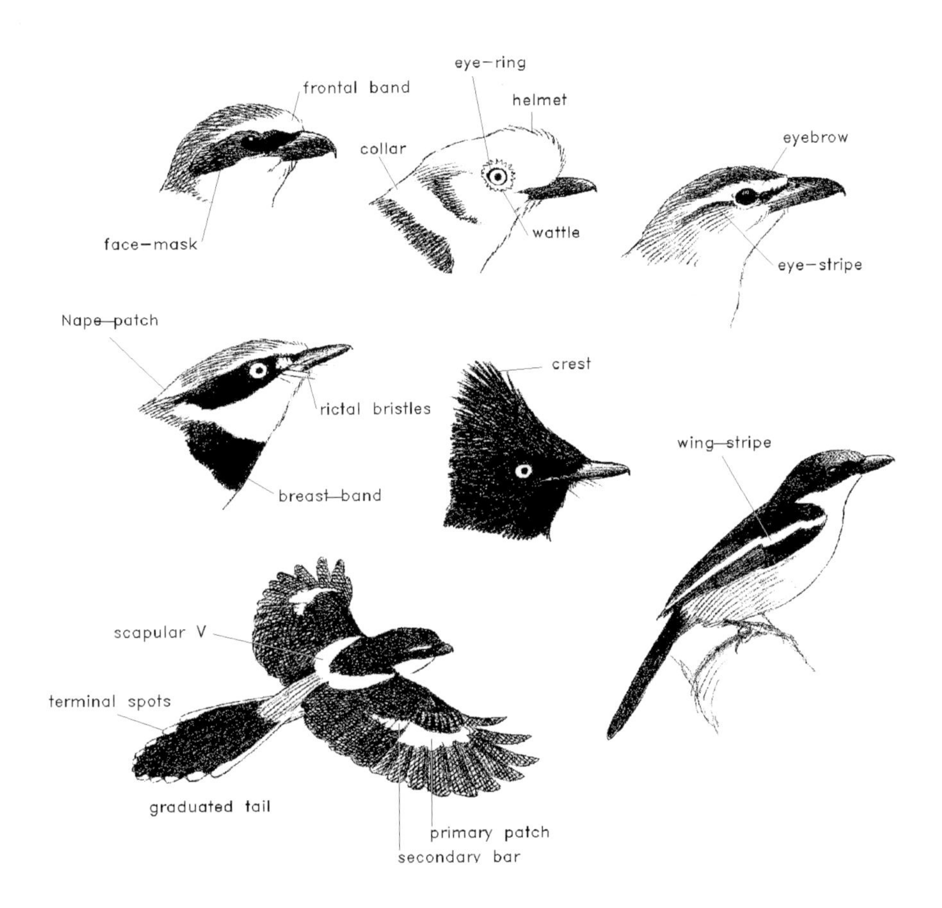

GENERA OVERVIEW

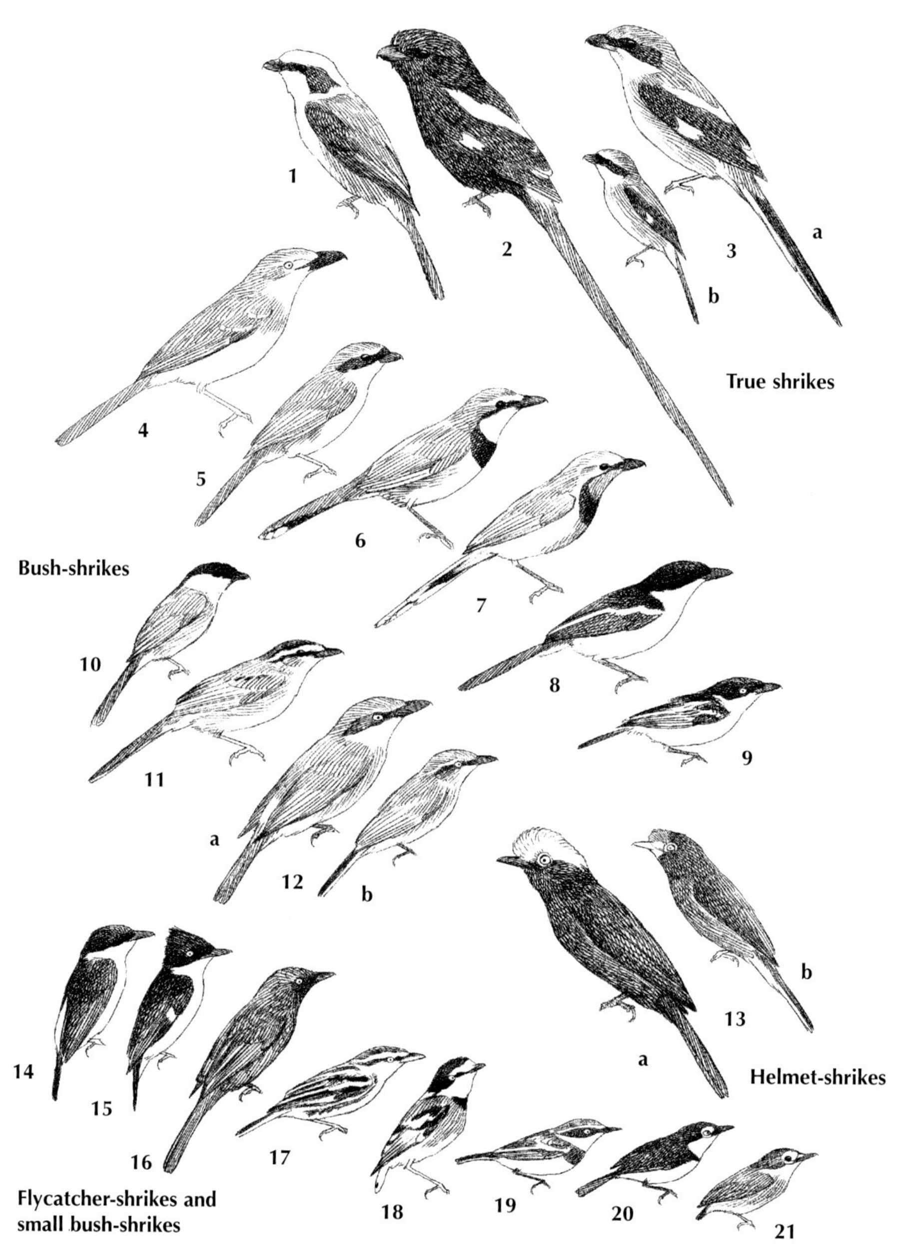

True Shrikes
1 *Eurocephalus*
2 *Corvinella*
3 *Lanius* - size range a. largest, b. smallest

Bush-shrikes
4 *Malaconotus*
5 *Chlorophoneus*
6 *Telophorus*
7 *Rhodophoneus*
8 *Laniarius*
9 *Dryoscopus*
10 *Antichromus*
11 *Tchagra*
12 *Tephrodornis* - size range a. largest, b. smallest

Helmet-shrikes
13 *Prionops* - size range a. largest, b. smallest

Flycatcher-shrikes and small bush-shrikes
14 *Megabyas*
15 *Bias*
16 *Philentoma*
17 *Nilaus*
18 *Lanioturdus*
19 *Batis*
20 *Platysteira*
21 *Dyaphorophyia*

PLATES 1–41

PLATE 1 TRUE SHRIKES 1

1 Northern White-crowned Shrike *Eurocephalus rueppelli* Text p.139

Large, sexes similar. Geographical variation slight. Gregarious, flight parrot-like, hunts from exposed perches in dry thornbush in NE and E Africa. Calls diagnostic (see Sounds).

1a Adult Distinctive. Stocky with black face-mask and ear-patches, white crown and rump diagnostic in flight. Throat, breast and belly white.
1b Juvenile Browner than adult, crown brown, lacks black ear-patches and has bill pale.

2 Southern White-crowned Shrike *Eurocephalus anguitimens* Text p.140

Large, sexes similar. Geographical variation slight. Gregarious, flight parrot-like, hunts from exposed perch in dry woodlands and thornbush in southern Africa. Calls diagnostic (see Sounds).

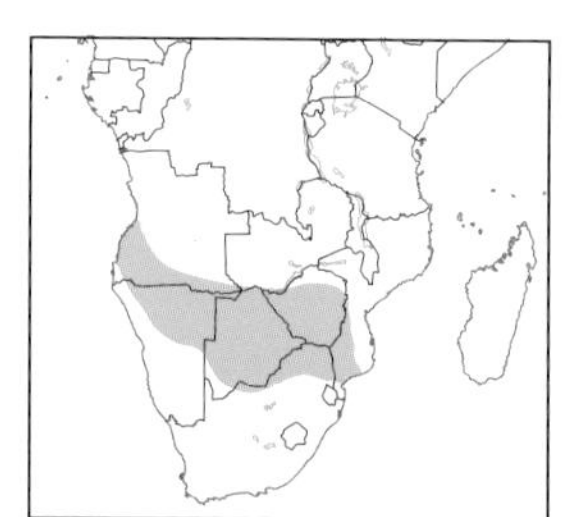

2a Adult Distinctive. Stocky with black face-mask, ear-patches and white crown. Throat and breast white, belly brown.
2b Immature Face whiter than adult, crown buffy-white, ear-patch whitish, bill pale.

3 Magpie Shrike *Corvinella melanoleuca* Text p.142

Very large, black and white with very long thin graduated tail. Sexes nearly similar. Geographical variation slight. Gregarious, performs group-bowing, wing-up displays. Hunts from exposed perches in woodland savanna in E and southern Africa. Whistled calls diagnostic (see Sounds).

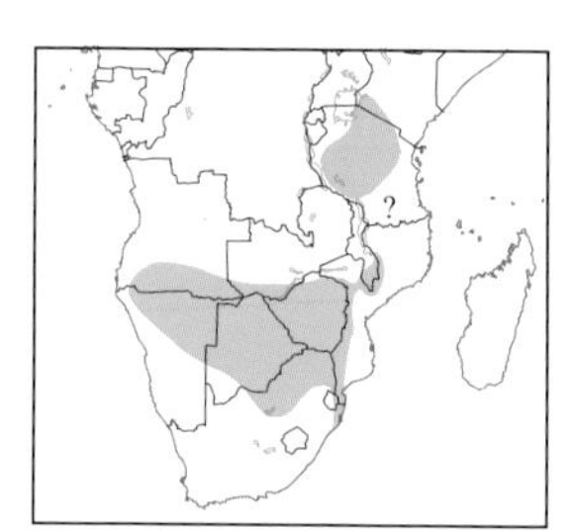

3a Adult ♂ Distinctive. In flight, black with long tail, white rump, wing-patches and V-shaped scapulars diagnostic.
3b Adult ♀ Like ♂, but with extensive white on flanks.
3c Juvenile Duller, browner, faintly barred below, and tail shorter than adult.

4 Yellow-billed Shrike *Corvinella corvina* Text p.144

Very large, distinctive, streaky brown, long tail, yellow bill and chestnut-brown wing-patches. Sexes different. Geographical variation moderate. Gregarious, often display in groups. Hunts from exposed perches in savanna woodland and thornbush. Mainly N of equator in Africa. Calls diagnostic (see Sounds).

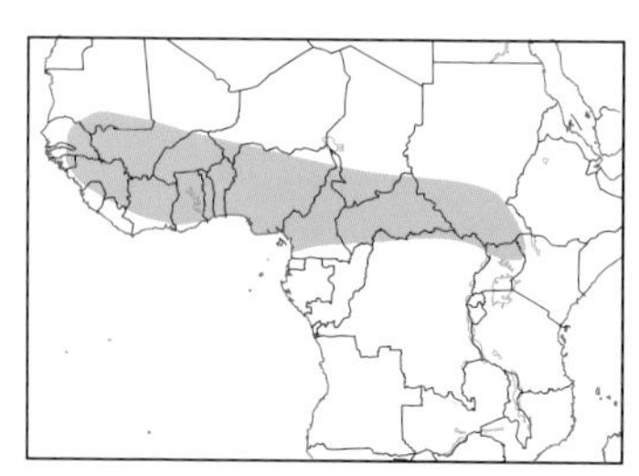

4a Adult ♂. Distinctive. In flight, pale with long tail, yellow bill and chestnut-brown wing-patches diagnostic.
4b Adult ♀. Like ♂, but with much darker maroon flanks.
4c Juvenile Duller than adult, mottled and barred (not streaked) blackish-brown above and below.

1a
1b
1a
2a
2a
2b
3a
3b
3a
3c
4a
4a
4b
4c

PLATE 2 TRUE SHRIKES 2

5 Chinese Grey Shrike *Lanius sphenocercus* **Text p.146**

Very large, sexes similar. Geographical variation marked. Solitary, hunts from exposed perches in open country with scattered trees, from E Asia in China, Russia and Korea. Boreal winter migrant in same area S to Hong Kong. Whistle call diagnostic (see Sounds). (Green stripe on yellow in map = resident or migrant.)

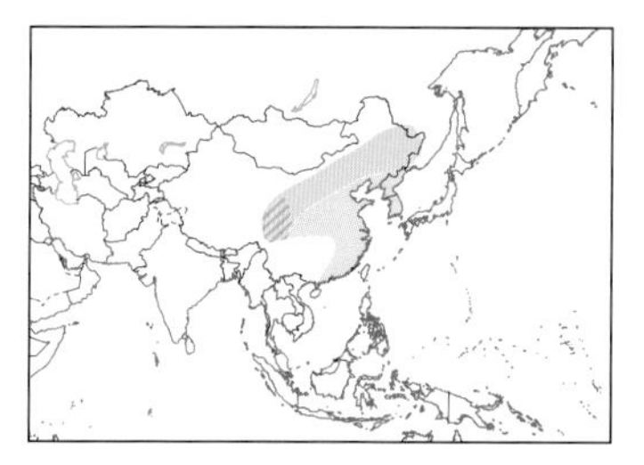

5a Adult *sphenocercus* Extensive double white wing-patch (on primaries and secondaries) and white on long, strongly graduated tail. White diagnostic in flight, often hovers. **Compare** Great Grey Shrike race *sibiricus*, somewhat similar to illustration of *borealis* (Plate 3), and Southern Grey Shrike race *pallidirostris* (Plate 4).
5b Juvenile Barred buffy-grey above, tinged buffy-white below. Wing-coverts tipped buff. Bill pale on lower mandible. **Compare** as for adult.
5c Adult *giganteus* Larger and darker than 5a, with less white in wings and tail and no white eyebrow. Underparts with slight grey tinge. At high elevations in central China and E Tibet.

6 Grey-backed Fiscal *Lanius excubitoroides* **Text p.148**

Very large, sexes different. Geographical variation slight. Gregarious, often in displaying groups. Hunts from exposed perches in thornbush from West Africa in Sahel region to NE and E Africa south to Burundi. Whistle calls diagnostic (see Sounds).

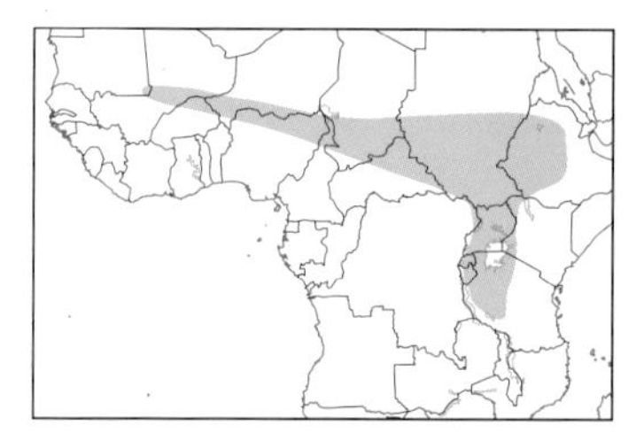

6a Adult ♂ Broad black forehead and face-mask to shoulder. Tail long with distinctive large white basal panels, black central and broad terminal band. Large white wing-patch, obvious in flight. **Compare** migrant Lesser Grey Shrike (Plate 5).
6b Adult ♀ Like ♂, but with dark chestnut-brown flanks, sometimes concealed by closed wing.
6c Juvenile Barred greyish-brown above, faintly barred below. Lacks black forehead, face-mask brownish-black. Wing-coverts tipped buff. Tail pattern like adult. Bill paler. **Compare** Long-tailed Fiscal (Plate 6) and Common Fiscal race *humeralis* (Plate 7).

5a
5a
5b
5c
6a
6a
6b
6c

PLATE 3 TRUE SHRIKES 3

7 Great Grey Shrike *Lanius excubitor* **Text p.150**

Large, sexes rather similar. Geographical variation marked. Solitary, hunts from exposed perches in wide variety of open habitats, taiga, tundra and forest edge in N and Central Europe, N and Central Asia and North America. Whistle call diagnostic, other calls like Southern Grey Shrike (see Sounds). (Blue striped area on map = presumed non-breeding distribution.)

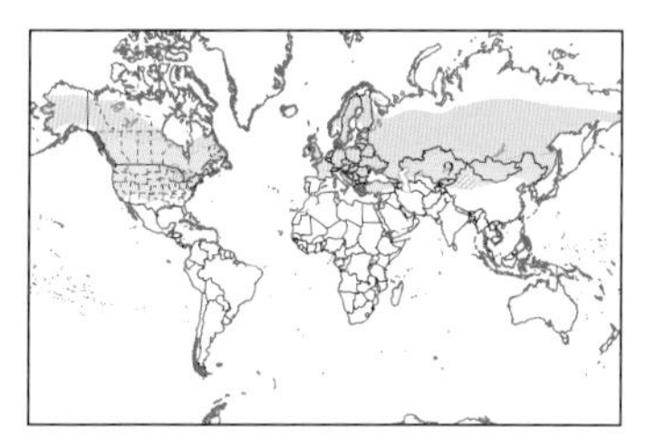

7a Adult *excubitor* Pale grey above, finely barred below. Narrow face-mask black, usually with narrow white eyebrow. Single white wing-patch (on primaries only). Tail black with white outer feathers. **Compare** Southern Grey Shrike (Plate 4) and Lesser Grey Shrike (Plate 5).

7b Adult *excubitor* Like 7a, but with double wing-patch (on primaries and secondaries). Plain white below. (Flight sketch.)

7c Adult ♀ *excubitor* with double wing-patch. Similar to 7b, but tends to show less white in wing, tail, scapulars and eyebrow. Underparts faintly barred on breast.

7d Juvenile Greyish-brown above, below same but with faint barring. Face-mask brownish, narrower than that of adult. Wing-coverts tipped buff. Bill paler, particularly on lower mandible. **Compare** as for adult.

7e Adult *leucopterus* (like *homeyeri*) Palest race, paler grey above than 7a, with white on forehead, prominent white eyebrow and rump. Extensive white in wings with double wing-patch (on primaries and secondaries). SW Russia.

7f Adult *borealis* (like *invictus* and *sibiricus*) Above like 7a, but rump paler. Single white wing-patch (on primaries only). Underparts greyer with fine barring. North America and Siberia. **Compare** Loggerhead Shrike (Plate 5) in North America and Chinese Grey Shrike (Plate 2) in E Asia.

7g Juvenile *borealis* Above buffy-brown, flight feathers brown. Face-mask brownish. Underparts buff, extensively barred. Wing-coverts buff. Bill pale. **Compare** as for adult 7f.

7a
7b
7b
7c
7d
7f
7e
7f
7g

PLATE 4 TRUE SHRIKES 4

8 Southern Grey Shrike *Lanius meridionalis* Text p.155

Large, sexes similar. Geographical variation marked. Solitary, hunts from exposed perches in hot dry open bush in SW Europe, North Africa, Middle East and Central Asia. Some double-note calls diagnostic, others like Great Grey Shrike (see Sounds).

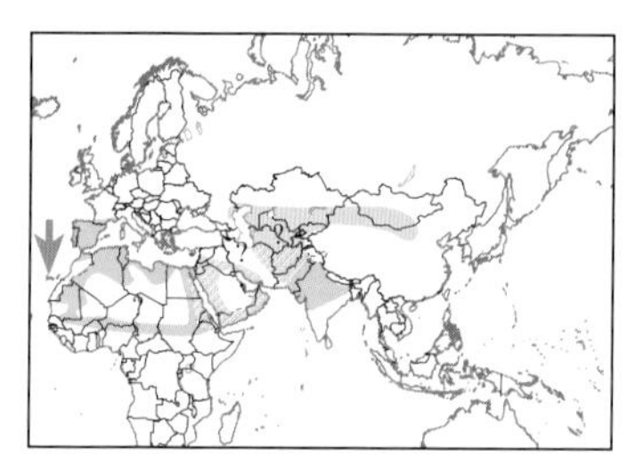

8a Adult *meridionalis* Dark grey above including rump. Obvious white eyebrow over bill and broad black face-mask. Single white wing-patch (on primaries only). Underparts pinkish-buff, chin white. S France and Iberian Peninsula. **Compare** Great Grey Shrike nominate race (Plate 3) and Lesser Grey Shrike (Plate 5).
8b. **Immature** Above pale greyish-brown without white eyebrow, face-mask brownish-black. Underparts buff, sometimes with faint barring. Bill with pale base to lower mandible.
8c Adult *leucopygos* Very pale. Pale grey above with whitish rump, lacks eyebrow. Secondaries broadly tipped white, large white wing-patch (on primaries only), white below. S Sahara.
8d Adult *lahtora* Darker grey above with broad black face-mask which extends over bill. Extensive white in wings, including tips of secondaries and broad wing-patch. W and N India, E Pakistan.
8e Adult *buryi* Darkest race with least white in wings. Dark grey above, scapulars and underparts pale grey. Yemen.
8f Adult *pallidirostris* Palest race with washed-out appearance. Face-mask small, forehead white, lores usually white. Bill pale grey-brown with flesh-coloured base and dark tip. Single large wing-patch (on primaries only). Underparts variable, white to faint pinkish tinge. Mainly Central Asia, migrating S as far as N Africa in boreal winter. **Compare** Great Grey Shrike (Plate 3) and Chinese Grey Shrike (Plate 2).
8g Immature *pallidirostris* Paler than adult, particularly brownish wings with pale buff coverts. Face-mask pale brown, smaller than adult. Lores and forehead whitish. Underparts buffy-white, usually without faint barring. Bill paler than adult. **Compare** as for adult 8f.

8a
8b
8a
8c
8d
8e
8f
8g
8f

PLATE 5 TRUE SHRIKES 5

9 Loggerhead Shrike *Lanius ludovicianus* Text p.159

Medium size, sexes similar. Geographical variation marked. Solitary, hunts from exposed perch in open country with short grass and scattered bushes and trees in North America. Northern populations migrate S. Calls diagnostic (see Sounds).

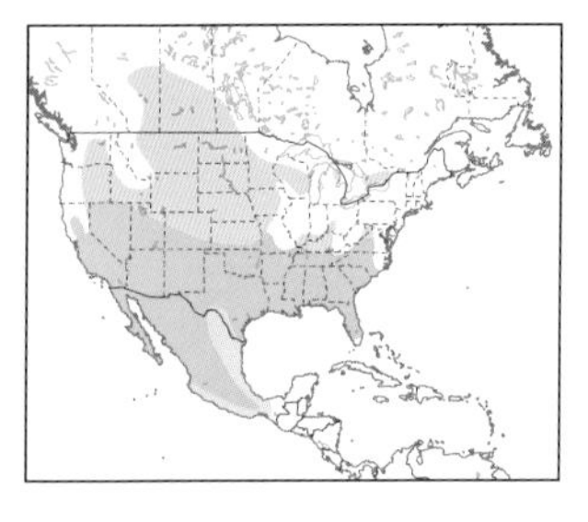

9a Adult *ludovicianus* Above darkish-grey, broad black face-mask extending over small black bill. Underparts variable, white to tinged grey. Scapulars white with single white wing-patch (on primaries only). SE USA. **Compare** Great Grey or Northern Shrike race *L. e. borealis*, particularly bill size, face-mask and underparts (insert and Plate 3).
9b Juvenile Above pale brownish-grey; finely barred above and below. Face-mask brownish and does not extend over bill. Wing-coverts tipped buff. Base of bill pale. **Compare** as for adult.
9c Adult *mexicanus* Darkest race. Above dark grey, below tinged grey with fine barring. West coast of North America.

10 Lesser Grey Shrike *Lanius minor* Text p.163

Medium size, sexes similar. Geographical variation slight. Solitary, hunts from exposed perches in open dry woodland and steppes in Eurasia, boreal winter migrant to southern Africa thornbush. Some calls diagnostic (see Sounds).

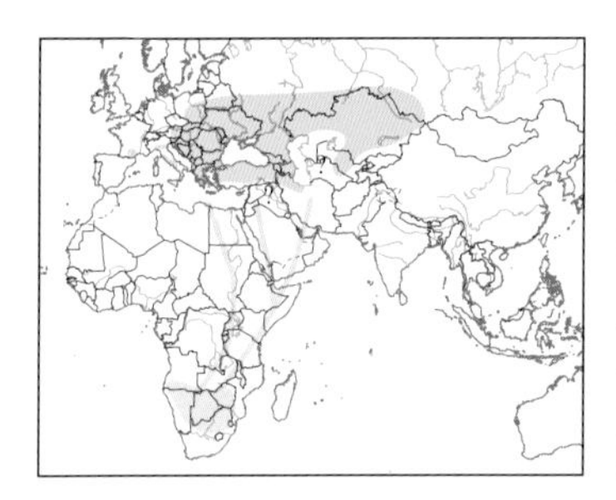

10a Adult ♂. Broad black face-mask including forehead. Long pointed wings black with white wing-patch. Underparts white with pinkish tinge, particularly in breeding birds. Short stubby bill and very upright stance. **Compare** in Europe and Asia Great Grey Shrike (Plate 3) and Southern Grey Shrike (Plate 4). In Africa Grey-backed Fiscal (Plate 2) and Mackinnon's Fiscal (Plate 6).
10b Adult ♀. Duller than ♂. Face-mask dull, lacks broad band on forehead which shows blackish-brown mottling. Underparts whiter.
10c Juvenile Above finely barred pale brownish-grey. Brownish-black face-mask does not extend onto forehead. Flight feathers brownish-black, these and wing-coverts tipped buff. Underparts cream to buffy-white, sometimes breast and flanks faintly barred. **Compare** as for adult and Woodchat Shrike (Plate 8).
10d Subadult 1st-winter (boreal). Duller than adult. Upperparts may show a little barring. Generally lacks black on forehead. Wing-coverts tipped buff. Base of bill pale. **Compare** as for adult.

9a
9a
9b
9c
L. excubitor borealis
10a
10a
10b
10c
10d

PLATE 6 TRUE SHRIKES 6

11 Mackinnon's Fiscal *Lanius mackinnoni* Text p.167

Medium size, sexes different. Solitary, hunts from exposed perches in forest edge and woodland on fringe of tropical forests in Central Africa. Some calls diagnostic (see Sounds).

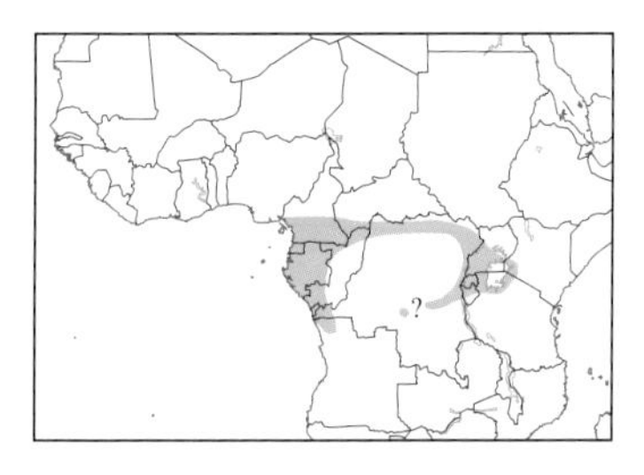

11a Adult ♂ Above grey with white scapulars. Black face-mask with distinctive white eyebrow, extending over bill. Wings black without white patch. Underparts white. **Compare** Grey-backed Fiscal (Plate 2), Lesser Grey Shrike (Plate 5).
11b Adult ♀ Like ♂, but flanks rufous, often concealed by wings.
11c Juvenile Above barred greyish-brown, scapulars whitish tipped buff. Face-mask brownish, eyebrow indistinct. Underparts barred greyish-white. Bill pale. **Compare** as for adult and Common Fiscal (Plate 7).

12 Long-tailed Fiscal *Lanius cabanisi* Text p.169

Large, sexes different. Gregarious. Hunts from exposed perches in dry savanna and thorn scrub of East Africa. Some calls diagnostic (see Sounds).

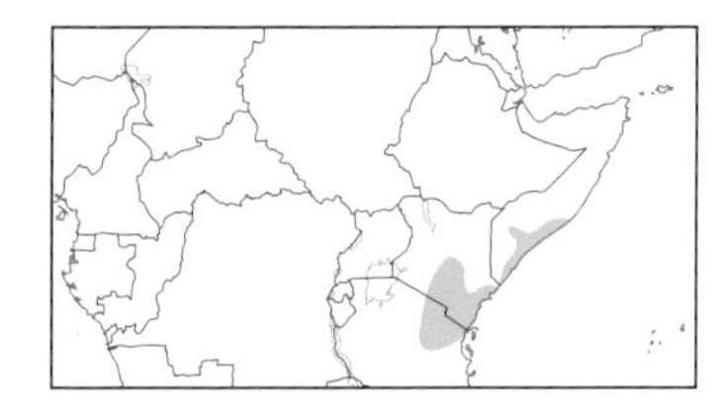

12a Adult ♂ Above black with dull greyish-black back and whitish rump. Wings black with white wing-patch, tail long. **Compare** Common Fiscal race *humeralis* (Plate 7).
12b Adult ♀ Like ♂, but small dark rufous flanks, usually concealed by wings.
12c Juvenile Above greyish-brown finely barred buff, rump pale. Face-mask brownish-black. Flight feathers and wing-coverts tipped buff. Whitish below with faint barring, flanks with rufous tinge. Bill paler. **Compare** as for adult and Grey-backed Fiscal (Plate 2).

13 Taita Fiscal *Lanius dorsalis* Text p.170

Medium size, sexes different. Solitary, hunts from exposed perches in dry thornbush in East Africa. Some calls diagnostic (see Sounds).

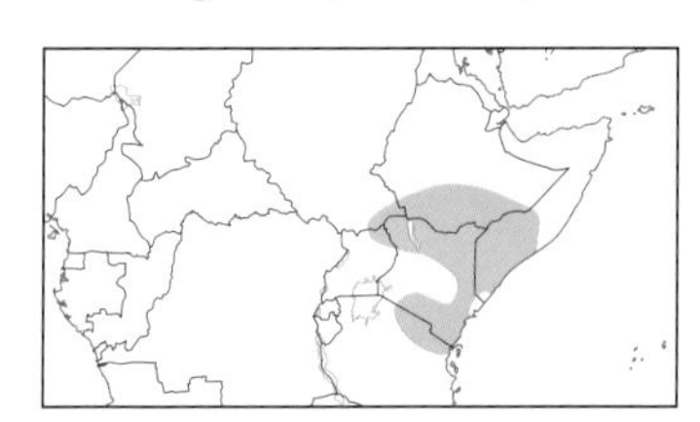

13a Adult ♂ Black head contrasts with pale grey back, white scapulars and grey rump. Wings black with small white patch. No white on secondaries. Tail with little white. Underparts white. **Compare** Somali Fiscal and Common Fiscal (Plate 7) in denser woodland.
13b Adult ♀ Like ♂, but with small dark rufous flank patch.
13c Immature Above greyish-brown, barred black on head, scapulars tipped buff, indistinct. Flight feathers and wing-coverts tipped buff. Whitish underparts barred. Bill pale. **Compare** as for adult.

11a
11b
11a
11c
12a
12a
12b
12c
13a
13a
13c
13b

PLATE 7 TRUE SHRIKES 7

14 Somali Fiscal *Lanius somalicus* Text p.171

Medium size, sexes similar. Solitary, hunts from exposed perches in dry thornbush of NE Africa. Calls little known (see Sounds).

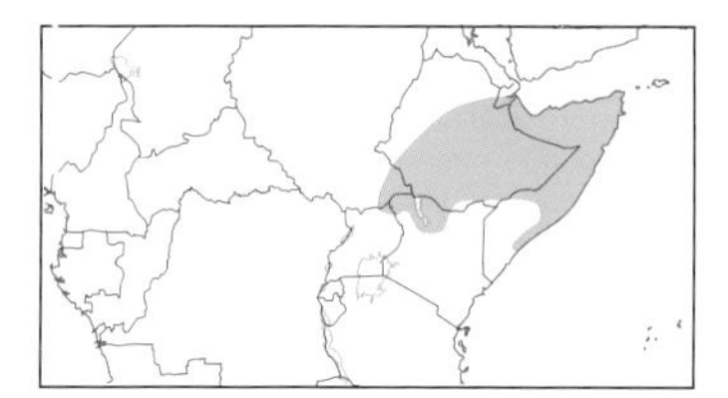

14a Adult Black head, grey back, white scapulars and rump. Large white wing-patch, secondaries and tertials tipped white. Underparts white. ♀ lacks rufous flanks. **Compare** Taita Fiscal (Plate 6) and Common Fiscal (this plate).
14b Juvenile Above pale greyish-brown, scapulars buffy-brown, back and rump barred pale buffy-brown. Face-mask brownish. Wing-coverts, tertials and secondaries broadly tipped buff. Underparts whitish with pale barring. **Compare** as for adult.

15 Common Fiscal *Lanius collaris* Text p.172

Medium size, sexes usually different. Geographical variation marked. Solitary, hunts from exposed perches in variety of open treed habitats, often associated with man. Widespread in sub-Saharan Africa. Calls diagnostic, some calls of N and S populations differ (see Sounds). (Area of light green in the map shows distribution of the northern group; dark green = southern group.)

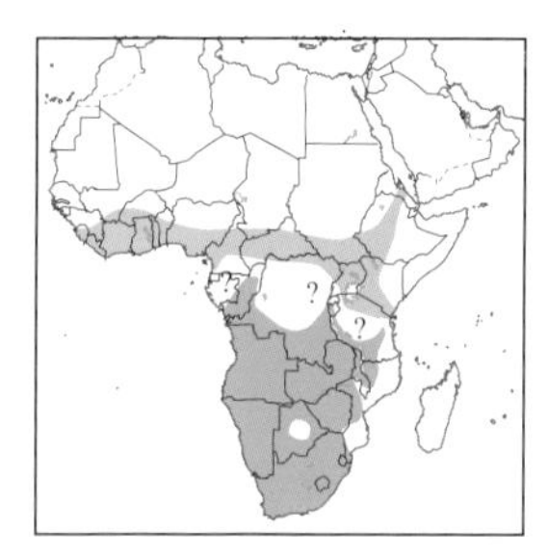

15a Adult ♂ *collaris* Distinctive. Above black with greyish rump. White scapulars and wing-patch. Underparts variable, dull white to greyish with fine barring. South Africa. **Compare** Fiscal Flycatcher *Sigelus silens.*
15b Adult ♀ *collaris* Like ♂, but duller, flanks rufous.
15c Juvenile *collaris* Above pale brownish-grey finely barred. Scapulars mottled buff brownish-white. Wings dark brown, tertials and coverts tipped buff. Underparts buffy-white finely barred greyish-brown. Flanks slightly rufous in both sexes.
15d Adult ♂ *predator* Like 15a, but above slate-black, below white. Tail relatively short and broad. ♀ with rufous flanks. Zimbabwe to E South Africa.
15e Adult *subcoronatus* Prominent white eyebrow and rump. Southern Africa.
15f Adult *marwitzi* Like 15e, but darker, rump grey. SW Tanzania on high ground.
15g Adult *smithii* Above black, rump greyish-white. Underparts white; ♀ rufous flanks absent or small. W Africa to Angola and W Uganda.
15h Adult ♂ *humeralis* Above duller black than previous races. Tail longer and thinner with more white. ♀ smaller than ♂ and has rufous flanks. East Africa. **Compare** Long-tailed (Plate 6), Taita (Plate 6) and Somali Fiscals (this plate).
15i Juvenile *humeralis* Above rufous-brown, densely barred blackish. Wings and coverts rufous-brown. Underparts buff coarsely barred blackish-brown. **Compare** as for adult.

16 São Tomé Fiscal *Lanius newtoni* Text p.177

Medium size, sexes similar. Solitary, hunts from exposed perches below closed-canopy of lowland forest. São Tomé Is. in Gulf of Guinea, West Africa. Calls diagnostic (see Sounds).

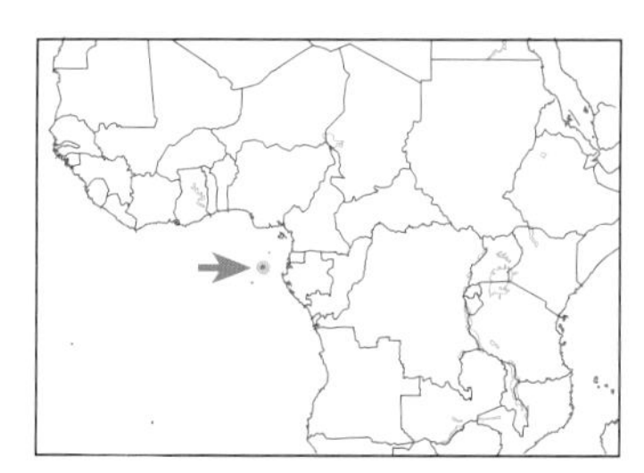

16a Adult Distinctive. Above black, scapulars yellowish. White wing-patch small or absent. Underparts pale yellow.
16b Juvenile Above brown finely barred, below tawny-yellow barred. Wings and tail brownish-black.

14b
14a
15a
14a
15a
15c
15b
15e
15i
15f
15d
15g
15h
16a
16b
16a

PLATE 8 TRUE SHRIKES 8

17 Masked Shrike *Lanius nubicus* Text p.178

Medium-small and slightly built, sexes different. Solitary, hunts from exposed perches and within trees in well-wooded areas of E Mediterranean and Middle East. Boreal winter migrant, mainly to NE Africa and Middle East. Some calls diagnostic (see Sounds).

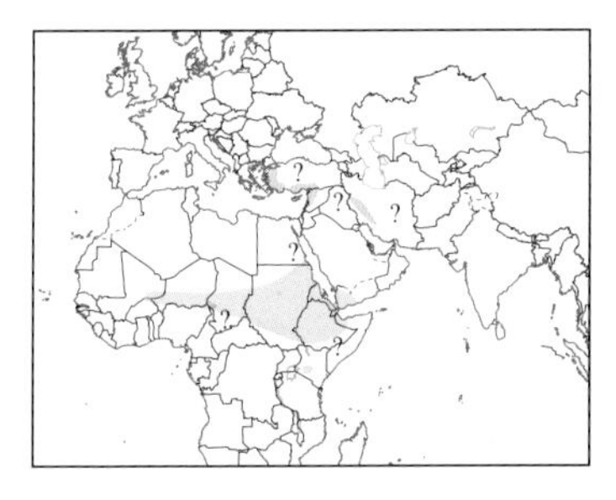

17a Adult ♂ Distinctive, above black with conspicuous white forehead, eyebrow, scapulars and wing-patch. Underparts rusty-buff, mainly on flanks.
17b Adult ♀ Like ♂, but duller, paler with less contrast.
17c Juvenile Above barred greyish-brown, including rump. Face-mask brownish, indistinct with faint buff eyebrow. Wings blackish-brown. Underparts whitish and heavily barred. **Compare** Woodchat Shrike (this plate).

18 Woodchat Shrike *Lanius senator* Text p.180

Medium size, sexes slightly different. Geographical variation marked. Solitary, hunts from exposed perches in open woodland and orchards in Mediterranean region E to Iran. Boreal winter migrant to N of equator in sub-Sahara. Some calls diagnostic (see Sounds).

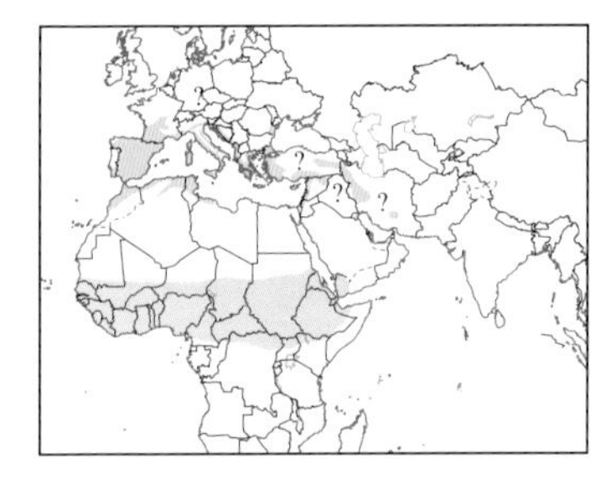

18a Adult ♂ *senator* Distinctive. Reddish-brown head, broad black forehead and face-mask, white lores, scapulars and rump.
18b Adult ♀ *senator* Like ♂, but paler, browner above with forehead and face mottled.
18c Juvenile Above barred greyish, rufous-buff with buffy-white scapulars and rump. Face-mask dull, indistinct. Wing, tail and coverts tipped and edged buffy-rufous. Underparts dull white with dark barring. **Compare** Red-backed Shrike (Plate 10), Lesser Grey Shrike (Plate 5), Brown Shrike (Plate 9) and Masked Shrike (this plate).
18d Adult *badius* Like 18a, but with little or no white wing-patch. W Mediterranean islands.
18e Adult *niloticus* Like other races, but larger white tail base and wing-patch. E Mediterranean and Middle East.

19 Bull-headed Shrike *Lanius bucephalus* Text p.184

Medium size, sexes different. Geographical variation in ♀ marked. Solitary, hunts from exposed perches in open woodland and mixed forest in far E Asia and Japan. Some migrate to S regions of breeding range. Some calls diagnostic (see Sounds).

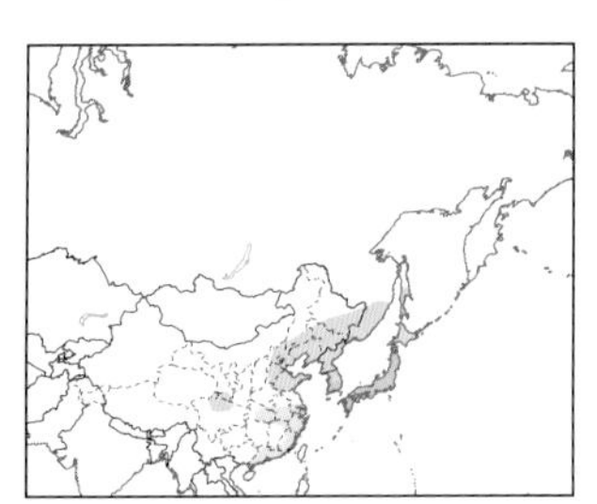

19a Adult ♂ *bucephalus* Head rufous-brown, face-mask black, narrow white eyebrow and grey back. Small white wing-patch. Underparts tinged rufous-buff. **Compare** Brown Shrike (Plate 9).
19b Adult ♀ *bucephalus* Like ♂, but browner without black face-mask or white wing-patch. Underparts barred. Base of bill pale.
19c Juvenile Like ♀, but darker and barred above. ♂ shows small white wing-patch. **Compare** Brown Shrike (Plate 9) and Thick-billed Shrike (Plate 10).

17a
17c
17b
17a
18b
18a
18c
18a
18d
18e
19a
19b
19c
19a

PLATE 9 TRUE SHRIKES 9

20 Brown Shrike *Lanius cristatus* Text p.186

Medium-small, sexes slightly different. Geographical variation marked. Solitary, hunts from exposed perches in open woodland and thorn scrub in NE Asia. Boreal winter migrant to Indian subcontinent and SE Asia. Some calls diagnostic (see Sounds).

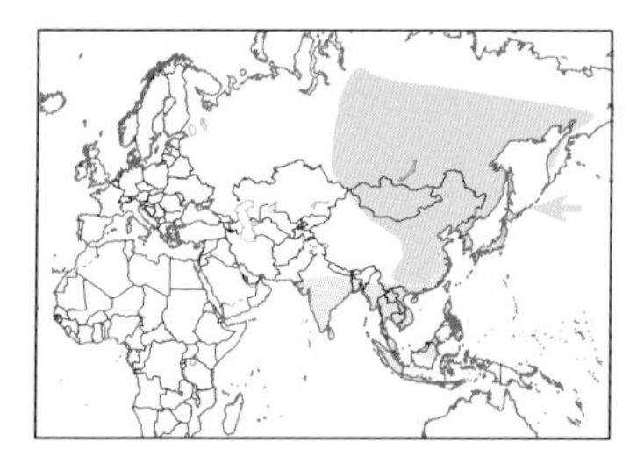

20a Adult ♂ *cristatus* Reddish-brown head, brownish back with black face-mask and broad white eyebrow. Rump and thin tail reddish-brown. Wings lack white patch. Underparts whitish tinged buffy-rufous. Central Russia to E Siberia. **Compare** Isabelline Shrike (this plate) and Red-backed Shrike (Plate 10).
20b Adult ♀ *cristatus* Like ♂, sometimes indistinguishable, but often duller above, less distinct face-mask with buffy eyebrow, and may have faint barring on underparts.
20c Juvenile Variable with age; first barred greyish-brown above, face-mask dull brown. Underparts buff with dark barring. Bill pale. **Compare** as for adult.
20d Adult *superciliosus* Bright reddish-brown head and back. Broad white frontal and eyebrow contrasting with black face-mask. Chin and throat white, rest of underparts buffy-rufous. ♂ white frontal broader than ♀. E Russia on S Sakhalin, Japan from Hokkaido to S central Honshu.
20e Adult *lucionensis* Head grey, back brownish-grey, rump and tail reddish-brown. Face-mask black. Underparts buff. China and Korea. Boreal winter migrant mainly to Taiwan and Philippines.

21 Isabelline Shrike *Lanius isabellinus* Text p.189

Medium-small, sexes different. Geographical variation marked. Solitary, hunts from exposed perches in open country with scattered bushes. Central Asia, migrating to NE Africa S of Sahara, Middle East and S Asia in NW India during boreal winter. Calls like Red-backed Shrike (see Sounds).

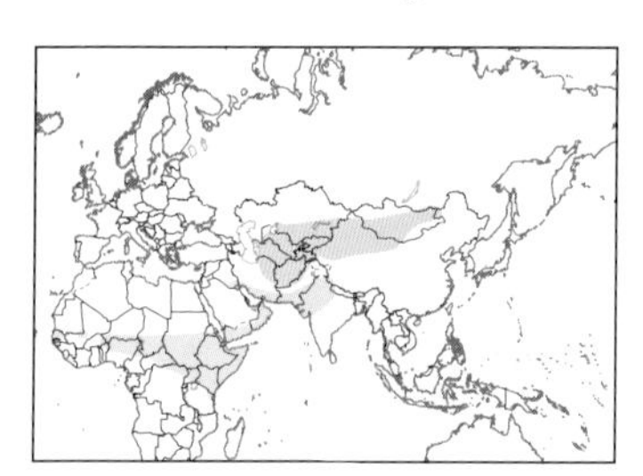

21a Adult ♂ *isabellinus* Very pale. Above pale buff-brown to sandy-grey, face-mask dark, lores pale. Underparts dull white. Pale base to bill. Breeds NW China, boreal winter migrant from NW India to Arabian Peninsula. **Compare** Red-backed Shrike (Plate 10) and Brown Shrike (this plate).
21b Adult ♀ *isabellinus* Above like ♂, but duller. Face-mask smaller, underparts often faintly barred on breast and flanks. Creamy wing-patch reduced or absent. Bill with pinkish base. Juvenile like ♀.
21c Adult ♂ *phoenicuroides* Head rufous-brown, eyebrow white, broad face-mask black. Back greyish brown, rump and tail rufous with dark terminal centres to feathers. Wing dark with white patch. Underparts white or pinkish. Bill black. Breeds Iran to W China, boreal winter migrant mainly to Africa. **Compare** as for nominate.
21d Adult ♀ *phoenicuroides* Like ♂, but duller, face-mask browner and smaller, lores buffy-white. Wing-patch smaller, and underparts with faint barring on breast and flanks.
21e Juvenile *phoenicuroides* Above barred greyish-brown. Face-mask brownish, indistinct. Underparts faintly barred, mainly sides of breast and flanks. Bill pale. **Compare** as for adult.

20a
20b
20c
20a
20d
20e
21a
21e
21a
21b
21c
21d

PLATE 10 TRUE SHRIKES 10

22 Thick-billed Shrike *Lanius tigrinus* **Text p.193**

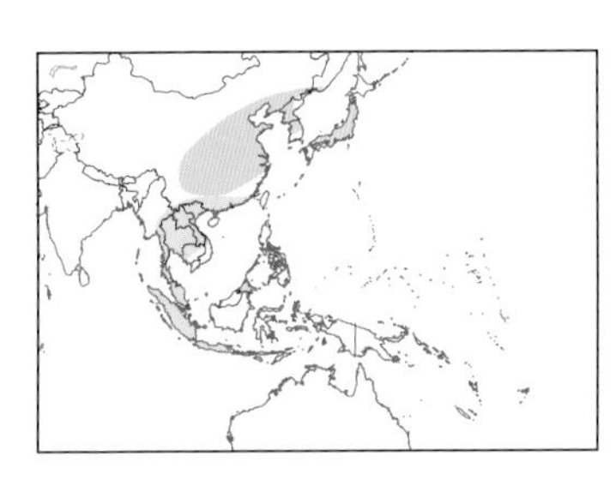

Medium-small, sexes different. Solitary, hunts from exposed perches in open forested areas with thick undercover in E Russia, China, E Asia and Japan. Migrates in boreal winter to Oriental region S to Bali. Some calls diagnostic (see Sounds).

22a Adult ♂ Distinctive. Thick bill, grey head, black face-mask, barred rufous back and rump. No white in wing. Underparts white. **Compare** Brown Shrike (Plate 9).
22b Adult ♀. Duller, browner than ♂, less grey above. Face-mask smaller, lores whitish, sometimes short buffy eyebrow. Underparts buffy-white , darkly barred on belly and flanks.
22c Juvenile Above rufous-brown, heavily barred. No face-mask but buffy indistinct ring around eye gives 'big-eyed' appearance. Underparts buff, heavily barred. Bill pale. **Compare** Brown Shrike (Plate 9) and Burmese Shrike (Plate 11).

23 Souza's Shrike *Lanius souzae* **Text p.195**

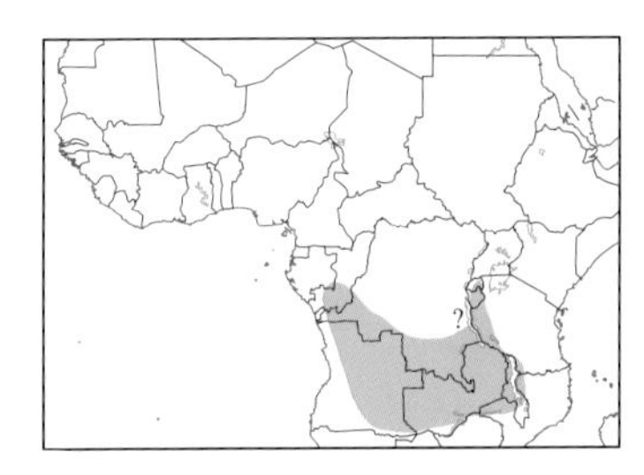

Medium-small, sexes different. Geographical variation slight. Solitary, hunts from exposed perches in miombo woodland in S Central Africa. Calls quiet, little known (see Sounds).

23a Adult ♂ Head pale grey, face-mask black. Back brown tinged rufous, finely barred black. Scapulars white. Wings-coverts barred, no white in wing. Long thin tail. Underparts dull white. **Compare** migrant Red-backed Shrike (this plate).
23b Adult ♀ Like ♂, duller and browner, flanks tinged rufous.
23c Juvenile Above rufous-brown finely barred black. Indistinct pale eyebrow and brownish face-mask. Underparts dull white, barred, flanks pale rufous. Bill brownish-black. **Compare** Red-backed Shrike (this plate) and Common Fiscal (Plate 7).

24 Red-backed Shrike *Lanius collurio* **Text p.197**

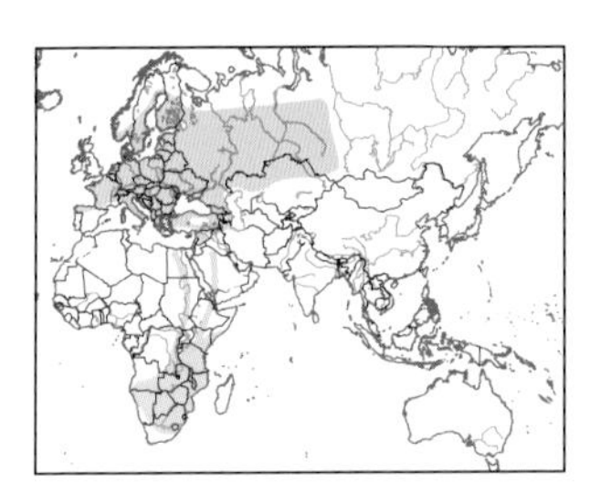

Medium-small, sexes different. Geographical variation slight. Solitary, hunts from exposed perches in open areas with scattered bushes. Europe and Central Asia, migrating in boreal winter to Africa S of equator in thorn savanna. Calls diagnostic, but check Isabelline Shrike (see Sounds).

24a Adult ♂ Distinctive, grey head, broad black face-mask extending over bill, and bright reddish-brown back. Rump grey. Wing usually lacks white patch. Underparts whitish, faintly tinged pink. **Compare** in Africa, Souza's Shrike (this plate) and Emin's Shrike (Plate 11).
24b Adult ♀ Above dull rufous-brown, head and nape tinged grey. Face-mask small, ear-coverts brownish. Underparts dull white with dark barring. Bill pale. **Compare** Brown Shrike and Isabelline Shrike (Plate 9).
24c Juvenile Like ♀, but extensively barred on head, back and underparts. Wing-coverts, tertials and tail have blackish subterminal bar on each feather. **Compare** as for adult ♀ and Woodchat Shrike (Plate 8).
24d Subadult ♂ Intermediate plumage, patchy grey developing on head and nape. Underparts may have some barring.

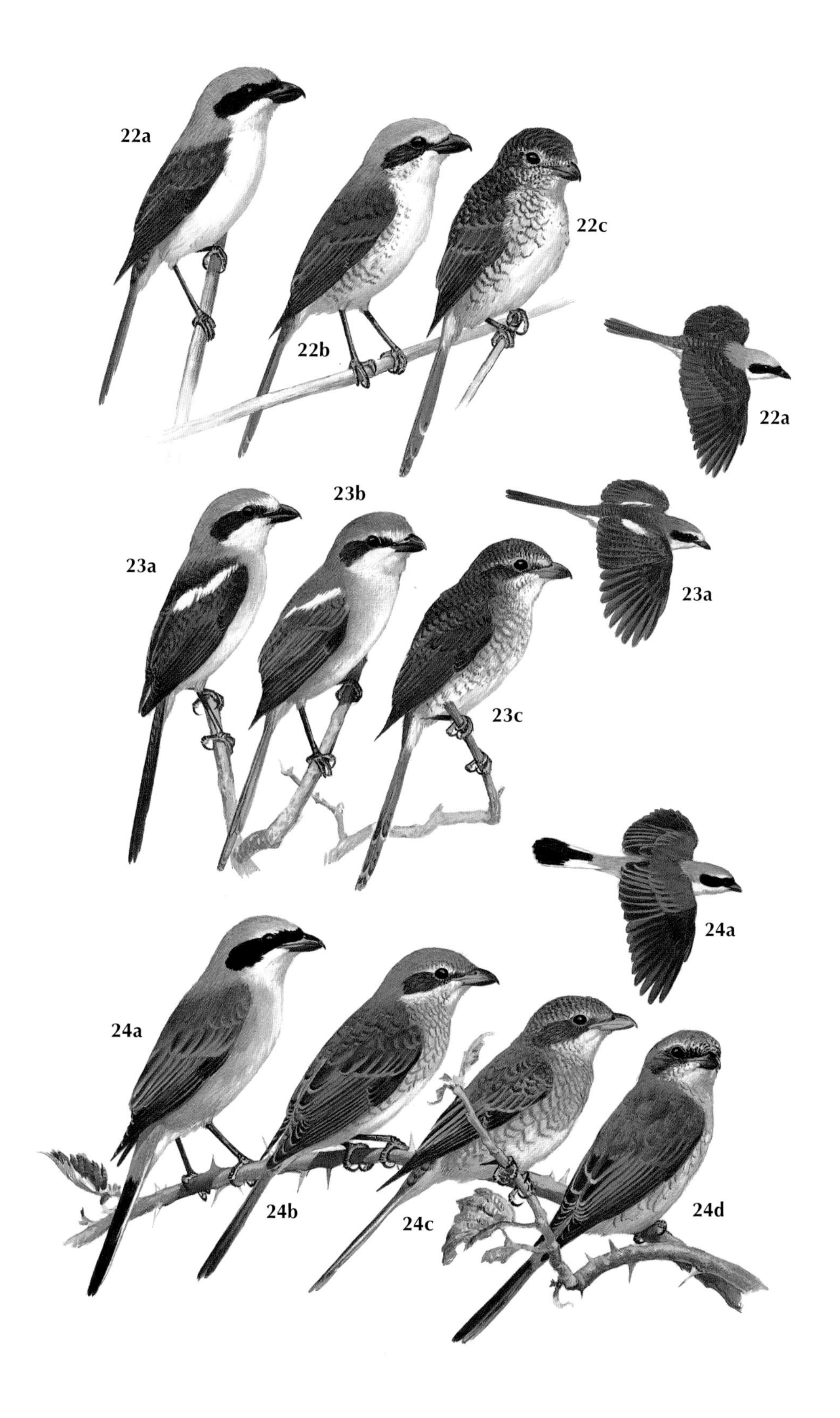
22a
22b
22c
22a
23b
23a
23a
23c
24a
24a
24b
24c
24d

25 Emin's Shrike *Lanius gubernator* Text p.202

Small, sexes different. Solitary or in small groups, hunts from exposed perches in open tree savanna of West and Central Africa, N of equator. Calls little known (see Sounds).

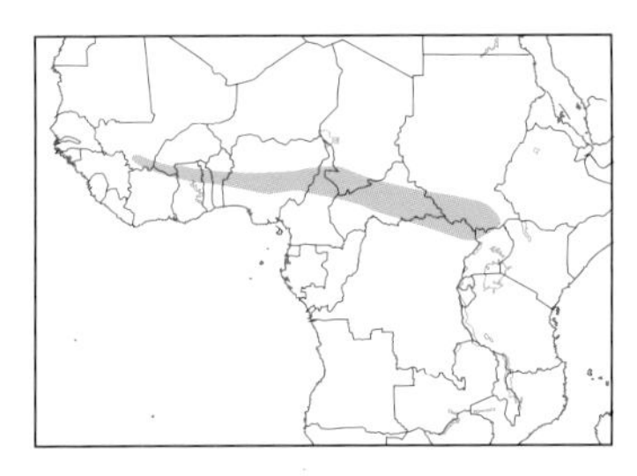

25a Adult ♂ Head grey, face-mask black. Back and rump reddish-brown. Wings with white patch. Underparts buffy rufous-brown, throat white. **Compare** migrant Red-backed Shrike (Plate 10) and Isabelline Shrike (Plate 9).
25b Adult ♀ Like ♂, but duller, above grey tinged brown, face-mask smaller and browner, white wing-patch smaller. Underparts variably tinged pale rufous.
25c Juvenile ♂ Above tinged rufous, darkly barred, no grey on head. Face-mask dull and small. Underparts rufous-brown, darkly barred. **Compare** as for adults and Common Fiscal (Plate 7).
25d Juvenile ♀ Like juvenile ♂, but greyish-brown above, finely barred buff-and-blackish. Underparts rufous-brown with dark barring. **Compare** as for juvenile ♂.

26 Bay-backed Shrike *Lanius vittatus* Text p.203

Medium size, sexes similar. Geographical variation slight. Solitary, hunts from exposed perches in variety of open habitats from SE Iran to India. Northern populations migrate S and SW in boreal winter. Some calls diagnostic (see Sounds). (Blue stripe on green in map = migrant and resident.)

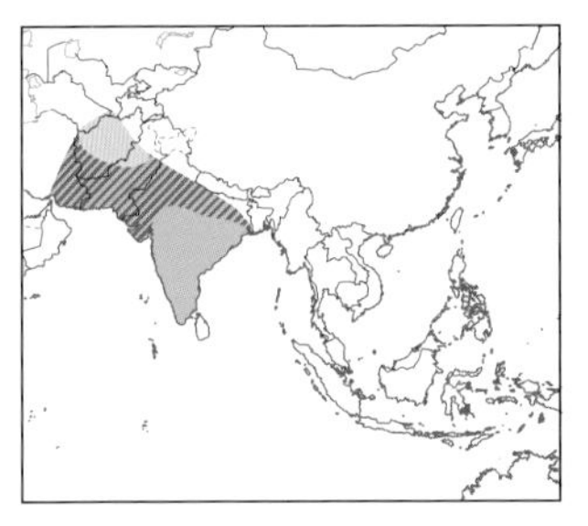

26a Adult Broad black frontal and face-mask, grey head, dark reddish-brown back and whitish rump. Wings black with large white patch. Tail black with white outer feathers. Underparts white, sides and flanks rufous. ♀ often slightly duller. N and central India. **Compare** Burmese Shrike (this plate) and Long-tailed Shrike (Plate 12).
26b Juvenile Above greyish-brown with buff and blackish barring. Ear-coverts brownish. Wing-coverts and tertials edged buff, wings lack white patch. Tail rufous. Underparts dull white, slightly barred. **Compare** as for adult, Brown Shrike and Isabelline Shrike (Plate 9).

27 Burmese Shrike *Lanius collurioides* Text p.205

Medium size, sexes similar. Geographical variation slight. Solitary or in groups, hunts from exposed perches in open country with scattered trees. NE India, S China and SE Asia. Boreal winter migrant W and S of breeding range in SE Asia. Calls little known (see Sounds).

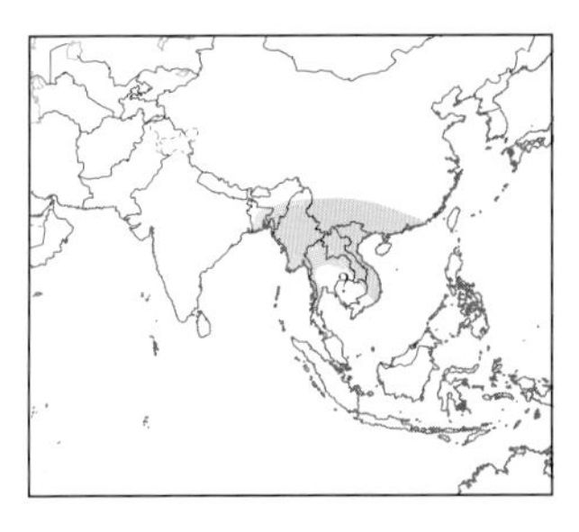

27a Adult Head dark grey with broad (variable) black frontal and face-mask. Back and rump deep reddish-brown. Wings black with white patch. Tail black, outer feathers white. Underparts dull white. ♀ usually has paler lores. India to N Vietnam. **Compare** Bay-backed Shrike (this plate) and Thick-billed Shrike (Plate 10).
27b Juvenile Head greyish-brown, barred and spotted. Back and rump barred rufous-brown. Wing-patch absent or indistinct. Tail rufous. Underparts buffy-white, barred brownish. **Compare** as for adult, Bull-headed Shrike (Plate 8) and Brown Shrike (Plate 9).

25a
25a
25b
25c
25d
26a
26a
26b
27a
27a
27b

28 Long-tailed Shrike *Lanius schach* **Text p.206**

Large, sexes similar. Geographical variation marked. Forms two groups based on head coloration. Solitary, hunts from exposed perches in wide range of open habitats from Central, SE and E Asia, India, Malay Archipelago and New Guinea. W and NW populations migrate to India in boreal winter. Some calls diagnostic (see Sounds). (Blue stripe on green in map = non-breeding migrant and resident; yellow stripe on green = breeding migrant and possible resident.)

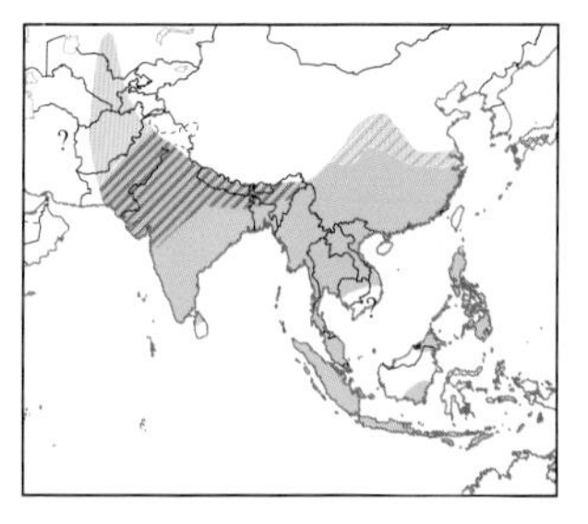

A. Black face-mask group

28a Adult *erythronotus* Black face-mask with narrow frontal, eyebrow white. Head and mantle pale grey, back and rump rufous. Small white patch on wings. Turkmenistan to NW India. **Compare** Grey-backed and Philippine Shrike (this plate) and Bay-backed Shrike (Plate 11).
28b Adult *schach* Like 28a, but black frontal broader and grey darker. S China, Hainan, Taiwan and N Vietnam.
28c Adult *bentet* Like 28b, but black frontal broader. Malay Peninsula, Sumatra to Lesser Sundas and probably SE Borneo.
28d Juvenile Head greyish-brown barred black. Face-mask blackish-brown. Back and rump like adult but barred, tail like adult. Bill pale. **Compare** as for adult.

B. Black headed group

28e Adult *longicaudatus* Distinctive. Head black, back and rump reddish-brown. Wings and tail black, large white wing-patch. E India to N Laos. **Compare** Burmese Shrike (Plate 11). **28f Adult** *stresemanni* Like 28g, but less grey. E New Guinea. **28g Adult** *nasutus* Like 28f, but back almost completely grey. Philippines, probably also N Borneo. **28h Juvenile** Paler than Group A juvenile. Head and mantle buff barred black. Face-mask blackish-brown. Back and rump like adult. Tail brown. Underparts dull white, flanks barred. Bill pale. **Compare** as for adults of both groups. **28i Adult** melanistic '*fuscatus*' Distinctive. Blackish, rump and vent rufous-grey. S China, Hong Kong, Hainan, Taiwan and N Vietnam.

29 Grey-backed Shrike *Lanius tephronotus* **Text p.210**

Large, sexes similar. Geographical variation moderate. Solitary, hunts from exposed perches in scrub and scattered trees at high elevations from N India, Nepal, Tibet and W China. Boreal winter migrant to SE Asia. Calls little known (see Sounds).

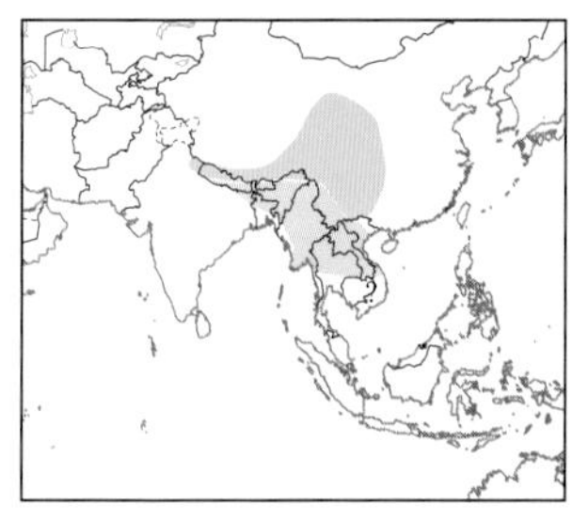

29a Adult ♂ *tephronotus* Above dark grey, black face-mask with narrow frontal, rump rufous. Wings black, white patch small or absent. Underparts white, sides and flanks rufous. **Compare** Long-tailed and Philippine Shrike (this plate).
29b Adult *lahulensis* Like 29a, but paler above, lower back and rump rufous. Small white wing-patch present. Tail darker. N India in N Kashmir to Himachal Pradesh, possibly W Tibet.
29c Juvenile (nominate) Barred greyish-brown above including rufous rump. Face-mask dull. Underparts whitish, extensively barred. Flanks tinged rufous. **Compare** as for adult.

30 Philippine Shrike *Lanius validirostris* **Text p.211**

Medium-large, sexes similar. Geographical variation slight. Solitary, hunts from exposed perches in forest edge and scattered trees in grasslands on Philippines in N and central Luzon, Mindoro and Mindanao. Calls little known (see Sounds).

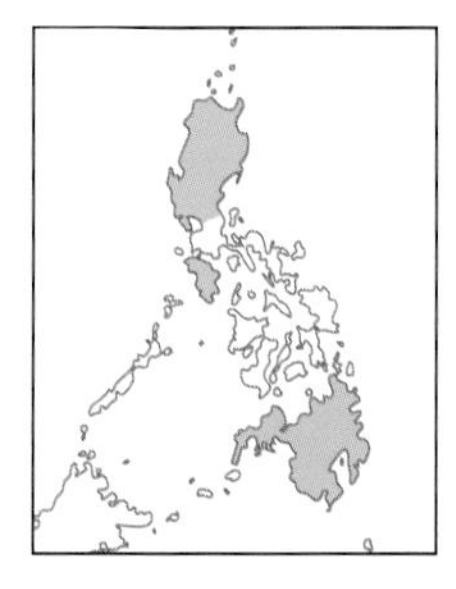

30a Adult Distinctive. Dark grey above, including rump. Thin white eyebrow above black face-mask. Wings and tail black with no white. Underparts white, flanks rufous. **Compare** Long-tailed Shrike (*nasutus*) (this plate).
30b Juvenile Above greyish-brown with dark barring. Face-mask brownish-black. Below greyish-white with dark barring. Bill pale. **Compare** as for adult.

28a

28d

28i

28b

28c

28b

28h

28e

28e

28f

28g

29b

29c

29a

30b

30a

PLATE 13 LARGE BUSH-SHRIKES 1

31 Lagden's Bush-shrike *Malaconotus lagdeni* Text p.212

Large, sexes similar. Geographical variation moderate, calls may differ. Solitary, skulking in mid- to upper canopy of lowland forest in West Africa from Sierra Leone to Ghana, and in montane forest in East Africa from E Zaïre, SW Uganda and Rwanda. Some calls diagnostic, but check Grey-headed and Fiery-breasted (see Sounds).

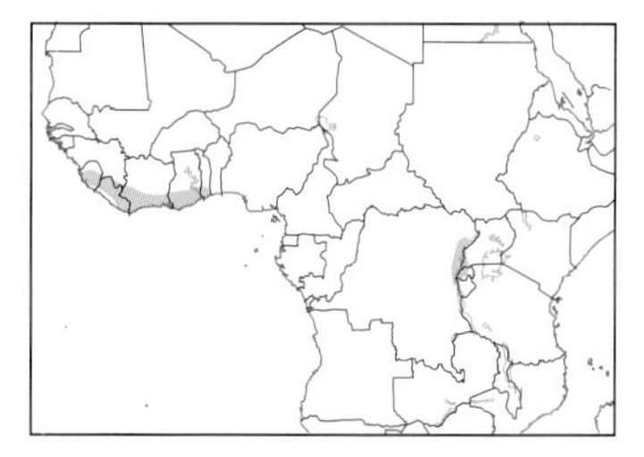

31a Adult *lagdeni* Head grey with massive black bill and whitish eye. Back, tail and wings olive-green. Wings with distinctive spotting, formed by wing-coverts and tertials tipped black and yellow. Underparts yellow, tinged orange. Lowland forest Sierra Leone to Ghana. **Compare** Fiery-breasted Bush-shrike (Plate 14) and Grey-headed Bush-shrike (Plate 14).
31b Adult *centralis* Like 31a, but with little or no orange on breast. Montane forest E Zaïre, SW Uganda and Rwanda. **Compare** as for nominate.
31c Juvenile Head greyish-brown, green duller. Spotting on wings less striking, wing-coverts and tertials tipped buffy-yellow. Underparts variable, greyish-white with faint barring, or with yellow streaking in older birds. Bill greyish-brown. Eye probably brown. **Compare** as for adult.

32 Uluguru Bush-shrike *Malaconotus? alius* Text p.214

Medium-large, sexes fairly similar. Solitary, skulking in montane forest canopy. Endemic to Uluguru Mountains in Tanzania, East Africa. Call diagnostic (see Sounds).

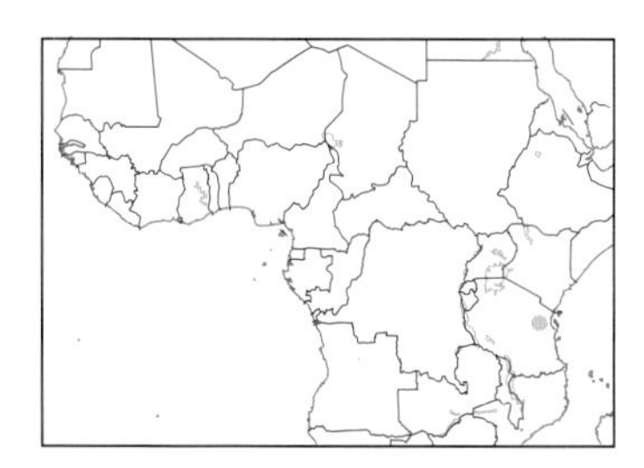

32 Adult ♂ Head black with a massive black bill and reddish-brown eye. Back, wings and tail olive-green. Underparts bright yellow. ♀ more greenish-yellow. **Compare** Yellow morph of Black-fronted Bush-shrike (Plate 17) and Grey-headed Bush-shrike (Plate 14).

33 Green-breasted Bush-shrike *Malaconotus gladiator* Text p.214

Large, sexes similar. Solitary, skulking in canopy of montane forest from W Cameroon and E Nigeria. Harsh calls of ♀ appear diagnostic (see Sounds).

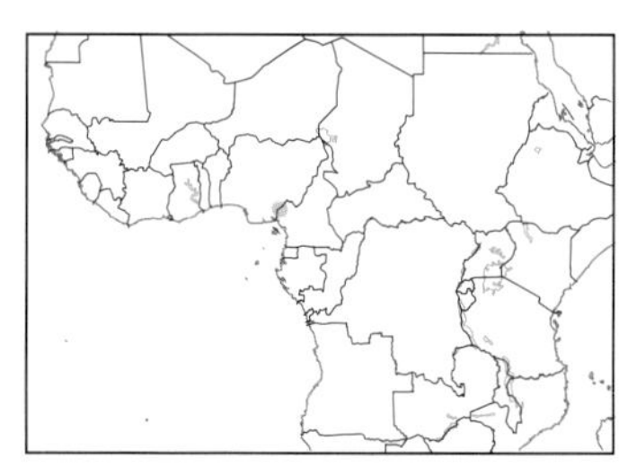

33 Adult Distinctive. Head dark grey with massive black bill and pale eye. Rest of plumage dull olive-green.

31c
31a
31b
32
33

PLATE 14 LARGE BUSH-SHRIKES 2

34 Fiery-breasted Bush-shrike *Malaconotus cruentus* Text p.215

Large, sexes similar. Geographical variation moderate, but polymorphism marked (red and yellow morphs with intermediates). Solitary, skulking at all levels of lowland forest from West Africa to Uganda. Whistle calls diagnostic (see Sounds).

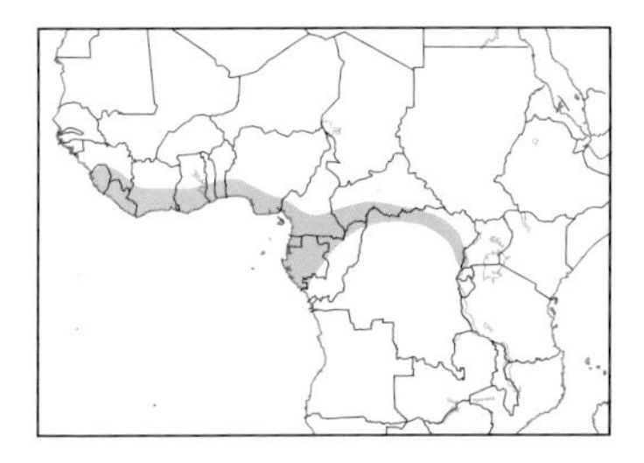

34a Adult *cruentus* Intermediate morph. Head and mantle pale grey with extensive white on face encircling pale eye, and massive black bill. Back, wings and tail olive-green. Tertials and tail broadly tipped black and yellow. Throat and breast orange, belly yellow. Sierra Leone to Cameroon.
34b Adult *cruentus* Yellow morph. Above like 34a. Underparts yellow with only a tinge of orange. **Compare** Lagden's Bush-shrike (Plate 13), Grey-headed Bush-shrike (this plate) and smaller Many-coloured Bush-shrike (Plate 16).
34c Adult *gabonensis* Red morph. Like 34b but deep scarlet red below with little yellow on lower belly. Cameroon to Gabon and NE Congo, E Zaïre to W Uganda.
34d Juvenile *cruentus* Head mottled greyish-brown, lores whitish. Throat and upper breast greyish-white, lower breast and belly greenish-yellow. Bill greyish-brown and eye brown. **Compare** as for adult.

35 Grey-headed Bush-shrike *Malaconotus blanchoti* Text p.217

Large size, sexes fairly similar. Geographical variation moderate. Solitary, skulking mainly in upper-levels in savanna woodland, widespread throughout sub-Sahara. Whistled calls like some other members of genus (see Sounds).

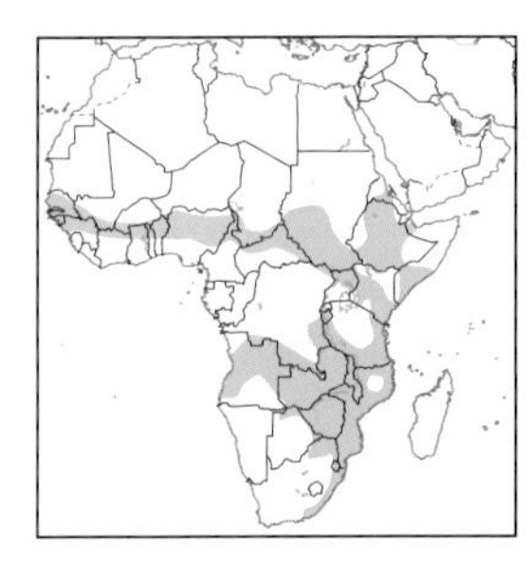

35a Adult *hypopyrrhus* Head and nape pale grey, lores white in front of pale yellow eye, massive black bill. Back, wings and tail olive-green. Wings spotted with yellow tips to coverts. Tanzania south to Zambia and southern Africa. **Compare** Monteiro's and Orange-breasted Bush-shrike (Plate 15) and Lagden's Bush-shrike (Plate 13).
35b Adult *approximans* Has darkest orange-brown underparts. East Africa from S Ethiopia, Kenya and N Tanzania.
35c Adult *catharoxanthus* (like *citrinipectus*) Both yellow-breasted morphs from N Central Africa in N Zaïre Uganda, W Kenya and Ethiopia, and from SW Central Africa in N Angola, W Zambia and N Namibia.
35d Juvenile *hypopyrrhus* Head mottled greyish-brown, lores dull white to yellowish. Back, wings and tail like adult. Underparts pale lemon-yellow. Bill greyish-brown, eye brown. **Compare** Lagden's Bush-shrike (Plate 13). Juvenile Monteiro's Bush-shrike unknown.

34a
34b
34c
34d
35a
35d
35b
35c

PLATE 15 LARGE and SMALL BUSH-SHRIKES

36 Monteiro's Bush-shrike *Malaconotus monteiri* Text p.220

Large size, sexes similar. Geographical variation moderate. Solitary, skulking in canopy of forests in Angola and Cameroon. Whistled calls like some other members of genus (see Sounds).

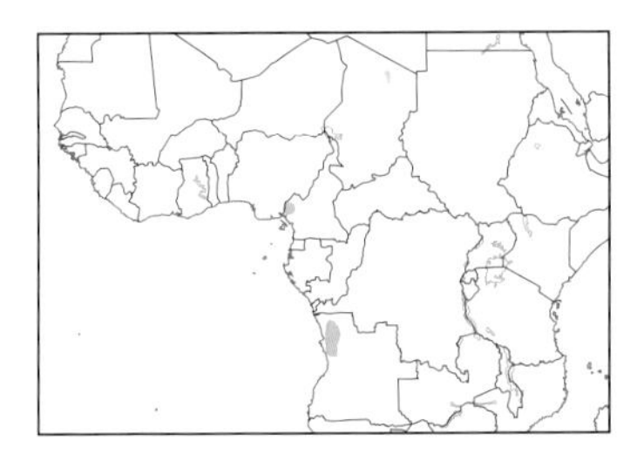

36a Adult *monteiri* Head grey, white on face almost encircling pale grey eye, black bill massive. Underparts bright lemon-yellow. Sometimes with brownish tinge as shown here. Escarpment and riverine forest, Angola. **Compare** Grey-headed Bush-shrike (Plate 14).
36b Adult *perspicillatus* Like 36a, but paler lemon below. Montane forest in Cameroon. **Compare** Grey-headed Bush-shrike and Fiery-breasted Bush-shrike (Plate 14).

37 Orange-breasted Bush-shrike *Chlorophoneus sulfureopectus* Text p.221

Medium size, sexes similar. Geographical variation slight. Solitary, skulking in canopy of savanna woodland, widespread in sub-Saharan Africa. Whistle calls diagnostic, but check Bocage's Bush-shrike (see Sounds).

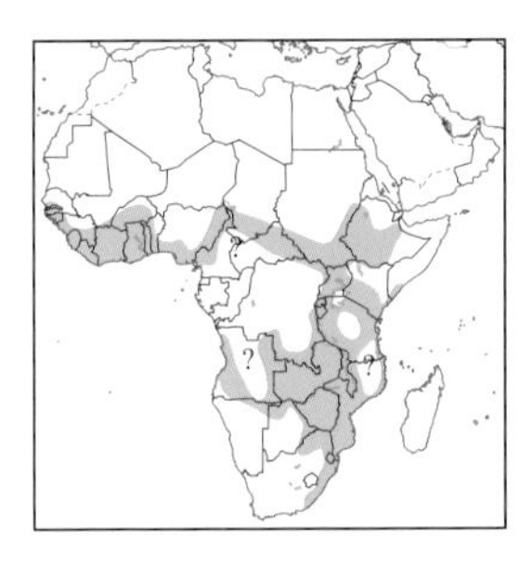

37a Adult Head and mantle pale bluish-grey, frontal and eyebrow yellow, face-mask black. Back, wings and tail olive-green. Underparts bright yellow with orange breast. Bill small, eye brown. **Compare** Grey-headed Bush-shrike (Plate 14) and other small forest *Chlorophoneus* bush-shrikes.
37b Adult Yellow-breasted morph. W region of southern Africa.
37c Juvenile Head and mantle whitish-grey with dark barring, back greenish barred. Wing-coverts tipped buff. Underparts dull white with heavy dark barring. Bill pale, eye brown. **Compare** Bocage's Bush-shrike (this plate) and other small forest *Chlorophoneus* bush-shrikes.
37d *'andaryae'* Possible hybrid, probably a 1st-year bird. Above grey, including forehead, face-mask and rump. Lores and eyebrow white. Wings brownish-green. Tail greenish with grey central feathers. Underparts buffy-white. Entebbe in Uganda.

38 Bocage's Bush-shrike *Chlorophoneus bocagei* Text p.223

Medium size, sexes fairly similar. Geographical variation slight. Solitary, skulking in canopy of secondary forest and thickets from Central Africa in Cameroon, N Angola, Zaïre, Uganda and Kenya. Whistle calls diagnostic, but check Orange-breasted Bush-shrike (see Sounds).

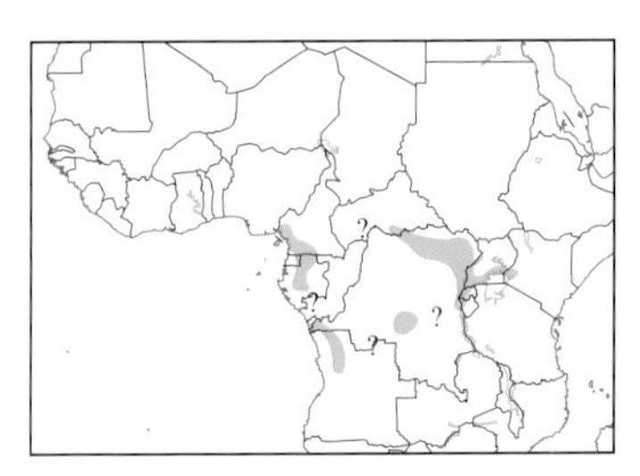

38a Adult Black head with contrasting white forehead and eyebrow. Back and wings dark grey, tail black, grey in ♀. Underparts buff, chin white. **Compare** Pink-footed Puffback Shrike (Plate 26) and ♀ Black-backed Puffback (Plate 25).
38b Immature Above like adult, but duller, head less black with eyebrow and lores buffy-white. Wing-coverts tipped buff. Underparts dull white with coarse grey barring. **Compare** Orange-breasted Bush-shrike and other small forest *Chlorophoneus* bush-shrikes.

36a
36b
37c
37b
37a
37d
38b
38a

PLATE 16 SMALL FOREST BUSH-SHRIKES 1

39 Many-coloured Bush-shrike *Chlorophoneus multicolor*

Text p.225

Medium size, sexes different. Geographical variation slight but polymorphism marked (red, orange, yellow, buff and black morphs). Solitary, skulking in canopy of lowland and montane forest from West Africa to NE Zaïre and Angola. Harsh ♀ call appears diagnostic, but check Black-fronted Bush-shrike (see Sounds).

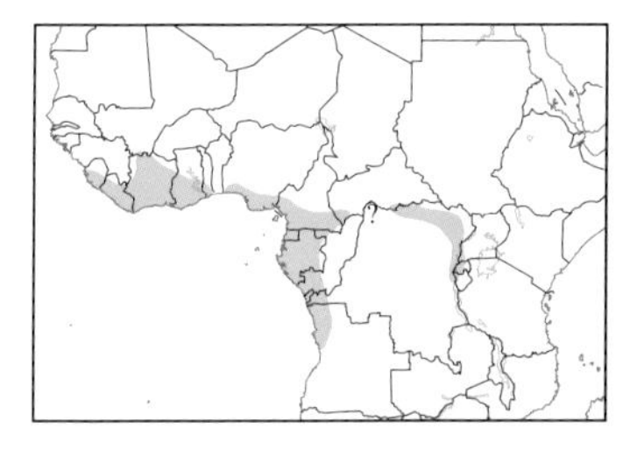

39a Adult ♂ *multicolor* Red morph. Head and mantle grey, broad black frontal and face-mask, eyebrow white. Back and wings olive-green. Tail mainly black with pale tips. Underparts scarlet-red. Bill small and black. W Africa to Zaïre. **Compare** Fiery-breasted Bush-shrike (Plate 14) and Black-fronted Bush-shrike (Plate 17).
39b Adult ♀ *multicolor* Red morph. Like ♂ but duller and lacking black face-mask, and has a green tail.
39c Immature ♂ Red morph. Like ♀ but with patchy black frontal and face-mask, some yellowish tips to wing-coverts, and patchy scarlet and yellowish-green underparts. **Compare** as for adult.
39d Juvenile: Red morph. Underparts vary according to colour morph. Barring below generally indistinct or absent (absent in W, occasional in E); may also show barred crown. Tertials and wing-coverts with distinct terminal yellow spots. Tail green like ♀. Underparts show traces of scarlet-red on throat and breast, with rest yellowish-green. Bill pale. **Compare** as for adult.
39e Adult ♂ *batesi* Yellow morph. W Africa to Zaïre and the only morph in Angola.
39f Adult ♂ *batesi* Orange morph. W Africa.
39g Adult ♂ Buff morph. E Zaïre.
39h Juvenile Buff morph. Underparts differ from other morphs. Whitish chin, throat, breast and upper belly, grading into olive-green on lower belly. Flanks greyish to olive-green and slightly barred. Bill pale. **Compare** Black-fronted Bush-shrike (Plate 17), Orange-breasted Bush-shrike and Bocage's Bush-shrike (Plate 15).
39i Adult ♂ Black morph. ♀♀ do not occur in this morph. W Africa.

39a
39b
39d
39c
39h
39e
39f
39g
39i

PLATE 17 SMALL FOREST BUSH-SHRIKES 2

40 Black-fronted Bush-shrike *Chlorophoneus nigrifrons* Text p.226

Medium size, sexes different. Geographical variation slight, but polymorphism marked (red, orange, yellow, buff and black morphs). Solitary, skulking in canopy of lowland and montane forest from Kenya to South Africa. Harsh ♀ call appears diagnostic, but check Many-coloured Bush-shrike (see Sounds).

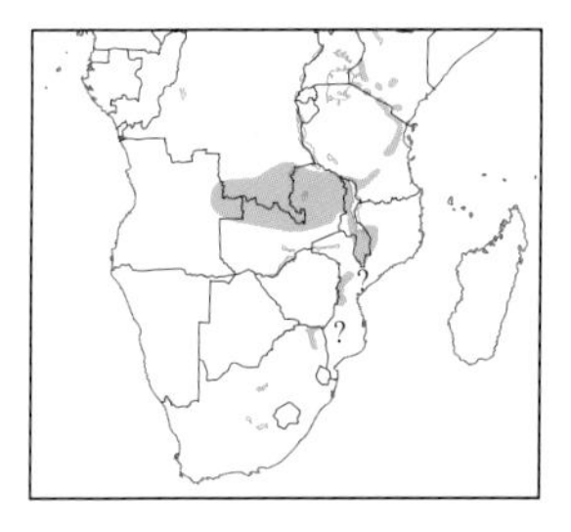

40a Adult ♂ *nigrifrons* Orange morph. Grey head with black frontal and face-mask. Back, wings and tail olive-green. Underparts orange. Kenya to South Africa. **Compare** Many-coloured Bush-shrike (Plate 16) and Olive Bush-shrike (Plate 18).
40b Adult ♀ *nigrifrons* Like ♂, but black face-mask does not extend onto frontal or ear-coverts. Underparts duller and less extensive than ♂, usually with faint barring on flanks. Occurs in all morphs except Black.
40c Immature Above like ♀, but without face-mask. Primary-coverts tipped buff. Development of underpart colour begins on chin, throat and breast. Flanks barred. **Compare** Buff morph Many-coloured Bush-shrike (Plate 16) and Olive Bush-shrike (Plate 18).
40d Juvenile Above like ♀, but without face-mask. Flight feathers and wing-coverts tipped buff. Underparts buff to yellowish-green with distinct grey barring. Bill pale. **Compare** as for immature.
40e Adult ♂ Red morph. Kenya to SE Zaïre.
40f Adult ♂ Yellow morph. Kenya to Tanzania.
40g Adult ♂ Buff morph. Kenya to Malawi.
40h Adult ♂ Black morph. ♀♀ do not occur in this morph. E Usambara Mts in Tanzania, and Namuli Mts in N Mozambique.

40a
40b
40c
40d
40e
40f
40g
40h

PLATE 18 SMALL FOREST BUSH-SHRIKES 3

41 Olive Bush-shrike *Chlorophoneus olivaceus* Text p.229

Medium size, sexes different. Geographical variation slight but polymorphism marked (olive and buff morphs). Solitary, skulking at all levels in forest edge and dense coastal bush from Malawi to South Africa. Whistled calls diagnostic (see Sounds).

41a Adult ♂ Olive morph. Head, back and wings olive-green, lores and eyebrow yellow, face-mask black. Tail black with yellow tips and edges. Underparts rufous-yellow. From SW South Africa to Zimbabwe. **Compare** Black-fronted Bush-shrike (Plate 17).
41b Adult ♀ Olive morph. Like ♂, but duller, lacks distinctive black and yellow face markings, and has a green tail without yellow tips or edges.
41c Juvenile Above like ♀, but with buff tips to primary wing-coverts. Underparts pale buffy-rufous with indistinct barring. Bill pale. **Compare** as for adult.
41d Adult ♂ Buff morph. Head pale grey with black face-mask, lores white and eyebrow behind eye white. Back and wings olive-green. Tail black with yellow tips and edges. Underparts buffy-rufous to salmon-pink. Throughout range from SW South Africa to Malawi. **Compare** as for olive morph.
41e Adult ♀ Buff morph. Like ♂, but duller, without distinctive face-mask and eyebrow. Lores whitish, ear-coverts darker grey. Tail green. Underparts buffy-rufous, less extensive than ♂, and belly greyish-green with more extensive barring.
41f Juvenile Buff morph. Like ♀, but without face markings. Head, face and mantle pale grey tinged greenish. Back, wings and tail green. Primary wing-coverts tipped buff. Underparts greenish-grey, faintly barred buffy-grey. Bill pale. **Compare** as for adult.

41a
41b
41c
41a
41d
41e
41f

42 Mount Kupé Bush-shrike *Chlorophoneus? kupeensis* Text p.230

Medium-large, sexes different. Solitary, skulking in low to mid-levels of montane forest in W Cameroon, West Africa. Calls diagnostic (see Sounds).

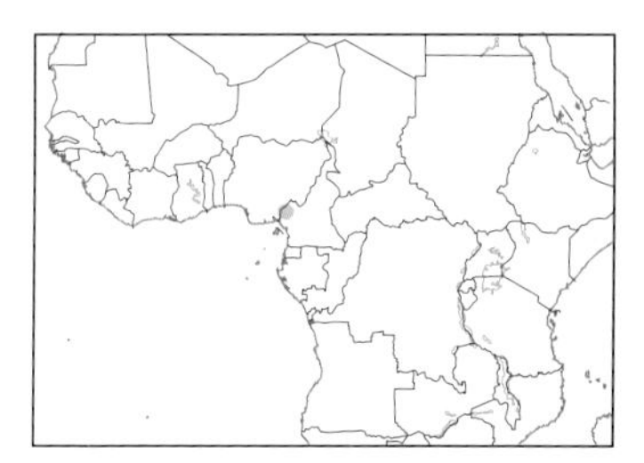

42a Adult ♂ Distinctive. Grey head, nape, breast and belly. Vent yellow. Black face-mask and white throat with narrow black necklace. Back, wings and tail bright olive-green.
42b Adult ♀ Like ♂, but with a single large round chestnut-brown spot in centre of white throat just above grey of breast. May show tinge of yellow around this spot when breeding.

43 Gorgeous Bush-shrike *Chlorophoneus viridis* Text p.232

Medium size, sexes different. Geographical variation marked. Solitary, skulking low down in dense undergrowth of forest edge and thickets. Two separate, distinct populations: S Somalia to E southern Africa, and Congo to NW Zambia. Calls diagnostic (see Sounds).

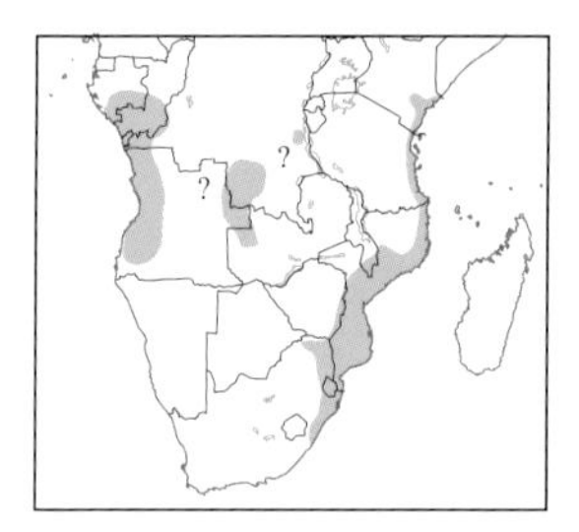

43a Adult ♂ *viridis* Bright olive-green above including wings. Head with yellowish frontal and short eyebrow, narrow black face-mask from lores, extending into broad black breast-band encircling scarlet-red throat. Remaining underparts dark green with maroon-brown lower edge to breast-band, stripe down mid-belly and undertail-coverts. Tail black. Congo, SE Gabon, Zaïre, N Angola and NW Zambia. **Compare** Doherty's Bush-shrike (this plate).
43b Adult ♀ *viridis* Like ♂, but duller, lores greenish-yellow and breast-band narrower. Tail mainly green.
43c Juvenile *viridis* Lacks frontal, throat and breast-band markings of adult. Above dull olive-green including wings and tail, face yellowish-green. Chin and throat yellowish grading to yellowish-green and finely barred below. Bill pale.
43d Adult ♂ *quadricolor* Like 43a, but brighter below without maroon-brown markings. Below breast-band yellowish-orange grading into bright reddish undertail-coverts. Tail mainly blackish. S Somalia to South Africa. **Compare** as for nominate.
43e Adult ♀ *quadricolor* Like ♂, but duller, lacks black and yellow facial markings. Lores greenish-yellow. Tail mainly green. Red throat-patch paler, breast-band narrower and belly without reddish tinge.
43e Immature *quadricolor* Like ♀, but with progressive development of red throat and black breast-band.

44 Doherty's Bush-shrike *Chlorophoneus dohertyi* Text p.234

Medium size, sexes fairly similar. Solitary, skulking in dense undergrowth of forests and thickets from E Zaïre, Rwanda, Burundi, W Uganda and W Kenya. Calls diagnostic (see Sounds).

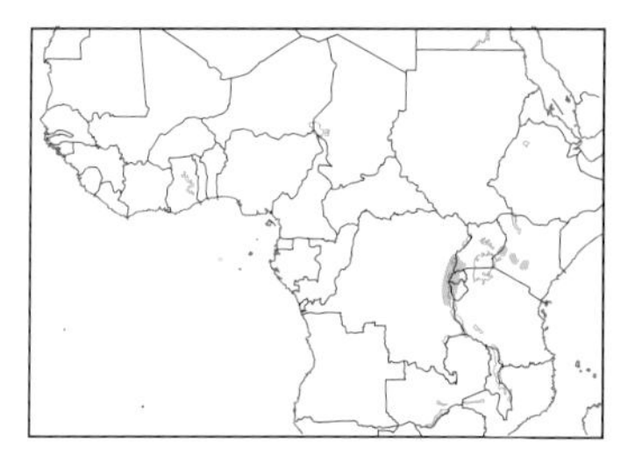

44a Adult Distinctive. Above olive-green, broad scarlet-red frontal. Black face-mask extends into broad black breast-band encircling scarlet-red throat. Below breast-band bright lemon-yellow. Undertail-coverts red. **Compare** Gorgeous Bush-shrike (this plate).
44b Adult: Yellow morph. Rare.
44c Juvenile Above dull tawny-green with fine barring, face greenish-yellow. Underparts pale yellow, finely barred. Undertail-coverts reddish. Bill pale. **Compare** as for adult.

42a
42b
43a
43b
43c
43d
43e
43f
44b
44a
44c

PLATE 20 MAINLY TERRESTRIAL BUSH-SHRIKES

45 Bokmakierie *Telophorus zeylonus* Text p.235

Large, sexes similar. Geographical variation slight. Solitary or in pairs, mainly terrestrial in open bush habitats in southern Africa, with an isolated population in E Zimbabwe. Calls diagnostic (see Sounds).

45a Adult Distinctive. Grey head with broad yellow eyebrow and black lores extending as a broad black breast-band encircling chrome-yellow throat. Lower back and wings olive-green. Black tail with broad yellow outer feathers diagnostic in flight. Underparts chrome-yellow, flanks greenish.
45b Juvenile Above dull olive-green, face and ear-coverts greyish. Underparts olive-green, finely barred grey. Chin and throat buff, belly and flanks yellowish-green. Wings and tail like adult.

46 Rosy-patched Shrike *Rhodophoneus cruentus* Text p.238

Large size, sexes different. Geographical variation marked. Solitary or in pairs, mainly terrestrial in arid thornbush of NE Africa. Whistle diagnostic (see Sounds).

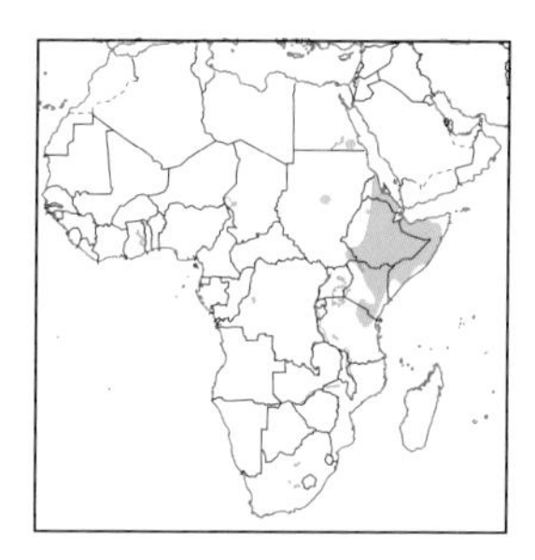

46a Adult ♂ *cruentus* Distinctive. Pale greyish-brown above with pale eyebrow. Reddish-pink back and black tail with broad white tips to outer feathers diagnostic in flight. Underparts dull white with reddish-pink stripe in centre from chin to belly, flanks pale rufous. SE Egypt, Eritrea, Djibouti, central Sudan and N Ethiopia.
46b Adult ♀ *cruentus* Like ♂ above but with broad black breast-band encircling white throat.
46c Juvenile Duller than adult with buff mottling on crown and buff tips to wing-coverts. Underparts dull white with buffy or pale rufous flanks. Bill pale.
46d Adult ♂ *hilgerti* Like 46a, but darker, reddish-brown above, without pale eyebrow. Underparts with darker rufous-brown flanks. Somalia, E Ethiopia and N Kenya.
46e Adult ♂ *cathemagmenus* Like 46d, but pinker above and has black breast-band encircling reddish-pink throat. S Kenya and E Tanzania.
46f Adult ♀ *cathemagmenus* Like ♂, but with white throat.

45a
45b
45a
46b
46a
46a
46c
46d
46f
46e

PLATE 21 BLACK BOUBOUS

47 Sooty Boubou *Laniarius leucorhynchus* **Text p.240**

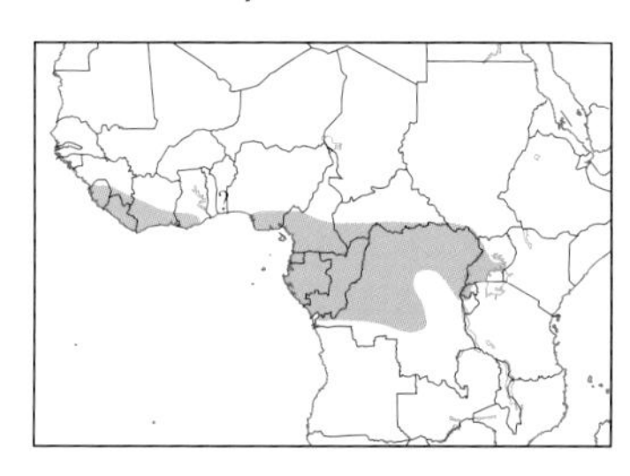

Medium-large, sexes slightly different. Solitary, skulking low down or on ground, mainly in lowland dense undergrowth of secondary forest and thickets from Sierra Leone to W Kenya, and in W down to Zaïre and Angola. Calls diagnostic (see Sounds).

47a Adult ♂ Stoutly built, uniform black with slight gloss. Rump without concealed white spots. **Compare** Mountain Sooty and Slate-coloured Boubou (this plate).
47b Adult ♀ Like ♂, but duller without gloss.
47c Immature Distinctive. Like ♀, but tinged brown with faint pale spotting on crown, and with whitish or ivory-coloured bill. Note juvenile has dark bill. **Compare** as for adult.

48 Mountain Sooty Boubou *Laniarius poensis* **Text p.241**

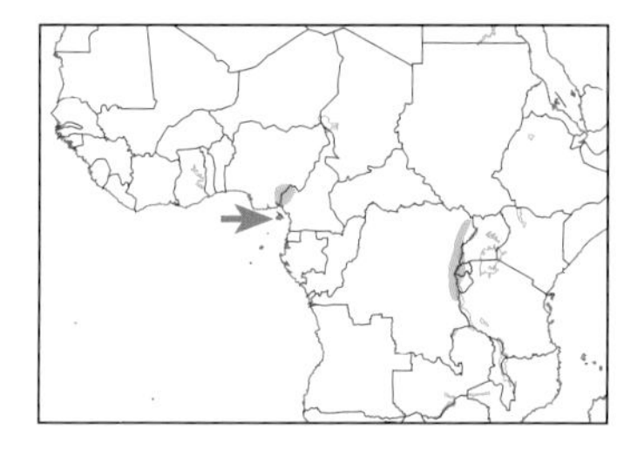

Medium-small, sexes similar with ♀ slightly duller. Geographical variation slight. Solitary, skulking low down or on ground in dense undergrowth of montane forests in two separate populations: SE Nigeria, S Cameroon and Bioko, and E Zaïre, SW Uganda, Rwanda and Burundi. Calls of separate populations differ (see Sounds).

48a Adult Completely black with slight gloss, appearing purplish or blue-black. Rump without concealed white spots. **Compare** Sooty and Slate-coloured Boubou (this plate)
48b Juvenile Completely brownish-black with faint pale spotting on crown. **Compare** as for adult.

49 Fülleborn's Black Boubou *Laniarius fuelleborni* **Text p.242**

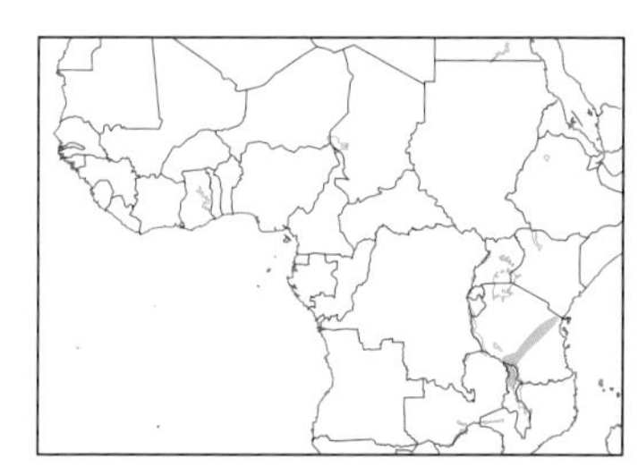

Medium size, sexes slightly different. Geographical variation slight. Solitary, skulking at all levels, mainly in dense undergrowth of montane forest from NE Tanzania to NE Zambia and N Malawi. Calls diagnostic (see Sounds).
49a Adult ♂ Completely greyish-black, rump without concealed white spots. **Compare** Slate-coloured Boubou (this plate).
49b Adult ♀ Like ♂, but head paler and underparts tinged olive.
49c Juvenile Dull olive-grey. **Compare** as for adult.

50 Slate-coloured Boubou *Laniarius funebris* **Text p.243**

Medium size, sexes slightly different. Geographical variation slight. Solitary, skulking low down or on ground in dense undergrowth of dry thickets in thornscrub and woodlands from S Sudan, Ethiopia, Somalia, Uganda, Kenya, Tanzania and Rwanda. Calls diagnostic (see Sounds).

50a Adult ♂ Completely dark grey, rump with concealed white spots. **Compare** all-black morph of Tropical Boubou (Plate 24), Sooty and Fülleborn's Black Boubou (this plate).
50b Adult ♀ Like ♂, but paler and smaller.
50c Juvenile Duller than adult, more blackish-brown. Above lightly spotted buff, wing-coverts edged buff. Underparts barred buffy greyish-black. Bill black. **Compare** as for adult.

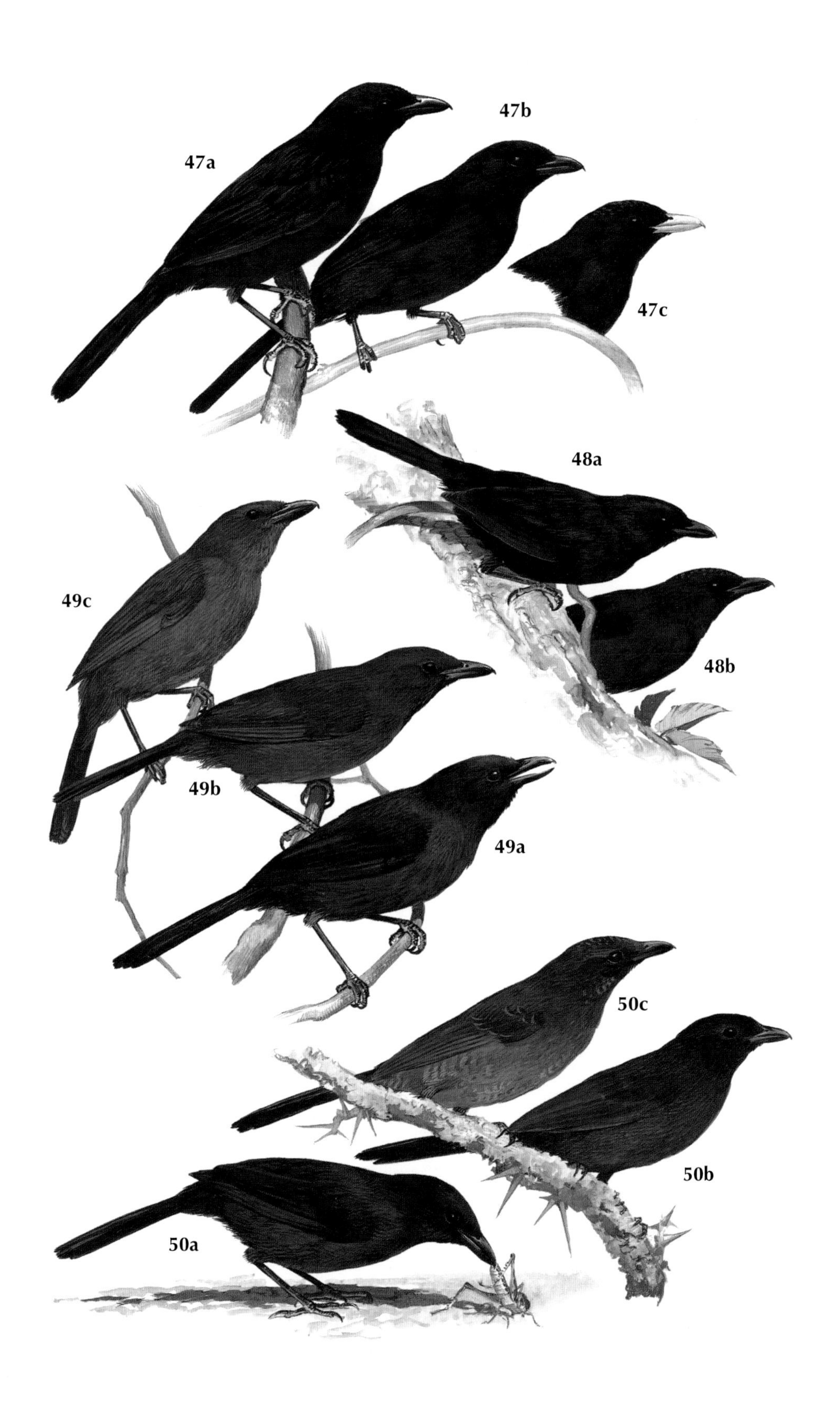

47a
47b
47c
48a
48b
49c
49b
49a
50c
50b
50a

PLATE 22 CRIMSON BOUBOUS

51 Crimson-breasted Gonolek *Laniarius atrococcineus* Text p.245

Large, sexes similar. Solitary, skulking low down or on ground in thornbush. From S Angola to southern Africa. Calls diagnostic (see Sounds).

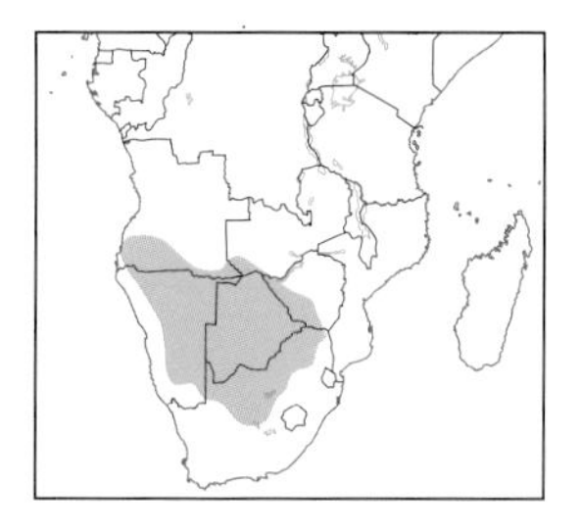

51a Adult Distinctive. Above black with white wing-stripe and dark eye. Underparts crimson-red.
51b Immature Above brownish-black, below greyish-buff with dark barring and patchy areas of pale crimson. Primary wing-coverts tipped buff. Bill black.
51c Adult Yellow morph. Rare.

52 Black-headed Gonolek *Laniarius erythrogaster* Text p.247

Medium-large, sexes similar. Solitary, skulking low down or on ground in thornbush from Chad to Eritrea and S in East Africa from Uganda, Kenya, Rwanda, Burundi and SE Zaïre. Calls diagnostic (see Sounds).

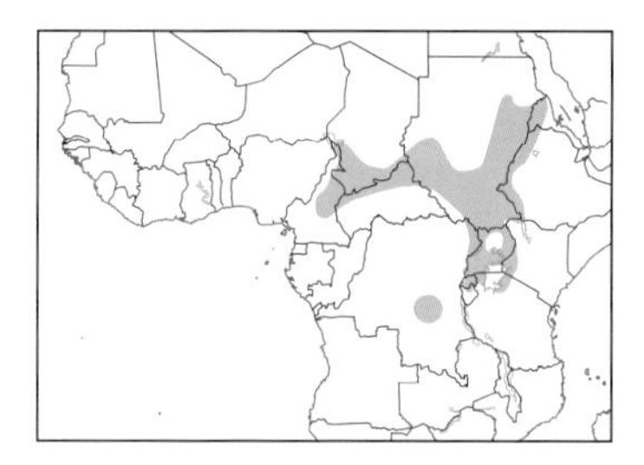

52a Adult Distinctive. Above completely black. Eye pale yellow. Underparts crimson-red, lower belly and undertail-coverts dark buff. **Compare** Yellow-crowned and Papyrus Gonolek (this plate).
52b Immature Above dull black, forehead, crown and wing-coverts tipped buff. Below buff with dark barring, progressively replaced with crimson-red. Eye brown. **Compare** as for adult and Slate-coloured Boubou (Plate 21).

53 Yellow-crowned Gonolek *Laniarius barbarus* Text p.248

Large, sexes similar. Geographical variation moderate. Solitary, skulking in dense undergrowth of thickets in savannas or papyrus in S Mauritania to N Cameroon. Calls diagnostic (see Sounds).

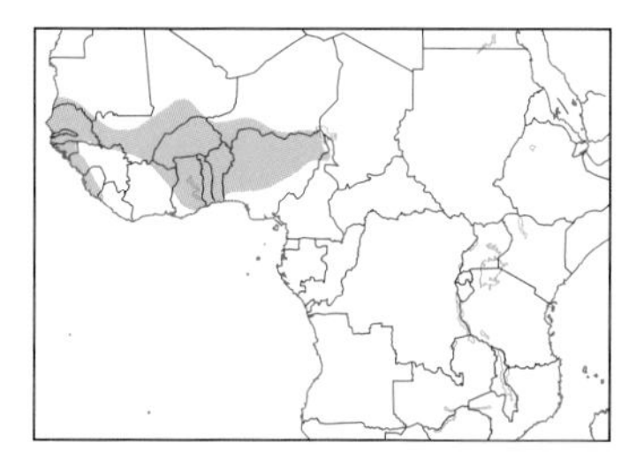

53a Adult *barbarus* Distinctive. Above black with golden crown. Eye brown. Underparts crimson-red (rarely yellow) with lower belly and tail-coverts dark buff. S Mauritania to Cameroon. **Compare** Black-headed Gonolek (this plate).
53b Adult *helenae* Like 53a, but crown deeper rufous-yellow. Inhabits papyrus swamp. Sierra Leone.
53c Immature Above like adult but duller black. Crown dull yellow and less extensive. Wing-coverts tipped buff. Underparts buff with dark barring, progressively replaced with crimson-red. **Compare** as for adult.

54 Papyrus Gonolek *Laniarius mufumbiri* Text p.249

Small-medium, sexes similar. Solitary, skulking in papyrus swamps from E Zaïre, W and S Uganda, W Kenya along Lake Victoria, Rwanda, Burundi and possibly NW Tanzania. Calls diagnostic (see Sounds).

54a Adult Distinctive. Above black, eye pale yellow. Crown dull yellow. Wings sometimes with short white stripe. Underparts pale crimson-red, lower belly and vent whitish. **Compare** Black-headed Gonolek (this plate).
54b Immature Above like adult, but duller, some feathers tipped buff. Crown broadly tipped dull greyish-olive or buff. Wing-coverts tipped and edged buff; small wing-stripe may be present. Underparts brick-red to yellowish-pink with yellowish-buff throat. Lower belly and undertail-coverts whitish-buff. Eye pale brown. **Compare** as for adult.

51a
51b
51a
51c
52a
52b
53b
53a
53a
53c
54b
54a

PLATE 23 BOUBOUS 1

55 Yellow-breasted Boubou *Laniarius atroflavus* Text p.250

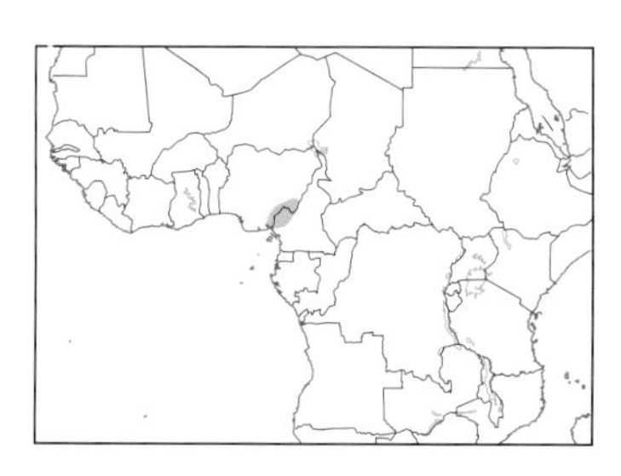

Medium size, sexes similar. Geographical variation slight. Solitary, skulking in undergrowth and mid-levels of montane forest in West Africa from E Nigeria and W Cameroon. Some calls diagnostic, others like Mountain Sooty Boubou (see Sounds).

55a Adult Distinctive. Above black, below deep yellow.
55b Immature Above dull brownish-black with buff-spotted crown. Wing-coverts and outer tail feathers tipped and edged buff. Underparts paler and duller than adult.

56 Lühder's Bush-shrike *Laniarius luehderi* Text p.251

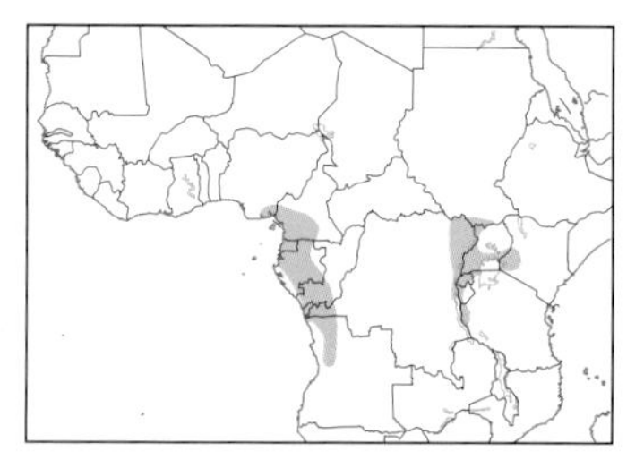

Medium size, sexes similar. Geographical variation marked. Solitary, skulking in undergrowth of mainly lowland forest in two separate populations: SE Nigeria to W Zaïre, Angola, and from S Sudan, W Uganda, W Kenya, NW Tanzania, W Rwanda, Burundi and E Zaïre. Calls generally diagnostic, but check Tropical and Swamp Boubou (see Sounds).

56a Adult *luehderi* Distinctive. Above black with rufous-brown crown. Wing black with thin white stripe. From chin to upper belly tawny-orange, lower belly white. **56b Immature** Dusky barring gradually lost. Above olive-brown, dull wing-stripe, wing-coverts tipped buff. Tail rufous. Underparts deep yellow tinged orange on breast. **56c Juvenile** Above olive-brown, finely barred. Rump and uppertail-coverts rufous barred black. Wing-coverts tipped buff, wing-stripe buffy-yellow. Tail dark rufous. Underparts buffy-yellow with heavy barring. Bill greyish-brown. **Compare** Tropical and Swamp Boubou (Plate 24). **56d Adult** *brauni* Distinctive. Sometimes considered a separate species. Like 56a, but throat and breast reddish-orange. Restricted to rainforest in NW Angola. **56e Adult** *amboimensis* Distinctive. Sometimes considered a separate species. Like 56a, but underparts completely white. Restricted to rainforest at Gabela in W Angola. **Compare** Tropical and Swamp Boubou (Plate 24).

57 Red-naped Bush-shrike *Laniarius ruficeps* Text p.253

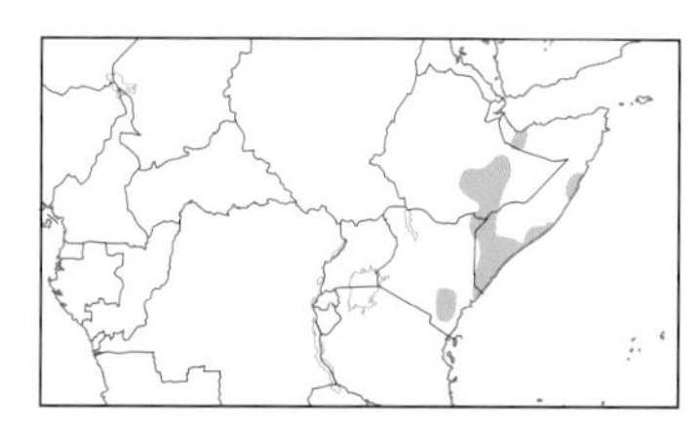

Medium size, sexes slightly different. Geographical variation moderate. Solitary, skulking low down in dense thickets in arid thornbush of NE and East Africa. Calls diagnostic (see Sounds).

57a Adult ♂ *ruficeps* Distinctive. Reddish-orange crown, black face-mask, white eyebrow and white wing-stripe. Underparts white or buff. NW Somalia and Eritrea.
57b Adult ♀ *ruficeps* Like ♂, but back more olive-grey.
57c Adult *rufinuchalis* Like 57a, but larger black forehead, underparts rufous. Ethiopia, central and SE Somalia, Kenya.
57d Immature Like adult, but duller, tinged brown above with dull reddish crown mottled black. Wing-coverts tipped buff. Underparts buffy-white.

58 Bulo Burti Boubou *Laniarius liberatus* Text p.254

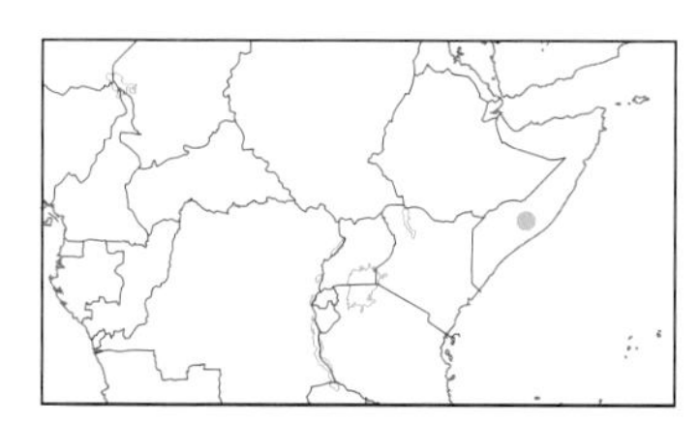

Medium size, only known from one individual of unknown sex. Skulks low down or on ground in thornbush. Only recorded at Bulo Burti, central Somalia. Calls little known (see Sounds).

58 Adult (presumed). Above black, long broad yellowish eyebrow, black face-mask and white wing-stripe. Underparts light yellow, belly white.

55a
55b
56e
56b
56c
56d
56a
57c
57d
57b
57a
58

PLATE 24 BOUBOUS 2

59 Southern Boubou *Laniarius ferrugineus* Text p.255

Medium-large, sexes different. Geographical variation marked. Solitary, skulking low down or on ground in moist dense bush from SE Zimbabwe to SW South Africa. Calls diagnostic, but check Tropical Boubou (see Sounds).

59a Adult ♂ *ferrugineus* Above black, wing-stripe white. Underparts white, flanks and belly rufous. SW to SE South Africa. **Compare** Tropical Boubou (this plate).
59b Adult ♀ Like ♂, but dull greyish above.
59c Adult *pondoensis* Darkest race, underparts deep buffy-rufous. Pondoland.
59d Juvenile Above dull brownish-black, pale mottling on head. Wing-stripe buffy-white, coverts tipped buff. Underparts pale buffy-rufous with fine barring. **Compare** as for adult.

60 Tropical Boubou *Laniarius aethiopicus* Text p.257

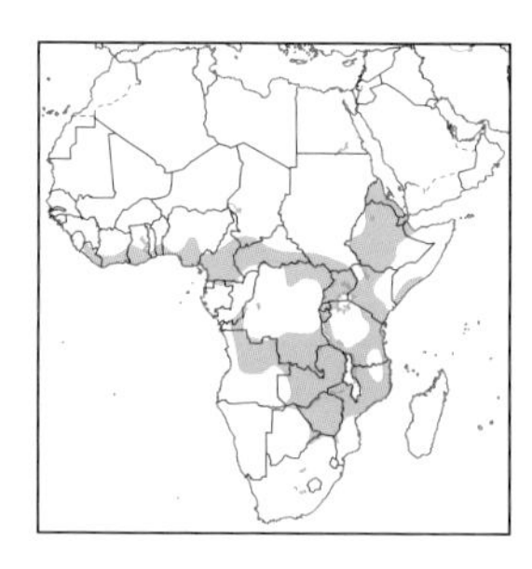

Large, sexes similar. Geographical variation in plumage and calls marked. Solitary, skulking at mid-levels or on ground in dense bush. Widespread in sub-Saharan Africa to border of South Africa. Some calls diagnostic, but check other boubous (see Sounds).

60a Adult *ambiguus* Above black with short white wing-stripe. Underparts white, tinged pink on breast and flanks. Kenyan highlands and NE Tanzania.
60b Juvenile *ambiguus* Above dull brownish-black barred tawny-buff with mottled appearance. Wing-stripe whitish, tertials and coverts tipped tawny. Underparts whitish, barred on flanks. **Compare** Southern Boubou (this plate).
60c Adult *sublacteus* Little to no white in wing. Coastal E Kenya and Zanzibar. **60d Adult** *mossambicus* More buffy-pink below than pinkish. S Zaïre, E Zambia, Mozambique, S Zimbabwe and N South Africa. **Compare** Southern Boubou (this plate). **60e Adult** *major* Usually pinkish below, but white (as illustrated here) in S central Zaïre and NW Angola. **Compare** Swamp and Turat's Boubou (this plate).**60f Adult** *sublacteus* Completely black morph. Tana River mouth, Lamu I, Manda I and lower Juba River. **Compare** Slate-coloured Boubou (Plate 21).

61 Turat's Boubou *Laniarius turatii* Text p.260

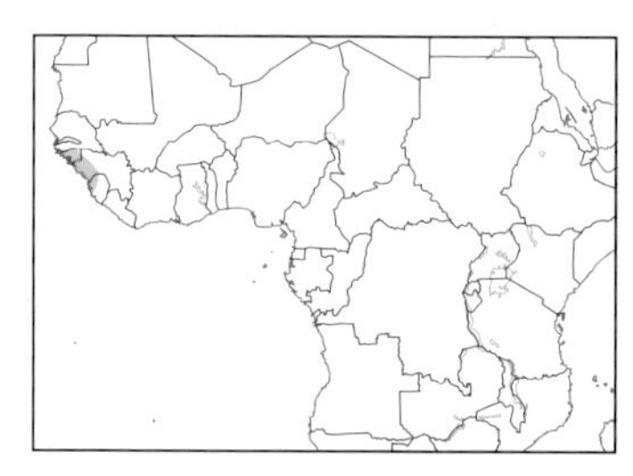

Large, sexes similar. Solitary, skulking in dense thickets and forest edge in West Africa, in Guinea-Bissau, Guinea and W Sierra Leone. Calls diagnostic (see Sounds).

61 Adult Distinctive. Above black without wing-stripe. Underparts whitish with pinkish-buff tinge, not always obvious. **Compare** Tropical Boubou (this plate).

62 Swamp Boubou *Laniarius bicolor* Text p.261

Large, sexes similar. Geographical variation moderate. Solitary, skulking at mid-levels or on ground. In N in savanna thickets and forest regrowth. In S in riverine thickets and reedbeds. From Cameroon to Botswana and NW Zimbabwe. Harsh ratchet call diagnostic (see Sounds).

62a Adult Above black with white wing-stripe. Underparts white. **Compare** Tropical Boubou (this plate).
62b Juvenile Above dull black, lightly spotted and barred tawny-buff. Underparts whitish lightly barred dusky. Bill pale. **Compare** as for adult.

59a
59b
59d
59c
60a
60c
60f
60d
60b
60e
61
62a
62a
62b

PLATE 25 PUFFBACKS 1

63 Black-shouldered Puffback *Dryoscopus senegalensis* Text p.262

Medium-small, sexes different. Solitary or in pairs, skulking in mid- to upper levels in forest clearings; avoids closed forest. Diagnostic white puffback display. From SW Nigeria to NE Angola and N equatorial belt to NE Zaïre and SW Uganda. Calls little known; check Black-backed Puffback (see Sounds).

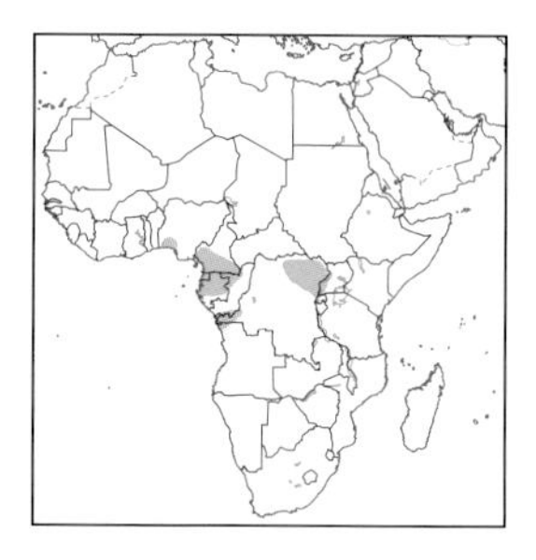

63a Adult ♂ Above glossy black with reddish eye and broad white rump. No white in wings. Underparts white. **Compare** Sabine's and Pink-footed Puffback (Plate 26) and Red-eyed Flycatcher-shrike (Plate 29) and Black-backed Puffback race *affinis* (this plate).
63b Adult ♀ Like ♂, but duller with short white eyebrow and greyish rump. **Compare** as for ♂.
63c Immature Like ♀, but duller above. Underparts dull white. **Compare** as for ♀.

64 Black-backed Puffback *Dryoscopus cubla* Text p.264

Medium-small, sexes different. Geographical variation marked. Solitary or in pairs, skulking in mid- to upper levels. Diagnostic white puffback display. Found in dense woodland and forest, widespread S of equator. Calls diagnostic (see Sounds).

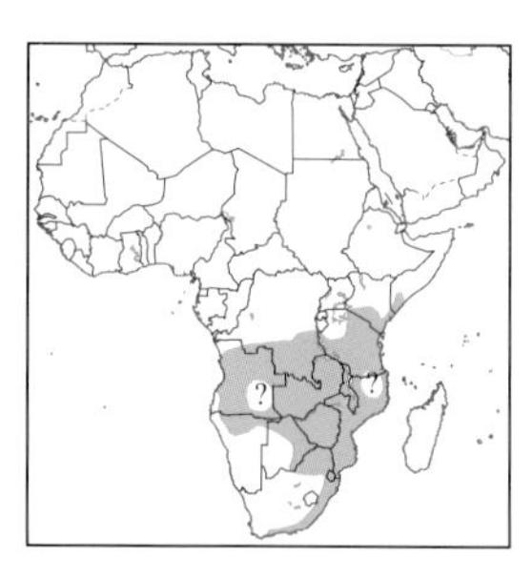

64a Adult ♂ *cubla* Glossy black above with reddish eye, white scapulars, wing-stripe and rump. Underparts white. S and E South Africa. **Compare** Pringle's and Northern Puffback (this plate).
64b Adult ♀ *cubla* Like ♂, but duller, whiter face and short eyebrow. Rump olive-grey. Underparts duller: dull white to buffy-grey.
64c Immature Like ♀, but white areas buff to buffy-grey. **Compare** as for adult.
64d Adult ♂ *hamatus* Whiter than 64a, particularly wings and underparts. Kenya, Tanzania, Zaïre and S Angola.
64e Adult ♂ *affinis* Like 64a, but lacks white scapulars and white in wings. Coastal E Africa. **Compare** note similarity to Black-shouldered Puffback, ranges separate (this plate).
64f Adult ♀ *affinis* Like ♂, but short white eyebrow, black loral spot, and greyish scapulars and rump. **Compare** as for 64e.

65 Pringle's Puffback *Dryoscopus pringlii* Text p.266

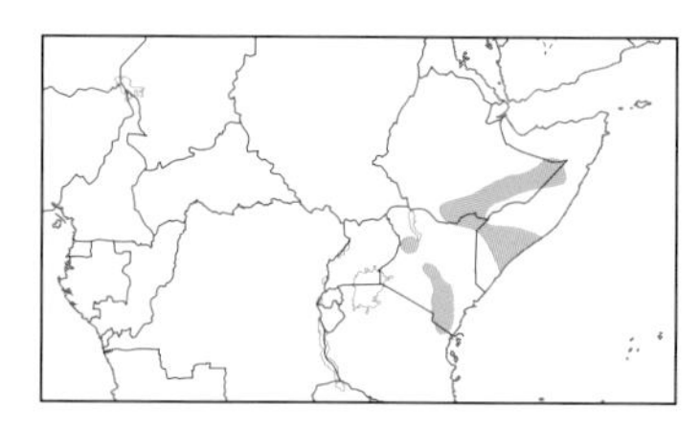

Small, sexes different. Solitary, skulking in bushes in arid thornbush in NE Africa from Ethiopia and Somalia to Kenya and NE Tanzania. Calls little known, but some diagnostic (see Sounds).

65a Adult ♂ Above black with red eye, rump greyish-white, wing-coverts edged white. Underparts greyish-brown. Diagnostic bicoloured bill. **Compare** Black-backed and Northern Puffback (this plate).
65b Adult ♀ Pale greyish-brown above and below. Wing-coverts whitish. Bill like ♂. **Compare** as for ♂.
65c Juvenile Like ♀, but duller, buffier below. Eye probably brown. **Compare** as for ♀.

63a
63b
63c
64a
64b
64c
64e
64f
64d
65a
65b
65c

PLATE 26 PUFFBACKS 2

66 Northern Puffback *Dryoscopus gambensis* **Text p.267**

Medium-small, sexes different. Geographical variation in ♀♀ marked. Solitary or in small groups, skulking in canopy of a variety of habitats from savanna woodland to forest edge. Widespread N of equator. Calls typically puffback, some diagnostic (see Sounds).

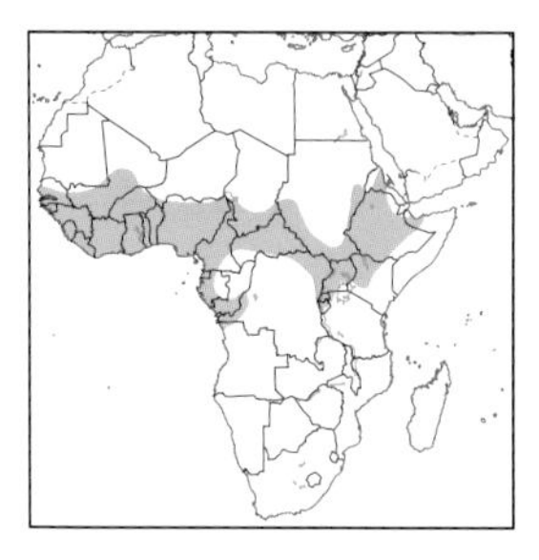

66a Adult ♂ *gambensis* Above glossy black. Rump, scapulars and wing-coverts greyish. Underparts dull white. Eye red, bill black. Senegal–Chad. **Compare** Sabine's and Pink-footed Puffbacks (this plate), Black-backed, Northern and Pringle's Puffbacks (Plate 25).
66b Adult ♀ *gambensis* Above greyish-brown with orange eye. Wing-coverts edged buff. Underparts tawny-buff. **Compare** as for ♂.
66c Immature ♀ Head and nape mottled greyish-brown, underparts more tawny-orange than adult, eye brown. **Compare** as for ♂.
66d Adult ♀ *erythreae* Above dark brown, below pale buff. E Sudan, Ethiopia and NW Somalia.

67 Pink-footed Puffback *Dryoscopus angolensis* **Text p.269**

Medium-small, sexes different. Geographical variation in ♂♂ moderate. Solitary, skulking in mid- to upper canopy of primary forest. Population fragmented: E Nigeria, Cameroon, Congo, SW Zaïre and N Angola. In E from SE Sudan, E Zaïre, W Uganda, W Kenya, W Tanzania and W Rwanda. Calls little known (see Sounds).

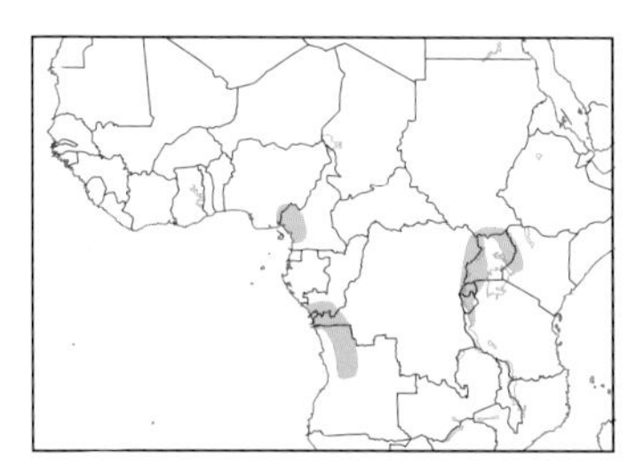

67a Adult ♂ *angolensis* Head and mantle bluish-black, back, rump, wings and tail grey. Underparts greyish-white. Legs pink, eye brown. Angola, W Zaïre. **Compare** Sabine's and Northern Puffback (this plate) and Black-shouldered Puffback (Plate 25).
67b Adult ♀ *angolensis* Head grey, short white loral stripe, eye brown. Back and rump olive-brown. Underparts buffy-orange. Legs pink. **Compare** ♀ Northern and Sabine's Puffback (this plate).
67c Immature Like ♀, but duller, more olive-brown above and brighter tawny-buff below. **Compare** as for ♀.
67d Adult ♂ *kungwensis* Head greyer than 67a. W Tanzania.

68 Sabine's Puffback *Dryoscopus sabini* **Text p.270**

Medium size, sexes different. Geographical variation in ♀♀ moderate. Solitary, skulking high up in canopy of lowland forest from Sierra Leone to Zaïre. Whistle call diagnostic (see Sounds).

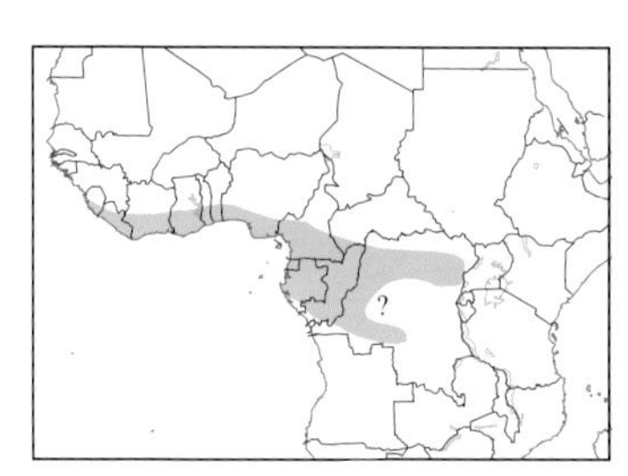

68a Adult ♂ *sabini* Above glossy blue-black, rump white. Eye reddish-brown, bill heavy. Underparts white. Sierra Leone to Nigeria. **Compare** Pink-footed and Northern Puffback (this plate) and Black-shouldered Puffback (Plate 25).
68b Adult ♀ *sabini* Head grey. Back, rump, wings and tail tawny-brown. Underparts similar but paler tawny-buff. Eye reddish-brown, bill heavy. **Compare** Pink-footed and Northern Puffbacks (this plate).
68c Immature ♀ Like 68b, but duller above with paler head and brown eye. **Compare** as for ♀.
68d Adult ♀ *melanoleucus* Above darker brown on head and back, bill longer. Cameroon to Zaïre and Angola at Cabinda.

66a
66b
66c
66d
67a
67d
67b
67c
68d
68a
68c
68b

PLATE 27 BUSH-SHRIKES and TCHAGRAS

69 Blackcap Bush-shrike *Antichromus minuta* Text p.271

Medium-small, sexes different. Geographical variation marked. Solitary, skulking in rank vegetation and reedbeds. Widespread from West, East and Central Africa as far S as E Zimbabwe. Whistle call diagnostic (see Sounds).

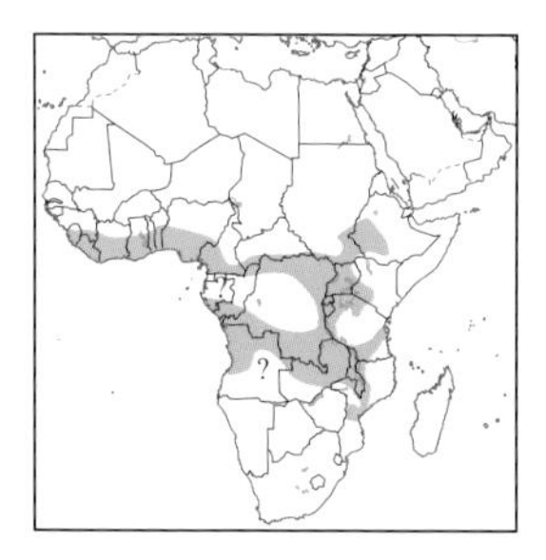

69a Adult ♂ *minuta* Distinctive. Head black, eye reddish, bill robust. Back and underparts reddish-brown, scapulars black. Wings bright chestnut-brown, tail black. Sierra Leone to Ethiopia, N and E Zaïre to Kenya and NE Tanzania.
69b Adult ♀ *minuta* Like ♂, but with broad white eyebrow and black stripe through eye. **Compare** Black-crowned Tchagra (this plate) and Brown-headed Tchagra (Plate 28).
69c Immature *minuta* Crown patchy, streaked black, brown and buff with buff eyebrow. Scapulars streaked black, rest of back and underparts like adult. Eye brown, bill pale, particularly on lower mandible. **Compare** as for adult ♀.
69d Adult ♂ *anchietae* Like 69a, but without black scapulars. Angola, S Zaïre, Zambia, S Tanzania, Malawi, Mozambique, E Zimbabwe.
69e Adult ♀ *anchietae* Like 69b, but without black scapulars.

70 Black-crowned Tchagra *Tchagra senegala* Text p.273

Medium-large, sexes similar. Geographical variation moderate. Solitary, skulking low down or on ground in variety of habitats. Widespread in Africa N and S of Sahara and in Arabian Peninsula. Whistle call diagnostic (see Sounds).

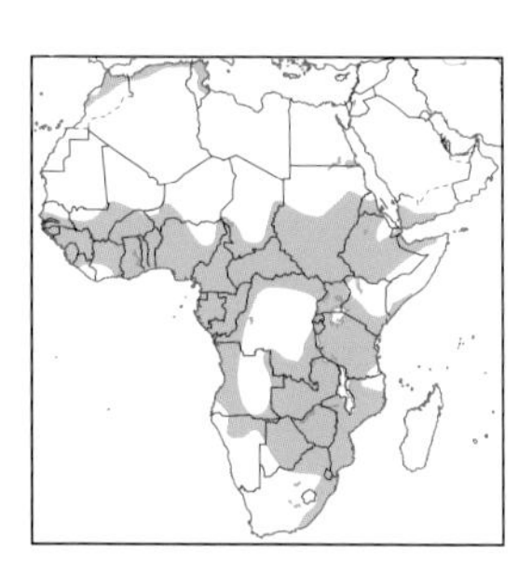

70a Adult *senegala* Crown and stripe through eye black with long broad white eyebrow. Bill relatively long. Wings bright chestnut-brown. Tail mostly black, broadly tipped white, diagnostic in flight. Senegal to Sierra Leone. **Compare** Brown-headed and Three-streaked Tchagra (Plate 28) and ♀ Blackcap Bush-shrike (this plate).
70b Immature Like adult, but crown mottled blackish-brown, eyebrow buff and underparts more buff than adults. Bill pale. **Compare** as for adult.
70c Adult *remigialis* Like 70a, but paler and almost white below. Chad to Sudan.
70d Adult *cucullata* Distinctive. Darker than 70a. North Africa from Morocco to Tunisia and Libya.
70e Adult *percivali* Distinctive. Darkest race. Grey-brown above, grey below. Lacks black scapulars and tertials and brownish central tail feathers of other races. SW Arabian peninsula in Yemen and Oman.

71 Southern Tchagra *Tchagra tchagra* Text p.275

Medium-large, sexes similar. Geographical variation slight. Solitary, skulking low down or on ground in dense scrub and coastal bush in southern Africa from S and SE South Africa and Swaziland. Whistle call diagnostic, but check Brown-headed Tchagra (see Sounds).

71a Adult Crown brownish with black streak through eye, long broad white eyebrow. Bill relatively long. Wings bright chestnut-brown. Tail mostly black, broadly tipped white, diagnostic in flight. Underparts pale grey. **Compare** Black-crowned Tchagra (this plate) and Brown-headed Tchagra (Plate 28).
71b Immature Like adult, but duller and paler with buffy-white eyebrow and pale bill. **Compare** as for adult.

69a
69d
69b
69e
69c
70a
70b
70c
70d
70e
71b
71a

PLATE 28 TCHAGRAS and ASIAN WOOD-SHRIKES

72 Brown-headed Tchagra *Tchagra australis* Text p.277

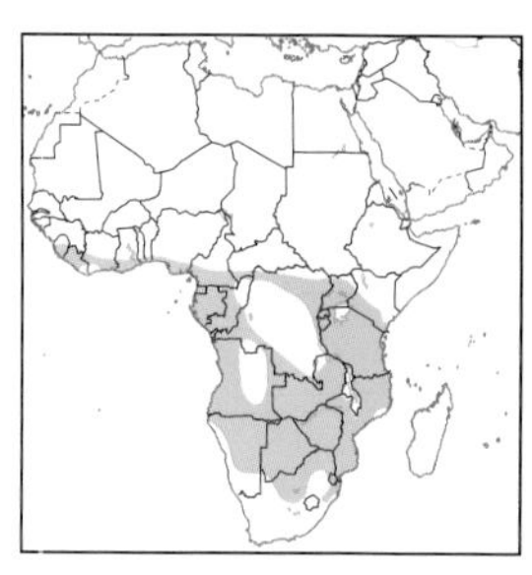

Medium size, sexes similar. Geographical variation moderate. Solitary, skulking low down or on ground in variety of wooded habitats. Widespread in Africa. Whistle call diagnostic, but check Three-streaked and Southern Tchagra (see Sounds).

72a Adult Crown brown, eyebrow white, bordered by black line through eye and above eyebrow. Bill small. Wings chestnut-brown. **Compare** Black-crowned Tchagra, Southern Tchagra and ♀ Blackcap Bush-shrike (Plate 27) and Three-streaked Tchagra (this plate).
72b Adult *souzae* Distinctive. Greyest race, with almost silvery-grey underparts. SE Zaïre to Angola.

73 Three-streaked Tchagra *Tchagra jamesi* Text p.279

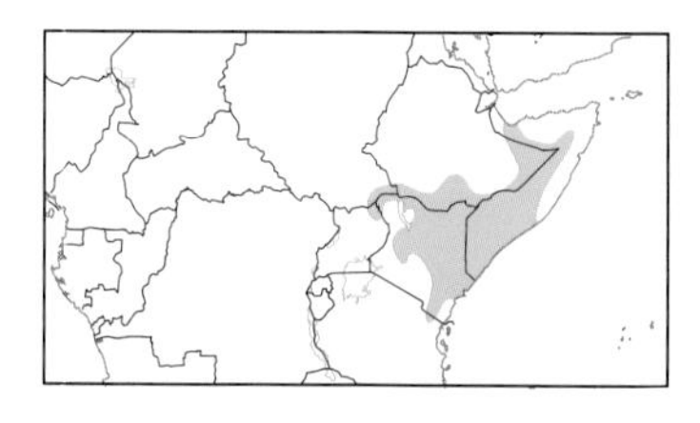

Small, sexes similar. Geographical variation slight. Solitary, skulking low down or on ground in semi-arid thornbush in E and NE Africa including Manda I and Lamu I. Whistle call diagnostic, but check Brown-headed Tchagra (see Sounds).

73 Adult Above and below greyish-brown. Head with three black streaks, one through each eye and one in centre of crown. Wings bright chestnut-brown. Tail broadly tipped white, diagnostic in flight. Bill small. **Compare** Brown-headed Tchagra (this plate).

74 Large Wood-shrike *Tephrodornis gularis* Text p.281

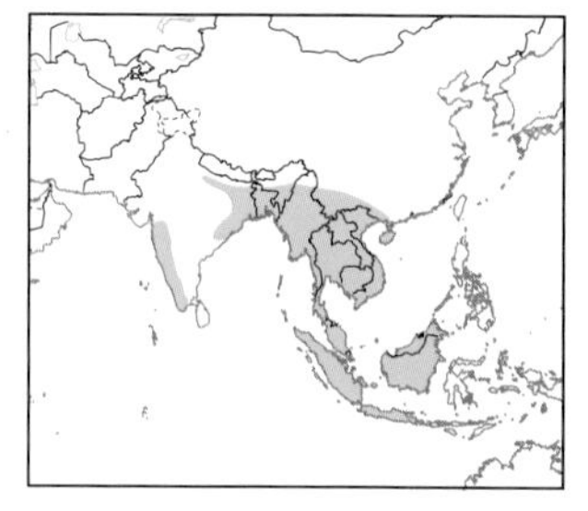

Medium-small to medium-large, stocky, sexes different. Geographical variation marked. Two groups with intermediates; in S small grey-backed, in N larger brown-backed. Often gregarious, groups small, larger in boreal winter. In canopy of forest edge and clearings. Widespread in Oriental region: India to S China, SE Asia to Java and Borneo. Whistles diagnostic, but check Common Wood-shrike (see Sounds).

74a Adult ♂ *gularis* S group. Head grey, face-mask black, eye brown. Bill relatively long. Back and wings brown tinged grey. Tail dark greyish-brown, rump white, diagnostic in flight. Thai Peninsula, S Malaysia, Sumatra and Java. **Compare** Common Wood-shrike (this plate). **74b Adult** ♀ *gularis* Above brown, including forehead and crown, small face-mask brown. **Compare** as for ♂. **74c Juvenile** Above pale brown. Head finely spotted buff, more coarsely spotted and barred on back. Wing-coverts tipped buff. Underparts like ♀. Eye brown. **Compare** as for ♂.
74d Adult ♂ *frenatus* Small race. Above grey with black face-mask, wings and tail, and white rump. On Java has whitish frontal (shown here). Java and Borneo. **74e Adult** *pelvica* N group. Like 74a, but paler and back browner. Eye variable yellow to olive. Nepal, W India, Pakistan and N Burma.

75 Common Wood-shrike *Tephrodornis pondicerianus* Text p.283

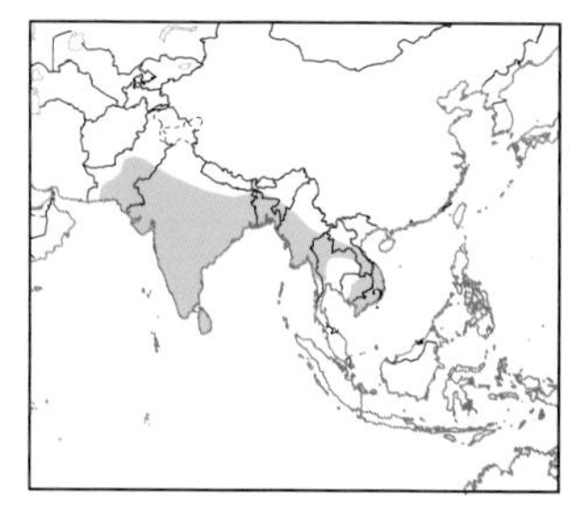

Medium-small, sexes slightly different. Geographical variation slight. Solitary or in small loose groups, skulking in canopy of open dry deciduous forest and woodland in Oriental region: Nepal, India, Pakistan, Thailand, Cambodia and Burma. Whistles diagnostic, but check Large Wood-shrike (see Sounds).

75a Adult ♂ Above pale grey-brown with indistinct dark face-mask and broad whitish eyebrow. Rump white, tail brown with white outer feathers. Underparts pale greyish-brown. Eye pale brown. **Compare** ♀ Large Wood-shrike (this plate).
75b Adult ♀ Like ♂, face markings indistinct, eyebrow shorter.
75c Juvenile Above pale brown spotted buff, mainly on head. Rump brown, tail like adult. Underparts dull white spotted brown. **Compare** Large Wood-shrike (this plate).

72a
72a
72b
73
74d
74e
74a
74b
74c
75b
75a
75c
74a
75a

PLATE 29 FLYCATCHING SHRIKES and ASIAN PHILENTOMAS

76 Red-eyed Flycatcher-shrike *Megabyas flammulatus* Text p.284

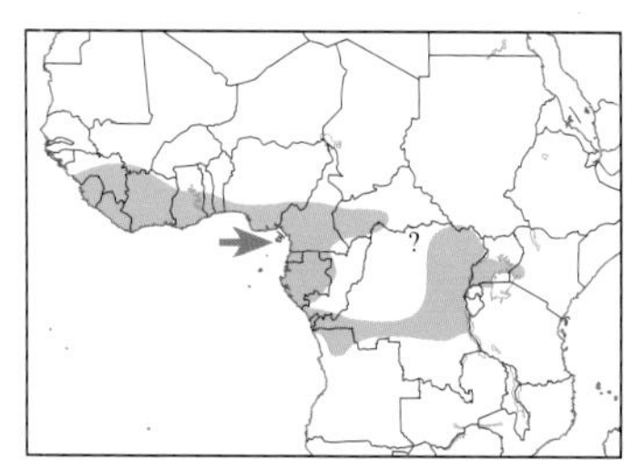

Small, thickset. Sexes different. Geographical variation slight. Solitary or in small groups, in forest edge and clearings of mainly lowland forest. From Senegal to N Angola, Zaïre to Uganda, S Sudan, W Kenya and NW Tanzania. Call diagnostic (see Sounds).

76a Adult ♂ Above bluish-black, rump and underparts white. Short tail wagged from side to side. Eye red, black bill broad. **Compare** Crested Flycatcher-shrike (this plate), Black-shouldered Puffback (Plate 25) and Sabine's Puffback (Plate 26).
76b Adult ♀ Head grey-brown, back wings and tail rufous-brown. Underparts whitish streaked dark brown. Eye like ♂. **Compare** Crested Flycatcher-shrike (this plate) and African Broadbill *Smithornis capensis*. **76c Subadult ♂** Immature like ♀. Eye reddish-brown.

77 Crested Flycatcher-shrike *Bias musicus* Text p.286

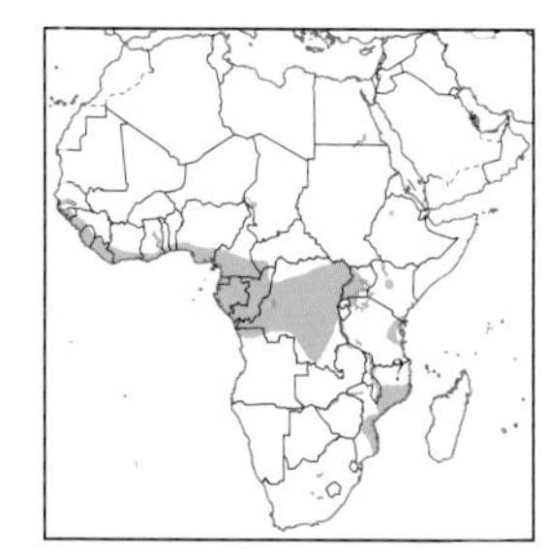

Small, sexes different. Geographical variation slight. Solitary, mainly in canopy of tall riverine woodland and forest trees. West, Central and East Africa to E Zimbabwe. Calls diagnostic (see Sounds).

77a Adult ♂ Distinctive. Glossy black with crested head, yellow eyes and legs. Belly and wing-patch white, diagnostic in flight. **Compare** Red-eyed Flycatcher-shrike (this plate).
77b Adult ♀ Distinctive. Crested brownish head, bare parts like ♂. Back, wings and tail bright rufous-brown.
77c Subadult ♂ Immature like ♀. Eye pale yellow.

78 Rufous-winged Philentoma *Philentoma pyrhopterum* Text p.289

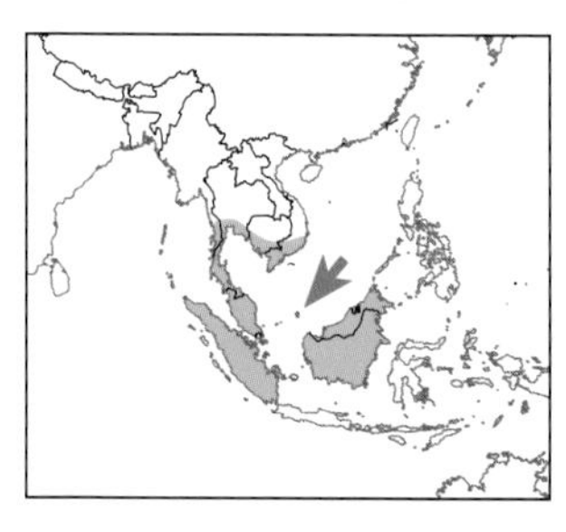

Small, sexes different. Geographical variation slight. Solitary in low to mid-levels of mainly lowland forest in SE Asia in S Thailand, S Vietnam, Thai–Malay Peninsula, Sumatra, Borneo and smaller islands. Whistles diagnostic (see Sounds).

78a Adult ♂ Common morph. Head, back and breast pale blue, rump greyish-brown. Eye crimson-red. Wings and tail bright rufous-brown, belly buffy. **Compare** Black-naped *Hypothymis azurea* or Indian Verditer *Eumyias thalassina* Flycatchers. **78b Adult ♀** Head greyish-brown tinged bluish. Eye red. Back and rump olive-brown. Wings and tail like ♂. Underparts rufous-buff. **Compare** as for ♂. **78c Juvenile** Like ♀, duller with browner head and mantle and pale rufous breast. Bill pale, eye brown. **Compare** as for ♂. **78d Adult ♂** Blue morph. Blue with no rufous-brown, eye red. Lower belly grey-brown. **Compare** Maroon-breasted Philentoma (this plate).

79 Maroon-breasted Philentoma *Philentoma velatum* Text p.290

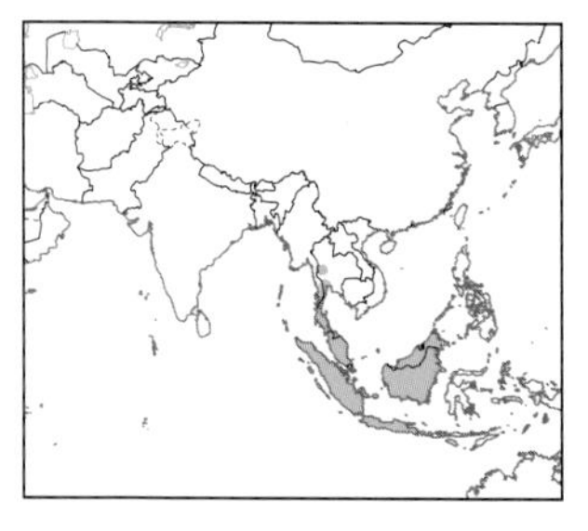

Medium size, sexes different. Geographical variation slight. Solitary, low down in dark, often moist forest in SE Asia in Burma, Thailand, Malay Peninsula, Sumatra, Java and Borneo. Whistles diagnostic (see Sounds).

79a Adult ♂ Appears black, but in good light indigo-blue. Broad frontal, face and ear-coverts black. Eye red. Underparts blue, chin and throat black, breast deep maroon. **Compare** rare blue morph of ♂ Rufous-winged Philentoma (this plate), Asian Fairy-bluebird *Irena puella* and Velvet-fronted Nuthatch *Sitta frontalis*.
79b Adult ♀ Like ♂, duller with indistinct face markings.
79c Juvenile Below, patchy blue, rich rufous. Tail and wings like adult, primary wing-coverts chestnut-brown. Eye brown. **Compare** as for ♂.

76a
76b
76c
76a
77a
77a
77b
77c
78a
78b
78c
78d
79a
79b
79c

PLATE 30 SMALL BUSH-SHRIKES

80 Brubru *Nilaus afer* Text p.291

Small, sexes different. Geographical variation marked in two woodland types: A) mainly broadleaved and *Acacia*; B) mainly miombo (*Brachystegia*). Solitary in canopy of larger trees in savanna woodlands. Widespread in sub-Saharan Africa. Whistle trill diagnostic (see Sounds).

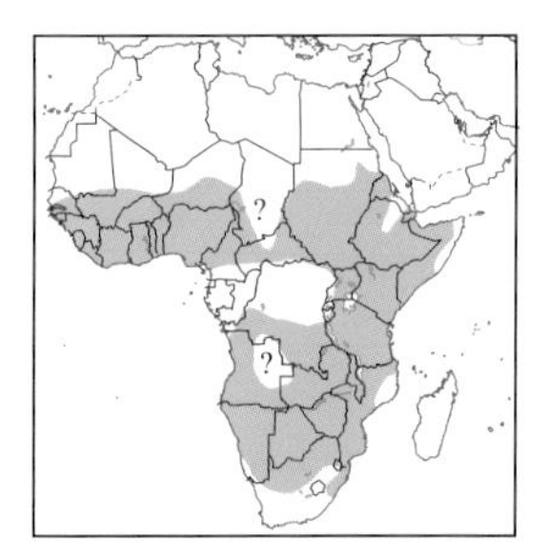

80a Adult ♂ *afer* Head, back and line through eye black. White eyebrow formed by frontal and lores to back of head. Eye brown. Nape-patch white and broad buffy stripe down middle of back. Wings black with buff stripe. Underparts white with rufous flanks. **Compare** batises (Plates 31–34).
80b Adult ♀ *afer* Like ♂, but duller and browner above. Underparts white with slight black streaking. Rufous flanks smaller. **Compare** as for ♂.
80c Juvenile *afer* Above mottled brown, buff and white. Flight feathers, wing-coverts, wing-stripe, and tail with buffy-brown edging. Underparts dull white barred brownish, lacks rufous flanks. Bill pale, eye brown. **Compare** Pallid Flycatcher *Bradornis pallidus*.
80d Adult ♂ *camerunensis* Larger and greyer above and below than 80a. Cameroon to Central African Republic.
80e Adult ♂ *affinis* Like 80f, but lacks rufous flanks in both sexes. N Angola.
80f Adult ♂ *nigritemporalis* Like 80a, but without white eyebrow. Pale areas on back and wing-stripe white not buff. Eye reddish-brown. NE Angola, S Zaïre, Tanzania, Zambia, Malawi, N and central Zimbabwe and Mozambique. **Compare** as for nominate.
80g Adult ♀ *nigritemporalis* Like 80b, but may have short eyebrow. Underparts heavily streaked black on throat and upper breast. Eye like ♂.
80h Juvenile *nigritemporalis* Like 80c, but buffier. Underparts heavily streaked. Eye brown. **Compare** as for nominate.

81 White-tailed Shrike *Lanioturdus torquatus* Text p.294

Small, sexes similar. Geographical variation slight. Solitary or groups at all levels, mainly on ground in semi-arid scrub savanna from SW Angola to central Namibia. Calls diagnostic (see Sounds).

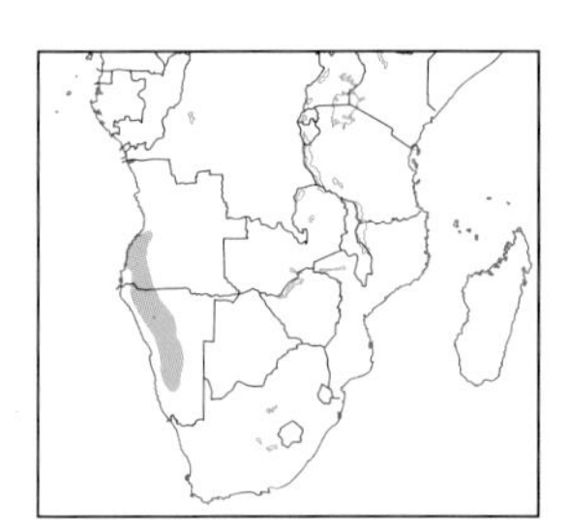

81a Adult Distinctive. Long legs and very short white tail. Head black with broad white frontal and black stripe through yellow eye. Large white nape-patch and wing markings. Wing-patches conspicuous in flight. Underparts grey with black breast-band and white throat. **Compare** ♂ Chinspot and Pririt Batis (Plate 32).
81b Juvenile Like adult, but duller with buffy-mottled nape, brown eye and narrower breast-band.

80a
80b
80c
80d
80e
80f
80f
80g
80h
81a
81b
81a

PLATE 31 FOREST BATISES 1

82 Cape Batis *Batis capensis* Text p.296

Very small, sexes different. Geographical variation marked. Solitary in mid- to lower levels of forests and gorges. Distribution fragmented from SE Tanzania to SW South Africa. Calls diagnostic, but check Forest Batis (see Sounds).

82a Adult ♂ *capensis* Head dark grey, face-mask black, eye orange-red. Back olive-brown, wing-stripe rufous. Underparts white, broad black breast-band, rufous flanks and white belly. SW to SE South Africa. **Compare** ♂ Forest Batis (this plate). **82b Adult ♀** *capensis* Like ♂, but thin whitish eyebrow, broad rufous-brown breast-band and white throat with rufous patch. **Compare** ♀ Woodwards' and Forest Batis (this plate). **82c Juvenile** Like adult ♀, but duller and darker above. Head without distinct face-mask, eye brown. Underparts paler than adult, throat-patch buffy-brown. **Compare** as for adult. **82d Adult ♂** *reichenowi* Above pale grey, wing feathers edged pale grey (not rufous), face-mask smaller (does not extend as far back as 82a), wing-stripe and flanks white. Tail short. Coastal SE Tanzania in Mikindani area. **82e Adult ♀** *reichenowi* Above like ♂, but wing-stripe rufous. Underparts white, tinged rufous on throat (not distinct patch). Broad rufous breast-band mixed with grey on sides. **82f Adult ♂** *dimorpha* Above dark grey, wing-stripe and flanks white (not rufous). S Malawi, adjacent Mozambique. **82g Adult ♀** *dimorpha* Above like ♂, but scapulars darker olive-brown. Underparts like 82b.

83 Margaret's Batis *Batis margaritae* Text p.299

Very small, sexes different. Geographical variation slight. Solitary in mid- to lower levels of dry evergreen forest, particularly *Cryptosepalum*. S Central Africa in NW Zambia, S Zaïre and W Angola. Whistles diagnostic (see Sounds).

83a Adult ♂ Above dark grey, face-mask black, eye orange. Wing-stripe white. Underparts white with broad black breast-band and white throat. **Compare** Chinspot Batis (Plate 32).
83b Adult ♀ Like ♂, but rufous wing-stripe and sides of breast. Eye redder. **Compare** as for ♂.

84 Forest Batis *Batis mixta* Text p.300

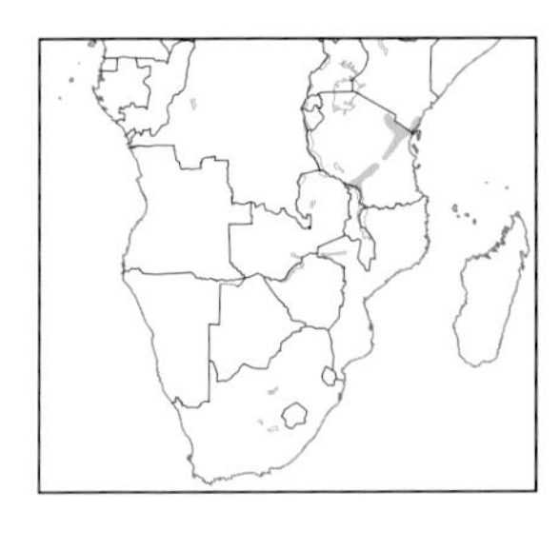

Very small, sexes different. Geographical variation moderate. Solitary, mainly at lower levels in coastal and montane forest and thickets in miombo woodland. SE Kenya to SW Tanzania and N Malawi. ♀ calls diagnostic, but check Woodwards' and Cape Batis (see Sounds).

84a Adult ♂ Above dark grey, face-mask black, short thin whitish eyebrow, eye red. Underparts white with broad black breast-band and white throat. N Malawi, Tanzania and Kenya. **Compare** Cape Batis (this plate).
84b Adult ♀ Above dark olive-grey, black face-mask with long white eyebrow, eye red. Wing-stripe buffy-rufous. Underparts white with pale buffy-rufous tinge on throat, breast and flanks. **Compare** ♀ Woodwards' Batis.

85 Woodwards' Batis *Batis fratrum* Text p.301

Very small, sexes different. Geographical variation slight. Solitary in mid to lower-levels of lowland dry or evergreen coastal and riverine forest and thickets. SE Mozambique, S Malawi, E Zimbabwe and SE coastal South Africa. Some calls diagnostic (see Sounds).

85a Adult ♂ Distinctive. Above dark grey, face-mask black, short white eyebrow, eye orange. Wing-stripe white. Throat white, breast, upper belly and flanks pale buffy-rufous. S Malawi, E Zimbabwe, SE South Africa.
85b Adult ♀ Distinctive. Above like ♂, but eyebrow longer, wing-stripe rufous. Underparts mainly pale buffy-rufous. **Compare** Forest Batis (this plate).
85c Immature Like 85b, but duller above. Eyebrow and side of face buffy-brown. Wing-stripe, coverts and flight feathers edged and tipped rufous-buff. Eye brown. **Compare** as for ♂.

82a
82c
82d
82b
82e
82f
82g
83a
83b
84a
84b
85a
85b
85c

PLATE 32 WOODLAND BATISES

86 Pririt Batis *Batis pririt* **Text p.303**

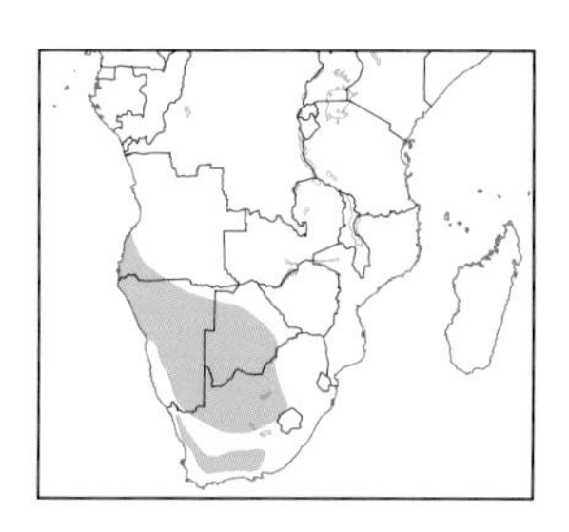

Very small, sexes different. Geographical variation slight. Solitary, in bushes and trees in dry savanna woodlands. SW Angola, Namibia, Botswana and NW and SW South Africa. Whistles diagnostic, but check Chinspot Batis (see Sounds).

86a Adult ♂ Above pale grey, face-mask black, eye yellow, eyebrow white. Wing-stripe white. Underparts white with broad black breast-band and white throat. Flanks barred grey. **Compare** Chinspot Batis (this plate).
86b Adult ♀ Distinctive. Above like ♂. Underparts buffy-orange with white belly and greyish flanks.
86c Juvenile Like ♀, but duller, head spotted buff, face-mask brownish-black, eye brown. Underparts dull white mottled black-and-buff on breast in both sexes.

87 Chinspot Batis *Batis molitor* **Text p.304**

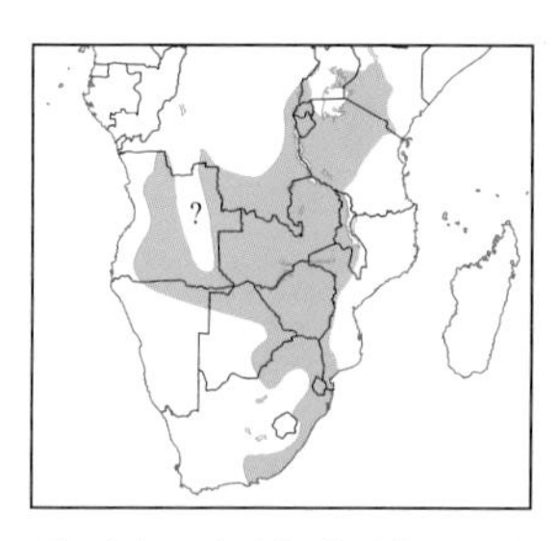

Very small, sexes different. Geographical variation slight. Solitary, at all levels, mainly in savanna woodlands. Widespread from Kenya to South Africa. Some calls diagnostic, but check Pririt, Mozambique, Grey-headed, Black-headed and Brown-throated Wattle-eye (see Sounds).

87a Adult ♂ Above dark grey. Face-mask black, eyebrow white, eye yellow. Wing-stripe white. Underparts white with broad black breast-band and white throat. SE South Africa, S Mozambique. **Compare** ♂ Pririt, Mozambique, Grey-headed, Black-headed, Pygmy, Margaret's and Ruwenzori Batis. **87b Adult ♀** Like ♂, but chestnut-brown breast-band and patch on chin. **Compare** Mozambique (this plate), Grey-headed and Black-headed Batis (Plate 33). **87c Juvenile** Above dull, mottled greyish-brown and buff. Face-mask blackish brown, eye brown. Underparts whitish with indistinct mottled brown-and-grey breast-band and throat-patch. **Compare** as for adult. **87d Immature ♂** Shows a combination of both sexes. Upperparts grey; may retain slight mottling. Face-mask black, eye pale yellow. Breast-band tawny with black developing progressively and indistinct rufous chinspot.

88 Mozambique Batis *Batis soror* **Text p.307**

Very small, sexes different. Solitary in mid-canopy of mainly lowland miombo woodland. SE Kenya to S Mozambique. Whistles diagnostic, but check Chinspot, Black-headed and Pygmy Batis (see Sounds).

88a Adult ♂ Above pale grey. Eyebrow white, face-mask black, eye yellow. Wing-stripe white. Underparts white with black breast-band and white throat. **Compare** ♂ Chinspot Batis (this plate), Pygmy and Black-headed Batis (Plate 33).
88b Adult ♀ Like ♂, but with narrower pale rufous breast-band and pale diffuse chinspot. **Compare** ♀ Chinspot (this plate) and ♀ Pygmy Batis (Plate 33).

89 Senegal Batis *Batis senegalensis* **Text p.309**

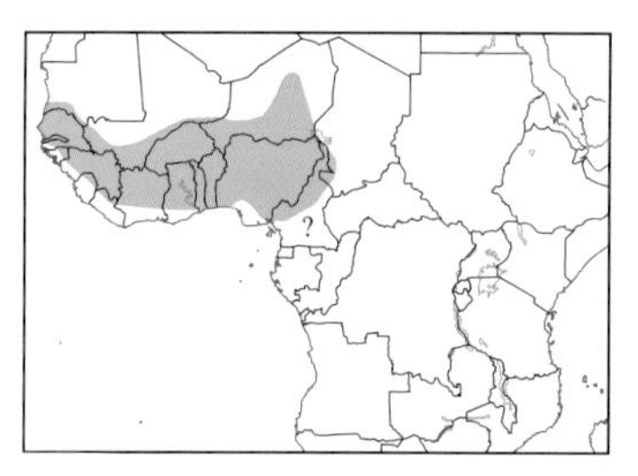

Very small, sexes different. Solitary in low to mid-levels of thorn savanna of West Africa from Mauritania to Cameroon. Whistles diagnostic, but check Black-headed and Grey-headed Batis (see Sounds).

89a Adult ♂ Above dark grey with long white eyebrow, face-mask black, eye yellow. Wing-stripe white. Underparts white with broad black breast-band and white throat. **Compare** Grey-headed and Black-headed Batis (Plate 33).
89b Adult ♀ Above like ♂, but duller with rufous-buff eyebrow, nape-patch and wing-stripe. Underparts white except for orange-buff tinge on throat and sides of neck. Orange-buff breast-band, broader on sides. **Compare** as for ♂.
89c Juvenile Like ♀, but duller above, eyebrow and wing-stripe rufous-buff. Underparts dull white mottled grey-brown on breast, eye probably brown. **Compare** as for ♂.

86b
86c
86a
87a
87d
87b
87c
87a
88a
88b
89a
89b
89c

PLATE 33 WOODLAND and SMALL FOREST-PATCH BATISES

90 Grey-headed Batis *Batis orientalis* Text p.311

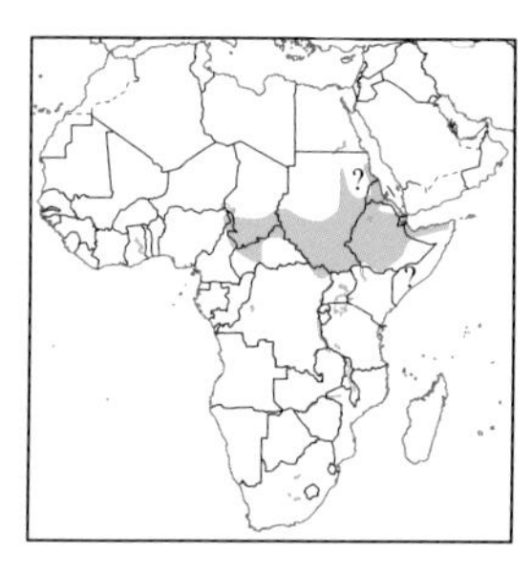

Very small, sexes similar. Geographical variation moderate. Solitary in dry savanna thornbush from E Chad to N Somalia, Ethiopia, NE Uganda and possibly N Kenya. Whistles diagnostic, but check Black-headed, Pygmy and Chinspot Batis (see Sounds).

90a Adult ♂ Above grey, face-mask black with long white eyebrow, eye yellow. Wing-stripe white. Underparts white with narrow black breast-band and white throat. **Compare** Senegal and Chinspot Batis (Plate 32), Black-headed and Pygmy Batis (this plate).
90b Adult ♀ Like ♂, but breast-band dark chestnut-brown. **Compare** as for ♂.
90c Juvenile Like ♀, but duller greyish-brown above. Below dull white, breast-band patchy chestnut-brown and black. Eye probably brown. **Compare** as for ♂.

91 Pygmy Batis *Batis perkeo* Text p.312

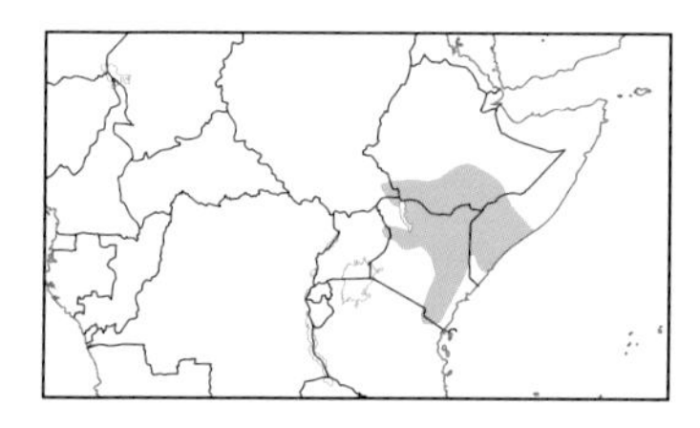

Very small, sexes different. Solitary in arid thornbush from SE Sudan, Somalia, Ethiopia, Uganda, Kenya and NE Tanzania. Some calls diagnostic, but check Black-headed and Grey-headed Batis (see Sounds).

91a Adult ♂ Above grey, short white eyebrow, face-mask black, eye yellow. Wing-stripe white. Underparts white with black breast-band and white throat. **Compare** Grey-headed and Black-headed Batis (this plate), Chinspot and Mozambique Batis (Plate 32).
91b Adult ♀ Like ♂, but eyebrow, nape-patch and wing-stripe rusty-buff. Underparts white with pale rufous-buff breast-band and buffy sides to throat. **Compare** as for ♂.

92 Black-headed Batis *Batis minor* Text p.313

Very small, sexes different. Geographical variation slight. Solitary in various habitats from arid to moist woodlands. Distribution fragmented: Nigeria to Eritrea, Gabon to SW Zaïre, and N Somalia to Tanzania. Some whistles diagnostic, but check Grey-headed, Mozambique, Pygmy and Angola Batis (see Sounds).

92a Adult ♂ Above dark grey to blackish, long white eyebrow, black face-mask, eye yellow. Wing-stripe white. Underparts white with broad black breast-band and white throat. **Compare** Grey-headed and Angola Batis (this plate), Chinspot and Mozambique Batis (Plate 32).
92b Adult ♀ Above like ♂, but breast-band dark chestnut-brown to russet-maroon. **Compare** as for ♂.
92c Juvenile Like adult ♀, but spotted buffy blackish-brown above. Eyebrow and wing-coverts tipped rusty-buff. Breast-band mottled blackish–chestnut. Eye brown.

93 Angola Batis *Batis minulla* Text p.315

Very small, sexes different. Solitary in canopy of small forest patches and thickets in woodland. SW Congo to Angola and W Zaïre. Whistles diagnostic, but check Verreaux's and Bioko Batis (see Sounds).

93a Adult ♂ Above dark grey, white spot in front of yellow eye, face-mask black to shoulder. Wing-stripe white. Underparts white with broad black breast-band and white throat. **Compare** ♂ Black-headed Batis (this plate) and Chinspot Batis (Plate 32).
93b Adult ♀ Above like ♂, but mantle slightly rufous and nape-patch smaller. Underparts white with dark chestnut-brown breast-band, broader on sides. **Compare** as for ♂.

90a
90b
90c
91a
91b
92a
92b
92c
93a
93b

PLATE 34 FOREST BATISES 2

94 Bioko Batis *Batis poensis* **Text p.317**

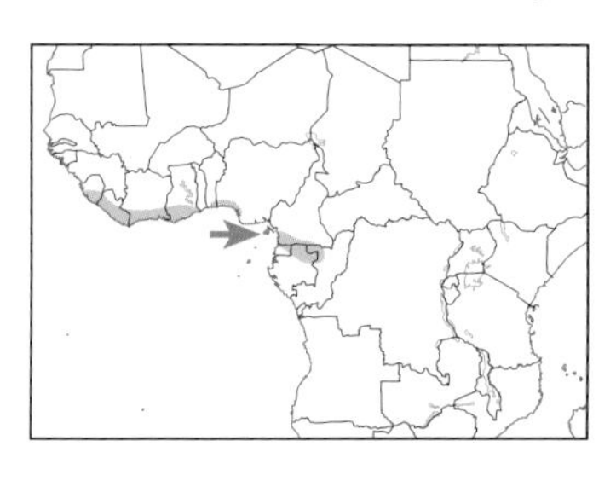

Very small, sexes different. Geographical variation in ♀ marked. Solitary in canopy of lowland and montane forest on Bioko and mainland from Sierra Leone to N Gabon. Some calls diagnostic, but check Gabon, Senegal and Black-headed Batis (see Sounds).

94a Adult ♂ *poensis* Distinctive. Above black, small white spot in front of yellow eye. Wing-stripe white. Underparts white with broad black breast-band and white throat. Bioko.
94b Adult ♀ *poensis* Distinctive, like ♂ above but duller. Below white, poorly defined breast-band chestnut-brown, diffuse with faint buffy barring.
94c Adult ♂ *occulta* Like 94a, but long thin white eyebrow and narrower black breast-band. Sierra Leone, Liberia, Ivory Coast, Ghana, SW Nigeria, S Cameroon and N Gabon. **Compare** ♂ Gabon Batis (this plate), Senegal (Plate 32) and Black-headed Batis (Plate 33).
94d Adult ♀ *occulta* Like ♂, but crown and mantle grey, tinged blue-black with whiter rump. Underparts white with clearly defined dark chestnut-brown breast-band. **Compare** as for ♂.
94e Juvenile *occulta* Like ♀, but sides of throat pale rufous, and white wing-stripe tinged rufous. Eye brown.

95 Gabon Batis *Batis minima* **Text p.319**

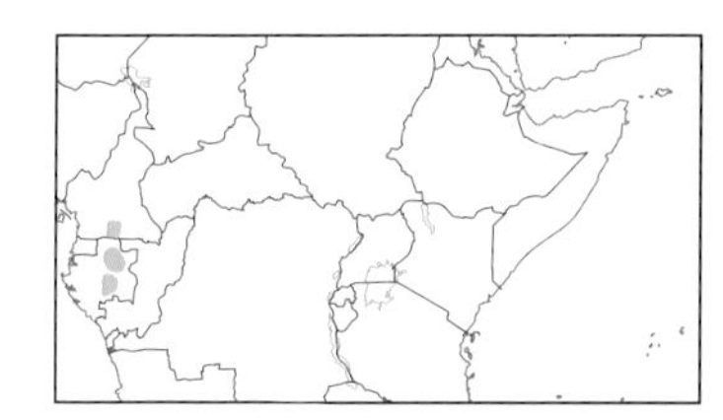

Very small, sexes different. Solitary in mid- to upper levels of lowland, mainly secondary forest from S Cameroon to Gabon. Calls little known, whistle call diagnostic, but check Bioko Batis (see Sounds).

95a Adult ♂ Above black with yellow eye. Wing-stripe white. Underparts white with broad black breast-band and white throat. **Compare** ♂ Bioko Batis (this plate).
95b Adult ♀ Distinctive. Like ♂ above, but breast-band grey.
95c Juvenile Above brownish-black with buff specks on head, back and wing-coverts. Wing-stripe tawny. Underparts whitish with breast-band mottled whitish-grey and indistinct if present. Eye probably brown.

96 Rwenzori Batis *Batis diops* **Text p.320**

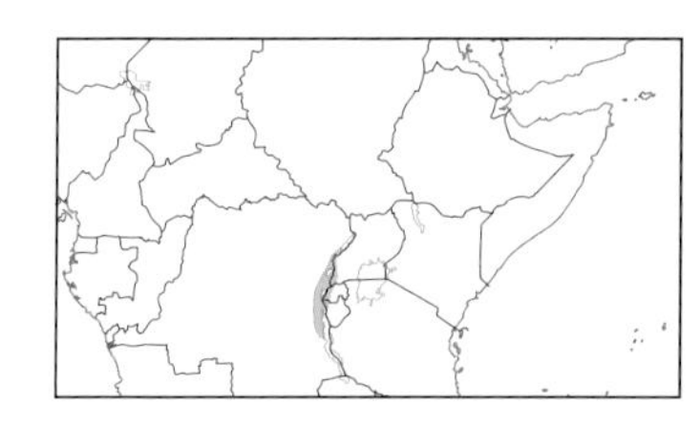

Very small, sexes similar except for eye colour. Solitary, mainly low down in dense undergrowth of montane and bamboo forest from SW Uganda, W Rwanda, W Burundi and E Zaïre in Rwenzori Mountains. Whistle diagnostic (see Sounds).

96a Adult ♂ Above bluish-black, face-mask black with white spot in front of golden-yellow eye. Underparts white with broad black breast-band and white throat. **Compare** Ituri Batis (this plate), Black-headed Batis (Plate 33), Chinspot Batis (Plate 32).
96b Adult ♀ Like ♂, but eye reddish. **Compare** as for ♂.

97 Ituri Batis *Batis ituriensis* **Text p.321**

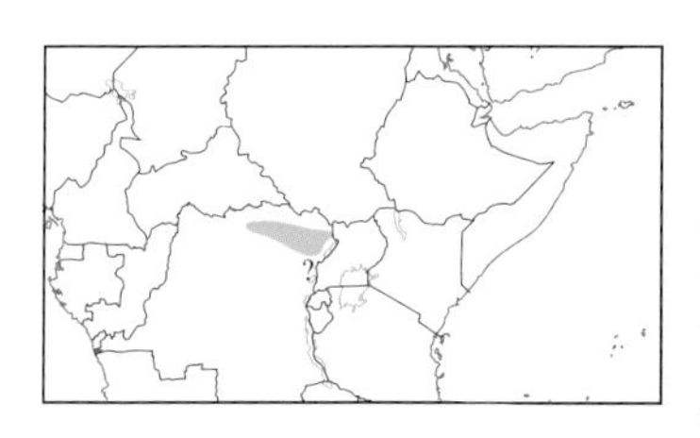

Very small, sexes very similar. Solitary in canopy of lowland degraded forest from E and NE Zaïre and W Uganda. Call unknown, predicted to have high-pitched cisticola-like whistles.

97a Adult ♂ Above dark bluish-black, face-mask black, large white spot in front of yellow eye. Wing-stripe white. Underparts white with broad black breast-band and white throat. **Compare** Rwenzori Batis (this plate) and Black-headed Batis (Plate 33).
97b Adult ♀ Like ♂, but may show indistinct white eyebrow. **Compare** as for ♂.

94a
94b
94c
94d
94e
95a
95b
95c
96a
96b
97a
97b

PLATE 35 LARGE WATTLE-EYES

98 Banded Wattle-eye *Platysteira laticincta* Text p.322

Small, sexes different. Solitary at all levels up to canopy, mainly low down in montane forest in Bamenda-Banso Highlands of W Cameroon. Calls little known, diagnostic (see Sounds).

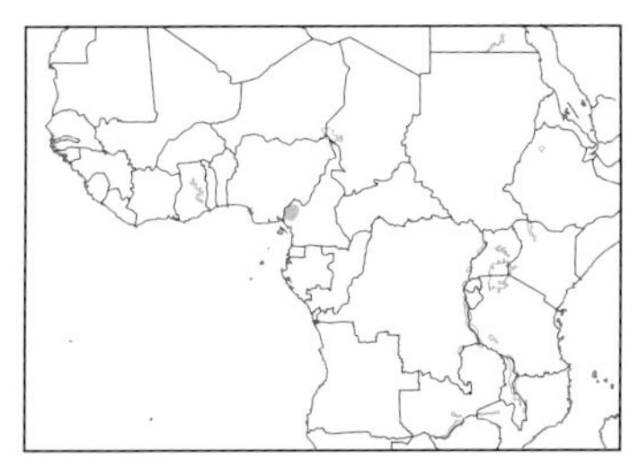

98a Adult ♂ Distinctive. Above glossy greenish-black, eye with bright red fleshy wattle. Underparts white with broad bluish-black breast-band and white throat. **Compare** Brown-throated Wattle-eye (this plate).
98b Adult ♀ Distinctive. Like ♂, but throat and upper breast greenish-black like upperparts. Chin white and wattle smaller. **Compare** as for ♂.

99 Black-throated Wattle-eye *Platysteira peltata* Text p.323

Small, sexes different. Geographical variation slight. Solitary in low- to mid-levels of riverine, lowland and montane forest. Somalia to E South Africa and Angola. Calls diagnostic (see Sounds).

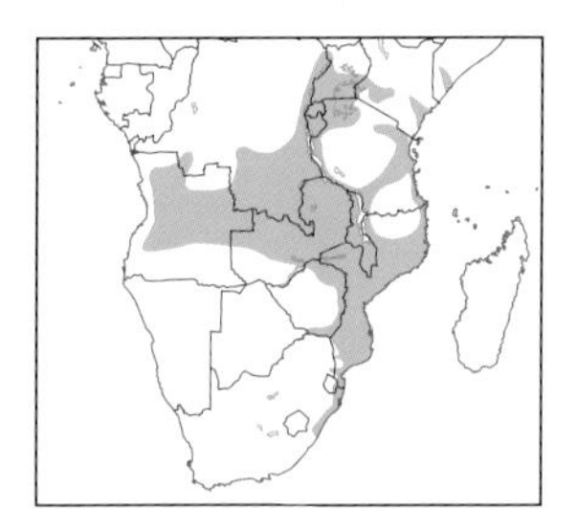

99a Adult ♂ Above glossy bluish-black. Eye with bright red fleshy wattle. Underparts white with very narrow black breast-band and white throat. **Compare** Brown-throated Wattle-eye (this plate), White-fronted Wattle-eye (Plate 36).
99b Adult ♀ Distinctive. Like ♂, but throat and upper breast blue-black like upperparts. Chin white and wattle smaller.
99c Juvenile Above pale greyish-brown spotted buffy-rufous on head and mantle, wing-coverts tipped buffy-rufous. Underparts dull creamy-white. Eye brown, bill pale.
99d Immature Above dull brown- to bluish-grey, lacks spotting of juvenile. Tertials, wing-coverts and inner secondaries edged rusty-brown. Underparts dull creamy-white with throat and sides of breast mottled tawny-and-buff, with progressive development of black. Eye brown; small wattle varies from pale orange to pink or dull red depending on age.

100 Brown-throated Wattle-eye *Platysteira cyanea* Text p.326

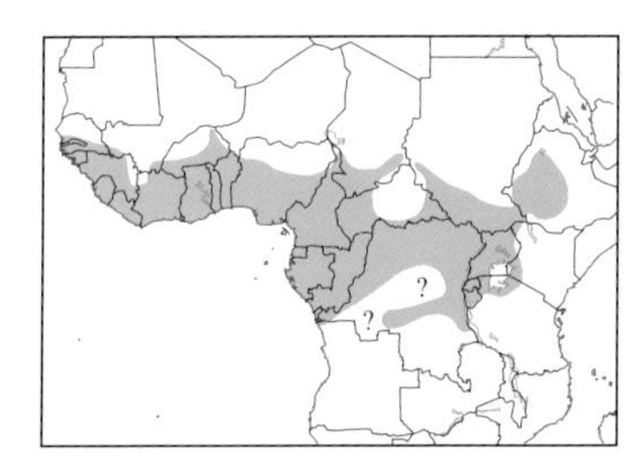

Small, sexes different. Geographical variation slight. Solitary in low- to mid-levels of riverine woodland and forest edge. Widespread; Senegal through Congo basin, N Angola and to Ethiopia, W Kenya and NW Tanzania. Calls diagnostic, but check Chinspot Batis (see Sounds).

100a Adult ♂ Above black with slight gloss, wing-stripe white. Eye with bright red fleshy wattle. Underparts white with broad black breast-band and white throat. **Compare** Black-throated and Banded Wattle-eye (this plate), and White-fronted Wattle-eye (Plate 36).
100b Adult ♀ Like ♂, but dark slate-grey above. Wattle smaller. Underparts white with deep chestnut-brown throat and breast. Chin white. **Compare** as for ♂.
100c Juvenile Above dull grey-brown, spotted rusty-buff. Wing-coverts and wing-stripe cream to rusty-buff. Underparts dull white tinged greyish-buff. **Compare** as for ♂.
100d Immature Above greyish-brown, lacks spotting of juvenile. Wing-stripe white or tinged rufous-buff, coverts tipped tawny. Underparts dull white, throat tinged pale chestnut-brown, darker on sides with lower edge greyish chestnut-brown. Bill paler, wattle small and pinkish. **Compare** as for ♂.

98b
98a
99a
99b
99a
99d
99c
100a
100a
100b
100d
100c

101 White-fronted Wattle-eye *Platysteira albifrons* Text p.328

Small, sexes different. Solitary in low- to mid-levels of dry thickets in lowland woodlands in NW Angola. Calls unknown.

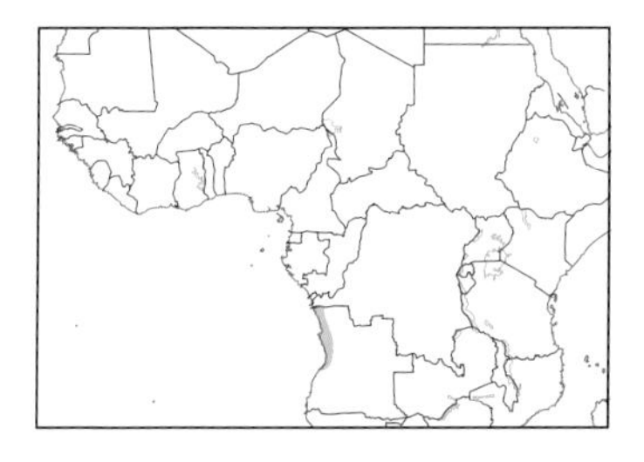

101a Adult ♂ Head black with narrow white frontal, eye with bright red fleshy wattle. Back grey, wing-stripe white. Underparts white with narrow black breast-band and white throat. **Compare** Brown-throated and Black-throated Wattle-eye (Plate 35).
101b Adult ♀ Like ♂, but head grey and wattle small. Underparts completely white. **Compare** as for ♂.
101c Immature ♀ Above like 101b, but buffy below, with pale rusty tips and edges to wing-coverts and inner secondaries. Immature ♂ shows mottled white, brown and black breast-band. **Compare** as for ♂.

102 White-spotted Wattle-eye *Dyaphorophyia tonsa* Text p.329

Very small, almost tailless, sexes different. Solitary, usually in mid- to upper levels and canopy of lowland forest. From SE Nigeria to NW Congo, and from NE to central E Zaïre. Calls diagnostic, but check Chestnut Wattle-eye (see Sounds).

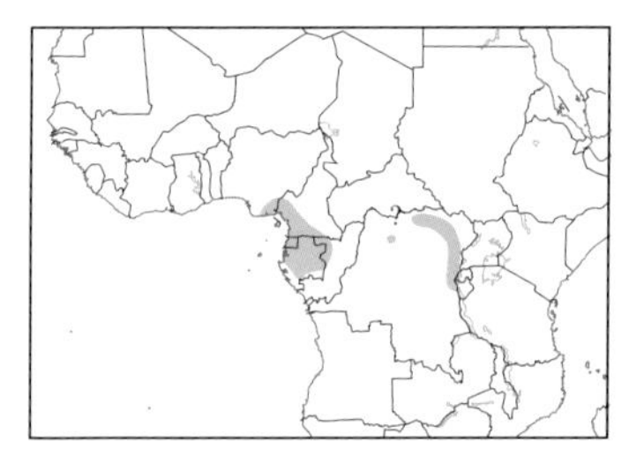

102a Adult ♂ Above black, short white eyebrow in front and behind eye with large fleshy dark purple wattle. White collar and rump conspicuous in flight. Underparts white with broad black breast-band and white throat. **Compare** Chestnut Wattle-eye (this plate).
102b Adult ♀ Crown and nape black, thin whitish eyebrow, face-mask grey, eye with small purple wattle. Back and wings bright chestnut-brown. Underparts white with throat and breast bright chestnut-brown, chin white. **Compare** as for ♂.
102c Juvenile Head greyish-brown, back and wings chestnut-brown. Throat and breast mottled greyish-buff tinged chestnut-brown with fine barring. Small greyish wattle. **Compare** as for ♀.

103 Chestnut Wattle-eye *Dyaphorophyia castanea* Text p.331

Very small, almost tailless, sexes different. Geographical variation moderate. Solitary at all levels, mainly mid- to lower levels in lowland forest from Sierra Leone to W Kenya, southward to NW Zambia. Calls diagnostic, but check White-spotted Wattle-eye (see Sounds).

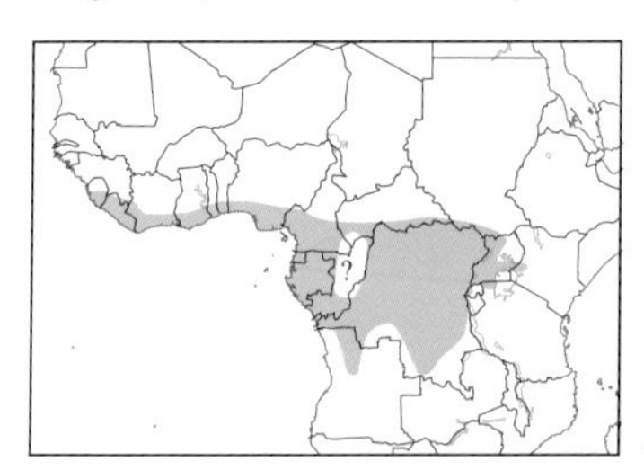

103a Adult ♂ *castanea* Above black, lacks white eyebrow and white collar. Eye with large fleshy dark purple wattle. White rump conspicuous in flight. Underparts white with broad black breast-band and white throat. **Compare** White-spotted Wattle-eye (this plate).
103b Adult ♀ *castanea* Head dark grey, eye with small fleshy purple wattle. Back and wings chestnut-brown. Underparts white with bright chestnut-brown throat and breast, chin white. **Compare** as for ♂.
103c Juvenile Head brownish spotted chestnut-brown with almost no wattle. Wings dull chestnut-brown. Throat whitish, breast finely barred greyish-white. **Compare** as for ♀.
103d Immature Like ♀, but head dull grey-brown with small dark grey wattle. Underparts developing chestnut-brown on throat, breast-band barred tawny blackish-brown. **Compare** as for ♀.
103e Adult ♂ *hormophora* Like 103a, but with distinct white collar. Sierra Leone to Togo. **Compare** as for ♂.

101a
101b
101c
102a
102a
102b
102c
103b
103e
103a
103d
103c

PLATE 37 SMALL WATTLE-EYES 2

104 Red-cheeked Wattle-eye *Dyaphorophyia blissetti* Text p.334

Very small, almost tailless, sexes slightly different. Solitary in dense undergrowth of lowland forest. E Guinea and Sierra Leone to S Nigeria and W Cameroon. Call diagnostic (see Sounds).

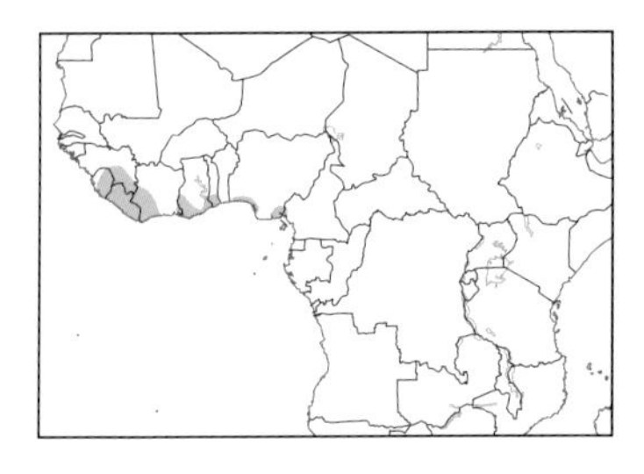

104a Adult ♂ Above black with greenish gloss. Eye with large blue-green fleshy wattle. Side of neck with large triangular chestnut-brown patch. Underparts white with throat and upper breast black like back. **Compare** Black-necked Wattle-eye and Jameson's Wattle-eye (this plate).

104b Adult ♀ Like ♂, but dark grey above with slight gloss and wattle smaller. **Compare** as for ♂.

104c Immature Above dull dark grey. Eye with small greyish wattle. Underparts dull white with sides of neck, throat and upper breast pale chestnut-brown, paler in centre of throat. **Compare** as for ♂.

105 Jameson's Wattle-eye *Dyaphorophyia jamesoni* Text p.335

See Red-cheeked Wattle-eye, ranges separate. From E and NE Zaïre to S Sudan, W Uganda, Rwanda, Burundi, W Kenya and NW Tanzania. Calls little known, diagnostic relative to Yellow-bellied Wattle-eye, but like Red-cheeked Wattle-eye (see Sounds).

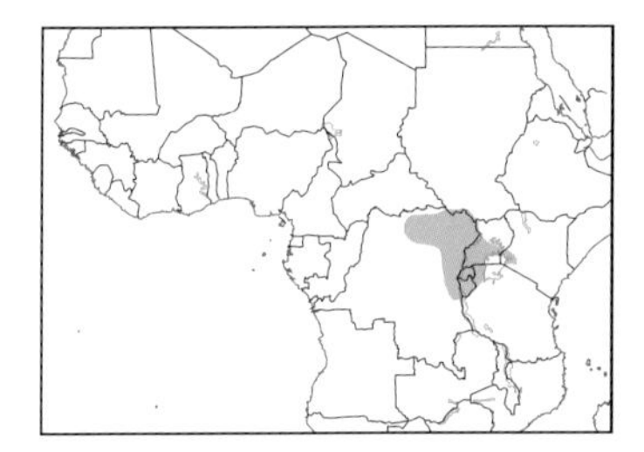

105a Adult ♂. Like Red-cheeked Wattle-eye, but chestnut-brown patches on sides of neck smaller and darker. **Compare** Yellow-bellied Wattle-eye (Plate 38).

105b Adult ♀. Like ♂, but duller above and wattle small. **Compare** as for ♂.

105c Immature Above greyer than ♀, lacks developed eye-wattle. Underparts white with sides of neck and throat pale chestnut-brown, with gradual development of glossy greenish-black in centre. **Compare** as for ♂.

106 Black-necked Wattle-eye *Dyaphorophyia chalybea* Text p.335

Very small, almost tailless, sexes slightly different. Solitary in dense undergrowth of lowland forest from W and S Cameroon, Bioko, Equatorial Guinea and Gabon, also NW Angola. Calls diagnostic, but check Red-cheeked and Yellow-bellied Wattle-eye (see Sounds).

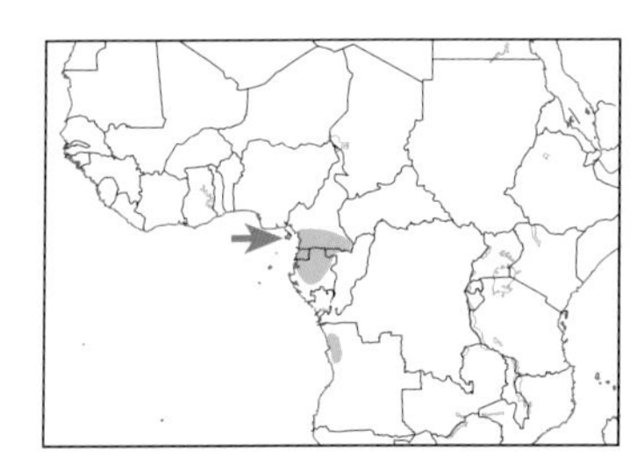

106a Adult ♂ Above glossy greenish-black. White rump conspicuous in flight. Eye with large fleshy emerald-green wattle. Underparts pale yellow with throat and breast like back. **Compare** Red-cheeked Wattle-eye (this plate) and Yellow-bellied Wattle-eye (Plate 38).

106b Adult ♀ Like ♂, but duller and grey above with less gloss. Wattle smaller. **Compare** as for ♂.

106c Juvenile Above dull dark grey without eye-wattle. Underparts dull greyish-white with broad tawny and chestnut-brown stripe down centre of throat.

106d Immature Above dark grey with little greenish gloss. Wattle small. Underparts whitish, throat and upper breast pale tawny, bordered by mottled chestnut-brown and blackish-brown. **Compare** as for ♂.

104a
104b
104c
105a
105b
105c
106a
106b
106d
106c

PLATE 38 SMALL WATTLE-EYES 3

107 Yellow-bellied Wattle-eye *Dyaphorophyia concreta* Text p.337

Very small, sexes different. Geographical variation moderate with marked polymorphism in ♂♂ (yellow, chestnut-brown and black morphs). In ♀♀ extent of chestnut-brown underparts variable. Solitary in dense undergrowth. Widespread, distribution fragmented; E Guinea to Ghana; SE Nigeria to W Zaïre and Angola; E and NE Zaïre to W Tanzania, and W Kenya. Calls diagnostic, but check Red-cheeked, Black-throated and Jameson's Wattle-eye (see Sounds).

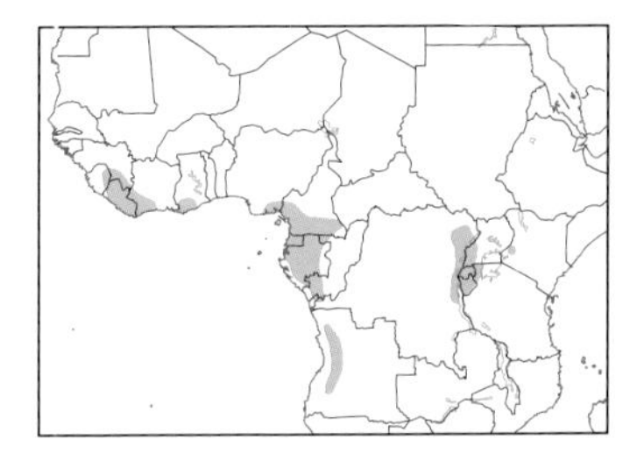

107a Adult ♂ *concreta* Chestnut-brown morph. Distinctive. Above dark glossy greenish-grey. Yellow spot in front of eye which has large fleshy bright emerald-green wattle. Underparts reddish chestnut-brown, chin yellow. Sierra Leone to Ghana.

107b Adult ♀ *concreta* Distinctive. Like ♂ above, but less glossy and wattle smaller. Underparts golden yellow with deep maroon chestnut-brown throat-patch.

107c Juvenile Above dull grey, spotted buff-brown, wing-coverts and tertials tipped rufous-buff. Wattle absent. Underparts dirty whitish-yellow tinged olive-grey. Bill browner.

107d Immature ♂ Above dull greenish-grey with small grey wattle. Underparts dull pale yellow tinged greyish-green with a few chestnut-brown feathers developing.

107e Adult ♂ *graueri* Yellow morph. Above like chestnut-brown morph. Underparts golden yellow. E Zaïre and SW Uganda.

107f Adult ♀ *graueri* Above like ♂, but duller with smaller wattle. Underparts yellow with reddish chestnut-brown throat and breast.

107g Adult ♀ *graueri* Like 107f, but underparts nearly completely reddish chestnut-brown, with only vent yellow.

107h Adult ♂ *kungwensis* Above pale slaty blue-grey. Eye with bright china-blue wattle. Underparts pale yellow, only occurring in yellow morph. Kungwe Mt, W Tanzania.

107i Adult ♂ *ansorgei* Black-breasted morph. Like 107e, but pale olive-grey above. Below yellow with bluish-black pear-shaped patch in centre on throat and upper breast. Angola.

107a
107a
107b
107d
107c
107f
107e
107g
107h
107i

PLATE 39 HELMET-SHRIKES 1

108 White Helmet-shrike *Prionops plumatus* Text p.340

Medium-large, sexes similar. Geographical variation marked. Gregarious, at all levels including ground in open woodland. Widespread in sub-Saharan Africa. Calls diagnostic, but check Grey-crested Helmet-shrike (see Sounds).

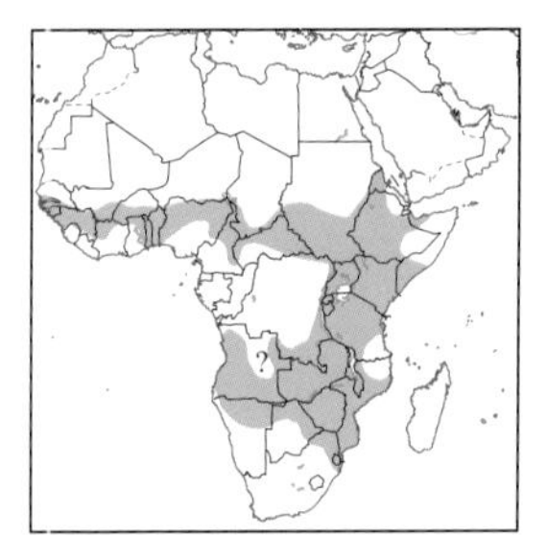

108a Adult *plumatus* Distinctive, head whitish with bushy frontal and long straight crest, ear-coverts with black crescent. Eye yellow with fleshy serrated yellow wattle. Back and wings black, wing-stripe and patch in primaries white. Tail black with white outer feathers. Underparts white. Bill black, legs red. Senegal and Gambia to Nigeria.
108b Juvenile *plumatus* Head dirty white without crest, eye brown without wattle, black crescent absent. Back and wings brownish-grey, wing-stripe dirty white, wing-coverts edged whitish. Underparts dull white. Bill brownish-black.
108c Adult *cristatus* Like 108a, but long white crest curls forward and lacks white wing-stripe. Ethiopia and SE Sudan.
108d Adult *talacoma* Like 108a, but with greyish head and no long white crest. S Uganda, NW Tanzania, S central Kenya, south to S Zaïre, Angola, Zambia and much of southern Africa. **Compare** Grey-crested Helmet-shrike (this plate).

109 Grey-crested Helmet-Shrike *Prionops poliolophus* Text p.344

Large, sexes similar. Little known. Gregarious at all levels , including ground in open woodland from SW Kenya to N Tanzania. Calls little known (see Sounds).

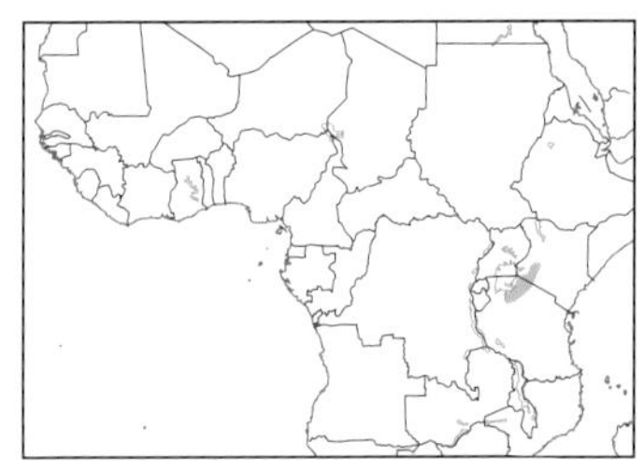

109 Adult Head grey with greyish crest, yellow eye with no wattle. Black crescent on ear-coverts, back and wings black. Wing-stripe and patch in primaries white. Tail black with white outer feathers. Underparts white with large black patches on sides of breast. Bill black, legs reddish. **Compare** White Helmet-shrike (this plate).

110 Chestnut-fronted Helmet-shrike *Prionops scopifrons* Text p.345

Small-medium, sexes similar. Geographical variation moderate. Gregarious in lowland and coastal forest. S Somalia, Kenya, NE Tanzania, Mozambique and E Zimbabwe. Calls diagnostic (see Sounds).

110a Adult *scopifrons* Above blackish-grey. Head darker with bright orange-brown frontal separated by pale grey band on crown. Eye yellow, with small greyish serrated wattle. White lores and reddish-orange bill. Wings with white patches in primaries. Tail like back with white outer feathers. Underparts like back, with chin, belly and undertail-coverts white. Legs red. SE Tanzania, Mozambique and E Zimbabwe. **Compare** Retz's Helmet-shrike (Plate 41).
110b Juvenile Head brownish-black mottled buffy-white, frontal greyish-brown, bill paler, eye brown, no wattle. Back greyish-brown finely barred buff-white. Wing-coverts and tertials tipped buff-white, wing-patch white. Underparts faintly barred greyish-brown, vent and undertail-coverts white. Legs dull red. **Compare** as for adult.
110c Adult *kirki* Like 110a, but paler crown and frontal and less white in wings. S Somalia, coastal E Kenya and NE Tanzania. **Compare** as for nominate.
110d Adult *keniensis* Like 110c, but frontal darker, very little white in wings, only obvious from below. Central Kenya at Meru and Ngaia forests.

108b
108a
108a
108d
108c
109
110b
110d
110d
110a
110b
110c

PLATE 40 HELMET-SHRIKES 2

111 Chestnut-bellied Helmet-shrike *Prionops caniceps* Text p.347

Medium size, sexes similar. Geographical variation marked. Gregarious in mid- to upper levels of lowland forest from Sierra Leone to Zaïre and W Uganda. Calls diagnostic (see Sounds).

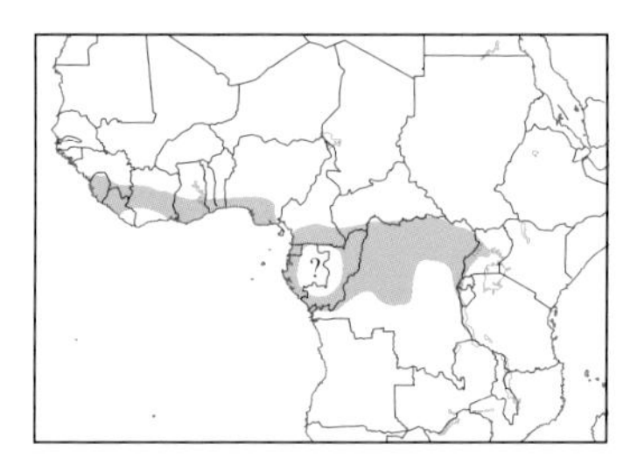

111a Adult *caniceps* Distinctive. Pale grey head, yellow eye with narrow reddish rim, and bill reddish-yellow. Back, wings and tail black with slight gloss, wings with conspicuous white patches in primaries. Underparts with throat and sides of face black, breast and upper belly white. Belly to undertail-coverts rufous-brown. Legs reddish. Sierra Leone to Togo.
111b Immature *caniceps* Above like adult, but frontal and crown greyish-white with dark lores. Eye yellow with orange rim. Wing-coverts tipped buff. Underparts initially with lighter sides to blackish throat. Bill pale reddish-orange, legs like juvenile.
111c Juvenile *caniceps* Above dull without gloss, frontal and crown whitish becoming streaky on hindcrown. Eye greyish-brown with dull rim, lores dark and ear-coverts greyish-brown. May have buffy-white collar extending around hindneck. Back, wings and tail black, wing-coverts tipped buff. Underparts with chin and throat buffy-white with slight streaking, breast and belly whitish to buffy-white, flanks and undertail-coverts darker. Bill blackish and legs dark orange.
111d Adult *harterti* Intermediate between 111a and 111e in head coloration, with bluish-grey more extensive on nape and extending to below eye. Chin and throat like 111a. Nigeria.
111e Adult *rufiventris* Like 111a, but blue-grey crown more extensive on nape and below eye to chin and upper throat. Underparts with only breast white, rufous-brown more extensive. Cameroon to Central African Republic.
111f Juvenile *rufiventris* Above like 111c, but more whitish on frontal, crown and ear-coverts. Underparts with mottled buff to blackish throat, whitish to buffy-white breast and belly. Flanks and undertail-coverts like adult.
111g Adult *mentalis* Like 111e, but head with more extensive blue-grey on nape and face. Eye greyish-brown with outer yellow rim and whitish eyelid. Underparts darker rufous with smaller greyish-black throat-patch which grades into white breast. E and S Zaïre, W Uganda.

111a
111a
111b
111c
111d
111g
111e
111f

112 Retz's Helmet-shrike *Prionops retzii* Text p.349

Medium-large, sexes similar. Geographical variation slight. Gregarious at mid- to upper levels of woodland and forest edge. S Somalia to Mozambique, Malawi, Zambia, Angola and southern Africa. Calls diagnostic, but check White Helmet-shrike (see Sounds).

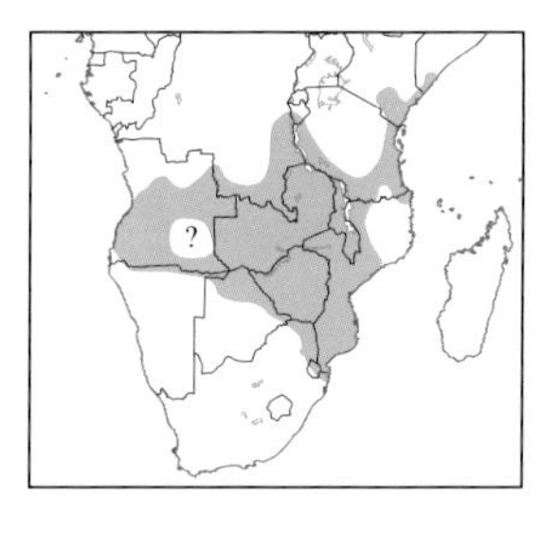

112a Adult Head black with yellow eye and red serrated wattle. Back and wings brown, wing-patch white. Tail black with white outer feathers. Underparts black, vent and undertail-coverts white. Legs reddish. **Compare** Gabela Helmet-shrike (this plate) and Chestnut-fronted Helmet-shrike (Plate 39).

112b Immature Like 112c, but dull brown without pale feather tips and barring. Eye and small wattle initially brown, bill developing reddish colour. **Compare** as for adult.

112c Juvenile Dull brown, undertail-coverts white barred brown. Back and underparts faintly spotted and barred buff, tertials and wing-coverts tipped buff. Eye brown, no wattle, bill greyish-brown, legs dull orange. **Compare** as for adult.

113 Gabela Helmet-Shrike *Prionops gabela* Text p.353

Medium size, sexes slightly different. Little known. Gregarious in canopy of secondary forest around Gabela in W Angola. Calls unknown.

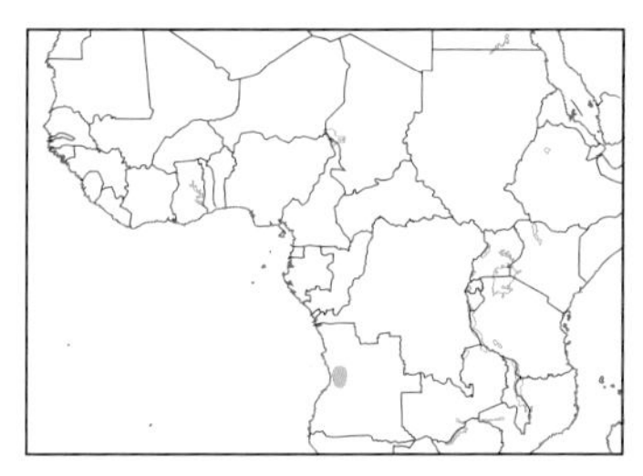

113a Adult Head black with small frontal crest. Yellow eye with small red serrated wattle. Back and wings dull brown. Tail black with white outer feathers. Underparts mainly brown with throat and upper breast black, undertail-coverts and vent white. **Compare** Retz's Helmet-shrike (this plate).

113b Adult ♀ Like ♂, but with small white wing-patch, possibly a juvenile feature.

114 Yellow-crested Helmet-shrike *Prionops alberti* Text p.353

Medium-large, sexes similar. Little known. Gregarious in mid-levels and canopy of montane forest in E Zaïre and SW Uganda. Calls little known (see Sounds).

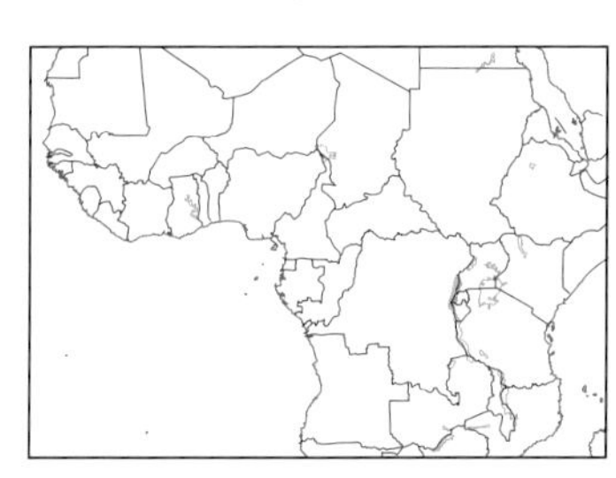

114a Adult Distinctive. Completely black with yellow frontal and crest, eye yellow with narrow orange wattle. Bill black, legs pale red.

114b Juvenile Duller than adult, entirely brownish-black with pale yellowish-white crown and small frontal. Bill and eye probably brown, legs probably orange.

112a
112b
112c
112a
113a
113b
114a
114a
114b

1 NORTHERN WHITE-CROWNED SHRIKE (White-rumped Shrike)
Eurocephalus rueppelli **Plate 1**

FIELD IDENTIFICATION Large (19–23cm), stocky brown and white shrike with white head and rump contrasting with dark brown side of head, back, wings and tail. White rump conspicuous in flight. Loud nasal bleating and chattering calls and round-winged, parrot-like flight distinctive. Sexes similar. Young has pale bill, with head and breast brown and ear-patch white. Gregarious, noisy and conspicuous, often in groups of *c.*3–6, sometimes up to 12 birds; forage mainly on ground. Resident in dry thornbush of E and NE Africa in Ethiopia, Somalia, Kenya and Tanzania. ***Flight characteristics***: Slow, direct with rapid shallow fluttering wingbeats, rather parrot-like, usually combined with short glides with wings uplifted in a shallow V above the back. Wings and tail rounded. White rump conspicuous.

COMPARISONS Distinctive. The only other white-crowned birds which may cause initial confusion include White-crowned Starling *Spreo albicapillus* and White-headed Buffalo-Weaver *Dinemellia dinemellia*. It is similar to Southern White-crowned Shrike *Eurocephalus anguitimens*, but ranges separate. Latter is larger, and lacks white belly and rump.

DESCRIPTION **ADULT** Sexes similar. ***Head*** Forehead, crown and nape white. Face-mask formed by dark line from bill, below the eye to large dark brown patches on ear-coverts and sides of neck, giving appearance of a medieval helmet with protective ear-plates. ***Back*** Brown, darker on lower back; rump and uppertail-coverts white. ***Wing and tail*** Dark brown. ***Underparts*** From chin to undertail-coverts white; sides of breast, belly and underwing-coverts dull brown. ***Bare parts*** Bill black; palate unknown; legs dark grey or brown; eye dark brown. **JUVENILE** Darker than adult with dark brown crown; ear-coverts, nape and rump creamy-white; sides of face blackish; wing-coverts and back feathers with pale edges and tips. Throat white, breast grey-brown with faint barring, forming narrow band; belly white. Bill pale grey-brown; legs paler than adult. **IMMATURE** Like juvenile, but head paling with development of white crown; develops through a stage with crown brownish, spotted buff, and ear-coverts and sides of neck spotted blackish.

GEOGRAPHICAL VARIATION Historically a number of races described, mainly on colour of mantle, underparts and size; however, variation is now known to be high, at least in both plumage characters, particularly as a consequence of feather wear. Birds in fresh plumage have paler upperparts compared to those in worn plumage, a situation complicated by paler immature plumage. Consequently the limits of races based on these characters are difficult to define. In body size there is a cline from small birds in the S (*rueppelli*: S Ethiopia, Kenya, Tanzania), to large ones in the N (*erlangeri*: Ethiopia, NE Kenya, Somalia). Thought by some authors to be monotypic[3, 40, 206, 223, 228, 237, 675].

MOULT Adult wing and tail Apr–May, July, Nov–Dec (mainly Ethiopia). Post-juvenile moult Aug (Kenya) and Jan–Mar (S Tanzania)[237, 832].

RANGE, HABITAT and STATUS **Breeding range** SE Sudan, Ethiopia except N and NW, central, NW and SW Somalia, NE Uganda, Kenya except SE and SW, Tanzania except NW and SE. **Habitat** Semi-desert to dry thornbush and open woodlands, favouring *Acacia* and *Commiphora* woodlands and thickets. Generally a lowland species of low to medium rainfall areas from sea-level to *c.*1600 m, occasionally higher to 2200 m (Kenya)[31, 242, 292, 318, 325, 420, 431, 631, 675, 859]. **Status** Common widespread resident, with possible local movements. **Conservation status** Unknown. Probably not threatened. Poisoning recorded during avicide spraying of Red-billed Quelea *Quelea quelea*[369, 1062].

MOVEMENTS Little known. Possibly some local seasonal movements (Sudan)[242].

SOCIAL ORGANISATION and GENERAL BEHAVIOUR Little known. Gregarious, noisy and conspicuous, often perched out exposed on tops of trees and bushes. Sometimes solitary or in pairs, more often in groups of 3–6 or more, occasionally up to 12 birds[238, 352, 420, 631, 675]. **Foraging behaviour** Hunts from exposed elevated perches, which in woodlands are *c.*6–7 m high. May perch in one place for extended periods while searching the ground below. Most prey is taken on the ground, where bird may hop about in pursuit. Large prey is usually carried back to a perch to consume, where it is held in the foot and torn apart with the bill. Also often takes aerial prey and occasionally gleans from foliage. Sometimes several birds can be seen feeding together on the ground or in the air. Birds have also been seen feeding like oxpeckers (Buphagidae) on the backs of Grant's Gazelles *Gazella granti*, but noticeably less agile, only working the back not the flanks[352, 420, 759]. **Food** Arthropods, mainly insects, including Coleoptera (beetles), Lepidoptera (butterflies) and Orthoptera (grasshoppers). Berries have also been recorded[2, 631, 675, 724, 733].

SOUNDS Little known. Repertoire complex, with a noisy, harsh, nasal, babbler-like quality, very similar to Southern White-crowned Shrike but speeded up. Sounds generally short, rather high-pitched, often a single squawk or squeak, or 2–3 chattering, repeated sharp *kek-kek*, *kak-kak* or *chee-chee* notes. Longer phrases consist of a rapid succession of notes running together: *chrrk, wirk-wirk, yerk-yerk, wuk-wuk, yerk...*, or *yerk yerk-yerk-yerk*. Also has a bleating *weeyer WOK, weeyer WOK* call (the *o* long). Juveniles give sharp, piercing *skeet*[420, 500, 631, 769].

BREEDING BIOLOGY Little known. Monogamous with suspected cooperative breeding. Although pairs are known to breed alone, there is also a report of three birds perched a few centimetres away from one that was incubating. This, combined with its gregarious social system, adds support to at least some cooperative breeding. Clutches of twice normal size may suggest possible extra-pair copulations and/or intraspecific nest parasitism. Cooperative breeding and clutches of twice normal size are known for its sister species the Southern White-crowned Shrike. Although breeding is rather protracted, it appears to be mainly in response to rain. Second broods are probably common, although unknown in the southern species[500, 936]. **Season** Mar–May, Oct and possibly Feb (Ethiopia)[237, 292, 558]; Aug and Dec (Sudan)[242]; Mar–Jun (Somalia)[237, 859, 933]; Jan–Apr, mainly May and Nov (Kenya)[201, 293]; Jun–Dec (Tanzania)[336]. **Displays** Unknown. **Nest** Role of members of group or sexes unknown. A neat, thick-walled, strong cup, densely built of fine grass stalks and vegetable down and heavily plastered with spider web, particularly on the rim. Usually moulded onto a horizontal fork of a slender branch near its end, but has also been reported up against the main trunk. Placed 4–6 m above the ground. Nests appear too small for the size of the bird. ***Size*** OD 100–120 mm, ID 75–90 mm, cup depth *c.*65 mm[2, 336, 420, 558]. **Eggs** 2–4, but up to 7 when two ♀♀ believed to have laid in same nest. White or faint lilac, variously blotched with up to 3 mm wide marks of yellow, brown, greys and purple. ***Size*** 25.5–28 x 21 mm[2, 336, 420, 859]. **Incubation** Unknown. **Nestling** Appearance and period unknown. Young have a dependency period of at least 3 months[574]. No further breeding information.

MEASUREMENTS and WEIGHTS *E. r. rueppelli* ♂ (18) wing 118.5–128.5 (122.7), tail 86–103 (94.4), bill (17) 16–18 (17.2), tarsus 20–23.5 (22.1); ♀ (9) wing 119–129 (124.9), tail 88–101 (96), bill 17–18.5 (17.7), tarsus 21.5–23.5 (22.6)[237]. **Weight** ♂♀? (16) 42–58 g (47.9)[509]. For additional data see [34, 237, 493, 583, 618, 768].

2 SOUTHERN WHITE-CROWNED SHRIKE (White-crowned Shrike)
Eurocephalus anguitimens **Plate 1**

FIELD IDENTIFICATION Large (24 cm), stocky brown and white shrike with white head contrasting with dark brown side of head, wings and tail. Loud nasal bleating and chattering calls and round-winged, parrot-like flight distinctive. Sexes similar. Young has pale bill, head brown, ear-patches white. Gregarious and noisy, usually in groups of *c.*5–6, sometimes up to 20 birds; forage mainly on ground. Resident in dry deciduous woodland in southern Africa from Angola, Namibia, Botswana, Zimbabwe and South Africa. ***Flight characteristics***: Slow, direct with rapid shallow fluttering wingbeats, rather parrot-like, usually combined with short glides, wings uplifted in a shallow V above the back. Wings and tail rounded.

COMPARISONS Distinctive. Similar to Northern White-crowned Shrike *Eurocephalus rueppelli*, but ranges separate. Latter smaller, darker above and with white rump and belly.

DESCRIPTION **Adult** Sexes similar. ***Head*** Forehead, crown and nape white. Face-mask formed by dark line from bill below the eye to large dark brown patches on ear-coverts and sides of neck, giving the appearance of a medieval helmet with protective ear-plates. ***Back*** Ash-brown, darker on lower back and rump. ***Wings and tail*** Dark brown. ***Underparts*** Chin, throat and breast white, gradually changing to ash-brown on belly and flanks; underwing and undertail-coverts pale brown. ***Bare parts*** Bill black, palate pinkish-flesh, legs dark brown, eye dark brown. **Juvenile** Head and back pale ash-brown, nape cream like underparts; brownish-black face-mask much reduced, lacks dark ear-coverts; bill pale, legs greyish. **Immature** Differs from adults by having crown mottled and faintly barred with pale brown; sides of neck, face, nape and ear-coverts whitish. Flight feathers and wing-coverts edged and tipped buff. Underparts: Chin and throat white, breast and belly edged ashy-brown. May show faint barring. Bill pale, legs greyish.

GEOGRAPHICAL VARIATION Two races of similar size. Nominate *anguitimens* (Angola, Namibia, W South Africa and W Zimbabwe) is slightly darker above than *niveus* (Zimbabwe except W, N and E South Africa, W Mozambique, NE Swaziland)[56, 168].

MOULT Apparently a single post-breeding moult, with wing and tail moult recorded in Jan (Botswana)[546].

RANGE, HABITAT and STATUS **Breeding range** SW Angola, Zimbabwe except N, Botswana except SW, central, N and E Namibia, SW Mozambique, N and E South Africa, possibly NE Swaziland. **Habitat** Dry savanna and open deciduous woodlands with sparse ground cover, including *Acacia*, miombo *Brachystegia*, baobab *Adansonia* and mixed broadleaved woodlands. In arid W range, restricted to riverine bush along dry watercourses[7, 26, 30, 48, 53, 205, 297, 639, 807, 907]. **Status** Widespread, locally common resident with some seasonal movements. **Conservation status** Habitat not threatened, population probably stable. Held in captivity[369, 655].

MOVEMENTS Local seasonal austral winter movements reported. In years of drought appear markedly nomadic and rather irruptive[48, 56, 205, 322].

SOCIAL ORGANISATION and GENERAL BEHAVIOUR Gregarious and conspicuous as birds chatter and bleat noisily. Sometimes solitary or in pairs more often in groups of *c*.5–6 when breeding (2–8, n=14), and up to 20 in non-breeding season. Little information on social organisation; however, their behaviour suggests a dominance hierarchy. Foraging direction and group movements appear to be initiated by dominant birds, who coordinate movements by calls and probably visual signals. When one bird calls it sets others off, and they frequently call on take-off and flick the tail on settling. Duetting is common between presumed dominant pair, and a distinctive display is used when certain individuals (status unknown) come together. This greeting display involves drooping the wings on landing, and then partly raising them, half-open above the back, followed by weakly fluttering them at the side of the body. Territorial displays are not well known, but groups perch loosely in exposed, prominent positions while calling. This is accompanied by much tail-flicking and wing-shuffling. One bird initiates calling, to which others respond in duet and chorus. The presumed dominant pair also have a high display-flight, interspersed with wing-up V gliding posture, a repeated *kikek-kikek* call and other rapid *tchetchetchetche* calls which grade into more squeaky notes. Threat is signalled with bill open, neck and crest raised, accompanied by growling call. They readily attack predators but are not pugnacious like *Lanius* shrikes. While foraging some birds appear to act as sentries, giving the alarm call in danger. Lone birds flying about above the trees calling *K-KaeeK...K-KaeeK*-repeatedly are thought to be lost and attempting to regain contact with their group. Like helmet-shrikes they are attracted to wounded members of the group, a behaviour exploited by early collectors. Allopreening takes place, possibly only between dominant pair. Night roosts are in dense foliage and repeatedly used. At roosts there is much calling and jostling for position as members sit huddled together on a branch. This is followed by auto- and allopreening, purring growls and chortling calls. Generally sleep with bill tucked under wing. On leaving the roost in the morning, birds chase each other about noisily, some appearing to nibble each other, and up to 5 birds have been seen hanging upside down like a bunch of grapes from the end of a trailing branch, nibbling each other and picking the leaves off the branch, while making a soft chortling *ka-ka-ka-kakrrrrr* sound. Flights from roost are high and in a tight flock, unlike during foraging. Bathes in dew-covered foliage and scratches indirectly[6, 205, 297, 500]. **Foraging behaviour** Hunts from elevated perch *c*.3–6 m above the ground, crouched squatting on a branch in a horizontal posture scanning the ground below, often stationary for some time. Moves through the woodland in loose groups, singly, in pairs or small sub-groups which tend to progress by a continual leap-frogging of individuals ahead of the birds in front. Most prey is taken on the ground. Here it is consumed, or in the case of larger prey birds return to a perch carrying the prey either in the bill or in the feet. Often hold prey down, or in one foot while tearing it apart. They also glean from thicker branches, trunks and occasionally from clumps of foliage, sometimes hanging by one leg upside down while investigating terminal seed pods, or feeding from prey held in the other foot. Frequently hawk insects in the air. Sometimes attempt to flush prey by fluttering about in thick foliage. Although woodlands are favoured, they often venture out into grassland with only a few scattered thornbushes. A soft chittering call is given when preferred prey is caught. They often forage in the company of *Tockus* hornbills, feeding on insects disturbed by these birds. Foraging is interrupted periodically when the group re-groups usually on some large conspicuous tree. No impaling or wedging of prey observed[1, 9, 205, 416, 500]. **Food** Arthropods, mainly insects. Appears to favour large prey like Orthoptera (locusts and grasshoppers), Lepidoptera (caterpillars), Hymenoptera (black bees), Isoptera (termites) and Coleoptera (beetles). Also feeds on millipedes and small fruits[9, 20, 205, 254, 500].

SOUNDS Repertoire varied and complex. Calls generally loud, some harsh or strident squeaks and squawks, others bleating with a nasal quality and often associated with stuttering, chattering and twittering calls which are usually given in chorus. Territorial calls are initiated by one bird (dominant bird?) with *Kaekaew*, a sound which has aptly been described as like a child's strident trumpet, to which others respond by chorusing with a variety of calls including stuttering and bleating *K-K-K-Kaew, skwee-kwee-kwee, Kaeeer, kwee-* and *Chuk-* or *chut* calls. Threat given with low *Krrrr* growling sounds. Alarm a noisy affair, one bird sounding the alarm with a loud nasal *Kaeeeer* to which others immediately respond with repeated *KeeKeeKee-* calls in chorus. Contact maintained with bleating *Kaee* and repeated *K-KaeeKe-* calls. Pairs duet, ♂ *Kaaeer*, ♀ *Kaekae*. Also have a stuttering *Kida-kida-kida-* call which appears to be used in greeting display or when approaching fledglings with food. Also an excited *tchetchetche*-chitter, apparently given when preferred food is found. Nestlings and fledglings beg with loud wheezy persistent *skea-skea-skea-* calls[48, 205, 297]. Sonagram[48].

BREEDING BIOLOGY Monogamous, cooperative and territorial with a single dominant breeding pair, sometimes assisted by helpers. Degree of cooperative breeding appears to vary between groups, sometimes involving only a pair, other times 3–5 helpers. Size of breeding territories unknown, but austral winter home range of one group estimated at *c*.200 ha. In support of monogamy, a breeding ♂ was observed ignoring a helper who solicited copulation, the breeding pair even allowing her to sit in the nest. However the occurrence of twice normal size clutches, which are presumably the result of a second ♀ laying in the same nest, suggests possible extra-pair copulations and/or intra-group brood parasitism. These nests are easily identified as there are inevitably broken eggs below the nest which cannot accommodate all the eggs. They do not appear to post a sentry near the nest like helmet-shrikes. Appear to be single-brooded[52, 53, 205, 500, 936]. **Season** Nest-building Oct, in breeding condition Nov (Angola)[7, 865, 907]; Sep–Jan, mainly Oct–Nov (Zimbabwe)[30, 359]; Oct–Dec (NE South Africa)[48, 320]; Apr (Namibia)[639]; Sep–Dec (Mozambique)[26]; egg-laying Nov–Jan (Botswana)[807]. **Displays *Courtship*** Pairs duet, ♂ *Kaaeer*, ♀ *KaeKae*, and often allopreen each other. A possible courtship display-flight involved two birds (dominant pair?) flying high and slow with exaggerated wingbeats, followed by a slow gliding descent with wings held in a rigid V. Copulation has been observed to take place on the nest. Courtship-feeding unknown[205]. **Nest** Built by the breeding pair, sometimes assisted by helpers. An extremely neat, perpendicular- and thick-walled cup, usually built of fine dry yellow grass and bark, plastered on the outside and rim with spider web, which gives it a silvery-grey appearance. It is occasionally lined with hair or feathers, and is moulded and secured to the branch with web. Sometimes old nests are re-used. Placed *c.*5 m (2–18, n=95) above the ground, usually near the end of a slender horizontal or downsloping branch, not necessarily on a lateral fork and in a variety of trees, including thorn trees. ***Size*** OD 115–125 mm, ID 85–92 mm, cup depth 35–47mm, height 50–70 mm (n=4). Built in *c.*7 days and often located in the same place in consecutive seasons[6, 20, 205, 500]. **Eggs** Usually 3–4 (2–5, n=21, exceptionally 10). White or creamy, sparsely blotched and spotted with greys and browns, mainly at the large end. ***Size*** 23.0–30.0 x 17.0–22.8 mm (27.2 x 21.3, n=94). Clutches of double normal size are probably laid by 2 ♀♀, and result in many falling out[6, 19, 48]. **Incubation** Assumed by dominant ♀; occasionally helpers sit for short periods. Sitting bird gives contact call from the nest. Estimated period *c.*18–20 days[205]. **Nestling** At least one record of asynchronous hatching. Hatch blind, naked with purple-pink skin, bright orange gapes and yellow gape-flanges. Mouth spots unknown. Usually attended by all members of the group. Young beg with loud persistent *skea-skea-* calls. Brooding ♀ observed feeding nestlings from prey caught below the nest. In another unusual observation 2 Icterine Warblers *Hippolais icterina* regularly fed 3 young. Nest sanitation apparently poorly developed, with nestlings usually defecating over edge of nest. Fledge after 18–20 days. Fledglings respond to adults giving the *kida-kida-kida-krrrr* food call by begging with the *skea-skea-* call accompanied by wing-fluttering in a crouched position[55, 203, 205, 500, 675, 853]. **Predation and longevity** unknown. **Brood parasite** None recorded, although an African Cuckoo *Cuculus gularis* has been seen calling near a nest and taking great interest in the activities there[205].

MEASUREMENTS and WEIGHTS *E. a. anguitimens* ♂ (16) wing 129–140 (137.0), ♀ (10) wing 133–142 (137.1); ♂♀? (28) tail 96–107 (101.8); ♂♀? (10) bill (to skull) 22–26 (24.5); ♂♀? (10) tarsus 24–28 (25.6)[500]. **Weight** ♂ (13) 55.7–76.8 g (68.0), ♀ (9) 59.0–84.0 g (70.1)[205], ♂♀? (3) 51–70 g (63.5)[48].

3 MAGPIE SHRIKE (Long-tailed Shrike)
Corvinella melanoleuca — Plate 1

FIELD IDENTIFICATION Large (45 cm includes tail of *c.*30 cm) pied black and white shrike with a very long tail, white rump and wing-patches and V on back. Fluttering flight distinctive. Sexes different; ♀ with extensive white flanks. Gregarious, noisy with harsh calls and loud whistling, often given in distinctive communal display. Usually in small groups of *c.*6 birds. Perch prominently, forage on the ground. Resident, mainly in thornbush from Kenya in E Africa to southern Africa. ***Flight characteristics***: Relatively fast and horizontal, consisting of rapid fluttering wingbeats. Birds tend to fly in single file, flight ending with an upward swoop to perch, similar to *Lanius* shrikes. Wings rounded with conspicuous white patch in primaries, white V on the back formed by scapulars and white rump.

COMPARISONS Distinctive, superficially similar to Yellow-billed Shrike *Corvinella corvina* in E Africa, but ranges separate, and Long-tailed Starling *Lamprotornis mevesii* in southern Africa.

DESCRIPTION **Adult ♂ *Head*** Black with slight gloss and with lanceolate feathers, particularly on frontal, but extending from crown to lower back. ***Back*** Black with slight gloss, with extensive white scapular feathers forming a V with the greyish-white rump; uppertail-coverts black. ***Wings*** Black with large white basal patch in primaries and white tips on secondaries and tertials. ***Tail*** Black, long and graduated (outer feathers less than half the length of central pair). ***Underparts*** Black, feathers lanceolate, throat and breast duller, flanks may show a few white feathers. ***Bare parts*** Bill and legs black, palate pinkish, eye brown. ***Abnormal plumage*** Partial albinos have been recorded[48]. **Adult ♀** Similar to ♂ but with extensive white on flanks. Breeding birds are thought to have more extensive white on flanks than non-breeders. Tail slightly shorter than ♂ (see Measurements)[205]. **Juvenile/Immature** Duller, browner and with shorter tail than adult. Above dull black, barred rufous-brown. Whitish scapulars tipped brown and smaller than adult, rump greyish-brown. Wings dark brown, coverts tipped buffy-brown.

Below blackish barred brown, flanks with some buffy-white feathers. Fledglings have much shorter tails than adults.

GEOGRAPHICAL VARIATION Four races, variation mainly in tail and wing length, extent of white terminal spots on wing feathers, greyness of rump and brownness of plumage. Nominate *melanoleuca* (S Zambia, Namibia, N South Africa, W Zimbabwe) largest in wing and tail size, *aequatorialis* (S Kenya, Tanzania) has shortest tail with deeper black on throat and breast; *expressa* (S Malawi, N Mozambique, E South Africa) has smaller body size, smaller white terminal wing spots and rump more greyish, rather than white; *angolensis* (Angola, NE Namibia) is similar to *aequatorialis*, has a shorter tail than nominate race, but its status requires further study. This and *expressa* have been regarded by some authors as synonyms of *melanoleuca*[3, 25, 30, 58, 168, 206, 675, 682].

MOULT Unknown.

RANGE, HABITAT and STATUS **Breeding range** Distribution fragmented; SW Kenya, N and central Tanzania, Malawi (breeding requires confirmation), SW Zambia, W and S Mozambique, Zimbabwe (except N and E), central and E South Africa, E Swaziland, Botswana (except SW), N Namibia, SE Angola. Apparently absent from S Tanzania and N Mozambique. **Habitat** Mainly in *Acacia* savanna and open dry woodland, thornbush and occasionally in broadleaved woodland and mopane *Colophospermum*[7, 26, 30, 48, 119, 291, 431, 481, 631, 639, 675, 807, 907]. **Status** Uncommon to locally common resident with local movements. **Conservation status** Generally not threatened, but some evidence suggests that it has become sparser, or has disappeared from some areas. Generally does not adapt well to man-made habitats or areas where extensive bush encroachment has occurred. Held in captivity[205, 369, 639, 655, 810].

MOVEMENTS Little known. Some seasonal movements suspected owing to apparent austral winter vagrants occurring out of normal breeding range. Believed to be a non-breeding visitor to Malawi (requires confirmation). Also known to move temporarily into areas recently cleared by fire[119, 291, 639].

SOCIAL ORGANISATION and GENERAL BEHAVIOUR Gregarious, sometimes solitary, more often in well-spaced groups of *c*.6 birds (2–11, n=9), with up to 19 in austral winter, but also in pairs associated with a few helpers during breeding season. Social organisation unknown, but appears to be based on a dominance hierarchy with the breeding ♀ being the most dominant. Generally shy and difficult to approach. It perches conspicuously on top of prominent trees, sits upright and often flicks and jerks its tail while calling. When group members come together, either in a tree or on the ground, they face each other and have what is believed to be a greeting display. This involves bowing, wing-raising and tail flicking while giving various whistling calls. Juveniles also have a similar display (appeasement?), during which they raise and flutter the up-held wing, with the head held up. Territorial behaviour is initiated by one or two birds (dominant pair?) giving loud melodious whistles, usually in duet, and flying towards the intruders. This attracts other members who join in with a variety of harsh and whistle calls in chorus. Groups may sit in adjacent trees displaying to each other, or merge, accompanied by a frenzy of body movements and calls similar to those described for the greeting display (see Sounds) . The display appears to emphasise the tail, scapulars and flank feathers. A group occupied a home range of *c*.70 ha, while breeding pairs defend a small area of only *c*.3 ha around the nest. Contact is maintained with various whistles and harsh calls. When moving, flies straight in single file, often calling in flight. During threat the head feathers are raised to form a crest, tails raised and expanded and wings opened and lowered. When one bird gives the alarm call it causes others to approach and call the same. Aggression between individuals takes the form of chases accompanied by alarm calls. When ♀♀ or young beg for food they adopt a horizontal, fluttering, wing-drooped posture. They scratch indirectly, but in spite of their social organisation, no allopreening has been recorded. Little is known about their roosting behaviour, but apparently they do not roost huddled together like other social shrikes, but sit *c*.1 m apart[6, 20, 205, 500]. **Foraging behaviour** Hunts from the top of a bush or tree, or on its outer branches, perched in a horizontal posture while scanning the ground below. When prey is spotted, flies or flutters down, often hopping about in search of prey. Also gleans prey from branches and leaf-clusters, sometimes hanging upside down by one foot while feeding off prey held in the other. Occasionally insects are hawked in the air. Most prey is carried in the bill, but they will also carry and manipulate prey with their feet like *Lanius* shrikes. **Food** Arthropods, mainly insects. Diet also includes millipedes, reptiles, mice, occasional small fruit, fresh or rotting meat. Nestlings are fed insects, reptiles and rodents[9, 20, 32, 48, 205].

SOUNDS Repertoire complex, loud and noisy, with various melodious whistles and harsh notes. Calls often combined in duets and complex choruses. Territorial call consists of various loud repeated *teelooo-teelooo*, *tlee-teeoooo* or *tweo-wheeo-weeo* whistles, the first note higher than the second, suggesting the phrase *needle-boom-needle-boom*. Some whistles also described as squeaky or squealing. This call, thought to be made by a dominant bird, is often used to initiate group territorial displays. The call has the effect of attracting members, who approach with whistle and harsh calls, joining in and calling in a complex whistling chorus, phrases repeated and variously combined. Breeding pairs duet with similar calls, *teelooo* by ♂, and a higher-pitched *tleeeu* by ♀. Contact is maintained with various harsh *tchzaaa-tchzaaa-* calls and whistles. Alarm call a harsh grating, scolding *Tchzrrr-Tchzrrr-* or *skaaa-*. A similar call is used in threat. Begging call by breeding ♀ on nest a repeated *tzzeeew-*, and that of young a loud repeated nasal *tzzeeeer-*. Whistled calls of young have a distinct quavering quality[20, 205, 631]. Sonagram[48].

BREEDING BIOLOGY Monogamous and territorial with some cooperative breeding. Groups appear to have only one breeding pair, who hold a small territory around the nest. During nest-building and incubation the breeding ♂ can be seen perched conspicuously near or on the nest tree. Sitting erect with scapulars and rump feathers fluffed out, he gives loud repeated whistles for long periods. When the ♀ is off the nest the pair often engage in duet singing. Apparently only certain members of the group are tolerated at the nest as only 1–3 helpers have been observed. In one observation 2 ♂♂ fed a ♀ on the nest, one ♂ (breeding ♂?) eliciting a much higher response from the ♀ than the other. Double broods are common, with first brood helping to feed second brood. On completion of breeding, parents and young gradually rejoin their group[52, 57, 205, 617]. **Season** In breeding condition Nov–Dec (Angola)[7, 865, 907]; Feb (Tanzania)[25]; Jan–Apr (East Africa)[675]; Jan–Mar, Oct–Dec, mainly Oct–Nov (Zambia)[291]; Aug–Mar, mainly Oct–Nov (NE South Africa)[48, 639]; Aug–Feb, mainly Sep–Dec (Zimbabwe)[48, 639]; Nov–Feb (Botswana)[675, 807]. **Displays** Little is known about courtship; ♂ feeds his mate and both often sing in duet. During nest-building ♂ frequently gives whistled calls from nest tree. ♀ begs in a crouched horizontal posture with wings slightly open, drooped and fluttering. She often calls from the nest. **Nest** Role of sexes unknown. An untidy bulky cup, built of thin thorny twigs and dried grass, often with dry asparagus *Protoasparagus* stems around the outside and a lining of fine grass and sometimes animal hair. Most are placed in thorn trees, particularly *Acacia*, at *c*.4 m (1.5–12, n=121) above the ground. ***Size*** OD *c*.250–300 mm, ID 75–100 mm, cup depth 25–38 mm[6, 205, 500]. **Eggs** Usually 3–5 (1–6, n=56). Buff or yellowish, spotted with browns and greys. ***Size*** 23.1–29.9 x 18.3–20.7 mm (26.8 x 19.7, n=166)[19, 48, 205, 359]. **Incubation** By ♀ only, period unknown[205]. **Nestling** Hatch synchronously, naked with dark pink colour, blind and lack mouth spots, gape yellow. Brooded by ♀ only, with mate and sometimes 1–3 helpers supplying food. Fledge after at least 15 days. Dependency period unknown[27, 53, 205, 500]. **Predation and longevity** Suspected nest predation by monkeys and raptors[500]. **Brood parasite** None.

MEASUREMENTS and WEIGHTS *C. m. melanoleuca* ♂♀? (42) wing 122–143 (134), tail ♂ (25) 225–350, ♀ (17) 215–340, ♂♀? (42) bill 16.5–20.5, ♂♀? (42) tarsus 31–35[548]. **Weight** *melanoleuca* ♂ (21) 54.8–97.1 g (82.1), ♀ (12) 70.9–96 g (82.4)[205]. For additional data see[58, 682].

4 YELLOW-BILLED SHRIKE *Corvinella corvina* — Plate 1

FIELD IDENTIFICATION Large (30 cm includes tail of *c*.18 cm), long ragged-tailed shrike, pale streaky brown with a yellow bill and distinctive chestnut-brown wing-patch, obvious in feeble fluttering flight. Sexes different: ♀ has dark maroon flanks, usually concealed when wing closed. Young like adult but mottled and barred blackish-brown above and below. Gregarious and noisy, with harsh chattering and whistled calls, often given in distinctive communal display. Usually in groups of *c*.6–15 birds; forage mainly on the ground. Resident with local movements, found in *Acacia* savanna and open woodland from Mauritania in West Africa to Sudan and Kenya in East Africa. ***Flight characteristics***: Low and straight, rather hesitant, feeble and fluttering. Wings rounded with bright rufous wing-patch and dark tips. Shows characteristic long-tailed, short-winged silhouette.

COMPARISONS Behaviour and build similar to larger black and white Magpie Shrike *Corvinella melanoleuca* in E and southern Africa. Ranges separate.

DESCRIPTION **ADULT** ♂. ***Head*** crown and nape tinged rufous and streaked, lores and ear-coverts blackish. ***Back*** Pale brown with dark streaks; rump paler and less heavily streaked. ***Wings*** blackish-brown, basal section of primaries rufous; coverts, tertials and secondaries dark brown with buff edging. ***Tail*** Long, graduated (outer feathers about half length of middle pair), dark brown fringed with rufous and whitish at tips. ***Underparts*** buffy-white with fine streaking on breast and flanks, sometimes with slight barring. Flanks pale reddish-brown, tipped dark grey with faint rufous barring in older birds. ***Bare parts*** Bill yellow; palate unknown; legs dark greyish-green; eye dark brown, rims of eyelids yellow. **ADULT** ♀ Similar to ♂ but with dark maroon flank feathers, tipped white in older birds. These feathers are tipped reddish-brown (like ♂, but with a maroon base) in younger birds[60]. **JUVENILE/IMMATURE** Mottled and barred blackish-brown above with no streaking, below dull white with blackish barring on breast and flanks. By about the seventh week of life the tips of the flank feathers are pale reddish-brown. Determination of sex, based on flank colour, is possible at about 11–12 weeks. Generally, the older the bird the more prominent the streaking below[60].

GEOGRAPHICAL VARIATION Little consensus on extent and validity of some races. At least five races, usually with only four accepted but not always the same. Main variation concerns the colour of upperparts and degree of streaking of this area, presence of faint barring below and extent of rufous patch in wings. Nominate *corvina* (Senegal, Gambia to Niger) retains traces of dusky barring on breast in adult and has a relatively large rufous primary wing-patch; *chapini* (NE Zaïre, W

Kenya) more greyish-brown above, rufous area in primaries more restricted and adults never show any barring on breast; *caliginosa* (SW Sudan) more heavily streaked and greyer above with a longer tail; *affinis* (SE Sudan, Uganda and W Kenya) like nominate but more greyish-brown, less reddish above with smaller rufous primary patch; *togoensis* (Guinea-Bissau to Sudan) like nominate but more heavily streaked above. Races *chapini*, *affinis*, and *togoensis* are sometimes considered synonyms of *corvina*[3, 206, 290, 564, 723].

MOULT Little known. Post-breeding moult Aug–Oct. Sexually distinct characters develop at post-juvenile moult[59].

RANGE, HABITAT and STATUS **Breeding range** Mauritania, Senegal, E Gambia, Guinea-Bissau, Guinea, N Sierra Leone, Ivory Coast, Ghana, Togo, Benin, Cameroon, N Nigeria, N Zaïre, S Mali, Burkina Faso, S Niger, S Chad, Central African Republic, W, central and S Sudan, N Uganda, W and NW Kenya. Northern limit *c.*15°N. **Habitat** Wide climatic tolerance, in northern Sahel zone in dry *Acacia* savanna, open grassland with scattered trees. Further S in more wooded, higher-rainfall areas, including open woodland, riverine forest, cultivated areas and gardens. Found up to 2200 m in Kenya[21, 22, 23, 37, 38, 234, 242, 290, 318, 431, 481, 482, 504, 631, 675, 848]. **Status** Widespread, locally common to uncommon resident with local movements. **Conservation status** Not threatened, and may have increased in certain areas, such as Ghana. However, in East Africa it was formerly more widespread. Its decline is thought to be due to replacement of habitat by cultivation[234, 369, 631].

MOVEMENTS Northern populations, particularly in the Sahel zone, exhibit strong seasonal movements, moving S during the dry season, with flocks of up to 150–200 birds reported from S Mauritania. In S Mali only common between Oct–May and in Chad and Sudan there is a general movement S with the advance of the dry season (Nov–Dec). A report of flocks of juveniles seen together requires confirmation[15, 318, 504, 675, 696].

SOCIAL ORGANISATION and GENERAL BEHAVIOUR Gregarious in groups of *c.*12 birds (6–25, n=18) throughout the year, with group size increasing in the dry season. Flocks of 150–200 birds having been recorded from the arid NW during the latter period. Social organisation apparently based on a dominance hierarchy, with breeding ♀ most dominant, probably followed by her mate. The rest of the hierarchy, involving helpers, is not well understood. Young remain in their natal territory as helpers for a few years before dispersing, sometimes in parties of the same sex. ♀♀ tend to move further than ♂♂. Intra-group aggression appears minimal, but does occur sometimes after territorial disputes, and sometimes when helpers are feeding young. These interactions may involve mainly ♂♂. Yellow-billed Shrikes usually sit on prominent perches scattered over a small area or move in follow-my-leader flights. Generally noisy and shy, except when associated with human habitation when more approachable, and active with movements accompanied by incessant chattering and whistling. They advertise and defend a territory of *c.*17 ha (10.6–27.1, n=18). Group and territory size are independent. In territorial interactions, one or two individuals moved to a nearby exposed, usually high position, while giving a distinctive warbling call. This attracts other members who join in with similar noisy calling, sometimes even attracting the breeding ♀ off the nest. The display takes the form of hopping from branch to branch or bowing up and down towards nearest neighbours, tails jerking up and down, in circular movements or from side to side, and with body feathers fluffed out exposing flank feathers. Bill-wiping frequently occurs at the same time, and is probably displacement behaviour. Displays may last up to 15 min, sometimes culminating in physical contact as individuals grapple in the air, falling and separating before hitting the ground. When one bird gives the alarm call it attracts others who call the same. Group members roost together in the same site throughout the year. Prior to entering the roost individuals give the warbling call, which is continued for a short period before stopping abruptly[22, 59, 455, 696]. **Foraging behaviour** Usually feed individually, but sometimes attracted to sources of food by the activities of other members, at which time feed communally. Hunt from exposed perches on top of small bushes or from edges of trees, low bushes or in undergrowth. Generally swoop down in a short flight to capture prey on the ground. Sometimes hops or bounces about turning over leaf-litter like a thrush. Also hawks insects in the air. Large ants are rubbed on a branch before being swallowed. **Food** Arthropods, mainly insects and some small vertebrates. Insects include Coleoptera (beetles), Orthoptera (grasshoppers), Mantodea (mantids), Hemiptera (bugs), Lepidoptera (caterpillars), Isoptera (termites) and Hymenoptera (ants, including large *Paltothyreus tarsatus*). Also recorded feeding on spiders, worms and small fruits. Known to attack young birds and feed on lizards and frogs. Nestlings were fed mantids, caterpillars, slugs and spiders. Not known to impale and cache prey[59, 290, 328, 455, 675].

SOUNDS Repertoire complex and noisy with a variety of harsh rasping, buzzing, chattering, chirping and twittering sounds, some resembling helmet-shrikes, others starling-like which are combined with distinctive whistle calls, similar to Magpie Shrike, but less sonorous. Calls are usually given in duet and chorusing, and often in flight. Harsh calls include a chattering *kzzzrkzzzr-* and a commonly heard, loud repeated hoarse *scis-scis*, *schiss--schiss* or *zrreetzrreet-* and hard *squee squee* in flight, or squealing notes with guttural rattling *drreee-too-*, *brrreeeu-*, *ksseeu-* and others which develop into a communal chattering racket. These displays are usually initiated by a distinctive warbling call, which is also used at communal roosts. Various modulated whistles are loud (audible up to 200 m) and rapidly repeated, sounding like *twee-dl-ooo*, *tluueet-tluueet-* and often given in a phrase suggesting 'may we, may we wait, may we' or 'maaay...we, may...we, wait we--eah---eah-

---eah'. Alarm a 2–3 note call, transcribed as a harsh *twe-kik...wee-ti-kik* or rasping *kzzzz-kzzzz-kzzzz*. The breeding ♀ has a distinctive harsh repeated call, given from the nest, and used to solicit food from her mate and helpers[22, 59, 290, 455, 500, 696, 769]. Sonagram[59].

BREEDING BIOLOGY Monogamous, cooperative and territorial. Groups have only one breeding pair who are assisted by group members. Sometimes two ♀♀ appear to compete for sole breeding status. No breeding takes place without helpers, who assist in nest-building, nest defence and the feeding of the breeding ♀ and young. The breeding ♀ gives a distinctive food-soliciting call from the nest, which causes her mate and helpers to supply food. Older birds tend to provision more. Nestlings are fed by all members, although the breeding ♂ may provision the most. Birds approaching the nest with food sometimes give what is thought to be an appeasement call, and which is also used when flying high over another territory. In one study in Ghana a density of 0.8 birds/ha has been recorded. In this population 25% of all eggs laid produced fledglings. Hatching success was 37–63% (av. 51.2%, n=5) and fledging success was 21–36% (av. 27.4%, n=5). Most breeding takes place during the rains, with second and sometimes third broods normal[59, 696]. **Season** Jun–Aug (Senegal)[482]; Mar–Oct, mostly Jul–Oct (Gambia)[39, 482, 696]; all months except Nov, mainly Feb–Apr (Ghana)[59, 234]; all months except Nov–Dec, in N Apr–Jul (Nigeria)[37, 290], Jul (Sudan)[242]; nestlings Feb (Uganda)[290]; Feb–Mar (Kenya); Feb (Tanzania)[293]. **Displays** Little known; see General Behaviour. Courtship feeding occurs, and during territorial displays flank feathers are exposed. When 2 breeding ♀♀ occurred in one group, both competed for the attention of the group by calling from the nest; eventually only one ♀ bred successfully[59, 60]. **Nest** Built by breeding pair assisted by some helpers. A substantial cup, rather loosely built of twigs, grass-stems and sometimes leaves, lined with finer rootlets and grass. Placed in a tree or bush, often thorny, usually at heights of 3–6 m (1–10), often concealed in thick foliage. ***Size*** OD 95 mm, cup depth 44 mm. Construction may take up to 4 weeks, but in the case of replacement clutches, only 3–4 days. Some nests are re-used in same season[22, 59, 290, 328]. **Eggs** Usually 3–5 (2–6, n=98), laid on consecutive days. Cream, buff, reddish or greenish-white, spotted with yellowish brown and grey, usually in ring around the large end. ***Size*** 22.3–25.0 x 17.7–19.4 mm (22.4 ±0.16 x 18.3 ±0.06, n=36)[15, 22, 38, 59, 290, 328]. **Incubation** Normally by breeding ♀ only. Period *c.*16 days (15–18, n=17). ♀ calls from the nest and is fed by mate and helpers[59]. **Nestling** Appearance unknown. Brooded for *c.*1 week by breeding ♀ only. Period 18–20 days. Nestlings fed by all members, who pass food to ♀, who in turn feeds nestlings. Although all members help, not all at the same time. Fledglings are independent by the 7th week after hatching, and are integrated into group activities by 10 weeks, feeding fledglings (from later broods) by 14 weeks and nestlings by 24 weeks[59]. **Predation and longevity** Alarm given to Shikra *Accipiter badius* and Pied Crow *Corvus alba*. Longevity at least 5 years[59]. **Brood parasite** African Cuckoo *Cuculus canorus* is a rare parasite (1 in 160 nests). Although the incubating and brooding ♀ persistently begged for food for the young cuckoo, helpers were often aggressive towards it[59, 619].

MEASUREMENTS and WEIGHTS *C. c. corvina* ♂ (5) wing 123–130, ♀ (5) wing 115–123, ♂♀? (9) tail 160–181, bill 17–19, tarsus 30–34[59]. **Weight** ♂♀? (11) 58.0–79.9 g (65.4) (Ghana)[59]; ♂♀? (1) juvenile 66.5 g (Ghana)[582].

5 CHINESE GREY SHRIKE (Chinese great Grey Shrike, Wedge-tailed Shrike) *Lanius sphenocercus* — Plate 2

FIELD IDENTIFICATION Large (29 cm) grey, black and white shrike with black face-mask and white eyebrow (absent in one race). Wings and long graduated tail black, showing much white, particularly in flight. Sexes similar. Young with buffy tinge, faintly barred above. Fast strong flyer, frequently hovering, perches prominently. Calls high-pitched 2-note whistle and grating sounds. Solitary in open country with scattered trees and bushes in E Asia from central China, E Russia and N Korea. Boreal winter migrant in same area, S to Hong Kong. ***Flight characteristics***: Fast, with rapid wingbeats. Flies low to ground, swoops up to perch. White wing-patch obvious in flight as well as long graduated black and white tail. Frequently hovers like a Kestrel *Falco tinnunculus*[191, 272].

COMPARISONS In field resembles Great Grey Shrike *Lanius excubitor*, but differs by larger size, including bill, and much longer, more strongly graduated tail with much white. Wings have much larger white patches. Most likely to be confused in boreal winter with Great Grey race *sibiricus*, which is a duller, browner-grey above and finely barred below. The Southern Grey Shrike *Lanius meridionalis* race *pallidirostris* may also overlap in W of range, but occurs in more arid steppe habitat[209, 212, 284, 651, 675].

DESCRIPTION ADULT Sexes similar. ***Head*** Forehead with narrow white band, crown and nape pale grey. Black face-mask extends from in front of eye to ear-coverts, bordered above with a white eyebrow to just behind the eye (lacking in *giganteus*). ***Back*** Mantle to rump and uppertail-coverts pale grey, scapulars white. ***Wings*** Black edged white, with very large white wing-patch (variable) at base of primaries and secondaries; secondaries and tertials broadly tipped and edged white; wing-coverts mostly black. ***Tail*** Markedly graduated, black with outer feathers broadly edged whitish. Usually central two feathers are black, but occasionally these also tipped white. ***Underparts*** Chin to vent whitish, often with pinkish tinge; underwing-coverts whitish. ***Bare parts*** Bill black, long, strong and well hooked, base of lower mandible pale; palate unknown; legs dark blackish; eye dark brown. **JUVENILE/IMMATURE** Distinguished from adult by buffy tinge and faint wavy barring on upperparts; flight feathers edged buff, wing-coverts tipped buff. Underparts whitish with buffy tinge on breast. Bill brownish, blackish on upper mandible only, legs brownish-black[214, 675, 913].

GEOGRAPHICAL VARIATION Two races differ in size, coloration and habitat preference. Race *giganteus* (central China, E Tibet) larger (20 mm longer in wing and tail), and darker above with no white on face or forehead. Tail with less white on outer feathers. Wings with no white on outer webs of secondaries. Underparts not as white, more lavender-grey compared to nominate *sphenocercus* (NE Asia in E Siberia, Korea, N and E China). Juvenile *giganteus* darker than nominate on upperparts and more distinctly tinged buff, particularly on underparts. Nominate race inhabits low-lying valleys and plains, *giganteus* in mountainous regions and high-lying valleys[197, 675, 913].

MOULT Little known. In adults, a complete post-breeding moult takes place from Jun–Oct, after which they may show a faint pinkish tinge on the breast. Post-juvenile moult of body feathers takes place soon after fledging (Aug–Sep)[214, 675, 835, 913].

RANGE, HABITAT and STATUS **Breeding range** Limits not well known; NE and central China, far E Russia to at least 50°N and probably NE Korea. Western limit at *c.*98°E and in S at *c.*28°N. Species may also be found to occur in E Mongolia. **Non-breeding range** See Movements. **Habitat** Nominate race occurs from sea-level to *c.*200 m in broad valleys, pastures and cultivated areas with small clumps of trees (Russia). Also found up to 1800 m in foothills, open steppes and semi-deserts (China). In Tibet *giganteus* breeds from *c.*3000–5200 m along or above the timber-line, usually in stunted vegetation like rhododendron scrub[188, 190, 197, 212, 214, 272, 284, 675, 913]. **Status** Uncommon resident and partial migrant. **Conservation status** Unknown.

MOVEMENTS Nominate race is a resident and partial migrant, with movements mainly to SE China, mostly N of Chang-jiang and up to *c.*105°E in China, and S to Korea (Oct–Apr, and mostly Nov–Dec). Occasionally to Kong Kong (Sep–Nov) and Japan (Nov–Mar). Migration routes not well known, but in autumn apparently in a S and SW direction. Some birds already in their non-breeding grounds in Jun–Jul, but most Siberian birds depart Aug–Oct, returning in Mar. In China at Hebei, occurs Aug–Mar, in Beidaihe area a few spring records, but mainly Aug–Nov, and in Nanking Dec–Mar. The mountainous race *giganteus* appears to be resident with only local, mainly altitudinal movements from breeding area to below 4000 m[188, 190, 191, 193, 195, 212, 214, 268, 269, 272, 284, 675, 687, 913].

SOCIAL ORGANISATION and GENERAL BEHAVIOUR Little known. Appears similar to the Great Grey Shrike, usually solitary and conspicuous as perches prominently in an upright posture in open country. Reported as shy, although mountainous race *giganteus* apparently very confiding. Advertises and defends a surprisingly small territory of *c.*4 ha (2.3–5.8, n=4) (Russia). Territories seldom overlap due to low population density[191, 284, 675, 913]. **Foraging behaviour** Hunts from exposed, relatively high perches, usually 4–6m (2–8) above the ground. Most prey caught on the ground, less frequently in low vegetation and sometimes in the air. Small insects are caught like a flycatcher, larger prey, including birds, are chased on the wing for up to *c.*100 m like a hawk. Often hovers like a Kestrel *Falco tinnunculus* for up to 30 sec at about 5–6 m above the ground, occasionally up 30 m. Often impales or wedges prey and forms caches in small bushes or trees. These are used mainly in spring. Pellets are large (20–40 x 8–15 mm) and often contain bones. When breeding both sexes hunt between 10 and 400 m, usually 40–70 m, from the nest. **Food** Diet seasonally variable and includes arthropods, mainly insects and small vertebrate prey, the latter forming a significant component of its diet. In boreal summer mainly insects, including Orthoptera (grasshoppers, crickets and mole-crickets), Coleoptera (beetles), Hymenoptera (bees, bumble bees and wasps), Lepidoptera (caterpillars), and Diptera (blood-sucking flies). Also takes spiders. In one study Orthoptera, Coleoptera and Hymenoptera made up *c.*95% of prey. Also frequently takes small vertebrates, 16% of prey items in one study. In boreal winter feeds mainly on vertebrates, particularly mammals (rodents). Also recorded are small amphibians, reptiles and birds. In one study nestlings were fed mainly small mammals, crickets and grasshoppers[105, 270, 271, 272, 559, 675, 812, 835, 913].

SOUNDS Little known. Repertoire consists of whistled sounds and harsh notes. Song described as similar to Great Grey Shrike. Main territorial call, given by both sexes, consists of loud repeated disyllabic *tri-rli*, *tree-rleee* or *tsveet-tsveet-* fluted whistles, increasing in pitch towards the end, with the second note drawn out and often the most prominent note. This sounds like *tschriii, rlu, rleee* or *chreee*. These calls have also been described as a trill, and are sometimes combined with a long, hardly audible warbling or twittering phrase. Another call has been described as a harsh *check-cherr*. Alarm a sharp nasal *keee* or *tscheee*, given in flight or when perched. Also described as a 'mew'-type call. ♂ heard to give *churr-churr* sounds while feeding young[105, 209, 270, 284, 600, 675, 835].

BREEDING BIOLOGY Monogamous and territorial. Migrants appear to return to the same area each year and breeders are very aggressive.

Generally occurs at low densities; varies in different years from 0.23–0.34 pairs/km² in central Amurland to 0.4–1 pairs/km² in the plains near Lake Khanka, where neighbouring pairs are 1–2.5 km apart (Russia). In one study of 11 nests, 74 eggs were laid of which 58 hatched (78.4%) and 45 young fledged (60.8%)[105, 284, 559, 675, 913]. **Season** Nominate race Mar–Jul (Russia)[105, 209, 284, 675, 835, 913]. **Displays *Courtship*** ♀ has been observed soliciting from ♂ in a crouched, open-bill posture[835]. **Nest** Role of sexes unknown. The cup is of variable size, sometimes appearing too large for the size of the bird, in other cases too small. It is built of twigs, leaves, dried grass stems and rootlets, and thickly lined with fine grass, vegetable down, feathers, sometimes including man-made materials and animal hair. Usually placed in a fork of tree (e.g. willow, elm, oak or birch) or bush 1.2–5 m above ground. ***Size*** OD 155–265 mm, ID 90–120 mm, cup depth 74–100 mm, height 105–220 mm (n=26). Nest is only used once, with a new nest built for replacement clutches, often quite close to the original site; a completed nest may remain empty for 7–8 days before egg-laying begins[105, 210, 214, 284, 835, 913]. **Eggs** Usually 6–8 eggs (5–9, n=21), laid at 24-hour intervals. Creamy or greyish-white, sometimes with a greenish or bluish tinge and spotted pale brown to reddish-brown or grey, often concentrated at the large end. ***Size*** 26.2–30.3 x 19.8–21.5 mm (28.16 ±0.16 x 20.72 ±0.06, n=56 from 11 clutches)[105, 210, 214, 284, 559, 665, 913]. **Incubation** By ♀ only. ♂ feeds ♀. Period 16–19 days. In final stages of incubation behaviour changes, ♂ moves away from nest and gives loud prolonged whistles, moves about agitatedly and vibrates tail; ♀ also gives penetrating whistles[105, 835, 913]. **Nestling** Hatch with pink skin; probably lacks mouth spots. Shells carried away or eaten. Attended by both sexes, and produce loud calls by 9–13 days. Fledge after 19–21 days. Independent after a further *c.*35–65 days and move away in mid-Jul[105, 835, 913, 789]. For development of nestlings see[105]. No further breeding information.

MEASUREMENTS and WEIGHTS *L. s. sphenocercus* ♂♀? (11) wing 119–126 (121.9), tail 130–145 (139.3), bill (to skull) 23.1–27 (25.5), tarsus 29–32.1 (30.5)[500]; wing ♂ (6) 117–125 (121.3), ♀(5) 112–125 (120)[214]; *giganteus* ♂ (1) wing 138, tail 161, bill (to skull) 24.5, tarsus 33[500]; wing 134–147, tail 160–173[212]; ♂(?) av. *c.*160, ♀ slightly smaller[675]. **Weight** *sphenocercus* ♂ (3) 87.2 g, 90.4 g, 100.0 g, ♀ (2) 87.2 g, 95.7 g[214, 835]; juveniles ♂♀? (5) 79.0–92.5 g (86.0)[835]; ♂♀? 80–100 g, generally 90–100 g[675].

6 GREY-BACKED FISCAL (Long-tailed Grey-backed Fiscal)
Lanius excubitoroides **Plate 2**

FIELD IDENTIFICATION Large (26 cm), robust, black, grey and white shrike, with broad black face-mask and forehead, black and white wings, and long black tail with broad white base. Sexes different; ♀ with rufous flanks, usually seen only in flight or display. Young barred greyish-brown above, lighter below, with small dark brown face-mask. Perch prominently, gregarious and noisy, often chorusing with whistle and chattering calls. Sometimes solitary or in pairs, more often in parties of *c.*5–6 birds, in active and noisy displays with much body, wing and tail movement. Resident with local movements. Found in *Acacia* and bush savanna from Mauritania to Ethiopia, Uganda, W Kenya, Rwanda, Burundi and NW Tanzania. ***Flight characteristics***: Groups disperse by following one another with a direct but rather laboured, slow and lazy flight. White in wings and tail pattern diagnostic, with tail appearing disproportionately long.

COMPARISONS Similar to much smaller migrant Lesser Grey Shrike *Lanius minor* with black frontal band (present in range from about Aug–Sep to Apr–May) and Southern Grey Shrike *L. meridionalis*, particularly *leucopygos* race. Differs from both in being larger, with longer tail which has distinctive basal white pattern, and in having the black on the head (frontal and face-mask) extending down the sides of the neck to wings. Southern Grey lacks black frontal. Behaviour also differs: Grey-backed Fiscal is gregarious in small groups, the other two species are solitary. Juvenile similar to juvenile Long-tailed Fiscal (*L. cabanisi*) except for tail pattern, both are gregarious. Juvenile Common Fiscal *L. collaris* race *humeralis* smaller, more rufous and lacks tail pattern.

DESCRIPTION ADULT ♂ ***Head*** Black face-mask extensive, from forehead through eye to ear-coverts and onto shoulder and wing; some individuals show slight white eyebrow; crown and nape pale grey. ***Back*** Pale grey, rump whitish-grey. ***Wings*** Black with large white patch on primaries. ***Tail*** Graduated, black with basal half white except for central 2 feathers, base of which are barred; all feathers show small white tips. ***Underparts*** White from chin to vent, including flanks. ***Bare parts*** Bill black; palate unknown; legs blackish; eye dark brown. ADULT ♀ like ♂ but with dark chestnut-brown flanks, concealed when wing closed. JUVENILE/IMMATURE Upperparts greyish-brown; head, mantle and back heavily barred with fine pale brown to dusky bars; rump buffy-white barred black. Small face-mask brownish-black and not extending onto forehead. Scapulars, tertials, flight feathers and tail edged with pale rufous. Wings and tail dark brown with adult white areas. Wing-coverts slightly barred and edged buff. Underparts dull white to buffy-white with faint dusky barring mainly on breast and flanks. ♀♀ rufous flank-patches develop *c.*50 day after fledging. Bill pale.

GEOGRAPHICAL VARIATION At least three races, varying in size, darkness of upperparts and extent of white in tail. The NE *intercedens* (NW Uganda, central Ethiopia, W Kenya) is slightly larger, longer-tailed and with less black on the tail than nominate *excubitoroides* (West Africa to Zaïre, Sudan and Uganda); *boehmi* (S central Uganda, W Tanzania, E Zaïre, Rwanda and Burundi) appears intermediate in size but with darker, duskier-grey upperparts[940].

MOULT Wing moult in May (Uganda)[762].

RANGE, HABITAT and STATUS Breeding range SE Mauritania, central Mali, N Nigeria, N Cameroon, Central African Republic, N Zaïre, S Sudan, SW Ethiopia, Uganda, W Kenya, W of Rift Valley, NW Tanzania, Rwanda and Burundi. **Non-breeding range** See Movements. **Habitat** In sub-Sahara from Sahel region in thornscrub and open *Acacia* savanna. Further S in wooded grasslands and open bushed woodlands, pastures and cultivated areas including gardens. In Kenya mainly from *c.*1000–1900 m[31, 37, 237, 242, 290, 292, 318, 338, 355, 356, 431, 481, 631]. **Status** Generally a common resident, but less common to rare in extreme W range, where undergoes local movements. **Conservation status** Unknown. Habitat probably not threatened. In E range population probably stable, but surveys recommended[369].

MOVEMENTS Little known with conflicting evidence. Earlier reports of great numbers migrating to Rift Valley in Kenya have subsequently been rejected, but some birds do appear in unexpected places, such as Mau Narok (3000 m). In W range definitely undergoes local migration, disappearing or becoming very rare in SE Mauritania and central Mali during the rains. Possibly also locally migratory in Sudan[11, 237, 242, 318, 431, 504].

SOCIAL ORGANISATION and GENERAL BEHAVIOUR Gregarious and tame, sometimes solitary, in pairs, more often in noisy groups from 2–15, occasionally up to 20 birds, but usually *c.*5–6 birds. Groups are seen only when defending a territory or feeding on swarming insects, at other times they are dispersed throughout the territory. Groups consist of family members with one breeding pair. Advertise and defend a territory of *c.*15 ha (*c.*9–34, n=23, Uganda). These are advertised by individuals perching prominently (static marking), or by patrolling a boundary. The whole group defends the territory in a noisy excited duetting or 'chorus' dancing display in which members sit close together, rocking back and forwards, waving, swinging and fanning tails and fluttering their wings while calling. Individuals change perch frequently, with the groups sometimes only a few metres apart. Territorial threat is initiated by a breeding bird with a metallic-sounding call which develops into a excited duetting with its mate or chorus with rest of group. Flight at intruders is direct with rapid wingbeats, followed by a glide, one bird following the other. The pursuers then present their contrasting black and white areas by lowering heads with bills open, wings outstretched and tails fanned. At still higher intensity this display is repeated as the defenders approach, duet and dance, alternately jumping up and down about a foot into the air. This is accomplished by taking off with wings flapping rapidly and then landing with tail gently waved up and down. All group members, except juveniles younger than *c.*6 months old, are involved in this display, which may last up to 30 min. Should the intruders remain, the interaction may develop into physical contact and even aerial battles. No intra-group aggression occurs, but they are clearly aggressive towards rival groups and competitors, like the Common Fiscal. ♀ rufous flanks are exposed in this display. Group members roost together, sometimes maintaining the same roost site for years. Allopreening does not occur[2, 15, 155, 237, 356, 357]. **Foraging behaviour** Individuals of a group forage alone, spread throughout the group territory. They perch in an exposed position on top or in edge of bush or tree *c.*2–4 m up, scanning the ground below. Most prey is caught on the ground; once caught the bird returns quickly to a perch. Some insects are also caught in the air and all group members converge on swarming prey, such as ants and caterpillars. Impales prey and forms caches[357, 675]. **Food** Little known. Arthropods, mainly large insects and vertebrate prey. Insects include Lepidoptera (*Cossus* caterpillars), Hymenoptera (ants *Dorylus*) and Isoptera (termites). Small vertebrates, including frogs and birds, are taken, and Quelea *Quelea quelea* nests are plundered[357, 675].

SOUNDS Little known. In one study repertoire thought to consist of *c.*6 different calls. Interestingly, it apparently lacks an obvious contact call, this function probably being achieved by visual cues. Its repertoire has been variously described as containing harsh notes, noisy chattering, rasping and shrill, jarring or screaming notes. High-pitched whistle notes, while superficially resembling Long-tailed Shrike *Corvinella melanoleuca* and Yellow-billed Shrike *C. corvina*, are varied and tend not to be clear, but to have a buzzy quality, rather starling- or drongo-like. Songs show individual variation, but whether these differences are due to sex or status are unknown. Two calls are commonly used in territorial interactions and appear to be initiated by the dominant bird: threat is initiated with a metallic-sounding *kyoir-l* whistle; this changes to the display call, which develops in the form of an excited duetting or chorus, uttered repeatedly by the displaying birds out of step with each other, and sounding like *kyoir-l, kyoi, kyo-ooh*. These calls have been variously described as a shrill and jarring chatter, ending in a squeak, a *teudleeoo-teudleeoo* whistle, a discordant medley of strident, often metallic notes, or a screaming *tiri-iri-tiri*. Alarm call is a loud and harsh *krrr-krrr*-or *zrrit-zzzrit*- and also used in the presence of an aerial predator. Begging call a loud repeated *pssh*, given by ♀ during courtship or begging young.

Adults often give a brief song while feeding fledglings. In juveniles, the first elements of adult song are heard *c.*75 days after fledging[2, 9, 155, 290, 357, 500, 675].

BREEDING BIOLOGY Cooperative and territorial. Only one breeding pair, with other group members acting as helpers. Only ♂♂ appear to inherit breeding status; ♀♀ must leave their natal group to attain breeding status. Only birds older than 6 months act as helpers at the nest. In one Kenyan study the following breeding success was reported: of 23 eggs laid in 17 nests, 21 (91.3%) hatched; 8 of 55 nests (14.5%) fledged young; 1.39 young/group, 2.65 young fledged/successful nest; 64–67% (41/61 and 34/53) individual adult survivorship. Breeding appears to be mainly in response to rains; apparently single-brooded[355, 356, 357, 896]. **Season** Feb–Mar (Mauritania and Mali)[675]; breeding condition Apr (Cameroon)[37, 338]; breeding condition all year (NE Zaïre)[290, 338]; Apr–May, Aug (Sudan)[242]; Apr, Jun (Ethiopia)[292]; May–Jul, Oct–Dec (NE Uganda)[2, 290]; Mar–Apr, Nov (E Kenya, N Uganda); Dec–Feb (central and S Uganda); Jan, Jun–Aug, Nov (NE Tanzania to E central Kenya)[293, 576]; attempted breeding all year, mainly May–Nov (S Kenya)[375]. **Displays *Courtship*** Mated pair separates from the group and ♂ feeds ♀ who solicits with wings drooped and *pssh* begging calls. He gives a brief song during courtship feeding. The combination of this song and begging call is a good indicator for the start of breeding. **Nest** Built mainly by breeding ♀; although breeding ♂ supplied material, he did not take part in construction. In one case the helpers of a group worked on a flimsy nest while breeding ♀ built another. A compact cup of small sticks, thorn twigs, grass stems, bark fibre and rootlets, lined with fine grasses and small feathers. Nests are apparently not re-used, although material from old nests and other species' nests is sometimes used. Placed *c.*1–12 m up at various locations in thorn trees, usually on horizontal branch, but also in centre of tree. May remain empty for up to 2 weeks before egg-laying[2, 237, 290, 357, 576]. **Eggs** Usually 3 (2–4, n=17), laid on successive days. Colour variable; creamy-pink, pale yellowish-grey or olive-buff with spots of brown, red-brown and grey mainly at the large end. ***Size*** Av. 25 x 18.5 mm (n=?)[2, 237, 290, 576]. **Incubation** By ♀ only; period 13–15 days, hatching usually synchronised. ♀ fed by group, with breeding ♂ provisioning more than helpers, but ♀ helpers provisioning more than ♂ helpers[357]. **Nestling** Appearance unknown. Brooded by ♀ only. Fledge after *c.*20 days. All members help feed and remove faecal sacs, although ♂ and ♀ breeders provision most. Young completely dependent for first 2 weeks and remain in their natal territory to become helpers in later years. For development of young see[357]. **Predation and longevity** In one study, Gabar Goshawk *Micronisus gabar* frequently predated nestlings. Longevity at least 3 years[357]. **Brood parasite** None.

MEASUREMENTS and WEIGHTS *L. e. excubitoroides* ♂♀? (7) wing 110–118 (113), tail 123–140 (130), bill (to skull) 20–23 (21.7), tarsus 28–30 (29.4)[500]. **Weight** ♂ (42) 47–63.5 g (55.32 ±SD 13); ♀ (26) 46.5–59 g (52.21 ±SD 3.34) (Kenya)[357]. For additional data see[237].

7 GREAT GREY SHRIKE (Northern Shrike in North America)
Lanius excubitor **Plate 3**

FIELD IDENTIFICATION Large (24–25 cm) grey, white and black shrike with narrow black face-mask, pale blue-grey head and back, white scapulars, black wings with obvious, usually double white wing-patch and long black tail with white outer feathers. Underparts variable from white to barred pale whitish-brown. White of scapulars, wing and tail conspicuous in flight. Sexes similar but ♀ has less white in wings and tail. Young similar to adults but duller and browner above with buff wing-coverts. Calls harsh and grating, whistles and warbling song with mimicry. Solitary, perches prominently, found in wide range of habitats from shrub tundra to forest edge. Widely distributed in Holarctic, mainly N of 50°N in Eurasia and North America, partial boreal winter migrant to S Eurasia and S North America. ***Flight characteristics***: Rapid and powerful, flies low with swoop up to perch, undulating over long distances, also hovers. White scapulars, wing-patch and black and white tail conspicuous.

COMPARISONS Very similar to and difficult to distinguish from some races of Southern Grey Shrike *Lanius meridionalis*. In Europe, Great Grey Shrikes spending boreal winter in the SW overlap with the range of nominate Southern Grey Shrike, while in Central Asia a number of races overlap the range of the Southern Grey race *pallidirostris*. Although the Great Grey Shrike has slightly longer wings, shorter, less robust bill and shorter legs, these characters are not obvious in the field. Careful attention to coloration, face and wing patterns, and presence or absence of barring, are essential for accurate identification. Nominate Great Grey more easily separated from nominate Southern Grey, which has dark lead-grey upperparts (pale grey in Great Grey), thin white eyebrow extending over the bill (absent in Great Grey), single wing-patch on primaries only (double in Great Grey, on primaries and secondaries), pinkish-buff underparts with a white chin and throat (uniform whitish in Great Grey) and black face-mask narrower and less extensive in Great Grey, particularly on the ear-coverts (Southern Grey has broader, more extensive face-mask). There is also a tendency for the bill to be darker in Great Grey, with a less extensive pale base than Southern Grey. Compared to central and E Asian Great Grey Shrikes, Southern Grey races lack a brownish tinge on upperparts and dark barring below (although some Southern Grey show traces of barring). Separation of juveniles difficult, based mainly on extent of barring below, but very variable. Generally barring is more distinct in Great Grey, but indistinct or absent in Southern Grey. Much more field work is required to refine differences between these two species, particularly for the little known Asian races. For additional information see[285, 453, 499, 521, 522, 651, 675, 667, 997]. Distinguished from Lesser Grey Shrike *L. minor* by larger size (Lesser Grey a smaller, more compact bird), face-mask without black frontal (also lacking in immature and first-winter [boreal] Lesser Grey), whitish eyebrow (lacking in Lesser Grey), longer, more hooked bill (stubbier, less hooked in Lesser Grey), longer tail (longer wings of Lesser Grey, extending well past tail-coverts, give it a shorter-tailed appearance). Tail pattern differs: black in centre of tail is wide at base and narrow towards end (opposite in Lesser Grey). Underparts generally less pink and stance less upright than Lesser Grey. In E Asia the Great Grey race *sibiricus* is distinguished from Chinese Grey Shrike *L. sphenocercus* by brownish tinge to grey upperparts, barred underparts (pale grey above, white below in Chinese Grey), smaller body and bill size, shorter, less graduated tail with much less white (very large body and bill, longer, more graduated tail with extensive white in Chinese Grey). Small white wing-patch compared to very large wing-patch in Chinese Grey. The Great Grey Shrike in North America, races *borealis* and *invictus*, is easily confused with the smaller Loggerhead Shrike *L. ludovicianus*. Best identified on size and shape of bill. Great Grey has a longer, heavier, more strongly hooked bill than Loggerhead. (For additional characters see Loggerhead species account p.159).

DESCRIPTION ADULT ♂ ***Upperparts*** Pale blue-grey (greyish-brown in E Asian races); rump and uppertail-coverts whitish-grey; black face-mask formed from lores, eye-stripe and large ear-covert patch; thin whitish eyebrow, extending over bill, but sometimes absent; scapulars white. ***Wings*** Black with white wing-patch at base of primaries and secondaries (latter sometimes absent); white tips to primaries and particularly to tertials and inner secondaries. For wing formula see[453, 675]. ***Tail*** Graduated, black wide at base, narrowing towards end, with large white edges to outer feathers, sometimes completely white. ***Underparts*** Whitish, may have faint rosy tinge on breast when fresh (barred greyish-brown in E Asian and North American races. ***Bare parts*** Bill black with pale base to lower mandible (seasonally variable), palate unknown, legs black to blackish-brown, eye dark brown. ADULT ♀ Similar to ♂, but has less white in plumage, particularly in wing, which has a smaller wing-patch and narrower white tips to secondaries and tertials. There is also less white in the tail. Underparts generally darker, usually with faint brown barring on breast in boreal winter. ***Bare parts*** Bill black with pale base to lower mandible (seasonally variable). These criteria appear to apply to all races[284, 285, 469, 484, 536, 675]. JUVENILE/IMMATURE European nominate *excubitor* above similar to adult, but more brownish-grey, usually faintly barred dark brown from lower crown to uppertail-coverts. Short, poorly differentiated dull white eyebrow, dark brownish-black face-mask (narrower than adult); wings and tail similar to adults but tertials and greater coverts tipped buffy-brown, all coverts showing dark subterminal bar. Underparts dull white to greyish-brown with faint greyish-brown barring. Bill brownish-grey with pale base. Juveniles attain adult plumage during their first autumn. First-winter (boreal) birds similar to ♀ except they retain brownish-tipped greater coverts (retained up to spring of second year). Juvenile *borealis* (North America) is very different to nominate, with browner upperparts, darker, more heavily barred underparts and browner flight feathers[257, 285, 675].

GEOGRAPHICAL VARIATION At least nine races, varying mainly in size, colour of upper- and underparts, extent of wing-patch, and presence or absence and extent of barring below. Two subgroups are recognisable: western group includes nominate *excubitor* (including *galliae* and *melanopterus*, W and N Europe, USSR to W Siberia), *homeyeri* (SE Europe in Bulgaria, Romania, Ukraine to W Siberia), and *leucopterus* (SW Siberia). In the series *excubitor–homeyeri–leucopterus* there is a gradual paling of upper- and underparts, an increase in size of white wing-patch, formed by basal white on both primaries and secondaries, and an increase in wing length from W to E. Adults are grey above and lack barring below. In the eastern subgroup variation is more complex: birds are generally darker, tinged brown above, all are extensively barred below and lack white on secondary bases (wing shows only one white wing-patch on primaries). This subgroup includes *borealis* (eastern North America in central and N Quebec and N Ontario) is similar to nominate, except underparts greyer with faint barring; *invictus* (western North America from N Alaska to N Alberta and possibly extreme NE Siberia) similar to previous race but paler; *sibiricus* (E Siberia and N Mongolia) browner above than nominate with barring below. Upperparts and barring get progressively darker and heavier from *mollis* (Russian Altai, NW Mongolia) to *funereus* (Russian Tien Shan, W China), which is the largest race and a high-mountain inhabitant; *bianchii* (Sakhalin and S Kurils) a small insular race with greyer upperparts and lighter barring below than *sibiricus*. Nominate *excubitor* is highly variable with some individuals appearing intermediate between both subgroups[212, 214, 257, 284, 285, 329, 453, 499, 521, 522, 651, 675, 997].

MOULT Central Europe and Siberian juveniles undergo a partial moult (Jul–Nov) of mainly head and body feathers into first-winter (boreal) plumage, at which time they resemble adults except for buffy-brown wing-coverts. North American juveniles have been recorded undergoing a pre-breeding spring moult (Mar–Apr). European adults undergo a complete post-breeding moult (Jun–Dec, mainly Oct–Nov) while still on their breeding grounds, and some may also undergo a partial pre-breeding moult from Mar–May, but this is not well understood[214, 255, 257, 284, 285, 484, 675, 814, 997].

RANGE, HABITAT and STATUS Breeding range Widespread in Holarctic taiga belt. In Eurasia N of *c*.50°N and in North America N of *c*.55°N. In Eurasia from central and E France, Belgium, Netherlands, Luxemburg, Germany, Poland, Romania, Denmark, Czech Republic, Faeroes, Slovakia, Moldova, Ukraine, Belarus, Lithuania, Latvia, Estonia, N Norway, N Sweden and Finland. A vagrant with no evidence of breeding in Iceland, British Isles, Hungary, Italy, Yugoslavia, Bulgaria, Albania, Greece or Cyprus. Widespread in Russia, where southern boundary in W Siberia lies at *c*.57°N, also further S in Kazakhstan and NW China, where possibly as far S as 43°50′N. Also in Mongolia and S Siberia with race *bianchii* on Sakhalin and possibly some Kuril Islands. No evidence of breeding in Siberian Kamchatka Peninsula, vagrant to Korea. In North America occurs from Alaska to Labrador in a relatively narrow belt, extending in the E as far S as N Ontario. Northern limit in Alaska similar to Eurasian population at *c*.70°N, but further S in Quebec to *c*.60°N. **Non-breeding range** Generally lies S of breeding range for the migrant high-latitude populations. The non-breeding range of some populations overlaps the breeding range of some resident populations further S, as well as extending beyond these limits. See Movements. **Habitat** Open country interspersed with trees, bushes, fence-posts and powerlines. N populations are found in clearings in taiga or in the transition zone from taiga to tundra and forest edge. Sparse or low vegetation is an important component, such as occurs in peat-bogs, heathland, clearfells and low-intensity cultivation. Typical perch densities in C and N Europe 5–15 perches/ha. Habitats used in non-breeding areas are similar, but not identical, to those used when breeding[212, 214, 255, 257, 284, 285, 373, 383, 395, 396, 675, 787, 964]. For additional data on habitat requirements see[397]. **Status** Variable depending on location, rare to locally common. Migrant or partial migrant. **Conservation status** European populations are relatively well known. In Sweden and Finland the breeding range expanded S in 1950s from its former N range. However, in the 1970s this trend reversed, with the populations declining, and now no longer breeding in Switzerland and Czech Republic, and extremely rare in Austria and SW Germany. Similar declines have been documented in Denmark and W Central Europe, particularly in Germany and France. Some populations further E also appear to be declining, such as in the Baltic and Volga regions of USSR. North American populations in the W appear stable, with those in the E showing an 8-year cycle in relative abundance, with an overall decline. Estimated populations (total or for pairs): mean 6,000 pairs (Arctic Alaska), 600–1,200 (Belarus), 130–160 (Belgium), 1,000–2,000 (Czech Republic), 10–11 (Denmark), 200–400 (Estonia), 5,000–10,000 (Finland), 1,000–10,000 (France), 1,200–1,500 pairs (Germany), 100–150 (Latvia), 25–50 pairs (Lithuania), 50–100 (Luxemburg), 15–40 (Netherlands), 5,000–10,000 (Norway), 4,000–4,500 pairs (Poland), 1,000–3,000 pairs (Romania), 100,000–1,000,000 pairs (Russia), 500–1,000 (Slovakia), 1,000–10,000 (Sweden), 1,000–2,500 (Transcaucasia), 900–1,200 (Ukraine). Declines appear to be due to a number of factors influencing the ecology of this species, including: habitat destruction through land-use changes, increased use of agricultural chemicals resulting in diminished diversity and quality of prey, and changes in agricultural practices causing an increase in ground-cover or a reduction in suitable numbers of perches. These combine to result in reduced carrying capacities, increased energetic requirements and decreased breeding success. Increased disturbance and climatic variation have a greater negative effect where prey availability is already diminished due to other causes[244, 247, 315, 317, 383, 396, 397, 480, 675, 787, 788, 936, 937, 938, 948, 962, 964, 977, 978, 1014].

MOVEMENTS Most populations are migratory or partially so, with the non-breeding range including most of the breeding range in addition to more southerly areas. Population movements appear primarily related to food shortages. In the W Palearctic individuals are resident, altitudinal, short- or long-distance migrants. In some populations, mainly ♀♀ migrate. Most birds leave their breeding territories from Jul–Oct, mainly Sep–Oct, overwinter for *c*.4–5 months and return in boreal spring from Mar–May, mainly Mar–Apr. Generally European populations migrate S of *c*.60°N in boreal winter, but in N Sweden and Norway birds move only slightly S to *c*.67°N, presumably not far from their breeding grounds. Similarly, many SW European birds (e.g. Germany, France) appear largely sedentary compared to populations further east (e.g. Czech Republic). Non-breeding range includes British Isles, W Norway, S Sweden, SW France, occasionally N Spain, Central Europe from N Italy, some Mediterranean islands and Balkans. In Central Asia ♀♀ tend to outnumber ♂♂. Some *homeyeri* migrate to Kazakhstan, N Iran, N Caucasus, Nepal, Tibet, N and NW India, N Pakistan and NW China. Also recorded as an occasional vagrant to Europe (Germany, Czech Republic and Sweden). In S Siberia and Mongolia race *mollis* undergoes altitudinal as well as some southerly movements to *c*.35°N in some places. Accidental in Japan (Honshu and Kyushu at turn of century). Race *sibiricus* moves S to SE Siberia, Inner Mongolia and NE Chinese provinces, and is a rare vagrant E to Europe (Norway). Race *bianchii* appears to be mainly resident, with some birds moving S in Kurils, as far S as N Japan (Hokkaido) where possibly breeds; occasionally further S on Honshu and in Korea. In North America breeding birds occasioanlly move S as far as central Alaska.

Non-breeding range extends S over Canada and N United States where in the E it occurs as far S as N Carolina at *c.*35°N, extending W through N Texas and central New Mexico to N central California. Generally migration routes are not well known, with most information coming from Europe. Scandinavian birds move S to SW in autumn, except for a few birds which take a SE route. Birds spending boreal winter in British Isles probably originate in Scandinavia, and Central European birds (e.g. Germany) also fly SW to non-breeding areas in France or N Italy. There is some evidence to suggest that the migratory strategy of some populations is changing (e.g. increasing numbers of birds remaining in S Fennoscandia)[193, 195, 212, 214, 255, 257, 276, 284, 285, 675, 687, 787, 848, 941, 997, 1015].

SOCIAL ORGANISATION and GENERAL BEHAVIOUR Generally well known. Found singly or in widely separated pairs, also sometimes in groups of up to 6. Sits out exposed on prominent perches, often for long periods. It is a bold and pugnacious bird, but usually difficult to approach. Both sexes defend a territory on breeding (joint territory) and non-breeding grounds (individual territory). In Central Europe the density of birds in boreal winter is higher than in summer (1:1.2–2.3), but local seasonal fluctuations are common. Where populations are partial migrants, most ♀♀ leave in boreal winter. However, where populations are resident, pairs separate and hold individual territories. In European summer and winter there is a tendency for 3–4 territories to be grouped together, with groups separated by *c.*4–6 km. Within these groups, territories in well-populated areas are *c.*200–300 m apart but in high latitudes several kilometres apart. Fidelity to non-breeding winter territories has been shown in some individuals, but not in others. Territories are defended by static marking in an upright position from an exposed perch and by giving a characteristic whistled *prrii* call. Throughout the year both sexes also make high display-flights (inspection flights) over the territory. These last up to a minute and are made in spiral, successive stages, often hovering before gliding down from 30–100 m above the ground. This behaviour appears to initiate group meetings of up to 6 birds, usually 4. These take place in spring (mainly migrants) as well as in autumn (mainly residents), may last from 0.25–2 hours and may occur within a few kilometres from participants' territories. Interactions involve much perch-changing and calling, ranging from contact to aggression and song duets (antiphonal). Throughout the species's range territory size varies considerably with habitat, from *c.*20–357 ha. Apart from habitat it also depends on whether occupied by lone birds or pairs, residents or migrants. Summer breeding territories are generally smaller than those in winter, and birds in high latitudes tend to have larger territories than further S. Home ranges may be up to three times the actual territory size. Visual and vocal signals are graded in intensity to signal intent. Threat and aggression are signalled at low intensity by upright posture and slight tail-fanning. At higher intensity greater tail-fanning, wing-jerking, -flicking or -fluttering, and at highest intensity by horizontal posture with fluffed-out body feathers and raised crest. Appeasement at close quarters and low intensity signalled by briefly turning bill away from opponent, at high intensity by upright bill-up posture. When further away usually adopts a crouched wing-fluttering posture combined with begging calls. Roosting sites are characterised, particularly in boreal winter, by being relatively low down (1–2 m) and with a high stem density. In winter birds may switch from deciduous to evergreen bushes or trees (e.g. junipers). Roost sites provide protection from predators, wind and cold, and are sometimes used during the day. Communal roosting has been recorded in spring[257, 284, 285, 373, 381, 383, 395, 399, 675, 788, 968].

Foraging behaviour Hunts from relatively high perches, between 3–8 m (1–18), spending long periods scanning the ground for prey, pouncing on quarry after a quick dive. Often changes perch while hunting. In bad weather may hop about on the ground in search of food. Often hovers, usually *c.*3–10 m above the ground for up to 20 minutes. Also takes insects on the wing. Small birds are usually captured on the ground or in trees and bushes, or less often pursued like a hawk and caught in the feet. Prey is also flushed from foliage or dislodged from thick vegetation by moving actively about among branches or on the ground with fluttering movements or by flashing open the wings and tail. It has also been shown to use song containing mimicry of local birds to attract these species close enough to be caught. Once prey is caught it is either consumed immediately, or transported to a perch, usually in the bill, but if heavier than *c.*20 g is carried in the feet. Kills vertebrates with bill in repeated blows to the skull. Holds prey in the foot and tears it apart with the bill, and often impales or wedges prey on branches 0.5–1.5 m above the ground to form caches. These are situated at varying distances from the nest site (3–1500 m). The Great Grey Shrike is estimated to require *c.*2–3.5 vertebrate prey/day.

Food Consists mainly of small vertebrates and arthropods. Voles appear to be the most frequently taken vertebrate prey, usually in excess of 50%, sometimes as high as 90% of total biomass taken. Shrews, lizards and frogs are also frequently taken. Small birds usually make up less than 10% of total biomass taken, with fledglings, exhausted migrants, handicapped birds and displaying ♂♂ of some species being the most susceptible prey. Occasionally takes larger prey, such as the downy chicks of gallinaceous birds (e.g. Willow Grouse *Lagopus lagopus*). Small mammals are taken in preference to birds, but when there is a covering of snow they are forced to take birds. A variety of other vertebrate prey has been recorded, including fish, newts, young rats, lemmings, and a young weasel *Mustela nivalis*. It also pursues bats. Arthropods, of which insects are the most common, are caught throughout the year, with a peak in summer. At this time they form a substantial portion of the prey delivered to nestlings.

Surprisingly, however, insects seldom represent more than 15% of the total biomass taken. Coleoptera (beetles), Orthoptera (grasshoppers and crickets) and Hymenoptera (wasps and bumblebees) are, in that order, the chief insect prey. Various other insects and invertebrates are taken, including arachnids (spiders and scorpions), worms, snails and crayfish. Carrion has occasionally been recorded, and small fruits are possibly rarely recoded[161, 214, 255, 257, 284, 285, 373, 395, 415, 484, 675, 787, 956].

SOUNDS Repertoire consists of harsh grating calls, fluted whistles and warbling song. In aggressive situations utters a loud shrill drawn-out, often raspy whistle, described as *prrii-*, *trrri-*, *treeu-*, *kwiet-*, *kwiecht* or *Tik-weep*. This call is heard when threatening intruders and appears to be used mainly in territorial advertisement and mate attraction. It is often directed at ♀ by ♂, often combined with song and used in duet with ♀ in boreal winter. During group interactions may duet antiphonally with other participants. Also has softer drawn-out *trüü*, *trüh* or *prrüt*. Alarm is signalled by repeated loud, harsh screeching, considered by some authors as a mew-type sound, but described as *kwäääà-*, *keee-*, *jaa-jaa-*, *grèè-grèè-* or *chek-chek-chek-*, which changes at higher intensity to a rapidly repeated rattling *tr-tr-tr-* or popping *aak-aak-aak*, often combined with bill-snapping, usually given in upright threat posture with tail swinging or in flight. Raptor alarm a whistled *breezeek*. Agitated adults with young give *knuk* or *kruk*. Contact call a harsh *gihrr-*, *kwä* or *wuut* with other variable *chliep* and *chli* calls. It is given during courtship and is often interspersed with song. Adults and young beg with persistent whining harsh nasal *waik-waik-waik-* sounds. Song is heard mainly in spring and consists of a repetition of single or double notes in short variable phrases like *Tu-Tu-krrr-pree-pree* or *trrr-turit- trrr-turit....* It probably does not serve a territorial function. Song changes during courtship to a softer, relatively melodious warble which contains harsh sounds and mimicry of other birds. It is combined with other calls when the ♂ attracts the ♀ to potential nest sites, where he uses a variety of calls including fluted *tli-tli-* whistles, trilling *prrr* and *kwiw....püh* sounds for a long time. During courtship partners also often duet with contact and begging calls. Song containing mimics has also been shown to attract the mimicked species, who are then attacked and sometimes caught[161, 214, 225, 244, 285, 373, 383, 440, 500, 956]. Sonagram[225, 257, 284, 373, 484, 600].

BREEDING BIOLOGY Monogamous and territorial, defence of territories lasting until a pair has young. Pair formation is a more drawn-out process than in Southern Grey Shrike. While breeding it tends to be more skulking and less conspicuous. Central European birds tend to have seasonal pair-bonds and first-year birds are known to attempt breeding. Preliminary pair-bonding takes place in non-breeding territory. In pairs with neighbours, the ♂ continuously follows his mate about (mate-guarding behaviour) a few days prior to egg-laying, at which time courtship feeding and copulations reach a maximum. He usually also perches higher than her during this period. In spite of guarding, about 30% of visits by neighbouring ♂♂ results in extra-pair copulations. Generally paired ♀♀ spend more time than ♂♂ in cover. Egg-dumping and occasional visits to broods with young from other individuals (helpers?) occurs infrequently. High display-flights cease on egg-laying. Normally only a single clutch is laid, with double broods very rare; however, replacement clutches often occur. In Central Europe density seldom exceeds 0.3 breeding pairs/km^2. Breeding success in one study showed 56 young hatched from 78 eggs (72%); of these 44 fledged (56%) (Central Europe), and in North America a study showed 60% nesting success and 72.4% fledging success. Pairs breeding in the centre of larger groups tend to show a higher breeding success. Obviously, infertitility, predation and adverse weather also decrease breeing success. In some parts it breeds in association with Fieldfares *Turdus pilaris*, with nests sometimes less than 10 m apart. Surprisingly fledglings are only taken occasionally. This association appears to be based on mutual protection against predators, especially Corvidae[257, 284, 373, 405, 537, 675, 787, 788, 789].

Season Well known in W and Central Europe, but little known in Eurasia. Egg-laying varies with latitude and with migratory status, being later in the migrant higher-latitude populations; breeding Mar–Jun (Central Europe)[257, 373, 285, 789]; egg-laying May–Jun (Finnish Lapland); hatching May (Moscow), fledglings Jun–Jul (USSR)[214], egg-laying Apr–May, fledglings Jun–Jul (Siberia)[284]; breeding Mar–Oct (North America)[255]; Jul (Ontario)[972]; May–Jul (Labrador)[244]; Apr–May (Alaska)[383].

Displays Note differences in probable signal areas on wing and tail of ♂ and ♀. ***Courtship*** A drawn-out process, which progresses through a number of phases as ♀ changes from aggressive to submissive/receptive with ♂ continually courtship-feeding her. ♀ may occasionally feed ♂. When being fed she begs with whining nasal sounds while in a crouched posture with wings quivering and fluttering. Initially ♂ give whistles and contact calls combined with wing fluttering, low bows, turning his head away from ♀ and tail-fanning. This is followed by display-flying (see General Behaviour) and wing-fluttering. ♂ calling increases and is combined with warbling song, wing-fluttering, begging calls with tail-fanning, sometimes turning to present his tail to her. He also frequently sits facing her at right angles. In time ♀ then adopts similar postures to ♂, including a bill-up, tail-fanned courtship posture. Much mutual begging in duet and wing-fluttering in crouched posture follows. ♂ continually courtship-feeds ♀ from courtship caches which he establishes in conspicuous places. Courtship displays occur at pair formation and at the break-up of pairs prior to boreal winter. ***Pre-copulation*** Both birds face each other, ♂ usually with prey in bill, begins wing-quivering and -fluttering accompanied by contact call. ♀ crouches and gives begging call. They approach each other with legs slightly bent and tails fanned. As ♂ almost touches ♀ he stretches his legs and neck and turns to the left and right. This is repeated a few times before he mounts, and offers prey to ♀. Both birds give loud begging calls during copulation. ***Nest-site display*** ♂ chooses the nest site, hops about through a particular bush or tree, sitting crouched while giving a distinctive nest- call consisting of trilling *prrr* combined with fluted *tli-tli-*, *kwiet* or *kwiw....püh* whistles while raising and lowering or swaying the head with tail fanned[161, 373, 398, 789].

Nest Site selected by ♂; both build with ♂ providing most material. Construct a solid bulky, rather untidy cup with a base of twigs, moss, grass and sometimes man-made materials. The cup is lined with rootlets, wool, hair, lichens and feathers. Nest height varies with habitat, from *c.*1.2 to 38 m; in alpine areas (North America) av. 1.8 m (n=40), in orchards av. 6.8 m (n=15) and 15–17 m (n=17) in poplars (Central Europe). A variety of trees are used, including fruit trees, oak, alder, spruce, poplars and conifers (Central Europe). The use of conifers appears to be increasing. Also occasionally use large thorny bushes or dense shrubs. Nests are usually well hidden, and often placed in mistletoe, ivy or other tree growths, in forks or on a lateral branch. In conifers usually against trunk. ***Size*** OD 200–280 mm, ID 80–120 mm, cup depth 100–150 mm. Built in 6–15 days, with some nests re-used[214, 285, 383, 675, 791].

Eggs Usually 6 (Central Europe) and 8 (North America) (3–9). Greyish-white, seldom bluish or whitish, spotted and blotched with olive-brown or dull olive, purplish-grey, buff, reddish-brown or brown, sometimes around the large end. ***Size*** *excubitor* 23.0–30.5 x 18.0–20.5 mm (26.3 x 19.5, n=117). Replacement broods begun 5–15 days from loss and contain fewer eggs[214, 257, 284, 373, 383, 454, 537]. **Incubation** Mainly by ♀. ♂ feeds ♀ on and off nest. Period usually 15–17 days (14–19, possibly to 21 days for very large clutches)[214, 257, 285, 373, 383]. **Nestling** Hatch blind and naked, flesh-coloured, becoming darker after a few days; mouth pink, gape flanges yellow; probably lack mouth spots. Brooded by ♀, fledge after 15–19 days (14–21). ♂ supplies most food initially, thereafter both sexes attend to young, remaining with them for 4–5 weeks. Brood division reported sometimes, occurring *c.*10 days after fledging, with one adult attending and feeding the same young for about another week. Young are independent and depart their natal territory *c.*20–45 days after fledging[214, 285, 399, 537, 789]. For development of young see[395]. **Predation and longevity** Corvids are important nest predators. Longevity 4.5 years[788]. **Brood parasite** Formerly regularly parasitised in certain areas of W Europe by Common Cuckoo *Cuculus canorus*; however, this has not been recorded for at least 20 years[285, 675].

MEASUREMENTS and WEIGHTS *L. e. excubitor* ♂ (35) wing 108–118 (113.8), tail 102–116 (109.1), ♂ (25) bill (to skull) 21.8–24.3 (23.0), ♂ (20) tarsus 26.0–28.8 (27.4), sex differences not significant[257]. **Weight** *excubitor* ♂♀? (44) 48–81 g (63.4 ±SD 5.96) (mainly Sep–Apr); *borealis* ♂♀? (6) 61.8–69.0 g (65.6) (W North America)[478]. For additional data see[257].

8 SOUTHERN GREY SHRIKE *Lanius meridionalis* — Plate 4

FIELD IDENTIFICATION Large (24–25 cm) grey, white and black shrike, rather variable, usually with black face-mask and white eyebrow, head and back variable from dark lead-grey (Europe and Africa) to pale sandy-grey (Central Asia), white scapulars, black wings with single white wing-patch, long black tail with white outer feathers. Underparts variable from pale buffy-pink (Europe) to greyish or pale whitish-buff (Central Asia). White of scapulars, wing and tail conspicuous in flight in dark-backed birds. Sexes similar. Young similar to adults but duller brownish-grey above, buffy below sometimes with faint barring. Calls mainly double-noted; harsh and grating sounds, whistles and warbling song with mimicry. Solitary, perches prominently, occurs in SW Europe, North Africa, Middle East and Central Asia to NW India. Central Asian population spends boreal winter in Middle East and North Africa. ***Flight characteristics***: Rapid and powerful; flies low with swoop up to perch, undulating over long distances; also hovers. White scapulars, single wing-patch and black and white tail conspicuous on darker races.

COMPARISONS In Eurasia very similar to Great Grey Shrike *Lanius excubitor*, from which it has only recently been separated. In Europe, only some Great Grey Shrikes spending the boreal winter in the SW overlap with the range of the Southern Grey Shrike (nominate *meridionalis*), but in Central Asia a number of races overlap the range of the Southern Grey Shrike race *pallidirostris*. For difference see Great Grey Shrike Comparisons p.150. It is also similar to Lesser Grey Shrike *L. minor* with which it overlaps in France, Spain and North Africa where Lesser Grey is a passage migrant. Distinguished by larger size (Lesser Grey a smaller, more compact bird), face-mask without black frontal, or in NE African races only a narrow frontal band (Lesser Grey has a very broad frontal, but note this is lacking in immature and first-winter [boreal] birds), usually a whitish eyebrow, but may be absent in some races (lacking in Lesser Grey), longer, more hooked bill (very stubby, less hooked in Lesser Grey), longer tail (longer wings of Lesser Grey extend well past tail-coverts, giving it a short-tailed appearance). Tail pattern differs, black in centre of tail is wide at base and narrow towards end (opposite in Lesser Grey). Underparts generally less pink and stance less upright than Lesser Grey. In E Central Asia, Southern Grey race *pallidirostris* distinguished from Chinese Grey Shrike *L. sphenocercus* by pale sandy-grey upper- and underparts (pale grey above, white below in Chinese Grey), smaller body and bill size, shorter, less graduated tail with much less white (very large body and bill, longer more graduated tail with extensive white in Chinese Grey). Small white wing-patch compared to very large wing-patch in Chinese Grey. In Africa confusion with Grey-backed Fiscal *L. excubitoroides*) unlikely as this bird is larger and darker with a broad black forehead, no white scapulars or tips to tertials and secondaries, and distinctive basal white in long tail; it is a gregarious species, unlike Southern Grey Shrike[552, 997].

DESCRIPTION **ADULT** Sexes similar. ***Upperparts*** Dark lead-grey, variable in other races; rump and uppertail-coverts paler grey; brownish-black face-mask formed from eye-stripe and ear-coverts; thin whitish eyebrow, usually extending over bill; scapulars white. ***Wings*** Black with white wing-patch at base of primaries only; secondaries narrowly, tertials broadly tipped white. For wing index see[453, 675]. ***Tail*** Broadly black at base, narrowing towards end, with large white edges to outer feathers. ***Underparts*** Buffy- to greyish-pink (particularly in fresh plumage) with white chin and throat. Underparts variable in other races. ***Bare parts*** Bill brownish-black with pale base to lower mandible (not consistent, e.g. *pallidirostris* pale grey-brown with flesh-coloured base with dark tip; shape also varies in other races), palate pinkish (*lahtora*), legs black to blackish-brown, eye dark brown. **ADULT ♀** Generally similar to ♂, but may have faint brown barring on breast in boreal winter[257, 469]. **JUVENILE/IMMATURE** Variation between races not well studied. Generally similar to adults but duller, with face-mask dark brown and lores whitish. Upperparts pale greyish-brown. Wing-coverts and tertials tipped buff. Underparts greyish or tinged buffy-pink, sometimes with faint dusky barring. Throat and sides of neck whitish. Bill paler than adult, that of Central Asian *pallidirostris* pale grey-brown with a dark tip, legs generally browner than adult, eye like adult.

GEOGRAPHICAL VARIATION At least 10 races, variation complex and generally clinal with intermediates common. Variation mainly involves colour of upper- and underparts, body size, structure of face-mask and extent of white in wings. Nominate *meridionalis* (Iberian Peninsula, SW France) has dark lead-grey upperparts, thin white eyebrow, single white wing-patch and pinkish-buff underparts. In relation to nominate, the populations across North Africa become gradually paler above from W to E. This is shown progressively in the order *koenigi* (Canary Islands), *algeriensis* (W Mauritania, Western Sahara, Morocco, Algeria and Tunisia), *elegans* (N and central Sahara from Mauritania to Egypt and Sudan) and *leucopygos* (S Sahara from central Mali, Niger, N Nigeria, Chad and N Sudan); *aucheri* (including *theresae* and *jebelmarrae*, N Sudan, N Ethiopia, Eritrea, N Egypt, S Israel, Syria, Iraq, S Iran, W central and E Saudi Arabia) similar to *elegans* but has a narrow black band at base of bill, less white in wings and darker underparts; *buryi* (Yemen) dark slaty-grey above like *algeriensis*, also darker below including throat; *uncinatus* (Socotra) like *aucheri* but less white in scapulars and bill longer; *lahtora* (E Pakistan, W, NW and NE India) similar to *aucheri* but with relatively wide black frontal band, more white in wings and tail, and white (not greyish) underparts, bill distinctly heavier. The 'Steppe Grey Shrike' *pallidirostris* (N Pakistan, Afghanistan, NE Iran, E of Caspian Sea to S Mongolia at *c.*40°N, and extending as far E as *c.*112°E in China; northern limit at *c.*50°N) has a distinctly washed-out appearance and differs from *aucheri* and *lahtora* by lacking black frontal band, has pale lores and a pale grey-brown bill, and usually a pinkish tinge to underparts, although in many characters rather variable[212, 214, 257, 284, 285, 329, 453, 462, 484, 499, 521, 522, 651, 675, 667, 997].

MOULT Partial juvenile moult begins soon after fledging, usually only affecting body feathers, but also includes some outer primaries, and in some desert races, including *pallidirostris*, a variable number of secondaries and tail feathers. Nominate adults undergo a complete post-breeding moult Jun–Oct, and a partial, weakly discernible pre-breeding head and body moult from Feb–Apr. Adults of Central Asian *pallidirostris* undergo a complete moult Jun–Oct[214, 257, 284, 285, 675, 997].

RANGE, HABITAT and STATUS **Breeding range** SW France, Portugal, Spain, Canary Islands, Morocco, Algeria, Tunisia, Libya, Western Sahara, Mauritania, Senegal, Mali, Chad, N Cameroon, N Nigeria, Burkina Faso, Niger, Sudan, Egypt, N Ethiopia, Eritrea, Djibouti, Socotra, Yemen, Oman, Saudi Arabia, Israel, Lebanon, Syria, Iraq, SW and NE Iran, Afghanistan, Turkmenistan, Uzbekistan, Kazakhstan eastwards to W and N China at *c.*112°E in Mongolia, and southwards in N and E Pakistan, N and NW India. **Non-breeding range** Most populations appear to be sedentary, except for an estimated 70% of those in Central Asia (*pallidirostris*) which are long-distance migrants, spending boreal winter S of breeding range, possibly in Iran, but generally SW as far as E Sudan, Eritrea, N Ethiopia and N Somalia. Vagrant further S to Kenya/Sudan border. Central African Republic record rejected[431]. Also recorded in SE Asia as far S as Borneo. See Movements. **Habitat** Occurs in a wide range of open bushed habitats in mediterranean, desert and tropical savanna climates. In SW Europe and particularly S France, occurs in dry open areas dotted with scrubby vegetation dominated by *Quercus coccifera*, evergreen spiny *Phyllirea* and *Rubus*. This habitat is characterised by exposed areas with bare soil, low grassy vegetation and scattered bushes. It is also found in dry cultivated areas, including vineyards and abandoned or fallow land with suitable bushes or trees. Usually found below 1000 m. In North Africa in dry woodlands and semi-desert characterised by clumps of thorny bushes and trees (e.g. *Acacia* and *Ziziphus*). In Central Asia, the 'Steppe Grey Shrike' (*pallidirostris*) occurs in a variety of arid habitats, including stony hilly areas and sandy or clay deserts with sufficient bushy vegetation (*Pistacia, Calligonum, Ammodendron* and *Tamarix*). In India and Pakistan found in sparse scrub jungle, and edge of thorn- and deciduous forest as well as more typical semi-desert areas. Oases also provide suitable habitat for all races in Asian and African deserts. The density of perches and caching sites has been shown to be important in territory size: the greater the density, the smaller the territory[284, 285, 595, 675, 944]. **Status** Not uncommon resident, migrant or partial migrant. **Conservation status** Little known. In SW Europe nominate *meridionalis* is possibly declining. Estimated population for Europe (total or for pairs); 1000–2000 pairs (SW France), 200,000–250,000 pairs (Spain); 10,000–100,000 (Portugal). Little information on population estimates or trends for North Africa, Middle East or Central Asia. Few thousand pairs in Israel, a tentative 1,000–2,000 pairs in Canary Islands. Reasons for possible decline in Europe assumed to be the same as for Great Grey Shrike. Other populations likely to be better off owing to their inhospitable arid semi-desert habitat, little influenced by man[285, 369, 480, 787].

MOVEMENTS Some populations of the Central Asian race *pallidirostris* are long-distance migrants, particularly those in N region of range. Western birds of this race leave their breeding grounds in September, returning Mar–Apr. They fly SW, with at least one-third of population remaining in boreal winter in Turkmenistan. Others spend winter in Middle East (Saudi Arabia, Iran, Iraq), W Pakistan (rarely to NW India) and NE Africa (Sudan, Ethiopia, N Somalia). Occasionally as a vagrant as far as Brunei and British Isles. Movements of SE populations not well known, with at least some local movements in Pakistan, and some populations of *lahtora* believed to move W to spend boreal winter in Saudi Arabia. European and African races undergo limited small-scale movements, which are not well understood. For example, in *meridionalis* in S France, some birds are clearly resident, but others regularly appear during boreal winter in areas where they are not known to breed. These birds also regularly occur on Gibraltar in Sep–Nov, occasionally in Italy and as a vagrant to Sicily, Malta and even the Baltic region. They may be found to reach North Africa as well. North African populations undergo local movements, but these are poorly understood. For example, *elegans* spends boreal winter in the lower Sénégal valley, and is more common at this time in Tafilalt region of Morocco. South of the Sahara in the Sahel region, *leucopygos* is a vagrant to Gambia (Dec–Apr) and Ghana (Mar–Apr). Local movements are also apparent in the Middle East for *aucheri*, particularly in Israel (Aug–Oct and Mar–Apr), Yemen and Saudi Arabia (Mar–Apr and Sep–Nov). Little is known about dispersal of young from their natal territory, but in one study one bird was recovered 230 km in a NW direction after 170 days, another 32 km in a SE direction after 155 days[21, 28, 37, 38, 45, 36, 182, 188, 212, 214, 216, 217, 220, 222, 224, 234, 237, 242, 246, 274, 278, 284, 285, 292, 305, 325, 327, 382, 431, 434, 449, 450, 453, 482, 631, 666, 675, 720, 746, 859, 933].

SOCIAL ORGANISATION and GENERAL BEHAVIOUR Solitary or in widely separated pairs. Generally less conspicuous than Great Grey Shrike as it perches upright on the highest points of bushes. General behaviour similar to this species, territorial and vocal, with ♂♂ advertising with double-noted harsh calls and song. Territorial disputes, including physical contact, are common. Harsh calls often accompanied by wing-fluttering, the movements and calls sounding similar to begging calls. Short repeated contact whistles are given by both sexes in a very upright posture. Display-flights performed in circles, arcs or more complex flight-path throughout the territory, but apparently absent in *pallidirostris*. Threat signalled by hunched, fluffed posture at low intensity and sleek horizontal posture at high intensity. Also has an erect, head-up posture. Holds non-breeding and breeding territories, which in nominate race vary from *c.*10–25 ha. Generally silent in non-breeding territories. Central Asian *pallidirostris* and North African *elegans* have breeding territories of *c.*10ha, while those of *aucheri* in the Negev Desert are much larger, averaging 62 ha (53–77, n=31). On non-breeding grounds 4 birds/ha (Djerba, Tunisia) and 10 pairs/km^2 (Turkmenistan). Some ♂♂ appear to show strong site-fidelity, possibly remaining in the same territory for life. This is in contrast to ♀♀ who rarely occupy the same territory twice[284, 454, 675]. **Foraging behaviour** Similar to Great Grey Shrike but hunts lower down owing to differences in habitat structure, usually 2–3 m above the ground. Also hovers less and impales fewer arthropod prey. Southern Grey Shrike forms caches of prey mainly during non-breeding period. In one study, cached items were consumed within 9 days, and 62% of cached prey was utilised[595, 675]. **Food** Arthropods, mainly insects and their larvae, and small vertebrates, particularly reptiles. Insects include predominantly Coleoptera (beetles, particularly Tenebrionidae), Orthoptera (grasshoppers and crickets), Lepidoptera (caterpillars, butterflies and moths) and Hymenoptera (bees, wasps and ants). Other arthropods include crustaceans and centipedes. The commonest vertebrate prey are reptiles (mainly lizards, snakes and frogs), small rodents (shrews, mice, voles, gerbils and jerboa), and small birds, even sandgrouse and nestlings. Reports of eggs being eaten require confirmation. In North Africa the species has been observed impaling ripe dates *Phoenix dactylifera* and young were fed peanuts obtained from tables. On Canary Islands this shrike has been shown to be important in the dispersal of *Lycium intricatum*, not by ingesting the fruits directly, but by preying on lizards that feed on the fruits. Under natural conditions does not drink water[15, 214, 224, 257, 278, 381, 454, 470, 595, 675, 946].

SOUNDS Repertoire consists of harsh calls, drawn-out whistles and warbling song. Calls graded in pitch and repetition rate. Territorial calls in *pallidirostris* are harsh repeated double-noted *kwi-rick* sounds, variously described as a more nasal *sheenk-sheenk* or *shihk-shihk* or *chree-chree* and metallic *schryck* or rolling *schrrik*. These change to nasal *kcha-kcha-* or *wche-wche-* and, at higher intensity, almost alarm-like *sheck-sheck, shek-shek*. Also *djerki-djerki-djerki,* probably of similar function. Has a short repeated rasping trill *ptriz-* or *zri-zri-* varying to *trr-trr-* or *dri-dri-dri-* given when fighting conspecifics. In at least western races (e.g. *aucheri*), the warning call or mate contact call is a drawn-out whistle *kwiet* or *kwiecht* or hard ringing double *trip-trip* or *tew-dew;* in *meridionalis* a piercing whistle consisting of harsh buzz and whistle combined, sounding like *tzzweeet* or *bzzweeet*. However, this call does not occur in the repertoire of *pallidirostris,* nor apparently *lahtora*. Alarm or threat a loud repeated harsh screeching, considered by some authors to be a mew-type sound, described as *gihr-gihr-gihr-* , *keeer-keer-* or grating *che-che-che-* and *chet-chet-chet-*, also harsh clicking *chack-chack-chack-* and bill-snapping. Agitated adults with young give *zeep-seep*. Contact a short *hui-hui-* whistle. Begging call a repeated harsh nasal *gaik-gaik-gaik-* or *pchee-ar, chee-chee-chee* accompanied by wing-fluttering. In breeding season ♂ has a repetitive short lively warbling, tinkling song interspersed with harsh chinking phrases and including trills and mimicry of birds[23, 28, 217, 224, 257, 276, 278, 338, 500, 504, 600, 631, 1039]. For development of calls see[729]. Sonagram for *pallidirostris*[284, 600].

BREEDING BIOLOGY Mostly monogamous, with ♂♂ generally sedentary and ♀♀ moving out of the area during boreal winter, and usually being replaced by a new ♀ the following season. This finding is contrary to an earlier study which predicted permanent pair-bonds in this species. Pair formation is rapid; breeds in greater densities than Great Grey Shrike. Low levels of polygamy (breeding with two ♀♀ simultaneously) also reported. ♀♀ start visiting ♂ territories in spring, at which time ♂♂ begin courtship-feeding. During nest-building ♂ is highly territorial. Most ♂ song is heard at this time; ceases after egg-laying. Mate selection by ♀ *aucheri* has been shown to be strongly influenced by ♂ cache size, and that reproductive success is increased in individuals with larger caches. In migrant *pallidirostris* ♂♂ usually return to their breeding grounds a few days before ♀♀. Breeding densities very variable, in nominate *meridionalis* *c.*1 pair/100 ha (S France and NW Spain), but in *elegans* inhabiting a date-palm grove as many as 5 pairs/4 ha (Algeria). Double broods normal; sometimes a third brood is laid and even a fourth attempted (Israel). However, at higher latitudes in range, such as in SW France and N range of Central Asian *pallidirostris,* only single broods are raised. In one study nesting success was 63% (range 31.7–82.8%, n=21), fledging success 81% with no more than 60% surviving past post-fledging stage. Some pairs lost up to 83% of fledglings to predation. In spite of ♂♂ feeding their mates and sometimes raising a brood simultaneously on their own, they have been shown to maintain the lowest reported energy costs for an adult bird feeding altricial young. Their caching behaviour probably helps reduce energetic costs[182, 381, 405, 454, 597, 666, 675, 746, 943, 971, 975, 1043].

Season Egg-laying Mar–Jun, mainly Apr (SW France); egg-laying Feb–Jun (Spain); egg-laying Feb–Jul (North Africa)[182, 675]; breeding Jan–Aug (Israel)[454, 746]; nestlings Mar (Somalia)[859]; breeding Mar–Apr (Russia)[284]; breeding Jan–Oct, mainly Mar–Jun (Pakistan, NW India)[224].

Displays Reasonably well known in *pallidirostris*. ***Courtship*** Similar to Great Grey Shrike, but appears more sensitive to close contact, members being reluctant to approach each other, even with food. Both birds may flutter wings and give adult begging calls. At higher intensity wings are held open and fluttered. Courtship in this species does not involve high display-flight. Much of courtship takes place in the prospective nest tree, birds hopping about, ♂ following ♀ and frequently courtship-feeding her. ***Pre-copulatory display*** ♂ stretches up in bill-up posture, ♀ crouches in fluffed-out, wing-drooped posture. Prey-exchange not obligatory before mounting. ***Nest-site display*** Appears similar to Great Grey, fluffs out feathers, stretches head forwards, fans tail and moves (nods) head deliberately up and down, giving double-noted call with each nod. Tail feathers may be fanned up and down[284].

Nest Built by both sexes usually of dried material, giving it an old appearance. Generally an untidy deep compact cup built of thorny twigs, grass, wool and feathers, often including man-made material (string and rags). Nests are usually hidden relatively low down in a fork or on a lateral branch at *c.*1–3 m (0.3–5) above the ground, depending on habitat. Sometimes nests are placed much higher in palm trees near oases in North Africa, or on pylons in Central Asia. In SW Europe appears to be positioned to avoid shade. Sometimes renovates old nest (in one case in the same position for five years) or uses old nest of Magpie *Pica pica*. Commonly uses thorny bushes or trees, also in pistachio, *Calligonum* and *Ammodendron* in Central Asia. ***Size*** *meridionalis* OD 170–270 mm (216), ID 85–154 mm, cup depth 55–75 mm (64), height 96–170 mm (125). Construction takes about a week (*c.*6–12 days, n=27)[224, 257, 284, 285, 454, 675].

Eggs Usually 5–6 (2–7). Coloration not known to differ from Great Grey Shrike. ***Size*** Nominate race 24.0–30.1 x 18.2–20.5 mm (27.3 x 19.6, n=120); *pallidirostris* 23.1–24.5 x 18.1–19.1 mm (23.8 x 18.6, n=8)[182, 284, 285, 454, 666, 675]. **Incubation** Begins after third egg, by ♀ only. Period 17–18 days (14–18). Fed by ♂ on and off nest. **Nestling** Appearance unknown. Brooded by ♀, remain in nest for 18–19 days (16–19, n=29). Monogamous ♂♂ help feed young, whereas polygynous ♂♂

appear not to feed young directly: they either feed ♀ or impale prey which she retrieves. An unusual behaviour has been observed in one study, where nestlings were forced out of the nest onto the ground by their parents, and coaxed some distance away to cover, apparently in response to nest disturbance by predators or humans. Dependency period estimated at *c*.35–40 days after fledging. Brood division sometimes recorded in *meridionalis*[216, 285, 454, 597, 675, 789, 942]. For captive breeding and development of young see[729]. **Predation and longevity** Little Owls *Athene noctua* are known to prey on fledgings frequently and on nestlings occasionally (Israel). Specimens of race *lahtora* survived at least 8.5 years in captivity[1003]. **Brood parasite** None.

MEASUREMENTS and WEIGHTS *L. m. meridionalis* ♂♀? (16) wing 102–112 (106.6), tail 101–118 (109.5), ♂♀? (15) bill (to skull) 23.2–25.3 (24.2), ♂♀? (17) tarsus 29.4–31.3 (30.0)[257]. *pallidirostris* ♂ (11) wing 108–114 (111.4), tail 96–107 (101.7), ♂ (9) bill (to skull) 20.3–23.8 (22.3), tarsus 29.6–31.7 (30.6); ♀ (11) wing 105–112 (108.4), tail 93–103 (96.5), bill (to skull) 21.1–24.2 (22.2), ♀ (10) tarsus 29.5–31.9 (30.8). Differences in sex significant for wing and tail[257]. **Weight** *meridionalis* ♂♀? (23) 53–93 g (70.0)[285]; *pallidirostris* ♂ (4) 60–68 g (64.3); ♀ 58 g[257]. For additional data see[216, 224].

9 LOGGERHEAD SHRIKE *Lanius ludovicianus* Plate 5

FIELD IDENTIFICATION Medium-sized (21–22 cm) grey, black and white shrike with a black face-mask over bill, black wings with small white patch, white scapulars and black tail with white outer feathers. Below white, or tinged grey in some races. Black and white pattern obvious in flight. Sexes similar. Young pale brownish-grey, barred above and below, wing-coverts tipped buff. Flies low and fast, swooping up to perch. Calls harsh, with whistles and warbling song. Solitary in open country with short grass and scattered trees or bushes in North America from Canada to Mexico. Southern populations resident, N populations migrate S in boreal winter. ***Flight characteristics***: Fast with rapid wingbeats, drops down low in horizontal flight, swoops up to perch. Long flight undulating. Contrasting plumage and white V on back conspicuous.

COMPARISONS Identification difficult where this species overlaps Great Grey Shrike *Lanius excubitor*. Many characters suggested for separation, including: body and bill size (larger in Great Grey), colour of bill base (paler in Great Grey), extent of barring on underparts (greater in Great Grey), extent of face-mask (narrower in Great Grey), amount of black above bill (lacking in Great Grey). However, many of these are only effective at close range, and apart from smaller size of Loggerhead, the best field characteristic appears to be the size and shape of the bill. Loggerhead has small stubby bill compared to the longer, heavier and more strongly hooked bill of Great Grey. Loggerhead has a completely black bill before mid-Mar (i.e breeding), Great Grey has light colour on bill base after mid-Feb and light colour on the upper mandible (any month). Separating immatures in boreal autumn and winter is easy: Loggerhead is greyish, Great Grey quite brownish. Barring is much finer and less conspicuous than in Great Grey Shrike. Reported behavioural difference is that Great Grey perches much higher and tends to fly level from one high perch to another. Loggerhead superficially resembles Mockingbird *Mimus polyglottos*, but has blacker wing, face-mask, heavy hooked bill and undulating flight with very rapid wingbeats (Mockingbird has slow wingbeats). For additional differences between these species see[421, 422, 440, 1054].

DESCRIPTION **ADULT ♂** ***Head*** Forehead with thin black frontal, lores and ear-coverts (black above and below eye); crown and nape pale grey extending to uppertail-coverts, which may be pale in some races. ***Wings*** Black with white patch on primaries, and white tips to scapulars, tertials and secondaries. Scapulars form a white V on the back. ***Tail*** Black with white outer feathers, white decreasing towards inner two feathers, which lack white. ***Underparts*** White to dirty white, some races greyish with fine barring (vermiculations). ***Bare parts*** Bill black (breeding), but has a brown base in boreal autumn and winter; palate greyish; legs black; eye dark brown[624, 1054]. **ADULT ♀** Similar to ♂, but in some populations ♀♀ appear to have a less extensive face-mask with brownish-black lores. May also have faint breast markings and browner primaries, giving a browner rather than the bluish appearance of ♂. ♀ also tends to have less white in the wings and scapulars than ♂. Bill, wing and tail significantly smaller than ♂[255, 406, 536, 624]. For pterylosis see[255]. ***Abnormal plumage*** Albinos recorded. **JUVENILE/IMMATURE** Face-mask brownish, lacks black on forehead. Upperparts brownish-grey finely barred. Scapulars finely barred buffy-white. Wings black with white patch at base of primaries, inner primaries, secondaries and tertials tipped whitish-buff, greater-coverts tipped rufous-buff. Tail edged white with buff tips. Underparts brownish-grey, finely barred on breast, sides and flanks. Chin, throat, belly and undertail-coverts dull white. Bare parts: Bill brownish-grey with flesh-coloured base, palate yellowish, eye brown. 1st-year birds retain buff-tipped primary coverts[255, 308, 440, 1054].

GEOGRAPHICAL VARIATION At least 11

races, described, with numerous intermediates; variation complex. Races have been described on body size and proportions (particularly wing : tail ratio), colour of back and underparts, and extent of breast-barring. Broadly separable into two groups based on paleness of back and underparts, and presence or absence of light-coloured rump and breast-barring. Mainly E coast group; nominate *ludovicianus* (SE to central Florida), *miamensis* (S Florida), *migrans* (central and NE USA to Quebec) and *excubitorides* (includes *nevadensis* and *sonoriensis* from central and more W and SW USA) occupy progressively more arid climates and show increasingly lighter upperparts. The underparts are also whiter than other races and lack a pale rump and breast-barring. West coast races inhabit moister areas, are generally darker above, some with pale rumps and breast-barring: *mexicanus* (includes *gambeli* and *nelsoni*, SW Canada to S California and Mexico), *anthonyi* (Santa Rosa, Santa Cruz, Santa Catalina and Anacapa), *mearnsi* (San Clemente Island) and *grinnelli* (SW California). The use of wing:tail ratios have been shown to be misleading, at least for Canadian birds[206, 230, 255, 307, 456, 624, 630, 675, 1054].

MOULT Adults and first-winter (boreal) birds undergo a partial pre-breeding body moult of mainly chin feathers from Feb–Apr. After breeding adults and first-summer (boreal) birds undergo a complete moult lasting about 3 months during Jul–Jan, mainly Sep–Nov. Post-juvenile moult takes rather longer, *c.*3–4 months during Apr–Nov. Races that migrate generally begin moult on breeding grounds, apparently suspending it and then completing it in non-breeding area[255, 308, 675, 1054].

RANGE, HABITAT and STATUS Breeding range From S Canada in SE Alberta, S Saskatchewan and SW Manitoba at *c.*55°N to S of Lake Superior. Distribution fragmented in S Ontario and S Quebec at *c.*45°N. In N USA rare in Wisconsin, Michigan and Ohio. In the E, commoner from North Carolina southwards to Florida. Throughout central USA to Mexico, as far S as Oaxaca at *c.*16°N. From here N, including some California islands (e.g. San Clemente) and Baja California islands up the W coast to Washington. Vagrant to British Columbia. **Non-breeding range** Northern populations spend boreal winter S of *c.*40°N within the range of resident populations. Vagrant to Guatemala, Bahamas (Great Exuma, Andros) and Bermuda. See Movements. **Habitat** Occurs in a wide variety of habitats from semi-desert areas with mesquite, yucca and agave cactus to scrublands with sagebrush, wooded savannas, woodland edge, orchards and other cultivated areas such as grazed pastures and grasslands with scattered bushes. Most habitat is characterised by widely spaced and often spiny shrubs and low trees interspersed with short grasses, forbs (generally greater than 50% herbaceous cover), and bare ground. Perch sites such as isolated bushes, trees and fences are essential, as well as suitable nest sites. Some cultivated areas (e.g. citrus groves) have been shown to be nutritionally poorer than pastures. Generally occurs below *c.*2000 m, and avoids forests and open treeless or scrubless areas[255, 256, 389, 400, 407, 440, 498, 675, 958, 959, 967, 973, 1054, 1059]. **Status** Rare to locally common resident, migrant or partial migrant. **Conservation status** Distribution and abundance has changed dramatically over the last 200 years, particularly having declined since 1920s, initially rather unevenly, but then more generally, especially in the NE. Average rates of regional declines vary from 2.5–3.4%, but locally up to *c.*9%. Virtually disappeared from most of its historical range in the NE, having formerly bred in Maritimes and New England. In E Canada it is classified as endangered in Quebec (*c.*10 pairs). In W Canada (SE Alberta, S Saskatchewan and SW Manitoba) more numerous, but still considered threatened. In NE USA it is considered threatened in Wisconsin, with only 9 pairs in Michigan, 10–20 pairs in Ohio, and in the E generally rare till North Carolina. SE populations also declining. SW populations also appear to be threatened, not only on the mainland but also on San Clemente (*mearnsi*), where it is now considered critically endangered with a population of less than 50 individuals. Causes of decline not well understood, but believed to be due to a number of factors including: changes in agricultural practices and land use, removal of hedgerows and fence lines, increased uptake of agricultural pesticides and herbicides, and the use of fertilisers. These combine to reduced prey diversity and abundance which directly impacts on survival of migratory as well as resident races, ultimately reducing their breeding success. This situation is aggravated with bad weather, interspecific competition and collisions with cars. The suggestion that introduced fire-ants *Solenopsis invicta* have contributed to the decline of this shrike has been dispelled in one study, but, the influence of these ants on arthropod abundance has not been studied. On San Clemente, declines have resulted from the loss of nesting habitat owing to feral herbivores and increased predation by natural and exotic predators. Held in captivity[247, 256, 310, 311, 312, 316, 407, 498, 655, 675, 925, 959, 960, 963, 966, 967, 969, 970, 974, 983, 1054, 1058].

MOVEMENTS Not well known; probably a diurnal migrant, with no stop-over concentrations recorded. Populations N of *c.*40°N with 10–30 days/year of snow cover are migratory, moving S into areas with resident populations. Central and NE birds of races *migrans* and *excubitorides* have been shown to migrate. Those in the NW (*gambeli*) and central W (*nevadensis*) were previously thought to migrate but evidence is lacking. Northern populations of the nominate SE race (*ludovicianus*) also undertake local movements. Migrants leave their breeding grounds in autumn, depending on latitude, between Jul–Dec, mainly Sep–Nov. Populations E of Rocky Mountains migrate partially or wholly to the SE. Movements of populations W of Rockies are largely unknown. Birds arrive in S non-breeding grounds from Jan–Feb (Missouri). Following spring migration, birds arrive back on their breeding grounds from

Jan–May, mainly from Mar–Apr[255, 386, 389, 577, 675, 984, 1054].

SOCIAL ORGANISATION and GENERAL BEHAVIOUR Usually solitary in all seasons, but also seen in pairs or small family groups in breeding season. Generally conspicuous as it sits upright, exposed on prominent perches surveying the ground for prey and advertising its presence by static marking. Pairs may defend the same territory throughout the year, or separate and defend individual territories, often adjacent areas, or in the case of migrants, establish individual territories on their non-breeding grounds. Migrant ♂♂ appear to show stronger breeding site-fidelity than ♀♀, but site-fidelity generally appears to be unusually low and rather variable. Territories are defended in boreal summer and winter with loud song while perched, and the often-heard territorial call, a series of repeated harsh *tcheeer-* or *bzeeet-* calls, given while perched or in flight. Territory size varies with habitat. The number of perches has been shown to be important (more perches result in smaller territories). Most mainland territories are smaller than *c.*10 ha (range *c.*1–18, rarely 24 ha) and show little seasonal variation, but those on San Clemente may be as large as 34 ha. During close aggressive interactions, resulting from territorial intrusions, participants adopt a crouched, horizontal posture, with head down, wings slightly drooped and fluttered rapidly, rump and back feathers erected and tail spread. Birds tend to face away from each other and often peck the ground or perch forcefully, remaining silent or giving a harsh begging-like call. This display usually lasts *c.*30 sec before one bird chases the other. Disputes seldom result in physical contact. In contrast to this, subordinate birds adopt an upright posture with head held up. Group meetings sometimes occur, probably consisting of adjacent pairs. When alarmed the tail is flicked sideways and up and down, and fanned. Feathers of head and body are raised and body usually crouched with head lowered and bill open. When mobbing may adopt an upright posture with wings open. Pairs roost apart in same tree or bush, well protected by foliage. Sleeps with body feathers fluffed out and bill tucked into scapulars (captive birds). Scratches indirectly, sun-bathes on ground, bathes in shallow pools of water, and produces pellets[196, 255, 387, 406, 407, 675, 970, 958, 984, 1054].

Foraging behaviour Opportunistic, hunts from an elevated perch *c.*2–10 m up on bushes, trees, fences and telephone lines. Most prey caught on the ground in a radius of *c.*12 m. Regularly changes perch and occasionally hunts up to *c.*400 m from the nest. Sometimes hovers before diving onto prey, particularly where ground cover tall or thick, and will hawk insects in the air. When on the ground it hops about; will flush prey by wing-flashing. Small prey is consumed immediately, larger prey is carried back to a perch, where it is held down by the foot or up in the foot and torn apart with the bill. Regularly impales or wedges prey, and forms caches, which in some studies remained mostly uneaten, but in others were used to feed the incubating ♀ and nestlings. May also function as mate attraction. Prey larger than *c.*30 g, such as rodents and birds, may be transferred from bill to feet in flight, or carried only in the feet. Readily attacks and carries prey up to at least 129% of own body mass. Experimentally determined preferred prey size *c.*7 g (4.6–16.5). Occasionally resorts to kleptoparasitism[107, 389, 418, 489, 498, 675, 976, 979, 1004, 1054].

Food Arthropods, mainly insects and their larvae, and small vertebrates. In one study 72% of diet consisted of arthropods, mainly insects. These include Lepidoptera (butterflies and moths), Orthoptera (crickets and grasshoppers), Coleoptera (beetles), Hemiptera and Homoptera (bugs), Hymenoptera (bumblebees, wasps and ants), Dermaptera (earwigs), Odonata (dragonflies) and Diptera (flies). Also takes spiders, harvestmen, Isopoda, snails, crabs, crayfish and some vegetable matter. Vertebrate prey, which is usually taken more frequently in boreal winter, in one study up to 76%, includes mice, reptiles (mainly lizards), amphibians and birds. Occasionally preys on bats and fish (minnows) and has been recorded raiding Cliff Swallow *Petrochelidon pyrrhonota* nests and attacking birds the size of California Quail *Callipepla californica*. Readily feeds on carrion and quickly learns to accept dead mice in supplementary prey experiments. Has not been recorded drinking water[196, 225, 389, 498, 675, 976, 980, 1054].

SOUNDS Repertoire consists of harsh calls, whistled notes and warbling song. Calls graded in pitch and repetition rate. Territorial call a repeated harsh screech *tcheeer-tcheeer-* or, in territorial threat, a sharper *bzeeek-bzeeek-* of 4–10 or 12 notes progressively diminishing in intensity, the first notes slightly higher-pitched and shorter than the terminal ones. A similar but more metallic-sounding version of this call is used in courtship and advertising displays (see General Behaviour). Another presumed territorial call consists of a repeated shrill high-pitched whistle combined with a harsh buzzy note, sounding like *tuubzzt-* or *tzzweet-*. The calls of mated and unmated ♂♂ reportedly different. Alarm consists of repeated harsh *keer-keer-keer-* or *kzzzz-kzzzz-* and rasping buzzy *aak aak aak* notes to aerial predators, or *jaa* to terrestrial predators, repetition rate varying with intensity of interaction; the higher the intensity the faster the repetition rate. Also has prolonged jay-like harsh *schgra-a-a* notes, variously repeated when defending the nest. The same call is given when attempting the dispatch of prey that cannot readily be killed. High intensity alarm includes bill-snapping, low buzzing and staccato notes. Raptor alarm a double whistle when at distance, single buzzier note when close, before making for cover. Contact call unknown. Duetting between mates has been recorded, but call-type not documented. Begging call a slightly quavering nasal buzzing or wailing *naaa-naaa-* call given by young, similar in adults but quality slightly different. Nestlings beg with thin *tsp* initially, this changing to a husky *tcheek-* or *tcheep-* later.

Apprehension or location call of abandoned young a repeated *screig-*. Song produced by both sexes, apparently mainly by ♂; consists of short trills or combinations of clear double- or triple-whistle notes, repeated rhythmically a number of times and varying in pitch and quality. Strangely, mimicry has not been recorded. Song is most frequently heard in late boreal summer. Immature subsong is continuous, consisting of short screeches, gurgles, trills and clear notes[255, 256, 387, 406, 440, 500, 1054]. Sonagram[1054].

BREEDING BIOLOGY Monogamous with a low incidence of polygyny. First-year birds may attempt breeding. Group interactions have been reported, and probably represent interactions between 2–3 neighbouring pairs. In monogamous pairs, ♀ may lay a second clutch 10–12 days after the first clutch has hatched. ♂ attends this brood and feeds ♀ on second clutch. Occasionally ♀ may desert mate once young of first brood have fledged and raise a brood with a new ♂. In the polygynous situation, a second ♀ lays only after the eggs of the other ♀ have hatched. ♂ feeds both ♀♀ and their young. ♂♂ of polygynous pairs capture more prey/hour, especially vertebrate prey; pairs lay more eggs, raise more young and feed their young more frequently than ♂♂ of monogamous pairs. Earlier (1930) reports of this species occasionally nesting in 'colonies', with nests less than 18 m apart, may be the result of more prevalent polygynous breeding. Normally nests are *c.*150–800 m apart. Second broods normally occur in S populations, rarely third broods, with N populations usually single-brooded. Up to five replacement clutches have been recorded. Reported fledging success varies from *c.*24–94%. Nest predation is believed to be a major cause of poor nesting success. This situation is aggravated by fenceline or hedgerow linear nesting because of the ease with which predators search such vegetation[404, 405, 407, 675, 961, 965, 970, 973, 980, 984, 985, 1054, 1058].

Season Throughout range, egg laying takes place from Feb–Jul, mainly Mar–Jun. Breeding in mountainous areas and high latitudes is generally later than average. In many areas it is one of the earliest passerines to nest[255, 386, 404, 972, 1054].

Displays ***Courtship*** Pair formation appears to consist of a repeated metallic screeching *bzeek-* call, probably by ♂, followed by excited hopping and flitting about together. This is followed by presumed ♂, crouching near ♀, tail fanned and cocked upwards while giving the same metallic screech. ♂ then flies back and forth above ♀ performing a display fight, consisting of erratic zigzagging with vertical undulations and changes in pace. Display-flights sometimes include hovering, which is performed higher above the ground than when hunting. Courtship may also include excited song given by the ♂ when perched a few metres from his mate. Occasionally ♀♀ also sing, but with softer simpler song, consisting mainly of trills. Other courtship displays involve head and bill up and tail fanned, usually combined with begging calls. courtship-feeding may or may not involve wing-fluttering or begging calls. Dance performed during pair formation not to be confused with appeasement display during agonistic interactions. ***Pre-copulation*** Usually preceded by courtship-feeding by ♂ and sometimes loud song. ♀ usually begs and flutters wings, apparently soliciting copulation, which takes place 2–4 days before egg-laying. During copulation ♀ holds prey in bill. ***Nest-site display*** Both birds inspect potential sites by hopping about through branches[406, 255, 675, 1010, 1054].

Nest Apparently selected and built by both sexes, mainly ♀. The rather bulky cup is built of sticks, grass and herb stems and lined with rootlets, plant fibres, moss, feathers, cattle hair, woolly material, cotton and man-made material like rags and paper. Material from an old nest may be used; birds occasionally build on top of their own old nest, or that of another species, such as Northern Mockingbird or Magpie *Pica pica*. Nests are usually placed in dense thorny shrubs, bushes or deciduous trees. Preferred bushes and trees include hawthorn, red cedar, blackberry, sagebrush, bitterbrush and greasewood. Cabbage palms are also used. One unusual nest was placed in amongst discarded fence wire. Nest height varies with habitat; usually placed 1–4 m (0.33–15) above ground. In one study second nests were placed higher than first nests. ***Size*** OD 80–200 mm, ID 80–90 mm, cup depth 30–76 mm, height 70–120 mm. Built in 7–12 days[255, 256, 386, 404, 440, 441, 675, 973, 981, 985, 1054].

Eggs Usually 4–5 (1–7), but variable with latitude. Colour varies from dull white, light neutral grey or buff, spotted with greys, yellowish-brown and umber, concentrated at the large end. ***Size*** *gambeli* 26.9–22.0 x 19.4–17.3 mm (24.1 x 18.1, n=94). Replacement clutches frequent and normally raises 2, occasionally 3 broods in S range[255, 386, 404, 440, 441, 973, 1054]. **Incubation** By ♀ only, begins with penultimate egg, fed by ♂ on and off nest. Period usually 15–17 days (13–20)[255, 256, 386, 404, 440, 1054]. **Nestling** Hatch blind and nearly naked, have neossoptiles (downy feathers) on ventral and sometimes spinal tract, lack mouth spots, mouth deep pinkish-orange. Initially beg with thin *tsp-tsp-* calls. Brooded by ♀, attended by both sexes. Fledge after *c.*16–18 days (16–21). Young begin feeding themselves after *c.*13 days and are independent at 26–35 days after fledging, but may remain with parents for up to 95 days (av. 50 days)[153, 255, 256, 386, 404, 789, 1054]. For development of young see[255, 1055]. **Predation and longevity** Main nest predators are thought to be Ravens *Corvus corax*, Magpies, racoons, feral cats, foxes (for *mearnsi*), weasels and snakes. Disturbance and bad weather known to affect nesting success. Weak adults and fledglings are probably caught by diurnal and nocturnal raptors. Road-kills may also be an important factor. Longevity believed to be only 3–4 years[255, 1054]. **Brood parasite** Occasionally parasitised by Brown-headed Cowbirds *Molothrus ater*[385].

MEASUREMENTS and WEIGHTS *L. l. ludovicianus* wing ♂ (39) 93.5–99.3 (97.0), ♀ (31) 90–96 (94.0); tail ♂ (44) 96.9–106.5 (102.8), ♀ (31)

96.6–104.5 (99.4); bill ♂ (43) 11.5–13.4 (12.4), ♀ (30) 11.2–13.1 (12.0); tarsus ♂ (43) 25.7–28.3 (26.8), ♀ (31) 25.0–27.8 (26.5). In N populations ♂♂ are larger than ♀♀[255]. **Weight** *ludovicianus* (n=103) mean 47.9 g ±SD 3.3(Florida)[489]. For additional data see[255, 478, 982, 1054].

10 LESSER GREY SHRIKE *Lanius minor* Plate 5

FIELD IDENTIFICATION Medium-sized (21 cm) grey, black and white shrike with a broad black face-mask which extends as a broad band on forehead. Sits very upright and has a short stubby bill. Sexes similar, but ♀ has smaller face-mask. Above blue-grey. Black wings long and pointed, crossing over above back and show white patch, conspicuous in flight. Tail black with white outer feathers. Underparts pinkish-white (particularly before breeding). Juveniles pale brown, barred above, cream to buff below, lack black frontal markings. Flies fast, interspersed with glides; hovers. Calls harsh; warbler-like song with mimicry. Solitary or in loose groups; perches prominently; found in hot dry open wooded country in Eurasia, migrating to thorn savannas in southern Africa. ***Flight characteristics***: Relatively long pointed wings produce a flight not entirely typical of *Lanius*. Flight faster and smoother, with quicker wingbeats, often interspersed with glides. Generally less undulating than other members of the genus. Frequently hovers like a Kestrel *Falco tinnunculus* before pouncing on prey. White wing-patch and black and white tail conspicuous in flight. Flies low to the ground and swoops up to perch.

COMPARISONS Similar to Great Grey Shrike *Lanius excubitor* and Southern Grey Shrike *L. meridionalis*. Distinguished from these by smaller and more compact size, broad black face-mask (but absent in immature and first-winter boreal birds), and noticeably stubbier, less hooked bill. Longer wings extend well past tail-coverts giving Lesser Grey a seemingly shorter tail. Tail is proportionally shorter and less rounded, with different pattern (see Comparisons of these two species). Underparts generally pinker, and Lesser Grey tends to have a more upright stance. On passage, confusion possible with Grey-backed Fiscal *L. excubitoroides* as both have similar black facial markings; however, Grey-backed is much larger with a longer tail, the terminal half completely black (Lesser Grey has white outer feathers), and it is a gregarious shrike with rounded wings and weaker flight. Lesser Grey is less distinctive in juvenile plumage, with pale edges to scapulars suggesting bolder-marked juvenile Woodchat Shrike *L. senator*, but Woodchat smaller and slighter with more obvious barring above and below, more diffuse face-mask, duller wing-patch and narrower white edges to tail. Great Grey Shrike juvenile distinguished mainly on larger size, wing structure (appears shorter-winged) and relative tail length; underparts are usually more heavily barred[522, 257, 747].

DESCRIPTION ADULT ♂ ***Head*** Black face-mask extensive, from forehead to above and behind eye (extent variable), including lores, eye-stripe (above and below eye) to ear-coverts; crown and nape pale grey to blue-grey. ***Back*** Mantle to rump grey, scapulars have whitish tips which form a pale patch on folded wing. ***Wings*** Black with conspicuous white patch in primaries; tertials and inner secondaries tipped white. For wing formula see[675]. ***Tail*** Graduated, black with almost all-white outer feathers. ***Underparts*** Chin and throat white, rest white with pinkish-mauve tinge (variable, more prominent in birds returning to breeding grounds), mainly on breast and flanks. ***Bare parts*** Bill black, short and stubby; legs dark grey; eye dark brown. ***Abnormal plumage*** Melanistic morph rare[218]. ADULT ♀ Similar to ♂, but all colours less pure, grey of upperparts less blue in tone and underparts less pink. Black face-mask with brownish tinge, has more grey speckles on forehead and brown on ear-coverts. These differences most marked following autumn moult[257]. **JUVENILE** Head: Pale brownish-grey, finely barred on forehead and crown; face-mask indistinct and frontal lacking (gradually changes to mixed grey and black), only lores and ear-coverts brownish-black. Back pale brownish-grey, less barring on mantle and back; scapulars grey-brown with pale edges. ***Wings*** Dark brownish-black, all feathers tipped buffy-white especially coverts and tertials, primary wing-patch white. Tail as in adult, not as dark and with less white. Underparts: Throat and chin white, rest creamy-white with faint barring on flanks and sides of breast, often tinged buff. Bare parts: Bill pale greyish-black with pale base; legs and eye as in adult. **IMMATURE/FIRST-WINTER** (boreal) Resembles less marked juvenile or drab adult; lacks black forehead, has pale bill, and upperparts are greyish, some tinged brown, and may still show a little fine barring. Wing-coverts and flight feathers with pale tips. Underparts creamy-white sometimes faintly barred. These birds can be recognised on their non-breeding grounds up to mid-January[510, 747, 923].

GEOGRAPHICAL VARIATION Two races, not always accepted; variation slight and clinal. Nominate *minor* (W populations from Spain, Central Europe, Balkans to W Russia) smaller and darker than *turanicus* (E populations in Asia). Juvenile and first-year *turanicus* more sandy-brown than nominate; this race is believed to outnumber nominate in Zimbabwe[30, 147, 211, 212, 257, 285, 675].

HYBRIDS Two hybrids known, both with Red-backed Shrike *Lanius collurio*. Lesser Grey has also been observed attempting to approach, presumably in courtship, a ♀ Bay-backed Shrike *L. vittatus*[257, 268, 379, 675].

MOULT Post-juvenile head and body moult begins soon after fledging, and is completed in 10–11 weeks by Aug–Sep. First-winter (boreal) birds are brownish-grey, with a variable amount of dark barring above and cream below. These birds undergo a complete moult on non-breeding grounds and are then similar to adults. Occasionally some first-summer (boreal) birds back on their breeding grounds have traces of juvenile plumage, such as pale secondaries and tertials. Adult post-breeding moult begins with tertials, is usually started in breeding area, suspended on migration, and completed in non-breeding grounds from Dec–Apr, mainly Jan–Mar. Plumage differences between sexes are most marked following this moult[140, 257, 284, 285, 675, 814].

RANGE, HABITAT and STATUS **Breeding range** Eurasia, distribution fragmented in W. Found from NE Spain, S France, Italy and Sicily, Austria, Hungary, Romania, Bulgaria, Czech Republic, E Poland, Balkan states, Turkey, N Syria, Lebanon, N Iraq, N Iran, NE Afghanistan, Transcaucasia, Caucasia, Russia in W and Central Asia to Altai in Siberia and NW China at *c*.85°E. Northern boundary lies at *c*.55°N. The range extends *c*.6000 km E–W and *c*.2000 km N–S. In Europe vagrant to Faeroe Isles, British Isles, Netherlands, Denmark, Norway, Sweden and Finland. **Non-breeding range** Migrant to southern Africa. Passage migrant to Cyprus, Saudi Arabia, United Arab Emirates, Afghanistan, Oman, Jordan, Israel, Libya, Egypt, Chad, Sudan, Djibouti, Somalia, Uganda, Kenya, Tanzania. Rarely to Gabon, Congo, Cabinda, Zaïre and Rwanda. Considered a vagrant to Pakistan, Mauritania, Tunisia, Mali, Cameroon, Nigeria, Príncipe, Niger, Burundi, Yemen, Lesotho, Madagascar and SW South Africa. Main non-breeding grounds in southern Africa centred in the Kalahari basin of Botswana, but also includes to a much lesser extent Namibia, S Angola, S Zambia, Malawi, S Mozambique, Zimbabwe and N South Africa. Virtually the entire world population spends the boreal winter in this region, in an area 5 times smaller than breeding range (1.5–1.75 million km^2 versus 8 million km^2). Its main distribution in the Kalahari coincides with an area from which the Common Fiscal *L. collaris* is virtually absent. Occasionally spends boreal winters in Middle East (Iraq, North Yemen), Gabon, Rwanda, Zambia, SE Zimbabwe and Botswana. See Movements.

Habitat ***Breeding range*** Requires drier and sunnier conditions than most other European shrikes with a mosaic of open grassy and bare ground with scattered tall trees and bushes characteristic of steppe, forest-steppe and Mediterranean regions. In Europe generally below 900 m, but up to 2200 m in E range. Adapts well to cultivated areas and pastures scattered with suitable trees, with *c*.5–15 trees/ha, or telephone wires. Also often found in orchards with well-spaced trees, vineyards, groves, parks and woodland edge. ***Non-breeding range*** Semi-arid open dry deciduous savanna and thornveld, especially open *Acacia* parkland with low bushes and taller trees, alternating with open short grassy areas. Also in fallow land with young sprouting *Acacia* bushes and along ecotone between arable land and bushveld. Generally avoids monotypic stands of the broadleaved deciduous *Terminalia* but is found in mopane *Colophospermum mopane*. Habitat segregation between this species and the Red-backed Shrike in the same area appears similar to that found in their breeding grounds (Italy), with Lesser Grey favouring the more open habitat. Ground cover (the avoidance of taller grass) may be a limiting factor determining the boundaries of its non-breeding range[7, 21, 22, 26, 30, 36, 37, 48, 119, 140, 190, 205, 212, 214, 216, 217, 218, 220, 222, 231, 242, 246, 257, 274, 278, 284, 285, 290, 291, 292, 305, 318, 320, 325, 382, 431, 434, 443, 449, 484, 504, 510, 631, 639, 675, 688, 703, 807, 819, 859, 907, 923, 933, 931, 952].

Status Migrant, rare to extinct in parts of W Europe. **Conservation status** Has drastically declined over the W part of breeding range in last 200 years. Formerly reasonably common in central and S Europe, including Germany and France. After 1850 populations began declining, and apart from a temporary recovery in the 1880s and 1930s, has continued to decline. It appears to be unusually susceptible to periodic climatic fluctuations, and therefore population estimates need constant review. Central and E Asian populations appear more stable, but little known. It has disappeared from most of France, no longer in Germany, Switzerland, Czech Republic and W Poland. Estimated population (totals or for pairs): 2,000–5,000 pairs (Albania), 5–10 pairs (Austria), 50–200 pairs (Belarus), 1,000–10,000 pairs (Bulgaria), 3,000–4,000 (Croatia), *c*.50 pairs (France), 2,000–3,000 (Greece), 5,000–8,000 (Hungary), 1,000–2,000 pairs (Italy), 10–20 pairs (Lithuania), 10,000–15,000 (Moldova), 10–50 (Poland), 30,000–70,000 pairs (Romania), 10,000–100,000 pairs (Russia), 400–600 pairs (Slovakia), 20–30 pairs (Slovenia), 45–90 (Spain), 10,000–100,000 pairs (Turkey), 3,000–3,500, with *c*.50 pairs in western regions (Ukraine). However, extrapolation from strip counts and distribution of optimal vegetation in its southern African non-breeding grounds indicated a world population of from *c*.5–7.3 to 10 million birds. Historic European population fluctuations are thought to have been linked to climatic fluctuations, but more recent declines are probably linked to changes in agricultural practices. The absence of food-caching makes this species vulnerable to prolonged cold or wet weather, at which times a ♀ has even been known to cannibalise her own brood. However, in E Europe, where the climate is becoming drier not wetter, the species continues to decline. Other threats include changing agricultural practices, a decline in large insect prey due to insecticides and pollution, high nest predation by natural predators, mainly corvids, and human disturbance including shooting; on passage, potential increased exposure to pesticides and drought. Threats in non-breeding grounds include drought, a reduction of habitat due to bush encroachment, and probable increased competition with the more numerous Red-backed Shrike. The restricted nature of its non-breeding distribution provides a unique opportunity to monitor the entire population and investigate whether factors in this area are contributing to its decline[257, 284, 285, 369, 480, 598, 599, 639, 675, 787, 923, 936, 937, 639, 938, 948, 952, 964, 1015].

MOVEMENTS All populations are migratory. In boreal autumn this long-distance night migrant departs from W and Central Europe, passing through the Balkans and over the Aegean Sea, entering Africa on a narrow front around Egypt (between Libya-Egyptian border and W Arabia). Central Asian populations migrate SW, with juveniles dominating the last few weeks of departure (Kazakhstan). Main migration route in North Africa appears to be along the Nile valley. Return route is further E with main exodus from Africa via Ethiopia and Somalia (loop migration). Leaves breeding grounds Jul–Oct, mainly Aug–Sep, passage to southern African non-breeding grounds takes 8–10 weeks. Arrival on non-breeding grounds is progressively later the further S, and remarkably punctual from year to year, from Oct–Dec, remaining in the area for 18–22 weeks. There is some indication that immatures may move further S than adults. Departure from non-breeding grounds in austral autumn (Mar–Apr) is fast and synchronised within a few nights. A few birds have been found to remain on their non-breeding grounds. Arrives back on Eurasian breeding grounds in boreal spring (Apr–Jun), the passage having taken only 6–8 weeks. In one study *c.*30% of birds returned to the same breeding grounds. Site-fidelity on non-breeding grounds has not been proved by ringing, but is expected to be high based on its early, fast and punctual arrival on non-breeding and breeding grounds. This, combined with the observation that several birds arrive together as a group on breeding grounds, has led to the suggestion that subpopulations may keep together on their non-breeding grounds. Builds up fat reserves prior to migrating[33, 48, 140, 141, 181, 257, 284, 285, 318, 375, 484, 546, 639, 703, 728, 923, 1015].

SOCIAL ORGANISATION and GENERAL BEHAVIOUR A largely solitary, conspicuous shrike which perches exposed on top of trees, fences, telephone wires and powerlines, characteristically with a very upright posture. In hottest time of day may seek shade. Sometines weakly gregarious, nesting in loose colonies, overlapping hunting areas and occasionally in loose groups of up to 10 individuals on non-breeding grounds. This reduced intraspecific aggression may have developed in response to predation or climatic fluctuations, allowing for improved vigilance and shared foraging areas. In breeding grounds it may also form loose associations with other birds, presumably for protection, such as with the Kestrel, Red-footed Falcon *F. vespertinus* and Fieldfares *Turdus pilaris*. Territory size is rather variable depending on habitat, ranging from 1.9–23 ha. This shrike spends only 35% of its life on its Palearctic breeding grounds, 65% in North Africa, of which 35% is spent on its non-breeding grounds and 30% on passage. Territories are advertised and defended by static marking from prominent post, calling and a distinctive display-flight, which consists of a straight or wide sweeping, slow undulating flight across its territory with tail spread. Variations on this include a gradual high ascent with shallow wingbeats alternating with glides, followed by a descending glide with tail and wings fully spread. The display is usually accompanied by loud *kerrib-kerrib* and *tschertscherb-tschertscherb* calls. It is performed by both partners, ♀ usually ahead of ♂, and may take place through neighbouring territories with two pairs involved in a ritualised flight, not a hectic chase. The sight of this display attracts others and stimulates similar flights. Unpaired ♂♂ repeatedly give this display accompanied by territorial calls. In mated birds the display ceases after egg-laying. On arrival and departure from non-breeding grounds it shows intraspecific aggression. It holds well-spaced territories with birds aggressively defending these areas, which are advertised by static marking, apparently with no territorial calling. Density on non-breeding grounds range from 2 birds/km on roads (Namibia), 1 bird/25 ha in Kalahari (Botswana), 1 bird/10–15 ha (E Botswana and W South Africa) or up to 8 birds/ha (Botswana); on passage up to 12 birds/ha. On breeding grounds predators are attacked vigorously and aerial predators pursued, often to great heights, after which the shrike glides back in a display-flight. When excited swings and flicks tail in all directions, in more aggressive context adopts a horizontal threatening posture, with body hunched and feathers on back and underparts markedly ruffled. Body bowing may also occur. Roosts in a tree or bush and scratches indirectly[205, 214, 284, 285, 373, 639, 703, 819, 869, 881, 923, 945, 952].

Foraging behaviour Hunts from elevated, exposed positions 1–8 m high, taking prey mostly on the ground, but will also take many slow-flying insects in the air. May fly 400–500 m in search of food. Also gleans from branches and foliage, particularly in cool or wet weather. Often hovers for 10–30 sec at 2–6 m above the ground. On the ground it hops about, often spending much time here in bad weather. Hunts well into dusk and has been recorded attacking small bats. Frequently changes perch, dropping down and flying low to the ground, before swooping up to perch. Prey is consumed whole, usually on return to perch, or if large may be held in one foot and torn apart. Unlike other shrikes it seldom caches food on breeding grounds. Impaling has been reported on its non-breeding grounds, but hovering is rarely observed. Although primarily insectivorous, the occasional vertebrates caught are wedged or impaled.

Food Arthropods, almost exclusively insects, including Coleoptera (beetles), Orthoptera (grasshoppers and crickets), Hymenoptera (bumblebees and wasps), Hemiptera (bugs and cicadas), Lepidoptera (caterpillars, butterflies and moths), Ephemeroptera (mayflies), Dermaptera (earwigs) and Diptera (flies). In one study beetles formed up to 97% of diet. Other less usual prey includes spiders, harvestmen, millipedes, snails, earthworms, fruits and seeds. Small vertebrates, such as voles, mice, lizards and even fish (possibly carrion) are occasionally taken, and it is known to attack small bats. Birds are rarely taken, although exhausted migrants up to the size of Quail *Coturnix coturnix* have been known to fall victim. One case of cannibalism of nestlings is known. It is not known to drink water on its non-breeding grounds[48, 214, 205, 257, 284, 285, 352, 373, 480, 484, 639, 675, 848, 949, 950, 951].

SOUNDS Repertoire consists of a wide range of harsh chattering and grating calls and whistles, which are combined with mimicry to form its song. Calls are graded and similar calls appear to be used in different contexts. Territorial call a repeated monosyllabic *kscha-* or disyllabic *ko-ick-* sound, described as *kerrib-*, *chrrit-* or *chey-ek...chey-ek-*, *tscherb-tscherb-* and *kueek-chok*, *chzhuck-chok*. Other variations include harsher disyllabic *tschertscherb,* shorter *tschsch*, *tsch* and *ksch* sounds. Also has a short double-noted whistle *tijü- tijü* or *tschilip-tschilip*. These are given while perched or in flight. In display-flight gives repeated *tshe-yek--dje-yek-* phrase (see Displays). Rival aggression calls and alarm calls often given in long repeated series producing a chattering effect and extensively graded in pitch and repetition rate. Rival aggression call is a harsh *rrre*-type sound, described as *keeeee* or *rrrre*. Alarm calls are repeated harsh chatters, like *teck-teck*, *check-*, *shek-*, *tscheck-tschek-*, *tschäckäck-*, *shrek-shrek-*, *schäck-* or *scharreck-* and *tchak*. At higher intensity a rapidly repeated *kshek-kshek-kshek-* and hoarse *gägägägä-* or *geer-geer-geer-* or forceful *kschvee*. Calls may develop into a rattling *tr-tr-tr-tr-* when attacking predators, when often combined with bill-snapping and 'wing-fripping' sounds. Contact call is a harsh *krett* given when nest-building, ♂ feeding ♀, and adult feeding young, with variations of *krje*, *wät*, *kwiä* or strangled *widiä-*. Contact-type calls appear to be given in combination with a number of other calls. Begging calls by adults and young are a repeated *gäh-gäh-* or *gaee-gaee-*, with variations such as a rapidly repeated *cha-cha-cha-cha-* coaxing call during courtship. Recently hatched chicks give a strident drawn-out penetrating *chip-chip*. At least two song types: (a) quiet and warbler-like, a combination of very fast chattering, grating and thin trilling whistles, mingled with mimicked calls of other birds, given by paired ♂♂ in courtship and birds on non-breeding grounds, and (b) loud song of similar composition given mainly by unpaired ♂♂ in boreal summer, probably serving mate-attraction function. Song contains excellent mimics of other birds and mammals and is often introduced with short *krje*-type calls[48, 181, 205, 209, 210, 225, 284, 285, 373, 500, 600, 728]. Sonagram[48, 225, 257, 284, 484, 600].

BREEDING BIOLOGY Monogamous and territorial, but weakly gregarious, often in loose clusters or colonies of 3–7 pairs (2–10 pairs), sometimes nesting in neighbouring trees, rarely in the same tree. More often *c.*30–180 m apart in widely scattered pairs. Breeding density of 23–26 pairs/10 km^2 or 4 nests/ha (Slovakia) have been recorded. Territory boundaries not well demarcated and tend to be overlapping with only the immediate vicinity of the nest being vigorously defended. At least *c.*30% of adults show breeding site-fidelity, although in one ringed pair, both had new mates the following season. Young have also been recorded breeding near their natal territory. Territories are defended only until eggs have hatched. When a brood is lost often may relocate to a new territory. Pair formation appears to take place, either in their non-breeding grounds or during the austral spring migration. This is supported by the presumed courtship-feeding observed in a pair on the non-breeding grounds in November, as well as the fact that most birds arrive on their breeding grounds already paired (Europe). However, in some Asian populations pair-formation apparently occurs on breeding grounds with 2–3 ♂♂ courting a single ♀. Loud song is rarely heard from paired birds, but is the dominant call of unpaired ♂♂. Soft warbling song is common in paired ♂♂, and prior to migration from non-breeding grounds. Nest-building and copulations can be observed from the day of arrival, but are more frequently from the second or third day. In one study breeding success was *c.*34%. The family remains in the territory for 10–14 days after the nestlings have fledged, and may move into larger areas up to 1 km away, where they remain for up to 8 weeks before departure. Normally only a single brood is laid. Tolerate and are tolerated by congeners in the same habitat, although Asian population appear to show greatest interspecific aggression, particularly towards Bay-backed Shrike *L. vittatus*[284, 285, 373, 480, 500, 675, 728, 949, 950].

Season Similar throughout range; egg-laying Apr–Jul, mainly May–Jun (Europe)[257]; May–Jun (Turkmenistan)[214]; Apr–Jun (Ukraine)[284, 1015].

Displays *Courtship* Initial mate attraction consists of loud song given mainly by unpaired ♂♂. This followed by at least two phases prior to egg-laying. Initially consists of much flying, ♀ leading, ♂ behind and below, continuously calling a repeated *tshe-yek--dje-yek*--phrase. ♀ remains silent. When ♂ perches close to ♀, he raises himself up, with head held up and turning from side to side while fanning his tail and usually accompanied by soft excited song. Then moves closer (20–30 cm away) in a horizontal posture with tail fanned, singing and fluttering his wings as he faces ♀. Fanned tail may be moved up and down. ♂ also observed to perch close to ♀ who has tail fanned; he faces away slightly with bill pointing down, tail widely fanned, then performs numerous rhythmic bows while fluttering wings, bill raised momentarily, then bows almost touching female's feet, fanned tail vertical. May give soft song during this display. Occasionally both sexes may bow simultaneously. Following courtship-feeding, ♀ recorded facing away from ♂ who nods head. This phase is followed by nest-building and then phase in which ♂ calls vigorously with loud hoarse *shek-shek-shek-* sounds and continuously chases ♀. This attracts other ♂♂ who are chased off. ***Pre-copulation*** May or may not be preceded by courtship-feeding, during which ♀ flutters and droops wings in a crouched posture while giving begging call. ♂ announces that he has food with a *krett* call, answered with same call by ♀. In one study, prior to copulation, the ♂ approached ♀ while giving loud *shek-shek-* calls, mounted, copulated then perched quietly giving a warbling song. Copulation begins 2–3 days before egg laying. ***Nest-site display*** Both sexes appear to choose a nest site, although ♂ believed to entice ♀ to selected sites with soft *kerrib* calls. Sits in prospective site, turns head from side to side. In early stages of construction ♂ can be seen lying in nest with wings spread out and tail slightly fanned and moved up and down while giving *tijü* call[181, 257, 284, 285, 728].

Nest Built by both sexes, initially by ♂, then by both: a cup with a loose foundation of twigs, grass, rootlets, man-made materials, often with a high proportion of green plant stems, especially aromatic species (e.g. chamomile), with leaves and flowers attached, with or without a lining of rootlets, hair and feathers. In Europe nearly always placed in trees at height of *c*.5 m (2–23, n=112) above the ground, usually in poplars, elms, alder and fruit trees, sometimes also conifers. In Asia, generally nests lower down owing to lack of large trees, using shelter-belts with various broadleaved bushes and trees, including pistachio *Pistacia* and honey-locust *Gleditsia* trees. Occasionally nests in reeds, apparently in response to habitat deterioration. Nests placed against the trunk, on a lateral branch or in the crown. ***Size*** OD 75–130 mm, ID 94 mm, cup depth 30–50 mm, height 95 mm. Built in 2–5 days. Occasionally built in an old crow or magpie nest, or repair an old nest. Egg-laying begins immediately or rarely within 1–2 days[181, 214, 257, 284, 285, 380, 728, 1015].

Eggs Usually 5–6 (3–9), laid on consecutive days. In one study in the afternoon (cf. other *Lanius* which usually lay in the early morning). Pale bluish-green, seldom cream or buff, with spots and small blotches of olive or olive-brown and lavender-grey, mainly at broad end. ***Size*** 22.0–28.2 x 16.6–20.0 mm (25.2 x 18.2, n=125)[214, 257, 284, 285, 373, 728]. **Incubation** Starts on 4th or 5th egg, by ♀ only. ♂ feeds ♀ on and off the nest. Period 15–16 days (range 12–16)[181, 257, 284, 285, 728]. For nestling development see[728]. **Nestling** Hatch blind but not naked (cf. most other *Lanius*), with whitish down on either side of abdomen and on uppertail-coverts. Mouth is light orange and apparently lacks mouth spots. Brooded by ♀, fledging after 16–18 days (13–19). Fed by both sexes, including after fledging. Brood division recorded irregularly, with each parent attending to specific young, who are independent *c*.14–20 days after fledging, although they may remain with parents for at least 8 weeks[257, 284, 285, 373, 728, 789]. **Predation and longevity** Predated on passage in S Aegean by Eleonora's Falcon *F. eleonorae*[257]. **Brood parasite** Rarely parasitised by Common Cuckoo *Cuculus canorus*[675].

MEASUREMENTS and WEIGHTS *L. m. minor* ♂ (26) wing 114–126 (119.3 ±SD 2.84), ♂ (20) tail 84–94 (88.6 ±SD 3.02), ♂ (20) bill (to skull) 19.1–22.5 (21.0 ±SD 1.10), ♂ (18) tarsus 24.1–26.4 (25.3 ±SD 0.69), difference between sexes not significant[257]. **Weight** Breeding grounds; Apr–May ♂ (7) 43–54.4 g (45.9), ♀ (5) 42–55 g (47.2)[257]; non-breeding grounds ♂♀? (33) 28.6–62.9 g (47.5)[48]. For additional data see[214, 257, 319, 478].

11 MACKINNON'S FISCAL (Mackinnon's Shrike)
Lanius mackinnoni — Plate 6

FIELD IDENTIFICATION Medium-sized (20 cm) grey, black and white shrike with grey head and back, black face-mask with contrasting white eyebrow, white scapulars and black wings with no white patch. Tail black with outer feathers tipped white. Sexes different; below white, ♀ with dark rufous flanks, usually concealed by wing. Young barred greyish-brown above with poorly defined pale eyebrow and scapulars, below barred dull white. Little known; calls harsh, rattling with warbling song. Solitary, found in forest edge and clearings and associated woodland. Resident on fringe of Central African tropical forests from SE Nigeria to N Angola, and N of forests eastwards to Kenya, south to Burundi and SE Zaïre. ***Flight characteristics***: Flight rapid and low, swooping up to perch. White V-shaped scapulars conspicuous. Wings black with no white patch in primaries.

COMPARISONS Resembles the larger Grey-backed Fiscal *Lanius excubitoroides* and migrant Lesser Grey Shrike *L. minor*, but Mackinnon's lacks broad black frontal and face-mask and white wing-patch, and has conspicuous white scapulars. Overlaps widely with similar Common Fiscal *L. collaris*, but is ecologically segregated where found together, Mackinnon's Fiscal in denser woodland and forest edge, Common Fiscal in more open habitats. Latter lacks the white eyebrow of Mackinnon's and has black upperparts and a white wing-patch. Juveniles similar but lack of white wing-patch separates the two species.

DESCRIPTION ADULT ♂ ***Head*** Forehead, crown and nape sooty-grey with white above bill which extends as an eyebrow to behind the eye; black of lores extend through eye (below only) to ear-coverts. ***Back*** Mantle and back sooty-grey, rump and uppertail-coverts lighter grey; scapulars white. ***Wings*** Black, without a white wing-patch, coverts and tertials black; ulna region white. ***Tail*** blackish-brown with white terminal spots on all feathers except central two. ***Underparts*** Whitish to dull white. ***Bare parts*** Bill and legs black; palate unknown; eye dark brown. **ADULT ♀** Like ♂ but with rufous or chestnut-brown flanks. **JUVENILE/IMMATURE** Upperparts greyish-brown with fine barring on buffy-brown, rump barred; face-mask brownish-black with pale, poorly defined eyebrow; scapulars white tipped buff with dark subterminal bar; wing-coverts tipped buff; tail brownish-black with dull white terminal spots; underparts greyish-white with dark crescent barring from chin to undertail-coverts and no rufous flanks. Bill paler than adult, eye grey-brown, legs slate-grey[646].

GEOGRAPHICAL VARIATION None. Monotypic.

MOULT Little known. Full moult in Aug, tail moult Jan–Mar (Ruwenzori Mts)[930].

RANGE, HABITAT and STATUS **Breeding range** SE Nigeria, S Cameroon, Equatorial Guinea, Gabon, N and S Congo, N, E and S Zaïre, Rwanda, Burundi, SW Uganda, W Kenya, NW Tanzania and NW Angola. Limits of range in S Zaïre not well known; appears fragmented. **Habitat** Forest-savanna mosaic species which prefers forest edge and clearings (lowland and montane), secondary growth, coffee plantations and woodland. Also found in wooded and bushed grassland, pastures, villages and gardens. Found from sea-level up to 3200 m in Ruwenzori Mts[7, 21, 37, 290, 295, 318, 431, 481, 504, 631, 865, 907, 930]. **Status** Resident, locally common to uncommon in far E of range. **Conservation status** Unknown. Deforestation within its range is known to occur, but effect unknown. Deforestation may be beneficial as it produces more secondary growth. Basic research and population surveys recommended[369, 675].

MOVEMENTS Unknown, probably sedentary.

SOCIAL ORGANISATION and GENERAL BEHAVIOUR Little known. Solitary or in pairs. Generally perches relatively low and unobtrusively on a bush or low branch at edge of forest or in clearings. Territories vary from 1–6 ha depending on bush density[22, 294, 504, 754]. **Foraging behaviour** Hunts from exposed perches *c.*2–5 m above the ground. Takes most prey on the ground, also some from foliage and in the air. Observed following swarming ants. Impales prey and forms caches. **Food** Arthropods, mainly insects and small vertebrates. Insects include Coleoptera (beetles), Orthoptera (grasshoppers), Lepidoptera (caterpillars), Hemiptera (bugs), Hymenoptera (ants *Dorylus*) and Isoptera (termites). Also takes small vertebrates, of which frogs, geckos, small birds and nestlings have been recorded[2, 15, 290, 294, 445, 675, 764].

SOUNDS Little known. Repertoire consists of harsh sounds, low musical warbler-like song and prolonged whistles. From recordings, territorial call probably a repeated *tzree-tzree-*, *bzrrre-bzrrre-* or *zrrre-zrrre-*. Also has a distinctive repeated stuttering phrase, more musical with clear strident notes, variable and sounding like *tuk-weez-wekiti* or *chickarea* or *chik-erea*. Function of this call unknown. Song combines hoarse *chruu* calls with stuttering, rich and variable warbler-like notes which include much mimicry. Alarm call a harsh chatter or rattling *ra-a-a-*, *zik-zik-* or *k-k-k-k-k-*, but also reported as a prolonged whistle. A repeated *cha-cha-cha-cha-* probably has a similar function. Begging call a repeated low plaintive *churr- churr.* Young heard to give this call continuously as they accompanied their parents[22, 338, 500, 631, 754].

BREEDING BIOLOGY Little known. Monogamous, territorial and pugnacious during breeding. Second clutches regularly laid[294]. **Season** Breeding condition Mar, fledglings and juvenile Apr, May (Angola)[7, 865, 907, 909]; Sep–Apr (Cameroon)[37, 338, 347]; displays and egg-laying Aug–Apr, dependent fledglings till May–Jun (Gabon)[294, 295]; nest-building Apr–Aug, fledged young May–Sep (NE Zaïre), Jun–Oct, Jan (SE Zaïre)[22, 290, 338, 688]; Feb–Aug (Kenya and central S Uganda)[293]. **Displays** ♂ with puffed-out plumage bows to ♀ after each song phrase[754]. **Nest** Role of sexes unknown. Bulky cup built of dry grass, rootlets, shredded bark, weed-stalks and lined with finer fibres. One nest had maize 'silk'. Placed *c.*3 m above the ground, generally in a thorny bush or small tree. ***Size*** OD 110 mm, ID 66 mm, cup depth 50 mm, height 75 mm[2, 25, 646, 675]. **Eggs** Usually 3 (2–3). Buff or cream speckled and spotted with yellowish-brown and various shades of grey and purple. ***Size*** *c.*23–23.5 x 17.5–18 mm[25, 34, 290, 338, 646, 688]. **Incubation** Apparently by both sexes. Period unknown[34]. No further breeding information.

MEASUREMENTS and WEIGHTS *L. mackinnoni* ♂♀? (7) wing 87–91 (88.7), tail 97–108 (102.0), bill (to skull) 20–21.4 (20.8), tarsus 21.5–25 (23.8)[500]; ♂ (4) wing 85–89 (87.5), tail 109–113 (110.8), bill 15–16 (15.5), tarsus 23–24 (23.8)[492]. **Weight** ♂♀? (5) 35.6–37 g (36.2)[457, 500]; ♂♀? (3) 34–37 g (Uganda)[764]; ♂♀? (3) 35 g each (Uganda)[765]. For additional data see[290].

FIELD IDENTIFICATION Very large (about 27 cm), robust black and white shrike, with black head, dark grey back and conspicuous white rump, black wings with white patch and long black tail. Sexes different; below white, ♀ with rufous flank-patch, usually concealed by wing. Young finely barred greyish-brown above, barred dirty white below with rufous flanks. Flight rather slow and heavy. Main calls, often in chorus, harsh chattering and scolding notes and whistles. Conspicuous and noisy, gregarious, usually in parties of *c*.4–5 birds. Resident in bush and wooded areas of East Africa in S Somalia, SE Kenya and NE Tanzania. ***Flight characteristics***: Rather slow and heavy with fast wingbeats. White rump conspicuous.

COMPARISONS Similar in size and gregarious behaviour to Grey-backed Fiscal *Lanius excubitoroides* but Long-tailed is mainly black not grey. Resembles Common Fiscal *L. collaris*, but is larger with a broader longer tail, and lacks conspicuous white V-shaped scapulars and broad white edges on tail. Juvenile differs from juvenile of this fiscal by lack of buff-edged whitish scapulars, and from Grey-backed Fiscal by lack of broad white patch in tail.

DESCRIPTION **ADULT ♂** ***Head* and nape** Black with indistinct face-mask. ***Back and mantle*** Dull greyish-black; rump and uppertail-coverts whitish-grey, coverts sometimes with dark terminal barring. ***Wings*** blackish-brown with conspicuous white patch in primaries, secondaries with narrow whitish edging. ***Tail*** Graduated, black with outer feathers faintly narrowly edged and tipped whitish, but black from below. ***Underparts*** White. ***Bare parts*** Bill and legs black; palate unknown; eye dark brown. **ADULT ♀** Similar to ♂ but with small dark rufous or chestnut-brown patch on flanks. **JUVENILE/IMMATURE** Face-mask brownish-black; upperparts greyish-brown finely barred buff; rump and uppertail-coverts buffy-white, heavily barred; primaries black, secondaries and wing-coverts edged buff, wing-patch white; tail brownish-black, narrowly tipped buff; underparts whitish with barring on breast; flanks tinged with pale rufous in both sexes. Bill blackish grey-brown.

GEOGRAPHICAL VARIATION None, Monotypic.

MOULT little known. Post-juvenile and post-breeding moult recorded in Aug (East Africa). Wing-coverts are the last feathers to moult into adult plumage[500].

RANGE, HABITAT and STATUS **Breeding range** S Somalia, central and SE Kenya and NE Tanzania to Dar es Salaam. **Habitat** Dry savanna, thorn scrub, bushed grassland, open woodland and edge of cultivation from sea-level to 1600 m[25, 46, 318, 325, 237, 431, 481, 631, 675, 859]. **Status** Common resident. **Conservation status** Unknown. Habitat probably not threatened, but survey recommended. Poisoning recorded during avicide spraying of Red-billed Quelea *Quelea quelea*. Held in captivity[369, 655, 1062].

MOVEMENTS Little known. Generally thought to be resident, but with a few records S of known breeding range suggesting some movements.

SOCIAL ORGANISATION and GENERAL BEHAVIOUR Little known. Gregarious, conspicuous and noisy. Social organisation of groups unknown, but probably consist of family members. Solitary or often in small groups of 2–6. Individual birds perch in a prominent position with upright posture. In groups, birds perch close together excitedly waving tails about and chattering noisily. Group territorial displays take the form of posturing with the body held upright, wings down or slightly open, and the long tail swinging in all directions, up and down, side-to-side, or in a figure of eight, then over the back and fanned. Forward-and-back body-rocking and head-down postures are thought to also occur. These movements are accompanied by noisy chattering and whistles. The display occurs throughout the year. ♀ rufous flanks are exposed in this display[2, 46, 357]. **Foraging behaviour** Hunts from a prominent perch *c*.2 m high and takes most of its prey on the ground. Some prey gleaned from foliage, but rarely takes aerial prey. Apparently impales prey and forms caches. It has been reported associating with a group of Red-billed Buffalo Weavers *Bubalornis niger* in a mutualistic relationship, the shrike benefiting from the insects flushed, the weavers from the shrike's vigilance and alarm calls[9, 352, 551, 675]. **Food** Arthropods, mainly insects and small vertebrates. Insects include Coleoptera (beetles) and Orthoptera (grasshoppers). Vertebrate prey includes lizards, snakes and small birds. Has also been recorded eating fruit (*Salvadora persica*), bread and cheese[9, 46, 352, 392, 1062].

SOUNDS Little known. Repertoire consist of harsh chattering or scolding notes, buzzy whistles and almost bell-like tinkling sounds. Call quality recalls helmet-shrike or starling. Structure of phrases recall Grey-backed Fiscal and *Corvinella*, with some repeated phrases reminiscent of very fast Taita Fiscal *L. dorsalis* phrase. Notes are combined in repeated phrases which are given simultaneously by 2–6 members of a group in duet and chorusing. Calling is characterised by much body, wing and tail movement. A chorus appears to be initiated by one bird with *cha-cha-raa*, to which another bird responds with *chit-er-row, chit-er-row*, both calling together. A commonly heard 3-note phrase combines harsh stem-sounds with whistled endings: *zzreele-tzzrulu-tzzreele*. Other harsh calls include a low in-drawn *chaak-*, *tzzzr*, a cackling *ae-ae* and a more musical repeated *kech-wa*. Alarm call a repeated harsh rasping *kerrr-kerrr-kerrr-* recalling Common Fiscal. Begging call a quavering nasal *naaae-naaae-*[9, 46, 500, 769].

BREEDING BIOLOGY Little known. Possibly cooperative, but no evidence; only pairs have been reported at nests. Their visual and vocal displays, combined with their gregarious gatherings, are similar to other cooperative-breeding shrikes, particularly Grey-backed Fiscal and Magpie Shrike *Corvinella melanoleuca*. Reportedly breeds in pairs, each holding a separate territory and congregating in the evening in groups of 4–6 birds[46, 52, 205]. **Season** Estimated laying dates Apr, May, Sep (n=4), breeding May–Jun (Somalia)[237, 859]; Jan–May, Aug–Oct, Dec (Kenya)[293]; Jan, Jun (Tanzania)[25, 237, 734]. **Displays** Little known. See General Behaviour. **Nest** Role of sexes unknown. A large cup is built of rootlets, sometimes exclusively, or with small twigs, bits of grass, bark fibre and lined with finer grass roots. Often spider web worked around the rim and sometimes as a felted mass in the bottom of the bowl. Placed 2–3 m (n=2) above the ground in a thick thorn tree on a horizontal fork or inclined branch. ***Size*** OD 127 x 114 mm, ID 102 x 89 mm, cup depth 38 mm[2, 25, 46]. **Eggs** Usually 3 (3–4). Pale olive to creamy-white, spotted and blotched variably with dark brown, yellowish- or purplish-brown, mainly round the large end. ***Size*** 23–26 x 19 mm[2, 25, 46, 859]. **Incubation** Begins with the first egg, but role of sexes unknown. Period 13–14 days[46]. **Nestling** Appearance unknown. Fledge after 16–18 days[46]. No further breeding information.

MEASUREMENTS and WEIGHTS *L. cabanisi* ♂♀? (7) wing 105–115 (110.7), tail 142–156 (152.1), bill (to skull) 23–27 (24.6), tarsus 30.5–34.5 (32.2)[500]. **Weight** ♂(1) 82 g[500]; ♂(1) 70 g, ♀(1) 69 g[509].

13 TAITA FISCAL (Teita Fiscal) *Lanius dorsalis* — Plate 6

FIELD IDENTIFICATION Medium-sized (21 cm) black and white shrike with a black head and white underparts, pale grey back with conspicuous white V-shaped scapulars, white rump and small white wing-patch. Black tail relatively short with white edge. White areas conspicuous in flight. Sexes different; ♀ with small rufous flank patches, usually concealed by wings. Young finely barred greyish-brown above, whitish with bars below. Little known; calls harsh and grating, also fluted whistles. Perches prominently, solitary. Resident in dry bushed grassland, thornbush and woodland in East Africa from SE Sudan, E Uganda, S Ethiopia, S Somalia to Kenya and NE Tanzania. ***Flight characteristics***: Wingbeats rapid, dropping down low to ground and swooping up to perch, white wing-patch and V of scapulars conspicuous. Long flights undulating, seldom high.

COMPARISONS Most likely to be confused with Somali Fiscal *Lanius somalicus* with which it overlaps in N range. Somali Fiscal is ecologically segregated in more arid regions. Taita Fiscal shows less white in wings (Somali has broad white tips to tertials and secondaries), and has a more robust bill and shorter tail with less white, which when closed and seen from below appears barred black-and-white (Somali Fiscal has a longer bill and excessive white on tail, which when closed and seen from below appears completely white). Somali ♀ lacks the rufous flanks of Taita ♀. Differs from Common Fiscal *L. collaris*, which occurs in moister habitats, by grey not black back. Juveniles of these three species difficult to separate; Common Fiscal generally more rufous above and below. Much larger Long-tailed Fiscal *L. cabanisi* lacks white scapulars and grey back, has all-black tail and is gregarious in moister habitats. Similarly, Grey-backed Fiscal *L. excubitoroides* is much larger, has grey head and back, and lacks white scapulars. Like the previous species it is gregarious and occurs in moister habitats. Range generally separate.

DESCRIPTION ADULT ♂ ***Head, crown and upper mantle*** Jet-black. ***Back*** Lower mantle pale grey, scapulars white, rump greyish-white. ***Wings*** Black with small basal white patch in primaries. ***Tail*** Graduated, black with outer feathers edged and tipped white, rest tipped white except central pair; uppertail-coverts whitish. ***Underparts*** White to dull white. ***Bare parts*** Bill and legs black; palate unknown; eye dark brown. ADULT ♀ Similar to ♂ but with small dark rufous or chestnut-brown flank-patch, usually concealed by wing. JUVENILE/IMMATURE Upperparts pale greyish-brown, finely barred black on head, neck and mantle, mantle becoming patchy black in older birds; face with brownish-black face-mask; scapulars not obvious, barred buffy-grey; rump barred greyish-buff. Wing-coverts, secondaries and tertials edged buffy-white; primaries dark brownish-black, white wing-patch conspicuous. Tail brownish-black, edges and tips buffy-white. Underparts dull white with some barring on breast and flanks. Bill grey-brown.

GEOGRAPHICAL VARIATION None. Monotypic.

MOULT Little known. Tail and wing moult Jun (Ethiopia)[237].

RANGE, HABITAT and STATUS **Breeding range** Not well known in N range; SE Sudan, S Ethiopia, S Somalia, NE Uganda, widespread in Kenya, except mainly central region and E highlands and NE Tanzania. **Habitat** Dry open bush, *Acacia* woodland and other dry open wooded habitats, from sea-level up to 1500 m[11, 239, 242, 292, 318, 325, 431, 481, 631, 859]. **Status** Common resident, less common in extreme S of range. **Conservation status** Unknown. Habitat probably not threatened. Basic biological and taxonomic research and population surveys recommended[369].

MOVEMENTS Little known. Few reports of local movements and birds in atypical habitat. At the turn of the century a 'great movement' was observed in S Somalia on the Juba River at Kismayo from May–Jul, suggesting post-breeding movements. In S of range recorded as a vagrant as far S as Dar es Salaam (Tanzania) and in the E at Kericho in moist atypical habitat (Kenya)[11, 237, 318, 336, 675].

SOCIAL ORGANISATION and GENERAL BEHAVIOUR Little known. Solitary, in pairs or family group, apparently shy and difficult to approach. Sits upright in a prominent position. General behaviour reportedly similar to Common Fiscal[1011]. **Foraging behaviour** Hunts from a prominent perch, in one study at 2.5m high, taking most prey on the ground. Also occasionally gleans from vegetation and takes aerial prey[352]. **Food** Arthropods, mainly insects and small vertebrates. Insects include Orthoptera (grasshoppers) and Lepidoptera (caterpillars). Also takes spiders in addition to small vertebrates, including lizards, snakes and rodents. Possibly takes nestlings in Red-billed Quelea *Quelea quelea* colonies[2, 352, 1011, 1062].

SOUNDS Little known. Repertoire apparently not unlike (East African) Common Fiscal, but quieter, with territorial call believed to be a flute-like whistle. However, known recordings do not support this; instead has short whistles and harsh buzzy notes combined with double *tzuptzup-* and corvid-like *klopklop-* or *wokwok-* and *tudil-* sounds to form a phrase, some variants sounding rather like Monotonous Lark *Mirafra passerina* e.g. *tzuptzup-bzzze-bzzze, wokwok-huuu, wukwuk-zzzer* or *tudil-zzeer* and *tcha-koko-wik*. This phrase is repeated many times. May give the harsh buzzy note repeatedly *bzzree-bzzree-buzzree-* or *zrrree...zrrree....* Whistled calls tend to have a bubbly quality. A descending display-flight with calls has also been recorded, but context unknown. Song described as low and chuckling or a quaint mixture of churrs, hollow sounds and tinkling note *chwaaa-pikereek-chrrrrrr-yoook-piker-chik...skyaaa-weeek-kiok-tiureek.* Alarm call a harsh grating churring sound[500, 631, 769, 879, 1011].

BREEDING BIOLOGY Little known. Apparently monogamous based on solitary habits and territorial behaviour. Breeding appears protracted and coincides with the rains. **Season** Mar–Jun, Dec–Jan (Kenya)[293, 675]; Jan, Jun (Tanzania)[293], May (Somalia)[859]. **Displays** A descending display-flight with calls may be related to courtship, but context unknown[879]. **Nest** Role of sexes unknown. Cup built of twigs and grass and placed in a thorn tree[336]. **Eggs** 3–4. Creamy or greyish-white, spotted and blotched with brown and grey mostly at the large end. ***Size*** *c.*23 x 14 mm[336, 859]. No further breeding information.

MEASUREMENTS and WEIGHTS *L. dorsalis* ♂♀? (8) wing 99–104 (102.1), tail 85–95 (91.2), bill (to skull) 21.0–23.2 (21.9), tarsus 25.0–28.5 (27.2)[500]; ♂ (2) wing 103–104, tail 90, bill 17.5–18, tarsus 28–28.5, ♀ (1) wing 94.5, tail 84.5, tarsus 26[237]; wing 94–106[336]. **Weight** ♂♀? (3) 45.5–55.0 g (49.5) (Somalia and Ethiopia)[870]; ♂ (1) 54 g, ♀ (1) 47 g[500].

14 SOMALI FISCAL *Lanius somalicus* — Plate 7

FIELD IDENTIFICATION Medium-sized (21 cm) black and white shrike with a jet-black head and white underparts, grey back with conspicuous white V-shaped scapulars, white rump, and much white in wings, with large white wing-patch and tips to secondary flight feathers. Tail black with extensive white outer feathers. Sexes similar. Young finely barred greyish-brown above, dirty white with little barring below. Flight distinctive due to extensive white areas. Little known; has harsh notes and short whistles; perches prominently, solitary. Resident in arid semi-desert regions of NE Africa, from SE Sudan, Ethiopia, N Kenya and Somalia. ***Flight characteristics***: Fast, drops down and flies low before swooping up to perch. White V-shaped scapulars, rump, tips of secondaries, tertials and tail feathers conspicuous. Longer flights undulating.

COMPARISONS Most similar to Taita Fiscal *Lanius dorsalis* with which it overlaps in S range. Taita Fiscal is ecologically segregated in denser, less arid regions. Somali Fiscal has tertials and secondaries broadly tipped white, a white rump and a longer tail with extensive white, which when closed and seen from below appears completely white (Taita has no white on secondaries, a greyish rump, a more robust bill and shorter tail with less white, which when closed and seen from below appears barred black-and-white). Similar to Common Fiscal *L. collaris*, particularly W race *smithii*, which lacks grey back and white on secondaries. Juveniles of these three fiscals are difficult to separate but Common Fiscal generally more rufous-coloured.

DESCRIPTION ADULT Sexes almost similar. ***Head,*** including crown and upper mantle Jet-black. ***Back*** Lower mantle pale grey, scapulars white, rump and uppertail-coverts white. ***Wings*** Black, primaries with large basal white patch, tertials and secondaries broadly tipped white. ***Tail*** Graduated, black with outer feathers completely white, others broadly tipped white except central pair. ***Underparts*** White. ***Bare parts*** Bill and legs black, palate unknown, eye brown. ADULT ♀ Like ♂ but with brownish ashy-grey, not black axillaries. Like ♂ lacks rufous on flanks[675].

JUVENILE/IMMATURE Upperparts pale greyish-brown; head and mantle unbarred, head and nape becoming patchy black in older birds; face with blackish-brown face-mask; scapulars, lower back, rump and uppertail-coverts barred brownish; tertials and wing-coverts barred and edged buff, white on secondaries less than adults and buffy-brown. Tail dark brown, outer feathers buff to dull white. Underparts dull white, throat white, breast finely barred pale greyish-brown. Bill grey-brown.

GEOGRAPHICAL VARIATION None. Monotypic.

MOULT Little known. Of 3 ♀♀ in late stage of moult Dec, Feb, at least 2 appear to be post-juvenile moult (Ethiopia)[237].

RANGE, HABITAT and STATUS **Breeding range** SE Sudan, SE, S and NE Ethiopia, Somalia except S, N Kenya. Vagrant to Djibouti. **Habitat** Open grassy plains, *Acacia* short-grass savannas, bushland including *Acacia–Commiphora* thornbush in arid regions and semi-deserts with little (*Acacia–Chrysopogon*) or no bush. Found from lowlands at sea-level up to 1570 m (Somalia)[11, 242, 292, 318, 325, 431, 631, 859]. **Status** Common to thinly distributed uncommon resident. **Conservation status** Unknown. Status of birds in Sudan require confirmation. Habitat probably not threatened. Basic biological and taxonomic research and population surveys recommended[369].

MOVEMENTS Little known. Possibly some local movements as birds occasionally wander S of breeding range in Kenya; recorded from Baringo, Wamba and Menti Districts. Records from SE Sudan and Djibouti (Mar) may be similar[631, 675].

SOCIAL ORGANISATION and GENERAL BEHAVIOUR Little known. General behaviour similar to Taita Fiscal. Usually solitary, perches prominently, exposed on top of bushes, trees or telephone wires[33, 631]. **Foraging behaviour** Hunts from exposed perches on top of bushes or on the outside edge of trees. Takes prey on the ground[33]. **Food** Arthropods, mainly insects and small vertebrates. Recorded prey includes large insects such as Coleoptera (beetles), Orthoptera (grasshoppers) and Mantodea (mantises). Also takes small birds. Often impales prey and forms caches[33].

SOUNDS Little known. Song consists of short phrases, rather complicated and variable, formed of initial buzzy notes followed by rapidly repeated more musical series, the two parts forming a distinctive phrase, of which a common form is *burer-er...lit-it-it* or *tchechetcher-brr-we-weet*. Also heard is an unmusical *thring-thring* call. Its presumed alarm call is a low churring note[336, 500, 558, 631].

BREEDING BIOLOGY Little known. Monogamous and territorial. Particularly aggressive and pugnacious at breeding time. Breeding season is protracted and takes place during the summer rains. **Season** Mar, May–Aug, Nov (Ethiopia)[292]; Jan–Jul, Nov–Dec (Somalia)[33, 859, 933]; May, Nov (Kenya and NE Tanzania)[293]. **Displays** Unknown. **Nest** Role of sexes unknown. Open shallow cup built of fine grass and fibrous material, supported by thorn twigs and lined with rootlets or finer material. Placed at 1–7 m, low down in a bush or higher in the centre of a thorn tree. ***Size*** OD 114 mm, ID 64 mm, height 50 mm[33, 336, 558]. **Eggs** 3–4. Creamy, sometimes greenish-white to dull yellowish-white with pale brown and pale grey spots forming a zone around one end. ***Size*** Av. 26.2 x 19 mm (n=12), commonest size 25 x 19 mm[33, 336, 859]. No further breeding information.

MEASUREMENTS and WEIGHTS *L. somalicus* ♂♀? (5) wing 95–108 (100.0), tail 88–107 (97.6), bill (to skull) 20.6–22.0 (21.4), tarsus 24.5–26.5 (25.9)[500]; ♂ (2) wing 99–108, tail 94–106, bill 15–16, tarsus 26.5–27; ♀ (3) wing 95.5–103 (99.8), tail 93.5–99 (96.2), bill 16, tarsus 26–27[237]. **Weight** ♂ (2) 40 g, 48 g[583]; ♀ (1) 48 g[500].

15 COMMON FISCAL (Fiscal Shrike, Butcher Bird)
Lanius collaris — Plate 7

FIELD IDENTIFICATION Medium-large (21–23 cm) black-and-white shrike with a black head and back contrasting with distinctive white V-shaped scapulars, white wing-patch and long thin tail with white outer feathers. May show a white eyebrow. Sexes different; below white, ♀ usually with rufous flanks. Young dull brownish, barred above and below. Pied plumage distinctive in flight. Calls harsh and grating with whistles and warbling song. Solitary, conspicuous, noisy and pugnacious. Resident in a wide range of wooded savannas and urban areas throughout most of sub-Saharan Africa. ***Flight characteristics***: rapid and powerful; drops down and flies low with swoop up to perch. Undulating over long distances; sometimes hovers briefly. Pied plumage with white of V-shaped scapulars, wing-patch and tail conspicuous in flight.

COMPARISONS In East Africa most similar to Taita Fiscal *Lanius dorsalis*, which occurs in more arid habitats and has a grey back (black in Common Fiscal). Also similar to Somali Fiscal *L. somalicus* which has a grey back and much more white in wings, particularly on secondaries. Where Common Fiscal overlaps these species it is ecologically segregated, occurring in moister habitat. Also resembles the much larger Long-tailed Fiscal *L. cabanisi*, which has a much longer, heavier tail and dark greyish back, lacks white scapulars and is a gregarious species which occurs in moister habitats. Separation of juveniles more difficult. Juvenile Common Fiscal more rufous than juvenile Taita and Somali Fiscals. Juvenile also similar to juvenile Souza's Shrike *L. souzae*, which is smaller and greyer with very thin tail and different barring. Also similar to juvenile Mackinnon's Fiscal *L. mackinnoni*, but distinguished by presence of wing-patch. In southern Africa superficially resembles Fiscal Flycatcher *Sigelus silens*, but is larger and more robust with a heavy hooked bill and white outer tail feathers (flycatcher has rectangular white panels in tail).

DESCRIPTION **ADULT ♂** ***Head,* crown and upper mantle** Jet-black. ***Back*** Lower mantle greyish-black, scapulars white, rump greyish-white. ***Wings*** Black with white patch on base of primaries. ***Tail*** Graduated, black with outer feathers almost completely white, rest tipped white except central pair (*humeralis* differs, see Geographical Variation); uppertail-coverts grey to whitish-grey. ***Underparts*** Variable from dull white to tinged grey with fine barring (vermiculations). ***Bare parts*** Bill and legs black; palate flesh-coloured; eye dark brown. ***Size*** Nominate similar to ♀, *humeralis* ♂ larger than ♀ (see Measurements). **ADULT ♀** Like ♂ but duller greyish-brown upperparts and always rufous to chestnut-brown patch on flanks (variable or lacking in some races; See Geographical variation). Flank-patch can be concealed or exposed. ***Abnormal plumage*** Partial albinos reported. **JUVENILE/IMMATURE** Nominate *collaris*, *predator* and *subcoronatus* (S group) have upperparts pale brownish-grey with fine buffy barring on head, back and rump; ear-coverts brownish-black (eyebrow buff in *subcoronatus*); wings dark brown, coverts barred and tipped buffy-brown, ulna white, wing-patch dull white, tertials buff-edged, small scapulars whitish with buffy and blackish-brown mottling; underparts buffy-white finely barred (vermiculated) greyish-brown; flanks slightly rufous in both sexes, may be retained for up to 18 months; *marwitzi* described as darker and much more heavily barred below; *smithii* and *humeralis* (N group) have upperparts rufous-brown, densely barred blackish, including on whitish scapulars; ear-coverts blackish-brown; wings and coverts rufous-brown with distinct subterminal black bar; wing-patch dull white; underparts whitish to buffy-white coarsely barred dusky blackish-brown, sometimes appearing mottled. 1st-year individuals in both groups can be identified by the presence of buff-tipped primary coverts (see Moult)[32, 205, 237, 336, 500, 504, 631].

GEOGRAPHICAL VARIATION Traditionally at least 10 races; morphological variation often rather slight with much intergrading. Races described on one or a combination of body size, coloration of upper- and underparts, extent of white on tail, length and extent of gradation of tail and presence or absence of rufous flank-patch in ♀, or white eyebrow in both sexes. Variation complex and limits of races not well known. Recent work suggests probably more than one species involved. Race *smithii* (West Africa from Sierra Leone to SW Sudan and W Uganda, including Angola at Cabinda) has upperparts glossy black, underparts snowy-white, tail similar to S populations, rufous flanks on ♀ small, sometimes absent; *humeralis* (NE and E from Eritrea, E Sudan, Ethiopia, Kenya, N Tanzania) has upperparts generally duller black, underparts dull white with rufous flank-patch in ♀, tail long, narrow and more graduated with completely white outer feathers; whistle calls differ from S populations (see below and Sounds). SW of this is *capelli* (including *dominator* Angola, N Namibia, Congo, S Zaïre, Zambia, Malawi and probably S and E Tanzania), similar to previous race, tail also long and narrow but with less white, underparts lack rufous flank-patch in ♀; this S central population occurs mainly in *Brachystegia* woodland. S of this is *predator* (formerly *pyrrhostictus*, Zimbabwe, W Mozambique, NE and E South Africa and Swaziland) upperparts deep sooty-black, underparts dull white with rufous flank-patches in ♀, tail broad and short. South of this is nominate *collaris* (including *vigilans*, S, central and E South Africa, Lesotho, S Namibia) upperparts slate-black, underparts dirty white, sometimes tinged greyish with fine flecking (vermiculated), tail short and broad, ♀ flanks rufous. Two other races with rufous flanks have distinctive white eyebrows, and both intergrade to varying degrees with contiguous races. In arid SW *subcoronatus* (including *aridicolus* N and E South Africa, Namibia, S Angola, Botswana) shows widespread integration. The other white-browed race *marwitzi* (central SW Tanzania on high ground from Mpwapwa and Ukaguru to Njombe and mountains N of Lake Malawi like Mt Rungwe) similar to previous race but darker upperparts and grey rump. Shows little intergrading, although intermediates have been seen in NE Zambia and as far S as Nyika in Malawi. Variation in vocalisations presents a different picture. At least two groups emerge, namely a N and S group. Northern group includes *humeralis* from Ethiopia to N Tanzania. This group probably also includes *smithii*, but few vocalisations are known from this race. Southern group includes *capelli*, *predator*, *subcoronatus* and *collaris*. The exact boundary between these two vocally distinct populations appears to be at *c.*5°S in central Tanzania. Vocalisations of *marwitzi* are unknown, but are predicted to be similar to the S group (see Sounds). This separation is also largely supported on juvenile plumage. Northern group are distinctly rufous-coloured, more heavily barred above and below, sometimes appearing mottled. This contrasts with the mainly greyish-brown, finely barred upper- and underparts of the S group[25, 32, 46, 168, 173, 174, 192, 205, 206, 237, 268, 291, 299, 402, 413, 425, 500, 504, 545, 557, 558, 568, 610, 631, 675, 785, 929, 987, 1008, 1012].

MOULT Post-juvenile moult takes place at about the same time as adult moult. In South Africa (*predator*) and West Africa (*smithii*) it begins between *c.*2–3 months of age and is completed by *c.*4–6 months. In one study in South Africa, wing and tail moult took place from Feb–Jun, with body moult recorded from Jan–Jun. 1st-year birds retained buff-tipped primary wing-coverts and sometimes rufous flanks for up to *c.*18 months. In East Africa (*humeralis*) post-juvenile moult begins at *c.*3 months of age and is reputed to be completed within about a month. Adults undergo a complete post-breeding moult. Moult of flight feathers Aug–Dec (East Africa), Jun–Nov, Dec–Mar (West Africa), Jan (Tanzania), Jan–Apr (South Africa). In South Africa body moult is recorded for most of the year (Jan–Oct), with lowest frequency recorded over breeding period[152, 164, 172, 176, 205, 413, 500, 628, 675, 832].

RANGE, HABITAT and STATUS Breeding range widespread in sub-SaharaNorth Africa, with N boundary *c.*10°N, locally extending further N in Mali, Niger and Eritrea. In Guinea, Sierra Leone, Ivory Coast, Ghana, Togo, Benin, Cameroon, Nigeria, Gabon, Congo, Zaïre, Rwanda, Burundi, Mali, Burkina Faso, Niger, Central African Republic, Sudan, Ethiopia, Eritrea, Uganda, Kenya, Tanzania, Angola including Cabinda, Zambia, Malawi, Mozambique, Namibia, Botswana, Zimbabwe, South Africa, Swaziland and Lesotho. Vagrant to Mauritania as far N as *c.*15°N. Absent from forests and deserts. Absence from areas such as central Kalahari of Botswana and SW Zambia thought to be due to competition with other shrikes, such as Long-tailed Shrike *Corvinella melanoleuca* and particularly migrant Lesser Grey *L. minor* and Red-backed Shrikes *L. collurio*. **Habitat** Wide habitat tolerance, including semi-desert, open grassland with scattered bushes, trees, fences or telephone lines, *Acacia* savanna, bushy hillsides, edges of miombo *Brachystegia* and other woodlands, edge of plantations, and particularly farmlands, cultivated areas, urban gardens, parks and along roadsides. Generally absent from low-lying major river valleys such as Zambezi. In E Central and East Africa commoner in highland areas up to 3350 m. The distinctive white-browed *marwitzi* only occurs on highland plateaus at 2600–2900 m. All races require low ground cover with open spaces and adequate perch and nest sites[7, 21, 22, 23, 26, 30, 31, 37, 48, 101, 119, 234, 242, 290, 291, 292, 295, 318, 425, 431, 481, 639, 631, 675, 807, 819, 848, 858, 907, 945]. **Status** Widespread common resident; in East Africa commoner in highlands than at lower elevations. **Conservation status** Generally not threatened. Adapts well to agricultural areas and towns and has increased in abundance in most areas since the early 1900s. However, the taxonomic status of some races requires further investigation, particularly the N and S groups and *marwitzi*. Held in captivity[205, 369, 655, 929, 974].

MOVEMENTS Generally sedentary, but local seasonal movements recorded in some areas, for example probably an austral winter visitor into semi-arid areas of Botswana and Kenya. In southern Africa the furthest recovery of a ringed adult is 110 km. Most movements are within 20 km (n=45). A juvenile relocated 5 km away returned to release site 6 months later[318, 639, 678, 703, 807].

SOCIAL ORGANISATION and GENERAL BEHAVIOUR A solitary, pugnacious and conspicuous bird which perches out exposed with upright stance. White underparts conspicuous from a distance as it advertises its territory by static marking or loud calls. Generally confiding where associated with man. When disturbed flies to top of nearby tree. Pairs and unmated ♂♂ maintain territories throughout the year. Unmated ♀♀ appear to roam about and not defend specific areas for long periods. Territories vary in size depending on habitat, from *c.*0.5 ha in urban environments to *c.*13 ha in semi-arid areas. Density of perches has been shown to be important in determining territory size: the more perches the smaller the territory. When defending its territory, perches on one of the highest points and gives loud repeated harsh double-noted calls (S group). Sits upright with white scapulars expanded. When excited wags and swings tail, and at higher intensity bows body, flicks wings and switches from side to side. Neighbouring pairs often countersing, each matching the call of the other. In East Africa also seen to give harsh calls with wings outspread and quivering as well as long-drawn-out whistles (see Sounds). In aggressive situations, at low intensity adopts an upright posture with body and crown feathers erected, but at higher intensity feathers become sleeker and posture more horizontal, finally lunging forwards with bill open, making bill-snapping sounds in attack. Alarm call is often heard in response to intruders and predators. Conspecifics are chased out of the territory, after which the owner swings back into his own territory with wings and tail spread displaying the striking pied pattern. Physical contact is rare, but occasionally chases progress through adjacent territories, resulting in much alarm and territorial calling as other birds join the chase. Most pugnacious in early stages of breeding, and frequently chases any birds. Consequently has acquired a bad reputation with garden-bird lovers and cage-bird owners. Well-foliaged sites are chosen for roosts, where pairs roost separately, usually sleeping with the bill tucked into scapulars. Sunbathing has been recorded, as well as orientation of back towards the sun on cold mornings. They have been seen to bathe in dew-soaked foliage; scratches indirectly and pairs sometimes allopreen[5, 46, 48, 163, 164, 167, 169, 170, 172, 205, 413, 500, 675, 872, 878, 929, 991, 994].

Foraging behaviour Opportunistic, taking virtually anything it is able to overpower. Hunts from elevated perches, usually at 3–5 m (up to *c.*10 m), taking most prey on the ground within a radius of *c.*10–20 m, occasionally up to *c.*80 m. Sometimes hovers briefly before pouncing on prey. Hovers more frequently in habitats with long grass. Sometimes also hawks insects in the air like a flycatcher. Larger prey, e.g. grasshoppers and birds, are occasionally caught with the feet like a hawk. In poor weather will glean from branches and foliage or hop about on the ground in search of prey. Sometimes flushes prey by adopting an upright stance and flashing wings and tail open. Known to plunge-dive for tadpoles. Most small prey is consumed immediately, or when larger carried to a perch, usually in the bill but, if too large, in the feet. Large prey is usually impaled or wedged. Impales prey but does not have specific caches. Appears to use cached prey mainly in adverse weather when normal foraging is impossible. Prey may be held down or in the foot while being torn apart with the bill. Sometimes obtains prey by kleptoparasitism and occurs in a feeding association with large mammals (domestic and wild), sometimes perching on an animal's back.

Food Mainly arthropods, less frequently small vertebrates. Arthropod prey consists mainly of insects, including Coleoptera (beetles, weevils and toxic cantharid blister-beetles), Orthoptera (grasshoppers, crickets and mole-crickets), Lepidoptera (butterflies, moths and hairy and smooth caterpillars), Odonata (damselflies). To a lesser extent Hemiptera (bugs and cicadas), Hymenoptera (bumblebees and ants), Isoptera (termites) and Diptera (flies and their larvae). Also takes spiders, ticks, millipedes, scorpions, worms and occasionally crabs. Vertebrate prey includes rodents, reptiles (snakes, blindworms, lizards, geckos, chameleons and young tortoises), frogs and small birds, including nestlings. Rarely fish and bats. Occasionally feeds on carrion and small fruits, impaling figs. Known to feed on a wide variety of cooked or processed food like bread, meal, chicken bones, cheese and others. Regularly drinks water, particularly in austral winter[2, 5, 46, 48, 152, 171, 172, 176, 205, 628, 675, 739, 872, 917, 929, 990, 992, 994, 998, 999, 1005, 1006, 1007].

SOUNDS Sounds of N and S populations are presented separately. Generally vocalisations are graded in tone and repetition rate. Similar calls are used in different contexts with different meanings. southern Africa repertoire consists of at least 10 types of call and a song. Calls consist of harsh grating notes, whistles and mimicked sounds. The differences in repertoire of East African and southern African Fiscals suggests that they are probably separate species. In East African *humeralis*, territories are defended with repeated, drawn-out harsh *tcheeeer-tcheeeer, tweeeeer, ghreeee, cheee-iii* or *chii-uirr* calls. This population also has a distinctive drawn-out whistle call, with no equivalent in southern African populations, frequently used during breeding season. The exact function of this call is unknown, with conflicting reports. Here thought to be an advertising call, delivered as mono- or disyllabic notes. Call variable from piercing to plaintive drawn-out whistle, which varies in pitch and is given in series of single, double or 3-note phrases, sounding like *tuuooooooo-, tuuuuuuu- or tuuuuweet-tuuuuweet* and *tweeeeeer-tweeeeeer.* Also described as *tuu-li-uu, tu-liii, chuu-liii* or *tee-wee-teewee.* Call given by both sexes, and often heard in countersinging between adjacent pairs. It may be delivered up to 24 times/minute over a 15-minute period. Aggression and alarm signalled by repeated harsh *keeer-keeer-* or *churrr-* calls. Contact maintained with *tchaa tchaa-* calls. Begging calls are quavering nasal *naaae-* sounds. Song consists of subdued warbling. Calls of West African *smithii* are little known, but published and unpublished descriptions suggest this population has similar calls, although possibly less vocal than the East African population[46, 299, 338, 413, 455, 500, 517, 545, 557, 558, 631, 879, 880, 1033]. In southern Africa (*predator, capelli, collaris* and *subcoronatus*) the main territorial call is a loud repeated, usually disyllabic harsh *terjert* or *Jerjert* sound which is most commonly used by unpaired ♂♂. A discrete loud repeated lower-pitched *tjutju* or *Jujuut* call is only used by unpaired ♂♂ when attracting an unpaired ♀. Alarm is signalled by loud repeated harsh *Keer-Keer-, ghreee-,* or *Skez-Skez-* calls. Raptor alarm is a distinct *sqwark* associated with a dash for cover. Contact call consist of single or repeated *tchaa-* or disyllabic *ktchaa-* notes. These are used in many contexts, ranging from initial courtship, nest approach to apparent pair-bond maintenance in austral winter, when given in antiphonal duet. These calls are frequently combined with whistles, producing a repeated *ktch-ktch-* whistle phrase. This develops with the inclusion of progressively more complex whistles into the song. It consists of at least three phrases: (1) initial *tcha-* type sounds, followed by (2) *ktcha-* type sounds with a few simple whistles included, and finally by (3) complex, rapidly modulated whistles including mimicry. Repeated whistles are used by paired and unpaired birds, either as subdued subsong or in louder advertisement combined with other calls. Whistles form the main part of the nest-site display, being rapidly modulated with, trills and mimicked sounds (see Display). The calls of birds, mammals and some human sounds are mimicked, most of which appear to be learnt on the natal territory. Subsong is first heard from fledglings within a few days of leaving the nest, and consists of a subdued warbling interspersed with harsh notes. Begging calls consist of repeated, insistent, rather querulous nasal *naaae-* or *cheee-cheee-* sounds used by adults and young. Fledglings also make a quiet chortling *chip-chip* when hopping about or feeding. Calls of *marwitzi* unknown but probably similar to southern population[22, 48, 152, 205, 500, 872, 929]. Sonagram[48, 929].

BREEDING BIOLOGY Monogamous, highly territorial and pugnacious, particularly when eggs hatch, and will chase most small birds and may destroy nests of other species in the vicinity. ♂♂ show higher site-fidelity to their territory than ♀♀, with one record of a ♂ remaining on its territory for at least 5 years. Pairs have been known to remain together for at least 3 years. However, mate changes and pairs moving to a new territory are not uncommon. A report of two pairs nesting within *c.*4 m of each other and sharing a territory is highly unusual. In general main breeding season appears to be in response to rains. May attempt breeding in first year and most populations lay multiple broods. There is one record of two nests being built by a pair; ♀ apparently laid in both and incubated and raised chicks in one, the ♂ doing the same at the other nest. Occasional records of twice nodal clutch size are thought to be due to dumping by another ♀. In cases of multiple broods, young from first brood are tolerated and fed while adults attend to second brood. Pair-bonds are believed to be maintained by mutual courtship-feeding and repeated contact calls, which are often given in duet (antiphonally), particularly in austral winter. Highest breeding densities of *c.*1 pair/2 ha occur in urban environments. In one study adult survivorship was recorded at 39%, but thought probably also to include the influence of dispersal (Kenya). Nesting success has been recorded at 15–50%[5, 6, 46, 52, 151, 163, 164, 169, 172, 176, 179, 205, 237, 290, 355, 413, 500, 675, 732, 858, 872, 929, 994, 996].

Season West Africa: Mar–May (Guinea)[101]; Feb–May (Sierra Leone)[338]; Feb–Aug, courtship display Dec onwards, nest-building and copulation Feb, egg-laying Feb–Mar, fledglings Mar–Apr, immatures Apr–Sep (Liberia)[628, 858]; throughout the year except Nov, peak egg-laying Jan (Ghana)[172, 234]; mainly Mar–May, also Jul and Nov–Dec (Nigeria)[37]; East Africa: May–Jun (Sudan)[242]; Apr–Jul (Ethiopia)[292]; Central Africa: Jun–Feb, mainly Jun–Aug (S Zaïre), Jan–May (N Zaïre)[22, 290]; Aug–Nov (Angola)[423, 907]. East Africa Jan, Sep–Nov (Tanzania), Jan–Dec (Uganda/Kenya)[293]. *marwitzi* nest-building Dec (Tanzania)[832]; mainly Sep–Nov (Malawi)[119]; Oct–Nov (Mozambique)[26]; Jun–Dec, mainly Oct (Zambia)[291]; Apr–Jan, mainly Aug–Dec (Zimbabwe)[30]; all months except possibly Feb, mainly Aug–Dec (southern Africa)[48, 205, 320, 151, 172, 639]; Aug–Sep (Botswana)[807].

Displays ***Courtship*** Differs between N and S groups. In *humeralis*, posturing, ruffling of breast and head feathers, and a bolt-upright stance with wings just out from the body, while giving a *chii-ur* call. ♂ chases ♀ from bush to bush, then whistles *tuu-li-uu, tuu-li-uu, tu-liii*. In *predator* and other S group members, when an unmated ♂ sees a roaming ♀ he advertises with a specific loud repeated harsh disyllabic *Jujuut* call, causing other unmated ♂♂ to give same call; the call is followed by excited song. When the ♀ moves close enough, ♂ immediately begins searching for food and gives repeated *tcha-* contact calls. After cautiously offering food, both birds adopt an aggressive horizontal posture which may develop into alternate bowing and head-up displaying. Following courtship-feeding, ♂ immediately performs a low exaggerated zigzag display-flight through the territory with white wing-patches flashing and tail spread. This is repeated after each exchange. If ♀ responds positively, ♂ becomes more excited, with much contact-calling, display-flying and whistled mimicked song which eventually culminates in a nest-site display. Rufous flanks of ♀ have been shown experimentally to be an important sexual signal area[46, 163, 205, 929]. ***Nest-site display*** (S group) ♂ flies to an old nest site, or prospective site, crouches down and gyrates in this position with tail cocked vertically upwards and quivered. At the same time the head is held upright and twisted from side to side. Display is accompanied by calls that reach a climax of rapidly modulated whistles and mimicked sounds. Display may be terminated by ♀ courtship-feeding ♂. At a later stage ♂ may entice ♀ to a nest site with whistle calls and pieces of nesting material which are placed at the site[205, 872, 929, 994]. ***Pre-copulation*** In S group copulation may take place within a few days of ♀ arrival. She appears to solicit this with repeated begging calls, given in a crouched posture with wings loosely fluttered and exposing her rufous flanks and grey rump. Copulation is usually accompanied by courtship-feeding or presenting nesting material, with contact-calling by the ♂[163, 176, 205, 929].

Nest Final site selection apparently made by ♀. Built by both sexes, mainly ♀. The rather bulky cup is placed *c.*3 m (0.6–6, n=789) above the ground in a wide variety of trees, particularly thorn trees, and occasionally on artificial devices. A wide variety of materials are used, including twigs, stems, fibres, cocoons, leafy herbs like *Helichrysum* and man-made materials (e.g. string, rags and plastic). It is usually lined with rootlets and finer material. ♀ attends to shaping, lining and completion. ***Size*** OD 100–180 mm, ID 65–90 mm, cup depth 35–75 mm, height 65–120 mm. Built in 3–8 days[2, 46, 48, 151, 162, 163, 164, 169, 176, 205, 872].

Eggs Usually 3–4 (southern Africa 1–5, rarely 8, n=958), with smaller clutches near equator: 2–3 (1–3, n=15 Ghana). Colour variable, from cream to pale green, speckled with pale browns, yellowish-olive and greys, mainly in a ring around the large end. ***Size*** 19.6–28.5 x 15.6–19.9 mm (23.5 x 17.7, n=630) (southern Africa). Egg-laying may commence immediately after nest completion or be delayed for up to *c.*2 weeks. In a case of protracted laying, the nest was only used the following season. Sometimes 2–3 nests are built before successful laying takes place, the ♀ destroying the nest each time. Usually the same nest is used for multiple broods[19, 46, 48, 52, 151, 163, 164, 172, 175, 176, 205, 290, 338]. **Incubation** Begins on last or second last egg, usually only by ♀, but a few records of ♂ sitting. In one case, ♂ incubated a clutch for full term. Usually ♂ feed ♀ on and off nest. Period 15–17 days (14–19, southern Africa), 14–15 days (12–16, East Africa)[46, 48, 163, 164, 172, 176, 205, 872]. **Nestling** Hatch blind, naked with a few neossoptiles present on abdominal, caudal and alar tracts. Lack mouth spots. Usually brooded by ♀, but one case of ♂ brooding for full term. Fledge after *c.*19 days (17–21). Fledglings feed themselves by *c.*14 days and are independent *c.*25–50 days after fledging, remaining in their parental territory for *c.*4–5 months (southern Africa) or 5–7 months (East and West Africa)[27, 46, 48, 153, 163, 164, 172, 176, 205, 355, 357, 789]. For development of young see[152, 164]. **Predation and longevity** Various avian and terrestrial predators reported taking nest contents or killing adults or young. These include mongooses, domestic cats, diurnal raptors, owls, crows, bush-shrikes, monitor lizard and snakes. Bad weather and nest parasites, such as larvae of the blood-sucking fly *Passeromyia heterochaeta* are known to cause death of nestlings. Roadkills also account for many deaths. Longevity 7 years, 8 months and 27 days[205, 806, 872, 995, 1000, 1079]. **Brood parasite** Fiscals do not reject foreign white eggs. Both morphs of Jacobin Cuckoo *Oxylophus jacobinus* recorded at low levels of parasitism. Chases most cuckoo species and has been recorded feeding a fledgling Diederik Cuckoo *Chrysococcyx caprius*[151, 205, 353, 872].

MEASUREMENTS and WEIGHTS S group: *L. c. predator* ♂ (47) wing 84–101 (94.7); ♀ (37) 88–98 (92.5); tail 61–116 (101.2); ♂♀? (56) bill (to skull) 15–18 (16.4, tarsus 24–28.1 (26.1)(NE South Africa)[500]; N group: *humeralis* ♂♀? (17) wing 88–101 (93.4), tail 95–131 (118), bill 14–16 (15.2), tarsus 2.5–25.5 (24.1) (Ethiopia and Kenya)[237]; ♂ wing 95.3 ±0.4 (SE), ♀ 93 ±0.4 (SE) (n=78) (Kenya)[413]; *smithii* ♂ (4) wing 87.5–90 (88.6), tail 109–115 (113.3), bill 16–17 (16.4); ♀ (3) wing 86.5–88 (87.2), tail 106–112 (108), bill 16, 16.5 (Cameroon)[412]. **Weight** southern Africa races combined (S group) ♂ (84) 24.7–51 g (41.8), ♀ (69) 27.7–52 g (39.8)[205]. ♂♀? (107) 31–58 g (41.6)[48]; N group *humeralis* ♂ (10) mean 38.8 g ±SD 2.4, ♀ (10) 35.7 g ±1.3[176]; *smithii* ♂ (22) 27–39 g (34.1 ±SD 3.2). ♀ (44) 27–36 g (31.1 ±SD 1.7) (Liberia)[628]. For additional data see[48, 64, 259, 319, 412, 413, 478, 732, 907].

16 SÃO TOMÉ FISCAL (Newton's Fiscal) *Lanius newtoni* Plate 7

FIELD IDENTIFICATION Medium-sized (19–21 cm), glossy black skulking shrike, rather flycatcher-like, with yellowish underparts, indistinct yellowish V-shaped scapulars, and a stumpy black bill. Sexes apparently similar. Young barred brown above buff below. Little known. Flight weak. Best located on loud repetitive nasal call or harsh chattering alarm call. Solitary or in pairs, found below canopy in closed-canopy lowland primary forest. Resident endemic to São Tomé island in Gulf of Guinea. ***Flight characteristics***: Flies weakly.

COMPARISONS Distinctive, the only Fiscal on São Tomé. Similar in build to the mainland Common Fiscal *Lanius collaris* but less robust; black rump, yellow underparts and forest habitat distinctive. Wings sometimes show slight wing-patch, evident on closed wing. Whitish tips to closed tail gives a barred appearance from below.

DESCRIPTION **Adult** Sexes apparently similar. ***Upperparts*** Glossy black; scapulars yellowish. ***Wings*** Glossy black with very small or no white patch on primaries. ***Tail*** Black with pale greyish-white to white tips and edging on outer feathers, central two feathers completely black. ***Underparts*** Throat to belly yellowish-orange to lemon-yellow (colour fades to white in museum specimens); vent and undertail-coverts lemon-yellow. ***Bare parts*** Stumpy bill black with pale pink base; palate unknown; legs pale grey; eye brown[427, 500, 836]. For wing formula see[427]. **Juvenile** Birds seen in mid-Jan had brown, finely barred upperparts and tawny-yellowish barred underparts; throat yellowish and bill grey-brown[507]. **Immature** (museum specimens) Upperparts brownish-black, lacking gloss of adults; scapulars buffy-brown; wings blackish-brown, coverts tipped buff; tail blackish-brown, outer feathers tipped greyish-buff. Underparts buffy-brown to tawny-orange without barring[500, 675, 836].

GEOGRAPHICAL VARIATION None. Monotypic.

MOULT Unknown, except Jul adult had no moult[427].

RANGE, HABITAT and STATUS **Breeding range** São Tomé Island in Gulf of Guinea, West Africa. **Habitat** Below canopy and in open, boulder-strewn undergrowth of closed-canopy lowland primary rainforest at low- to mid-elevations, below *c.*700 m, and restricted to undisturbed virgin forest. Suggestions that it may prefer ridge areas require confirmation[432, 479, 507]. **Status** Rare endemic resident. **Conservation status** There are fewer than *c.*30 records of this species. Originally discovered by F. Newton in 1888 when he collected 6 specimens, one from São Miguel, three from the Rio Quija, one locality known as 'Zungui' and one unknown locality. The species was not seen for a further four decades until Correia collected 13 specimens in 1928, 12 in the Roca Jou and Rio Quija area, and one in the hills above the Rio Io Grande. There were no further sightings until 1990 when a bird was trapped in a dry tributary near the source of the Rio Xufexufe. Subsequently, several birds have been seen in the SW (Rio Xufexufe and Rio Quija valleys) and in more central E areas (Rio Ana Chaves and Rio Io Grande). Its population is thought to number in the hundreds. The rarity of this species remains baffling, and the future of the island's forests, particularly lowland forests, remain uncertain. This shrike would be seriously threatened by any loss of lowland primary rainforest. As the least-known and most threatened *Lanius* shrike in the world it is in urgent need of basic biological research and population surveys. Red Data Species now considered Critical[343, 369, 403, 427, 428, 466, 479].

MOVEMENTS Unknown, probably sedentary.

SOCIAL ORGANISATION and GENERAL BEHAVIOUR Little known. Solitary, quiet and inconspicuous. Although relatively tame, it is difficult to locate unless calling. Perches below the canopy from *c.*2–5m above the ground. It has a typical *Lanius* upright posture. When disturbed ascends into the lower canopy. Territories are thought to be relatively large[427, 432, 507]. **Foraging behaviour** Searches while perched below the canopy where it remains motionless for a few minutes before descending to the ground for prey. Also hops about on the ground and between boulders searching for prey. Also thought to skulk about in low bushes and has been seen attempting to hawk insects in the air: an early collector described it as a 'yellow-bellied flycatcher'[432, 629]. **Food** Apparently insectivorous, once seen taking Coleoptera (beetles). Its relatively small weak bill with very small hook on tip of upper mandible suggests that it probably does not take small vertebrates[427, 432, 466].

SOUNDS Little known. Presumed territorial call a loud, rather nasal, monotonously repeated *juurt-juurt-juurt-*, *tuurt-tuurt-* or described as well-separated, fluted, far-carrying *tiu-tiu-tiu-tiu-* notes, sometimes repeated up to 250 times, delivered at *c.*1.25 notes/sec. A young bird has also been observed giving a repeated 3–4-note *tieu-tieu-tieu* similar to adult, but more nasal in quality. Presumed alarm call a rapidly delivered, harsh rasping *kerkerkerkerker-* or *kikikikikiki-* and rapidly repeated harsh *tzk-tzk-tzk-* or *tsink-tsink-tsink-*. Other sounds reported include a low squawk, and when being handled a scolding *churr*[427, 500, 507, 675].

BREEDING BIOLOGY Virtually unknown. Territorial, and observations of pairs and family groups suggest it is monogamous. **Season** Singing birds have been heard in Dec, Jan and Aug[675]; 2 ♂♂ with enlarged gonads Nov–Dec, and 2 ♀♀ showing traces of juvenile plumage in same months[343]; juveniles reported in Jan and Aug[507]. No further breeding information.

MEASUREMENTS and WEIGHTS *L. newtoni* ♂ (10) wing 91.5–96 (*c.*93), tail 110–117.5 (*c.*114), ♂ (7) bill 13–14.5 (13.8), ♂♀? (14) tarsus 23–26; ♀ (5) wing 87–96 (89.5), ♀ (2)[100, 115], ♀ (4) bill 12–13 (12.5)[675]; ♂♀? (9) wing 87–95 (92.2), tail 102–116 (111.0), bill (to skull) 17.2–20 (18.9), tarsus 21–25 (23.8)[500]. For additional data see[427]. **Weight** ♀ (1) 22.4 g[427]. Sexing criteria require confirmation[500].

17 MASKED SHRIKE (Nubian Shrike) *Lanius nubicus* Plate 8

FIELD IDENTIFICATION Medium-small (17–18 cm) slim, slightly built, black and white shrike with a small bill, rusty underparts and a conspicuous white forehead, eyebrow, scapulars and wing-patch, which contrasts with black upperparts. Sexes similar but ♀ duller and paler. Tail appears long. Young barred greyish-brown above, barred dull white below. Flight flycatcher-like, showing conspicuous black and white pattern. Gives short harsh notes and warbling song. Solitary or in family group, often skulking in light forest and well-wooded areas. Breeds in E Europe from Balkans to Israel, Iraq and Iran in Middle East. Migrates in boreal winter mostly to N of equator in sub-Saharan Africa, mainly in NE and SE Arabian Peninsula. ***Flight characteristics***: Light, flycatcher-like with conspicuous black and white pattern formed by white forehead, scapulars, wing-patch, tertials and outer tail feathers, which contrast against the completely black upperparts. Long flights generally not undulating.

COMPARISONS Adults distinctive with pale head and scapulars and dark rump. Most similar to Woodchat Shrike *Lanius senator*, but Masked slightly smaller and slimmer, with finer bill and longer tail. Juveniles more likely to be confused; Masked separated by more whitish face and more greyish (not sandy) barred upperparts with rump same as back (paler in Woodchat). Longer tail of Masked, which is often slightly cocked and waved up and down, helps separate young of these two species. In flight Masked shows larger white wing-patch[305, 747, 866].

DESCRIPTION ADULT ♂ ***Head*** Crown black; frontal and eyebrow white; face-mask formed by stripe through eye to ear-coverts. ***Back and rump*** Black; scapulars white. ***Wings*** Black with white patch at base of primaries; secondaries and tertials edged white, as are lesser and median-coverts; ulna area white. ***Tail*** Black with outer feathers edged white. ***Underparts*** Reddish-brown to rusty-rufous, darker on flanks; chin and throat paler; undertail-coverts white. ***Bare parts*** Bill and legs black; palate unknown; eye brown. ADULT ♀ Similar to ♂ but much paler, lacks the contrasting black and white of the ♂; frontal area dull white to buff; upperparts are brownish-black, scapulars whitish to buff; light areas on wing tinged buff; tail similar to ♂ but not as black; underparts off-white, less rusty and concentrated mainly on flanks. JUVENILE Lacks the contrasting head pattern of adults, with brownish face-mask with pale eyebrow and little white on forehead. Upperparts greyish-brown, barred (mottled) on head, back and rump. Wings dark brown with white wing-patch; coverts, secondaries and tertials edged buff. Underparts dull white and heavily barred. IMMATURE/FIRST-WINTER (boreal) Forehead, eyebrow and scapulars whitish; wings and tail similar to adult ♀; underparts greyish-brown to dull white with crescent barring. Lack rufous flanks. Bill and legs greyer than adult. See Moult for details of first-summer (boreal) plumage[866].

GEOGRAPHICAL VARIATION None. Monotypic.

MOULT Juvenile moult begins a few weeks after fledging, and involves head and body feathers, lesser and median-coverts and sometimes tertials. If not completed by the autumn migration, it is suspended and completed on the non-breeding grounds, where it intergrades with the moult into first-summer (boreal) plumage. This may be completed before the spring migration, but usually some juvenile feathers are retained (usually some primaries and their coverts). Old feathers are distinctly browner than the new black ones, less marked in duller ♀♀, but still making the identification of first-summer (boreal) birds possible. In adults a complete post-breeding moult starts on the breeding grounds, and if not completed, suspended and completed on the non-breeding grounds (Oct–Dec)[214, 257, 675, 814, 866].

RANGE, HABITAT and STATUS Breeding range not well known, particularly in the E. Found in Balkan countries, possibly in S Macedonia; NE Greece and some islands in E Aegean Sea, SW Bulgaria; also in W, S and SE Turkey, Cyprus, NW Syria, Lebanon, N, NW and central Israel, possibly NW Saudi Arabia. Further east in N Iraq and W Iran. Known also from Turkmenistan, where possibly accidental, but may represent NE limit of range, which may include NW Afghanistan. Vagrant from Mar–May in France, Spain, Turkmenistan, Malta, Algeria, Libya and Mauritania. Also in countries to the N of breeding range, such as Sweden and Finland in Oct[214, 216, 217, 218, 222, 257, 285, 305, 317, 377, 443, 480, 675, 746, 747, 787]. **Non-breeding range** In sub-Saharan Africa N of equator, mainly S to *c.*10°N in Ethiopia, Sudan, Chad. Recorded less frequently as a passage migrant or boreal winter visitor in E Mali, N Cameroon, N Nigeria, S Niger, Central African Republic, Zaïre, S Egypt, Eritrea, Djibouti, NW Somalia, N Kenya, Yemen, Saudi Arabia. Known to spend boreal winter in United Arab Emirates, as well as some birds remaining on their non-breeding grounds during breeding season, with suspected breeding in Sudan. See Movements. **Habitat *Breeding range*** In open park-like and hilly terrain, forest dominated by oak, pine and juniper, light forest with thorny undergrowth, scrub with scattered large trees, orchards, citrus and olive groves, cyprus, poplar plantations, cherry and apple orchards, vineyards and gardens. This shrike differs from most western Palearctic shrikes in being more arboreal and inhabiting areas of high tree cover. Found up to 2000 m (Turkey). ***Non-breeding range*** Also favours terrain with high tree cover, common in hot *Acacia* lowlands and riverine woodland, Sahel thornscrub near streams and sometimes in gluegum *Eucalyptus* plantations[21, 22, 36, 37, 216, 242, 246, 257, 290, 292, 305, 318, 325, 375, 376, 431, 504, 554, 631, 675, 787, 933]. **Status** Migrant, breeding status variable depending on locality. **Conservation status** In Europe populations are declining in Turkey and Greece, but showing a possible increase in Bulgaria. Status in non-breeding range virtually unknown. In Somalia, formerly known to be not uncommon, now rare. Population estimates (total or for pairs); 5,000–50,000 pairs (Turkey); 600–2,000 pairs (Greece); 2,000–4,000 (Cyprus); 50–100 pairs (Bulgaria). Little data for Middle East, but showed a widespread decline in Israel in 1950s and 1960s, apparently due to pesticides; in 1970s and 1980s population estimated at a few thousand breeding pairs. In Europe major threats include the disappearance of groves and individual large trees from traditional farmland, and the general degradation of these habitats. Decreased levels of grazing create denser ground cover and undergrowth, reducing feeding opportunities. Its occupation of plantations, which have replaced natural woodlands, is a recent adaptation and may be of long-term conservation benefit. In Turkey, the Middle East and Africa this shrike is shot during autumn migration (Aug). Also shot on breeding grounds in Syria and Greece, where locally considered a bird of ill-omen. Habitat preservation and legal protection from shooting urgently required. Monitoring of trends in breeding and non-breeding range and attempts to establish limits and status of E populations combined with implementation of conservation measures a priority. Provisionally considered Vulnerable[285, 369, 480, 675, 787, 859].

MOVEMENTS All populations are migratory, spending *c.*3 months each on breeding grounds, autumn migration, non-breeding grounds and spring migration. Believed to migrate (boreal autumn and spring) through E Mediterranean; however, it is much commoner in spring (Mar–Apr) in countries like Egypt, Jordan and Israel, suggesting a clock-wise migration route. Boreal autumn migration may begin as early as Jun, but main migration recorded from Aug–Sep when common in Iraq, Israel, the Arabian Peninsula and Egypt. Nov and Dec records from the breeding range are exceptional. Boreal spring migration may begin as early as Jan on non-breeding grounds, but main migration occurs Feb–Mar, in Arabian Peninsula mainly Feb–May, in Egypt Mar–Apr. Most birds are back on their breeding grounds in Apr, but arrivals are very protracted. Density at staging sites on migration can be very high, in excess of 100/day. Birds hold very small temporary territories (*c.*0.5 ha) at migration stopovers, and in general these territories are held for a shorter duration on the spring migration than in autumn. This species apparently concentrates more than other migrant shrikes[216, 257, 675, 939].

SOCIAL ORGANISATION and GENERAL BEHAVIOUR Usually solitary, relatively tame, but generally less conspicuous than other European shrikes as it tends not to perch out exposed, except at the start of breeding, when ♂♂ can be seen perching on top of trees and bushes, static marking or calling. Calls often accompanied by tail cocking and characteristic swinging of the tail sideways and up and down with U-shape movements. At other times it perches inside or low down on the edge of trees, bushes or in shrubs, *c.*2–6 m above the ground. It is generally more skulking and arboreal than other European shrikes. Advertises and defends a small breeding territory of 2–5 ha. Small territories of *c.*3 ha are also kept on non-breeding grounds. In this area calls are restricted to contact and alarm notes. It is aggressive towards own and other species, sometimes resulting in physical contact[257, 285, 394, 675]. **Foraging behaviour** Prey captured on the ground and within the crown of trees and inside bushes and shrubs, where it gleans from branches and leaves. It hunts for prey on the ground from perches on the edge or below the crown of trees and bushes, from where it drops or flies down to the ground, often hovering briefly before pouncing.

Often quite confiding, taking prey at an observer's feet. Also catches prey in the air like a flycatcher, and often impales prey. Uses the foot to hold prey. **Food** Arthropods, mainly insects and small vertebrates. Insects include Odonata (dragonflies), Orthoptera (crickets and grasshoppers), Lepidoptera (moths and caterpillars), Hymenoptera (ants) and Coleoptera (beetles). Also occasionally takes vertebrates like lizards and birds, including nestlings. Exhausted migrants probably form a major component of birds caught on passage, like records of the Lesser Whitethroats *Sylvia curruca* and even a Little Swift *Apus affinis*[214, 257, 675].

SOUNDS Little known. Repertoire consists of plaintive whistles and harsh calls. Main territorial call a short repeated harsh *tsr-* or *tzr-* note, also *krret, shek,* hoarse *kihr-* or subdued low *rad.* Others described as double *chek-chek, crrt-crrt* or *tset-set* notes. Alarm a rattling or scolding *krrrr* or *krrrt,* sometimes given as a double note *krrrr-krrrr.* When very aggressive snaps bill. ♀ gives a trembling begging call, while young give an insistent screeching, variable from a churring *skerr-skerr-skerr-* to a low grating *scirp-scirp.* ♂ song, given from an elevated perch, is a rather quiet but rich warble with chattering, jerky, scratchy notes, given in bursts of up to *c.*1 minute. Recalls *Hippolais* warblers, but apparently does not mimic[33, 225, 246, 257, 394, 500, 504, 631]. Sonagram[225, 257].

BREEDING BIOLOGY Little known. Monogamous and territorial. In Apr ♂♂ generally arrive a few days before ♀♀ and establish territories, initially creeping about in very upright posture. At this time they can be seen exposed on tops of trees and bushes advertising by calling and static marking, and generally relatively approachable at this time. Singing ♂♂ sometime countersing with neighbours and are frequently seen chasing each other. Nothing is known about courtship, except courtship-feeding recorded. Highest reported breeding density 2 nests 55m apart (Cyprus), 10 pairs along an 800 m edge of open oak *Quercus* forest (N Iraq), *c.*6 pairs/km^2 (Greece) and 2.3 pairs/km^2 (Israel). Replacement clutches frequent and two broods probably normal. Breeding success: of 13 nests, 10 failed due to predation, possibly by lizards (Cyprus)[218, 257, 285, 675]. **Season** Apr–May (Greece)[257]; Mar–Oct, mainly Apr–Jun (Cyprus)[218, 257]; Apr (Iran)[257]; Apr–Jul (Israel)[746]. **Displays** ***Courtship*** ♂ courtship-feeds ♀, who crouches down, begging in spread-wing posture. **Nest** Built by both sexes, ♂ sometimes more than ♀. Small, often inconspicuous, compact cup built of rootlets, bark strips, pine needles, plant down, plant stems, man-made material, and lined with wool, hair, rootlets and fine stems. Usually placed *c.*5 m (1.5–10) above the ground, either far out on a lateral branch, or against the trunk. Prefers deciduous trees for nesting, not necessarily thorny, but also uses conifers and mixed woods. ***Size*** OD 157 mm, ID 75 mm, cup depth 35 mm, height 60–70 mm (n=3). In replacement clutches, often demolishes old nest for material to build new one[214, 218, 257, 284, 285, 675, 787]. **Eggs** 3–7. Colour variable from creamy to pale buff or yellowish, rarely white or greenish-grey, with ring of pale to dark brown blotches towards broad end and large background blotches of pale and dark grey. ***Size*** 19.4–22.3 x 15.2–16.6 mm (20.7 x 16.0, n=40)[257]. For additional data see[214, 257, 284, 746]. **Incubation** Little known. Probably by ♀ only, ♂ thought to guard. Period 14–16 days[218, 257, 746]. **Nestling** Appearance unknown; attended by both sexes. Fledge after 18–20 days. Fledglings fed for at least a further 12 days. By 24 days brood ventured up to 800 m from the nest and independent *c.*25–30 days after fledging[257, 789]. **Predation and longevity** Crows and cats believed to prey on nestlings and young[257]. **Brood parasite** None.

MEASUREMENTS and WEIGHTS *L. nubicus* ♂ (48) wing 87–95 (90.7), (31) tail 83–92 (86.6), (51) bill (to skull) 16.7–19.9 (18.2), (18) tarsus 22.0–23.6 (22.7), differences in sex not significant[257]. **Weight** ♂♀? (16) 14.5–23.1 g (20.1) (Cyprus Mar–Apr), ♂♀? (11) 23–30 g (25.0) (Cyprus Jun–Aug)[257]; 21–26 g[216]; ♂♀? (23) 20–37 g (23.0) (N Chad)[257]. For additional data see[478].

18 WOODCHAT SHRIKE *Lanius senator* — Plate 8

FIELD IDENTIFICATION Medium-sized (19 cm) brown, black and white shrike with distinctive reddish-brown head and nape, black forehead and face-mask with white spots in front of eye, whitish rump and white V-shaped scapulars. Underparts white. Wing-patch white (absent in one race), conspicuous in flight. Sexes different; ♀ duller above with smaller face-mask. Gives harsh notes and warbling song with mimicry. Solitary, in pairs or family group, perches prominently, found in open woodland with scattered trees and orchards. Breeding migrant from W Europe in Mediterranean and S Central Europe to Balkans, Middle East, Iran and NW Africa. Migrates in boreal winters to N of equator in sub-Saharan Africa. ***Flight characteristics***: Similar to other *Lanius* but less undulating. Flies with rapid wingbeats, drops down low and swoops up to perch, displaying prominent white V-shaped scapulars, white in tail and wing-patch (except in one race).

COMPARISONS Adults distinctive. Young chestnut-buff birds resemble ♀ and young Red-backed Shrike *Lanius collurio,* but Woodchat somewhat larger and thickset, particularly about the head, less rufous-brown colour to upperparts which are whiter and greyer. Face-mask is more obvious, scapulars pale, dull buffy-white wing-patch (lacking in race *badius*), pale rump and shorter dark brown tail. Also noticeably bulkier than Masked Shrike *L. nubicus*, which appears darker above in flight, with a blackish not whitish rump, and is a slimmer, longer-tailed bird. Immature Masked generally greyer with larger wing-patch and pale forehead, which from about Sep begins to resemble adult. Immature Woodchat intermediate between immature Lesser Grey *L. minor* and Brown Shrike *L. cristatus*, but differs by being generally greyer, with finer bill, longer tail and paler forehead. Differs from juvenile Lesser Grey by smaller size, more heavily barred crown and back, less well developed rear face-mask, barred sides to throat, more contrasting pale scapular patch, smaller or no wing-patch (as in *badius*), less black wings and duller tail with narrower white edge. Immatures more barred than Isabelline Shrike *L. isabellinus*, with whitish shoulder-patches evident and darker face-mask[257, 747, 866].

DESCRIPTION **Adult ♂** ***Head*** Crown, nape and upper mantle rich chestnut-brown (paler in race *niloticus*), often with some white on forehead; lores white (producing two distinctive white spots on the head when viewed from the front); broad black frontal (variable) forms face-mask extending through eye (above and below) to ear-coverts and continuing to shoulder. ***Back*** Variable from black to greyish-black or dark brown; scapulars white; rump grey with whitish uppertail-coverts. ***Wings*** brownish-black with conspicuous white wing-patch at base of primaries (lacking or very small in *badius*); secondaries and tertials with whitish-buff edging. ***Tail*** Black with white outer feathers which have a large black spot two-thirds down on the inner web (white most extensive in *niloticus*), base of central feathers white. ***Underparts*** Buffy-white, darker on flanks; chin and throat whitish. ***Bare parts*** Bill and legs black; palate unknown; eye brown. **Adult ♀** Similar to ♂ but generally paler; also differs in narrower black face-mask with forehead and lores usually mottled. Back browner with variable dusky barring on breast and flanks (occasionally present on ♂). **Juvenile/Immature** Above rufous-buff to greyish-buff (particularly *niloticus*), finely barred black, brown and white on head and back, with reddish-brown tinge on nape and upper mantle, barring broader on buffy-white rump. Face-mask indistinct, darker on ear-coverts. Scapulars pale buffy-white. Wing-coverts edged buff and white; wing-patch buffy. Tail dark brown, outer feathers buffy-white. Underparts dull white with crescent barring, chin whitish. Bill paler, particularly at base of lower mandible, legs dull grey not black. See Moult for additional information on immature plumage[866].

GEOGRAPHICAL VARIATION Four races considered here, with variation based on plumage characteristics and wing length. White in tail increases towards SE Europe and Middle East. The width of this band, and that of the white wing-patch, increase progressively from W–E; also a slight increase in wing length. Nominate *senator* (including *hensii* on Sicily, breeds in Europe from Spain, France, Italy, Sicily, Greece and W Turkey; spends boreal winter in West and Central Africa to W Sudan); *rutilans* (Iberia and NW Africa) is similar to nominate race but with shorter wing (most authors consider it a synonym of *senator*); *niloticus* (breeds in E Turkey, Syria, Israel and Iran; spends boreal winter in NE and East Africa and Arabian Peninsula) differs from other races by always having a broad band of white at base of tail feathers, and with the white wing-patch larger than in nominate race; it is also duller with a pale chestnut-brown crown and nape, and often some white on forehead, underparts whiter with less buff on flanks; *badius* (breeds in Balearic Is, Corsica, Sardinia and Capraia; spends boreal winter in West Africa from Ivory Coast, Ghana, Togo and Benin to SW Nigeria) is not part of this cline; shows very little or no white at base of tail feathers, and differs from *senator* in having narrower black forehead and only very little or no white at base of primaries, which is often hidden[183, 212, 257, 285, 484, 675, 787, 866].

HYBRIDS At least six cases of hybridisation known to occur involving ♂ Red-backed Shrike x ♀ Woodchat Shrikes. Three pairs are known to have produced offspring. In the field the young hybrids are easily mistaken for young Red-backed Shrikes. They lack a white wing-patch and scapulars are only slightly paler than rest of upperparts. What is believed to be a ♂ Woodchat Shrike x ♀ Red-back Shrike hybrid has also been seen, as well as their display documented. The hybrid has grey upperparts, including grey rump and uppertail-coverts, white scapulars, a black face-mask which did not extend as a broad frontal, black wings with white wing-patch, black tail with white outer feathers and dull white underparts with buffy sides of breast and flanks[284, 285, 374, 675].

MOULT Boreal autumn moult complicated and not well understood. Adult *senator* undergoes a partial post-breeding (Jun–Aug) moult of body feathers, some tertials and sometimes some tail feathers. This is suspended and continued with a complete moult on non-breeding grounds (Oct–Jan). However, apparently some previous-year birds (2nd calendar year birds), whose first pre-breeding 'complete' moult on non-breeding grounds was incomplete, begin a partial moult of primaries on their breeding grounds, suspend it before migration, and resume it on non-breeding grounds. Consequently the complete renewal of wings and tail may only take place in the birds' second boreal winter. The contrast between old abraded and new feathers is obvious in ♂♂, but less so in ♀♀. Second-year adults may also show some barred juvenile body feathers. In another variation, E *niloticus* apparently undergoes a complete post-breeding moult before migrating S. Juveniles undergo a partial moult soon after fledging, involving some head, body and wing-covert feathers. The extent of this moult is variable, sometimes being suspended, and resumed on non-breeding grounds into a first-summer (boreal) plumage[284, 285, 645, 675, 786, 814, 866].

RANGE, HABITAT and STATUS **Breeding**

range Fragmented, mainly limited to SW Palearctic in Mediterranean region. In North Africa from N Morocco, N Algeria, Tunisia and NE Libya. In Europe the main population occurs in Portugal, Spain, France, Italy and former W Yugoslavia in Croatia, Albania, Bulgaria, Greece, Turkey. Almost all Mediterranean islands are occupied. In Central Europe, where its distribution is fragmented, it is rare or possibly no longer a breeding bird in Germany, Switzerland, Poland, Czech Republic and Romania. No longer breeds in Netherlands, Belgium, Luxemburg, Austria and Hungary. Further E known to breed in Georgia, Armenia, Azerbaijan, Syria, Lebanon, Israel, N Iraq and in NW and possibly SW and SE Iran, where eastern limit in the province of Kerman at *c*.58°E[36, 45, 212, 214, 218, 257, 284, 285, 382, 449, 484, 675, 746, 787]. **Non-breeding range** Migrates mainly to Africa N of the equator, occurring in a broad belt across S Sahara between *c*.15°N and 5°N in W and between *c*.13°N and 2°N in E, extending into SW Arabian Peninsula. Some birds may spend boreal winter at oases in Algeria. In North Africa it is a passage migrant or boreal winter visitor in the following countries: Mauritania, Senegal, Gambia, Guinea, Sierra Leone, Liberia, Ivory Coast, Ghana, Togo, Benin, Cameroon, Nigeria, Gabon, Zaïre, Mali, Burkina Faso, Niger, Chad, Central African Republic, Sudan, Ethiopia, Eritrea, Yemen, Uganda, Kenya. Further S or W African vagrants, some of which require confirmation, have been recorded in Angola, Somalia, Burundi, South Africa and Madagascar. In Europe vagrants have been recorded between Mar–Sep from countries like the Netherlands, Denmark, Norway, Sweden and the British Isles as far N as Shetland. In E range vagrant to Dagestan, Afghanistan and Oman. See Movements.

Habitat ***Breeding range*** In Europe found in scrub on dry hillsides, open ground or heathland scattered with shrubs or trees, olive groves, orchards, gardens, open forest and forest edge and clearings, hedges, roadsides and cultivation with scattered trees. Normally breeds below 1000 m, except in mountains of S France, Spain, Morocco and Israel. Generally habitat characterised by low ground cover. African and Middle East populations inhabit desert oases, forests of *Quercus ilex*, cultivated areas with trees, open grassy scrubland in dry steppes or semi-desert areas. ***Non-breeding range*** In Africa occur in open bush country, dry *Acacia* savanna, cultivated areas with trees and bushes and sometimes forest clearings[21, 22, 28, 37, 39, 101, 205, 216, 217, 220, 222, 234, 242, 246, 257, 274, 290, 292, 318, 327, 375, 376, 431, 450, 482, 504, 554, 631, 696, 848, 858, 859, 907, 931, 952, 1015].

Status Migrant, not uncommon, rare in N of range. **Conservation status** Declines have occurred virtually throughout Europe. It has declined by over 20% in 90% of its European population, particularly in the N and W, and has disappeared from Netherlands, Belgium and Czech Republic, with severe declines in S France and N Spain. Other range contractions have occurred in Luxemburg, Germany, Poland, Austria, Switzerland, Romania, Bulgaria and Malta. In Europe, main population inhabits the Mediterranean region. The Iberian Peninsula may hold over 600,000 breeding pairs, representing 85% of total European population. Population estimates (total or for pairs) for countries with *c*.50 or more individual; 2,000–5,000 pairs (Albania); 300–3,000 (Bulgaria); 200,000–300,000 (Croatia); 6,000–12,700 (France); 1–50 (Germany); 5,000–20,000 (Greece); 5,000–10,000 pairs (Italy); 10–50 (Poland): 10,000–100,000 (Portugal); 10–20 pairs (Romania); 1–10 pairs (Slovakia); 390,000–860,000 (Spain); 30–50 (Switzerland); 5,000–50,000 (Turkey). Loss and degradation of habitat through agricultural intensification, afforestation and fires, together with long-term climatic changes bringing wetter springs, are thought to be the main threats in the breeding range. Prolonged drought and changing agriculture in its non-breeding range also thought to influence survival. This shrike is regularly shot in Italy, Spain and North Africa. Monitoring trends in breeding and non-breeding range and the implementation of conservation measures a priority. Considered Vulnerable[257, 285, 369, 480, 675, 787, 937, 938, 948, 952].

MOVEMENTS All populations are migratory with the different races migrating at slightly different times, in different directions and to different non-breeding areas (see Geographical Variation). Boreal autumn migration begins in Jul–Aug, sometimes with pre-migratory movements taking place as early as Jun. Records from breeding range as late as Sep or even Oct are exceptional. Birds arrive in main African non-breeding area in mid-Aug–Oct. Spring migration may begin as early as Jan, but is mainly in Mar–Apr, rarely as late as May. Most birds arrive in their breeding grounds Apr–May, however in some areas this is protracted, with birds returning as late as Jun. Autumn movements of Central European populations occur in a WSW or SW direction towards Iberian Peninsula. Italian birds move SE. In northern spring they appear in SE Mediterranean countries, where they were relatively scarce in autumn. Although possible non-stop flights in autumn may account for this, direct observations and ringing suggest that at least some western populations make an anti-clockwise loop-migration, returning E of their southward route. In one study no significant weight difference existed between autumn and spring migrants[375, 675, 939]. For additional information see references in Breeding and Non-breeding ranges.

SOCIAL ORGANISATION and GENERAL BEHAVIOUR Solitary, in pairs or small family groups. Generally a conspicuous shrike which perches upright on an exposed site advertising its territory by calling or static marking. However, sometimes it can be shy and difficult to locate as it has the habit of skulking within the canopy. Excited bird typically ruffles forecrown, causing white forehead patches to be particularly prominent. ♂♂ advertise and defend territories from *c*.0.5–12 ha depending on habitat. Individual territories may vary during the breeding season. ♂♂ give repeated harsh territorial calls from top of tall trees, frequently changing singing perch. High-intensity threat signalled with a rattle call, and heard when ♂ and ♀ attempt to displace another pair or individual from an already occupied territory. Physical contact is not unusual. Unmated ♂ appears to direct calling towards paired birds, and often intrudes into their territory, giving persistent contact calls. It also tends to associate with a specific pair, following it if it moves. In threat ♂ adopts an upright posture with ruffled feathers, wings slightly open and drooped showing prominent white scapulars and wing-patch. When about to attack, adopts a forward, sleek posture, head lowered and swaying from side to side. Also bows down and slowly nods head down and up in a bobbing threat display. Opponents may remain upright and only nod head forward until bill is on the breast, showing the chestnut-brown crown. In this display opponents remain in the head-down posture for a few seconds, alternately giving the *grüg* call. The display is typically used between ♂♂ and in courtship. In juveniles, appeasement signalled by crouch and wing-fluttering, but adults usually adopt a bill-up posture with head turned away, or at higher intensity with head laid back and bill vertical while hopping about. When alarmed swings tail from side to side. On non-breeding grounds birds hold small territories but are generally silent, except for occasional warbling song. Little known about roosting behaviour; a pair have been seen lying flat on the nest together during high winds[257, 284, 285, 373, 387, 484, 675].

Foraging behaviour Hunts from exposed perches 1–6 m high, usually on the edge of a bush or tree, scanning the ground below for food. Most of its prey is taken on the ground, occasionally hovering before pouncing, or taking prey off the surface of water. In wet weather recorded hopping on the ground in search of food. Also sometimes takes aerial prey. Prey is apparently rarely impaled; unrecorded in some studies. Large prey carried in bill and sometimes transferred to foot in flight. Recorded robbing food from wheatears *Oenanthe* on non-breeding grounds.

Food Mainly arthropods, particularly insects and small vertebrates. Coleoptera (beetles) and Orthoptera (grasshoppers and crickets) constitute bulk of prey, to a less extent Hymenoptera (wasps, bumble-bees and ants), Lepidoptera (moths, butterflies and larvae), Hemiptera (bugs), Diptera (horse-flies), Odonata (damselflies and dragonflies), Dermaptera (earwigs), Dictyoptera (cockroaches) and Mantodea (mantises). Spiders and scorpions are also taken as well as other invertebrates such as larval millipedes, worms and snails. Small vertebrates are occasionally caught, including shrews, voles, mice, lizards and frogs. Bird nests are robbed and small passerines, particularly young ones or exhausted migrants are caught. Small fruits like mulberries *Morus* and berries *Prunus* have also been recorded[223, 257, 284, 285, 290, 373, 401, 484, 675].

SOUNDS Repertoire consists of a variety of harsh calls and warbling song. Main territorial call a harsh repeated *kscha-* sound, described as *dschär-rt, dsschä-dschä* or *grüg-*. Territorial warbling song often initiated by loud *grüg* call which may be given repeatedly. Alarm calls are loud, harsh chattering sounds, variously described as *gegegegeg-* or commonly heard 3-syllable *gräck-kjäck-käck,* also *gäck-gäck-, hek-hek-hek-* or *kra-kra-* repeated at varying speeds depending on level of excitement, at high intensity a rattling *tr-tr-tr-* when attacking conspecifics or predators. Snaps bill during attack. Advertising and contact calls are often repeated disyllabic *ko-ick*-type sound, described as *pitquür-, kwikwik* or trisyllabic *pitpitquür.* Also has *rrre*-type sounds like *rretts* and shorter *crex* advertising calls. The di- and trisyllabic calls are also used by adults when bringing food to the nest. Begging call a loud hoarse drawn-out *tschärp-tschärp-* or a softer *gagagaga-*. A specific contact call *kreck-kreckekeck* is repeated at short intervals and used to keep adults and young in contact over large distances. The same call is thought to be used by pairs for maintaining contact during the spring migration. Song given mainly by ♂, occasionally in duet with ♀, consists of a rather quiet, extremely varied, continuous fine, rich and musical warbling, or a lower-pitched harsher, scratchy chattering with few high-pitched whistles like *zrlui-* and trills, containing much mimicry[28, 225, 257, 284, 285, 373, 484, 600]. Sonagram[225, 257, 284, 373, 484, 600].

BREEDING BIOLOGY Monogamous and territorial. Most birds arrive on breeding grounds already paired, or less often ♂♂ arrive a few days before ♀♀. If pair-bond strong these birds do little calling, but immediately begin nest-building, sometimes laying within *c.*6 days. In contrast, unpaired ♂♂ give repeated *grüg* and contact calls associated with loud prolonged warbling song. Many unpaired ♂♂ arriving on breeding grounds do not succeed in holding territories. Highest density recorded in Spain in open forest are 1.5–3 birds/10 ha. Sometimes breeds close to other shrikes (Lesser Grey and Red-backed) as well as an unusual association with Fieldfare *Turdus pilaris* and Orphean Warbler *Sylvia hortensis,* where occupied nests of either species have been found in the same bush as the shrike's nest. It shows strong breeding site-fidelity but apparently little mate-fidelity. Length of pair-bond unknown, but in one case a ♂ bred with 3 different ♀♀ over 3 consecutive years. Young remain with parents for 4–6 weeks until start of migration. Breeding success estimated to be between 36.5–82%. Replacement clutches are common. Southern populations (North Africa, Israel) known to raise two broods. Nestling mortality due mainly to bad weather[257, 373, 484, 675, 689, 957].

Season Egg-laying Apr–Jul (Maghreb, Spain and W Mediterranean Isles)[675]; Apr–May (Algeria)[257]; May–Jul (Greece)[675]; May–Jun (France, Central Europe)[675]; Mar–Jul (Israel)[216, 746].

Displays ***Courtship*** Unmated ♂♂ perform zigzag or curved display-flights accompanied by much song and contact-calling. Similarly in a newly formed pair with weak pair-bond, the ♂ sings, calls and builds nest alone until the ♀ is actively involved in nest-building. In courtship and pair-bonding, ♂ flies to many different trees, singing and calling, and at times performing a head-nodding display accompanied with song and call notes *(kwikwik* and *grüg)* from within cover. ♀ approaches and calls, which causes ♂ to wing-flutter. This behaviour may lead to mutual bobbing display and duetting. In the bobbing display ♂ and ♀ lower bill alternately (or simultaneously), head feathers ruffled and body feathers sleeked while bending legs, then rapidly stretching up to full height. This display is variable, sometimes only incorporating head-nodding. Pair sometimes sing in duet. ♂ may lure ♀ from tree to tree by wing-fluttering and loud-calling. ♂ gives disyllabic *pitquür* contact call prior to courtship-feeding; ♀ turns head away from ♂ before receiving food. Once nest-building begins in earnest, ♂ song decreases dramatically. ***Pre-copulation*** Usually preceded by contact call and wing-fluttering, sometimes by courtship-feeding and accompanied by singing. ***Nest-site display*** Song by ♂ at site[257, 284, 339, 373].

Nest ♂ selects site, both build. A compact cup of plant material, often green (unlike other *Lanius*), fine twigs, roots and lined with wool, hair, fine roots, spider web, moss and lichen. Often incorporates fresh flowers and sometimes man-made materials. Placed in a variety of trees, especially oak, poplar, pine, fruit and olive trees on thick horizontal branch away from the trunk. Nest height is unusually variable from season to season, in early to late breeders and between first and replacement clutches. It is usually less than 5 m (range 1–20) above the ground, but in Mediterranean often low down in dense bushes or brambles. ***Size*** OD 100–156 mm, ID 55–90 mm, cup depth 35–67 mm, height 60–90 mm (n=131). Building takes *c.*4–6 days. On completion of the nest, egg-laying may be delayed for up to a few weeks[216, 257, 284, 285, 373, 401, 484, 675, 689, 936, 957].

Eggs 1–8, usually 5–6, rarely 7 or 8. Northern populations tend to lay larger clutches. Pale to olive-green, also sandy- or greyish-yellow or more rarely reddish-yellow or -brown, speckled and blotched with brown and greys usually around the large end. ***Size*** 23.4 x 17.2 mm (20.0–27.8 x 14.1–19.2, n=437)[257, 284, 285, 484, 668, 675, 746, 957]. **Incubation** Usually by ♀, fed by ♂ mainly on the nest. Period 14–16 days (n=10). For additional data see[257, 284, 285, 373, 484]. **Nestling** Appearance unknown; hatching partially synchronised, closely brooded by ♀ for *c.*9 days, fed by both sexes; initially ♂ brings food, ♀ feeds nestlings. Fledge after 15–20 days, usually *c.*17 days. Follow parents about after 10–14 days, remaining with them for *c.*25–45 days after fledging, independent just before migration. Brood division recorded irregularly[257, 373, 789]. For additional data see[285, 484]. **Predation and longevity** Nest predation by snakes high in Israel, particularly following touching of nest by researcher. Fires also destroyed nests[746]. **Brood parasite** None.

MEASUREMENTS and WEIGHTS *L. s. senator* ♂ (24) wing 98–102 (100.5 ±SD 1.31), tail (17) 75–82 (78.0 ±SD 2.11), bill (to skull) (34) 17.6–20.2 (18.8 ±SD 0.76), tarsus (17) 23.5–25.4 (24.6 ±SD 0.63); sex differences not significant[257]. **Weight** ♂ (49) 28–45 g (34.6), ♀ (44) 33–52 g (37.4)[257]; passage birds *niloticus* ♂♀? (94) 20–38 g (29.1 ±SD 2.8) (Israel)[939]; ♂♀? (65) 21.0–41.0 g (29.1)[478]; 2 non-breeding birds 27.5–29.5 g (Nigeria)[494]. For additional data see[284, 484].

19 BULL-HEADED SHRIKE (Japanese Shrike)
Lanius bucephalus **Plate 8**

FIELD IDENTIFICATION Medium-sized (20 cm) brown, grey and black shrike with a reddish-brown head and nape and grey back. Black face-mask extends through eye, bordered above by white eyebrow. Sexes different; tinged reddish-buff below, ♂ plain, ♀ barred. ♂ also has small white wing-patch, absent in ♀. Young like ♀, but darker, barred above and below. Calls harsh and grating, including trills and chattering; song warbler-like. Solitary, in pairs or family group; perches prominently. Found in open woodland with scattered trees or forest edge in far E Asia and Japan. Some migrate in boreal winter to S of range. ***Flight characteristics***: Flies with rapid wingbeats; drops down and flies low before swooping up to perch. White in wing of ♂ conspicuous. Longer flights tend to be undulating.

COMPARISONS Adults similar to Brown Shrike *Lanius cristatus* but differ by having pale grey back (grey-brown to reddish-brown in Brown), and a grey rump and dark tail (Brown has rufous rump and tail). ♂ Bull-headed has a conspicuous white wing-patch (indistinct or lacking in Brown). More difficult to separate ♀♀ and juvenile from juvenile Brown. Adults unlikely to be confused with Thick-billed Shrike *L. tigrinus* as latter has a grey head, rufous back and white underparts, no eyebrow and no white wing-patch. Young of these two species may be confused, but Bull-headed distinctly larger with a proportionately smaller bill.

DESCRIPTION ADULT ♂ ***Head*** Crown, nape and mantle rufous-brown (variable from greyish- to dark reddish-brown); forehead whitish extending as an eyebrow to beyond eye; black face-mask extends from lores through eye to ear-coverts. ***Back*** Mantle to rump pale grey. ***Wings*** blackish-brown with small white wing-patch at base of primaries; secondaries and coverts black with buff to reddish-brown edging. ***Tail*** Graduated, greyish black with small white tips on outer feathers. ***Underparts*** Buff- to reddish-brown, throat whitish, flanks darker, sometimes with faint barring. ***Bare parts*** Bill and legs black; palate unknown; eye brown. **ADULT ♀** Browner than ♂ with sides of head rufous like crown, without black face-mask and back tinged rufous. Eyebrow less distinctive. Underparts whitish to rufous-buff with extensive wavy barring. Wings without white patch at base of primaries. Bill black with pale base to lower mandible. **JUVENILE/IMMATURE** Tinged reddish-brown all over. Forehead, crown, nape and mantle barred black on reddish-brown (paler brown than adults); ear-coverts dark reddish-brown, pale dull white eyebrow; back and rump grey, tinged with reddish-brown; primaries and secondaries black with buff reddish-brown edging; coverts edged with buff reddish-brown (buff-tipped greater primary coverts indicate first-year bird). Juvenile ♂♂ show small whitish wing-patch. Tail pale reddish-brown with black subterminal bar. Underparts including flanks off-white to pale reddish-brown and finely barred black. Bill brownish-black with pale base[370].

GEOGRAPHICAL VARIATION Two races, nominate *bucephalus* (E Asia, Japan and China), and *sicarius* (S China in W Kansu [Gansu]), in which ♂ differs from nominate in having a darker grey back and less conspicuous white wing-patch, and ♀ in being distinctly more heavily and extensively barred below and having the bill all black, not pale below[188, 212, 820].

MOULT In E Russia moult begins on breeding grounds, as early as Jul, others Aug. In Japan, juvenile moult involving body and wing-coverts is completed as early as Aug, at which time it is difficult to tell juveniles from adults. However, young retain unmoulted buff-tipped primary wing-coverts until the following May[284, 370].

RANGE, HABITAT and STATUS **Breeding range** Far-eastern Palearctic extending N to *c.*50°N in E Russia and on adjacent Kuril Islands, and S to NE China, including an isolated population in the SW (Kansu [Gansu] Province), Korea and Japan, including Kyushu, Shikoku, Honshu and Hokkaido and numerous smaller islands as far S as Chichijima on the Ogasawara Islands[188, 198, 212, 214, 284, 433, 675]. **Non-breeding range** See Movements. **Habitat** Generally a lowland species, but in some localities will ascend to 1500 m, occasionally 2700 m (Japanese Alps) or 2750 m (S China). Occupies open habitats with scattered trees, often areas modified by man (cleared, logged and cultivated areas, in addition to parks, gardens and roadsides). Also in sparse deciduous and mixed forest and forest edge and denser areas along watercourses, including reedbeds in boreal winter. On Kuril islands in man-made clearings in taiga forest or bamboo stands[193, 195, 212, 270, 284, 370, 675]. **Status** Resident and partial migrant, not uncommon. **Conservation status** In Japan a population has been recorded declining over a 20-year period, particularly in modified habitats on Hokkaido. Causal factors need to be investigated. Held in captivity[408, 655, 824].

MOVEMENTS Little known. Generally populations are migratory, moving S, although some do not move out of the breeding range, and others undertake only local, particularly altitudinal movements. N populations in Russia and NE China appear to leave these areas completely, moving S to Japan (Kyushu, Shikoku, Honshu, occasionally to Hokkaido), central Korea and S China, where they occur as passage migrants or non-breeding birds. In Japan N birds and those at high elevations move to warmer regions or lower elevations, where they remain for boreal winter. Some birds occur as vagrants to Hong Kong and Taiwan. Most breeding birds depart their breeding grounds from Aug–Sep, occasionally as late as Oct, returning in Apr, ♂♂ generally arriving first[188, 191, 212, 267, 270, 284, 372, 675].

SOCIAL ORGANISATION and GENERAL BEHAVIOUR Solitary, in pairs or family groups. A rather conspicuous and often noisy shrike, which tends to perch in a prominent position with tail frequently waved, fanned or rotated when agitated. Some populations migratory, others resident with individuals either strictly sedentary (breeding and spending boreal winter in the same territory), or known as 'floaters' — birds which leave their non-breeding territory to breed elsewhere. In resident populations in central Japan both sexes have individual non-breeding territories. Advertises and defends a territory of *c.*2–12 ha with repeated harsh calls. Adjacent territories often overlap slightly[284, 348]. **Foraging behaviour** Hunts from a prominent perch, flying down to the ground to capture prey. Prey is often impaled and caches formed throughout the year[687]. **Food** Arthropods, mainly insects and small vertebrates, seasonally variable. Insects include Coleoptera (beetles and weevils), Orthoptera (crickets and grasshoppers), Lepidoptera (butterflies and caterpillars), Hymenoptera (flying ants and wasps), Neuroptera (lacewings) and Hemiptera (bugs and cicadas). Also takes spiders, worms, centipedes and crustaceans. Small vertebrates include birds, mice, voles, frogs, lizards and fish. Berries have also been recorded. In one study nestlings were fed Noctuidae caterpillars, crickets and cicadas. In another study Arachnoidea (spiders), Orthoptera and the larvae of Lepidoptera formed the bulk of the diet[193, 271, 284, 675, 687, 821, 822].

SOUNDS Little known. Repertoire consists of harsh notes and warbling song. Main territorial call of ♂ a noisy harsh repeated *tscha*-type sound, described as a repeated short, high-pitched *tzert-tzert-*, *tchuk-*, *kew-kew-*, and rapid high-pitched chattering *ju-ju-ju-* or *gi-gi-gi-*. This may be followed by a higher-pitched trill *kurrrrrirri* or *tschurrr*, which is heard mainly at beginning of breeding season. ♀♀ also give trill call. Variations include *chi-chi-chi* terminating in brief *tyo-tyo-tyo* and a falcon-like *gygygygy*. Alarm a repeated harsh chattering *kkkkkkk-*, *krrr-krrr-* or *kerrr-*. Begging call a querulous nasal *naaae-naaae-*.

Young begging call a repeated *jiá-jiá-jiá-* or *biá-biá-biá-*. ♂ copulation call during migration a high-pitched *Tururu-* or *Tihihi-*. Also has a loud warbling song reminiscent of Marsh Warbler *Acrocephalus palustris* with imitations of other birds and insects like cicadas[193, 214, 271, 284, 372, 500, 600, 675, 687]. Sonagram[284, 600].

BREEDING BIOLOGY Monogamous and territorial, attacking not only congeners (particularly Brown Shrike) but also other birds. Has a protracted breeding season and often raises two broods. In one study, ♀♀ begin wandering through ♂ territories in Jan until they select a mate, most settling within 1km of their non-breeding territories; *c.*30% of them select the same mate in subsequent seasons, while *c.*40% choose a new mate. In central Japan densities varied from *c.*1 pair/2 ha in summer, to *c.*1.3 ha per individual bird in boreal winter. In migrant populations ♂♂ usually arrive first, pair formation taking place rapidly when the ♀♀ arrive; however, in many cases birds appear to be already paired on arrival. In resident populations (e.g. central Japan) ♂♂ and ♀♀ hold individual non-breeding territories. Generally ♀♀ remain in ♂ territories for 50–90 days, occasionally up to 150 days when raising two broods. One study showed 10% of nestlings had extra-pair paternity, a result thought to be a consequence of extra-pair copulations[371, 675, 822, 827]. **Season** Pair formation Jan (Japan), Apr (E Russia); egg-laying from late Feb–Mar (S and central Japan); end of Apr in Sakhalin (Russia) and further N beginning May (N Japan, Hokkaido and Kuril Islands). Occasionally replacement clutches still evident in Jul[284, 438, 675]. **Displays** ***Courtship*** At start of breeding season unpaired ♂♂ sing loudly from prominent perches, frequently changing perches and performing zigzag display-flights accompanied by loud trilling call. On sighting a ♀ it gives 3–4 short, harsh *kew-kew-* calls, sometimes accompanied by a trill. ♂ performs a courtship dance next to ♀, during which he turns his upward pointing head from side to side, cocks the tail and bows the body, while uttering subdued subsong. Tail also slightly fanned. Courtship-feeding by ♂ frequent. ***Pre-copulation*** On migration ♂ gives a high-pitched *Tururu-* or *Tihihi-* accompanied by wing-quivering, ♀ begs continuously in a crouched, wing-fluttering posture. On mounting, ♀ ceases begging and ♂ changes call to subsong, continuing this after copulation. There is apparently no courtship-feeding associated with copulation. ***Nest-site display*** Unknown. ♀ has a characteristic flight and soft call during nest-building, a call similar to *tschurrr* call of ♂ as he approaches nest[284, 372, 600]. **Nest** Built by both sexes, ♀ most. A bulky cup of twigs, dry bark, grass stalks, leaves and moss. It is lined with rootlets, fine grass, wool and fur. It may be placed in isolated bushes or trees, or in dense thickets composed of bushes, shrubbery, trees or bamboo, and usually at a height of 0.3–4.5 m above the ground. In one study early breeders nested lower than later breeders. Thorns and nettles may be placed around the nest. ***Size*** OD 125–160 mm, ID 80 mm and cup depth *c.*50–100 mm. Built in *c.*5–10 days. The relatively large bulky nest with thick walls is probably related to the early breeding season[284, 372, 675, 822]. **Eggs** Usually 4–7 (2–7, n=8) (E Russia). Populations in N may have larger clutches than in S. Yellowish-white over pinkish- or purplish-green with brown and grey markings concentrated mainly at the large end. ***Size*** 20.5–25.7 x 16.3–18.7 mm (23.07 x 17.47, n=50)[284]. Apparently double brooded throughout its range, with replacement clutches of N populations still evident in Jul[822]. **Incubation** By ♀ only, fed by ♂ on and off the nest. Period usually 14–15 days (*c.*13–16)[193, 214, 284, 372, 687]. **Nestling** Appearance unknown; attended by both sexes. Fledge after *c.*14 days. Fledglings fed for at least a further *c.*15 days[193, 372]. For additional information see[845]. **Predation and longevity** Little known. Oldest retrap 2.7 years[267]. **Brood parasite** Commonly parasitised by the Common Cuckoo *Cuculus canorus* and the Himalayan Cuckoo *C. saturatus*[284, 438].

MEASUREMENTS and WEIGHTS *L. b. bucephalus* ♂ (25) wing 79–88 (85.0), tail 81–91, bill ♂♀? *c.*20 mm; ♀ (18) wing 79–87 (81.7), tail 83–91[214]; ♂♀? (11) wing 84–90 (87.1), tail 78–96 (87.7), bill (to skull) 20–21.5 (20.7), tarsus 24–27 (25.4)[500]. **Weight** Breeding ♀ (66) 37.3–54.4 g (44.8 ±3.67 g); non-breeding ♀ (37) 35.2–43.2 g (39.2 ±1.73 g) (Japan)[372]; *c.*40 g[284].

20 BROWN SHRIKE (Red-tailed Shrike) *Lanius cristatus* Plate 9

FIELD IDENTIFICATION Medium-small (17–19 cm), variable brown, reddish-brown or greyish-brown and white shrike, usually with reddish-brown above contrasting with lighter rufous rump and tail, broad white eyebrow and black face-mask. Underparts whitish with buffy-rufous tinge. Reddish rump and tail obvious in flight, no white wing-patch. Sexes similar. Young dull greyish-brown, barred above and below, tail and rump reddish-brown. Calls harsh and grating, song warbler-like. Solitary, perches prominently in open woodland and thorn scrub in E Asia. Migrant to NE Africa, SE Asia as far S as Lesser Sundas. ***Flight characteristics***: Flies low, swoops up to perch; tail appears very thin. Reddish tail and rump obvious in flight, and no white wing-patch. Longer flights undulating[257, 280].

COMPARISONS Identification often difficult owing to similarities with Isabelline Shrike *Lanius isabellinus* and ♀ and juvenile Red-backed Shrike

L. collurio (see Hybrids). Brown has a bulkier, big-headed, heavier-billed appearance with a longer, slimmer more rounded tail. Combined with this, adults differ from ♀ and juvenile Red-backed by redder upperparts, (greyer in Red-backed, an exception being the very grey *lucionensis* race of Brown), more prominent white eyebrow, underparts rufous-buff with very little or no barring (whitish with extensive barring in Red-backed). Tail and rump redder and generally lighter (darker brown in Red-backed). This creates greater contrast in Brown between the back and the rump/tail. The Brown race *superciliosus* is an exception as it is brighter reddish-brown above with a darker tail. Field differences between juveniles of Brown, Red-backed and Isabelline very difficult and little studied. Generally Brown juveniles have a better defined eyebrow and face-mask, less barring on upperparts, more rufous tail without pale tips, and rufous-buff underparts with less heavy barring, especially on breast. Differs from adult nominate Isabelline by relatively browner, less rufous tail, darker reddish-brown back and rump (*isabellinus* has pale rufous-red rump like the tail), and rufous-buff underparts. Most similar to *phoenicuroides* race of Isabelline Shrike, but Brown distinguished by pale forehead and broader white eyebrow, reddish-brown crown and mantle (mantle greyish-brown in *phoenicuroides*), and darker tail. Underparts usually with rufous-buff tinge (lacking in *phoenicuroides*). In addition, *phoenicuroides* usually has a small pale wing-patch (seldom found in Brown). Distinguished from Bull-headed Shrike *L. bucephalus* by more slender build and lack of prominent white wing-patch, even in young. Superficially similar to brown races of Larger Wood-shrike *Tephrodornis gularis*. Brown Shrike is smaller, shorter-billed and lacks the white rump of this species, and has different habits. Separation of juvenile Isabelline very difficult and little studied in field; apparently differs by deeper buff colour below, and narrow, rather indistinct pale tips to flight feathers and coverts. Juvenile Long-tailed Shrike *L. schach*, is much larger and longer-tailed and has white wing-patch. Distinguished from young Thick-billed Shrike *L. tigrinus* by black face-mask and little or no barring below (Thick-billed has heavy barring above and below)[158, 198, 257, 278].

DESCRIPTION **Adult ♂** ***Head*** Forehead buff-white, crown and nape reddish-brown; broad white eyebrow; blackish face-mask from lores through eye to ear-coverts. ***Back*** Mantle, scapulars, back and rump pale russet-brown to isabelline-brown (contrasting with rufous crown and light rufous tail). ***Wings*** Flight feathers dark brown, tertials and coverts similar but edged rufous; visible wing-patch usually absent. ***Tail*** Narrow, graduated, light rufous with pale tips. ***Underparts*** White with rufous-buff tinge. ***Bare parts*** Bill heavy, black in ♂ and most breeding ♀♀, otherwise greyish horny-brown with pinkish base; palate unknown; legs bluish-grey; eye brown. **Adult ♀** Very similar to ♂, usually duller above, less distinct face-mask, may have buffy eyebrow and show faint barring (vermiculations) on breast and flanks. In *superciliosus* ♀ has a narrower white frontal band than ♂[681]. **Juvenile/Immature** Plumage varies with age, initially grey-brown and barred above and below, lacking rufous-brown on back and head. Changes to ♀-like back and rump with some barring; facial makings pale, barred and spotted black, ear-coverts dark brown to reddish-brown; underparts rufous-buff with sides of breast and flanks heavily barred; bill greyish-brown, pale at base. First-year birds show indications of subterminal dark cross-bars on the upper surface, most marked on the rump, and narrow black edges to the feathers of the breast and flanks (similar to immature Red-backed). This plumage retained for a full year[279, 281].

GEOGRAPHICAL VARIATION Four races, with clinal variation in size and colour, mainly of upperparts, size varying from small *cristatus* (in N from central Russia to E Siberia) to large *lucionensis* (N, E and SE China, Korea, possibly S Japan), upperparts varying from rufous-brown on *cristatus* to bright reddish-brown on *superciliosus* (far E Russia on S Sakhalin, Japan from Hokkaido to S central Honshu). The race *confusus* (E Siberia) is intermediate between these two and difficult to separate, having paler upperparts and wider frontal; *lucionensis* is a dull grey-brown; *superciliosus* is the only race in which the sexes are easily distinguished, ♂♂ having a broader white frontal band than ♀♀[214, 284, 675, 681].

HYBRIDS Only a few hybrids are known between this species and Red-backed and Isabelline Shrikes, in spite of wide overlap with the latter species. Occasional hybridises with Thick-billed Shrike *L. tigrinus*, a species which has similar mating displays[284, 364, 600, 675, 721, 722, 1052].

MOULT Moult strategy adopted by a particular race or population depends on the length of its migration. Populations with short migrations (those in S range including *lucionensis, superciliosus*, some *confusus* and most non-breeding *cristatus*) undergo a complete post-breeding moult while still on their breeding grounds, beginning once their young are independent. Most *cristatus* and late-breeding *confusus* begin moult on breeding grounds, completing it during stop-overs. Northern *cristatus* and late-breeding *confusus* adopt a different strategy. They begin moulting on the breeding grounds. The extent of this moult is variable, but it is suspended until they reach the non-breeding grounds, where it is completed. While on the non-breeding grounds all races undergo a second complete moult (migratory–breeding). Within *Lanius* shrikes this characteristic is shared only with Thick-billed Shrike. The Brown Shrike is also unusual in that its primary moult sequence starts with P3, P4, P5 or P6 instead of P1, and proceeds simultaneously in both directions. Post-juvenile moult of mainly body feather begins when young 40–55 days old. It is interrupted during migration and resumed on non-breeding grounds, where complete or near-complete moult occurs[284, 323, 675, 691, 731, 814, 1049].

RANGE, HABITAT and STATUS **Breeding**

range Widely distributed in Central and NE Asia, including E Russia (Siberia), Mongolia and SE China, with N boundary lying within the Arctic Circle at *c.*70°N. In the N, the western boundary lies at *c.*81°E. Southern boundary extends from the Russian Altai N of Nan Shan to SE in China where S limit at *c.*24°N. In NE extends from about the Arctic Circle southwards along W Kamchatka Peninsula, then southwards along the coast to Korea, including Sakhalin and Japanese islands. **Non-breeding range** S Korea, SE China, Taiwan, Hainan, Hong Kong, Vietnam, Laos, Thailand, Cambodia, Burma, Andaman, Nicobar, Laccadive and Maldive islands, Bangladesh, India (possibly to Pakistan, but requires confirmation), Sri Lanka, Nepal, Malay Peninsula, Sumatra, Java, Bali, Sumba, Flores, Philippines, Borneo, Sulawesi and Moluccas. Vagrants recorded from E Kazakhstan, British Isles, Denmark, far NE Russia and W Alaska on St Lawrence Island and Aleutians, as well as further S on Farallon Is. (California). In SE Asia from Tobi Is. (SW of Palau) and New Guinea (see Movements)[189, 191, 194, 195, 196, 198, 209, 212, 221, 224, 248, 250, 252, 257, 261, 262, 263, 264, 265, 268, 276, 278, 281, 284, 414, 435, 437, 442, 472, 675, 687, 694, 782]. **Habitat *Breeding range*** Unique in *Lanius* for unusually wide habitat tolerance, from tropical forests of S China, desert steppes, taiga and open tundra forest in Siberia, particularly in deforested and burnt areas, border of tundra and edge of open mixed forest and woodland, avoiding thick forest. Basic requirements similar to Red-backed Shrike, i.e. open areas with scattered bushes and small trees. In the N the highest densities occur along steppe river valleys, clear-cuts and burns. Also found in meadows with thickets and scattered groves, cultivated areas, rice plantations and parks. In the S in plains and mountainous areas up to *c.*1800 m in Altai region. ***Non-breeding range*** Generally in open country in lowlands, often associated with cultivation (e.g. paddyfields), otherwise found in forest edge and clearings, secondary scrub jungle and grass-covered hillsides with scattered bushes and small trees[188, 189, 190, 193, 207, 214, 221, 224, 257, 263, 279, 281, 284, 414, 437, 675, 822]. **Status** Mainly an E Palearctic migrant; S populations partial migrants. **Conservation status** Little known. Declining in Japan (*superciliosus* and *lucionensis*). Since 1970s has declined by 80% in Japan (Hokkaido). Causes unknown, but thought to be due to a number of factors in the non-breeding range. Of particular importance are habitat destruction through increased cultivation, fires and pesticides, and the extensive autumn and spring harvest of migrants in Taiwan (now outlawed effectively) and Philippines. Requires a monitoring programme to assess population trends[193, 267, 442, 824].

MOVEMENTS Most populations migratory, moving S in E Asia, with older birds leaving first; generally travels in small groups of 2–3 birds. Each race has a distinct non-breeding area with some overlap. In S breeding range some populations possibly only partially migratory. For example *lucionensis* probably spends boreal winter from Aug–Apr within its breeding range in SE China and S Korea. Other populations move further S in Taiwan, Hainan, Hong Kong, Philippines, N Borneo and Sulawesi. Nominate *cristatus* spends boreal winter from Jul–Sep in Indian subcontinent, including Nepal and Sri Lanka. Also found in Bangladesh, Burma, Thailand, S China, Malay Peninsula and possibly Borneo. Arrives Jul–Sep, departs Mar–May, mainly Apr, occasionally remaining to Jun. Race *confusus* spends boreal winter in Malay Peninsula and Sumatra; *superciliosus* spends boreal winter in SE China, Vietnam and Laos. It appears to be mainly a passage migrant to Malay Peninsula, and further S in Sumatra to Lesser Sundas from Sep-May. In boreal spring birds increase in weight before migrating. Nominate race arrives back on breeding grounds in May–Jun; more southerly birds (*lucionensis*) arrive the earliest. Migration routes are generally poorly known. Nominate race moves S and SW on broad front. Race *superciliosus* moves mainly SW and *lucionensis* mainly SE[157, 188, 191, 214, 221, 224, 250, 252, 257, 267, 284, 442, 472, 675, 677, 694, 1049].

SOCIAL ORGANISATION and GENERAL BEHAVIOUR Little known. Solitary except during migration when may occur in small groups of 2–3 birds. General behaviour similar to Red-backed Shrike, but tends to perch less prominently, uses more concealed perches and tail-swinging less pronounced. Also possibly more crepuscular, at which time it may be particularly noisy. Apart from breeding territories, both sexes hold non-breeding territories, which in one study were *c.*0.25 ha. These are defended with aggressive calling and physical fighting occurs frequently. Non-breeding site-fidelity recorded at 25% in one study. Breeding territories are defended by calling from prominent perches and display-flights through the territory. Threat is signalled by hunched, crouched, fluffed-out posture. In one Japanese study territory size ranged from 1–2 ha. Highest density in Siberia *c.*80 pairs/km². Roost sites generally situated 4–5 m above the ground[191, 196, 224, 267, 284, 675, 677, 694, 822]. **Foraging behaviour** Hunts from exposed perches, usually 1–3m above the ground. Where natural perches are absent, will use telephone wires. In open habitats, flies down to capture prey on the ground within a radius of *c.*1.5 m, exceptionally up to 22 m. In thicker habitats usually drops vertically onto prey. Rarely gleans from vegetation or hawks insects in the air. Reportedly swoops into bird flocks like a raptor, a behaviour common during autumn migration. Impales prey on breeding and non-breeding grounds and actively forages till after dark[822, 1053]. **Food** Arthropods, mainly insects and small vertebrates. In one study, most prey was too small to identify, the rest consisted mainly of insects, including Orthoptera (locusts, grasshoppers and crickets), Coleoptera (beetles), Lepidoptera (butterflies, moths and caterpillars), Hymenoptera (bees and wasps), to a lesser extent Isoptera (termites), Odonata (dragonflies), Diptera (flies), Ephemeroptera (mayflies), Dermaptera (earwigs), Hemiptera (bugs); also takes earthworms and spiders. Occasionally feeds on small vertebrates such as rodents, birds (including occasional nestlings), reptiles (lizards and geckos) and amphibians[214, 224, 261, 263, 273, 284, 675, 687, 822, 1053].

SOUNDS Little known. Repertoire apparently similar to Red-backed Shrike. Main territorial calls are harsh repeated *kscha*-type sounds, described as *zcha-zcha-zcha-scha-schah* repeated 5–6 times, also *chr-r-r-* or *shark* calls. During mate attraction, and particularly during zigzag display-flight gives a *kriki-kriki-kriki...tschef...tschef* phrase. Alarm a loud harsh repeated chatter, variously described as *je-je-je-je-je-jeeeet,* staccato *chak-ak-ak-ak-ak, tck-tck-tck-tck-tck, krech-krech-krech-, check-check-* or *jaya-jaya* and high-pitched squawking notes. At high intensity gives rapid bill-snapping. On non-breeding grounds gives an occasional chattering *tzih-tzih-tzih* call. Contact calls unknown, probably *kscha*-type. Song varied and warbler-like with mimicry. On non-breeding grounds, particularly before boreal spring migration, gives quiet subsong-like warbling with mimicry, moving tail up and down while singing[252, 257, 261, 262, 263, 276, 281, 284, 414, 500, 600]. Sonagram[284, 600].

BREEDING BIOLOGY Little known. Monogamous and territorial, with unmated ♂♂ usually arriving first on breeding grounds, at which time they are highly motivated. Due to lack of obvious sexual dimorphism, mate-attraction appears to be a case of trial and error, where unmated ♂♂ court each other as well as other shrikes. Nests in close proximity to Bull-headed Shrike, with territories sometimes overlapping. In these cases interspecific aggression occurs. No information on breeding success, except hatching success given as 88.2% in one study. Although replacement clutches are common, it is not known whether more than one brood is raised[284, 675, 731, 822]. **Season** Breeding occurs later at higher latitudes; Jun–Aug (Siberia, Russia)[214, 284]; May–Aug (E and central China)[273, 731]; Apr–Jul, mainly May–Jul (Japan)[193, 687]. **Displays *Courtship*** An unmated ♂, on seeing an intruder (♂ or ♀), does a zigzag display-flight, rolling from side to side and giving *kriki-kriki-kriki...tschef....tschef* calls. Approaches other bird with rapid shallow wingbeats, lands beside it, sits erect in bill-up posture while turning head from side to side. This display accompanied by muffled song. Does not bow. If both ♂♂, they perform similar displays. When approaching ♀, ♂ may glide towards her, and on landing may perform bill-up, head-turning display, with or without food. ***Pre-copulation display*** Unknown. ***Nest-site display*** Crouches with legs bent and tail slightly spread, moving in this position through the bushes. ♂ may follow ♀ about through bushes, singing loudly with head and tail slightly raised. At higher intensity, much singing and bowing with tail almost vertical, accompanied by various displacement activities. **Nest** Initial selection by ♂, with both building, mainly by ♀. Cup made of small twigs, grass stems, roots, stalks, moss, cotton, and feathers, lined with fine grass and horse hair. Nest height regionally variable according to habitat. May be placed relatively low at 0.5–3 m (*cristatus*), sometimes even on the ground (*confusus*) in grass or leaves; other sites are higher from 6–9 m (*superciliosus*), exceptionally up to 18 m in a tree. Usually well concealed in a shrub, bush or tree. ***Size*** OD 115–130 mm, ID 79 mm, cup depth 55 mm, height 120 mm. May take up to *c.*6 days to complete[193, 210, 214, 273, 284, 675, 731, 822]. **Eggs** Clutch size geographically variable, usually 4–6 (3–8). Ground colour variable from similar to Red-backed Shrike eggs to greenish-white or milk-white with uneven spots of grey-blue and yellow-brown. ***Size*** *cristatus* 21.0–24.8 x 16.3–18.3 mm (22.8 x 17.3, n=18)[193, 214, 273, 284, 687, 731]. **Incubation** By ♀ only, period *c.*15 days (13–16 days)[193, 284, 675, 681, 731]. **Nestling** Appearance unknown; fledge after 14–15 days (13–16), remaining within a radius of *c.*400 m for at least 2 weeks. Brood division recorded irregularly[284, 675, 731, 789]. For prey fed to nestlings see[822]. **Predation and longevity** Little known. Oldest retrap 5.2 years[267]. **Brood parasite** Known to host Common Cuckoo *Cuculus canorus* and the Indian Cuckoo *C. micropterus* in E Russia, and Common Cuckoo and Oriental Cuckoo *C. saturatus* in Japan[284, 675].

MEASUREMENTS and WEIGHTS *L. c. cristatus* and *confusus* combined: wing ♂ (13) 86–90 (87.9) ±1.23; tail ♂ (14) 81–89 (84.5) ±2.57; bill (to skull) ♂ (14) 19.1–20.9 (20.1 ±SD 0.57); tarsus ♂ (14) 24.2–26.7 (25.2 ±SD 0.79; no significant difference between sexes[257]. **Weight** *cristatus* ♂ (15) 31–38 g (34.5) ±2.20; ♀ (8) 30–36 g (33.1) ± 2.10[257], ♂♀? (14) 21–35 g (28.0)[224]. For additional data see[214, 273, 783, 828].

21 ISABELLINE SHRIKE (Red-tailed Shrike) *Lanius isabellinus* Plate 9

FIELD IDENTIFICATION Medium-small (17–19 cm), rather variable pale buff-brown shrike with a dark face-mask, pale eyebrow, small white wing-patch (♂) and reddish rump, tail and undertail, these contrasting strongly with brownish back. Sexes rather similar, ♀ duller, usually with sparse fine barring below. Young like ♀. Palest of all Eurasian shrikes with marked racial variation. Solitary, perches prominently in open semi-arid areas with scattered bushes and small trees. Found in Central Asia. Migrates in boreal winter to S Asia (Indian subcontinent) and Africa S of Sahara and roughly N of equator. ***Flight characteristics***: Flies low, swoops up to perch. Small white wing-patch conspicuous, particularly in ♂. Longer flights undulating.

COMPARISONS Identification of ♀♀ often difficult between ♀ and juvenile Red-backed Shrike *Lanius collurio* and Brown Shrike *L. cristatus*. Some individuals appear not to be assignable to any species. Breeding range of Isabelline and Red-backed overlap marginally, with hybridisation (see Hybrids). Also overlap on migration, particularly in Middle East and NE Africa. Isabelline is a rare but regular vagrant to W Europe. Eastern part of Isabelline breeding range overlaps with W breeding range of Brown Shrike with limited hybridisation. Both overlap on their non-breeding grounds in N India. Adult Isabelline, particularly first-winter (boreal), easily confused with ♀ and juvenile first-winter (boreal) Red-backed. Isabelline slightly larger and paler than Red-backed with slightly longer, more rufous tail, which is more often cocked at an angle to the body. Isabelline shows a marked contrast between tail and back colour (lacking in Red-backed), also has fine, sparse barring on sides of breast and flanks (extensive in ♀, and more so in juvenile Red-backed), and a pale rufous undertail (greyish in Red-backed); tail sides more ginger (Red-backed has clearer, whiter fringes). Creamy wing-patch visible in many adult Isabelline ♀♀ (races *phoenicuroides* and *speculigerus*). ♀♀ or nominate *isabellinus* are particularly pale and sandy, with very faint barring. Juvenile Isabelline typically paler, buffier above with sparse faint barring below (Red-backed pale grey-brown to dark rufous and usually prominently barred below); however, some first-year *phoenicuroides* very similar to first-year Red-backed, though slightly paler, greyer and less heavily barred above. Undertail chestnut-brown in Isabelline (greyish in Red-backed). Isabelline separated in the hand from Red-backed on non-breeding grounds by having 9th primary much shorter than 6th (greater or equal in Red-backed), and more extensive emargination of outer web of 6th primary (numbered descendantly or outwardly). Tips of tail feathers in all ages are rounded in Isabelline, more pointed in Red-backed[200, 305, 631, 675, 747]. Separation of Isabelline and Brown Shrike more difficult in the field, particularly *phoenicuroides* group. Brown Shrike has a bulkier, big-headed, heavier-billed appearance, with proportionately shorter wings and tail. Tail of nominate Isabelline tends to be redder than Brown Shrike (being more russet-brown or ochrous rather than rufous). Brown also tends to have a rufous tinge below (but underparts whiter in boreal winter), but certain E races are greyer above and have a visibly rufous-tinged rump. Isabelline race *phoenicuroides* usually has a pale wing-patch (generally lacking in Brown). Separation of immatures appears virtually unstudied; Brown Shrike are barred warm brown above, tail brown and face-mask black (generally darker than Isabelline). They lack white wing-patch (present in Isabelline). The general lack of distinctive plumage characters makes reliable field identification extremely difficult. In the hand, wing formula rather similar. Isabelline is appreciably paler than immature Woodchat Shrike *L. senator* which has a darker crown and large white shoulder marks (scapulars)[158, 212, 214, 257, 305, 675].

DESCRIPTION **Adult ♂** (see Geographical Variation). ***Head*** Crown variable, buff to sandy-grey (*isabellinus*) or rufous (*phoenicuroides*); face with cream to buff eyebrow (*isabellinus*), or whitish (*phoenicuroides*); face-mask brownish-black and poorly defined with pale lores (*isabellinus*), face-mask blackish from lores to ear-coverts (*phoenicuroides*). ***Back*** Pale isabelline-buff to sandy-grey (*isabellinus*), grey-brown (*phoenicuroides*); rump rufous, paler in *isabellinus*. ***Wings*** Grey-brown with buff-edged tertials, secondaries and coverts; sometimes wing-patch at base of primaries buff-cream, inconspicuous to absent (*isabellinus*) with very pale flight feathers. White wing-patch present on dark flight feathers (*phoenicuroides*). For wing formula see[675, 814]. ***Tail*** Pale rusty-rufous without distal centre shading (*isabellinus*), darker with distal centre shading (*phoenicuroides*); undertail pale rufous-brown. ***Underparts*** Sandy-buff (*isabellinus*) or whitish-cream (*phoenicuroides*), usually tinged pink, particularly in fresh plumage. ***Bare parts*** Bill pink-based (*isabellinus*), black (*phoenicuroides*); palate unknown; legs grey-black; eye brown. **Adult ♀** Similar to ♂ but duller; upperparts pale earth brown or isabelline (some *phoenicuroides* are more chestnut-brown on head); face-mask smaller with pale lores; underparts cream with slight, often indistinct barring; wings with reduced or absent creamy wing-patch. Bill light brown, base tinged pink. ♀♀ generally more difficult to assign to race than ♂♂. **Juvenile/Immature** Little known. First-winter (boreal) bird resembles ♀, but with remnants of juvenile barring above and below; crown variable like adult, but seldom rufous; greater and median-coverts and tertials fringed buffy with subterminal dark markings; underparts creamy with fine brown barring (vermiculations), except on centre of throat, breast, belly and undertail-coverts; bill light brown, base tinged pink[257, 675].

GEOGRAPHICAL VARIATION At least four races, with variation in size and colour, mainly of upperparts. Geographical variation complicated and not well understood, and beset with taxonomic and nomenclative problems, particularly with *isabellinus* (includes *arenarius*) and *speculigerus*. Recent behavioural evidence (signals and breeding biology) supports earlier attempts to separate *phoenicuroides* (Red-tailed or Turkestan Shrike) as a distinct species[211, 284, 600, 671, 1052]. However, while such recognition characters are supported, it is here retained within *isabellinus* awaiting published details of the behavioural differences. The four races appears to form two main groups: *isabellinus* (central range from NW China), including *tsaidamensis* (SE range from N central China); and *phoenicuroides* (W range from Iran and Transcaspian plains E to Tien Shan, Afghanistan and W Pakistan), including *speculigerus* (E range from N China, SE USSR,

Mongolia). They range from small *isabellinus* to larger *tsaidamensis* and *speculigerus*. Colour varies from sandy-buff *isabellinus* in centre of range to darker grey *phoenicuroides* in W, with other races intermediate. Comparison of ♂♂: *phoenicuroides* has a warm to grey-brown mantle and typically (but not always) a chestnut-brown upper head. Face-mask well defined and black. Lower back with chestnut-brown uppertail-coverts, uppertail and undertail. Primaries black with a prominent white wing-patch; underparts white; *speculigerus* differs from *phoenicuroides* in being sandier above without the chestnut-brown on head, and in being creamy (not white) below; *isabellinus* and similar but larger *tsaidamensis* differ from *speculigerus* in having a dark brown (not black) face-mask and paler primaries, usually without a visible white wing-patch. In wing formulae, *phoenicuroides* approaches Red-backed Shrike rather than *isabellinus*. For details see[200, 211]. Generally *isabellinus* has a shorter wing, has sexual size dimorphism and inhabits the plains, while *phoenicuroides* has a longer wing, lacks sexual size dimorphism and occurs on higher ground. For distribution map of races and additional information see[157, 158, 200, 212, 214, 257, 364, 284, 285, 484, 600, 675, 1052].

HYBRIDS Regularly hybridises with Red-backed Shrike in at least four zones, resulting in very confusing identification of 'buffy' shrikes, which in the past led to the naming of at least 13 forms, which have since been invalidated. A single hybrid zone occurs between *speculigerus* x *collurio* in far-eastern range of Red-backed in the SE Altai Chua region. Three known zones occur between *phoenicuroides* x *collurio* in the S and SE range of Red-backed Shrike. These occur just SE of Caspian Sea in S Turkmenistan and N Iran, NE of Aral Sea in Kazakhstan, and in E Kazakhstan NE of Lake Balkash. Single hybrids may be found breeding throughout the range of *phoenicuroides*. The race *isabellinus* occasionally also hybridises with Brown Shrike[257, 284, 285, 318, 364, 675, 1052]. For distribution map of hybrid zones see[284, 364, 600, 675, 1052].

MOULT Pattern rather variable, but basically two strategies with intermediates; in the general pattern (*phoenicuroides*), adults undergo a partial post-breeding moult from Jul–Sep involving body, tertials, wing-coverts and tail feathers. Then in non-breeding grounds from Nov–Feb, adults and most first-winter (boreal) birds undergo a complete moult. A few young birds may retain some inner primaries until following boreal winter. However, E populations of *isabellinus* which spend boreal winter in Pakistan and India, and most *speculigerus* have a different pattern. They undergo a complete moult in summer while still on breeding grounds, and do not moult in non-breeding grounds. Post-juvenile moult of nominate and *phoenicuroides* similar to Red-backed Shrike (see this species Moult p.198) as well as some individuals following general pattern described for adults[157, 198, 214, 224, 253, 364, 675, 786, 814].

RANGE, HABITAT and STATUS **Breeding range** Central Asia, E of SE Caspian Sea and N Aral Sea to N and NW China, W and NW Mongolia to *c.*120°E. S limit on boundary of Nan Shan, and in W extending S to E Iran as far S as *c.*29°N, Afghanistan and W and NW Pakistan. **Non-breeding range** Passage migrant through Turkmenistan, N Pakistan, central Iran, Iraq, Saudi Arabia, Israel and Egypt. Main non-breeding grounds in central and S Pakistan and NW India, in Middle East from S Iran to S Iraq, E, S and SW Saudi Arabia, United Arab Emirates, Oman and Yemen. In North Africa S of Sahara mainly in Sahel where distributed N of Red-backed non-breeding grounds. Here found as far W as the Gambia, Senegal, S Mauritania and Mali, where rare or vagrants. Further E more common in S Niger, S Chad, N Nigeria, N Cameroon, N Zaïre, Rwanda, S Sudan, Ethiopia, Eritrea, Djibouti, Somalia, Kenya, NE Uganda and NE Tanzania. Vagrants recorded in Gabon, Malawi and Zambia. In Europe, vagrants (probably *phoenicuroides* on geographical grounds) recorded from Britain, Ireland, France, West Germany, Denmark, Norway, Sweden, Finland, Latvia, Austria, Italy, Greece, Cyprus, Turkey, Poland, Spain and Canary Islands. In Indian subcontinent vagrant to Nepal. See Movements. **Habitat** ***Breeding range*** Fairly uniform, occurs in semi-desert, dry steppes and arid mountainous regions usually between 200–2500 m, occasionally to 3500 m (*phoenicuroides*). Habitat characterised by being very dry, open and with scattered shrubs, bushes (e.g. peabush) and trees, even woodland, cultivated areas and parks. Also found in river valleys with *Acacia*, tamarisks and pistachio groves, and in juniper and wild almond on mountain slopes. ***Non-breeding range*** Similar, in open dry savanna country with scattered, mainly thorn scrub, bushes and trees from sea level to *c.*2000 m. Also in cultivated areas and parks[38, 119, 188, 189, 190, 198, 212, 216, 217, 220, 221, 222, 239, 246, 257, 278, 284, 292, 305, 317, 318, 325, 364, 375, 431, 443, 631, 690, 746, 859, 933, 1051]. **Status** Not uncommon migrant. **Conservation status** Unknown.

MOVEMENTS Not well understood, all populations migratory, moving SW or S and SE in autumn (Aug–Sep), except far-eastern populations which may have to skirt the high mountains before turning SW. Nominate race spends boreal winter from NW India, Pakistan, S Afghanistan, S Iran, S Iraq and Arabian Peninsula where less common. Adults depart before young, leaving breeding grounds from Jul–Oct, mainly Aug–Sep, returning from Feb–Apr. Race *phoenicuroides* leaves before *isabellinus*, and appears to be widespread throughout non-breeding range, with an apparent long stop-over in Arabian Peninsula, as only reaches E African non-breeding grounds in Nov, where remains until Mar–Apr. Returns in spring to breeding grounds between Mar–May. Race *speculigerus* spends boreal winter mainly in Arabian Peninsula and NE Africa, with a few birds remaining in these areas during breeding season. Movements of *tsaidamensis* little known; through S Iraq so probably similar to nominate. Autumn and spring migration routes believed to be similar[212, 214, 257, 278, 284, 285, 364, 675, 696, 746, 747, 933].

SOCIAL ORGANISATION and GENERAL BEHAVIOUR Generally not well known; nominate and *tsaidamensis* virtually unknown, *phoenicuroides* and *speculigerus* similar to Red-backed Shrike. Solitary; sits conspicuously on prominent perches *c.*2 m above the ground; often swings tail. Visual and vocal displays also generally similar to Red-backed Shrike. ♂♂ advertise territories with display-flights which in *speculigerus* consists of a long glide with wings extended. Generally *phoenicuroides* appears to ignore *isabellinus* on breeding grounds. Territories in the former race tend to overlap extensively. When giving alarm *tschek*, rhythmic *krkrkrkr-* or *ktschaaa* calls, fluffs out crown and body feathers. At higher intensity tail partly fanned, body bowed and low hoarse *ksss...ksss* calls given. Tail also fanned when disturbed at the nest. In non-breeding grounds, birds are territorial and in E Africa sing and give chattering *chak-chak-* alarm calls[278, 284, 305, 352]. **Foraging behaviour** Similar to Red-backed Shrike, but appears to feed more on the ground (*c.*73%), from lower shrubs and leaves (11%) and less frequently hawks insects in the air (9%). Impales prey[257, 352]. **Food** Similar to Red-backed Shrike; arthropods and small vertebrates. In non-breeding grounds, presence around Red-billed Quelea *Quelea quelea* colonies may indicate predation on chicks[214, 222, 257, 278, 284, 352, 675, 733, 1062].

SOUNDS Repertoire similar to Red-backed Shrike. Main difference found in courtship calls and softer, less nasal main advertising call. Main territorial call a harsh repeated *kscha*-type sound, described as *tsch-ef...tsch-ef, zech-zeck-, zea-zea.* When disturbed gives *zeee*, also *dzhikh-dzhikh-dzhikh-* or a nasal mewing rasp. Territorial calls appear to change to *ko-ick*-type mate-attraction calls: *zautzat...zautzat, tzautzat...tzautzat* or *ko-ick.* This advertising call is given by ♂ while perched or in flight display as well as during nest-building (*phoenicuroides*). The call is often combined with repeated harsh contact-like *kscha-kscha-* (*speculigerus*) or *zea-zea-* sounds. During display-flights ♂ flies with emphasised wingbeats, back and forth in various directions. May also glide at different heights, and fan tail and wings fully on landing. Low-intensity threat at close quarters a quiet hoarse *ksss...ksss-*. Alarm a harsh *ktschaaä* and protracted sparrow-like chattering *chak-chak-chak-* or low buzzy *chat-, chet-, keck-* or rapid rhythmic and toneless rattling *krkrkrkr-*, and at higher intensity snaps bill. Reportedly also gives a series of *tschek-tschek-* or *tschre-tschre-* calls in threat as well as in courtship. A muted trill given by *speculigerus* during courtship is also widely used during pair formation and other interactions with ♀. This call is sometimes combined with song. ♀ gives contact *z-cha...z-cha* calls between bouts of courtship. Begging call a series of insistent *kikikiki-* or *keee-keee-keee-* given by both sexes, particularly by ♀ soliciting food, copulation or during nest-building. Similar to juvenile begging call. Song described as a continuous quiet and varied warble, a melody of harsher and squeakier sounds, at times quite melodious, containing much mimicry. Generally a much better singer than Brown Shrike. A toneless trill given by *speculigerus* apparently does not occur in *phoenicuroides*[214, 257, 278, 284, 600, 631]. Sonagram[284, 600].

BREEDING BIOLOGY Little known; monogamous and territorial. Generally territories overlap extensively (*phoenicuroides*) but few aggressive interactions. In three main races, ♂♂ usually arrive a few days before ♀♀; in some cases may arrive already paired. Pairing observed on stopover in United Arab Emirates. On arrival, initially subdued with little aggression for a few days. Normally single brooded although double broods suspected for nominate race.

Season Apr–May (*isabellinus*) (Sinkiang, China)[214]; May–Jun (*phoenicuroides*)(Turkmenistan) and for same race Apr–Jun (Pakistan)[214, 278]; May–Jun (*speculigerus*) (Altai region in Russia)[214, 675].

Displays *Courtship* ♂ calls loudly with repeated nasal-sounding *tschre...tschre-* (*isabellinus*) or *zauzat-zauzat-* (*phoenicuroides*). When competing with another ♂ for a ♀, both ♂♂ indulge in gliding display-flights. ♂ performs flight-display, flying back and forth combined with high intensity *zauzat-*. Also during courtship gives softer *zech...zech* and more drawn-out begging *zeee...zeee* calls with wing-fluttering. After a while these calls give way to song, which is given from the top of bush. When ♂ close to ♀, he fans the tail, adopts upright, bill-up stance, turns head from side to side, then makes repeated deep bows, tail pointing upwards, turning the head at same time. In *isabellinus* this display not accompanied by calls. Then both may fly through the territory with a peculiar fluttering flight. ♂ begins courtship-feeding ♀ and creeping through branches of upper branches of bushes in search of nest site. Display-flying continues throughout courtship. ***Nest-site display*** ♂ attracts ♀ into potential sites; with much singing he crouches down, with breast in fork and tail slightly raised. Performance repeated and combined with courtship bowing-display. Nest-site display intensifies, at this time ♂ often seen in erect, bill-up stance (*phoenicuroides*). Also continues to creep about in bushes, with tail now fanned even more and moved up and down. Generally signals start of nest-building. While building ♂ will fly towards nest with *tschef...tschef* calls, which changes to song while building. ♂ may also lie in, or next to nest with wings spread out showing primary patch, tail fanned and moved up and down, giving *tschef-* call and flicking wings. ♂ on sighting ♀ coming to nest begins singing excitedly. During this time both birds are heard to give repeated contact-like *z-cha* calls, even in flight. ***Pre-copulation*** On migration ♂ fans tail and gives begging call with wing-fluttering. In *speculigerus*, as intensity increases, opens wings to extended position while fluttering. This display has not been seen in *phoenicuroides.* Also seen to sit in bill-up posture with wings slightly open. Copulation may also follow courtship display or take place without any display, as ♂ flies in from behind ♀ and mounts her[675, 284].

Nest Site apparently selected by ♂, who also

initiates building, but in other observations ♀ does most work. A deep cup built of small twigs, bark, leaves, rootlets, grass, shreds of wool and feathers. Usually placed 1–2 m (0.3–*c*.3) above the ground, often in thorny bushes or trees such as peabush or pistachio, sometimes in reeds. ***Size*** (*phoenicuroides*) OD 122–240 mm (165), ID 65–70 mm, height 70–85 mm (82)[214].

Eggs 4–5 (*isabellinus*), usually 5 (3–7, n=58) (*phoenicuroides*), and usually 5–6 (4–8) (*speculigerus*). Colour in *isabellinus* as for *Lanius cristatus* (see Brown Shrike p.189). In *phoenicuroides* most eggs have a reddish ground colour of various shades, some creamy or ochrous, markings of reddish-brown superficially, and greyish underlying markings with larger patches at large end. From Pakistan described as normally glossy whitish or pinkish in ground colour, liberally spotted with pale brown in a zone at the broad end. ***Size*** (*phoenicuroides*) 21–24 x 15.6–17.8 mm (22.15 x 16.73, n=87)[214, 278, 675]. **Incubation** By ♀ alone, fed by ♂. Period 13–17 days[214, 278, 675]. **Nestling** Appearance unknown; fledge after 12–16 days, fed by both sexes for *c*.1 month after fledging[214, 278, 675]. **Predation and longevity** Unknown. **Brood parasite** *phoenicuroides* host to Common Cuckoo *Cuculus canorus*. In one study level of parasitism 14%. One record of host feeding two cuckoo fledglings[214, 284, 675].

MEASUREMENTS and WEIGHTS *L. i. isabellinus* ♂ (13) wing 89–94 (91.1 ±SD 1.17); tail ♂ (13) 76–82 (79.7 ±SD 2.03), ♂ (11) bill (to skull) 18.1–19.8 (18.8 ±SD 0.58), ♂ (13) tarsus 23.9–25.7 (25.0 ±SD 0.54); ♀ (12) wing 88–92 (89.5 ±SD 1.02), tail 74–80 (77.2 ±SD 2.26), bill 17.3–19.3 (18.3 ±SD 0.67), tarsus 24.1–25.5 (24.7 ±SD 0.47). Significant difference between sexes for wing, tail and bill, but not tarsus[257]; *phoenicuroides* ♂ (10) wing 91–97 (93.7 ±SD 1.62); ♂ (9) tail 74–82 (78.2 ±SD 2.80); ♂ (10) bill (to skull) 17.4–18.8 (17.9 ±SD 0.56); ♂ (10) tarsus 24.2–25.3 (24.8 ±SD 0.34). No significant difference between sexes[257]. **Weight** *isabellinus* ♂ (3) 30.8–33 g (32.1), ♀ (7) 26–33.5 g (29.5)[257]; *phoenicuroides* ♂ (6) 25–31.8 g (29.5), ♀ (1) 25.4 g[214]; ♂ (20) 25–38 g, ♀ (8) 26.3–34 g[257]. For additional data see[214, 257].

22 THICK-BILLED SHRIKE (Tiger Shrike) *Lanius tigrinus* Plate 10

FIELD IDENTIFICATION Medium-small (18 cm) brightly coloured reddish-brown, grey and white shrike with a small, squat, very thick-billed appearance. Sexes different. ♂ has grey head with broad black face-mask; less extensive in ♀, contrasts with reddish-brown upperparts with characteristic dark barring ('tiger' effect). Underparts white (♂) or cream with distinctive dark barring (♀). Young duller and paler, extensively barred, lack grey crown and black face-mask. No white in wings or tail. Calls harsh and grating. Solitary, less conspicuous than other shrikes, found in relatively closed habitat of mixed forest and forest edge in E Russia, China, Japan and E Asia. Migrates S in boreal winter to S China, SE Asia and Malaysia. ***Flight characteristics***: Flies low and swoops up to perch. No white in wing or tail.

COMPARISONS Easily confused with other shrikes during migration; tends to be less conspicuous than Brown Shrike *Lanius cristatus*, keeping more to forest edge. Differs from Brown by slightly smaller size, shorter tail and heavier bill. Thick-billed also lacks prominent white eyebrow (obvious in *superciliosus* race of Brown), lacks white in wings and tail and has grey, not brown head. Juvenile Thick-billed, Brown and Burmese Shrike *L. collurio*ides difficult to separate. Best identified by lack of contrast in facial pattern, showing barred ear-coverts, usually not darker than crown, and only a short buffy eyebrow (sometimes absent), and buffy lores. Frequently shows a pale crescent on ear-coverts. Also shows a whitish eye-ring and/or a small white area behind the eye, giving a 'big-eyed' effect, and has an obvious pinkish base to bill. Superficially resembles Bull-headed Shrike *L. bucephalus*, but is smaller, with shorter tail and grey not rufous head. Differs from Burmese by barred plumage, rufous wings without wing-patch, and lack of white in tail. Separate ranges eliminate confusion with similarly coloured Red-backed Shrike *L. collurio*[281, 324].

DESCRIPTION Adult ♂ ***Head, crown, nape and upper mantle*** Light grey; face-mask formed by black narrow frontal band, lores, sides of head and ear-coverts. ***Back*** Lower mantle, back, scapulars, rump and uppertail-coverts rufous-brown coarsely barred with black. ***Wings*** Dull brown, inner feathers edged reddish-brown and tertials paler; coverts pale tipped with black subterminal bar similar to back. ***Tail*** Dull reddish-brown, graduated and with paler edges and tips. ***Underparts*** White, flanks faintly barred. ***Bare parts*** Bill particularly heavy, blue-black with black tip; palate unknown; legs greyish-black; eye dark brown[435]. See Moult for unusual adult post-breeding plumage. Adult ♀ Duller than ♂, appears browner with less grey crown and nape, black face-mask less extensive, lores whitish (not black), sometimes with short buffy to whitish eyebrow. Underparts buff-white with extensive dark barring on belly and flanks. Juvenile/Immature Crown, forehead, lores and ear-coverts dark reddish-brown, narrowly barred with black, side of face spotted black, white and brown, pale eyebrow giving a 'big-eyed' appearance. Barring on buffy reddish-brown mantle and back becomes wider, heavier and brighter rufous on lower back, rump and uppertail-coverts. Flight feathers similar to adult, coverts edged buff-brown; rump and tail like adult. Underparts: Throat white, rest including flanks dirty white, resembling ♀, but with more extensive barring[191]. First-winter (boreal): Head and nape entirely brown, no face-mask, underparts heavily barred.

HYBRIDS One hybrid known from E Russia: a breeding pair consisting of ♂ Tiger x ♀ Brown Shrike. In another case ♂ Brown Shrike observed courtship-feeding and nest-building with a ♀ Thick-billed Shrike in Japan. Both species have similar mating displays[675, 722, 284, 1052].

GEOGRAPHICAL VARIATION None. Monotypic.

MOULT Has a complete moult twice a year, one (post-breeding) on the breeding grounds in late summer (Jul–Sep), and one (pre-breeding) in the non-breeding grounds (Dec–Apr); affects birds of all age groups. In Malay Peninsula there are two plumage categories of birds arriving in autumn: (1) First-winter (boreal) — head and nape entirely brown, heavily barred, no face-mask; (2) Adult — head and nape a mosaic of barred brown and plain pale grey feathers, face-mask partially developed, the black feathers with white shaft-streaks. Extent of post-breeding moult in adults is variable; ringed birds recaptured during their 2nd and 3rd boreal winters in almost entirely juvenile-type plumage[252, 284, 323, 691].

RANGE, HABITAT and STATUS Breeding range Extreme E Palearctic as far as 44°N in Siberia, E Russia; main population in NE and S provinces of China, as far W as Sichuan and Guizhou at about 101°E, Korea, Japan on Honshu island[188, 190, 193, 195, 212, 214, 262, 273, 675, 687]. **Non-breeding range** See Movements. **Habitat** Breeds in temperate climate, mainly in lowlands in well forested areas with thick undercover and small open areas in deciduous or mixed woods (e.g. conifers, elms, alders and oaks), forest edges, thickets, wooded cultivated areas, orchards, and occasionally suburban parks. Usually below *c.*150 m (E Russia) and below 800 m (Japan). In non-breeding grounds in tropical or sub-tropical climates, where avoids open country, preferring edge or clearings in primary and secondary deciduous and evergreen forests, cultivated areas, mangroves and gardens, usually below 1000 m[190, 193, 195, 214, 252, 281, 284, 414]. **Status** Migrant; rare in extreme N breeding range (China and Russia), fairly common (Korea), to uncommon and local (Japan); in non-breeding range locally uncommon to common[193, 195]. **Conservation status** Little known, but in NE breeding range (Russia and Japan) has declined markedly over last 30–40 years[193, 675].

MOVEMENTS Migratory in boreal winter to low elevations in Oriental region, with occasional records of migrants remaining in Japan. Northern populations depart breeding grounds in Aug, returning May–Jun. Japanese birds depart Aug–Sep, returning May. Northern boundary of non-breeding range lies just S of breeding range, passing through SE China, E Burma, N Vietnam, N Laos, Thailand, throughout Malay Peninsula (where immatures more common) to Singapore and surrounding islands. Also non-breeding visitor throughout Greater Sundas as far S as Bali. Vagrant to Hokkaido (Japan), Hong Kong, N and E Sulawesi, Philippines and S Tenasserim (Burma). Taiwan record requires confirmation. Non-breeding site fidelity recorded[191, 193, 194, 214, 248, 249, 252, 261, 263, 265, 267, 268, 280, 281, 284, 324, 414, 435, 675].

SOCIAL ORGANISATION and GENERAL BEHAVIOUR Little known. Solitary, in pairs or family groups and rather inconspicuous in its relatively closed habitat. Territorial ♂♂ perch in prominent positions and, while calling, adopt an upright posture with wings fluttering[414, 675]. **Foraging behaviour** Unusual in that it combines the typical sit- and-wait method as well as frequently skulking in trees and shrubs to glean prey from branches and leaves at all levels, from ground to canopy. Food caches have not been recorded[263, 675]. **Food** Arthropods, mainly insects, including Orthoptera (grasshoppers and crickets), Coleoptera (beetles, Elateridae, Scarabaeoidae), Hemiptera (bugs, Pentatomidae) and Lepidoptera (caterpillars, moths and butterflies). Attacks small birds and thought to take other small vertebrates like frogs, lizards and rodents[263, 271, 272, 273, 675].

SOUNDS Little known. Repertoire consists of harsh calls and warbling song. Main territorial call a loud, harsh, repeated *tscha*-type sound, described as *tschcha-tschcha-*, *tcha-tcha-tcha-* or *gichi-gichi-*. Alarm a grating or scolding chatter similar to Brown Shrike and Bull-headed Shrike, but louder and harsher. Also gives a more subdued harsh trill-type sound, described as *tschick, tchik* or rapidly repeated *tsik-tsik-tsik-tsik-* notes. Birds arriving on their breeding grounds give repeated shrill *kai-kai-kai-kai-* reminiscent of a small hawk. Song resonant and musical, but at start of courtship may be subdued. Mimicry unknown[262, 263, 271, 284, 414, 500, 600, 675]. Sonagram[284, 600].

BREEDING BIOLOGY Little known. Monogamous and territorial. ♂♂ outnumber ♀♀ on arrival on breeding grounds and pair formation takes place quickly. Some birds appear to pair on passage. Generally single-brooded, with replacement clutches often recorded. Nest failure is high due mainly to the Magpie *Pica pica* and high winds. Densities in far N estimated at *c.*1 pr/2.5–3 km². However in same region pairs have been recorded nesting 10–12 m apart, which suggests territory size is relatively small[284, 675]. **Season** May–Jul, egg-laying Jun (Japan and E Russia). Northern birds breed earliest[193, 214, 270, 272, 284]. **Displays *Courtship*** ♂ sits beside ♀, singing a soft muffled scratchy subsong, head pointing upwards and moved from side to side; body bows up and down with tail straight, not cocked. Then flies to top of tree and gives harsh grating call. ♂ performs powerful fast jinking display-flight which is usually accompanied by harsh calling. Unmated ♂♂ sit on top of trees and give grating call or sing softly. Unmated ♂♂ may attempt to court other shrikes (e.g. Brown Shrike). At least one hybrid is known. ***Pre-copulation*** Pairing on migration (?copulation) may take place in the absence of any courtship display. ***Nest-site display*** When excited on the nest, swings tail up and down, fanning it on the down-stroke, no side to side movements. ♂ courtship-feeds ♀ during nest-building; she begs in typical crouched wing-fluttering manner[284, 600]. **Nest** Built by both sexes. A small compact, thick-walled cup composed of weed stems, grasses, twigs, roots, pliable bark, other herbaceous material; sometimes covered on the outside with flowers and fresh leaves. Nest lining of fine grass, seeding grass heads and occasionally moss. Usually placed 1.5–5 m, occasionally higher, in a deciduous tree (oak, elm, fruit tree), usually on a horizontal lateral branch 1–4.5 m from trunk in top of tree. Nests in S China recorded low down in brambles and low bushes. ***Size*** OD 100–140 mm (120), ID 65–80 mm (70), cup depth 35–50 mm (45), height 60–85 mm (75). Built in 5–7 days. Some half-finished nests are abandoned and a new nest started[214, 270, 272, 273, 284, 687]. **Eggs** Usually 5 (3–6, n=11)(E Russia). Colour variable; whitish, pinkish, pale orange or bluish-green, usually with dark brown, grey or violet spots, patches and streaks mainly around large end. ***Size*** 21.2–24.1 x 15.3–17.8 mm (22.2 x 16.7, n=60)[214, 270, 272, 273, 284, 687]. For additional data see[273, 284]. **Incubation** By ♀ alone, beginning with last egg. Period 14–16 days[193, 272, 284, 675]. **Nestling** Appearance unknown; ♀ broods continuously for first 6 days. Nestling eyes open after 3 days. Fledge after *c.*14 days, and remain in the vicinity of nest for a further 2 weeks. Two ♂♂ observed feeding a single young bird[284]. **Predation and longevity** Little known. Oldest retrap at least 2 years[252, 267]. **Brood parasite** Unknown.

MEASUREMENTS and WEIGHTS *L. tigrinus* ♂ (10) wing 77.8–83.9 (80.9), tail 66.9–75.0 (70.8), tarsus 21.7–23.9 (23.0), bill 14.1–15.9 (15.3); ♀ (10) wing 79.5–85.3 (82.3), tail 66.3–79.1 (72.5), tarsus 22.2–23.4 (22.8), bill 14.8–16.7 (15.5)[273]; ♂♀? (11) wing 80–88 (83.5), tail 68–77 (70.8) tarsus 19.8–24 (22.0), bill (to skull) ♂♀? (10) 18.8–21 (19.9)[500]. **Weight** ♂ (10) 27–29 g (28.3), ♀ (10) 29–37 g (32.1)[273]. For additional data see[478].

23 SOUZA'S SHRIKE *Lanius souzae* — Plate 10

FIELD IDENTIFICATION Medium-small (17–18 cm) greyish, brown and white shrike looking like a dull Red-backed Shrike, but has white V-shaped scapulars on back (sometimes concealed), and fine barring on brownish back, wings and tail. Tail very thin, appearing relatively long. Dull grey head with black face-mask and pale eyebrow. Sexes different. Below creamy-white in ♂, similar but flanks tinged pale rufous in ♀. White of scapulars and outer tail feathers conspicuous in flight. Young like dull ♀ but extensively barred above and below. Little known. Calls soft, harsh and grating with whistles. Inconspicuous, perches on edge or below woodland canopy. Solitary, in pairs or groups, found mainly in miombo woodland, sometimes other broadleaved woodlands. Resident with presumed local movements in S subtropics of Africa from S Congo, S Zaïre, Angola, N Namibia, N Botswana, Zambia, Malawi, Rwanda, Burundi and W Tanzania. ***Flight characteristics***: White V-shaped scapulars and outer tail feathers conspicuous as bird swoops up to perch.

COMPARISONS Similar to Red-backed Shrike *Lanius collurio* but Souza's appears duller in the field, is a slighter bird with a very thin longish tail and a white V on the back formed by the scapulars. Care needed as these can sometimes be concealed. At close range the fine barring on back, wings and tail distinguish it from Red-backed. Emin's Shrike *L. gubernator* similar but ranges separate. Juvenile Souza's differs from juveniles of Red-backed and Common Fiscal *L. collaris* by smaller size, smaller bill, thinner tail and lack of contrast between upper- and underparts, which usually have rufous tinge. Differences in habitat are also important, with Souza's occurring in miombo and broadleaved woodland, not in thornbush.

DESCRIPTION ADULT ♂ ***Head*** Crown, nape and mantle pale grey; face-mask formed by black stripe through eye extending to the ear-coverts; whitish eyebrow. ***Back*** Brown tinged rufous, finely barred with black; rump like back, less barred and sometimes greyer; scapulars white. ***Wings*** Flight feathers dull brown, coverts tinged rufous-brown and finely barred black. No white at base of primaries. ***Tail*** Narrow, dull brown, finely barred with rufous-brown and black, tipped white on all but central two feathers, outer feathers partially white. ***Underparts*** Cream to whitish-buff, sometimes with faint barring. ***Bare parts*** Bill black with a pale base to lower mandible; palate unknown; legs dark grey; eye brown. ADULT ♀ Similar to ♂ but duller, browner and with pale to dark rufous-brown tinge on flanks. JUVENILE Face-mask brown with whitish eyebrow, lacks grey of adult and has upperparts, including crown and nape, finely barred black on rufous-brown, similar to lower back of adults. Scapulars whitish, barred pale rufous-brown. Underparts buffy-white, extensively barred blackish-brown with pale rufous tinge on flanks like ♀. Bill brownish-black, eye brown. IMMATURE Resembles dull ♀ and is slightly barred below.

GEOGRAPHICAL VARIATION Little studied. At least three races, with variation mainly in size and colour of upperparts and flanks. Western nominate *souzae* (S Congo, S Zaïre and Angola, except SE) is larger, has darker grey head, browns are more chestnut-brown and flanks paler compared with smaller *burigi* (SE Zaïre, W Tanzania, Rwanda, Burundi). Race *tacitus* (SE Angola, S Zaïre, N Namibia, N Botswana, Zambia, W Malawi, N Mozambique) intermediate with mantle dull olive-brown and less rufous on flanks of ♀. A cline of decreasing wing size exists from W to E[89, 360, 362].

MOULT Little known. Appears to undergo a complete post-breeding moult from Mar–May. Primary moult recorded in Jun[319, 675].

RANGE, HABITAT and STATUS **Breeding range** S Congo, S Zaïre, Angola, Rwanda, Burundi, W and SW Tanzania, Malawi, Zambia, NW Mozambique. Possibly also in SE Gabon and NW Zimbabwe. Burundi record requires confirmation. Vagrant to N Namibia and N Botswana. Central Namibian record rejected[266]. **Habitat** Virtually endemic to more open miombo *Brachystegia* woodlands with short grass, but also in other more open savanna and mixed broadleaved woodlands not necessarily dominated by *Brachystegia*, including *Uapaca*, *Burkea* and, in extreme S, *Baikiaea*. In Rwanda confined to *Pericopsis* savanna and extends into *Acacia-Combretum* savanna. Generally found at mid-altitudes from *c.*750–1800 m[5, 7, 30, 89, 119) 205, 290, 291, 295, 361, 431, 456, 481, 631, 675, 774, 907]. **Status** Uncommon resident with probable seasonal movements. **Conservation status** Population trends unknown, but because it is primarily an endemic miombo woodland species, degradation of this habitat within its range would have a negative effect. Deforestation is known to occur in Malawi. Basic research into the biology and conservation status are considered a priority[369].

MOVEMENTS Little known. Generally considered resident, but seasonal records from N Namibia and N Botswana and the absence of birds from certain parts of Malawi in austral winter suggest at least some seasonal movements[205, 338].

SOCIAL ORGANISATION and GENERAL BEHAVIOUR Little known. Solitary or often in small groups of 3–5 individuals throughout the year. It is an inconspicuous, shy, silent shrike which keeps to the lower canopy of woodland trees. When disturbed moves into the upper canopy foliage and disappears. However, some birds are confiding and easy to approach. When calling, adopts an upright posture while sitting exposed atop smaller trees or at the edge of tree canopy. White scapulars can be concealed[6, 205, 502]. **Foraging behaviour** Hunts from perches below woodland canopy, sitting immobile in an inclined to horizontal posture as it searches for prey on the ground. Dives down to capture prey, consuming small food items immediately, or carrying larger prey back to a perch before eating. Holds prey down with one foot while tearing prey apart with the bill. Food caches have not been recorded and it does not join mixed foraging parties. **Food** Little known. The few items recorded include only Hemiptera (cicadas) and spiders. Probably also feeds on small vertebrates and has been seen attacking a Violet-backed Sunbird *Anthreptes longuemarei*[150, 834].

SOUNDS Little known. A seldom-heard species with quiet vocalisations. Most frequently heard call is a soft muted drawn-out *tzzeeee*, *tzzer* or shorter *ziz* whistled sound, also described as a grating *chirp*. Louder harsh repeated *Tzz-jert* calls are given in response to playback of repeated *tzzeeee* call; both are thought to serve a territorial function. Alarm described as a scream, scold or low scraping sound, also a low chattering sound was made by ♀ while an observer inspected the nest. Begging call appears to be *tzzzzzick*, given on the nest or while perched and accompanied by wing-fluttering. Adults heard giving *tzzer* food call to fledglings. During the breeding season has a quiet scratchy chattering whistled song[6, 35, 150, 205, 338, 503, 878]. Sonagram[48].

BREEDING BIOLOGY Little known. Apparent prevalence of small groups throughout the year suggests a possible cooperative breeding system, but this has not been documented and no more than 2 birds have ever been seen at a nest together. At one nest an incubating bird was fed by another bird in a nearby tree. Number of broods and reproductive success unknown. **Season** Sep–Nov (Zaïre)[6, 22, 290]; Sep–Dec, mainly Oct (Malawi)[119]; Sep–Nov (Zambia)[291]; Sep (Angola)[423, 907]. **Displays** Presumed ♀ begs in crouched position with wings fluttering and accompanied by *tzzzzzick* call[150]. **Nest** a pair of birds has been seen collecting spider web, but only one of them was seen to sit in the nest and shape it. A small, compact, relatively deep cup, built of leaf petioles, small twigs and grasses bound together and lightly plastered with spider web, and with an internal lining of fine roots, tendrils and grass. It is usually decorated with vegetable down, fluffy seed-heads, moss or lichens, causing it to be relatively well camouflaged. Placed *c.*5 m (1.5–8, n=9) above the ground in a tall shrub or small tree, usually in a fork or on a horizontal branch, sometimes on a lichen-covered branch or in a leafless tree. ***Size*** OD 104 mm, ID 59 mm, cup depth 33 mm, height 52 mm (av. of n=4). One nest took about 3 weeks to complete[6, 22, 35, 150, 205, 290, 500]. **Eggs** Usually 3–4 (1–4). Pale greenish-grey or buff and flecked with brown, purple and grey round large end. ***Size*** 19.5–23.2 x 15.6–17.1 mm (21 x 16.4, n=10)[6, 19, 48, 423, 290]. **Incubation** Apparently by ♀ only; she begs from nest with a drawn out *tzzzzick* call, and is fed off the nest by presumed mate. Period unknown[6, 150, 205, 290]. **Nestling** Appearance and period unknown. An adult with food in its bill heard giving a *tzzer* food call to fledglings[205, 500]. No further breeding information.

MEASUREMENTS and WEIGHTS Races combined ♂ (22) wing 78–87 (81.3), ♀ (24) 78–85 (81.6); ♂♀? tail 72–87, ♂♀? bill 12.5–14, ♂♀? tarsus 19–23[48]; ♂♀? (12) wing 75–85 (80.8), 69–86 tail (80.2), bill (to skull) 16–18 (17.1), tarsus 19–22.5 (21.5)[500]. **Weight** *souzae* ♂ (12) 21–30 g (26.9); ♀ (11) 22–30 g (25.7) (Angola)[89]. For additional data see[89, 319, 360].

24 RED-BACKED SHRIKE *Lanius collurio* Plate 10

FIELD IDENTIFICATION Medium-small (17–18 cm), reddish-brown, grey, black and white shrike. Sexes different. ♂ distinctive with bright reddish-brown back, blue-grey head with black face-mask, grey rump, whitish underparts with pink tinge and white-edged black tail. ♀ and young brownish and barred below. White in tail of ♂ conspicuous in flight. Calls harsh and grating, song warbler-like. Solitary, perches prominently (♀ less so) in areas with low scattered bushes or trees in Europe and W Asia. Migrates in boreal winter to Africa S of equator into thorn savanna. ***Flight characteristics***: Direct, low and rapid; swoops up to perch. White in tail of ♂ conspicuous. Flight over long distances markedly undulating.

COMPARISONS Separation of ♀♀ and juveniles of Red-backed, Brown *Lanius cristatus* and Isabelline Shrike *L. isabellinus* difficult, particularly given the few atypical Red-backed individuals with a rufous rump and tail. The presence or absence of a white wing-patch, mainly in young ♂♂, is of little use in separation, as found occasionally in both Red-backed and Brown Shrikes, and frequently in some races of Isabelline Shrike. Isabelline most difficult to separate, requiring scrutiny of mantle, rump and tail. Mantle and coverts of Red-backed are redder (grey to sandy brown in Isabelline). Tail of typical Red-backed ♀ and immature is darker and browner (rump and tail more rufous in Isabelline). Consequently Isabelline shows marked contrast in colour of rump and tail to body. Tail usually tipped and edged white (only tipped white in Isabelline, with pale ginger sides). Undertail-coverts whitish (rufous in Isabelline). Base of bill pale to yellowish (pink in Isabelline). Separation from immature Isabelline more difficult, particularly (*phoenicuroides*), for example; rump of juvenile Red-backed always barred (unbarred in first-winter [boreal] Isabelline, except some *phoenicuroides*). In the hand adults separated from *isabellinus* by having the 6th and 9th primary of similar length; *isabellinus* has the 9th much shorter than 6th, which also has more extensive emargination than 6th in *collurio* (numbered from inner wing outwards). Tail in Isabelline is rufous above and below. Confusion with juvenile Woodchat Shrike *L. senator* also possible, but Red-backed juvenile often more rufous above and lacks pale scapulars and wing-patch, also noticeably less bulky. Immature Masked Shrike *L. nubicus* is greyer, slimmer and has large white primary patch (see Woodchat Shrike Comparisons p.180). Brown Shrike separated more easily, as it has a bulkier, big-headed, heavier-billed appearance, with proportionately shorter wings and longer, slimmer, more rounded tail. Brown has underparts usually tinged with rufous-buff (lacking in Red-backed), and with very little barring, mainly on sides of breast and flanks (much heavier and extensive barring in ♀, and even more so in juvenile Red-backed), more sharply defined face-mask and paler tail. Hybrid ♂ Red-backed x Isabelline has greyish upperparts and a black and white tail. ♀ similar to ♂ Red-backed but with a rufous tail. ♂♂ in North African non-breeding range superficially resemble Emin's Shrike *L. gubernator*, which has more tawny to rufous underparts (not pinkish) and a chestnut-brown rump (not greyish). Black face-mask extends onto the forehead (lacking in Emin's Shrike). Also resembles Souza's Shrike *L. souzae*, which has white scapulars and barred upperparts. In Middle East superficially resembles Bay-backed Shrike *L. vittatus*, which has extensive black on forehead, a large white wing-patch and whitish rump[158, 257, 631, 866].

DESCRIPTION ADULT ♂ ***Head*** Crown, nape and upper mantle bluish-grey; forehead pale grey with face-mask formed by black band above bill extending through lores and eye to ear-coverts, sometimes bordered above with a thin faint pale eyebrow. ***Back*** Bluish-grey of upper mantle grades into chestnut-brown on back; rump and uppertail-coverts grey. ***Wings*** Flight feathers hair-brown, coverts and tertials edged with buff rufous-brown, very small white patch at base of primaries sometimes present. ***Tail*** Black, all but central pair with white base and outer pair fully edged white. Feathers tipped white in fresh plumage. ***Underparts*** Variable pinkish-white to greyish-pink; throat and chin whitish; undertail-coverts whitish; flanks occasionally barred. ***Bare parts*** Bill black; palate unknown; legs grey-black; eye brown. ADULT ♀ ***Head*** Variable; a few show male-like head colours, others dull with reddish tails. Typical form has brown to rufous-brown upperparts, with rear crown, nape and upper mantle tinged grey; buff band above bill extends through lores to form eyebrow; ear-coverts brownish. ***Back*** Variable, brown to rufous-brown with variable barring; rump greyish-brown, lightly barred. ***Wings*** Primaries dark hair-brown, secondaries and coverts dark rufous-brown, edged with buffy-rufous, no white wing-patch at base of primaries. ***Tail*** Dark blackish-brown (some show a more rufous tail, and occasionally even ♂-like tail), outer feathers with dull white to buff outer web and narrow edging on entire feather. ***Underparts*** Cream to dull white or buff with dark crescent barring; chin whitish; undertail-coverts whitish. ***Bare parts*** Bill paler than ♂, dusky with pale base; palate unknown; legs brown to brownish-grey; eye brown. JUVENILE Resembles ♀, but upperparts, including wing-coverts and tertials, have less variable ground colour: buff- or rufous-brown and (except on ear-coverts) closely barred with black crescents. Underparts dull cream, completely covered with greyish bars, generally more heavily barred than ♀. IMMATURES All first-year birds retain a large proportion of coverts and upper body feathers with recognisable dark subterminal marks. First-winter (boreal) plumage like ♀ but with crown, rump and sometimes tail more rufous (similar to Isabelline), upperparts still barred, underparts less so. Subadult ♂♂ moulting into adult plumage have an intermediate mixed plumage. In non-breeding grounds young can be sexed by Feb[257, 364, 786].

GEOGRAPHICAL VARIATION Controversial, with little agreement between workers. Usually at least three races commonly recognised, with only slight variation in both sexes. Probably best considered monotypic. Extreme E race *pallidifrons* (W Siberia) paler on upperparts (forehead sometimes whitish), and with deeper pink-brown underparts than nominate *collurio* (including *juxtus* in Britain, Europe and Asia Minor). Both have a brighter rufous-brown back than the duller *kobylini* (S European Russia in Crimea, Caucasus, E through Transcaucasia to Iran), which also has the grey of head and nape extending onto the back. All three races spend the boreal winter in North Africa S of equator. In southern Africa, non-breeding *collurio* is found throughout the subregion, *pallidifrons* mainly in the Kalahari and adjacent areas, and *kobylini* in N Namibia, E Zimbabwe to E South Africa[148, 206, 211, 213, 214, 257, 284, 285, 484, 600, 675, 1013].

HYBRIDS Hybridisation not uncommon; occasional (6 cases) between ♂ Red-backed x ♀ Woodchat Shrike, one with ♀ Red-backed x ♂ Woodchat Shrike (see this species p.180), rare (2 cases) Red-backed x Lesser Grey Shrike (see this species p.163), and a few (2 cases) between Red-backed x Brown Shrike, and regularly between Red-backed x Isabelline. Hybrids reported in breeding as well as non-breeding range (East Africa) (see this species p.186)[158, 212, 257, 284, 285, 318, 364, 365, 379, 675, 1052]. For distribution map of hybrid zones see[284, 364, 600, 675, 1052].

MOULT In autumn on breeding grounds, some adults undergo a partial post-breeding moult of head and body, occasionally tertials and a few central tail feathers. These birds suspend moult until they reach their non-breeding grounds. Others do not start moult before migration, although they may begin on stop-overs before reaching non-breeding grounds. Missing flight feathers are usually replaced before migration. Post-juvenile moult concerns body feathers, lesser and median coverts, and occasionally some greater coverts, but highly variable. Takes place 3–4 weeks after fledging, sometimes before the flight feathers are fully grown. On non-breeding grounds all birds undergo a complete moult, adults beginning before first-year birds. Moult, including primary moult takes *c.*3 months and in South Africa young can be sexed by Feb, with *c.*50% of birds in moult by December, and all birds completing moult by mid-Apr. During moult the bill becomes lighter[157, 257, 253, 675, 786, 814, 954].

RANGE, HABITAT and STATUS Breeding range Widely distributed in Europe and Central Asia. In W Palearctic throughout Central and E Europe from N Portugal and N Spain in the west. Absent from N and NE France, W Belgium and Netherlands. In Scandinavia, occurs in SE Norway, and in S Sweden and Finland as far north as *c.*67°N. Throughout E Europe, in Russia it extends eastwards to upper Ob and central Altai in W Siberia at *c.*85°E, with N limit at *c.*64°N and S limit at *c.*48°N. In W Palearctic limit in S generally follows the N Mediterranean coastline to W Turkey. Present on Corsica and Sardinia, rare in Sicily, Crete and Cyprus. Absent from S Turkey, with S limit extending eastwards at *c.*38°N through NE Iran to W coast of Caspian Sea. Absent from coastal low-lying areas in the N of Caspian Sea. In the Middle East, isolated populations occur in the mountainous areas of Syria, Lebanon and Israel. ***Non-breeding range*** From about the equator S, generally avoiding forested Congo Basin, S to southern Africa. In North Africa a passage migrant to Libya, Egypt, Sudan, W Chad, NE Zaïre, Ethiopia, Eritrea, Djibouti, Somalia, N Kenya and N Uganda. Birds spend boreal winter from SE Kenya and NE Tanzania southwards in Tanzania, Rwanda, Burundi, S and SE Zaïre, Angola, Zambia, Malawi, Mozambique, South Africa, Botswana and Namibia. Birds recorded from NW and W Africa are generally considered to be vagrants (but see Movements). Here recorded from Tunisia, Algeria, Morocco, Mauritania, Canary Islands, Gabon, Mali, Ivory Coast, Cameroon, Nigeria, Congo, Niger, and Central African Republic. S of subregion a vagrant to Madagascar and Marion Island in sub-Antarctic. In southern Africa, main concentrations occur in Kalahari basin, Limpopo drainage and lowveld of the NE and SE, and Swaziland. In this region stragglers recorded as far as S South Africa, rare in Lesotho. Occasionally non-breeding birds remain during breeding season as far N as Somalia, Uganda, W Kenya, more frequent further S in central Tanzania, and also known from Botswana (see Movements)[26, 30, 48, 119, 205, 291, 320, 366, 318, 431, 502, 631, 639, 675, 703, 746, 807, 810, 819, 882, 884, 887, 907, 931, 945, 1041].

Habitat *Breeding range* Warm dry or even semi-arid areas with low (1–3 m) scattered or open growth of thick bushes, shrubs or low trees with short grass, heath or bare ground, including steppe and scrub desert areas. Found in low-intensity farmland interspersed with heaths, hedgerows, orchards, vineyards, young forest plantations (particularly spruce and conifer), shrubby meadows, river valleys, traditional pastures, bogs and moors, edge of cultivation, parks and gardens. Frequently found in forest clearings, along forest/field ecotone, roads and railways. Favours areas with hawthorn and blackthorn in Europe, and peabush, honeysuckle, juniper and light forests of birch, pine and aspen in Central Asia. Optimum habitat contains a perch every *c.*20 m. Breeds from sea level to *c.*3200 m in subalpine meadows in Caucasus. Avoids hot low-lying coastal plains and is generally one of the most cold-tolerant of European shrikes, but avoids cold rainy areas. ***Non-breeding range*** Occurs in arid savannas with a strong preference for dry *Acacia* thornveld. ♂♂ prefer more open habitats with fewer and smaller trees, compared with ♀♀ which skulk in taller woodland. Core distribution is on periphery of Kalahari basin[26, 30, 48, 242, 257, 284, 285, 290, 291, 366, 639, 675, 787, 819, 884, 887, 952, 1017, 1023, 1025]. **Status** Rare to not uncommon migrant.

Conservation status Has declined dramatically over the W and NE breeding range, particularly from 1970–1990. During this period major declines occurred in Sweden, Netherlands and Belgium, and from 1989 no longer breeds in Britain. Population estimate (totals or for pairs): 10,000–30,000 (Albania), 50–70 pairs (Andorra), 10,000–15,000 pairs (Austria), 50,000–70,000 (Belarus), 550–900 (Belgium), 100,000–1,000,000 pairs (Bulgaria), 200,000–300,000 (Croatia), 25,000–50,000 (Czech Republic), 1,500–3,000 (Denmark), 50,000–80,000 (Finland), 160,000–360,000 (France), 50,000–140,000 (Germany), 20,000–50,000 (Greece), 60,000–90,000 (Hungary), 30,000–60,000 pairs (Italy), 20,000–40,000 (Latvia), 20,000–30,000 (Lithuania), 300–500 (Luxembourg), 60,000–80,000 (Moldova), 150–220 (Netherlands), 5,000–10,000 (Norway), 80,000–300,000 (Poland), 100–1,000 (Portugal), 600,000–1,000,000 pairs (Romania), 100,000–1,000,000 pairs (Russia), 65,000–130,000 pairs (Slovakia), 20,000–30,000 (Slovenia), 240,000–500,000 (Spain), 20,000–100,000 (Sweden), 8,000–12,000 (Switzerland), 50,000–500,000 pairs (Turkey), 200,000–210,000 (Ukraine). Many of the above estimates are *c.*10 years old, and in urgent need of update. Populations in E and SE Europe appear to be stable. The recent local increases reported for Norway, France, Belgium, Netherlands and Germany should be viewed cautiously, particularly in view of known fluctuations and improved censusing techniques. Currently, the European population is estimated at *c.*2.2 million breeding pairs with southern African non-breeding grounds supporting a few tens of millions. Declines have also been noted in numbers of passage birds in Ethiopia, as well as on non-breeding grounds in Namibia. On its breeding grounds, the destruction and deterioration of habitat through increased cultivation, afforestation and the heavy use of pesticides and inorganic nitrogen fertilisers are thought to be the major causes of declines in Europe. However, declines have also occurred in some areas where there is still suitable habitat. In some areas there is a trend towards occupying habitats at higher elevations. In the non-breeding grounds, overgrazing by livestock reduces prey availability, but also results in bush encroachment and expansion of preferred habitat. Climatic change is also thought to be important, and temperature is known to influence clutch size. The wetter, cooler summers in breeding grounds, and the 20-year drought in non-breeding grounds, have probably reduced prey diversity and abundance. On its breeding grounds, population fluctuations are common and, at least in one long-term study, are probably influenced by a number of factors, including vegetation structure, increased predation, behavioural adaptations, temperature, dispersal of young and immigration. Average densities of 5–30 birds/10 ha, exceptionally up to 80 birds/10 ha are recorded for optimal non-breeding areas. These compare favourably with densities in optimal breeding habitats. In Europe, innovative conservation strategies and habitat improvements in some areas have resulted in increased numbers[285, 317, 366, 369, 452, 480, 639, 650, 675, 703, 787, 819, 882, 884, 936, 937, 938, 948, 952, 964, 1014, 1016, 1017, 1019, 1023, 1024, 1025].

MOVEMENTS All populations are migratory, spending boreal winter mainly in E and southern Africa, the highest concentrations occurring from S Zambia southwards. Migration in autumn and spring follow different routes, a displacement known as 'loop' migration, characteristic of this species and the Lesser Grey Shrike. Birds leave their breeding grounds in autumn from Jun–Sep, mainly Jul–Aug. Generally adults leave first, initially ♂♂ followed by ♀♀ and then young. European populations move in a SE direction, including far-western birds from Iberian Peninsula, travelling E and then SE, crossing the E Mediterranean to enter Africa on a narrow front from E Libya to the Suez Canal in Egypt (*c.*20°–33°E). Birds recorded from NW and W Africa are generally considered vagrants (see Non-breeding range), but may represent either a much smaller migration through W Mediterranean, or a westward movement in the Sahel from the main E route. Some records from W Africa are probably misidentifications of young Woodchat Shrikes. Far-eastern (W Siberian) populations move SW over Kazakhstan, NW India, W Pakistan, N Afghanistan, Iran, Oman, Arab Emirates and Saudi Arabia to cross the Red Sea into Africa. Arrival in the southern African non-breeding grounds is remarkably synchronised throughout the region from Oct–Dec, mainly Nov, a trip of *c.*10–14 weeks. Migrants show high site-fidelity with peak density of up to 8 birds/ha. Sexes have different habitat preferences, resulting in areas with differing sex ratios (see Habitat). They remain in this region until mid-Apr, when the whole population departs in a few nights. Even at this latitude there is evidence of its loop migration, with higher concentrations in the W in early austral summer, and in the E in autumn. Northward movements are displaced eastwards, being more numerous in the Horn of Africa, including Somalia, Ethiopia, Eritrea, Red Sea area and W Saudi Arabia. European birds arrive on their breeding grounds in Apr–May, arrival dates earlier at low latitudes (e.g. Israel), later at high latitudes (e.g. Sweden). The return trip takes *c.*6–8 weeks. Migration routes of far-eastern birds appear to be similar in spring and autumn. Migrates at night with estimated speeds of 43–70km/hour. Apparently feeds on other small migrants to supplement low fat reserves which are built up prior to migration and under endogenous control[48, 64, 148, 205, 212, 222, 224, 257, 284, 285, 320, 325, 366, 443, 631, 639, 650, 747, 884, 885, 939, 954].

SOCIAL ORGANISATION and GENERAL BEHAVIOUR Solitary, ♂♂ perching conspicuously on prominent perches usually 1–5 m above the ground. Sits in upright stance defending and advertising territory by static marking and calling. Territories are usually 1–2 ha (0.25–6), with mainly core area defended, other areas shared with neighbours. Although most unmated ♂♂ roam about, those that settle hold territories 2–3 times larger than mated ♂♂. Also hold small feeding territories on passage and in non-breeding grounds, where generally perch 1.5–2 m above the ground and show high site-fidelity. After breeding, occurs in temporary concentrations before migrating; on passage sometimes a few hundred individuals together. Song and territorial calls heard on non-breeding grounds on arrival and before departure. When excited both sexes swing, flick and move tail up and down, often fanning only half the tail as it swings to one side (right side fanned as it swings to right and vice versa). This movement often accompanied by *chack-* alarm calls with throat puffed out. When anxious, bows forward with tail held up and wings flicked slightly. When a person approaches nest, adopts a concealing-threat posture: ♂ crouches down, remaining motionless with body flattened, head staring straight ahead and tail hanging vertically down. Hunched threatening posture similar but less crouched, with head, back and rump feathers fluffed out and tail spread. Roosts in dense foliage; on breeding grounds usually in nest tree or in vicinity; on migration roosts communally. Scratches indirectly[64, 205, 257, 268, 284, 285, 373, 620, 675, 1018, 1026, 1045]. For study in captivity and wild see[620].

Foraging behaviour Hunts from exposed, usually low (1–5 m) perches on side of tree or bush, taking most prey from low herbs and grass or on the ground, either dropping directly onto it, or gliding down within a radius *c.*5–10 m, sometimes up to 30 m. May hover briefly before pouncing on prey. Most prey carried back to perch in the bill or, if very large, in the feet. Larger prey is held down or in foot while tearing it apart with the bill. Prey often impaled, rarely wedged, and caches established on breeding grounds, usually less than *c.*30 m from nest. Impales less frequently in non-breeding grounds. Generally only ♂♂ impale prey, rare in ♀♀ and young. Frequently hawks insects in the air, sometimes after lengthy pursuit. In this niche, competition may occur with Marico Flycatcher *Melaenornis mariquensis* in non-breeding grounds. Also gleans insects from vegetation, even clinging to bark to extract larvae. In poor weather will hop about on the ground. Venomous insects (bees and wasps) are de-venomed by wiping.

Food Well known. Opportunistic and seasonally variable; mainly arthropods, particularly insects and small vertebrates. Most frequent insect prey includes Coleoptera (beetles), Orthoptera (grasshoppers and crickets), Lepidoptera (butterflies, moths, caterpillars), Odonata (dragonflies) and Hymenoptera (bumble bees, bees, wasps and ants). Less frequently Dermaptera (earwigs), Dictyoptera (cockroaches), Hemiptera (bugs), Neuroptera (lacewings), Trichoptera (caddisflies) and Diptera (flies). Other invertebrates include spiders, mites and wood lice, millipedes, centipedes, earthworms, snails, slugs and small fruit and seeds. Vertebrate prey includes small mammals (mainly mice, voles, shrews, rarely bats), small birds (mainly nestlings, fledglings or exhausted migrants), reptiles (lizards and snakes), amphibians, and rarely carrion. Mainly insectivorous in non-breeding grounds; occasional small mammal or reptile, birds unrecorded. Known to cannibalise own young. Drinks water regularly, but may go without[48, 205, 257, 284, 285, 317, 352, 373, 595, 620, 639, 803, 964, 1024, 1026, 1027, 1028, 1047].

SOUNDS Repertoire consists of harsh notes and whistled sounds, graded in tone, duration and repetition rate. Main territorial call of ♂♂ a repeated harsh *kscha*-type sound, described as *kscha-kscha-*, *tchaa-tchaa-*, *chah-chah-*, *Jert-Jert*, *tzert-tzert*, *tche`-tche`* or *gäck-gäck*. Given from exposed perch or in flight and usually combined in song. Neighbouring ♂♂ respond with similar calls. Courting ♂ repeatedly gives loud drawn-out advertising calls, such as *dschid*, *dscha*, *dschried* or excited *tschock*, these often associated with display flying, during which disyllabic *chee-uk* and *ko-ick* calls are also given (see Display). Alarm a short, harsh, repeated chatter, sounding like *chack-*, *chak-*, *Tsak-*, *Tsik-*, *gek-*, *tek-tek-*, *cht-cht-*, *ch-ch-ch-*, *wett-wett-* or *trrtr-trrt*, usually combined with tail wagging and fanning on down-stroke. Also described as repeated noisy *dschrää-*, *tchraaa-*, *dschro-* or *grèè-*. Raptor alarm a few rapid *chack-* calls followed by dive for cover. At higher intensity also snaps bill. Contact call a graded disyllabic nasal-sounding *chee-uck*, *chu-ik*, *chch-ik*, *chääik*, *ko-ick*, *gu-äck*, *tschuäg*, *dschried* or more drawn-out loud *dschid*. This call used between mates and by adults feeding young. Similar call used in flight during switchback-display, a thin *kièk-kièk-* or rapid *ki-jet..ki-jet*. Begging call graded, at low intensity a soft *chee-ay-*, at higher intensities a querulous *quee-ee-ee*, *kwee-ee-ee*, *chi-ee-i* or nasal *naee-naee-*, also rendered *hiää-* or piercing *quää-*. Nestlings initially beg with *chuk-yuck-yuck* and *ee-uk..ee-uk*, later *chic-chic-* or *cheec-cheec-*. Fledglings beg with *Kee-uk*, *Kee-uk-*. Rarely heard advertising song of ♂ a subdued warble consisting of a jumbled phrase of jerky, chattering, often buzzy notes with much mimicry, given during initial pairing in spring. Develops into courtship song once ♀ in territory. This is usually combined with advertising calls before and after song. Only heard in sexual displays, like parading display, when gives a soft sweet twittering. Song heard in non-breeding grounds, particularly just before migration, a jumble of chirping harsh notes and trills with mimicry of mainly European species. At this time also noted occasionally to flutter wings slightly as it sings. No duetting recorded in this species[48, 201, 205, 214, 257, 268, 284, 285, 373, 500, 600, 631, 1045]. Sonagram[48, 225, 257, 284, 600].

BREEDING BIOLOGY Monogamous and territorial. In spring ♂♂ arrive either 1–5 days before ♀♀ or already paired. This behaviour possibly varies geographically as W populations apparently pair on breeding grounds, while those in the E already paired. Unmated ♂♂ are very aggressive and spend much time in territorial calling, song and chasing intruders (see Displays). Territories usually *c.*20–50 m apart, occasionally at a density of 1 pair/ha in small loose groups. ♂♂ show a much higher site-fidelity than ♀♀ and young; in one study c.50% of ♂♂ returned, compared to 25% of ♀♀. Consequently most appear to mate with same ♂ for one season only. Usually single-brooded, but occasionally overlapping broods by same pair. Extra-pair copulations are not uncommon; in one study up to 50% of copulations were with strangers. Both sexes defend territory, mainly ♂, until young are independent. ♂ most aggressive during nest-building and egg-laying. This probably related to marked mate-guarding behaviour during ♀ fertile period. ♂ chases almost all intruders at this time. Interestingly, the Barred Warbler *Sylvia nisoria* is tolerated in the territory, occasionally nesting within 1 m of the shrike. This association possibly derived from the warbler's superficial resemblance to ♀; both species probably benefit from greater nest protection. ♀ fertile period and most copulations occur from 3 days before egg-laying until laying of penultimate egg. ♂ provides most of the food to ♀ during incubation and early brooding, supplying her direct or from cached food. Occasionally unmated ♂♂ or ♀♀ help raise a brood, sometimes even taking over completely from the parents. Birds may attempt to breed in their first year. Clutch size and laying date are correlated with temperature. In Poland, 16.5°C is the optimal laying temperature, resulting in clutches of 6 eggs; lower or higher temperatures resulted in smaller clutches. Usually single-brooded, rarely two broods. Up to 4 replacement clutches may be laid, a new nest built each time and clutch size decreasing[214, 257, 268, 284, 285, 373, 484, 620, 668, 675, 787, 843, 937, 952, 964, 1017, 1018, 1021, 1026, 1045, 1048].

Season Egg-laying May–Jul, mainly May–Jun[257, 284, 285, 373, 675, 964]. **Displays** ***Mate attraction*** Advertising song thought to attract ♀, rather than having a territorial function. Song combined with territorial calls to attract ♀. Once mate attracted most advertising song ceases. ***Courtship*** Performs a zigzag fluttering display-flight accompanied by repeated *chee-uck* or *ko-ick* calls; may land with gliding flight and slightly spread tail. Also makes rapid straight flights to different points giving advertising call, sometimes in flight, often when perched. When ♀ approaches, ♂ pursues her and performs display-flights, wing-fluttering and *chee-uck* or *ko-ick* calls. This followed by a switchback display in which he flies back and forth on a deeply undulating path in front of her, showing off wing and tail pattern as he rolls from side to side, giving these calls repeatedly. May then perch near ♀, give similar call in erect posture with wings slightly drooped and quivering on nearest side to ♀, repeats this several times and may offer food. This signifies the start of main courtship phase. ♂ may also make short display-flights, flying up c.5 m, then gliding down while giving courtship song. During intense courtship, performs a parading display: perched next to ♀, ♂ flutters wings, patters feet excitedly and begins courtship song in upright stance with head turned from side to side, then switches from bill-up posture to rapid series of stiff, deep bows, singing and head-turning while swaying body from side to side. May fan tail while bowing. During display ♂ patters towards ♀. This display may continue for days. Courtship-feeding may be initiated with ♂ offering a green leaf. After a while ♀ begs in typical crouched, wing-fluttering display accompanied by begging calls. ***Pre-copulation*** Intensity of solicitation varies from little or no display to intense wing-fluttering by ♂; sometimes follows switchback display-flight where ♂ circling ♀, mounting while still giving *chee-uck* or *ko-ick* call. After copulation, heard to give a repeated *di-di-di-di-wett* phrase. ***Nest-site display*** Usually ♂ selects site giving *chee-uck* or *ko-ick* calls to entice ♀. Either sex may also give *dschried* call, ♂ sometimes with nesting material[257, 268, 284, 285, 373, 620, 1026].

Nest Built by both sexes, mainly ♀. A rather untidy cup built with plant stems, leaves, grass, roots and lichen, lined with finer material, grass, hair, moss, fur or feathers. Main structure often contains man-made materials (e.g. string, cloth and plastic). Occasionally repairs and re-uses old nest or even Barred Warbler nest. Uses a variety of bushes and trees, often thorny, including hawthorn, blackberry, rose, blackthorn, peabush, poplars, firs, pines, willows, spruce, juniper. Occasionally uses reeds, woodpiles or roles of fencing wire. Usually placed low down at c.1 m (0.1–5, exceptionally on ground or up to 25 m), well concealed in darker, shaded area of bush. Occasionally building continues during egg-laying, sometimes resulting in an egg being built into the nest. ***Size*** OD 100–180 mm, ID 60–90 mm, cup depth 45–80 mm, height 75–115 mm. Built in 3–7 days (1–8)[257, 284, 285, 373, 964, 1015, 1017, 1020].

Eggs Usually 5–6 (range 1–9, exceptionally 12 due to 2 ♀♀ laying in same nest), geographically variable with clutches of 7 eggs more common in E Europe than in the W, except Corsica. Colour variable; pale green, pinkish, buff, or creamy-white speckled and blotched with light brown, olive, brownish-red, greys or purple mainly at large end. ***Size*** 18.3–26.0 x 14.0–18.5 mm (22.3 x 16.7, n=500)[257, 284, 285, 373, 964, 1021, 1056]. **Incubation** Usually only by ♀, rarely by definite ♂, but some misidentification of ♀♀ with male-like plumage possible. ♀ may sit from the penultimate egg or when clutch complete. ♂ feeds ♀ on and off nest, announcing arrival with food by repeated *Chee-uck* calls. In one case ♀ laid a second clutch 2 days after last egg hatched in first nest; ♂ brooded and fed chicks in this nest and fed ♀ who laid and incubated a second clutch. In one exceptional case, where two ♀♀ had laid in the same nest, both sometimes attempted to cover the eggs simultaneously. Period 13–15 days (12–16 days, exceptionally to 20 days in bad weather)[257, 373, 284, 285, 675, 1026, 1056]. **Nestling** Hatch blind, naked and without mouth spots, mouth yellow. Brooded by ♀, fed by ♂ for first week; later both sexes feed young. Occasionally nestlings fed by non-breeding bird and particularly late in the season unpaired ♂♂ or unsuccessful ♀♀ breeders occasionally help raise broods from a few successful pairs, sometimes actually taking over a brood. Adults seen taking a pellet out of a nestling's gape. Fledge after 14–15 days (9–20) at which time fledgling weighs c.22.5 g. Brood division recorded irregularly. Fledglings independent at c.14–35 days after fledging and are defending own feeding territory by 6–8 weeks, just before migration[257, 284, 285, 373, 426, 675, 789, 1015, 1022, 1024, 1026, 1027, 1042, 1045]. **Predation and longevity** Predation by fox, stoat, weasel, dormouse, feral cats and diurnal and nocturnal raptors. Nest predators include snakes, crows, jays and magpies. Cannibalism of young during severe weather, which in heavy rain causes nests to become water-logged or too heavy, resulting in contents being tipped out. Human disturbance also a serious cause of nest failures. Longevity 7.5 years[373, 484, 843, 964, 1017]. **Brood parasite** Parasitism by Common Cuckoo *Cuculus canorus* not uncommon in some parts of range. In one study this shrike was able to discriminate and reject cuckoo and conspecific eggs, a behaviour which is apparently learnt. In other areas up to 12% egg loss due to parasitism[257, 675, 1030].

MEASUREMENTS and WEIGHTS *L. c. collurio* ♂ (54) wing 91–99 (94.9 ±SD 1.84), ♀ (32) wing 89–98 (93.2 ±SD 2.49); ♂ (23) tail 73–79 (75.5 ±SD 1.75), ♀ (19) tail 69–79 (73.1 ±SD 3.30); ♂ (61) bill (to skull) 17.1–19.8 (18.5 ±SD 0.75), ♀ (32) bill (to skull) 16.5–20.2 (18.2 ±SD 1.10); ♂ (27) tarsus 22.7–25.1 (24.0 ±SD 0.72), ♀ (20) tarsus 22.3–24.4 (23.6 ±SD 0.76)[257]. **Weight** Europe (*collurio*) (during nest-building) ♂ (34) 25.2–32.5 g (28.9 ±SD 1.8), ♀ (11) 28.0–39.0 g (32.5 ±SD 2.9)[257]. On migration ♂♀? (308) av. 22.9–25 g for two different years (Sudan)[841]; ♂♀? (60) 21.7–37.5 g (30.2) (Uganda)[1057]; ♂ (38) 23.8–46.0 g (29.5), ♀ (21) 20.7–36.4 g (28.2) (southern Africa)[205]. For additional data see[214, 257, 319, 484].

25 EMIN'S SHRIKE *Lanius gubernator* — Plate 11

FIELD IDENTIFICATION Small (15 cm), dumpy, reddish-brown, grey and black shrike with grey head and black face-mask contrasting with deep reddish-brown back and rump. Small white patch in wing. Sexes different: ♂ buffy rufous-brown below with white throat, ♀ similar but duller above. White in wing and edge of tail conspicuous in flight. Young barred grey-brown or rufous above, below barred and tinged buffy-rufous. Little known. Calls unknown, apparently rather silent. Solitary, in pairs or small groups of 4–5 birds. Resident in N tree savannas from Ivory Coast in West Africa to N Uganda in East Africa. ***Flight characteristics***: White wing-patch and whitish edges to outer tail feathers conspicuous in flight.

COMPARISONS Similar to larger migrant ♂ Red-backed Shrike *Lanius collurio*, but easily separated above on rump and uppertail-coverts, which are reddish-brown (greyish in Red-backed). Below tinged rufous (pinkish-white in Red-backed). In boreal winter also overlaps with migrant Isabelline Shrike *L. isabellinus*, race *phoenicuroides*, which also has a reddish-brown rump, but tail red (black in Emin's). Juvenile Emin's distinguished from other juvenile and immature *Lanius* shrikes by rufous on underparts.

DESCRIPTION ADULT ♂ ***Head*** Crown and nape grey, face-mask black, extending from narrow frontal (width variable), lores, through eye to ear-coverts, with a slight whitish eyebrow. ***Back*** Grey of head grades into reddish-brown of mantle, scapulars, back, rump and uppertail-coverts. ***Wings*** Primaries grey-brown, coverts and tertials broadly edged rufous-brown, secondaries edged reddish-brown, white wing-patch at base of inner primaries. ***Tail*** Brownish-black with white outer feathers. Central two fringed with rufous, remainder tipped and edged white, outer feathers broadly edged white. ***Underparts*** Chin, throat and upper breast white, lower breast, belly and flanks tinged rufous to reddish-buff (variable). ***Bare parts*** Bill small and black; palate unknown; legs greyish-black; eye brown. ADULT ♀ Similar to ♂ but duller; face-mask smaller (absent from frontal) and browner, less well defined; frontal whitish-grey; upperparts duller grey tinged brown; rump and uppertail-coverts pale reddish-brown; wing with smaller white patch; underparts variably tinged pale rufous, darker on flanks. **JUVENILE/IMMATURE** ♂ More rufous over whole upperparts, ♀ greyer. Upperparts grey-brown barred black, rufous and buff; face-mask similar to ♀ but browner; inner flight feathers tipped and edged buffy-white, coverts barred, tipped and edged buff; rump greyish barred rufous and buff; tail reddish-brown, edged rufous-buff; underparts dull white tinged with rufous-buff, with fine dark barring on breast, coarser on belly and flanks; bill pale[290].

GEOGRAPHICAL VARIATION None. Monotypic.

MOULT Little known; ♀ in complete post-breeding moult in Oct (Congo)[755].

RANGE, HABITAT and STATUS Breeding range Locally in sub-Saharan Africa N of Equator in Mali, N Ghana, Ivory Coast, Nigeria, N Cameroon, NE Zaïre, Central African Republic, S Sudan and N Uganda. Probably overlooked in Togo, Benin and Burkina Faso. **Habitat** Grassland savannas with scattered bushes, open woodland, forest clearings and edge of cultivations up to 1500 m. In Ghana and Nigeria in degraded Guinea savanna[21, 22, 37, 242, 290, 431, 504, 675, 710, 711, 742]. **Status** Resident, apparently uncommon to rare in most localities, possibly a non-breeding visitor in some areas[710, 742]. **Conservation status** Unknown;

habitat probably not threatened. Basic research and population surveys are recommended[369].

MOVEMENTS Little known. Suggested movements require confirmation[234, 338, 710].

SOCIAL ORGANISATION and GENERAL BEHAVIOUR Little known. Solitary or small parties flying from tree to tree. Groups vary from 4–5 birds and, although sex usually not specified, at least one group consisted of ♂♂ only. Perches in exposed positions on top of bushes or telephone lines[338, 502, 504, 742]. **Foraging behaviour** Hunts from elevated perches, takes food on ground, or searches in mid- and upper levels. Also hawks insects in air. Occasionally joins mixed foraging parties[15, 504]. **Food** Insects including, Coleoptera (beetles), Orthoptera (grasshoppers) and Mantodea (mantises)[22, 290].

SOUNDS Little known; apparently a rather quiet species. ♂ calls while in company of 3–4 individuals sitting on a branch. Call described as pleasant, also a low hissing note and ♂ noted as having a loud clear call. Also various twitterings and whistles together with low harsh *zut zut, chuzzoo-wit* and low *chark chark* as a bird landed in a tree[338, 567].

BREEDING BIOLOGY Little known. Apparently monogamous, although reports of groups of birds (see General Behaviour) suggestive of a more social system associated with possible cooperative breeding. **Season** beginning of rains, nest-building Mar–Apr, juveniles Jul (NE Zaïre); recently fledged juveniles from Jun–Jul (Nigeria)[22, 37]; possible breeding Mar–Apr (Sudan)[242]. No further breeding information.

MEASUREMENTS and WEIGHTS *L. gubernator* ♂♀? (15) wing 74–87 (78.9), tail 58–67 (62.5), bill (to skull) 15.2–18.2 (17.2), tarsus 19.7–24 (21.6)[500]. **Weight** 23.5 g[500]. For additional data see[34, 675].

26 BAY-BACKED SHRIKE *Lanius vittatus* Plate 11

FIELD IDENTIFICATION Medium-sized (19 cm), plump, large-headed, grey, black, reddish-brown and white shrike: broad black forehead and face-mask, grey head and dark reddish-brown back with whitish rump. Black wings with large white patch on primaries, and black tail edged white. White of rump, wing-patch and tail conspicuous in flight. Below white with sides and flanks rufous. Sexes similar. Young barred dull greyish-brown above, pale below with barring. Calls harsh and grating; warbling song. Solitary, perches prominently, found in dry open scrub habitat in S Asia, Iran to India. Northern populations migrate S in boreal winter. ***Flight characteristics***: Flies low, swooping up to perch. White of rump, wing-patch and tail conspicuous.

COMPARISONS Superficially similar to a few other reddish-brown, grey, black and white shrikes; in extreme E range Burmese Shrike *Lanius collurioides* has a darker grey head and a rufous rump (pale grey head and whitish rump in Bay-backed). Differs from Long-tailed Shrike *L. schach* by shorter white-edged square tail (not long, graduated and buff-edged), and dark reddish-brown back (usually pale rufous in most Long-tailed races), and whitish rump (pale rufous in Long-tail), and generally prefers drier habitats. Juveniles with greyish-brown rump, reddish tail and no wing-patch resemble juveniles of a number of other shrikes, particularly Brown Shrike *L. cristatus* and Isabelline Shrike *L. isabellinus*. Bay-backed has contrasting rufous greater coverts and grey lower rump. Differs from juvenile Burmese by grey-brown upperparts (reddish tinge in Burmese). From juvenile Long-tailed Shrike by grey-brown rump (rufous in Long-tailed)[224, 747].

DESCRIPTION ADULT ♂ ***Head*** Extensive black face-mask, formed by broad black frontal (extends to behind eye, but variable), eye-stripe and ear-coverts; whitish border (sometimes extensive) between black face-mask and pale grey of crown and nape. ***Back*** Upper mantle and back reddish-brown; rump greyish-white. ***Wings*** Black, primaries with very large wing-patch at base; tertials edged white. ***Tail*** Black with white outer feathers. ***Underparts*** White with buff-brown to rich rufous-brown sides; flanks same but darker; throat white. ***Bare parts*** Bill and legs black; palate unknown; eye dark brown. ADULT ♀ Similar to ♂ but duller, with slightly narrower black frontal. Northern race generally more easily separable from ♂, being duller and greyer, with less striking upperpart colours[224, 675]. JUVENILE Upperparts greyish-brown, head and mantle grey-brown barred with black and buff; frontal barred greyish-brown, ear-coverts brownish; rump barred greyish-brown; wings greyish-brown, coverts and tertials edged rufous-buff; no white wing-patch; tail pale reddish-brown; underparts dull white to pale brown with barring, mainly on breast and flanks. IMMATURE Head and mantle similar to juvenile, but back reddish-brown like adult; wings like adult, greater coverts and tertials edged rufous-buff; wing-patch evident; tail black with buff outer feathers; rump grey, upper tail-coverts whitish; underparts similar to adult but may show slight barring. First-winter (boreal) bird similar to adult but duller with some black wavy barring on flanks and upperparts; forehead usually lacks black[305].

GEOGRAPHICAL VARIATION Two races, with variation in size of bill and wing, and colour of upperparts. Northern and W birds are largest. Compared to nominate *vittatus* (N and central India), *nargianus* (SE Iran, Turkmenistan,

Afghanistan, E Pakistan) is larger and paler above in both sexes, and appears to show greater individual variation[212, 284, 675].

MOULT Adults have a single post-breeding moult which is generally completed by Aug. Post-juvenile moult includes body, tertials, wing-coverts (except primary coverts) and some tail feathers. First-summer (boreal) birds retain a variable number of unmoulted feathers[214, 675].

RANGE, HABITAT and STATUS Breeding range Irregularly distributed in S Asia from central S Turkmenistan, SE Iran, E Afghanistan, Pakistan and India (except Assam and Bangladesh) and S Nepal. **Non-breeding range** See Movements. **Habitat** Northern populations found in semi-desert, dry rocky areas with scrub, bush and scattered trees, pistachio woods and cultivated areas in lowland plains, foothills, valleys, slopes to 2000 m. Avoids open desert. Southern populations occur in a variety of habitats from open scrub and thorny tree-jungle to wasteland, grazing land and cultivated areas around villages, canal-bank tree plantations as well as in parks and gardens. Avoids better wooded areas. Its habitat appears to be intermediate between the semi-desert favoured by the *lahtora* race of the Southern Grey Shrike *L. meridionalis*, and the relatively more wooded, well-watered areas favoured by the Long-tailed Shrike and Grey-backed Shrike *L. tephronotus*[183, 209, 212, 214, 224, 276, 278, 305, 449, 675]. **Status** S populations common and widespread resident, N populations less common and migratory, either with local or more widespread seasonal movements. **Conservation status** Little known, probably not threatened.

MOVEMENTS Generally resident, but with marked seasonal movements, particularly in NW populations, but little studied. Populations in E Pakistan and India may be migrants, but in most cases appear to be resident with local movements. Pakistan birds leaving in Oct and returning in Mar are thought to spend boreal winter along the Makran coast. Turkmenistan birds leave their breeding grounds from Aug–Sep, migrate to India, returning in Apr–May. In Nepal mainly an uncommon boreal winter visitor or passage migrant, but with regular summer and winter sightings at Surkhet. In Middle East (SE Iran) birds are resident with some local movements. Vagrant to United Arab Emirates (Apr, Nov and Feb), Saudi Arabia (Apr), Oman (Apr) and Bhutan[209, 214, 217, 221, 222, 224, 675, 747].

SOCIAL ORGANISATION and GENERAL BEHAVIOUR Solitary or in pairs; perches in exposed positions; relatively tame. Territorial and aggressive in all seasons, adopting an upright posture with tail often swung from side to side as it calls. Advertise and defend a territory of *c*.1–2 ha. ♂♂ and ♀♀ perform display-flights, often accompanied by *zea-* calls. Display-flights are generally similar to Red-backed and *phoenicuroides* race of Isabelline Shrike. During high-intensity interactions with conspecifics, ♂ performs a high flight display, remaining aloft and circling around in a gliding flight interspersed with rapid shallow wingbeats. This display-flight is reminiscent of Lesser Grey Shrike *L. minor*. Readily chases congeners like Long-tailed and Lesser Grey Shrike. **Foraging behaviour** Hunts from prominent perch, usually 2–2.5 m high, and captures food mainly on ground within a radius of 10 m. Hops on the ground. Larger prey carried to perch, held by foot and torn apart. Known to form caches. **Food** Arthropods, mainly insects and their larvae, and vertebrates. Insects include Orthoptera (crickets and grasshoppers), Coleoptera (beetles), Hymenoptera (wasps and ants), Lepidoptera (caterpillars, moths and butterflies). Also occasionally takes nestling birds, young mice and lizards[224, 278, 552, 675].

SOUNDS Little known. Repertoire consists of harsh calls and warbling song; calls distinctively nasal in quality. Main territorial call a harsh nasal grating di- or trisyllabic *kscha*-type phrase, described as *chur-r* or *chee-ur, keechew-keechew-, keekekuw-, jeejeejweet-, tchchejeewt-* or *chew-chew-chew*; also *ko-ick*-type calls. Contact a more melodious *zea-zea-zea* call or rhythmically repeated *rrre*-type sound, like *rrre-rrre...* during courtship. Song consists of loud warbled whistles, rather high-pitched and lark-like, combined with harsh notes and much mimicry. Alarm call a harsh, rough, rapid chatter or ratchet-like *tzrrr, krrrr-krrrr-, trrrr-trrrr-* or *cha-a-a-a-a* and a scolding *chirr-chirr*. Begging calls repeated quavering nasal *naaae-naaae-*[284, 224, 278, 500, 600]. Sonagram[284, 600].

BREEDING BIOLOGY Monogamous and territorial. In migrant populations ♂♂ arrive before ♀♀. Initially they are quiet, but once a territory is established they sing loudly and persistently, giving a repetitive *zea-zea-zea-*. Before breeding activities really start, the sexes keep in touch with various softer *zea-* calls. Two ♂♂ may court a single ♀. Breeding densities range from 25–30 breeding prs/km^2 (N India) to 12–14 prs/4 km^2 (Turkmenistan). Sometimes nest up to 50 m apart in optimal habitats (India); 150 m apart in poorer habitats (Turkmenistan). In one study reproductive success was *c*.40% (n=8), with a hatching success of 69%. Breeding behaviour is different to other small brown shrikes, with both sexes being unusually active, and ♀ behaviour initially being similar to ♂. Double broods are common, occasionally three, and are usually laid in a new nest. Up to three replacement clutches have been recorded[224, 278, 284, 552, 675]. **Season** Apr–Jul (NW India), Feb–Sep (central India), Feb–Apr (S India)[224, 552]; Mar-Aug (Pakistan)[278]; May (Turkmenistan)[209, 284]. **Displays** ***Courtship*** ♀ sits close to ♀, body erect, bill up and facing away from her, sometimes with his back to her and tail partially cocked. ♂ then makes rhythmical deep body-bows, almost touching her feet and accompanied by loud song while keeping his head turned away from her. ♂ may display-fly around territory before repeating courtship display. Display usually begins with excited *zea-* or characteristic rhythmic *rrre....rrre-* calls and then changes into song. Whole display may take as lit-

tle as 4 min. ♀ may respond with harsh *chee-ur* calls. ♂ courtship-feeds ♀. ***Pre-copulation*** unknown. ***Nest-site display*** Apparently performed by either sex, bird sitting in prospective sites, body feathers fluffed out, head held up while rotating body sideways with tail slightly spread and moved up and down. This display is accompanied by calling, including begging calls[224, 284, 675]. **Nest** Built by both sexes. A small neat cup of grass, rags, wool, tow and feathers, with the exterior smeared with web, and usually lined with soft grass. Usually placed in fork or crotch of bush or small tree, often thorny, 1.5–4 m (0.9–10) above ground. ***Size*** OD 83–101 x 95–109 mm, ID 52–56 x 56–63 mm, cup depth *c.*30 mm (n=3). Completed in 5–8 days (n=9)[214, 224, 276, 278, 552, 675]. **Eggs** Usually 4 (3–5), laid on consecutive days. Colour variable; whitish or pinkish-white to greenish-white with brown spots and blotches forming a zone at broader end, plus some secondary greyish markings, others salmon pink, densely speckled with reddish or purplish brown. ***Size*** 19.7–23.1 x 14.1–17.1 mm (20.8 x 15.7, n=100)[209, 214, 224, 278, 552]. **Incubation** Mostly by ♀, ♂ feeds ♀ on nest. Period 14–15 (n=4)[278, 552]. **Nestling** Hatch blind and naked. Mouth spots unknown. Attended by both sexes, ♂ supplying most food, and passing it to ♀ who feeds young. Fledge after 14–15 days (n=4)[278, 552, 675]. For development of nestling see[552]. **Predation and longevity** Oldest retrap 7 years[267]. **Brood parasite** None.
MEASUREMENTS and WEIGHTS *L. v. vittatus* ♂ (10) wing 82–88 (85.5), bill 15.5–18 (16.5)[212]; ♂♀? wing 82–90, tail 81–96, usually less than 90, bill (to skull) 15–18, tarsus 21–24[224]; races combined ♂♀? (14) wing 80–91 (85.5), tail 79–93 (85.8), bill (to skull) 16–18.5 (17.0), tarsus 21.5–24.5 (22.8)[500]. **Weight** ♂♀? (17) 18–24 g (20.8) (India)[224]. For additional data see[224, 274].

27 BURMESE SHRIKE (Chestnut-rumped Shrike)
Lanius collurioides **Plate 11**

FIELD IDENTIFICATION Medium-sized (20cm), black, deep reddish-brown and white shrike with broad black head and face-mask, dark grey head and deep reddish-brown back and rump. Wings Black with white patch (usually only seen in flight); tail long, black with white edge. Below cream with faint rufous tinge. Sexes similar. Young dull greyish-brown, barred above and below. Little known; calls harsh and grating, song includes whistles. Solitary or sometimes gregarious in noisy groups, perches prominently. Resident or migratory, found in open woodland and forest edge in NE India, S China and SE Asia. Some populations migrate S in same area in boreal winter. ***Flight characteristics***: Short rounded wings with white wing-patch, and long black tail tipped and edged white distinctive.
COMPARISONS Superficially similar to Bay-backed Shrike *Lanius vittatus* in extreme W, but has a dark blackish head (contrasting black and grey in Bay-backed), a small white wing-patch (broad in Bay-backed), and less white in tail. Differs from Thick-billed Shrike *L. tigrinus* by slimmer appearance, longer tail, broader black frontal and presence of white wing-patch. Differs from Long-tailed Shrike *L. schach* by white outer tail feathers, darker grey crown and lack of rufous-sided underparts. Juvenile differs from other brown shrikes, Burmese being darker reddish-brown above and heavily barred below (Bay-backed more greyish with little barring below). Differs from juvenile Long-tail by darker rump and absence of orange-buff in plumage, from juvenile Brown *L. cristatus* by lack of buffy eyebrow and greyer head and nape, and from juvenile Bull-headed *L. bucephalus* by slimmer, longer-tailed appearance and lack of heavy barring on back.
DESCRIPTION **ADULT ♂** ***Head*** Forehead black (extent variable), lores, ear-coverts and around eye black, shading to dark grey crown and nape, which grades into paler grey mantle. ***Back*** Rich dark reddish-brown ; rump same. ***Wings*** Primaries blackish-brown with white patch; greater coverts and tertials edged rufous-brown. ***Tail*** Black with outer feathers completely white, grading inwards. ***Underparts*** White to dull white. ***Bare parts*** Bill small, grey-brown with black tip; palate unknown; legs greyish-black; eye reddish-brown. **ADULT ♀** Similar to ♂, duller and paler, lores and nasal feathers whitish, black on forehead less extensive[224]. **JUVENILE** Head spotted and barred greyish-brown and buff, ear-coverts brownish; mantle, back and rump barred rufous-brown; tail brown with outer feathers pale buff, rest buff-tipped; flight feathers buff-edged, without white wing-patch (or just developing); coverts buff-tipped, greater and tertials buff-edged; tail dull brown, pale outer feathers; underparts dirty white to buff, breast and flanks barred with blackish-brown; undertail dull white[437]. **IMMATURE** Similar to ♀, but barred above.
GEOGRAPHICAL VARIATION Two races; *nigricapillus* (S Vietnam) similar to *collurioides* (E India to N Vietnam) but with frontal black more extensive, and grey darker on head, nape and mantle; back richer chestnut-brown; ear-coverts not so distinct[324].
MOULT Post-juvenile and, more remarkably, post-breeding moults are completed from Aug–Oct[224].
RANGE, HABITAT and STATUS **Breeding range** Little known; S Asia, NE India, Burma, S

China, Thailand and SE Asia (except Malay Peninsula) and South Vietnam. Probably also in Laos, Cambodia and N Thailand where usually only considered a visitor[188, 189, 190, 194, 224, 281, 437, 444, 600, 675]. **Non-breeding range** See Movements. **Habitat** Found from plains at sea-level up to 1800 m (Burma), 2400 m (S Vietnam) and 2500 m (China), in scrubby open woodland, edge of secondary forest, and edges of cultivated land, paddies and gardens in villages. Often found along roads[188, 189, 190, 261, 281, 324, 437]. **Status** Little known, generally not uncommon local resident and partial migrant with some seasonal movements. **Conservation status** Population trends unknown; at least in Thailand not at risk[444].

MOVEMENTS Populations are either migratory or resident with local or altitudinal movements. Breeding and non-breeding ranges overlap broadly, with non-breeding range tending to be more southerly at lower elevations. It is a passage migrant and probably a boreal winter visitor to the plains and foothills of Assam (India), rarely to SE Bangladesh. It is a common boreal winter visitor to N and E plains of Thailand, where often in paddies and other cultivation. Occurs as far S as Prachuap Khiri Khan at *c.*12°N but is apparently absent from the central and SE provinces. In NE Thailand commonest from Jul–Mar. Some birds migrate to NE Burma, but apparently more common in central and S plains from Dec–Mar. Generally birds depart S from Jun–Aug, returning from Mar onwards. In irrigated areas of Shwebo district they move out in Mar and return in June. In boreal winter birds regularly appear as far S as Henzada, sometimes to Amherst at *c.*16°N, and will probably also be found to occur in Tenasserim. Chinese, and probably other eastern populations down to S Vietnam appear to be resident, with only local altitudinal movements recorded. Vagrant to Hong Kong in Mar[224, 261, 267, 281, 675].

SOCIAL ORGANISATION and GENERAL BEHAVIOUR Virtually unknown; solitary as well as reportedly often collecting into noisy parties, squatting on tops of bushes flapping their wings and screeching loudly. However, it is unclear whether this refers to a family group with dependent young or to a more social gathering. Perches out exposed, apparently confiding and easy to approach. Migrating birds show non-breeding site-fidelity[224, 261, 675]. **Foraging behaviour** Hunts from prominent perch, diving to ground for prey, returning to same or different perch; hops on ground. Probably impales prey, although unrecorded[224]. **Food** Insects, including Orthoptera (grasshoppers). Also takes lizards and other small terrestrial vertebrates[224].

SOUNDS Little known. Repertoire consists of harsh, grating calls and warbling song. Also described as having a staccato rattle similar to Brown Shrike. Song musical, recorded as 'sweet and full'. Also recorded as having an unusual whining call (begging?), and apparently collects into noisy parties[189, 224, 261, 281, 560].

BREEDING BIOLOGY Little known. Apparently monogamous and territorial. May lay two broods. **Season** Mar–Jun, egg-laying Apr–May (Burma); Jun (SE China)[261]. **Displays** Unknown. **Nest** Role of sexes unknown. Built of flowering grass heads, leaves, lichen and feathers, covered with spider webs, and lined with fine grass stalks. Some nests are much larger than others. Recorded 2 m above the ground in a fir tree, or small tree, against trunk[261, 270]. **Eggs** 3–6. Colour variable, pale greenish-white spotted all over chiefly at large end with pale ashy-purplish and yellow brown, other ground colour yellowish-white. ***Size*** Av. 21.1 x 16.4 mm (n=100) (China)[189, 270]. No further breeding information, except for a single retrap after 12 months[267].

MEASUREMENTS and WEIGHTS Races combined ♂ (5) wing 82–88 (85.0), tail 82.5–93 (88.3), bill (to skull) 17.8–18.5 (18.1), tarsus 23–24.5 (23.5)[500]; ♂♀? wing 85–94, tail 92–102, bill 17–19, tarsus *c.*25[224]. **Weight** ♀ Imm 26 g[495].

28 LONG-TAILED SHRIKE (Black-headed, Black-capped, Schach or Rufous-backed Shrike) *Lanius schach* Plate 12

FIELD IDENTIFICATION Large (23–27 cm), rufous, grey, black and white shrike with a relatively long black, buff-edged tail and large rufous rump. Much geographical variation in colour of head, mantle and back. Two prominent head patterns and a melanistic form: (A) distinctive black face-mask contrasting with grey head and mantle, sometimes with thin white eyebrow, back rufous; (B) face-mask absent, head completely black (black cap); mantle and back grey, rufous or reddish-brown. Below whitish with rufous flanks. Wings black, usually with conspicuous white wing-patch. Melanistic form has head and body greyish-black. Sexes similar. Young barred dull brownish-grey above, with indistinct face-mask and lightly barred below. Calls harsh, grating with buzzing quality; warbling song with mimicry. Solitary or in family group, perches prominently, found in wide range of habitats from lowlands to mountains at 3000 m, and from semi-arid, open scrub, steppe and semi-desert areas in W, to better wooded, wetter areas, forest clearings and cultivated areas in E. Distributed from NE Iran to SE Asia, Malay Archipelago, Indonesia and New Guinea. Northern populations migrate SE in boreal winter. ***Flight characteristics***: Flies low to ground, swooping up to perch. White in wings and tail conspicuous in flight in some races, pale rufous rump conspicuous.

COMPARISONS Black face-mask group, particularly race *caniceps*, most similar to Grey-backed Shrike *Lanius tephronotus* race *lahulensis* and Philippine Shrike *L. validirostris*, which have grey to dark grey (not rufous-brown) upperparts, and indistinct wing-patch. Grey-backed also has a heavier bill. This group also resembles Bay-backed Shrike *L. vittatus* in head coloration, but Long-tailed differs by being much larger with rufous-brown rump (Bay-backed greyish-white), small (sometimes absent) white wing-patch and only little (depending on race), white or pale tips on longer tail (Bay-backed has very large wing-patch and much white on shorter tail). Black-headed (capped) group superficially like smaller Burmese Shrike *L. collurioides*, which has a dark grey and black head (not completely black), deep reddish-brown back (not rufous) and much white in outer tail feathers. Separation of juvenile Long-tailed from juvenile Grey-backed unstudied in field. Study skins similar, although Grey-backed tends to show more extensive barring below. Best identified from other smaller brown shrikes on greater size, greyer upperparts and greater contrast between black wings and body. First-winter (boreal) birds similar to Bay-backed, but have rufous-buff rump and uppertail-coverts and lack chestnut-brown on shoulder[747].

DESCRIPTION **ADULT Group A** (*schach, erythronotus, caniceps*). Sexes generally similar. ***Head*** Face-mask formed by black forehead, extending back on crown to at least level of eye; black lores and ear-coverts; thin whitish eyebrow separates face-mask from crown; face-mask contrasts with pale grey crown, nape and mantle. ***Back*** Mantle grades into rufous-brown to tawny back and rump. ***Wings*** Black with small white wing-patch at base of primaries; secondaries tipped buff-white, tertials with broader buff-white edging, ulna white. ***Tail*** Black with pale buff to whitish tips and edges to outer feathers. ***Underparts*** White to dull white tinged with reddish rufous-brown, darkest on flanks and side of breast; breast, throat and chin whitish. ***Bare parts*** Bill black, pale at base of lower mandible (bill browner in ♀); palate flesh-coloured; legs black to greyish-black, generally browner in ♀; eye dark brown. **Melanistic forms** *'fuscatus'* Head, throat, wings and tail black, rest of body dark, dusky grey grading to dull rufous-brown on rump and tail-coverts; lacks white wing-patch; underparts dull grey, sometimes mottled dull buff and rufous[500, 692]. **ADULT Group B** (*longicaudatus, tricolor, nasutus, suluensis, stresemanni; bentet* somewhat intermediate). Sexes generally similar. ***Head*** No face-mask as entire head black from frontal, crown, nape, upper mantle, lores to ear-coverts (hindcrown, nape and mantle grey in *bentet*). ***Back and rump*** Reddish rufous-brown. ***Wings*** Black with large white wing-patch at base of primaries; secondaries and tertials edged and tipped rufous-brown, like back. ***Tail*** Long, thin and black with small rufous-buff edging. ***Underparts*** **and bare parts** Similar to Group A races. **ADULT ♀** Generally similar to ♂ in both groups; sometimes greyer on back and more extensive rufous-brown flanks, but variable and not consistent. Bill may be paler. **JUVENILE/IMMATURE (Group A)** Brownish-grey above with distinct dark barring, less extensive dark face-mask (restricted to sides of face), dark barring on breast and flanks, and dark subterminal bands and pale fringes to coverts and tertials. Head: Forehead dark spotted buff, lores and ear-coverts dark brown; crown, nape and mantle spotted and barred grey-buff, grading into back. Back to rump: Rufous-brown (similar to adult) barred. Wing: Brown-black with rufous-buff edging on coverts and tertials, small wing-patch buff, often absent. Tail: Black like adult, but terminal spots buff-brown (not white). Underparts: Similar to adult, usually with some barring, particularly on flanks. Apparently more prominent in some races. Bare parts: Bill horny-brown with flesh-coloured base; legs dark brown; eye brown. **(Group B)** Similar, but with small buff-tipped black bars on head, larger on mantle; lower back and rump with little barring; tail brown (not black), pale-edged; underparts creamy-white without barring. Subadults have mottled greyish-black heads. First-year birds distinguished on juvenile tail. Young assume adult plumage after about 10 weeks[224, 498]. For difference between juvenile, first-winter (boreal) and first-summer (boreal) plumage see[719].

GEOGRAPHICAL VARIATION Variation complex with many races described and many intermediates. Variation mainly in body, wing, tail, and bill size, and colour of head, mantle and back. Nine races considered here. Different groupings possible using head, mantle or back colour. Using head colour, two basic groups can be identified: (A) grey head with distinctive black face-mask — *schach* (S and E China, Hainan, Taiwan, N Vietnam), *erythronotus* (Central Asia in Afghanistan, Turkmenistan, SE Kazakhstan, S Uzbekistan, Kyrgyzstan, Tajikistan, Pakistan, NW India) and *caniceps* (S and W India, N Sri Lanka); (B) head completely black, no face-mask — *longicaudatus* (SE and central Thailand), *tricolor* (including *nigriceps* (E India, Himalayas in Nepal, N Burma, S China, N Laos, N Thailand), *nasutus* (Philippines except Sulus, probably also on N Borneo), *suluensis* (Sulu Archipelago) and *stresemanni* (central highlands of E New Guinea). Race *bentet* (Malaya Peninsula, Sumatra, Java, Lesser Sundas, and probably SE Borneo) appears intermediate between groups. Birds from E Java, Bali and SE Borneo are sometimes strikingly different from typical race, and may constitute a separate race, while others show variable amount of black, and may be intermediate. For detailed distribution map see[284, 675, 600]. Within black face-mask group (A) there is also a general increase in grey on the back from *schach–erythronotus–caniceps*. Similarly, in the black-headed group (B) there is an increase in grey on the back, from the completely reddish-brown of *longicaudatus* through *tricolor* and *stresemanni* to the predominantly grey-backed *nasutus*. The three insular races (*nasutus*, *suluensis* and *stresemanni*) are most similar. The dark greyish-black melanistic form '*fuscatus*' (S and SE China, Hong Kong, Hainan, Taiwan, N Vietnam) shows intermediates with *schach*[186, 190, 191, 212, 261, 284, 268, 449, 496, 600, 675].

MOULT Adults have a complete post-breeding moult beginning with body feathers, with the western migratory populations completing this at the start of the autumn migration. Appears to have a complete post-juvenile moult from Jul–Oct as boreal winter birds tend not to show juvenile plumage[436, 675]. For additional details see[257].

RANGE, HABITAT and STATUS **Breeding range** (Group A: grey-headed, black face-mask races). S Asia and W Indonesia from NE Iran, Afghanistan, S Kazakhstan and Turkmenistan, Pakistan, India (N to Himalayan foothills), S China, Taiwan, N Vietnam, Malaya, Sumatra, Java and Lesser Sundas. (Group B: black-headed races) E Central Asia in N India, SE Tibet, SW China, Burma, Thailand, Laos and central Vietnam, N Malay Archipelago in N Borneo and Philippines (including Sulu Archipelago) and New Guinea. **Non-breeding range** NW populations migrate SE to India. See Movements. **Habitat** Occurs in diverse range of habitats from lowlands to 4300 m in Himalayas, including semi-desert, steppe, open country, grassland with scattered bush, willow scrub, plantations and occasionally in evergreen forest, cultivated lands, orchards, gardens and parks, paddies, marshes, tall grass and reedbeds. Appears to favour vegetation associated with rivers and canals. Avoids very arid areas[188, 190, 191, 197, 212, 220, 221, 224, 248, 251, 252, 257, 260, 261, 262, 263, 265, 271, 273, 274, 276, 277, 278, 281, 284, 324, 435, 442, 449, 484, 675, 692]. **Status** Common to uncommon resident, but with N populations partially or entirely migratory. **Conservation status** Little known, but changes in relative abundance have occurred, with a general decrease in W and an increase in E. Marked decrease noted in S Turkmenistan since end of last century, at which time it was common, but today is rare. Similarly it has disappeared from Tajikistan. In S Burma the race *tricolor* may have disappeared as a breeding species, while the race *bentet* was more numerous on Sumatra half a century ago. However, local increases in this race were noted in the Malay Peninsula in the 1960s. In spite of the potential gain in breeding areas due to the large-scale deforestation of the Himalayan midlands, it appears to be only sparsely distributed along these enormous terraced slopes. Climatic changes and habitat destruction are probably the main causes of changes in relative abundance. The use of mandibles of this species in Nepali 'rice feeding ceremony' for six-month-old children is probably of minimal conservation concern. Estimated population in Kabul (Afghanistan) is 1,000–1,500 breeding pairs[284, 276, 305, 675, 792, 928].

MOVEMENTS Most populations resident, but some migratory or subject to local (including altitudinal) movements. It is a nocturnal migrant. W and NW populations (*erythronotus*) leave breeding range (Central Asia in Turkmenistan, SE Kazakhstan, Tajikistan and Afghanistan) from Aug–Nov, returning in Apr–May. In Afghanistan some populations are migratory from Sep–Mar, some returning as early as February. Populations in Pakistan and N India are also migratory or partially so, departing in Sep. Migrants appear to spend boreal winters in plains of India. S China population (*schach*) is either resident or descends to the plains in the S in Sep. In Nepal (*tricolor*) birds undergo altitudinal movements to below 1700 m, with some remaining in the foothills and others moving S to India. Central Indian populations (*caniceps*) appear to be subject to local seasonal movements only. Vagrants have been recorded in Western Palearctic from Hungary, Turkey, Israel and Oman, and in the far east in Japan and Korea from Jan–Mar[221, 257, 272, 274, 284, 675, 719, 746, 874, 928, 1040].

SOCIAL ORGANISATION and GENERAL BEHAVIOUR Little known. A loud, noisy, conspicuous and pugnacious bird. Solitary; usually perches prominently with upright posture, particularly when calling. Foraging posture more horizontal, when also perches low down. During calling head is raised and tail moved, the wings are flicked during song. Both sexes sing. Remarkably, in S China it is active at night, calling and feeding, particularly on crabs which come out at night[224, 260, 271, 273]. **Foraging behaviour** Hunts from prominent perch; food mainly taken on ground, where hops about. Prey usually taken back to perch before being eaten. Also hawks insects in air and will pirate food from other birds (kleptoparasitism). **Food** Arthropods, mainly insects and their larvae, and vertebrates. Insects include Orthoptera (locusts and crickets), Lepidoptera (butterflies and caterpillars), Hymenoptera (wasps, bees and ants), Coleoptera (beetles), Mantodea (mantises), Odonata (dragonflies) and Hemiptera (cicadas). Also takes earthworms, centipedes, scorpions, crabs, and small vertebrates including fish, frogs, lizards, young birds and rodents. Fruits also recorded. Not all populations impale and form caches, although these are frequently found in some areas[224, 260, 273, 271, 278, 477, 813, 928].

SOUNDS Repertoire consists of noisy, harsh and unmusical calls, often with a slightly nasal and querulous quality, and includes whistles and warbling song. Calls apparently graded with at least two types of main advertising call and characteristic threatening rustling sound. Commonly heard territorial call a loud, harsh repeated *kscha*-type sound, described as *scha-scha-scha-schi---schi----schi*, and *scha----schach-schach* (*nasutus*), *ketsch-ketsch-* or *tchert-*. Also a more disyllabic harsh repeated *ko-ick*-type note, described as *tch-ick*, *cha-dit* or *kerr-ick* (*schach*) or *ger-lek...ger-lek*, *jülek-jülek* (*erythronotus*), and sometimes followed by a yapping *yaou-yaou* or *choo-wee* (*stresemanni*) or *keoo-keoo-* (*nasutus*). Variations include loud raucous rhythmic *krre....krri-krre krre-krri-krret* (the last part sounding similar to the Common Quail *Coturnix coturnix*) and repeated harsh *kech-kech-kech-* (*erythronotus*). Other distinctive advertising calls have a harsh buzzy or rustling quality and are of the *rrre*-type sound, variously described as *grennh-grennh-*, *rrrre-* or *terrrr* (*bentet*). Alarm signalled by a repeated harsh *kerrr-kerrr-*, *zerrr-zerrr-* or *sre-sre-* (*erythronotus*) and at higher intensity a cackling chatter (*schach*) or *keek-keek-keek-keek-* (*nasutus* and *bentet*). Snaps bill in threat. Scolding sounds recall distant rasping of Corncrakes *Crex crex*. Begging call a harsh nasal rasping (*erythronotus*). Song a melodious subdued whistling interspersed with grating notes, producing a scratchy warbling like a reed warbler *Acrocephalus*, often with a metallic quality, and includes mimicry of other species. It may continue for up to 15 minutes (*erythronotus*). Singing is accompanied by irregular flicking of wings (*erythronotus*)[209, 224, 250, 252, 260, 262, 271, 273, 276, 278, 284, 305, 474, 476, 484, 498, 500, 600, 675, 694, 747, 813]. Sonagram[284, 600].

BREEDING BIOLOGY Monogamous and highly territorial. ♂♂ of NW migrant population (*erythronotus*) usually arrive before ♀♀, although some birds may pair on migration. In this population breeding densities have been recorded from 8 pair/40 ha and 6–7 pairs/8 ha to 4 pairs/ha (Afghanistan) and 26 pairs/7 ha (Turkmenistan) in orchards. In resident populations second broods are normal (occasionally three in central India), while NW populations usually only produce single, rarely two broods. ♂ has been recorded feeding fledglings from previous brood as well as feeding incubating ♀. In one study of 26 nests only 6 fledged young (23%) (*nasutus*)[224, 278, 498, 675, 813, 928].

Season *erythronotus* May–Aug, mainly May–Jul (Turkmenistan)[209, 294]; Apr–Jul, nest-building and eggs Apr–May, fledglings Jun–Jul (Afghanistan)[928]; *schach* Mar-Jun (Hong Kong)[675], Apr–Jul (S China)[273]; Mar–Jul (India)[224]; *caniceps* Mar, Dec–Jun (Sri Lanka)[224], May–Jun (Sikkim)[275]; Mar (Pakistan)[278]; *tricolor* Apr–Jul (India)[224], Mar (Nepal)[792]; *bentet* Feb, Jun–Sep, Dec (Malay Peninsula)[252]; Apr–Jun Wallacea[264]; Jun–Jul, young in Oct, Dec, Feb (Sumatra)[248]; Java all months, peak May–Aug (Java and Bali)[263]; *nasutus* Mar-Jun, mainly Apr (Philippines)[265, 813]; *stresemanni* Jun–Nov (New Guinea)[260]. **Displays** Little known. ***Courtship*** In *nasutus* ♂ chases ♀, often accompanied by other ♂♂; both sexes give loud harsh calls. ♂ courtship-feeds ♀ and has been observed apparently attacking her, both falling fluttering down with much calling, separating before reaching the ground. ***Pre-copulation*** In captive birds, copulation follows after much submissive bowing and clucking. ***Nest-site display*** Unknown. In captivity selection by ♀[224, 278, 284, 498, 813].

Nest Built by both sexes (*erythronotus*). Cup variable; in *schach* compact, but in *erythronotus* loosely built and bulky. Built of thorny twigs, grasses, bamboo leaves, moss, roots, papery bark, man-made materials and lined with fine grasses. Usually placed in bushes, *Acacia* and other thorn trees, poplars, bamboo, fruit trees, conifers, or low down in brambles, sword-grass, vines or reeds. Height above ground varies with habitat and human presence. In Central Asia and India it is usually placed at 3–5 m (1.5–10, exceptionally at 24 m). In areas of high human disturbance it is usually placed higher at 4–12 m. On Luzon *nasutus* nests at a mean height of 1.7 m (0.75–3, n=46), while on Malay Peninsula *bentet* recorded from 0.9–3.5 m from the ground. ***Size*** OD 150–200 mm, ID 70–95 mm, cup depth 50–60 mm, height 95–121 mm; (*nasutus*) OD 115–135 mm, ID 80–90 mm, cup depth 50–65 mm, height 95–121 mm (n=46). Nest Built in 4–8 days (*erythronotus*)[284, 224, 273, 278, 477, 675, 813].

Eggs Clutch size variable, usually 3–4 (2–6, occasionally 7 or 8 Central Asia). Clutch size appears to decrease with latitude, with the smallest clutches of 2 recorded from New Guinea (*stresemanni*). Egg colour variable from whitish or greyish-green to pale olive-green, spotted with pale rust to pale reddish-brown over underlying spots of greyish or lavender often forming a zone at the broad end. In *nasutus* newly laid eggs apparently have a whitish ground colour, changing to greenish in older eggs. ***Size*** Average ranges from 22.5 x 17.1 mm (n=96) (*nasutus*) to 23.6 x 17.9 mm (n=200) (*tricolor*)[209, 224, 251, 252, 260, 272, 278, 813, 928]. **Incubation** by ♀ only, although ♂ may assist sometimes. Period 13–16 days (n=12). In captivity 18 days, by ♀ only[224, 278, 498, 813]. **Nestling** Hatch blind and naked (*nasutus*), and probably lack mouth spots. Attended by both sexes, who also give elaborate distraction displays in presence of predators. Fledge after *c.*15–17 days (14–19). Range from 14–15 days (*tricolor*) to 17–19 days (n=5) (*nasutus*). Captive birds 16 days. If disturbed may leave the nest after 13 days. Young are able to feed themselves when 25 days old, and remain with adults for at least 10 weeks[224, 278, 498, 813]. For nestling development see[498, 813]. **Predation and longevity** Predators include crows, monitor lizards, civets, cats and humans. Oldest retrap 1 year[267, 278, 813, 928]. **Brood parasite** Commonly parasitised by Common Cuckoo *Cuculus canorus*, Common Hawk-cuckoo *C. varius* and Jacobin (Pied) Cuckoo *Oxylophus jacobinus*[224].

MEASUREMENTS and WEIGHTS *L. s. schach* ♂ (10) wing 96.5–102.0 (99.8), tail 108–134 (125.9), bill 17.8–19.6 (18.9), tarsus 27.5–30.1 (28.9); ♀ (10) wing 92–99 (96.3), tail 110–127 (118.7), bill 17–19.5 (18.3), tarsus 26.6–30 (28.7)[273]. **Weight** ♂ (10) 51–61 g (53.4); ♀ (10) 43–60 g (49.7)[273]. For additional data see[214, 224, 274, 478, 484, 495, 496, 695, 828].

29 GREY-BACKED SHRIKE (Tibetan Shrike)
Lanius tephronotus **Plate 12**

FIELD IDENTIFICATION Large (22–23 cm), grey, rufous, black and white shrike, with black face-mask, dark grey back with small rufous rump. Below whitish with rufous sides and flanks. Wings black, sometimes with small white patch; tail dark brown. Sexes similar. Young barred greyish-brown above, barred dull white below. Calls harsh and grating; song with mimicry. Solitary or in pairs; perches prominently, noisy and conspicuous. A high-elevation shrike found in open scrub with scattered bushes or small trees to 4000 m. Resident and migratory in S Asia from N India, Nepal, Tibet, W and central China; spends boreal winter in SE Asia, S China, India, Burma, Thailand and Cambodia. ***Flight characteristics***: Flies low to ground, swooping up to perch; shows very little to no white in wing or tail.

COMPARISONS Very similar to slightly larger races of Long-tailed Shrike *Lanius schach* with black face-mask and grey head. Generally not as conspicuous and tame as Long-tailed in same area. Grey-backed has much darker grey upperparts and a small indistinct rufous rump (pale grey upperparts and extensive rufous rump in Long-tailed); also has shorter browner, dark rufous-edged tail (long black tail with paler edges in Long-tailed), and a slightly heavier bill than Long-tailed. Most similar to Philippine Shrike *L. validirostris* but ranges separate. Juveniles difficult to separate from juvenile Long-tailed, and not well studied in the field. Tend to be greyer above. Study skins of Grey-backed tend to have more barring below than Long-tailed. Best identified from smaller brown shrikes on larger size, heavier bill and deeper rufous on flanks.

DESCRIPTION ADULT Sexes similar. ***Head*** Face-mask formed by narrow black frontal extending through eye-stripe to ear-coverts, sometimes with a thin white eyebrow and band above black frontal; crown, nape, mantle and back variable, dark to light grey; rump has small patch of rufous-brown, uppertail-coverts reddish rufous-brown. ***Wings*** Primaries black, with insignificant to absent white wing-patch at base, secondaries pale edged, and tertials buff-edged. ***Tail*** Dark brown with dark rufous-brown edges. ***Underparts*** Throat, breast and belly white, sides of breast and flanks rich reddish rufous-brown. ***Bare parts*** Bill black to blackish-brown, paler at base of lower mandible; palate unknown; legs blackish; eye brown[224, 792]. JUVENILE/IMMATURE Browner above than adult; upperparts brown to greyish-brown with dark barring, finer on head; black face-mask reduced to blackish-brown on ear-coverts; rump and uppertail-coverts light rufous barred blackish; underparts greyish-white with narrow dark barring and a rufous tinge on flanks and breast. Bill grey-brown.

GEOGRAPHICAL VARIATION Two races, differing in size and upperparts. Nominate *tephronotus* (Nepal, Sikkim, Bhutan, Arunachal Pradesh, Tibet, China) larger, darker, more slate-grey above, sometimes with small white wing-patch and eyebrow. Race *lahulensis* (N India in N Kashmir east to Himachal Pradesh, also possibly W Tibet) smaller and paler, with weaker, slender bill. Upperparts tinged brown; usually has a small white wing-patch; tail brown like nominate, although also described as black like Long-tailed Shrike. This race has also been considered to be a hybrid of Grey-backed and Long-tailed Shrikes[224, 491, 675].

MOULT little known. A partial post-juvenile moult of flight feathers has been recorded. Post-breeding moult appears to be completed by Dec, and some apparently first-year birds have a complete moult in Mar–May[224, 436, 496, 675, 792].

RANGE, HABITAT and STATUS **Breeding range** S Asia in Himalayas from Kashmir in India to Nepal, Sikkim, Bhutan, central and SE Tibet, W, central and S China. In China N limit *c.*40°N Kansu [Gansu], E limit *c.*110°E (Shaanxi)[190, 197, 221, 224, 675]. **Non-breeding range** See Movements. **Habitat** A high-elevation species which breeds between 2200–4500 m in Himalayas in open dry country, plateau plains or mountain meadows with groups of bushes or scattered trees, forest clearings, secondary growth and open scrub. On non-breeding grounds in valleys and plains in a variety of habitats including abandoned cultivation, gardens and orchards[224, 324, 675, 792]. **Status** Not uncommon resident, or altitudinal and regional migrant. **Conservation status** Population trends unknown; apparently not threatened.

MOVEMENTS Little known. Not all populations are migratory in boreal winter from Sep–May. Some are resident, others only undertake local, usually altitudinal movements down to lower elevations, and still others undertake larger regional movements. In W range *lahulensis* appears to be resident or with altitudinal movements to the foothills of the Himalayas. In Sep–Apr nominate *tephronotus* descends locally to lower elevations. Chinese birds appear to be mainly altitudinal migrants within their breeding range. In Nepal and Tibet birds move from 2745–4575 m down to between 275–2560 m, usually remaining above 365 m and at Kathmandu are found mainly from Oct–Mar. Others travel further S in India as far as West Bengal. In Bangladesh it is a local non-breeding visitor from Oct–May. Generally the regional migrants move southwards to SE Asia, the plains of S China, India, Burma, Laos, N Vietnam and N Thailand[188, 197, 224, 221, 261, 675, 792].

SOCIAL ORGANISATION and GENERAL BEHAVIOUR Little known. Solitary or in widely separated pairs. Perches prominently with upright stance, noisy and conspicuous. On non-breeding grounds a few birds have been observed gathering together at dusk to roost[224, 261]. **Foraging behaviour** Hunts from exposed perch, taking food mainly on the ground. May occasionally hawk insects in the air. Impales prey and forms caches[224, 277]. **Food**

Arthropods, mainly insects, and small vertebrates. Insects include Coleoptera (beetles), Orthoptera (grasshoppers, crickets) and Lepidoptera (caterpillars). Small vertebrates include lizards, nestling birds and rodents (baby mice)[224, 276, 277].

SOUNDS Little known but probably similar to Long-tailed Shrike. Main territorial call appears to be a repeated harsh *zzert-zzert-*, *tchert-tchert-* or *tzert-tzert-*. Has a harsh repeated *ktcht-ktcht-ktcht-* call at dusk or when alarmed. Harsh scolding or grating calls have been likened to the cries of a bird as if seized by a hawk, or the squealing of a frog caught by a snake! Song in breeding season subdued and musical with mimicry of other bird calls and continuing for several minutes[224, 261, 276, 277, 500].

BREEDING BIOLOGY Little known. Monogamous and territorial. Like other *Lanius* they are particularly pugnacious during breeding, and apparently also territorial on their non-breeding grounds. Their behaviour is thought to be similar to the Long-tailed Shrike. Migrants are back on their breeding grounds in May. Second broods may be reared, but confirmation required[224, 675]. **Season** Mainly Jun–Jul (India)[224]; Apr, May, Jul, mainly May–Jun, exceptionally to Aug, suggesting second broods (Tibet)[221, 675, 792]. **Displays** Unknown. **Nest** Role of sexes unknown. An untidy bulky cup, largely composed of wool mixed with thorny twigs, grass and feathers bound with fibres and lined with finer grass. Those near human habitation often contain man-made materials such as rags. Placed relatively low down in a small tree or bush, often of a thorny type, from 1.5–3 m above the ground (India). Nest height of 8 m requires confirmation. ***Size*** OD 130–200 mm and height *c.*85 mm[224, 675]. **Eggs** 4–6. Ground colour variable, commonly pale grey-green blotched and spotted with grey-brown or brown, with numerous secondary markings of lavender and grey. ***Size*** av. 24.9 x 18.7 mm (n=200)[224]. **Incubation and nestling** Appearance and period unknown, but probably similar to Long-tailed Shrike. No further breeding information.

MEASUREMENTS and WEIGHTS *L. t. tephronotus* ♂ (25) wing 98–106 (100.7), tail 110–123 (115.5), bill (to skull) 21–23 (22); ♀ (12) wing 97–105 (99.7), tail 109–116 (114.8), bill (to skull) 21–24 (22.1)[496]. **Weight** ♂ (8) 39–51 g, ♀ (4) 43–54 g (India)[224, 478]. For additional data see[197, 212, 224, 496].

30 PHILIPPINE SHRIKE (Mountain or Strong-billed Shrike)
Lanius validirostris **Plate 12**

FIELD IDENTIFICATION Medium-large (21–22 cm), grey, rufous, black and white shrike, with narrow black face-mask, dark grey head, back and rump. Wings and tail blackish-brown with no white. Below white with rufous sides and flanks. Sexes similar. Young barred greyish-brown above, barred greyish-white below. Little known; calls harsh and grating. Solitary, perches prominently in open secondary growth, clearings, forest edge and scrubby grassland in mountains over 1000 m in Philippines. ***Flight characteristics***: Flies low and swoops up to perch; no white in wings and tail.

COMPARISONS Superficially similar to larger Long-tailed Shrike *Lanius schach*, which in this region has a black head (*nasutus*). Philippine Shrike differs by having a grey head with black face-mask, is smaller with shorter brown tail and grey back and rump (tail long and black, rump and lower back pale rufous-brown in Long-tailed, which also generally occurs at lower elevations). Differs from vagrant Thick-billed Shrike *L. tigrinus* by greater size and grey back (dark reddish-brown in Thick-billed). Most similar to Grey-backed Shrike *L. tephronotus* but ranges separate. Juvenile similar to juvenile Long-tailed Shrike, but greyer above with grey rump and no wing-patch.

DESCRIPTION Adult Sexes similar. ***Head*** Black face-mask extends from a narrow band (variable) above bill, through eye-stripe to ear-coverts; thin whitish eyebrow sometimes extends onto forehead. Crown, nape, mantle and back dark grey, sometimes tinged brown on lower back; rump dark grey (sometimes tinged brown). ***Wings*** Brownish-black with no white wing-patch at base of primaries. ***Tail*** Brownish-black like wings; undertail-coverts rufous-brown. ***Underparts*** White to greyish-white with rich reddish-brown flanks, sides of breast and belly; breast, throat and chin white. ***Bare parts*** Bill heavy and black; palate unknown; legs blackish-brown; eye dark brown. Juvenile/Immature Upperparts brown to greyish-brown with dark barring; black face-mask reduced to blackish-brown on ear-coverts; wings and tail brown like adult; underparts greyish-white with narrow dark barring, rufous tinge on flanks and breast. Resembles Grey-backed Shrike[410].

GEOGRAPHICAL VARIATION At least four races with minor differences mainly in body size, and extent and darkness of rufous underparts. Race *tertius* (Mindoro) is smaller, has more rufous on breast and belly, and flanks and undertail-coverts darker rufous than nominate *validirostris* (Luzon); *hachisuka* and *quartus* (both Mindanao) similar to *tertius* but darker below, and intermediate in size between nominate and *tertius*[393, 409, 410, 411, 435, 468].

MOULT Unknown.

RANGE, HABITAT and STATUS Breeding range Endemic to Philippines, restricted to N and central Luzon, Mindoro and Mindanao islands. **Habitat** Clearings and edges of oak and pine forests, open secondary growth, open woodland, scrub in grasslands above 1000 m to *c.*2250 m[265, 411, 468, 473, 488]. **Status** Not uncommon resident. **Conservation status** Little known and with little consensus. In 1994 thought to Near-Threatened, but now known to be fairly common in upland habitat that is currently under little human pressure. Requires basic biological research and population surveys[488, 479].

MOVEMENTS Unknown.

SOCIAL ORGANISATION and GENERAL BEHAVIOUR Virtually unknown; solitary, perches with upright stance, and behaves in typical *Lanius* manner. **Foraging behaviour** Hunts from exposed perches on top of bushes and trees; behaviour believed to be similar to Bull-headed Shrike *L. bucephalus*. Probably hops on the ground. **Food** Arthropods, mainly insects, of which small and medium-sized Coleoptera (beetles) appear important. Some beetles are extremely hard-bodied, for which the thick bill is possibly adapted[473].

SOUNDS Virtually unknown; said to be similar to Bull-headed Shrike. Recordings indicate a repertoire consisting mainly of harsh and whistled calls. Harsh calls tend to be repeated, short, abrupt notes like *tzik-tzik-tzik-;* in alarm it gives abrupt, harsh *chrr-chrr-chrr-* sounds. Song warbler-like with high-pitched whistles[500, 473].

BREEDING BIOLOGY Virtually unknown; probably monogamous and territorial based on behaviour. **Season** ♀ collected in February had slightly enlarged ovaries[411], and a pair were seen feeding juveniles 15 May[488]. No further breeding information.

MEASUREMENTS and WEIGHTS *L. v. validirostris* ♂ (12) wing 86–94 (89.3), tail 94–102 (96.8); ♀ (6) wing 85–88 (86.5), tail 91–93 (92.0)[472]; ♂♀? (12) wing 80–93 (85.9), tail (86–95 (89.1), tarsus 25–26.5 (25.7), bill (to skull) 19.3–23.8 (21.5)[500]. **Weight** Unknown. For additional data see[393, 409, 410, 411, 468].

31 LAGDEN'S BUSH-SHRIKE *Malaconotus lagdeni* Plate 13

FIELD IDENTIFICATION Large (23 cm), dark grey-headed bush-shrike with a massive bill and grey eye. Sexes similar. Back, wings and tail green; wings with two lines of black and yellow spots. Tertials and secondaries also boldly tipped black and yellow. Underparts variable; bright yellow or yellow with orange tinge on breast. Young duller and greyish-white below, becoming yellow; bill and eye brown. Shy and skulking, more often heard than seen. Calls variable: drawn-out and mournful, short, hollow and barbet-like; also disyllabic whistles and harsh sounds. Solitary in mid-levels and canopy of lowland and montane forest. Two separate populations, E montane in E Zaïre, SW Uganda and Rwanda, and W lowlands in West Africa from Sierra Leone to Togo. ***Flight characteristics***: Short and heavy, wings rounded, sometimes makes loud flapping ('fripping'?) sounds with wings[524].

COMPARISONS Range overlaps Fiery-breasted Bush-shrike *Malaconotus cruentus* which has a pale grey head with extensive white on face and no spots on wing-coverts. Tail and tertials tipped black and yellow and underparts crimson red (orange-yellow in Lagden's). Grey-headed Bush-shrike *M. blanchoti* also has conspicuous white on face, but lacks the distinctive black and yellow tertials and spots on wing-coverts, although it does have plain yellow spotted wing-coverts. Caution required in use of calls, as some, particularly drawn-out mournful whistles, are similar to those of some other large bush-shrikes. However, best identified from these by combination of a series of 3–4 short barbet-like *toot-* calls and often-repeated melodious disyllabic whistles (see Sounds).

DESCRIPTION Adult Sexes similar. ***Head*** Frontal, lores, sides of face and ear-coverts, crown and upper mantle dark grey. Forehead may show a few small whitish feathers. ***Back*** Lower mantle to rump olive-green; rump feathers long and fluffy. ***Wings*** Olive-green, flight feathers with green outer web, hair-brown inner, appearing green when closed; primary coverts, tertials and secondaries black, broadly tipped yellow. ***Tail*** Olive-green, tipped and edged yellow. ***Underparts*** Throat and upper breast bright orange-yellow (W population), yellow (E population), merging into yellow belly and undertail-coverts; flanks pale green. ***Bare parts*** Bill black; palate unknown; legs blue-grey; eye light grey, faintly tinged bluish[290, 1061]. Juvenile Upperparts similar to adult but duller. Crown, face and upper mantle dark brownish-grey. Wing markings less striking, with less obvious black and narrower buff-yellow tips. Underparts variable, from chin to upper belly whitish to greyish-white; may show light barring and yellow streaking; lower belly greyish-green, undertail-coverts greenish-yellow, flanks greenish. Bill greyish-brown. Eye unknown, probably brown[500]. Immature Wing markings more distinct like adult and progressively more yellow on underparts; bill black. Transition to adult plumage rapid[290, 460, 500, 504, 524].

GEOGRAPHICAL VARIATION Two widely separated races, differing mainly on colour of underparts. Western nominate *lagdeni* (Liberia to Ghana) is a lowland bird with orange-yellow breast, while eastern *centralis* (E Zaïre, SW Uganda and Rwanda) is a montane forest bird with little or no orange on breast. Calls of the two populations may differ, but little known.

MOULT Worn plumage Sep–Oct, new or starting wing moult in Dec, suggesting post-breeding moult (Liberia)[858].

RANGE, HABITAT and STATUS Breeding range Fragmented, W population found in Sierra Leone, Liberia, Ivory Coast, S Ghana and Togo. Eastern population from central E Zaïre, Rwanda and SW Uganda in Bwindi (Impenetrable) Forest. **Habitat** In West Africa in lowland mature primary forest, gallery forest, secondary growth and lightly logged forest from 100–700 m (Liberia). In Central Africa, occurs in montane forest, including disturbed secondary growth, from 2100–2800 m on Ruwenzori Mts[22, 234, 259, 290, 431, 479, 481, 504, 524, 688, 697, 712, 717, 848, 858, 930, 1061]. **Status** Uncommon to rare resident. **Conservation status** Unknown. Liberian population may be well above 6,000 pairs and therefore possibly the largest known population. Use of disturbed areas suggests a reasonably wide habitat tolerance. Survey required of Central African populations. Considered Near-Threatened[858, 479].

MOVEMENTS Unknown.

SOCIAL ORGANISATION and GENERAL BEHAVIOUR Little known. Solitary, in pairs or sometimes in groups of 2–4 birds, probably family parties. Elusive, skulking and slow-moving. Found at all levels, mainly in mid-canopy, where keeps to dense thickets and tangles. Often in the company of Many-coloured Bush-shrike *Chlorophoneus multicolor*. **Foraging behaviour** Gleans prey at all levels, mainly in mid- to upper levels at 10–30 m, rarely below 5 m. Searches in dense creeper tangles and open forest canopy, keeping to thinner branches, where hops or bounces from branch to branch. Often a member of mixed foraging parties. Large insect prey is immobilised by beating vigorously on a branch before swallowing. **Food** Arthropods, mainly large insects and small vertebrates. Insects like large Orthoptera (grasshoppers) are taken. Recorded vertebrates include an *Agama* lizard and small birds[290, 504, 524, 688, 717, 858].

SOUNDS Little known. Eastern and W populations possibly differ, although both have a repertoire consisting of low-pitched whistles and harsh rasping sounds. Some calls similar to Grey-headed Bush-shrike, but generally more variable with shorter notes and often-heard disyllabic whistles with inflections. Some disyllabic notes have first part higher-pitched, others reversed. Length of notes and repetition rate variable. Sequences seldom longer than *c.*14 notes. Simple low-pitched whistles vary from a slowly repeated, 3–4 short-note series, each note more resonant, beginning and ending more abruptly than drawn-out notes, and sounding barbet-like, and consequently similar to Fiery-breasted Bush-shrike, a *hoop...hoop...hoop* or *toot..toot-*. Where Lagden's and Fiery-breasted occur together, this whistle appears slightly lower-pitched. Also has a longer, drawn-out mournful *uuuuuuuh.....uuuuuuuh* or *whoooooooo-* whistle similar to Grey-headed Bush-shrike, sometimes with a terminal inflection *whooooo-lwe* or *whooooo-up*. Others are higher-pitched *heeeeew...heeeeew*. Many whistles are disyllabic and more melodious, *heeewoo*, often with a marked inflection, *heejwoo-*, *heeet-huuuu-* or *huu-jwoo-*. Simple and disyllabic whistles also occur together in combined series, e.g. *hoop..hoop..hoop.......hweet-huuuu....* Pairs may also duet with these calls, sounding like *heejwoo-heeew* or *hlwee-hooo*; however, details require confirmation. Other calls are harsh and raucous, including grating *chaarr-chaarr-*, *chrrrr-* and staccato *KKK-K-K-KKK-* sounds. Probably snaps bill and known to produce loud flapping noise with the wings ('wing-fripping'?) when agitated[431, 500, 501, 504, 524, 712, 717]. Sonagram[717].

BREEDING BIOLOGY Little known. Apparently monogamous. Densities may locally reach 0.5–1.5 pairs/km^2 (Liberia)[858]. **Season** Aug fledglings (Liberia)[858]; Nov–Dec (Ivory Coast)[712]; Mar ♀ gonads slightly enlarged (Ruwenzori Mts); Jan, Sep–Oct, Dec (W Ruwenzori [E Zaïre])[234, 290]. **Displays** Known to duet while nest-building[712]. **Nest** Role of sexes unknown. A bulky bowl of dry leaves, bracken and long thin, barely visible fibres, well hidden at 3.5–*c.*6 m (n=2) above ground in fork of a small tree in secondary growth, or in leafy re-growth on top of a broken-off tree[290, 712]. **Eggs** At least 2 (n=2). Dull light grey with specks and spots of dark brown slightly tinged with purplish, concentrated densely at the large end. ***Size*** 30.2 x 20.9 mm (n=1)[290]. **Incubation** Unknown. **Nestling** Appearance and period unknown. Fledglings remain with parents for at least 25 days. Evidence of brood division, with each of two young remaining with one parent[858]. No further breeding information.

MEASUREMENTS and WEIGHTS *M. l. centralis* ♂ (5) wing 110–113.5 (111.5), tail 100–106.5 (104.2), bill 27–30 (29.0); ♀ (6) wing 109–113 (110.9), tail 102–108 (104.2), bill 27–29.5 (28.0)[458]; ♂♀? (6) wing 111–115 (112.8), tail 97–113 (105.2), bill (to skull) 30–32 (30.8), tarsus 33–34 (33.6)[500]; *lagdeni* ♂ wing 115, tail 100, bill 35[259]. **Weight** *lagdeni* ♂ 97 g, unsexed adult 96 g (Liberia)[259]; *centralis* 84 g (SW Uganda)[1061]. For additional data see[460].

32 ULUGURU BUSH-SHRIKE *Malaconotus? alius* Plate 13

FIELD IDENTIFICATION Medium-large (21–22 cm), black-headed bush-shrike with a massive bill and reddish-brown eye. Sexes different. Back, wings and tail dark olive-green; underparts bright yellow (♂), greenish-yellow (♀). Young unknown. Little known, very rare, shy and skulking, more often heard than seen. Call a distinctive double or treble whistled note. Solitary in canopy of montane forest only in Uluguru Mountains in Tanzania. ***Flight characteristics***: Short-distance; wings rounded.

COMPARISONS Most similar to yellow morph of smaller Black-fronted Bush-shrike *Chlorophoneus nigrifrons*, which has a much smaller bill and lacks completely black head. Differs from all other members of its large-billed genus by having a black, not grey head and reddish-brown eye. Grey-headed Bush-shrike *Malaconotus blanchoti* is the only other large bush-shrike with a massive bill within range. However, Grey-headed is a savanna species, with grey head, white lores, yellowish eye, yellow-spotted wing-coverts and yellowish-orange underparts. Main call of Uluguru Bush-shrike distinctive compared to monotonous drawn-out, low-pitched and mournful *whooooooo* whistle of Grey-headed Bush-shrike or hollow single and disyllabic whistles of Black-fronted Bush-shrike (see Sounds).

DESCRIPTION **ADULT ♂** ***Head*** Nape to upper mantle glossy black with bluish tinge, including below eye and ear-coverts. ***Back*** Including lower mantle and rump dark olive-green, rump feathers long and fluffy. ***Wings and tail*** Uniformly dark olive-green. ***Underparts*** Rich yellow on throat and breast, yellow on belly and greenish-yellow on flanks. ***Bare parts*** Bill black; palate unknown; legs blue-grey; eye reddish-brown. **ADULT ♀** Similar to ♂ but underparts generally duller and greener. **JUVENILE/IMMATURE** Unknown.

GEOGRAPHICAL VARIATION None. Monotypic.

MOULT Unknown.

RANGE, HABITAT and STATUS **Breeding range** Very restricted, endemic to the Uluguru Mountains in central E Tanzania. **Habitat** Restricted to montane forest, widely but very thinly spread from 1300 m to at least 2100 m, in an area probably less than 260 km^2 [343, 431, 459]. **Status** Rare resident. **Conservation status** Discovered in 1926, 2 specimens collected in Uluguru Mts. at Bagilo at 1830 m on E slopes. In 1948 one bird seen in forest above Bunduki on W slopes. Subsequently at least 15 specimens collected. Rediscovered in 1981 when heard and seen on both sides of Lupanga Mountain at 1600–1650 m and on the W escarpment of the Lukwangule Plateau at 2100 m. Its occurrence on the E slopes of the of Uluguru North Forest Reserve appears to coincide with best quality forest and the highest precipitation. In this area there is still a good area of flat forest between 1200–1500 m. Virtually all other subtropical forest, which is thought to be its core habitat, has now been cleared. Recently observed and tape recorded in 1996. Felling known to occur on Ulugurus, but E Ulugurus less disturbed due to more difficult access. Red Data Book species now considered Critical[343, 378, 388, 479, 535].

MOVEMENTS Unknown.

SOCIAL ORGANISATION and GENERAL BEHAVIOUR Virtually unknown. A solitary, skulking, canopy species where extremely difficult to see, as it keeps to dense foliage. Reported often in company of Grey-headed Bush-shrike, but this requires confirmation in view of their different habitat preference[336, 500]. **Foraging behaviour** Appears to occur mainly in the canopy, where probably gleans prey like other members of the genus. Has been seen in mixed foraging parties[343]. **Food** Insects and probably small vertebrates.

SOUNDS Little known. A distinctive series of strident low-pitched disyllabic whistles of at least two types: (i) *huw-teew....huw-teew-* or *HuuKew...HuuKew*, and (ii) *KoKok-teew...KoKok-teew* or *WokWok-teew-teew....WokWok-teew-teew*. Responds to call-up of recordings of same call. Earlier described as a repeated *ku-ku-kua-kua*. Calls are unlike other members of the genus[336, 500, 699].

BREEDING BIOLOGY No information available. Probably monogamous like other members of genus. Breeding season likely to be between Oct–Feb.

MEASUREMENTS and WEIGHTS *M.? alius* ♂♀? (3) wing 101–107 (104.0), tail 96–99 (97.0), bill (to skull) 31–33 (31.7), tarsus 28–31.5 (30.2)[500]. **Weight** unknown.

33 GREEN-BREASTED BUSH-SHRIKE *Malaconotus gladiator* Plate 13

FIELD IDENTIFICATION Very large (25 cm), dark olive-green bush-shrike with a dark grey head and pale grey eye (no white on face). Sexes similar. Back, wings, tail and underparts dark olive-green. Wings and tail narrowly tipped yellow. Young unknown. Little known, shy and skulking, more often heard than seen; call a series of mournful whistles and harsh calls. Found in canopy of montane forest, restricted to W Cameroon and E Nigeria. ***Flight characteristics***: Short-distance; wings rounded.

COMPARISONS Unlikely to be confused with other members of the genus as it is the only large bush-shrike with dark green underparts; all others are yellow or orange-yellow below. Caution required in use of calls, as drawn-out mournful whistles similar to most other large bush-shrikes. Best identified by raucous, harsh, rasping or tearing *haaarrrrr-* call, which appears lower-pitched than similar call in other large bush-shrikes (see Sounds).

DESCRIPTION **ADULT** Sexes similar. ***Head*** Dark grey from crown to lower mantle, including frontal, lores, ear-coverts, sides of neck and below eye. ***Back*** Including rump and uppertail-coverts dark olive-green; rump feathers long and fluffy. ***Wings*** Olive-green, primaries dark brown, secondaries olive-green on outer webs, tertials olive-green with pale yellow inner edges; some yellowish tips to wing-coverts. Underwing-coverts yellowish-green. ***Tail*** Dark greenish-brown. ***Underparts*** Chin greyish-green, rest including belly and undertail-coverts, dark olive to yellowish olive-green. ***Bare parts*** Bill black; palate unknown; legs blue-grey; eye pale grey. **JUVENILE/IMMATURE** Unknown

GEOGRAPHICAL VARIATION None. Monotypic.

MOULT Unknown.

RANGE, HABITAT and STATUS **Breeding range** Restricted to W Cameroon and E Nigeria. **Habitat** Montane forest in Cameroon on Mount Cameroon (950–1500 m), Rumpi Hills (1300–1520 m), Mount Kupé (1100–1950 m), Mount Manenguba (1500–1900 m), Mount Nlonako (1400–1600 m), Mount Oku (=Kilum) (2200–2300 m), Bakossi Mts and Bamenda-Banso Highlands, and E Nigeria on Obudu Plateau (1500 m)[21, 37, 343, 431, 504, 864]. **Status** Rare resident. **Conservation status** Known from only 5 specimens and a few sight records. At known localities in montane forest, occurs at very low densities. Although there is considerable loss of habitat on the Bamenda-Banso Highlands and on the Obudu Plateau, there are conservation measures being applied in these areas as well as on Mount Kupé. Red Data Book species considered Vulnerable[343, 378, 479, 485].

MOVEMENTS Unknown.

SOCIAL ORGANISATION and GENERAL BEHAVIOUR Little known. Found singly or in pairs, an elusive, skulking species, occurring at very low density in montane forest. Possibly some competition with Mount Kupé Bush-shrike *Chlorophoneus? kupeensis*, as Green-breasted occurs at lower elevations where this species is absent. Although recorded between 2–20 m above the ground, it appears to be mainly a canopy species. When agitated gives a bill-rattling call (bill-snapping) accompanied by throwing head back with a staccato movement downwards. In Grey-headed Bush-shrike this call is given while head is thrown backwards[345, 504, 515, 864]. **Foraging behaviour** Appears to glean prey mainly in canopy[864]. **Food** Insects, including Orthoptera (large green locusts)[347, 605, 626].

SOUNDS Repertoire similar to Grey-headed Bush-shrike, particularly whistle-call of ♂; however, a raucous call, believed to be given by ♀, appears different. Main call consists of a series of slowly repeated ventriloquial, drawn-out, low-pitched, mournful whistles. Each note begins softly, increases in volume and ends abruptly. Note duration variable from *c*.0.7–1.4 sec. Other calls include harsh rasping or tearing sounds and loud bill-snapping. Whistles are given in variable series of at least 4 types: (i) series of 5–10 plain whistles at same pitch, described as an in-drawn *uuuuuu-uh....uuuuuuh-*, *whoooooo* or *phooooooo*; (ii) shorter series at same pitch with an upward-terminal inflection, *uuuuh-lwe....uuuuh-lwe*; (iii) a broken series of whistles, undulating with one half, or different sections at slightly different pitch, *uuuu-uh...uuuuuh...oooooh...*; and (iv) a combination of plain whistles and those with an upward-terminal inflection. Responds to imitations of whistle calls. A call, believed to be given by ♀, consists of raucous, harsh, rasping or tearing *haaarrrrr-haaarrrrr-* notes given in a series of up to 5 notes. These are probably given sporadically in duet with the ♂. When agitated gives a few strident, rapidly delivered, buzzy *Tziktzu-* sounds. Alarm signalled by loud bill-snapping *Tik!-Tik!-* and unmusical staccato chattering[338, 345, 431, 500, 501, 504, 515, 626, 864]. Sonagram[846].

BREEDING BIOLOGY Unknown.

MEASUREMENTS and WEIGHTS *M. gladiator* ♂ (2) wing 119, 120.5, tail 112, 121, bill 30, 31.5, tarsus 33[458]; ♂ (3) wing 117–121 (119.3), tail 112–114 (113.0), bill 29–31 (30), ♂ (2) tarsus 34–36 (35)[347, 626]; ♂ (1) wing 119, tail 111, bill (to skull) 35.5, tarsus 37[500]. **Weight** 99 g[500].

34 FIERY-BREASTED BUSH-SHRIKE *Malaconotus cruentus* Plate 14

FIELD IDENTIFICATION Large (25 cm), brightly coloured bush-shrike with pale grey head, extensive white face with greyish eye, and massive black bill. Sexes similar. Upperparts, wings and tail green. Tertials and tail broadly tipped black and yellow. Underparts variable; two colour morphs; yellow and scarlet-red, with intermediates. Young duller with pale brownish-grey head, brown eye, and whitish-grey and yellow underparts. Shy, skulking and slow-moving. More often heard than seen; call a series of short, hollow, barbet-like whistles and harsh sounds. Solitary at all levels from dense undergrowth to canopy of lowland forest. Resident from West Africa to W Uganda and Zaïre. ***Flight characteristics***: Short-distrance; wings rounded with black inner webs to primaries and secondaries, and black and yellow terminal band on tail visible in flight.

COMPARISONS Generally ecologically segregated from most members of this genus, except Lagden's Bush-shrike *Malaconotus lagdeni*, which in West Africa also occurs in lowland forest. Easily separated as Lagden's lacks white on the face and black in the tail, and has two lines of yellow spots on the wing-coverts. Unlikely to overlap with the savanna Grey-headed Bush-shrike *M. blanchoti* or montane Monteiro's Bush-shrike *M. monteiri*, but best identified from these species by the more extensive white face, which continues above and below the grey eye (eye yellow in Grey-headed), and lack of yellowish spots on wing-coverts. Also similar to much smaller Many-coloured Bush-shrike *Chlorophoneus multicolor* which shows remarkable plumage similarity, but its smaller body and bill size, maroon eye and different calls are distinctive. While whistle-calls of many large bush-shrikes are similar, those of Fiery-breasted are more distinct and sound rather barbet-like (see Sounds).

DESCRIPTION **ADULT** Sexes similar. ***Head*** Frontal whitish, extending to lores, above and below eye; crown to mantle and upper back pale grey, including below eye and ear-coverts. ***Back*** including rump and tail-coverts Olive-green, feathers long and fluffy. ***Wings*** Olive-green, flight feathers black with yellowish-green outer webs on primaries, olive-green edges on outer webs of secondaries which have yellowish terminal band; tertials and primary coverts are black with broad terminal yellowish band. ***Tail*** Olive-green with broad yellowish tips on a black subterminal band. ***Underparts*** Variable, red and yellow morphs with intermediates. Chin yellow to yellowish-orange; throat, breast and upper belly yellow to deep orange-red or scarlet red (so-called *gabonensis*); lower belly to vent yellow to yellowish-orange; undertail-coverts deep yellow; flanks yellowish-green. ***Bare parts*** Bill black; palate unknown; legs blue-grey; eye grey, blue-grey or greyish-white[342, 646]. **JUVENILE** Head greyish-brown, more tawny on nape and mantle with buff tips to feathers; lores whitish; frontal and crown with faint pink tinge. ***Underparts*** Throat to upper breast greyish-white, lower breast to undertail-coverts yellow to greenish-yellow. Bill greyish to dark grey-brown and smaller than adult, legs blue-grey, eye brown. **IMMATURE** Head becomes greyer and underparts progressively mottled with orange (*cruentus*), or deeper red (*gabonensis*)[460, 646].

GEOGRAPHICAL VARIATION Complex, poorly differentiated and not well understood. At least three races described, variation mainly in the intensity of red underparts and in size. However, variation also considered by some workers to be due to polymorphism in a monotypic species with at least two colour morphs (yellow and red) with numerous intermediates. This view is supported here. Nominate *cruentus* (Sierra Leone to Cameroon) is yellower below, and supposed *gabonensis* (including *adolfi-friederici* Cameroon to Gabon and NE Congo, E Zaïre to W Uganda) has more extensive and darker scarlet-red underparts with less yellow[458, 460].

MOULT Wing moult Apr, Jun–Jul and Oct. In fresh plumage Nov–Mar (Liberia)[259, 858].

RANGE, HABITAT and STATUS **Breeding range** SE Guinea, Sierra Leone, Liberia, Ivory Coast, Ghana, Togo, S Cameroon, Nigeria, Central African Republic, Equatorial Guinea, Gabon, Congo, N Zaïre, SW Uganda and W Kenya (requires confirmation). Bioko record rejected[431]. **Habitat** A lowland forest species from *c.*900–1500 m, rarely to 1900 m. Found in primary, secondary and riverine forest, forest edge, also secondary growth, plantation regenerated growth in abandoned farms, thickets and well-wooded gardens. In E from Bwamba Forest at 700 m (Uganda)[22, 37, 101, 234, 259, 290, 294, 330, 424, 431, 456, 504, 688, 697, 848, 858, 864]. **Status** Locally common to uncommon resident. **Conservation status** Unknown. In Ivory Coast appears to be much rarer now than in the past[711].

MOVEMENTS Unknown.

SOCIAL ORGANISATION and GENERAL BEHAVIOUR Little known. Solitary or in pairs and once recorded in a party of four birds. An unobtrusive, shy, skulking and slow-moving species, very wary and often hiding behind trunks and in dense thickets. In spite of coloration, more often heard than seen. Vocal throughout the year. Found at all levels from undergrowth to forest canopy (2–15 m). Occupies territories of *c.*6–10 ha[15, 22, 294, 330, 338, 504, 690]. **Foraging behaviour** Forages by creeping slowly about, gleaning prey at all levels, occasionally on the ground, more usually in undergrowth and mid-levels, sometimes in high canopy. In secondary growth and abandoned farms often seen low down. Searches dense thickets and tangles, often remaining motionless for 10 minutes before moving on. Joins mixed foraging parties. Prey is held down with the foot and ripped apart with the bill[294, 330, 688, 858]. **Food** Arthropods, mainly insects and their larvae, and small vertebrates. Insects include, Coleoptera (beetles), Orthoptera (grasshoppers), Hemiptera (cicadas), Lepidoptera (butterflies, caterpillars and moth eggs). Also known to feed on small tree frogs and seeds. In captivity accepts small bits of meat[259, 290, 294, 347, 616, 765, 526].

SOUNDS Little known. Repertoire consists of clear, low-pitched, hollow whistles and harsh notes. Series of whistles different from Grey-headed and Green-breasted Bush-shrikes *Malaconotus gladiator*, more resonant, hollow-sounding and barbet- or trogon-like. These calls sometimes described as cooing. Generally notes shorter and less ventriloquial than other large bush-shrikes, with an abrupt start and end. Length of notes and repetition rate variable, usually with *c.*1 sec interval. Described as a series of *c.*5–6 notes, sounding like *toot-toot-*, *tout-tout-*, *poop-poop-*, *hoop-hoop-* or *coo-*. Some series have slightly longer notes *hooop-*, and notes in some series may increase in volume from start to end. Has various harsh, rasping, chattering and frog-like notes, piercing *kik-ik-kik* calls and bill-clicking or snapping sounds. Known to make 'fripping' sounds with the wings[22, 23, 34, 290, 338, 504, 500, 501, 765].

BREEDING BIOLOGY Little known. Monogamous. Recorded at a density of 6 calling birds in 2 km of ridge forest (Liberia)[858]. **Season** Birds in song mainly Sep–Mar, courtship display and copulation Oct, ♀ with developed gonads Jul, enlarged gonads Nov, dependent downy young Nov (Liberia)[259, 858]; ovaries with yolking eggs Jun and Nov, breeding Aug (Cameroon)[37, 234, 616, 646]; Mar–Jul, and Oct–Nov (Zaïre)[290, 688]. **Displays** ***Nest-building*** When carrying nest-building material, vibrates (flutters) wings like a young bird soliciting food[294]. **Nest** ♀ appears to build the nest, collecting material within 10–15 m of nest site. ♂ remains silent nearby. Construction takes place for *c.*20 min in the early part of the day before it gets too hot, working material into the nest for *c.*1.5–2 min at a time. Nest described as a basic platform of dry twigs on which a shallow, loosely built, bulky cup is built of fibres, dry vines, tendrils, smaller twigs, leaf petioles and dried leaves with a lining of black rootlets. One nest was placed low down in the small branches of a thicket, another was in entangled vines and a third was 4 m above the ground in the fork of a cacao tree[15, 22, 290, 294, 646]. **Eggs** 2–3. Colour variable, from creamy to pinkish-white, finely speckled, spotted and blotched with pale yellowish-brown, rich maroon and pale purple or lilac-grey, mainly at large end. ***Size*** 28–28.5 x 20.5 mm[15, 22, 290, 500, 646]. No further breeding information, except for young killed by a snake[526].

MEASUREMENTS and WEIGHTS Races combined ♂♀? (10) wing 104–115 (110.0), tail 94–104 (100.9), bill (to skull) 30–35 (32.3), tarsus 30–34 (32.5) (West Africa)[500]. **Weight** *cruentus* ♂ (7) 76.5 ±6.8 g, ♀ (4) 70.1–91.2 g (77.0) (Liberia)[259]; 79.5 g (Central African Republic)[424]; *gabonensis* ♂♀? (2) 70–75 g (Uganda)[765]; 72 g (Congo)[500]. For additional data see[342, 259, 458, 460].

35 GREY-HEADED BUSH-SHRIKE *Malaconotus blanchoti* Plate 14

FIELD IDENTIFICATION Large (25 cm), brightly coloured bush-shrike with pale grey head, white spot in front of yellowish eye, and a massive black bill. Sexes similar. Back, wings and tail green with yellow tips to wing and tail, and two lines of yellow spots on wing-coverts. Below variable, yellow or tinged orange or orange-brown. Young have greyish-brown head with pale bill and pale yellow underparts. Shy and skulking, slow-moving. More often heard than seen, call a series of hollow, drawn-out mournful whistles, and explosive harsh calls. Resident, solitary at all levels, mainly mid- to upper canopy of woodland savanna, riverine and forest edge throughout Africa. ***Flight characteristics***: Short-distance; wings rounded, makes 'wing-fripping' sounds when excited. Usually glides between trees, swooping up to perch.

COMPARISONS Similar to congeners which, however, are all primarily forest birds. The rare Monteiro's Bush-shrike *Malaconotus monteiri* differs by being structurally heavier, especially the bill, and in having a darker grey head, more extensive white on face, extending above and below the grey eye (eye yellowish in Grey-headed), and yellower underparts. Lagden's Bush-shrike *M. lagdeni* (montane forest) distinguished by lack of white lores. Head darker grey, wing-coverts, tertials and inner secondaries tipped black and yellow and eye grey. Plumage similarity with much smaller Orange-breasted Bush-shrike *Chlorophoneus sulfureopectus* remarkable; however, latter has a distinct yellow eyebrow, brown eye, small bill and short repetitive higher-pitched whistles. In possible overlap areas of these large bush-shrikes, caution is required when using calls for identification, as most have poorly known, similar hollow-sounding, mournful whistles.

DESCRIPTION ADULT Sexes similar. ***Head*** including ear-coverts, nape and mantle Grey; lores white. ***Back*** including uppertail-coverts Yellowish-green. ***Wings*** Green, outer webs green, inner hair-brown, appearing green when closed. Secondaries and tertials tipped light yellow, as well as greater and median coverts. ***Tail*** Greenish-yellow narrowly tipped light yellow. ***Underparts*** Chin and throat yellow; breast and upper belly colour variable from bright yellow (*catharoxanthus*), tinged bright orange (*hypopyrrhus*) or brownish-yellow (*approximans*); lower belly to undertail-coverts yellow; flanks greenish-yellow. ♀ breast duller. ***Bare parts*** Massive bill black; palate black; legs bluish-grey; eye yellow to orange-yellow. ***Abnormal plumage*** The occurrence of abnormal plumage is not uncommon. A report of canary-yellow upperparts (back and tail) and ochre underparts was published as an albino. A specimen with a grey breast-band also recorded; another with no yellow or green, having the whole upperparts grey like the head, tips of coverts and flight feathers and tail white, underparts white, breast-band and flanks tawny, also published[500, 615, 623].

JUVENILE/IMMATURE Has head mottled pale brown and grey. Face greyish with lores variable yellowish to whitish. Back, wings and tail like adult, with primaries, tertials and greater wing-coverts tipped buffy-yellow. Rump faintly barred. Underparts pale lemon without barring, often with a few orange feathers on breast in immature. Bill grey-brown or greyish, usually with paler base; eye variable from brown in juvenile, to grey or whitish in immature, depending on age[32, 205].

GEOGRAPHICAL VARIATION At least 7 races, varying mainly in colour of underparts, although there is also a decrease in size from N to S. Variations range from bright yellow to yellow tinged with tawny or orange-brown. Yellow-breasted birds occur in NE range, *catharoxanthus* (N Zaïre, Uganda, W Kenya, Ethiopia) and in SW range *citrinipectus* (Angola, S Zaïre, W Zambia, N Namibia). In West Africa *blanchoti* (Senegal to Cameroon) varies from yellow to a faint tinge of tawny or orange-brown, as does *interpositus* (N Angola, S Zaïre, W Tanzania, NW Zambia). An increase in orange-brown occurs in the E and southern African populations, with *approximans* (S Ethiopia, Kenya, N Tanzania) having the darkest underparts. South of this *hypopyrrhus* (Tanzania southwards to South Africa, including Zambia, S Angola, Zimbabwe, N Namibia and NE Botswana), shows less intense orange-brown on the underparts. At S limit *extremus* (SW to SE South Africa) is distinguished by darker head and back[130, 622, 623].

MOULT Little known. Adults have a complete post-breeding moult. Juveniles reported to undergo a complete moult; however, immature specimens suggest a second moult before acquiring adult plumage[25, 108, 500, 832].

RANGE, HABITAT and STATUS Breeding range Widespread in Africa from Senegal, Gambia, Guinea-Bissau, Guinea, Sierra Leone, Ivory Coast, Ghana, Togo, Benin, Cameroon, Nigeria, Zaïre, Rwanda, Mali, Burkina Faso, Niger, Chad, Central African Republic, Sudan, Ethiopia, Eritrea, Somalia, Uganda, Kenya, Tanzania, Zambia, Malawi, Mozambique, Angola, NE Namibia, Zimbabwe, N and E Botswana, N, E and SE South Africa and Swaziland. **Habitat** Savanna woodlands, in medium-dense *Acacia*, miombo *Brachystegia* and other broadleaved woodlands, often favouring the larger trees in these habitats. Also occurs in mature riverine bush, forest edge, thickets, suburban gardens and occasionally interior of lowland forest and rarely in plantations[7, 21, 26, 30, 37, 48, 119, 130, 234, 242, 290, 291, 325, 431, 481, 482, 504, 631, 639, 807, 810, 848, 859, 907]. **Status** Uncommon resident with local movements. **Conservation status** Not threatened, and apparently expanding into suburban habitats, at least in S of range[205, 622].

MOVEMENTS Appears to undertake some local seasonal movements, ranging widely in austral winter in S of range or expanding into more arid regions during the rains in W Africa. Mournful whistle-calls heard during austral winter as a bird passed through a non-breeding area[37, 39, 48, 119, 205, 234, 338, 500, 639].

SOCIAL ORGANISATION and GENERAL BEHAVIOUR Little known. Solitary; an extremely wary, agile but slow-moving, skulking and inconspicuous bird, with only fleeting glimpses caught of it as it creeps, almost rodent-like, about in mid- to upper canopy. More often heard than seen. Usually calls from within the crown of larger trees, also sometimes from a more conspicuous perch near top of a large tree. Territories are large, at least 50 ha, increasing in non-breeding season to a home range of at least 200 ha. ♂ advertising call a repeated low, mournful, drawn-out whistle. During calling adopts an inclined posture displaying orange breast, tail hangs vertically down and head bows downwards with each call. This call sometimes also given in flight. Rival ♂♂ may deliver this call simultaneously or alternately. Threat signalled by distinctive slow bill-snapping (clicking) combined with short hollow whistles; clicks produced as bill raised, whistles as bill lowered onto breast with nape slightly raised. Neighbouring pairs may interact at close quarters with this display. At higher intensity adopts a crouched, hunched posture, back feathers raised, the bill held open, with head swayed menacingly from side to side and tail fanned. A bird heard to give whistles in flight, combined with 'wing-fripping' sounds, is thought to be responding to rival aggression. At still higher intensity, produces harsh explosive squawks and dive-bombs an intruder. Known to bathe by fluttering about in dew-soaked foliage. Scratches indirectly[205, 504, 631, 696, 872]. **Foraging behaviour** Mainly arboreal; forages by gleaning at all levels, mainly in dense mid- and upper canopy, occasionally on the ground. Creeps slowly along branches peering and twisting head about, above and below branches, appearing less interested in foliage than branches. Often raids nests of eggs or young. Tends to forage from low down in a tree, moving upwards and then flying (usually gliding) to another tree low down to repeat the process. Prey is captured in the bill, usually with a lunge. When nesting appears to use a preferred killing tree where prey is immobilised before delivering to nest. Large prey is wedged into a fork or, when smaller, held in the foot like 'true' shrikes; also caches food. When prey is dropped, dives to ground to retrieve it. Seen to attack large galls, presumably to extract grubs. Occasionally hawks insects in the air, capturing them with an audible bill snap. Sometimes pursues prey on the ground in large leaps or clambers about on trunk. Although often mobbed by smaller birds, joins mixed foraging parties, particularly during non-breeding season. **Food** Arthropods and small vertebrates. Most prey consists of arthropods, mainly insects such as Orthoptera (grasshoppers) and Hymenoptera (wasps, particularly mason wasps Eumenidae); also feeds on centipedes and scorpions. Frequently takes a wide variety of vertebrate prey, sometimes almost up to own body weight, including rodents, birds (including eggs and particularly nestlings), reptiles (lizards, snakes, chameleons), amphibians and even bats. Recorded eating dried meat[17, 22, 32, 33, 48, 133, 205, 290, 504, 871, 872].

SOUNDS Repertoire consists of low-pitched ventriloquial whistles, harsh drawn-out sounds and sharp metallic clicking. Main advertising call of ♂

is a far-carrying, low-pitched, monotonously repeated, mournful and haunting, drawn-out whistle, described as an in-drawn *uuuuuuuh*, *whoooooo* or *phoooooo-*. This call sometimes also delivered at a slightly higher pitch, sounding like *pheeeeeu-*. Each note starts softly, rises in volume and stops abruptly. Note duration variable from *c.*0.4–1 sec, and repeated sometimes up to *c.*50 times, interval *c.*5 sec, but variable. The sequence sometimes contains a similar-sounding but disyllabic note due to a terminal inflection, resulting in a higher-pitched ending, sounding like *whooooo-lwe* or *whooooo-up*. Other variations include series which have a distinct break in the middle, with the second half being higher-pitched. Reportedly also has a single metallic bell-like note heard in E Africa, but unknown in S Africa. ♀ may occasionally duet with 4–5 harsh, rasping, tearing drawn-out *Skeeeeer-Skeeeeeer-*, *Skwaaar-skwaaar-* and *skreeep-skreeep-* notes. Threat signalled by loud bill-snaps resembling sound made by hedge-clippers, followed by a short soft hollow whistle, and described as *Klip!-Klip!-phoou*. This phrase often given in duet, probably between partners, and also between rivals in bouts of counter-calling. At higher intensity only bill-snapping *Klip!-Klip!-*, *tuk-tuk-* or *Tik!-Tik!-* sounds. Alarm signalled by repeated harsh *Ke-Ke-Ke-*, *kr-a-a-a-a* or *wik-uraaanh-uraaanh-uraaanh...* and loud explosive *SquoK-SquoK-*, *Squot-tot-squot-tot* or *skwaark* calls, often uttered in flight, and heard once to be accompanied by 'wing-fripping' sounds. Contact given by repeated soft plaintive mewing *phouu-phouu-* or slightly higher-pitched *phoee* whistle. Adults, nestlings and juveniles beg with soft buzzing *zzhoreer-zzhoreer-* sounds. See General Behaviour for postures accompanying calls[9, 48, 205, 504, 631, 696, 864, 872]. Sonagram[43, 48].

BREEDING BIOLOGY Little known. Monogamous and territorial, occasionally with an additional bird in vicinity of nest, probably a member of previous brood. Exceedingly wary in vicinity of nest, approaching it by hopping through adjacent vegetation with minimal flight. Aggressive towards other birds in vicinity of nest. Contact and possible greeting display between the sexes characterised by much loose wing-fluttering, with or without food, and often while some distance from nest. Apparently single brooded, with replacement clutches frequent. In one case, a destroyed nest was rebuilt in 10 days, and in another rebuilt and re-laid in 14 days after eggs had been taken. Nests appear too small for the large chicks. The only breeding success recorded is 22%. In spite of 3–4 eggs being laid, usually only one or two survive to fledging, with overall fecundity of 0.8 (fledglings/pair/year). Occurs at low densities, in one study at less than 1 pair/200 ha[67, 131, 133, 205, 320].

Season West Africa: Jun–Jul, nestling in Nov (Gambia)[38, 39, 482, 696]; Jan, May, fledglings Feb, May, Jul (Ghana)[234]; Jan–Apr, Jun and Sep (Nigeria)[37, 328]; Sep–Nov (NE Zaïre), Sep–Oct (SE Zaïre)[22, 290]; East Africa; possibly May, definite Jun (Ethiopia)[292]; Feb–Mar (Somalia)[33, 859]; Jul, Sep–Dec (East Africa)[293]; Aug (Tanzania)[299]; Jan, Apr–May, Sep–Dec mainly Dec (Malawi)[119]; Sep–Oct, Dec, mainly Sep (Zambia)[291]; nestlings and eggs Sep (Angola)[7, 423]; Jul–Apr, mainly Sep–Nov (Zimbabwe)[30]; Aug–Jan (South Africa)[48, 320, 639].

Displays ***Courtship*** Conspicuous when courting, which appears similar to territorial threat, as one bird chases another, the first bird frequently raising its head, either bird or perhaps both, uttering a rapid bill-snapping (rattle) *Klip-Klip-* followed by short *phoou-* whistle. ♂ also seen doing a fluttering display-flight with tail fanned, interspersed with gliding flight in which wings held back and slightly elevated, and combined with short *whooo-* whistles. In another observation ♂ moved about in crouched posture, fluttering wings in half-spread position, and occasionally breaking off a pencil-thick dry twig, then flying over and passing it to the other bird without vocalisations. Courtship-feeding takes place, during which ♂ loosely flutters slightly open wings while giving a soft mewing *phouu-* or *phoee-* contact call. ♀ also flutters wings and begs with soft buzzing *zzhoreer-zzhoreer-*. ♀ duets occasionally with repeated harsh drawn-out *Skeeer-Skeeeer-* calls in response *whooo* whistle of ♂. Pairs maintained contact with soft plaintive mewing *phoee-phoee-* whistles[205, 529, 1031]. ***Nest-site display*** A member of a pair observed sitting repeatedly in a prospective nest site which was later used[131].

Nest Selection appears to be done by both sexes; ♂ observed passing twigs to ♀ who incorporated these into nest. Both birds add the lining. The rather untidy shallow cup consists of a base of coarse twigs on which a cup of finer material, such as grass stems and leaf petioles is built, and lined with tendrils, rootlets or dry leaves. Has been noted to use the nests of other species such as dove, lourie or goshawk. Nests are usually placed *c.*4 m (1.2–12, n=125) above the ground, and most often in thornless deciduous trees, in a fork or frequently in a parasitic growth, like *Loranthus* sp. ***Size*** OD 152–170 mm (158), ID 70–102 mm (88), cup depth 45 mm. May nest in same tree annually[6, 20, 22, 35, 133, 205, 290, 328, 338, 500].

Eggs 3–4, usually 3 (2–5, n=33). Colour variable, pinkish, greenish, cream or buff, finely spotted and blotched with chestnut-brown, purplish-brown and grey, especially at the large end. ***Size*** 26.5–32.1 x 19.3–21.8 mm (29.4 x 20.6, n=69)[6, 19, 48, 67, 119, 205, 290, 299, 359]. **Incubation** Apparently by ♀ only, ♂ feeding her on and off nest. Period *c.*16–17 days, (15–18, n=3). Generally sitting bird is difficult to flush. ♀ utters a soft repeated *phoee-phoee-phoee* on approach of ♂[48, 131, 205, 500]. **Nestling** Hatch blind, naked and lack mouth spots. At a week old still blind and naked. Bill fleshy grey, dark brown at tip, gape yellowish-white; tongue and palate orange-yellow[328, 331]. Attended by both sexes. Initially ♂ supplies food to ♀ who feeds nestlings. Normally only one adult at a time arrives to feed nestlings, but often one only approaches when the other has also arrived. Before flying to the nest, may adopt a horizontal posture, with wings rapidly fluttering while held slightly away from the body. Similar display occurs at the nest when one adult approaches the other. Sitting bird also observed to flutter wings. Nest guarding is believed to take place. Fledge after c.20 days (20–21, n=2). Nestlings and fledglings beg with buzzing *zzhoreer* calls and are uttering squeaky quavering whistles c.2 months after leaving nest. Young remain in parental territory for at least one year[48, 133, 205, 331, 644]. **Predation and longevity** Little known, snakes known to predate nestlings[859]. **Brood parasite** None.

MEASUREMENTS and WEIGHTS *M. b. catharoxanthus* (Zaïre) ♂♀? (9) wing 116–124 (118.8), tail 101–112 (107.1), bill (to skull) 31–35 (32.5), tarsus 33–36.5 (35.1)[500]; *hypopyrrhus* (southern Africa) ♂♀? (30) wing 107–121 (114), tail 106–117, bill 26–31, tarsus 29–35[48]. **Weights** southern Africa ♂ (17) 72.9–83.9 g (77.8), ♀ (16) 65.0–99.2 g (76.0)[205]; *interpositus* unsexed 81 g (Angola)[907]. For additional data see[622].

36 MONTEIRO'S BUSH-SHRIKE *Malaconotus monteiri* Plate 15

FIELD IDENTIFICATION Large (25 cm), colourful, yellow and green bush-shrike with massive black bill and extensive white on face, above and below grey eye. Sexes similar. Head dark grey; back, tail and wings olive-green with distinctive yellow tips to flight feathers and two lines of yellow spots on wing-coverts. Underparts bright lemon-yellow. Little known, shy and skulking in canopy, more often heard than seen; call a series of drawn-out mournful whistles. Solitary in primary montane or escarpment forest. At least two separate populations; probably resident on Mount Cameroon and Kupé in Cameroon, and on NW Angola escarpment. ***Flight characteristics***: Wings rounded.

COMPARISONS Most similar to savanna Grey-headed Bush-shrike *Malaconotus blanchoti*, which differs by having paler grey head, less extensive white on the face (white almost encircles the eye in Monteiro's) and a yellow eye (grey in Monteiro's). Monteiro's appears a larger, heavier bird, with a more massive bill. Also similar to the Fiery-breasted Bush-shrike *M. cruentus* in face and eye coloration, but this bush-shrike has reddish underparts (yellow in Monteiro's), distinctive black and yellow terminal markings on wing and tail, while lacking the two lines of yellow spots on wing-coverts of Monteiro's. Occurs in the same habitat as distinctive Green-breasted Bush-shrike *M. gladiator*. Caution required in use of calls, as drawn-out, mournful whistle similar to equivalent calls of most other large bush-shrikes within its range (see Sounds).

DESCRIPTION **Adult** Sexes similar. ***Head*** Grey from frontal to upper mantle. Face white from lores to above and below eye. ***Back*** Lower mantle to uppertail-coverts olive-green. Rump feathers long and fluffy. ***Wings*** Olive-green with broad yellow tips to secondaries, tertials, median and greater coverts. ***Tail*** Olive-green with yellow tips. ***Underparts*** Lemon-yellow to dark yellow, some showing brownish tinge on breast; flanks greenish-yellow. ***Bare parts*** Bill black and massive, palate unknown, legs blue-grey, eye grey in nominate and *perspicillatus*[113, 458]. **Juvenile/Immature** Unknown.

GEOGRAPHICAL VARIATION Two races in widely separate areas. Variation mainly in underparts and size of bill. Nominate *monteiri* (Angola) darker yellow below, sometimes with brownish tinge on breast; *perspicillatus* (Cameroon) lighter lemon-yellow below with a heavier bill[113, 458].

MOULT Unknown.

RANGE, HABITAT and STATUS **Breeding range** Fragmented distribution with breeding unconfirmed. In Angola from Gabela in Cuanza Sul, N along escarpment through southern Cuanza Norte to Bengo. If a specimen in Zoologisches Institut und Zoologisches Museum, Hamburg, Germany, is correctly identified, the distribution would be extended south to NW Huambo. One historical record and one recent sighting from Cameroon, and a historical record from W Kenya (specimen subsequently lost)[7, 343, 345, 402, 431, 622, 907, 989]. **Habitat** In Angola mainly on the escarpment in riverine, gallery forest and forest underplanted with coffee. May extend into lowland forest. In Cameroon from primary montane forest at 1000 m on Mount Cameroon and 1450 m on Mount Kupé. Kenyan specimen was from Kakamega Forest[7, 79, 343, 345, 622, 907]. **Status** Rare, apparently resident. **Conservation status** Described in 1870 from a specimen collected along the Rio Dande near Luanda, next collected in 1900s from Dondo and Ndalo Tando on the Angolan escarpment. In 1954 collected from Mucoso (near Dondo) and from Gabela. No recent records from Angola. A single specimen was collected on Mount Cameroon at 1000 m and described in 1894 as *Laniarius perspicillatus*. A similar bird was sighted in 1992 on Mount Kupé (Cameroon). A similar bird was collected in the Kakamega Forest in W Kenya in 1922, but the specimen was subsequently lost. In Angola it appears threatened by major habitat destruction and was not seen in a 1992 survey of the escarpment. A Red Data Book species considered Endangered[343, 345, 431, 479, 586, 989].

MOVEMENTS Unknown.

SOCIAL ORGANISATION and GENERAL BEHAVIOUR Little known; solitary, skulking and difficult to see. In Cameroon recorded once from upper-levels of primary montane forest. This bird responded to initial imitations of Green-breasted Bush-shrike whistle, and then to own call. In response to tape playback, made bill-rattling sounds, throwing head back with a 'staccato' movement downwards — here interpreted as bill-snapping while the head is thrown backwards, an aggressive behaviour commonly seen in Grey-headed Bush-shrike[205, 345]. **Foraging behaviour** Probably mainly a canopy gleaner. Also reported occasionally foraging on the ground, where hops about amongst the leaves[338]. **Food** Insects and small vertebrates such as mice, and reptiles[338].

SOUNDS Little known. In Cameroon, a series of low-pitched, mournful whistles. Originally described as similar to but distinct from those of Green-breasted Bush-shrike (with which it was interacting). Gave longer repeated series of 5 whistles, whereas Green-breasted gave shorter series of 3 whistles. Each note was shorter than those of Green-breasted, and lacked a terminal upward-inflection. However, Green-breasted now known to have various whistle phrases, some of which appear identical to those of Monteiro's and Grey-headed Bush-shrike (see Sounds of these species). Known to respond to imitations of Green-breasted Bush-shrike. Rattles or snaps the bill when agitated, a sound probably similar to the *Klip!-Klip!-* of Grey-headed Bush-shrike[205, 345, 431, 500].

BREEDING BIOLOGY Unknown.

MEASUREMENTS and WEIGHTS *M. m. monteiri* ♂ (3) wing 117, 118, 119, tail 110, 112, 109, bill(2) 32, 33, tarsus(3) 36, 36, 35; ♀ (2) wing 110, 114; tail 101, 107, bill 31, 34; tarsus 34.5, 36[458]; ♂ (1) wing 117, bill 33; ♀ (2) wing 109, 115, bill 31, 34[113]; *perspicillatus* ♀ (1) wing 115, tail 115, bill 30, tarsus 35[989]; re-measured wing 118, tail 109, bill 34, tarsus 36[458]. **Weights** unknown.

37 ORANGE-BREASTED BUSH-SHRIKE (Sulphur-breasted Bush-shrike)
Chlorophoneus sulfureopectus **Plate 15**

FIELD IDENTIFICATION Medium-sized (19 cm), colourful bush-shrike with grey head, prominent yellow eyebrow, black face-mask, brown eye and small black bill. Back and wings green, tail green with yellow tips. Underparts yellow, usually with orange tinge on breast. Sexes similar. Young barred above and below with a pale whitish-grey head. Shy and skulking, more often heard than seen; call a series of slowly or rapidly repeated short whistles. Solitary in canopy of savanna woodland and riverine bush throughout Africa, except arid areas, most of SW and S Central Africa and equatorial forests. ***Flight characteristics***: Flies short distances; frequently glides between trees, entering a tree with a characteristic final twisting movement. Flight is jerky with shallow wingbeats, sometimes accompanied by 'wing-fripping' sounds when excited.

COMPARISONS Most similar to much larger Grey-headed Bush-shrike *Malaconotus blanchoti*, but separated on smaller size, prominent yellow eyebrow (absent in Grey-headed), small weak bill (massive in Grey-headed), brown eye (yellowish in Grey-headed), and repeated piping whistles (slow low-pitched mournful whistles in Grey-headed). Also similar to some colour phases of Many-coloured Bush-shrike *Chlorophoneus multicolor*, which have a whitish eyebrow, or Black-fronted Bush-shrike *C. nigrifrons*, which lacks an eyebrow, or Olive Bush-shrike *C. olivaceus*, which has a yellow eyebrow. Details of head, particularly the more extensive black face-mask, and colour of underparts, in addition to forest habitat, help separate the bush-shrikes. Orange-breasted juvenile is paler grey on head, paler yellowish-white below and more extensively barred than the forest bush-shrikes. Juvenile Bocage's Bush-shrike *C. bocagei* darker greyish and barred above, with coarse grey barring below. Calls very similar to Bocage's Bush-shrike, and some superficially resemble Olive Bush-shrike.

DESCRIPTION ADULT ♂ ***Head*** Forehead yellowish-green grading into bluish slate-grey crown, nape and upper mantle (in East Africa some birds have crown, nape and upper mantle speckled black[237]; bright chrome-yellow eyebrow extends from forehead to behind eye; lores black. ***Back*** Bright pale olive-green, including rump. ***Wings*** Darker olive-green, coverts, tertials and secondaries edged and tipped pale yellow. ***Tail*** Bright olive-green tipped and edged pale yellow. ***Underparts*** Chin, throat, belly and vent bright yellow; breast bright orange, virtually lacking in W birds. ***Bare parts*** Bill small and black, palate black, legs bluish-grey, eye dark reddish-brown. ADULT ♀ Similar to ♂ except generally duller, has less yellow on forehead, orange on breast, and black on face. Also shows faint barring on flanks. JUVENILE Head and mantle whitish-grey with dark barring, lacks yellow and black on face. Remaining upperparts similar to adult but with dark barring. Wings greenish-grey, coverts tipped buff to yellowish-white. Upper- and undertail-coverts barred. Tail greenish tipped and edged pale yellow. ***Underparts*** Chin grey, finely barred, breast and flanks greyish- to whitish-yellow with heavier dark dusky barring, belly pale yellow with fine barring; eye brown. This plumage apparently retained for *c.*6 months[35, 500]. IMMATURE Progressive development of orange on breast and adult-like head, but lacks yellow forehead, eyebrow and black lores. First-winter (austral) plumage differs from adult in having the forehead and lores whitish, the throat paler, little if any orange breast-band, and wing-coverts tipped whitish. Adult plumage attained in about 1 year;

barred throat and sides of face and buff-tipped coverts are the last areas to attain adult plumage. Bill blackish, with pale base to lower mandible; eye brown[205, 500, 546].

GEOGRAPHICAL VARIATION At least 6 races; variation slight involving mainly size and colour intensity of face, upperparts, breast and flanks. Northern nominate *sulfureopectus* (Senegal to NE Zaïre) and *modestus* (N Angola, probably to N Namibia and S Zaïre) distinguished from others by darker ear-coverts. Eastern *terminus* (SE South Africa to SE Tanzania) and *suahelicus* (S Somalia, coastal Kenya, Tanzania and central Mozambique) are small races, compared to *similis* (Ethiopia to Angola, N Namibia, Botswana, Zimbabwe) from interior which has greyer ear-coverts and more extensive orange on the breast than nominate or previous two races; *fricki* (S Ethiopia to Kenya) has a greenish forehead. Birds in the W region of southern Africa have very pale breasts, appearing almost yellow-breasted[114, 168, 528, 621].

HYBRID or ABNORMAL PLUMAGE A possible hybrid Orange-breasted x Bocage's Bush-shrike was originally described in 1919 as *Chlorophoneus andaryae* from near Entebbe, Uganda. It has also been suggested as a possible colour morph of Orange-breasted Bush-shrike, but is here thought simply to represent an abnormal plumage of this species. **Description** Upperparts grey from forehead to uppertail-coverts, including scapulars; lores and long eyebrow white; face-mask grey. ***Wings*** Primaries and secondaries greenish-brown; tertials and secondaries tipped yellow-buff; lesser, median and greater coverts greyish-green, narrowly tipped buffy-yellow; primary coverts darker olive-green broadly tipped buffy yellow. ***Tail*** Central pair grey with faint greenish tinge, remainder green to greenish-grey, outer feathers edged and tipped pale buffy yellow. ***Underparts*** Chin and throat whitish, breast buffy; belly to undertail-coverts whitish. ***Bare parts*** Bill black, palate unknown, tarsus blue-grey, eye brown. The tipped primary coverts suggest a first-year bird. Size: wing 81, tail 70, exposed bill 13, tarsus 23[112, 180, 500, 775, 776].

MOULT In Jan immature completing moult from first-winter (austral) into adult plumage. Adults at same time in post-breeding moult (Botswana). Tail moult recorded in Aug (Kenya)[237, 546].

RANGE, HABITAT and STATUS Breeding range Widespread from Senegal, Gambia, Guinea, Sierra Leone, Ivory Coast, Ghana, Togo, Benin, Cameroon, Nigeria, Mali, Burkina Faso, Niger, Chad, Central African Republic, Gabon, Zaïre, Rwanda, Burundi, Sudan, Ethiopia, Somalia, Uganda, Kenya, Tanzania, Zambia, Malawi, Mozambique, Angola including Cabinda, N and NE Namibia, N and E Botswana, Zimbabwe, Swaziland and N, E and SE South Africa. Bioko record rejected[431]. **Habitat** Wide variety of woodlands, including bushveld, broadleaved and *Acacia* woodland, particularly mixed riverine woodland, occasionally in miombo *Brachystegia*. Also in thickets on termitaria, forest edge, gallery forest and occasionally entering lowland forest. Up to 3000 m in East Africa[7, 21, 22, 26, 30, 37, 38, 48, 114, 119, 234, 242, 290, 291, 292, 295, 297, 318, 320, 325, 431, 481, 482, 504, 631, 639, 807, 848, 907]. **Status** Locally common to not uncommon resident. **Conservation status** Unknown, probably not threatened.

MOVEMENTS Appears sedentary in southern Africa, but possible seasonal movements recorded in Kenya and from the Sahel, particularly from S Sudan, N Nigeria and N Ghana, where moves into N dry areas during the rains, retreating S again in dry season[37, 234, 242, 318, 639].

SOCIAL ORGANISATION and GENERAL BEHAVIOUR Little known. Usually solitary or in pairs, shy and skulking and difficult to see. More often heard than seen. Territory size thought to be relatively large, probably 20–30 ha. Advertises territory by calling in an inclined to upright posture. Before calling, bows forward then bends head backwards with bill inclined upwards, showing off the yellow throat and orange breast. Most calling done from within the upper canopy of prominent trees, rarely perching in more exposed positions, possibly in static-marking. Main territorial call a loud series of repeated clear piping whistles. During territorial threat, adopts a more horizontal, sleek posture and sways body from side to side while making harsh tearing and bill-clashing sounds. Scratches indirectly[5, 15, 22, 111, 205, 631, 872]. **Foraging behaviour** Searches from mid- to upper canopy, where hops about in horizontal posture, pauses and peers about, then darts at prey, gleaning from branches, twigs and leaves. Works its way to the top of a tree then glides to the base of the canopy of another tree. Often joins mixed foraging parties, particularly in non-breeding season[48, 26, 205, 504, 631]. **Food** Arthropods, mainly insects and their larvae, particularly Hymenoptera (bees and wasps). Other insects include Lepidoptera (smooth and hairy caterpillars), Mantodea (mantids) and Coleoptera (beetle larvae). Possibly takes chicks in Red-billed Quelea *Quelea quelea* colonies[8, 48, 205, 290, 1062].

SOUNDS Repertoire consists of repeated series of far-carrying, often monotonous, pure ringing whistles and harsh tearing sounds. Calls show little geographical variation but may differ in repetition rate and length of series from *c.*3 slow melodious *hu-hu-hooo, hooi-hooi-hoooi,* to *c.*15 rapid higher-pitched *hehehehehe-, kew-tee-tee-tee-tee-tee-tee* whistles. Most series begin or end with slightly different notes, either lower- or higher-pitched or of longer duration, variously described as *poo-ti-ti-ti-ti-ti-, twit-o-o-o-o-o, hwe-hwe-hwe-, hu-hu-hu-hu-hweet, hu-hu-hu-hoooo twi-twu-twu-twurrr, whi-whi-whi-whi-her* or *fwee-fwee-fwee-her.* In West Africa two immatures noted counter-singing with single *puwheet* whistles. Duetting poorly developed, the ♀ occasionally responding with soft husky harsh *skizzz* or double-noted *tzzrrik-tzzrrik* or *sswoor-swearzz* calls. Threat signalled with a harsh drawn-out call, usually followed by two bursts of rapid bill-clashing (clicking), producing *Tzzrrrrr-KilliKilliK* or reversed as in *tititeeezz.* During alarm and very aggressive interactions the call becomes even more extended and higher-pitched, sounding like *Tzzrrreeeer*, usually interrupted by short jerky, 'wing-fripping' flights. Short range contact maintained with soft low *chrrr* calls, which also signal anxiety. Young beg with high-pitched *seee-seee* or *tseep-tseep* sounds. Responds to imitation of whistle call[5, 48, 205, 299, 339, 504, 631, 696, 872]. Sonagram[43, 48].

BREEDING BIOLOGY Little known. Monogamous and territorial. Second broods have been recorded; in one case a second nest was built for this purpose[6, 205]. **Season** Juvenile in Jan (Gambia)[38]; May, Jul–Aug (Ghana)[234]; May nest-building, eggs (Nigeria)[37]; Jan, Sep–Oct (Zaïre)[22, 290]; Aug–Sep (Sudan)[242]; Jan, Mar, May–Jun, Oct (East Africa)[25, 293]; Feb (Uganda)[2]; Dec–Jan (Tanzania)[25, 237]; Jan–Feb, possibly Mar, Oct–Dec (Malawi)[119]; Oct–Dec, Feb (Zambia)[291]; Jan–Mar, Apr, Jun–Jul, Sep–Dec, mainly Oct–Dec (Zimbabwe)[30]; probably Oct–Dec (Mozambique)[26]; Nov and Jan breeding condition, juvenile in Jul (Angola)[7, 907]; southern Africa; most S populations appear to breed slightly earlier; Aug–Mar (South Africa)[48, 320, 639]; egg-laying Dec–Jan (Botswana)[807]. **Displays** Unknown. Possible courtship involves ♂ giving repeated high-pitched, monotonous *hoytee-tee-tee-tee-tee-tee*, with ♀ occasionally responding in duet with harsh *skizzz* call. ♂ may vary call with less musical, quieter *cha-cha-cha-cha-cha-cheer* sounds, accompanied by heavy, jerky 'wing-fripping' flights combined with a series of quiet *tzzerkwa-tzzer-* sounds. ♂ chases ♀ through the canopy, both hopping or bouncing in tandem. Courtship feeding apparently does not occur[205]. **Nest** Built by both sexes. Structure consists of a transparent, frail platform, like a dove's nest, with a shallow cup of tendrils, fine rootlets, leaf petioles, grass or twigs as well as spider web; lined with finer material. It is usually placed in a thorn tree, typically an *Acacia* (often before the tree has come into leaf), in a lateral position on a well-supported horizontal branch, multiple fork or in creeper tangles at *c.*4 m (1.8–10.0, n=67). Some nests placed in parasitic growths like *Loranthus*. Often nests in the same vicinity each season[6, 22, 48, 205, 290]. **Eggs** Usually 2 (1–3, n=33). Dull light green or greenish-white, thickly streaked and spotted with shades of brown and grey mainly at the large end. ***Size*** 19.5–24 x 14–18 mm (22 x 16.1, n=51)[48, 359, 234, 19, 119, 205]. **Incubation** By both sexes, period unrecorded. ♂ gives whistle-calls from nest, probably to initiate nest relief[48, 205]. **Nestling** Hatch blind, naked, pinkish-orange and have mouth spots. They give repeated high pitched *seeeep-seeeep* or *tseeeep-* begging calls with a ventriloquial quality, and are attended by both sexes. Period 12 days (n=1). Fledglings give similar calls accompanied by crouched wing-fluttering movements[48, 205, 331]. **Predation and longevity** Taken by Wahlberg's Eagle *Aquila wahlbergi* in East Africa and a nestling taken by a boomslang *Dispholidus* sp. Ringed bird 7–7.5 years old[657, 855, 1002]. **Brood parasite** None.

MEASUREMENTS and WEIGHTS Races combined ♂♀? (89) wing 82–94 (88.9), tail 79–94 (86.6), ♂♀? (88) bill (to skull) 12.2–20.5 (16.0), tarsus 21.8–27 (25.0)[500]. **Weight** *sulfureopectus* ♂ (2) 31.0–34.0 g; ♀ (2) 28.0–29.5 g; ♂♀? (2) 29.6–30.0 g (Ghana)[582]; races combined ♂ (34) 24–30.5 g (27.5), ♀ (21) 19.5–30.2 g (26.4); ♂♀? (13) 26–32 g (29.1) (southern Africa)[48, 205]. For additional data see[319].

38 BOCAGE'S BUSH-SHRIKE (Grey Bush-shrike, Grey-green Bush-shrike) *Chlorophoneus bocagei* Plate 15

FIELD IDENTIFICATION Medium-small (16–17 cm) dull-coloured bush-shrike with a black head, contrasting white forehead and long white eyebrow. Back and wings dark grey, tail black. Underparts buff, chin and belly white. Sexes similar. Young greyish-brown barred above, underparts buff with coarse grey barring. More often heard than seen; gives loud repetitive short whistles. Solitary in canopy of forest, forest edge, thickets and secondary growth. Resident in Central Africa on periphery of equatorial forest from S Cameroon, N Angola, Zaïre, to Uganda and W Kenya. ***Flight characteristics***: Short-distance; wings rounded.

COMPARISONS Most similar to Pink-footed Puffback *Dryoscopus angolensis* in coloration, but which lacks the white eyebrow strip and has pinkish, not grey legs. Superficially similar to ♀ Black-backed Puffback *D. cubla*, which has white lores. General behaviour and calls very similar to Orange-breasted Bush-shrike *Chlorophoneus sulfureopectus*. Caution required when identification is based on calls alone. Juvenile similar to juvenile Orange-breasted, distinguished by darker barred buffy greyish-brown upperparts (barred greyish in Orange-breasted) and darker greyish wings (green in Orange-breasted).

DESCRIPTION Adult ♂ ***Head*** Crown and nape glossy black; forehead and lores whitish, eyebrow white extending behind eye to above ear-coverts; face-mask black from eye to ear-coverts and neck. ***Back*** Mantle to rump dark grey, rump feathers long and fluffy. ***Wings*** dark grey (outer webs), inner webs black (no white in wings). ***Tail*** Black (darker than wings); uppertail-coverts dark grey. ***Underparts*** Chin and throat white, breast and upper belly creamy-buff, lower belly and vent whitish. ***Bare parts*** Bill black; palate unknown; tarsus blue-grey; eye dark reddish-brown to dark brown[290, 764]. Adult ♀ Similar to ♂ except tail greyer (not black), also apparently has less distinct head pattern; eye greyish-brown[180, 500]. Juvenile

Upperparts from forehead to rump greyish-brown barred buff-yellow on head and mantle, becoming more tawny on back, each feather with a subterminal black bar; head and mantle with greenish tinge; buffy eyebrow indistinct. Wings: Pale brown with greenish tinge on outer webs, broad tawny to buff-white tips on secondaries, tertials and primary coverts. Tail: Greyish-brown with greenish tinge on outer margins, tipped buff. Underparts: Whitish to buffy-white tinged pale green with coarse grey barring. Bare parts: Bill grey-brown; palate unknown; legs like adult; eye pale brown[25, 338, 500].
IMMATURE Upperparts, wings and tail similar to adult, but with buff tips to wing-coverts, particularly primary coverts; eyebrow whitish to buffy-white and not as extensive as adult; ear-coverts blackish and less extensive than adult. Underparts: Whitish-buff to light yellow, with greyish barring mainly on flanks; throat dull white; thighs greyish[112, 290, 500, 646]. For development of plumage see[576].
GEOGRAPHICAL VARIATION Three races described. Variation slight, mainly in intensity of tail and back coloration. ♀ *jacksoni* (W Kenya) apparently has dark tail like ♂ nominate *bocagei* (Cameroon to N Angola), while *ansorgei* (N Angola) is paler grey on back[112, 350].
HYBRID or ABNORMAL PLUMAGE A possible hybrid Bocage's x Orange-breasted Bush-shrike described. See Orange-breasted Bush-shrike, Hybrid (p.222).
MOULT Recorded for Sep (Kenya) and Mar, Sep–Oct (Uganda)[237, 576].
RANGE, HABITAT and STATUS Breeding range S Cameroon, Central African Republic, Equatorial Guinea, Gabon, Zaïre except central regions, W and S Uganda, W Kenya and NW Angola. Formerly in Rwanda. Congo record rejected[431]. **Habitat** Mainly in secondary forest, overgrown forest clearings, edges, gallery forest, wooded savannas with dense bush, particularly in areas modified by man, such as old overgrown plantations. Also in cacao and coffee plantations and bordering thickets. Less frequently in primary forest. Up to 2200 m in East Africa[7, 21, 22, 290, 294, 295, 318, 347, 431, 481, 504, 631, 664, 688, 907]. **Status** Rare to not uncommon resident. **Conservation status** Unknown, but apparently disappearing in E range, as formerly in Rwanda and in Kenya from Nyarondo and Kericho[431, 631].
MOVEMENTS Unknown, probably sedentary.
SOCIAL ORGANISATION and GENERAL BEHAVIOUR Little known. Solitary or in pairs in middle and upper levels. Behaviour reportedly similar to Orange-breasted Bush-shrike; shy and skulking, easily overlooked, more often heard than seen. Defends a territory of 2–3 ha or smaller. Moves slowly and deliberately[112, 294]. **Foraging behaviour** Searches foliage in mid- to upper levels at 8–20 m above ground, occasionally in crown of very large trees or low down in subcanopy at forest edge. Gleans prey as it moves slowly and deliberately through the vegetation[294, 456, 504, 631]. **Food** Arthropods, mainly insects and their larvae, including Mantodea (mantids), Hemiptera (cicadas) and Lepidoptera (caterpillars). Orthoptera (grasshoppers) and Lepidoptera (butterflies, moths and caterpillars) fed to nestlings[290, 294].
SOUNDS Little known. Repertoire varied, consisting mainly of clear, rapidly repeated, often monotonous, fairly high-pitched whistles and harsh notes resembling Orange-breasted Bush-shrike but delivered more rapidly, sometimes with a bubbling apalis-like quality. Main advertising call a repeated series of whistles at the same pitch. May vary in pitch, rate of delivery and number of notes and have a longer note at beginning or end of series. Variously described as *peeeee-pee-pee-pee-pee-pee-pee-pee-pee*, *hu-hu-hu-hu-hu-huuu* or *uwee-wee-wee-wee-wee*. Also commonly repeats a double-noted call: *wewewewit-wewewewit, peeeu-peeeeu, pureet-ureet, tuootweeet,* sometimes *tweee-teeeeu* or *teeeeuooo-teeeeuoo-, Twee-ti-ti-teer,* with the second note lower. ♀ duets occasionally with harsh tearing batis-like *zreeekk, tzrrerr* or shorter *Zzzzz* or *zwik* sounds, while other phrases recall the sound of Gorgeous Bush-shrike *C. viridis*. Has other harsh scolding notes[22, 290, 294, 347, 500, 501, 504, 631].
BREEDING BIOLOGY Little known. Apparently monogamous and territorial. **Season** Most vocal Nov–Feb (Gabon)[294]; Oct breeding condition (Angola)[7, 907]; Aug–Sep (Zaïre)[290]; Aug–Sep and Feb (East Africa)[293]. **Displays** Unknown. **Nest** Similar to Orange-breasted Bush-shrike. Role of sexes unknown. Shallow cup built of strong tendrils. Placed in a fork on a branch of an *Acacia* at *c.*10 m (n=1) above the ground[290]. **Eggs** 2. Pale green, heavily smeared and blotched with olive-brown, dark brown and greyish-purple. ***Size*** 21.9 x 16 mm[290]. **Incubation** Apparently by both sexes, as ♂ recorded sitting. Period unknown[290]. **Nestling** Hatch blind, naked and appears to have mouth spots, although poorly defined. When feathered, extensively barred, brownish-buff above, whitish barred greyish below. Tongue and inside of mouth orange[500, 646]. No further information.
MEASUREMENTS and WEIGHTS Races combines ♂♀? (10) wing 72–84 (78.0), tail 62–70 (66.2), bill (to skull) 16–18.5 (17.2), tarsus 20–24 (22.2)[500]. **Weight** *bocagei* ♂ (1) 28.0 g (Angola)[911]; ♂ (1) 29.0 g (Cameroon)[478]; ♀ (2) 27 g (Uganda)[764]. For additional data see[34].

39 MANY-COLOURED BUSH-SHRIKE
Chlorophoneus multicolor — Plate 16

FIELD IDENTIFICATION Medium-sized (20 cm), brightly coloured bush-shrike with greyish head, green back and wings and bright colourful underparts. Sexes different. ♂ has broad black frontal and face-mask, and blackish tail with broad pale tips. ♀ lacks black face-mask and has a green tail. Underparts variable; 5 colour morphs (red, orange, yellow, buff and black) with intermediates. Up to 3 morphs recorded from same area. Young like dull ♀, sometimes barred below. Shy and skulking, more often heard than seen; call a slowly repeated series of hollow single short or double whistles, often with harsh drawn-out snarl. Solitary or in pairs in canopy of mainly lowland evergreen forests in W, but in montane forest in E. Resident in Central and West Africa. ***Flight characteristics***: Short-distance; wings rounded.

COMPARISONS In E range most similar to smaller Black-fronted Bush-shrike *Chlorophoneus nigrifrons*, with which sometimes considered conspecific, but ranges separate (see latter for comparison, p.226). Many-coloured also similar to other larger brightly coloured forest bush-shrikes, particularly Fiery-breasted *Malaconotus cruentus*. However, all members of this genus are much larger with a massive bill and pale eye (Many-coloured has small bill and dark eye).

DESCRIPTION The 5 colour morphs have similar upperparts and face markings but differ on colour of underparts (red, orange, yellow, buff and black) and colour of terminal tail spots. **ADULT ♂ *Head*** Crown to mantle blue-grey, face-mask black from frontal through lores, eyes to ear-coverts; usually bordered above by white eyebrow, extending over frontal (white absent in some red and most buff morphs). ***Back*** including rump and uppertail-coverts olive-green. ***Wings*** Coverts olive-green, flight feathers green on outer web, hair-brown on inner; appears green when closed. Secondaries and tertials tipped yellow. ***Tail*** Greenish-black to black, broadly tipped yellow or orange-red depending on colour morph. ***Bare parts*** Bill and palate black; legs blue-grey; eye deep purple or violet (Liberia) or reddish mauve with a narrow whitish rim (Zaïre)[79, 259, 290]. ***Underparts*** Variable, 5 colour morphs: RED: brilliant scarlet from chin to lower belly where it becomes more orange; undertail-coverts yellow-orange to orange. White of white eyebrow variable, from extensive to lacking. ORANGE: variable from reddish-orange to brownish-orange, extending from chin to undertail-coverts. Throat and breast brightest. White frontal and eyebrow variable, but extensive. Flanks reddish-green. Tail with broad yellow terminal spots. YELLOW: bright yellow from chin to undertail-coverts. Flanks greenish-yellow. BUFF: chin and throat white, breast and upper belly buffy-white darkening to greenish-yellow on flanks; lower belly whitish; undertail-coverts yellowish. White eyebrow usually absent. BLACK: black of face-mask extends onto throat, breast and upper belly; lower belly variable from yellow to orange-yellow or reddish; undertail-coverts and tail tips orange-yellow. White eyebrow usually absent[112, 113, 115, 347]. **ADULT ♀** General coloration similar to ♂, occurring in all colour morphs except Black. Differs with head completely grey, often paler around eye. Lacks black face-mask. Amount of white on eyebrow and frontal variable. Underparts duller and less extensive, usually grading into greenish-yellow flanks and lower belly. Tail green, above and below, with smaller yellow or orange tips depending on colour morph. Wing length slightly smaller than ♂. Eye reported as greyer-mauve or -blue than ♂[115, 646]. **JUVENILE** Head pattern, back and tail resembles ♀; wing also similar but with distinctive yellow terminal spotted primary and median coverts. Tail like ♀. Underparts variable depending on colour morph. Barring below generally indistinct or absent (absent in W, occasional in E); may also show barring on crown. Underpart colour, depending on morph, initially evident on throat and upper breast. Rest of underparts yellowish-green, darker on flanks. Buff morph birds have whitish chin, throat, breast and upper belly, grading into olive-green on lower belly. Flanks olive-green and slightly barred. Bare parts: Bill blackish-brown, paler at base; palate unknown; legs like adult; eye brown to greyish-blue. **IMMATURE** Shows progressive development of face-mask in ♂, underpart coloration, loss of pale buff-tipped wing-coverts, and blackening of bill in both sexes[79, 112, 113, 115, 500, 646].

GEOGRAPHICAL VARIATION Variation confused by polymorphism and intermediates, as well as variation within a colour morph. At least 3 races, separated mainly on the basis of presence or extent of white on the head, extent of black in the tail and the occurrence of either black or buff morphs. Race *multicolor* (Sierra Leone to Cameroon) has variable amount of white on head, *batesi* (Cameroon to W Uganda, N Angola) has most white on head, both being lowland forest species; *graueri* (including *ituriensis*, E Zaïre) has least amount of white on head, and inhabits montane forest only. The blackish-green tail coloration of ♂♂, apart from terminal spots, varies from mainly green in extreme west of W Africa (Sierra Leone–Togo) to mainly black in rest of range. Birds in Cameroon are largest, those in Angola and East Africa smallest. Distribution of morphs as follows: red (W Africa to Zaïre), orange (W Africa), yellow (W Africa to Zaïre and the only morph in Angola), buff is less common than other morphs except black (E Zaïre); black rare (W Africa). Bill length decreases southwards in W populations[3, 22, 79, 112, 113, 115, 341, 670, 688, 1061]. For proportional distribution of colour morphs see[113, 115, 670].

MOULT Wing moult recorded in Apr–May, with one individual completing wing moult in Jul, suggesting post-breeding moult. Most Jun–Oct birds in fresh plumage (Liberia)[259].

RANGE, HABITAT and STATUS Breeding

range Sierra Leone, Mali, Liberia, Ivory Coast, Ghana, Togo, Nigeria, Cameroon, Central African Republic, Equatorial Guinea, Gabon, Congo, Zaïre, Rwanda, SW Uganda and N Angola. **Habitat** Mainly lowland primary, secondary and gallery forest, but not restricted to these, and found in older secondary forest and degraded areas, forest-grassland mosaics, dense bush around villages and in gardens up to 1100 m (Liberia). Eastern population (*graueri*) occurs in highlands (montane forest) up to 2200 m. In Gabon in similar but more degraded habitat than Bocage's Bush-shrike *C. bocagei* [7, 21, 22, 37, 79, 101, 112, 115, 259, 290, 294, 338, 431, 481, 504, 670, 713, 848, 858, 907, 993]. **Status** not uncommon resident. **Conservation status** unknown. Estimated population in Liberia 200,000 pairs[858].

MOVEMENTS Unknown, apparently sedentary.

SOCIAL ORGANISATION and GENERAL BEHAVIOUR Little known. Solitary or in pairs, a shy and skulking bird, inconspicuous in spite of bright coloration, and difficult to see. More often heard than seen, with ♂ more vocal than ♀. Calls throughout the year[341, 504]. **Foraging behaviour** In some areas forages high up in mid- to upper canopy, mainly between 8–30 m (Liberia), in others lower down at 2–10 m (Gabon) in shrubs and bushes. Searches and gleans prey in foliage and smaller branches in the shaded interior of treetops and dense creeper tangles, occasionally in open canopy. Often a member of mixed foraging parties[294, 341, 858]. **Food** Arthropods, including large insects and their larvae, Orthoptera (grasshoppers and mantids), Lepidoptera (moths and caterpillars), Phasmatodea (stick insects), Hemiptera (bugs) and Coleoptera (beetles)[15, 259, 290, 294, 688, 858].

SOUNDS Little known. Repertoire appears similar to Black-fronted Bush-shrike, but ♂ call more hollow-sounding, and that of ♀ much harsher and lower-pitched. These are given as a series of slowly repeated, single, melodious, hollow *huwo.....huwo-, hooui....hooui-, whoop....whoop-* or *whoup-* whistles. Length of note and repetition rate variable. Whistled calls are sometimes also repeated as a series of double *huo-huo, hwo-hwo* or *huwa-huwa* notes. Disyllabic calls may also sometimes consists of a low and high note, sounding like *whoo-op, fu-fee* or with a terminal inflection *huolo.* ♀ answers ♂ in duet with drawn-out, harsh, rasping *kzzrrrr, tzzerrr, zzrrrrr* or still lower-pitched *harrrrrrr* calls, which appear lower-pitched and lack the characteristic nasal quality of Black-fronted Bush-shrike, the combination sounding like *hoou-kzzrrrrr* or *hooi-kzrrrrr.* Alarm signalled by harsh repeated rasping *zzreeeu-zzreeeu-.* Other harsh calls of unknown function include *chak-chak* and possibly represent bill-clashing or clicking sounds[15, 22, 336, 347, 500, 501, 504, 908].

BREEDING BIOLOGY Little known. Monogamous and territorial. No selective mating occurs, with pairs sometimes made up of different morphs. Estimated density based on calls 3–9 pairs/km² (Liberia)[112, 115, 341, 858]. **Season** Gonads suggest breeding condition in Oct (Liberia)[259]; Nov–Dec (Nigeria)[37]; most vocal Oct–Mar (Gabon)[294]; nest-building in rainy season, Jan, Mar–Jun, Sep and juveniles in Aug and Oct (E Zaïre)[22, 688]; Feb–Mar (central and S Uganda)[293]. No further breeding information except that the nest is concealed[294].

MEASUREMENTS and WEIGHTS *C. m. multicolor* ♂(21) wing (100.5 ±3.7), tail (86.8 ±3.4), bill (22.7 ±1.4); ♀ (3) wing 90–96 (92), tail 82–86 (84.3), bill 20–23 (21.8) (Liberia)[259]; races combined ♂♀? (15) wing 90–100 (94.7), tail 85–94 (88.9), tarsus 23.5–27 (24.6), bill (to skull) 19.9–23 (21.1)[500]. **Weight** *multicolor* ♂ (21) 51.0 g ±4.4; Imm ♂ (2) 48.1–48.4 g (48.3); Adult ♀ (3) 46.2–54.8 g (51.6); Imm ♀ (1) 42.3 g (Liberia)[259]; ♀ 37.0 g (Cameroon)[478]; *graueri* ♂ (3) 41 g each, ♀ (2) 36–39 g[1061]. For additional data see[15, 79, 670, 688].

40 BLACK-FRONTED BUSH-SHRIKE
Chlorophoneus nigrifrons **Plate 17**

FIELD IDENTIFICATION Medium-sized (19 cm), brightly coloured canopy bush-shrike, with grey head and black face-mask. Upperparts, wings and tail green. Underparts variable; 5 colour morphs (red, orange, yellow, buff and black). Sexes different. ♀ with smaller black face-mask. Young dull, without face-mask, pale below with faint barring. Shy and skulking, more often heard than seen; call a slowly repeated series of hollow short single or double whistles, often with a drawn-out nasal snarl. Solitary, found in canopy of montane and lowland evergreen forest from Kenya, Tanzania, SE Zaïre, N Zambia, Malawi, E Zimbabwe, W Mozambique and NE South Africa. ***Flight characteristics***: Short-distance; rounded wings, heavy with rapid wingbeats, sometimes accompanied by 'wing-fripping' sounds.

COMPARISONS Most similar to the Many-coloured Bush-shrike *Chlorophoneus multicolor*, with which sometimes considered conspecific, but ranges separate. ♂♂ of all morphs distinguished by green tail feathers with narrow yellow tips (black with broad yellow, orange or reddish tips in W Many-coloured). Most Many-coloured, except buff morph, have a white eyebrow (absent in Black-fronted). Many-coloured has yellow terminal spots on secondaries and tertials (absent in Black-fronted). Adult ♀♀ of both species have green tails, but easily separated on presence of black face-mask in Black-fronted (absent in ♀

Many-coloured). Separation of juveniles difficult, and not well studied. Both have barred underparts where ranges close. Many-coloured has prominent yellow-tipped secondaries, tertials and wing-coverts (tipping absent or only weakly developed in Black-fronted). Identification based on calls requires caution, as both species have similar repertoires. Harsh rasping call of ♀♀ sound the most different, nasal in Black-fronted, very harsh and low-pitched in Many-coloured. In S range overlaps with Olive Bush-shrike *C. olivaceus*. Easily distinguished by lack of yellow or white on face (Olive has white or yellow lores and eyebrow). Although buff morph Black-fronted closely resembles Olive Bush-shrike, they do not overlap. Calls very different: Olive has loud rapidly repeated and often descending whistles[113, 115, 205].

DESCRIPTION The 5 colour morphs have similar upperparts and face markings, but differ on colour of underparts (red, orange, yellow, buff, black). Intermediates between red, orange and yellow also occur. **Adult ♂** ***Head*** Crown to mantle blue-grey, face-mask formed by broad black frontal band extending through lores and eye to ear-coverts. ***Back*** Grey mantle grades into olive-green of back, rump and tail-coverts. ***Wings*** Coverts olive-green, flight feathers green on outer web, hair-brown on inner, appearing green when closed. ***Tail*** Olive-green with small terminal yellow spots, mainly on outer feathers. ***Bare parts*** Bill and palate black, legs blue-grey, eye maroon. ***Underparts*** Variable, 5 colour morphs. RED: chin to upper belly pale scarlet, grading through yellow into yellowish-green lower belly and undertail-coverts; flanks greenish. ORANGE: chin to upper belly orange, grading into yellowish-green on lower belly and undertail-coverts; flanks greenish. YELLOW: chin to lower belly bright yellow, undertail-coverts yellowish-green; flanks greenish. BUFF: chin and throat whitish, breast to upper belly cream-buff; lower belly and undertail-coverts greyish-white to greyish-yellow; flanks greyish-green. In all buff birds yellow is absent from the underparts except the underwing-coverts and undertail-coverts. BLACK: black of face-mask extends to underparts, including chin, throat, breast and upper belly, where it grades into a completely dark olive-green lower belly, flanks and undertail-coverts. Has yellow underwing-coverts, but no yellow tips to tail feathers[5, 113, 115, 121]. **Adult ♀** General coloration similar to ♂, main difference being in the black face-mask which is less extensive and does not extend onto frontal or ear-coverts. Underparts duller and less extensive, occurring in all morphs except black. Usually shows faint barring on flanks. **Juvenile** Resembles dull-coloured ♀, but lacks black face-mask. Underparts buff or yellowish-green with fine but distinct grey barring. Flanks barred greenish-grey. Flight feathers and wing-coverts narrowly tipped yellowish-white. Bill dark grey-brown with a pale base, eye brown[205]. **Immature** Colour morph is identifiable on the underparts in all but the red morph occurring in SE Zaïre (Upemba), where apparently barred pale greenish-yellow below, but confirmation required. Progressive development of black face-mask and underpart coloration, which begins on chin, throat and breast region. Primary wing-coverts retain narrow buff tips[115].

GEOGRAPHICAL VARIATION Variation confused by polymorphism and variation within morphs. Three races considered here. The races named *elgeyuensis*, *munzneri* and *nigrescens* are regarded as synonyms of *nigrifrons* because they are based, respectively, on red, buff and black morphs. Variation described mainly on colour of underparts and extent of terminal spots on tail. The S populations (Malawi to South Africa) have similar underpart coloration. Nominate *nigrifrons* (Kenya to N Malawi and N Zambia) is larger in wing length and body mass than *manningi* (E Angola, SE Zaïre, N and NE Zambia) and *sandgroundi* (E Malawi to South Africa). Morph distribution as follows: red (Kenya to SE Zaïre); Orange (Kenya to South Africa); yellow (Kenya, Tanzania); buff, less common than other morphs except black (Kenya to Malawi); black rare, only found in ♂♂ (E Usambara Mts in Tanzania, and Namuli Mts in N Mozambique). Intermediates between some morphs known to occur in W Kenya[112, 113, 115, 319, 334, 335]. For proportional distribution of colour morphs see[113, 115].

MOULT Jul post-breeding wing moult (Tanzania)[309].

RANGE, HABITAT and STATUS **Breeding range** Consists of many fragmented populations in Kenya, Tanzania, E Angola, SE Zaïre (Upemba), N and E Zambia, Malawi, E Zimbabwe, central W and N Mozambique and NE South Africa. **Habitat** A species of montane, escarpment, lowland and riverine evergreen forest. Lowland birds occur in SE Zaïre, E Angola, N Zambia, E Zimbabwe and W Mozambique. Montane birds found in Kenya, Tanzania, Malawi, E Zambia, E Zimbabwe and South Africa found mainly from 2300 m. E Angolan, SE Zaïre and N Zambian populations less ecologically restricted, and are found in drier wooded plateaus, miombo *Brachystegia* woodland and thickets associated with termite mounds[5, 7, 22, 26, 30, 48, 79, 115, 119, 146, 205, 290, 291, 299, 318, 319, 320, 431, 448, 459, 481, 631, 639]. **Status** Rare to locally common resident with local movements. **Conservation status** Unknown, but locally threatened by continued deforestation, particularly in lowland forest of Zimbabwe, and no longer occurs at Taita Hills in Kenya. Classified as an Indeterminate Red Data Book Species in South Africa[144, 205, 631, 825].

MOVEMENTS Widespread evidence from East Africa, Malawi and possibly South Africa of regular local seasonal movements, particularly altitudinal movements, where birds move down to lower elevations in non-breeding season. Movements of 60–100 km from breeding areas recorded in Malawi[205, 291, 320, 459, 448, 631].

SOCIAL ORGANISATION and GENERAL BEHAVIOUR Little known. Solitary or in pairs; a shy, wary and skulking species, more often heard than seen. Keeps mainly in mid- to upper canopy, where in spite of its coloration is often difficult to see as it creeps about. Vocal throughout the year;

maintains a territory of *c*.3–10 ha with slowly repeated resonant hollow whistles and a combination of whistles and harsh *Kzzeeerrr* sounds. During territorial calling ♂ adopts an inclined upright posture, bowing slightly with each call. ♂♂ often heard to counter-sing against each other with similar single whistle-calls. Territorial threat signalled by increased rate of both call types, culminating in bill-clashing, high-pitched screams and deep churring sounds. These are given in a horizontal posture and accompanied by wing- and tail-flicking. When excited makes 'wing-fripping' sounds in flight. ♀ duets with tearing sounds (see Sounds). Dew-bathing recorded, and scratches indirectly[205, 448, 500]. **Foraging behaviour** Forages in mid- to upper levels of tall forest, gleaning mainly from smaller branches and foliage, particularly in dense leafy thickets and matted creeper entanglements. Creeps and hops about in a crouched position peering around in search of prey. Also gleans from larger moss-covered branches and occasionally from trunks. Generally works its way upwards in one tree, then glides down to mid-levels of next to repeat cycle. Occasionally hawks insects in the air. Often joins mixed foraging parties, particularly during breeding season[146, 205, 448]. **Food** Arthropods, mainly insects and their larvae, including Coleoptera (beetles) and Hymenoptera (wasps)[9, 205].

SOUNDS Repertoire consists of hollow whistles and harsh tearing sounds. Main territorial call usually a slowly repeated, low-pitched, hollow resonant series of whistles, variously described as *hou....hou-*, *whoop-*, *hoi*, *kwo-* or *quoh-* and sometimes combined with 2–3 similar notes *hohoho* given in a short rapid series. Length of series and note interval variable, in non-breeding season single whistles given sporadically, but in breeding season may be given in a series of up to 20 notes, with an interval of as little as 3–4 sec, but more usually 15–20 sec or longer. The whistle may also be combined with a second higher-pitched note, usually given immediately after, but also sometimes reversed, particularly in N populations. The combination produces a disyllabic note, sounding like *hou-ho*, *whu-koooo*, *whoo-heeu*, *whoop-tweeup*, *whie-kou*, *whoop-WEEup*, *haw-kwoi* or, when reversed, *WHEEo-worik*. Both call types may be followed in duet by ♀ giving a long-drawn-out nasal tearing or rasping snarl, which begins softly and increases in volume, sounding like *Kzzeeerrr*, *screeee*, *NYAAAAA* or *SHNARR*. Usually the call is given as a single note, but sometimes also as a series of up to *c*.3 *zzweeerrr-zzweeerrr-* notes. ♂ reportedly capable of producing entire 'duet' on his own. In East Africa mates apparently also duet with mellow *woo* whistles. Has a variety of other whistle notes, include a plaintive resonant *rooooo* or *qurooooo*. Territorial threat signalled by an increase in *hou-* whistles and combined *hou-Kzzeeerrr* phrase, culminating in a combination of rapid bill-clashing (clicking) *KillliK-* sounds, high-pitched *ZzreeE-ZzreeE-* screams and deeper *gruk-gruk-* churring sounds. Alarm signalled with harsh repeated drawn-out *Kzzeeerrr-*, *dzik-skaaa-aaa* or *CHAAAAAAAA* sounds and snarling, rapid bill-clashing, sounding like *KilllIK-*, clicking *chit-ick* or repeated *click-clack* sounds. These are often combined with low, guttural *grrr-* or *zor-* sounds, which appear to signal anxiety. The same churring sounds are used in short range contact between mates. Young beg with high-pitched drawn-out *seeeeep-seeeeep-* calls. When excited makes 'fripping' sounds with wings in flight. Responds well to imitations of whistle call[5, 22, 48, 205, 298, 299, 337, 500, 501, 515, 575, 631, 831]. Sonagram[43, 48].

BREEDING BIOLOGY Little known. Monogamous and territorial, showing aggression towards Olive Bush-shrike, and both respond to playback of each other's calls, particularly during breeding season with territorial threat[205]. **Season** Probable breeding condition Apr (E Angola)[7, 865]; Oct–Dec (SE Zaïre)[22, 338]; Feb (Tanzania)[293, 832]; breeding Feb–Mar, Oct, gonads active Jan, Nov, Dec[291, 500]; Oct–Nov (Zambia/Malawi)[359]; Oct–Nov (Malawi)[119, 575]; Feb, Nov–Dec (Zimbabwe)[30, 707]; probably from about Oct, nest-building Jan (Mozambique)[26]; nest-building Jan, oviduct egg Oct, fledglings Mar–Apr (South Africa)[500, 632]. **Displays *Courtship*** Possible courtship involves ♂ bowing and swaying body while rapidly calling *hou-hou-hou-* and accompanied by short flights with loud 'wing-fripping' sounds. ♀ performed a similar display, but without 'wing-fripping', accompanying ♂ in duet with harsh *kzzweer-kzzweer-* calls[205]. **Nest** Both sexes collect material, and probably both build the shallow flimsy saucer-shaped structure, using dried twining twigs and tendrils, and lined with fibre-lichen (*Usnea*). Concealed in dense site from 12–20 m (n=3) in mid- to lower canopy. ***Size*** OD 80–120 mm, ID 45 mm, cup depth 8.5–15 mm, height 40–57 mm (n=2)[19, 48, 575, 707, 853]. **Eggs** 2 (n=3). Pale greenish, heavily, evenly and uniformly smeared in elongated streaks of dark brown and light chocolate all over on underlying blue-grey, mauve and french grey. Underlying markings well distributed all over, though sparingly, with concentrations around the large end. ***Size*** 22.3–22.4 x 17–17.3 mm (22.4 x 17.2, n=2)[19, 205, 575]. **Incubation** By ♀, with ♂ probably also participating[575]. **Nestling** Appearance and period unknown. In one observation where the nest was at 12 m, the fledglings were fed lower down. They beg with high-pitched *seeeeep-seeeeep-* calls accompanied by crouched posture and wing-fluttering. Attended by both sexes[205, 707]. **Predation and longevity** Unknown. **Brood parasite** An early report of Black Cuckoo *Cuculus clamosus* parasitising this shrike requires confirmation. It is considered highly unlikely as no other members of this genus are parasitised[353].

MEASUREMENTS and WEIGHTS Races combined ♂♀? (91) wing 85–98 (90.5), tail 74–95 (85.7), ♂♀? (87) bill (to skull) 13.5–23 (18.0), tarsus 22.5–27.5 (25.1)[500]. **Weight** races combined ♂♀? (18) 32.2–39.4 g (34.8) (Kenya–South Africa)[500]. For additional data see[146, 205, 299, 319].

41 OLIVE BUSH-SHRIKE *Chlorophoneus olivaceus* Plate 18

FIELD IDENTIFICATION Medium-sized (18 cm), greenish bush-shrike found in two colour morphs (buff and olive) with similar green back and wings. Sexes different. Buff morph: ♂ head grey with black face-mask, white lores and white eyebrow behind eye. ♀ head duller, lacks prominent face-mask and eyebrow. Underparts buffy-rufous, brighter and more extensive in ♂. Tail of ♂ black with yellow outer feathers, ♀ green. Olive morph: back, wings and tail like buff morph. Head olive-green not grey, ♂ has black face-mask, yellow lores and eyebrow, lacking in ♀. Underparts rufous-yellow, brighter and more extensive in ♂. Skulking, more often heard than seen; call a series of short liquid whistles varying in rate of delivery and pitch. Found at all levels of evergreen and riverine forest and dense bush (montane and coastal) from SW South Africa to Mozambique, Zimbabwe and Malawi. ***Flight characteristics***: Short, slow and heavy with rapid shallow wing-beats, often making 'fripping' sounds in flight. Wings rounded.

COMPARISONS Buff morph most likely to be confused with Black-fronted Bush-shrike *Chlorophoneus nigrifrons*, particularly ♀. Olive morph does not occur together with Black-fronted. Best identified on presence of white lores in both sexes and similarly coloured eyebrow behind the eye in ♂. Loud whistled calls different; Olive Bush-shrike gives rapidly repeated calls, Black-fronted gives a slowly repeated single or double whistle. Immatures difficult to separate and not well studied. Also resembles Orange-breasted Bush-shrike *C. sulfureopectus*, particularly Olive morph with yellow lores and eyebrow. However, this morph has a green not grey head. Orange-breasted is primarily an *Acacia* savanna species. Identification based on calls requires caution as some calls similar.

DESCRIPTION Two colour morphs (buff and olive). **ADULT** BUFF ♂ ***Head*** Crown to mantle blue-grey; lores white to buffy-white; face-mask formed by black eye-stripe through eye to ear-coverts; eyebrow behind eye white to buffy-white. ***Back*** Including rump and uppertail-coverts olive-green. ***Wings*** Olive-green on outer web, hair brown on inner web, appears green when folded. ***Tail*** Black with pale yellowish tips and edging. ***Underparts*** Chin and throat whitish, breast buffy rufous to salmon-coloured; flanks greyish-green, faintly barred; belly whitish. ***Bare parts*** Bill blackish-brown, palate black, legs blue-grey, eye reddish-brown. **ADULT** BUFF ♀ Duller than ♂. ***Head*** Crown to mantle light grey. Face-mask less distinctive, eye-stripe and ear-coverts greyish-black, lores whitish. No white eyebrow. ***Back and wings*** Like ♂. ***Tail*** Olive-green. ***Underparts*** Like ♂, duller buffy rufous and less extensive, flanks greyish-green with more extensive barring. ***Bare parts*** Like ♂. **ADULT** OLIVE ♂ ***Head and mantle*** Olive-green; lores yellow; black of face-mask like Buff morph; eyebrow behind eye yellow. ***Back, wings and tail*** Like buff morph. ***Underparts*** Breast to belly rufous-yellow, flanks greenish, faintly barred, belly greenish. ***Bare parts*** Like Buff morph. **ADULT** OLIVE ♀ Duller than ♂. ***Head*** Crown to mantle olive-green. Lacks face-mask, lores pale yellowish extending as an eyebrow to above ear-coverts. ***Back, wings and tail*** Like ♀ buff morph. ***Underparts*** Like ♂ but duller. ***Bare parts*** Like ♂. **JUVENILE** BUFF ***Head, face, ear-coverts and mantle*** Pale grey tinged greenish. ***Back, wings and tail*** Pale olive-green. ***Underparts*** Greenish-grey, faintly barred buff-grey. Olive morph lacks grey on head, is more buffy below with less distinct barring. Both morphs have back, wings and tail olive-green similar to respective ♀, but primary wing-coverts tipped buff. ***Bare parts*** Bill grey-brown, paler on lower mandible, palate unknown, legs like adult, eye pale brown. **IMMATURE** Plumage held for at least 1 year, barring remains longest on belly and flanks[500].

GEOGRAPHICAL VARIATION At least 5 races, with slight variation in bill size and coloration. Nominate *olivaceus* (South Africa, S Mozambique), *taylori* (Swaziland), *interfluvius* (E Zimbabwe, Mozambique) paler than *bertrandi* (Milanja Hills, Malawi) and *makawa* (Mount Chirobwe, Malawi); *interfluvius* and Malawi birds have heavier bill than nominate or *vitorum* (coastal Mozambique), which has a more prominent white eyebrow than *interfluvius*, and a grey, not black face-mask. Buff morph occurs throughout the range and is more common, it is the only morph in N of range. In Zimbabwe, of 145 netted only 1 was olive morph[112, 113, 120, 607, 608, 707].

MOULT Complete post-breeding moult. Adults recorded moulting from Dec–Apr, and subadults Jan–Mar (Zimbabwe)[205, 875].

RANGE, HABITAT and STATUS **Breeding range** Malawi, Mozambique, E Zimbabwe, and N, E and S South Africa. **Habitat** In riverine, coastal, submontane and montane primary and secondary forest, forest edge, thickets and dense, moist woodland and heath (*Philippia*). Occasionally in alien plantations[25, 26, 30, 32, 48, 119, 120, 320, 322, 431, 448, 639]. **Status** Not uncommon resident. **Conservation status** Unknown, probably locally threatened due to deforestation[639].

MOVEMENTS Altitudinal movements in Malawi and Zimbabwe, where it descends to low-lying areas in non-breeding season[30, 119, 205].

SOCIAL ORGANISATION and GENERAL BEHAVIOUR Usually solitary or in pairs; agile, skulking and difficult to see. More often heard than seen; one of the loudest forest birds. Moves about in crouched, horizontal posture. ♂ advertises and defends a territory as small as 1.5 ha by calling from mid- to upper canopy. Main territorial call a rather variable, often monotonous series of piping whistles, with ♂♂ often counter-singing with each other using the same calls. Calling posture consists of an inclined upright stance with tail slightly fanned. During territorial threat ♂ adopts a more horizontal posture with excited bowing and swaying of the body from side to side, flicking the tail and making loud 'fripping' sounds with wings in flight. Maintenance behaviour includes scratching indirectly, and bathing by fluttering through dew-laden foliage[8, 48, 205]. **Foraging behaviour** Forages at all levels in forest from within a metre of the ground in secondary growth to high canopy; mostly mid-levels. However, where it overlaps with Black-fronted Bush-shrike it tends to forage lower down. Agile, swift and silent as it hops and bounds about peering and darting at prey, most of which is gleaned from branches, twigs and leaves. Usually glides from one tree to another, and frequently joins mixed foraging parties, particularly in non-breeding season[32, 205, 448]. **Food** Arthropods, mainly insects and their larvae, including Coleoptera (beetles), Orthoptera (grasshoppers), Hymenoptera (bees, wasps and black ants), Mantodea (mantids). Also spiders and small fruits[8, 48, 205, 500].

SOUNDS Repertoire consists of loud clear piping whistles and harsh notes. Territorial call unusually variable in repetition rate and tonal quality, both individually and geographically. Territorial calls range from a few descending, slowly delivered *hew...hew...huw-*, *teu...teu...tuu-*, *tew...tew-* or bubbling *poy-poy-poy-poy-* whistles, to more rapid *hwe-hwe-hwe-*, *wheet-wheet-wheet* or *poo-poo-poo-poooo* calls that remain on the same pitch, to very fast descending, bubbling, tripping and ringing *hehehuuuuuuu-* notes. Some descending whistle series begin with 1–2 higher-pitched notes, followed by up to *c*.7–8 quick notes *peep-whit-whit-whit-whit-* or *Kwheeee! Kwhee-kwhee-Kwhee, kwhee, kwhee....* Duetting is poorly developed, with the ♀ joining in occasionally with a few harsh, tearing *zzrrree-zzrrree, girrrrp-girrrrp-* or *zizz* calls. During territorial interactions ♂ signals threat by adopting a more horizontal posture, bowing and swaying the body from side to side, and flicking the tail. Territorial threat signalled by a variety of tearing discordant notes, sometimes combined with piping whistles. Alarm signalled by harsh scolding sounds, rapid bill-clashing (clicking) *KillliKillliK* sounds and guttural *Kruk-Kruk-*, *Krrr-Krrr-* or *crock* sounds, and 'wing-fripping' sounds in flight. Harsh rasping sound made in the hand. Short range contact maintained by soft guttural *grrr-* calls which appear also to be used in anxiety. Fledglings solicit with high-pitched *seee-seee-* calls[5, 6, 8, 48, 117, 205, 337, 872]. Sonagram[43, 48].

BREEDING BIOLOGY Little known. Monogamous and territorial. No selective mating takes place as birds of different morphs breed together. Apparently attempts breeding in first year and is single-brooded. Occurs at a density of 3 pairs/4.5 ha in escarpment forest (South Africa)[205, 320]. **Season** Oct (Malawi)[119]; Oct–Jan, mainly Nov (Zimbabwe)[30]; Nov–Dec (W Mozambique)[26]; Sep–Feb (South Africa)[48, 320]. **Displays** During nest-building ♂ particularly vocal in vicinity of nest[875]. **Nest** Built by both sexes. A flimsy, often transparent (eggs visible from below), shallow saucer-shaped structure, roughly built of grass tendrils, stems (including asparagus *Protoasparagus* stems), leaf petioles, rootlets (including aerial rootlets) and twigs. Sometimes lined with a little fine dark fibrous material. Placed at *c*.3 m (0.6–6.0, n=15) from ground in the fork of a sapling, bush (including *Philippia, Widdringtonia*) or creeper in thick matted undergrowth, quite often in a thornbush or tree, and frequently at the edge of forest or clearing. ***Size*** OD 95–115 mm, ID 65–90 mm, cup depth 25–32 mm, height 60–87 mm[8, 205, 500, 875]. **Eggs** 2 (1–3, n=12). Pale greenish-white, heavily streaked with brown and grey. ***Size*** 19.4–23.0 x 14.3–17.0 mm (21.6 x 15.9, n=18)[19, 26, 30, 48, 119, 205, 359]. **Incubation** By both sexes. Nest relief signalled by ♂ with various piping whistles, which either summons ♀ back or indicate that he is approaching nest to relieve his mate. Approach nest indirectly. Period at least 18 days (n=1)[205, 331, 872, 875]. **Nestling** Hatch blind, naked and pinkish in colour. Mouth spots unknown. Attended by both sexes; at one nest only ♂ brooded at night. Initially appear to feed the nestlings by regurgitation, and only when they are older do they bring more solid food. Nestlings beg with high-pitched *seeeeep-seeeeep* calls. Fledge after *c*.16–17 days (n=1)[117, 331, 875]. **Predation and longevity** At one nest Burchell's Coucal *Centropus superciliosus* thought to have taken chicks. ♂ ringed as an adult survived 9 years 135 days[707, 875]. **Brood parasite** None.

MEASUREMENTS and WEIGHTS Races combined ♂♀? (111) wing 77–92 (84.0), ♂♀? (110) tail 72–89 (80.3), bill (to skull) 15–24.5 (19.3), tarsus 22–28 (25.6)[500]. **Weight** Races combined ♂ (103) 31.1–38.8 g (34.5), ♀ (56) 24.6–43.6 g (32.76)[48]. For additional data see[48, 113, 120, 205, 478].

42 MOUNT KUPÉ BUSH-SHRIKE (Serle's Bush-shrike)

Chlorophoneus? kupeensis **Plate 19**

FIELD IDENTIFICATION Medium-large (21–22 cm) bush-shrike with a distinctive white throat and broad black face-mask. Sexes different; head to mantle grey; back, wings and tail bright olive-green; chin and throat pure white, ♂ with narrow blackish necklace at line between throat and grey breast. ♀ has deep maroon chestnut-brown spot in white above grey breast; belly greenish-grey. Little known; shy and skulking, more often heard than seen; call a 3-note ascending whistle, continuous insect-like grating and harsh babbler-like chatter. Solitary or in pairs, mainly in lower and mid-levels of primary montane forest. Rare resident, only found in Cameroon, West Africa. ***Flight characteristics***: Wings rounded; makes 'fripping' sounds in flight, particularly when excited.

COMPARISONS Confusion unlikely due to distinctive white throat. Intermediate in size between Many-coloured Bush-shrike *Chlorophoneus multicolor* and larger Green-breasted Bush-shrike *Malaconotus gladiator*. Seen from behind it could be confused with Grey-headed Greenbul *Phyllastrephus poliocephalus*[508].

DESCRIPTION ADULT ♂ ***Head*** Broad black face-mask extends from forehead, above and below eye to ear-coverts, bordered above by thin faint white eyebrow; crown to upper mantle and sides of neck grey. ***Back*** Including rump and uppertail-coverts bright olive-green; rump feathers long and fluffy. ***Wings*** Olive-green, outer web of flight feathers green, inner hair-brown, outer primaries fringed yellowish-olive at base; closed wing appears green. ***Tail*** Olive-green. ***Underparts*** Chin and throat pure white, with a broken necklace of 3–4 dark blackish spots forming a necklace (15 mm long, 2–4 mm wide), often broken with a neat metallic purplish-black pear-shaped spot bordering white on upper breast at junction with grey of breast and belly; flanks olive-green; lower belly dark olive-green with bright yellow patch; vent and undertail-coverts bright yellow. ***Bare parts*** Bill black; palate yellow; legs blue-grey; eye violet[349, 500, 508]. ADULT ♀ Like ♂; often appears cleaner and brighter, and instead of a row of small spots and black pear-shaped spot, it has a single large round dark chestnut-brown spot (*c*.6 mm) in centre between throat and breast, in the white of throat just above grey of breast. The apparent seasonal development of a yellow tinge around the breast-spot is thought to coincide with breeding. Thighs and flanks appear yellower than in ♂. The only known photograph is of a bird trapped in Nov 1994 and thought to be a non-breeding adult ♀. Bare parts similar to ♂[508]. For photograph see[914]. JUVENILE Unknown, but probably olive-green judging from the greenish flecks occurring on upper and lower parts of museum specimens. IMMATURE Similar to adult, but crown and mantle flecked with olive-green; black forehead incomplete and sides of neck tinged yellowish-green. ***Underparts*** Throat flecked with pale yellow; necklace and spot dull yellow-brown or absent; yellow-olive patches, streaks or flecks on breast; flanks and undertail-coverts olive[349, 500, 508].

GEOGRAPHICAL VARIATION None. Monotypic.

MOULT Unspecified Jun[349].

RANGE, HABITAT and STATUS **Breeding range** Mt Kupé and Bakossi Mts (W Cameroon). **Habitat** In primary pre-montane forest, apparently preferring ridges, steep slopes and similar elevated areas. Appears not to tolerate secondary growth, even relatively small areas within primary habitat. On Mt Kupé from 900–1500 m, and on Bakossi Mts from 1150–1200 m[21, 349, 431, 508, 864]. **Status** Rare, apparently resident. **Conservation status** Since its discovery in 1949 it has been seen a number of time and mist-netted once. The forest on Kupé is now the subject of a major conservation programme. Red Data Book species considered Critical[343, 479].

MOVEMENTS Unknown.

SOCIAL ORGANISATION and GENERAL BEHAVIOUR Solitary, in pairs or occasionally in presumed family group of 3 individuals. Extremely secretive, wary and difficult to observe. Two presumed adjacent pairs have been observed exchanging calls and then feeding closely together for 30 min, before returning to their respective territories. Territories appear large, with 2 pairs covering a circuit on the mountain slopes of *c*.200 m in altitude. Territorial calls thought to consist of whistle phrases. Suspected territorial threat involves rapidly repeated harsh babbler-like calls combined with excited 'wing-fripping'. Sits in a very upright posture when giving loud, rapidly fluctuating whistles. In threat, body held upright and forward, wings drooped and flicked with tail fanned. Neck slightly extended with body bowed more to sides, probably combined with body-swaying. Alarm call given in upright posture with tail fanned[343, 349, 500, 508, 589]. **Foraging behaviour** Favours mid-levels between 0.5–12 m, rarely to 18 m and usually between 3–4 m. During feeding moves slowly and deliberately through dense foliage. Observed with mixed foraging parties on a number of occasions, and seen low to the ground (0.5 m) hanging in curious fashion from vertical stems in tit-like behaviour. Once prey located bird moves to lower more horizontal position beneath prey. With body held low, tail down and head up, the bird launches itself vertically upwards to snatch prey in a slightly free-fall, twisting motion. Large prey is beaten on the branch before swallowing. Birds also search the foliage diligently like a greenbul (*Andropadus*), and sometimes hawk prey in flight[344, 349, 508, 515, 589, 864]. **Food** Arthropods, mainly insects and their larvae, including Coleoptera (small beetles), Orthoptera (grasshoppers) and Lepidoptera (caterpillars)[349, 508].

SOUNDS Little known. Repertoire consists of at least 6 different calls, including whistles, insect-like grating and harsh, scolding sounds. Three different whistles reported. (1) a single quiet clear liquid *crooa* rising and falling in pitch, was made by a ♀, believed to be in breeding condition (yellow tinge on breast); also given in a series of 3–4 notes. (2) Rarely heard, distinctly trisyllabic series of 3 ascending whistles, with a slight inflection at the end of each note (sounding somewhat out of tune) and usually repeated up to 6 times, although persistent calling also reported. Tone of call more like Many-coloured Bush-shrike than the lower notes of Green-breasted Bush-shrike. (3) A loud, rapidly fluctuating nasal whistle repeated several times by ♂. When disturbed (alarm?) makes a distinctive harsh scolding *ke-ke-ke-*, often ending with a *churr*. Contact between pairs appears to be signalled almost continuously with a distinct grating, reminiscent of a distant cicada *gr-i-i-i-k..gr-i-i-i-k-* or *grrr-grrr-grrr-*, and repeated every 3–5 sec. This call is useful initial indicator of the presence of a pair and a helpful aid in following birds, but is apparently not made by solitary birds. The call is sometimes initiated with bill-clashing sounds similar to those heard in *Chlorophoneus* species. A third harsh call is thought to be used in territorial defence, and consists of a loud harsh babbler-like chatter with a few short introductory notes *thec-thec-kh-kh-kh* followed by 3–4 rapid *tchrraa-tchrraa-tchrraa-* notes repeated at *c*.2–3 notes/sec for up to *c*.30 notes. Length of notes also variable. Responds excitedly to this call on playback, giving similar calls combined with loud 'wing-fripping' produced in series of 4–6 frips. The call is made in flight and while foraging, and was once heard in Mar, when 2 birds (sex unseen), separated by *c*.10 m, called repeatedly to each other for 10 mins. Wing-fripping also heard at other times not associated with playback, and thought to have occurred when observer close to nest. Juvenile believed to beg with harsh sounds. Also produces noisy harsh bill-clattering or -snapping[349, 500, 508, 515, 589].

BREEDING BIOLOGY Territorial and apparently monogamous, but requiring confirmation, with most pairs observed during periods Apr–Jul and Sep–Oct. Once 4 birds, believed to be two pairs, seen foraging together. ♀♀ appear to develop a yellow tinge on the breast around the chestnut-brown patch from mid-May. Both members of a pair aggressively chase other species during the presumed breeding season[508]. **Season** Persistent trisyllabic whistling for 2 days in late Mar, and call believed to be territorial threat, heard Mar–Apr. Yellow tinge on ♀ breast mid-May. Nesting believed to occur Apr–Jun. Fledged young observed being fed by adults and independent at two sites from Apr–May, immature accompanying adults in Jun, and suspected first-year bird with green flecking seen in Oct[349, 508, 515]. **Displays** ***Courtship*** In other bush-shrikes, signals used in territorial threat are commonly used in courtship. In a pair considered close to breeding, the ♀ persistently behaved in a submissive fashion towards the ♂, continually crouching in a presumed mating posture with wings drooped and fluttering, head up and bill open. This suggests courtship-feeding probably takes place. The display is similar to food-begging by young. In one pair the ♂, and occasionally ♀, regularly defended a low dense block of tangled vegetation at the top of a steep incline against Brown-chested Alethe *Alethe policephala* and Fork-tailed Drongo *Dicrurus adsimilis*. When not in direct confrontation, the birds sat in an upright position with tail fanned and giving the alarm call *ke-ke-ke-* and *churrr.* Once the pair successfully drove out a small bird party from the area. Once a ♀ was observed tugging at leaves, but none was removed[508]. **Nest** unknown, but suspected to be low at 1–3 m in dense thickets, based on territorial defence and food-carrying behaviour[508]. No further breeding information.

MEASUREMENTS and WEIGHTS *C.? kepeensis* ♂ (1) wing 98, tail 81, tarsus 29, bill (to skull) 27; Imm ♀ (1) wing 98 tail 83, bill (to skull) 26, tarsus 28.5[500]. **Weight** unknown. For additional data see[349].

43 GORGEOUS BUSH-SHRIKE (Four-coloured or Perrin's Bush-shrike)
Chlorophoneus viridis **Plate 19**

FIELD IDENTIFICATION Medium-sized (19 cm), strikingly colourful, skulking green bush-shrike with bright red throat and black breast-band. Sexes different; ♂ with broad black breast-band, ♀ narrow. Young dull yellowish-green without red and black breast-band, finely barred below. Solitary, shy, inconspicuous and skulking, more often heard than seen; distinctive loud 5–6 note whistle. Occurs low down in dense, often impenetrable undergrowth of lowland forest, riverine bush and thickets. Resident in two separate, distinct populations; eastern (E Africa to southern Africa), and western (Congo, Gabon, Angola, Zaïre and NW Zambia). ***Flight characteristics***: Heavy with short rapid wingbeats, seldom flying long distances. When excited makes short flights with 'wing-fripping' sounds[205].

COMPARISONS Most similar to Doherty's Bush-shrike *Chlorophoneus dohertyi*, which has forehead, throat, and undertail-coverts deep crimson-red, and underparts bright lemon-yellow. Doherty's occurs in montane forest (Gorgeous in lowland forest). Juvenile similar to other forest canopy *Chlorophoneus* bush-shrikes but ecologically segregated. Calls rather similar but Doherty's lacks the lower-pitched initial notes and tends only to give phrases of repeated terminal rising notes.

DESCRIPTION ADULT ♂ *quadricolor* ***Head*** Upperparts olive-green; face with short yellow to golden-brown (sometimes orange) eyebrow from bill to eye; lores black, continuing as a line down side of neck to form broad black breast-band which encloses vivid crimson-red (scarlet) chin and throat. ***Back*** Olive-green, including rump and uppertail-coverts. ***Wings*** Coverts olive-green, flight feathers green on outer web, hair brown on inner; appears green when closed. ***Tail*** Mainly black. ***Underparts*** Black breast-band edged below by reddish-yellow (*viridis* crimson) which grades into yellowish-green belly and olive-green flanks. *viridis* darker olive-green below with irregular maroon-brown stripe down mid-belly. Undertail-coverts reddish-yellow (*viridis* maroon). ***Bare parts*** Bill and palate black; legs blue-grey; eye dark brown. **Adult ♀** Generally duller, upperparts similar to ♂; face lacks black lores and black line down the neck connecting with the black breast-band, which is narrower and less distinct. Chin and throat yellowish-red. ***Wings*** Like ♂. ***Tail*** Olive-green, may have darker terminal section. Underparts more yellowish-green, (*viridis* darker olive-green with dull maroon-brown mid-line). Undertail-coverts yellowish-green (*viridis* maroon). **Juvenile** Lacks facial, throat and breast-band markings of adult. Upperparts: Dull olive-green including wings and tail; face yellowish-green. Underparts: Chin and throat yellowish grading to yellowish-green, finely barred on throat, breast and flanks (*quadricolor* with more obvious and extensive barring). Bare parts: Bill grey-brown with pale lower mandible; legs blue-grey; eye grey-brown[500]. **Immature** *quadricolor*: Upperparts like ♀, underparts show progressive development, initially of yellowish red throat and indistinct small greyish-black breast-band. Adult plumage attained after 1 year, the black breast-band and red throat taking about two months to appear[205].

GEOGRAPHICAL VARIATION At least 4 races in the two eastern and western fragmented populations, which were formerly separated as distinct species. Main difference between the two concerns the darker scarlet throat, darker and more extensive olive-green underparts with dull maroon-brown mid-line belly markings, and maroon undertail-coverts of western birds (*viridis*) (Congo, E, W and S Zaïre, Angola, NW Zambia). There is little variation within this population. The E populations, represented by *quadricolor, quartus* and *nigricauda,* show greater variation. Compared to *quadricolor* (South Africa, Swaziland, S Mozambique), *quartus* (Zimbabwe, Malawi, N Mozambique) is paler and more yellow-green above, and generally lacks scarlet undertail-coverts. *nigricauda* (E Africa) has greater amount of black in central tail feathers and a redder belly. The two populations are united as one species on plumage and vocal similarities[129, 145, 431, 831].

MOULT Unknown.

RANGE, HABITAT and STATUS **Breeding range** two disjunct populations, formerly separated as distinct species. In the W, *viridis* occurs in Congo, SE Gabon, E, W and S Zaïre, Angola including Cabinda and NW Zambia. In the E, *quadricolor* from S Somalia, E Kenya, E Tanzania, S Malawi, Mozambique, and in southern Africa from E Zimbabwe (including Zambezi Valley), Swaziland and N and E South Africa. **Habitat** *viridis* in edges of clearings in primary and secondary forest, gallery forest, coffee plantations and dense thickets associated with edge of woodland and forest, undergrowth of dense thickets and shrubbery in wooded savanna and along gallery forest, forest clearings, edges of secondary growth, *Cryptosepalum* woodland and overgrown cassava gardens[7, 22, 143, 290, 291, 338, 431, 504, 740, 907]. Race *quadricolor* in undergrowth of dense thickets and impenetrable tangles in riverine forest, dense edges and clearings in moist forest, coastal forest and thickets in quite dry country, dense vegetation along escarpment and mountain foothills. Mainly below 600 m, although found locally up 1200 m (Mt Endau) and even to 2000 m (N Pare Mts) in East Africa[26, 30, 80, 119, 129, 297, 318, 320, 322, 325, 431, 459, 481, 631, 810, 859, 888]. **Status** Not uncommon to locally common resident. **Conservation status** Unknown. Probably not threatened, although range contraction recorded in Kenya, where no longer present in some areas, e.g. Voi and Taita Hills. Similarly it appears formerly to have been distributed further S in South Africa, although the records in question may represent misidentifications based on calls. However it may also have benefited locally from bush encroachment due to overgrazing in parts of E South Africa and Swaziland[129, 481, 631, 810, 825].

MOVEMENTS Race *quadricolor* undertakes local movements out of drier parts of range in non-breeding season[205].

SOCIAL ORGANISATION and GENERAL BEHAVIOUR Little known. A solitary, shy, retiring but inquisitive, skulking and highly secretive bush-shrike. Creeps about in the undergrowth, silently and swiftly in a crouched position, and very difficult to see in its gloomy tangled habitat. More often heard than seen, but occasionally shows itself for a few seconds before disappearing again. Calls throughout the year, with an increase in austral summer. Race *quadricolor* advertises and defends a small territory of *c.*1.5 ha with a repeated loud, penetrating *kong-koit-koit* whistled phrase. Before calling, ♂ jinks his way to an elevated position, and calls with an inclined, head-up posture, bobbing the head with each call and expanding the throat, which produces flashes of yellow and red as the yellow feather-bases are exposed. ♀ responds erratically with harsh calls in duet. ♂♂ may counter-sing in unison or antiphonally, sometimes separated by less than a metre. Territorial threat signalled by a faster rate of calling, excited bowing, side to side jerking of the body, and by wing- and tail-flicking, and accompanied by bill-clashing sounds made in a more horizontal posture with the neck stretched out. Also makes short 'wing-fripping' flights. Roosting behaviour unknown. Observed sun-bathing with one wing extended and tail fanned. Scratches indirectly[205, 290, 504, 631]. **Foraging behaviour** Forages low down, gleans prey from trunks, branches and leaves, also hops and creeps about on the ground turning over leaves and forest litter. Occasionally takes aerial prey. Tends to work its way upwards, peering about and darting at prey[32, 205]. **Food** Both populations take arthropods, mainly insects and their larvae, including Lepidoptera (moths and caterpillars, hairy and smooth types), Coleoptera (beetles), Hymenoptera (parasitic wasps). Also feeds on spiders. An early report of it sometimes attacking small birds requires confirmation[9, 20, 143, 205, 500].

SOUNDS Repertoire consists of a repeated loud clear whistled phrase, harsh tearing and guttural notes and bill-clashing sounds. Whistled phrase shows individual and geographical variation. The most frequently heard territorial call consists of a repeated phrase formed by 5–6 whistled notes, in *quadricolor* usually consisting of a single low-pitched *kong, hu* or *pom* note followed by two disyllabic notes, formed of a similar but shorter low-pitched *kow, ko, hu,* or *po* note and second higher-pitched rising *it* or *wit* note. The combination sounds like *kong-kowit-kowit,* with the emphasis on the second syllable *wit.* Other descriptions include *kong-koit-koit, kong-kong-koit, pom-puwe-puwe* or *hu-huwit-huwit.* Variations include *wewit-wewit-wewit, witwit-witwit-witwit* or *hooi-hooi-hooi-hooi.* The similar whistled phrase of the ♂ in *viridis* is of identical tone, quality and structure, except that it tends to have longer and more initial low-pitched *kong* notes. It is described as a four-noted *kong-kong-kong-kowit,* or trisyllabic *kong-kowit-kowit,* bubbling *wo-wo-pree, wo-wo-pree, hu-huwit-huwit, hew-hew-wheet, hew-hew-wheet, ko-ko-kwi* or *jou-jou-wit.* ♀ calls unknown for this population. The phrase may be delivered slowly and deliberately, with individual notes well spaced, or very fast with almost no break between notes. It is often preceded by a soft *ti* or *klink* note which is only heard at close range. In *quadricolor* ♀ duets irregularly with a single or double harsh tearing *zzrrrer-zzrrrer* note. Territorial threat signalled by rapidly repeated phrases, followed by a double soft rattling or bill-clashing *trrrip-trrrip* or *thrrr-rrrup* sound made by clattering or vibrating the mandibles. This is often accompanied by short 'wing-fripping' flights. ♀ joins these interactions by duetting with soft, low-pitched *zzrrr* and guttural sounds. Alarm to terrestrial or avian predator a louder *grrr-grrr-, graak-graak, graad-graad, grod-grod, chunk-chunk-* or *churr.* May also be accompanied by bill-clashing. Contact call a low guttural croaking, grunting or growling *grrr-grrr* sound, only heard at close range. Juvenile contact is slightly higher-pitched[6, 8, 9, 43, 48, 79, 127, 128, 145, 171, 205, 290, 338, 431, 500, 501, 504, 631, 831]. Sonagram[43, 48, 145].

BREEDING BIOLOGY Little known. Monogamous and territorial. ♀♀ attempt breeding in first year. Probably single-brooded. Breeding details refer to *quadricolor* unless specified otherwise[32, 205]. **Season** *viridis* Jun–Jul juveniles, breeding condition Mar, May (Angola)[7, 865]; nest-building Sep(Zaïre)[22]; gonads active in Sep–Oct (Zambia)[291, 780]; *quadricolor* Oct–Feb, mainly Oct–Dec (Zimbabwe)[30, 359]; Aug, Nov–Dec, Feb (Mozambique)[26, 297]; Apr (Malawi)[119]; Oct–Nov (South Africa)[48, 320]. **Displays** A presumed courtship display resembled high intensity threat, and involved ♀ bowing in front of ♂, while he gave whistled phrase, she gave bill-clashing sounds[205]. **Nest** Role of sexes unknown. A shallow, sometimes transparent, flimsy saucer made of twigs, stalks, dry grass, weed stems, roots, thin twisted tendrils, and lined with leaf petioles. Placed *c.*1 m (0.6–1.5, n=10) above the ground, usually well concealed in the centre of a creeper or thorny bush. ***Size*** OD 100–118 mm, ID 65–100 mm, cup depth 15–17 mm, height 49–70 mm (n=3). Nest appears very small for size of bird[6, 32, 205, 500]. **Eggs** Usually 2 (n=13). Light greenish-blue or whitish-blue, streaked and spotted with grey-brown and purplish-grey. ***Size*** 22.4–24.6 x 15.9–18.3 mm (23.3 x 16.9, n=10)[6, 19, 48]. **Incubation** By both sexes; ♂ gives whistle call from nest, probably a nest-relief signal[8, 297, 500]. **Nestling** Hatch naked, blind and have mouth spots. Fledging period unknown. ♂ calls in vicinity of nest and feeds nestlings. Begging call unknown. Young remain with adults for at least 4 months, maintain contact with parents with a call that is a higher-pitched *grr-grr-* version of contact call[205, 331]. **Predation and longevity** Young caught by Little Banded Goshawk *Accipiter badius.* One individual remained in same territory for 6.5 years[205, 806]. **Brood parasite** Unknown.

MEASUREMENTS and WEIGHTS Western population *C. v. viridis,* ♂ (5) wing 85–90 (86.6), tail 83–88 (84.4), bill (to skull) 23–25 (24.0), tarsus 28–31.5 (28.9); ♀ (5) wing 81–86 (84.0), tail 70–82 (76.6), bill (to skull) 21.5–22 (21.9), tarsus 28.5–29 (28.7)[500]. Eastern population *quadricolor,* ♂ (18) wing 78–83.5 (81.4), ♂♀? (17) wing 78–85 (81.0), ♂ (18) tail 81.5–90 (84.9), ♂♀? (17) 81.5–88.5, bill ♂ (13) 19–21.5, ♀ (4) 17–19, ♂♀? (17) tarsus 23–28[48]. **Weight** Western population *viridis* ♂ (2) 49–50 g (Angola)[907]. Eastern population, races combined ♂ (19) 29.6–40.5 g (38.0), ♀ (7) 31–39.5 g (35.7) (southern Africa)[48]. For additional data see[15, 79, 129, 205, 290, 870].

44 DOHERTY'S BUSH-SHRIKE *Chlorophoneus dohertyi* Plate 19

FIELD IDENTIFICATION Medium-sized (19 cm) strikingly colourful, skulking green bush-shrike with a bright red forehead and throat, broad black breast-band, and brilliant lemon-yellow belly. Sexes similar. Young pale green above, finely barred yellowish-green below. More often heard than seen; call distinctive loud 4–5 note whistle. Solitary, shy, inconspicuous and skulking. Occurs low down in dense undergrowth of forest, forest edge and thickets. Resident in highlands of W Kenya, Rwanda, Uganda and E Zaïre. ***Flight characteristics***: Short-distance; wings rounded.

COMPARISONS Most similar to Gorgeous Bush-shrike *Chlorophoneus viridis,* which lacks red forehead and yellow underparts. Juveniles rather similar and probably best separated on habitat. Doherty's Bush-shrike is a montane species, Gorgeous a lowland species. Calls are also similar, except that Gorgeous gives low-pitched notes combined with rising terminal notes (low-pitched notes generally lacking in Doherty's).

DESCRIPTION **Adult ♂** ***Head*** Frontal to above eye deep scarlet-red (rarely yellow); lores black, extending through eye and down neck to join broad black breast-band which encloses deep scarlet red chin and throat (rarely yellow). Upperparts from crown to uppertail-coverts olive-green. ***Wings*** Coverts olive-green; flight feathers have outer web green, inner hair-brown; appear green when closed. ***Tail*** Mainly black. ***Underparts*** Lower breast to belly bright lemon-yellow; flanks greenish; undertail-coverts scarlet-red. ***Bare parts*** Bill black, palate unknown; legs blue-grey; eye dark brown. **Adult ♀** Similar to ♂ but appears darker above. Tail of East African population may have outer webs and tips dark olive-green. Flanks with more extensive olive-green[238, 631]. ***Abnormal plumage*** Rarely occurs with red forehead and throat replaced by yellow[631]. **Juvenile** ***Upperparts*** Olive tawny-green with fine blackish barring from crown to uppertail-coverts. ***Wings*** Brownish-grey, outer web greenish, coverts and tertials tipped tawny-buff with blackish subterminal band. ***Tail*** Greenish-grey. ***Underparts*** Pale yellowish-green, chin, breast and flanks finely barred; belly yellowish-green; undertail-coverts pinkish-red. ***Bare parts*** Bill grey-brown and narrow yellow eye-ring[338, 500, 631]. **Immature** ***Upperparts*** Greenish like adult but with some remnant barring on head, neck and face. ***Wings*** Coverts and some tertials retain buff tips. ***Underparts*** Yellowish-green; throat may retain some barring, but breast-band development progressive, initially finely barred black with a few reddish feathers showing on throat; undertail-coverts like adult[500].

GEOGRAPHICAL VARIATION None. Monotypic.

MOULT Unknown.

RANGE, HABITAT and STATUS **Breeding range** Central E Zaïre, Rwanda, Burundi, W Uganda, W and central Kenya. **Habitat** In thick scrub and undergrowth, edge and clearings of primary and secondary forests, dense secondary growth and moist thickets, especially where mixed with bracken and bamboo. Generally found above 1500 m, up to *c.*3350 m[11, 22, 290, 306, 318, 431, 481, 637, 688, 631, 717]. **Status** Uncommon local resident. **Conservation status** Unknown.

MOVEMENTS Unknown.

SOCIAL ORGANISATION and GENERAL BEHAVIOUR Little known. Solitary, shy and retiring as it skulks and creeps about in dense undergrowth. More often heard than seen. Territorial call a loud repeated whistled phrase, which can be heard throughout the year. Occasionally confiding, when easily seen as it moves about on the ground. Observed being chased by a black boubou *Laniarius*[318, 631, 717]. **Foraging behaviour** Searches dense undergrowth, where gleans from vegetation as well as feeding on the ground[631, 717]. **Food** Arthropods, apparently mainly insects like Coleoptera (beetles) and Orthoptera (grasshoppers)[290, 761].

SOUNDS Little known. Repertoire consists of variable phrases of 3–6 repeated loud piercing flute-like whistles, harsh rasping and probable bill-clashing sounds. Calls superficially resemble Gorgeous Bush-shrike but lacks the repeated lower-pitched notes of that species. Calls show individual and geographical variation. Main territorial call a phrase composed of rising whistles, variously described as *huwit, fou-ic, u-week, kwit, quit-* or *pui-* repeated in different ways and at different rates. Also sounds like *huwit-huwit-huwit, quit-quit-quit-work* or *quick-quick-quick-work, we-week u-week-u-week, kwit-kwit-kwit-work,* an almost liquid *wurk-wurk-wurwurwurwurk* or *weeo-weeo-weeo-weeo-werk,* with slightly accented ending. Other variations include *tip-witwit, tip-witwit* or *tip-wokwok, tip-wokwok.* Some phrases initiated by a short, softer *gr* or *kr* note. Also reportedly gives a *quip-whee-u* whistle. A prolonged low rasping *krrerr* is possibly given by the ♀ in erratic duet, and a sound described as a scolding rattle *crrrrr* could possibly be bill-clashing, both characteristic of other *Chlorophoneus* bush-shrikes. Alarm signalled with a sharp harsh *tchrak, tchrak, jeb* or rasping *krrerr*[22, 290, 336, 348, 500, 501, 631, 717]. Sonagram[43].

BREEDING BIOLOGY Virtually unknown. **Season** Apr, Jul (Zaïre)[22, 290]; May and Jun (Uganda and W Kenya)[293]; Nov–Mar young in barred plumage, Jul ♀ breeding (Kenya)[290]; Aug and juvenile being fed Oct (Rwanda)[717]. No further breeding information.

MEASUREMENTS and WEIGHTS *C. dohertyi* ♂ (5) wing 79–84 (81.4), tail 74–80 (77.2), bill (to skull) 20.5–23 (21.6), tarsus 28–30.5 (29.4); ♀ (7) wing 78–82 (79.9), tail 74–80 (76.3), bill (to skull) 22–22.5 (21.6), tarsus 27.5–32 (29.4)[500]. **Weight** ♂ (1) 43.0 g, ♀ (1) 30.9 g[500]. For additional data see[238, 338].

45 BOKMAKIERIE *Telophorus zeylonus* — Plate 20

FIELD IDENTIFICATION Large (23 cm) green and grey bush-shrike with bright yellow underparts, black breast-band and black tail broadly tipped yellow (distinctive in flight). Sexes similar. Young dull greenish above, barred greyish-green below. Shy and retiring, more often heard than seen. Gives loud ringing whistles and trill, usually in duet. Solitary or in pairs, largely terrestrial.

Resident in varied open scrub and bush habitats in southern Africa from S Angola, W Namibia, SE Botswana, South Africa, Swaziland, Lesotho and E Zimbabwe. ***Flight characteristics***: Relatively slow and laboured with rapid wingbeats, combined with short glides. Usually flies low to the ground with black tail fanned, showing the distinctive yellow tips on all but the central two feathers. Wings rounded.

COMPARISONS Superficially resembles Yellow-throated Longclaw *Anthus chloris* and Golden Pipit *Tmetothylacus tenellus* with their yellow underparts and black breast-band. Easily identified from these on calls and by uniform olive-green back and long tail with yellow tips. Some repeated loud whistled calls are similar to forest-dwelling Olive Bush-shrike *Chlorophoneus olivaceus*.

DESCRIPTION ADULT ***Head*** Grey including sides of neck and ear-coverts; eyebrow chrome-yellow; lores black. ***Back*** Mantle greyish-green, back, rump and uppertail-coverts olive-green. ***Wing*** Olive-green; underwing greyish-yellow. ***Tail*** Graduated, central pair dull olive-green with faint fine cross-barring, others black broadly tipped chrome-yellow, increasing in extent on outer feathers. ***Underparts*** Black stripe below eye to sides of neck forming broad breast-band which encircles chrome-yellow chin and throat; rest of underparts yellow, flanks greyish-green. ***Bare parts*** Bill and palate black, legs and feet blue-grey, eye mauve-brown. ***Abnormal plumage*** Rarely recorded. In one case greys replaced by white, and face, breast, wings and tail lemon-yellow, with belly and flanks white[817, 818]. JUVENILE Upperparts: Dull dark olive-green; face and ear-coverts greyish. Underparts: Chin and throat buffy to dirty white, breast olive-green, finely barred with grey. Belly and flanks yellowish-green with more prominent dusky barring; wings and tail like adult. ***Bare parts*** Bill pale greyish-brown with pale base, palate unknown, legs and eye like adult. IMMATURE ***Upperparts*** Head, nape and mantle pale grey; dirty yellowish-white eyebrow; face-mask from lores to below eye and below ear-coverts turning black. ***Underparts*** Chin to throat whitish with few yellow feathers; black breast-band patchy from sides of neck to breast. Breast-band and yellow throat-patch start appearing after 70 days; breast greyish-white, lower breast and belly yellow; bill greyish-brown with pale base, palate unknown, legs as in adult, eye greyish-brown[124, 500].

GEOGRAPHICAL VARIATION Four races, with variation slight and clinal, concerning body size and colouring. Nominate *zeylonus* (South Africa); *thermophilus* (NW South Africa) paler above and below; *phanus* (S Angola, Namibia) paler than former race and with a slightly heavier bill. *restrictus* (E Zimbabwe and W Mozambique) occurs at 1350–2000 m in the Chimanimani Mts on E border of Zimbabwe and Mozambique, being isolated from rest of the southern African populations. Differs from nominate race in being darker above with greyer flanks, larger breast-band, with shorter wing and longer tail[125, 126, 429].

MOULT Post-breeding moult of wing, tail and contour feathers in Mar[500].

RANGE, HABITAT and STATUS **Breeding range** Distribution fragmented; main range from SW Angola, W and S Namibia, SE and SW Botswana, South Africa except NE. Also found in Lesotho and W Swaziland. Isolated population in E Zimbabwe and neighbouring Mozambique. **Habitat** In a variety of habitats ranging from arid boulder-strewn bushy mountain slopes and sparse bush-covered dunes in Namibia, to thickets in open grassland, dense protea scrub, areas with aloes, euphorbias, fynbos, exotic plantations, parks and gardens. In all habitats it appears to require bushes with associated open areas. In marginal areas at edge of its range, it occurs at low densities in light mixed woodland and thorn savanna. Found from sea-level to *c*.2500 m in the Drakensberg highlands. Isolated E Zimbabwe and W Mozambique population occurs in well-wooded, boulder-strewn ravines and steep slopes with scattered rocks, small trees, bushes and *Philippia* heath of *Hymenodyction* scrub[7, 26, 30, 32, 48, 123, 205, 300, 320, 322, 431, 639, 807, 810, 639, 907, 945]. **Status** not uncommon resident. **Conservation status** Not threatened. Isolated population in Chimanimani Mts and adjacent Mozambique estimated to be *c*.400 birds[429].

MOVEMENTS Sedentary, with 10 ringed birds recovered within 5 km of the ringing site[639].

SOCIAL ORGANISATION and GENERAL BEHAVIOUR Solitary or in pairs, an alert, shy and retiring bird. Often perches exposed on top of a rock, bush or small tree giving a wide range of loud ringing calls, usually in duet. Spends most of its time running around on the ground among bushes. Moves with long swift strides, head tucked in, generally creating the impression of being in a hurry. More often heard than seen, with pairs frequently indulging in unusually varied duets, unsurpassed in bush-shrikes. During territorial advertisement, adopts inclined, upright stance, with head and bill pointing up, exposing the bright yellow throat and black breast-band, while fanning the mainly yellow and black tail. Territories vary in size according to habitat and season. When breeding, pairs defend areas of about 5 ha in suburban habitats, but larger in more arid areas. In non-breeding season occupies much larger areas. Advertises and defends territory throughout the year with a wide range of calls, often in duet, given from an exposed perch, sometimes lasting for several minutes. Duetting pairs are often widely separated in the territory, and neighbouring pairs often counter-sing with each other. Territorial threat involves typical calling posture, but with bowing, side to side and tense, jerky body movements, wing-flicking and tail-fanning. Neighbouring pairs may chase each other about on the ground or in a bush, with much posturing and tail-fanning combined with complex duetting, culminating in tearing and slashing sounds. Display may be accompanied by short 'wing-fripping' flights. Known to react to its own reflection by posturing and making harsh threatening sounds. Pairs roost separately or together in a dense bush or creeper. Scratches indirectly[6, 32, 48, 122, 205, 500, 872].

Foraging behaviour Most prey taken on or near the ground as the bird zigzags, running to and fro, always remaining close to cover. Small prey is eaten immediately, larger items are first immobilised by beating or wiping as in the case of hairy caterpillars, and then carried to a concealed spot where consumed. Birds tend to move between one concealed spot and another, gleaning from the base of grass clumps, bushes and trees, often jumping up to secure food just out of reach. When it gets to a bush it may hop up through the branches searching the trunk, twigs and leaves for prey. On reaching the top it will either glide down to continue foraging in a new direction, or fly low above the ground to the base of another bush. Occasionally hawks insects in the air. Drinks water.

Food Arthropods, mainly insects and their larvae, and small vertebrates. Insects include Coleoptera (beetles), Lepidoptera (moths, smooth and hairy caterpillars), Orthoptera (grasshoppers), Phasmida (stick insects), Mantodea (mantises). Also takes spiders and centipedes. Vertebrate prey includes small reptiles (geckos, lizards, young chameleons, snakes) and amphibians, and attacks and kills birds the size of prinias *Prinia* and white-eyes *Zosterops*, but not seen to feed on them. Small seeds and fruit taken and it reportedly takes assorted food from feeding tables and nips off buds[48, 124, 205, 500, 1065, 1068].

SOUNDS Repertoire complex and not well understood, consists of repeated ringing whistles, trills, stuttering, croaking, tearing, slashing and bill-clicking sounds. It is characterised by extensive antiphonal duetting, which is unsurpassed in the bush-shrikes. At least 12 different song types have been identified, with calls and duet patterns showing marked individual and geographical variation, resulting in motifs which can be used to identify different pairs. Although either sex may initiate duetting, the ♂ appears to take the lead most of the time. In the case of mate loss, individuals are capable of singing complete duet sequences on their own. In duets, members of a pair may utter a variety of sounds simultaneously or antiphonally in rapid succession. ♂ and ♀ appear to have distinct repertoires, with a number of other calls being shared. ♂♂ tends to give loud ringing whistles, which vary from single, slowly repeated *houuuu* notes and double *hu-hu-*, *hoe-hoe* or *hwe-hwe* calls, to rapidly delivered multi-note phrases, of which the low, slowly delivered 4-note *huu-huhuhu* and double, rapidly delivered 3-note higher-pitched *hehehe-hehehe* phrases are particularly common. The latter call reminiscent of a modern telephone. ♀♀ tend to respond in duet from afar or at close range, with longer, rapidly repeated whistled series which vary from high-pitched *teuteuteuteuteu* and *hwehwehwehwe-* to lower-pitched *wikwikwikwikwikwik-* and *wokwokwokwokwok-* sounds. Like the ♂, she has various other calls which are used in more complex duet sequences, in which they may change from one phrase to another. For example, its common name is derived from a duet consisting of *bok-bok-* or *wok-wok-*, followed by trilling *trrrreee*, or *bok-bok-ma-kierie*. Territorial threat is signalled by elaborate visual displays accompanied by complex duets that include rising *trrrrrrrree-* or *prrrrrrree* trills, low croaking *grrrrr* or *krrrrrr-* sounds, tearing *zzzzeeee* or *tzzrrreeo-* sounds, slashing *zzzz-zzzz-* and *K-K-K-K-* bill-clicking sounds, many of which defy transcription. When one member of a pair changes its note, the other pair change theirs too. Alarm at terrestrial predator signalled by slowly repeated low-pitched *Tok-Tok*, *Tock-* or *chock* notes, or *krrrr-* at raptors and various other harsh scolding sounds. When excited makes fripping sounds with wings in flight. Contact maintained at long range by duetting, and at short range by softer whistles, croaking *grrrr* and tearing *skizzzz-* sounds. Nestlings beg with soft, guttural, hissing *gherrr-* sounds, and fledglings beg with higher-pitched *zzrrreee-* or *zzrrriii-* sounds. One fledgling recorded making a hissing sound when seeing prey, the noise attracting an adult who then caught the prey and fed the fledgling. After about 55 days immatures indulge in duets with their parents, resulting in trios 'duetting' together. Whistles of young are off-key and quavering. Mimicry reported once in wild and captive birds requires confirmation[48, 61, 122, 124, 136, 205, 245, 500, 818, 872, 1067]. Sonagram[43, 48].

BREEDING BIOLOGY Monogamous and territorial. Highly secretive when breeding and nests difficult to find. Pair bonds thought to be relatively long in view of elaborate duetting, which continues during nesting. Duet and solo vocalisations decline at the start of breeding. Duets are more frequently given than solo vocalisations in months before breeding, reaching a peak before egg-laying. This trend is reversed in the last half of the breeding season. Apart from an obvious territorial and contact function, their elaborate duetting is thought also to function in pair-bond maintenance and stimulation and synchronisation of reproductive condition. Replacement clutches frequent, and in one case old nest destroyed and new one built, with pair sitting within two weeks. Second broods not uncommon[61, 122, 205, 500]. **Season** Recorded breeding throughout the year with a peak in late austral winter and early summer, but varies geographically. Breeding condition Aug–Sep, nesting Nov–Jan (Zimbabwe)[30, 48, 429]; oviduct egg Apr (Namibia)[123]; all months except Apr (South Africa)[48, 320, 639]. **Displays *Courtship*** Little known, with display appearing similar to territorial threat, possibly fluffs out rump feathers. Courtship feeding apparently does not occur[205]. **Nest** Built by both sexes. A compact cup built from twigs, roots, grasses, stems, woolly plant down, and herbs such as *Helichrysum*, and usually lined with fine rootlets or grass. Occasionally man-made materials are incorporated. It is concealed in a thick bush or creeper, usually less than 2 m (0–6, n=441) above the ground, often less than half a metre, particularly in the macchia vegetation in SW range. Often built in the same vicinity as (and occasionally on) an old nest. Sometimes a number of incomplete nests are built before the birds settle on a site. ***Size*** OD 127–142 mm, ID 80–89 mm, cup depth 38–58 mm, height 76–96 mm (n=3)[6, 32, 48, 205]. **Eggs** Usually 3 (2–6, n=64), laid on consecutive days. Bright greenish-blue, spotted with reddish-brown, violet-grey or lilac, sometimes in a ring around the large end. ***Size*** 22.6–29.3 x 16.5–20.8 mm (25.6 x 19.3, n=194)[19, 48, 63, 205, 1066]. **Incubation** By both sexes, ♀ usually at night. Nest-relief is usually signalled by calling from the nest or on approach to it. Birds seldom approach the nest directly, generally very secretive and usually along the ground. Period *c.*16 days (14–19, n=21)[48, 63, 124, 205]. **Nestling** Hatch naked, blind and apparently lack mouth spots (confirmation required); mouth bright yellow. Upperparts purplish, below orange. Eyes take about 10 days to open. Attended by both sexes, who carry more than one food item in the bill. Egg shells and faeces dropped away from nest. Nestlings beg with guttural, hissing *gherrr* sounds. Fledge after *c.*18 days (14–21, n=13). Dependency period unknown, but young tolerated well into following breeding cycle[205, 331, 506, 872].

Predation and longevity Adults have been known to destroy their own eggs. Eggs and nestlings are taken by various predators, including snakes, mongooses, other shrikes such as Common Fiscal *Lanius collaris* and probably Southern Boubou *Laniarius ferrugineus*. Red-breasted Sparrowhawk *Accipiter rufiventris* recorded taking an adult. Ringed bird still alive after almost 8 years[205, 806, 1032]. **Brood parasite** Although an occasional egg of the Jacobin Cuckoo *Oxylophus jacobinus* has been found in the nest, no cuckoo nestlings or fledglings have been reported to provide confirmation[94, 353, 926].

MEASUREMENTS and WEIGHTS All races except *T. z. restrictus* ♂♀? (86) wing 89–105 (98.2), tail 86–107 (94.7), bill (to skull) 23–30 (26.3), tarsus 31–37.5 (33.7)[500]; *restrictus* ♂ (5) wing 96–97 (96.8), tail 100–103 (100.8), bill 24.5–26 (25.4), tarsus 32–34 (33.2); ♀ (4) wing 92–94 (92.8), tail 94–98 (96.0), bill 24–25 (24.5), tarsus 31–33 (32)[429]. **Weight** All races except *restrictus* ♂ (12) 57–71.3 g (65.1), ♀ (11) 48–76.1 g (61.2); ♂♀? (19) 52–76 g (66.6)[48, 205]; *restrictus* ♂ (5) 67.8–71.3 g (69.4), ♀ (4) 63.8–76.1 g (68.4)[429]. For additional data see[125, 126, 478].

46 ROSY-PATCHED SHRIKE (Rosy-patched Bush-shrike)
Rhodophoneus cruentus **Plate 20**

FIELD IDENTIFICATION Large (23 cm) greyish-brown bush-shrike with long black tail broadly tipped white and bright reddish-pink rump, both distinctive in flight. Sexes different; ♂ variable, below bright pink with or without black breast-band; ♀ always with black breast-band encircling white throat. Young dull, lacks black breast-band and pink below. Little known. Easily located on monotonous loud ringing whistles, usually in duet. Solitary, in pair or family groups. Noisy, restless and largely terrestrial. Resident in arid thornbush of NE and E Africa. ***Flight characteristics***: Heavy, combined with long glides, flies low to the ground. Fanned tail showing black and white pattern, and bright pinkish-red rump distinctive. Wings rounded.

COMPARISONS Distinctive. Tail pattern similar to Black-crowned Tchagra *Tchagra senegala*, but easily separated on rump colour and calls.

DESCRIPTION **ADULT ♂** races different (see Geographical Variation). ***Head*** Pale greyish with whitish lores, eyebrow and sides of face; may have a pinkish tinge to crown. ***Back*** Pale brownish-grey, sometimes with a pinkish tinge; rump reddish-pink. ***Wings*** Pale brownish-grey. ***Tail*** Graduated, central two feathers as back, but with fine cross-barring; outer feathers black broadly tipped white, increasing in extent towards outer feathers, which are almost half white. ***Underparts*** Whitish with buff to rufous-buff on sides of breast, flanks and belly; chin whitish, grading into a central reddish-pink stripe from throat to mid-belly (variable). No black breast-band except in southern *cathemagmena*. ***Bare parts*** Bill and palate black; legs pale grey; eye greyish-purple or brownish. **ADULT ♀** Similar to ♂, but with a black breast-band and white chin and throat. **JUVENILE** Head and mantle pale greyish-brown, with fine buffy spotting; lower back and rump buffy with some pinkish feathers; wings grey-brown, tertials, secondaries and coverts edged and tipped buff, greaters tipped and edged tawny; ulnar area whitish; tail similar to adult; underparts whitish from chin to belly; flanks, thighs and undertail-coverts buffy, paler than adult. Bill paler than adult[500]. **IMMATURE** Similar to adult on upperparts except paler and greyer with buff edges to crown feathers. Rump as in adult. Wing-coverts and secondaries have quite broad pale buff edges, which form two distinct wingbars. Underparts generally greyish-buff; initially lack pink or black, although development of these progressive with breast-band initially mottled greyish-brown. Chin and throat white. May take 2 years to attain adult plumage, but confirmation required[237].

GEOGRAPHICAL VARIATION Three races described, two fairly similar, one distinct. Northern nominate *cruentus* (SE Egypt, Sudan and N Ethiopia) palest with greyish-brown back, whitish eyebrow and sides of face and pale rufous-brown flanks. Central *hilgerti* (Somalia, E Ethiopia and N Kenya) is darker, lacks the whitish eyebrow, has a richer reddish-brown back and darker rufous-brown flanks. Southern *cathemagmena* (S Kenya and E Tanzania) is distinctive and possibly warrants specific status. Similar to *hilgerti* but pinker above, both sexes with black breast-band (restricted to ♀ in other two races). Chin and throat bright reddish-pink in ♂ and white in ♀.

MOULT Unknown.

RANGE, HABITAT and STATUS Breeding range Central, SE and S Sudan, SE Egypt, Ethiopia, Eritrea, Djibouti, Somalia, Kenya and NE Tanzania. **Habitat** Found in arid regions, semi-desert savannas with thornbushes and thickets, thorn and aloe scrub in arid areas and wadis with *Acacia* groves. From sea-level to *c.*1300 m, locally up to 1800 m[11, 33, 36, 231, 242, 292, 318, 325, 351, 431, 481, 631, 859]. **Status** not uncommon to locally common resident. **Conservation status** Unknown, probably not threatened.

MOVEMENTS Unknown.

SOCIAL ORGANISATION and GENERAL BEHAVIOUR Little known. Solitary, in pairs or small noisy family groups like babblers. Restless and shy; spends most of its time on the ground, where runs quickly between cover, or creeps about in undergrowth. Flies low, just above the ground, with distinctive tail and rump pattern. Its active behaviour and bright plumage renders it quite conspicuous, sometimes tame and confiding. Territorial calling usually done from top of low bushes or boulders, members of a pair duetting with disyllabic whistles near to each other, often in the same bush, where they may face each other, stretching up with bill pointing upwards on first note, wings drooped at sides, then bow or bob down with second note. Continue duetting in this manner monotonously for long periods. Territorial threat takes the form of ♂♂ perched close together, either on the ground or in a bush or tree, counter-singing with similar whistles and stretching and bowing movements. At higher intensity chase each about with outstretched wings and tails fanned, or perch in a bush, bobbing up and down to each other, alternately flashing the pink throat and rump while calling. During this performance, displaying birds are very confiding and may be approached to within a few metres. Most calling takes place in early morning or evening, and birds readily respond to imitations of their call. Roosting behaviour unknown[33, 36, 237, 246, 305, 631, 1033, 1034, 1035]. **Foraging behaviour** Feed mainly on the ground (92% of 50 items) by running about picking up insects from bare ground or in grass, and always appears to be in a great hurry. Usually keeps within 5 m of cover of bushes, avoiding large open areas. Also creeps about in bushes gleaning prey[2, 237, 352]. **Food** Insects, including Coleoptera (beetles)[500].

SOUNDS Little known. Repertoire consists of piercing, thin, high-pitched, quavering, melodious whistles, of similar quality to Rufous-naped Lark *Mirafra africana*. Also described as metallic, ventriloquial, shrill piping or chirping. Calls are often given in duet, and monotonously repeated. Also has harsh rasping sounds. Commonest territorial call is a whistled duet: ♂ appears to initiate with high-pitched single *tzee* or disyllabic *Twee-u, tee-u, tzee-u* or *tzwee-wee* notes, sometimes reversed *tu-wee* or *tu-ee*. These are responded to in quick succession antiphonally by ♀ with slightly lower-pitched *tu-ea, tzee-ur, tzwee-ur* or *ter-ee* notes. Combined sequence sounding like *tee-u..tzee-ur..tee-u..tzee-ur..* alternating indefinitely. Alarm consists of harsh grating *krrrr-* notes and scolding *zwerrrrk-zwerrrrk-*[4, 9, 33, 237, 305, 336, 500, 558, 631, 769, 879, 1035, 1036].

BREEDING BIOLOGY Little known. Monogamous and territorial. Breeding appears to be in response to rains, with duetting common in austral spring and early summer[231, 293]. **Season** Mainly Apr–Jul, peak in Jun, also Jan (Somalia)[33, 859]; Mar and Jun (Egypt)[231]; Nov–May (Ethiopia)[237, 292, 558]; Apr–Jun, Nov (Kenya)[293, 237]. **Displays** ***Courtship*** Possible courtship involved two ♂♂ counter-singing, stretching and bowing and then following a ♀[558]. **Nest** Role of sexes unknown. A shallow flimsy saucer-shaped platform resembling a dove's nest, sometimes with a base of twigs, or built only with plant fibre, rootlets and fine dry grass stalks. Placed low down at *c.*1.5 m (*c.*0.6–4.4, n=13) above the ground in a thornbush or tree. Usually well concealed, sometimes at the top of a bush. OD *c.*102 mm[33, 36, 500, 558]. **Eggs** Usually 2–3. A report of 5 requires confirmation. Colour variable, from pale green, bright apple green, green-blue or bluish, densely spotted and streaked over entire surface, but more boldly at large end with various browns, reddish-brown, greys or purples. ***Size*** 22–26 x 16–19 mm (24.2 x 17.7, n=13)[33, 36, 500, 558]. No further breeding information, except young have mouth spots and adult seen carrying faecal sac[500].

MEASUREMENTS and WEIGHTS Races combined ♂ (22) wing 89–99 (92.9), tail 103–121 (112.8), bill (to skull) 18–27 (22.9), tarsus 31–35.5 (33.1); ♀ (13) wing 87–96 (90.7), tail 100–120 (108.8), bill (to skull) 18.5–26 (23.1), tarsus 30–33 (31.5)[500]. **Weight** Races combined ♂♀? (5) 50–60 g (53.2)[500, 509, 768]. For additional data see[237].

FIELD IDENTIFICATION Medium-large (20–22 cm), stoutly built bush-shrike, completely black or blackish-brown with slight purplish gloss in ♂, duller, less glossy in ♀. Young browner with whitish bill. Secretive, usually in pairs, more often heard than seen. Calls consist of loud whistles and harsher notes, usually in duet. Resident, found low down in thick undergrowth of lowland forest and forest patches (also montane forest in Cameroon) in West Africa from Sierra Leone across to S Sudan and East Africa in Uganda (accidental in W Kenya), southwards through Congo basin to NE Angola. ***Flight characteristics***: Wings rounded, tail relatively broad, flight weak; makes 'fripping' sound with wings in flight[15, 754].

COMPARISONS In West and Central Africa similar to the Mountain Sooty Boubou *Laniarius poensis*, which has a bluer gloss and is a smaller montane forest species. At least in W Africa, this latter occurs at higher elevations than the Sooty Boubou. In East Africa other back boubous within range are non-forest birds. Calls similar to Yellow-breasted Boubou *L. atroflavus*, which generally occurs at higher elevations. Some calls also similar to Tropical Boubou *L. aethiopicus*. Separation of young generally not difficult as Sooty Boubou has a whitish bill, Slate-coloured Boubou *L. funebris* is dull blackish barred brown below and Mountain Sooty Boubou resembles its dull adult. Other all-black birds such as drongos, flycatchers, cuckoo-shrikes, cuckoos and starlings have different habits and are generally not skulking species of dense undergrowth.

DESCRIPTION **Adult ♂** Entirely uniform black or brownish-black throughout with slight gloss; rump with long fluffy feathers, and no concealed white spots; underside of primaries dark brown: ***Bare parts*** Bill black; palate unknown; legs dark bluish-black to black; eye dark brown to dark reddish-brown. **Adult ♀** Similar to ♂ but duller without gloss. **Juvenile** Entirely sooty-black with blackish bill; eye dark brown[290]. **Immature** Similar to adult ♀, but tinged browner with very faint pale spotting on crown, and with whitish bill (ivory-colour), tinged pink in one ♀; legs bluish. Tail sometimes with whitish tips. Bill colour may be retained for some time after fully grown. Scientific name derived from bill colour[34, 180, 290].

GEOGRAPHICAL VARIATION None. Monotypic.

MOULT In West Africa flight feathers moulted Mar–Apr (Liberia), Sep in East Africa[259, 330, 576, 858].

RANGE, HABITAT and STATUS **Breeding range** From Sierra Leone, SE Guinea, Liberia, Ivory Coast, Ghana, Cameroon, Nigeria, Central African Republic, S Sudan, SW and S Uganda and W Kenya (where accidental) southwards through Equatorial Guinea, Gabon, Congo and Zaïre to N Angola and Cabinda. Bioko record rejected[431]. **Habitat** Generally a lowland species of low dense impenetrable undergrowth of secondary forest, forest edge and clearings, dense thickets, coastal scrub, open swamp vegetation, tangles, rank vegetation, and overgrown cultivation in clearings. Sometimes penetrates primary forest. Ascends to 700 m in montane forest in Liberia and Cameroon. In Congo also in thickets in mixed papyrus marsh, and clearings in swamp forest[7, 21, 22, 34, 37, 101, 110, 207, 234, 242, 259, 290, 294, 318, 431, 481, 504, 631, 717, 848, 852, 858, 907]. **Status** Resident, generally uncommon to rare, but may be not uncommon in West Africa, and probably overlooked. In Kenya accidental, based on single specimen collected at Kaimosi Forest in W Kenya, Apr 1931[37, 242, 504, 631]. **Conservation status** Widespread, does not appear to be threatened.

MOVEMENTS Sedentary (Gabon)[294].

SOCIAL ORGANISATION and GENERAL BEHAVIOUR Little known. Solitary or in pairs; a shy skulking species of dense thickets and undergrowth, where difficult to observe. More often heard than seen. Remains close to ground, seldom higher than *c.*15 m. Creeps around, clumsily emerging for a moment, then plunging back into undergrowth. Highly vocal, usually in duet; calls all year. Advertises and defends a territory of *c.*6–8 ha with loud ringing calls and duets[15, 294, 504]. **Foraging behaviour** Creeps and hops about gleaning food in lower branches of thickets and undergrowth and on ground. Joins mixed foraging parties[294, 688]. **Food** Arthropods, mainly insects, including Coleoptera (beetles), Lepidoptera (butterflies and caterpillars), Hymenoptera (black ants and wasps), Orthoptera (grasshoppers), Hemiptera (cicadas), Mantodea (mantises) and Isoptera (termites). Also spiders and bits of snail recorded. Termites, cicadas, mantids and caterpillars fed to nestlings[259, 290, 294].

SOUNDS Little known. Dialects of birds from West Africa and E Central Africa (Uganda and Rwanda) show very little variation, in spite of the large distance separating these populations. Repertoire consists of very low-pitched, slowly delivered whistles (resembling flufftails *Sarothrura*) and harsh tearing sounds, usually in duet. Territorial call of ♂ a series of up to *c.*10 loud, very low-pitched (less than 1 kHz), quavering, ringing whistles *huoo-huoo-* or *Ooo-Ooo-Ooo-* or longer drawn-out *huuuoo-huuuoo*. Double notes sometimes given with different pitches. Rate of delivery varies from slowly repeated *ho–ho–ho-*, to faster *hohohoho* notes, sometimes in short series, at other times for up to *c.*50 notes. These may start softly and get louder or remain the same. ♀ responds in duet with protracted harsh grating or tearing *hzzrrrrrit-hzzrrrrrit*, *skaaaa* or *crèèk-crèèk* call. Also may answer with a vibrating, hoarse or trembling note. ♀ reportedly may also respond with drawn-out plaintive *hweeeew* or *Hwe-e-e-e* whistle. Some duets are antiphonal, others synchronous, and either sex may initiate calling. Variations include bubbling and gurgling *blop-blopblop-* or *blpblpblpblp-* calls, apparently given while feeding, and slowly repeated nasal twanging *tzzaa-naa-naa-naaa* typical of territorial threat and courtship in the genus. Alarm signalled with sharp *Tik-Tik-* or sharp harsh *hoik* sounds. Ticking sounds sometimes precede tearing sounds[23, 110, 290, 294, 500, 504, 530, 631, 717, 754]. Sonagram[43].

BREEDING BIOLOGY Little known. Monogamous and territorial. **Season** West Africa, probably throughout the year; nest-building May (Guinea)[101]; nest-building Mar, also breeding Oct, enlarged gonads Mar and Nov (Liberia)[37, 234, 330, 858]; breeding condition May, Dec, nest Dec (Gabon)[294, 295, 338, 456]; enlarged ovaries Mar and Nov (Cameroon)[234]; Feb, Jun and Aug (Zaïre)[22, 290, 688]; East Africa young by Nov (Uganda)[576]. **Displays** Unknown. Long rump feathers probably fluffed out in display like other members of genus. **Nest** Role of sexes unknown. Builds a large nest in proportion to its size. Shallow, dove-like cup, loosely built of thin twigs entwined with rootlets, lined with fine roots. Usually placed in a fork 1–5 m above the ground in thick bush, small tree or sapling. One nest was placed above water[15, 22, 290, 294, 515, 858]. **Eggs** Usually 2. Greenish-grey or greenish-white, spotted with grey, ochreous-brown or reddish-brown, mostly around large end. ***Size*** 24–25 x 17–18 mm[15, 22, 294, 290]. **Incubation** Apparently only by ♀. Period unknown[294]. No further breeding information.

MEASUREMENTS and WEIGHTS *L. leucorhynchus* ♂ (5) wing 95–102.5, ♀(5) 92–96, ♂♀? (10) tail 81–92, bill 24–27, tarsus 29–31.5 (West Africa)[34]. **Weight** ♂ (5) av. 57.1 ±5.1, ♀ (2) 57.6–59.5 g, imm 56.6 g (Liberia)[259]; ♀ (1) 49 g (Angola)[569]; ♂♀? (14) 45–55 g (Uganda)[765]. For additional data see[15, 259].

48 MOUNTAIN SOOTY BOUBOU *Laniarius poensis* Plate 21

FIELD IDENTIFICATION Medium-small (17–18 cm), completely black bush-shrike with slight gloss giving a blue-black appearance. Bill relatively heavy. Sexes similar. Young duller and browner. Little known; a shy and skulking species more often heard than seen. Calls very variable; mainly whistles and harsh sounds in duet. Solitary or in pairs; resident in dense undergrowth of montane forest in two separate populations: West Africa from E Nigeria, W Cameroon and Bioko, and E Central Africa from E Zaïre, Uganda, Burundi and Rwanda. ***Flight characteristics***: Short-distance; wings rounded.

COMPARISONS Very similar to Sooty Boubou *Laniarius leucorhynchus*, with which it overlaps, but which is larger and duller, more slaty black (less glossy), and generally inhabits lowland, not montane forest. Calls different: Sooty Boubou has very low-pitched, slowly delivered, flufftail-like whistles and tearing notes. Some calls similar to those of Yellow-breasted Boubou *L. atroflavus*, which usually occurs at higher elevations, although overlaps widely. Mountain Sooty Boubou and Fülleborn's Boubou *L. fuelleborni* similar (sometimes considered conspecific), but Fülleborn's has a finer bill and is very dark grey, rather than black. Calls different and ranges separate. Slate-coloured Boubou *L. funebris* is smaller and deep bluish-slate rather than black, has a finer bill and is a non-forest species. Juveniles are more distinct, Mountain Sooty Boubou wholly brownish black, immature Sooty Boubou has a whitish bill, and Fülleborn's Boubou is dark grey, heavily tinged with olive. Slate-coloured Boubou is barred (not wholly black). For confusion with other all-black species see Sooty Boubou Comparisons p.240.

DESCRIPTION **Adult ♂** Completely black with slight gloss giving a purplish or blue-black appearance. Rump greyish-black without concealed white spots. Feathers long and fluffy. ***Bare parts*** Bill and legs black; palate unknown; eye dark brown to blackish-brown[2, 15, 492]. **Adult ♀** Slightly duller and smaller than ♂[2, 338]. **Juvenile/Immature** Little known. Young dull brownish-black with very pale spotting on crown and back, duller than ♀. Bill black[2, 22, 290, 338, 533, 500].

GEOGRAPHICAL VARIATION At least two races described, with variation mainly in depth of colour and size. Nominate *poensis* (Mt Cameroon and Bioko) is smaller and deeper glossy-black than *holomelas* (E Zaïre, SW Uganda on Mt Ruwenzori) which is ashier and greener. Calls of the two races appear different. E population appears to have lower-pitched longer whistles and rattling notes[15, 533, 500, 717].

MOULT Unknown.

RANGE, HABITAT and STATUS **Breeding range** Fragmented into two separate populations; West Africa from SE Nigeria, S Cameroon, Bioko. E Central Africa from NE, E, SE Zaïre, SW Uganda, Rwanda, Burundi on slopes of Ruwenzori and Virunga Mts. **Habitat** Primary and secondary montane forest up to about 3000 m in dense undergrowth, tangles, forest edge and bamboo zone. In West Africa not at highest elevations of montane forests[22, 37, 412, 431, 492, 504]. **Status** Common resident. **Conservation status** Potentially threatened due to isolated montane distribution[343].

MOVEMENTS Unknown, probably sedentary.

SOCIAL ORGANISATION and GENERAL BEHAVIOUR Little known. Solitary or in pairs, difficult to see, a shy and skulking species, more often heard than seen as it remains in thick undergrowth. Calls very variable, usually in duet[347, 717]. **Foraging behaviour** Remains low down, usually within 5 m of ground. Probably hops like other members of the genus. Joins mixed foraging parties[290, 688]. **Food** Arthropods, mainly insects including Coleoptera (beetles), Lepidoptera (caterpillars, including hairy ones) and isopod crustateans (pill-bugs)[290, 688].

SOUNDS Little known. Complex and geographically highly variable, and not well understood. Situation compounded by plumage similarities and previous classification with Fülleborn's Black Boubou. Calls of W and E populations differ. Like other members of this genus the repertoire consists of a variety of whistles and harsh tearing or rattling sounds, usually in duet. In West Africa, ♂ nominate (*poensis*) commonly gives whistled *whoo-ee, Wee, wit* or repeated short whistles *wokwok-wok-wok, wik-wikwik, kwoni-wou* or faster *vu-vu-vu* and even more rapid bubbling *bobobobo.* These are followed in duet by ♀ with long-drawn-out harsh tearing *tzzzeeerrr* or *zweeeerr* notes, or in rapid duet with shorter, abrupt buzzy *Wizz, Hzz, ze* or nondescript *eng, ang* or *earp* sounds. Also produces harsh duet sequences like *chik-a-chaka, Tk!-a-Tk!a, KcheKcher!* or *wad-ju-wad.* A guttural *choork* sound is reputed also to be given by ♀. The speed of response in duets varies; some short-note duets are very rapid, e.g. *Wee-ze,* with a distinctly buzzy quality. In some sequences, ♂ may respond to ♀ call a second time, producing a 3-note sequence. Alarm probably signalled by drawn-out harsh notes and clicking sounds. In E Central Africa (*holomelas*), ♂ gives short low-pitched *huu* or longer *hooo* whistles, and even longer-repeated, low-pitched deeper ringing *huu-uuue* or *fuuuuue* whistles of 1–2 sec, with or without an initial click. This is followed by ♀ in duet with *wee-wee, hweehwee, tzweet* or *tzrrwe* whistles, as well as repeated low harsh slow hollow rattling *kr-r-r-r-r-r,* or faster *kerrrrrr, tzwrrrrrrreee* or tearing *heerrrzzz* or *tzweeeerrr* sounds. In another variation (sexes unknown) short harsh low-pitched crow-like croaking sounds are repeated in a sequence of 4 notes, sounding like *kowkowkowkow.* Generally calls appear lower-pitched and more drawn-out than W population. A nasal twanging *zzazanananana* sound is also produced by this species and typical of other members of the genus. It is believed to be given in territorial threat and courtship. Alarm is a short or more drawn-out scolding or rasping note. Young in nest have an insect-like *fru frur* begging call[2, 22, 290, 347, 412, 445, 500, 504, 530, 717, 1070]. Sonagram[717].

BREEDING BIOLOGY Virtually unknown. Apparently monogamous and territorial. **Season** Dry season breeder, in breeding condition Mar–Apr, Oct–Dec (Cameroon)[37, 347, 412, 664]; Dec–Feb (Uganda)[293, 336]; Oct (Rwanda)[717]. **Displays** Unknown. **Nest** Role of sexes unknown. A mossy cup built in a cypress bush, covered with *Gouania* creepers[717]. No further breeding information, except that a pair was observed feeding nestlings[717].

MEASUREMENTS and WEIGHTS *L. p. poensis* ♂♀? (8) wing 76–81 (77.8), ♂♀? (7) tail 63–69 (66.7), ♂♀? (8) bill 21.5–24 (22.7), ♂♀? (4) tarsus 28–31 (29.3)[533]; ♂♀? (12) 79–88 (81.8)[347]; *holomelas* ♂♀? (8) wing 78–86 (81.0); tail 67–79 (72.3); bill 16–18 (17.4); tarsus 24–28 (26.6)[492]. **Weight** ♂ (1) 44 g, ♀ (1) 40 g[500].

49 FÜLLEBORN'S BLACK BOUBOU *Laniarius fuelleborni* Plate 21

FIELD IDENTIFICATION Medium-sized (18–20 cm), entirely slaty-black bush-shrike, ♀ with less black on head and with faint olive tinge on breast. Young dull sooty black to olive-grey. Skulking and difficult to see, more often heard than seen. Gives loud fluted whistles and trills in duet. Resident in dense undergrowth of moist montane forests from NE Tanzania to N Malawi and NE Zambia. ***Flight characteristics***: Short-distance; wings rounded.

COMPARISONS Similar to Slate-coloured Boubou *Laniarius funebris* but ecologically segregated, being a non-forest species. Other black boubous have separate ranges further N.

DESCRIPTION **Adult ♂** Uniformly slaty- or greyish-black; no concealed white spots on rump. ***Bare parts*** Bill and legs black; palate unknown; eye brown to dark brown. **Adult ♀** Similar to ♂, but head not as black and underparts faintly tinged olive. ♀ may also be smaller[838]. **Juvenile/Immature** Dull sooty-black or olive-grey above, throat and breast dull olive-grey or dusky-olive; more buff on belly[500, 533, 631].

GEOGRAPHICAL VARIATION Three races; variation slight, concerning general greyness and size. Nominate *fuelleborni* (SW Tanzania, Malawi and N Zambia) largest and greyest race; *uluguren-sis* (Uluguru Mts) darker slate-grey above and below, and smaller than nominate; *usambaricus* (Usambara Mts) more sooty-grey rather than black and smallest race[533].

MOULT Completed in late Sep (Rwanda)[717].

RANGE, HABITAT and STATUS **Breeding range** From NE, S central and SW Tanzania in W Usambaras and Ulugurus Mts, N Malawi and NE Zambia. **Habitat** Moist montane and submontane forest in dense undergrowth, creeper tangles, forest edge and regrowth, bamboo, cultivated areas clearings and valleys up to 3000 m[146, 291, 431, 448, 459, 631]. **Status** Common resident. **Conservation status** Probably threatened due to isolated montane distribution[343].

MOVEMENTS Small local movements, ranging up to 250 m, as well as possible altitudinal movements (Malawi)[119, 660].

SOCIAL ORGANISATION and GENERAL BEHAVIOUR Little known. Solitary or in pairs; a shy skulking species of thick undergrowth, very vocal, and more often heard than seen; duets frequently. **Foraging behaviour** At all levels from ground to canopy, most often low down. A foliage and bark gleaner. **Food** Known to feed on swarming carnivorous ants[74, 146, 291, 445, 448].

SOUNDS Show little geographical variation. Repertoire consists of whistles and harsh notes, usually in duet. Calls generally sex-specific, with ♂ giving loud liquid fluted whistling and ♀ rattling trills, with either sex initiating duets. Typical duet consists of series of 1–3 short loud flute-like liquid descending whistles by ♂: *whee-whee-whee-*, *fweet-fweet-*, *wick-wick-*, or *pui-*. ♂ also has longer rising whistle *hooi-* or *huwee-*. Long and short sounds are variously combined with *hu* or *pui* notes. ♀ sometimes responds in duet to ♂ whistles with a rattling *turrrrrrr* or *P-r-r-r-r-r-* trill, which may descend or rise sharply at first, then trail off gradually. ♀ may also respond with a bubbling rapid *u-u-u-u-u-u*, to which ♂ may then respond with another 1–3 whistles, the combination sounding like *whee-whee-whee-u-u-u-u-u-u-whee-whee-whee.* Also give a harsh *nyaaaa-skereeeee* duet. ♂ sometimes gives a solo rapidly repeated 5-note whistle. Alarm call a repeated hard *click-click-* or, in response to swarming carnivorous ants, a rapid *a-a-a-a-a-a-a-* rattle, also *scaic-ack*, a scolding *raaj-raaj-raaj-* and grunting *chack*[299, 445, 500, 530, 631, 717, 832]. Sonagram[530, 717].

BREEDING BIOLOGY Little known. Monogamous and territorial; territory size varies from as small as 0.6–1 ha, usually 2–3 pairs/10 ha, av. 1 pair/4 ha. Known to remain in territory for at least 8 years[74, 146, 448, 660]. **Season** Dec–Feb (S Tanzania)[832]; Dec–Jan (Malawi)[119, 359], gonads active Sep (Zambia)[291]. **Displays** Unknown. **Nest** Role of sexes unknown. A shallow cup of grass, tendrils and rootlets in fork of shrub or among creepers[336]. **Eggs** 2. Pale greenish-blue sparingly spotted or freckled with brown and olive-brown, and with slate or lead-grey undermarkings. ***Size*** c.25 x 19 mm[336]. No further breeding information, except incubation probably by both sexes as both have brood patches[1001]. **Predation and longevity** Ringed bird 7 years 2 months[534].

MEASUREMENTS and WEIGHTS Races combined ♂♀? (15) wing 82–88 (84.6), ♂♀?(14) tail 75–82 (78.0), ♂♀?(16) bill 22–26 (23.8), ♂♀? (7) tarsus 31–33.5 (32.4)[533]; *fuelleborni* ♂ (6) wing 87.5–91.0 (88.9), ♀ (5) wing 81–84 (82.9)[838]. **Weight** *fuelleborni* ♂ (6) 46.0–53.0 g (48.9), ♀ (4) 43.0–47.0 g (45.2) (N Malawi)[838]; ♂♀? (20) 37–53 g (46.4)[146, 876]. For additional data see[809].

50 SLATE-COLOURED BOUBOU *Laniarius funebris* Plate 21

FIELD IDENTIFICATION Medium-sized (18–20 cm), entirely dark bluish slate-grey bush-shrike with a blackish, slightly glossy head, wings and tail. Appears completely black in field, in good light ♂ bluish-slate, ♀ paler. Young duller and more blackish-brown barred below. Very vocal, shy and skulking, sometimes confiding. More often heard than seen. Calls varied, usually in duet; loud flute-like whistles and snarling notes. Solitary or in pairs; resident in dry bush, scrub, thickets and *Acacia* woodland in E and NE Africa. ***Flight characteristics***: Heavy; flies reluctantly. Wings rounded.

COMPARISONS Similar to larger coastal all-black morph of Tropical Boubou *Laniarius aethiopicus*, which is glossy black (not bluish-slate) but ecologically segregated, Slate-coloured occupying drier habitats. Overlaps widely with normal morph of Tropical, and is known to counter-sing with this species. Some whistled calls similar. Also overlaps and counter-sings with Black-headed Gonolek *L. erythrogaster*, which is unmistakable. In W Kenya similar to Sooty Boubou *L. leucorhynchus*, which is a larger black or brownish-black (not bluish-slate) forest species with a heavier bill; calls different. In S of range similar to Fülleborn's Black Boubou *L. fuelleborni*, which is a moist montane forest species with a heavier bill and different calls. Care needed in separation of immature from all-black morph of larger Tropical Boubou. Slate-coloured has similar barring below and buffy spotting above, but has a much finer bill. Normal morph of Tropical has a white wing-stripe. Other all-black boubous lack barred plumage[325]. For confusion with other all-black species see Sooty Boubou Comparisons p.240.

DESCRIPTION ADULT ♂ Entirely dark greyish to slate-grey. ***Head, wings and tail*** Blackish with slight gloss; lower back and rump slate-grey with concealed white spots, feathers long and fluffy. Underwing dark brown. ***Underparts*** Dark slate-grey. ***Bare parts*** Bill, palate and legs black; eye brown to dark reddish-brown[519, 832]. ADULT ♀ slightly smaller and paler than ♂. ***Abnormal plumage*** Partial albinism recorded[618]. JUVENILE/IMMATURE Duller and more blackish-brown than adult. Upperparts lightly spotted buff, wing-coverts edged buff to greyish-brown, uppertail-coverts barred. ***Underparts*** Throat, breast, belly and flanks and undertail-coverts barred buffy greyish-black. Eye dark brown, bill black. Adult plumage attained in 6–7 weeks. One captive ♀ retained juvenile plumage for 4–6 months[43, 237, 500, 631, 832].

GEOGRAPHICAL VARIATION Two races; variation slight, mainly in size and greyness. Race *degener* (S Ethiopia, S Somalia and E coastal Kenya) differs from nominate *funebris* (N Somalia, central Ethiopia, S Sudan, E Uganda, W Kenya and

N Tanzania) in being paler and smaller[237, 618].

MOULT Unknown.

RANGE, HABITAT and STATUS Breeding range S Sudan, NE, SE and S Ethiopia, NW and SW Somalia, SW and E Uganda, Kenya, Tanzania and Rwanda. **Habitat** In dense undergrowth of dry bush country, including thick *Acacia* scrub and woodlands, thickets and overgrown cultivation. Often associated with thicker vegetation in riverine woodland[237, 242, 325, 292, 318, 431, 481, 631, 859, 933]. **Status** Common resident throughout most of range. **Conservation status** Not threatened. Held in captivity[655].

MOVEMENTS Unknown, probably sedentary.

SOCIAL ORGANISATION and GENERAL BEHAVIOUR Solitary or in pairs; noisy, shy and skulking, but sometimes inquisitive and confiding. More often heard than seen, duets frequently. Found on or near ground in thick vegetation. Advertises and defends a territory of from *c*.1.5–3.5 ha throughout the year, with loud whistles and snarling sounds. Generally ascends to the top of a bush to call, stretches up, and while calling depresses head and body in a bow. Duets are performed throughout the day, usually with partners widely separated and obscured by dense vegetation. Most calling takes place in the early morning and evening. Pairs have a number of duet types, each tending to serve either territorial advertisement, synchronisation of breeding or mate-guarding (contact). Threat signalled with horizontal stance and bill open. Frequently counter-sings with Black-headed Gonolek. Roosting and maintenance behaviour unknown[43, 46, 302, 531]. **Foraging behaviour** Searches for food on ground and in undergrowth of thick vegetation. Hops on ground and gleans food from trunks, branches and foliage. **Food** Arthropods, mainly insects including Isoptera (termites), Hymenoptera (ants, bees and wasps), Lepidoptera (butterflies, caterpillars and moth larvae), Orthoptera (grasshoppers), Mantodea (mantids) and Coleoptera (beetles). Also feeds on ticks and occasionally fruits. Green caterpillars fed to young. Possibly takes young in Red-billed Quelea *Quelea quelea* colonies[43, 46, 299, 531, 733, 1062].

SOUNDS Repertoire loud and very variable, usually in duet with metallic gong-like notes, clear flute-like ringing whistles or a series of whistles and harsh snarling notes. Generally duets consist of 3 notes (elements), of which at least 24 have been identified. Elements appear to be sex-specific and either sex may initiate duets, but not all calls are answered, and ♂♂ often produce long series of solo song. Territories are advertised and defended with a number of song types. In one study, ♂♂ had at least 4 song types ranging from 1–3 elements, while ♀♀ had only one. Generally ♂ gives *ko-ko-* and *whee-you* notes, ♀ *whee* or *wit-wit* notes, repeated up to 8 times. These combine in commonly heard duets such as: *ko-ko-whee* or *whee-ko-ko-whee, whee-ko-ko* or single *wheee-e-e-e*. In a different song type, these may be preceded by ♂ with drawn-out low guttural snore or croaking, *zrraaw, ah-horr, ah-haw, horr,* guttural crow-like *kwrroo, whoy* or wheezing *brrrrreee* and *kzzzweee* notes. Other variations include ♂ giving triple whistles of three tones, followed by ♀ with snarling or croaking *CHUERR, urr* or *huerr* call. Also rapidly delivered double notes by ♀, sounding like *quick-quick* and followed by a *squee* from ♂ with variations. Bubbling calls are also produced. In alarm or when excited, as in threat at nest, a noisy harsh *kch-kch-, teck-teck-* or shrill *rrrh*, guttural *CHERKK, churr* or *krrrr* sounds. Many of these probably represent different levels of intensity. Full duet may follow these calls. Long-range contact maintained by duetting, short-range contact by soft, barely audible calls. Nestlings beg with plaintive *seee* calls. Known to counter-sing (duet) with Tropical Boubou and Black-headed Gonolek. The number of different song types varies individually and geographically with individual repertoire size, stabilising after 1 year old. Newly fledged young produce a mixed babble of high and low sounds which bear no relationship to adult song[2, 4, 33, 43, 46, 136, 302, 500, 519, 530, 531, 532, 558, 631, 811]. For additional information on development of song and duet sequences see[725]; influence of sex hormones on duetting see[726], and function of three different duets see[531]. Sonagram[43, 106, 136, 531, 532].

BREEDING BIOLOGY Monogamous and territorial with no evidence of courtship-feeding. Breeding initiated by rains. Sometimes nests are abandoned before completion, and a new nest built using the original material. New nests are usually built for replacement clutches, and in one case a pair began building three nests simultaneously, before concentrating on one[43, 46, 531]. **Season** Oct (Sudan)[242]; Apr (Ethiopia)[292]; Apr–Jun[33], nest-building Oct (NW Somalia)[859, 933]; Jan, Mar–Jun, Oct–Nov (Uganda and Kenya)[290, 293, 336]; Dec–Mar, Oct–Nov (Tanzania)[336, 832]. **Displays *Courtship*** ♂ calls, stretches up, and while calling depresses head and body, and may swing from side to side. He then bends forward, depresses wings and raises long fluffy rump feathers (white under-feathers give a piebald effect) like a puffback *Dryoscopus*. Tail is raised and fanned; may take a short flight; the wings are quivered rapidly and rump feathers expanded. In another observation two birds *c*.30 cm apart, presumed ♂ (nearly black) gave deep guttural calls as he bowed forward, answered by presumed ♀ (greyer) giving repeated hoarse cough, thrusting down and forwards with each note, display lasting *c*.2 minutes. No courtship feeding known to take place. ***Pre-copulation*** ♀ crouches and quivers wings before ♂ mounts. After copulation birds may give noisy *kch-kch-* or, rarely, shrill *rrrh* sounds. Copulations only observed in the nest tree. ***Nest-site display*** Unknown[43, 46, 631, 531, 759]. **Nest** Both sexes build, ♂ less, sometimes not at all. Cup built of shreds of bark fibre or dry grass, lined with fine grass and rootlets. Occasionally a frail shallow structure poorly bound. Outer wall sometimes covered with spider web. In one study 70% placed *c*.1.5 m (30% were either lower than 1 m or higher than 2 m, n=24) above the ground, usually in fork, or on horizontal branch near the end, in small lateral branches of a small bush on the fringe of a thicket. Most nests are well concealed, some occasionally exposed. ***Size*** OD 60–70 mm, ID 30 mm, cup depth 25 mm, height 60 mm. May take up to a week to build (1–7 days, n=9)[2, 33, 43, 46, 531]. **Eggs** Usually 2 (2–3, n=21), laid on consecutive days. Pale blue with reddish-brown spots becoming more concentrated at the large end, forming a solid brownish-grey patch. ***Size*** 21–24.4 x 16–17.5 mm. In cases of nest predation, up to 4 clutches may be laid[33, 46, 290, 336, 531]. **Incubation** Shared by both sexes, sometimes only ♀. Nest relief coordinated by duets. Period 17 days (n=4)[43, 46]. **Nestling** Hatch blind, naked with black skin and yellow gape. Mouth spots unknown. Fully feathered by 12 days, wings and tail still short. At fledging, coloured black with each feather tipped buff. Attended by both sexes. Eggshells are removed. In first few days faecal sacs are eaten, thereafter removed, and nestlings are initially fed only on green caterpillars. Nestlings are brooded continuously for up to a week, ♀ spreading wings over them to protect them from rain. Beg with plaintive *seee* calls. Fledge after 14–15 days, attended by both sexes[43, 46]. For growth details see[43]. **Predation and longevity** Unknown for certain, but nest contents believed to be plundered by predators like snakes, monitor lizards, mongooses and hornbills. Fledglings predated by mongooses and genets[46, 531]. **Brood parasite** Unknown, although observed giving harsh call when a cuckoo (unspecified) appeared near the nest[531].

MEASUREMENTS and WEIGHTS Races combined ♂ (19) wing 81–95 (88.1), tail 78.5–93 (85.0), bill 20.5–24.0 (22.3), tarsus 28.0–32.0 (30.5); ♀ (17) wing 82–92 (86.1), tail 74–87 (81.1), bill 20–24 (21.9, tarsus 27.7–32 (30.2)[237]. **Weight** ♂♀? (123) 32.2–50.4 g (40.35) (Ethiopia)[870]; ♂♀? (37) 28–47 g (39.9) (Kenya)[509]; captive birds ♂ (26) 42.3 ±2.9 g, ♀ (23) 37.8 ±2.4 g[861]. For additional information see[583, 857].

51 CRIMSON-BREASTED GONOLEK (Crimson-breasted Shrike, Burchell's Gonolek, Crimson-breasted Boubou)

Laniarius atrococcineus **Plate 22**

FIELD IDENTIFICATION Large (22–23 cm), distinctive jet-black, brilliant crimson and white bush-shrike with explosive whistle-calls. Sexes similar; above black, including tail and wings which have a white wing-stripe. Below crimson-red (rarely bright yellow). Young brownish-black above, barred below with patchy areas of pale crimson. More often heard than seen. Rapidly repeated, loud explosive ringing whistles and tearing calls, usually in duet. Solitary or in pairs, shy and skulking, mainly in lower levels or hopping on ground in thornbush. Resident in southern Africa from S Angola, Namibia, Botswana, Zambia, Zimbabwe and South Africa. ***Flight characteristics***: Heavy with shallow rapid wingbeats. Seldom flies far, gliding between bushes or trees. When excited makes 'fripping' sounds with wings in flight. White wing-stripe conspicuous. Concealed white spots on lower back exposed when rump fluffed out. Wings rounded.

COMPARISONS Distinctive. Upperparts and wing pattern resembles other boubous in the region, but crimson underparts diagnostic.

DESCRIPTION **Adult** Sexes similar. ***Head, including sides of face, back, wings, and tail*** jet-black with slight glossy sheen; lower back and rump feathers long and fluffy with concealed white spots; wings with long white wing-stripe, formed by edges of outer secondaries and outer webs of median-coverts. ***Underparts*** Bright crimson including undertail-coverts (rarely bright yellow); thighs black. ***Bare parts*** Bill, palate and legs black; eye greyish-brown with narrow rim of pale violet. **Abnormal plumage** Rarely occurs with crimson underparts replaced completely by golden yellow. **Juvenile** Mottled and barred greyish buff-brown above and below. Primary wing-coverts tipped buff. Bill, palate and legs greyish-black; eye mauve[500]. **Immature** Progressive development of black upperparts followed by crimson underparts, beginning at the vent, taking *c.*35 days. White wing-stripe is similar to adults at 20–25 days. Primary wing-coverts tipped buff. Bill pale at base[44, 205]. For additional information on plumage development see[44].

GEOGRAPHICAL VARIATION Monotypic, but shows slight clinal variation. Populations in N and W paler than those in the E. Birds in W Namibia have slightly paler underparts than those in NE South Africa[654].

MOULT Apparently a complete post-breeding moult. Wing and tail moult recorded in Mar (NE South Africa), adult in post-breeding moult Jan (Botswana). Partial post-juvenile moult results in outer greater primary wing-coverts retaining juvenile plumage[500, 546, 656].

RANGE, HABITAT and STATUS **Breeding range** SW Angola, Namibia (except coastal desert and S), S Zambia, W and SW Zimbabwe, Botswana and central N South Africa. **Habitat** *Acacia* savanna, bushveld and woodland, riverine thornbush and semi-arid scrub[7, 30, 48, 291, 320, 431, 639, 807, 907]. **Status** Common to locally fairly common resident. **Conservation status** Not threatened. Bush encroachment as a result of overgrazing probably creates additional habitat. Held in captivity[655].

MOVEMENTS Local movements recorded, particularly in non-breeding season when it moves into better riverine woodland[205, 639].

SOCIAL ORGANISATION and GENERAL BEHAVIOUR Solitary or in pairs; exceedingly quick, wary and difficult to see, but confiding while nesting. More often heard than seen. Generally more conspicuous in austral winter, when often seen feeding on the ground. Tail flicked while moving, occasionally also when stationary. Bounces (hops) along with little flicks of the tail which exposes undertail-coverts, tail often cocked. Also swings and wags tail. Advertises and defends territory by giving explosive whistles and tearing sounds in duet from within the crown of trees or bushes. Calls throughout the year, but reaches a peak before breeding. Calling posture upright, often with tail cocked. Territories vary from 4–5 ha in optimal habitat to 9–12.5 ha in poorer habitat. During territorial threat, ♂♂ often counter-sing against each other, accompanied by excited body-bowing, side to side movements and tail jerking. Roosts in a dense thorn tree. Scratches indirectly. Body temperature 42.2°C at 25.6°C ambient[44, 205, 320, 639, 798]. **Foraging behaviour** Forages low down, often on the ground, where hops about, flicking debris aside with the bill like a thrush and peering under loose pieces of bark. Frequently gleans from trunks, sometimes from branches and leaves, and occasionally hawks insect in flight. Generally works its way from base of bush or tree towards the top, where it flies out to base of next tree. Appears to form a feeding association with a number of ground or near-ground feeders, using them to flush prey. **Food** Arthropods, mainly insects and their larvae, including Hymenoptera (ants), Coleoptera (beetles), Lepidoptera (caterpillars). Also takes centipedes and occasionally berries and nuts. Captive birds recorded killing other species in same cage[44, 205, 701, 704].

SOUNDS Repertoire consists of loud, explosive, ringing whistles and harsh tearing sounds, usually in duet. Antiphonal duet sequences are delivered at incredible speed. Unmated birds are more vocal than pairs. Birds with fledged young exceptionally silent. Many calls defy transcription. Calls show geographical and individual variation between pairs. Territorial call of ♂ an explosive high-pitched whistle, either a single *Quip, cheop* or double *QwipQwip* also *Qwiwip.* ♀ responds immediately in duet with a harsh, tearing *tzui, CHUI, TJERR* or *TSEEO* call, producing a sequence sounding like *QwipQwip-tzui-QwipQwip*. Territorial threat signalled by repeated *QwipQwip* and a harsh snarling twanging *Tzananana* call, which is also used in courtship. ♀ may join in with tearing *tzui* and double-noted *tz-ui*. *Qwiwip* or *kwewiep* used by both mated and unmated birds, but seldom in duet, and often uttered continuously. When in duet *Qwiwip-TJERR-Qwiwip* during stress when nest checked. *TJERR* used in similar way to *Qwiwip.* Although either sex may initiate duetting, ♂ appears to do so more often. Counter-singing common in territorial encounters. Alarm signalled with loud *Qwip* calls and slowly repeated harsh *Tik-Tik-* calls. Long-range contact maintained by duetting, short-range contact by soft low-pitched churring *Guur-r-r-r* calls. Unmated birds (and sometimes mated birds) occasionally call *QwipQwip* for extended periods, also frequently *tzui-QwipQwip*, often continued for several minutes. An unmated bird recorded calling complete duet sequence a few days after losing its mate. Also has a loud penetrating repeated *Tseeoo* whistle of unknown function. When excited makes 'fripping' sounds with wings in flight. Nestlings beg with plaintive high-pitched *pseee* or *wo-siee* calls, which develop into loud *peeep* calls in fledglings[44, 205, 500]. In the field this species responds positively to calls of Black-headed Gonolek *L. erythrogaster*, with which it has recently been considered conspecific[431]. For additional information see[44]. Sonagram[43, 48, 145].

BREEDING BIOLOGY Monogamous and territorial, sometimes with additional bird, probably a member of a previous brood, observed at nest and during fledging period of second brood, but not seen helping. Breeding occurs in response to rain, and is confined to the wet season. Calling reaches a peak before egg-laying, but is much reduced during incubation and fledging periods. Average densities of 2 birds/10 ha in Kalahari bushveld, and 1 bird/ha in tall *Acacia* woodland. Breeding birds are susceptible to disturbance, and may destroy their own nest. They also destroy their own nests at all stages, from nest-building to brooding, apparently for no reason; possibly nest parasites may trigger this response. Breeding success recorded at 30–62% for two seasons (n=38 nests). May raise two broods, and in one case relaid 14 days after first nest had fledged. Replacement clutches not uncommon; in one study up to 4 clutches laid[44, 205, 234, 320, 639].

Season Dec, Nov nest-building, Nov–Dec breeding condition (Angola)[7, 865, 907], gonads active Oct–Nov (Zambia)[291], Oct–Mar (Namibia); Sep–Apr (mainly Oct–Nov in E), peaking later in W (southern Africa)[48, 639]; egg-laying Jul, Sep, Feb–Mar (Botswana)[807]. **Displays** ***Courtship*** Unmated ♂♂ use repeated *QuipQuip, tsh-QuipQuip, kwewiep* and *tjerr* calls in mate attraction and territorial defence. Having attracted a ♀, much duetting and nasal twanging *Tzananana* calling. ♂ chases ♀, both hopping in tandem through branches, or in flight with 'wing-fripping' sounds. ♂ rump fluffed out exposing white spots. Newly formed pair seen vigorously attacking each other, tails jerking up and down. No courtship-feeding takes place. Occasionally observed to attack species occupying the same habitat. In one case it took at least a month between attracting a mate and egg-laying. ***Pre-copulation*** No elaborate display and no courtship-feeding recorded, but ♂ quivers wings during copulation[44, 205].

Nest Built by both sexes. Built almost entirely of broad (*c*.6–10 mm) shreds of bark, woven with some spider web, with inner lining of fine grass or root material. Placed *c*.3 m (1–7.6 m, n=61) above the ground in fork of tree, usually a thorn tree and generally not particularly well concealed. ***Size***

OD 100–130 mm, ID 90–110, cup depth 50–65 mm, height 120–150 mm. Built in *c*.5 days, and may remain empty for up to 2 weeks[44, 205, 500]. For additional information see[44].

Eggs Usually 2–3 (1–4, n=62), laid at 24 hour intervals. Colour unusually variable, being either buff, pale green, blue or occasionally pure white, normally spotted with shades of brown and grey, concentrated at the large end. ***Size*** 22.0–25.5 x 16.3–19.7 mm (23.7 x 17.5, n=69)[19, 48, 359]. **Incubation** May start with first egg, but usually with second or third egg. Both sexes incubate, nest relief initiated by calls, usually from the relieving bird, *QuipQuip* or *tzui* depending on sex; sitting bird responds from nest. Period *c*.17 days (15–19, n=7)[44, 48, 137, 205]. **Nestling** Hatch blind, naked, pinkish then black, and have a yellow gape, palate and tongue, and probably have mouth spots. Later, uniform buffy brown above and below, each feather tipped light buff, especially above. Undertail-coverts crimson (not so bright as adult), bill grey-brown. Tail, primaries and coverts black tipped buff. Attended by both sexes and beg with high-pitched *pseee*. Fledge after *c*.19 days (18–20, n=6), and are independent by at least 51 days (n=1)[42, 44, 331]. **Predation and longevity** Recorded causes of nest failure include: nest parasites, self destruction of nest at all stages (mostly during incubation), human disturbance and probable predation by Small Spotted Genet *Genetta felina*. Recorded once in nest remains of Bateleur *Terathopius ecaudatus*. Ringed bird recovered after 2 years 168 days[30, 44, 54, 205]. **Brood parasite** Only Black Cuckoo *Cuculus clamosus*, with 2.6% of recorded nests parasitised. Shrikes mob this species, and the same pair are often repeatedly susceptible, while neighbours not. Eggs of cuckoo resemble host's but are slightly larger[94].

MEASUREMENTS and WEIGHTS *L. atrococcineus* ♂ (23) wing 98–105 (100), ♀ (13) 93–101 (97), tail ♂♀? (36) 90–109, tarsus ♂♀? (36) 30–34, bill ♂♀? (36) 20.5–26[48]; bill (to skull) ♂♀? (10) 23–25 (24)[500]. **Weight** ♂♀? (32) 40.0–56.4 g (48.8)[205, 500].

52 BLACK-HEADED GONOLEK (Ethiopian or Abyssinian Gonolek, Black-headed Bush-shrike) *Laniarius erythrogaster* Plate 22

FIELD IDENTIFICATION Large (20–23 cm), jet-black and brilliant crimson bush-shrike with pale yellow eye, black head and no white wing-stripe. Sexes similar; above jet-black, below crimson-red with dark buff lower belly and undertail-coverts. Young barred blackish-brown above, yellow-buff below, often with patchy pale crimson areas. More often heard than seen; explosive loud percussive ringing whistles and tearing calls, usually in duet. Solitary or in pairs, shy and skulking, usually in lower-levels or on ground. Resident across N savanna thornbush from Eritrea in NE Africa to Chad in West Africa, where also in papyrus and grassy riverbanks. In East Africa from Uganda, Kenya, NW Tanzania to Rwanda, Burundi and SE Zaïre. ***Flight characteristics***: Short and rather heavy. Concealed white spots on lower back exposed when rump fluffed out. Wings rounded.

COMPARISONS In W of range in West Africa similar to Yellow-crowned Gonolek *Laniarius barbarus*, which has a yellowish-brown forehead to nape and a brown eye. Whistled calls similar, harsh calls different, with a tearing note in Black-headed (clicking or rattling note in Yellow-crowned). In East Africa similar to much smaller Papyrus Gonolek *L. mufumbiri*, which has a golden-yellow forehead and crown, and lemon-yellow eye, less heavy bill and longer toes, and is restricted to papyrus swamps and marshes. Other *Laniarius* bush-shrikes have similar black upperparts but lack the brilliant crimson underparts. Juvenile similar to juvenile Yellow-crowned and probably Papyrus Gonolek, and superficially similar to juvenile Slate-coloured Boubou *L. funebris*.

DESCRIPTION Adult Sexes similar, except ♀ possibly smaller. **Upperparts including sides of face, wings and tail** Back with slight glossy sheen. Rarely individuals show a few yellowish feathers on frontal and crown. Lower back and rump feathers long and fluffy with concealed white spots. ***Wings*** Black without wing-stripe, but may occasionally have a few white spots on wing-coverts. ***Underparts*** Crimson, except for dark buff lower belly and undertail-coverts; thighs buff and black. ***Bare parts*** Bill black, palate unknown, legs dark grey, eye whitish to lemon-yellow. **Juvenile** Upperparts blackish-brown, tipped buff with faint barring; underparts yellowish-buff narrowly barred dusky and black. Eye brown. **Immature** Upperparts similar to adult but duller black and with buff tips to forehead, crown and wing-coverts. Underparts like juvenile with barring gradually replaced with crimson, beginning from lower belly, giving a very mottled patchy appearance[504, 631].

GEOGRAPHICAL VARIATION None. Monotypic.

MOULT Unknown.

RANGE, HABITAT and STATUS **Breeding range** East and NE Africa including W and S Ethiopia, Eritrea, Sudan to Uganda, NW Kenya, NW Tanzania, Rwanda, Burundi. In Central Africa from NE and SE Zaïre and Central African Republic, and in West Africa in NE Nigeria, N Cameroon and S Chad. **Habitat** Thornbush, thickets, gardens and scrubby cultivation and belts of trees bordering lakes and streams, including papyrus swamps and grassy riverbanks[21, 22, 37, 242, 290, 292, 431, 481, 504, 631]. **Status** Locally common to fairly common resident. **Conservation status** Unknown, probably not threatened.

MOVEMENTS Only local movements documented (Kenya)[631].

SOCIAL ORGANISATION and GENERAL BEHAVIOUR Little known. Solitary or in pairs, very shy and difficult to observe, never seen for more than a few seconds in open before disappearing into undergrowth. Sometimes inquisitive and responsive, but more often heard than seen, with loud calls given in duet. Territories advertised with loud *whee-yoo* calls. **Foraging behaviour** Searches low down, gleaning from branches and trunks, and often on the ground where it hops about. **Food** Mainly insects, including their larvae. Lizards and eggs also recorded[134].

SOUNDS Little known. Territorial and most frequently heard call a loud, double *whee-yoo, hweeu, whee-u, yoick* or *howeo* whistle by ♂, usually answered immediately by ♀ in duet with short harsh rasping or tearing *Tzzz, Turrrr* or *Kssrrr* sounds, a call sounding like the violent tearing of cloth. Duets delivered at incredible speed and sounding like one bird. Another reported duet consists of a hollow whistle *chuyo-chuyo, chyochochocho* involving both members of pair. Alarm call a loud harsh, rapidly repeated *ChK-ChK-ChK-*, the notes run together in a continuous rail-like chatter. A juvenile observed joining in duets with adults at 3 months old, synchronising perfectly with ♀, giving ♀ part of the duet; developed the ♂ call after about 6 months. ♂ and its offspring appear to compete for ♀, who responds to both originally, but later only to the older bird. Recordings of calls of this species do not sound as clear and ringing as other crimson-breasted gonoleks[134, 136, 500, 530, 631]. Sonagram[106, 145, 530].

BREEDING BIOLOGY Little known. Monogamous and territorial. **Season** Jan, Mar–Jul and Sep–Dec (East Africa, plus NE, E and SE Zaïre)[293, 576]; Mar–Apr, Jun–Jul (Sudan)[338, 242]; Jul (Central African Republic)[338]. **Displays** Little known. Only documented display concerns one bird wing-quivering and begging while other collected nesting material[134]. **Nest** Role of sexes unknown. A loosely built structure of roots, grasses and pieces of fibre and fragments of bark, lined with finer rootlets. Usually placed in a fork or on an outer branch, either in a thick bush or thorntree from 4–8.5 m above the ground. In some instances the eggs are clearly visible from below[22, 134, 530]. **Eggs** Usually 2. Pale blue or bluish-green, heavily blotched with reddish-brown and grey. ***Size*** 22.9–25 x 17.8–18 mm[290]. No further breeding information, except that young resemble adults after 4 months[134].

MEASUREMENTS and WEIGHTS *L. erythrogaster* ♂♀? (15) wing 93–110 (101.1), tail 83–106 (92.5), ♂♀? (14) bill (to skull) 21–28 (24.3), tarsus 29–34 (31.6)[500]. **Weight** ♂♀? (5) 42–45 g (42.8) (S Zaïre)[319]; ♂♀? (44) 35–56 g (48.8) (Kenya)[509]. For additional data see[238, 319, 492, 554].

53 YELLOW-CROWNED GONOLEK (Common Gonolek, Gonolek or Barbary Shrike) *Laniarius barbarus* Plate 22

FIELD IDENTIFICATION Large (22–23 cm), jet-black and brilliant crimson bush-shrike with golden-yellow crown, black face-mask and brown eye. Sexes similar; above jet-black, except for golden-yellow forehead, crown and nape; below crimson (rarely yellow) with lower belly, thighs and undertail-coverts dark buff. Young dull brownish-black above barred buff below with crimson patches. More often heard than seen; explosive loud ringing whistles and rasping rattles, usually in duet. Solitary or in pairs, shy and skulking in lower levels or on ground. Resident in savanna thornbush and dense thickets, also near watercourses and sometimes in mangroves and papyrus swamp from S Mauritania to N Cameroon in West Africa. ***Flight characteristics***: Short and rather heavy. When excited makes 'fripping' sounds with wings. Concealed white spots on lower back exposed when rump fluffed out. Wings rounded.

COMPARISONS Similar to Black-headed Gonolek *Laniarius erythrogaster*, which has a completely black head and yellowish eye. Some whistled calls also similar, but harsh calls different: rattling sounds in Yellow-crowned (tearing in Black-headed).

DESCRIPTION **ADULT** Sexes similar. Upperparts slightly glossed, jet-black, except for golden olive-yellow forehead, crown and nape. Lower back and rump with long fluffy feathers and concealed white spots. ***Wings and tail*** Black. ***Underparts*** Crimson, rarely yellow[662]; thighs, lower belly and undertail-coverts dark buff. ***Bare parts*** Bill black; palate unknown; legs dark grey; eye dark brown. **JUVENILE** Upperparts blackish-brown, feathers tipped buff. Wing-coverts tipped buff. Underparts yellowish-buff narrowly barred dusky. **IMMATURE** Upperparts like adult but duller black, forehead, crown and nape dull yellow and less extensive. Wing-coverts tipped buff. Barred underparts gradually replaced with crimson, beginning at sides of belly, feathers tipped buff.

GEOGRAPHICAL VARIATION Two races. In southwest of range *helenae* (Sierra Leone) differs from nominate *barbarus* (S Mauritania to Cameroon) in being deeper-coloured, with more rufous-yellow forehead, crown and nape. It is an inhabitant of papyrus swamp, unlike nominate[180, 338].

MOULT Unknown.

RANGE, HABITAT and STATUS Breeding range West Africa from S Mauritania, Senegal, Gambia, Guinea-Bissau, Guinea, Sierra Leone, Liberia, Ivory Coast, Ghana, Togo, Benin, Nigeria, Mali, Burkina Faso, Niger, Chad and N Cameroon. **Habitat** Throughout savanna zone, including sandy coastal country in undergrowth of riverine woodland, *Acacia* thornbush, dense thickets in semi-arid areas and scrub, gardens and mangroves (Sierra Leone), often near water and water-courses[21, 23, 37, 39, 180, 207, 234, 327, 431, 455, 482, 504, 848]. **Status** Resident, common to fairly common, but rare or overlooked in Liberia. **Conservation status** Little known, probably not threatened. Held in captivity[655].

MOVEMENTS Some dry-season movements suspected (Gambia)[39].

SOCIAL ORGANISATION and GENERAL BEHAVIOUR Little known. Solitary or in pairs. Shy and difficult to observe, skulks in thick cover, occasionally emerging to perch in the open. More often heard than seen. Territorial and most frequently heard call a whistle followed by harsh rattling notes in duet. **Foraging behaviour** Mainly on the ground where hops about, also gleans from trunks and branches. Aggressive and probably robs nests regularly, as observed attacking weaver nest and impaling a waxbill on a thorn[529]. **Food** Arthropods, mainly insects, including Coleoptera (beetles) and Lepidoptera (caterpillars). Some vertebrate prey also taken; nestlings and small birds recorded[9, 529].

SOUNDS Little known. Repertoire consists of whistles and harsh rattling notes given in duet, and delivered at incredible speed, sounding like one bird. Territorial and most frequently heard call a distinctive loud resonant double *huweeu, whee-oo, whee-u* or *too-lioo* whistle by ♂, followed instantaneously in duet by 2–4 harsh dry rasping rattles or clicks *KKK, ch-chacha, Tik-Tick* or *Tic-Tac* notes from ♀. Apparently either sex may initiate duet, the sequences being unusually variable (within and between pairs), e.g. *huweeu-KKK-huweeu* or simply *huweeu-KKK*. A second often heard call is a series of 1–10 clicking sounds *KKKKKKKK-K-K* produced by one bird and answered similarly by mate. Given from deep cover, these clicks have half the duration of those given in the *whee-u* sequence. Repeated solo rhythmic *huwelo–huwelo- or twoo-woo–* whistles are also sometimes heard. Another call, apparently part of courtship, is described as being similar to Tropical Boubou and probably refers to the metallic twanging sound typical of the genus. It is given in flight, with 'wing-fripping' sounds, and may involve a second bird in duet. Alarm probably harsh ticking notes. Various other harsh calls recorded[136, 500, 501, 530, 540, 661]. Sonagram[106, 136, 540].

BREEDING BIOLOGY Little known. Monogamous and territorial. **Season** During rainy season, from Jan–Sep and Nov[37, 234, 338, 482, 696]. **Displays** Observed chasing each other 'leap-frog' fashion, hopping up and down in a bush. A call, thought to be part of courtship, is apparently a metallic twanging sound given in flight with 'wing-fripping' sounds. This call is characteristic of the genus *Laniarius* and given in territorial threat and courtship. Mates call in duet[529, 540]. **Nest** Role of sexes unknown. A deep cup of small rootlets with a lining of fine tendrils, some unlined. Nests often flimsy and transparent. Placed in dense bush or tree[15, 338]. **Eggs** Usually 2 (2–3). Pale blue-green or grey-green sparingly marked with dark brown, orange-brown and lilac spots and blotches. ***Size*** 22.8–24.4 x 17.2–18 mm[15, 38]. No further breeding information.

MEASUREMENTS and WEIGHTS *L. b. barbarus* ♂♀? (13) wing 95–108 (102.0), tail 93–105 (99.0), bill (to skull) 24.5–27.5 (25.7), tarsus 33–35.5 (34.3)[500]; ♂ (5) wing 104–112, ♀ (4) wing 102–108, ♂♀? (9) tail 101–111, bill 22–24, tarsus 32–35[34]. **Weight** *barbarus* ♂♀? (9) 42–56 g (48.8)[500]. For additional data see[494, 582, 652].

54 PAPYRUS GONOLEK (Papyrus Bush-shrike, Mufumbiri Bush-shrike)
Laniarius mufumbiri **Plate 22**

FIELD IDENTIFICATION Medium-small (17–19 cm), jet-black and crimson bush-shrike with dull yellow crown, black face-mask, pale yellowish eye and usually white wing-stripe or few spots. Sexes similar; above black, except for crown and wing-stripe. Below orange-crimson with lower belly, thighs and undertail-coverts whitish. Young like adult but duller above and with pale throat. More often heard than seen; main call rapidly repeated whistles and harsh notes in duet. Solitary or in pairs; shy and skulking. Resident, restricted to papyrus swamps and marshes from E Zaïre, Rwanda, Burundi, NW Tanzania, W Kenya and S Uganda. ***Flight characteristics***: Short-distance; wings rounded, wing-stripe (if present) conspicuous. Concealed white spots on lower back exposed when rump fluffed out.

COMPARISONS Overlaps slightly on edges of swamps with Black-headed Gonolek *Laniarius erythrogaster*, which is considerably larger with a heavier bill and lacking yellow crown, white wing-stripe and white undertail-coverts. Similar to West African Yellow-crowned Gonolek *L. barbarus*, which is considerably larger, has a brown eye and lacks white wing-stripe and white undertail-coverts; also ranges separate. Papyrus Gonolek has distinctly longer toes and claws than Black-headed Gonolek, presumably an adaptation for clinging to reeds.

DESCRIPTION ADULT Sexes similar. **Upperparts** Black with slight glossy sheen; head, including sides of face, black with forehead and crown dull golden-yellow. ***Back*** Black; lower back and rump with concealed white spots, feathers long and fluffy. ***Wings*** Black with median-coverts broadly tipped white (variable, occasionally almost absent), forming distinctive wing-stripe. ***Tail*** Black. ***Underparts*** Crimson with slight orange tinge, particularly on throat; thighs, lower belly and undertail-coverts whitish-buff. ***Bare parts*** Slender bill and palate back; legs dark grey; toes and claws long; eye lemon-white to straw-yellow[553]. **IMMATURE** Dull black without gloss above, some feathers showing pale tips; crown broadly tipped dull greyish-olive or buff; wing-coverts tipped and edged buff, wing-stripe present; underparts brick-red to yellowish-pink with throat yellowish-buff; lower belly and undertail-coverts whitish-buff; eye pale brown[553, 631, 658].

GEOGRAPHICAL VARIATION None. Monotypic.

MOULT Probably post-breeding, wing moult recorded Sep–Feb (Kenya)[562].

RANGE, HABITAT and STATUS Breeding range Endemic to the interior of papyrus swamps from E Zaïre to NW Tanzania (requires confirmation), W and S Uganda, W Kenya along Lake Victoria, Burundi and Rwanda. **Habitat** In pure and mixed papyrus swamps and marshes from 1100–1600 m[318, 431, 479, 481, 604, 631]. **Status** Common to locally common resident. **Conservation status** Unknown. Considered Near-Threatened due to restricted habitat[479].

MOVEMENTS Unknown; probably sedentary.

SOCIAL ORGANISATION and GENERAL BEHAVIOUR Little known. Solitary or in pairs; exceptionally shy and difficult to see, but inquisitive as it skulks about in reedbeds. More often heard than seen. In one study an estimate of two singing birds/ha was recorded at Kadenge (W Kenya) in Feb–Mar. Surprisingly, in the same study based on retraps, the population density is given as 9 birds/ha[530, 562, 631]. **Foraging behaviour** Apparently obtains all its food from papyrus, where probably hops about. Occupies mid-levels, occasionally using upper and lower levels to acquire its food from emergent vegetation. Seldom leaves papyrus except for short flights over open water[343, 631]. **Food** Arthropods, mainly insects, including Hymenoptera (ants, Formicinae and Myrmicinae), Coleoptera (beetles and weevils, Carabidae, Curculionidae, Elateridae, Lagriidae and Staphylinidae), Diptera (flies), Lepidoptera (caterpillars). Also takes small snails and small fruits and seeds[554, 763].

SOUNDS Little known. Short whistles and harsh tearing notes usually given in duet. ♂ probably gives whistles and ♀ harsh sounds. Commonly heard duet consists of 2–3 repeated high-pitched whistled notes in various combinations, *weyo-weyo, U-U, yo-yo yoo-yo, yoyo-yo* or *yo-yip*, also *yong-yong, chyo-chyo* or *yoo yong-yong*. These are sometimes immediately responded to by ♀ with harsh single or double tearing *Tzeu* notes, sounding like *U-Tzeu-U-Tzee, Tzeu-U* or *TzeuTzeu-U* with either sex initiating duet. During counter-singing, presumed ♂♂ respond to each other with similar *weyo-weyo* phrase. Other whistles are given in series of rapid bursts of *c.*4 notes *tU-tU-tU-tU* or *qU-qU-qU-qU* at varying speeds. Possibly counter-sing with these calls as well. Probably has harsh ticking alarm[22, 145, 500, 501, 631].

BREEDING BIOLOGY Little known. Monogamous and territorial. **Season** Jun, Sep–Dec, Feb (Kenya)[562]. No further breeding information, except nest probably placed in small shrub in reedbeds[2].

MEASUREMENTS and WEIGHTS *L. mufumbiri* ♂ (5) wing 88–98 (94.2), tail 76–84 (80.2), bill (to skull) 24.5–25.5 (25.0), tarsus 30–34 (32.2); ♀ (5) wing 88–93 (90.2), tail 81–77 (78.8), bill (to skull) 23–24.5 (24.0), tarsus 31–33.5 (32.4)[500]; ♂♀? (10) wing 87–98 (92.3) ±3.30[562]. **Weight** ♂♀?(12) 34.4–46.0 g (41.5 ±SD 3.62)[562]. For additional data see[509, 553, 554].

55 YELLOW-BREASTED BOUBOU (Mountain Gonolek)

Laniarius atroflavus **Plate 23**

FIELD IDENTIFICATION Medium-sized (18–19 cm), distinctive black and yellow forest bush-shrike with explosive whistle-calls. Sexes similar; above jet-black, below deep yellow; thighs and undertail-coverts buff. Young paler below. More often heard than seen; usually 3 loud explosive ringing whistles and chattering calls in duet. Solitary or in pairs, skulking and shy. Resident in dense undergrowth of montane forests of E Nigeria and W Cameroon in West Africa. ***Flight characteristics***: Heavy and usually short between trees. Wings rounded.

COMPARISONS Distinctive. Unlikely to be confused with other boubous due to yellow underparts. However, Mountain Sooty Boubou *Laniarius poensis* has many similar calls, and though generally occurring at lower elevations, shows wide overlap. Calls of Yellow-breasted Boubou generally shorter and more explosive, duetting occurring at incredible speed compared to longer, slower duets of Mountain Sooty Boubou.

DESCRIPTION **ADULT** Sexes similar. ***Upperparts*** Head including sides of face, back, rump, wings and tail black with slight gloss giving a blue-black appearance. Rump with long fluffy feathers and concealed white spots. ***Underparts*** Deep yellow, chin and throat paler yellow. Undertail-coverts and thighs buff. ***Bare parts*** Bill black, palate unknown, legs dark grey, eye brown to dark brown. **JUVENILE** Unknown. **IMMATURE** Above dull brownish-black with yellowish-green to buffy tips of crown feathers, edges of wing-coverts and outer tail feathers; underparts paler and duller than adult[500, 757].

GEOGRAPHICAL VARIATION Two races: *craterum* (Cameroon highlands) differs from nominate *atroflavus* (Mt Cameroon) in being larger, with duller yellow underparts and greenish tinge on throat[347, 412, 669].

MOULT Unknown.

RANGE, HABITAT and STATUS **Breeding range** Endemic to montane forest in E Nigeria (Obudu and Mambilla Plateaus; Chappal Hendu, Gashaka-Gumti National Park) and W Cameroon (Mt Cameroon; Mt Manenguba; Bamenda Highlands) in West Africa[21, 37, 431, 504]. **Habitat** Montane forest in dense undergrowth of clearings, along streams, bracken thickets and brambles, secondary scrub, small forest remnants and bamboo above 2000 m[347, 530]. **Status** Uncommon to locally common resident. **Conservation status** Possibly threatened due to restricted montane and highland habitat[343, 756].

MOVEMENTS Unknown, probably sedentary.

SOCIAL ORGANISATION and GENERAL BEHAVIOUR Little known. Solitary or in pairs; shy and restless, low down or in mid-canopy. Advertises and defends territory with whistles and explosive calls in duet. While giving whistled calls bows forward[530]. **Foraging behaviour** Mainly in lower and mid-levels[23, 504]. **Food** Insects.

SOUNDS Little known. Repertoire consists of short high-pitched explosive whistles and short harsh tearing sounds usually in duet, delivered and responded to at incredible speed. Call tone and structure similar to the crimson gonoleks *Laniarius*. Territorial calls consist of duets initiated by either sex. In a duet the ♂ component is a loud whistled *whee-oo, hweeu* or *hwee*, followed immediately by various short harsh sounds from ♀, described as clicking *chook*, tearing *Tzik, Tzz* or *Kzzr*. Typically a duet sounds like *hweeu-Kzzr-hweeu*. ♂ also has a loud ringing *Quick-Quick-Quick* and prolonged *hweeu-hweeu-* series. A sound described as a startling double swishing note, is probably a nasal twanging sound produced in territorial threat and courtship by members of this genus. Other whistles are less tonal, e.g. *quelch* from ♂, instantly answered by *ich* from ♀. Also has a variety of harsh calls including series of explosive stuttering or rapidly repeated *cha-kick-kick-kick-kick, Tik-Tik-* or *KiKiKiKi-*, rattling and harsh grating notes. Bill-clashing sounds, similar to *Chlorophoneus* bush-shrikes, are also made. Alarm a sharp *tuk-tuk-*, or *cha*, often followed by *ich-ich-ich-ich*. Many calls are similar the Mountain Sooty Boubou[15, 23, 34, 145, 338, 500, 504, 555, 754]. Sonagram[145].

BREEDING BIOLOGY Little known. Monogamous and territorial. **Season** Cameroon Nov–Mar[37]. **Displays** Unknown. **Nest** Role of sexes unknown. It is a roughly made, semi-transparent cup of fibres and roots placed about 1 m above the ground in dense undergrowth, bushes, brambles or bracken on edge of forest. One nest at 10 m[37, 338, 515]. **Eggs** Clutch and egg size unknown. Pale green, speckled with brown, often in a zone round the large end[338]. No further breeding information, except both adults feed nestlings[515].

MEASUREMENTS and WEIGHTS *L. a. atroflavus* ♂ (9) wing 81–85 (83.6), ♀ (4) 81–83 (82)[412]; ♂ (1) wing 84, ♀ (1) 81, tail ♂ (1) 81, ♀ (1) 79, bill ♂ (1)18, ♀ (1)20, ♂♀? (2) tarsus 30[34]; *craterum* ♂ (3) wing 87–90 (88.7); ♀ (2) 87, 90 ♂♀? (5) tail 77–81, bill 18–19, tarsus 31–32[669]. **Weight** ♂♀? (4) 41.5–46.9 g (43.7) (Cameroon)[757]; ♂♀? (2) (40.0 g) (Cameroon)[478]; ♂♀? (3) 40.6–44.5 g (42.6) (Cameroon)[756]. For additional data see[15, 347, 412, 616, 669].

56 LÜHDER'S BUSH-SHRIKE *Laniarius luehderi* Plate 23

FIELD IDENTIFICATION Medium-sized (18–19 cm), distinctive black, brown and white bush-shrike with a dark chestnut-brown head, black face-mask and heavy bill. Back, tail and wings black with white wing-stripe. Below variable, from throat to upper belly reddish-brown to orange-buff (one rare Angolan population bright reddish-orange below, another completely white below). Lower belly white. Sexes similar. Young buffy olive-brown with barring and a rufous tail. More often heard than seen; resonant whistles, guttural calls and harsh clicking sounds in duet, given from undergrowth or treetops. Solitary, or in pairs, skulking mainly in dense undergrowth of secondary forest, riverine and forest edge. Resident in two widely separate populations in W and E Central Africa. ***Flight characteristics***: Heavy; wings rounded; brown, black and white plumage conspicuous in flight.

COMPARISONS Distinctive, except for some calls which resemble those given by Swamp Boubou *Laniarius bicolor* and Tropical Boubou *L. aethiopicus*. Neither of these is a forest bird. May be found alongside Mountain Sooty Boubou *L. poensis* but feeds higher up in trees. Juvenile superficially similar to juvenile boubous, but has a rufous-brown tail[717].

DESCRIPTION ADULT Sexes similar, races different. ***Head* including crown and nape** rufous-brown to chestnut-brown or orange-tawny, occasionally with buff edges to crown; face-mask black, including lores, below eye and ear-coverts. Extends onto black shoulder, mantle and back; rump black with concealed white spots, feathers long and fluffy. ***Wings*** Black with narrow white wing-stripe formed by some greater coverts and outer margin of two secondary feathers; uppertail-coverts black. ***Tail*** Black. ***Underparts*** Chin to upper belly rufous-buff to orange-tawny, sometimes quite yellowish (bright reddish-orange in race *brauni*, white in race *amboimensis*); lower belly, vent and undertail-coverts white. ***Bare parts*** Bill black, with thick deep shape, palate unknown; legs light blue-grey to slate; eye brown to dark reddish-brown, dark brownish-grey in *brauni*[290, 500, 541]. **JUVENILE** Rather yellowish-brown appearance, particularly below. Upperparts: Olive-brown, finely barred; uppertail-coverts rufous-brown barred black. Wings: Flight feathers and coverts brown with yellowish-green to buff edging; wing-stripe buffy-yellow. Tail: Dark rufous-brown. Underparts: Chin and throat finely barred dark greenish-white; breast to vent buffy-yellow to greenish-yellow on lower belly, strongly barred dusky. Bare parts: Bill grey-brown to dark grey; legs light blue to greyish; eye reddish-brown[290, 504, 631, 646, 680]. **IMMATURE** Dusky barring gradually lost. Upperparts olive-brown; wing-stripe dull white to yellowish. Tail dark rufous-brown. Underparts deep yellow with orange tinge on breast[504]. For stages of immature plumage see[618].

GEOGRAPHICAL VARIATION Four races from two widely separate E and W populations, two of these from two isolated localities in Angola. Variation mainly in colour of head and underparts and body size. Nominate *luehderi* (SE Nigeria, Cameroon to Zaïre and Kenya) with chestnut-brown to orange-tawny head, throat and breast; *castaneiceps* (S Uganda, W Kenya) is similar to nominate but smaller and paler; *brauni*, sometimes considered a separate species, has a reddish-orange throat and breast, and is restricted to rainforest of Cuanza Norte in NW Angola; *amboimensis*, also sometimes considered a separate species, has the underparts completely white, and is known only from Gabela in W Angola[7, 25, 79, 479].

MOULT Jan–Feb birds moulting into adult plumage (Gabon/Congo)[456].

RANGE, HABITAT and STATUS Breeding range Two disjunct populations; in West Africa from SE Nigeria, Cameroon, Equatorial Guinea, Gabon, Congo, W Zaïre, NW and W Angola and Cabinda; in East Africa from S Sudan, W Uganda, W Kenya, NW Tanzania, W Rwanda, Burundi, and E Zaïre. Bioko and Central African Republic records rejected[431]. **Habitat** Nominate race mainly in lowlands in undergrowth of riverine and secondary forests, forest patches, thickets, overgrown clearings, dense scrub and abandoned cultivation with dense tangles; *brauni* in tropical evergreen rain forest in secondary growth and gallery forest on Angolan escarpment; *amboimensis* known only from evergreen escarpment forest around Gabela[7, 22, 79, 242, 290, 294, 318, 431, 504, 631, 717, 907]. **Status** Resident; nominate race generally uncommon, other three races rare. **Conservation status** *amboimensis* known only from restricted evergreen forest areas around Gabela in the Amboim Escarpment of Cuanza Sul region of Angola, last seen in 1992; *brauni* known only from rainforest at a few sites (Camabatela, Canzele and Quibaxi) within a 50 km radius of Quicolunge in Cuanza Norte region on the northern part of the scarp of Angola. Deforestation has proceeded steadily in recent years and resulted in severe habitat fragmentation. Due to their uncertain taxonomic status (elevated to species level by some authors), restricted distribution and destruction of habitat, both are potential Red Data Book species considered Endangered[7, 108, 423, 479].

MOVEMENTS Unknown; probably sedentary.

SOCIAL ORGANISATION and GENERAL BEHAVIOUR Little known. Usually solitary or in pairs; a shy skulking species, remains hidden in thick cover near or on the ground. Sometimes inquisitive but more often heard than seen. Moves about in a crouched position. Calls given from low down as well as treetops. Quite vocal, throat extending out while calling, head and neck bent forward at each call. In at least one call, head is suddenly raised up, then retracted and thrown forward and accompanied by a swelling of the throat. Most vocal at dawn and dusk[290, 294, 456, 530, 631, 646]. **Foraging behaviour** Hops about on the ground and searches lower levels in thickets and creeper tangles, occasionally higher up in treetops where gleans prey. Joins mixed foraging parties[479]. **Food** Arthropods, mainly insects, including Coleoptera (beetles), Hemiptera (leafhoppers), Lepidoptera (caterpillars), Orthoptera (grasshoppers), Mantodea (mantises) and Isoptera (termites). Also takes spiders, isopods and snails[290, 294, 764].

SOUNDS Very variable, although dialects similar between widely separated populations in West Africa and E Central Africa. Repertoire complex and not well understood. Consists of low metallic guttural sounds, whistles, harsh calls or clicking notes, usually in duet. Territorial advertisement and pair contact is maintained with a commonly heard 'croak' or 'snore' by ♂, being a very low-pitched hoarse metallic resonant rather guttural *worr, horrr, whaw, k-kaw, whook, wurrk, crrrou* or softer *prru*. The call has a rather throaty, somewhat rolling or bubbling and frog-like quality. It is sometimes repeated at long irregular intervals. These may be answered immediately by ♀ in duet, either with similar notes or with harsh sounds, typically up to *c*.5 dry harsh *k!-k!-k!-k!-k!* or *kè-kè-kè-* cackles, protracted *K-KKKrrrr* or *kiurrrr* rasping, or strident *Tzik!, tlk-* or *kek-* notes. Another duet consists of ♂ giving shorter whistles, such as a sudden hollow *co* or *Yo*, followed by a rapid *hohoho* or *YoYoYo*, also double *YoYo*, to which ♀ answers with strident clicks. A further duet consists of a soft tremulous *keow* by ♂, sometimes followed by low churring *cha-cha* or *chee-uu-graa* notes from ♀. The ♂ may initiate duets with sharp *Tzik-Tzik* notes. Same-note croak duets without clicking appear to be used in territorial threat between neighbours, as well as when the nest is threatened. A nasal twanging *tzaanana-tzaanana, tszowarrr* or *tzowarr* (*brauni*) like a releasing spring, is believed to be made during territorial threat and courtship, as in other members of the genus. Alarm signalled by short harsh repetitive *Ki-Ki-Ki-Ki-, Tik-Tik-* or *tut-tut-* sounds. Contact maintained with duets. Begging calls unknown. Duetting structure and some low notes similar to Tropical Boubou and Swamp Boubou[22, 34, 290, 294, 336, 456, 500, 504, 530, 631, 717, 754, 908]. Sonagram[530, 717].

BREEDING BIOLOGY Little known. Monogamous and territorial at densities of 2–3 pairs/10 ha (Gabon)[294]. **Season** Eastern population: Jan–Apr, Nov–Dec (Sudan)[242]; Jun–Jul (East Africa)[293, 336]; Apr–Jul (NE Zaïre)[22]. Western population: Sep–Oct, juvenile in Apr (Nigeria)[37]; Jul–Oct (Cameroon)[336, 338, 646]; Apr, Jul, May–Jun to Dec in S (Zaïre)[290, 688]; Sep–Nov, Dec, Feb (NE Gabon)[294]; Mar (*brauni*)(Angola)[7]. **Displays** Unknown. **Nest** Role of sexes unknown. In nominate race a shallow, flimsy, loosely built cup made of dried weed stems, grass interlaced with creeper fibres and rootlets, lined with fine rootlets. Usually placed 1.8–2.5 m above the ground in fork of dense bush or low tree and well concealed[294, 338, 646]. **Eggs** Usually 2 (1–2), laid at 24 hour intervals (n=3). Colour variable, from pale-blue, pale greenish-blue to creamy-buff with reddish-brown, yellow-umber or bluish-grey markings distributed evenly or confined to large end. ***Size*** 22–27 x 16–19 mm (n=9) (Cameroon)[37, 290, 646]. **Incubation** In nominate race by both sexes, sometimes by ♀ only. Period at least 15 days[34, 294]. **Nestling** Appearance unknown. Attended by both sexes. Fledge after 15 days[294]. No further breeding information.

MEASUREMENTS and WEIGHTS *L. l. luehderi* ♂ (8) wing 91–95, ♀ (6) 87–90, ♂♀? (13) tail 83–90, bill 20–23, tarsus 31–33 (West Africa)[34]; ♂ (5) wing 85–89 (87.0), tail 76–82 (78.4), bill (to skull) 23.5–25.5 (24.4), tarsus 30–32 (31.2); ♀ (6) wing 84–87 (86.0), tail 74–80 (76.5), bill (to skull) 23.5–25 (23.9), tarsus 27.5–30 (28.7) (Zaïre)[500]; *amboimensis* wing 90; *brauni* wing 92–93[337]. **Weight** *luehderi* ♂(3) 52–55 g (54.0) (Cameroon)[478]; ♂♀? (37) 36–50 g (43.1) (East Africa)[509]. For additional data see[764, 765].

57 RED-NAPED BUSH-SHRIKE *Laniarius ruficeps* Plate 23

FIELD IDENTIFICATION Medium-sized (18–19 cm), pied black, white and grey bush-shrike with a striking reddish-orange crown, black face-mask and narrow white eyebrow. Wings black with white wing-stripe, tail black with white outer feathers. Underparts whitish, tinged pink or rufous-brown. Sexes slightly different; ♂ back greyish-black, ♀ olive-grey. Young olive-grey above, dull white below. White in wing conspicuous in flight. More often heard than seen; gives loud whistles and harsh notes in duet. Usually in pairs; skulking and shy. Resident in arid thornbush in NE Africa from Eritrea, Somalia, Ethiopia and E Kenya. ***Flight characteristics***: Heavy and short; wings rounded; white outer tail feathers and wing-stripe conspicuous in flight.

COMPARISONS Adults distinctive with reddish crown. Smaller than other black and white boubous. Tropical Boubou *Laniarius aethiopicus* has glossy black upperparts. Both species may show pinkish-white underparts, but are ecologically segregated with Tropical occurring in less arid habitats.

DESCRIPTION **ADULT** Sexes similar, except for colour of back. ***Head*** White eyebrow extends above eye to sides of neck. Forehead shiny black (extent variable) extending to front of crown in nominate race, or onto crown to behind eye in *rufinuchalis*; crown and nape orange- to rufous-red. Lores black, extending through and below eye to ear-coverts and shoulder. ***Back*** Scapulars black with white under feathers giving a spotted appearance; mantle to lower back grey to greyish-black; rump spotted black and white, feathers fluffy; uppertail-coverts black. ***Wings*** Brownish-black with white stripe formed by covert tips and edging of two secondary feathers. ***Tail*** Black with white tips except central pair, and white edges to outer feathers. ***Underparts*** Chin and throat white; breast and flanks whitish or cream tinged pink (nominate) or buffy-rufous (*rufinuchalis* and *kismayensis*); belly white (nominate) or buffy. ***Bare parts*** Bill black; palate unknown; legs dusky-grey; eye brown. **ADULT ♀** Similar to ♂, but back more olive-grey. **JUVENILE** Head: Crown, nape and mantle dull greyish olive-brown, rather mottled. Face dull greyish-black with dirty white eyebrow. Scapulars and rump mottled white with olive-brown edges. Wings olive-brown with buffy edges. Wing-stripe indistinct buffy-white. Tail: Greyish-olive, outer two pairs broadly tipped and edged tawny. Underparts: Brownish-grey tinged buff, paler on centre of belly and throat. Bare parts: Bill horn-brown, legs grey-brown, eye brown[500, 618, 631]. **IMMATURE** Crown mottled with blackish, nape becomes dull reddish; face-mask to ear-coverts become dull blackish. Wing and tail become blacker than juvenile. Underparts dull white to buffy; *rufinuchalis* more buffy rufous-brown below. Bare parts: Bill grey-brown. For additional details on development of adult plumage see[618].

GEOGRAPHICAL VARIATION Three races, varying mainly in extent of black on forehead and the colour of back and underparts. Race *rufinuchalis* (Ethiopia, central Somalia, central and N Kenya) has most extensive amount of black on forehead and rufous underparts; nominate *ruficeps* (NW Somalia, Eritrea) has less black on forehead and whitish underparts; *kismayensis* (NE Kenya, coastal SE Somalia) considered by some authors to lack black forehead, while others regard it to be similar to *rufinuchalis*, but with a paler grey mantle, also described as having less orange-red on crown and more black[3, 33, 336, 500, 631].

MOULT Unknown.

RANGE, HABITAT and STATUS Breeding range E and S Ethiopia, Eritrea, NW, central and SE Somalia, and E and SE Kenya. **Habitat** Dry arid and semi-arid areas below 1000 m; favours denser bushland and woodland, thickets and dense *Acacia* thornscrub[33, 292, 318, 325, 431, 631]. **Status** Uncommon to locally common resident. **Conservation status** Unknown, probably not threatened.

MOVEMENTS Possibly local seasonal movements in Kenya and Somalia[33, 318].

SOCIAL ORGANISATION and GENERAL BEHAVIOUR Little known. Solitary or in pairs; a shy, secretive and skulking species of dense thorn thickets, usually on or near the ground, occasionally out exposed. More often heard than seen, sometimes calling from top of bush in early morning[33, 336, 631, 670]. **Foraging behaviour** Feeds mainly on ground or low in bushes[336]. **Food** Insects[336].

SOUNDS Little known. Repertoire varied, consisting of loud whistles and harsh crow-like, creaking, chuckling and an early unconfirmed report of distinctive whip-lash or 'whip-crack' sounds in duet. Duets like other members of the genus, except an early account suggests that ♂ 'growls', while the ♀ notes are more liquid and described at that time as *terra-kuid*. This is opposite to all other members in the genus *Laniarius* and requires confirmation. It was probably assumed that the ♂ calls first, but recordings suggest that either sex may intitiate duets. These take the form of a short low-pitched whistle followed immediately by a descending series of loud harsh clicking or ticking sounds, described as *ho-TicTicTicTicTic* or *ho-KKKKKKK* and reminiscent of clicking in puffbacks *Dryoscopus*. Also makes a repeated low-pitched guttural crow-like snore *gwaaar* or *grrrra*, which is also combined in duet, *grrrra-KKKKKKK*, the number of clicks being variable. During solo calling, has low-pitched, repeated *kwoi kwoi kwoi...* or longer *whooi-whooi...* and *cheo-oo* whistles. Alarm appears to be signalled with loud bursts of clicking *TiK-TiKKKKK* or *KKKKK...KKK-* and repeated harsh scolding *kwerrr-kwerrr* sounds. The report of whip-lash calls suggests a possible relationship to the crimson gonoleks[2, 336, 500, 530, 631, 760].

BREEDING BIOLOGY Little known. Apparently monogamous and territorial. **Season** May in Somalia, Ethiopia and Kenya[292, 318, 325, 859]. **Displays** Unknown. Fluffy rump feathers suggestive of similar fluffed-out rump displays characteristic of the genus. **Nest** Role of sexes unknown. A slender dove-like structure, consisting of twigs, sticks, rootlets and grass stems, placed in low bush or tree, up to 1.5 m above the ground, usually in the centre of dense *Acacia* thorn tree[2, 33]. **Eggs** 2–3. Greenish-white, dirty green or pale blue-green ground colour, streaked and spotted with red-brown, lilac and pale greys, which form a zone around the large end. ***Size*** 20.5–22.0 x 15.5–16.0 mm (n=4)[2, 33]. No further breeding information.

MEASUREMENTS and WEIGHTS Races combined ♂♀? (12) wing 68–83 (76.2), tail 69–86 (77.2), bill (to skull) 19.2–24 (21.7), tarsus 25–30 (27.8)[500]. **Weight** Race unknown ♂♀? (2) 29.2–33.4 g[509].

58 BULO BURTI BOUBOU (Bulo Burti Bush-shrike)

Laniarius liberatus **Plate 23**

FIELD IDENTIFICATION Medium-sized (*c*.17–18 cm) black, white and yellowish bush-shrike with black face-mask and long broad yellowish eyebrow and spotted rear crown. Back, tail and wings black with white wing-stripe. Species described on basis of single unsexed individual. Skulking, remains low or on ground. Calls boubou-like: fluted double whistles and harsh notes. Habitat preference uncertain: originally found in riverine *Acacia* thicket at Bulo Burti in central Somalia. ***Flight characteristics***: Flies low between bushes; wings rounded; white wing-stripe probably conspicuous in flight.

COMPARISONS General patterning similar to Red-naped Bush-shrike *Laniarius ruficeps*, but has yellow (not red) on rear crown, and yellow and white (not white) underparts. Also superficially resembles Tropical Boubou *L. aethiopicus*, but Bulo Burti Boubou differs in facial and underpart coloration, in addition to having a markedly deeper bill than the Tropical Boubou[542].

DESCRIPTION **ADULT** Described from single individual of unknown sex. ***Head*** Crown matt-black, rear crown with pale yellow feather tips giving a mottled appearance. This area also has 6–8 bristle-like feather shafts emerging *c*.10 mm above general plumage surface; nape dark grey, occasional black feathers with dull white tips. Broad pale yellow eyebrow from bill to sides of nape, where it becomes white and squared off; matt-black face-mask (from bill through and slightly above eye to ear-coverts) and shoulder. ***Back*** Matt-black; rump with broad white spots, normally concealed when plumage is sleeked, but gives a spotted appearance when they are fluffed out during roosting. ***Wings*** Black with white wing-stripe formed from white tips on outer webs of median coverts and inner greater coverts with broad white tip to outer web. Tertials and secondaries dull brown-black with white edges on outer webs of nos. 4–6 (for wing formula see[542]). ***Tail*** Black, white tips on all except central pair. ***Underparts*** White with light yellow sides of throat, upper breast and sides of lower breast. ***Bare parts*** Bill blue-grey; palate black; legs dark grey; eye red-brown with a black rim[542, 680]. Colour photograph[932]. **JUVENILE/IMMATURE** Unknown.

GEOGRAPHICAL VARIATION Unknown as only one bird has ever been seen.

MOULT Bird completed a moult while in captivity[542].

RANGE, HABITAT and STATUS **Breeding range** Unknown. Located only at Bulo Burti, central Somalia (3°50'N, 45°33'E), but may have wandered from another locality[542]. **Habitat** Originally found in disturbed *Acacia* thicket in the grounds of a hospital. **Status** Unknown but controversial. Rare or local, and possibly on the edge of extinction. First seen in Aug 1988, held in captivity and released elsewhere in 1989, not seen since[542, 862, 863]. **Conservation status** Tsetse fly *Glossina pallidipes* eradication has resulted in an increase in livestock and farming practices, and hence extensive habitat degradation, in the Bulo Burti region. Considering only a single individual has ever been seen it is important to try and establish whether a resident population actually exists. Somalia generally is poorly known ornithologically, but the existence of a population close to Bulo Burti seem remote in view of the apparent considerable bird-watching and mistnetting conducted in the area. This suggests that the specimen was a vagrant, and that populations should possibly be sought further afield. Red Data Book species considered Critical[479, 542], but see Appendix A (p. 379).

MOVEMENTS Unknown, but it is thought that the single bird was a wandering or displaced individual.

SOCIAL ORGANISATION and GENERAL BEHAVIOUR Unknown. Its behaviour is typically boubou-like, remaining in dense cover. Flights low and brief. **Foraging behaviour** Remained in dense vegetation, generally keeping below *c.*3 m above ground. Foraged low down, or on the ground, hopped about in search of food[542]. **Food** In captivity fed on insects and small vertebrates, including Orthoptera (crickets), Dictyoptera (cockroaches), geckos and lizards[542], but see Appendix A (p. 379).

SOUNDS Generally silent. Uttered low harsh *churr* when flying to and from roost. While feeding gave single or repeated low *chack-* warning or alarm calls. In captivity, frequently uttered a high-pitched disyllabic *poo-eeh* or *tuwe....tuwe-* whistle repeatedly. Recordings of this call are reminiscent of the off-key notes produced by immatures in this genus. Some authors consider this to be a contact call. This call was not heard in the wild. The two low-pitch calls are similar to Slate-coloured Boubou *L. funebris*. Recordings sound like a harsh *TikTikTikTik-*[500, 542, 680]. Sonagram[680].

BREEDING BEHAVIOUR Unknown.

MEASUREMENTS and WEIGHTS *L. liberatus* Adult (1 unsexed), wing 89–92 (pre-and post moult), bill 20.5, tarsus 34[542]. Apparently tail length and weight unrecorded.

59 SOUTHERN BOUBOU *Laniarius ferrugineus* Plate 24

FIELD IDENTIFICATION Medium-large (21–23 cm), black and white bush-shrike with rufous flanks and belly, and bold white wing-stripe. Sexes different, ♂ black above to below the eye, ♀ dark grey. Young similar to ♀, but more buffy above and finely barred below. Solitary or in pairs; shy and skulking, more often heard than seen. Main calls are whistles and harsh sounds, usually in duet. Found at all levels, mainly low down and on ground, in variety of dense habitats from thickets, woodlands and forest edge. Widespread resident in southern Africa from SE Zimbabwe, E Botswana, South Africa and S Mozambique. ***Flight characteristics***: Short and heavy with rapid shallow wingbeats; glides between bushes; wings rounded. When excited makes 'fripping' sounds with wings.

COMPARISONS Confusion with Tropical Boubou *Laniarius aethiopicus* most likely in N edge of range. Tropical, although slightly larger, is smaller-billed, cream below (lacks rufous tinge), glossy blue-black above in both sexes with a whitish rump, and easily distinguished on sounds during duets: ♀ responds with distinctive nasal snarling or tearing *Weer-* calls (Southern ♀ has whistle-calls). Caution required in overlap zone where hybridisation recorded. Separation of juvenile Southern and Tropical Boubous difficult as plumage similar. Habitat and vocalisations helpful[205].

DESCRIPTION **ADULT ♂** ***Head*** **including sides of face and mantle** Black with slight gloss. ***Back*** **and rump** Duller grey-black with olive tinge, rump with indistinct white spotting, feathers long and fluffy. ***Wings*** Black with white wing-stripe formed by inner 3 secondaries and median and greater secondary coverts. ***Tail*** Black. ***Underparts*** Variable; throat and breast cream to buffy-white, flanks rich rufous to reddish-brown buff. ***Bare parts*** Bill and palate black; legs bluish-grey; eye brown to dark brown. **ADULT ♀ *Head,* sides of face and back** Dark grey. ***Tail* and wings** Dull black. Wing-stripe as in ♂. ***Underparts*** Variable, throat and breast buffier than ♂; lower belly and flanks rufous to brownish-buff. ***Bare parts*** Like ♂. **JUVENILE** Brownish-black upperparts tipped with tawny or buffy-brown, giving a mottled appearance. Wing-stripe buffy-white, wing-coverts tipped buffy. Underparts pale with fine rufous-brown barring. Bill dark greyish-brown. **IMMATURE** Similar to adult ♀ but duller; may show slight barring on breast; wing-coverts tipped buff and wing-stripe dirty white, coverts tipped buffy-rufous.

GEOGRAPHICAL VARIATION At least 6 races with variations in body size, coloration of upperparts, extent of rufous colour below and degree of sexual dimorphism. Some variation is restricted only to ♀♀. Nominate and most southerly race *ferrugineus* (SW South Africa from W Cape to Humansdorp) is dark above and below. East of this (*natalensis*, SE South Africa) there is a lightening of the upperparts in ♀♀, and rufous in both sexes, the rufous underparts of some ♂♂ reaching their palest in this race. Within the range of this race occurs *pondoensis* (Pondoland, SE South Africa), a small enclave of dark-coloured birds, underparts completely dark buffy-rufous. Race *tongensis* (E South Africa, S Mozambique) is similar to, but smaller than *natalensis*. Further N the rufous underparts darken. The smallest population occurs still further N, *savensis* (Mozambique-Zimbabwe border, Sul do Save, between Lundi and Limpopo rivers). Finally *transvaalensis* (E to NE South Africa and Swaziland) shows the least sexual dimorphism. Calls show much geographical variation in number of notes, tonal quality of whistles and duet sequences[3, 26, 30, 109, 122, 138, 205, 500, 538, 548].

MOULT Post-breeding moult of flight feathers and body moult recorded at beginning of austral winter (May–Jun)[205, 500].

RANGE, HABITAT and STATUS Breeding range SE Zimbabwe, E Botswana, S, SE and E South Africa, Swaziland and Sul do Save region of Mozambique. Overlaps with Tropical Boubou in NE. **Habitat** Sea-level to high elevations of Drakensberg Mts. A species of dense bushy tangles in a wide range of woodland types, also coastal and riverine bush, including mangroves, scrub thickets, forest patches and forest edge, gardens and exotic plantations. In drier habitats confined to thickets along watercourses[26, 30, 48, 205, 320, 431, 550, 639, 807, 810, 953]. **Status** Common resident. **Conservation status** Not threatened. Adapts well to human habitation in suitably dense habitats. Held in captivity[655, 974].

MOVEMENTS Sedentary with small local movements. One bird known to have remained in same territory for 11 years. The furthest a ringed bird has moved is 15 km[122, 205, 639].

SOCIAL ORGANISATION and GENERAL BEHAVIOUR Solitary or in pairs; a shy and secretive, skulking species, usually in dense vegetation. Highly vocal, more often heard than seen; duetting common. Calls in upright stance, bobs head and makes a shallow bow while calling. Creeps through vegetation in crouched horizontal posture. Advertises and defends a territory of *c*.3 ha with repeated loud ringing whistles throughout the year, with a peak before breeding. Usually given from an elevated perch, sometimes exposed. ♀ may join in duet with repeated higher-pitched whistles. During territorial threat, ♂♂ counter-sing with repeated whistles and nasal metallic sounds, accompanied with tail-fanning and fluffed-out spotted black-and-white rump feathers. This call often given in flight, while descending with slow exaggerated wingbeats and head held up. Bows and sways body from side to side. This display is also given during courtship. Roosts in dense tangles, giving alarm ticks before settling. Scratches indirectly[122, 205]. **Foraging behaviour** Creeps about gleaning prey from trunks, branches and leaves; also hops on ground, often flicking debris aside with bill like a thrush. Large prey held down with foot, some prey wedged for stripping, impaled prey recorded in captivity. Known to drink water[43, 205, 872]. **Food** Arthropods, mainly insects and their larvae, and small vertebrates. Insects include Coleoptera (beetles), Orthoptera (grasshoppers), and Hymenoptera (bees, wiping sting off before swallowing). Also regularly feeds on small fruits, grain and porridge in urban habitats. Other prey includes snails, birds eggs, small vertebrates such as nestlings, fledglings and reptiles[48, 205, 549, 872].

SOUNDS Repertoire consists of repeated fluted whistles and harsh sounds, usually in duet, which show individual and geographical variation. Main territorial and advertising calls are loud ringing whistles, usually given in antiphonal duet. Duets may be initiated by either sex and many calls appear to be sex-specific with a number of song types. In territorial interactions, ♂ gives loud repeated ringing *houu-houu-*, or slightly higher-pitched *houue* whistles. ♀ respond in duet with loud higher-pitched *huwee* or double *huwehuwe* whistles. During aggressive interactions and courtship gives repeated *hou-* or *boo-* whistles and snarling, nasal, clashing, metallic-sounding *Tchzananan-tchanana* or *bizzykizzkizz* calls, with tail fanned and rump fluffed out. Flies about excitedly making 'fripping' sounds with the wings. ♀ usually accompanies in duet with *huwehuwe* whistles and explosive harsh scolding *Kzaak-Kzaak*, *Chak-Chak-* and *skhaaa* calls. Alarm a repeated harsh *Tik-*, *Tuk-* or *Tschok-*, rattling *KriKriKri-*, guttural *cha-aa-aa* and scolding notes similar to those used in threat. *Tik-* notes also given prior to roosting and while plundering nests. Another call of unknown function is a repeated high-pitched *squee-squee-squee-Tik-Tik-Tik* which may be responded to by a similar call from mate. Contact maintained with duetting, and with often-heard lower-pitched *hou-hou-*, *bou-*, *boo-boo-* or *bobobo* whistles (origin of Boubou), repeated a number of times by ♂, usually responded to by ♀ with *huhuwee, hoowhee, wheeo,* with variations. Chicks beg with high-pitched *pseep* sounds[48, 122, 205, 500, 872]. Sonagram[43, 48, 136].

BREEDING BIOLOGY Monogamous and territorial. An austral summer breeder in response to rain. Secretive but aggressive, chases other birds and plundering nests in its territory. Duetting reaches a peak prior to egg-laying. Breeding is attempted in first year, and possibly attempts two broods in a season[205]. **Season** Austral summer breeder: Aug–Feb (South Africa)[48, 320, 639]; Oct–Dec (Mozambique)[26]. **Displays *Courtship*** ♂ chases ♀, both hopping in tandem through branches, accompanied by 'wing-fripping' in flight. ♂ performs a descending display-flight with slow exaggerated wingbeats, head held up and white-spotted rump feathers fluffed out. This is accompanied by a snarling nasal metallic call (see Sounds) similar to territorial threat. Courtship-feeding apparently does not occur[205]. **Nest** Built by both sexes, mainly by ♀. A flimsy, shallow, loosely built structure similar to dove's nest, or a more substantial shallow bowl built of roots, twigs and grass, crudely woven together and bonded lightly with spider web; may also have a lining of spider web. Usually placed in a creeper or dense bush *c.*2 m (0.25–8.0, n=80) above the ground, and well hidden, rarely in exposed leafless fork. ***Size*** OD/ID 127–135 mm, cup depth 15–25 mm, height 28–50 mm. Completed in about 6 days[6, 205, 500]. **Eggs** Usually 2 (2–3, n=77). Pale greenish-white, finely speckled with shades of brown and grey forming a ring around the large end. ***Size*** 22–27.4 x 16–19.2 mm (24.6 x 18.1, n=90)[19, 48]. **Incubation** By both sexes. Nest relief signalled by calls from both sexes. Period 16–17 days (n=1)[27, 48, 205, 331]. **Nestling** Hatch blind, naked and probably have mouth spots. Back blackish, rest orange-red. For development of nestlings see[872]. Attended by both sexes. Nestlings beg with high-pitched *pseep-*. Fledge after *c.*16 days (n=1). Fledglings beg with same call, remain dependent for *c.*8 weeks. At about 13 weeks either sex can make both ♂ and ♀ calls. Remain with parents for about 11 weeks[42, 48, 205, 331, 354]. **Predation and longevity** Ringed bird in same territory for 11 years[122]. **Brood parasite** 2.1% of nests parasitised by Black Cuckoo *Cuculus clamosus* and a single record of two fledgling cuckoos being fed. Mobs this species and Klaas's Cuckoo *Chrysococcyx klaas*. Possibly an accidental host of Jacobin Cuckoo *Oxylophus jacobinus*[94, 872].

MEASUREMENTS and WEIGHTS *L. f. ferrugeneus* ♂ (13) wing 92–99.5 (97.9), (14) tail 92.3–100 (96.4), ♀ (11) wing 90.5–99 (94.0), (8) tail 90–97.2 (93.2)[138]. *transvaalensis* ♂ (9) wing 95–101 (99.9), ♀ (10) 92–97 (94.5), ♂♀? (33) tail 85.9–102.5 (93), ♂♀? (11) bill (to skull) 24.5–27.5 (25.7), ♂♀? (11) tarsus 32–35.2 (33.8)[48, 138, 500]; *savensis* ♂ (1) wing 88, tail 88, tarsus 32, bill 25; ♀ (1) wing 87, tail 86, tarsus 31, bill 23[539]; ♀ (1) wing 88, tail 82[30, 538]. **Weight** *ferrugineus* and *natalensis* ♂ (11) 53–68.8 g (60.2), ♀ (7) 54.1–61.9 g (57.5), S Mozambique *savensis* ♂ (3) 44.2–53.2 g (50.0), ♀ (5) 42.1–51 g (44.7)[48]. For additional data see[109, 205]

60 TROPICAL BOUBOU (Bell Shrike)
Laniarius aethiopicus **Plate 24**

FIELD IDENTIFICATION Large (23–25 cm), glossy black and white bush-shrike with conspicuous white wing-stripe (variable in extent, absent in restricted East African coastal population, which also has an all-black morph). Above glossy blue-black, below whitish with faint pinkish or buffy tinge. Sexes similar. Young duller and browner above with fine barring below. White-spotted rump conspicuous in display. More often heard than seen; duets with loud ringing whistles and harsh snarling or tearing sounds. Solitary, or in pairs; shy and skulking. Found in mid- to lower levels and on ground in a variety of dense habitats, from thickets and woodlands to forest edge. Widespread resident throughout sub-Saharan Africa to N South Africa. ***Flight characteristics***: Short and heavy with rapid shallow wingbeats. Glides from upper branches to base cover of undergrowth, white spotted rump conspicuous in flight (lacking in all-black morph); wings rounded. When excited makes 'fripping' sounds with wings in flight.

COMPARISONS Southern and W populations most similar to Swamp Boubou *Laniarius bicolor* from which it is identified with difficulty. Tropical Boubou is smaller and has cream to pinkish tinge below. Swamp Boubou has pure white underparts and is usually found in moister habitats, and has a shorter wing-stripe in West African populations. Where they occur together they are generally ecologically segregated, Tropical Boubou in the drier habitat fringing riverine vegetation. More easily identified on ♀ calls during duets. Tropical ♀ responds to ♂ whistle with a nasal snarling or tearing sound (Swamp ♀ responds with a harsh staccato ratchet-like call). A possible hybrid zone occurs in W Angola where some Tropical Boubous show very white underparts. S populations may be confused with smaller Southern Boubou *L. ferrugineus*, which usually has a rufous tinge (variable) on flanks and ♀ is dark grey above, lacking glossy black of ♂. Presence of hybrids in overlap zone makes positive identification difficult in some areas. In West Africa may be confused with Turat's Boubou *L. turatii*, which is much smaller, lacks white on wing and has a darker pinkish tinge below. Vocally distinct (♀ responds with staccato ratchet-like call, rather similar to

Swamp Boubou). In coastal East Africa the all-black morph may be confused with smaller Slate-coloured Boubou *L. funebris*, which is bluish-slate, not glossy black. This species is known to duet with Tropical Boubou. Puffbacks, while superficially resembling boubous, are arboreal feeders and much smaller. Separation of young difficult as plumage similar, except for presence or absence of wing-stripe. Habitat preference and vocalisations helpful[108, 180, 205, 504, 530, 550, 631].

DESCRIPTION **ADULT** Sexes similar. ***Head, back and tail*** Slightly glossy blue-black, including sides of face; lower back and rump with concealed white spots, feathers long and fluffy; tail sometimes with white-tipped outer feathers. ***Wings*** Slightly glossy blue-black with variable amount of white on median and secondary coverts and inner edge of secondaries. Lacking in some races (see Geographical Variation). ***Underparts*** White with variable amount of pinkish or pinkish-buff tinge on breast and flanks. Note all-black form (see below). ***Bare parts*** Bill and palate black; legs bluish-grey; eye dark reddish-brown. **Abnormal plumage** An all-black morph of *sublacteus* has bluish-black upperparts, rump black with no concealed white spots, and tail with no white tips on outer tail feathers, in contrast to normal *sublacteus*; underparts black, bluish-black on throat and breast. **JUVENILE** Dark dull head and upperparts strongly tipped with yellowish-ochre or tawny, giving mottled appearance; ear-coverts and eyebrow brownish; lower back and rump broadly barred with yellowish-ochre or tawny; wing-stripe white to dirty white, except tertials and coverts tipped tawny; underparts dull white with some dusky barring, particularly on flanks (except *sublacteus*); undertail-coverts buff. Bill greyish-brown, paler on lower mandible. **IMMATURE** Yellowish-ochre tips to feathers on upperparts are lost except on wing-coverts, wing-stripe dull white; underparts remain dull without pinkish tinge, flanks buffy to pale brown. Young of some races may have white tips to outer tail feathers[25, 238]. See Geographical Variation. Birds remain with parents till about the time of this plumage change[46] (see Breeding).

GEOGRAPHICAL VARIATION At least 7 races. Variation mainly in body size, amount of white forming wing-stripe and in tail, amount of pink or buffy pink on underparts, and in vocalisations. Eye colour also variable. One race has a completely black morph. Variation in wing-stripe ranges from white on median and greater coverts and edges of inner secondaries in widespread *major* (Sierra Leone to Sudan, and S Congo basin, Angola). Race *aethiopicus* (Ethiopia, Somalia, N Kenya) similar but with less white on secondaries; *ambiguus* (highlands of Kenya, NE Tanzania) and small *erlangeri* (S Somalia) have only median coverts white, and *sublacteus* (coastal E Kenya, Zanzibar) has very little to no white in wing; *major*, *ambiguus* and *sublacteus* may also show white-tipped outer tail feathers; *sublacteus* also has a completely black morph which occurs in coastal E African (Tana River mouth, Lamu Island, Manda Island and lower Juba River). Northern populations of *major* have more intense pinkish underparts, similar to *aethiopicus*, but birds in S central Zaïre and NW Angola are markedly whiter. This race merges with smaller and buffier S populations represented by *mossambicus* (S Zaïre, E Zambia, Mozambique), with variable pale pinkish-buff underparts. Southernmost population *limpopoensis* (S Zimbabwe, N South Africa, W Mozambique) buffier below. A hybrid zone exists between this race and the Southern Boubou in Limpopo Valley. Vocalisations of the Tropical Boubou show marked geographical variation in tonal quality and phrases used in duet sequences. NE populations tend to have more resonant whistles and to use them more frequently. They also use more same-note duet sequences than S birds. Croaking notes are apparently only found in S birds, while rattling notes (resembling Swamp Boubou) apparently only occur in NE populations[3, 31, 109, 205, 299, 500, 501, 530, 556, 558, 631].

MOULT Complete post-breeding moult recorded in S population[205, 500].

RANGE, HABITAT and STATUS **Breeding range** Widespread in Africa, avoiding arid and dense forest regions. In W from as far N as Senegal, where a vagrant, replaced in far W by Turat's Boubou. Mainly S of 10°N, from Liberia, Ivory Coast, Ghana, Togo, Benin, Cameroon, Nigeria, Chad, Central African Republic, Equatorial Guinea (requires confirmation), Zaïre, Rwanda, Burundi, Sudan, Ethiopia, Eritrea, Djibouti, Somalia, Uganda, Kenya, Tanzania, Malawi, Mozambique, as far south as N South Africa along Limpopo River. Throughout most of central regions except equatorial rain forests. Absent from W coast from about 5°N where replaced by Swamp Boubou, but found inland in this region to as far S as N Namibia, joining up with central and E populations through Angola, S Zaïre, Zambia, Botswana, Zimbabwe, South Africa. Replaced in S by Southern Boubou (*L. ferrugineus*). Bioko record rejected[431]. **Habitat** Requires thick cover from highland forests, including juniper forests and bracken-briar to lowland coastal scrub. Found on edge of primary, gallery and riverine forest. Also in savanna woodland, miombo *Brachystegia*, thickets and gardens up to *c*.3000 m (Kenya). In more arid areas restricted to riverine vegetation[7, 21, 26, 30, 37, 46, 48, 119, 180, 207, 291, 234, 242, 292, 318, 325, 337, 402, 431, 481, 482, 504, 631, 807, 873, 848, 859, 907, 933]. **Status** Resident and widespread, not uncommon to locally common. Rare or overlooked in Liberia. Occurrence in Gambia requires confirmation[431, 858]. **Conservation status** Not threatened; adapts well to human habitation[1071].

MOVEMENTS Local seasonal movements recorded in Kenya, and possibly some altitudinal movements in Ethiopia[237, 325].

SOCIAL ORGANISATION and GENERAL BEHAVIOUR Solitary or in pairs; secretive and shy, occasionally confiding, skulking in dense cover, usually within a few metres of or on the ground, occasionally in canopy. Sometimes gathers in loose noisy groups, possibly similar to the 'parliaments' described for some batises. More often heard than seen; fluted ringing whistles and duetting common. Advertises and defends a territory of *c.*1–3 ha, and up to 8 ha in non-breeding season, with repeated fluted whistles and harsh calls in duet. Call from elevated position, sometimes exposed, and while calling bobs head and bows the body. During territorial threat gives nasal metallic snarl or twanging sound accompanied by a descending flight with slow exaggerated wingbeats, head held up and rump feathers fluffed out exposing white spots. This display is also used in courtship. Roosts in dense bush and entanglements. Scratches indirectly and pairs sometimes allopreen each other[5, 46, 205, 348, 530, 631]. **Foraging behaviour** Usually forages on ground or lower levels, occasionally in canopy; hops and creeps about searching for food, also gleans from trunks, branches and foliage. On the ground stands with legs at full length, tail slightly raised above wing tips, and body feathers drawn close. Frequently robs birds' nests. Large prey held down with foot. Recorded wedging prey as well as impaling prey in captivity[43, 46, 205, 530]. **Food** Arthropods, mainly insects and their larvae, and small vertebrates. Insects include Isoptera (termites), Hymenoptera (*Dorylus* ants), Coleoptera (beetles), Lepidoptera (moths and caterpillars), Orthoptera (grasshoppers) and Mantodea (mantises). Also takes eggs. Vertebrates include nestlings, rodents, reptiles (snakes, lizards including geckos) and amphibians. Occasionally small fruits and snails[46, 48, 205, 455, 500, 871, 1062].

SOUNDS Repertoire consists of repeated low or higher-pitched whistles, longer low resonant drawn-out whistles, and harsh tearing, snarling and croaking sounds, usually in antiphonal duet. Duets consisting of 2–3 notes are most common, those with 5–8 notes are less common; occasionally up to 14 notes. Most duets last from 0.5–3 sec and are made up of a combination of notes, such as short-short whistles, long-short whistles, croak-whistles, snarl-whistles, snarl-snarl or croak-snarl combinations. Although either sex may start or end a duet, it appears that ♂♂ initiate most. Calls are probably sex-specific, although a number appear to be shared. Individuals who have lost a mate are capable of producing a complete duet sequence alone. The ♂ is thought to give short and long low-pitched whistles and harsh croaking sounds, while ♀ gives higher-pitched whistles, harsh tearing and rattling sounds. In addition there is extensive geographical variation in tone of fluted whistles and in predominant duet patterns, with a general trend from mainly whistles in the N to mainly harsh croaks and snarls in the S. Flute-like whistles range from short single low-pitch *bou* or *hou* notes to double *boubou* (origin of Boubou name) or longer series, like rapid bubbling or quavering *bobobobo* notes. Other whistles are longer, louder and far-carrying, with a resonant, ringing, bell-like quality. They vary from *hoou* or *hooo* to longer *hoooooooo* notes. Harsh notes vary from tearing *Weeer* or *krzzzz* notes to croaking or low-pitched nasal snoring *Haaw* and chattering (rattling) *Ke-Ke-Ke-* sounds. ♂ also produces metallic hissing or twanging *Tchanananana* or *SCHRANG! SCHRANG!* sounds in territorial threat and courtship. Typical duets sound like *hoho-u-ho hoou-Weeer-hoou, hoo-hii-hoo, hoooooo-ho-ho, houhou-Weeer, bobobobo-Weeer, haw-Weeer-haw, Weeer-Weeer* and others. ♀ responds with 1–3 snarling *Weeer-* notes. ♂ also makes a repeated buzzing *Ho-Kzzz* in intense interactions. Alarm signalled with single or repeated harsh chattering *Ke-Ke-Ke-, Chuk-, Tuk-Tuk, teuch-, zzweo, krrrr* or explosive *Tchak* notes. Repeated *Tuk-* notes given prior to roosting. Loud 'wing-fripping' accompanies many intense interactions. Territorial countersinging (duetting) common as well as trio 'duetting', particularly when young birds are learning. Contact is maintained by lower-pitched, softer *bou* notes and general duetting. Nestlings beg with thin high-pitched repeated *pseep-* or *tseep-* calls[5, 46, 48, 106, 110, 205, 229, 299, 419, 455, 500, 501, 504, 527, 631]. For development of calls see[354, 530]. Sonagram[43, 48, 106, 530].

BREEDING BIOLOGY Monogamous and territorial. Some duets repeated monotonously up to 75 times. Nest relief usually signalled by either incoming bird or sitting bird, once it has left the nest. Density varies with habitat, recorded at 1 bird/ha (N Botswana) to *c.*34 birds/km² (NE South Africa)[5, 46, 205, 530, 639, 1071]. **Season** North Africa S of Sahara: Jun–Sep (Sudan)[242]; Apr–Jun (Somalia and Ethiopia)[33, 859]; West Africa: Jun, ♀ sitting Feb–Mar (Nigeria)[37, 328]; Feb–May, Sep–Dec (Zaïre)[290, 338]; enlarged gonads Aug–Sep (Angola)[7]; all year (East Africa)[293]; Sep–Apr (Tanzania)[336, 737, 832]; Dec–Apr (Mozambique)[5, 26, 336]; southern Africa: Dec–Apr Sep–Apr, mainly Oct–Dec (Zambia, Zimbabwe, Malawi, South Africa)[48, 119, 291, 320, 359, 639]; egg-laying Nov (Botswana)[807]. **Displays *Courtship*** ♂ chases ♀, pair hopping rapidly in tandem through branches. ♂ gives croaking *haw* call (southern Africa), preceded by shallow head-bob and accompanied by body-bowing with neck extended. ♂ also makes short flights which include 'wing-fripping' and glides with rump feathers exposed. Display climaxes with repeated metallic twanging *schrang-* or *Tchananana-* calls sometimes followed by loud *kit-tuu-iii* (East Africa), wings drooped, tail fanned and rump feathers raised. Also makes descending flight with slow exaggerated wingbeats and white-spotted rump feathers exposed. ♂ gives long-drawn-out *hoooooooooo* whistle, to which ♀ usually responds in duet. Courtship-feeding apparently does not occur[46, 205, 530, 631]. **Nest** Both sexes construct nest, mainly by ♀. A shallow, thin-walled, transparent bowl, built of twigs, tendrils and rootlets, occasionally some grass or bark strips worked in, bound lightly with spider web and sometimes lined with finer material. Usually placed *c.*3 m (0.5–15.0 m, n=130) above the ground, in climbing plant, parasitic growth or lateral fork on horizontal branch, relatively exposed, and often in an isolated bush. ***Size*** OD 100–200 mm, ID 76–85 mm, cup depth 20–50 mm, height 47–64 mm. Known to pull old nest to pieces[8, 46,

[205, 500, 871]. **Eggs** Usually 3 (2–3, n=7). Bluish-green to greenish-buff, spotted brown and lilac. ***Size*** 22.3–26.8 x 16.7–19.1 mm (25.0 x 18.3, n=19) (southern Africa)[19, 48]. For additional information see[15, 33, 46]. **Incubation** By both sexes, ♀ most. Nest relief initiated with whistled *hou* by ♂ or snarl by ♀ (southern Africa). Give low alarm *Tuk-* notes on approaching nest. Period 15 days (14–16, n=2)[46, 48, 205]. **Nestling** Hatch blind, naked, pinkish-brown and apparently with mouth spots. Attended by both sexes. Beg with repeated high-pitched *pseep-* calls. Fledge after *c.*15 days (14–16, n=2). Dependency period; capable of feeding themselves by *c.*7 weeks; remain with adults for about 5 months[27, 42, 46, 48, 205, 331, 354]. **Predation and longevity** Ringed bird 9–10 years[282]. **Brood parasite.** Parasitised by Black Cuckoo *Cuculus clamosus* at level of 2.1%. Host mobs this species. Same pair often repeatedly susceptible, often in same season[94].

MEASUREMENTS and WEIGHTS Races combined ♂♀? (14) wing 89–102 (97.6), tail 90–107 (96.3), bill 20.5–23.5 (22.0), tarsus 29.5–34 (32.4) (East Africa)[237]; *limpopoensis* ♂ (25) wing 86.5–108 (98.8), ♀ (21) 89–101.5 (94.1), ♂ (22) tail 89.3–113.1 (103.9), ♀ (18) 91.1–107.3 (99.4), ♂♀? (10) bill (to skull) 25–27.8 (26.4), tarsus 32–36.5 (34.2) (southern Africa)[500]. **Weight** *ambiguus* ♂ (2) each 50 g; ♀ (3) each 50 g[768]; ♂♀? (39) 38.8–66.0 g (48.7) (Kenya)[478, 808]; *major* ♂ (8) 56–66 g (64.4); ♀ (9) 55–71 g (61.4)[319]; *mossambicus* ♂♀? (69) 37.9–56.0 g (47.1 ±4.8 g) (Mopeia, Mozambique and Nchalo, Malawi); ♂♀? (52) 42.9–61.0 g (50.0 ±4.5 g) (Zimbabwe)[561]; ♂♀? (104) 44–66 g (50.2) (southern Africa)[500]. For additional data see[48, 319, 478, 538].

61 TURAT'S BOUBOU (Turati's Boubou) *Laniarius turatii* Plate 24

FIELD IDENTIFICATION Large (23 cm) black and white bush-shrike with no white wing-stripe. Above black (with slight gloss) to below eye, below creamy-white with pale pinkish-buff tinge (not always obvious in the field) contrasting with whitish belly. Sexes similar. Young duller and browner above with faint barring below. Solitary or in pairs, shy and skulking in dense vegetation. Difficult to see and little known. More often heard than seen; duets frequently, ♂ giving ringing whistles, ♀ responding with harsh grating or rattling calls. Resident low down in dense bush and forest edge in West Africa from Guinea-Bissau to Sierra Leone. ***Flight characteristics***: Wings rounded, rump pale in flight.

COMPARISONS Overlaps with similar Tropical Boubou *Laniarius aethiopicus*, which has a white wing-stripe. Calls also similar, but those of Turat's Boubou less variable, more stereotyped. Recordings suggest they are also delivered much slower than Tropical Boubou. Habits also similar but Turat's tends to be more terrestrial than Tropical and is less likely to ascend into canopy. In overlap zone, occur in similar habitats, but tend to be segregated altitudinally, Turat's in lowlands and Tropical in highlands. Juveniles separated on basis of presence or absence of wing-stripe. Superficially resembles ♂ Sabine's Puffback *Dryoscopus sabini*, which is black and white and lacks a white wing-stripe. However, puffback is smaller with a distinctive white rump, and is an arboreal forest species[110]. See Tropical Boubou Comparisons for other similar species p.257.

DESCRIPTION ADULT Sexes similar. ***Head and back*** Black with slight gloss to below eye; rump greyish-black with large concealed white spots and tips of rump feathers whitish; feathers long and fluffy. ***Wings*** Black without wing-stripe. ***Tail*** Black. ***Underparts*** creamy-white with pinkish-buff tinge on breast and upper belly; lower belly and undertail-coverts white; thighs white. ***Bare parts*** Bill black, palate unknown; legs blue-grey; eye brown to dark brown[109]. **JUVENILE/IMMATURE** Similar to adult but duller, with dusky barring below and feathers of head and upperparts tipped buff; bill dark grey-brown[504].

GEOGRAPHICAL VARIATION Monotypic, with only slight size variation; smallest individuals occur in Sierra Leone[109].

MOULT Unknown.

RANGE, HABITAT and STATUS Breeding range Restricted to West Africa from Guinea-Bissau, Guinea and W Sierra Leone. **Habitat** Mainly lowlands with dense tangles and thickets in wooded savanna, forest regrowth and forest edge, not true forest[110, 343, 431, 479, 504]. **Status** Common resident. **Conservation status** Unknown, but due to its restricted distribution considered Near-Threatened. Occurs in captivity[343, 479, 542].

MOVEMENTS Unknown, probably sedentary.

SOCIAL ORGANISATION and GENERAL BEHAVIOUR Little known. Solitary or in pairs, a skulking species found low down in dense habitat, where difficult to observe. More often heard than seen, duets frequently[23, 110, 338]. **Foraging behaviour** Low down in undergrowth and on ground. Probably gleans from trunks and branches and hops on ground like other boubous. **Food** Unknown, probably similar to other boubous.

SOUNDS Little known. Repertoire consists of low-pitched whistles, harsh tearing and nasal twanging calls, often in duet. Calls probably sex-specific and similar to other members of genus, in which ♂ usually whistles and ♀ give harsh calls. Either sex known to initiate duets. ♂ recorded giving a slow series of drawn-out, resonant and ringing metallic *hoo, hoou–hoou-* or *whoooooo* whistles, responded to by ♀ in duet with harsh tearing *k-kchchnerr* or nasal *k-k-zzeerrr*, grating *gkrzzz* or strident clicking *K-K-K-KKK* notes. Slowly delivered duet sounds like *houu-k-k-zzeerrr-houu.* Also has loud, explosive *kek-*, often in long series, and a slowly delivered, nasal twanging *Wa-wa-zzzn-errrrr* call typical of the genus, and used in territorial threat and courtship[15, 110, 500, 501, 504, 530].

BREEDING BIOLOGY Little known. Monogamous and territorial. **Season** May (Guinea Bissau)[338]. **Displays** Unknown. **Nest** Role of sexes unknown. A flimsy structure of grass-stems and fine rootlets, one nest contained dried leaves. Placed 2 m above the ground in a fork[15, 338]. **Eggs** 2. Turquoise-blue and unmarked. ***Size*** 25 x 19 mm[15, 338, 500]. No further breeding information.

MEASUREMENTS and WEIGHTS *L. turatii* ♂♀? (9) wing 89–105 (96.0), tail 82–99 (90.2), bill (to skull) 23.5–29 (26.3), tarsus 31.5–36 (33.7)[500]. **Weight** Unknown. For additional data see[15].

62 SWAMP BOUBOU (Gabon Boubou) *Laniarius bicolor* Plate 24

FIELD IDENTIFICATION Large (23–25 cm) black and white bush-shrike with broad white wing-stripe. Above glossy bluish-black to below eye. Below pure white (diagnostic). Northern birds have less white in wing than in S. Sexes similar. Young mottled brownish-black above, finely barred dusky below. A bolder bird than other boubous, although more often heard than seen. ♂ whistles, ♀ responds in duet with harsh ratchet-like staccato calls. Solitary or in pairs, skulking low down in dense vegetation, sometimes in canopy. Resident from West Africa in savanna thickets, forest regrowth and mangroves. Further S more often associated with riverine vegetation, including reedbeds. Found from Cameroon along coast to SW Angola, inland to N Namibia, N Botswana, SW Zambia and NW Zimbabwe. ***Flight characteristics***: Sometimes quite long when flying out into reedbeds; rather heavy with rapid shallow wingbeats. White wing-stripe distinctive in flight; wings rounded. When excited makes 'fripping' sounds with wings in flight.

COMPARISONS Overlaps and is similar to Tropical Boubou *Laniarius aethiopicus*, which is cream to pinkish-cream below (pure white in Swamp Boubou). In S overlap zone, Tropical tends to have buffier underparts. Swamp is bolder and often calls in an exposed position, also slightly larger with smaller bill, and in West Africa usually slightly less white in wing, but similar to Tropical in overlap zone. Easily separated on duet call of ♀, being a harsh ratchet-like staccato *Ka-Ka-Ka-KaKKKK.* Whistle of ♂ similar to Tropical. Where both occur together they tend to be ecologically segregated. Swamp in riverine vegetation, Tropical in fringing drier thickets. Special care required in W Angola where Tropical shows very little pink below, and Swamp found in a wider range of habitats. Whistled and ratchet calls similar to Lühder's Bush-shrike *L. luehderi.* Separation of young Swamp and Tropical difficult as both are spotted buffy above and barred dusky below[109, 205, 504]. See Tropical Boubou Comparisons for other similar species p.257.

DESCRIPTION **Adult** Sexes similar. ***Head and back*** Deep blue-black with slight glossy sheen to below eye; rump with concealed white spots, feathers long and fluffy. ***Wings*** Black with pure white wing-stripe formed by white on inner secondaries (variable), greater and median coverts. ***Tail*** Black, sometimes tipped white. ***Underparts*** Pure white. ***Bare parts*** Bill and palate black; legs dark bluish-grey; eye brown to dark brown. **Juvenile** Upperparts dull black, spotted buffy to tawny on head, barred same on back and rump; below lightly barred dusky. Outer tail feathers tipped buff and the white wing-coverts blotched with greyish-brown. Bill greyish-brown[48, 79, 338, 616]. **Immature** Similar to adult but duller, coverts tipped buff, bill less black.

GEOGRAPHICAL VARIATION Three races, with variation in size and extent of white in wing. Nominate *bicolor* (Gabon–Congo, including Angola at Cabinda) has least white on edges of inner secondaries, occasionally lacking altogether, and is the smallest race. Merges with *guttatus* (Congo–W Zaïre and Angola), which shows white on 1 or 2 secondaries, rarely 3. Replaced inland in S by *sticturus* (Angola, Namibia, Botswana, Zimbabwe), the largest race with white in 3 secondaries, tail may also show white tips[3, 109, 402].

MOULT Adults recorded in post-breeding moult in Nov. Juveniles in post-juvenile moult in Nov. Young birds in Jan in first-winter (austral) plumage (Botswana)[546].

RANGE, HABITAT and STATUS **Breeding range** West Africa from coastal Cameroon, Gabon, Congo and Zaïre; southwards to Cabinda, coastal and escarpment Angola, and along major rivers of N Namibia, Botswana, SW Zambia and NW Zimbabwe. **Habitat** In West Africa found in savanna thickets, including dry thickets, coastal scrub, forest regrowth and mangroves. In thick riverine in montane valleys on Angolan escarpment. Further S in riverine *Acacia* thickets, reedbeds and papyrus associated with lakes, rivers and swamps, from where it derives its common name[7, 21, 22, 48, 109, 290, 291, 431, 504, 639, 708, 717, 807, 907]. **Status** Not uncommon resident. **Conservation status** Unknown, but in S range the clearing of riverine woodland and thickets is likely to impact this species negatively.

MOVEMENTS Unknown; probably sedentary.

SOCIAL ORGANISATION and GENERAL

BEHAVIOUR Little known. Solitary or in pairs; bolder bird than other boubous, often calling from exposed perches on top of vegetation. Still, however, essentially a shy, skulking bird of dense undergrowth, sometimes ascending into canopy of large trees. Territories of *c.*2 ha are advertised and defended for most of the year, with loud whistled calls by ♂. Calls in upright posture, with head up and tail slightly fanned. ♀ responds in duet with harsh ratchet-like clicking sounds, her tail vibrating as she calls. ♂ bobs head while giving the initial *grr-* sound, then bows body during whistle. Territorial threat signalled with whistles and harsh calls accompanied by bowing, tail-flicking and 'wing-fripping' and rapidly repeated harsh *Kawkaw-* sounds and nasal twanging calls accompanied by a descending flight with head up, tail fanned and slow exaggerated wingbeats, with white-spotted rump fluffed out. A similar display is used in courtship. Roosts in dense bush tangles, making harsh alarm ticking sounds prior to entering roost site. Scratches indirectly[205, 500]. **Foraging behaviour** Searches for food from ground level to upper canopy. Hops on ground flicking debris aside with bill like a thrush. In dense undergrowth, gleans from foliage, branches and trunks, working up into canopy, from where it glides to base of adjacent vegetation. Ventures into the edges of reed beds. Occasionally hawks insects in flight[205, 500]. **Food** Arthropods, mainly insects, including Lepidoptera (moths and caterpillars), Coleoptera (beetles) and Hemiptera (bugs and cicadas). Also recorded taking millipedes, thin worms and small fruits[290, 500, 544].

SOUNDS Repertoire consists of loud ringing flute-like whistles and harsh ratchet clicking sounds. Duetting generally synchronous, calls overlapping substantially. Either member of a pair may initiate duets. Repertoire appears less diverse than many other black and white boubous. Main territorial, and most commonly heard call, a loud repeated ringing *houuu* whistle, usually preceded by a softer short guttural *grr-* sound. ♀ responds in duet with harsh staccato ratchet-like rattling *Ka-Ka-Ka-KaKKKK*. Length of rattle call variable. Territorial threat signalled by loud, harsh and rapidly repeated *KawKaw-* and nasal twanging *Tchzenenene* call, usually given in a flight display. Alarm a slowly repeated *Tik-* or *Tuk-Tuk-Tuk-*, also given prior to roosting. Contact maintained with duets consisting of shorter repeated whistles *hou-hou-hou* by ♂ in duet with ♀ giving a few harsh ratchet *Ka-KaKa-*, *K-KKK* or tearing *tcherrr* calls[205, 500, 501, 504, 530]. Sonagram[43, 48, 136, 530].

BREEDING BIOLOGY Little known. Monogamous and territorial. Pair bonds appear to be maintained by duetting. Density varies from 1 pair/2 ha to 1–2 birds/10 ha in Botswana[205, 639]. **Season** Breeding condition Sep (Angola)[907]; throughout the year, mainly Sep–Mar, and where it overlaps with Tropical Boubou, breeding may peak in austral winter (Botswana)[48, 205, 546, 639, 807]; Aug (Zambia)[780]. **Displays** ***Courtship*** ♂ chasing ♀, bouncing rapidly in tandem through vegetation, pausing to call. ♂ gives drawn-out whistles and glides after ♀. Flight-song display appears similar to territorial threat (see Sounds and General Behaviour)[205]. **Nest** Role of sexes unknown. A flimsy saucer-shaped structure made of fine twigs loosely woven together placed 2–3 m (n=3) above the ground in small bush or tangle, possibly also breeds in reedbeds. ***Size*** OD 120 mm, ID 76 mm, cup depth 45 mm, height 70 mm[500, 1037, 1038]. **Eggs** 2 (n=1). Pale cream or greenish, lightly speckled rufous. 23.0–23.7 x 19.8–19.9 mm (23.4 x 19.9, n=2)(Botswana)[19, 205, 1037, 1038]. **Incubation** By both sexes. ♀ gives *Tuk-Tuk* calls on nest prior to nest relief, ♂ responds in duet. Period unknown[1037]. **Nestling** Appearance unknown. Attended by both sexes. Fledging period unknown[1037]. **Predation and longevity** Unknown. **Brood parasite** Black Cuckoo *Cuculus clamosus* recorded once[544].

MEASUREMENTS and WEIGHTS *L. b. bicolor* ♂ (2) wing 102–103, tail 90–92, bill 35–36, tarsus 24; ♀ (3) wing 94–100, tail 85–90, bill 23–24, tarsus 35–36 (Cameroon)[616]; ♂♀? (5) wing 95–100[109]; *guttatus* ♂ (14) wing 91–103 (97.0), ♀ (12) 88–102 (97.9)[109]; *sticturus* ♂ (5) wing 102.3–110.0 (107.4), tail 100.0–109.0 (106.0), ♀ (2) wing 102.5–108.0 (105.2), tail 101.0–104.6 (102.8)[138]; ♂♀? (23) wing 103–111 (106.8) (Zambia)[240]; ♂♀? (12) bill (to skull) 23.0–28.2 (26.3), tarsus 34.0–38.5 (35.9)[500]. **Weight** *sticturus* ♂ (5) 47.8–56.7 g (53.3), ♀ (4) 43.0–58.2 g (52.1)(southern Africa)[346]; *guttatus* ♂ (10) 52–65 g; ♀ (8) 45–57 g[912].

63 BLACK-SHOULDERED PUFFBACK (Red-eyed Puffback)

Dryoscopus senegalensis **Plate 25**

FIELD IDENTIFICATION Medium-small (17 cm), glossy black and white arboreal bush-shrike. Sexes different; ♂ has pure white rump and underparts. ♀ duller, greyer with short white eyebrow and grey rump. ♂ rump fluffed out in display. Young similar to dull ♀. Little known; secretive, more often heard than seen. Gives loud, explosive whistles, clicking and rasping sounds. Usually in pairs or family group, inconspicuously skulking in canopy of forest edge, secondary forest and clearings (avoids closed forest). Resident from Nigeria in West Africa, including down to N Angola, and across N equatorial belt to SW Uganda and E Zaïre. ***Flight characteristics***: Wings rounded. White rump conspicuous in display.

COMPARISONS Most similar to ♂ Sabine's

Puffback *Dryoscopus sabini*, which has a heavier bill, giving the bird a more elongated form. ♀ Sabine's is distinctive tawny-orange below. ♂ Pink-footed Puffback *D. angolensis* also has dark unmarked wings, but has a black head and mantle contrasting with greyish back and rump, and greyish-white underparts. Also has a dark brown eye. All other ♂ puffbacks have wings with white markings. See Black-backed Puffback Comparisons p.264 for identification of immatures and other possible confusing species, particularly ♂ Red-eyed Flycatcher-shrike *Megabyas flammulatus*. Use calls with caution as puffbacks share many rather similar harsh rasping notes, clicking and disyllabic explosive whistles. Some calls similar to Black-backed Puffback *D. cubla* and ratchet-like sounds of Swamp Boubou *Laniarius bicolor*[22, 500].

DESCRIPTION ADULT ♂ ***Upperparts*** Glossy black; lower back and rump pure white. ***Wings*** Black, rarely with pale greyish-white edging to coverts and secondaries (Cameroon). ***Tail*** Glossy black. ***Underparts*** Pure white to whitish. ***Bare parts*** Bill black, lower mandible heavy and pale; palate unknown; legs bluish-grey; eye orange-red[616]. ADULT ♀ Similar to ♂ but duller, head black with whitish eyebrow from nostril to above eye (variable); dark loral spot. ***Back*** Dark grey; rump grey. ***Wings* and tail** Like ♂. ***Underparts*** White to dirty white; thighs whitish barred black. ***Bare parts*** Bill (upper madible) black (lower mandible) blue-grey at base, dark on tip; palate unknown; legs and eye similar to ♂. JUVENILE Little studied. Apparently much like adult ♀ but duller, and with buff tinge on wings and underparts. Lower mandible grey-brown; eye probably brown. IMMATURE Like adult ♀ but duller, dusky black above; whitish stripe over lores; rump greyish-white; below dull white to buffy. The rare pale wing markings reported from Cameroon may represent an immature character[338, 456, 616, 646].

GEOGRAPHICAL VARIATION Monotypic, with only the rare occurrence of individuals with greyish-white edging to coverts and flight feathers (Cameroon)[616].

MOULT Unknown.

RANGE, HABITAT and STATUS **Breeding range** West Africa from SW Nigeria, S Cameroon, SW Central African Republic, Congo, NE Zaïre, Equatorial Guinea, Gabon, Cabinda and NE Angola. In East Africa from W Uganda and Rwanda (requires confirmation). **Habitat** Clearings in primary and secondary forest (avoiding closed forest), gallery forest and coffee plantations, open secondary growth, riverine forest and thick bush of old plantations[7, 11, 21, 22, 37, 290, 294, 295, 431, 456, 481, 504, 664, 717, 907]. **Status** Resident, rare to locally common. **Conservation status** Unknown, but probably not threatened due to habitat preference.

MOVEMENTS Unknown.

SOCIAL ORGANISATION and GENERAL BEHAVIOUR Little known. Solitary, in pairs or small family groups in upper-levels. Behaviour similar to Black-backed Puffback; shy and difficult to observe. ♂ highly territorial, regularly moving around the territory advertising and defending it by loud whistles and harsh calls from canopy, often accompanied by puffback display and 'wing-fripping' sounds[15, 22, 294, 504]. **Foraging behaviour** Similar to Black-backed Puffback, gleans from foliage 10–25 m above the ground, sometimes higher, but rarely lower. May sometimes hawk insects in the air and is often a member of mixed foraging parties[294]. **Food** Arthropods, mainly insects and occasional small vertebrate. Insects include, Lepidoptera (large caterpillars), Coleoptera (beetles), Hemiptera (bugs), eggs of Mantodea (mantids) and Isoptera (termites). Also spiders, and small frog recorded[294, 290, 765].

SOUNDS Little known. Repertoire appears similar to Black-backed Puffback, with loud, explosive repetitive whistles, clicking and harsh rasping notes. Territorial call of ♂ a loud, explosive and frequently repeated *KYow!-KYow!-KYow!-, tu!-tu! tu!-, ptiou-ptiou-* or monotonous *chew-chew-chew-, TewTewTew, Tzuw-Tzuw-, TzewTzewTzew-* whistles, also harsh disyllabic *KurrrWEERrr, KzzkWeeU-* or *TzWrrrooo* and drawn-out *Tzrrrree* or *krrièèè* combined with snapping and scolding sounds. ♀ responds in duet with rasping, weaver-like notes, low *churr* and ratchet *KKKKK-* sounds reminiscent of Swamp Boubou. Other calls include loud clicking *TikTikTikTik-* and harsh alarm notes. Apparently makes 'wing-fripping' sounds in flight[22, 34, 290, 294, 500, 501, 504].

BREEDING BIOLOGY Little known; territorial and probably monogamous. In NE Gabon occurs at density of 2–4 pairs/10 ha. In Gabon unusually aggressive towards Bocage's Bush-shrike *Chlorophoneus bocagei*, but also occasionally attempts to court this species[294]. **Season** Aug, Nov (Cameroon)[37], Dec–Mar (Gabon)[294]; all year (NE Zaïre), mainly Jun–Jul (S Zaïre)[22, 290, 688]; breeding condition Aug (Uganda)[336]. **Displays *Courtship*** Rump and lower back feathers fluffed out in typical puffback display, accompanied by loud explosive *ptiou-* and rasping *krrièèè-* calls. Courtship feeding unknown[290, 294]. **Nest** Built by ♀ with ♂ escorting her. A small shallow compact cup built of strips of bark, plant fibres and rootlets which are held together and secured to the branch with spider web. Some bark wrapped around branch as well, and nest decorated with lichens. Resembles nest of Crested Flycatcher-shrike *Bias musicus* but is a little bigger. Usually placed *c.*10 m (4–16) above the ground in a fork on outer edge of trees[22, 34, 294]. **Eggs** 2 (n=1). Whitish with large contrasting reddish spots in a band around the large end. A single museum specimen is whitish, with small reddish and mauve spots and blotches in a band around the large end. ***Size*** 22.5 x 10.6 mm (n=1)[294, 500, 516]. **Incubation** By ♀ only. Period 16 days[294]. **Nestling** Little known. Develops plumage similar to juvenile, lacking barring and buff-tipped wing-coverts. A report of a nestling with dark chocolate-brown crown, back, wings and tail, and pure white rump and underparts, requires confirmation. Nestling ♂ also reported similar to adult but shows no barring or light tips to wing-coverts. Attended by both sexes. Period unknown. Young remain in their natal territory until following breeding season[294, 295, 456]. No further breeding information.

MEASUREMENTS and WEIGHTS *D. senegalensis* ♂♀? (10) wing 74–83 (78.3), tail 61–71 (65.1), bill (to skull) 21.5–23 (22.0), tarsus 21–25 (22.3)[500]; ♂ (6) wing 75–83, ♀ (3) 75–80, tail ♂♀? (9) 65–73, bill 17–20, tarsus 21.5–23.5[34]. **Weight** ♂ (1) 28.0 g (Cameroon)[478]; ♂♀? (2) 30–34 g (Uganda)[765]; ♂♀? (3) 23 g, 29 g, 32 g[500].

64 BLACK-BACKED PUFFBACK (Southern Puffback)

Dryoscopus cubla **Plate 25**

FIELD IDENTIFICATION Medium-small (*c.*17–18 cm), black and white arboreal bush-shrike with reddish eyes. Sexes different; ♂ head and mantle glossy black; scapulars, rump and underparts white to greyish-white. Rump fluffed out in spectacular white puffback display. ♀ duller, greyish-black above, rump greyish. Sides of face and underparts dull white. Young similar to dull ♀. Secretive, more often heard than seen. Flights short with loud 'wing-fripping'. Gives loud, explosive whistles, loud clicking and rasping sounds. Usually in pairs or family group; skulks mainly in canopy of woodland, riverine and montane forests. Resident in Africa S of equator, absent from Congo basin and arid regions of continent. ***Flight characteristics***: Bouncy, makes loud 'fripping' sounds with wings. Wings rounded, ♂ white rump conspicuous in display.

COMPARISONS In NE range similar to ♂ Pringle's Puffback *Dryoscopus pringlii* and ♂ Northern Puffback *D. gambensis*. Northern distinguished by larger size, more robust build, heavier bill, and grey rump (like ♀ Black-backed, but latter has white facial marking). Pringle's smaller, with bicoloured bill, more extensive white in wings, white edging to tail feathers, and occurs in very arid country. ♀ Black-backed distinguished from ♂ Pringle's by whiter face markings. Identification of immatures requires caution as all have a dull buffy-brown ♀-like plumage with dark eye. Adult ♀ Pringle's Puffback resembles some immatures, but has a reddish eye. Careful use of wing and facial markings, underpart and leg colour and bill size, in conjunction with habitat are recommended. Immature Northern, Pink-footed and Sabine's are richer tawny-buff below than other immature puffbacks. In addition Pink-footed has pink legs and Sabine's a very heavy bill. Other species which it superficially resembles include the much larger, more terrestrial Tropical *Laniarius aethiopicus* and Southern Boubous *L. ferrugineus*, ♂ Red-eyed Flycatcher-shrike *Megabyas flammulatus* and Bocage's Bush-shrike *Chlorophoneus bocagei*.

DESCRIPTION **Adult ♂** ***Head*** To lower back and face blue-black with slight glossy sheen (some races have greyish back: see Geographical Variation); scapulars white to greyish-white (lacking in *affinis*); rump white with greyish tinge. ***Wings*** Black, coverts edged and broadly tipped white, flight feathers narrowly edged white (little or no white in wing of *affinis*). ***Tail*** Black, tipped white; uppertail-coverts black. ***Underparts*** Including cheek and throat white to greyish-white; flanks tinged grey. ***Bare parts*** Bill and palate black (base of lower mandible pale in *affinis*); legs slate-blue; eye red to reddish-orange. **Adult ♀** Like ♂ but duller and greyer; greyish-black above with olive-grey rump and flanks. Loral surface and areas around eyes whitish (*affinis* has black loral spot, whitish eyebrow from nostril to eye and indistinct greyish scapulars). Underparts more buffy-grey than ♂. ***Bare parts*** Bill greyish-black, lower mandible paler; palate black; legs blue-grey; eye yellowish to orange-yellow. **Juvenile** Similar to adult ♀ but with upperparts blackish-grey with buff tips to most feathers; rump grey-brown. White in wings buff. Eye brown to greyish, bill grey-brown. Underparts dull white from chin to undertail-coverts. **Immature** Upperparts like adult ♀. Wings with buff-grey tips to coverts and flight feathers. Underparts various shades of tawny-buff (depending on race), flanks greyer. Bill blackish-grey with paler lower mandible; eye brown. First-year birds resemble adult ♀ but are more strongly tinged with olive-buff, especially over rump; underparts finely barred (vermiculated), eye more yellowish-orange[71, 72, 832].

GEOGRAPHICAL VARIATION At least 5 races, based on variation in physical proportions, intensity of whiteness of rump and underparts in adult ♂♂, amount of white in wings in both sexes, the presence or absence of black loral spots and the colour of mantle and rump in ♀♀. Eye colour in both sexes has also been used; however, in southern Africa this appears to vary from orange-red in forest to red in woodland populations. Northern populations inhabit woodland habitats while those in S also in this habitat, as well as evergreen forests. Nominate *cubla* (South Africa) and *affinis* (coastal E Africa) represent extremes in some characters: rump and underparts greyish-white in nominate morph, pure white in *affinis*. Others, like *hamatus* (Kenya, Tanzania, Zaïre, S Angola), *nairobiensis* (S Kenya, N Tanzania), *chapini* (Mozambique, S Tanzania) and *okavangensis* (W Angola, SW Zambia, Namibia, N South Africa, E Botswana, Zimbabwe) are intermediate. Race *hamatus* has more white in wing and less grey below than nominate. Nominate morph has extensive white in wings while this is lacking in *affinis*, which also has a black loral spot in ♀♀.

This character is also shared by *nairobiensis*, which is otherwise very similar to *hamatus*. In ♀♀ forehead and back colour variable, for example very grey in *okavangensis*[3, 72, 205, 523].

MOULT Adults undergo a post-breeding moult of flight and tail feathers. Post-juvenile moult appears to take place soon after leaving the nest, possibly within 10 days[71, 500].

RANGE, HABITAT and STATUS Breeding range From about the equator, including S Somalia (*affinis*), Kenya, Tanzania, S Zaïre, Rwanda, Burundi, Angola, N Namibia, E Botswana, Zambia, Malawi, Mozambique, Zimbabwe and N, E and SE South Africa. Absent from Congo basin and arid SW desert and semi-desert regions. **Habitat** In canopy of well wooded areas including various deciduous woodland types, thickets, plantations and gardens. More common in the denser woodlands and edge of forest, but also in evergreen montane, riverine, lowland and coastal forest, including mangroves. Southern population tends to occur more frequently in forest habitats than the more northern birds[7, 22, 26, 30, 48, 72, 119, 290, 291, 299, 318, 320, 325, 431, 448, 481, 631, 639, 807, 907]. **Status** Fairly common to common resident. **Conservation status** Not threatened; however, in South Africa much of its natural habitat has been destroyed in SE and E areas[639].

MOVEMENTS Sedentary, with 4 ringing recoveries within 10 km of ringing site[639].

SOCIAL ORGANISATION and GENERAL BEHAVIOUR Solitary or in pairs; restless, skulking about in crouched position usually in canopy. Also in groups of 5–7 birds chasing each other about. Advertises and defends a territory of *c.*4–12 ha. Territorial behaviour includes repeated *K-weeU* (click followed by a whistle) by ♂, responded to by ♀ in duet with single rasping or tearing *tzzerrr*, or similar double- or triple-noted call. May be accompanied by a descending, whirring-fluttering display-flight with tail fanned and lower back and rump feathers fluffed out to form a 'puff-back'. This display usually accompanied by 'wing-fripping' sounds. On landing ♂ inclines body downwards and sways from side to side. At higher intensity, calls given more frequently with loud 'wing-fripping' and percussive bill-clicking, combined with body-bowing and side to side body movements, sometimes with bill partly open. Alarm signalled with percussive sounds, 'wing-fripping' and rump fluffed out. Roosting behaviour unknown. Observed bathing in dew-covered foliage and scratches indirectly[46, 146, 205, 448, 500]. **Foraging behaviour** Arboreal, hops about swiftly and silently, gleaning from foliage and branches in canopy of trees and bushes, seldom lower down, rarely on ground, usually to retrieve fallen prey. Sometimes hawks insects. Some foraging behaviour reminiscent of tits and occasionally holds prey in the foot. Often a member of mixed foraging parties[205, 506, 737]. **Food** Arthropods, mainly insects and their larvae, and small vertebrates. Insects include Coleoptera (beetles), Lepidoptera (moths, butterflies and caterpillars), Odonata (dragonflies), Orthoptera (grasshoppers and crickets), Isoptera (termites), Hymenoptera (ants). Also small vertebrates (lizards), young birds and eggs, as well as young buds[46, 48, 69, 205, 338, 566].

SOUNDS Repertoire consists of loud calls, repeated explosive single and disyllabic whistles, clicking, clashing and rasping sounds. Duetting complex; basically consists of ♂ giving whistles and ♀ rasping calls. Territorial call consists of loud whistles repeated up to *c.*10 times. These vary from simple *cheew, weeo-, teeoo-, tchew, tyew, stchew-* or *twhew-* notes, to distinctly disyllabic *Tu-weeeo, trrk-wheeu, tip-wheep, q-weeu* or *K-weeU*, all representing a percussive click followed by a whistle. ♀ responds in duet with scolding rasping sounds, variously described as *tsuik, zkit-, tzzerrr-, Tzk-tzzerrrr, chikerrrr-, ki-eeeh or ki-erk* and an often rather drawn-out *kirr-r-r-r*. Similar rasping calls are used for contact by both sexes. Territorial threat signalled with repeated *K-weeU*, as well as rapidly repeated *teeu-teeu-teeu-teeu-* whistles and tearing *Tzk-Tzzerrrr* calls. At higher intensity, include numerous tearing rasping *Tzzrrrr* (often drawn-out *Tzzr-r-r-r-*) threat calls and strident *Ki-Ki-Ki-Ki-* bill-clicks. Alarm signalled with harsh *Kzzzrrrr* notes and *Ki-Ki-Ki-Ki-* strident bill-clicking (snapping). 'Wing-fripping' and bill-clicking frequently accompany calls given in flight. Nestlings and fledglings beg with repeated high-pitched strident *Tzzeeee-* calls. During nest-building ♂ utters high-pitched, strident *Tzeet* calls[5, 46, 48, 205, 290, 500, 631]. Sonagram[48].

BREEDING BIOLOGY Monogamous and territorial. Frequent calling by ♂ and striking display-flights conspicuous. Density of 1 pair/42 ha in broadleaved woodland. Nesting success 40%, breeding success 29% in one study. Appears to be single-brooded[6, 46, 205, 320, 871]. **Season** Recently fledged young Oct (Somalia)[859]; throughout most of year Dec–May, Aug–Oct (East Africa)[293]; Jan–Mar (S Tanzania)[832]; Sep–Oct, also Jan–Mar and Jun–Jul (Zaïre)[22, 290]; Oct–Dec (Angola)[7, 865, 907]; Sep–Dec (Zambia)[291]; egg-laying Nov, Jan (Botswana)[807]; all months, mainly Sep–Jan (South Africa), all months except May, mainly Sep–Nov (Zimbabwe)[48, 639]. **Displays *Courtship*** ♂ gives repeated *K-weeU-K-weeU-* and *teeu-teeu-teeu-*, also changing to slower, more rolling *K-weeU-* calls, or calls *chak-chak-chak* on the wing. Most calls given during steeply descending puffback display, during which the feathers of the lower back and rump are fluffed out. ♀ responding in duet with *tzzerrr, Tzk-tzzerrr* calls. On approaching ♀, ♂ utters *weeU-weeU-* or *teeu-teeu-* whistles and *ki-erk kirrrrr* notes. Puffback display includes bowing, drooping and vibrating of wings and spreading of tail. ♂ makes short butterfly flights with puff expanded, and may drop vertically through the air with raised wings. Also chases ♀ about with 'wing-fripping', and fast zigzag display-flight. Courtship-feeding takes place[46, 205, 631]. **Nest construction** Generally ♂ does not help in building the nest, but escorts ♀ back and forth, with loud 'wing-fripping' and repeated *K-weeU-K-weeU-* whistles. Also utters high-pitched, strident *Tzeet* calls at this time, to which ♀ responds in duet with harsh *tzzerrr* or *Tzk-tzzerrr* calls[205]. **Nest** Built mainly by ♀, with ♂ escorting her. Deep thin-walled cup of grass, roots and bark bound with web, with some fine lining. Occasionally lichen, pieces of bark or dried leaves added to outside. Web apparently carried in the mouth. Placed in upright fork near the top of a tree or bush about 6 m (2–15, n=109) above the ground. ***Size*** OD 81 mm, ID 50 mm, cup depth 32 mm, height 94 mm. Completed in about 10 days (6–11, n=3)[46, 68, 205, 576]. **Eggs** Usually 2 (2–3, n=40). Pale white, cream or pinkish with fine spots and streaks of brown and grey, often concentrated at large end. 19.2–24.4 x 14.9–17.7 mm (22.2 x 15.9, n=52)[19, 48]. **Incubation** May start with first or last egg, mostly by ♀, relieved by ♂ for short periods. ♂ feeds mate on nest, announcing arrival with *weeU-weeU-*. Both appear to initiate nest relief with their respective calls. ♀ gives *Tzk-tzzerrr* with or without ♂ around. Increased camouflage may be added to the nest during this period. Period 13 days (n=1)[46, 48, 205, 872]. **Nestling** Hatch naked, flesh-coloured, blind and with mouth spots. Eyes brown, bill grey-brown. Develops blackish-grey upperparts with buffy tips to feathers and whitish underparts which change to buff within days of fledging. Nestlings beg with repeated high-pitched strident *Tzzeeee* calls. Attended by both sexes. Adults announce that they have food with the *Tzeet* call. Fledge after 17 days (n=1), and solicit for at least a further 3 weeks. Immature remains with adults for at least a year, and has been observed feeding a fledgling (probably of previous brood) during this period[27, 46, 67, 205, 320, 331]. **Predation and longevity** Adult killed by African Goshawk *Accipiter tachiro*. Nest contents taken by Grey-headed Bush-shrike *Malaconotus blanchoti* and killed by ants. Both sexes recorded surviving 5.5–10 years[205, 657, 714, 855]. **Brood parasite** Emerald Cuckoo *Chrysococcyx cupreus* confirmed; one record of Black Cuckoo *Cuculus clamosus* and records of Klaas's Cuckoo *Chrysococcyx klaas* require confirmation. Chases Red-chested Cuckoo *Cuculus solitarius*[5, 94, 156].

MEASUREMENTS and WEIGHTS Southern races combined ♂ (62) wing 76.5–88 (81.8); ♀ (41) wing 75–85 (78.8); ♂ (36) tail 60–73 (66.7), ♀ (36) 61–74.5 (66.7); bill ♂♀? (31) 17.5–21, tarsus ♂♀? (31) 21–24 (southern Africa)[48]. **Weight** ♂ (125) 19.3–36 g (27.1), ♀ (98) 21–30.4 g (25.4) (southern Africa)[48]. For additional data see[72, 146, 205, 319, 346, 478, 618, 830, 870].

65 PRINGLE'S PUFFBACK *Dryoscopus pringlii* Plate 25

FIELD IDENTIFICATION Small (13–14 cm) dry-country bush-shrike with white wing markings, bicoloured bill and reddish eye. Sexes different. ♂ has glossy black head and mantle, grey scapulars and back, and greyish-white rump. Tail black with white edging (obvious only in fresh plumage). Wings dark with broad whitish edging to coverts and flight feathers. Below greyish-brown. Black bill distinctly lighter at base of lower mandible. ♀ pale greyish-brown all over, tail dark brown, eye crimson. Young like dull ♀. Little known; calls include repeated whistles and churring sounds. Usually in pairs, skulking in tops of low bushes in arid thornbush and woodland. Resident NE Africa, from NE Tanzania, Kenya, Ethiopia and Somalia. ***Flight characteristics***: Wings rounded.

COMPARISONS ♂ resembles a diminutive Northern Puffback *Dryoscopus gambensis*, but has basal half of lower mandible pale, more white in the wing with broader white edging to coverts, secondaries and tertials. Outer tail feathers narrowly edged and tipped whitish. Distinguished from ♂ Black-backed Puffback *D. cubla* by smaller size, bicoloured bill, grey scapulars and rump. From ♀ Black-backed by lack of white facial marking. Other ♂ puffbacks have no white in wings and are forest or forest-edge species. Flycatchers with similar coloration to the ♀ have a smaller bill, slimmer build and different habits. See Black-backed Puffback Comparisons p.264 for identification of immature puffbacks and other possible confusing species.

DESCRIPTION Adult ♂ ***Upperparts*** Glossy black, lower back greyer; scapulars dirty grey; rump greyish-white. ***Wings*** Blackish-brown with broad creamy-white edges to coverts, secondary and tertiary feathers, narrower edging on outer webs of primaries. ***Tail*** Black with narrow creamy-white edging to outer feathers, inner feathers tipped white. ***Underparts*** Chin whitish, rest dirty creamy-white with a brownish-grey tinge across breast and along flanks. ***Bare parts*** Bill black with basal half of lower mandible pale; palate unknown; legs blue-grey; eye crimson. **Adult ♀ Upperparts** Pale greyish-brown; rump greyish-brown with white feather bases; face with inconspicuous white eye-ring and white lores. ***Wings*** Like ♂ but duller. ***Tail*** Dark greyish-brown with white tips. ***Underparts*** Pale buffy-cream from chin to upper belly; belly vent and undertail-coverts white; thighs barred brown. ***Bare parts*** Similar to ♂. **Juvenile** Resembles ♀ but duller and has a slight buff tinge on breast. Eye probably brown[336, 500, 631]. **Immature** ♂ similar to ♀ but head and mantle brownish, becoming progressively more black and having a mottled appearance; bill with upper mandible black, lower whitish; legs purplish; eye crimson[500].

GEOGRAPHICAL VARIATION None. Monotypic.

MOULT Unknown.

RANGE, HABITAT and STATUS Breeding range NE Africa in S and central Somalia and S Ethiopia, southward to E and NE Kenya; also a fragmented population in NW Kenya and another in NE Tanzania. **Habitat** Arid thorn scrub, thornbush and woodlands and wooded grasslands, particularly dry *Acacia* and *Commiphora* bush[292, 318, 325, 431, 558, 631, 859]. **Status** Local and uncommon resident. **Conservation status** Unknown, probably not threatened.
MOVEMENTS Unknown.
SOCIAL ORGANISATION and GENERAL BEHAVIOUR Little known. Solitary, in pairs or small groups, moving about in vegetation, often low to the ground. **Foraging behaviour** Arboreal, active foliage-gleaner, usually with mixed foraging parties, hopping through undergrowth, in bushes or low trees; may keep close to ground[631, 352, 631, 760]. **Food** Insects.
SOUNDS Little known. A sharp repeated *keu-*, which may be given by several birds; also a low-pitched *churr* sound and a short monotonous harsh song of rather low pitch. Nasal rasping *cheeeTzrrrr-* and rapidly repeated *ZiiiitZiiiitZiiiit-* and *chup-chup-chup*. Nestlings utter a low chattering[420, 500, 631, 760].
BREEDING BIOLOGY Little known; probably monogamous. **Season** One record Nov (East Africa)[293]. **Displays** Unknown. **Nest** Role of sexes unknown. A neat cup moulded on an almost horizontal branch and anchored to a vertical twig. Placed 1.3 m above the ground in sapling, some concealed, others exposed. ***Size*** OD 60 mm, cup depth 50 mm[336, 420]. **Eggs** 2. Colour unknown[420]. **Incubation** Unknown. **Nestling** Skin of young nestlings dull purplish, mouth yellow, edges of gape cream, blind. Utter a low chatter. Adults sit very tight, and both feed young. Period unknown[420]. No further breeding information.
MEASUREMENTS and WEIGHTS *D. pringlii* ♂♀? (9) wing 62–73 (69.3), tail 52–65 (58.8), tarsus 19.5–21.5 (20.2), bill (to skull) 17.5–20 (18.6)[500]. **Weight** ♂ (8) 19.0–22.6 g (19.7); ♀ (5) 18.4–20.6 g (19.6)[509].

66 NORTHERN PUFFBACK *Dryoscopus gambensis* Plate 26

FIELD IDENTIFICATION Medium-small (17–18 cm), restless arboreal bush-shrike with an orange-red eye. Sexes different. ♂ glossy black above with grey rump and scapulars, streaky whitish-brown wings and dull white underparts. ♀ greyish-brown above, tawny-orange below. Young like ♀ but more intensely orange below. Flight noisy with loud 'wing-fripping'. Gives loud, explosive whistles, strident clicking and rasping sounds. More often heard than seen. Solitary, in pairs or small groups in mid- to upper levels of larger trees in wooded savannas and forest edge (avoids closed forest). Resident, mostly N of equator from NE Africa to W Africa, also E and W of Congo basin. ***Flight characteristics***: Wings rounded, noisy 'wing-fripping'. Pale rump conspicuous, particularly when fluffed out in display.
COMPARISONS ♂ most similar to ♂ Black-backed Puffback *Dryoscopus cubla*, including calls, but distinguished by larger size, heavier bill, grey rump and scapulars (as in ♀ Black-backed, but latter has white facial markings). Also similar to Pringle's Puffback *D. pringlii*, which is smaller, has a conspicuous pale base to lower mandible, white edges and tips to tail feathers, and occurs in much drier bush. Slight resemblance to ♂ Black-shouldered *D. senegalensis*, Sabine's *D. sabini* and Pink-footed *D. angolensis*, but all these lack the white wing markings. Northern Puffback ♀ most similar to ♀ Sabine's and Pink-footed Puffback, which are more orange-brown all over and lack wing markings. In addition Pink-footed has pink legs and a brown eye, Sabine's has a much larger bill, and both are forest species. Immatures of these two species identified from Northern immature on the same basis as their ♀♀. ♀ Pringle's Puffback has pale wing markings but lacks greyish head and buffy-orange underparts. See Black-backed Puffback Comparisons p.264 for identification of other immature puffbacks and other possible confusing species. Calls should be used with caution as puffbacks share many rather similar harsh rasping notes, clicking and disyllabic explosive whistles. Sparrow-like notes of Northern more nasal and hoarse than corresponding notes of Black-shouldered. Disyllabic notes similar to Black-backed Puffback and nasal sounds similar to Sabine's[290, 500, 545].
DESCRIPTION ADULT ♂ ***Upperparts*** Glossy black; rump and scapulars grey. ***Wings*** Greyish-brown with dull white to greyish-white edging and tips to coverts and flight feathers. ***Tail*** Glossy black above, dark blackish-brown below. ***Underparts*** Whitish tinged buffy grey. ***Bare parts*** Bill and palate black; legs blue-grey; eye orange-red. ADULT ♀ **Upperparts** Head and nape dark grey to greyish-brown; lores dirty greyish-white; mantle to rump dull brown. ***Tail*** Dark blackish-brown, contrasting with paler upperparts. ***Wings*** Dull brown, coverts and flight feathers edged and tipped buff. ***Underparts*** Chin to upper belly variable, tawny-buff to tawny-orange depending on race; lower belly and flanks buffy-white. ***Bare parts*** Bill black on upper mandible, paler base to lower mandible; palate unknown; legs bluish-grey; eye more yellow-orange than ♂. JUVENILE At least two juvenile plumages. First plumage grey-brown to chocolate-brown on head and mantle with sparse pale spot-

ting, rump grey; scapulars broadly streaked buff and brown; tertials, secondaries and coverts broadly edged buff to tawny-buff; tail edged and tipped buff; below white, tinged buff on breast. Second plumage more like ♀ but greyer and paler on the head with brown tinge. Wings: Coverts and flight feathers edged and tipped buff. Underparts: Greyish-buff. Bare parts: Bill brownish-grey, paler at base of lower mandible; legs like adult; eye dark to greyish-brown[500]. **IMMATURE** ♂ Head, nape and mantle mottled greyish-black; underparts buffy-white; wing-coverts and flight feathers with buff tips and edges. ♀ head and nape mottled greyish-brown, underparts more tawny-orange than adult, and wing like immature ♂. Eye brown.

GEOGRAPHICAL VARIATION At least 5 races, with variation mainly evident on upper- and underparts in ♀♀. Slight size variation with *erwini* (E Zaïre to N Tanzania) being the smallest. In ♀♀, head colour varies from dark brown in *erythreae* (E Sudan, Ethiopia and NW Somalia) and *malzacii* (Central African Republic, Sudan and Kenya) to a grey slate-brown in *congicus* (Gabon to SW Zaïre), still paler in nominate *gambensis* (Senegal–Chad). Similar variation in underparts, with *congicus* and *malzacii* having richest buffy-orange and nominate and *erythreae* palest buff[15, 237].

MOULT Wing moult Mar–May, tail Jan (West Africa); wing moult Nov (Rwanda)[330, 717, 858].

RANGE, HABITAT and STATUS Breeding range In West Africa from Mauritania, Senegal, Gambia, Guinea-Bissau, Guinea, Sierra Leone, Liberia, Ivory Coast, Ghana, Togo, Benin, Mali, Nigeria, Cameroon, Equatorial Guinea, Gabon, Burkina Faso, Niger, Chad, Ethiopia, and Congo, Zaïre south to Angola and Cabinda. Through Central African Republic, S Chad, S Sudan to East Africa, generally N of equator; Ethiopia, Eritrea, Uganda, NW Kenya, NW Tanzania, Rwanda, Burundi. Formerly occurred, but now a rare straggler, in NW Somalia[325, 859, 933]. Bioko record rejected[431]. **Habitat** Canopy of variety of savanna woodlands, particularly better woodlands with large trees, forest-grassland mosaic, also edges of gallery forest, in primary and secondary forest clearings (avoiding closed forest), bamboo, mangroves, isolated thickets and gardens[22, 31, 37, 234, 242, 259, 290, 292, 294, 330, 431, 481, 504, 631, 717, 848, 858, 907]. **Status** Widespread, uncommon to common resident. **Conservation status** Not threatened, although formerly found in NW Somalia[933].

MOVEMENTS In West Africa some evidence of local S movements in dry season, and in NE Gabon only observed in Jul[37, 294, 858].

SOCIAL ORGANISATION and GENERAL BEHAVIOUR Solitary, in pairs or small groups of 4–6 birds; restless, stealthy and secretive, contact being maintained with persistent scolding calls. Noisy 'wing-fripping'. Pale rump conspicuous, particularly when fluffed out in territorial and courtship display[455, 572]. **Foraging behaviour** Arboreal, usually fairly high in trees; also in tops of tall undergrowth, hopping about gleaning insects from foliage and branches. Often a member of mixed foraging parties[631, 455, 504, 688]. **Food** Arthropods, mainly insects, including Coleoptera (beetles) and Lepidoptera (caterpillars). Small buds also recorded[9, 15, 688].

SOUNDS Repertoire consists of persistent loud calls, explosive whistles, strident clicking, harsh and rasping sounds. Calls given while stationary or foraging, also in flight and flight display, where accompanied by loud 'wing-fripping' sounds. Main territorial call a repeated harsh *tchrep-tchrep-, tzzit* and other calls, often delivered rather slowly, e.g. *Chip-chip-chip-, chuik..chuik.., tuk-tuk-, tchik, tchik, tic tchak, tchak-tchak, Cherp-Cherp-, Churc-Churc-, wrrich, wrrich-* and a rasping *zhiuu, zhrraanh* or *tzzik, tzzik or tzzk-tzzk-chee-chee.* Also repeated nasal *krim-krim-* and higher pitched, rather querulous *weer-weer.* These interspersed with nasal disyllabic explosive whistles, *pi-chew-, tchew-* or *ptkew* and *ptkik,* including *keow* or *keewu* repeated several times after a short pause. Calls often accompanied by strident clicking and chattering notes. Has a prolonged metallic trilling when handled. Alarm described as sharp repeated *kek-kek-, chuck-chack or tuk-tak.* Pairs maintain contact with repeated scolding, grating or rasping calls, some rather sparrow-like. See Comparison for similarity to other species[22, 23, 290, 455, 500, 501, 504, 558, 572, 631, 696, 717, 754].

BREEDING BIOLOGY Little known; probably monogamous. **Season** West Africa probably throughout the year, recorded from Jan, Apr–Jul and Sep–Dec[22, 23, 37, 234, 338, 455, 482, 688, 690, 858]; Feb, Jun–Jul (Sudan)[242], Mar–Jul, Dec–Jan (Uganda)[290]; rest of East Africa Jan, Apr–May and Oct[33, 293]. Apr, possibly Jan, Mar and Dec (Ethiopia)[292]. **Displays** ***Courtship*** Elaborate; birds indulge in noisy chasing accompanied by calling, puffed-out rump feathers and loud 'wing-fripping'. **Nest** Role of sexes unknown. A compact cup composed of fine bark strips plastered with spiders web, camouflaged with lichens or mosses and lined with rootlets. Secured firmly in a fork with spider web at *c.*6.5–23 m above the ground[2, 15, 22, 23, 455, 576]. **Eggs** Usually 2. Greyish-white, spotted and streaked with brownish-grey and grey mostly about the large end (East Africa). In West Africa, white to pinkish-white, (a) speckled all over with dark stone-colour or (b) dotted and speckled with sepia with grey shell markings. ***Size*** 16 x 10 mm[2, 15]. No further breeding information.

MEASUREMENTS and WEIGHTS *D. g. malzacii* ♂ (5) wing 88–94, tail 80–86, bill 18–20, tarsus 23.5–25; ♀ (6) wing 85–90, tail 79–85, bill 17–20.5, tarsus 23–24[238]. **Weight** Race unknown ♂♀? (7) 27.2–39.0 g (33.5)[478]. For additional data see[34, 259, 330, 457, 494, 582, 652, 688, 758, 768, 870].

FIELD IDENTIFICATION Medium-small (15–18 cm), arboreal forest bush-shrike with pink legs and dark brown eye. Sexes different; ♂ head and mantle black, contrasting with slate-grey back and rump; tail and wings greyish-black. Below greyish-white. ♀ head and mantle pale grey; face with inconspicuous white loral stripe and eye-ring. Back, rump, tail and wings olive-brown; below rich tawny-buff to pale orange, white on belly. Bill black in both sexes, ♀ with pale lower mandible. Young like dull ♀. Little known; secretive, more often heard than seen. Gives harsh churring and repeated explosive whistles. Usually in pairs; forage by skulking mainly in upper canopy of dense forest and forest edge. Resident in Congo basin lowlands, Angola and Central and East African mid-altitude highland forests. ***Flight characteristics***: Wings rounded.

COMPARISONS No other ♂ puffback has a black head with plain grey back, wings and tail. In addition all other adult ♂ puffbacks have reddish eyes (not brown) and blue-grey legs (not pink). ♂ similar to Bocage's Bush-shrike *Chlorophoneus bocagei*, which has a prominent white eyebrow. In ♀, the brown eye distinguishes it from the larger ♀ Northern Puffback *Dryoscopus gambensis* which has an orange eye. The lack of pale buff wing markings and pink legs, also helps distinguish Pink-footed Puffback. ♀ Sabine's Puffback *D. sabini* has dark eyes, grey legs and a much heavier bill, and is more of a primary forest, canopy bird. Immatures have pink legs which distinguish them from Northern and the much larger-billed Sabine's Puffback. See Black-backed Puffback Comparisons p.264 for identification of other immature puffbacks and other possible confusing species.

DESCRIPTION ADULT ♂ ***Upperparts*** Blue-black with slight glossy sheen; lower back and rump pale grey. ***Wings and tail*** greyish-black. ***Underparts*** Chin and throat white; rest greyish-white, belly and flanks darker. ***Bare parts*** Bill black; palate unknown; feet flesh to lavender-pink; eye dark brown, narrowly edged with bright cobalt-blue; eyelids reddish grey. ADULT ♀ ***Head and mantle*** Grey to blue-grey. Face with narrow white loral stripe and eye-ring. ***Back, rump, wings and tail*** Olive-brown; rump grey tinged olive. Secondaries edged tawny. ***Underparts*** Tawny-buff to buffy-orange; belly, vent and undertail-coverts white. ***Bare parts*** Similar to ♂, except lower mandible pale. JUVENILE/IMMATURE resembles adult ♀ but duller above, with slight tinge of olive-brown over the mantle. The tawny-buff of underparts more developed. Bill pale, legs flesh-coloured and eye brown.

GEOGRAPHICAL VARIATION At least 4 races in two fragmented populations. In ♂♂ variation mainly in extent of grey tinge on head and mantle, increasing in extent from W nominate *angolensis* (Angola, W Zaïre) to *boydi* (Cameroon), and in the E from *nandensis* (E Zaïre, Sudan, W Kenya) to *kungwensis* (W Tanzania). Race *boydi* is darker grey on back and breast than nominate. Race *nandensis* has greyer head than nominate and *kungwensis* is even greyer[3]. ♀♀ vary slightly in brightness of underparts and extent of white on lower belly.

MOULT Unknown.

RANGE, HABITAT and STATUS Breeding range Distribution fragmented. In E from SE Sudan, NE, central and E Zaïre, W Uganda, W Kenya, W Tanzania, W Rwanda. In W from E Nigeria, Cameroon, Congo, SW Zaïre and N Angola. Central African Republic record rejected[431]. **Habitat** Upper and middle canopy of mature primary forest at intermediate altitudes, also in secondary growth, forest edge, coffee plantations and clearings down to sea-level[347, 431, 504, 631, 717, 907]. **Status** Resident, generally localised, uncommon to rare[37, 631]. **Conservation status** Unknown.

MOVEMENTS Unknown.

SOCIAL ORGANISATION and GENERAL BEHAVIOUR Little known. Solitary or in pairs. Skulks about in a crouched position like a large warbler, rather silent, but more often heard than seen, and located on its harsh contact note. **Foraging behaviour** Arboreal, mainly in mid- and upper canopy, gleaning prey off high foliage and large subcanopy branches, hopping about in search of food. Often a member of mixed foraging parties[22, 631, 688, 717]. **Food** Insects.

SOUNDS Little known. Not very vocal. Has an emphatic *TCHEW, TCHEW, TCHEW..* or *tzeu-tzeu-* whistle note, repeated up to 30 times. Also harsh churring or jarring *Tzzik-Tzzik* contact calls, given by both sexes, a call on which it is usually located. Three ♂♂ chasing each other gave *pik-pik-krrraa* calls[347, 500, 501, 571, 631, 717].

BREEDING BIOLOGY Little known; territorial and probably monogamous. **Season** In East Africa Mar–May, Jul[70, 293]; West Africa probably throughout year, recorded Jan, Apr, Jun, Oct–Dec[22, 37, 338]; Jan, Apr–Jun, Nov (Zaïre)[688]. **Displays** Unknown. **Nest** Built by ♀. A fairly large cup incorporating spider web and covered with lichen. One nest placed *c.*7 m above the ground in a dead tree covered with creeper, a metre from trunk on horizontal branch, well hidden in thick foliage[70, 571]. **Eggs and incubation** Unknown. **Nestlings** Appearance unknown; apparently only ♀ feeds nestlings, who beg noisily. ♂ often accompanies ♀. Period unknown[70]. No further breeding information.

MEASUREMENTS and WEIGHTS *D. a. boydi* wing ♂ (7) 80–86 (81.7); ♀(7) 78–83 (80.2); tail ♂ (7) 63–65.5 (64.6); ♀ (7) 62.5–65 (64.5); bill ♂ (7) 18–21.5 (19.4); ♀ (7) 18–19 (18.3); tarsus ♂ (3) 23–24 (23.7); ♀ (4) 23–24 (23.3)[347, 412]. **Weight** *boydi* ♂♀? (7) 35–40 g (37.1) (Cameroon)[412]; *angolensis* ♀ 27 g[907]; *nandensis* ♂♀? (2) 36–37 g (Uganda)[425].

FIELD IDENTIFICATION Medium-sized (18–19 cm), arboreal lowland forest bush-shrike with very heavy bill and dark eye. Sexes different. ♂ glossy blue-black above, including wings and tail, which contrast with white lower back, rump and underparts. ♀ head and nape grey; back tawny-brown, including wings and tail. Below rich tawny-buff to pale orange. Young like ♀. White rump of ♂ conspicuous in flight; makes 'fripping' sounds with wings. Little known. Secretive, more often heard than seen. Gives loud, explosive repeated descending whistles, clicking and rasping sounds. Difficult to observe, usually in pairs skulking in high forest canopy. Resident from Sierra Leone to Central African Republic and Zaïre to Angola. ***Flight characteristics***: Makes loud 'fripping' sound with wings; wings rounded, and white rump of ♂ conspicuous.

COMPARISONS ♂ most similar to ♂ Black-shouldered Puffback *Dryoscopus senegalensis*, which has much smaller bill and occurs in different habitat, generally avoiding closed forest. Some calls also similar but ♂ and ♀ alike in this species. ♂ Pink-footed *D. angolensis* also has a dark eye but lacks black wings and conspicuous white rump. Where ranges overlap, usually found at lower elevations. ♂ Red-eyed Flycatcher-shrike *Megabyas flammulatus* is smaller with shorter bill and tail, and different posture and calls. ♀ Pink-footed most similar to ♀ Sabine's, including dark eye, but has smaller bill, darker upperparts and pink legs. It is a bird mainly of secondary forest. ♀ Northern Puffback *D. gambensis* has smaller bill, streaked wings and an orange eye. Ranges separate and habitat different. Immatures of these three ♀♀ identified on the basis of bill size, leg colour, range and habitat. See Black-backed Puffback. Comparisons p.264. for identification of other immatures and other possible confusing species. Use calls with caution as puffbacks share many rather similar harsh rasping notes, clicking and disyllabic explosive whistles. The harsh grating trill is similar to one of the calls of Northern Puffback. Descending whistles recall Yellow Longbill *Macrosphenus flavicans*[294].

DESCRIPTION ADULT ♂ ***Head to upper back*** Glossy blue-black. ***Lower back and rump*** Silky white. ***Wings and tail*** Glossy blue-black. ***Underparts*** White; flank and thighs white. ***Bare parts*** Bill greyish-black, with paler base on upper and lower mandible; palate unknown; legs bluish-grey; eye dark reddish-brown. ADULT ♀ ***Head*** Crown and nape grey, shading into tawny-brown on rest of upperparts, wings and tail; face with pale loral stripe and whitish narrow eye-ring. ***Underparts*** Tawny-buff to pale orange, paling to white in centre, lower belly and undertail-coverts. ***Bare parts*** Like ♂. JUVENILE Little known, apparently similar to adult ♀. IMMATURE ♀ Like adult ♀ but with paler head. ♂ head to mantle greyish mottled with black. Scapulars patchy black, rest of back brown with white patches; uppertail-coverts brown like ♀. Underparts whitish mottled tawny-brown as plumage changes. Eye brown[330, 500].

GEOGRAPHICAL VARIATION Two races with variation in wing and bill size in both sexes, and colour of ♀♀; ♂♂ indistinguishable. ♀ nominate *sabini* (Sierra Leone to Nigeria) is paler with smaller wing and bill. ♀ *melanoleucus* (Cameroon to Zaïre and Angola at Cabinda) is darker brown on head and back, and has a longer bill.

MOULT Wing feathers moulted May–Jun (Liberia)[330, 259].

RANGE, HABITAT and STATUS **Breeding range** West Africa in Sierra Leone, Liberia, Ivory Coast, Ghana, Benin, Nigeria, Cameroon to Central African Republic, southward to Equatorial Guinea, Gabon, Congo, Zaïre, Angola (Cabinda). In Central Africa from central, E and S Zaïre. Record from Bioko rejected[431]. **Habitat** Mainly in lowland primary and secondary forest and forest edge. Occasionally in secondary and logged forest, thick bush and edge of clearings, towns and gardens[37, 234, 259, 298, 431, 451, 504, 848, 858]. **Status** Resident, uncommon to locally common. **Conservation status** Unknown.

MOVEMENTS Sedentary (Gabon)[294].

SOCIAL ORGANISATION and GENERAL BEHAVIOUR Little known. Solitary or in pairs; secretive and skulking, moving about in a crouched position like a large warbler. Apparently members of a pair remain closer together than other bush-shrikes. Makes loud 'fripping' sound with wings. Home range *c.*20 ha. **Foraging behaviour** Gleans insects from foliage high up in canopy, usually higher than 8 m, mostly from 20–45 m. Searches outer branches, twigs and vines, often on edge of clearings or in gloomy interior, where it keeps to dense foliage and creeper tangles, hopping about in search of food. Also searches extremities of branches, picking prey off upper and lower surface of leaves. Often joins mixed foraging parties[294, 347, 505, 858]. **Food** Arthropods, mainly insects, including Orthoptera (grasshoppers and crickets), Coleoptera (beetles), Lepidoptera (caterpillars and moths), Isoptera (termites)[259, 294, 505].

SOUNDS Little known. Repertoire consists of loud calls, explosive repetitive whistles, clicking and harsh rasping notes. Whistled notes include a prolonged descending sequence, variable in length, of loud pealing notes, the sequence lasting up to 2–3 minutes: *tsee-tsu-tsu-tsu-tsu-tsu...*, *Tew-tew-tew...*, *Tzeeeu-Tzeeeu-* or *WeetWeet---tuu---tuu-*. Series may begin with very high-pitched notes, like squeaky bicycle pump, descending in pitch and repetition rate, *hihihi-he-he-hee-hee-her–her...*, or *tWeetWeet–tu-tu–tuur-*. Descending sequence recalls some batis sequences or notes of Yellow Longbill. Nasal rasping *Tzrrrrrr*, *TzweeTzwee*, *zzreet-zzreet*, *Zzz* or *Tzrrreeeeu* notes similar to Black-backed Puffback but longer. Harsh notes include a grating trill, or long rattling series (up to 4 sec) *trtrtrtrtr-* (possibly alarm), often given in flight with much 'wing-fripping' and white puffback display, also *tok-tok-tok-* in similar display, and a drawn-out *weeeer* and loud clicking sequence of rapid percussive notes *Tick-Tick-Tick*. Three ♂♂ chasing each other gave loud *krrraa* rattles, preceded by *pik pik*. Contact signalled with grating *krrriéé* call[34, 294, 500, 501, 504, 572, 717].

BREEDING BIOLOGY Little known; territorial and probably monogamous. Estimated 2–5 pairs/km² (SE Liberia) and 8–10 pairs/km² (Gabon)[294, 858]. **Season** West Africa Jun–Dec[37, 259, 338, 858]. Nestbuilding also recorded in dry season (Zaïre)[22]; family parties at end of short dry season (Gabon)[294]. **Displays** ***Courtship*** ♂ fluff out white rump in an elaborate display[37]. No further breeding information, except immature changing into adult plumage in May (Liberia)[330].

MEASUREMENTS and WEIGHTS Races combined ♂ (9) wing 88–94 (90.0), tail 70–77 (74.0), bill (to skull) 24.5–27.5 (26.2), tarsus 23–24 (23.5); ♀ (8) wing 85–88 (86.6), tail 73–81 (76.3), bill (to skull) 25–27 (25.9), tarsus 22–24 (23.0)[500]. **Weight** *sabini* ♂ (3) 31 g, 40.7 g, 43.9 g (38.5); ♀ (3) 32.4 g, 39 g, 39.2 g (35.8) (Liberia)[259]. For additional data see[259, 330, 494].

69 BLACKCAP BUSH-SHRIKE (Blackcap or Marsh Tchagra)

Antichromus minuta **Plate 27**

FIELD IDENTIFICATION Medium-small (16–18 cm), chestnut-brown, black and whitish bush-shrike with a stocky, short-tailed, big-headed and heavy-billed appearance. Black head with reddish eye, chestnut-brown wings, short black tail and buffy-white underparts distinctive. Nominate race has a black V on back formed by scapulars. Sexes different. ♀ has broad white eyebrow. Young similar to ♀ but buffier, with mottled and streaked crown and back. Flight short with loud 'wing-fripping'. Short whistled song bulbul-like, often in duet. Display-flight distinctive. Solitary or in pairs; skulking but often perches in open with distinctive upright posture. Resident in moist, marshy, rank grass habitat. Distribution fragmented from W, Central, E and central southern Africa as far south as E Zimbabwe; absent from central Congo basin. ***Flight characteristics***: Generally flies only short distances, except in display-flight, which is rather jerky, with 'wing-fripping' during ascent, followed by descending glide, then dives into cover. Wings broad and rounded.

COMPARISONS ♀ and young resemble Black-crowned Tchagra *Tchagra senegala*, especially the black crown, whitish eyebrow and chestnut-brown wings. Separated on short black tail which lacks conspicuous white tips, deeper bill, habit of perching in the open (Black-crowned seldom perches exposed for long periods), short song (Black-crowned has drawn-out lilting song), reddish eye and rank habitat.

DESCRIPTION **ADULT ♂** ***Head*** Upper half of head including eye, but not ear-coverts, glossy jet-black; ear-coverts and cheeks white. ***Back*** Reddish-brown, paler on rump; scapulars streaked with black, giving the appearance of a V (lacking in southern races). ***Wings*** Coverts bright chestnut-brown, quills brown with narrow chestnut-brown outer web. ***Tail*** Short, completely black with very small whitish tips. ***Underparts*** Chin and throat white grading into buff to buffy-white on breast, belly and flanks. ***Bare parts*** Bill and palate black, legs slate-grey, eye reddish-pink to pale purple. For pterylosis see[49]. **ADULT ♀** Similar to ♂ except has a prominent broad white eyebrow and a black stripe through the eye. **JUVENILE** resembles a dull ♀ but with buffy-white eyebrow and mottled and streaked crown. Mantle and scapulars have a black-streaked appearance in nominate race, also present to a lesser extent in other races which lack this character in adult plumage. Wings like adult. Tail dark brownish-black. Underparts buffier. Bill pale at base of lower mandible, legs grey, eye grey-brown. **IMMATURE** Gradual transition to adult plumage. Crown developing through a more patchy black and buff appearance to glossy jet-black of adult. Buffy-white eyebrow disappears in ♂, becoming whiter in ♀. Scapulars become more prominent in nominate race, but disappear in other races. Pale base to lower mandible steadily disappears and eye becomes like adult.

GEOGRAPHICAL VARIATION At least four races, variation mainly in body size and presence or absence of black scapulars. Northern nominate *minuta* (Sierra Leone to Ethiopia, N and E Zaïre, Angola [Cabinda], S Sudan, Kenya and NE Tanzania) has black scapulars. This character is not found in other races, which show slight variation in size and coloration from larger, paler *remota* (SE Zimbabwe) to darker *anchietae* (Angola, S Zaïre, S Tanzania, Malawi) and smaller *reichenowi* (coastal E Kenya, NE Tanzania), which has white at base of crown. Nominate race sometimes considered distinct species, and *remota* not recognised by some authors[3, 24, 184, 303].

MOULT Post-breeding moult recorded; Feb wing moult (Liberia), Aug–Nov (Kenya); Jun (Tanzania)[25, 205, 562, 858].

RANGE, HABITAT and STATUS **Breeding range** Widespread but fragmented. West Africa from Sierra Leone, SE Guinea, Liberia, Ivory Coast, Ghana, Togo, central and S Nigeria, S Cameroon, S Gabon, S Central African Republic, lower and N Congo, N, E and S Zaïre, S Sudan east to SW Ethiopia, Uganda, W Kenya, W, central and S Tanzania, Rwanda, Burundi, Malawi,

Mozambique, E Zimbabwe, N Zambia, S Zaïre and central and N Angola and Cabinda. **Habitat** Generally occurs at low to medium altitudes, from sea-level on edge of lagoon up to *c.*2000 m. Found in moist, humid areas with tall grass and scattered bushes or in reeds and papyrus on edge of streams and marshes, damp edges of forest or secondary growth. Does not penetrate far into papyrus swamps. Also in overgrown old cultivation and cotton, coffee, sugarcane and maize plantations. At higher elevations in bracken-briar and herbaceous scrub on hillsides[5, 7, 13, 15, 21, 23, 26, 30, 37, 101, 119, 242, 259, 290, 291, 296, 301, 318, 319, 431, 504, 631, 848, 858, 907]. **Status** Locally common to uncommon resident. **Conservation status** Unknown. The fragmented nature of its distribution facilitates the identification of range contraction. Some populations in East Africa appear to be threatened. In Kenya the ranges of nominate race and coastal *reichenowi* have contracted in the last decade[2, 318, 631].

MOVEMENTS Little evidence, although in Nigeria N records are mostly during the rainy season when they breed, suggesting possible seasonal movements. The interpretation of Mozambique coastal records (May and Jul) as possible non-breeding visitors requires confirmation[13, 15, 26, 37].

SOCIAL ORGANISATION and GENERAL BEHAVIOUR Usually solitary, in pairs or small family group, particularly at end of breeding season. A rather slow-moving bird, often seen sitting upright for long periods exposed on taller bushes, reeds or grass stems, especially in early morning and evening. When disturbed prefers to creep away, or flies a short distance before dropping back into thick cover and disappearing. Territory advertised and defended with short whistled phrase given in flight or occasionally while perched. Flight-song display consists of a level flight, during which the bird does a sudden upward check, rising with muffled 'wing-fripping'. At apex of flight, raises head and crest and gives whistled phrase, followed by downward glide with tail fanned. ♀ often accompanies ♂ in duet, giving nasal *cherrruu*. She also occasionally does a less elaborate flight-song display, giving her nasal call a few times. Defends a territory of *c.*1–1.5 ha. Aggressive territorial interactions consist of repeated flight-song displays and, when perched, birds move about excitedly bowing, jerking the body from side to side, flicking wings and cocking the tail. ♀ joins in these interactions in duet. Alarm usually accompanied by similar body movements. Contact appears to be maintained by duetting and soft, harsh, nasal or mewing calls. Roosts low down in small bush. Scratches indirectly[101, 205, 304, 631]. **Foraging behaviour** Most prey is gleaned from the stems of reeds and grass and from the trunks, branches and leaves of bushes. Some prey is caught on the ground. Also occasionally hawks insects in the air[205]. **Food** Arthropods, mainly large insects, including: Orthoptera (grasshoppers), Coleoptera (beetles), Odonata (dragonflies) and Hemiptera (bugs and cicadas)[205, 290, 319].

SOUNDS Repertoire consists of a short whistled phrase and harsh, nasal, mewing or bleating sounds. At least two types of ♂ territorial call given in flight display and occasionally when perched: a short cheery whistle (i) *tuweetwertuweet* or *tuwertuwee*, and (ii) *tuweetilweuu* (*remota*) or *hwehwerttweo*, also transcribed as *pirree ti-weep peeeu, chillep-chee-chin, hetutlweuu* or *tewayo-tuwaro*, suggesting the words 'today or tomorrow' (*minuta*). The phrase sounds rather bulbul-like, and is often responded to by ♀ in duet with nasal *cherrrruu*. In aggressive territorial threat ♂ and ♀ calls often followed by rapid harsh *tzzerrr-tzzerrr-, tzzrrrr-tzzrrrr-* and *Tzik-Tzik-* calls. Alarm signalled by repeated harsh *Tzik-Tzik-Tzik-* and rattling *Kzrrrr-* calls, hoarse *charr, churr, chuck* or scolding *kiop* or *tchup* notes. Prior to roosting gives low harsh *tzrr-tzrr-* calls. Contact maintained with softer *tzik-tzik-* and *chirp* calls by ♂, answered by ♀ with nasal *maeeer-, naae* or *maa* mewing or bleating calls. Fledged young beg with similar nasal mewing call. Makes 'fripping' sounds with wings at start of flight display[5, 15, 48, 205, 290, 299, 500, 501, 631]. Sonagram[48].

BREEDING BIOLOGY Little known. Monogamous and territorial[205, 304]. **Season** Jun–Jul (Nigeria)[15, 37, 328]; dependent young Oct (Ghana)[234]; Mar–Apr (Cameroon)[347]; Oct (Sudan)[242]; Feb–Jun, Sep–Nov (East Africa; Uganda, Kenya and Tanzania)[9, 25, 293, 318, 832]; Jul–Oct in NE, Sep–Mar in SE (Zaïre)[22, 290]; Nov (Malawi)[119]; Nov–Dec (Zambia)[291]; Nov–Mar (Zimbabwe)[12, 19, 30, 304, 359]; Jan–Mar, in north Dec (Mozambique)[5, 26]. **Displays** ***Courtship*** Little known, appears to resemble territorial threat. In addition to duetting and repeated flight-song displays by ♂, in which rump feathers are fluffed out, both sexes also make nasal mewing *maeeer-* calls while ♂ chases ♀. Not known to courtship-feed[205, 304, 500]. **Nest** Both sexes build. A rather bulky, deep cup, often decorated externally with snake skin. Built of tendrils, stems and rootlets, bound on the edge with a little spider web. Some nests have a lining, usually consisting of fine grass pieces, sometimes moss or vegetable down and occasionally a feather. Usually placed less than 1 m (n=8) above ground, occasionally up to *c.*1.6 m, in fork of a small bush, or woven onto upright stems, usually at edge of marshy area or in secondary growth on edge of forest. ***Size*** OD 76–95 mm, ID 64–75 mm, cup depth 38–52 mm, height 61–110 mm (n=3)[2, 5, 20, 22, 25, 205, 299, 304, 500, 934]. **Eggs** Usually 2–3 (1–3, n=5). White, spotted and streaked with reddish, purplish-browns and greys mainly in zone at large end. ***Size*** 19.4–26.6 x 15.7–18.9 mm (22.5 x 17.0, n=12)[19, 48]. For additional information see[5, 6, 15, 242]. **Incubation** By both sexes. Period unknown. **Nestling** Hatch naked and blind, skin pinkish after 6–7 days. Mouth spots unknown. Role of sexes unknown. Young beg with nasal mewing *maeeer-maeeer-* calls. Period unknown[12, 27, 205, 506]. No further breeding information.

MEASUREMENTS and WEIGHTS Races combined ♂ (36) wing 70–81 (75.6), tail 70–84 (75.0), bill (to skull) 17.6–23 (20.3), tarsus 24.6–30.5 (26.8); ♀ (21) wing 69–79 (74.5), tail 70–90 (76.4), bill (to skull) 18.2–28.6 (21.5), tarsus 24.1–29.5 (27.1)[500]. **Weight** Races probably combined ♂ (13) 30–36.5 g (33.0); ♀ (5) 32.2–36.5 g (34.7)[48]. For additional data see[299, 259, 319, 478, 582, 764].

70 BLACK-CROWNED TCHAGRA *Tchagra senegala* Plate 27

FIELD IDENTIFICATION Medium-large (20–23 cm), brown and black bush-shrike with bright chestnut-brown wings, long black graduated tail broadly tipped white (distinctive in flight). Head with black crown, prominent whitish eyebrow, long black line through eye and long black bill. More often heard than seen. Easily identified on slow mournful lilting whistle. Sexes similar. Young similar to adult but buffier, crown mottled brown and black. Usually solitary; largely terrestrial and skulking. Widespread resident in tree and bush savannas of Africa. Resident N and S of Sahara and in S Arabian Peninsula, absent from forests and arid desert areas. ***Flight characteristics***: Flies low between bushes; flight rather heavy and jerky, often with 'wing-fripping' sounds followed by a glide and dash into cover. Wings broad and rounded; graduated tail fanned displaying conspicuous broad white tips.

COMPARISONS Easily confused with other tchagras on wing and tail coloration. Southern Tchagra *Tchagra tchagra* is similar size, but has dark brown back and crown and darker underparts. Brown-headed Tchagra *T. australis* is smaller, has a brown crown, white eyebrow bordered above and below with a black stripe and smaller bill. Three-streaked Tchagra *T. jamesi* is smaller still and has a black stripe in the centre of brown crown as well as through eye. ♀ Blackcap Bush-shrike *Antichromus minuta* has a heavier bill, broad white eyebrow, reddish eye and short black tail without broad white tips. Black-crowned generally bolder and more conspicuous than other tchagras. Care required in separating young tchagras as most tend to have crowns of similar colour. Best separated on body and bill size, black and buffy-white head markings and colour of underparts. Ecological segregation: appears to be ecologically segregated from Brown-headed in some areas but not others. Tends to occur in less dense bush, and at S limit does not extend into the more arid areas occupied by Brown-headed, a trend which is reversed at its N limit. In the centre of its range, when in *Brachystegia*, the separation is more obvious, with Brown-headed Tchagra being confined only to denser thickets within this woodland. Broad overlap occurs in mixed and *Acacia* woodlands. Where overlapping they do not appear to compete. The larger body and bill size of Black-crowned suggests a difference in preferred prey[139, 205, 481, 515].

DESCRIPTION **ADULT** Sexes similar. ***Head*** Forehead, crown and nape black to deep blue-black, eyebrow from bill to back of head varies from white (*senegala* only) to varying amounts of buff on sides and back of head; black stripe through the eye to buffy brown ear-coverts. ***Back*** Tawny-brown, scapulars rufous-brown with dark centres, rump and uppertail-coverts greyish. ***Wings*** Coverts bright chestnut-brown, flight feathers brown with narrow outer web chestnut-brown. ***Tail*** Graduated, central pair greyish-brown with fine cross-barring, others black broadly tipped white, increasing in extent in outer feathers. ***Underparts*** Chin and throat cream to greyish-white; rest light grey to whitish on belly. ***Bare parts*** Bill and palate black; legs grey; eye greyish-mauve, some individuals having a number of white spots surrounding the pupil. In East Africa eye of ♂ purplish-blue, ♀ dark blue[631]. **JUVENILE/IMMATURE** Appears to lack distinctive plumage, basically similar to adult, except crown mottled brown and blackish; cheeks, sides of head and whole eyebrow buffy. Underparts buffier, tail buff-tipped and more pointed, bill grey-brown, lower mandible paler. In East Africa juveniles have brownish-grey eyes[631].

GEOGRAPHICAL VARIATION At least 14 races with variation in size and coloration, mainly on back, underparts and eyebrow. At least three main groups recognisable: large dark North African birds, smaller dark NE African and S Arabian Peninsula birds, and those from the rest of Africa. Variation ranges from large, dark *cucullata* (North Africa from Morocco to Tunisia and Libya) to smaller dark *habessinica* (including *warsangliensis*) (NE Africa from Sudan, Ethiopia, N Somalia, Eritrea, Djibouti) and *percivali* (SW Arabian Peninsula in Yemen and Oman). Arabian race is unique in that it lacks the black scapular and tertial markings, and brown central tail feathers of other races. At the other extreme *remigialis* (Chad to Sudan) and *kalahari* (Zimbabwe, S Angola, Namibia) are paler, particularly below, than nominate *senegala* (Senegal to Sierra Leone), the only race with an almost completely white eyebrow. The rest, including *camerunensis* (Cameroon to S Sudan, Uganda), *pallida* (Ghana, Ivory Coast to Central African Republic), *armena* (S Uganda to SE Zaïre, Zambia), *rufofusca* (SW Zaïre, N Angola), *notha* (Mali to Chad), *confusa* (South Africa), *orientalis* (S Somalia, E Tanzania), and *mozambica* (Mozambique) are intermediate and rather similar[3, 23, 180, 238, 290, 291, 326, 500].

MOULT Complete adult post-breeding moult, primaries descendent. Moult in first-adult plumage appears complete[257].

RANGE, HABITAT and STATUS **Breeding range** Widespread, mainly in Africa with a small population in Middle East from SW Arabia (Yemen and Oman). Populations occur N and S of Sahara. In North Africa mainly coastal in Morocco, Algeria, Tunisia and Libya. Occurs S of the Sahara in the Sahel region from c.17°N southwards, except from Congo basin and arid NE and SW areas of the continent. In West and Central Africa from S Mauritania, Senegal, Gambia, Guinea-Bissau, Guinea, Sierra Leone, Liberia, Ivory Coast, Ghana, Togo, Benin, Cameroon, Nigeria, Gabon, Congo, Zaïre, Rwanda, Burundi, Mali, Burkina Faso, Niger, Chad and Central African Republic eastwards into Sudan, Ethiopia, Eritrea and Djibouti. In East Africa absent from arid areas in SE Ethiopia, N and NE Kenya and most of Somalia, except S. Occurs in Uganda, Tanzania, Zambia, Malawi, Mozambique, Zimbabwe, SE South Africa, Botswana (except SW), NE Namibia, Angola except arid SW and Cabinda. **Habitat** In North Africa and Middle East, found in scrubby semi-desert, dense macchia, tamarisk, euphorbia and thickets, dry open forest, plantations and gardens. Prefers bushy slopes and ravines at base of mountains. Rest of Africa in wide range of habitats from dry thorn and savanna woodlands at N and S limits to moister deciduous broadleaved woodlands, including *Brachystegia* and forest edge, in central areas. Generally requires good ground cover and is less common in thornbush. In Ethiopia up to 3000 m in forested habitats dominated by olive, juniper and *Podocarpus*, and in lowland *Ficus–Acacia* habitats. Also found in overgrown cultivations, exotic plantations and gardens[7, 26, 30, 37, 39, 45, 48, 182, 183, 217, 234, 257, 285, 290, 291, 292, 318, 325, 330, 431, 514, 631, 639, 807, 848, 858, 859, 907]. **Status** Resident; local and uncommon in North Africa; rest of Africa uncommon to locally common. **Conservation status** Not threatened, but does not adapt well to man-made habitats.

MOVEMENTS Local seasonal movements recorded in Morocco, Gambia and South Africa. A single ringed adult was retrapped within 1 km of the ringing site[39, 205, 257, 639].

SOCIAL ORGANISATION and GENERAL BEHAVIOUR Solitary or in pairs; shy and retiring and difficult to observe. Usually seen on ground or flying low between bushes with conspicuous black and white tail spread as it dives for cover. Prefers to creep about, rodent-like, rather than fly. More often heard than seen, calls usually given from within a bush, or on an exposed perch near the top of bush, also in flight-song display. Occasionally from ground or nest. ♀ usually perches below ♂ during duets. When calling, adopts a very upright posture. Song heard mostly in morning and evening, mainly in austral spring and early summer. Territorial calling reaches a peak prior to breeding with lilting whistle consisting of at least three phrases. In non-breeding season this is reduced to a single phrase. Defends a territory from *c*.4 ha and larger. In territorial flight display, ♂ flies steeply to *c*.15 m while making loud 'fripping' sound with the wings. In upward flight, tail held depressed and body very upright. At the highest point raises crest, holds head up, and begins lilting whistle as it glides, sometimes in an arc, jerkily down, fanning tail near end of flight, which may cover up to 70 m. ♀ sometimes accompanies ♂ in similar flight display without calling, but often responds to ♂ in duet. During territorial threat birds observed walking about on the ground with head held up, tail tensely wagging, raised and lowered, or rotated, sometimes with slight fanning. When alarmed adopts a more horizontal posture, moving about excitedly, flicking tail and bowing body while giving harsh calls. Roosting behaviour unknown. Scratches indirectly[6, 46, 48, 205, 257]. **Foraging behaviour** Forages low down, mainly on ground in the vegetation around the base of trees and bushes, where it creeps, hops and runs about, also flicks debris aside with its bill like a thrush and will turn dung over in search of food. Also gleans from trunks, branches and leaves, sometimes taking aerial prey. Noted using root structures for securing a snake while stripping flesh. Occasionally joins mixed foraging parties, particularly in non-breeding season. **Food** Arthropods, mainly insects and their larvae, also small vertebrates. Insects include Coleoptera (beetles), Orthoptera (grasshoppers, crickets), Mantodea (mantises), Isoptera (termites), Hymenoptera (wasps), Hemiptera (bugs and cicadas), Lepidoptera (caterpillars). Also feeds on spiders, worms and small fruits (*Lycium*). Recorded vertebrate prey includes tadpoles, tree-frogs, lizards and snakes. Will attack small mammals and birds, but not recorded killing and eating them. In East Africa young are fed moth larvae, nymphal grasshoppers and other Orthoptera, beetles, spiders, and tadpoles[46, 205, 217, 246, 257, 285, 290, 916, 1009].

SOUNDS Repertoire consists of lilting whistles, trills and harsh notes. Main song is a loud lilting or slurred drawn-out mellow whistle with much individual, seasonal and geographical variation. Territorial call usually consists of a series of 1–3 repetitive phrases, each successive syllable and phrase falling in pitch and volume: *ha-wee-tee ha-wee-too ha-woo-too* or *hweeheoow-hweooheuuw-hwuuhuuuw*. ♀ duets with long rattling *trrrrrrrr-* trill, sometimes initiating duet with this call. Song usually delivered from a perch or in flight display, where initiated by loud 'wing-fripping' sounds as bird flies up. Other duets consist of rattling trill and a single whistled phrase followed by another trill in quick succession. During more aggressive territorial interactions, pairs counter-sing with excited and complex duetting including explosive whistling, growling, rolling, bubbling, chuckling, tearing, clashing *sswr-rrrreeeeeeo* and whooping *trrrreeeo* or *whu-heeuw* whistles and much 'wing-fripping'. Interactions may involve one giving a throaty *chrrrrwee* to which the other bird replies with a low, drawn-out *whoooo*. Mild alarm is signalled by *chrrrrr* or slowly repeated *Chuk-Chuk-*, *Tsuk-Tsuk-* or *tchuk-* and rattling *Krrrrr-* or *chrrrrrrrr* and guttural *churr* calls. More intense alarm signalled by harsh tearing *Kzzzrrr-* sounds. Apparently different in East Africa where recorded as a clear liquid *chu-tu-woi* or *chu-ti-boi*. Long-range contact maintained by duetting; short range contact appears to be maintained with barely audible, soft throaty sounds. Nestlings beg with soft guttural hissing *ghuurr* sounds[2, 5, 46, 48, 205, 500, 501, 504, 631]. Sonagram[43, 48].

BREEDING BIOLOGY Monogamous and territorial. In Morocco recorded breeding at densities of 1.3–8 pairs/km², or 1 pair/10 ha depending on habitat. In South Africa 1 pair/25 ha. Very secretive in vicinity of nest. Apparently single-brooded[320, 257, 285].

Season May (Oman, S Arabia)[217]; May–Jun (Morocco), Apr–May (Tunisia)[28, 182, 257]; Aug–Nov (Sudan)[242]; Apr–Jun (Somalia)[33, 859]; Apr–Jul

(Ethiopia)[292]; Jul (Senegal)[482]; Oct–Dec (Gambia)[38, 39, 482]; Dec (Liberia)[858]; display-flights most frequent in wet season Apr–Jun in S and Jul–Sep in N, dependent young Apr and Aug (Ghana)[234]; Feb–Sep, mostly May–Sep (Nigeria)[37, 328, 529]; Mar in N, May–Jun in E, Sep–Nov in S (Zaïre)[6, 290, 319]; Aug–Oct (Angola)[7, 865, 907]; all year (East Africa)[293]; Nov–Dec, Jun (Tanzania)[293, 832]; Jan–May, Oct–Dec (Malawi)[119, 359]; Jan–Mar, May–Jun, Sep–Dec (Zambia)[291, 502]; Aug–Apr, mainly Oct–Dec (Zimbabwe)[30]; Sep–Mar (Mozambique)[26, 48, 297]; Sep–Feb, mainly Oct–Dec (South Africa)[48, 639]; egg-laying Dec (Botswana)[807].

Displays *Courtship* Little known, but flight-song displays are common and probably contain rump-fluffing as in other tchagras. Pairs perform elaborate duet sequences resembling those used in territorial threat, during which calling is complex and they adopt very upright postures and wag, rotate, raise and lower the tail, sometimes fanning it as well. Displays also involve slow head and body side to side movements and bowing. Not known to courtship-feed. Several ♂♂, while chasing a ♀, may interact with each other to the point of physical contact[205].

Nest Built by both sexes. A shallow cup built of fine twigs, rootlets and tendrils, and lined with fine grass stems or rootlets. Sometimes bound with a little spider web and occasionally decorated with dry leaves or snakeskin. Placed *c.*2 m (0.6–5.4, n=185) (southern Africa) above the ground, sometimes higher, in vertical or horizontal fork in bush or small tree, usually well concealed, but sometimes exposed. ***Size*** OD 88–125 mm, ID 72–88 mm, cup depth 25–53 mm, height 50–78 mm. Built in *c.*7 days[6, 20, 28, 205, 237, 328, 500].

Eggs 2–3 (1–4, n=100) (southern Africa). Colour variable; pure white, slightly glossy ground colour, well marked with spots and lines of bunting type (North Africa); white to pinkish-white, spotted and blotched with dark red-brown, grey and lavender concentrated at large end (southern Africa) or scrawled, streaked and smudged with claret, red-brown markings forming a ring at large end (West Africa), with two types identified, Nigeria (either scrawled, irregularly streaked or smudged with claret, red-brown, and purplish-brown, with underlying greyish-purple markings of the same character, markings forming ring at large end; or markings the same colour, but lacks scrawls, with only blotches and spots, concentrated mainly at the large end; white with rather large grey and brown blotches and freckles (*percivali*). ***Size*** Geographically variable; 21.9–27.5 x 17.0–19.4mm (24.6 x 18.0, n=184) (southern Africa)[15, 19, 36, 48, 246, 328]. For additional data see[6, 15, 33, 36, 237, 290, 328]. **Incubation** By both sexes, but mostly by ♀. Sitting bird leaves before mate arrives; apparently no nest relief calling. Reaction of birds to intruder variable, from skulking away to preening in nearby bush. Period 12–15 days (n=2)[205, 805]. **Nestling** Hatch blind, naked, brownish-pink or mauve and without mouth spots. Later become covered in light greyish-brown feathers. Gape yellow with pale fringes. Attended by both sexes, and fed on large insects, mostly grasshoppers. Nestlings beg with soft guttural hissing *ghuurr-ghuurr-* sounds. Fledge after *c.*15 days (14–16, n=2). Recently fledged young keeps in thick cover until able to fly. Dependency period unknown but family groups remain together for most of non-breeding season[27, 46, 205, 331, 328, 500, 506, 513]. For nestling development see[872]. **Predation and longevity** Predation unknown. Ringed bird 6 years old[257]. **Brood parasite** None.

MEASUREMENTS and WEIGHTS Races combined ♂♀? (79) wing 76–97 (86.0), tail 82–107 (94.5), bill (to skull) 17.5–25 (23.0), tarsus 26.5–32.5 (30.0)[500]. **Weight** ♂ (46) 33.0–59.0 g (53.5), ♀ (34) 35.0–59.7 g (53.4), ♂♀? (4) 32–67 g (51.8) (southern Africa)[205]. For additional data see[238, 257, 290, 319, 346, 478, 494, 509, 808, 815].

71 SOUTHERN TCHAGRA *Tchagra tchagra* — Plate 27

FIELD IDENTIFICATION Medium-large (20–22 cm), greyish-brown and black bush-shrike with bright chestnut-brown wings and black tail broadly tipped white (distinctive in flight). Head with rufous-brown crown, prominent white eyebrow, long black stripe through eye and long black bill. Sexes similar. Young similar to adults but duller, paler and buffier. More often heard than seen. Song a rapid series of single whistles at same pitch, usually given in flight display with 'wing-fripping'. Little known, solitary, largely terrestrial, skulking. Resident in dense scrub, thorny riverine and coastal bush of southern Africa from S and SE South Africa and Swaziland. ***Flight characteristics***: Heavy, usually short and low with rapid wingbeats, tail spread with conspicuous broad white tips; wings broad and rounded. Flight-song display initiated with rapid wingbeats associated with 'fripping' sounds as it rises up, followed by song in a descending glide with tail fanned and final dive for cover.

COMPARISONS Similar in structure and overlaps extensively with larger Black-crowned Tchagra *Tchagra senegala*, which has a black crown, white underparts and a mournful slow lilting whistle. Care needed with juvenile Black-crowned Tchagra, as it also has a brown crown. Black-crowned favours more open habitats and occurs at higher elevations. Also similar to smaller Brown-headed Tchagra *T. australis*, which has a dull brown crown (not reddish-brown) with a narrow black line above white eyebrow, and a smaller bill. Overlap with this species restricted to N KwaZulu-Natal. Southern Tchagra is generally darker than both these tchagras. Calls similar to Brown-headed Tchagra, which has double-noted whistles that fall in pitch (Southern Tchagra has single-noted whistles with more constant pitch). Separation of young of these three species requires care. Best identified on body and bill size, black and buffy-white head markings and colour of underparts (darker grey in Southern Tchagra).

DESCRIPTION **ADULT** Sexes similar. ***Head*** Crown olive-brown tinged deep rufous, broad eyebrow almost to nape and sides of face white, line through eye black, ear-coverts greyish-white. ***Back*** Dark olive-brown, rump olive-grey. ***Wings*** Coverts bright rufous-chestnut brown, formed by rufous outer webs, except for median and lesser coverts which are entirely rufous; primaries and secondaries brown with narrow outer web chestnut-brown. ***Tail*** Graduated, central pair greyish-brown with fine cross-barring, others black broadly tipped white, increasing in extent in outer feathers. ***Underparts*** Vary from pale to dark grey, flanks darker, more olive-grey; chin and throat greyish-white. ***Bare parts*** Bill and palate black; legs grey; eye brown[500]. **JUVENILE/IMMATURE** Resembles adult but generally duller and paler on upperparts, more olive-tinged. Eyebrow buffy-white. Underparts and wings have a buffy tinge. Tail more pointed with buffy tips. Bill dark brown, paler on base of lower mandible[32].

GEOGRAPHICAL VARIATION Three races, varying in bill length and darkness of upper- and underparts. Northern birds browner above with underparts more olive; S birds have greyer underparts. Nominate *tchagra* (Western Cape in SW South Africa) is darkest below with longest bill, *caffrariae* (Eastern Cape in South Africa) is lighter below with smallest bill, *natalensis* (KwaZulu-Natal to Mpumalanga in E South Africa, Swaziland) has the lightest underparts but crown redder than previous race[3, 51, 500].

MOULT Unknown.

RANGE, HABITAT and STATUS **Breeding range** Mainly coastal South Africa from S Western Cape at Hermanus to KwaZulu-Natal. In S, inland to Beaufort West, Graaf-Reinet and Cradock, in the N to Swaziland and SE Mpumalanga Province. Probably S Mozambique. Confusion with Brown-headed Tchagra is known to have influenced historical records. **Habitat** Mainly occurs within 100 km of coast, penetrating inland up rivers. Found on dense drier vegetation, including coastal bush, thorny scrub, edge of coastal dune forest, in clearings, lantana tangles, thorny thickets, brush piles at edge of rural cultivation and fynbos. In dry country found in dense *Acacia* riverine bush. At northern limit in bracken and scrub at interface between montane grassland and forest[26, 32, 50, 51, 205, 320, 322, 431, 512, 639]. **Status** Resident, locally uncommon in N to fairly common in S. **Conservation status** Not threatened, and appears to have benefited from the spread of alien trees in some areas. Some evidence of a range expansion over the last 25–30 years in S range[332, 639].

MOVEMENTS Sedentary[639].

SOCIAL ORGANISATION and GENERAL BEHAVIOUR Usually solitary or in pairs in austral summer, or small family groups mainly in winter. Keeps to thick cover, where difficult to see, shy and skulking low down or on the ground. Seldom emerges from cover, except to fly low, diving for cover with black and white tail fanned, from one thicket to another. Calls with head and bill held up. Advertises and defends a territory of *c*.4 ha. Territorial behaviour consists of a flight display which usually consists of 'wing-fripping' followed by repeated whistles while in flight, but may consist only of 'wing-fripping' followed by whistles once the bird has landed. Flight display usually low over bushes, sometimes circular; consists of a rapid ascent combined with loud 'wing-fripping' and rump fluffed out. At apex of flight, head and crest are raised before descent begins, calling as it glides down with tail broadly fanned. High-intensity threat in aggressive interactions involves excited 'wing-fripping', tail-fanning and jerky body movements. It may also take the form of slow head and body side to side movements and bowing, tail cocking and flicking. Whistle and rattling calls also made in display-flight[205, 332, 872]. **Foraging behaviour** Low down, mainly terrestrial where it creeps, runs and hops about, turning over debris like a thrush, also gleans prey from lower branches and stems[48, 205, 872]. **Food** Arthropods, mainly insects and their larvae, including Coleoptera (beetles) and Orthoptera (corn crickets). Also takes small fruits and small land molluscs[1, 48, 205, 872].

SOUNDS Repertoire consists of a series of single-note whistles and various bubbling, chuckling and harsh tearing sounds. Sounds geographically variable. Territorial flight display initiated with 'wing-fripping' followed by a series of stuttering croaking notes which change into loud liquid repetitive whistles, slowing in tempo towards the end but remaining at same pitch. Usually about 10–15 notes, sometimes as many as 30. Whistling often continues after the bird has landed *ttttrtr-te-te-teu--teu—teuu-teuuu* or *trrr-t-t-t-tew-tew-tew*. After such displays the ♂ often gives a harsh tearing *tzzerrr-tzzerrr-* or *sskwirrr-* (similar to *Dryoscopus* puffbacks). Similar call occasionally used by the ♀ in duet. During more aggressive interactions 'wing-fripping' usually combined with complex purring, trilling and tearing sounds including harsh *TziK-* or *Tzock-*, chuckling *ChoK-*, tearing *tzzerrr-* or *jee jeee* and rattling *KiKiKiKiKi-* calls which are also used in alarm. Contact a quiet single *twet* while birds foraging close together, or louder harsh *tzzerrr-* calls and duetting when further apart. Nestlings beg with quiet tippering sound. Name of genus derived from Levaillant's description of call *tcha-tcha-tcha-gra*[9, 48, 205, 332, 500, 872]. Sonagram[43, 48].

BREEDING BIOLOGY Little known. Monogamous and territorial. Calling reaches a peak prior to breeding. Sometimes double-brooded[205]. **Season** Aug–Dec, mainly Sep–Nov (South Africa)[48, 205, 639]. **Displays** ***Courtship*** Little known, appears similar to high-intensity threat and involves frequent excited display-flights by ♂ with grey rump fluffed out, also excited posturing with tail fanned and repeated body-bowing and stretching. Not known to courtship-feed[205]. **Nest** Probably built by both sexes. A shallow cup of stems, twigs and rootlets lined with finer rootlets, hair also used sometimes. Placed *c.*1 m (0.3–3, n=41) above the ground, in a fork of matted bush or shrub, usually well hidden and often in an isolated bush or thicket. Sometimes repairs old nest or may build on top of old nest of other species. ***Size*** OD 113–127 mm, ID 70–101 mm, cup depth 50 mm[48, 205, 332, 506, 872]. **Eggs** Usually 2 (2–3, n=17). White, spotted and scrolled with dark red-brown and purplish-grey. ***Size*** 22.9–26.7 x 17–19.7 mm (24.3 x 18.4, n=19)[19, 48]. **Incubation** Role of sexes unknown. Incubating bird very confiding. Period *c.*16 days (15.5–16, n=2)[27, 48, 205, 331]. **Nestling** Hatch blind, naked and without mouth spots. Skin initially orange, later darkening to mauve-pink. Nestlings and fledglings attended by both sexes. Fledge after *c.*14 days (13–15, n=2)[27, 48, 205, 506, 872]. For nestling development see [872]. **Predation and longevity** Unknown. **Brood parasite** One nest appeared to be parasitised by Jacobin Cuckoo *Oxylophus jacobinus*, and in an experiment a pair accepted a white Jacobin-type egg[512, 802].

MEASUREMENTS and WEIGHTS Races combined ♂♀? (31) wing 75–86 (81.1), tail 82–92.3 (87.9), bill 25.5–30.8 (27.9), tarsus 27–31 (29.0)[500]. **Weight** ♂♀? (22) 38–54.3 g (47.2)[48]. For additional data see[51, 205, 478].

72 BROWN-HEADED TCHAGRA *Tchagra australis* Plate 28

FIELD IDENTIFICATION Medium-sized (18–20 cm), brown and black bush-shrike with bright chestnut-brown wings and black graduated tail broadly tipped white (conspicuous in flight). Head with white eyebrow bordered above and below by a black line (useful at close range), brown crown and small bill. Sexes similar. Young like adult, but head markings duller and buffier below. More often heard than seen. Song a rapid series of descending double whistles given in flight display initiated with 'wing-fripping'. Solitary, largely terrestrial, skulking. Widespread resident in Africa S of Sahara. Absent from Congo basin, forests and arid NE and SW regions of continent. ***Flight characteristics***: Short; flies low and jerkily between bushes, black and white tail conspicuous as it dives for cover; wings broad and rounded. Flight-song display consists of a jerky upward flight initiated with rapid wingbeats associated with 'fripping' sounds, followed by song in a descending glide with tail fanned and final dive for cover.

COMPARISONS Easily confused with three other tchagras; generally a shier species. Black-crowned Tchagra *Tchagra senegala* is larger with longer tail and bill and a black crown (not brown). Calls distinctive; Black-crowned has slow mournful lilting whistled song. For ecological difference see Black-crowned Tchagra Comparisons p.273. Southern Tchagra *T. tchagra* also larger, with long bill and generally much darker plumage and darker rufous-brown crown with no black line above eyebrow. Flight-song display also similar, but lacks double whistled notes of Brown-headed and pitch remains more constant. Brown-headed overlaps this species in SE range where generally ecologically segregated, occurring in *Acacia* and mixed woodland, while Southern is confined to forest edge and broadleaved thickets. Similar in size and song to Three-streaked Tchagra *T. jamesi*, which has a black stripe in centre of crown, a less distinct eyebrow (lacks upper black stripe) and is generally paler. Overlap with this more arid species possible in E Uganda and SE Kenya. Calls similar. For separation of young of these species see Black-crowned Tchagra Comparisons p.273.

DESCRIPTION ADULT Sexes similar. ***Head*** Forehead and crown brown, eyebrow white, bordered above and below by black line (diagnostic at close range), side of face and ear-coverts brownish. ***Back*** Light brown, rump greyish-brown. ***Wings*** Coverts bright chestnut-brown, quills brown with narrow outer web chestnut-brown, tertials dark brown edged with rufous-brown and buff. ***Tail*** Graduated, central pair greyish-brown with fine cross-barring, others black, broadly tipped white. ***Underparts*** Vary from buff-brown to greyish, flanks similar but darker, chin whitish-buff. ***Bare parts*** Bill and palate black, legs grey, eye light brown with pale inner rim. JUVENILE/IMMATURE Appears to lack distinctive plumage, basically similar to adult but duller and browner, particularly underparts and flanks. Black and white head markings less pronounced, black absent in very young. Tail tipped buff and more pointed, bill light greyish-brown, lower mandible lighter.

GEOGRAPHICAL VARIATION At least 9 races, varying mainly in size and coloration of underparts. Southern and E populations have strong buff tinged underparts and include *australis* (including *tongensis*) (N South Africa, E Swaziland, SE Zimbabwe, S Mozambique), *damarensis* (including *rhodesiensis*) (Angola, Namibia, Botswana, SW Zimbabwe, NW South Africa), *ansorgei* (including *bocagei*) (W Angola) and *littoralis* (coastal E Kenya to S Mozambique). Northern and western populations are whitish below with grey or brownish flanks and include *ussheri* (Sierra Leone to SW Nigeria), *frater* (Nigeria to Gabon, W Zaïre), *emini* (E Zaïre to S Sudan, W Kenya) and *minor* (including *congener* and *littoralis*) (SE Kenya, Tanzania, Malawi, Zambia). Race *souzae* (SE Zaïre to Angola) has the greyest, almost silvery-grey underparts, and differs from all other races in having brown of inner secondaries merging with rufous edges. Visually distinct but vocally similar to nominate race[3, 145, 149, 291, 500].

HYBRIDS or ABNORMAL PLUMAGE An adult ♂ collected W of Lodwar, Turkana (Kenya) has been suggested as a hybrid Brown-headed x Three-streaked Tchagra. It is the size of, and has similar back and tail of Brown-headed. Top of head with white appearance, no black border to brown crown, white eyebrow and lores broader and more pronounced than Brown-headed, extending back and onto nape. Feathers on side of head above eye-stripe tipped brown with white bases. There is a patch of black on middle of nape, but not on crown[1060].

MOULT Post-breeding moult recorded. Flight feathers replaced in Apr–May (Liberia), Nov (Botswana)[205, 330, 546, 858].

RANGE, HABITAT and STATUS Breeding range Widespread in Africa S of *c*.8°N except in Congo basin and arid NE and SW areas of continent. West Africa from Sierra Leone, Liberia, Ivory Coast, Ghana, Togo, Benin, Mali, S Nigeria, S and central Cameroon, S Central African Republic, Gabon, Congo, N, E, W and S Zaïre, S Sudan, Uganda, W Kenya, Tanzania, Rwanda, Burundi, Malawi, Zambia, Zimbabwe, Mozambique, E Swaziland, N and E South Africa, Botswana, Angola including Cabinda, and Namibia except S and W. **Habitat** In a variety of wooded habitats with thick undergrowth, from arid thornbush and scrub (in SW of range), through bush savannas, miombo *Brachystegia, Acacia*, mopane and other broadleaved woodlands to secondary bush, forest edge, gallery forest and clearings. Occurs mainly at low to medium altitudes, but where higher, e.g. Malawi (1800 m) and E Zaïre (*c*.2500 m), found in bracken-briar. Also found in old cultivations and gardens[7, 21, 26, 30, 37, 119, 234, 242, 259, 290, 291, 294, 320, 431, 504, 631, 639, 807, 848, 858, 907]. **Status** Resident, locally common throughout range. **Conservation status** Not threatened, but susceptible to disturbance[294].

MOVEMENTS Sedentary, except possibly some small local movements in more arid areas like Sudan. In southern Africa, 3 ringing recoveries were within 1 km of ringing site[242, 639].

SOCIAL ORGANISATION and GENERAL BEHAVIOUR Usually solitary or in pairs, occasionally in family parties after breeding and in non-breeding season. A shy, skulking species, more often heard than seen. Much calling done in flight display, less frequently while perched, usually concealed in thick vegetation. Keeps low down in bushes and on the ground, creeping about in a crouched posture, movements rodent-like. Seldom sits out exposed; flies reluctantly, preferring to creep or run away. Flight short, low and jerky. Advertises and defends a territory of *c*.4 ha with a distinctive, repeated territorial flight-song display or while perched, where it moves head slowly from side to side. Before giving flight display, ♂ usually zigzags its way to top of small bush or tree. Takes off in a steep jerky upward flight of *c*.15–20 m making loud 'fripping' sounds with wings. Just before reaching apex of flight, raises head and crest, and begins calling while gliding jerkily down. Initially call consists of a rapidly delivered stuttering trill, later developing into a series of double-noted liquid whistles that gradually slow down and drop in pitch. Roosting behaviour unknown. Scratches indirectly[46, 205, 290]. **Foraging behaviour** Mainly on the ground around and under bushes in thick undergrowth, where creeps, runs and hops about. Gleans prey from branches and leaves and occasionally takes aerial prey. Often in mixed foraging parties and forms feeding association with a number of ground or near-ground feeders, taking prey flushed by these species[205, 297, 704]. **Food** Mainly arthropods, occasionally small vertebrates, particularly reptiles. Bulk of prey consists of insects and their larvae, including Orthoptera (grasshoppers), Lepidoptera (caterpillars), Coleoptera (beetles), Mantodea (mantis egg-cases). Also takes spiders. Small hairless mouse fed to chicks[8, 46, 205, 294, 290, 871]. For diet of nestlings see[46].

SOUNDS Repertoire varied, consist of a series of simple or complex whistles, trills and harsher chucking notes. Geographically variable. Territorial song usually given in display flight, accompanied with loud 'wing-fripping'. Sometimes given while perched or on ground. Song has an explosive beginning, initially consisting of a rapidly delivered stuttering trill which develops into a series of double-noted liquid whistles that gradually slow down, dropping in pitch but rising in volume in the middle and fading away at end. Typically consists of 12 notes but may occasionally continue for up to 30 notes: *ttttr-tre-tre-treu–treu—treeuu-*, also *WEEo, WEwo-wo, WEEwo-kew-kew-kew-tu-tut-tu-tu, chero-che-rochererreri-ri-t-ri* and other variations. Notes sometimes rather wheezy. Flight-song display often begun and ended with *tchuk-* notes. ♀ sometimes responds in duet with soft nasal *cheru-cheru*. In southern Africa aggressive interactions include more complex sounds, often in duet, such as nasal *pitcheuu-pitcheuu-* and tearing *Tzk-tzzer-rr-* and *zzweet*, bubbling trilling *trrreeeeee-* whistles, and scolding *tchuk* sounds, sometimes rather warbler-like, with ♀ giving nasal *cheru-* duet. Alarm signalled by harsh repeated *Chuk-Chuk-Chuk-* and *Tzzerrrrrr-, krrrrr-, churr* or *chiii* calls, often combined with short 'fripping' flights. In East Africa gives a low *cheerk* or *chierk* call note as well as a single oriole-like *quweeo*. Contact maintained with *ptchew* and *chuk* or *tuk* calls. During courtship ♂ has warbling song consisting of typical flight-song and courtship calls (see Displays). Nestlings beg with low squeaks and soft guttural *gherrr-* sounds. Fledglings use louder nasal *tzzerrr-* begging calls[5, 22, 46, 48, 205, 290, 294, 500, 501, 504, 631]. Sonagram[48].

BREEDING BIOLOGY Little known. Monogamous and territorial with breeding density of 1 pair/20 ha in *Acacia* and 1 pair/25 ha in broadleaved woodland. Apparently single brooded[6, 46, 205, 320]. **Season** Young in Sep (Liberia)[858]; May–Jun (Ghana)[234]; Feb, Jun–Sep (Nigeria)[37]; Mar, Aug–Oct (Cameroon)[290, 646]; thought to occur all year, definite Oct, Dec (Zaïre)[290]; Aug–Feb (Gabon)[294]; Dec (Sudan)[242]; most months in East Africa (Uganda, Kenya and Tanzania)[293, 832]; Jan–Mar, Oct–Dec (Malawi)[119]; Sep–Apr, mainly Oct–Dec (Zimbabwe)[48]; Jan–Mar, Sep–Dec (Zambia)[291]; Aug–Oct (Angola)[7, 423]; Sep–Nov (Mozambique)[26]; Jan, mainly after Dec (Namibia)[63, 639]; Sep–Mar, mainly Oct–Dec (South Africa)[48, 639]; egg-laying Nov (Botswana)[807]. **Displays *Courtship*** Involves repeated flight-song displays with rump fluffed out and tail fanned on descent. ♂ also postures in front of ♀ while uttering a variety of complex calls resembling those given in territorial threat, including an excited nasal *pitcheuu-pitcheuu-*, tearing *zzweet-* and *trrreeeee-* whistles. Posturing consists of bowing, stretching body up with bill upwards, fanning, cocking and flicking the tail in addition to jerky side to side body movements. Courtship-feeding not known to occur. During this period the ♂ has been observed foraging and collecting nesting material on the ground while giving a warbling song consisting of typical flight-song and territorial threat calls[46, 205, 631]. **Nest** Built by both sexes. A neat, shallow cup of rootlets, leaf petioles or coarse grass, lightly bound with spider web around the outside. Some nests are so thin that the eggs can be seen from below. May contain a little lining of fine grass stems or rootlets. Usually well concealed, placed in a vertical or outer horizontal fork of a sometimes isolated bush or small tree, about 1 m (0.2–3.6, n=166) (southern Africa) above the ground. ***Size*** ID/OD 60–75 mm, cup depth 20–30 mm. Takes about a week to build[46, 205, 294, 500]. **Eggs** 2–3 (2–4, n=72) (southern Africa), laid at 24–48 hour intervals. White to pinkish-white with brown and grey spots and blotches concentrated at the large end (southern Africa). ***Size*** 19.4–25.3 x 14.9–18.3 mm (21.7 x 16.3, n=133) (southern Africa)[19, 48, 294]. For additional data see[290, 347, 646]. **Incubation** By both sexes, mostly by ♀, some reports only by ♀. May sit very tight and start with first egg. ♂ continues flight-song displays, often in the direction of the nest, and may signal nest relief. He feeds ♀ on nest. Period *c.*15 days (14–17, n=3)[27, 46, 205, 294, 500, 805, 832]. **Nestling** Hatch blind, naked and brown, and lack mouth spots. Mouth is bright orange with pale gape flanges. Eyes open in 4–5 days. Attended by both sexes and fledge after *c.*15 days (14–16, n=2). Nestlings beg with soft coarse hissing *gherrr-gherrr-* and nasal *naaa-* sounds and give alarm *tchuk* calls. Later their begging calls are loud nasal *tzzerrr-* sounds which resemble some adult calls. Adults also use this call to attract the young to them. Adults and young also frequently give *Chuk-Chuk-* warning calls during this stage. Dependency period unknown, but young remain in family parties for at least 5 months[27, 46, 205, 294, 331, 500, 506, 646, 805]. **Predation and longevity** Adult preyed on by African Hawk Eagle *Hieraaetus spilogaster*, eggs and nestlings preyed on by rats, mongooses, ants and Grey-headed Bush-shrike *Malaconotus blanchoti*. Ringed bird 7–7.5 years old[46, 205, 806, 1002]. **Brood parasite** None.

MEASUREMENTS and WEIGHTS Races combined ♂♀? (113) wing 71–88 (76.1), tail 74–95 (85.5), ♂♀? (110) bill (to skull) 15–21.8 (18.7), tarsus 23.8–29 (26.2)[500]. **Weight** Races combined ♂ (91) 27–45.8 g (32.8); ♀ (68) 25–40 g (31.7); ♂♀? (22) 27–33.6 g (31.7) (southern Africa)[48]. For additional data see[34, 48, 149, 478, 509, 808, 815].

73 THREE-STREAKED TCHAGRA *Tchagra jamesi* Plate 28

FIELD IDENTIFICATION Small (16–17 cm), slender pale greyish-brown bush-shrike with bright chestnut-brown wings and black graduated tail broadly tipped white (conspicuous in flight). Head with narrow black line in centre of greyish-brown crown and through eyes (three streaks) with faint whitish eyebrow. Sexes similar. Young similar to adults but buffier. More often heard than seen. Main call a repeated series of whistles on a descending scale combined with flight display and 'wing-fripping' sounds. Little known, solitary or in pairs, skulking low down or on ground in thick undergrowth. Resident in arid and semi-arid dry bush in E and NE Africa. ***Flight characteristics***: Short jerky flights between bushes, black tail broadly tipped white fanned and conspicuous as it dives for cover; wings broad and round. Tail also fanned during display-flight, consisting of a gradual climb with 'wing-fripping', followed by a gliding descent[509].

COMPARISONS Most similar to slightly larger and darker Brown-headed Tchagra *Tchagra australis*, which lacks the black streak on centre of crown, but has a more prominent whitish eyebrow due to contrast of black line above and below it. Crown brown (greyish-brown in Three-streaked) and underparts buffier (greyish-buff in Three-streaked). Main display call also similar, but differs by being more mellow and musical (see Sounds). Three-streaked Tchagra replaces Brown-headed in more arid areas. Also similar to much larger Black-crowned Tchagra *T. senegala*, which has an entirely black crown, broad conspicuous white eyebrow, longer bill and different calls. For separation of young see Black-crowned Tchagra Comparisons p.273[500, 509, 558].

DESCRIPTION **ADULT** Sexes generally similar, although ♀ underparts possibly more buff. ***Head*** Greyish-brown with whitish eyebrow, black line through eye to sides of neck and a central black streak (variable width) on crown extending from bill to nape. Sides of face whitish. ***Back*** Olive to greyish-brown, rump grey. ***Wings*** Carpal area whitish; primary coverts brown, outer webs and remaining coverts chestnut-brown; flight feathers brown; base of narrow primary outer webs and whole of secondary outer web chestnut-brown; tertials brown. ***Tail*** Graduated, central pair grey, with fine cross-barring, rest black broadly tipped white. ***Underparts*** Chin whitish, rest greyish-white to greyish-buff (♀ or Imm?); flanks slightly darker. ***Bare parts*** Bill and palate black; legs grey; eye brown with inner ring of 5–10 white or silvery spots. **JUVENILE/IMMATURE** General plumage similar to adult, particularly ♀ except breast, belly and flanks more buff. Tail more pointed, white areas usually buffy to dull white. Bill lighter, particularly lower mandible[237].

GEOGRAPHICAL VARIATION Two races. N nominate *jamesi* (SE Sudan, NE Uganda, SW Ethiopia and Somalia) darker than S *mandana* (Manda and Lamu Is and adjacent coast of Kenya and NE Tanzania). The latter differs slightly by being buffier on back and underparts, with a broader central stripe and paler sides of crown[2, 3, 237].

HYBRIDS or ABNORMAL PLUMAGE Possible Three-streaked x Brown-headed Tchagra hybrid. See Brown-headed Tchagra Hybrids p.278[1060].

MOULT Unknown.

RANGE, HABITAT and STATUS **Breeding range** E and NE Africa in SE Sudan, NE Uganda, S Ethiopia, Somalia (absent from extreme N and NE with one record from NW), N and E Kenya including Manda and Lamu islands, with patchy distribution. Southern limit in NE Tanzania. **Habitat** Arid and semi-arid bushland, bush grasslands, thickets, thornbush (*Acacia–Commiphora* woodland), dense thorn scrub in semi-desert savanna. Generally found below 1100 m in Kenya, and below 2000 m in Ethiopia[237, 242, 292, 318, 325, 431, 481, 467, 859, 933]. **Status** Resident, locally common to widespread and common. **Conservation status** Unknown, probably not threatened.

MOVEMENTS Some local seasonal movements suspected in Kenya[318].

SOCIAL ORGANISATION and GENERAL BEHAVIOUR Little known. Usually solitary or in pairs; shy and skulking low down, movements almost rodent-like. Dives for cover fanning conspicuous black and white tail feathers. Advertises territory in flight display similar to Brown-headed Tchagra, consisting of an ascent with 'wing-fripping', followed by a gliding descent accompanied by rapidly repeated short whistles which descend in pitch. **Foraging behaviour** Usually gleans prey low down in thick thorny thickets and probably on ground[33, 631]. **Food** Mainly insects, including Dictyoptera (cockroaches), Mantodea (mantis eggs) and Lepidoptera (moths). Possibly takes chicks in Red-billed Quelea *Quelea quelea* colonies[733, 1062].

SOUNDS Little known. Repertoire appears similar to Brown-headed Tchagra. Song given in flight display, consisting of emphatic series of whistles on a descending scale (downslurred) *wi-weo-weo-weo-weo* or *chweeo-chweeo-chweeo-*. Differs from Brown-headed Tchagra in being more mellow and musical. Also has harsh tearing, rasping *tzzeeerrr-* notes. Alarm a nasal scolding *chuwaa, chwaa-chwaa* and *cherraa-cherraa.* 'Wing-fripping' sounds accompany flight display[336, 500, 558, 631].

BREEDING BIOLOGY Little known. Monogamous and territorial. **Season** Dec (S Sudan)[242]; Mar–May, egg-laying estimated at Apr and Jul (Somalia)[33, 859]; Mar–Jul (Ethiopia)[292]; May (coastal Kenya including Manda I)[2, 293, 513]. **Displays** Unknown. **Nest** Role of sexes unknown. A small shallow compact cup composed of dry grass or leaf stalks, shreds of grass-like bark, roots or twigs interwoven with some spider web and lined with fibrous material. Placed in a thorn tree *c*.1–3 m (n=3) above ground, sometimes in an isolated small bush. Nest placed in a fork, sometimes exposed. ***Size*** OD 75–100 mm, ID 70–75 mm, cup depth 30–35 mm, height 50 mm[9, 33, 237, 601, 826]. **Eggs** 2–3. White to pinkish-white ground colour, heavily flecked and spotted with red-brown and lilac. Large end sometimes almost completely brown. ***Size*** 22.9–23.8 x 15.2–18.1 mm[9, 33, 601, 859]. **Incubation** Both sexes incubate, period unknown[237]. No further breeding information, except found in prey remains of Tawny Eagle *Aquila rapax*[804].

MEASUREMENTS and WEIGHTS Races combined ♂♀? (15) wing 65–79 (69.9); tail 75–88 (83.8); bill 19–21 (19.9); tarsus 22.5–25.5 (24.2)[237]; ♂♀? (13) wing 66–74 (70.8), tail 71–87 (80.1), bill (to skull) 15–18 (16.2), tarsus 21.8–25 (23.6)[500]. **Weight** Race unknown ♂ (5) 22–30 g (27); ♀ (2) 26–27 g; ♂♀? (9) 24–32 g (27.9)[509]. For additional data see[768, 870].

74 LARGE WOOD-SHRIKE (Hook-billed, Chinese, Nepal or Brown-tailed Wood-shrike) *Tephrodornis gularis* Plate 28

FIELD IDENTIFICATION Small–large (*c*.17–22 cm), variable, restless bulky brown or grey bush-shrike with a relatively long hooked bill, distinctive broad black face-mask, white rump and rather square tail. Shows much geographical variation, mainly in colour of upperparts and size. Two main groups. N larger birds are brown above with a pale grey head and greyish-white underparts. Southern birds are smaller and completely grey above. Sexes different. ♀ generally duller and brown above, most similar to ♂ in N birds. Young brownish, spotted buff above. Calls and white rump distinctive, more often heard than seen. Main call rapid, short series of high-pitched whistles, also constant harsh chattering. Gregarious and noisy, usually in pairs or small groups, larger in winter. Found mainly in canopy of deciduous and evergreen forest and woodland. Resident in SE Asia from S China, Nepal, India, Pakistan, Thailand, Malay Peninsula to Java. ***Flight characteristics***: Slow and undulating, with a few rapid wingbeats followed by a downward dip. Glides or parachutes from branch to branch. White rump conspicuous, wings rounded, tail rather square[224].

COMPARISONS Differs from Common Wood-shrike *Tephrodornis pondicerianus* by larger size and lack of white eyebrow and white in tail. Large Wood-shrike prefers wetter areas and is more arboreal than Common Wood-shrike. Main whistled calls similar except delivery much faster in Common Wood-shrike. Superficially resembles smaller Brown Shrike *Lanius cristatus*, but has a longer bill, a white rump, is gregarious and occurs in forest canopy. Also superficially resemble cuckoo-shrikes, and in behaviour most similar to minivets *Pericrocotus*, with which it sometimes associates in mixed foraging parties. Juvenile identified from juvenile Common Wood-shrike by larger size and lack of white outer tail feathers and buffy eyebrow[281].

DESCRIPTION **Adult ♂** N large group *pelvica* ***Head*** Black face-mask formed by thin black band over bill continuing through lores, above and below eye to ear-coverts; forehead, crown and nape pale grey, sometimes tinged brown. ***Back*** Upper mantle and back pale brown to reddish brown; rump white with some barring, feathers fairly long and fluffy. ***Wings*** Dark brown, tipped and edged rufous-brown to chestnut-brown (*hainanus*); coverts and tertials like back. ***Tail*** Dark brown to rufous-brown; uppertail-coverts brown with dark edging; undertail-coverts white; ***Underparts*** Chin, throat and sides of face whitish to greyish-white, grading to pale greyish-buff (ashy) on breast and flanks; belly and vent whitish. ***Bare parts*** Bill black to horny-black; mouth (palate?) greyish-pink to pale creamy-yellow and pink; legs dark grey, soles of toes bright yellow; eye apparently variable including yellow (*pelvica*), lemon-yellow or greenish-yellow (*sylvicola*), light brown or olive (*latouchei*), or reddish-brown. Variation probably due to age[188, 224, 500, 750]. **ADULT ♀** N large group *pelvica* Similar to ♂ but with forehead and crown brown like back; lores greyish, eye-stripe and ear-coverts dark brown and less extensive. Underparts generally darker than ♂. Bill dark brown to light grey-brown; eye light bluish-green to olive (*pelvica*), khaki (*sylvicola*) or grey-brown[188, 224]. **ADULT ♂** S small group (*frenatus*) ***Head*** Forehead grey to whitish; broad black face-mask like N group; rest of upperparts grey to dark grey with faint dark streaking; rump broad white, feathers fairly long and fluffy. ***Wings and tail*** Black, wing-coverts like upperparts; tail-coverts white. ***Underparts*** Greyish-white (ashy) to white, chin white in ashy birds. ***Bare parts*** Bill black, legs dark grey to black, eye brown (*gularis*), light yellowish-green to light olive (*frenatus*)[263, 773]. **ADULT ♀** S small group (*frenatus*) Upperparts brown, similar to ♀♀ of N group, except Java ♀♀ tend to be greyer and more like ♂. **JUVENILE** Both groups have similar buff to white-spotted brown upperparts, particularly on head. Brown back spotted and barred. Tertials edged rufous-buff; primary coverts tipped buff, remaining coverts and uppertail-coverts barred buff; rump brownish-white; tail tipped and edged buff-brown. Underparts: Similar to ♀, except most S birds tend to be white. Fledglings (*pelvica*) on leaving nest are speckled grey-brown all over, especially on head[224]. **IMMATURE** First-year birds indistinguishable from ♀, except for pale tips to primary coverts, and have been recorded with grey-brown to greyish-yellow eye[224].

GEOGRAPHICAL VARIATION At least 11 races. Variation mainly in colour of upperparts and in overall body size. Colour variation more obvious in ♂♂. Two main groupings: large brown-backed N birds and smaller grey-backed S birds. Variation in brown-backed group ranges from pale brown *pelvica* (including *sylvicola* in W India; ranges from Nepal, W and E India, Pakistan, N Burma) with buff spotting on outer edge of secondaries and lower back, to darker *latouchei* (S China) and *hainanus* (Hainan Island, Vietnam, N Laos). Intermediates between these and the second, greyer group are evident in *annectens* (including *jugans, vernayi, mekongensis*) (S Burma, N Malaysia, Thailand, Cambodia, Vietnam, Laos) and the more S *gularis* (including *fretensis*) (Sumatra, Java, Thailand peninsula and S Malaysia), which have the brown upperparts tinged grey. The second group of smaller greyer birds (*frenatus*, Borneo) have mainly dark grey upperparts with some brown streaks and a darker tail. This morph includes an even smaller, paler grey population (Java) with a white forehead and obvious white rump. ♀ similar to ♂, but back browner due to fine brown streaking. ♂ tail black, dark blackish-brown in ♀.

MOULT Post-breeding moult of primaries recorded in Oct (Malay Peninsula). Post-juvenile moult includes body and all coverts except primary, tertials and tail. Primary coverts moulted last[224, 252, 500].

RANGE, HABITAT and STATUS Breeding range Widespread in Oriental region as far W as Nepal and W India. Absent from central India, but occurs again in E, Pakistan, Burma, Thailand, Vietnam, Cambodia, S China (Yunnan Province), Hainan, Malaysia, Borneo, Sumatra and Java. **Habitat** Usually found in forest edge and clearings, mainly in canopy of open moist deciduous and evergreen primary and secondary forest and well wooded country, including old teak plantations. In Nepal found in broadleaved forests and well-wooded country up to *c.*1200 m, preferring wetter areas than the Common Wood-shrike. In China generally a lowland species, but may occur up to 1850 m. Found in dry and well-wooded country, evergreen and deciduous forests, including teak and scrub forest. In Malay Peninsula and Greater Sundas found in lowland and montane rainforest and secondary forest up to 1500 m on Java[188, 190, 221, 224, 248, 262, 263, 276, 277, 281, 414, 563]. **Status** Resident, generally uncommon to locally common. **Conservation status** Unknown, probably not threatened.

MOVEMENTS Local, including altitudinal boreal winter movements (India and Burma)[224, 261].

SOCIAL ORGANISATION and GENERAL BEHAVIOUR Social organisation unknown. A canopy bird, usually in pairs when breeding, or small loose groups of 4–10 birds, or in non-breeding season up to 30 individuals. More often heard than seen; active, restless and quite tame. Individuals follow one another among the trees, gracefully dropping, gliding or parachuting down from one branch or leafy cluster to another. Moves between trees with a slow dipping flight. Birds seen bathing by dipping into water in flight[224, 261, 563]. **Foraging behaviour** Arboreal, mainly in crown of trees; favours forest edge and clearings. Gleans insects off leaves, branches and trunks, often clinging to the bark in search of food. Also favours thin branches on the edge of the canopy in leafy clusters. May hang upside down at the end of a branch like a tit. Moves slowly along branches in bouncing clumsy hops; sometimes descends to ground or takes insects off water, and hawks insects in air like a flycatcher, returning to the same perch or moving on. Flutters through vegetation to dislodge prey. Often in mixed foraging parties in association with minivets, drongos and other insectivorous birds[189, 224, 262, 560, 751]. **Food** Arthropods, mainly insects and their larvae, including Coleoptera (beetles), Odonata (dragonflies), Orthoptera (locusts, grasshoppers and crickets), Mantodea (mantids), Lepidoptera (moth grubs and caterpillars, including hairy type) and Melolonthinae (leaf chafers)[224, 263, 751, 773].

SOUNDS A noisy bird more often heard than seen. Repertoire consists of a series of loud, ringing, rapidly repeated, high-pitched whistles and harsh scolding notes. Whistled notes geographically variable. Groups keep up an incessant, rather musical chorus of repetitive, *c.*4–7 rapidly delivered series of loud clear whistles *tutututut*, *wewewewewewe*, *kew-kew-kew-kew-*, *wit-wit-wit-wit-*, *pui, pui, pui-* or *pipipi-pii-pii-pii*, often starting softly and slowing down towards end. Notes have quality of small sparrowhawk, and recall Black-naped Monarch *Hypothymis azurea* and Asian Flycatcher *Terpsiphone paradisi*, but with shorter interval between notes. Repetitive notes also elaborated to loud sharp woodpecker-like *pew-ti-ti-te-te-tew*, and *witoo..witoo..witoo-*, *wehu-wehu-wehu* or *kee-a, kee-a*. These calls occasionally punctuated by a single harsh querulous *Tzzurr, tzerrrr, chak* or *chrr*, possibly in duet. Members of a group also maintain contact with harsh shrike-like notes, chattering and scolding *kra-cha-cha-cha-cha-*, *chreek-chreek-chreek*, *chee-ree* or *tra-a-a-a*, sometimes combined with whistles like *chee-ree-ree--chee-ree-reeoo-reeoo*. Also uses various softer *wik-*, *tit-tiu*, *thul-thul*, *chup...chup* and *grrreuuu* notes, some reminiscent of helmet-shrikes[224, 252, 261, 262, 276, 281, 500, 563, 748].

BREEDING BIOLOGY Little known, apparently monogamous in spite of gregarious foraging and winter flocking, which breaks up into pairs in Apr–May (India). Breeding attempted in first year. In one study hatching success 27%, nesting success 13%, productivity 0.33/pair (n=12)[224, 778]. **Season** Dec–Jun, mainly Mar–Apr (India and Pakistan)[224, 748]; Mar, May (Nepal)[221]; Jul (China)[270]. **Displays** Unknown. No information on courtship-feeding. **Nest** Probably built by both sexes. A shallow cup of grass or weed stems, rootlets, tendrils, pieces of bark. Sometimes decorated with moss and lichens. Secured to branch and plastered on outside with spider web and lined inside with thin fibres, grass or leaf-stems. Placed from 3–13 m up, one study at 10 m (8–13, n=12). In Nepal placed fairly low down. Usually on top of horizontal branch of a medium-sized tree, at base of main stem or at fork, and difficult to locate. Sometimes in fork of bush. ***Size*** OD 100 mm. Built in 8–12 days[224, 272, 276, 500, 778]. **Eggs** usually 2–3 (2–5). Whitish to cream ground colour, some pale greenish-buff, fairly evenly marked, mottled and spotted all over with dark and pale browns, greys and lilac-greys. In some, marking more restricted to large end. ***Size*** *hainanus* av. 24.1 x 18.8 mm (n=11)[189, 224, 500]. For additional data see[224, 270]. **Incubation** By both sexes, mainly by ♀, who sits with head back and bill pointing vertically up, resembling a broken branch. Period 15–16 days[224, 748, 778]. **Nestling** Little known. Race *latouchei* has head, mantle and lower back spotted and barred whitish-buff, underparts white. Probably hatch blind, naked and have mouth spots. Role of sexes unknown. Fledge after 17 days[270, 500, 778]. No further breeding information.

MEASUREMENTS and WEIGHTS Northern races ♂♀? (39) wing 97–124 (111.0), tail 63–90 (77.2), ♂♀? (38) bill (to skull) 24–28 (25.9), tarsus 16.5–21.4 (19.1)[500]. Southern race (Java) *frenatus* ♂♀? (11) wing 91–96 (93.5), tail 59–68 (63.2), bill (to skull) 21–24 (22.7), tarsus 16.5–19.0 (17.7)[500]. **Weight** ♂♀? (4) 38.0–46.0 g (India)[478].

75 COMMON WOOD-SHRIKE (Wood Shrike, Lesser Wood-shrike)
Tephrodornis pondicerianus **Plate 28**

FIELD IDENTIFICATION Medium-small (17–18 cm), drab pale greyish-brown bush-shrike with broad pale eyebrow, indistinct dark face-mask, white rump, and short square tail with diagnostic white outer feathers. Sexes similar. Young brown, spotted buff above. White in tail conspicuous in flight. Whistled trill distinctive. In pairs or small groups, tame, mainly in canopy of open dry deciduous forest, woodland and scrub in SE Asia, from Nepal, India, Pakistan, Thailand, Cambodia and Burma. ***Flight characteristics***: Wings rounded, white outer tail feathers conspicuous in flight. Groups fly in follow-my-leader fashion between trees[278].

COMPARISONS Similar to Large Wood-shrike *Tephrodornis gularis*, but smaller with distinctive white outer tail feathers, a broad buffy-white eyebrow, and a smaller less distinct white rump-patch. The tail is proportionately longer and the bill less heavy. Occurs in drier areas and is less arboreal than Large Wood-shrike. Whistled call similar to Larger Wood-shrike and Common Iora *Aegithina tiphia*. Bares superficial resemblance to Grey Bushchat *Saxicola ferrea* and Isabelline Shrike *Lanius isabellinus*, but behaviourally more like a minivet *Pericrocotus*. Immature similar to that of Large Wood-shrike, but separated by smaller size, presence of buffy eyebrow and white outer tail feathers[281, 749].

DESCRIPTION ADULT ♂ ***Head*** Crown and nape pale grey-brown; indistinct face-mask formed by dark brown stripe from lores, below eye to ear-coverts; broad whitish eyebrow extends to behind eye, variable in length. ***Back*** Pale grey-brown, lower back feathers faintly spotted buff with slight barring; rump white, feathers fairly long and fluffy. ***Wings*** Pale brown, ulna region white; tertials and coverts edged pale buff. ***Tail*** darker brown with white outer feathers having a brown subterminal spot on narrower outer web; uppertail-coverts dark brown, undertail-coverts white. ***Underparts*** Pale greyish-brown to creamy-brown from neck to lower breast; belly whitish; chin and sides of face whitish, chin sometimes streaked. ***Bare parts*** Bill horn-brown, palate greyish-flesh or pale yellowish grey and pink, legs greyish-brown, eye pale brown to greenish-brown or yellow-brown (*affinis*)[500, 224, 278]. ADULT ♀ Similar to ♂ but with less extensive eyebrow and paler brown face-mask[278]. JUVENILE Upperparts, including wing-coverts and tertials, brown spotted buff, particularly on crown; face similar to adult ♀; rump brown; tail dark brown; outer feathers white; underparts whitish spotted brown; chin whitish. Bill pale horn-brown, palate pale lemon-yellow, legs bluish-slate, eye brown[224]. IMMATURE First-year birds like adult, except for pale margins of inner secondaries and pale tips to primary coverts[224].

MOULT Has a complete post-breeding moult, but no pre-breeding moult (Jul–Aug). Post-juvenile moult includes body feathers, all coverts except primaries 3–4, innermost secondaries, tertials and tail[224, 750].

GEOGRAPHICAL VARIATION At least 3 races, plumage variation slight, mainly in colour of upperparts and extent of eyebrow. Race *affinis* (Sri Lanka) greyer with shorter eyebrow and shorter tail; *pallidus* (W Pakistan, NW India) lighter than nominate *pondicerianus* (includes *orientis*) (E India, Burma, Thailand, S Laos, Cambodia and S Vietnam).

RANGE, HABITAT and STATUS **Breeding range** SE Asia in central and S Burma, NW, NE and SW Thailand, Cambodia, Vietnam, S Laos, India and Sri Lanka, S, central and N Pakistan and SW, S central and SE Nepal. **Habitat** Generally a lowland species of plains and foothills below 400 m, exceptionally to 1600 m at base of mountains. Occurs in rather dry areas of secondary forest, open, lightly wooded country (sal, teak and other deciduous forest), scrub, roadsides and rambling jungly gardens in and around towns and villages. In Pakistan in better wooded regions, also tropical scrub, relic patches of riverine forest and especially in man-made irrigated forest plantations. Characteristic bird in *Olea cuspidata* scrub forest in the Salt Range; also found in tree-planted avenues alongside many of the older larger canals. In Nepal occurs in dry forests, lightly wooded areas and scrub. In Thailand occurs in dry diptocarp and mixed deciduous woodlands, open country with scattered trees[221, 224, 261, 276, 278, 281, 324]. **Status** Generally common resident. **Conservation status** Unknown, apparently not threatened.

MOVEMENTS Unknown.

SOCIAL ORGANISATION and GENERAL BEHAVIOUR In pairs or small loose parties of 5–6, in tops of trees and bushes or flying in a follow-my-leader fashion between trees. Rather tame. Has an upward glide to perch, where it remains immobile for a while, before looking around and starting to move. Main whistle call often heard as birds move between trees calling to each other[276, 748]. **Foraging behaviour** Mainly arboreal; creeps about gleaning from leaves and branches and searching for food in crevices of bark. Works quickly and efficiently from tree to tree. Sometimes descends to ground or hawks insects on the wing like a flycatcher. Frequently seen in mixed foraging parties, often with minivets, sometimes with Large Wood-shrike. Observed drinking on the wing[224, 258, 261, 276, 278, 560]. **Food** Arthropods, mainly insects, including Coleoptera (beetles), Lepidoptera (moths and caterpillars), Mantodea (mantids), Orthoptera (grasshoppers), Hymenoptera (bees), Hemiptera (bugs and cicadas). Spiders also taken[224, 278, 750, 752].

SOUNDS Little known. ♂ gives a distinctive rich liquid whistle throughout the year. Territorial call consists of a series of rapidly accelerating piping whistles. This is usually initiated by 1 or 2 brief, well spaced plaintive whistled *weet--weet* notes,

followed by a (usually) descending trill of *c.*3–5 piping notes: *whi-whi-whi-whi-* or *pi-pi-i-i-i* or *tweee-twee-twee-twee-twee.* Variations include *chuwee-wee-wee-wee-wee, wewewewewert,* a high-pitched cuckoo-like *tututweet-tututweet-* and an ascending *whi-whi-whi-whee.* Notes have a peculiar peevish or burry quality. A brief song is heard in breeding season, consisting of longer phrases of quickly repeated whistles and softer trills; ♂ also reported giving a shrill warbling song in breeding season. Other calls include a repeated, moderately loud *chaa—chaa,* soft *tik* notes, and a buzzy helmet-shrike like *Zrreet, Zrrreee-Zruuu,* probably in duet[224, 276, 278, 324, 500, 750].
BREEDING BIOLOGY Little known. Monogamous; parental duties shared by both sexes. **Season** Mar–Jul (Burma)[261]; Feb, Apr (Nepal)[221]; Jan–Sep mainly Mar–May (India)[224, 748]; Mar–May, nestlings sometimes found as late as end of Jun (Pakistan)[278]. **Displays** Unknown, no information on courtship-feeding. **Nest** Built by both sexes. A neat thick-sided cup of soft bark, fibres, bound and plastered with spider web and camouflaged with lichens, spider egg cases or bits of paper-like bark. Cup lined with silky vegetable down and fibres. Comparatively small for the size of the bird. Usually placed 2–6 m up, occasionally 9 m. Usually completely exposed in a fork of leafless sapling, or wedged tightly into the angle of a horizontal forked branch. Sometimes concealed in thick foliage. ***Size*** ID *c.*50 mm, cup depth 30 mm. Completed in 4–10 days[224, 748, 750, 278, 752]. **Eggs** 3, rarely 4. Pale greenish-grey or cream, marked and spotted fairly evenly, but sparsely with reddish-brown, purple-browns and grey, often forming a ring round broad end. ***Size*** av. 19 x 15.1 mm (n=50)[224, 500]. **Incubation** By both sexes. Period 14 days[278]. **Nestling** Hatch blind and naked, later covered in grey down. Mouth spots unknown. Nestlings observed to bury heads into fluffed out breast feathers of adult to avoid sun. Nestlings covered in grey down, the same colour as the nest. Fed by both sexes. Period unknown[224, 752, 278]. No further breeding information.
MEASUREMENTS and WEIGHTS *T. p. pondicerianus* ♂♀? (9) wing 81–90 (85.4), tail 63–69 (64.7), bill (to skull) 20–22.5 (21.7), tarsus 17–19.8 (18.5)[500]. **Weight** ♂♀? (17) 18.0–27.0 g (20.2) (India)[478]. For additional information see[224, 563].

76 RED-EYED FLYCATCHER-SHRIKE (African Shrike-Flycatcher, Common Shrike-Flycatcher) *Megabyas flammulatus* Plate 29

FIELD IDENTIFICATION Small (15–16 cm), thickset flycatcher-like bird with broad hooked bill and reddish eye. Rather quiet with upright stance, short legs and characteristic slow side to side swinging of short tail. Sexes markedly different. ♂ glossy blue-black above, including wings and tail, with rump and underparts pure white. ♀ head and mantle dull-brown shading into rufous-brown on back, wings, rump and tail. Below white with heavy brown streaking. Young similar to ♀ but duller. Flight strong and powerful, ♂ white rump conspicuous. Main call a double-noted high-pitched whistle or often repeated series of rising double notes. Usually in pairs or small groups in mid-canopy of mainly lowland forest, edge of clearings, disused plantations or riverine woodland. Resident and local migrant from Senegal in West Africa through central Zaïre and N Angola to Uganda, S Sudan, W Kenya and NW Tanzania. ***Flight characteristics***: Direct, strong and powerful, rapid with short glides. Has irregular wingbeats, resulting in rhythmic droning. Also apparently a slow flight with rapid wingbeats in aerial display. Wings pointed; white rump conspicuous in flight[336, 456].
COMPARISONS Differs from Crested Flycatcher-shrike *Bias musicus* in having no crest, narrower bill, dark eye (not yellow), direct flight (not butterfly-like), and distinctive tail-swinging behaviour. ♀ and young have paler head and rump, and dark streaks on whitish underparts. Calls similar to this species but higher-pitched. ♂ superficially resembles ♂ Black-shouldered Puffback *Dryoscopus senegalensis* and Sabine's Puffback *D. sabini.* Distinguished from them by shorter legs, more upright stance and general behaviour. ♀ and young superficially resemble African Broadbill *Smithornis capensis,* which is a small, squat, shorter-billed bird with black streaks on underparts, and which occurs low down in dense vegetation[289, 456].
DESCRIPTION **ADULT ♂ Upperparts** Head to below eye, crown, mantle and upper back, wings and tail blue-black with slight gloss. Rump feathers white with black bases, giving a spotted appearance; feathers long and fluffy. ***Underparts*** Including underwing and undertail-coverts white, except flanks which are mottled black-and-white, and thighs which are black narrowly barred white. ***Bare parts*** Bill black and noticeably hooked; prominent rictal bristles; palate colour unknown; legs grey, brown to pink or reddish-purple; eye scarlet, reddish-orange to reddish-brown. **ADULT ♀ Upperparts** Head, including sides and hindneck to upper mantle, greyish-brown; lores whitish, ear-coverts mottled white and grey-brown. Lower mantle, back and scapulars dark rufous-brown (reddish-brown); rump and uppertail-coverts paler. ***Wings*** Primaries and secondaries dark brown, coverts and outer webs of secondaries and tertials,

greater and primary coverts rufous-brown. ***Tail*** Dark rufous-brown, edged rufous. ***Underparts*** White with broad blackish steaks (feathers have white centres and brown edges), lower belly whitish, less streaked; sides with few rusty crescent marks, vent and undertail-coverts buffy-white. ***Bare parts*** Bill black to blackish-brown; palate colour unknown, legs and eye like ♂. **JUVENILE** Similar to adult ♀ but duller, with buff-white spotting on head and back. Lower back and rump rufous-brown including outer edges of secondaries. Primary coverts and secondaries tipped white. Eye probably brown[500]. **IMMATURE** Like adult ♀ but duller, head and neck browner; upperwing- and uppertail-coverts edged and tipped whitish. Subadult ♂ moulting into adult plumage shows patchy black head and mantle; rump white with rufous-brown patches; tail with some feathers black, others rufous-brown. Bare parts: Bill black; legs pale purplish pink; eye deep reddish-brown[500, 676].

GEOGRAPHICAL VARIATION At least two races. Variation slight and concerned mainly with ♀ tail and upperpart colours. Race *aequatorialis* (including *carolathi*) (N Angola, Zaïre to East Africa) differs from nominate *flammulatus* (Senegal and Gambia to Gabon and Bioko) in that ♀ is darker above with blackish tail, not rufous[18, 289, 338, 676, 682].

MOULT Wing moult recorded for Apr, Jul, Aug and Oct (Liberia)[259], and Mar (Angola)[682].

RANGE, HABITAT and STATUS **Breeding range** Mali, Guinea, Sierra Leone, Liberia, Ivory Coast, Ghana, Togo, S Nigeria, Bioko, Cameroon, Central African Republic, Equatorial Guinea, E Gabon, Congo, N Angola, Zaïre, S and W Uganda, NW Tanzania, W Kenya, S Sudan. Vagrant to Mauritania, Senegal and Gambia[431, 696]. **Habitat** Found mainly in primary lowland rainforest, secondary growth and coffee forest, also old clearings and disturbed areas with tall trees, disused plantations and riverine woodland. May also be found around villages. Recorded up to 2150 m (Uganda)[7, 22, 31, 37, 234, 242, 318, 431, 465, 481, 631, 696, 848, 907]. **Status** Resident with some evidence of local movements, generally uncommon, except in Guinea and Ghana where not uncommon[676]. **Conservation status** Unknown. Occurrence in habitats modified by man suggests it may not be affected too seriously by deforestation.

MOVEMENTS Little known, but probably an Afrotropical migrant; local movements observed in NE Gabon where only recorded Nov–Mar; also thought to be a post-breeding visitor to Kakamega Forest (Kenya)[456, 676].

SOCIAL ORGANISATION and GENERAL BEHAVIOUR Little known. Solitary, in pairs, family parties or sometimes gregarious in small groups of *c*.4 birds, often with 2 ♂♂ and a juvenile or ♀ together. Territorial behaviour unknown. A rather quiet flycatcher-like bird with a very upright stance, remaining motionless apart from characteristic habit of slowly swinging or twitching closed tail from side to side. Generally silent, calling only when on the move or when closely approaching a conspecific[294, 456, 465, 688, 847]. **Foraging behaviour** Arboreal, in mid- to upper levels of mature forest and secondary growth from *c*.10–45 m, typically near the edge of forest clearings. Often found in vicinity of flowering and fruiting trees. Pairs or group members forage silently together, very mobile, changing perch from one large tree to another with direct fast flight. Perches in lowest part of tree crown, usually on leafless branches, but avoids twigs and thinner branches. Forages by hopping and running along branches, and flies up and down among branches, frequently pausing to look around. At rest peers about warily, often glancing from side to side. Sallying flights are direct, fluttering, looping or hovering as prey is picked from underside of leaf or in the air. These flights are usually *c*.12 m, occasionally up to 20 m. Sometimes joins mixed foraging parties, remaining higher up avoiding undergrowth, and regularly feeds on swarming ants and termites. Also seen to follow butterflies and falling leaves[15, 456, 465, 631, 648, 676, 858]. **Food** Arthropods, mainly insects, including many Coleoptera (beetles), also Lepidoptera (moths), Orthoptera (grasshoppers and cockroaches), Hemiptera (bugs and cicadas), Hymenoptera (winged ants) and Isoptera (termites). Prey size 15–25 mm[259, 289, 676].

SOUNDS Repertoire consists of whistles and harsh, often metallic-sounding calls. Territorial song of ♂ a long powerful series of repeated brief phrases, usually consisting of 2–3 notes separated by silences, with the emphasis on the last note of each phrase: *titiwit...titiwit...titiwit...piwit... piwee...tit...tit...pityew...pityew...piwit...piwit...tut uwit...tutuwit...pirrit...tutuwit...tuwit...pirrit-*. A variation consists of a series of phrases composed of dry, tuneless upslurred notes which gradually ascend the scale, becoming shorter and higher-pitched towards the end: *chewy-chewy-chewy...chewy-chewy-chewy...chui-chui...teesy-teesy...ticlik...ticlik,* or *chi-ki-tik, chi-ki-tik, chiki-tik-tik.* The metallic clicking notes which often end the series are probably produced by the bill. Both sexes produce a melodious rapid disyllabic whistle *tuwick* or *chuick-chuick* and include variations like *tsu-tsu, tsuee-tsueet* and *chichi-jwejuwe,* or simply *jwe-juwe.* ♀ apparently answers ♂ with churring or rasping note, suggesting possible duets. Contact call by both sexes a very high-pitched repeated thin penetrating whistle *tseee, pseet,* with variations like *zeet . . zeet-* or *zit--zit-,* also a harsh nasal *tsit.* Pre-flight call a short *psit.* Flight call by both sexes a rolling *tsrrrt,* and thought to be similar to the insect-like rasping trill *prrrt* recorded at the nest. ♀ known also to give brittle *chip-chip* calls near the nest (see Incubation). During mobbing gives harsh grating screams[22, 336, 338, 465, 500, 504, 648, 676, 696, 849].

BREEDING BIOLOGY Little known. Monogamous, possibly with helpers, as 2 ♂♂ and a ♀ attended one nest during the incubation period. Territorial, aggressively chasing own species and other birds in vicinity of nest. Density in Kenya (Kakamega Forest) 2–5 adults and 1 immature in 8 ha. Calls suggest densities of 2–4 pairs/km² (Liberia)[847, 858]. **Season** Increased song activity Dec–Apr, nest-building Mar, enlarged gonads Oct (Liberia)[259, 858]; Mar (Guinea)[101]; Dec, also juveniles in Mar and May (Ivory Coast)[465]; Feb ♂ display-flying, juveniles in Mar (Ghana)[234]; ♀ with active gonads Apr, pair with enlarged gonads Jun (Nigeria)[37, 690]; May, nest-building Feb (Cameroon)[21, 676]; Jan (Gabon)[676]; enlarged gonads Mar–Nov, mainly Jun–Sep (Zaïre)[22, 289, 688]; juvenile Mar, in breeding condition Jun (Angola)[865, 907]; Apr and Jun (East Africa)[293, 676]. **Displays *Courtship?*** Aerial display by both sexes apparently consists of slow flight with rapid wingbeats resulting in rhythmic droning ('wing-fripping'?) while calling on the wing. A description of ♂ singing during pipit-like courtship flight requires confirmation (see Eggs). Courtship feeding unknown[336, 456]. **Nest** Built by both sexes. A small, compact, neat, smooth grey cup built mainly of thin vegetable fibres and moss, also rotten wood, flakes of bark and lichen, tightly bound and secured to branch with spider web. One exposed nest placed in a fork on a horizontal branch, another resembling a bump on a branch. One nest placed at *c*.15 m above the ground in an *Albizzia sassa*, another *c*.35–40 m up near the top of a leafless *Klainedoxa* tree. ***Size*** OD 40 mm, height (cup depth?) 15 mm. Nest resembles that of Crested Flycatcher-shrike[676, 858]. **Eggs** Not known for certain; previously described as 3. Reported as bluish or greenish grey with small spots and blotches of umber-brown and lilac grey, tending to form a zone round the middle of the egg. ***Size*** *c*.21 x 16 mm[336]. The same authors later say this description probably refers to Crested Flycatcher-shrike. Requires confirmation[338]. **Incubation** By both sexes; period unknown, but at least 16 days[676]. At one nest, at least 3 birds were in attendance (2♂♂, 1♀). At this nest incubation change-overs were always between ♂ and ♀, replacing each other roughly every 30 min, with the nest left unattended for periods of 15–60 mins. A second ♂ was seen within 50 cm of nest while other ♂ incubated. Both gave *chuick-chuick* call and non-incubating ♂ combined this with a dipping or nodding display (head and upper body repeatedly tilted downwards towards other bird). On one occasion incubating ♂ drove other ♂ away to 3 m. At incubation change-overs, birds would begin either without a display or do a dipping and tail-wagging display with *chuick-chuick* calls or an insect-like rasping trill *prrt*. All 3 birds seen to give this display and the 2 types of call. ♀ also gives a brittle *chip-chip* on arrival at nest[465, 676]. **Nestling** Mouth spots unknown. Greyish-brown above with buff spotting all over. Wings, coverts and tail with rufous-buff edging. Underparts white with greyish tinge on breast. Attended by both sexes. Period unknown. Young apparently stay for a long time with their parents. Dependent young being fed by ♀ showed typical tail-swinging behaviour[289, 500, 676]. No further breeding information.

MEASUREMENTS and WEIGHTS Races combined ♂ (5) wing 86–91 (88.8), tail 57–65 (61), bill (to skull) 23.1–26.5 (24.3), tarsus 15–16.8 (15.3); ♀ (5) wing 87–91 (89.2), tail 64–67 (65.6), bill (to skull) 23.8–25.8 (24.6), tarsus 15.5–16.8 (16.0)[500]. **Weight** *flammulatus* ♂ (7) mean 27.6 ±1.7 g; ♀ (5) mean 25.7 ±2.2 g Liberia[259]; *aequatorialis* ♂ (12) 29–34 g (30.7), ♀ (12) 22–32 g (28.1) Uganda[676]. For additional data see[259, 425, 676, 682, 907].

77 CRESTED FLYCATCHER-SHRIKE (Black-and-white Shrike-Flycatcher, Vanga Flycatcher) *Bias musicus* — Plate 29

FIELD IDENTIFICATION Small (15–17 cm), distinctive, chunky flycatcher-like bird with a big flat crested head, broad bill, yellow eye and short tail. Sexes markedly different. ♂ above, including throat and breast, glossy blue- to greenish-black; below white. Legs yellow. Large white patch in broad rounded wing conspicuous in flight. ♀ crested head brownish-black; back, wings and tail bright rufous-brown; below white with rufous-tinged flanks, yellow legs. Young like ♀ but duller. Characteristic butterfly-like flight. Noisy and conspicuous. Calls loud, sharp and musical in repeated series of whistles and harsh clicking notes. Solitary, in pairs or small family group, mainly in outer crown of tallest trees in clearings of evergreen and riverine forests. Resident, from West Africa in Senegal and Gambia through Congo basin to Uganda and S Sudan. Isolated populations in central Kenya, E Tanzania, S Malawi, E Zimbabwe to S Mozambique. ***Flight characteristics***: Normal flight slow and flapping; appears to parachute from branch to branch, reminiscent of helmet-shrike, sometimes quivering or undulating. Also capable of swift direct flight. Wings broad and rounded, ♂ with conspicuous white wing-patch. In display a slow hovering circular flight accompanied by butterfly-like fluttering with more rapid wingbeats and 'fripping' sounds. Concealed white in rump conspicuous when fluffed out in display[15, 31, 506, 631].

COMPARISONS Crested appearance distinctive. Coloration similar to ♂ and ♀ Red-eyed Flycatcher-shrike *Megabyas flammulatus*, which is a much less active species, lacks a crest and has a dark reddish eye (not yellow). ♂ Red-eyed Flycatcher-shrike is completely white below and lacks white wing-patches, ♀ has broad brown streaks below, and this species has a characteristic side to side tail-swinging behaviour.

DESCRIPTION ADULT ♂ ***Upperparts*** Including throat and upper breast, wings and tail glossy blue- to greenish-black. Feathers of hindcrown long and lanceolate, forming crest. Rump with concealed white spots, feathers long and fluffy. Wing with white patch at base of primaries. ***Underparts*** White from lower breast, belly and undertail-coverts; flanks mottled black-and-white. ***Bare parts*** Bill black, broad and flat; gape lemon-yellow; palate colour unknown; legs greenish to straw yellow; eye chrome to golden-yellow. **ADULT ♀** ***Head*** Crown and ear-coverts brownish-black, feathers of hindcrown long and lanceolate forming crest, shorter than ♂; lores buff. ***Back*** Including sides of neck mottled dark rufous-brown and brownish-black. Rest of upperparts bright rufous-brown (chestnut-brown) with indistinct dark streaks on upper mantle and concealed whitish spots on rump. ***Wing and tail*** Including wing-coverts and uppertail-coverts dark rufous-brown. Primaries dark at ends, rufous-brown at bases. ***Underparts*** Chin white, rest creamy white with breast, flanks and undertail-coverts tinged rufous. Flanks faintly spotted black-and-white. ***Bare parts*** Bill and legs like ♂; eye pale yellow with outer edge green-grey[259, 425]. **JUVENILE** Resembles adult ♀ but head and mantle brown with buff spotting, breast scalloped with narrow dark crescents. Bare parts: Apparently similar to ♀, but eye probably dark[500, 676]. **IMMATURE** Like adult ♀ but duller, head and neck browner, upper mantle streaked, wings with small buffy spots. ♂ moulting into adult plumage has patchy rufous-brown mixed with glossy black above. Below dull white with patchy black-and-white throat and breast; eye pale yellow[299, 631, 676, 500, 504].

GEOGRAPHICAL VARIATION At least three races. Variation slight and mainly involving ♀. In nominate *musicus* (including *feminina* and *pallidiventris*) (West and Central Africa, N Angola, S and W Uganda, NW Tanzania) ♀♀ are predominantly rufous below in W of range, with an increasing trend to paler underparts in E and SW. ♂ *changamwensis* (Kenya and E Tanzania) smaller and paler above and below than nominate; ♀ paler, except for head, and without blackish centres to feathers of mantle; *clarens* (Mozambique, Malawi and Zimbabwe) similar to *changamwensis* but ♀ and young ♂ paler, whiter below, with crown matt-black (not sooty-brown) and malar streaks with only slight rusty tinge[18, 676].

MOULT Little known. No moult recorded in Jan and Apr, but Aug early stages of wing moult (Liberia)[330, 858].

RANGE, HABITAT and STATUS **Breeding range** Widespread in Central, W and southern E Africa. West Africa from Gambia, Guinea-Bissau, Sierra Leone, Guinea, Liberia, Ivory Coast, Ghana, Togo, Benin, Nigeria, S Cameroon, Equatorial Guinea, Gabon, Congo, Central African Republic, Zaïre, Cabinda and N Angola, S Sudan, Somalia (requires confirmation), S and W Uganda, Kenya (isolated population in central region), NW and E Tanzania, S Malawi, Mozambique, E Zimbabwe. Bioko record rejected. Vagrant in Gambia and status in Guinea requires confirmation[431]. **Habitat** Large trees on edge of clearings and openings or along streams in primary lowland and montane rainforest, gallery forest, second growth, edges of riverine woodland and open miombo *Brachystegia* woodland. Also in man-made habitats, including plantations and recently logged areas with at least some tall trees, gardens and farms. Up to 1700 m in Uganda[5, 22, 23, 26, 37, 101, 234, 242, 289, 318, 330, 425, 431, 649, 676, 848, 858, 907]. **Status** Resident, locally common to rare. **Conservation status** Threatened by deforestation in smaller forest patches, particularly in E part of range, such as the fragmented population on NE edge of central highlands in Kenya and E Zimbabwe. It has already disappeared from coastal Kenya[318, 481, 631].

MOVEMENTS Local movements evident in E Zimbabwe, leading to suggestions that Mozambique birds possibly migratory[30, 48, 639].

SOCIAL ORGANISATION and GENERAL BEHAVIOUR Solitary, in pairs or family groups of up to 3–5 birds. A noisy, active, conspicuous and aggressive bird which is difficult to overlook. Active all day, members of a pair usually remaining close together, but may be up to 300 m apart, particularly in non-breeding season, when they maintain looser contact. ♂ defends a territory of *c.*42 ha (n=4) (Gabon) by regular patrols and territorial song, combined with erratic flight and acrobatics, which give the impression of a large black-and-white butterfly. Display-flight consists of shallow, slow, flapping flight, with rounded wings fully extended exposing white patches, crest erect and rump feathers fluffed out. When intruder detected, perches in exposed position, usually on top of very tall tree, where adopts an upright posture with crest fully erect and neck extended, flicks wings and wags head from side to side and gives loud territorial song, followed by display-flight, sometimes diving at the intruder. Pair-greeting display consists of ♂ giving territorial song and acrobatic display-flights. During this ♀ perches on an exposed branch in upright posture, with bill pointing upwards, flicks wingtips and wags tail, then crouches in horizontal posture, fans and closes outer tail feathers in jerky manner and bobs head up and down. Perched birds maintain a minimum distance of *c.*30–60 cm. If one comes too close, the other erects crest, rapidly fans outer tail feathers, flicks wingtips, and give hoarse flight calls. May also point bill at partner and make biting intention movements. When anxious, crouches in hunched posture, sleeks plumage, lowers flattened head and extends neck forward. When alarmed, stretches legs and body upwards, erects crest, jerkily flicks both wings, nervously fans outer tail feathers and gives territorial song (♂) or rasping call (♀). Roosting behaviour conspicuous: ♂ leads, sings in tallest trees, then makes steep spiral glides above roost site, a bush or small tree; gives loud scolding territorial songs; ♀ then joins him, followed by young, which roost a little apart from adults. Roosting bird fluffs out plumage and tucks bill into scapulars. In ♂ white rump-spots are exposed, giving a speckled appearance. Dives into water to bathe[5, 22, 259, 289, 294, 676]. **Foraging behaviour** Arboreal, at all levels, but mainly in crown of tallest trees at 20–40 m. Moves about actively on the outside of tree crowns and frequently changes trees. Adopts an upright or hunched posture during which the head is slowly moved from side to side as it searches for and gleans prey. Usually perches at the end of leafy branches and makes short descending butterfly-flights, or hovers to capture prey from underside of leaves. Known to flutter among vegetation to flush insects, which are captured in flight. Behaves like a typical flycatcher when aerial prey abundant, hawking insects on the wing, occasionally near the ground. Does not appear to join mixed foraging parties[259, 299, 456, 653, 676, 688, 754]. **Food** Arthropods, mainly insects, occasionally small vertebrates. Insects include Lepidoptera (moths and caterpillars), Diptera (flies), Orthoptera (grasshoppers), Hymenoptera (wasps, bees and winged ants), Odonata (dragonflies), Isoptera (alate termites), Coleoptera (beetles), Dictyoptera (cockroaches and mantids) and Heteroptera (bugs). Also spiders and small lizards. Mean prey size 20 mm (n=186)[259, 456, 676].

SOUNDS Repertoire consists of loud percussive whistles and harsh notes. Territorial song of ♂ very variable, individually and geographically. May be given while perched, but more often in flight. Song consists of an often repeated, variable sequence of 1–4 loud, energetically delivered whistles and sharp percussive notes, sounding like *tit-tiu-, wit-ti-tu, wee-tew-tew* or *tiew-tyip-tiewp-tiewp.* Phrases often begin or end with harsh notes, like rattling *churrr* or *Tchzz* notes and strident *chi-tk-* or *Tch* clicking sounds; *chi-chi-cheeri, chi-chi-twoo, chi-KIK-yoo, che-chik-choo Tch-TchiTcheu, Tch-HeHew* or *chip-we-chip.* Also gives single long notes like *Hweeet* or downslurred *cheeeyuw.* In high intensity territorial calling phrases are longer, speeding up and rising in pitch: *tit-tiu-.....wit-ti-tu...wit-ti-tu..wit-tu-wit-tu-tui-tui-tu-.* Variations include: *wheet-tee-tee-tiuw-tiuw, tee-tiu-tee-tiu Pitchee-witchee-witchee-pitchew, pee-tzub, pee-tzub-tzub, We-chip! chip-chip! chee-chee-chee-ee-ee!, triddee-tree-tree-tree-ree-ree, Hwee-HweHweHweHweHwe-* or *Tzheheew-HweHweHwe-.* The sequence often ends with a prolonged *wurp-weep-weep-cheew-cheew-cheew-cheew.* In aggressive situations ends song with separate lower-pitched *tyew-tyiew*, first note sharply downslurred, and when fighting gives long whistle *tyiew.* In these situations ♂ and ♀ give 3–4 brief guttural notes followed by a descending grating *zzrrr* call. Alarm also described as a harsh swearing call; heard to give buzzy bill-clashing and bill-snapping. The normal call of ♀ is a long rasping *kchchew*, possibly in duet. Fledglings and immatures also give this call. Begging nestlings give a long nasal call. Many notes are reminiscent of puffback shrikes and wattle-eyes[5, 23, 48, 289, 299, 500, 504, 676, 696, 706, 754]. Sonagram[48].

BREEDING BIOLOGY Monogamous and territorial. Although a second ♂ has been seen in vicinity of the nest, this was probably young from the previous breeding season. Pairs remain together for 3–5 years. Density of 2.1 pairs/km² (Gabon); 1–4 pairs/km² (coastal Liberia). ♂ guards nest site and greets ♀ with territorial display-flights and calling. Defends nest against a wide variety of birds and mammals. Breeding success: out of 11 nests in which eggs were laid, 10 produced 1 or more fledglings (av. 1.64 young/nest); 13 of 14 eggs hatched and 17 of 21 nestlings fledged[294, 676, 518, 858].

Season Generally in rainy season. Apr, song Feb–Jul, nest-building May, juveniles Dec (Liberia)[330, 858]; ♀ with ovary egg Mar (Ghana)[234]; nest-building Mar, ♀ with enlarged ovary Apr (Nigeria)[37, 584]; Feb–Jun, nest-building Feb (Cameroon)[21]; Sep–Mar, May (Gabon)[294, 295, 338]; displaying May (Equatorial Guinea)[101]; Mar (Central African Republic)[676]; Apr–Aug N of equator, Aug–Dec S of equator, ♀ in breeding condition Sep, fledglings Nov–Dec(Zaïre)[22, 289]; Sep, Feb, very noisy Sep–Jan (Congo)[338, 717]; Nov–Jan, juveniles Feb (Angola)[865, 907]; Nov–Jan, nest-building Oct (Zimbabwe)[649, 706, 639]; nest-building Nov (Mozambique)[500]; Jan, Mar–Jul, Sep–Nov (East Africa)[293]; Sep–Mar (Uganda)[25, 289]; Jan (Tanzania)[336].

Displays ***Courtship*** ♂ display appears similar to high-intensity territorial flight-song display, except wingbeats much slower and combined with circling, swooping flight around ♀. At close range he frequently displays white underparts and fluffed-out rump, flying away from ♀ with undulating motion. Courtship-feeding not recorded, but predicted to be present[634]. ***Nest-site display*** Although ♀ prospects for nest sites, ♂ apparently chooses final site, where he crouches, neck and head horizontal, conceals crest, spreads forward and quivers wings, and fluffs out rump feathers exposing white spots[5, 294, 634, 676, 754, 767].

Nest Built by ♀ only in about a week, ♂ accompanying her to and from nest calling *che-chick-choo* or *chip, we-chip* with territorial display-flights. A small, neat, shallow, compact thick-walled cup built of thin stems, rootlets, leaf stalks and pieces of leaf skeleton, dry pieces of bark, vegetable fibres and small bits of decaying wood. Sometimes lined with leaf petioles. Covered on the outside with spider web and lichens, giving it a silvery-grey appearance. It is moulded onto the branch and resembles a small bump. Usually placed 1.2–30 m up; in one study most nests were below 10 m. In another series (n=9), nests were 3–20 m (9.0) above ground. Usually placed at extremity of branch in crotch on a stout horizontal branch in dense foliage, but sometimes completely uncovered. ***Size*** OD 76–90 mm, ID 53–80 mm, cup depth 18–35 mm, height 28–45 mm. Nest resembles that of Brubru *Nilaus afer*[2, 15, 338, 289, 294, 576, 706].

Eggs Usually 2 (2–3, n=9), laid at 1-day intervals, beginning 4–8 days after completion of nest. Dirty white or whitish-grey to very pale blue-green, heavily blotched and spotted with dark brown, rufous-brown, grey and/or lilac, forming a conspicuous ring or cap at large end. ***Size*** 19–21 x 15–16 mm. Observed to re-lay 14 days after young predated shortly before fledging[2, 15, 19, 22, 330, 338, 500, 576, 646, 706, 709, 676]. **Incubation** Starts with last egg. Both sexes share incubation during the day, changing about every 30 min. ♀ incubates at night, with ♂ roosting 50–120 m away. During nest relief, ♂ much noisier than ♀, giving long series of loud territorial songs and making butterfly-flights, also *te-heuw, te-heuw-* as nest approached. ♀ makes soft buzzing sound on approach, also gives sharp buzzing *tzzz* calls. ♂ also recorded giving soft *weet weet weet* in vicinity of nest. ♂ guards nest even during brooding period. Occasionally sings from the nest, but more often leaves it to give territorial display. Period 18–19 days[294, 500, 584, 646, 676]. **Nestling** Hatch blind and naked. In older birds skin greenish-yellow with sparse greyish down. Later has dark brown head with buffy-rufous spotting on crown and back; wings and tail rufous-brown. Chin and throat dirty white, tinged brown and grey. Belly white, tinged pale brown. Mouth spots unknown, predicted to be absent. Attended by both sexes; faeces removed from nest. For first 5–6 days young beg only when adults arrive. From 5–10 days they respond to calls of approaching adults, thereafter giving a nasal begging call almost continuously. Fledge after 18–23 days. Fledglings remain near the nest for 3–4 days, then follow parents around, each parent caring for a particular young, which are dependent for *c.*6 weeks and may be fed for 1–2 (occasionally 3) months. Young observed to stay in canopy and remain with parents until next breeding season, in one case still with adults 18 weeks after nest-building[289, 294, 500, 506, 584, 634, 676, 709]. **Predation and longevity** Frequently one fledgling in a brood dies in the first 15 days. Adults survive at least 5 years[676]. **Brood parasite** Unknown.

MEASUREMENTS and WEIGHTS Races combined ♂ (7) wing 82–92 (86.9), tail 45–50 (47.6), bill (to skull) 22.0–24.1 (22.9), tarsus 12.3–14.3 (13.4); ♀ (12) wing 80–88 (84.3), tail 47–53 (50.4), ♀ (11) bill (to skull) 21.1–23.5 (22.2), ♀ (11) tarsus 12.5–14.5 (13.2)[500]. **Weight** *musicus* ♂ (10) 20–25 g (22.1), ♀ (3) 21–22 g (21.3) (Uganda)[676]. For additional data see[259, 299, 425, 676, 911].

78 RUFOUS-WINGED PHILENTOMA (Chestnut-winged Flycatcher, Rufous-winged Flycatcher) *Philentoma pyrhopterum* Plate 29

FIELD IDENTIFICATION Small (15–17 cm), active, slim flycatcher-like bird with a dark head, distinctive rufous wings and tail, and reddish eye. Sexes different. ♂ has two colour morphs: (1) above pale blue including upper breast, contrasting with greyish-white belly (common); (2) entirely pale blue, except lower belly grey-brown (rare). ♀ head greyish-brown, back brown, below buffy. Young similar to ♀ but browner above and with a brown eye. More often heard than seen; main call a repeated series of soft high-pitched whistles, also harsh scolding notes. Resident, usually in pairs in lower to mid-levels of mainly lowland evergreen and heath forests in SE Asia from S Thailand, S Burma, S Vietnam, Malay Peninsula, Sumatra, Borneo and smaller islands. ***Flight characteristics***: Flight bounding with rapid deep undulations; makes 'fripping' sounds with rounded wings in flight[500, 771].

COMPARISONS Distinguished from similar blue flycatcher-like birds by red eyes, except ♀ Maroon-breasted Philentoma *Philentoma velatum* which also has red eyes. Easily distinguished from this species by rufous wings and tail, and pale underparts. Blue morph ♂ like ♀ Maroon-breasted Philentoma but smaller with a shorter tail, paler blue and without a dark throat; lower belly and undertail-coverts usually more greyish-brown; whistled notes longer. They also tend to be ecologically segregated with Rufous-winged, foraging higher up in more open parts of forest. Superficially resembles Black-naped Flycatcher *Hypothymis azurea* or Indian Verditer Flycatcher *Eumyias thalassina*. General behaviour resembles *Terpsiphone* flycatcher[262, 520].

DESCRIPTION ADULT ♂ Common morph. ***Head and back*** Including throat and breast pale blue (indigo-blue); lower back and rump buffy to rufous-grey, feathers long and fluffy. ***Wings*** Tertials and most of outer webs of secondaries bright rufous-brown (chestnut-brown), remainder dark brown. Outer webs of primaries edged with rufous-grey; lesser and primary coverts indigo-blue with blackish centres; greater wing-coverts rufous-brown (chestnut-brown); ***Tail*** Uppertail-coverts and tail bright rufous-brown (chestnut-brown). ***Underparts*** From breast pale buff, becoming paler on vent and undertail-coverts, often greyish with white streaks. ***Bare parts*** Bill broad and black; palate unknown; legs pale purplish-blue to olive-grey; eye crimson-red. ADULT ♂ Blue morph. Completely indigo-blue with no rufous-brown; underparts indigo-blue grading to grey-brown on lower belly. Belly sometimes streaked whitish[262, 500]. ADULT ♀ ***Head*** Forehead, crown, nape and sides of head olive- to greyish-brown with slight bluish tinge. ***Back*** mantle, scapulars and rump rufous-grey to pale olive-brown. ***Wings and tail*** Like ♂ but with lesser wing-coverts pale olive-brown. ***Underparts*** Chin to breast variable dull white to pale rufous-buff, sides of breast greyer, belly whitish. ***Bare parts*** Like ♂. JUVENILE Similar to ♀ but with brownish head, mantle and orange-rufous breast. Bill with upper mandible pale horn-brown, lower mandible fleshy-white, legs like adult, eye dark brown[187, 252, 281, 500]. IMMATURE ♂ similar to adult ♀ but with buff chin and throat and buff-grey breast. One ♀ specimen had legs and feet pale horny-red and eye pale red, speckled with white[187, 500].

GEOGRAPHICAL VARIATION Two races. Nominate *pyrhopterum* (S Vietnam, S Thailand, Malaysia, Sumatra and Borneo) differs from *dubium* (Natuna Islands) by having a longer wing and duller underparts[685].

MOULT May–Nov adult flight feathers, with post-juvenile moult recorded as early as May[252].

RANGE, HABITAT and STATUS Breeding range SE Asia in peninsular Burma and Thailand, Malay peninsula, S Vietnam, Sumatra including Lingga Archipelago, Bangka and Batu Islands, Borneo (including Natunas) and intervening islands. **Habitat** Generally a lowland species, occasionally up to 1600 m in Borneo. Prefers mid- to lower levels in interior of evergreen primary and secondary forest, mature logged forests, peatswamp and heath forests and scrub, rarely in plantations. Often associated with wet and waterlogged areas, including in the vicinity of streams and rivers[248, 252, 262, 281, 324, 414, 483]. **Status** Resident, uncommon to locally common[262, 414]. **Conservation status** Appears locally threatened, as previously recorded from Singapore but now extinct. Reportedly does not adapt to man-made clearings and plantations, and is known to be exported in bird trade[414].

MOVEMENTS Unknown.

SOCIAL ORGANISATION and GENERAL BEHAVIOUR Little known. Solitary or in pairs. It is a tame active flycatcher-like bird, moving quietly through mid- to lower levels of forest, pairs usually foraging together. Makes 'fripping' sounds with wings in flight and flicks wings slightly when perched[414]. **Foraging behaviour** Catches prey on the wing in short sallies from an exposed perch in low- to mid levels at 2–4 m above the ground, or in bounding, undulating flight. Joins mixed foraging parties[483, 771]. **Food** Insects, including Hemiptera (bugs)[483].

SOUNDS Little known. Repertoire consists of soft disyllabic high-pitched whistles and harsh scolding notes. Whistled calls given in series, varying in rate from slowly repeated drawn-out and rising disyllabic *hweeet......hweeet-* or *hweeeee....hweeeee-*, *huw-weee... huw-weee* to rapidly repeated, cuckoo-like *hwee-hwee-hwee-hwee-*, or *tew-ii* whistle. Also has softer *tu-huuuuu* whistle, with emphasis on the lower, second syllable, and various harsh metallic scolds. Fledglings beg with repeated high-pitched *tzeet-tzeet-* or *huweet-huweet-* calls[262, 281, 500, 520].

BREEDING BIOLOGY Unknown, probably monogamous and territorial. **Season** Juveniles Apr–Oct (Malay Peninsula)[252]. No further breeding information, except nestling has upperparts dark greyish-brown, streaked and spotted with rufous-brown. Back more rufous-brown, wing grey-brown with outer web rufous-brown. Coverts, tail and underparts rufous. Fledglings observed being fed by ♀[500]. Oldest bird 4 years 11 months[252].

MEASUREMENTS and WEIGHTS *P. p. pyrhopterum* ♂♀? (11) wing 76–84 (80.1), tail 63–69 (66.5), bill (to skull) 19.5–21 (20.2), tarsus 15.5–17.5 (16.3)[500]. **Weight** *pyrhopterum* ♂♀? (32) mean 16.9 g[483].

79 MAROON-BREASTED PHILENTOMA (Maroon-breasted Flycatcher, Maroon-breasted Monarch) *Philentoma velatum* Plate 29

FIELD IDENTIFICATION Medium-sized (19–20 cm), dark indigo-blue stocky flycatcher-like bird with red eye. Sexes different. ♂ completely indigo-blue with black face-mask and maroon breast, appearing black in poor light. ♀ completely dark slaty-blue, appearing black in field. Young similar to ♀. In flight makes 'fripping' sounds with wings. More often heard than seen; main call a series of slowly repeated whistles, also harsh calls. Resident, solitary or in pairs in lower levels of dark, often swampy, mainly lowland forest in SE Asia. Resident from S Thailand, Burma, Malay Peninsula, Sumatra, Java, and Borneo. ***Flight characteristics***: Wings rounded; makes loud 'fripping' (fluttering) noise in flight[281].

COMPARISONS ♀ very similar to rare blue morph of ♂ Rufous-winged Philentoma *Philentoma pyrhopterum*, which is a smaller, paler blue bird with a shorter tail and greyish-brown lower belly and undertail-coverts. Whistled notes shorter than Rufous-winged Philentoma. Differs from Asian Fairy-bluebird *Irena puella* by much smaller size and having wings same colour as body; Asian Fairy-bluebird occurs in groups and tends to be a canopy species. The Velvet-fronted Nuthatch *Sitta frontalis* is also indigo-blue but smaller with reddish bill and yellow eye; also lacks flycatcher-like behaviour. Drongos larger with distinctive tails.

DESCRIPTION Adult ♂ indigo-blue. ***Head* and back** Forehead, lores, chin, cheeks to above eye black; crown to rump indigo-blue, feathers long and fluffy. ***Wings*** Flight feathers black, outer web broadly edged indigo-blue. Tertials indigo-blue, but with the shafts black. ***Tail*** Central tail feathers indigo-blue, rest black on the inner web and blue on the outer. ***Underparts*** Chin black, throat and breast rich maroon, rest of underparts indigo-blue. ***Bare parts*** Bill black, broad; palate unknown; legs bluish- to purplish-black; eye crimson-red. Adult ♀ Completely dusky or slaty indigo-blue, duller than ♂. ***Head*** Darker on forehead, lores, cheeks, chin and throat. Rump, belly and undertail-coverts with greyish tinge. ***Bare parts*** Like ♂[252, 261, 262, 263,

[500]. **JUVENILE** Head, upper and underparts patchy indigo-blue and rich rufous-brown (chestnut-brown). Tail and wings as adult, wing-coverts chestnut-brown. Eye probably brown like nestling[500]. **IMMATURE** Similar to ♀[187, 500].

GEOGRAPHICAL VARIATION Two races. Variation mainly in coloration of head of ♀. Compared to nominate *velatum* (Java and Timor), *caesium* (Malaysia, Burma, Thailand, Borneo and Sumatra) ♀ is slightly darker above than ♂, and has darkish-grey to blackish frontal band and face-mask as well as chin, throat and upper breast, which grade into indigo-blue on belly[206, 500].

MOULT Flight feathers Jul and Oct, probably post-breeding[252].

RANGE, HABITAT and STATUS **Breeding range** SE Asia. Thailand from SW and peninsular provinces from Prachuap Khiri Khan to extreme S, Burma from Tenasserim as far N as Mt Mulayit, Malay Peninsula, Greater Sundas (except Bali) including Sumatra throughout mainland from Alas Peurba, Aceh to the Barisan ranges of Bengkulu and Selatan, Java and Borneo[194, 248, 252, 262, 263, 324]. **Habitat** a lowland species, exceptionally up to 1400 m. Found in mid- to lower levels of primary and secondary evergreen forest and forest edge. Often associated with dark swampy areas[248, 261, 263, 414, 483]. **Status** Resident, generally locally common, but uncommon in Java and Thailand. **Conservation status** Unknown.

MOVEMENTS Unknown.

SOCIAL ORGANISATION and GENERAL BEHAVIOUR Little known. Solitary or in pairs in mid- to lower levels of lowland forest, often in rather dark areas. Makes 'fripping' sounds with wings in flight. Has a rather hunched calling posture. Bathing recorded[263, 281]. **Foraging behaviour** Like a flycatcher, taking insects in flight during short sallies in undergrowth, usually from 4–6 m above ground, occasionally higher[281, 483, 511]. **Food** Soft insects and occasional Orthoptera (cricket)[263].

SOUNDS Little known. Repertoire consists of clear whistles and harsh grating notes. Territorial call a long (up to *c.*2 min) descending series of clear, slowly repeated (interval variable), loud ringing whistles *hu....hu....hu-* or *hou--hou--hou--* with pitch varying from high-pitched *he...he...he-* or *hwee...hwee-* to more plaintive lower-pitched *ho...ho...ho-*. Also double-noted whistles *hwe-weer.* Noisy harsh calls, probably alarm, vary from sharp grating metallic *churr, tzkerr,* scraping *Zrrr Zrrr-,* loud harsh squirrel-like *chuck-uk* or *cheechee-chakchak* to chattering *chik-chik* and *chi-chi-chick-chick* or *chi-chi-chi–chak-chak.* Whistled calls similar to African bush-shrikes (*Laniarius* and *Chlorophoneus*) and batises[252, 262, 281, 500].

BREEDING BIOLOGY Virtually unknown. Apparently monogamous. **Season** Jun, two young in nest (Java)[263, 772], Jan (Borneo) but see comments under Eggs[772]. **Displays** Unknown. **Nest** Role of sexes unknown. A shallow cup with thick-wall, built of vegetable fibres, moss and spiders webs, loosely attached to a low branch fork[263]. **Eggs** (the following information requires confirmation as the description of the eggs does not fit any known fly-catcher-like bird): 2 (n=2). Colour greyish and unmarked. ***Size*** 20.9 x 14.9 mm (n=2)[516, 772]. No further breeding information, except nestling initially rufous-brown, with upperparts mottled dark grey from head to rump. Wings dark grey. Bill black, gape whitish, legs grey, eye brown. Mouth spots unknown[500]. ***Bare parts*** Bill black, gape whitish; legs grey; eye brown[500]. .

MEASUREMENTS and WEIGHTS *P. v. caesium* ♂♀? (10) wing 92–99 (95.9), tail 80–86 (83.7), bill (to skull) 19.8–21.5 (20.7), tarsus 17.1–19 (17.9)[500]. **Weight** *caesium* ♂♀? (2) 25.0–27.2 g (26.1) (Borneo)[478].

80 BRUBRU (Brubru shrike) *Nilaus afer* — Plate 30

FIELD IDENTIFICATION Small (12–15 cm) black, white and chestnut-brown elusive arboreal bush-shrike with white or buff wing-stripe, broad buff stripe down back, buff or white-tipped outer tail feathers and chestnut-brown flanks. Much variation in presence, absence or extent of broad white eyebrow, chestnut-brown flanks and streaking below. Three basic forms occupy two habitat types. (A) *Acacia* and broadleaved woodland: ♂ black above with long broad white eyebrow; below white with broad rufous-brown flanks. ♀ like ♂ but duller, browner above, lightly streaked below. (B) mainly miombo woodland: ♂ without white eyebrow, usually with rufous-brown flanks, but absent in both sexes of one race (third form). ♀ like ♂ but duller, browner above with heavy streaking below. Young similar to ♀ but mottled above and barred (A), or streaked (B) below. Restless and unobtrusive in canopy; habits rather tit-like, flight undulating. More often heard than seen; ♂ far-carrying whistled trill, usually answered by ♀ in duet with short nasal call. Widespread resident, usually solitary or in pairs in canopy of larger trees of savanna woodlands throughout sub-Saharan Africa except central equatorial forest and extreme S regions of continent. ***Flight characteristics***: Undulating, often quite long as it flies from one large tree to another. Has a pied appearance and makes 'fripping' sounds with wings in flight.

COMPARISONS Distinctive, but superficially resembles batises with black, white and chestnut-brown plumage. Care required in separating young from young of some flycatchers, e.g. Pallid

Flycatcher *Bradornis pallidus*. In East Africa the forest-inhabiting Chestnut-throated Apalis *Apalis porphyroleama* has a rather similar trilling whistle.

DESCRIPTION **Adult ♂** *afer* (habitat A). ***Head*** Crown, eye-stripe to hindneck black with slight gloss; black stripe from bill through eye and ear-coverts to nape; lores and eyebrow white, extending behind eye to back of head (length variable; see Geographical Variation); sides of face and large nape-patch white. ***Back*** Black with broad mottled buff-brown (tawny) streak down centre, grading into mottled buff-and-black rump; feathers long and fluffy. ***Wings*** Coverts black with slight gloss; flight feathers dark blackish-brown; has a broad buff-brown wing-stripe formed by median and secondary coverts and inner secondaries. ***Tail*** Relatively short, central feathers black, rest black tipped white, outer feathers edged and tipped white or buff. ***Underparts*** Plain white (sometimes streaked; see Geographical Variation); sides of breast and flanks streaked with dark rufous-brown (chestnut-brown) (absent in *affinis*). ***Bare parts*** Bill black with paler grey base to lower mandible; palate black; legs grey; eye dark brown (see Geographical Variation). **Adult ♀** *afer* (habitat A) Similar to ♂ but duller, upperparts dark brown to blackish-brown. Nape-patch smaller. White of tail more buff. Underparts duller white, usually lightly streaked blackish on throat (see Geographical Variation); rufous flanks duller, paler and less extensive (absent in *affinis*). **Adult ♂** *nigritemporalis* (habitat B) Differs from nominate by lack of white eyebrow, resulting in completely black temporal region. Lores white. Rufous-brown flanks much paler and wing-stripe and stripe down centre of back whiter, not buff-brown or tawny. ***Bare parts*** Like nominate but eye reddish-brown. **Adult ♀** *nigritemporalis* (habitat B) Duller than ♂, but may have a white eyebrow, but this does not extend beyond the eye. Rest of plumage similar to nominate ♀, except whitish underparts are more heavily streaked black on throat and upper breast. ***Bare parts*** Like ♂. **Juvenile** Apparently plumage of short duration. Upperparts mottled brown, buff and white; flight feathers, coverts and tail with buffy-brown edging; wing-stripe buffy-white. Underparts dull white barred brownish, lacks rufous-brown flanks. Bill greyish-brown, lower mandible paler; eye brown. **Immature** *afer* Generally similar to adult ♀, but variable with race. Flight feathers and coverts edged and tipped buff, wing-stripe buff; tail tipped buff. Underparts dull white, irregularly barred brown, throat more speckled than barred. Rufous-brown flanks develop progressively as adult plumage acquired in about 60 days after leaving nest. Bare parts: Bill greyish-black; eye brown[61]. **Immature** *nigritemporalis* Upperparts and tail buffier-brown than ♀. Underparts differ from other races (except possibly *miombensis* and *affinis*) in having fine longitudinal streaks rather than heavier transverse bars below. Similar to ♀ of this race, but streaking heavier from throat to belly. Flanks and side of body rusty-buff. Bare parts: Bill dark greyish-black, paler on lower mandible; legs grey; eye reddish-brown[5, 66].

GEOGRAPHICAL VARIATION Variable, irregular and rather complex; at least 10 races. Three basic forms separable into two broad habitat types, (A) *Acacia* and broadleaved woodland, (B) mainly miombo *Brachystegia* woodland. Variation mainly in wing size, colour of upperparts and flanks, extent of eyebrow, presence or absence of streaking below in ♀♀, barring or streaking of juveniles and the presence or absence of adult chestnut-brown flanks. Habitat A supports one basic form, represented by at least 7 races: *camerunensis* (Cameroon to Central African Republic) larger and more greyish-tinged than nominate *afer* (Senegal to Ethiopia) and less pure white below, with a streaky greyish throat, grey loral spot and darker tone of brown in plumage; *massaicus* (E Zaïre, Rwanda to SW Kenya) paler above and on flanks than nominate, flanks broader and less streaked; *minor* (E Eritrea to E Kenya) similar to nominate but flanks much paler (tawny not chestnut-brown), broader and less streaked, the smallest race (this and *hilgerti* of central Ethiopia included by some authors with nominate); *brubru* (S Angola, Namibia, Botswana and NW South Africa) similar to *minor* but larger (largest race), ♀ with throat and breast slightly streaked; *solivagus* (SE Zimbabwe, E South Africa and Swaziland) has white eyebrow extending well beyond eye, ♀ slightly streaked below. Habitat B supports 2 basic forms represented by at least 3 races: *nigritemporalis* (NE Angola, S Zaïre, Tanzania, Zambia, Malawi, N and central Zimbabwe and Mozambique) ♂ differs from nominate by lack of white eyebrow resulting in white face with no black stripe through reddish-brown, not brown eye; central stripe on back and wing-stripe whiter, not buffy-brown; ♀ usually with short eyebrow, always streaked below; *miombensis* (Mozambique) similar to previous race, but darker above and with narrower, paler rufous-brown flanks, ♀ pure white below; secondly, *affinis* (N Angola) similar to *nigritemporalis* but lacks chestnut-brown flanks in both sexes. Intergradation occurs between *affinis* and *brubru*, and *affinis* and *nigritemporalis*[3, 30, 33, 34, 48, 53, 59, 66, 180, 290, 338, 402].

MOULT Post-breeding moult in Dec, completing wing and tail moult in Jan. Immatures begin post-juvenile moult in Jan. Evidently there is a female-type first-winter (austral) plumage in ♂♂ (Botswana). In Tanzania complete post-breeding moult recorded Jan–Mar[546, 832].

RANGE, HABITAT and STATUS **Breeding range** Widespread in sub-Saharan Africa from *c.*17°N, except in Congo basin and S tip of continent. From S Mauritania, Senegal, Gambia, Guinea-Bissau, Guinea, Sierra Leone, Ivory Coast, Ghana, Benin, Cameroon, Nigeria, Zaïre, Rwanda, Burundi, Mali, Burkina Faso, Niger, S Chad, Central African Republic, Sudan, Ethiopia, Eritrea, Somalia, Uganda, Kenya, Tanzania, Zambia, Malawi, Mozambique, Namibia, Angola, Botswana, Zimbabwe, E Swaziland and N South Africa. Vagrant to Liberia. **Habitat** Occupies two distinct habitat types (see Geographical Variation). (A) Savanna woodlands, tall *Acacia* woodlands, mixed woodlands, mopane *Colophospermum mopane* and mosaics of different woodlands. Ranges from tall well-developed woodlands and forest edge to arid woodlands and arid thornbush savanna. (B) Miombo *Brachystegia* and mixed woodlands. Occurs up to *c.*2000 m[4, 7, 21, 22, 23, 26, 30, 37, 39, 61, 234, 242, 290, 291, 292, 318, 325, 431, 481, 482, 504, 558, 631, 639, 807, 810, 848, 858, 859, 907]. **Status** Not uncommon; widespread resident with local movements in N range. **Conservation status** Unknown, probably not threatened.

MOVEMENTS Some evidence of seasonal movements in Sahel region with birds moving N during rains and S during dry season. In E Africa reportedly wanders. Southern African population sedentary[15, 23, 37, 38, 481, 504, 639].

SOCIAL ORGANISATION and GENERAL BEHAVIOUR Solitary or in pairs, members often widely separated. Unobtrusive, restless and agile, continuously on the move, often flying long distances with undulating flight, between suitable large foraging trees within its territory. ♂ advertises and defends an unusually large territory, of *c.*35 ha in broadleaved woodland, by giving a repeated high-pitched whistled trill from the top of large trees throughout the year. Calling posture upright, throat expanded, tail slightly fanned, crest raised slightly and eyebrow expanded. ♀ may respond in duet with a few short high-pitched notes, fanning tail while calling. In non-breeding season, apart from normal duets, ♂ also gives a repeated short single-note whistle, which is occasionally answered by ♀ in duet with her normal high-pitched call. Territorial threat involves counter-singing, bowing, tail-flicking, rapid side to side body movements, and zigzag display-flights with exaggerated wingbeats, usually accompanied by loud 'wing-fripping'. ♀ joins in erratic duet, flicks tail open and closed and bows rapidly. Roosting behaviour unknown. Scratches indirectly[61, 205]. **Foraging behaviour** Arboreal, mainly in the mid-to upper canopy of larger trees, occasionally lower down. Its preference for the larger trees in woodlands probably explains why it has such an unusually large territory. Captures most prey by gleaning from twigs and leaves, flitting and hopping about, constantly on the move. While searching terminal pods, sometimes hangs upside-down like a tit. Often attracted to insect-rich flowering trees and often joins mixed foraging parties. Occasionally hawks insects in the air. Larger prey is held down with one foot and torn apart with the bill like a true shrike. Ecologically most similar to the larger Black-backed Puffback *Dryoscopus cubla*, with which it may compete in some woodland habitats[48, 61, 205, 352, 574, 631, 639]. **Food** Arthropods, mainly insects and their larvae, including Lepidoptera (butterflies and caterpillars), Coleoptera (beetles), Hymenoptera (ants), Orthoptera (grasshoppers) and Diptera (flies). Also feeds on spiders[4, 48, 290, 500].

SOUNDS Repertoire consists of at least 10 distinct calls, including commonly heard loud, far-carrying, repeated high-pitched whistled trill of slightly metallic quality, like a pea whistle and somewhat ventriloquial. Also has nasal sounds and short harsh notes. Main territorial call a loud drawn-out trilling or purring sound *c.*0.5–0.8 sec long, varying in tone within one individual, from a very high-pitched short rapid trilling *prrriiii* to lower-pitched slower and longer *b-r-r-r-r-u-u-u-u-u* (from which its common name is derived). It has been variously described as *pir-r-r-r-r*, *brrruuuuu*, *prrruuuuu*, *prrrrreeeee* or *kuuurrrrrrr*. It may be repeated up to *c.*40 times, and is usually preceded by up to 6 softer *tch-*, *tchu-* or *chuk-* notes, which are also used by ♀. She responds erratically in duet with a few short, high-pitched squeaky *eeeu*, *teeeu*, *wheeu* or *skweeu* calls. These are sometimes also given synchronously rather than antiphonally. The duet has been likened to *Wherrrre-Herrre*. Only ♂ appears to initiate duets. Territorial threat consists of excited posturing, rapidly repeated high-pitched, short trills and 'wing-fripping'. Counter-singing ♂♂ often use trills of different pitch, producing a see-saw effect. ♀♀ join these interactions in duet with repeated *eeeu-eeeu-* and *tu-tu-* calls. Long-range contact maintained with duets, at short range with softer pipping *tu-*, *tu-wit*, *pe-wit*, *chip-chip-* and harsh rasping *tzzrr* calls. During nest-building, nest relief and while bringing food to nest use *pe-witor tuet* contact calls. In non-breeding season both sexes give repeated high-pitched penetrating *piep-piep-piep-*, *pe-pe-pe-pe-pe-*. A *wutitititititi* probably also given in this context. ♀ may respond to these in duet with normal *eeeu* call. Alarm signalled by rapidly repeated *chiK-chiK-chiK-* or *chK-chK-*, harsh rasping *tzzrr*, *kirr* or *krrr* notes and excited 'wing-fripping'. ♀ also gives repeated *eeeu-* notes in alarm when threatened on the nest, and both sexes give a nasal *naaa-naaa-* call in this context. Begging call unknown, although recently fledged young give *tu-wit* contact call of adults[4, 5, 6, 22, 61, 64, 35, 205, 290, 500, 504, 558, 631, 696]. Sonagram[48].

BREEDING BIOLOGY Monogamous and territorial. ♂ calling peaks in early spring. Pair-bonds probably maintained by duetting. Breeding appears to be in response to rain in spring. General location of nest fairly easily determined as ♂ calls from nest, but actual location of nest more difficult as extremely well camouflaged. This species appears unusually sensitive during nest-building, abandoning and destroying a number of its own nests without laying in them. In one study only 3 clutches out of 10 hatched successfully. Apparently single-brooded. Occurs at densities from 1 pair/30–50 ha in broadleaved woodland, to 1 bird/4 ha in *Acacia* woodland[61, 320, 639].

Season Jun–Jul, Nov (Mali)[338]; Feb (Chad)[338]; Jan–Feb requires confirmation, adults feeding young Nov (Gambia)[37, 696]; Jan, juveniles Jul–Aug (Ghana)[234]; Apr–May, Nov (Sudan)[242]; Apr (Ethiopia)[292]; Apr–May (Somalia)[237, 859]; in East Africa Feb–Jun, Aug–Nov[293]; Oct–Dec (Tanzania)[336]; Mar (Kenya)[237]; Sep–Nov, Feb–Apr in E, Dec–Jan in N (Zaïre)[22]; Sep–Oct (Angola)[7, 865]; Sep–Dec mainly Nov (Zambia)[291, 359]; Mar, Aug–Dec (Malawi)[119, 359]; in southern Africa, Aug–Apr, mainly Sep–Nov (South Africa); Sep–Jan

(Zimbabwe)[30, 359]; apparently any time in arid SW of central and S Namibia[639]; egg-laying Oct–Nov, Jan–Feb (Botswana)[807].

Displays ***Courtship*** ♂ utters high-pitched repeated *prrriiiii* trill, also high-pitched *tuet-tuet-tuet-* and *weep-weep-weep-*, both calls given with food in bill. Surprisingly, courtship-feeding has not been reported, but in view of the behaviour described, probably does occur. A record of a ♂ bowing to ♀ was probably given during courtship. ***Pre-copulation*** ♂ gives repeated trills, ♀ sitting fluffed up, wings drooped. ♂ sidles up alongside, mounts and copulates. He continued calling before and after copulation. ***Nest-site display*** Both sexes duet, then ♂ with prey makes quiet *tu-et....tu-et* while standing in what was thought to be a possible prospective nest site[5, 61, 205, 500].

Nest Built by both sexes. A small neat compact shallow cup of twigs, tendrils, grass and leaf petioles, bound with web and usually decorated with lichens. Spider web collected on the leaf petioles before adding to the nest. The nest is smoothed off and extremely well camouflaged. It is usually placed in a fork near the top tree at *c*.5 m (2.5–9, n=21) above the ground. Often uses pale-barked or lichen-covered branches. ***Size*** OD 65–89 mm (75), ID 38–45 mm (43), cup depth 19–20 mm (20), height 50 mm (n=3). Built in *c*.6 days. Nests appear too small for the chicks[2, 61, 575].

Eggs usually 2 (rarely 1–3, one nest record card indicating 4, n=60). Coloured dull white, greenish or greyish, lightly spotted or heavily streaked with dull greyish-brown and grey. ***Size*** 18.6–22.3 x 14.3–16.8 mm (20.2 x 15.4, n=44)[6, 19, 48, 290, 575].

Incubation By both sexes; starts with first egg. ♀ sits at night. Only ♂ signals nest relief regularly on the nest; however, if ♀ sitting and ♂ approaches calling, she will duet from nest. She gives repeated *eeeu-eeeu-* calls when threatened on the nest. At change-over they give soft *tuet-* and *pe-wit* contact calls. Period 19 days (n=1)[6, 61]. **Nestling** Hatch on consecutive days, blind and naked. Mouth spots unknown. Attended by both sexes; brooded continuously for *c*.7 days, next 3–4 days only sporadically, then not at all, except at night when ♀ broods. Faeces removed and apparently always eaten. Begging call unknown. Fledge after *c*.22 days (21.5–22.0, n=2). Develop adult plumage by 2 months but have brown eye; give similar contact *tu-wit* calls. Dependency period *c*.8 weeks[27, 61, 205].

Predation and longevity Nests frequently destroyed by the birds themselves, particularly when disturbed. Tree squirrels *Paraxerus cepapi* probably also destroy nest contents as do snakes, such as Bird Snake *Thelotornis capensis*. Fledgling killed by Common Fiscal *Lanius collaris*. Ringed bird 8–8.5 years[779, 1002]. **Brood parasite** None.

MEASUREMENTS and WEIGHTS *N. a. brubru* ♂ (10) wing 87–90.5 (88.4); ♀ (10) 83–91.5 (86.0)[66]; ♂♀(60) wing 80–91 (84); tail 52–63; bill 14–17.5, tarsus 20–24[48]; *nigritemporalis* ♂ (10) wing 80–87 (85.1); ♀ (10) 81–85 (83.6)[66]; ♂ (10) wing 80–86 (83.2), tail 47–58 (52.1); ♀ (8) wing 80–85 (82.6), ♀ (7) 48–55 (52.4)[319]. **Weight** ♂ (32) 17.0–32.0 g (23.2); ♀ (26) 18.0–30.0 g (22.8) (southern Africa)[48]. *nigritemporalis* ♂ (9) 21–27 g (24.6); ♀ (7) 21–25 g (23.0)[319]. For additional data see[48, 66, 205, 237, 346, 478, 494, 582, 912].

81 WHITE-TAILED SHRIKE *Lanioturdus torquatus* Plate 30

FIELD IDENTIFICATION Small (14–15 cm) black, white and grey bird with very short tail, long legs and a yellow eye. Distinctive; appears big-headed particularly when crest raised. Sexes similar. Young similar to adult but with brown eye. Pied plumage conspicuous in flight, particularly large white wing-patches. Noisy; loud ringing whistles and harsh tearing calls in duet. Solitary, in pairs in austral summer or small groups in winter. Found at all levels, mainly terrestrial with very upright stance. Resident with local movements, occurs in arid savanna bush from S Angola to central Namibia. ***Flight characteristics***: Direct, heavy, laboured and ungainly, rather butterfly-like. Pied plumage conspicuous, particularly large white wing-patches; wings rounded.

COMPARISONS Distinctive, superficially resembles large ♂ batis with pied plumage and yellow eye, but is much larger and mainly terrestrial (batises arboreal).

DESCRIPTION **ADULT** Sexes similar. ***Head*** Forehead white; crown, hindneck, ear-coverts and sides of face to below eye and lores black with slight blue-black gloss. ***Back*** Nape with white patch; mantle, back and scapulars grey; rump and uppertail-coverts grey with white spots; feathers long and fluffy. ***Wings*** Primaries and secondaries black with white bases and usually tipped white; tertials black with white tip; primary coverts black, alula black usually with small white tip, secondary coverts white; underwing-coverts black with white tips. ***Tail*** Very short, white, central two feathers with subterminal black tear-shaped patch; unusually stiff. ***Underparts*** Chin, throat and sides of neck white; narrow breast-band black with slight blue-black gloss; below belly and vent white, flanks and sides of lower breast grey. ***Bare parts*** Bill and palate black; legs black; eye yellow to greenish-yellow. **JUVENILE/IMMATURE** Similar to adult but with narrower breast-band, buffy-mottled nape and brown eye.

GEOGRAPHICAL VARIATION Two races; variation slight. Nominate *torquatus* (S Angola and Namibia) smaller and lighter than *mesicus* (Angola)[3, 62].

MOULT Body feathers appear to be moulted

throughout the year, with post-breeding moult of flight feathers in non-breeding season[205].

RANGE, HABITAT and STATUS Breeding range From Angola W of 15°E, from about 12°S in Benguela, S to about 15°S, in Mossamedes and W Huila, S to Namibia in Kaokoland, Ovamboland and Damaraland to Naukluft Mts S of Windhoek at *c*.25°S on Tsondab and Sossus Rivers. **Habitat** In S in semi-arid scrub savanna on the escarpment above 1000 m. In denser scrub, *Commiphora* and *Acacia* thornbush. Particularly abundant in mopane *Colophospermum mopane* and leadwood *Combretum imberbe* woodlands. Often found on rocky hillslopes and by watercourses. In Angola also occurs in mopane, miombo *Brachystegia* and other woodlands, including silver terminalia *Terminalia sericea* and teak woodlands on sands[7, 48, 62, 63, 64, 79, 180, 205, 431, 639, 676, 865, 907]. **Status** locally common resident and partial migrant. **Conservation status** Not threatened; as desertification occurs on the E border of its range, it may expand into these areas. Population in Namibia estimated at *c*.1.5 million[639, 889, 890].

MOVEMENTS Seasonal movements into urban areas and dry riverbeds during austral winter in Namibia, and suspected N movements in Angola into miombo woodland during Apr–Aug, where less common in Sept, and uncommon in Oct[205, 639, 676, 907].

SOCIAL ORGANISATION and GENERAL BEHAVIOUR Solitary or in pairs when breeding, in groups of 2–5, sometimes up to 12 birds in austral winter when it becomes less territorial and tends to forage more often in the vicinity of riverbeds. Looks and behaves like a large long-legged batis, appearing rather plump when perched, but has a very upright stance on ground, where often raises small crest, giving it an odd-looking, big-headed appearance. Crest-raising also often observed by only one individual of a nesting pair (♂?). Moves rapidly on the ground in long hops, with short tail pointing vertically down. Restless, active and conspicuous with pied plumage, broad black and white wings and butterfly flight, but shy and difficult to approach in open habitat; sometimes inquisitive. When flushed, flies into a bush or tree and calls. In austral summer ♂ advertise and defends a territory of *c*.5 ha with loud crescendo ringing whistles from an exposed perch. ♀ responds in duet with a harsh tearing descending call. Both sexes stretch the neck and raise the bill while calling. Most calling done from bushes and trees, some from ground. During territorial threat ♂♂ counter-sing with crescendo whistles, ratchet-like sounds and repeated nasal calls. ♀♀ join in duet with tearing call. Adopts a crouched horizontal posture in threat, glaring at the intruder. Pairs roost separately in a dense site in canopy of larger trees, and ♂ seen to roost in nest tree during breeding. Before entering roost site a pair will move about giving low *Chuk-* or *Tok-* notes. Scratches indirectly[48, 63, 64, 205, 490]. **Foraging behaviour** Mainly on the ground, where it hops about, also at all levels including canopy of large trees up to 25 m, but generally keeping to denser vegetation. Picks prey off the ground, or jumps up to glean from low vegetation, particularly around the base of bushes, sometimes hanging upside-down in its attempt to obtain food. Also gleans from trunks, branches and leaves. Occasionally hawks insects in the air. Joins mixed foraging parties, particularly in non-breeding season[48, 205, 639, 676, 743]. **Food** Arthropods, mainly insects including Coleoptera (beetles), Lepidoptera (moths, butterflies and caterpillars), Mantodea (mantids) and Orthoptera (grasshoppers). In one study nestlings fed grasshoppers (20%), caterpillars (10%), butterflies and moths (5%), remaining 65% unidentified small insects, mainly beetles. Rarely drinks water[500, 676, 743].

SOUNDS Repertoire complex and not well understood. Consists of various loud, penetrating, often querulous high-pitched whistles, nasal notes, harsh churring, tearing and ratchet notes, mostly given in duet. Various whistles are used by ♂♂ in territorial advertisement and defence. Commonly heard whistles include a repeated loud clear *huuuu, poo-eee* or *oo-eee*, lasting *c*.0.5 sec, or repeated downslurred, liquid crescendo whistles *heeeU-, hoooU-, cheeeu-, cheeuwr-*, or shorter *chiu-* whistles. Others are loud, abrupt and explosive *tewp-* or *qwup*. Most whistles are repeated up to *c*.5 times. ♀ usually responds in irregular duet with churring harsher lower-pitched *tchzrrr* or *kirrrrr* calls, and other more tearing sounds, generally with downslurred endings, *tchzrree, tchzeeu* or *treeuw*. Nasal *krrank* notes are interspersed with whistles, and apparently made by ♂, who appears to initiate duetting. Threat signalled with rapid whistles, often with counter-singing, and various loud harsh ratchet-like *Chuk-Chuk-K-K-KKK-* and harsh nasal *Kzzzp-Kzzzp-* or *krrank-* by ♂ and *ktchzrrr* by ♀. Alarm call a stuttering nasal-sounding *chiKchiKchiKchiK, chuk-k-k-k-k-* or *chk-chk-ckk-* and harsh *TzuKzuK-* notes. High-intensity alarm involves harsh *WrWr-WaWaWa, Cha-Cha-Cha-Cha-* and explosive *Skzeer-Skzeer-* or *skwee-skwee* sounds. At low intensity signalled by slowly repeated *Chuk-Chuk-* or *Tok-Tok-*, also made as bird goes to roost and by nestlings. ♂ usually gives *heeeU* whistle on approaching and while guarding nest. Long-range contact maintained with duetting, short-range contact with hollow metallic *chink....chink* notes, which are often heard when pairs are in the vicinity of the nest. Sometimes *chink* notes are responded to with whistles. Nestlings give soft high-pitched *seee-seee-* calls, fledglings harsh *cheerr-cheerr-* accompanied by wing-fluttering. When excited ♂ makes 'fripping' sounds with wings in display-flight[48, 205, 490, 676, 743]. Sonagram[48].

BREEDING BIOLOGY Monogamous and territorial. Although gregarious in non-breeding season, cooperative breeding has not been recorded. Groups break up into pairs for breeding. After the eggs have hatched ♀ continues to solicits food from ♂ for *c*.3 days with mouth open and wings fluttering. During first 3 days of nestling period, presumed ♂ gives whistled *cheeuwr* while waiting to pass food to his mate near the nest. ♀ responded with *treeuw* before also arriving with food. Having fed the nestlings both fly off giving metallic *chink-* call. Nesting birds tend to approach the nest cautiously and indirectly. ♂ has been observed guarding nest while ♀ away, giving frantic *heeeU-* whistles if mate remained away too long. Pair bonds apparently maintained, at least in part by duetting. Recorded at a density of 26 birds/km² in mopane woodland. Double broods have been recorded[205, 639, 743, 744, 890, 1063, 1064]. **Season** Nov–Dec, breeding condition Nov–Dec (Angola)[865, 907]; Sep–Apr, mainly Feb–Mar (Namibia)[48, 64, 205, 639]. **Displays *Courtship*** ♂ display-flight consists of a steep upward climb, followed by a descending, bouncing glide with rump feathers fluffed-out and repeated *tchuee-tchuee-tchuee-* whistles. ♂ pursues ♀ with low flying and rapid hopping on ground and up through bushes, birds bowing during interactions. Pairs perform fast duets, initiated by ♂, and sounding like *heeeU-tchzrrr-heeeU-tchzrrr-*. Courtship-feeding unknown, although ♂ feeds ♀ during incubation and early brooding period. ***Pre-copulation*** Copulation takes place without obvious display[205, 1063]. **Nest** Built by both sexes, ♀ doing most work. A deep, neat, smoothed and well-moulded cup of fine dry grass, hair and bark strips, bound and plastered with spider web. May have lining of finer dry vegetable material. Placed *c.*2.5 m (0.4–8, n=18) above the ground, on horizontal branch or in a fork near the top of a tree, often thorn trees and frequently exposed in trees devoid of leaves. ***Size*** OD 70–80 mm, ID 60 mm, cup depth 30–40 mm, height 55–80 mm. Nest completed in about 6 days. Nest placed in same vicinity each year[64, 205, 500, 590, 639]. **Eggs** Usually 2 (1–3, n=16), laid at 24 hour intervals. Whitish or pale greenish, sparsely spotted with red-brown and blue-grey mainly around the large end. ***Size*** 20.2–20.9 x 15.4–16.8 mm (20.4 x 15.8, n=9)[19, 64, 205, 500, 590]. **Incubation** By ♀ only, very confiding. ♂ feeds her on and off nest. At one nest ♂ remained on guard when ♀ off. Period 15 days (n=1). ♀ duets from nest[205, 1063]. **Nestling** Hatch blind, naked, turning blackish-purple. Develops grey, black and white plumage in *c.*12 days. Eye dark. Mouth bright orange-yellow with no mouth spots. Apparently only ♀ broods; initially she does all the attending, passing food solicited from ♂ to nestlings. ♂ feeds them directly after a few days. Begging call a soft high-pitched *seee-seee-*. Nestlings develop grey, black and white plumage by *c.*13 days. Fledge after *c.*19–20 days (16–21, n=5); may remain on the ground before strong enough to fly. Attended by both sexes. Dependent for at least 2 weeks, remaining in territory for at least 4.5 months. In an unusual observation, this species seen feeding two fledged Lark-like Buntings *Emberiza impetuani*[205, 500, 743]. **Predation and longevity** Nests destroyed in bad weather[63]. **Brood parasites** Unknown.

MEASUREMENTS and WEIGHTS *L. t. torquatus* ♂ (24) wing 80.0–90.0 (86.7), ♀ (21) wing 84.0–91.0 (86.0); ♂♀? (44) tail 39.8–48.0 (44.2), ♂♀? (39) bill (to skull) 20.6–24.0 (21.8), ♂♀? (44) tarsus 25.6–32.0 (29.5)[500, 676]; *mesicus* ♂♀? (20) wing 83–93 (87.9)[62]. **Weight** *torquatus* ♂♀? (26) 22.5–45.0 g (29.0)[205, 500]; *mesicus* ♂♀? (16) 23–38 g (30.9)[62]. For additional data see[48, 64].

82 CAPE BATIS *Batis capensis* — Plate 31

FIELD IDENTIFICATION Very small (11–12 cm), dumpy, restless, black, white and rufous flycatcher-like bird with greyish head, black face-mask and reddish eye. Sexes different. white below; ♂ with broad black breast-band, white (northern) or rufous (southern) wing-stripe and flanks. ♀ rufous chinspot, broad breast-band, flanks and wing-stripe. Young like ♀ but darker above, with double rufous wing-stripe and brown eye. More often heard than seen, main call a slowly repeated, plaintive, short, low-pitched whistle. Solitary, in pairs or family group, inconspicuous, occurs at all levels, mainly low down in evergreen forests and densely wooded gorges and plantations, from sea-level to montane forests. Resident with local movements, from SE Tanzania, Malawi and adjacent Mozambique, E Zambia, Zimbabwe, Lesotho, Swaziland and South Africa. ***Flight characteristics***: Short; has pied appearance and makes 'fripping' sounds with wings in flight. Wings rounded.

COMPARISONS In S population (S of Zambezi River), ♂ differs from other batises by broad black breast-band, rufous wing-stripe and flanks, and lack of white eyebrow. ♀ like ♂ but has chestnut-brown throat or chinspot and breast-band and short narrow white eyebrow. Only other ♀♀ with rufous wing-stripe in its range are Woodwards' *Batis fratrum* and in the N, Forest Batis *B. mixta*. Woodwards' is also distinguished by white eyebrow extending beyond eye, and diffuse underpart colour without a defined throat patch. In N population (N of Zambezi River), wing-stripe and flanks of ♂ are white (not rufous). ♀♀ similar to S birds. Cape Batis ♂ differs from ♂ Forest Batis in lack of white lores and eyebrow (Forest Batis white in these areas) and a longer tail. ♀ Forest Batis has buffy-rufous (not chestnut-brown) breast-band extending onto throat without a distinct break to form a chinspot. Eye red and tail very short in Forest Batis. Whistled calls of the three forest species ♂♂ are rather similar, stone-rubbing (chuntering) sounds and ♀♀ churring calls different.

DESCRIPTION **ADULT ♂** ***Head*** Forehead, crown and hindneck dark bluish-grey; face-mask black. ***Back*** Mantle, scapulars, back, rump and uppertail-coverts olive-brown, feathers long and fluffy. ***Wings*** Primaries and secondaries blackish, narrowly edged white; wing-stripe formed by broad rufous tips to tertials, inner greater coverts and median coverts (variable; see Geographical Variation). Underwing-coverts whitish. ***Tail*** Black with white outer feathers, rest except central pair tipped white. ***Underparts*** Chin and throat white, broad breast-band black, belly and undertail-coverts white; flanks chestnut-brown (variable; see Geographical Variation); thighs blackish. ***Bare parts*** Bill, palate and legs black; eye variable; lemon-yellow, orange-red to red (includes *dimorpha*). Probably influenced by age, with yellow eye indicative of young birds, as well as seasonal changes and habitat differences. **ADULT ♀** Differs from ♂ by having narrow whitish eyebrow, and chin and throat rufous to chestnut-brown in middle, white at sides, and breast-band rufous to chestnut-brown. Bare parts like ♂; however, *dimorpha* may be dimorphic in this character, with ♀ having a paler eye than ♂[500]. **JUVENILE/IMMATURE** Like adult ♀, but upperparts more olivaceous dark grey, mantle spotted buffy-brown, greater and median wing-coverts broadly tipped rufous forming a double wing-stripe; black face-mask absent and throat buffy brown. Later breast-band partially developed mottled brown and black in ♂. Eye initially brown to dark brown, later becoming pale yellow[32, 205]. For development of plumage see[83, 872].

GEOGRAPHICAL VARIATION At least 7 races. Variation mainly in coloration of upperparts, width of breast-band, extent, saturation and inclusion of grey in rufous underparts, and absence of rufous flanks. Broadly separable into two main groups: (a) southern population S of Zambezi River; (b) northern population in Malawi and SE Tanzania. Southern population ♂♂ have top of head grey and mantle deep olive-green; lack white lores and eyebrow; tertials and wing-coverts edged chestnut-brown, flanks chestnut-brown. Included here are *hollidayi* (E South Africa, Swaziland, Mozambique), like nominate *capensis* (S and SE South Africa) but crown blue-grey, mantle and rump greyish-olive, and flanks lighter; *erythrophthalma* (E Zimbabwe, W Mozambique), like nominate but mantle grey, with little contrast between crown and mantle, breast-band wider in ♂, mantle of ♀ more olive-brown, and breast-band wider and darker, eye of both sexes with inner and outer rings; *kennedyi* (SW and central Zimbabwe), like nominate but larger and rufous areas paler. Northern population ♂♂ have top of head and mantle grey, tertials, wing-coverts and flanks white, and like S birds lack white lores and eyebrow; ♀ wing-coverts and flanks chestnut-brown like S population. Included here are *dimorpha* (S Malawi, adjacent Mozambique) ♂ has white wing-stripe and flanks, ♀ has scapulars blackish olive-brown. *sola* (N Malawi) ♂ like previous race, ♀ having greyer mantle and lesser coverts black not brown, tertials fringed white not rufous. Finally, *reichenowi* (coastal SE Tanzania, restricted to the Mikindani area) which some authors consider a race of Forest Batis or as a separate species, is shorter-tailed than nominate, and upperparts of ♂ pale grey, wing feathers edged pale grey (not rufous), face-mask less extensive (does not extend as far back), wing-stripe and flanks white. ♀ with tinge of rufous on throat and breast-band mixed with grey on sides. Its relationship remains controversial (see Relationships, p.44)[18, 85, 86, 287, 578, 632, 906].

MOULT Post-breeding primary moult starts soon after breeding (Oct–Mar) (South Africa and Zimbabwe), with juveniles in moult from Dec–Feb (Zimbabwe)[205, 875].

RANGE, HABITAT and STATUS **Breeding range** Fragmented with numerous isolated populations. In South Africa mainly coastal from SW to E, and inland to isolated populations in NE, NW Lesotho, Swaziland, SW to E Zimbabwe, S and W Mozambique, Malawi (S of but not including Misuku Hills) and E Zambia on Nyika Plateau and SE Tanzania (*reichenowi*). **Habitat** Evergreen forest from sea-level to 2450 m, occurring in lower to mid levels. In southern Africa, found in forest edge and clearings, wooded gorges, riverine fringes, dense bush and bracken at high elevations. Also found in adjacent woodland, secondary growth, dense succulent scrub, wattle, pine and other plantations and gardens. Requires forest patches of at least 0.3–0.35 ha, occasionally as low as 0.25 ha (Malawi)[5, 48, 205, 448, 459, 578, 639, 676, 945]. **Status** Resident with local movements, generally common. **Conservation status** Although adaptable and wandering during non-breeding season, the fragmented nature of its distribution results in numerous small isolated populations which are potentially more vulnerable, particularly in N of range.

MOVEMENTS In non-breeding season, wanders into adjacent woodlands and undertakes downward altitudinal movements in E Zimbabwe and Malawi. In South Africa there appears to be some W–E austral winter movements in SW of range. Its ability to wander in the non-breeding season may assist in maintaining the many apparently isolated populations[30, 83, 119, 448, 578, 639, 660].

SOCIAL ORGANISATION and GENERAL BEHAVIOUR Solitary, in pairs or family groups, restless and constantly on the move. A dumpy, tame and inquisitive bird. Prior to breeding may congregate in small flocks of *c*.10, occasionally up to 30 birds, sometimes of same sex, known as 'parliaments'. Birds in these gatherings chase each other about with much 'wing-fripping' and excited calling. In ♂ gatherings they give churring 'stone-rubbing' call with heads pointing upwards. Advertises and defends a territory of *c*.1 ha (0.3–1.0), in which it may remain for at least 10 years, with repeated *hui-* whistles from a perch, adopting a squat inclined posture, head slightly inclined, throat expanding as a conspicuous white signal while calling, and tail fanned slightly. Pairs defend territory with bouncy, zigzag flights with tail fanned, 'wing-fripping', bill-snapping and a wide variety of calls including grating, rolling 'stone-rubbing' calls during which rump feathers are fluffed-out and tail fanned. They may also fan the tail to one side, with head cocked pointing upwards, or crouch with head up, swaying body from side to side, and tail fanned. Roosting behaviour unknown. Scratches indirectly[146, 205, 448, 506, 660, 872, 875]. **Foraging behaviour** Arboreal, at all levels from undergrowth to canopy of large trees at 20–25 m. Gleans prey mainly from underside of leaves, also branches and trunks in short flights of 1–2 m, usually capturing prey with an audible bill-snap. Will take prey in flight or glean off branch while perched; hops along branches. Make light bouncy flights between bushes. Joins mixed foraging parties, particularly in non-breeding season[5, 205, 448]. **Food** Arthropods, mainly insects and their larvae, including Diptera (flies), Coleoptera (beetles), Hemiptera (bugs), Lepidoptera (moths and caterpillars). Young fed flies, Dictyoptera (small cockroaches), moths and spiders[8, 83].

SOUNDS Repertoire consists of plaintive whistles, harsh churring and bill-snapping sounds. Territorial call of ♂ a series of up to *c*.12 loud, short, plaintive, slowly repeated *hui—hui—hui–* or *tu-*, *fu-* or *whew-* whistles delivered at same pitch. Sometimes the last few notes are slightly higher-pitched. Notes have a similar quality to the call of Grey-headed Bush-shrike *Malaconotus blanchoti*, but are much shorter. Number of notes/series varies geographically (fewer in S). Delivery rates vary from *c*.1–3 notes/sec. The length of the whistle also varies from short *hu-* to longer *hueet-* or disyllabic *huWit-*, sometimes with a ringing quality. Counter-singing ♂♂ often use whistles of slightly different pitch, producing a *hee-huu-hee-huu-* see-saw effect. Reports of ♀ occasionally making similar whistle sounds requires confirmation. She usually joins in duet with various churring calls, ranging from *jjwrr* and *jjwee* to softer more rolling *jjizjjizjjiz-* phrases. Territorial threat signalled by both sexes with harsh, grating or churring *chi-chi-chch-chi-ri-ri-ri-* or buzzy *kerick-ick-ick-ick* calls, and others impossible to describe adequately, but sounding like two stones being rubbed together. These vary from low-pitched rolling *jirrowirrowirr-* and *jk-jk-jjwrjjwrjjwr-* phrases (chuntering) to more intense, higher-pitched *jrrr-jrrr-jrreeE* and *jrreeE-jrreeE-* sounds. ♀ joins in duet with a few *Jrrr-Jrrr-* or buzzing *Zizz-Zizz-* calls combined with softer ticking sounds. During these interactions the birds make bouncing, jerky, zigzag display-flights with tail fanned and noisy 'wing-fripping'. ♂ also fluffs out rump feathers, and both sexes bow and give excited *jk-jk-jk-* calls with bill-snapping. Other calls of unknown function include repeated *tsett-tsett-* and *tjewett*. Alarm signalled with harsh *ChikChik-* and rapid bill-snapping, often accompanied by 'wing-fripping'. Contact maintained with soft *chik-chik-* or *jk-* calls and churring. Begging call of nestlings a quiet chattering *chizchizchiz-*. Young and ♀ solicit with louder chattering *KisshKissh-* calls[5, 48, 83, 145, 205, 676, 872]. Sonagram[48].

BREEDING BIOLOGY Monogamous and territorial. A second ♀ sometimes present in breeding territory, probably an immature from previous breeding attempt, and suggestive of possible low incidence of cooperative breeding. In S of range known to breed within 20 m of Pririt Batis *Batis pririt*. No hybridisation recorded[676, 801]. **Season** Sep–Jan, mainly Oct–Dec (South Africa)[48]; Oct (Mozambique)[26]; Sep–Feb, mainly Oct–Dec (Zimbabwe)[30, 359]; Sep–Feb, mainly Sep–Dec (Malawi)[74, 119]; gonads active Sep–Nov (Zambia)[291]. **Displays *Courtship*** Similar to high-intensity territorial display, ♂ flying about constantly with much 'wing-fripping', body-bowing and excited calling. ♂ display-flight is jinking and undulating, accompanied by 'wing-fripping'; on landing flashes out rump feathers, fans tail and raises wings above the back. At the same time gives rolling or churring calls. ♀ solicits in crouched position, bill pointing upwards, wings fluttering, and gives a chattering *KisshKissh-* or *skizzskizz-* call. ♂ known to courtship-feed[205]. **Nest** Built by both birds, mainly by ♀ closely attended by ♂. A small strong thick-walled deep cup of bark strips and plant material camouflaged with leafy or filamentous lichens (*Usnea*) and moss, whole structure being moulded onto branch and bound together with spider web. Both sexes apply web with side to side weaving or wiping movements of the head. Nest is usually lined with fine dry plant material. Nest placed on horizontal branch or against trunk or in fork, also once in tree hollow, and usually 3–4 m above ground (0.8–9.5 [3.0], n=138). ***Size*** OD 60–76 mm, ID 50 mm, cup depth 30–50 mm, height 40 mm. Completed nests sometimes remain empty for a few weeks before egg-laying, and are often built in same area each year, and occasionally re-used[5, 75, 83, 84, 205]. **Eggs** Usually 2 (1–3, n=65). Eggs of 2 distinct types: (a) very pale green with dark brown spots and blotches; (b) white or very pale pink, spotted and blotched with purple-grey and red-brown. Both types have markings concentrated in a well-defined belt around the broad end. Pale green eggs less common. ***Size*** 16.0–21.0 x 12.6–15.2 mm (18 x 13.9, n=40). Lays 1–2 broods[5, 8, 19, 48, 75]. **Incubation** By ♀ only; starts with last egg. ♂ feeds her on and off nest, announcing his arrival with contact or stone-rubbing call. ♀ unusually confiding when incubating. Period 18 days (17–21, n=4). Shells dropped over side of nest, faeces removed away from nest[48, 83, 872]. **Nestling** Hatch blind, naked and without mouth spots; gape creamy, tongue plain yellow, eye brown, skin blackish. Fledge after *c*.16 days (n=2); attended by both sexes, but fed mainly by ♀. They make a quiet *chizchizchiz-* begging call. Young may remain in parental territory for at least 1 year[83, 84, 205, 872]. For nestling development see[83]. **Predation and longevity** Known predators of adults include Fork-tailed Drongo *Dicrurus adsimilis* and Bat Hawk *Machieramphus alcinus*; of nestlings, boomslang *Dispholidus* and probably monkeys. Ringed bird at least 10.8 years old[205, 500, 505, 707, 660]. **Brood parasite** Klaas's Cuckoo *Chrysococcyx klaas*; levels unknown, but in one study 3 out of 5 nests parasitised[75].

MEASUREMENTS and WEIGHTS *B. c. capensis* ♂ (113) wing 56.5–66.5 (61.6), tail 40.5–49.5 (45.1), bill 14.0–18.0 (16.6); ♀ (97) wing 56.5–67.0 (60.5), tail 40.0–48.0 (44.3), bill 14.5–17.5 (16.1), ♂♀? (38) tarsus 18–22 (18.8) (South Africa)[287, 676]; *reichenowi* ♂ (3) wing 60.5–62.5 (61.5), tail 34.0–35.0 (34.5), bill 16.5–17.0 (16.8); ♀ (5) wing 58.0–60.0 (59.0), tail 31.0–32.0 (31.5), bill 14.0–16.5 (15.2) (SE Tanzania)[287]. **Weight** *capensis* plus other southern races ♂ (101) 9.3–14.5 g (11.8); ♀ (200) 8.9–13.9 g (11.5) (southern Africa)[48]. For additional data see[146, 205, 287, 478, 838, 875].

83 MARGARET'S BATIS *Batis margaritae* Plate 31

FIELD IDENTIFICATION Very small (11–12 cm), dumpy, black and white flycatcher-like bird, grey above with black face-mask and reddish eye. Sexes different. White below, ♂ with broad black breast-band and white wing-stripe, ♀ with rufous wing-stripe. Young like ♀, but duller with brown eye. Little known. Main call a long series of low-pitched whistles on same pitch. Solitary or in pairs, rather confiding and less active than other batises in its range. Occurs at mid levels, mainly in dry evergreen forest, especially *Cryptosepalum*. Resident with some seasonal movements, in W Angola, NW Zambia and S Zaïre. ***Flight characteristics***: Wings rounded; appears pied in flight.
COMPARISONS Similar to ♂ Chinspot Batis *Batis molitor*, but easily distinguished on call. ♂ Margaret's gives a long series (up to *c.*26) of short whistled notes at same pitch. Chinspot Batis usually having a short series of 2–3 whistle notes on descending scale; however, it is also known to give longer series, particularly in overlap zones with other batises. Margaret's Batis is a bulkier and dumpier bird, with a squat puffed-out appearance. It is also less active than Chinspot. ♂ Margaret's breast-band is broader and lacks the slight narrowing or nick in centre of ♂ Chinspot's breast-band. ♂ Margaret's also lacks a distinctive eyebrow (Chinspot has a long white eyebrow) and it has an orange-yellow eye (yellow in Chinspot). ♀♀ unlikely to be confused as ♀ Margaret's has a black breast-band and rufous wing-stripe (♀ Chinspot has chestnut-brown breast-band and chinspot, and white wing-stripe). Where found together, Margaret's Batis usually forages below the canopy, Chinspot above it in the canopy[635, 700].
DESCRIPTION **ADULT ♂** *kathleenae* ***Head and back*** Dark grey including uppertail-coverts; rump paler grey with concealed white spots, feathers long and fluffy; face-mask black; lores grey. ***Wings*** Primaries and secondaries black, narrowly edged white on outer edge; tertials black broadly edged and tipped white forming a wing-stripe extending onto middle greater and median coverts; other coverts black. Underwing-coverts white. ***Tail*** Black, outer feathers edged white, all except central pair tipped white. ***Underparts*** Chin and throat white; broad (*c.*15 mm) black breast-band; belly and undertail-coverts white; flanks white tinged grey; thighs grey. ***Bare parts*** Bill black; palate unknown; legs black; eye golden-yellow tinged orange. **ADULT ♀** **Upperparts** Like ♂ but white wing feathers rufous not white; lores whitish, sometimes extending to form an indistinct eyebrow. ***Tail*** Outer feathers tipped buff. ***Underparts*** White; possibly slightly narrower black breast-band, with small rusty patch on sides; flanks buffy. ***Bare parts*** Like ♂ but eye claret-red[831]. **JUVENILE/IMMATURE** Like adult ♀, but upperparts olive-brown (slate-grey in adults) and flight feathers edged buff not white and coverts more rufous. Eyebrow pale greyish and longer, extending behind eye. Underparts: Throat tinged tawny, breast-band duller and slightly narrower, lower breast darker buff-brown to pale rufous; flanks tinged same; eye brown[635, 831].
GEOGRAPHICAL VARIATION Two races, variation mainly in body size and colour of upperparts and wing-coverts. Nominate *margaritae* (W Angola) is larger and has ♂ upperparts darker and ♀ wing-coverts edged rich rufous-brown compared to *kathleenae* (NW Zambia and S Zaïre).
MOULT Unknown.
RANGE, HABITAT and STATUS **Breeding range** S Central Africa in NW Zambia, S Zaïre (Shaba) and W Angola (Mt Mocco=Manje Mts)[907]. **Habitat** Mainly in *Cryptosepalum* forest, also in other dry evergreen and drier riverine forest, wet forest and man-induced thickets[7, 291, 431, 635, 907]. Its absence from some evergreen habitats may be due to competition with Black-throated Wattle-eye *Platysteira peltata*[291]. **Status** Generally common resident. **Conservation status** Considered Near-Threatened; however, generally common[343].
MOVEMENTS In Zambia, although possibly resident in riverine forest, apparently has seasonal movements out of *Cryptosepalum* forests during rains from about Oct or Nov–Apr[291, 635, 676, 831].
SOCIAL ORGANISATION and GENERAL BEHAVIOUR Little known. Solitary or in pairs; very confiding and much less active than Chinspot Batis, but social organisation and general behaviour similar to this species. Tends to keep below the canopy. **Foraging behaviour** Arboreal, searches for prey in mid levels from 2–5 m above the ground. Often remains motionless for 1 min or more. Joins mixed foraging parties and may be found in the same party as Chinspot Batis[635, 865]. **Food** Insects.
SOUNDS Little known. Repertoire consists of whistles and harsh churring calls. Territorial call a

series of short soft thin *huu-huu-huu-, hooit...hooit...hooit-* whistles repeated every *c.*2/sec, but variable, for *c.*3–26 times, usually up to about 10 times. First note higher than rest, which are often thin, weakly delivered and remain at the same pitch. ♀ duets with *chhrweet....chhrweet....* Also makes churring *chchchchrrrr* stone-rubbing sounds and in alarm a harsh scolding rattle *grragr-ragra...grraa.* Whistle notes similar to Cape Batis *Batis capensis* but slightly higher-pitched[500, 635, 865].
BREEDING BIOLOGY Unknown. Probably monogamous and territorial. **Season** Probably from late Sep (Angola)[7, 865, 907]; gonads active Sep (Zambia)[291, 780, 831]. No further breeding information.
MEASUREMENTS and WEIGHTS *B. m. margaritae* ♂ (5) wing 65.0–68.0 (66.38), tail 45.0–46.5 (46.00), bill 16.0–17.0 (16.25), ♂ (1) tarsus 20; ♀ (5) wing 66.0–69.0 (67.40), tail 45.5–47.5 (46.60), bill 15.5–16.0 (15.9), ♀ (1) tarsus[20, 287, 500]. **Weight** *kathleenae* ♂ (4) 11.5–13 g (12.3); ♀ (4) 12.5–15.5 g (14.1); Imm ♀ 10.2 g[635]. ♂♀? (16) 9.8–13.0 g (11.0)[876]. For additional data see[287, 831].

84 FOREST BATIS *Batis mixta* — Plate 31

FIELD IDENTIFICATION Very small (9.5–10 cm), dumpy, restless, black and white flycatcher-like bird with grey back, black face-mask and reddish eye. Sexes different. White below, ♂ with broad black breast-band and white wing-stripe and flanks, ♀ with chin and breast mottled buffy-rufous and wing-stripe pale rufous. Young like ♀ but darker above and with pale eye. Little known. More often heard than seen; main call a slowly repeated short low-pitched whistle. Solitary or in pairs at all levels and in a range of habitats from woodland, thickets and forest at sea-level to montane forests. Resident from SE Kenya, Tanzania to N Malawi. ***Flight characteristics***: Short-distance; wings rounded. ♂ has a pied appearance. Makes 'fripping' sounds with wings in flight.
COMPARISONS Similar to Cape Batis *Batis capensis*, their ranges approaching but not overlapping in N Malawi. ♂♂ similar except that Forest Batis has white lores (absent in Cape Batis) and a shorter tail. ♀ Forest separated from ♀ Cape on paler buffy-rufous underparts with chinspot and breast-band poorly defined and separated (Cape has distinct chestnut-brown to rufous breast-band and chinspot, which in *reichenowi* from coastal SE Tanzania has a poorly defined chinspot). ♀ similar to ♀ Woodwards' Batis *B. fratrum.* Main whistle call of ♂ similar to Cape Batis and Ruwenzori Batis *B. diops*, but nasal churring calls different. Call also superficially resembles Chestnut Wattle-eye *Dyaphorophyia castanea.* Range overlaps 3 other savanna woodland batises, all of which have distinctive white eyebrows, yellow eye and white wing-stripes in ♀♀[448, 500].
DESCRIPTION **Adult ♂ Upperparts** Head to uppertail-coverts dark bluish-grey; lores white, may extend back slightly; face-mask black; rump feathers long and fluffy with concealed white spots. ***Wings*** Primaries and secondaries blackish, narrowly edged white; tertials black broadly edged white, forming part of wing-stripe, which extends forwards through tips of inner greater and median coverts. Underwing-coverts white. ***Tail*** Black with outer feathers edged and tipped white, rest except central pair tipped white. ***Underparts*** Chin and throat white, breast-band black (*c.*14–23 mm wide); flanks and belly white; thighs blackish. ***Bare parts*** Bill black; palate unknown; legs black; eye red[287, 676]. **Adult ♀ Upperparts** Head to rump dark olive-grey, scapulars blackish olive-brown. **Wing** Feathers olive-brown with russet outer webs; wing-stripe pale rufous. ***Underparts*** Chinspot, breast-band and flanks tawny to pale buffy-rufous, feathers tipped white, giving a mottled appearance. Chinspot and breast-band poorly separated, practically merging; rest of underparts white. ***Bare parts*** Like ♂. **Juvenile** Similar to adult ♀, but speckled with buff above[631]. **Immature** Like adult ♀ but upperparts more olivaceous and face-mask not well differentiated; eye paler. In ♂, development of black breast-band simultaneous with whitening of underparts and wing-stripe. ♀ initially with buffy eyebrow and paler breast[618].
GEOGRAPHICAL VARIATION Two races, variation mainly in body size and plumage details of head, throat and breast. Occurs as two population groups: those in the isolated mountain chains of Tanzania, where in NE descend to lower elevations, and those in the coastal population in S Kenya. Race *ultima* (coastal SE Kenya) differs from nominate *mixta* (N Malawi, Tanzania and Kenya) by being smaller, ♂ with white lores, a narrow white eyebrow and a narrower breast-band (8–14 mm), ♀ with breast-band feathers having more white on tips[287, 676].
MOULT Post-breeding moult recorded in Feb (S Tanzania)[832].
RANGE, HABITAT and STATUS **Breeding range** SE coastal Kenya, NE to SW Tanzania from Kilimanjaro to coastal forests, Usambara and Uluguru Mts to N Malawi at Karonga and Misuku Hills. **Habitat** From sea-level in coastal forest, thickets and miombo *Brachystegia* woodland to isolated montane evergreen forest, up to *c.*2300 m on Kilimanjaro. Within this habitat it is found in lower levels from undergrowth to mid-levels, sometimes canopy[287, 431, 448, 578, 448]. **Status** Generally common resident. **Conservation status** Unknown. However, general trend of forests

becoming more fragmented suggests the situation requires attention[515].

MOVEMENTS Some evidence of seasonal altitudinal movements (Tanzania)[737].

SOCIAL ORGANISATION and GENERAL BEHAVIOUR Little known. Solitary, in pairs or small family groups. Behaviour appears to be similar to Cape Batis. Calling ♂ raises head and puffs out white throat feathers with each whistle. **Foraging behaviour** Arboreal, recorded at all levels, mostly below mid levels. Race *ultima* forages low down, while *mixta* is at least partially a bird of forest canopy[2, 299, 448, 631, 737]. **Food** Insects, including Isoptera (termites)[676].

SOUNDS Repertoire consists of plaintive whistles and harsh churring and bill-snapping sounds. Territorial song of ♂ a persistently repeated slow series of short low-pitched hollow *hu-hu-hu-hu-* or *yeo-yeo-* or *ooo-ooo-* whistles, also described as piping *eee...eee...eeeuk...eee-*. Notes have a ringing metallic quality, sometimes ventriloquial, and are repeated regularly at *c*.1–4 sec intervals. Quality similar to Grey-headed Bush-shrike *Malaconotus blanchoti*, note much shorter. Said often to alternate with identical call of mate, but this is contrary to other batises and is thought to represent ♂♂ counter-singing. ♀ responds in duet with a curious rough nasal *rrannh* call, or softer *nyemp* given at intervals during the whistled series. Other calls include *chik-*, *chrrr* and chuntering, sounding like two stones being rubbed together repeatedly: *shrurrshreee-*. Alarm signalled by a rapid mechanical-sounding *ch-ch-ch-ch-* or *ch-ch-ch–chchch-cheenh* combined with 'wing-fripping' and bill-snapping[299, 448, 500, 500, 515, 631, 676].

BREEDING BIOLOGY Little known. Monogamous and territorial. **Season** oviduct egg May (Kenya)[676]; May–Jun (East Africa)[293]; Dec (Tanzania)[734, 832], ♀♀ with brood patches Sep and Oct[737]. **Displays** Unknown. **Nest and eggs** Unknown. One record of 2 eggs[734]. No further breeding information, except that fledging period is *c*.15 days[805].

MEASUREMENTS and WEIGHTS *B. m. mixta* ♂ (33) wing 59.0–64.5 (62.58), tail 31.5–38.0 (35.63), bill 14.5–17.5 (15.59), tarsus 17.9–19.4 (18.6); ♀ (30) wing 58.0–66.0 (61.73), tail 31.0–38.0 (34.96). bill 14.0–16.5 (15.29), tarsus 18.0–19.0 (18.7)[287, 676]. **Weight** *mixta* ♂ (14) 11.7–13.5 g (12.5); ♀ (24) 10.5–13.6 g (12.1) (Tanzania)[299, 676]. For additional data see[287, 299, 676, 777].

85 WOODWARDS' BATIS (Zululand Batis) *Batis fratrum* Plate 31

FIELD IDENTIFICATION Very small (10.5–11.5 cm), dumpy, restless, grey, black and white flycatcher-like bird. Blue-grey above with short whitish eyebrow, black face-mask and orange-red eye. Sexes different. ♂ wing-stripe, chin and throat white, breast and upper belly pale buffy-rufous; ♀ wing-stripe and chin to upper belly tawny to buffy-rufous. Young like ♀ but eyebrow buff, face-mask indistinct and eye brownish. More often heard than seen; main call a series of slowly repeated, low-pitched plaintive whistles made with distinctive frog-like posture. Solitary, in pairs or family group, inconspicuous, occurs in lowland dry or evergreen coastal and riverine forest, thickets and dense *Acacia* stands. Resident from S Malawi, E Zimbabwe, Mozambique to SE South Africa. ***Flight characteristics***: Short-distance; wings rounded. Has pied appearance and makes 'fripping' sound with wings.

COMPARISONS Separated from most other batises by lack of distinct breast-band in both sexes, and presence of pale buffy-rufous wing-stripe in ♀. ♂ distinctive, ♀ most similar to Forest Batis *Batis mixta*. Calls of ♂♂ similar, those of ♀♀ more distinct compared to Forest Batis[631, 700].

DESCRIPTION **ADULT ♂** ***Head*** Forehead blue-grey, short white eyebrow; crown and nape dark bluish-grey; no white nape-patch; face-mask black, extending almost to back of neck. ***Back*** Mantle and back dark bluish-grey; scapulars edged bluish-black; rump and uppertail-coverts blue-grey, rump feathers long and fluffy with concealed white spots. ***Wings*** Primaries and secondaries black with narrow white edges; wing-stripe formed by median coverts broadly tipped white, linking up to narrow white tips along the outer webs of black tertials. Underwing-coverts white. ***Tail*** Black, outer feathers edged white, all except central two tipped white. ***Underparts*** Chin, throat and sides of neck white, breast, upper belly and flanks tawny to buffy-rufous, feathers tipped buffy-white; lower belly and undertail-coverts white; thighs dark grey. ***Bare parts*** Bill legs and palate black; eye orange to red, sometimes with a yellow inner ring. **ADULT ♀** Like ♂ but has a narrow white eyebrow extending back behind eye to nape; crown lighter than ♂; mantle, back and scapulars olive grey. ***Wings*** Pale reddish-brown wing-stripe and outer edge of primaries. ***Underparts*** Chin, throat, breast and flanks pale buffy-rufous; belly buffy dull white. **JUVENILE** Fledgling has upperparts spotted buff and brown; eye grey-brown; underparts with slight pale rufous tinge. **IMMATURE** Like adult ♀, but eyebrow buffy, face-mask buffy-brown, and broad rufous-buff edging and tips to wing-coverts and flight feathers; legs dusky flesh-coloured. Eye brown[32, 205].

GEOGRAPHICAL VARIATION Two races, variation slight and concerned mainly with colour of upperparts. Nominate *fratrum* (S Malawi, E

Zimbabwe, South Africa) is darker and less rufous above than *sheppardi* (Mozambique) and ♂♂ are smaller in wing and tail than nominate. This race is not recognised by some authors[603, 641].

MOULT Unknown.

RANGE, HABITAT and STATUS Breeding range S coastal and central Mozambique lowlands, S Malawi, E Zimbabwe and coastal E South Africa. **Habitat** Generally a lowland coastal forest species, ascending to *c.*900 m in S Malawi. Found in low and mid levels of lowland forests, evergreen thickets in deciduous dry forest, riverine forest, thick low bushes in dune forests, forest-savanna woodland mosaic and dense stands of *Acacia*. Wanders into adjacent woodlands in austral winter[26, 30, 80, 205, 322, 639, 676, 955]. **Status** Resident, locally not uncommon. **Conservation status** In South Africa, historical distribution extended further S. This combined with the threat of coastal dune mining in this area and the loss of habitat in S Mozambique poses a serious threat. A South African Red Data Book species listed as Indeterminate, which now requires urgent conservation of remaining dune forest[26, 32, 144, 639, 867, 868].

MOVEMENTS Only small-scale local movements into adjacent woodland habitats in non-breeding season[205].

SOCIAL ORGANISATION and GENERAL BEHAVIOUR Solitary, in pairs or family groups, also noisy social 'parliaments' of up to *c.*12 birds of both sexes. Shy, restless and constantly on the move, but rather less tame, active and vocal than savanna woodland batises. Tends to have a more crouched posture than other batises. ♂ advertises and defends a territory of *c.*0.5–1 ha (coastal forest) by uttering slowly repeated plaintive *hui—hui–* whistles. Adopts an inclined, crouched posture, with the neck stretched to the extent that the feathers in this region part and form a stiff ruff, resulting in a strange treefrog-like appearance. Tail is fanned slightly at the same time. During ♂ counter-singing, each gives whistles of slightly different pitch, producing a seesaw effect. ♀ joins in irregularly in duet with an abrupt, harsh *Krjjer* call. Contact appears to be maintained by visual signals (wing, tail and body movements), and calls. Readily mobs predators. Roosting behaviour unknown. Scratches indirectly[205, 506]. **Foraging behaviour** Arboreal, at all levels from 1–18 m; hover-gleaner, feeding from a few centimetres above the ground to lower canopy. Makes short sallies to snap up insects from leaves, twigs and branches, often hovering momentarily before seizing prey with audible bill-snap. Movements are accompanied by a flick of the tail, possibly facilitating the flushing of prey. Hops through the vegetation. Joins mixed foraging parties, particularly in non-breeding season[32, 80, 205, 448]. **Food** Insects.

SOUNDS Repertoire consists of repeated whistles, churring sounds and bill-snapping. Territorial call of ♂ a rather monotonous series of short plaintive *hui--hui--hui--*or *poo-poo-poo-* or *whhhh-* whistles, repeated up to *c.*10 times at a rate of a note per *c.*1–2.5 sec, delivered at the same pitch. Tone varies from mournful and 'spooky', slowly repeated *huu–huu–* notes to faster, higher-pitched *huet-huet-huet-* notes, often with a slight quavering quality. Quality similar to call of Grey-headed Bush-shrike *Malaconotus blanchoti*, but much shorter. Sometimes notes have a slight echo at the end *whhhh-wh* or *hui*. ♀ responds in duet, often rather erratically, with an abrupt harsh *Krjjer* call, to which ♂ responds immediately with *hui-* whistle. ♀ calls appear randomly spread throughout the sequence. When excited during high-intensity territorial interactions, they give rapidly delivered *chik, chuk* and nasal mechanical-sounding drawn-out *jnananaee* or higher-pitched *jneeeu* notes, which may also be accompanied by 'wing-fripping'. Also gives chuntering calls (sounds like two stones being rubbed together). Alarm signalled by rapid bill-snapping and harsh repeated *ChikChik-* or rasping, jerking *prer-rer-rert* notes. Contact maintained by soft *chik* or *chuk* calls and probably 'wing-fripping' sounds[5, 48, 205, 676]. Sonagram[48].

BREEDING BIOLOGY Little known. Monogamous and territorial. Recorded densities include 7 pairs/2–3 ha, 1 pair/0.5–1 ha (KwaZulu-Natal, South Africa) or 10 pairs/10 ha (Malawi)[80, 205, 448, 512]. **Season** Oct–Dec (SE South Africa)[48], Nov (Mozambique)[26, 833], Nov (Zimbabwe)[30]. **Displays** ***Courtship*** Similar to high-intensity territorial interactions, which involve much zigzag display-flying, 'wing-fripping', *chik* and *chuk* calling and a nasal mechanical-sounding *jnananaee* calls, becoming higher-pitched *jneeeu* at the height of the display. White-spotted rump feathers are suddenly fluffed-out and the wings dropped on landing[205]. **Nest** Role of sexes unknown. Structure less tidy than in other forest batis nests, more loosely built, of dry grass, bark and moss, bound with spider web and sometimes decorated with lichen. Usually well hidden in a fork or on a horizontal branch of a tree or bush at *c.*2 m (0.8–3, n=5) above the ground. One nest appeared to have been placed on top of that of another species. ***Size*** ID 45 mm, cup depth 13 mm[205, 500, 649, 833]. **Eggs** Usually 2–3 (1–3). Creamy-white or bluish-white, spotted and blotched with red, brown and grey, mainly around the broad end. ***Size*** 16.3–19.3 x 12.4–14.1 mm (18.1 x 13.1, n=8)[19, 48]. For additional information see[649]. No further breeding information, except ♀ known to incubate and brood, and fledglings attended by both sexes[205].

MEASUREMENTS and WEIGHTS Races combined ♂ (17) wing 58.5–64 (61.2), tail 33–38 (34.8), bill 15.5–17.5 (16.5), ♂♀? (8) tarsus 17.5–19; ♀ (19) 57.5–62.5 (60.0), tail 32–35 (33.2), bill 15–16 (15.4), tarsus (see ♂)[676]. **Weight** ♂ (43) 10.4–13.8 g (12.2); ♀ (23) 10.3–13.6 g (11.7) (southern Africa)[205]. For additional data see[48, 88, 287, 603].

FIELD IDENTIFICATION Very small (11–12 cm), restless, grey, black and white flycatcher-like bird with black face-mask, yellow eye, white eyebrow and white wing-stripe. Sexes different. Below white, ♂ with black breast-band and greyish flanks, ♀ with throat and breast orange-buff. Young like ♀ but dull and spotted above. Flight bouncy. Main call a very long series of plaintive whistles on descending scale. In pairs or family group foraging at all levels in dry thornbush savanna or trees and scrubs associated with dry watercourses. Resident from SW Angola, Namibia, W Botswana and W and SW South Africa. ***Flight characteristics***: Rapid and bouncy; wings rounded. Has pied appearance and makes 'fripping' sounds with wings.

COMPARISONS ♂ Pririt and Chinspot Batis *Batis molitor* extremely difficult to separate in field, ♂ Pririt tending to have a paler crown and dark marks on flanks (Chinspot darker crown and flanks unmarked). Best identified on distinctive ♀♀. ♀ throat and breast-band orange-buff (distinct chestnut-brown breast-band and throat patch in Chinspot). Song of ♂♂ different: Pririt has very long, up to *c*.50 slightly descending notes (Chinspot usually 2–3 descending notes, occasionally longer series); however, in overlap areas this species is known to deliver up to *c*.8 notes on same pitch, in an apparent display of interspecific song-matching. Also overlaps marginally with Cape Batis *Batis capensis* in S of range, where it occurs in dense evergreen vegetation (Pririt in arid bush)[700, 801].

DESCRIPTION **ADULT ♂** ***Head*** Forehead, crown and nape pale grey with long narrow white eyebrow; hindneck with white nape-patch. ***Back*** Grey, including mantle, scapulars and uppertail-coverts. ***Wings*** Primaries and secondaries black, narrowly edged white; tertials black, broadly edged white forming part of wing-stripe; greater and median primary coverts black, except two near middle which are broadly edged white; median coverts white and lesser coverts black. Underwing-coverts blackish. ***Tail*** Black, outer feather on each side edged and tipped white, rest except central pair tipped white. ***Underparts*** Chin to undertail-coverts white, except for broad (*c*.10–14 mm) glossy black breast-band; flanks with indistinct dark grey bars; thighs grey. ***Bare parts*** Bill, palate and legs black; eye pale yellow. **ADULT ♀** **Upperparts** Like ♂, but crown with olivaceous tinge and white eyebrow less distinct. ***Underparts*** Chin, throat, breast and lower sides of neck buffy-orange, shading to white on belly and greyish-white on flanks. ***Bare parts*** Like ♂. **JUVENILE** Dull, above spotted black-and-buff on head, face-mask brownish-black. Wing-coverts tipped buff. Underparts dull white mottled black and buffy-ochre on breast (in both sexes). Eye probably brown[48, 137]. **IMMATURE** Like adult ♀, but breast progressively loses buffy-orange in ♂ and develops black breast-band. In ♀ black mottling is lost on breast; crown mottled with white, and eye pale yellow[137, 676].

GEOGRAPHICAL VARIATION Two races, variation mainly in body size, darkness of upperparts and extent of white in secondaries. Nominate *pririt* (South Africa) smaller and darker above; *affinis* (Angola, Namibia, W Botswana and NW South Africa) larger and paler above, black face-mask not forming a complete collar, and secondaries are broadly edged white. The isolated population in S of range warrants taxonomic investigation[81, 639].

MOULT Unknown.

RANGE, HABITAT and STATUS **Breeding range** SW Africa from coastal lowland plain in SW Angola, Namibia, except NE and coastal desert, Botswana, except N and E, and NW and SW South Africa. Recorded once in W Lesotho. In S there is a marked break in distribution resulting in an isolated population. It shares a common boundary in the N and E with Chinspot Batis, suggesting mutual competitive exclusion. **Habitat** Savanna grasslands with scattered *Acacia* and *Commiphora* trees, dry open woodland, scrub and riverine bush, especially dense stands of wild tamarisk *Tamarix usneoides* associated with dry watercourses in desert and mesquite *Prosopis*[7, 48, 241, 320, 578, 639, 676, 807, 907]. **Status** Common to locally common resident. **Conservation** Not threatened and probably benefits from bush encroachment in response to overgrazing.

MOVEMENTS In southern Africa undergoes local movements with some evidence of a N–S movement in SW of range, and easterly movement in W part of range[205, 639].

SOCIAL ORGANISATION and GENERAL BEHAVIOUR Solitary, in pairs or family party. Restless and constantly on the move, flicking tail at each move. In austral winter may occur in 'parliaments' of up to 12 birds, often of single-sex gatherings. During these, the birds fly about excitedly making chattering *chikchik-chik* calls, 'fripping' wings and snapping bills. ♂ defends large territory in austral summer, although vocal throughout the year. Territorial call a long series of short whistle notes on a descending scale, usually accompanied in duet with *Wik* calls by ♀. ♂ calls from a prominent perch, sits with body crouched in an inclined position, bill raised, white throat extended and tail fanned. Territorial threat signalled with higher-pitched whistles, and croaking calls usually given during a bouncy or jinking flight display above treetops, accompanied by loud 'wing-fripping' and rump-fluffing. ♀ duets erratically with loud *Wik* calls and excited *ckikchikchikchik*- calls, bill-snaps and 'wing-fripping'. Readily mobs Pearl-spotted Owl *Glaucidium pearlatum*, which probably preys on this batis. Body temperatures range from 40.3–42°C for ambient temperatures of 17–30°C respectively. Roosting behaviour unknown. Scratches indirectly[205, 580, 798]. **Foraging behaviour**

Arboreal, similar to Chinspot Batis; searches for food mainly within canopy in lower and mid levels of bushes and trees, searching the surrounding and overhead vegetation. Also forages in tops of large *Acacia* trees. In S of range, generally in scrubbier growth than other savanna woodland batises. Feeds by hover-gleaning (flights 1–2 m) off branches and leaves, often with audible bill-snap. Hawks insects in short flights. Tail-flicks constantly, possibly acting as a prey-flushing mechanism or a visual contact signal. In 75 feeds, hawked 33%, hawk-gleaned 60%, and gleaned 7%. Hovers before seizing prey more than Chinspot Batis. Holds large prey down with foot in manner of true shrikes. Hops on branch and readily joins mixed foraging parties[48, 676, 797]. **Food** Insects, including large Lepidoptera (moths)[797].

SOUNDS Repertoire consists of whistles, harsh calls and bill-snapping. Territorial song of ♂ a loud series (up to *c.*50 notes) of short repeated whistles on a descending scale. Begins with high-pitched *he-he-he-* and descends evenly and slowly through *ho-ho-ho-* to slower and more mournful *hu-hu-* notes, ending with a more rolling quality *trrop–trrop*. Repetition rates vary from *c.*1–1.5 notes/sec. Much seasonal, individual and contextual variation in the number and tone of notes. ♀ duets with up to 10 strident *Wik* or *chip* calls during ♂ song. During territorial threat uses higher-pitched whistles, *preet-preet-preet-* whistles and deeper croaking *gruu-gruu-* calls accompanied by loud 'wing-fripping'. ♀ accompanies with loud *Wik* calls and excited chattering *chikchikchikchik-* calls, bill-snapping and 'wing-fripping'. During courtship gives slower, rolling *trrop–trrop-* calls in addition to calls similar to territorial threat. Calls of ♀ thought to be different to those of Chinspot. Alarm signalled by bill-snapping, chattering *chikchik-* or sharp *chuk* notes. ♀ begs with a chattering *KisshKisshKissh-* sound. Contact maintained between pairs with quiet *chik-chik-*, *chuk*, *chek* or *tsip*[48, 205, 676, 700, 872]. Sonagram[48].

BREEDING BIOLOGY Monogamous and territorial. Breeding has been recorded for 9 months of the year over entire range, and appears to be mainly in response to rain, although breeding also recorded in its absence. Known to have bred within 20 m of Cape Batis *Batis capensis* and overlaps widely with Chinspot Batis, but with no hybridisation reported. Appears to be single-brooded[137, 205, 241, 801]. **Season** Sep–Mar, mainly Oct–Feb (Namibia); Aug–Dec (Botswana)[676, 807]; Jul–Mar, mainly Oct–Dec, fledglings late Jan (South Africa)[48, 320, 676]. **Displays *Courtship*** Little known, but thought to be similar to other savanna batises in which they use many of the calls and displays used in high-intensity territorial threat. ♂ courtship-feeds ♀, who assumes a submissive, crouched posture with wings fluttering. **Nest** Built by both sexes but mostly by ♀. Small neat cup built of fine grass, rootlets and plant fibres, neatly bound with spider web and cocoon threads. Usually decorated with bark chips, dead leaves and occasionally lichen (2 out of 24 nests). Lining normally consists of fine roots and sometimes animal hair. Placed at *c.*2 m (0.7–8, n=60) above ground, usually on a slender horizontal branch, often in *Acacia* tree or tamarisk bush, and often built against a small vertical stick, usually in shade but may be exposed. ***Size*** OD 60 mm, ID 40 mm, height 30 mm[137, 205]. **Eggs** Usually 2 (1–4, n=35). Colour varies from white or cream to greenish-white, spotted and blotched with shades of brown and grey. ***Size*** 15.7–18.1 x 12.0–13.3 mm (16.5 x 12.7, n=24)[19, 48, 205]. **Incubation** By ♀ only. She solicits with loud *KisshKissh-* begging calls. Period *c.*17 days (n=1)[48, 205]. **Nestling** Hatch blind and naked; probably lack mouth spots. By 14 days completely feathered with mottled plumage similar to other batis nestlings. Attended by both sexes. At one nest fully exposed to the sun, ♀ shaded young by crouching over them with head and body feathers ruffled and wingtips constantly quivering, this interpreted as fanning. Fledge after 17 days (n=1). Brood division recorded in 5 out of 7 observations, a fledgling was noted to follow an adult of the opposite sex. Independent after *c.*6 weeks, during which they attain adult plumage characteristics[61, 137, 205, 800]. For plumage development see[137]. **Predation and longevity** Little known; one young bird impaled by a thorn through the wing[137, 205]. **Brood parasite** Klaas's Cuckoo *Chrysococcyx klaas*, 7% of 76 Namibian clutches affected. In one locality, inland of Walvis Bay, 8% of 48 clutches affected. Known to mob this cuckoo[94, 137, 676].

MEASUREMENTS and WEIGHTS Races combined ♂ (23) wing 55–58 (56.4); ♂ (10) tail 44–48; ♂ (10) bill 14–15; ♂♀? (45) tarsus 16–19; ♀ (22) wing 52–57.5 (55.0); ♀ (8) tail 42–45; ♀ (8) bill 13–14[48]. **Weight** Races combined ♂ (12) 8–10 g (9.0), ♀ (21) 8–14 g (9.7)[48]. For additional data see[88, 205, 286, 478, 676].

87 CHINSPOT BATIS *Batis molitor* — Plate 32

FIELD IDENTIFICATION Very small (12–13 cm), dumpy, restless, grey, black and white flycatcher-like bird with black face-mask, yellow eye, short white eyebrow and white wing-stripe. Sexes different. Below white with broad breast-band, ♂ black, ♀ chestnut-brown with chestnut-brown spot on throat. Young like ♀ but spotted above, breast-band, wing-stripe and eyebrow tawny. Main call 2–3 short whistles on descending scale, or *c.*8 notes at same or slightly descending pitch. In pairs or family group in wide variety of savanna woodlands, as well as in open montane forest of high mountains in Central Africa. Widespread resident from East Africa to South Africa, westward to Angola and Namibia. ***Flight characteristics***: Rapid and bouncy; wings rounded. Has pied appearance and makes 'fripping' sounds with wings.

COMPARISONS ♂ similar to at least 5 other ♂ batises, ♀ more distinctive. (1) Pririt Batis *Batis pririt*: Chinspot has white flanks (Pririt speckled grey, ♀♀ distinctive); main Chinspot call a short *c.*3-note descending series or longer *c.*8-note series at a constant or slightly descending pitch (Pririt has very long series, up to 50 medium-pitched, slightly descending, slowly repeated notes), but note the occurrence of interspecific song-matching in overlap zones. (2) Mozambique Batis *B. soror*: Chinspot breast-band broad, back plain and eyebrow short (Mozambique breast-band narrow, back dappled white and eyebrow long, ♀ with a narrower, paler breast-band and less distinct chinspot); Mozambique has long series of up to *c.*12 rolling notes at the same or slightly descending pitch, and occurs in moister broadleaved and miombo *Brachystegia* woodlands. (3) Black-headed Batis *B. minor*: Chinspot has a grey crown, short eyebrow and broad breast-band (Black-headed has darker crown, long distinct white eyebrow and narrower breast-band; ♀ lacks chinspot and has a narrower maroon-coloured breast-band); Black-headed has similar calls which tend to be more drawn-out, less sharp, and series also tend to be longer and include an ascending as well as a descending 3-note phrase. (4) Grey-headed Batis *B. orientalis*: Chinspot has a short eyebrow (Grey-headed long; ♀ lacks chinspot); main call rather similar to long Chinspot series, but short descending series longer. (5) Pygmy Batis *B. perkeo*: Chinspot, larger, paler above with a longer eyebrow (♀ Pygmy lacks chinspot and has paler buffy-rufous breast-band, face and wing-stripe tinged buff); has a long series of high-pitched whistles, rather cisticola-like. Chinspot also similar to some forest batises like ♂ Margaret's Batis *B. margaritae*, which is a less active, dumpier bird with a broader breast-band (both ♂ and ♀ have black breast-band) that lacks the slight nick (narrowing) in centre found in Chinspot; it also lacks a distinctive eyebrow (Chinspot has a short white eyebrow). ♀ more distinctive with rufous wing-stripe (white in Chinspot). Margaret's has a long series of whistles delivered at the same pitch. ♂ Chinspot also superficially similar to Ruwenzori Batis *B. diops*, which is dark grey above with a white spot in front of eye (Chinspot grey above with short white eyebrow). ♀ Ruwenzori like ♂ but with reddish eye. Where Chinspot occurs with either of these forest species it generally forages above them. Its whistled calls are also reminiscent of Brown-throated Wattle-eye *Platysteira cyanea*[635, 700, 717].

DESCRIPTION **ADULT ♂** ***Head*** Forehead, crown and nape blue-grey; short white eyebrow, wide at front, narrow over eye (absent in one race); small white nape-patch. Face-mask glossy black. ***Back*** Mantle, scapulars and back blue-grey; rump and uppertail-coverts grey, rump feathers long and fluffy. ***Wings*** Black with white stripe formed by broad white ends to median and inner greater coverts and broad white edges to inner secondaries. Underwing-coverts blackish. ***Tail*** Black, outer feathers edged and tipped white. ***Underparts*** Chin to undertail-coverts white, except broad glossy black breast-band (*c.*10–14 mm); flanks white; thighs dark grey. ***Bare parts*** Bill, palate and legs black; eye bright lemon-yellow. **ADULT ♀** Like ♂, eyebrow sometimes longer and underparts with triangular patch on chin and breast-band chestnut-brown, slightly narrower than ♂. **JUVENILE** Superficially like adult ♀ but duller and mottled greyish-brown, particularly on forehead, crown, nape, mantle and back, feathers tipped buff. Face-mask less distinct and eyebrow and sides of neck tinged buff. Wing-stripe white to buffy-white, wing-coverts tipped buff. Underparts whitish with indistinct mottled brown-and-grey breast-band and throat-patch. Eye brown. This plumage retained for *c.*2 months[205]. **IMMATURE** More like adult ♀ but with progressive development of adult plumage. Upperparts grey with slight mottling. Face-mask black, eye pale yellow. ♂ may have breast-band tawny with a few black feathers and indistinct chinspot. Determination of First-year birds by clear contrast between the jet-black (or brighter blue-grey) new greater upper-wing-coverts and the paler, rather browner (or slatier) old outer coverts[656].

GEOGRAPHICAL VARIATION At least 5 races, variation mainly in colour of upperparts and breast-band, and extent of white in wings. Compared to nominate *molitor* (SE South Africa, S Mozambique), *palliditergum* (S Angola, S Zambia, Zimbabwe, Botswana, N Namibia, NW South Africa) has crown and mantle paler and tail slightly shorter; *pintoi* (N and central Angola, NW Zambia) intermediate in upperpart coloration between former two races, also has crown tinged glossy blue-black and breast tinged glossy green-black, not blue-black; *puella* (Angola, Zaïre, East Africa) has mantle more glossy blue-black, white on edge of primaries and secondaries narrower, sometimes lacking in ♂♂; breast-band and chinspot in ♀ a darker maroon-chestnut; tail slightly shorter than nominate[676].

MOULT In southern Africa post-breeding moult of flight feathers in autumn (Jul–Oct)[88, 205].

RANGE, HABITAT and STATUS **Breeding range** Widespread, from Uganda, W and S Kenya, Rwanda (requires confirmation), Burundi, Tanzania (except coastal and SE), SE Gabon and Congo, E and SE Zaïre, Angola (except coastal) and Cabinda, N Namibia, Zambia, Malawi, Zimbabwe, S and W Mozambique, N and E Botswana, NE and E South Africa (absent W of 24°E). Apparently a rare vagrant to N Lesotho. SE Sudan records require confirmation. **Habitat** savanna woodlands in a wide variety of deciduous woodlands including *Brachystegia*, riverine thickets, bushveld and edges of forest, open scattered scrub, orchard bush, gardens, farmland and some plantations. Ascends mountains to *c.*3000 m in Central Africa, where in open types of montane forest. Tends to be more habitat-specific in northern range where it overlaps with other batises[48, 242, 295, 320, 431, 504, 578, 631, 676, 717, 807, 873, 907, 945]. **Status** Resident, generally common, but uncommon in Central Africa (Zaïre) and rare in Lesotho[676]. **Conservation status** Not threatened.

MOVEMENTS Local seasonal movements possible at N limit of range (Kenya), as well as possible altitudinal migration during non-breeding season in East Africa[318, 578].

SOCIAL ORGANISATION and GENERAL BEHAVIOUR Solitary, in pairs or family group. Restless and very active, moving head constantly to search for prey, twisting and jerking body and flicking tail at each move, and cocking head at all angles. In austral winter and early spring groups of up to 10 birds congregate to form noisy 'parliaments', often consisting of single-sex gatherings with much flying about, 'wing-fripping' and excited *chiKchiKchiK-* calling. These displays sometimes include physical fights. Territorial throughout year; advertises and defends an area of *c.*5 ha with repeated loud 2–3 note descending whistle. ♀ may join in duet with *Wik* notes. Calls from prominent perch, head up exposing conspicuous white throat, tail fanned slightly. In high-intensity territorial aggression ♂ performs jerky, jinking flight display and short circular flights above tree tops with tail fanned, white spotted rump fluffed-out and head held up. This is combined with noisy 'wing-fripping', frog-like *grrruu-grrruu* sounds and rolling whistled *prrreeo-* calls. When perched head swayed slowly from side to side. ♀ joins in duet with *Wik* and excited *chiKchiKchiK-* calls. Alarm varies from low intensity strident, rapidly repeated *WikWikWik-* notes to high-intensity with rapid bill-snapping, crest raising and 'wing-fripping'. Aggressive towards predators, particularly owls and boubou shrikes *Laniarius*. Contact maintained with *wik* calls and probably visual signals (movements of body and wings, and tail-flicking). Prior to roosting a presumed family group flies about 'wing-fripping' with excited *chikchik-chik-* calling. Generally roosts low down in bush, sitting apart hunched up. Scratches indirectly[205, 793, 872]. **Foraging behaviour** Mainly arboreal, at all levels, 80% inside open tree canopy, 20% on outer edge in mid- to lower levels, where forages by hover-gleaning (60% hawk-gleaning), prey caught with an audible bill-snap, and general gleaning (13%). Tends to forage higher in Central African montane forest edge. Constant movement and tail-flicking may help flush prey. Also hawks (24%) insects in the air and occasionally descends to ground. Holds large prey down with one foot against branch for stripping; other large items beaten against branch. May hang upside-down like a tit. Frequently joins mixed foraging parties[5, 205, 352, 580, 717, 702]. **Food** Arthropods, mainly insects and their larvae, including Diptera (flies), Hymenoptera (wasps and ants), Coleoptera (beetles), Orthoptera (small grasshoppers) and Isoptera (termites). Small Lepidoptera (noctuid caterpillars and moths) and spiders fed to nestlings[8, 46, 205, 676].

SOUNDS Repertoire consists of repeated whistles, harsh notes and bill-snapping. Territorial song of two types: a commonly heard 2–3 note whistled phrase repeated a number of times, and a longer series (up to *c.*15 notes) of repetitive whistled notes at the same or slightly falling pitch. The short slowly repeated phrase, usually trisyllabic, has the first note higher pitched than the second, which may be the same or higher pitched than the third. This phrase is characterised by the mnemonic 'three blind mice' or transcribed as *he-ho-hu*, *weep-woop-wurp*, sometimes with a rolling quality *kreep-kroop-chowp*. Sometimes, particularly in non-nreeding season, the phrase consists of only the first, or first and second notes *hii-her*. ♀ joins in duet with strident *Wik* notes, the pair producing *he-ho-Wik-hu-Wik* sequence. In southern Africa, the second song type is less frequently heard. This series has also been recorded in the overlap zone between this species and Pririt Batis. Here ♂ gives up to 15 whistles (usually 7–10) in response to play-back, the notes matching Pririt Batis calls. In Rwanda and Kenya this series is apparently not as rare. Here known to give up to 8 monotonous whistles at a rate of 2/sec, preceded by a higher one (very like the song of Black-headed Batis). Other calls include frog-like *grrruu-grrruu* or *querk-querk-querk* sounds and rolling *prrreeo* or *kreew* whistles. Contact maintained with softer *chik*, *tik* or *wik* and *skizskiz-* notes, also recorded as *phut* or *phit* and believed to be different to those of Pririt Batis. Contact call during nest-building a quiet *tsit* or *tsittsit-*. Begging call a buzzing *ksshkisshkissh-* or *skizskizskiz-*. Alarm a strident chattering *WikWikWik-* or *ch-chk-* with bill-snapping and 'wing-fripping'. Young ♂ can give adult whistles at *c.*4 months[46, 48, 205, 631, 700, 717]. Sonagram[48].

BREEDING BIOLOGY Monogamous with a possible low incidence of cooperative breeding based on observations of an additional bird present in territory, probably offspring of earlier breeding. Third bird usually chased out eventually by breeding ♀. Records of twice normal clutch size probably involved more than one ♀, and are also suggestive of possible cooperative breeding. Mated pairs bond at least 3 years. Occurs in densities ranging from 5 pairs/100 ha to 1 pair/5 ha in *Acacia* and 1 pair/15 ha in broadleaved woodland. Nesting success 25%, breeding success 26% (Zimbabwe)[46, 52, 67, 205, 320, 566].

Season Ruwenzori Dec–Jan, Lubumbashi Sep–Oct (Zaïre)[676]; Sep–Nov, breeding condition Oct (Angola)[7, 423, 865, 907]; Jan–Jun and Oct–Feb, peak Oct–Jan and Apr–Jun (East Africa)[293]; Mar, Jun, fledglings in Jan (NW Tanzania)[239]; Oct–Nov (Malawi)[119]; Aug–Nov, peak Sep–Oct (Zambia)[119, 291]; Aug–Feb (South Africa); Aug–Feb, peak Sep–Nov (Zimbabwe)[30, 48, 320, 639]; Sep–Feb, mainly Dec (Botswana)[676, 807]; Mar–Apr, Nov (Mozambique)[26, 676].

Displays ***Courtship*** ♂ display is like high-intensity territorial defence, except that flight is lower down. It is characterised by frog-like *grrruu-grrruu* or *querk-querk-querk* sounds and rolling *prrreeo* or *kreew* whistles by ♂. These are combined in duet with ♀: *chik-prrreo* by ♂ and *weeeo-tik* by ♀, in addition to normal duetting. ♂ flicks tail up and down, bends forward and fluffs out rump feathers, flies in bouncing flight with 'wing-fripping' at each bounce, alights in front of ♀ in upright posture with wings quivering, gives croaking *grrruu*. With rump fluffed-out he flies around and in front of ♀ who responds with bill-snaps and clicks. Courtship-feeding present. ***Pre-copulation*** ♀ gives harsh begging calls in crouched position and flutters wings; copulation may follow accompanied by much wing-vibrating by both birds. Copulation may also occur after courtship-feeding[46, 205].

Nest Both members appear to choose site and build nest, but ♀ does most work, and may be solely responsible for adding lining. Material collected away from nest tree. Nest moulded on branch or in fork and well camouflaged. Cup built from bark and grass fibres bonded and plastered with web, decorated on outside with lichen, dried leaves or pieces of bark. Lined with fine material such as rootlets, leaf petioles or hair. Sides of neck and throat used to smooth web-covered edge of nest. Placed at *c*.3 m (0.45–12, n=263), in middle of horizontal branch or vertical fork, usually on lichen-covered branch. Some placed on down-hanging branch. ***Size*** OD 50–70 mm, ID 40–45 mm, cup depth 20–35 mm, height 25–45 mm. May take up to 2 weeks to complete and may remain empty for up to 10 days[5, 205, 676, 872]. For additional information see[46, 872].

Eggs Usually 2 (1–4, n=88), laid on consecutive days. Clutches of 4 thought to be due to two ♀♀ laying in same nest. Pale greenish or blue-green, spotted and blotched with blackish, brown and grey sometimes concentrated into a ring around the large end. ***Size*** 15.4–19 x 11.9–14.2 mm (17.3 x 13.0, n=92) (southern Africa)[19, 48, 52, 359]. **Incubation** By ♀ only; ♂ once recorded relieving. Very tight-brooded; ♀ can sometimes be touched. ♀ sits low in nest with only bill and tail above rim. She is fed on and off nest by ♂, who announces arrival with *chik-chik-* or whistles from a distance. ♀ usually begs loudly and flutters wings. She will also forage for herself. Period usually *c*.17 days (16–18, n=6)[46, 205]. **Nestling** Hatch naked, skin pink turning black, blind and without mouth spots. Opens brown eyes after 5 days. Fed by ♀ initially, who makes soft *whoit-whoit* calls; later fed by both sexes, mainly with caterpillars. Parents eat faecal sac or carry it away. Nestlings are well camouflaged, their mottled appearance resembling white-spotted lichen. Fledge after *c*.17 days (15–18, n=5). Eyes turn whitish at fledging. Dependency period *c*.8 weeks (6–14 weeks, n=6), but can remain with adults until start of next breeding season[27, 46, 205, 331, 506, 676]. For nestling development see[872]. **Predation and longevity** Monkeys and cold wet weather are known causes of nestling mortality. ♀ retrapped after almost 5 years[205]. **Brood parasite** Klaas's Cuckoo *Chrysococcyx klaas* in East and southern Africa. Known to chase this and Diederik Cuckoo *C. caprius*[94, 500].

MEASUREMENTS and WEIGHTS *B. m. molitor* ♂ (94) wing 55.5–66.5 (61.97), tail 41.0–51.5 (46.86), bill 14.50–18.0 (16.10); ♀ (68) wing 54.0–66.0 (60.84), tail 41.5–52.5 (46.71), bill 14.5–17.0 (15.57)[286]; ♂ (60) wing 57.5–65 (60.5); ♀ (64) 56–62.5 (59.2), ♂♀? (124) tail 42–52, ♂♀? (124) bill 11–14.5, ♂♀? (124) tarsus 16–20 (southern Africa)[48]. **Weight** ♂ (95) 8–14 g (11.2); ♀ (95) 8–14 g (12.1) (southern Africa)[48]. For additional data see[88, 205, 237, 286, 478, 676].

88 MOZAMBIQUE BATIS (East Coast Batis, Pale Batis)

Batis soror **Plate 32**

FIELD IDENTIFICATION Very small (10–11 cm), restless, black, grey and white flycatcher-like bird, pale grey above with black face-mask, yellow eye, white wing-stripe and white mottled back. Sexes different. Below white, ♂ with narrow black breast-band, ♀ with diffuse chinspot and pale narrow rufous breast-band. Young similar to ♀ but with rusty-buff breast-band and wing-stripe. Pied appearance in bouncing flight; makes 'fripping' sound with wings. Main ♂ call a long series of medium-pitched whistles, slowly repeated, usually at same or slightly descending pitch. Solitary or in pairs foraging in mid-canopy of lowland miombo woodland. Resident from SE Kenya to S Mozambique. ***Flight characteristics***: Undulating and bouncy; wings rounded. Has pied appearance in flight and makes 'fripping' sounds with wings.

COMPARISONS Overlaps marginally with similar larger Chinspot Batis *Batis molitor*. Mozambique Batis has a narrower, less clearly defined breast-band and chinspot, which in the ♀ is pale rufous (not chestnut-brown); ♂ has white dappling on the back and a more prominent white eyebrow. Mozambique Batis is ecologically segregated from Chinspot and generally occurs in moister low-lying broadleaved and miombo *Brachystegia* woodland. Mozambique has long series (up to *c*.12 notes) of slowly repeated short medium-pitched notes on same or slightly descending pitch (Chinspot has a shorter 'long' series and a short series of 2–3 descending notes). Note the occurrence of interspecific song-matching by Chinspot. Black-headed Batis *B. minor* also similar, but has dark crown and back, and longer eyebrow; ♀ lacks chinspot. Black-headed has similar series of whistles but higher-pitched. In northern range similar to Pygmy Batis *B. perkeo*, which has a short white eyebrow, darker grey upperparts, and in ♀ a buff tinge to face, chin and wing-stripe and no chinspot; calls high-pitched, cisticola-like. Grey-headed Batis *B. orientalis* occurs in coastal Somalia, slightly north of Mozambique Batis range. It has a paler grey crown and mantle and broad eyebrow with no chinspot; calls similar to Black-headed Batis but phrases shorter[700].

DESCRIPTION **ADULT ♂** ***Head*** Forehead whitish-grey; crown and nape blue-grey; glossy black face-mask with thin white eyebrow, extending almost to white nape-patch. ***Back*** Mantle, scapulars and back blue-grey, faintly dappled white; rump and uppertail-coverts grey, feathers of rump fluffy. ***Wings*** Black with white stripe formed by white tips to median and inner greater coverts and broad white outer edges to inner secondaries. Underwing-coverts blackish. ***Tail*** Black with outer feathers broadly edged and tipped white. ***Underparts*** Chin to undertail-coverts white, except for glossy black breast-band (*c.*7–10 mm wide, but variable); flanks white; thighs grey. ***Bare parts*** Bill, palate and legs black; eye bright lemon-yellow. **ADULT ♀** Like ♂ but with diffuse pale rufous spot on chin and upper throat, and breast-band pale rufous, slightly narrower in the centre than in ♂[88]. **JUVENILE** Unknown. **IMMATURE** Like adult ♀ but breast-band tawnier, white areas of face, throat and wing tawny to rusty-buff[88].

GEOGRAPHICAL VARIATION Monotypic, with slight variation[76, 88, 796].

MOULT Unknown.

RANGE, HABITAT and STATUS **Breeding range** SE Africa from S Kenya to S Mozambique, including SE Tanzania, Malawi and E Zimbabwe. The Limpopo River valley appears to form the S boundary. **Habitat** Typically in lowland miombo *Brachystegia* woodland, most common below 500 m in coastal, undisturbed woodland which forms mosaics with thickets and forest. Also in *Acacia* and mopane on edge of range. Also up to 1500 m in E Zimbabwe in tall stands of *Uapaca kirkiana, Philippia* thickets and mountain acacia *Brachystegia glaucescens* woodland[286, 431, 639, 676, 795, 873]. **Status** Resident, generally common, but in Malawi only locally common. **Conservation status** Unknown, probably not threatened.

MOVEMENTS Local seasonal movements, probably altitudinal in E Zimbabwe[639].

SOCIAL ORGANISATION and GENERAL BEHAVIOUR Little known. Appears similar to Chinspot Batis (see that species General Behaviour p.306). Solitary, in pairs or family group. Prior to breeding sometimes occurs in mainly single-sex gatherings or 'parliaments' flying about excitedly 'wing fripping', bill-snapping and giving *wik* calls. Territorial behaviour consists of repeated series of whistle notes, tempo varying according to intensity of interaction. ♀ joins in duet with a strident *Wik-* notes. During calling ♂ holds head up, white throat expanded and tail slightly fanned. Territorial threat signalled by frog-like *GruuK-GruuK* calls, uttered in a jinking flight with 'wing-fripping'. Home range covers at least *c.*3 ha; apparently only a small area around nest site is defended. Threat and alarm signalled by bill-snapping, excited *Wik-* calls and 'wing-fripping'. Contact maintained with soft *wik* notes, 'wing-fripping' sounds and possibly flicking of white outer tail feathers. Roosts low down in dense bush. Scratches indirectly[205]. **Foraging behaviour** Similar to Chinspot Batis; arboreal hover-gleaner, feeding at all levels, most often in mid-canopy of small-leaved trees. Prey caught with audible bill-snap. Flights between trees generally only 5–15 m. In non-breeding season often joins mixed foraging parties[26, 205, 580, 639, 676]. **Food** insects and their larvae.

SOUNDS Repertoire consists of repeated whistles, harsh calls and bill-snapping. Territorial call of ♂ a long series (up to *c.*12 notes) of short, high-pitched whistles at the same pitch *hu-hu-hu-hu-hu-, tlop-tlop-tlop-tlop, choi-choi-choi-* or *pl'k-pl'k-*, also described as soft metallic piping *yeenk-yeenk-yeenk-*, or an almost creaking *trree-trre*, and likened by some to a squeaky bicycle pump. The series may begin with first note slightly higher-pitched and may also descend the scale slightly. Delivery rates vary from *c.*6–9 notes/5 sec. ♀ joins in duet with strident *Wik-, whit, wit-wit* or *pik-pik-* notes. Long whistled series similar to Black-headed Batis and long series given by Chinspot Batis in overlap zones with other savanna batises. In courtship ♂ gives strident *WeeeK-WeeeK-WeeeK-* and *Klop-Klop-* notes, muted *prrrup-prrrup-* and slow deliberate croaking *Grrruk-GrrruK-* combined with 'wing-fripping'. ♀ duets repeatedly with excited *Wik-Wik-* calls. Alarm or threat signalled by bill-snapping, excited *wikwikwik-*, harsh jarring notes and 'wing-fripping'. Contact maintained with soft *wik* notes. ♀ begs with chattering *KisshKissh-, chi-chiur, cheer-chir-chir* sounds[48, 78, 205, 299, 631, 676, 700, 717]. Sonagram[48].

BREEDING BIOLOGY Little known. Monogamous with possible incidence of cooperative breeding based on observation of an additional ♀ in breeding territory, probably representing an immature from previous season[78, 205]. **Season** Nov (Mozambique)[26]; Oct–Nov (Zimbabwe)[30]; Jan, May (East Africa)[293]; Sep–Oct (Malawi)[119]. **Displays** ***Courtship*** ♂ does rapid zigzag display-flight, accompanied by 'wing-fripping', tail-fanning and fluffing out of white-spotted rump feathers. During display gives strident *WeeeK-WeeeK-WeeeK-* calls. Other calls made in this context include *Klop-Klop-* notes, muted *prrrup-prrrup-* and slow deliberate croaking *grrruk-grrruk-* in flight. ♀ joins in duet with excited *Wik-Wik-* calls repeatedly. On landing ♂ turns from side to side, flicking tail and giving rapid *hu-hu-hu-* whistles. Two ♀♀ appeared to be competing for a ♂ by making short 'fripping' flights. ♀ solicits from ♂ with *KisshKissh-* chattering, also described as *cheer-chir-chir* and *chi-chiur*, associated with wing quivering[78, 205, 299]. **Nest** Role of sexes unknown. Neat cup made of plant fibres and bark, bound with spider web and decorated on outside with bits of lichen. Placed in fork at *c.*8 m (4–15, n=4) above ground, higher than most savanna batises, in upper canopy of solitary trees in woodland and edge of forest. One completed nest was first used only the following season. ***Size*** Unknown[205, 299]. **Eggs** Usually 2 (2–3, n=3), two nests with 2 eggs each, one (East Africa) with 3 eggs. Colour and pattern typical batis[78, 205]. ***Size*** 18.3–19.1 x 13.8–13.9 mm (n=2) (E Zimbabwe), requires confirmation[26]. **Incubation and nestling** Only ♀ incubates; ♂ observed escorting ♀ back to nest. Periods unknown. Initially nestlings fed only by ♀, later by both sexes. ♀ gives bill-snapping and chattering *chi-chiur* notes in vicinity of nest[78, 299]. No further breeding information.

MEASUREMENTS and WEIGHTS *B. soror* Cline of increasing wing and tail lengths from N to S[88]. ♂ (64) wing 52.0–59.5 (56.20), tail 34.5–42.5 (38.77), bill 14.0–16.5 (15.27), tarsus ♂♀? (?) 17.5–19; ♀ (27) wing 51.0–58.0 (54.94), tail 34.0–42.0 (38.36), bill 14.0–16.0 (14.87), tarsus see ♂[48, 578]. **Weight** ♂ (36) 8.8–11.0 g (9.6); ♀ (38) 8.0–13.1 g (9.5) (Zimbabwe, Mozambique)[205]. For additional data see[48, 88, 299].

89 SENEGAL BATIS (Senegal Puff-back Flycatcher)
Batis senegalensis **Plate 32**

FIELD IDENTIFICATION Very small (10–12 cm), dumpy, restless, black and white flycatcher-like bird with greyish head, white eyebrow above black face-mask with yellow eye. Back darker grey, wings black with white stripe. Sexes different. Below white, ♂ with broad black breast-band, white eyebrow and wing-stripe, ♀ with orange-buff breast-band (narrow in centre, broad on sides), rusty-buff chin, eyebrow and wing-stripe. Young similar to ♀ but browner. Main call a series of medium-pitched double and treble-note whistles on same pitch, often with buzzy introductory notes. Solitary, in pairs or family group. Resident in lowland dry thorn savanna in West Africa from Mauritania to Cameroon. ***Flight characteristics***: Darts about with rapid wingbeats, seldom flying far. Flight dipping, sometimes with 'fripping' sounds from wings. Wings rounded; has a pied appearance in flight[455, 696].

COMPARISONS In E range similar to Grey-headed Batis *Batis orientalis* and ♂♂ difficult to separate: Grey-headed has pale grey crown (darker grey in Senegal Batis). ♀♀ more easily separated, Grey-headed has deeper chestnut-brown breast-band and white eyebrow and wing-stripe (Senegal has pale chestnut-brown [orange-buff] breast-band, eyebrow and wing-stripe). Also in E range similar to Black-headed Batis *B. minor*, which has a narrower white eyebrow and apparently less white in wing. ♀♀ more easily separated, and distinguished as for ♀ Grey-headed Batis. Calls of Senegal Batis distinctly disyllabic (long series and short phrase) compared to the high-pitched (squeaky pump) whistles of Black-headed and Grey-headed Batises.

DESCRIPTION **Adult ♂** ***Head*** Forehead and crown blackish slate-grey; very long broad white eyebrow, reaching almost to white nape-patch; face-mask glossy blue-black. ***Back*** Mantle, upper back and scapulars slate-grey with brownish tinge; lower back and rump mottled grey, white and black, feathers fluffy; uppertail-coverts glossy blue-black. ***Wings*** Black to brownish-black with white wing-stripe formed by white tips to median coverts and broad white outer edges to inner secondary coverts, and broad white edges to tertials. Primaries and secondaries brownish-black. Underwing-coverts black. ***Tail*** Black, outer 2 feathers on each side edged and tipped white. ***Underparts*** Chin to undertail-coverts white, broad breast-band (*c.*7–11 mm) glossy blue-black; flanks whitish-grey; thighs black, faintly barred white. ***Bare parts*** Bill black; palate unknown; legs black; eye golden-yellow. **Adult ♀** ***Head*** Forehead and crown sooty grey-brown with broad tawny to rufous-buff eyebrow extending back to join buff nape-patch; face-mask black. ***Back*** Mantle and upper back greyish tinged brown and mottled white. Lower back, rump and uppertail-coverts like ♂. **Wing** Slightly browner than ♂ and wing-stripe cream to tawny. ***Tail*** Like ♂. ***Underparts*** Chin, throat and lower sides of neck white, chin and upper throat with pale orange-buff tinge, rest of underparts including tail-coverts white, except pale chestnut-brown to orange-buff breast-band, which is twice as wide on sides as centre. ***Bare parts*** Like ♂. **Juvenile** Like ♀ but duller, head and wing-coverts with pale rusty-buff tips, white parts of head and wings tawny to rufous-buff; underparts white mottled grey-brown on breast, eye probably brown[500, 676]. **Immature** Like adult ♀ but browner, wing-coverts tipped rusty-buff; white in outer tail feathers tinged buff[676].

GEOGRAPHICAL VARIATION None. Monotypic.

MOULT Unknown.

RANGE, HABITAT and STATUS **Breeding range** W Africa from Mauritania, Senegal, Gambia, Mali, Niger, Guinea, Sierra Leone, Ivory Coast, Ghana, Togo, Benin and Nigeria, Burkina Faso, Niger and Cameroon. Vagrant to Liberia. **Habitat** Inhabits lowland dry thornscrub, grasslands with sparse trees and bushes and woody savannas, including open *Acacia* and baobab woodland[21, 23, 37, 38, 234, 455, 482, 286, 431, 287, 504, 578, 676, 848, 858]. **Status** Resident, generally common and widespread but uncommon in Niger. **Conservation status** Unknown, thought to be decreasing in Gambia due to loss of habitat[676].

MOVEMENTS Unknown.

SOCIAL ORGANISATION and GENERAL BEHAVIOUR Solitary, in pairs or family group. Restless and continually on the move. Territorial all year, advertising and defending an area of *c*.4–16 ha depending on habitat. ♂ patrols entire territory daily, giving advertising songs and sitting on high exposed perches. Territorial threat includes song while perched, or more often in bouncing flight with bill up, crown ruffled, rump feathers fluffed-out, tail half-spread and 'wing-fripping'. Aggressive behaviour includes upright posture with bill up, breast and crown plumage fluffed-out and carpals exposed; bird swings rear end, makes slow, jerky, sweeping movements of tail up and down, and from side to side, the tail half-spread and opened and closed erratically. In high-intensity threat, crouches with ruffled crown, exposed wrists, slightly hunched back, half-spread tail, and bill pointing at opponent. ♀ may approach calling and making 'fripping' sounds with wings. Pairs thought to maintain contact through calls and visual signals (body and wing movements and tail-flicking). Anxious bird quivers tail and, when alarmed, swings body jerkily from side to side, with tail swinging. Aggressively mobs shrikes, particularly Brubru *Nilaus afer* with bill-snapping and 'fripping' wings; also mobs hornbills, cuckoos and Pearl-spotted Owl *Glaucidium perlatum*. When facing the owl, crouches, raises foreparts, inclines bill and flicks tail jerkily up and down. Aggressively mobs tree-snakes, hovering and making rattling calls and bill-snapping. Roosts low down in isolated bush or small tree, usually near end of thin leafy branch, fluffs out plumage, resulting in a speckled appearance[676]. **Foraging behaviour** Arboreal, mainly 1–5 m above ground; typical foliage-gleaner, searching outer parts of branches and sometimes around trunks and stems, apparently not on the ground. Moves over entire territory each day but uses a core area and rotates over the rest in 3–5 days. Hops on branches and makes sallies of up to 2 m to pick up prey, sometimes after a brief hover. Hawks insects in the air. Large prey items rubbed or hit on perch, and a large caterpillar reportedly impaled on thorn. Fork-tailed Drongo *Dicrurus adsimilis* known to pirate food from this batis. Often joins mixed foraging parties[455, 676, 690, 696]. **Food** Small arthropods, mainly insects, including Coleoptera (beetles), Lepidoptera (caterpillars and moths), Mantodea (young mantids), Diptera (flies), Hymenoptera (small wasps, bees and ants), Orthoptera (grasshoppers), Homoptera (bugs and cicadas), Neuroptera (lacewings) and Isoptera (termites). Also takes spiders. Regularly feeds on swarming ants and termites. Prey size range 5–55 mm, mostly 20–30 mm[676].

SOUNDS Repertoire consists of repeated whistles, harsh buzzy calls and bill-snapping. Calls rather variable, with at least two main types of territorial song. One type is a simple series of 3–10 clear short disyllabic whistled notes *tlut-tlut-tlut-* or *tlwet-tlwet-* at a rate of *c*.2.5/sec, the series repeated 5–10 times. Second type consists of a series of repeated, longer, more complex di- or trisyllabic notes *yoo-beet-, chu-weet-, pew-pweeet-* or *zituwit-zituwit-*, with variations, e.g. *pew-pwit, ju-veet* or *chu-peeu* and also elaborated into more complex phrases *chewp----chwurp-chwurp-chwurp*. Some notes have a buzzy quality. Duetting and ♀ component unknown. Territorial threat consists of harsh downslurred repeated *ptiu-urrr* notes or higher-pitched, upslurred repeated *puuiiit-, peweeeet-* or *chch-zzeet-* scolding notes. Other notes include *klop-zheet, cherp-chup-zheet*, sometimes reversed: *peet-jit*. Responds to playback with agitated *zizi-YEEEER, zzweeeE-, chichi-zzeeet-* or *chichi-ZZurri–ZZurri-*. ♀ calls and duetting apparently not recorded. Contact call a soft *pui* or *piew* and aggressive or annoyance call a chat-like *tec-tec-tec-*. Mobbing or harassing call a harsh, buzzy vibrant *zrrrt-, zit-zit-zit-* or *tsit-tsit-* call and downslurred notes, usually combined with bill-snapping and 'wing-fripping'. Other calls include *jwit-jwit-jwit-*, a frequently heard low *p(h)eerk* and various dry, frog-like notes[15, 500, 648, 676, 696].

BREEDING BIOLOGY Monogamous and territorial, with pairs remaining together for at least 2 years. In Ivory Coast pairs produce on average 1.8 fledglings, while in Senegal, of 6 nests (from 4 pairs), only 4 received eggs and 2 fledged young. May produce two broods[676]. **Season** Mar, May–Jul (Senegal/Gambia)[38, 39, 482, 696]; Feb–Jun (Mali); Apr–May (Niger); Jan–Jun (Ivory Coast); May, Jul, Aug and ♂♂ with enlarged testes in Feb and ♀ with oviduct egg Apr (Ghana)[37, 234, 690]; Feb–Jun (Nigeria)[328, 579, 676]. **Displays *Courtship*** Rump feathers fluffed out in display, probably similar to territorial threat. Courtship-feeding probably present[500, 676]. **Nest** Built by both sexes. A tiny, neat, compact cup of small pieces of dried grass and bark fibre, decorated with leaves, small bits of lichen and bark, bound with spider web, well secured to support. Nest site variable, either placed in fork of scrub (once in bamboo stem) 0.6–1.5 m above ground, or at *c*.2 m (1–4, n=6) above the ground, in a fork, on thick stem or branch of small tree or bush up to 6 m tall. Nest is exposed but well camouflaged, resembling a knob. Favourite nesting trees in Senegal are *Grewia* and *Ziziphus*. ***Size*** OD 50–57 mm, ID 43 mm, cup depth 35 mm, height 41 mm. One pair began nest-building less than 24 hours after first shower of season. In other cases, rebuilding began 2–3 days after original nests destroyed (n=2)[15, 579, 676]. **Eggs** 2 (n=4), laid at one-day intervals. Pale greenish or blue-green, distinctly spotted with red-brown and violet almost all over, but towards large end spots larger, more violet and thicker, forming a cap or ring on underlying small rusty or lilac dots and blotches. ***Size*** 15.1–15.2 x 11.8–12.1 mm (n=2)[15, 676]. **Incubation** By ♀ only; usually begins when clutch is complete. ♀ sits at night and 80–90% of day; eggs shaded in hottest part of day. ♂ guards nest and feeds ♀ on and off the nest. All other birds near nest are attacked, and mobs Tree Squirrel *Heliosciurus gambianus* but not Ground

Squirrel *Xerus erythropus*. Period 15 days[676]. **Nestling** Hatch naked, skin dark purple-grey with sparse pinkish-brown down. Mouth spots unknown. ♂ provides food for nestlings and ♀ in first week, passing food to ♀ who feeds nestlings. After a week young fed by both sexes. Fledge after 18 days. Dependency period unknown; young remain in parental territory until next breeding season. They are repelled by day but tolerated in roost[500, 676]. For additional details see[676]. No further breeding information.

MEASUREMENTS and WEIGHTS *B. senegalensis* ♂ (11) wing 56.5–61.5 (58.04), tail 40.0–45.5 (42.30), bill 15.0–16.5 (15.75), ♂♀? (36) tarsus 16–17; ♀ (7) wing 54.0–58.5 (55.78), tail 39.0–43.0 (40.92), bill 15.0–17.0 (16.07)[286, 676]. **Weight** ♂ (9) 9.8–10.5 g (10.0 ±SD 0.2); ♀ (9) 9.0–10.0 g (9.3 ±SD 0.3); significant difference between sexes, ♂ 8% heavier than ♀ (Nigeria)[494].

90 GREY-HEADED BATIS *Batis orientalis* — Plate 33

FIELD IDENTIFICATION Very small (10–11 cm), restless, black, grey and white flycatcher-like bird, grey above contrasting with black face-mask and long white eyebrow to behind yellow eye. Wings dark grey with white stripe. Sexes different. Below white with narrow breast-band, black in ♂, russet chestnut-brown in ♀, which has no chinspot. Young like ♀ but mantle and wing-coverts tinged greyish-brown. Little known; main call a short series of 4–7 high even-pitched whistles or a similar lower-pitched, slightly descending series. In pairs or family group, foraging in centre of thorn trees. Resident in dry savanna woodland and thorn scrub from Chad to N Somalia, including NE Cameroon, Central African Republic, Sudan, NE Zaïre, N Uganda and N Kenya. ***Flight characteristics***: Wings rounded and has pied appearance in flight.

COMPARISONS Similar to Black-headed Batis *Batis minor*, but Grey-headed is generally grey above on crown and mantle (not black) with crown contrasting with ear-coverts (crown and ear-coverts similar in Black-headed). It also has a slightly broader breast-band, which is darker in ♀. However, in E Kenya and Somalia the two species are often mistaken (even in the hand) because crown of Black-headed varies from black to medium-grey. Calls rather similar, with Grey-headed's constant-pitch series being generally shorter, and short descending series being similar, but ascending series distinctive. Tends to occur in drier country than Black-headed Batis. Overlaps with tiny Pygmy Batis *B. perkeo* in S Ethiopia, but differs by having a long white eyebrow to behind eye (short eyebrow in Pygmy, only to eye); ♀ Grey-headed has a darker breast-band and no rusty tinge on face and chin. Pygmy Batis generally in drier habitat and has high-pitched cisticola-like song. In W range similar to Senegal Batis *B. senegalensis*, best separated on ♀, which in this species has a distinct pale rufous (tawny) eyebrow, chin and buffy wing-stripe, and tawny-rufous (orange-rufous) breast-band. Senegal has distinctly di-and trisyllabic notes often with buzzy introductory notes. In S of range similar to Chinspot Batis *B. molitor*, which has a narrower, shorter white eyebrow, broader breast-band and, in ♀, a rufous chinspot. Chinspot Batis calls similar but lower-pitched and known to elicit immediate response in Grey-headed. Mozambique Batis *B. soror* occurs on E coast slightly S of Somalia population. It is paler grey above and ♀ has a diffuse chinspot. Mozambique calls similar but lower-pitched[578, 631].

DESCRIPTION Adult ♂ *bella* (including *somaliensis*). ***Head*** Forehead, crown and nape bluish-grey; small white loral spot extends to form a long broad white eyebrow; small white patch on nape; face-mask glossy blue-black. ***Back*** Mantle and back dark grey, tinged glossy blue-black; scapulars blackish; rump whitish with fluffy feathers; uppertail-coverts black. ***Wings*** Black with white stripe formed by white median coverts and outer webs of inner greater coverts and inner secondaries and tertials; primaries and secondaries narrowly edged white; axillaries white. Underwing-coverts blackish. ***Tail*** Black, two outer feathers on each side tipped white, outer feathers edged white. ***Underparts*** Chin to undertail-coverts white, except for glossy black breast-band, width variable (*c.*4–9 mm). ***Bare parts*** Bill black; palate unknown; legs black; eye yellow. Adult ♀ Similar to ♂ but with breast-band russet or dark chestnut-brown, width variable (see Geographical Variation). Juvenile Similar to nestling, above greyish-brown speckled buff. Underparts dull white with russet-black breast-band. Eye probably brown[338, 500, 504]. Immature like adult ♀ but eyebrow and median wing-coverts tinged tawny-brown, mantle tinged brownish, breast-band probably black and russet chestnut-brown[338, 631, 676].

GEOGRAPHICAL VARIATION At least 5 races, with variation in body size, colour of upperparts and breast-band, and extent of eyebrow. Nominate *orientalis* (N Ethiopia, interior Eritrea) is largest race with darkest upperparts; *bella* (E, central and S Ethiopia, N Somalia, N Eritrea and possibly N Kenya) similar to nominate, smaller and with the palest upperparts; *chadensis* (Nigeria, Zaïre, Central African Republic, Sudan and W Ethiopia) similar to nominate but smaller; ♀ has a narrower breast-band than other races and upperparts tinged brown, flight feathers brown not black, and has a bold white eyebrow; *lynesi* (Red Sea province of Sudan) similar to *bella* but ♀ has breast-band paler with yellowish tinge[286].

MOULT Unknown.

RANGE, HABITAT and STATUS Breeding range Northern tropics; E Chad, E Niger (confirmation required), NE Cameroon, NE Nigeria, Central African Republic, S Sudan, Ethiopia, N Somalia (records in SW require confirmation), Eritrea, NE Uganda and possibly N Kenya. Distribution in E Africa controversial due to confusion with Black-headed Batis. **Habitat** Dry savanna woodlands, thornbush, subdesert steppe, open wooded grasslands and dense thorn-scrub, from sea level to 2100 m (Ethiopia). Keeps to low-growing *Acacia* and *Ziziphus* bushes and other thorn trees[242, 286, 325, 431, 558, 578, 631, 676, 860]. **Status** Resident, common to locally fairly common. **Conservation status** Unknown, probably not threatened.

MOVEMENTS Unknown.

SOCIAL ORGANISATION and GENERAL BEHAVIOUR Little known. Similar to other savanna batises; solitary or in pairs; arboreal and restless. Spends much time in shade in centre of trees where it evidently forages. Song heard mainly Dec–Apr (N Somalia), uttered while perched or in flight[676]. **Foraging behaviour** Forages in lower to mid-levels of savanna woodland and thorn scrub. Makes short sallying flights inside tree, gleaning from vegetation[504, 676]. **Food** Insects.

SOUNDS Little known. Apparently has two main song types. The first has various descriptions, from bell-like, usually *c.*4 notes, or a penetrating metallic clicking *tink-tink-tink-tink*, also a series of *c.*4–5 very high-pitched *eep-eep-eep-eep* notes at the same pitch (sounds like a squeaky bicycle pump). Second type is similar, but descends the scale slightly *eep-eep-eap-erp-erp*, also described as 6–7 mournful notes on a descending scale or *WEET-weet-weet-seeerr*, first note more emphatic than next two, the last note softer. The constant-pitch series sounds similar to Black-headed Batis. Recent Ethiopian recordings are clear piping whistles, almost indistinguishable from those of Kenyan Chinspot Batis, and which stimulate immediate vocal response from that species. ♀ calls and duetting apparently not recorded[33, 338, 500, 558, 631, 637].

BREEDING BIOLOGY Little known. Apparently monogamous and territorial. **Season** Apr–May (Uganda)[338]; Feb–Apr, Jul, some evidence for Feb–Apr (Ethiopia)[292, 676]; Apr (Sudan)[242]; Feb, May–Jun (N Somalia)[33, 237, 859]. **Displays** ***Courtship?*** A record of ♂ doing a high aerial flight, going round and round loudly giving 4 *peeps*, was originally reported as Pygmy Batis, but is here thought probably to have been Grey-headed Batis[500, 769]. **Nest** Role of sexes unknown. Neat cup made of fine shreds of fibre and dry bark, with large strips of bark on the outside, bound together with spider web and lined with fine grass. Well concealed in a central fork of thorn tree at *c.*2 m[33]. **Eggs** 2–3. Pale blue ground colour, finely dotted with purple-brown spots in zone round upper half, or flecked with black-brown and with underlying splashes of lilac confined to the top. ***Size*** Av. 17.5 x 13 mm (n=4)[33]. No further breeding information, except feathered nestling like adult but pattern indistinct, duller above with crown and mantle speckled whitish and breast-band partly dull chestnut-brown and black[676].

MEASUREMENTS and WEIGHTS *B. o. orientalis* ♂ (2) wing 63.5–64.5 (64.0), tail 48.0–48.5 (48.25), bill 16.5; ♀ (2) wing 60.5–61.5 (61.0), tail 45.0, bill 16.0[286]; *bella* ♂ (30) wing 56.0–60.0 (57.9), tail 37.0–45.5 (40.4), bill 14.0–17.0 (15.3), ♂ (5) tarsus 15.5–17 (16.1); ♀ (20) wing 55.0–60.0 (56.8), tail 36.5–41.5 (40.0), bill 14.0–15.5 (15.0), ♀ (5) tarsus 15.5–16 (15.5)[286, 500]. **Weight** *orientalis* ♂♀? (33) 8.8–13.4 g (11.1) (Ethiopia)[870]; ♀ (2) 9–10 g (Kenya); ♂ (1) 9 g (Uganda)[676].

91 PYGMY BATIS *Batis perkeo* — Plate 33

FIELD IDENTIFICATION Tiny (8–9 cm; smallest batis in region), dumpy, restless, black, grey and white flycatcher-like bird with bluish-grey head and back, contrasting with black face-mask and short white eyebrow to above yellow eye. Wings black with white stripe. Sexes different. Below white, ♂ with narrow black breast-band, ♀ with breast-band and chin pale rufous-buff, eyebrow and sides of face and wing-stripe tawny-buff. Young probably similar to ♀ but tawnier. Little known. Main call a long series of repeated sharp high-pitched whistles. In pairs, foraging in thorn scrub and *Acacia* trees in arid and semi-arid regions of Ethiopia, S Sudan, Somalia, E Uganda, Kenya and NE Tanzania. ***Flight characteristics***: Wings rounded, has pied appearance in flight and makes 'wing-fripping' sounds.

COMPARISONS Similar to Grey-headed Batis *Batis orientalis*, Chinspot Batis *B. molitor* and Mozambique Batis *B. soror*, but differs from these by very small size (smallest batis in E Africa) and shorter white eyebrow which ends above eye. ♂ Grey-headed and Chinspot have broader breast-band, ♂ Mozambique has paler grey top of head and mantle (Pygmy darker with mantle glossy blue-black). Differs from ♂ Black-headed Batis *B. minor* by grey (not black) crown (but variable; see species account p.313.). More easily separated on ♀♀. Pygmy Batis ♀ distinctive, with buffy tinge on face and sides of throat, pale rufous-buff breast-band and lack of distinctive chinspot. ♀ Chinspot and Mozambique Batis have rufous chinspot, ♀ Grey-headed and Black-headed Batis lack chinspot but have darker chestnut-brown breast-bands (Pygmy ♀ pale rufous-buff). Where range overlaps with Chinspot and Mozambique, Pygmy found in drier habitat. Calls high-pitched and cisticola-like, similar to Black-headed and Grey-headed Batis, but higher-pitched than Mozambique or Chinspot Batis[237, 286].

DESCRIPTION **ADULT ♂** ***Head*** Forehead, crown and nape bluish-grey; white loral stripe extends as an eyebrow; small white nape-patch; face-mask glossy black. ***Back*** Mantle, scapulars, back, rump and uppertail-coverts grey; rump and lower back spotted white, rump feathers fluffy. ***Wings*** Black with white stripe formed by broad white ends to median and inner greater coverts and broad white edges to inner secondaries and tertials. Underwing-coverts black. ***Tail*** Black with outer feathers edged and tipped white. ***Underparts*** Chin to undertail-coverts white, except for glossy black narrow breast-band (*c*.9–11 mm). ***Bare parts*** Bill black, palate dark grey and legs black; eye bright lemon-yellow, with dark outer rim[500]. **ADULT ♀** Similar to ♂ but front of eyebrow tinged rusty; nape-patch smaller and buffy; wing-stripe buffy; throat white in centre, buffy on sides; breast-band pale rufous-buff. ***Bare parts*** Like ♂. **JUVENILE/IMMATURE** Young ♂ resembles ♀, but upperparts tinged buffy-brown, eye probably brown[500].

GEOGRAPHICAL VARIATION None. Monotypic.

MOULT Unknown.

RANGE, HABITAT and STATUS **Breeding range** Dry E African savannas, from SE Sudan, central and SW Somalia, S of 9°N and W of 48°E, E and S Ethiopia, N and E central highlands in Kenya, E Uganda and NE Tanzania[242, 286, 325, 431, 467, 676, 631, 859]. **Habitat** *Acacia*, *Commiphora* and thorn scrub in arid and semi-arid low-lying regions, mainly within 250–500 mm annual rainfall area. In Tsavo National Park in wooded and bushy grassland, and woodland, but not riverine woods[242, 286, 325, 631, 676]. **Status** Resident; common to fairly common. **Conservation status** Unknown.

MOVEMENTS Apparently sedentary; however a single bird mist-netted with migrants in early Dec at Ngulia (Kenya) suggests possible movements[676].

SOCIAL ORGANISATION and GENERAL BEHAVIOUR Little known. Solitary, in pairs or family groups. A restless, arboreal species. Habits apparently similar to other savanna woodland batises. In flight sometimes makes 'fripping' sounds with wings[769]. **Foraging behaviour** Feeds mainly within bushes and trees. In one study, 55% prey taken from leaves, 31% from twigs and 14% in air; 50% caught deep inside foliage, 21% just inside and 29% at edge. Perch height av. 3.4 m. Often a member of mixed foraging parties[352, 859]. **Food** Insects, including small Coleoptera (beetles)[676].

SOUNDS Little known. Repertoire consists of repeated high-pitched whistles and harsh notes. Territorial call a series of repeated short sharp penetrating high-pitched whistles of up to *c*.20 notes at the same pitch, with rates of *c*.1–1.5 notes/sec. Some notes rather cisticola-like, *ting-ting-ting-*, or notes slightly more extended *zeet-zeet-zeet-*, *zleet-zleet-*, *pee-pee-pee-*, or *een-een-een-*. Alternatively described as weak *peeps*. Also makes chattering *chchchch-* and harsh churring sounds. Notes suggestive of Black-headed Batis, but typically sharper, higher-pitched, more ringing and less drawn-out[500, 631, 676].

BREEDING BIOLOGY Virtually unknown. Probably monogamous. **Season** Breeding indications Feb (Ethiopia); soft egg in dead bird late Mar (SE Kenya)[676]. **Displays** A report of ♂ doing a high aerial flight, going round and round loudly giving 4 *peeps*, is here thought to have probably been Grey-headed Batis[500, 769]. No further breeding information.

MEASUREMENTS and WEIGHTS *B. perkeo* ♂ (25) wing 48.5–55.0 (52.0), tail 30.0–37.5 (33.9), bill 14.0–16.5 (15.3); ♀ (13) 49.0–53.5 (50.7), tail 30.0–35.5 (32.8), bill 13.5–15.5 (14.5), ♂ (6) tarsus 15–17 (16.0); ♀ (13) wing 49–53.5 (50.7), tail 30–35.5 (32.7), bill 13.5–15.5 (14.5), ♀ (6) tarsus 14.5–15.5 (15.3)[500, 578, 676]. **Weight** ♂ (6) 8.0–9.0 g (8.2) (Kenya)[583]; ♂ (7) 5–8 g (6.2), ♀(3) 7–8 g (7.7) (Kenya)[676]. For additional data see[76, 676, 762].

92 BLACK-HEADED BATIS *Batis minor* — Plate 33

FIELD IDENTIFICATION Very small (10–11 cm), dumpy, restless, black, grey and white flycatcher-like bird with variable dark grey to blackish (sometimes glossy) head, long white eyebrow to behind yellow eye, and black face-mask. Back grey, wing-stripe and outer tail feathers white. Sexes different. Below white with breast-band, black in ♂, dark chestnut-brown in ♀ with no chinspot. Young like ♀ but spotted above and with blackish-brown breast-band. Flight bouncy with 'wing-fripping' sounds. Little known. Main call a long series of high-pitched whistles, also a short descending or ascending series. Usually in pairs or family group foraging in mid levels of trees and bushes in a wide range of wooded savannas. Distribution widespread but fragmented, populations resident; N tropics from Nigeria to Sudan, Ethiopia to Burundi; S tropics from S Gabon, SW Zaïre and N Angola; coastal lowlands in East Africa from SW Somalia to S Tanzania. ***Flight characteristics***: Bouncy and undulating; wings rounded. Has pied appearance in flight and makes 'fripping' sounds with wings.

COMPARISONS In N of range, similar to Grey-headed Batis *Batis orientalis*, which occurs in more arid thorn scrub and woodland at lower elevations (Black-headed in moister habitats). Grey-headed is greyer on crown and mantle, making contrast with ear-coverts, and generally has a broader breast-band, which is darker in ♀. Generally crown and ear-coverts are similar in Black-headed, but caution is required, because crown colour in this species varies from black to medium grey. Consequently, these two species are often confused, even in the hand. Calls are also rather similar, with Grey-headed's constant-pitch series being generally shorter, and short descending series similar, but ascending series distinctive. Best distinguished on ♀ and habitat. Chinspot Batis *B. molitor* also similar but has a shorter white eyebrow (does not extend to back of neck) and ♀ Black-headed Batis has darker maroon breast-band and no chinspot. Some calls also similar, except for a short (*c.*3-note) ascending phrase of Black-headed. Notes tend to be more drawn-out, less sharp, than those of Chinspot. Similar to Mozambique Batis *B. soror*, which is paler grey above, ♀ with pale rufous breast-band and chinspot; calls similar, lacks short phrase and notes lower-pitched. In NE of range similar to tiny Pygmy Batis *B. perkeo*, which has short eyebrow ending above the eye and ♀ has narrow pale tawny breast-band, and tawny tinge to face and chin. This species has high-pitched cisticola-like calls. In NW of range similar to smaller savanna grassland Senegal Batis *B. senegalensis*, which has a broader white eyebrow and ♀ with tawny eyebrow, faint chinspot, and tawny rufous breast-band. Senegal calls are distinctly di- or trisyllabic, often with buzzy introductory notes. In East Africa, where overlapping with Chinspot and Pygmy Batis, Black-headed tends to be restricted to riverine bush, occasionally in woodland along river courses. In SW of range overlaps widely with Angola Batis *B. minulla*, which is smaller with more white in wing but less white in tail, and a shorter less conspicuous white eyebrow. Calls appear rather similar. In the hand underwing-coverts are white in Angola Batis and blackish in other savanna batises. Black-headed tends to occupy more open savanna (Angola in more dense vegetation)[180, 289, 352, 500, 578, 631, 676].

DESCRIPTION ADULT ♂ *erlangeri* (including *congoensis*, *nyansae* and *batesi*) ***Head*** Forehead, crown and nape blackish-grey, with bluish gloss (see Geographical Variation). White loral spot extends back in form of broad eyebrow reaching back of neck; white nape-patch; face-mask glossy blue-black. ***Back*** Scapulars blackish, mantle and back dark grey; rump whitish, feathers tipped grey and white, giving spotted appearance; uppertail-coverts black. ***Wings*** Black with white stripe formed by white tips to median coverts and broad white outer edges to inner secondary coverts, and broad white edges to tertials and inner secondaries. Primaries and outer secondaries narrowly edged white. Underwing-coverts blackish. ***Tail*** Black, two outer feathers on each side tipped white, outer feathers edged white. ***Underparts*** White with glossy black breast-band (*c.*6–10 mm). ***Bare parts*** Bill black; palate unknown; legs black; eye yellow. ADULT ♀ Similar to ♂ but mantle blackish and breast-band dark chestnut-brown to russet-maroon, width variable (see Geographical Variation). ***Bare parts*** Like ♂. JUVENILE/IMMATURE Like adult ♀ but buffy blackish-brown above with each feather tipped buff; eyebrow and wing-coverts rusty-buff; underparts with blackish to dark chestnut-brown breast-band, later turning russet. Eye changes from whitish, through greenish to yellow; probably brown in juvenile. Immature ♂ retains russet breast-band for about 6–7 months[289, 500, 504, 676].

GEOGRAPHICAL VARIATION Occasionally treated as comprising 6 races, but only 3 accepted here; variation slight and concerned mainly with crown and mantle coloration, and size. Race *erlangeri* (W Kenya, NW Tanzania) (here including *congoensis*, *nyansae* and *batesi*) (West African, Angolan, Zaïre and N populations) is largest race with darker mantle and top of head jet-black, less glossy than nominate, ♀ mantle tinged olive-brown; nominate *minor* (S Somalia) and *suahelicus* (E Kenya, NE Tanzania) are smallest, with a glossier greyer crown and greyer mantle, ♀ with mantle less olive, *suahelicus* ♀ having a narrower breast-band, *minor* occurring in drier habitats than *suahelicus* and *erlangeri*[286, 631].

MOULT Unknown.

RANGE, HABITAT and STATUS **Breeding range** Distribution fragmented, main range in 3 parts: (i) northern tropics from Nigeria, Cameroon, Chad, Central African Republic, N Congo, N Zaïre, to S Sudan, with outlying populations in Darfur highlands and Gebel Elba, Ethiopia to Eritrea and N Somalia, Uganda, W Kenya (Kongelai Escarpment), Rwanda (requires confirmation) and Burundi; (ii) southern tropics from SE Gabon, Cabinda and N Angola, with outlying populations to SW Zaïre; (iii) coastal lowlands of E Africa from SE Kenya and NE and E Tanzania. Outlying populations in Eritrea and N Somalia require confirmation against Grey-headed Batis. **Habitat** Tolerant of a wide range of habitats from relatively dry to moist savanna woodlands, including wooded grassland, woodland edge, riverine bush, bushlands, moist savanna–forest mosaic woodlands, cultivated areas and gardens, tall grass and secondary growth. Also occurs in semi-deciduous forest, patches of mist forest and edge of juniper areas in association with evergreen forest[7, 21, 88, 242, 286, 295, 325, 431, 578, 676, 859, 860, 907, 909]. **Status** Resident; common to locally common. **Conservation status** Generally not threatened; however, in Somalia there are indications that numbers may have decreased[859].

MOVEMENTS Unknown.

SOCIAL ORGANISATION and GENERAL BEHAVIOUR Little known. Like other savanna batises, solitary, in pairs or family group. Arboreal and restless, flicking tail upwards at every change of position. Calls given from perch and in flight[22, 289, 504, 676]. **Foraging behaviour** Arboreal, feeds mainly just inside bush at all levels, but mostly in lower and mid levels, sometimes to canopy. Head constantly on the move, peering from side to side and upwards before making short flycatching sallies to glean prey from underside of foliage, branches or in the air. In one study 53% gleaned from leaves, 18% from twigs, 24% in flight; 29% deep inside vegetation, 53% just inside and 18% at edge. Forages at *c.*10 m above ground. In Chad, searches for minute insects in foliage, particularly of *Acacia raddiana*[2, 352, 504, 774, 676, 907]. **Food** Insects.

SOUNDS Repertoire consists of repeated whistles, harsh sounds and bill-snapping. Two main territorial song types, often given in flight. One type is a monotonous series of *c.*3–20 very high, even-pitched short whistles (sounds like a squeaky bicycle pump), with repetition rates usually varying from *c.*2–2.5 notes/sec. The other is a short phrase consisting of 2–3 notes. Song preference appears to be geographically determined, with predominantly long series in the W and central range, and the shorter phrase in the extreme E population. Western *erlangeri* has a penetrating, monotonous rapidly repeated whistle *eent-eent-eent-*, *reehn-reehn-* or *weet-weet-weet-*. In West Africa recorded as *heet-heet-heet-heet-*. Also produces slower, more drawn-out series at same pitch *zweet---zweet---*. Presumed ♀ accompanies in duet with softer *zwit* or *zit* notes. High-pitched notes reportedly given by both sexes, members of pair duetting (antiphonally), the notes well separated and unhurried. This is contrary to other batises and the occurrence of see-saw *eee-zee-eee-zee-* calling is thought more likely to represent counter-singing between ♂♂. Second song type consists of a repeated short phrase of usually up to *c.*3 high-pitched notes: *uteet-eet-* or *seent-wree-wree-* (first note appears higher than rest). Eastern *minor* has slower, longer, high-pitched notes, usually in groups of 2 or 3, first note usually lower and upslurred, producing an ascending phrase with second two notes on the same pitch *dooey-sweet-sweet*, *ureet-weet-weet* or *yeeo-eet-eet*, or in *suahelicus* a double or triple *thwi-thwe-thwee*. Alternatively third note may be higher *zwuu-zwee-zweet* or *thwi-thwe-thwee*. ♀ has rough *shaow* in alarm or annoyance. Alarm also recorded as *tchak*. Other sounds include buzzy *preeu*, churring *tserr*, chattering *chikchikchik-* (possibly alarm) and *kikkisskiss-* or buzzing *zz-zz-zz-* (possibly begging), *dzip-dzip* and 'wing-fripping' sounds. The descending 3-note phrase is similar to Chinspot Batis, but notes of Black-headed Batis tend to be more drawn-out and less sharp. Chinspot Batis is also known to produce long series in overlap zones with other batises[420, 500, 504, 631, 676, 700, 758].

BREEDING BIOLOGY Little known. Apparently monogamous and territorial[420, 676]. **Season** probable breeding Apr (Somalia)[336]; Jun, Oct (Kenya)[336]; Jan–Apr (Sudan)[242]; Jun (Tanzania)[336]; Jun, Nov (Uganda)[237]; Mar–Jun, Oct (East Africa)[293]; fledgling Apr (Cameroon)[676]; Mar–May (NE Zaïre)[289], Jul–Oct (S Zaïre)[22]; Mar, May, Aug, Sep (Ethiopia)[15, 292]. **Displays** Unknown. **Nest** Role of sexes unknown. Small neat cup of fine vegetable material or moss bound with spider web and decorated with flat pieces of bark or lichen fixed to exterior. Built in shrub, bush or small tree on branch or fork, usually only *c.*1 m above ground, sometimes sited on top of stump, once in fork of dead *Acacia* sapling 50 cm high. Records of higher nests at *c.*5 m in baobab *Adansonia*, require confirmation. ***Size*** OD *c.*50 mm[2, 22, 289, 338, 420]. **Eggs** Usually 2. Greyish-green or whitish, covered thickly with small reddish spots forming a zone around large end; pale greenish-grey with dark grey and umber spots and blotches. ***Size*** 15.3–16.2 x 12–12.8 mm (15.7 x 12.5, n=3)[22, 289, 420, 676]; a record[2] of 2 eggs measuring 16 x 12.5 and 17 x 11.5 mm requires confirmation. **Incubation** By ♀ who sits tight, allowing approach to within 1 m. Period unknown[420]. **Nestling** Hatch naked; mouth spots unknown. Young have irregular whitish blotches on upperparts giving the appearance of lichens or droppings on a grey branch. Attended by both sexes. At one nest fully exposed to sun, ♀ shaded young. Period unknown. Dependent young cared for by both sexes[420, 500, 676]. No further breeding information.

MEASUREMENTS and WEIGHTS *B. m. minor* ♂ (4) wing 54.0–56.0 (55.25), tail 34.5–39.0 (36.25), bill 15.0–15.5 (15.17); ♀ (5) wing 52.0–53.0 (52.50), tail 34.0–36.5 (35.50), bill 14.0–15.5 (14.80)[286]; *erlangeri* (including *congoensis*, *nyansae* and *batesi*) ♂ (66) wing 57–67.5 (61.8), tail 38–51 (44.2), bill 14–17.5 (16.5), ♂ (20) tarsus 16–17; ♀ (49) wing 57–64.5 (61.0), tail 40–50 (44.1), bill 15–17.5 (16.0); ♀ (13) tarsus 15–16[286, 676]. **Weight** *minor* ♂♀? (35) 9.3–13.8 g (9.3) (Ethiopia)[870]; *erlangeri* ♂♀? (4) 11.0–14.0 g (12.5) (Cameroon)[478].

93 ANGOLA BATIS *Batis minulla* — Plate 33

FIELD IDENTIFICATION Very small (9.5–10 cm), dumpy, restless, black and white flycatcher-like bird with yellow eye, black face-mask, white spot in front of eye, white wing-stripe and no white collar. Sexes different. Above dark grey, rump spotted white; below white with broad breast-band, black in ♂, chestnut-brown in ♀. Little known; main call a series of high-pitched whistles like a squeaky bicycle pump. Resident canopy forager in forest patches, gallery forest, thickets and thick woodland. Occurs in SE Gabon, S Congo, W and SW Zaïre and W Angola. ***Flight***

characteristics: Wings rounded, has a pied appearance in flight.

COMPARISONS Overlaps marginally with Chinspot Batis *Batis molitor*, with which it is thought to be similar in behaviour. Chinspot is more of a savanna woodland species and is considerably larger with a more conspicuous white eyebrow, partial white collar and less white in tail; ♀ has rufous chinspot (lacking in Angola Batis). Calls different: Angola has a series of high-pitched whistles, sounding like a squeaky bicycle pump, Chinspot usually has 3 descending whistles, although it is also known to produce longer series, particularly in areas of overlap with other batises. Overlaps widely with Black-headed Batis *B. minor*, which is also larger, has less white in wing but more white in tail, and a longer, more conspicuous white eyebrow. Calls appear rather similar. In the hand underwing-coverts are white in Angola Batis and blackish in Black-headed Batis. Probably does not overlap with Verreaux's Batis *B. minima*, which is a forest canopy species[289, 631, 676, 700, 717].

DESCRIPTION **ADULT ♂** ***Head*** Forehead and crown bluish-grey with small white loral spot; face-mask glossy black extending back to nape and running down sides of neck; small nape-patch white. ***Back*** Mantle grey; scapulars blackish; back, rump and uppertail-coverts blackish-grey with white spots; rump feathers long and fluffy. ***Wings*** Primaries and secondaries black, narrowly edged white on both webs; white stripe formed by white tips to median coverts and broad white outer edges to inner secondary coverts, and broad white edges to tertials and inner secondaries; greater and median primary coverts black; greaters narrowly edged white. Underwing-coverts whitish. ***Tail*** Short, black with white outer edges to outer two feathers on both sides. ***Underparts*** Chin and throat white, extending back to black stripe on side of neck; broad (*c*.11–13 mm) black breast-band; rest of underparts white including undertail-coverts; flanks greyish; thighs black. ***Bare parts*** Bill black; palate unknown; legs black; eye bright yellow or lemon-yellow. **ADULT ♀** Like ♂ but breast-band chestnut-brown; nape-patch smaller and mantle with rufous tinge[500, 676]. **JUVENILE/IMMATURE** Unknown.

GEOGRAPHICAL VARIATION None. Monotypic.

MOULT Unknown.

RANGE, HABITAT and STATUS **Breeding range** SW Congo basin from SE Gabon (requires confirmation), S Congo, W Zaïre widespread N of Congo R. near mouth, also Kwango Province and W Kasai Occidental Province, Angola from Cabinda, Cuanza Norte, W Malanje, S along escarpment to N Mossamedes and Capangombe, and in Quissama National Park, Luanda[7, 295, 504, 578, 676]. Originally listed for Cameroon but not included by subsequent authors; details cannot be traced[21, 23, 431]. **Habitat** Found in vestigial patches of forest, secondary and gallery forest, thick *Croton* woodland and adjacent bush, thickets and patches of young forest on edge of savanna. Sometimes in dry woodland, e.g. below escarpment in Angola, coffee plantations and along rivers and near S borders of rainforest in SW Congo basin[7, 180, 289, 295, 504, 774, 907]. **Status** Resident, local and uncommon. **Conservation status** Unknown.

MOVEMENTS Unknown.

SOCIAL ORGANISATION and GENERAL BEHAVIOUR Virtually unknown. Habits apparently similar to other batises; solitary or in pairs[676]. **Foraging behaviour** Arboreal, a canopy feeder, observed in larger trees[402, 515]. **Food** Insects.

SOUNDS Little known. Territorial call a rapid series of very high-pitched short whistles *fe-fe-fe-fe-fe-* or *zee-zee-zee-* sounding like a squeaky bicycle pump and rather cisticola-like. Also described as weak sucking *heep-heep-*. Series delivered at variable rates (e.g. *c*.2 notes/sec), and may get very long and monotonous (e.g. *c*.3–40 notes), particularly in response to playback. Pitch of series may descend slightly at the beginning and tends to get louder towards the end. Also gives churring sounds and buzzing short *zrrit-zrrit* or *frret-* calls. Calls are similar to Verreaux's and Bioko Batis but lack the buzzy introductory notes of the long whistled series in these two species[500, 504, 515].

BREEDING BIOLOGY Little known; apparently monogamous and territorial. **Season** Jul, including nest-building (Zaïre)[289, 676]. **Displays** Unknown. **Nest** Built by both sexes. Small neat compact deep cup of soft bark strips and spider web in fork of small tree, placed *c*.2 m (n=2) above ground. Both nests in recently burnt trees[22, 289]. **Eggs** 2. Colour and pattern unrecorded[22]. No further breeding information.

MEASUREMENTS and WEIGHTS *B. minulla* ♂ (17) wing 53.0–57.5 (55.12), tail 35.5–39.5 (38.00), bill 14.0–16.0 (15.25), ♂ (5) tarsus 14–15 (14.6); ♀ (19) wing 50.5–56.0 (54.05), tail 36.0–40.5 (37.97), bill 14.0–15.0 (14.64), ♀ (5) tarsus 14–14.5 (14.3)[287, 500]. **Weight** ♂ 10.4 g, ♀ (2) 9.3–10 g (Angola)[907, 911].

94 BIOKO BATIS (West African Batis, White-browed Puff-back Flycatcher) *Batis poensis* Plate 34

FIELD IDENTIFICATION Very small (9.5–10.5 cm), restless, black and white flycatcher-like bird with a black head, yellow eye and conspicuous long white eyebrow and white nape-patch (not in Bioko race). Back dark grey, wing-stripe and outer tail feathers white. Sexes different. Below white, ♂ with narrow black breast-band, ♀ with dark chestnut-brown (mainland) or diffuse buffy-chestnut (Bioko) breast-band. Young like dull ♀ with indistinct rufous breast-band and buffy wing-stripe. Little known. More often heard than seen; main call a series of high-pitched plaintive whistles usually with buzzy introductory notes (mainland). Solitary, in pairs or family group high up in canopy of tall trees in lowland and montane evergreen forest. Easily overlooked. Rare resident on Bioko and on mainland from Sierra Leone, Liberia, Ivory Coast, Ghana, SW Nigeria, S Cameroon and N Gabon. ***Flight characteristics***: Rather hesitant; makes 'fripping' sounds with wings in flight. Flies across large open spaces rapidly. Wings rounded, has a pied appearance.

COMPARISONS ♂ mainland race may be confused with similar but smaller ♂ Gabon Batis *Batis minima*, which has more conspicuous white spot in front of eye, less conspicuous white nape-patch and greyish-black (not black) back. ♀ Gabon Batis has grey (not buffy-chestnut) breast-band. Where both species occur together, Gabon Batis found lower down, in mid levels of smaller trees, while Bioko Batis in highest trees feeding inside the canopy. Their calls are also different: Gabon Batis usually lacks buzzy introductory notes of Bioko Batis. The situation is complicated as they seem to copy one another when they meet, like other batises. ♂ also resembles ♂ Senegal Batis *B. senegalensis* and Black-headed Batis *B. minor*, but these are thorn scrub and woodland species respectively, with greyer upperparts. ♀♀ have chestnut-brown breast-bands. Shows a superficial resemblance to Rufous-crowned Eremomela *Eremomela badiceps*, but Bioko Batis has more upright stance, bigger head, longer tail and black and white plumage with wide breast-band[294, 456, 676, 740].

DESCRIPTION Adult ♂ *poensis* ***Head and mantle*** Glossy blue-black, with small loral spot and usually lacks white eyebrow. ***Back*** blackish-grey with white spots on lower back and rump. Rump feathers long and fluffy. ***Wings*** Black with long white stripe formed by white tips to median coverts, broad white outer edges to inner secondary coverts, and narrow white edges to tertials and inner secondaries. Underwing-coverts whitish. ***Tail*** Black with narrow white edges to outer feathers. ***Underparts*** White except for broad black breast-band (*c.*10–11 mm). ***Bare parts*** Bill black; palate unknown; legs black; eye yellow. Adult ♂ *occulta* (sometimes separated as a distinct species; see Relationships p.44) ***Head*** Forehead bluish-black with large white loral spot in front of eye; crown and face-mask bluish-black; thin white eyebrow extends to behind eye and meets conspicuous white nape-patch. ***Back*** Mantle to rump slate-grey, back and rump mottled and spotted with partly concealed white spots. Rump feathers long and fluffy. ***Wings*** Including scapulars black with long white stripe formed by white tips to median coverts, broad white outer edges to inner secondary coverts, and broad white edges to tertials and inner secondaries. Underwing-coverts whitish. ***Tail*** Including upper-tail-coverts black, rectrices with broad white edges to outer feathers. ***Underparts*** Chin and throat white with slightly narrower glossy bluish-black breast-band (*c.*9–10 mm); rest of underparts white; flanks greyish; thighs black. ***Bare parts*** Bill black; palate black, legs black; eye lemon- or golden-yellow[500, 581, 676, 895]. Adult ♀ *poensis* Like ♂, slightly duller above; below white with breast-band dark chestnut-brown with faint buffy barring, breast-band diffuse and not clearly defined, extending as a tinge of chestnut-brown onto upper flanks and upper abdomen[287]. Adult ♀ *occulta* Similar to ♂ of this race, except crown and mantle are grey tinged blue-black; rump whiter; breast-band a more clearly defined dark chestnut-brown[287, 581]. Juvenile/Immature *poensis* Like adult ♀ but back tinged olive-ochre, white on wing tinged ochre, upperwing-coverts tipped buff, throat tinged rufous-buff, breast-band paler and more orange-chestnut. Young *occulta* similar to adult ♀ but sides of throat pale rufous, and white wing-stripe tinged rufous. Breast-band on ♂ progressively black. Eye probably brown[412, 500, 676].

GEOGRAPHICAL VARIATION Two races (sometimes separated as distinct species; see Relationships p.44), variation mainly in body size, amount of white on head, wings and tail and in distinctiveness of breast-band in ♀♀. Nominate *poensis* (Bioko) is a larger bird with a smaller loral spot, no white eyebrow, less white in wings and tail, ♂ with broader breast-band and a darker blue-black crown and mantle than *occulta* (mainland from Sierra Leone to Gabon). In this race ♂ has conspicuous white loral spot and eyebrow, broad white edge to tertials and tail feathers and a narrower breast-band. ♀♀ are more distinctive: nominate race has a less clear breast-band, which blends into upper belly and flanks; *occulta* has a darker, clearly defined breast-band with white flanks (see Description). Bill of *occulta* is narrower than nominate[259, 287, 500, 581].

MOULT Apparently post-breeding moult, body moult in Sep (Bioko) and wing moult Oct (Liberia)[259, 412, 858].

RANGE, HABITAT and STATUS Breeding range West Africa. Nominate on island of Bioko, mainland population from Sierra Leone, Liberia, Ivory Coast, Ghana and SW Nigeria to S Cameroon and N Gabon. Possibly also from Congo and Benin (require confirmation). **Habitat**

Forest; on Bioko in lowland forest up to border with montane forest. On mainland in tall trees in evergreen gallery forest, including lowland and primary montane forest, overgrown cultivation in rainforest where vegetation not uniform or dense, and large clearings with plantations of cacao or cassava, often with scattered tall trees and shrubs found along roadsides and around villages. Less frequent along primary forest edge and in degraded secondary growth with scattered trees. Lowland up to 1350 m, possibly 2500 m in Cameroon[37, 207, 234, 259, 287, 294, 412, 431, 451, 496, 504, 578, 664, 676, 848]. **Status** Mainland and island populations resident; generally considered rare. **Conservation status** Possibly threatened, although some indication that young readily colonize new clearings and other degraded forested habitats in Gabon[343, 676].

MOVEMENTS Unknown.

SOCIAL ORGANISATION and GENERAL BEHAVIOUR Little known. Solitary, in pairs or small family group of 2–5 birds. Restless and shy, constantly on the move and easy to overlook because it occurs high up in the lower canopy of tall trees, where moves from tree to tree. More often heard than seen. Advertises and defends a territory of *c.*27 ha (n=3)(Gabon) with display-flights. These consist of rather bouncy, circular flights (diameter 10–20 m) above treetops, calling and with lower back and rump feathers fluffed-out and crown feathers erect, accompanied with 'wing-fripping' and bill-snapping[294, 664, 676, 858]. **Foraging behaviour** Arboreal, in dense leafy canopy of very tall trees, mainly at 35–40 m, rarely down below 25–30 m or above 40 m. It is a foliage-gleaner, moving among branches hopping from twig to twig, making short inclined sallies or jumps to snatch prey in flight or to pick at underside of leaves, usually after a brief hover. Often feeds from a horizontal branch by flying up to leaves above it, returning to different places on the branch. Also makes short irregular zigzag, whirring flights, apparently to dislodge prey. Large, hard insects are rubbed and hit on a perch and dismembered. Often joins mixed foraging parties. **Food** Arthropods, mainly insects 5–20 mm long, including Hymenoptera (black flying ants), Coleoptera (small beetles), Lepidoptera (moths and caterpillars) and Hemiptera (cicadas)[259, 294, 412, 456, 515, 676, 858].

SOUNDS Little known. Repertoire consists of repeated high-pitched whistles, harsh notes and bill-snapping. Nominate race virtually undescribed; reportedly makes a quiet rasping sound. Mainland race *occulta* has at least two territorial song types, both very high-pitched, sounding like a squeaky bicycle pump and usually introduced by a dry grating or buzzy trill. One series consists of a short repeated phrase of *c.*2–3 whistled notes, usually beginning with a buzzy trill *trrrr-ztztzt-eep-eep-eep.* A second more variable type consists of a long series of up to *c.*40 similar repeated high-pitched, often plaintive whistles *eep-eep-eep-* or *weep-weep-*, *tee-tee-* or *see-see-*. These series may also have the grating or buzzy introductory trill *trrrrr-ztztz-* or *juririri-weep-weep-weep-weep.* In what appears to be territorial threat, the whistles are repeated more slowly, often rapidly di- or trisyllabic (buzz followed by whistles) *zzzueep---zzzueep--*or *zeze-ze–zeze-ze* with the emphasis on the last note. Also delivers more rolling whistles, apparently in similar context, *jirrreeet-*, *prreet-*, *jurrweep-*, *juriririweep-*, also repeated many times at variable rates. Variations include *trrruuu-*, *churr-weee-pitpit*, or simply *weee-pitpit.* ♂♂ chasing each other repeat the churring note many times. Other sounds include bill-snapping and 'wing-fripping'. Many calls recall high-pitched, rapidly repeated camaroptera notes[412, 500, 504, 515, 664, 676].

BREEDING BIOLOGY Little known. Monogamous and territorial; defends territory all year. Density of 2.3 pairs/km^2 (Gabon)[294]. **Season** enlarged gonads Sep–Jan, fledged young Oct (Bioko)[412, 676]; ♂♂ enlarged testes Jan, Jun, nest-building Oct (Nigeria)[37]; nest-building Mar (Cameroon)[664]; ♀ incubating Jan, family parties Nov–Mar, mainly Feb–Mar (Gabon)[294]. **Displays *Courtship*** Three birds 'dancing' around each other thought to form part of courtship display[858]. Courtship-feeding probably present. **Nest** Built by both birds, ♂ giving a quiet, high-pitched *see-see-see-see-* call while building. A small neat cup, tightly built and well camouflaged, made of fibres and covered outside with pieces of bark. Placed in a tree, sometimes leafless, situated at the extremity of a branch in a fork 1–30 m (n=4) above ground[294, 515, 664, 676]. **Eggs** Unknown. **Incubation** Probably by ♀ only. ♂ feeds ♀ on and off nest. Period unknown[294, 515, 676]. No further breeding information, except that young appear to remain in parental territory, almost until the next breeding season[676].

MEASUREMENTS and WEIGHTS *B. p. poensis* ♂ (7) wing 50.5–54 (52.7), tail 30–31.5 (30.2); ♀ (4) wing 50–53 (51.6), tail 30–31 (30.4)412; ♂ (9) wing 50–57.0 (53.39), tail 29.0–32.0 (30.33), bill 15.0–17.0 (15.67), tarsus 14–15 (14.6); ♀ (4) wing 51.5–54.0 (52.38), tail 29.0–33.0 (31.12), bill 14.0–15.5 (15.00), tarsus 14–15 (14.3)[581, 676]; *occulta* ♂ (9) wing 47.0–52.0 (49.83), tail 27.0–31.5 (30.11), bill 13.5–15.5 (14.33); ♀ (4) wing 48.0–51.0 (49.50), tail 28.5–31.0 (29.83), bill 13.0–15.0 (14.50)[581]. **Weight** *poensis* ♂♀? (11) 9–10 g (9.6)[412]; *occulta* ♂ (2) 8.8–9.4 g (9.1), Imm. ♂ 9.2 g; ♀ (2) 8.7–9.0 g (8.9) (Liberia)[259].

95 GABON BATIS (Verreaux's Batis, Grey-headed Puff-back Flycatcher)
Batis minima **Plate 34**

FIELD IDENTIFICATION Very small (9–10 cm), restless, black and white flycatcher-like bird with black head and small white spot in front of yellow eye. Back grey, wing-stripe and outer tail feathers white. Sexes different. Below white, ♂ with broad black breast-band, head black with white spot in front of eye, white collar, white eyebrow indistinct, ♀ similar but with narrower grey breast-band and little white on face. Young like ♀ but with buff-tipped wing feathers. Little known; main call a long series of rapid short high-pitched whistles. In pairs or family group foraging in mid- to upper canopy in lowland forest, mainly secondary forest. Rare resident, restricted to S Cameroon and NE Gabon. ***Flight characteristics***: Fast with rapid wingbeats; wings rounded. Has a pied appearance and makes 'fripping' sounds with wings in flight.

COMPARISONS Similar to ♂ Bioko Batis *Batis poensis* (mainland race *occulta*), but ♀ of latter has a chestnut-brown (not grey) breast-band. Bioko Batis is slightly larger and has a blacker back (not greyish-black), a less distinct loral spot but a more distinct nape-patch. Main call also similar but slower, lower-pitched and often without the introductory buzz of Bioko Batis. Situation complicated by interspecific song-matching where both occur. When found together, Bioko Batis tends to feed higher up and inside the canopy, Gabon Batis on the periphery. ♂ also resembles ♂ Senegal Batis *B. senegalensis* and Black-headed Batis *B. minor*, but these are thornscrub and woodland species respectively, with greyer upperparts. ♀♀ have chestnut-brown breast-bands[676].

DESCRIPTION Adult ♂ ***Head*** Forehead and forecrown velvety-black with white spot on either side of bill at base (loral spot); face-mask velvety-black; hindcrown blackish-grey; very narrow white eyebrow; hindneck and centre of nape white; white on throat extending around sides of neck in the form of a collar. ***Back*** Mantle and upper back velvety-black; upper rump mottled dark slate-grey, white and black; lower rump white, feathers long and fluffy. ***Wings*** Primaries, secondaries and tertials velvety-black, outer webs and tips of secondaries and tertials broadly edged white forming white wing-stripe with tips of median coverts and broad white outer edges of inner secondary coverts; flight feathers fringed white on inner web. Underwing-coverts whitish. ***Tail*** Including uppertail-coverts velvety-black, outer feathers with narrow white edge. ***Underparts*** Chin and throat white, extending back almost to nape, rest white except for glossy blue-black breast-band (*c.*10–12 mm); flanks white mottled blackish-grey; thighs black faintly barred white; undertail-coverts white. ***Bare parts*** Bill black; palate unknown; legs black; eye golden-yellow[676]. Adult ♀ Like ♂ but duller, loral spot smaller and white eyebrow less distinctive. Underparts white with a dark grey, slightly narrower (*c.*8 mm) breast-band. Juvenile Upperparts brownish-black with creamy-buff specks on head, back and upperwing-coverts; wing-stripe tawny; underparts whitish with breast-band mottled whitish-grey and indistinct if present. Eye probably brown[500, 676]. Immature Like adult ♀ but lower throat, lower breast and edges of median upperwing-coverts tipped buffy-white; two outer tail feathers edged and tipped buffy-white. Eye yellow[456, 464, 500, 676].

GEOGRAPHICAL VARIATION None. Monotypic.

MOULT Unknown.

RANGE, HABITAT and STATUS **Breeding range** Restricted to N and S Gabon and S Cameroon in the lowland Dja area[295, 431, 715]. **Habitat** Lowland forested areas, usually below 800 m. Not found in primary forest except on borders. Found mainly in secondary forest with ill-defined vegetation layers, a dense low undergrowth and dense but discontinuous canopy, also bushes bordering heavy forest and old plantations (cacao and coffee). Avoids open cultivated lands, even with scattered tall bushes and trees; also avoids neighbourhood of villages and other man-made habitats. Possibly also avoids forest 'saturated' with wattle-eyes, particularly White-spotted Wattle-eye *Dyaphorophyia tonsa*[289, 295, 456, 676]. **Status** Local and uncommon resident. **Conservation status** In Gabon originally believed to be reasonably tolerant of forest disturbance, but now thought to be rare and localised, and known only from the Makokou region. In Cameroon it is an uncommon bird of second growth. Requires additional data; formerly listed as Data Deficient[294, 343, 378, 479, 715].

MOVEMENTS Unknown.

SOCIAL ORGANISATION and GENERAL BEHAVIOUR Solitary, in pairs or family groups. Restless but unobtrusive, moving over almost entire territory daily, individuals maintaining constant contact, mostly by sight. ♂ leads and irregularly gives short territorial song, particularly in morning and late afternoon. Home range varies from 18–20 ha (Gabon). Regularly attacked and repelled by Bioko Batis; reacts to it by ruffling crown feathers and, in upright or crouched posture, moves body from side to side, with jerky tail- and sometimes also wing-flicks. Sun-bathes during hottest hours of day, back feathers fluffed-out and wings half-spread and drooping[294, 456, 676]. **Foraging behaviour** Arboreal, in foliage 5–40 m from ground in bushes and canopy, mainly at 14–24 m. Moves about in highest part of tree canopy, but does not frequently change trees. Favours small-leaved trees with foliage not too dense, and is attracted by flowering trees. Typically hover-gleans below and on side of canopy. Moves about from twig to twig and makes short upward sallies or jumps (usually 0.5–2 m) to snatch prey in flight or from under leaves, usually after a brief hover, or makes short circular whirring flights and snaps up moving prey. Also actively moves through foliage to dislodge prey, which is then caught after a rapid swoop. Hawks insects in the air. Large prey items are rubbed and hit on perch and dismembered before ingestion. It often joins mixed foraging parties. **Food** Arthropods, mainly insects, including many Coleoptera (beetles) and Hymenoptera (wasps, bees and ants), also Isoptera (termites) and spiders. Most prey items appear to be 5–15 mm long[22, 294, 456, 504, 676].

SOUNDS Little known. Territorial song a long series of very high, even-pitched thin short notes *pti-pti-pti..* or *eep-eep-eep-eep-* sounding like a squeaky bicycle pump. Rate of delivery varies, but generally 2–3 notes/sec. Sometimes gives a buzzy introductory phase similar to Bioko Batis. Call described as lower-pitched (0.7–1.0 kHz) and usually slower (intervals between 0.5 not 0.35 sec) than Bioko Batis. Similarity in calls complicated as they seem to copy one another when they meet, countersinging like other batises. Contact calls a variety of soft, clucking, buzzing, downslurred or upslurred notes emitted by both sexes. Countersings with White-spotted Wattle-eye[456, 500, 515, 676, 740].

BREEDING BIOLOGY Little known. Monogamous and territorial. Occurs in densities of 3 pairs/2 km² in old plantations or only 1 pair/km² in younger growth (Gabon)[294]. **Season** Young observed during rainy season following a short dry season. Probably Sep and Feb (Gabon)[294]. No further breeding information, except young stay with parents almost to next breeding season; some solitary and probably dispersing immatures seen in Jul–Aug during long dry season[676].

MEASUREMENTS and WEIGHTS *B. minima* ♂ (4) wing 49–50 (49.5), tail 31–33 (32.1), bill 11.5–13.5 (12.1), tarsus 11.5–13.5 (12.5); ♀ (4) wing 47.5–49 (48.0), tail 29–33 (31.75), bill 11.5–12 (11.75), tarsus 12–13 (12.5)[676]. **Weight** ♂♀? (5) 8–12 g (10.0) (Gabon)[676]; ♂ (1) 12 g, ♀ (1) 10 g, Imm ♂ (1) 11 g, Imm ♀ (1) 9 g[464]. For additional data see[287, 464, 578].

96 RUWENZORI BATIS *Batis diops* — Plate 34

FIELD IDENTIFICATION Very small (11–12 cm), dumpy, restless, black and white flycatcher-like bird with broad black breast-band and conspicuous white spot in front of eye. Above dark bluish-black with conspicuous white wing-stripe. Sexes similar, except eye colour: ♂ yellow, ♀ orange-red. Young similar to adults but with brown eye and buff spotting on head and upper back. Flight rapid with 'fripping' sounds. Little known; more often heard than seen; main call a series of low-pitched whistles. Solitary or in pairs at all levels, mainly low down in dense undergrowth of montane and bamboo forest. Resident from SW Uganda, W Rwanda, W Burundi and E Zaïre in Ruwenzori Mountains. ***Flight characteristics***: Fast, dipping with rapid wingbeats; wings rounded. Has a pied appearance and makes 'fripping' sounds with wings.

COMPARISONS Similar to Ituri Batis *Batis ituriensis*, which is a much smaller lowland forest species. Ruwenzori Batis replaces Ituri at higher altitudes, from *c.*1300 m. Both species lack sexual plumage dimorphism, although ♀ Ituri Batis sometimes has a thin whitish eyebrow. Also similar to woodland ♂ Chinspot Batis *B. molitor* and Black-headed Batis *B. minor*, which have conspicuous white eyebrow (Ruwenzori only has a small white spot in front of eye). Where Ruwenzori meets these species, it tends to forage lower down, under cover. ♀ Chinspot and Black-headed have a chestnut-brown breast-band (not black as in ♀ Ruwenzori Batis). The whistled calls of both these species are much higher-pitched. Some ♂ wattle-eyes show a superficial resemblance with their broad black breast-band[717].

DESCRIPTION ADULT ♂ ***Head*** Forehead glossy bluish-black with white spot on either side (loral spot); rest of head, sides of face to below eyes and ear-coverts glossy bluish-black. This colour extends back to form a narrow black line around lower hindneck; hindcrown and nape dark bluish-grey. ***Back*** Mantle dark grey with some glossy bluish-black feathers; scapulars black; rump dark grey to blackish, with concealed white spots, feathers long and fluffy; uppertail-coverts dark grey to blackish. ***Wings*** Primaries bluish-black with slight gloss on outer webs; white wing-stripe formed by white tips to median coverts, broad white outer edges to inner secondary coverts, and broad white edges and tips to tertials and inner secondaries; greater and median primary wing-coverts black; outer and inner greater coverts black, middle and median coverts white, lesser coverts black. Underwing-coverts white. ***Tail*** Black, outermost feathers with white edges and tips, rest tipped white. ***Underparts*** Chin white with small black spot at top; throat white, extending back to form a broken collar; broad breast-band glossy bluish-black (*c.*15–18 mm wide); belly, flanks and undertail-coverts white; sides below wings grey; thighs black. ***Bare parts*** Bill black, palate unknown; legs dark slate-grey to black; eye golden-yellow with dark rim[500, 676]. ADULT ♀ Like ♂ but with red or orange eye. Reports of ♂♂ with this eye colour are probably incorrectly sexed[289, 717]. JUVENILE/IMMATURE Similar to adult, but with crown, mantle, back and rump heavily spotted rusty brown to buff-brown. Scapulars, tertials and wing-coverts tipped buff, inner secondaries edged white. Breast and wing-stripe probably with some rufous. Initial eye colour probably brown, this changing to orange in young ♂[22, 289, 500, 676].

GEOGRAPHICAL VARIATION None. Monotypic.

MOULT Sep–Oct (Rwanda)[717].

RANGE, HABITAT and STATUS **Breeding range** Rift mountains: Ruwenzori to Itombwe and NE Shaba in SW Uganda, W Rwanda, W Burundi and Zaïre in W Ruwenzori. **Habitat** In lower levels of montane evergreen forest from 1340–3300 m. Most abundant in low closed bamboo forest on ridges. Also in mixed forest and scrub country. Optimum habitat in Rwanda is low closed forest on ridges[22, 314, 431, 481, 492, 676, 717]. **Status** Resident, common to very common[676, 688]. **Conservation status** Possibly threatened due to restricted distribution; however, within its range it is generally common[343].

MOVEMENTS Unknown.

SOCIAL ORGANISATION and GENERAL BEHAVIOUR Little known. Solitary or in pairs. A dumpy, shy and restless bird, constantly on the move. Tends to keep under cover[22, 676, 717]. **Foraging behaviour** Usually at low (1–3 m) and mid levels of undergrowth, often 2–6 m above ground, also in middle growth of high trees and their tops. Hops about, snatching insects from bark and undersides of leaves; also takes prey in the air during short flights[289, 676, 717, 767]. **Food** Arthropods, mainly insects, including many Coleoptera (beetles), Diptera (small flies) and other flying insects and Lepidoptera (caterpillars)[289, 676].

SOUNDS Repertoire consists of drawn-out whistles, harsh and churring sounds and bill-snapping. Territorial song a series of slowly delivered, low-pitched, ventriloquial, eerie, rather drawn-out whistles *theeoooo....*, *heeoooo...* or *fuu...* or *tuuu....tuuu....* with intervals of *c.*2–4 sec between notes. Pitch may change towards end of series. Notes reminiscent of Grey-headed Bush-shrike *Malaconotus blanchoti*. This whistle often followed by a sharp *chik*, *zik* or *Wik* to produce *tuuu-zik*, possibly also in duet by ♀, although known to be given by same individual, and often heard when bird is excited. Other short call notes include sharp *ch-k!* or *ck-k-k* and chuntering or compressed churring (probably similar to stone-rubbing sounds of other forest batises), *ch-k-oick-k-k-* or *chchchchrrrrr* and *tweer-tweer*, apparently used by ♂, to which ♀ responds with bill-snapping. Both sexes produce the churring sounds, and birds respond to each other with stone-rubbing *chchchurrr-* calls. Contact call a rather deep *tcweer tcweer*. Churring call used in alarm and aggression by both sexes. Whistled notes similar to Forest Batis *Batis mixta*, churring notes different[22, 289, 500, 515, 672, 676, 717, 767]. Sonagram[717].

BREEDING BIOLOGY Virtually unknown. Probably monogamous and territorial as neighbouring pairs dispute territorial boundaries. Found in densities of 2–3 pairs/10 ha in optimum habitat[676, 717]. **Season** Probably throughout the year; Jul–Nov, also Mar–Jun, juveniles Aug, Oct (Zaïre)[22]; Aug–Jan (Rwanda)[717]; juvenile Aug (Uganda)[676]. No further breeding information, except breeding ♀ is regularly fed by ♂. Although nests have been found, neither the nest nor its contents has been described[676, 717].

MEASUREMENTS and WEIGHTS *B. diops* ♂ (23) wing 60.0–66.5 (63.09), tail 38.0–43.0 (40.87), bill 14.5–16.0 (15.52), ♂ (4) tarsus 18–19 (18.5); ♀ (16) wing 61.0–66.0 (63.25), tail 40.0–43.0 (41.60), bill 14.0–16.0 (15.43), ♀ (2) tarsus 19[287, 676]. **Weight** ♂ (19) 11–15.5 g (12.8); ♀ (6) 8–15 g (12.4) (Uganda)[676]; ♂♀? (4) av. 12.7 g (Rwanda/Burundi)[457]; ♂♀? (5) 12.1–14.4 g (12.9)[876].

97 ITURI BATIS *Batis ituriensis* Plate 34

FIELD IDENTIFICATION Very small (9.5–10 cm), black and white flycatcher-like bird, white below with a broad black breast-band, black head with conspicuous white spot in front of yellow eye and a distinct white collar. Back black, wing-stripe and outer tail feathers white. Sexes similar, except ♀ has thin white eyebrow. Young spotted buff above, below dusky-grey on breast, and wing feathers tipped buff. Little known; call unknown, probably a series of high-pitched whistles. In pairs or family group foraging in canopy of degraded lowland forest, secondary growth and cultivated areas with scattered high trees. Resident, uncommon in E Congo basin in E and NE Zaïre and W Uganda. ***Flight characteristics***: Wings rounded, has pied appearance.

COMPARISONS Similar to montane forest Ruwenzori Batis *Batis diops*, both species lacking sexual plumage dimorphism, although ♀ Ituri Batis sometimes has a thin whitish eyebrow. Ituri differs in being a much smaller lowland forest species with black upperparts (not grey as in Ruwenzori Batis) and less pronounced white spots at base of bill and with distinct white collar. Ituri Batis is the only batis in lowland forests of E Zaïre. Ruwenzori Batis replaces Ituri at higher altitudes, from *c.*1300 m. Where the two occur together, Ituri tends to forage higher up. Calls of Ruwenzori Batis are repeated low-pitched whistles, those of Ituri Batis are unknown, but will probably be found to consist of a series of high-pitched whistles[500]. Also similar to drier woodland ♂ batises like Chinspot Batis *B. molitor* and Black-headed Batis *B. minor*, which have conspicuous white eyebrows and much greyer upperparts. ♀♀ of these woodland species have a chestnut-brown breast-band (not black like ♀ Ituri Batis).

DESCRIPTION ADULT ♂ ***Head*** Forehead glossy

bluish-black with white spot at base of bill (loral spot); forecrown, sides of crown, lores, cheeks and ear-coverts glossy bluish-black, including area below lores and above eye, and extending backwards; hindcrown and nape dark bluish-grey with pale nape-patch which is linked to the underparts by a white collar; hindneck dark grey. ***Back*** Mantle glossy bluish-black or dark grey; scapulars blackish; rump and uppertail-coverts dark grey, rump fluffy with indistinct white spots. ***Wings*** Primaries black with slight gloss, secondaries black, narrowly tipped white, tertials black. White wing-stripe formed by white tips to median coverts and broad white outer edges to inner secondary coverts; tertials and a few inner secondaries with broad white edging on outer web; greater and median coverts and alula black, outer median coverts white, lesser coverts black. Underwing-coverts whitish. ***Tail*** Black with outer feathers edged white and sometimes tipped white. Other feathers, except central pair, sometimes also tipped white. ***Underparts*** Chin to undertail-coverts white except for broad (*c*.9–13 mm) glossy bluish-black breast-band; flanks white; thighs black. ***Bare parts*** Bill black; palate unknown; legs black; eye yellow[676]. **ADULT** ♀ Like ♂; may have a thin whitish eyebrow, but not always obvious in field. Young and adult ♀♀ tend to show more white[500, 676, 735]. **JUVENILE** Upperparts dark greyish, densely spotted cream-white on head; ear-coverts and sides of nape blackish; underparts white, sides of breast dusky-grey; tail and wings blackish with creamy edging to wing-stripe; eye dark[492]. **IMMATURE** Like adult ♀ but duller; sides of throat and neck and edges of upperwing-coverts buff, primary wing-coverts tipped buff[676].

GEOGRAPHICAL VARIATION None. Monotypic.

MOULT Unknown.

RANGE, HABITAT and STATUS Breeding range E Congo basin: NE Zaïre from Buta (2°48′N 24°47′E) in N to Kakanda (3°14′S 28°20′E) and W Uganda in Budongo Forest. **Habitat** Lowland forests (900–1300 m), particularly degraded lowland forest, secondary growth and cultivated areas with scattered high trees; avoids primary forest[431, 492, 676]. **Status** Rare, apparently resident[289, 676, 688]. **Conservation status** Unknown.

MOVEMENTS Unknown.

SOCIAL ORGANISATION and GENERAL BEHAVIOUR Little known. Solitary, in pairs or small family group. Groups of *c*.6 birds also recorded. Restless and very active in tops of trees[688]. **Foraging behaviour** Arboreal, mainly in canopy of tall trees and mid-canopy down to 5–6 m above ground. Hops from twig to twig to glean foliage. Frequently joins mixed foraging parties[289, 338, 735]. **Food** Insects, including Isoptera (termites)[676, 735].

SOUNDS Unknown; erroneously reported as possibly similar to Bioko Batis *B. poensis*[515, 676]. Based on the comparison of visual characters and its relationships to other batises, it is predicted that Ituri Batis will be found to have a high-pitched cisticola-like call similar to the W forest and N savanna woodland batises[500].

BREEDING BIOLOGY Unknown, probably monogamous. ♂ seen to feed ♀ (Uganda)[676]. **Season** breeding Feb–Apr and Aug, juvenile Jun, nestling Jul (Zaïre)[22, 289, 492, 688]; ♂ feeding ♀ Mar (Uganda)[676, 735]. No further breeding information.

MEASUREMENTS and WEIGHTS *B. ituriensis* ♂ (8) wing 47–52 (49.1), tail 29–32.5 (30.5), bill 14–14.5 (14.1), ♂ (3) tarsus 13.5–14 (13.7); ♀ (4) 47–51.5 (49.6), tail 27–33 (30.2), bill 13.5–14.5 (14.0), tarsus 12.5–14.5 (13.2)[676]. **Weight**: unknown. For additional data see[287, 289, 464, 492, 578, 688].

98 BANDED WATTLE-EYE (Bamenda Wattle-eye)

Platysteira laticincta **Plate 35**

FIELD IDENTIFICATION Small (11–12 cm) black and white flycatcher-like bird with fleshy red eye-wattle. Sexes different. ♂ glossy blue-black above, white below with broad glossy blue-black breast-band. ♀ like ♂ above, below with white chin, glossy blue-black throat and breast, and white belly. Young dark brown above, white below with brownish-buffy to blackish throat and breast. Little known; main call a repeated series of rather harsh high-pitched unmusical notes. Usually in pairs foraging at all levels up to canopy of montane forest. Resident, localised to Bamenda-Banso Highlands of W Cameroon. ***Flight characteristics***: Wings rounded, makes 'wing-fripping' sounds in flight.

COMPARISONS Distinctive. Similar to more southern Black-throated Wattle-eye *Platysteira peltata*, but differs above by being blue-black (not greenish-black) (unlikely to be visible in field) and in ♂ a much broader breast-band. Calls appear higher-pitched. Ranges separate. Overlaps with Brown-throated Wattle-eye *P. cyanea*, which is a much more vocal species, with a white wing-stripe in both sexes and a brown throat in ♀. Generally Banded Wattle-eye replaces Brown-throated at higher elevations, although sometimes they are found together. Young separated by narrow rufous to rusty-buff wing-stripe in Brown-throated (lacking in Banded Wattle-eye). Other wattle-eyes are smaller, appear almost tailless and do not have red eye-wattles[605].

DESCRIPTION Adult ♂ See Description of Black-throated Wattle-eye p.323. Similar to *Platysteira peltata* race *mentalis*, which also has a glossy bluish-black, not grey- or greenish-black mantle. The main distinguishing character in ♂ is the much broader breast-band (*c.*15 mm). Banded Wattle-eye also has a slightly shorter, broader bill and shorter tail than Black-throated Wattle-eye. ***Bare parts*** Bill black; palate unknown; legs purplish-black; eye variable from reddish-brown, brownish-grey or bluish; wattle bright red and fleshy. **ADULT** ♀ Similar to ♂ but with throat to upper breast blue-black as upperparts; chin white. **JUVENILE** Unknown, probably similar to Black-throated Wattle-eye. **IMMATURE** Head and upperparts dark brown; flight feathers edged and upperwing-coverts tipped tawny to pale brown. Underparts: Chin white; brown throat and upper breast, latter mixed with black; rest of underparts white tinged buffy-grey on flanks. Bare parts: Bill black, legs purplish-black; eye reddish-brown; wattle small and red[347, 504].

GEOGRAPHICAL VARIATION None. Monotypic.

MOULT Unknown.

RANGE, HABITAT and STATUS **Breeding range** Endemic to Bamenda–Banso Highlands in the Kilum (Oku) Mountain forests, W Cameroon. **Habitat** Montane forest and forest edge, often associated with *Podocarpus* and bamboo forest. Also found in forest underplanted by subsistence crops. Occurs from *c.*1700–2400 m. Generally replaced at lower elevations by Brown-throated Wattle-eye[15, 343, 347, 431, 643]. **Status** Resident, locally common. **Conservation status** Habitat on the Bamenda-Banso Highlands was reduced by half, due to rapid deforestation, in the period 1965–1985. Its best chance of survival is thought to be on Mt Oku (Kilum-Ijim), which covers *c.*100 km² of suitable habitat and is currently the target of a major BirdLife International conservation and development project. Red Data Book species now considered Vulnerable[343, 479, 485, 756].

MOVEMENTS Unknown.

SOCIAL ORGANISATION and GENERAL BEHAVIOUR Little known. Solitary or in pairs. General behaviour known to be similar to both Black-throated and Brown-throated Wattle-eyes. In territorial interactions birds are generally silent as they posture in front of each other with the neck stretched up[515]. **Foraging behaviour** Arboreal, at all levels up to canopy, usually in undergrowth, where hops or makes short flights to snatch insects off foliage. Also hawks insects in flight[15, 343, 347, 504]. **Food** insects.

SOUNDS Little known. Apparently a rather silent bird. One recording of a call has similar structure to Black-throated Wattle-eye but is higher-pitched. Begins with harsh single repeated *zit-zit-zit-* notes, followed by double *huweet-huweet-* or *zrrhuweet-zrrhuweet-*. The terminal *weet* notes are high-pitched and sound like a squeaky bicycle pump. Contact call described as a soft grating noise. Alarm a repeated *tsit-tsit-* combined with 'wing-fripping'[15, 347, 500, 504, 515].

BREEDING BIOLOGY Little known. Apparently monogamous and territorial. **Season** Oct–May, mainly Dec–Feb[338, 343, 347, 636]. **Displays** Unknown. **Nest** Role of sexes unknown. A small open cup of felted moss and lichen, lined with material like thistledown, wrapped with spider web and dry bark. Placed 0.4–6 m from the ground in fork of tree[15, 338, 636]. **Eggs** 1–3. Colour and pattern unrecorded[15, 636]. **Incubation** Role of sexes unknown. Period 15–17 days[636]. No further breeding information.

MEASUREMENTS and WEIGHTS *P. laticincta* ♂ (11) wing 64–70, tail 48–52, bill 11–13, tarsus 16–20; ♀ (6) wing 65–69, tail 47–54, bill 11–13, tarsus 18–20[347]; ♂ (2) wing 65–68 (66.5), tail 49–50 (49.5), bill (to skull) 16.5–17.5 (17.0), tarsus 18–19 (18.5)[500]. **Weight** ♂♀? (9) 13.2–15.2 g (14.3) includes juveniles (Cameroon)[676]; ♂♀? (2) 11.4–11.2 g (Cameroon)[757]. For additional data see[757].

99 BLACK-THROATED WATTLE-EYE *Platysteira peltata* Plate 35

FIELD IDENTIFICATION Small (12–13 cm) black and white flycatcher-like bird with fleshy bright red eye-wattle. Sexes different. ♂ glossy greenish blue-black above, white below with narrow glossy black breast-band. ♀ white below with glossy greenish blue-black throat and breast. Young pale brown and spotted above, white below with mottled buff throat and breast. More often heard than seen. Calls a series of squeaky, rasping notes usually in duet. In pairs active and noisy, foraging in lower and mid levels of montane and lowland evergreen and riverine forest. Resident with local austral winter movements. Occurs from Somalia through East Africa and Mozambique to South Africa and W through S Zaïre and Zambia to Angola. ***Flight characteristics***: Rather jerky and short. Makes 'fripping' sounds with wings in flight, especially in display. Wings rounded, white in rump conspicuous when rump feathers fluffed-out.

COMPARISONS Most similar to more northern Banded Wattle-eye *Platysteira laticincta* in West Africa, which is glossy blue-black (no greenish gloss), and ♂ with a much broader breast-band. Ranges separate. Confusion with Brown-throated *P. cyanea* and White-fronted *P. albifrons* unlikely as both have distinctive white wing-stripes (lacking in Black-throated). ♀ Brown-throated has a brown throat and ♀ White-fronted has a white throat (throat black in Black-throated). Black-throated Wattle-eye usually found at higher elevations where they overlap. Other wattle-eyes are smaller, appear almost tailless and lack red eye-wattles.

DESCRIPTION ADULT ♂ ***Head*** Crown, nape and sides of head black with slight metallic bluish-green gloss. ***Back*** including mantle and scapulars Dark slate-grey with slight metallic greenish blue-black gloss; rump slate-grey, whitish at base, feathers long and fluffy. ***Wings*** Upperwing-coverts and tertials glossy greenish blue-black; primaries and secondaries dull black. ***Tail*** Uppertail-coverts and tail glossy green-black. Outer feathers narrowly edged and tipped white, remainder with small white tip decreasing inwards. ***Underparts*** Chin to undertail-coverts white, except for a narrow (*c*.2–5 mm) glossy greenish blue-black breast-band; flanks greyish-white; thighs black faintly barred white. ***Bare parts*** Bill black; palate pink to reddish (previously erroneously described as black); legs blackish slate-grey; eye brown, outer ring purplish or grey, white around pupil; fleshy wattle above and in front of eye bright red to scarlet-vermilion[90, 205]. ADULT ♀ Like ♂ but chin white, throat and breast glossy greenish blue-black. Wattle may be slightly smaller. **JUVENILE** Upperparts pale brown to greyish-brown, feathers (including wing-coverts) tipped buffy-rufous giving a spotted appearance; underparts dull creamy-white; eye brown; small orange-red wattle, evident after about a month[91, 676, 871]. **IMMATURE** Upperparts dull brownish- to bluish-grey; wings and tail blackish-brown; upperwing-coverts, tertials and inner secondaries edged tawny to rusty-brown; underparts creamy-white; throat and sides of breast mottled tawny-and-buff, progressively developing black; eye brown; palate pink; eye-wattle small, varying from pale orange, pink or dull red depending on age. Adult plumage attained after 12–14 months. Between 25–40 days pale orange wattles begin to develop, as well as pale brown smudges on breast. At 55 days upperparts greyer, edges of wing-coverts pale golden-brown. Sexes identifiable at *c*.95 days and wattles dark red at *c*.115 days[90, 91, 93, 676].

GEOGRAPHICAL VARIATION At least three races, variation being mainly in colour of upperparts. Nominate *peltata* (E Zambia, S Malawi, E lowlands of Zimbabwe, Mozambique S of Zambezi River, E South Africa) has glossy green tinge to upperparts; *mentalis* (including *jacksoni*) (W Kenya, W Tanzania, Uganda, Zaïre, N, W Zambia and Angola) has upperparts, breast-band of ♂ and throat and breast of ♀ with glossy blue-black tinge; *cryptoleuca* (Somalia, E Kenya, E Tanzania, Mozambique N of Zambezi River, S, SE Zambia, N, W and S Malawi, E highlands of Zimbabwe) has mantle darker and blacker than nominate and strongly glossed green[30, 291, 601, 631, 676, 851].

MOULT Contour feather moult takes place soon after fledging, resulting in a dull blue-grey plumage above, and below a pale grey or grey-buff throat, incomplete tawny breast-band, and usually tawny flanks. Rest of underparts white. Post-juvenile moult begins on head and tail, with the primaries and their coverts the last adult feathers to appear. At this stage sexual plumage dimorphism evident[90]. For additional data see[93].

RANGE, HABITAT and STATUS Breeding range mainly S of equator. In W from central and N Angola, S and E Zaïre, Rwanda, Burundi, S and W Uganda, W and SE Kenya, S Somalia, N, central and E Tanzania, Malawi, Zambia, N, E and S Zimbabwe, Mozambique, E Swaziland, E South Africa, vagrant further S to East London. **Habitat** N populations inhabit montane forest up to 3000 m. East and S populations mainly in lowland and escarpment evergreen forest, gallery and riverine forest often near water. Also in remnant forests, thickets, coffee plantations, mangroves and gardens. Southern birds wander into drier habitats in non-breeding season. There is some evidence that in E Zambia, Malawi and Zimbabwe it appears to be replaced by Cape Batis *Batis capensis* in moist montane forests, suggesting competitive exclusion. Woodwards' Batis *B. fratrum* may also be in competition with the wattle-eye[7, 26, 30, 119, 291, 325, 431, 481, 631, 639, 676, 717, 907]. **Status** Uncommon to locally common resident with local movements. **Conservation status** In S many populations appear dependent on riverine and coastal forests for breeding and seasonal movements. Deforestation of riverine woodlands and the threat from mining in coastal forests in South Africa could result in populations becoming more isolated. Situation in Mozambique unknown, but conservation areas are likely to be under threat due to political instability[500, 859, 1071].

MOVEMENTS Northern populations apparently sedentary; S populations undergo some seasonal movements, including downward altitudinal movements in non-breeding season, often into drier habitats. Some movements are extensive[205, 850].

SOCIAL ORGANISATION and GENERAL BEHAVIOUR Little known. Solitary, in pairs or family group. Restless, seldom sitting still for long. Noisy in breeding season with much territorial calling and duetting by pair, who advertise and defend a territory as small as *c*.1 ha in mangroves. Often calls from an exposed perch beneath the canopy, adopts an upright posture, tail slightly fanned, and in ♂ white throat expands as a conspicuous visual signal, and head is swayed purposefully from side to side. Also seen to interact silently, opponents posturing in front of each other with the neck stretched up. During intense territorial interactions opponents bow and oscillate rapidly from side to side. Species also engage in zigzag display-flights accompanied by loud 'wing-fripping'. In aggressive interactions flies directly at intruder with loud 'wing-fripping' and bill-snapping. Roosting behaviour unknown. Scratches indirectly[205, 500, 515]. **Foraging behaviour** Arboreal, mainly in mid- to lower levels of forest. Continually on the move, hopping and creeping with head moving rapidly about while searching for prey. Birds dart upwards to pick prey off lower surface of leaves or from branches, often hovering briefly before capturing items with an audible snap of bill. Also hawks insects on the wing, often with audible 'wing-fripping' sounds. Occasionally the wings are used to flush prey as it moves through vegetation, and it will often join mixed foraging parties[46, 205]. **Food** Arthropods, mainly insects including, Lepidoptera (moths, butterflies and caterpillars), Diptera (flies), Orthoptera (grasshoppers and crickets). Small caterpillars fed to nestlings[8, 46, 500].

SOUNDS Repertoire consists of repeated squeaky and harsh sounds, and bill-snapping. Territorial song variable, both individually and geographically. Consists of a series of rather harsh rasping unmusical squeaky sounds in a phrase with a slight nasal quality. Both sexes give similar, but slightly different-pitched calls, ♂ lower than ♀. Phrase usually begins with a few single simple notes, followed by more complex double notes; *zit-zit-zit-wich-wich-wichy-wichy-wichy-*, also described as *djip-djip-djip-dijp-zipweet-zipweet-* or *tek-tek-tek-tedaah-tedaah.* Variations include *chewy-chewy-chewy-*, *chik-cluk-cluck-jeeery* or longer *cluck- cluk-clik-cluk-cluk-jeeery*, *clo-jeeery* and *jip-jip-zik-keek-zik-keek.* ♀ duets with higher-pitched *weech-weech-* notes in combination with ♂. In high-intensity territorial interactions calls are mainly higher-pitched, ♂ *wech-wech-*, ♀ *weechy-weechy-*. Also rapidly repeated *ptec-ptec-ptec-* followed by long unbroken series of harsh sawing *-jutzy-jutzy-jutzy-* or *dzitta-dzitta-dzitta-* accompanied by loud 'wing-fripping'. Also reported giving a tinkling song *er-er-fee, er-er-fee-fu.* In alarm rapidly snaps or clicks bill, producing a sharp staccato *chit-chit-chit-*. Contact maintained with *juk, zuk* or metallic-sounding *zing, jing* or *zee* calls. Begging call a nasal persistent rapid harsh chattering or buzzing *chchchchchch-* or slower *ch-ch-ch-ch-*[8, 46, 48, 91, 205, 289, 338, 500, 676]. Sonagram[48].

BREEDING BIOLOGY Little known. Monogamous and territorial with possible helpers, probably immatures from previous brood. Very aggressive during nest-building. Estimated density in NE South Africa 45 birds/km^2. May breed in first year, and lay multiple clutches. In 25 nests in Zimbabwe, 31 of 48 eggs produced fledglings[90, 205, 676, 871, 1071].

Season Sep (Zaïre)[289]; Sep–Oct, ♂ enlarged gonads Aug (Angola)[7, 865, 907]; Apr–Jun, Aug–Nov, Dec (East Africa)[293]; Dec, Jan, breeding condition Aug (Tanzania)[336]; Aug–Mar (Mozambique)[26]; May–Dec (Malawi)[119]; Sep–Dec, Apr–May (Zambia)[291]; Sep–Feb, mainly Sep–Dec (Zimbabwe)[30]; Jul–Mar, mainly Oct–Nov (South Africa)[48].

Displays *Courtship* Courtship-feeding common, beginning before nest-building, with ♂ feeding mate continuously; she begs with incessant harsh chattering *chchchchchch-*, in crouched, wing-fluttering posture. Courtship display thought to be similar to high-intensity territorial display, and includes fluffed-out rump feathers, zigzag flights, 'wing-fripping' and excited *weechy-weechy-* calling. ♂ has also been seen to dive repeatedly to the ground below the nest, returning to the same perch while ♀ begs nearby. In between nest-building ♀ observed to fly above nest, bobbing and hovering over it, and then flying to ♂ for food. During early incubation she has also been seen to do a zigzag display-flight away from nest. ♂ fluffs out rump feathers prior to copulation. ♀ also observed to attempt reversed copulation with the ♂[91, 205, 500].

Nest Built by both sexes, mainly by ♀. A small shallow neat cup of fine plant material, grass, fibres and small pieces of bark bound with spider web, and sometimes camouflaged on the outside with lichens or dry leaves. Cup may be lined with *Usnea* beard-lichen, bark fibres, plant down or small feathers. Placed at *c.*5 m (0.3–12, n=24) above ground in fork of branch in a small tree, sometimes on drooping branch below thick foliage. Occasionally placed over water. ***Size*** OD 58 mm, ID 43 mm, cup depth 25 mm, height 56 mm. Pair has a strong fidelity to nest site[90, 91, 205, 299, 500, 676].

Eggs Usually 2 (1–2, n=25). Pale green or blue, or grey-green to greenish-white, densely marked with spots and blotches of reddish-brown, browns or grey-brown, with pale purple, slate, lilac and grey-blue undermarkings, particularly around large end, the rest mostly finely speckled pale brown. ***Size*** 16.5–18.5 x 13–14.3 mm (18.0 x 13.7, n=8) (southern Africa)[19, 46, 48, 90, 676]. **Incubation** By both sexes, mainly by ♀ who is fed on and off nest by ♂, who provides most of her food during the period from nest-building to hatching. ♂ gives a *juk-juk-* contact call on approach to nest, to which ♀ responds by begging. Period 16–18 days. **Nestling** Hatch blind, naked and pink, gape yellow and lacks mouth spots. Attended by both sexes, initially ♀ feeds nestlings with food provided by herself and ♂. Nestlings sheltered from the hot sun by ♀. Food obtained from nearby by ♀, further away by ♂. Fledge after 13–16 days. Dependency period unknown, but at least a few weeks. Young remain with parents for *c.*6 months[27, 46, 634]. For development of plumage and eye wattle see Immature. **Predation and longevity** Nestlings known to be predated by Tropical Boubou *Laniarius aethiopicus* and Grey-headed Bush-shrike *Malaconotus blanchoti*, as well as possibly by monkeys and snakes, which are both aggressively mobbed. Ringed bird ♂ 7–7.5, ♀ 5–5.5 years old[205, 657, 855, 1002]. **Brood parasite** Parasitised by African Emerald Cuckoo *Chrysococcyx cupreus*, possibly also Klaas's Cuckoo *C. klaas* in southern Africa. In Central and E Africa parasitised by Cassin's Honeybird *Prodotiscus insignis*, possibly also Eastern Honeyguide *Indicator meliphilus*, which is known to be chased by the wattle-eye[46, 94, 676, 856].

MEASUREMENTS and WEIGHTS *P. p. peltata* ♂ (38) wing 63–70 (65.1), ♀ (32) wing 62–67 (64.6), ♂♀? (5) tail 51–54, ♂♀? (5) bill 14–16, ♂♀? (5) tarsus 17–19[48]. **Weight** *peltata* ♂ (60) 11.4–17 g (13.6), ♀ (56) 10–18.8 g (13.8) (southern Africa)[48, 93, 205]. For additional data see[90, 486, 676, 851, 911].

100 BROWN-THROATED WATTLE-EYE (Common, Scarlet-spectacled Wattle-eye) *Platysteira cyanea* Plate 35

FIELD IDENTIFICATION Small (12–14 cm) black and white flycatcher-like bird with bright red eye-wattle and conspicuous white wing-stripe. Sexes different. ♂ black above with broad black breast-band, white throat and belly. ♀ grey-black above with dark chestnut-brown throat and breast, and white belly. Young browner and spotted buff above; eye-wattle small pinkish-grey; wing-stripe and throat pale rusty-buff. Flight jerky, wing-stripe distinctive. Usually heard before seen: far-carrying short series of descending whistles interspersed with harsh notes in duet. Bill-snapping and 'wing-fripping' common. Solitary, in pairs or family group, mainly foraging in mid-levels of variety of lowland habitats, usually forest edge, clearings or riverine. Widespread resident with seasonal movements from Senegal across Central Africa, including Congo basin and N Angola to Ethiopia, Uganda, Kenya, Rwanda and NW Tanzania. ***Flight characteristics***: Rather slow, hesitant and jerky; makes 'fripping' sounds with wings. White wing-stripe conspicuous.

COMPARISONS ♀ separated from Black-throated *Platysteira peltata*, Banded *P. laticincta* and White-fronted Wattle-eyes *P. albifrons* by deep chestnut-brown throat and breast. ♂ distinguished from Black-throated and Banded by white on wing and broad black breast-band, from White-fronted by entirely black (not grey) upperparts and narrow white edges of outer tail feathers. All other wattle-eyes are very small, almost tailless and do not have white wing-stripes or red eye-wattles. Batises are smaller and lack eye-wattles. Some calls of Brown-throated Wattle-eye similar to descending whistles of Chinspot Batis *Batis molitor*.

DESCRIPTION ADULT ♂ ***Head and back*** Including crown, lores, mantle and scapulars black with purplish-blue to steel-blue sheen or gloss; rump slate-grey becoming white on lower rump (feathers grey edged white). Feathers long and fluffy. ***Wings*** Upperwing-coverts glossy blue-black, most median and inner greater coverts broadly edged (outer) and tipped white; primaries, secondaries and tertials black, inner secondaries and outer tertials narrowly edged white along outer web. ***Tail*** Glossy blue-black, including uppertail-coverts, outer feather edged and tipped white, remainder tipped white, extent decreasing on inner feathers. ***Underparts*** White except for broad glossy blue-black breast-band; flanks grey, thighs black. ***Bare parts*** Bill black; palate unknown; legs brownish-grey to purplish-black; eye pale blue-grey with pale inner ring around pupil; fleshy eye-wattle around eye, coral-red to orange-red above eye, dull grey rim below[425, 500, 676]. ADULT ♀ Like ♂ but upperparts dark slate-grey, rump paler; chin and narrow malar stripe white; throat and sides of neck deep chestnut-brown, bordered black on upper breast; eye-wattle similar to ♂ but smaller. JUVENILE Upperparts dull grey-brown, spotted buff to rusty-buff particularly on crown, nape and sides of head. Axillaries and upperwing-coverts tipped buff; wing-stripe dirty cream to rusty-buff. Broad white margins on tail feathers. Underparts whitish with greyish-buff tinge on sides of throat and breast[500, 504, 676]. IMMATURE Upperparts greyish-brown, more olive-grey on back and upperwing-coverts. Flight feathers narrowly edged tawny on outer web; wing-stripe white to tinged rufous-buff; greater upperwing-coverts tipped tawny. Underparts: Throat and foreneck whitish, tinged pale chestnut-brown, sides of throat and neck chestnut-brown; narrow breast-band greyish chestnut-brown; throat and breast becoming progressively more chestnut-brown, initially with scattered chestnut-brown feathers; Bare parts: Bill dark grey, paler at tip; legs brown; eye olive to grey-brown; small eye-wattle pinkish-grey to greyish-yellow, developing through orange-red to adult colour[500, 504, 576, 631, 676, 696].

GEOGRAPHICAL VARIATION Three races, variation in body size, presence or absence of white frontal line, and greyness of upperparts. Race *nyansea* (E Central African Republic to Sudan, Uganda, W Kenya and NW Tanzania) similar to nominate (Senegal, Gambia to W Central African Republic, E Zaïre and Angola) but has narrow white frontal line in both sexes, variable in ♀♀; *aethiopica* (SE Sudan, Ethiopia) greyer than nominate and smaller than *nyansea*[237, 295, 481, 500, 631].

MOULT Jun, Aug wing moult (Liberia)[330, 858].

RANGE, HABITAT and STATUS Breeding range Widespread in W, Central and NE Africa. Occurs from Senegal, Gambia, Guinea Bissau, Mali, Guinea, Sierra Leone, Liberia, Ivory Coast, Ghana, Togo, Benin, SE Burkina Faso, W Niger, Nigeria, Cameroon, S Chad, W Central African Republic, Equatorial Guinea (Rio Muni), Gabon, Congo, N Angola including Cabinda, Zaïre, Rwanda, Burundi, NW Tanzania, Uganda, W Kenya, S Sudan and Ethiopia. **Habitat** Edge of lowland forest, forest clearings and regenerating forest, forest–grassland mosaics, lowland open woodland, riverine forest in wooded savanna, moist savanna, wooded grassland and bushland, coastal woods, thickets, mangroves, mixed swamp forest and tall swamp grass, gardens, coastal farmland, plantations and around villages. Also occurs occasionally in montane forest (Liberia and Cameroon) and *Juniperus* and *Podocarpus* forests (Ethiopia). Found up to *c.*2200 m. Absent from arid Sahel and closed forest. In Cameroon replaced by Banded Wattle-eye above *c.*1500 m[7, 21, 23, 39, 101, 234, 239, 242, 347, 425, 431, 482, 676, 717, 829, 848, 858, 907]. **Status** Resident, generally common. **Conservation status** Not threatened. Held in captivity[655].

MOVEMENTS Local seasonal movements recorded in W Africa, e.g. in Gambia more common during rains in May–Sep[15, 39, 336, 338, 696].

SOCIAL ORGANISATION and GENERAL

BEHAVIOUR Solitary, in pairs or small family groups of *c.*4 birds. Confiding, restless, noisy and active all day. Occasionally in larger groups of *c.*30 birds (Jul, Liberia), gatherings probably similar to 'parliaments'. Pairs advertise and defend a territory of *c.*4 ha (n=4); an unmated ♂ defended 2.5 ha. Territorial song given by both sexes, includes duetting, and is given throughout the day from perches at all levels. Calling birds adopt a stiff posture with plumage fluffed-out. When an intruder is detected, territorial pair, particularly ♂, gives an irregular series of grunts while moving towards the intruder with loud 'wing-fripping' and bill-snapping, fluffed-out plumage and gives rasping song. ♂ gives territorial defence song from perch in upright posture exposing throat and breast. Increased aggression signalled by ruffling plumage, crouched posture, flicking wings and tail while scolding opponent with flight song, often accompanied by ♀. Mates maintain close contact all year, probably with movements (body, wing and tail) or by duetting. When anxious, calls and crouches with sleeked plumage, jerking head rapidly from side to side and wagging tail. When more alarmed, erects crown feathers and flies about with noisy 'wing-fripping' and tail-flicking. Mobbing bird swoops toward predator with crest erect, eye-wattles exposed while vigorously flapping wings and bill-snapping, making a rattling noise. Roosting behaviour unknown. Has been reported sunning on the ground[330, 500, 676, 688, 754, 849]. **Foraging behaviour** Arboreal, active all day foraging amongst foliage, mostly low down in undergrowth, in Gabon between 8–16 m, Liberia 3–10 m above ground, sometimes lower, rarely higher. Moves among branches, often working through clusters of leaves in erratic whirring flight to dislodge prey. Hops from twig to twig looking upwards in search of prey, head constantly moving, then sallying or jumping to snatch insects from underside of leaves, sometimes after a brief hover or swoop. Foraging behaviour often reminiscent of a tit as it searches foliage. Hawks insects in flight. Prey usually taken 0.5–1.5 m from perch, occasionally up to *c.*5 m. Large, venomous, or hard-bodied insects rubbed and pounded. Often joins mixed foraging parties[23, 294, 676, 688, 717, 858]. **Food** Arthropods, mainly insects and their larvae; mainly Coleoptera (beetles), Lepidoptera (caterpillars, moths and butterflies), Hymenoptera (bees, wasps, ants, including winged ants) and Isoptera (termites), Orthoptera (grasshoppers), Diptera (flies), Hemiptera (cicadas), Mantodea (mantises), Dictyoptera (cockroaches). Small snails also recorded. Prey size 5–40 mm, mainly 10–20 mm[15, 294, 456, 676, 758].

SOUNDS Repertoire consists of repeated whistles, harsh rasping sounds and bill-snapping. Territorial song remarkably variable, individually and geographically. It is given while perched or in flight, and consists of a slowly delivered series of 3–6 loud, far-carrying, musical whistles, variously arranged, the overall phrase being on a descending scale: *he-her-her-hur, hee-hee-hu-hu* or often in two parts separated by a long pause: *hee-huhuu-ho....hee-hu-ho, teee-tu-tee-tu- too, heepu-heepu-heep, huit-eee-yew-yeew* with variations. Whistled series are often combined with harsh, often nasal buzzing notes, reminiscent of Forest Weaver *Ploceus bicolor*: *zurr-* or double *zurr-zurr, churr, tcha- tcha-, zik, chikchikchurr- or zikzikzurr, zurrik*, also described as *EENH*. Other harsh calls reminiscent of batis stone-rubbing or chuntering sounds. At least some of these calls appear to be given in duet: *he-he-her-zurr-her-ho* or *eee-tee-EENH-eu*. Other longer duets consist of a wide variety of notes given by both partners. In the usual pattern, the ♀ combines her notes with those of ♂ in both parts of the song, to produce a complex duet. Sometimes the first part is given by ♂ and second part by ♀, in most cases with almost no break, so that the listener hears only one song: *ptip-tip-tee-way-way....hee-hee-hu-hu, hu-ho-he-he-hoo-chu, ptick-ptick-tick-twaa-psee-tsic-tsuc-tee-tuu*. Also gives a rhythmic *ptiup...touay- touay* changing to *ptyup...toway- toway...ptip-tyay*. High-intensity territorial song given in flight. Aggressive call a nasal rasping *toc-roway-roway* or *ptoc-rouay-oway*, and when excited a harsh rasping *cray-cray-cray-cray-...* and rattling sounds accompanied by bill-snapping and 'wing-fripping'. Bill opened wide when snapping bill. Begging call of ♀ a low, hardly audible snapping of the bill, that of young a rapid nasal *tzrray-tzzray*. Many notes resemble those of batises and *Dyaphorophyia* wattle-eyes[2, 22, 23, 294, 289, 504, 500, 631, 646, 676, 696, 754, 758, 767].

BREEDING BIOLOGY Little known. Monogamous and territorial. Density of *c.*12.5 pairs/km^2, also 4–5 ♂♂/10 ha recorded; 3–4 ♂♂/10 ha in high montane forest (Liberia). Birds are aggressive during breeding, chasing cuckoos, coucals and shrikes[294, 456, 676, 858]. **Season** Jan, Mar, Apr–Jul, Nov–Dec, mainly during rains (Gambia)[38, 39, 482, 696]; Nov, Dec; ♂♂ with enlarged gonads Apr (Sierra Leone)[338]; Jul, Oct; ♀♀ in breeding condition, independent young Dec, very vocal Oct–Jul (coastal) and Feb–Apr (Mt Nimba) (Liberia)[259, 858]; Apr–Aug (Ivory Coast)[676]; Jun, Aug; dependent young Nov (Ghana)[234]; fledglings being fed Sep (Togo)[697]; Dec–Aug, possibly all year (Nigeria)[37, 648, 690]; Feb, Mar, May, Dec; ♂♂ with enlarged gonads Mar and Nov, juveniles Mar, May, Aug (Cameroon)[676]; Feb, Aug; ♂♂ with enlarged gonads Oct–Feb; young Feb–Apr, Jun, Oct (Gabon)[294]; Sep (Equatorial Guinea)[338]; Aug–Sep (Congo)[295]; Aug–Sep, Dec (Rwanda)[676]; ♀♀ with enlarged gonads Mar, Jul–Aug (Central African Republic)[676]; Aug–Sep (Congo)[908]; Mar; ♂♀ with enlarged gonads Jan, Mar, Jul (Zaïre)[22, 289]; juvenile Mar, breeding condition Cabinda Sep (Angola)[907]; Jan–Apr, Jul, Dec (Sudan)[242, 336]; Feb, Apr–Jun, Aug, Nov–Dec (East Africa)[25, 293]. **Displays *Courtship*** ♂ flies around ♀ with 'wing-fripping' sounds, uttering a low-pitched churring song *tchi-chur-chur, tchi-chur-chi- chur* followed by *chii-chii-chii-chii*. Fluffing out of rump feathers and courtship-feeding of ♀ by ♂ common, beginning just before nest-building; ♀ begs with a low, hardly audible bill-snapping[767]. **Nest** Built by both sexes. A small neat cup made of coarse and fine vegetable fibres, moss, lined with fine grass stems, bound with spider web and camouflaged with lichens. Usually placed low down at *c.*2–8 m above ground in small fork near end of a thin leafy or hanging branch of small tree. ***Size*** OD 65–75 mm, ID 45–50 mm, cup depth 25–30 mm, height 55–65 mm[2, 289, 455, 676]. **Eggs** 2, laid at 1-day interval. Creamy, pale olive-brown, pale greenish or brownish-white, with dark brown and purplish-brown spots all over, more concentrated at the large end. ***Size*** 18–19 x 14 mm[15, 23, 289, 576, 676]. **Incubation** By ♀ only. She is regularly fed by ♂ and he guards her with scolding notes, bill-snapping and 'wing-fripping'. Period unknown[289]. **Nestling** Probably hatch blind and naked, mouth spots unknown. Later covered in soft woolly feathers, blackish-grey, finely spotted above with buffy tips; below white; wing-coverts tipped buff. Attended by both sexes. In first week ♂ brings food which ♀ passes to young. Period unknown. Once fledged, young fed by both sexes for at least 1 month, and may remain in parental territory almost until next breeding season[500, 500, 576]. No further breeding information.

MEASUREMENTS and WEIGHTS *P. c. cyanea* ♂ (8) wing 62–66 (64.0), tail 47–49 (47.6), bill 16–18 (16.9), tarsus 18–20 (19.4); ♀ (8) wing 63–66 (64.4), tail 48–52 (50.2), bill 16–18.5 (17.2), tarsus 18–20 (19.2)[676]. **Weight** ♂ (4) 13.5–15.0 g (14.3 ±0.6 g); ♀ (8) 11.6–14.5 g (13.0 ±0.9 g (Ghana)[582]. For additional data see[259, 494, 478, 582, 676].

101 WHITE-FRONTED WATTLE-EYE *Platysteira albifrons* Plate 36

FIELD IDENTIFICATION Very small (10–11 cm), dark grey and white flycatcher-like bird with bright red eye-wattles and white wing-stripe. Sexes different. ♂ with black head and white below with narrow black breast-band. ♀ greyer above and completely white below. Young grey-brown above, throat and breast buffy. Little known; calls unknown. In pairs or family group, forages in mid levels of thickets, gallery forest in lowland wooded savannas and mangrove forest. Recorded only from W Angola; may also occur further N in W Zaïre and W Congo. ***Flight characteristics***: Wings rounded, white wing-stripe distinctive.

COMPARISONS Similar to Brown-throated Wattle-eye *Platysteira cyanea* in extreme N of range. Both species have a white wing-stripe, but ♂ White-throated distinguished by grey (not black) upperparts, and ♀ by completely white underparts. Throat and upper breast dark chestnut-brown in Brown-throated. Also overlaps with Black-throated Wattle-eye *P. peltata* in E of range. ♂♂ both have black breast-band on white underparts, but greyer upperparts, broader breast-band, paler eye and presence of white wing-stripe distinguishes White-fronted; ♀ White-fronted distinguished by grey (not black) upperparts, presence of white wing-stripe and completely white underparts (throat black in ♀ Black-throated).

DESCRIPTION **Adult ♂** ***Head*** Including crown and nape dark greyish-black; hindneck mottled black-and-white; lores, ear-coverts and sides of hindneck black, slightly glossed steel-blue; forehead with narrow white frontal band at base of bill. ***Back*** Mantle and back grey; scapulars dull black; rump grey with concealed white spots, feathers long and fluffy. ***Wings*** Flight feathers dull black, narrowly edged pale greyish-white along outer web; outer tertials edged white along outer web forming part of wing-stripe, extending onto median coverts with broad white tips, innermost greaters with broad margin or entire outer web and tip white; upperwing-coverts glossy blue-black; axillaries white. ***Tail*** Uppertail-coverts and tail deep glossy blue-black; outer feathers edged and tipped white, remainder tipped white decreasing inwards. ***Underparts*** White except for narrow glossy blue-black breast-band (*c.*6–7 mm); flanks greyish; thighs blackish narrowly barred white. ***Bare parts*** Bill black; palate unknown; legs dark purple; eye pale greyish-blue with narrow white inner ring; wattle above eye bright red to scarlet-vermilion, lower eye-lid dull olive[15, 676]. **Adult ♀** Like ♂ but upperparts duller and greyer, dark pearl- to slate-grey without black. Tail appears to have broader white edges to outer feathers. Underparts entirely white. **Juvenile** greyish-brown above; wings rufous-buff including upperwing-coverts. Underparts whitish; chin to breast tawny to rufous-buff; bill brownish; legs dark purple; eye bluish-grey with small fleshy wattle above eye[289, 338, 500]. **Immature** Like adult ♀ above but buffy below, with irregular pale rusty tips and edges to upperwing-coverts and inner secondaries. Subadult ♂ breast-band mottled whitish-brown and black[500, 676].

GEOGRAPHICAL VARIATION None. Monotypic.

MOULT Unknown.

RANGE, HABITAT and STATUS **Breeding range** Restricted range, known only from NW Angola, from Congo River mouth to Benguela and inland E in the Cuanza River drainage to Dondo, mostly along the escarpment. Probably also occurs in Congo. Presence in Zaïre on Kwango River and Ngombe Lutete requires confirmation[7, 343, 402, 431, 676, 907]. **Habitat** Found in dry thicket woodland and gallery forest in lowland wooded savannas, also in coffee plantations and mangrove forest. Common in *Croton* thickets in Quicama National Park[7, 774, 676, 907]. **Status** Apparently resident, not uncommon, at least in Kishama National Park and Barra do Cuenza[774, 676]. **Conservation status** Little known; potential Red Data Book species considered Near-Threatened[343, 479].

MOVEMENTS Unknown.

SOCIAL ORGANISATION and GENERAL BEHAVIOUR Virtually unknown. Apparently habits similar to Brown-throated Wattle-eye. Solitary, in pairs or family groups. **Foraging behaviour** Actively gleans foliage, hopping from twig to twig, makes short sallies to capture prey on or under leaves, sometimes hovering. Joins mixed foraging parties[676]. **Food** Small arthropods, particularly insects[676].

SOUNDS Unknown.

BREEDING BIOLOGY Unknown. Probably monogamous and territorial. **Season** Juveniles Nov (Angola)[7, 907]. No further breeding information.

MEASUREMENTS and WEIGHTS *P. albifrons* ♂ (4) wing 59.5–62 (60.7), tail 46–49 (47.5), bill 16.5–18 (17.5), tarsus 18–19.5 (18.6); ♀ (5) wing 59.5–62.5 (61.0), tail 47–51 (49.0), bill 16–17 (16.5), tarsus 18.5–19.5 (19.0)[676]. **Weight** ♂ 11.7 g, ♀ 12.6 g (Angola)[911].

102 WHITE-SPOTTED WATTLE-EYE *Dyaphorophyia tonsa* Plate 36

FIELD IDENTIFICATION Very small (9.5 cm), plump, almost tailless flycatcher-like bird with a big round-headed appearance and purple eye wattle. Sexes different. ♂ black and white; head, back, wings, tail and broad breast-band glossy black; white spot in front and behind eye; throat, neck-collar, rump and underparts white. ♀ rufous-brown, black and white; head black; throat, breast, back and wings rufous-brown (chestnut-brown). In both sexes purplish eye-wattle only above eye. White rump in ♂ conspicuous in flight. Young similar to ♀ but duller brown above and faintly barred below. More often heard than seen, main call a regularly repeated whistle, also grunts and churring sounds. Makes 'fripping' sound with wings. Very active, in pairs or family group usually in the canopy. Found in thick, mainly lowland primary forest. Resident with populations fragmented. In West Africa from SE Nigeria to Gabon and NW Congo, and in central E and NE Zaïre. ***Flight characteristics***: Fast, generally short, with rapid continuous wingbeats. Makes a continuous buzzing, whirring or 'fripping' sound with wings in flight. Wings rounded, white rump of ♂ conspicuous in flight, particularly when fluffed-out[15, 648, 676].

COMPARISONS Most similar to larger Chestnut Wattle-eye *Dyaphorophyia castanea* (particularly race *hormophora*) with which it overlaps. Generally, White-spotted is ecologically segregated, foraging higher up, mainly in canopy. It is also less noisy. Eyebrow extends as a large white spot behind eye in ♂ (diagnostic) (Chestnut Wattle-eye also has white eyebrow which does not extend behind eye and is concealed by wattle). White collar more prominent in White-spotted. Both have similar-coloured eye-wattles, but shape different: White-spotted mainly above eye (larger and encircles eye in Chestnut Wattle-eye). ♀ has a black (not grey) crown and nape. Young similar and probably impossible to separate in the field. In flight makes a continuous buzzing or 'fripping' sound, while sound in Chestnut Wattle-eye is more rhythmic. Some whistled calls are similar, and known to countersing with this species[289, 500, 504, 676].

DESCRIPTION ADULT ♂ ***Head*** Lores and anterior crown velvety-black, remainder of crown, nape, sides of face and ear-coverts dark glossy blue-black, short white eyebrow appearing as a spot in front and behind eye. ***Back*** Bluish-black; lower back and rump white, feathers long, silky, hair-like with dark bases; uppertail-coverts bluish-black. ***Wings* and *Tail*** Blackish with slight gloss. ***Underparts*** White with chin and throat forming a semi-collar around sides to hindneck; bordered below by broad blue-black breast-band (*c*.15–18 mm); belly and vent white. Thighs black barred white. Underwing-coverts black edged white, axillaries white, undersides of primaries and secondaries dark grey edged white along inner web. ***Bare parts*** Bill black; palate unknown; legs black to dark purplish-grey; eye brown to chestnut-brown; large fleshy dark purple wattle above eye[492, 676]. ADULT ♀ ***Head*** Forehead, crown and nape velvet-black; thin white to buffy-white eyebrow above eye and wattle; face-mask and ear-coverts grey. ***Back*** Mantle, back and scapulars rufous-brown to bright chestnut-brown; lower rump greyish, feathers long and hair-like. Uppertail-coverts black. ***Wings*** Lesser and median upperwing-coverts bright chestnut-brown; primaries and secondaries blackish-brown edged tawny (primaries) and chestnut-brown (secondaries); primary coverts dark grey-brown. ***Tail*** Black. ***Underparts*** Chin to breast rufous-brown; chin with small amount of white; belly and vent white; flanks grey. ***Bare parts*** Bill black; legs blackish-grey; eye brown to blackish with smaller fleshy greyish to purple-brown wattle above eye[289, 492]. JUVENILE Upperparts grey-brown with little chestnut-brown. Head and breast dark grey tinged tawny to pale rufous; throat and breast pale grey with buff barring[456, 500, 676]. IMMATURE Like adult ♀, but head more rusty-brown, with only a little black on crown. Throat and breast mottled greyish chestnut-brown, white and rufous with dark vermiculations. In ♀ throat and breast become progressively more chestnut-brown with a few light feathers. In ♂ throat becomes whiter, with only a few chestnut-brown feathers; breast-band becomes progressively more black, with only a few chestnut-brown feathers; chestnut-brown of back and wings browner; eye light brown to reddish-brown, purple eye-wattle small[456, 500, 676].

GEOGRAPHICAL VARIATION None. Monotypic.

MOULT Unknown.

RANGE, HABITAT and STATUS **Breeding range** distribution fragmented, in W from SE Nigeria, W and S Cameroon, Rio Muni, Gabon and NW Congo (requires confirmation). Also in central E and NE Zaïre. Probably more widespread in Congo basin. Reports from Liberia and Ivory Coast require confirmation due to confusion with Chestnut Wattle-eye (race *hormophora*). Record from Central African Republic rejected[431]. **Habitat** In lowland primary forest with thick and continuous high canopy with tall emergents; dense undergrowth not a prerequisite. Also in overgrown plantations, edge of riverine forest, in regenerating forest and tall secondary growth. Avoids clearings and open forest. Found up to 1500 m[21, 22, 37, 289, 294, 347, 431, 456, 676, 690, 688, 848]. **Status** Resident, rare in Nigeria, but common in some localities elsewhere in range. **Conservation status** Considered possibly threatened[343].

MOVEMENTS Unknown; probably sedentary as in NE Gabon[676].

SOCIAL ORGANISATION and GENERAL BEHAVIOUR Solitary, in pairs or family groups which maintain constant visual and vocal contact. Behaviour similar to Chestnut Wattle-eye, but more of a canopy bird; more often heard than seen. Pair cover entire territory daily, an area of 6.4 ha (n=22). Advertise and defend territory with repeated series of whistles, rate and pitch varying with context. In high-intensity interactions, like territorial defence, pairs raise crest, expand eye-wattle and move rapidly and noisily below or in canopy, giving grunts and high-intensity territorial songs. They make 'wing-fripping' and bill-snapping sounds before engaging in territorial fight or chasing intruders. Flies with rapid, continuous wingbeats. Territorial displays are much less formalised than in Chestnut Wattle-eye. Maintenance and aggressive behaviour similar to Chestnut Wattle-eye. Where ranges overlap, it is frequently found in association with this species[234, 294, 456, 676]. **Foraging behaviour** Forage mainly in the canopy, sometimes in undergrowth, but generally higher than 20 m. Often joins mixed foraging parties, particularly in non-breeding season. Forages among foliage of tree-crowns and leafy tangles. These two species exclude each other when foraging together, with White-spotted generally higher up in canopy. **Food** Arthropods, mainly insects, including Coleoptera (beetles), Lepidoptera (moths and caterpillars), Hemiptera (cicadas), Hymenoptera (bees, wasps and winged ants), Isoptera (termites), Diptera (flies) and Neuroptera (lacewings). Also takes spiders. Most prey 7–15 mm long, occasionally larger[294, 456, 676].

SOUNDS Repertoire consists of various calls including repeated whistles, harsh churrs, grunts and explosive sounds. ♂ territorial call a regularly repeated whistle, varying in pitch and repetition rate depending on the context: *hu-hu-hu-hu- or ou-ou-ou-* (60–70/min), with a cisticola- or batis-like quality. At higher intensity, by ♂ and often by both sexes in duet, a disyllabic whistle *tlet-tlet-tlet-* or repeated *ou-u-* (second note shorter and higher-pitched) at 65–70/min, with a similar triple note regularly interspersed. At still higher intensity, by either sex, a rhythmic *u-u-u-u-* at rate of 80–85/min, which may accelerate to higher-pitched, very rapid *uuuuu-* at 165–170/min. Territorial threat or defence song a series of hollow *tok- tok-*, *ptoc-ou* or more intense *ptoc-u* notes, followed by aggressive, scolding *ku-lee* or *ku-li*, sometimes *kulili*. Pairs countersing using notes of differing pitch, producing a seesaw effect. Other calls include churrs, an explosive *tong*, slightly reminiscent of Moorhen *Gallinula chloropus* call, and other short mellow whistles, *kwu* or *kwuu*, ascending in pitch. Courtship call a repeated nasal *ptooee-ptooee-*, which is also used in flight. When excited or aggressive gives churring calls and a harsh *prrrt* or scolding *ptec* or *ptedetec* irregularly repeated, followed by a prolonged grunt *krrkrrkrrk* or *gägägägä*. Alarm a repeated guttural *ptek*, *ptick* or *ptck* by ♂, or harsh *krrr* by ♀. 'Wing-fripping' and bill-snapping sounds also. Contact call a soft *pec*, *prrek*, *piup* or *tuctucpiup*. Young give harsh nasal *kwet*. Known to countersing with Chestnut Wattle-eye and Gabon Batis *Batis minima*[15, 22, 289, 338, 500, 648, 676].

BREEDING BIOLOGY Little known. Monogamous, with helpers made up of young of previous brood(s). Helpers assist parents, at least in nest-building and feeding older fledglings. Occurs in density of 13.7 pairs/km² (Gabon)[234, 294]. **Season** Mar, young being fed Apr, ♂♂ with enlarged gonads in Oct and Nov (Nigeria)[37, 718, 676]; Apr–May; ♂♂ with enlarged gonads Mar and Sep, and ♀♀ with slightly enlarged gonads in Dec (Cameroon)[676]; Dec–Feb, Apr, Sep–Oct (Gabon)[294, 676]; Feb, Mar, possibly Apr, juveniles in Feb, ♂ and ♀ with enlarged gonads Feb, Mar, May (Jan–Jul), Sep, Nov (Zaïre)[22, 676, 688]. **Displays** ***Courtship*** Main call a repeated nasal *ptooee-ptooee-*, similar to flight call[676]. Courtship-feeding probably present. **Nest** Built by both sexes, assisted by young of previous brood. Nest similar to Chestnut Wattle-eye (p.333). The only nest found was placed 15 m up at the end of a horizontal leafy branch of undergrowth tree in forest[294]. **Eggs** Unknown. **Incubation** By ♀ only. Behaviour similar to Chestnut Wattle-eye, with ♀ sitting for long periods and being fed by ♂ on and off nest. Period unknown[676]. **Nestling** Appearance and period unknown. Fledglings fed by both sexes and helped by young of previous brood. Dependent for at least 2 months and remain with family for almost 2 years[676]. No further breeding information.

MEASUREMENTS and WEIGHTS *D. tonsa* ♂ (10) wing 52.5–57.5 (54.2), tail 20.5–24 (22.1), bill 14–15 (14.3), tarsus 14.15.5 (14.9); ♀ (5) wing 52.5–55.5 (54.5), tail 22–23.5 (22.6), bill 13–15 (14.0), tarsus 14.5–15.5 (15.0)[676]. **Weight** ♂ (1) 11.5 g (Gabon)[676]. For additional data see[289].

103 CHESTNUT WATTLE-EYE *Dyaphorophyia castanea* Plate 36

FIELD IDENTIFICATION Very small (9–10 cm), active and noisy, plump, almost tailless black and white or grey, brown and white flycatcher-like bird with eye-wattle. Has a big-headed appearance with brown eye encircled by large fleshy purplish-grey wattle. Sexes different. ♂ black and white; head, wings, tail and broad breast-band glossy black; throat, rump and belly white. ♀ grey, chestnut-brown and white; head grey; back, wings, throat and breast chestnut-brown; belly white. Young similar to ♀ but with rufous-spotted head and rufous-mottled black breast. ♂ white rump conspicuous in flight. Calls variable; monotonous series of tinkerbird-like whistles, hollow frog-like calls and others with whip-lash quality; in flight makes noisy 'wing-fripping'. In pairs or family group, shy and difficult to see. Occurs mainly in lowland primary and secondary forest, usually in low to mid levels. Resident from Sierra Leone in West Africa to S Sudan, Uganda, Kenya and NW Tanzania in East Africa, southwards in W Africa to Congo, Zaïre and N Angola. ***Flight characteristics***: Fast, generally short, with rapid wingbeats. Makes a rhythmic buzzing, whirring or 'fripping' sound with wings. Wings rounded, white rump of ♂ conspicuous in flight, particularly in display when fluffed-out[676].

COMPARISONS Similar to quieter and smaller White-spotted Wattle-eye *Dyaphorophyia tonsa*. Chestnut Wattle-eye has larger eye-wattle which extends further backwards, and crown feathers longer. The white spot behind the eye is less evident, being partially obscured by the wattle. It also lacks the extensive white collar in ♂♂ (except in W race *hormophora*). Has different habitat preference, occurring lower down, in undergrowth and mid levels rather than canopy. In ♀♀ crown is grey, not black. Separation of young probably not possible in field; both have white throat. Flights different, Chestnut Wattle-eye making a rhythmic buzzing sound, White-spotted Wattle-eye a continuous, less rhythmic sound. Some whistled calls are similar, and it is known to countersing with this species. Other small black and white tailless wattle-eyes have distinctive large bright bluish-green eye-wattles and a black throat in both sexes. Young Red-cheeked Wattle-eye *D. blissetti* have tawny throat, and tend to occur at higher elevations. Young Jameson's Wattle-eye *D. jamesoni* have pale chestnut-brown throat bordered below by dusky, and dark grey upperparts. Where Chestnut Wattle-eye overlaps with distinctive Yellow-bellied Wattle-eye *D. concreta*, it tends to occur higher up in vegetation. Some calls are reminiscent of the longer-tailed *Platysteira* wattle-eyes, batises and tinkerbirds. In W Africa the Red-rumped Tinkerbird *Pogoniulus atroflavus* sometimes responds to playback of wattle-eye call[631, 676].

DESCRIPTION ADULT ♂ ***Head*** Crown, sides of head and lores glossy steel-blue. Small white spot above eye obscured by wattle. ***Back, wings and tail*** Steel-blue with slight gloss; scapulars black edged white; rump white, feathers long and hairy. Underside of primaries and secondaries dark grey with narrow white edge along inner web; axillaries white. ***Underparts*** Including sides of neck white (variable; see Geographical Variation) except for broad glossy blue-black breast-band (*c*.15–20 mm); thighs black barred white. ***Bare parts*** Bill black; palate unknown; legs reddish-blue to dark purple; eye chestnut-brown to purple-brown; large fleshy wattle encircles and extends above and behind eye, coloured purplish blue-grey, dark liver or purplish-black. ADULT ♀ ***Head*** Forehead, crown, nape, lores and ear-coverts dark slate-grey separated from underparts by narrow white line from chin to under eye; small spot above eye white and chestnut-brown, concealed by wattle. Feathers of hindcrown rather long and erectile, forming a low crest in display or alarm. ***Back*** Mantle and scapulars bright chestnut-brown; rump mottled grey, white and chestnut-brown, feathers long and hairy. ***Wing*** Upperwing-coverts bright chestnut-brown; primary coverts dark brown; primaries and secondaries blackish-brown, narrowly edged chestnut-brown to reddish-brown along outer web; tertials chestnut-brown. ***Tail*** Uppertail-coverts brown-black, tail feathers black with narrow whitish tips when fresh. ***Underparts*** Chin white, throat, neck and sides of neck and breast bright chestnut-brown; belly, vent and undertail-coverts white; flanks dark grey; thighs brownish-grey. ***Bare parts*** Bill black; palate unknown; legs reddish to dark purple; eye chestnut-brown to purple-brown; fleshy wattle above eye purple-grey to purple-black. JUVENILE head brownish to grey-brown, spotted with tawny chestnut-brown on crown; grey-brown extends to upper mantle; back chestnut-brown. Wings like adult ♀. Underparts: Chin and throat whitish; breast from lower throat to upper belly greyish-white with fine barring (vermiculations); flanks grey; eye reddish-brown; eye-wattle barely visible[500, 676]. IMMATURE Like adult ♀ but head browner, throat and breast chestnut-brown mottled white with blackish fine barring (vermiculations). In ♂ black breast-band develops progressively; upperparts and wings browner, not bright chestnut-brown; upperwing-coverts and tertials dark brown with chestnut-brown edges, not uniformly chestnut-brown; eye grey-brown to reddish-brown; eye-wattle smaller and greyer, only developing in second year; legs dark brown[412, 456, 504, 676].

GEOGRAPHICAL VARIATION Two races, with variation in size of body, crest, breast-band and possibly eye-wattle, as well as extent of white collar on neck. Nominate *castanea* (S Nigeria, Cameroon, Gabon, S through Congo basin and Zaïre to Angola, E to SE Sudan, Uganda and Kenya) is larger with longer crest feathers and broader breast-band. Also lacks the distinctive broad white collar which encircles the neck in *hormophora* (Sierra Leone to Togo). This W race also appears to have larger eye-wattles[289, 412, 500].

MOULT Early stages of wing moult Oct, Dec–Jan, medium stages Mar–Jul; most Jul–Dec birds were not moulting. Immature ♂♂ acquiring black adult breast-band Sep–Oct (Liberia)[259, 858].

RANGE, HABITAT and STATUS **Breeding range** W and Central Africa from Sierra Leone, Guinea, Liberia, Ivory Coast, Ghana, Togo, Benin, S Nigeria, S Cameroon, Equatorial Guinea, Bioko, Rio Muni, Gabon, Congo, Zaïre, Cabinda and N Angola, S Central African Republic, S Sudan, Uganda, W Kenya, NW Tanzania and NW Zambia. **Habitat** In lowlands up to 1800 m, in primary and secondary forest, including swampy and flooded forest. Usually in mature forest, avoids open undergrowth. Also found in regenerating forest and old plantations (cacao), forest-grassland mosaics, isolated thickets and gardens[7, 21, 22, 37, 101, 234, 242, 259, 294, 295, 289, 318, 330, 347, 412, 431, 456, 481, 504, 631, 676, 688, 690, 829, 848, 852, 907]. **Status** Resident, uncommon to locally abundant. **Conservation status** Not threatened; estimated population in Liberia 400,000 pairs[858].

MOVEMENTS Unknown, probably sedentary.

SOCIAL ORGANISATION and GENERAL BEHAVIOUR Solitary, in pairs or family groups, with members maintaining permanent and close visual and vocal contact. Restless and inquisitive, active throughout the day and noisy when disturbed. Non-breeding members always moving together. ♂ advertises and defends a territory of 2.4 ±0.3 ha (n=64) (Gabon) by singing, usually in upper levels of undergrowth or lower canopy, with crest erected. Both sexes defend the territory against individuals of the same sex. In high-intensity interactions, resident pair emit irregular series of alarm calls, move towards opponents with noisy 'wing-fripping', then while perched give territorial defence song with upright posture, exposed throat and breast, fluffed-out rump and erect eye-wattles. This is followed by intense grunting calls, bill-snapping, 'wing-fripping', exposed rump feathers, erect crown feathers and bright red eye-wattles swollen with blood and protruding like horns on the side of the head. On closer approach adopts crouched threat posture and emits scolding territorial flight song, *ptick* note while facing opponent and *kwow* with head turned to one side. Opposing ♂♂ and ♀♀ counter-sing in duet so that when one bird give the *ptick* call the other gives *kwow*. Territorial disputes often attract several other pairs and unpaired birds, with unpaired ♂♂ courting ♀♀ in a general chorus. Anxiety expressed by calls, rapid head movements and sleeked plumage while in a crouched posture. When alarmed erects crown feathers and calls while flying with 'fripping' wing sounds. Mobbing bird flies with vigorous 'wing-fripping' directly at intruder, crest erect, eye-wattles expanded and bill-snapping. Bathes in water trapped in trees or flutters through wet foliage. Roosts under leaf at extremity of exposed thin twig[2, 294, 456, 572, 631, 676, 688]. **Foraging behaviour** Arboreal, active all day covering entire home range, searching foliage at all levels up to lower canopy, 2–30 m, mainly 3–10 m. This behaviour is seasonally variable, with breeding birds feeding low down in undergrowth. Spends most of the time searching the extremity of branches, hopping from twig to twig in upright or crouched posture, head constantly moving. Most prey captured in short upward sally, snatched from under-surface of leaves, hovering briefly or hawking insects on the wing. Insects dislodged from leaves in noisy flapping flight. While foraging, sometimes aggressive towards other insectivorous birds, but will often join mixed foraging parties, particularly in dry season. **Food** Arthropods, mainly insects, including Coleoptera (beetles), Lepidoptera (caterpillars and moths), Orthoptera (grasshoppers), Hymenoptera (bees, wasps and ants), Mantodea (mantises), Hemiptera (cicadas and bugs), Dictyoptera (cockroach)es, Isoptera (termites). Also Neuroptera (lacewings) and to a lesser extent arthropods like spiders, millipedes and scorpions, as well as small fruits[259, 294, 412, 456, 640, 676, 688, 753, 849, 858].

SOUNDS Repertoire consists of a wide variety of different notes ranging from ringing and metallic to wheezing, bleating, grunting, nasal and hollow ventriloquial frog-like croaks, also various loud cracking, popping and 'fripping' sounds produced by the wings as well as bill-snapping. Calls are delivered in a rather unobtrusive, seemingly patternless medley, some inaudible at a distance. Territorial song a long, regular, slowly repeated, monotonous series of 6–10 tinkerbird-like sounds *tlu...tlu-*, *tlop...tlop-* or *tonk- tonk-* (95–110/min), varying to higher-pitched, much faster *tetetetetete-* or *weet-weet-weet-* notes (*c*.2/sec). Repeated notes also described as *tuck-*, *pti-*, *kak-*, *pink-* or *tink-*, often with a metallic ringing quality. Territorial flight song a rhythmic frog-like series consisting of a guttural note followed by an explosive sound: *ptik-kwow* or *pqwonk* (1/sec), variations including *wuK!-wuK!-*, *gwoK!gwoK!gwoK!-* and *KluzzT-KluzzT-* or *zzK!-zzK!-*, the ending sounding like a sharp explosive click. Also delivers a more complex phrase *kpwai-kpwai-k-k-k-pwai-wai-wai*. These calls are often given in same-sex duets, with some interactions developing into a chorus of several birds. Another more guttural territorial song involves a monotonous series of regularly uttered rough *ptock-ptock-* or *hwuK-hwuK-hwuK-*, *Grruk-Grruk-Grruk-*, *kuuk-kuuk-*

kuuk or *womp-womp-* notes (*c*.80/min). At higher intensity in territorial defence gives frog-like *kwow* or *kwonk* and in more aggressive interactions a strident whip-lash *TluuE!-TluuE!-* or higher-pitched *TleU!-TleU!-*, usually combined with chattering calls, bill-snapping and 'wing-fripping'. Courtship an explosive, hiccup-like *kwow, pkwup* or ascending *TuuE!zzglU* by ♂ above ♀ in flight. Nasal chattering frequent. Contact call a soft irregular *wa, tchwa, wo* or *wop*. Anxiety calls are nasal *kowo, koway* or *kowet- kowet-*, alarm a rapid *pop-pop-pop-*, then nasal *pop-pway-pop-pway-*. In appeasement gives irregular series of soft *u-u-u-u-*. In excitement (e.g. during nest-building) thin high-pitched *tstssts-* or crackling *tititit*. Begging calls of young and ♀ a harsh *kchay-kchay-kchay-*, also a rather *Lanius*-like nasal *naaat...naaat-*. Some calls bear a resemblance to *Platysteira* wattle-eyes, others to batises. In W Africa the Red-rumped Tinkerbird sometimes responds to playback of the territorial call of this wattle-eye[15, 22, 289, 412, 500, 515, 572, 631, 676, 767, 781, 849].

BREEDING BIOLOGY Monogamous, with helpers at some nests, and territorial. Densities of 42.3 pairs/km^2 in primary forest and 20–25 pairs/km^2 in regrowth and disused plantations (Gabon); 8–11 adults and 2 immatures in 8-ha census tract (Kenya). Breeding success; of 27 nests, eggs laid in 13, young hatched in 6 and fledged in 4. Of 13 nests, 25 eggs laid, 11 hatched, 8 fledged (Gabon). Apparently single-brooded[294, 456, 631, 676, 847].

Season Dependent young fed in all months Dec–Apr; ♀♀ with enlarged gonads Apr and Jul, ♂♂ with enlarged gonads Jan–Jul (Liberia)[259, 858]; Jan, Jul–Nov, juveniles Feb–Nov (Ivory Coast); Dec, Jan, fledgling Fed, imm Jul (Ghana)[234]; May, Dec (Nigeria)[37, 606]; May, Oct, with both sexes having enlarged gonads in Jan–Mar, Aug, Dec (Cameroon)[338, 347, 676]; ♂♂ enlarged gonads Sep–Nov, Jan; ♀ enlarged ovary Sep (Bioko)[338, 676]; Jul–Apr, mainly Sep–Oct and Dec–Feb (Gabon)[38, 295, 676]; Aug–Sep (Congo); Feb–Jul, Sep–Nov and ♂♂ with enlarged gonads Feb–Nov, juveniles in Jan–Jul, Oct; suggests egg-laying from Apr–Jul and Oct–Dec (Zaïre)[22, 289, 688]; Oct–Mar, ♀ enlarged gonads Feb, juveniles in Mar, Nov, Dec; breeding condition Jun, Aug–Oct and Feb (Angola)[7, 676, 865, 907]; imm May, ♀ enlarged gonads Apr–May, ♂♂ and ♀♀ enlarged gonads Jun (Central African Republic)[424]; Mar, May (Uganda)[293, 576]; Jun, Aug (Sudan)[242, 676].

Displays ***Courtship*** Display described as a dance, in which both sexes dart back and forth at great speed, producing a loud whirring or 'wing-fripping' sound. ♂ also flies around ♀ uttering a short sharp piercing whistle *slit-slit-slit*. He crouches and approaches her, often faces away, giving contact calls and appeasement song, hops about branches, passes behind ♀, perching less than 1 m above her, crouches, bends body forward and downward, fluffs out rump, droops wings, expands blood-swollen eye-wattles, then swoops down in front of her giving a single loud whip-lash *p'kwup* or ascending *TuuE!zzglU* call and perches below her. Display repeated several times over a few days. Courtship-feeding takes place and is then followed later by nest-building. Displays are characterised by loud 'wing-fripping', the display often attracting other ♂♂ and ♀♀[15, 295, 676, 767, 858].

Nest Built by both sexes, often helped by young of previous brood. Small compact deep cup of vegetable fibres, dried grasses, small stems, fine rootlets, pieces of bark and lichens, bound with spider web. Cup lined with thinner material, particularly fungus *Marasmius*, sometimes vegetable down. Use broadleaved trees, usually placed in fork at end of small branch, sometimes at top of young sapling, always partly hidden with a broad leaf (at least 6 cm wide) very close above nest, acting as a roof. Tip of leaf secured by spider web or fungus to rim. During construction and incubation birds very particular about distance of leafy roof from rim. Nest placed from 0.3–16 m above ground. In one study at *c*.6 m (1.5–16, mostly 3–8 m, n=37) (Gabon). ***Size*** OD 55–65 mm, ID 41–42 mm, cup depth 21–25 mm, height 25–35 mm. Built in 14–16 days[2, 294, 606].

Eggs Usually 2 (1–2, n=13), laid at 1-day intervals, beginning 1–4 days after nest completion. Bright blue to green or blue-green or bluish-white, finely spotted with dark browns and greys, mainly as a cap at broad end. ***Size*** 16–18 x 12–13.5 mm[2, 289, 294, 606, 647]. **Incubation** By ♀, begins with first egg, ♂ feeds ♀ on and off nest. Although she occasionally feeds herself, ♂ provides most of her food. ♂ sings appeasement song if he approaches nest without food. Period 17 days. **Nestling** Hatch naked, skin blackish; develops brownish down. Mouthspots unknown. Brooded initially only by ♀. ♂ also passes food to her to feed nestlings. Later fed by both sexes, and often helped by young of previous brood. Fledge after 14–16 days. Fledglings fed by members of family for at least 2 months, remaining in family group for almost 2 years, and help parents build nest and feed young. Young attain adult plumage at the end of second year (see Juvenile/Immature)[676]. **Predation and longevity** Predation unknown. Bird ringed as a juvenile still present in same place 4 years later (Kenya)[676]. **Brood parasite** Emerald Cuckoo *Chrysococcyx cupreus* observed being fed by family members (Gabon)[234, 463].

MEASUREMENTS and WEIGHTS *D. c. castanea* ♂ (15) wing 56–61 (58.7), tail 24.5–27.0 (25.6), bill 14–16.5 (15.0), tarsus 15–16 (15.4); ♀ (10) wing 55.5–60.5 (58.8), tail 24.5–26.5 (25.6), bill 14–15 (14.7), tarsus 15–16 (15.4)[676]. **Weight** ♂ (29) 12–16 g (14.3); ♀ (18) 11–15 g (13.9) (Uganda)[676]. For additional data see[259, 295, 412, 424, 425, 676, 876, 908].

104 RED-CHEEKED WATTLE-EYE *Dyaphorophyia blissetti* Plate 37

FIELD IDENTIFICATION Very small (8–9 cm), plump, almost tailless flycatcher-like bird with bright blue-green eye-wattles and large triangular chestnut-brown cheek or neck-patches. ♂ glossy blackish-green above, including throat; rest of underparts white. Sexes similar except ♀ greyer, less glossy with smaller eye-wattle. Young like ♀ except throat and upper breast tawny. More often heard than seen; call a rapid series of high-pitched whistles at same pitch, also loud 'wing-fripping' and bill-snapping. Usually in pairs or family group, active and noisy. Found in dense undergrowth of lowland secondary forest and abandoned plantations. Resident from Guinea and Sierra Leone to Nigeria and W Cameroon. ***Flight characteristics***: Rapid and short; wings rounded Makes loud whirring and 'fripping' sounds with wings.

COMPARISONS Overlaps in E of range with Black-necked Wattle-eye *Dyaphorophyia chalybea,* which tends to occur at higher elevations. This species differs by having emerald-green eye-wattles, pale yellow underparts and no chestnut-brown neck-patches. Most similar to Jameson's Wattle-eye *D. jamesoni,* which differs only in having smaller, darker cheek or neck-patches. Ranges separate. Separation of young Red-cheeked and Black-necked Wattle-eyes difficult; sides of throat darker in Red-cheeked. See Black-necked Wattle-eye Comparisons for possible confusion with other similar species p.335.

DESCRIPTION **ADULT ♂** ***Head and back*** Black with metallic bottle-green gloss. Rump feathers long and hair-like, basal feathers white; sides of neck chestnut-brown from below eye to sides of breast, forming a distinct triangular patch. ***Wings*** Like back, gloss confined to outer web on flight feathers. ***Tail*** Like back, underside grey-black. ***Underparts*** Throat and upper breast like back, forming a bib; lower breast to undertail-coverts white; flanks greyish; thighs blackish. ***Bare parts*** Bill black, broad and flat; palate unknown; legs greyish-blue to purple; eye dark brown to reddish-brown with silvery ring around pupil; large bright blue-green to turquoise-blue wattle around eye. **ADULT ♀** Similar to ♂ but duller, dark grey above with less gloss; eye-wattles much smaller. Throat-patch black with greenish gloss. **JUVENILE** Unknown. **IMMATURE** Above dull dark grey, sides of face dark greyish chestnut-brown. Underparts with throat and upper breast tawny, sides of neck and upper breast reddish-brown to chestnut-brown, with black feathers on sides of throat and sides of breast. Lower breast tinged tawny. Throat and breast darken progressively to adult plumage. Tail glossy green. Bare parts: Bill black; legs purplish; eye deep brown; wattle initially lacking, then small greyish-blue[500, 504, 676, 986].

GEOGRAPHICAL VARIATION None. Monotypic. Sometimes considered conspecific with Jameson's Wattle-eye.

MOULT Wing moult recorded Feb–Jun, Jul–Oct (Liberia)[259, 858].

RANGE, HABITAT and STATUS **Breeding range** West Africa from E Guinea, Sierra Leone, Liberia, Ivory Coast, Ghana, Togo, S Nigeria and W Cameroon. **Habitat** In dense undergrowth of lowland primary and secondary forest, forest edge, riverine forest, coastal thickets, plantations and relic forest patches in savanna. In Liberia also ascends into primary montane forest to 1500 m. Where range overlaps with Yellow-bellied Wattle-eye *D. concreta* it is usually found only in dense undergrowth of secondary forest[21, 23, 37, 234, 259, 295, 347, 412, 431, 676, 848]. **Status** Resident, uncommon to locally common. **Conservation status** Unknown; earlier thought to be potentially threatened, but no longer. Held in captivity[343, 655].

MOVEMENTS Unknown; probably sedentary.

SOCIAL ORGANISATION and GENERAL BEHAVIOUR Similar to Black-necked Wattle-eye (see this species p.335). Solitary, in pairs or family groups of 4–6 birds. Restless and inquisitive; can fly silently, but often produces sputtering series of loud wing-snaps or 'fripping' sounds[504, 572]. **Foraging behaviour** Forages low down in undergrowth, usually below 1 m, often in layers between dead twigs and branches, where it captures insects. Known to join mixed foraging parties. Behaviour similar to Black-necked Wattle-eye. For additional information see[259, 858]. **Food** Insects.

SOUNDS Little known. Territorial call a frequent series of 3–7 rapidly repeated high, even-pitched whistles, sounding like a squeaky bicycle pump: *heheheheheheh-, hihihihihi-* or *hee-hee-hee-hee-, peep-peep-peep-peep.* This call is loud, far-carrying and difficult to locate. Also a harsh chirp as birds chase each other about, and a nasal *chuwwchuwwchuw,* sometimes in duet *hehehehe-chuwwchuww-hehehe.* Other calls include a sharp whip-cracking sound, hoarse grating *k-k-sh-sh-sh,* churring, bill-snapping and noisy 'wing-fripping'[500, 504, 572, 849].

BREEDING BIOLOGY Little known. Probably monogamous. Thought to be similar to Black-necked Wattle-eye. **Season** Immatures in all months from Feb–Jul, ♀♀ with enlarged gonads Mar–Apr, Aug–Sep, Nov; ♂♂ with enlarged gonads Apr, Aug–Sep (Liberia)[259, 858]; ♂ enlarged gonads Feb (Ghana)[676]; Dec–Feb (Nigeria); Feb–Apr, Sep, ♂ and ♀ with enlarged gonads Jan (Cameroon)[676]. No further breeding information.

MEASUREMENTS and WEIGHTS *D. blissetti* ♂ (14) wing mean 53.3 ±1.4, tail mean 20.5 ±0.7, bill mean 15.2 ±0.4; ♀ (8) wing mean 53.1 ±0.8, tail mean 20.3 ±0.7, mean bill 15.1 ±0.4 (Liberia)[259]; ♂♀? (5) wing 49–53 (51.6), tail 17–23 (19.8), bill 14.8–15.8 (15.3), tarsus 17.2–17.6 (17.5)[500]. **Weight** ♂ (14) mean 11.0 ±1 g, Imm ♂ (1) 11.9 g; ♀ (8) mean 11.0 ±0.9 g (Liberia)[259]; ♂ 11.0 g, ♀ 11.5 g[676].

105 JAMESON'S WATTLE-EYE *Dyaphorophyia jamesoni* Plate 37

FIELD IDENTIFICATION Similar to Red-cheeked Wattle-eye *Dyaphorophyia blissetti*, except chestnut-brown cheek or neck-patches smaller and darker-coloured. ♀ like ♂ but greyer above with little green gloss. Young greyer than ♀ with throat and upper breast rufous-chestnut with black patches. Ranges are separate but habitat preference and calls similar. Resident from E Zaïre to S Sudan, W Uganda, Rwanda, Burundi, W Kenya and NW Tanzania. ***Flight characteristics***: Rapid and short; wings rounded. Makes loud whirring and 'fripping' sounds with wings.

COMPARISONS See Black-necked Wattle-eye below.

DESCRIPTION Adult ♂ ***Head and back*** Black with metallic greenish gloss; rump greyish, end of feathers white, feathers long and hair-like. ***Wings*** Coverts black like upperparts. ***Tail*** Like back, very short. ***Underparts*** Chin, throat and upper breast like back, rest white; a dark chestnut-brown patch on sides of neck. ***Bare parts*** Bill black, broad and flat; palate unknown; legs mauve; eye brown; wattle turquoise-blue. Adult ♀ Resembles ♂ but has dark grey above with very little green gloss on upperparts. Juvenile/Immature greyer and duller above than ♀, throat and breast pale tawny-brown to rufous-chestnut including sides of neck, which are slightly darker chestnut-brown. The black on the chin, throat and breast gradually appears initially as a bar below breast, then gradually invading breast and throat; eye mauve[2, 500].

GEOGRAPHICAL VARIATION None. Monotypic. Sometimes considered conspecific with Red-cheeked Wattle-eye.

MOULT Unknown.

RANGE, HABITAT and STATUS **Breeding range** Central and E Africa: E and NE Zaïre, S Sudan, W Uganda, Rwanda, Burundi, W Kenya and NW Tanzania. **Habitat** Mainly in secondary forest, sometimes also undergrowth in primary forest, where it occurs together with Yellow-bellied *Dyaphorophyia concreta* and Chestnut Wattle-eyes *D. castanea*. Jameson's Wattle-eye tends to occupy the lowest levels, where it prefers thicker, darker forest and keeps more to overgrown, creeper-clad smaller trees and undergrowth[431, 676, 767]. **Status** Apparently resident, fairly common in Kenya. **Conservation status** In Kenya, the long term preservation of Kakamega and South Nandi Forests is critical to this species.

MOVEMENTS Unknown; probably sedentary.

SOCIAL ORGANISATION and GENERAL BEHAVIOUR Little known. Solitary, in pairs or small family groups of *c*.4 members. Behaviour thought to be similar to Red-cheeked Wattle-eye, for details see Black-necked Wattle-eye *D. chalybea* p.335. Shy and difficult to see, more often heard than seen. Makes loud buzzing and 'fripping' sounds with wings in flight. A mechanical-sounding *wippy* note is produced by the ♂ when perched by making rapid jerky upward movements of its head and neck, as though actuated by a spring, the sound being produced with each upward movement. Territory size unknown[576, 631, 688, 767, 847]. **Foraging behaviour and Food** See Black-necked Wattle-eye.

SOUNDS Little known. Apparently similar to Red-cheeked Wattle-eye, although reputed to be less vocal than other *Dyaphorophyia* wattle-eyes. Main territorial song a long series of rapid high-pitched whistled *te-te-te-te-*, *hee-hee-hee-hee* or *ptee-dee-deee-* notes, accelerating from *c*.20 notes in 25 sec to *c*.20 notes in 17 sec. High-intensity territorial defence song introduced by hoarse *trr-trr* or harsh buzzy *ZrrZrr*, *Krr-Krr-* notes followed by a long series of whistled notes at same pitch, at a rate of *c*.3 notes/sec, like weak version of Olive-green Camaroptera *Camaroptera chloronota*, and ending in nasal *hee*. Other sounds include a subdued *chawuk-chawuk-chawuk-*, soft *wuk, wuk, wuk-* only audible at close range, and a mechanical-sounding *wippy* note. Also produces loud 'wing-fripping' and bill-snapping sounds[500, 515, 631, 676, 767].

BREEDING BIOLOGY Virtually unknown; thought to be similar to Red-cheeked Wattle-eye (see Black-necked Wattle-eye). Density of 10–11 adults and 3 young recorded in 8 ha census tract (Kenya). **Season** ♂♂ enlarged gonads May, Sep, Nov (Zaïre)[22, 298, 688, 676]; Jun (East Africa)[293]; Jul (Uganda)[767]. No further breeding information, except 2 birds ringed as juveniles were retrapped 2 years 7 months later[847].

MEASUREMENTS and WEIGHTS *D. jamesoni* ♂♀? (10) wing 52–57 (53.9), tail 21–24.8 (22.8), tarsus 16.5–18.5 (17.4), bill (to skull) 14.5–15.8 (15.0)[500]. **Weight** ♂ (29) 10–13 g (11.5), ♀ (28) 9–15 g (11.6), ♂♀? (6) 9–15 g (11.2) (Uganda)[676]; ♂♀? (14) 10–14.9 g (Uganda)[425]. For additional data see[583, 676].

106 BLACK-NECKED WATTLE-EYE *Dyaphorophyia chalybea* Plate 37

FIELD IDENTIFICATION Very small (9 cm), plump, almost tailless flycatcher-like bird with bright emerald-green wattle around eye. ♂ glossy blackish-green above including throat and breast; rump white, conspicuous when fluffed-out. Below pale yellow. Sexes similar, except ♀ duller with smaller eye-wattle. Young like ♀ except throat and breast tawny bordered by narrow chestnut-black band; below whitish. Flight rapid with whirring or 'fripping' sounds. Usually heard before seen; call a short series of descending high-pitched whistles and longer series at same pitch, often with bill-snapping. Usually in pairs or family group, active and noisy. Found in dense undergrowth of primary and secondary forest and overgrown cultivations. Resident in S Cameroon, Bioko, Equatorial Guinea, Gabon and Angolan escarpment. ***Flight characteristics***: Rapid and short; wings rounded; white of rump exposed in display. Makes whirring, buzzing and 'fripping' sounds with wings.

COMPARISONS Similar to Red-cheeked Wattle-eye *Dyaphorophyia blissetti* with which it overlaps in W of range. However, tends to be ecologically segregated, with Black-necked Wattle-eye at higher elevations. Red-cheeked Wattle-eye has large chestnut-brown patches on sides of neck, white underparts and blue-green eye-wattles. Also similar to Jameson's Wattle-eye *D. jamesoni*, which is very similar to Red-cheeked Wattle-eye, but has smaller darker chestnut-brown cheek-patches, and ranges separate. All other tailless wattle-eyes have chestnut-brown or yellow underparts, or a white throat with a distinctive black breast-band. Separation of young Black-necked and Red-cheeked Wattle-eye difficult and little studied; sides of throat appear darker in Red-cheeked. Young identified from ♀♀ Chestnut Wattle-eye *D. castanea* and White-spotted Wattle-eye *D. tonsa* by lack of chestnut-brown above and on wings. Descending whistle call reminiscent of Brown-throated Wattle-eye *Platysteira cyanea*.

DESCRIPTION **ADULT ♂** ***Upperparts*** Black with metallic bottle-green gloss. Lower rump white, feathers long and hair-like. ***Wings*** Like back, gloss confined to outer web on flight feathers. ***Tail*** Like back; underside grey-black. ***Underparts*** Throat and breast like back; lower breast, belly to under-tail-coverts creamy-yellow to pale yellow (fades in museum specimens); flanks greyish-black, thighs black. ***Bare parts*** Bill black, broad and flat; palate unknown; legs greyish-blue to greyish-purple, claws white; eye chestnut-brown with large bright flat-topped emerald-green wattle around eye, larger above than below eye. **ADULT ♀** Similar to ♂ but duller, grey above and less glossy; eye-wattle much smaller. **JUVENILE** Upperparts dull greyish to sooty-black; entire underparts dirty white with broad tawny stripe down centre of throat with chestnut-brown borders[504, 676]. **IMMATURE** Above dark grey to sooty-black with little greenish gloss; underparts lacks pale yellow of adult; chin, throat and upper breast pale tawny to rufous-buff, bordered by mottled chestnut-brown, blackish-brown and black, forming a narrow breast-band. Rest of underparts whitish with greyish flanks. Pale throat and breast area darkens in patches progressively to adult plumage with rest of underparts changing to creamy-yellow. Bill blackish, tipped pale; legs grey-brown to greyish-purple; eye greyish-brown, wattle very small[412, 500, 504, 676].

GEOGRAPHICAL VARIATION None. Monotypic.

MOULT Wing moult recorded in Sep (Bioko)[412].

RANGE, HABITAT and STATUS **Breeding range** Distribution fragmented; N population in W and S Cameroon, Bioko, Equatorial Guinea and Gabon; S population in NW Angola. **Habitat** In dense undergrowth of primary and secondary lowland forest. In Cameroon also found in primary forest, but where it overlaps with Yellow-bellied Wattle-eye *Dyaphorophyia concreata* it is usually found only in dense undergrowth of secondary forest at 1050–1950 m. In Gabon, typically a bird of secondary forest, also early-stage regenerated flooded forests on islands, overgrown vegetation around villages, plantations and in fallow ground with dense low vegetation[7, 21, 23, 207, 344, 412, 431, 504, 664, 676, 907]. **Status** Uncommon resident.

Conservation status Unknown.

MOVEMENTS Unknown; probably sedentary.

SOCIAL ORGANISATION and GENERAL BEHAVIOUR In pairs or family parties, members maintaining regular and close visual and vocal contact, with ♂ singing and both sexes giving contact calls and 'wing-fripping' sounds in flight. Defends territory of 7–10 ha (n=7) throughout year. Due to rapid habitat changes in some areas, pairs are rarely together or present in the same spot for more than one breeding season (Gabon). ♂ regularly patrols entire territory, singing from more open areas above undergrowth, where he flies from perch to perch with whirring wings and fluffed-out rump feathers. Sings with upright posture, bill pointing up, and swollen eye-wattles bright green. On approach of an intruder, ♂ gives long territorial advertising song, flying back and forth with whirring or 'fripping' wing sounds and fluffed-out rump feathers. Intruders are chased with high-intensity calls, rump fluffed-out, whirring, 'fripping' flight and bill-snapping[412, 456, 676]. **Foraging behaviour** Low down in dense undergrowth, among low shrubs, broadleaved herbs, tangles of leafy lianas, in piles of branches with dead leaves. Also inspects fallen and decaying trunks and large stems in thickets. Hops from twig to twig in upright or crouched posture, carefully inspecting vegetation with nervous lateral movements of the head and body. Often flies with whirring wings among tangles and thickets to dislodge insects. Then from a perch below, stretches to pick insects off leaves, or makes short sallies, sometimes hovering to capture prey. Often joins mixed foraging parties, particularly during non-breeding season. **Food** Arthropods, mainly insects, including Coleoptera (beetles), Lepidoptera (moths and caterpillars), Orthoptera (grasshoppers), Hymenoptera (ants), Diptera (large flies), Isoptera (winged termites). Also takes spiders. Prey mostly 10–15 mm long, sometimes up to 30 mm[294, 412, 456, 676].

SOUNDS Little known. Repertoire consists of high-pitched whistles, churring, grunting and bill-snapping sounds. Two types of territorial song: a short, often repeated phrase of 3–6 high-pitched, thin descending notes *fi-fi-fu, he-he-her-her-hur,* sometimes preceded by excited *wikwik-, ptiucteedee* or *ptiuc-ti-di-tititìtu*. This call is reminiscent of Brown-throated Wattle-eye. Second call type, used in high-intensity territorial defence, consists of a long series (over 1 min) of ringing notes on same pitch (*c*.3/sec) *fu-fu-fu-fu-*, *teer-teer-teer-teer-* and reminiscent of Olive-green Camaroptera *Cameroptera chloronota*. Flight call a *kweck-kweck-* accelerating to *ptedecptedecpt-edec-*, also nasal churring and grunting *gehgehge-hgeh-*. When excited a repeated high-pitched *ptick-ptick-*. In alarm a rapid *pwit-pwit-pwit-*, faster *chikchikchik*, *pwickpwickpwick-* or hard *pteckpteckpteck-*, bill-snapping and harsh 'wing-fripping'[412, 500, 515, 676].

BREEDING BIOLOGY Little known. Monogamous, with helpers, known at least to assist in feeding young. ♂ keeps close to the ♀ and regularly feeds her. Helpers believed to be from previous brood. Density estimates varied from *c*.7–13.5 pairs/km² depending on habitat[294]. **Season** Jan, Jul (Gabon)[294, 676]; gonads enlarged Oct–Nov (Bioko)[412]; ♂ breeding condition Aug (Angola)[865, 907]. **Displays** Unknown, except known to courtship-feed. **Nest** Role of sexes unknown. Small neat cup of vegetable fibres, small stems, rootlets, pieces of bark and dead leaves, with lichens and pieces of decaying leaves on outside, bound with spider web. Lined with finer material. Usually placed in fork of a sapling, or at a point where thin, low large-leaved vines cross. Nest placed under a leaf (not as close as in Chestnut Wattle-eye) at 0.4–1 m above ground. ***Size*** OD 45 mm, ID 40–45 mm, cup depth 30 mm, height 45 mm[294, 646, 676]. **Eggs** 2 (n=2). Pale greenish or greenish-white with cap of heavy brown to grey-brown spots and blotches mainly at large end. ***Size*** 17.5–18 x 12–12.5 mm (n=2)[646]. **Incubation** By ♀ alone, who sits for long periods and is regularly fed by ♂ on and off nest. ♂ closely guards ♀ while she is on the nest, also sings nearby. Period unknown, but at least 14 days[294, 676]. **Nestling** Dull blackish-brown to greyish-black above without spotting or chestnut sides of head. Wings similar with coverts tipped buff. Underparts white. Fed by both sexes, as well as by young from previous brood. Fledge after 15 days (n=1). Young remain with parents for several months, probably until next breeding season[294, 500, 676]. **Predation and longevity** Unknown, but see Jameson's Wattle-eye p.335. **Brood parasite** Unknown.

MEASUREMENTS and WEIGHTS *D. chalybea* ♂ (10) wing 51–54 (52.3), tail 22–25 (23.5), bill 14–15.5 (14.5), tarsus 17–18 (17.5); ♀ (3) wing 52–54 (51.8), tail 23–24 (23.8), bill 14–15 (14.5), tarsus 17–18 (17.3)[676]. **Weight** ♂♀? (10) 11–13 g (11.7) (Gabon)[676]. For additional data see[412, 676, 876].

107 YELLOW-BELLIED WATTLE-EYE (Golden-bellied, Chestnut-bellied or Kungwe Wattle-eye) *Dyaphorophyia concreta* Plate 38

FIELD IDENTIFICATION Very small (9–10 cm), plump, colourful, almost tailless flycatcher-like bird with a big head and bright green or blue eye-wattle and bright yellow, or yellow and chestnut-brown below. Sexes different. ♂ above glossy greyish blue-green, below variable from completely pale yellow (rarely with black bib in Angola) to bright reddish chestnut-brown with bright yellow chin. ♀ duller above, with throat, or throat and breast, dark chestnut-brown contrasting with bright yellow belly. Young above spotted buffy-brown, below whitish to yellowish-grey. More often heard than seen, particularly 'fripping' sounds of wings; calls variable, usually 2–4 loud, rapidly repeated whistles, often on a descending scale, and usually combined with guttural grunts, chuckling and scolding notes. In pairs or family group, usually foraging low down in undergrowth of primary and secondary lowland forest. Resident with fragmented distribution: in West Africa from E Guinea to Ghana; SE Nigeria to Central African Republic, southwards to W Zaïre; Angola; E Zaïre and W Uganda to W Burundi, W Kenya and NW Tanzania. ***Flight characteristics***: Fast; wings rounded, appears tailless. Often makes a whirring, buzzing, snapping or 'fripping' sound with wings in flight. Rump yellowish when exposed in display.

COMPARISONS Distinctive. From other wattle-eyes by bright yellow or yellow and chestnut-brown underparts.

DESCRIPTION Adult ♂ *graueri* ***Head and back*** Pale greenish blue-grey, head darker glossy bluish-green. Pale to golden-yellow line across base of upper mandible and above lores as a spot in front of eye. Back and rump feathers long and hair-like, lower rump feathers broadly tipped pale yellow, conspicuous only in display. Uppertail-coverts metallic steel-blue. ***Wings*** Primaries, secondaries and tertials blackish, edged greenish blue-grey on outer webs. ***Tail*** Below metallic steel-blue, underside grey. ***Underparts*** Variable with three morphs (see Geographical Variation). YELLOW morph; bright golden-yellow from chin to vent. CHESTNUT-BROWN morph; rich chestnut-brown except for golden-yellow chin and throat. In E Zaïre 19% ♂♂ have only chin yellow with rest of underparts chestnut-brown to rich reddish orange-brown. BLACK morph; only in *ansorgei* some ♂♂ show a black pear-shaped patch with a slight bluish gloss on yellow throat and breast. ***Bare parts*** Bill broad and black, palate unknown, legs purplish- to bluish-grey, claws whitish; eye colour variable — dark brown, red-brown to purplish or grey-brown with inner ring whitish, pale bluish or lavender; large fleshy flat- topped wattle around eye, wider in front, colour variable from light yellowish-green to bright emerald- or apple-green, bright china-blue in *kungwensis*[289, 471, 569, 674, 676]. **ADULT ♀** *graueri* Like ♂ but ***Upperparts*** including wings greyer with less metallic gloss; rump grey. Head not as dark and with whitish narrow forehead and loral stripe, chin and moustachial stripe whitish or pale yellow. ***Underparts*** Throat, breast and uppersides of belly chestnut-brown to deep reddish-brown, rest yellowish tinged pale chestnut-brown, with some specimens completely reddish-brown below; flanks grey. ***Bare parts*** Similar to ♂ but legs blue-grey (*graueri* W Kenya) and eye apparently dark grey with smaller eye-wattle[289, 631, 676]. **JUVENILE** *concreta* Upperparts dull grey, spotted rusty to buffy-brown, particularly on head and back. Loral streak dirty yellowish. Lower back feathers with pale olive edgings. Underparts dirty white to yellowish-white, tinged olive-grey particularly on breast; throat and sides of breast tinged dull yellowish. Wing-coverts and tertials tipped rufous-buff; bill browner, no eye-wattle[471, 504, 676]. **IMMATURE** Like adult ♂ but duller; upperparts greenish-grey, greyer on head, greener on mantle. Underparts dull pale golden-yellow (brighter in ♂) with grey-green tinge on throat, breast and flanks. Shows progressive development of chestnut-brown. In ♀ throat and upper breast with some chestnut-brown feathers. Wings: Coverts and tertials broadly edged rufous-buff, forming a double bar. Bill blackish; legs dark brown; small grey eye-wattle[259, 456, 471, 676].

GEOGRAPHICAL VARIATION At least 7 races, with three colour morphs (polymorphism restricted to ♂♂). Very variable and not well understood. Variation mainly in colour of underparts of ♂♂, in amount and intensity of chestnut-brown in underparts of ♀♀, and amount of green in upperparts. The colour of the wattle is important in one race. Variation in ♂ underparts: reddish chestnut-brown (chestnut-brown morph) in nominate *concreta* (including *lomaensis*, Sierra Leone to Ghana). Yellow or golden (yellow morph) in *silvae* (W Kenya) and *kungwensis* (Kungwe Mt., W Tanzania); *harterti* (Cameroon, SE Nigeria, Congo, Gabon) a deeper orange-yellow, and *kumbaensis* (SW Cameroon) intermediate. Both yellow and chestnut-brown morphs only found in *graueri* (E Zaïre and SW Uganda), chestnut-brown morph forming 19% of ♂♂ collected. Black-breasted morph, characterised by a bluish-black pear-shaped patch on the throat and breast, found only in *ansorgei* (Angola), where ♂♂ are normally yellow-bellied, although some ♂♂ also recorded with chestnut-brown tinge on breast and belly. Upperparts: compared to *graueri*, nominate race is darker greenish-grey above, *ansorgei* paler and more olive-grey, *silvae* lighter green with greyish nape, and *kungwensis* with a more slaty blue-grey with metallic tinge. This race is also paler below and has a distinctive bright china-blue eye-wattle (emerald-green in other races). In ♀♀ throat and breast intensity ranges from a distinct deep maroon chestnut-brown patch in *concreta*, to a more diffuse area which grades onto belly and flanks in other races. Yellow and green colours are known to fade in museum specimens[180, 471, 500, 569, 674].

MOULT Believed to have a complete post-juvenile moult. In adults, early stages of wing moult from Mar–May, mid-stages Apr–Aug, and late stages Jun–Nov (Liberia)[259, 757, 858].

RANGE, HABITAT and STATUS Breeding range Distribution widespread but fragmented: (1) E Guinea, Sierra Leone, Liberia, Ivory Coast and Ghana; (2) SE Nigeria, W and S Cameroon, W Central African Republic, Rio Muni, Gabon, Congo and W Zaïre; (3) W Angola; (4) NE and E Zaïre, Rwanda, Burundi, W Uganda, NW Tanzania; (5) W Kenya. **Habitat** Undisturbed primary and secondary lowland forest, but in SW Cameroon also extends into montane forest. Also found in forest patches in forest–grassland mosaic, thickets and sometimes in plantations and logged areas. In Gabon mainly in primary forest, rarely in secondary forest where replaced by Black-necked Wattle-eye. Avoids clearings and open areas where forest has been disturbed by storms, also areas of low and liana-rich forest. In Kenya in deep shady forest with well-developed layer of low trees and little ground cover. In Tanzania in forest and bamboo. Recorded up to 2500 m in Uganda[7, 23, 37, 234, 259, 294, 295, 318, 347, 431, 456, 471, 631, 637, 674, 676, 688, 713, 717, 848, 858, 907]. **Status** Resident, at least in Liberia and NE Gabon. Rare in some areas, locally common in others. **Conservation status** Unknown; however, its fragmented distribution and poorly understood taxonomy combine to warrant investigation. Estimated population in Liberia 80,000 pairs[858].

MOVEMENTS Unknown, appears sedentary in NE Gabon[676].

SOCIAL ORGANISATION and GENERAL BEHAVIOUR Solitary, in pairs or family groups. Shy and difficult to see, more often heard than seen as it keeps low down in dark shaded undergrowth. More easily seen when in mixed foraging parties. Active all day, partners always moving together, maintaining regular but not close or continuous vocal and visual contact like other *Dyaphorophyia*, except when breeding. Advertise and defend a territory of 17.0 ±3.7 ha (n=7) throughout the year. ♂ advertises territory from open undergrowth at *c.*2–4 m above ground. On approach of intruding pair, territorial ♂ rapidly repeats *houit-* note and makes lengthy, fast, whirring or 'fripping' flights with fluffed-out rump feathers and aggressive flight calls. Then perches in open, exposing bright yellow underparts, fully extending emerald-green eye-wattles and giving advertising song with bill tilted upwards. Intruding ♂♂ are chased by resident ♂ with his rump fluffed-out and aggressive bill-snapping. ♀ is usually passive in such encounters, although she may chase intruding ♀. When anxious, crouches with sleeked plumage and makes rapid lateral movements with head and body. When alarmed, ♂ stretches up with legs extended, grunts and flies off rapidly, ♀ usually remaining crouched among leaves. Roosting and maintenance behaviour unknown[294, 456, 676, 717]. **Foraging behaviour** Arboreal, in undergrowth, usually less than 4 m, mostly less than 2 m. In dry season higher up at 5–15 m, occasionally to 20 m. Gleans from foliage, hops in upright or crouched posture from twig to twig in saplings and small trees or dense leafy tangles, among dried leaves and dead or decaying twigs. Snatches prey from vegetation, either stretching upward from perch or hovering briefly to capture prey on the wing or from beneath a leaf. Sometimes moves through vegetation with whirring flight to dislodge insects. Frequently joins mixed foraging parties, particularly in non-breeding season[294, 456, 676, 688, 717, 858]. **Food** Arthropods, mainly insects, including Coleoptera (beetles), Hymenoptera (bees, wasps and ants), Lepidoptera (moths and caterpillars), Orthoptera (grasshoppers), Diptera (flies), Isoptera (winged termites), insect eggs and pupae. Also takes spiders and once small fruits. Prey 8–35 mm, mostly 12–18 mm, occasionally grasshoppers up to 70 mm[294, 676, 688, 858].

SOUNDS Repertoire variable and not well understood, with whistles, guttural clucks, chuckles, bill-snapping and 'wing-fripping' sounds. The presence of duetting between partners requires confirmation, but family members are known to chorus with hoarse calls. Whistled calls rather batis-like, other notes nasal or with a quality similar to the alarm call of Common Bulbul *Pycnonotus barbatus*. Generally calls are loud and far-carrying. Main advertising song geographically variable; in Angola a rapid trisyllabic melodious whistle *tututu,* third syllable sometimes strongly accentuated, producing a call reminiscent of Orange-breasted Bush-shrike *Chlorophoneus sulfureopectus*, also a whistled *phee-phee-pheat* or longer *pih-pih-puh-puh-puhh.* In Uganda a descending 4-syllable melodious whistle *ti-ti-ti-tyew* or *ptit-ti-ti-tyew,* last note the longest. In Kenya gives 3 short notes *kikiki,* followed by 2 whistled ones, each a third lower than the last, and a final loud, grating, upslurred one; *kikiki-pee-pur-GWICK* or *whick! whick! tchwee WHERNK!* In Gabon, a high-pitched 2-note whistle *eee- eee,* very often followed by some scolding *houit-, whick- or hwuK-* notes. Also has a longer series of 1–4 descending whistles *heet-whot* or *he-he-hu-ho-.* When very excited ♂ gives *eee-eee-houit-houit,* which is often preceded and combined with more hoarse, often buzzy notes *trr-trr-trr-ptipptip-eee-eee-houit-houit, wwikwik-he-he-hwuK- hwuK-* or *hip-hip-hip-huu-hu-WHIP.* Gabon birds do not respond to songs from Uganda. When ♂♂ countersing, each gives notes of slightly different pitch, *he-he-* by one, *hu-hu-* by another. The difference in pitch, volume and character between *eee-* or *he-* and *houit-* or *hwuK-* produces a ventriloquial effect, which has sometimes led to speculation about possible duetting. In Gabon, high-intensity territorial song is produced by ♂, and consists of a long series of distinctive, loud, emphatic *jik-, houit-, pwick-, tch-wik!, whick!* or *hwuK-* notes. Uganda birds have similar song, to which birds in Gabon show only a mild reaction to playback. Aggressive flight call consists of a series of regular, hoarse *gehgehge-hgeh-* notes followed by rapid *pwick-pwick-pwick-.* Contact calls by both sexes consist of irregular chattering of various soft notes: *hit, ptic, pwik, peep, pwayt, plup, pilup* or *prec,* mixed with hard, nasal *kckt, treck, tchek* or *terwit.* Also makes chattering *chchchchch-* and strident tinkling *tzik-tzik-tzik-* notes. Anxiety and alarm calls, irregular series or rapid, grating *pweck-* or *taytayk-* mixed with softer buzzy *twaytwi, turrit* or *pririt* sounds. Call of young *tictic-* or *pwick.* In hand adults give nasal *kwee-kway-kwee* and *coïk,* young softer *pwee-pway-pwee.* When excited, makes rapid bill-snapping, and in flight both sexes make loud 'fripping' sound with wings[79, 289, 500, 504, 515, 569, 631, 676, 865].

BREEDING BIOLOGY Monogamous and territorial; appears to have life-long pairs bonds (NE Gabon). Mean density in NE Gabon 5.1 pairs/km^2, but varies between 2.6–6.4. In Kakamega Forest (Kenya) 2 adults in 8 ha. In Gabon, of 12 nests, 8 contained a total of 15 eggs. Only 2 nests produced fledglings for a total of 4 young[294, 456, 676, 847]. **Season** ♀ enlarged gonads Apr (Sierra Leone)[15]; courtship display Dec–Feb and Apr, juvenile Dec, Feb, ♂ and ♀ with moderately enlarged gonads Jan–Aug (Liberia)[234, 259, 858]; ♂ and ♀ slightly enlarged gonads Apr (Nigeria)[676]; Nov–Feb, Apr, Jun (Cameroon)[757]; all months except Dec, mostly Aug–Oct and Jan–Feb (Gabon); Oct (Congo)[676]; ♂ and ♀ enlarged gonads Feb–Jun, juveniles Aug, Dec (Zaïre)[22, 289, 688]; juvenile Mar, enlarged gonads Aug, Jul–Nov (Angola)[7, 865, 907]; Nov (East Africa)[293]; Aug breeding condition (Tanzania)[336, 676]. **Displays** ***Courtship*** Unknown, but thought to be similar to ♂ high-intensity territorial display, in which he fluffs out rump feathers and makes loud 'fripping' sounds with wings during excited flights. Courtship-feeding takes place. **Nest** Built by ♀, escorted by ♂ who sings and often feeds her. The small neat cup is built of vegetable fibres, small stems, fine rootlets, pieces of bark, with pieces of dried leaves on outside, bound together with spider web. Lining consists of thinner material, particularly blackish *Marasmius* fungus. In NE Gabon, placed *c.*2 m (1–3, n=17) above the ground in middle of *Alchornea floribunda* (Euphorbiaceae), a common undergrowth plant whose leaves form receptacles for dead and decaying vegetable material, providing a camouflaged nest site. ***Size*** OD 55–75 mm, ID 46–48 mm, cup depth 25–36 mm, height 40–55 mm[294, 676]. **Eggs** Usually 2 (1–2, n=8), laid at 1 day intervals. Cream with slight pinkish, or pale green, ground colour with ring of dark brown-grey and rusty brown spots at large end (once near centre), and faint smaller brown-grey to lavender-grey speckles. ***Size*** 18–21 x 12–14 mm (19.3 x 12.9, n=5). Second or replacement clutches not recorded, but birds laying in Aug–Oct, if unsuccessful may lay again in Jan–Feb (NE Gabon)[294, 676]. **Incubation** begins with last egg, by ♀ alone, who sits for long periods, and is regularly fed by ♂. Although ♀ also feeds herself, ♂ remains with her, both keeping up an almost continuous babble of squeaking notes as they forage low down, sometimes almost on the forest floor. Period 16 days[294, 676]. **Nestling** Hatch blind and naked, skin pinkish-brown with sparse pale brown down. Mouth spots unknown. Upperparts grey with rufous buff-brown spotting from head to rump. Wing feathers tipped same. Underparts: Chin whitish with some orange spots, breast greyish-white, belly whitish. Initially ♀ does all the feeding, ♂ supplying her; later both feed young. Fledge after 12–13 days. Young remain with parents for 3–5 months, although dependent from *c.*10 weeks. Usually each parent cares for a particular young. When immatures move into adjacent territories, they are only threatened not attacked[294, 500, 676]. For nestling development see[676]. **Predation and longevity** Predation unknown. Live for at least 9 years, with pairs retaining the same partners[676]. **Brood parasite** Unknown.

MEASUREMENTS and WEIGHTS *D. c. graueri* ♂♀? (10) wing 59–65 (60.9), tail 23–26 (24.4), tarsus 14–16.5 (16.1), bill (to skull) 14–15.5 (14.8)[500]; *kumbaensis* ♂ (4) wing 57–61 (58.1), tail 25–28 (26.3), bill 12–13 (12.8); ♀ (3) 57–61 (59.0), tail 24–27.5 (25.8); bill 13–14 (13.5) (Cameroon)[412]. **Weight**: *concreta* ♂ (23) mean 11.7 ±1 g, Imm ♂ (5) 11.5 ±3.1 g; ♀ (22) mean 11.1 ±1.2 g, Imm ♀ (2) 8.8–9.8 g (Liberia)[259]; *ansorgei* ♂ (6) 9–12 g (10.9); ♀ (2) 10.5–0.5 g, juvenile ♂ 12.5 g (Angola)[569]; ♂ (7) 9–12.5 g (11.1) (Angola)[676]; *kumbaensis* ♂♀? (7) 12–14 g (13.1) (Cameroon)[412]. For additional data see[478, 569, 676, 682, 686, 757, 908].

108 WHITE HELMET-SHRIKE (White-crested Helmet-shrike, Curly-crested Helmet-shrike) *Prionops plumatus* Plate 39

FIELD IDENTIFICATION Medium-large (19–25 cm), black, white and grey helmet-shrike with bushy white to greyish frontal feathers and a bright yellow eye encircled by fleshy yellow wattle; bill black; legs reddish. Head variable, crest formed by frontal feathers ranging from whitish straight or curled to very small and greyish. Sexes similar, face variable from white to greyish with dark crescent shape on ear-coverts, nape-band white, back black, wings and tail black and white. Broad white wing-stripe and large white wing-patch, conspicuous in flight. Young tinged brown above, wing-coverts tipped white and eye brown, without wattle. Flight rapid, buoyant and undulating. Groups chorus and duet with descending nasal rolling, chattering, churring and growling notes, often with bill-snapping. Gregarious, in groups of less than *c.*10 members, foraging at all levels, including ground. Found in open woodland, riverine and dry bush. Resident with extensive local movements, occurring throughout deciduous woodlands of sub-Saharan Africa, except forested areas and SW arid region of continent. ***Flight characteristics***: Rapid, usually buoyant and undulating, rather butterfly-like. Groups move in leap-frog manner from tree to tree, each bird taking a perch ahead of the one in front. Wings broad and rounded; white wing-stripe, band across primaries and outer tail feathers conspicuous in flight, giving a pied appearance.

COMPARISONS Distinctive, confusion unlikely over most of range, except East Africa, where similar to larger Grey-crested Helmet-shrike *Prionops poliolophus*. This species lacks an eye-wattle but has a yellow eye, a white wing-stripe and a long, rather straight grey crest, with hindpart dark grey, and has distinctive blackish patches on sides of breast, when seen from front; occurs in better woodlands with higher rainfall. White Helmet-shrike often found in association with Retz's Helmet-shrike *Prionops retzii*[318].

DESCRIPTION **Adult** Sexes similar. ***Head*** Variable (see Geographical Variation), frontal bushy, white to greyish-white with long plumes, curled forward (*cristatus*), straight up to 38 mm (*plumatus*) or grey and very small (*talacoma*); hindcrown grey, darkening on hindneck; side of face white to greyish-white in fan shape around eye, bordered at back with dark greyish-black crescent on ear-coverts; nape white forming a collar over upperparts. Feather pigments known to be unstable[596]. ***Back*** Mantle to rump and uppertail-coverts blue-black with slight greenish gloss. ***Wings*** Black with slight gloss, broad white stripe (lacking in some races, see Geographical Variation) formed by coverts and outer web of outer secondaries and tertials. Broad wing-patch formed across inner webs of primaries. Secondaries tipped white. ***Tail*** Outer feathers completely white, rest with broad terminal white spot, decreasing inwards (see Geographical Variation). ***Underparts*** White to greyish-white; undertail-coverts white, unusually large. ***Bare parts*** Bill black; palate flesh-coloured; legs reddish- to pinkish-orange; eye bright yellow, surrounded by yellow fleshy scalloped wattle. **Juvenile** Upperparts duller than adult, head dirty white, without crest in *plumatus* and *cristatus*, frontal small; back tinged brownish-grey, feathers tipped whitish-buff; lacks distinctive crescent mark on ear-coverts. Wing: Similar to adult but primary coverts tipped and edged whitish. Underparts: Dull white to greyish-white. Bare parts: Bill brown to dull black; legs paler than adult; eye brown without surrounding wattle, eye-rim dark[2, 205, 504, 631]. **Immature** Duller than adult; head mottled grey-and-white or plain white, including nape; primary coverts tipped pale whitish, tertials broadly tipped white. Bill black; legs paler than adult; eye brown developing through grey or greenish-grey to yellow of adult. Wattle dark, developing through slight yellowing to greenish-yellow and finally bright yellow. Young attain adult plumage at one year old. Subordinate adults may have smaller wattles than dominant birds[2, 205, 290, 500, 506].

GEOGRAPHICAL VARIATION Variation extensive with at least nine races of which only six recognised here, intermediates common. Variation mainly in size, presence or absence of white wing-stripe, extent of white in tail and the length and character of the crest and frontal feathers. Nominate *plumatus* (includes *adamauae*, Senegal, Gambia to Nigeria and N Cameroon) has longest, straightest and whitest crest and frontal feathers. These are progressively shorter in *concinnata* (Cameroon to Sudan, N Uganda); *vinaceigularis* (includes *melanoptera*, Ethiopia, N and E Kenya, Somalia) and shortest in southernmost populations *poliocephalus* (E Tanzania, Malawi, SE Zambia, Mozambique to Zululand in South Africa) and *talacoma* (includes *angolica*, Zimbabwe, Botswana, Namibia, Angola, Zambia, S Zaïre, NW Tanzania, S Uganda and S central Kenya). These E and S races also have greyer heads and show the greatest amount of white in the tail; *talacoma* is longer-winged and longer-tailed than *poliocephalus*. Race *cristatus* (E and S Ethiopia, SE Sudan) has a long curly crest, *plumatus* and *cristatus* are the largest races. All races, except the large *cristatus* and smaller *vinaceigularis*, have white wing-stripes, or nearly so, with intermediates occurring between these and adjacent races[3, 96, 180, 206, 631].

MOULT Little known. A complete post-breeding moult recorded for Jan, Mar (S Tanzania), body moult Feb (Zimbabwe) and Jul (South Africa)[500, 832].

RANGE, HABITAT and STATUS Breeding range Widely distributed S of *c.*15°N; from West to East and southern Africa in Mauritania, Mali, Senegal, Gambia, Guinea-Bissau, Guinea, Sierra Leone, Ivory Coast, Burkina Faso, Niger, Chad, Ghana, Togo, Benin, Cameroon, Nigeria, Central African Republic, NE Zaïre, S Sudan, Eritrea, N and SW Somalia, Ethiopia, Uganda, Kenya, Tanzania, Rwanda, Burundi, Malawi, central and S Mozambique, Zambia, Angola, N Namibia, N, central and E Botswana, Zimbabwe, Swaziland and NE South Africa[7, 21, 26, 31, 37, 48, 96, 119, 242, 318, 325, 431, 482, 504, 631, 639, 697, 807, 848, 859, 907]. **Habitat** Found in a wide range of wooded savannas and woodlands, particularly deciduous broadleaved woodlands such as miombo (*Brachystegia* and *Julbernardia*), *Baikiaea*, *Burkea*, mopane *Colophospermum*, *Combretum*, *Pterocarpus* and *Terminalia*, as well as baobab and riverine woodland. Although sometimes found in *Acacia* woodland, this is usually during the non-breeding season when it disperses into a wide variety of habitats including suburban gardens. Occasionally also found on forest edges. Recorded up to 1800 m (Kenya) and 1900 m (E Zaïre)[22, 318, 320, 325, 506, 639]. **Status** Not uncommon to local resident with seasonal movements. **Conservation status** Not threatened. Held in captivity[655].

MOVEMENTS Undertakes local movements in non-breeding season. These are sometimes extensive, at least in southern Africa, with irruptions of groups in places where they are not usually found. Altitudinal movements on the E escarpment also recorded in austral winter, and assumed to be from high to low ground. The magnitude of these movements in the region remains unknown, but may be part of much larger-scale movements into the region from further N. The longer wing of the southernmost race suggests that it may undertake longer movements. During drought years groups tend to become more nomadic. Some races appear to move more than others, e.g. *poliocephalus* from Tanzania is mainly a non-breeding visitor to SE Kenya (May–Sep), overlapping with *vinaceigularis*. In West Africa groups tend to break up into smaller, less coherent groups in non-breeding season, whereas groups in southern Africa tend to increase their size[96, 97, 205, 320, 500, 631, 639, 891].

SOCIAL ORGANISATION and GENERAL BEHAVIOUR Gregarious; found in permanent groups of *c.*7 birds in austral summer, with winter groups generally larger (range 2–22, n=1096, southern Africa). A group consists of a dominant pair (alpha ♂ and ♀), which are usually the largest individuals, and the rest consisting of closely related birds. Social organisation appears to lack obvious signs of sexual dimorphism, aggression or status signalling, except for dominant birds which are larger and may have larger eye-wattles. Some correlation also exists between weight and age of other members and their status. Group structure appears to be established and maintained by a dominance hierarchy, with the most dominant ♀ at the top, followed by her mate, the most dominant ♂. Below these come adult ♀♀, who are usually the sisters of the dominant ♀, then adult ♂♂, who are usually brothers of the dominant ♂. These are followed by adult offspring, first-year offspring and finally fledglings. The dominant pair can usually be identified by their behaviour, particularly during courtship and breeding, when they often perch together and occasionally preen each other (allopreen). Visually they also appear to have larger eye-wattles. New groups are formed when up to 4 brothers leave their parental group and team up with a similar number of sisters from another group. The dominant ♂ mates with the dominant ♀, and only they hold breeding status within group. This status is passed on to other brothers and sisters on the death of one or both of the dominant birds. Offspring do not inherit the breeding opportunity in their parental group, they must first leave and form a new breeding group. Before the establishment of such a group they usually form wandering unisex subgroups. They leave their parental groups any time after they are a year old, and also return any time. Most immigration and emigration takes place at the beginning and end of the breeding season. At least half the offspring leave by the time they are 3 years old. Established groups last *c.*10 years. Within the system there are occasional power struggles for dominance, dominant pair separations, expulsion of a widowed dominant, and the breakaway of members to form new groups. Groups generally disintegrate when none of the original brothers and sisters are left, the remaining members usually joining another group. Restless, bold and inquisitive, with group behaviour coordinated, members acting in unison, e.g. territorial defence, feeding, preening or flight. Much of the behaviour is initiated by calls. They have a characteristic squat or crouched, horizontal posture in non-aggressive situations, or an upright stance in aggressive territorial interactions. Groups advertise and defend a home range of *c.*18 ha (4.5–30, n=140) which may overlap that of other groups. Within this they defend a summer breeding territory of *c.*12 ha (1.7–19.5, n=14) When calling, adopt an upright posture with tail slightly fanned. Group territorial display consists of members sitting closer together than normal, usually below dominant ♀, with bodies held upright, heads swayed from side to side, and tails fanned. Calling is usually initiated by dominant ♀ with *chi- chi-chi-cherow-cherow*, followed by duetting and chorusing with head and neck stretched upwards (see Sounds). Some calls probably given by individuals of a particular status. Groups attempt to displace each other by individuals flying (swooping) at opposing group. Occasionally resort to physical contact. Interaction ceases when one group suddenly departs, flying off in a tight flock. Prior to these interactions, individuals can be seen flying slowly, but with rapid wingbeats and body feathers fluffed out. Aggression is signalled by low-pitched *grrr-* sounds and rapid bursts of bill-snapping. Sometimes shows interspecific aggression towards Retz's Helmet-shrike, in spite of foraging together with this species. Exceptionally aggressive towards all predators, particularly owls, eagles and rollers, mobbing them with continuous dive-bombing and bill-snapping. They are attracted to injured conspecifics, and when alarmed will suddenly explode out of a tree twittering. A group progresses through woodland by a leap-frogging movement of members, those behind flying past others to settle ahead of them. Certain members appear to act as sentries while others forage, particularly when on the ground. Short-range contact and group cohesion is probably maintained by visual cues (white flash patterns) and by soft contact *tpweet-tpwee-* calls, chorusing, duetting, bill-snapping and *whit-whit-* flight calls. Some of these calls also used in greeting displays. Individuals separated from the group repeatedly utter a loud distinctive *treeu-* call. In maintenance behaviour, scratch indirectly; allopreening rare in wild, but known for captive birds; bathe in dew or rain caught in leaves; roost together, huddled up in a leafy tree, individuals showing no particular preference for the direction they face. There is even a record of birds perching on top of each other! The lower eye-wattle folds up when the bird sleeps and the head is tucked under the wing. Roost sites used for only a few nights[78, 97, 103, 205, 290, 500, 506, 575].

Foraging behaviour Forages in a group, flying from one tree to another. When perching they squat horizontally, remaining motionless for a moment before peering intently about or tilting (cocking) the head to one side as they search for prey, apparently using one eye, in a manner suggestive of listening for prey. Search for food at all levels from ground to canopy, mainly in mid- and lower levels. In one study 41% taken from twigs and stems, overall 32% when perched, 49% in flight and 19% on ground. In summer most food is gleaned from trunks, branches and foliage, sometimes foraging like a tit, hanging upside-down by one leg at the end of a branch. In austral winter this strategy changes to perch-hunting, scanning the ground below and dropping down to prey. On the ground they hop about. Prey is captured with an audible snap of the bill, and some insects are hawked in the air. Large prey is beaten vigorously against branch. A group will follow the same foraging route for a number of days, and often join or form the nucleus of mixed foraging parties.

Food Arthropods, mainly insects; occasionally small vertebrates. Insects include particularly Lepidoptera (caterpillars, moths and butterflies) (60%), rest made up of Hemiptera (cicadas), Mantodea (mantids), Orthoptera (grasshoppers), Coleoptera (beetles), Hymenoptera (ants) and Isoptera (termites, including alates). Also spiders and centipedes. Occasionally take small reptiles (geckos)[97, 205, 290, 352, 500, 506, 566].

SOUNDS Complex and variable; many defy transcription. Repertoire contains at least 20 different calls, many with a rather nasal quality. Phrases usually combine whistle notes with rolling, gobbling, twittering, buzzing, chattering, churring and growling sounds, often combined with bursts of rapid bill-snapping. Some sounds are sexually distinguishable with most calling in the form of duets and chorusing. Structure and function of calls in relation to status are not well understood, although dominant ♀ believed to initiate much of the calling. The most frequently heard calls are those given in chorus. These consist of variable descending sequences, usually beginning rapidly, high-pitched and complex, ending more slowly, lower-pitched and simple, often with a gobbling, rolling quality. A full sequence has at least 4 call types, which are each repeated a few times. Typically begins with a series of rapidly delivered, short, chattering *tz-tz-* or *ch-ch-ch-* notes (a), followed by rolling *cherow-cherow-*, *kerero-*, *krawow-*, *KWEE-we- wiro* or *chyow-* notes (b), then more buzzy sounds *zrrreeeeu-*, *krrreew-* or *zheeeeeeayh-* (c), then by growling *gruu-gruu-* notes (d), and finally ending in slower rolling *cheroop-* or *kloop-* sounds, which are thought to be modified *cherow* (b) sounds. Sequences are graded, variable and usually interspersed with chattering *tztz-* notes and bill-snapping, sounding like *tztztz-cherow-cherow-tztz-zrrreeeu-zrreru-tztz- gruu-gruu-cheroop*. The *cherow-* note appears a common stem-sound which is modified according to context. It is used by dominant birds to initiate chorusing and on the nest. A sentry will give a *chirule-* call before and after the departure of a group to feed. During incubation exchange, a sitting bird will call *cherow-* or *kchow-*, and the relieving bird gives *chitule-* or *cherow-* before settling. This call is also used by birds approaching the nest. Sitting bird also known to summons an exchange with *zrrreeeu-zrrreeeu-* call. Dominant pair duet with *yuki-yuki* by ♂, *Kidoki-doki* by ♀. Contact is maintained with chorusing, duetting and softer *tpweet-tpwee-* calls, bill-snapping and high-pitched *whit- whit-* or *zit-zit-* flight calls. Birds which appear to have lost their group give a repeated high-pitched loud *treeu-* call. Young beg with buzzing or chattering *tzzrrree-tzzrrree-* calls. Alarm and aggression signalled by rapid bill-snapping, the rate indicative of the intensity. At higher intensity this is also combined with loud, high-pitched, shrill *skree-skree-skree-* or *tzzee-tzzee-* calls[6, 48, 78, 136, 205, 290, 297, 500, 504, 506, 631, 769]. Sonagram[48].

BREEDING BIOLOGY Monogamous, cooperative and territorial, with a single dominant breeding pair assisted by helpers. Group density may reach 1 group/10 ha and estimated to be 5 times more numerous than Retz's Helmet-shrike. Groups indulge in group territorial displays. As autral winter approaches, the home range gradually enlarges until the birds move completely out of the area, returning at the beginning of the next summer. Bonds between dominant members last at least 2.5 years. In one study, 30% nesting success, 25% breeding success, 2.6 nesting attempts/season, 2.3 fledglings/pair/year (fecundity), 83% survival rate of 200 adults and 60% of 70 fledglings. Nesting cycle lasts *c.*45 days[67, 205, 506, 566].

Season Jan, Mar, May–Jun, Oct (Senegal and Gambia)[482]; egg laying Jan, fledglings Aug, Mar (Ghana)[234]; Mar–Jun, Oct–Nov (Nigeria)[37, 290]; Jul–Jan, mainly Sep–Oct (SE Zaïre)[22, 290]; Apr–Jun (Sudan)[242]; recently fledged young May, Oct (Somalia)[859]; Aug–Sep, juvenile and breeding condition Nov (Angola)[7, 423, 907]; Feb–Mar, Jun, Aug, Oct–Nov (East Africa)[293]; Mar (Tanzania)[25]; Sep–Apr, mainly Sep–Dec (Zambia/Zimbabwe/Malawi)[359]; Sep–Dec mainly Sep–Oct (Malawi)[119]; Mar, Aug–Nov, mainly Sep (Zambia)[291]; Aug–Apr, mainly Sep–Oct (Zimbabwe)[30, 48]; Sep–Jan, mainly Oct–Nov (South Africa)[48, 320]; egg-laying Oct–Feb (Botswana)[807].

Displays ***Courtship*** Behaviour occurs during formation of a new group, or start of breeding season in existing group. No elaborate courtship display takes place and courtship-feeding has not been recorded. The breeding pair separate from the group, court and copulate in silence and return within a few minutes. Courting birds perch close together, ♂ adopts a horizontal posture, opens and slowly flap wings close to the body. Sometimes ♀ adopts a similar posture, but ♂ movements more exaggerated. Pair-bond appears to be maintained, at least in part, by duetting, e.g. *yuki-yuki* by ♂, *Kidoki-doki* by ♀. ***Nest-site display*** Selection performed by the dominant pair, who sit in prospective sites, call and make movements resembling nest-building and shaping[97, 205, 506].

Nest All members help construct. Nesting material collected during foraging, individuals giving an excited chattering call when suitable material located, which appears to act as a signal for others to start gathering. The nest is built of bark, which is stripped from dead twigs. This is cemented with spider web collected off trunks and draped onto the frontal feathers. Members of a group will return to the nest, where each bird in turn adds material. Dominant pair do most building, which takes *c.*4 days to complete. The nest is usually placed *c.*5 m (2–10, n=113) above ground in a tree with greyish or lichen-covered bark. Placed on a horizontal branch or sometimes in an upright fork, to which it is securely bonded with web. Once completed it is a neat, compact, shallow, perpendicular-sided cup. The rim and outer wall is profusely plastered with spider web, giving it a smooth greyish appearance; some are camouflaged with small leaves. Lining consists of a few rootlets or dry grass fibres. ***Size*** OD 81–90 mm, ID 63–71 mm, cup depth 24–28 mm, height 35–65 mm (n=11). Nests may remain empty for up to a week before laying commences. Reports of several nests close together require confirmation[20, 32, 205, 290, 506, 697].

Eggs Usually 4 (2–5, n=29), but occasionally 2 ♀♀ lay in the same nest, with 9 eggs recorded, and in such cases some of the eggs may fall out. In one study, mean clutch size was 3.9 (3–9, n=109). Pale greenish or less commonly bluish, pinkish or buff with spots and blotches of purple, chestnut-brown, brown and grey, mainly at the large end. ***Size*** 18.5–23.5 x 14.5–18.0 mm (20.6 x 16.0, n=271)[6, 19, 48, 67, 119, 205, 290, 506]. **Incubation** All members help incubate and brood, with the breeding pair probably doing most. An incubating bird can summon the group to return with *cherow-*, *zrrreeeu-zrrreeeu-* or *chikurr-chair-chair* calls or, in the case of a predator present, prevent them from returning by bill-snapping. May also give the alarm call from the nest. Nest exchange takes place in confusion as group moves past nest tree, with one bird dropping out and exchanging with bird on nest. On settling the new bird calls *ch-cherow-* or *chi-chirule-*, often combined with bill-snapping. Wing fluttering also recorded during change-over. Period 18 days (17–21 days, n=8)[6, 78, 205, 500, 506]. **Nestling** Hatch naked, blind and have mouth spots. Attended by all members, who feed, brood, guard and remove faecal sacs, which are eaten when nestlings are small. Occasionally nestlings void faeces over side of nest. Nestlings beg with chattering *tzzrrree-tzzrrree-* calls and wing quivering. While foraging, when a few members have food for the nestlings, they give an excited chattering call, to which the group responds by returning to the nest, where members with food await their turn to feed the nestlings. The last one with food remains either to brood or to guard them. This bird can summon the group (see Incubation). Fledge after *c.*20 days (17–22, n=8). Fledglings will accompany the group after *c.*3 weeks. Still fed by *c.*10 weeks, at which time they are also feeding themselves. Independent by *c.*5 months and resemble adults when 1 year old[97, 205,

[331, 506]. **Predation and longevity** Adults taken by avian predators, such as Gabar Goshawk *Micronisus gabar*, Ayres's Hawk-eagle *Hieraaetus ayresii* and Bateleur *Terathopius ecaudatus*. Nestlings preyed upon by reptilian, mammalian and avian predators, of which the Gymnogene *Polyboroides typus* is probably the most important. Starvation and bad weather also thought to cause mortality. Oldest record *c*.5 years[205, 506, 806]. **Brood parasite** Only appears to be an accidental host, with one Black Cuckoo *Cuculus clamosus* recorded in a nest and one fledgling Red-chested Cuckoo *C. solitarius* travelling with a group. The high nest attendance may reduce brood parasitism (but see Retz's Helmet-shrike p.349)[5, 205, 506].

MEASUREMENTS and WEIGHTS *P. p. poliocephalus* and *talacoma* ♂ (82) wing 98–116 (106.3), ♂ (81) tail 78–90 (84.7), ♂ (78) bill 18.5–22 (19.9), ♂♀? tarsus 19–23; ♀ (73) wing 103–115 (108.9), ♀ (73) tail 70–91 (86), bill ♀ (70) 18.5–22 (19.9), tarsus see ♂[48]. **Weight** *plumatus* ♂♀? (12) 40.0–48.5 g (43.0 ±3.0 g) (West Africa)[582]; *poliocephalus* and *talacoma* ♂ (44) 27.3–35.8 g (32.7), ♀ (41) 29.7–39.8 g (34.9); ♂♀? (25) 24.5–37 g (29.5) (southern Africa)[48, 205]. For additional data see[96, 319, 346, 478, 494, 583].

109 GREY-CRESTED HELMET-SHRIKE *Prionops poliolophus* Plate 39

FIELD IDENTIFICATION Large (23–26 cm), black, white and grey helmet-shrike with bushy white face and frontal feathers and distinctive dark grey crest and a bright yellow eye without a wattle. Bill black, legs reddish. Below has distinctive (when seen from front) black patches on either side of white breast. Sexes similar, nape-band white, back black, wings and tail black and white. Broad white wing-stripe and large white wing-patch, conspicuous in flight. Young duller and browner above. Little known. Flight rapid, buoyant and undulating. Groups chorus with single (and series of) rolling, descending, churring notes, often with bill-snapping. In groups of *c*.7 members in open woodland, wooded grassland and bushland. Resident with considerable local seasonal movements. Restricted range from SW Kenya to NW Tanzania. ***Flight characteristics***: Wings broad and round. White wing-stripe, band across primaries and edges and tips of tail conspicuous in flight, giving pied appearance.

COMPARISONS Confusion likely only with the smaller White Helmet-shrike *Prionops plumatus*, which has a yellow wattle around the eye, no black breast-patches (black breast-patches are only really obvious when viewed from the front) and head without a distinctive crest; prefers poorer, more arid woodland. Behaviour similar but calls of Grey-crested Helmet-shrike unknown.

DESCRIPTION ADULT Sexes similar. Bushy frontal and feathers on side of face white to greyish-white; crest at back of head dark grey; blackish crescent on ear-coverts; nape white forming collar over upperparts: ***Back*** Mantle to rump and uppertail-coverts black with slight gloss. ***Wings*** Black with slight gloss, broad white stripe formed by coverts and outer webs of outer secondaries and tertials. Broad white wing-patch formed across inner webs of primaries. Secondaries tipped white. ***Tail*** Outer feathers completely white, rest with broad terminal white spot, decreasing in size inwards. ***Underparts*** Chin and throat greyish, rest white to greyish-white with broad blackish patches on either side of breast; undertail-coverts white, unusually large. ***Bare parts*** Bill black; palate unknown; legs reddish-orange; eye bright yellow, eyelids black, no eye-wattle. JUVENILE Little known. Young apparently dingier, upperparts tinged brown; white on wings not so extensive and crest feathers dull slate. Bare parts: Unknown, eye probably brown[2]. IMMATURE Forehead with small grey-brown crest; crown pale brown; nape dirty white; ear-coverts grey-brown. Mantle and back black with some brown feathers. Primaries black, secondaries and tertials brownish-black, wing-stripe dirty white; primary coverts tipped buff; tail black, feathers tipped white, which increases in extent outwards; underparts dirty white, flanks brownish; undertail-coverts white, side breast patches greyish-black; bill black; palate unknown; legs reddish; eye yellow[500].

GEOGRAPHICAL VARIATION None. Monotypic.

MOULT Unknown.

RANGE, HABITAT and STATUS **Breeding range** Found in a restricted area of SW Kenya and N Tanzania. Endemic to woodland E and S of Lake Victoria, formerly ranging from Naivasha and Kedong, SE to Mwanza and N Tabora (S to 5°S). Now found in Serengeti National Park, Mara Game Res., Loliondo, Loita and Nguruman Hills, north to Narok District. In the Rift from Kedong Valley N to Lake Elmenteita and Lake Nakuru National Park[11, 318, 431, 479, 591, 592, 627, 631]. **Habitat** Occurs at 1200–2200 m in moist open woodland, wooded grassland and bushland, typically in Whistling Thorn *Acacia drepanolobium* or *Tarchonanthus*, and also recorded in riverine *Acacia*[318, 479, 591, 631]. **Status** Local uncommon resident with seasonal movements. **Conservation status** Despite evidence that it is recolonising the Rift Valley, it is generally considered uncommon to rare. Until recently, considered extinct in the Naivasha–Kedong area, and apparently still extinct in the area S of Lake Victoria (Mwanza–Tabora), where reported at the turn of the century. It appears to have suffered decline due to habitat destruction, noted as early as 1922.

Requires additional data to make a meaningful assessment, particularly since it moves erratically through poorly observed areas and is subject to misidentification with the White Helmet-shrike. Red Data Book species considered Vulnerable[318, 479, 591, 592, 627].

MOVEMENTS Thought to be highly mobile due to range fluctuations and erratic occurrences, wandering great distances into lower-lying country from apparent breeding area. Post-breeding movements recorded for Jul and Oct–Feb. Recorded from Serengeti in Jun–Oct[180, 239, 318, 591, 592, 627].

SOCIAL ORGANISATION and GENERAL BEHAVIOUR Little known; gregarious, restless and noisy, occurs in groups of *c.*7 (4–9 or 12, n=6). Groups composed of adults and immatures, or newly fledged young. Behaviour reportedly similar to White Helmet-shrike, with which it sometimes flocks. Group members are attracted to wounded members. Feeds quietly, but noisily scolds intruders and group members chorus together. Known to perch in low bushes and join mixed foraging parties[2, 11, 309, 318, 591, 592, 618, 627, 631].

SOUNDS Little known. Description appears similar to White Helmet-shrike; noted as single *chw-err* notes and rolling descending, chattering and churring phrases, such as *chichi-cherrrro.* Chorus consists of additional harsh, scratchy and chattering sounds combined with bill-snapping, e.g. *chikiki-chi-chirrrow chi-chirro che-chiwow-cherrow chk chk skrrk cherrk...*[2, 631].

BREEDING BIOLOGY Virtually unknown; probably monogamous, cooperative and territorial like other helmet-shrikes. **Season** Only 3 breeding records (Apr–May): juvenile Apr, nest and newly fledged young May[2, 318]. **Displays** Unknown. **Nest** Role of sexes and group members unknown. Cup built of grass-stalks and spider web. Nest placed in fork of tree *c.*3.5 m above ground[2]. **Eggs** Only one egg recorded. Bluish-green with zone of dull greyish-brown and red-brown spots. ***Size*** 21 x 17 mm[2]. No further breeding information, except young in nest appear largely brownish-white[631].

MEASUREMENTS and WEIGHTS *P. poliolophus* ♂♀? (4) wing 131–134 (132.8), tail 104–106 (104.8), bill (to skull) 21.5–23 (22), tarsus 22.5–26.5 (24.8); Imm ♂ wing 118, tail 100, bill (to skull) 20, tarsus 24.5[500]; wing 130–135 mm[2, 336]. **Weight** ♂ (1) 49 g[509].

110 CHESTNUT-FRONTED HELMET-SHRIKE
Prionops scopifrons **Plate 39**

FIELD IDENTIFICATION Medium-small (16–18 cm), dark grey, black and white helmet-shrike with bristly orange-brown forehead, coral-red bill and legs, and bright yellowish-orange eyes encircled by small bluish-grey wattles. Sexes similar. Above slaty-black to greyish-black; wings black with small white wing-patch and tail black with broad white edges conspicuous in flight; underparts slate-grey; lower belly and large undertail-coverts white. Young uniform greyish, spotted buff above, faintly barred below and more white in wings; eye brown, no wattle or bristly forehead. Flight rapid, buoyant and undulating. Calls: Chorus with rolling descending, buzzing, nasal and lilting notes, often with bill-snapping. In groups of about 7 members in canopy of lowland and riverine forest, adjacent woodland and mangroves. Resident with local movements, range fragmented from S Somalia, through Kenya, E Tanzania, E Zimbabwe, N and central Mozambique. A straggler further S. ***Flight characteristics***: Rapid, buoyant and undulating. Wings broad and rounded. White band across primaries, particularly in young birds, and white in tail, lower belly and undertail-coverts conspicuous in flight, giving a pied appearance.

COMPARISONS The smallest helmet-shrike; has appearance of a pale Retz's Helmet-shrike *Prionops retzii*, which is larger with black bushy frontal feathers, a red bill and conspicuous red wattle encircling yellow eye. General plumage black and brown (not grey and black as in Chestnut-fronted). Both species often flock together.

DESCRIPTION **Adult** Sexes similar. ***Head*** Frontal with short dense bristly bright chestnut-brown (orange-brown) feathers, separated from crown by narrow band of grey; rest of head, nape and sides of neck and face blackish-slate grading into back; lores white (not all races). ***Back*** Mantle to rump and uppertail-coverts greyish-black with olive tinge. ***Wings*** Greyish-black, primary coverts with slight greenish gloss; narrow white wing-patch formed across primaries on inner web; underwing-coverts blackish. ***Tail*** Blackish, outer feathers edged white, all feathers tipped white, size decreasing towards central pair. ***Underparts*** Chin white (not all races); sides of throat blackish, rest including flanks dark grey, whitening on lower belly; undertail-coverts white, feathers unusually large. ***Bare parts*** Bill coral-red with paler yellowish tip; palate unknown; legs coral-red to bright orange; eye bright yellow with outer orange rim; serrated wattle encircling eye slate-grey to bluish-grey. May assume grotesque proportions in old birds[32]. **Juvenile** Head brownish-black to mottled white, frontal blackish- to greyish-brown, rest of upperparts greyish-brown finely barred buff-white. Wings: Alula, coverts and tertials tipped buff-white, primaries with conspicuous white patch across inner webs. Tail: Like adult. ***Underparts*** Faintly barred and mottled buff greyish-brown; lower belly and undertail-coverts white. Bare parts: Bill and legs dull yellow-orange; eye brown to grey-black without wattle[104, 500, 506, 618]. **IMMATURE** Head with black crown, frontal patch, which in time increases in size, becoming dark grey, progressing through brown tinge, then chestnut-brown dulled with dark grey to bright chestnut-brown. Underparts grey. Bare parts: like adult. Eye and wattle colour only attained in second year. At least 3 age-classes: drab juveniles with brown eye, first-year birds resembling adults but lacking chestnut-brown frontal, and adults with chestnut-brown frontal[48, 205, 297, 500].

GEOGRAPHICAL VARIATION Three races; variation slight, mainly in head coloration and amount of white in wings and tail. Nominate *scopifrons* most widespread (SE Tanzania, Mozambique, E Zimbabwe, straggler to E KwaZulu-Natal in South Africa); *kirki* (S Somalia, coastal E Kenya, NE Tanzania) lacks white lores and chin, has paler chestnut-brown frontal patch and whitish-grey crown-band, and less white in wings; *keniensis* (central Kenya in Meru and Ngaia forests) like *kirki* but has dark grey crown-band, white in wings greatly reduced, only evident from below, but has more white in tail and darker chestnut-brown frontal[500, 631].

MOULT Little known; in immature to adult development, complete body moult takes place before wings and tail are replaced. Straw-coloured frontal patch is not replaced with light chestnut-brown until the following moult[618].

RANGE, HABITAT and STATUS **Breeding range** distribution fragmented from S Somalia, isolated central (Meru), NE and SE Kenya, NE and SE Tanzania, N and central Mozambique and E Zimbabwe. Vagrant to N KwaZulu-Natal in South Africa. Malawi record rejected[431]. **Habitat** Moist lowland coastal and riverine forest, adjacent miombo *Brachystegia* woodlands, thickets and mangroves. Usually below 500 m, seldom inland to *c.*1200 m[26, 48, 205, 318, 322, 325, 431, 481, 631]. **Status** Uncommon to locally common resident over most of range, but rare in Kenyan isolated inland population. **Conservation status** Previously not considered threatened, but at least in southern Africa, because it occurs in low densities in a restricted range, it is threatened due to deforestation for logging and clearing for subsistence farming in E Zimbabwe and S Mozambique. In Kenya the rare isolated inland population (*keniensis*), which was formerly more widespread is now reduced to small numbers in the remnant Meru and Ngaia forests. Status needs reassessment[479, 631].

MOVEMENTS Appears to undertake local seasonal movements, as evident from sporadic sightings outside normal range in non-breeding season[205, 322, 631].

SOCIAL ORGANISATION and GENERAL BEHAVIOUR Gregarious species occurring in groups of *c.*7 (3–12, n=17), occasionally up to 30 birds in non-breeding season. Social organisation little known, but some evidence to suggest that groups consist of closely related individuals in a dominance hierarchy similar to other helmet-shrikes (see White Helmet-shrike *Prionops plumatus* p.340). A restless, noisy and gregarious canopy species, less shy than Retz's Helmet-shrike. In groups their behaviour is coordinated with members acting in unison, e.g. territorial defence, feeding, preening and flying. Much of their behaviour is initiated by calls. Rather inconspicuous in dense forest or woodland habitat, as groups tend to spread out over a wider range than White or Retz's Helmet-shrikes. Typically adopts squat, horizontal posture when perched and a more upright posture when calling. Territory size unknown. During group territorial interactions members sit close together while chorusing. One bird appears to initiate chorusing with *tzetzetzepre-churroe-churroe*-call. Responded immediately to by rest of group with complex calls, including *tueWee- whit-whit,* low *gro* sounds and frequently heard *chair-chair*-sounds, and often heard bursts of rapid bill-snapping. Readily mob predators, dive-bombing them and snapping the bill aggressively or opening it in threat. Contact apparently maintained by both visual and vocal cues, including *chuck- chairrer-chairrer-* and *whit-* calls, some of which are used in greeting displays in which birds bow and spread their wings. Often in association with Retz's Helmet-shrike, over which appears to be dominant, also associate with Green Wood-hoopoes *Phoeniculus purpureus.* Maintenance behaviour includes allopreening and indirect scratching. Roosts on a horizontal branch, bunched up with individuals showing no preference for the direction they face. Make low-pitched chuckling sounds as they compete for roosting positions[48, 205, 506, 585, 631, 649, 736, 833, 859, 905]. **Foraging behaviour** Arboreal, usually in canopy, but birds do descend low enough to be caught in mist-nets and occasionally to ground level. They show a preference for small-leaved trees, where they creep about in a crouched position, peering about and gleaning from trunks, branches, creeper tangles and foliage, often hanging upside-down, rather tit-like, in their efforts to secure prey. While foraging they cock the head to one side, giving the impression that they are listening for prey. Prey is often caught on the wing, more so than White or Retz's Helmet-shrikes, often hovering in the process. They flop into leaf-clusters, probably in an attempt to flush prey. Sometimes part of mixed foraging parties. They are often found foraging with Retz's Helmet-shrike, rarely with White Helmet-shrike. **Food** Arthropods, mainly insects and their larvae, and occasionally small vertebrates. Insects include Lepidoptera (moths and caterpillars). Also takes spiders. *Ochna* fruits fed to young[104, 205, 500, 506, 585].

SOUNDS Complex and variable, many defying transcription. Repertoire includes whistling notes and whirring, buzzing, gobbling, chuckling, grating and growling sounds, often with a distinct nasal quality. Calls are often given in duet or more usually in chorus and frequently combined with rapid bursts of bill-snapping. Structurally they begin rapidly, high-pitched and complex, ending more slowly, low-pitched and simpler. A chorus typically begins with short chattering *tz-tz-* or *ch-ch-ch-* notes followed by descending, repeated *cherrU-cherrU-*, *chrrre-chrrre-*, *chair-chair-* or more rolling *chirro-roe–chirro-roe* calls. Sequences may end with sharp *tzip-ip-ip-*. Other sounds include whistled phrases like *fyew-dyew-dewt* and repeated high-pitched *tuWee- tuWee-*, *tree-tree-*, *tzzea-tzzea-* and *whit-whit-*, or lower-pitched growling *grro* calls. Some appear to be greeting signals. They also have a distinctive trilling, tinkling *bitillwe-bitillwe-* or *bdddddt, bdddddt, ddddt-* and short sharp *shuK!* Incubating bird gives repeated descending *tree-tree-* or *tze-tze-tze-* and contact *chairrer-* from the nest. Begging call of young a repeated chattering *tzzrrree-*. Mild alarm signalled with rapid bursts of bill-snapping, more intense alarm with *tze-zee-zeeep* and rapidly repeated high-pitched *ZeeZee-* squeals with bill-snapping. Make a low chuckling sound when roosting. Finally, known to respond to playback of Retz's Helmet-shrike calls[48, 205, 299, 506, 585, 631, 698].

BREEDING BIOLOGY Little known. Monogamous, cooperative and territorial. Groups have a single dominant breeding pair, assisted by at least some members. Home range and territory size unknown, but groups appear to occupy large territories as their density is low. Although cooperative, their behaviour differs from White and Retz's Helmet-shrikes in that one or at most a few members incubate, the rest of the group supplying food[205, 506, 833, 854]. **Season** Jan–Jul, mainly Apr, nest-building Dec (Kenya)[104, 293, 585]; Feb (Tanzania)[336]; Nov (Mozambique)[48, 833]; Oct–Dec (Zimbabwe)[30, 48, 205]. **Displays** ***Courtship*** Little known, consisted of bowing and spreading of head feathers. Two individuals observed displaying and bowing to each other while carrying spider web. Soliciting bird called *eek* while crouched and spreading and waving its wings in a circle to each side for 10 min, reminiscent of ♂ European Starling *Sturnus vulgaris*[585]. Courthship-feeding unknown. **Nest** possibly not built by all members of group, as in one case 2 birds carried material, others accompanied them, and at least 3 moulded nest. Cup consists of bark strips and grass secured and plastered with spider web, sometimes incorporating lichen and moss, well camouflaged and silver-grey in colour. Placed high up on a horizontal branch or saddle in fork at *c.*12 m (4.5–23, n=8). Favours small-leaved trees like *Newtonia* and *Brachystegia spiciformis*. ***Size*** Diameter (not specified but probably OD) 62 x 65 mm, cup depth 24 mm[104, 205, 585]. **Eggs** 3 (n=2). Very pale grey, tinged turquoise and spotted with reds, greys and blues mainly in a band close to large end. ***Size*** 19–20 x 15.2–15.3 mm (19.5 x 15.3, n=3)[104]. **Incubation** Begins with last egg. Most, but possibly not all, members of group take part in incubation. This species differs from White and Retz's Helmet-shrikes in that there appears to be less division of labour, with only a few individuals coming to the nest for change-overs, e.g. 3 of group of 5, 4 of group of 8 and 4 of group of 10. In other cases only single birds are involved in incubation, during which they are fed on the nest by other members of the group. Calls given from the nest include contact *chairrer-*, a descending *tze-tze-tze-tze-* and *tzetzetzet-zeprechurroe-churroe*. Period unknown[833, 205, 500, 506, 585, 854]. **Nestling** Appearance and period unknown; young fed by all members of group. Fledglings solicit with a chattering *tzzrrree-* begging call[205]. No further breeding information.

MEASUREMENTS and WEIGHTS *P. s. scopifrons* ♂♀? (?) wing 97–104, tail 75–79, bill 17–18.5, tarsus 18–20[48]; *kirki* ♂♀? (6) wing 93–100, tail 75–81, bill 19–20, tarsus 19[297]. **Weight** *scopifrons* ♂ (19) 26.8–32.9 g (29.1); ♀ (20) 25.8–37.5 g (29.1)(southern Africa)[48, 205, 500]; *kirki* ♂ (3) 29.8 g, 30.1 g, 30.7 g; ♀ (3) 29.7 g, 30.7 g, 33.3 g (NE Tanzania)[299]; ♂♀? (1) 29 g (Kenya)[583].

111 CHESTNUT-BELLIED HELMET-SHRIKE (Northern Red-billed Helmet-shrike) *Prionops caniceps* Plate 40

FIELD IDENTIFICATION Medium-sized (18–20 cm), black, white and rufous helmet-shrike with greyish head, bright reddish-orange bill, legs and ring around yellow eye. Sexes similar, geographically variable. Nominate race with greyish-white head, black throat, back, wings and tail. Below white with rufous belly. Distinctive E race with bluish-grey head and upper throat, and deeper, more extensive rufous below. Young have greyish-brown heads and dark bill, legs and eyes. White in wings conspicuous in flight. Little known; calls complex, including noisy, rolling, chattering sounds and whistles in chorus with bill-snapping. In groups of *c.*3–6 members in mid- to upper levels of lowland forest. Resident from Sierra Leone to Zaïre and W Uganda. ***Flight characteristics***: Butterfly-like with mechanical 'wing-fripping' sounds. Wings broad and rounded, white band across primaries conspicuous in flight.

COMPARISONS Distinctive and unlikely to be confused with other helmet-shrikes. In flight broad wings with white patch combined with harsh calls superficially resembles ♂ Crested Flycatcher-shrike *Bias musicus*.

DESCRIPTION **Adult** *caniceps* Sexes similar. ***Head*** Small bushy frontal and forecrown, lores, sides of face to eye level whitish-grey to bluish-grey. ***Back*** Including sides of face from below eye, neck, nape, mantle, rump and uppertail-coverts black with slight gloss. ***Wings*** Black, coverts like back; primaries with broad white wing-patch formed across inner webs; secondaries black. ***Tail***

Black with slight gloss. ***Underparts*** Chin and throat black; breast and upper belly white; lower belly deep buff to rufous, darker on flanks and undertail-coverts, which are unusually large; underwing-coverts black. ***Bare parts*** Bill red, lighter at tip; palate unknown; legs reddish; eye bright yellow with outer reddish to reddish-orange ring. Narrow reddish rim around eye[259, 504]. **ADULT** *rufiventris* Similar to nominate but head and lower parts differ. ***Head*** Frontal white with deeper, more extensive blue-grey on crown which extends below eye to chin and upper throat. ***Underparts*** Only breast white, rest deep rufous-brown to orange-chestnut. Eye of *mentalis* dull brownish-grey with yellow outer ring; lacks obvious wattle[290]. **JUVENILE** Both population groups duller than adult and lack the sheen on upperparts. Head: *caniceps* Frontal and crown whitish becoming streaky on hindcrown. This area becomes blackish-grey to brownish and mottled; lores dark; ear-coverts greyish-brown to whitish mottled grey. May have a buffy-white collar extending around hind neck (*rufiventris* specimens more whitish on frontal, crown and ear-coverts). Back, wings and tail: Like respective adults. Underparts: Chin and throat buffy-white with slight streaking (*rufiventris* specimens have mottled buff to blackish throat); breast and belly dirty to buffy-white; flanks and undertail-coverts darker like respective adults. Bare parts: Bill blackish, or black mixed with red; legs dark orange; eye grey-brown to grey-green without outer ring, rim of eyelids blackish[259, 290, 500, 504, 646, 683]. **IMMATURE** Similar to respective adults, except Head: Frontal and crown whitish with little grey, lighter on frontal; lores dark; sides of face greyish-brown; neck with pale patches on either side. Wing-coverts tipped buff. Underparts: Progressively develop adult rufous-brown underparts. Bare parts: Bill orange to orange-red; legs like juvenile.; eye bright yellow with outer orange ring[500].

GEOGRAPHICAL VARIATION Four races in two distinct populations. Variation mainly in coloration of head, bare parts and underparts of W nominate *caniceps* (Sierra Leone to Togo) and E *rufiventris* (Cameroon to Central African Republic) (see above). Race *harterti* (Nigeria) is intermediate with the bluish-grey more extensive on nape and extending to below eyes, chin and throat like nominate; *mentalis* (E and S Zaïre, W Uganda) similar to *rufiventris* but rufous underparts darker; head with more extensive blue-grey around eye, ear-coverts, nape and chin; underparts darker rufous with smaller black throat-patch, which extends as a thin collar to mantle; below collar blue-grey, grading into white of breast. In *mentalis* eye is greyish-brown with outer yellow rim, sclerotic ring orange, bare rim of eyelid whitish[3, 34, 180, 290, 338, 500].

MOULT Little known; *caniceps* wing moult recorded from Feb–Jul, early moult Feb–Mar, advanced Mar–Jul (Liberia). Race *rufiventris* appears to have a single post-juvenile moult, beginning with wing-coverts and retarded longest on head[259, 330, 683, 858].

RANGE, HABITAT and STATUS Breeding range nominate *caniceps* (including *harterti*) in West Africa from Sierra Leone, Guinea, Mali, Liberia, Ivory Coast, Ghana, Togo, Benin, Nigeria and W Cameroon. Bioko record rejected[431]. More eastern *rufiventris* from Nigeria–Cameroon border at Calabar and approximately E of Sanaga River in S Cameroon, S Central African Republic, Equatorial Guinea, Gabon, Congo, Angola in Cabinda, Zaïre and W Uganda. Formerly in Rwanda. **Habitat** Generally a lowland forest species in mature primary, gallery and relic forest patches, old secondary forest and dense bush. Sometimes found on edge of forests. Ascends to 1450 m (Zaïre). In Gabon favours sloping sides of valleys[7, 21, 22, 37, 234, 259, 290, 294, 330, 431, 481, 492, 504, 587, 688, 697, 848, 858]. **Status** Not uncommon to locally common resident. **Conservation status** Apparently not threatened, although nominate race recorded declining around Lagos (Nigeria), and *rufiventris* no longer found in Rwanda[37, 431].

MOVEMENTS Unknown.

SOCIAL ORGANISATION and GENERAL BEHAVIOUR Little known. Usually occurs in pairs or small noisy groups of *c*.3–8 members, occasionally up to 15 (range 2–15, n=9). Groups in breeding season smaller than during dry non-breeding season. Found mainly in mid-levels at heights of *c*.10–20 m, less frequently in canopy. Social organisation unknown, but probably similar to other helmet-shrikes (see White Helmet-shrike p.340). Appears to comprise subgroups of adults with young, even in non-breeding season. Compared to White Helmet-shrike, groups move slower from tree to tree, in a sluggish way, one at a time, where they then sit motionless for a long time before continuing searching for prey. They also tend to be more spread out while on the move, less vocal, and their calls do not appear to be correlated with their movements (see White Helmet-Shrike). Foraging behaviour also different (see below). Occupy a territory of *c*.20 ha (n=2) which is defended by the group. Members maintain contact with frequently heard calls, bill-snapping and 'wing-fripping' sounds. **Foraging behaviour** Arboreal, forages between 10–50 m, mostly from 10–30 m. Prey caught on the wing in short fluttering forays. Also gleans from small branches, avoiding thicker ones near the trunk and small terminal twigs. Less frequently gleans from foliage. Frequently joins mixed foraging parties. **Food** Arthropods, mainly insects, including Lepidoptera (caterpillars), Coleoptera (beetles), Hemiptera (small cicadas), Orthoptera (large locusts) and Mantodea (mantids). Also takes spiders[34, 97, 259, 290, 294, 500, 587, 646, 688, 765, 858].

SOUNDS Complex and variable; some sounds defy transcription. Repertoires of E and W races share many elements, but may be found to differ with additional study. Western nominate *caniceps* has whistles and high-pitched chattering and buzzing sounds, and lower-pitched nasal chuckling and growling notes in duet or chorus sequences. Its calls are described as louder than White Helmet-shrike. A chorus may begin with high-pitched chattering calls like *tchee-tchee-* or more rolling *tzweer-tzweeer-*, ending with rapidly delivered shorter *tz-tz-tz-tz-* notes. Other sequences are distinctly disyllabic, e.g. often heard *chok-rrr*, explosive *chack-ack* or *tik-tew* in which the second syllable is accentuated and descending in tone. Still others are low-pitched, nasal, guttural and crow-like, e.g. *Waaar-Waaar-*, *Kaaa-* or *Quar-*, in duet *Kaaa-Wa* or *Waaar-gogo.* Most sequences are combined with whistles, *tiuk* and *weeaw* sounds, or short hard *chek* notes. Calls often combined with bursts of rapid bill-snapping. Immatures have a rapidly delivered querulous *Wee-wee-wee-* call[97, 294, 500, 504, 572, 646]. Eastern *rufiventris* has similar chattering, buzzing, chuckling and growling notes, with chorus sequences of high-pitched chattering notes, whistles and lower-pitched harsh notes. Some calls similar to White Helmet-shrike, others rather quail-like, with a rhythmic song of 2–3 similar notes repeated. Duet or chorus may begin with a buzzy rolling *kzz-weero-kzzweero-* or *zrrreeeu-zreeee-* followed by chuckling descending nasal *kree-kree-kree.* A common call consists of a series of 2–6 repeated disyllabic *hiyu-yu, hiu-yu, ch-we* or *chewy-you.* Also a repeated puffback-like *Kwe-U-* and single *zek* whistles. These often combined with rapidly delivered high-pitched *tz-tz-tz-* or more subtle low *chi-chi-chi-* notes. Also makes nasal low-pitched babbler-like *gwaarr-gwaarr-* or muffled jackdaw-like *tjok-air* and strange mewing and swishing sounds. Calls often combined with bursts of rapid bill-snapping. Alarm signalled by a shrill call and bill-snapping. Makes mechanical 'wing-fripping' sounds in flight[22, 290, 294, 338, 492, 500, 516, 646]. A comparison at this level suggests the two races have similar repertoires. Both have high-pitched chattering calls, disyllabic whistles and harsh nasal calls, a crow-like *Waaar-* in *caniceps* and a babbler-like *gwaarr-* in *rufiventris*[500].

BREEDING BIOLOGY Little known. Apparently a cooperative territorial breeder. Groups appear to have a dominant breeding pair assisted by helpers. Five birds have been observed nest-building, and fledglings have been observed being fed by a pair assisted by group members. Plumage development of young may be unique in helmet-shrikes (see Nestling)[858]. **Season** *caniceps* juveniles May–Nov (Ivory Coast)[712]; ♀ just finished laying Feb (Ghana)[234]; nest-building Jan, independent young Jan and Mar, immatures Jul and Oct (Liberia)[858]; young being fed Oct, groups with juveniles Jan–Mar (Nigeria)[37]; *rufiventris* May, Jul–Aug, Oct and Dec, juveniles seen in Jan, Jun and Aug (Zaïre)[22, 688]; gonads active Dec, dependent juveniles Nov and Feb (Gabon)[294]. **Displays** Unknown. **Nest** Only 2 nests described. Five birds built nest at 40 m above ground in *Sarcoglottis* tree (Liberia). Other nest was a neat, solid, greyish-green cup placed in a fork just below the canopy at 15 m above ground, in an isolated patch of secondary growth; appeared too small for the sitting bird (Ivory Coast)[663, 858]. **Eggs** Unknown. No further breeding information except: **Nestling** *rufiventris* has white head with two large bare patches on hindcrown and white nape which later both become covered by black feathers. Although plumage development is generally not well known in helmet-shrikes, this feature has not been recorded in the other species. Wings have white greater and median coverts. These are rapidly replaced by black feathers. Throat buffy-white. Bare parts: Bill black with corners of gape yellow; mouth spots unknown; legs dull yellowish; eye brownish-grey[500, 290, 683]. Young are fed by all members of the group, even during the dry non-breeding season[294]. **Brood parasite** No definite evidence, but since Thick-billed Cuckoo *Pachycoccyx audeberti* occurs in West Africa and ignores White Helmet-shrikes, it is assumed to parasitise Chestnut-bellied Helmet-shrike[705, 717, 816].

MEASUREMENTS and WEIGHTS *P. c. caniceps* ♂ (6) wing 105–118 (111.3), tail 68–77 (73.8), bill (to skull) 24–26 (25.2), tarsus 18–20.5 (19.1); ♀ (6) wing 109–121 (115.8), tail 68–80 (74.6), bill (to skull) 24.5–25.5 (25.1), tarsus 18–23 (20.4)[500]; *rufiventris* ♂♀? (7) wing 105–113 (109.8), tail 68–77 (72.4), bill (to skull) 24–26 (25.0), tarsus 18–19.5 (18.6)[500]. **Weight** *caniceps* ♂ (1) 55.7 g ; ♀ (5) 52.4 ±7.4 g[259]; ♀ (7) 42.3–52.3 g (48.6) (West Africa)[500]; *mentalis* ♂♀? (14) 37–50 g (Uganda)[765]; ♂ (3) 59.4 g (juvenile), 55.7 g, 63 g. For additional data see[34, 259, 330, 338, 492].

112 RETZ'S HELMET-SHRIKE (Red-billed Helmet-shrike)

Prionops retzii **Plate 41**

FIELD IDENTIFICATION Medium-large (19–24 cm) black, brown and white helmet-shrike with bright orange-red bill, legs and wattle encircling a yellow eye. Sexes similar; head and underparts black with slight gloss; back and wings brown with white band across primaries; tail black with broad white tips; large undertail-coverts white. White in wings, tail and undertail-coverts conspicuous in flight. Flight rapid, buoyant and undulating. Young brown with dark bill and eye without wattle. Chorus with musical churring, grating, rolling and often descending lilting sounds, often accompanied by bill-snapping. In groups of *c.*5 members in mid- to upper canopy of woodland and forest edge. Resident with local movements. Occurs from S Somalia to Mozambique, Malawi, Zambia, southern Africa and Angola. ***Flight characteristics***: Rapid, rather weak and fluttering, but buoyant and undulating. Wings broad and rounded. White band across primaries, broad white tips on tail and large white undertail-coverts conspicuous in flight, giving pied appearance.

COMPARISONS Similar to smaller little-known Gabela Helmet-Shrike *Prionops gabela* in Angola, which has much less black on underparts, a longer bushy frontal and very little white in wings. Ecologically segregated, with Retz's in *Brachystegia* woodland and Gabela usually in richer escarpment vegetation. Juveniles probably very similar, but note smaller size and amount of white in wing of Gabela Helmet-shrike. Also commonly found with the even smaller forest Chestnut-fronted Helmet-Shrike *P. scopifrons*, which has a chestnut-brown frontal and indistinct dark eye-wattle (not red). General plumage grey and black (black and brown in Retz's). Both species sometimes flock together.

DESCRIPTION **ADULT** Sexes similar. ***Head*** Frontal to upper back, face, sides of neck black with slight bluish gloss. ***Back*** Including rump brown to greyish-brown. ***Wings*** Secondary coverts and tertials brown like back, primary coverts black; flight feathers greyish-brown. Primaries with white patch on inner web (one race lacks white in wings). ***Tail*** Black with all feathers except central pair having large white tips, decreasing inwards. ***Underparts*** Black; vent blackish-white; undertail-coverts white, unusually large. ***Bare parts*** Bill deep pinkish-crimson to orange-red with a yellowish tip; palate unknown; legs reddish like red sealing wax; eye deep yellow to orange-yellow encircled with a serrated red wattle. **JUVENILE** First plumage completely dull brown to grey-brown, body feathers faintly tipped buffy-white above and below giving a slightly barred appearance; wing and tail similar to adult but duller, coverts and tertials tipped buffy-white. Vent and undertail-coverts white with brown terminal bar. Bill dull greyish-brown; legs dull pinkish-red to orange; eye brown without wattle. **IMMATURE** Similar to juvenile, but plumage replaced in first year by similar plumage but lacking pale feather tips. This second plumage progressively develops black of adult on head, breast and belly. Vent and undertail-coverts white without terminal bar. Bare parts: Similar to adult but duller; eye-wattle small, initially brown gradually changing to red. Full adult plumage attained only after 24 months, although museum specimens suggest 12–13 months[205, 237, 506, 509].

MOULT First brown spotted plumage replaced through a partial moult to a first-winter (austral) uniform brown plumage which lasts 12 months. During this period the bare parts change to dull adult colours. During late austral winter and early spring there is a prolonged first annual moult through immature into adult plumage, during which colour of bare parts intensify and wattle develops. However, note comments under Immature[48, 506, 546].

GEOGRAPHICAL VARIATION At least 6 races. Variation slight, mainly concerning body size, colour of upperparts and extent of white in wings. Length of frontal feathers also sometimes used. Race *tricolor* (S Tanzania, N, S Mozambique, Malawi, SE Zambia, E and SE Zimbabwe, E Swaziland, E South Africa) smaller and paler on mantle and rump less blackish than nominate *retzii* (SE Angola, N Namibia, N Botswana, NW South Africa, Zimbabwe and Zambia). Race *graculina* (S Somalia, E Kenya, NE Tanzania) similar to *tricolor* but much paler above, including wing-coverts, and with less white in wings (variable), sometimes completely absent from primaries and secondaries. Races *intermedia* (NW Tanzania) and *neumanni* (S Somalia) appear intermediate and are included by some authors in *graculina*, although *intermedia* has longer frontal feathers. Race *nigricans* (W Tanzania, S Zaïre, N Zambia to Angola) greyer, darker and larger than nominate race[3, 102, 290, 297, 299, 500, 576, 588].

RANGE, HABITAT and STATUS **Breeding range** S Somalia, E Kenya, W, E and S Tanzania, N and S Mozambique, Malawi, Zambia, N and E Botswana, S and SE Zaïre, Angola, N Namibia, Zimbabwe, NE South Africa and E Swaziland. **Habitat** Typically in mature deciduous broadleaved woodlands, including miombo *Brachystegia* mopane *Colophospermum* and *Baikiaea* woodland. Also found in wooded groves, tall riverine woodland, where restricted to this in drier habitats, but sometimes also found in dense dry woodland. Also occurs in forest edge and sometimes forest proper, including juniper forest in N range, and plantations. Ascends up to 1200 m (Tanzania) and 1900 m (Zaïre). In austral winter disperses into wider range of habitats, including mixed woodlands, *Acacia* savannas and more frequently found in forest[7, 22, 30, 99, 102, 119, 290, 291, 318, 320, 325, 431, 459, 631, 639, 807, 859]. **Status** Not uncommon to locally common resident with seasonal movements. **Conservation status** Currently not threatened, but at least in southern Africa the destruction of woodlands may threaten this species in the future[639].

MOVEMENTS Not well understood; disperses into drier woodland types in non-breeding season in southern Africa. East populations apparently increase in austral winter, while W populations increase in summer. This pattern may indicate a regional E–W movement[48, 205, 639].

SOCIAL ORGANISATION and GENERAL BEHAVIOUR Gregarious, occurring in permanent family groups of *c.*5 members. Breeding groups tend to be smaller (2–11, av.4.7, n=52) than non-breeding groups (2–15, av.4.9, n=220), with occasional groups up to 30. Group structure appears similar to White Helmet-shrike *Prionops plumatus*, although not as well known. It is established and maintained by a dominance hierarchy, with most dominant ♀ at top. She is the heaviest individual, followed by her mate, the dominant ♂. Both probably have larger eye-wattles and brighter-coloured bare parts than other members. Below them are subordinate adults of both sexes, who are usually inter-related, and finally fledglings. There does not appear to be any obvious sexual plumage dimorphism, or aggression in the group. Fledglings remain in the group for at least 2 years, the time required to attain adult plumage. The dominant pair can usually be identified by their behaviour, and although specific calls have not been identified, pair-bonds appear to be maintained, at least partially, by duetting and allopreening. Behaviour similar to White Helmet-shrike (see General Behaviour p.340 for this species), but Retz's generally more arboreal, quicker on the wing, occupies larger territories, flies greater distances and has louder, more musical calls, also unlike White they bow the body, raise the crest and spread the voluminous undertail-coverts, usually in aggressive interactions. Typically adopts a squat or crouched horizontal posture in non-aggressive circumstances. Group activities appear initiated and coordinated by calls. Groups appear to occupy a home range in which they defend a large, *c.*30 ha or more, summer breeding territory which is defended in group territorial displays. After breeding the group moves out of the home range. Territorial defence consists of group members perching close together, some birds calling, others posturing. Postures include fanning the tail, holding the wings slightly open or lowering them and rocking back and forth as though bowing. Body and rump feathers are fluffed-out and crest raised. In East Africa, display consists of whistled series of notes *tweeooh-tweew* combined with a slow deep bow with crest erect, the anterior body feathers fluffed-out and wings held slightly away from body. The deep bow is followed by a slow raising of the head, almost to the vertical, with bill pointing skywards. This display is repeated a few times. Sometimes individuals perform a display-flight during which they call, erect the crest and fluff the body feathers out. Calls are given in both horizontal and upright postures; in the latter stance, the bill is slightly raised and undertail-coverts are sometimes spread to form a conspicuous signal. In one observation this species participated in a display, apparently intended to distract attention from a young White Helmet-shrike in a group of these birds, suggesting interspecific co-operation. However, White Helmet-shrikes are also known to show interspecific aggression towards Retz's Helmet-shrike. Like White Helmet-shrikes, they are attracted to injured members of their group, but have also been reported pecking such individuals. They readily mob terrestrial and avian predators, dive-bombing, calling and bill-snapping at them. Roost communally, huddled in a row on branch in a leafy tree, individuals showing no apparent preference for which way they face, where generally silent except for low growling *grrr* sounds. Scratch indirectly[5, 9, 30, 48, 98, 99, 205, 290, 459, 506, 631].

Foraging behaviour Similar to White Helmet-shrike but more arboreal, rarely in low bushes or on the ground. Forages mainly in canopy and mid-levels where continuously on the move, clinging at all angles, creeping and peering about as they glean prey from (in order of priority) branches, trunks, and canopy foliage, sometimes behaving rather tit-like, as they hang upside-down by one leg at the end of a branch. While foraging they often tilt the head to one side, almost as if listening for prey. They give a *chucker* call when preferred prey is found, and will hawk insects in flight. Groups often form the nucleus for mixed foraging parties and frequently associate with groups of Chestnut-fronted or White Helmet-shrikes, occasionally both at the same time.

Food Mainly insects and their larvae include Orthoptera (grasshoppers), Lepidoptera (butterflies, moths and caterpillars), Coleoptera (beetles), Hemiptera (cicadas), Mantodea (mantids), Isoptera (alate termites). Also takes spiders and occasionally small vertebrates (lizards and geckos)[32, 78, 205, 290, 352, 500, 506, 566, 859, 877].

SOUNDS Complex and variable, with a repertoire of at least 16 different calls, consisting of whistles and harsh notes, often with a nasal quality, many defying transcription. Phrases usually combine whistle notes with rolling, guttural, grating, chattering and churring sounds, which are usually given in duet or chorus and often accompanied by bursts of rapid bill-snapping. Territorial phrases begin complex and fast, ending simple and slower. Structure and function of calls in relation to status are not well understood, although dominant ♀ believed to initiate much of the calling. Chorusing initiated with rolling *Jor-rrreeeea* or *krreeeer* call, followed immediately by group with *hu* or *hoo* whistles, nasal *grrr-* or *gooria-gooria-* growls and harsh *zrrreeeea-*, *tzzeee-* or *crrrrrrreeeeeeo* sounds with bill-snapping. Often-heard duets include *pechew-pechew* responded to by growling *tuuurrw*, or a high-pitched *tuurrrrr*, also *truuuwee* responded to with *tu* or *hu* whistles. Other phrases include *tu-whit-*, *tchuwee-tchuwee-tchwrrrr*, *tsurrEEoo-errrEEo*, *weetch-week-tchwerrr* and *tyew-tyow-dyeeeew-dyeeeeew*. Some are delivered more slowly, and include repeated *cheer-cheer-* or *chair-chair-*, *cherr-weeu- whip-reer*, *whip-reer-*, *chiwirew-chiwirew-* and *RRRREEO cko-wo*, *cho-wo*, *cho-wo*, *or choCHO*, *cho-CHO*, *cho-CHO*. Alarm a repeated *Jor-rrreeea* or *cherr- weeu* accompanied by bill-snapping. At high-intensity short sharp squeals or screaming *chirrr.* Some calls appear associated with particular actions, e.g. greeting calls include *weerr-Wik*, *weerrwe-hin* and *tyee-ow*, *tyeeee-owp*, and on settling a *trrrru*. Contact maintained with variety of calls, including *chuk*, *Wik-horr*, *chewherrrr-* and *Chullit*. Lost birds give repeated *Chullit* or *jor- rrreeeea* calls. Give a *chucker* call when preferred food is found, also *chuck-chuck* on feeding nestlings and at nest exchange. A low growling *grrr-* or *churr-* given at roosting. Begging call a chattering *tzzereeee tzzzereee-*, also described as a *chirrr*, *chirrr*. Calls made in flight include *twwaaaa* and *witchew-witchew-* [5, 48, 78, 99, 205, 299, 500, 585, 631]. Sonagram[48].

BREEDING BIOLOGY Monogamous, territorial and usually cooperative breeder; very rarely only a pair. Groups have a single dominant breeding pair assisted by helpers. Timing of breeding may be linked to trees coming into leaf. The species is susceptible to disturbance during nest-building and early incubation, resulting in the destruction of nest, probably by the birds themselves. Brood parasitism may result in exceptionally low breeding success. In one study nesting success reduced from 30 to 17%, 1.9 nesting attempts, 0.6 fledglings/pair/year based on 40 groups. This was half the success of other insectivores in the same woodland. Survival rate was 79% for fledglings (n=14) and 85% for adults (n=39)[67, 99, 205, 558].

Season Aug–Mar, mainly Sep (SE Zaïre)[22, 290]; Feb, Mar, Nov (East Africa)[293]; Sep–Nov (Zambia)[291], Sep–Dec, mainly Sep–Oct (Zambia/Zimbabwe/Malawi)[359]; Sep–Dec (Malawi)[119]; nestlings Aug, juveniles Sep–Oct, breeding Nov–Dec (Angola)[7, 423, 865, 907]; probably Oct–Dec (Tanzania)[336]; Oct–Nov (Mozambique)[5, 336]; Jun, Aug–Dec, mainly Sep–Nov (Zimbabwe)[30]; Mar, Sep–Dec, mainly Oct (South Africa)[48, 320]; egg-laying Nov (Botswana)[807].

Displays ***Courtship*** Initiated by the dominant ♂ who approaches dominant ♀ with large quantities of nesting material in his bill, and with wings drooped and half-open. Apparently courtship-feeding absent. ***Pre-copulation*** Before copulation the breeding pair separate from the group. During pre-copulatory display they perch together, either facing each other or side by side, and slowly flap their open and lowered wings. Before mounting they face each other, ♂ slowly arches his neck, fanning wings and tail, moves closer to the ♀, who also has her tail and wings fanned open. The whole display is carried out slowly and in silence. ***Nest-site display*** ♂ actively prospects for a nest site, squatting horizontally in an appropriate place and shuffling about as if shaping a nest. He has also been heard to utter subdued juvenile-like soliciting calls while perched close to the ♀. Nest site selection is by the dominant pair; prospective sites are tested in the same way as the ♂ does before copulation, except that both birds usually carry nesting material or spider web to the site. This behaviour is often accompanied by silent, subdued wing-lowering and -quivering display[205, 506].

Nest Members of group help in construction. Material carried in bill, including spider web, which is also draped over frontal feathers. Generally deposit material as a group. The neat cup is built of leaf petioles, tendrils, lichen, grass and bark, firmly bound and cemented to the branch with spider web. Lining consists of fine strips of grass and bark. Placed *c.*7 m (3–17, n=42) above the ground, often in a large dominant tree, favouring ones such as round-leaved kiaat *Pterocarpus rotundifolia*. Nest usually placed on horizontal, often lichen-covered branch, at a point where it forks. ***Size*** OD 100–133 mm, ID 70–77 mm, cup depth 15–30 mm, height 35–50 mm (n=10). One nest took 7 days to complete. Nests often destroyed as a result of disturbance. The nest differs from that of White Helmet-shrike in being broader, shallower and squatter with thicker walls, which are not smoothly finished[6, 48, 205, 500, 506].

Eggs Usually 3–4 (2–5, n=33), probably laid on consecutive days and left relatively unattended until the full clutch is laid (see Brood parasites). Pale bluish to greenish or buffy green, spotted and lined with blacks, browns, reds and greys mainly at the large end. ***Size*** 22.7–25.8 x 15.6–18.2 mm (24.4 x 17.1, n=36)[19, 48, 205]. **Incubation** All members help incubate, which begins after last egg. Sitting bird can summon group with loud *shur-rrreeea* call. Nest change-overs are performed without ceremony; group flies into the nest tree, one member replaces the sitting bird, accompanied by *chuck-* and *chiwirew-* calls. Incubating birds sit tight, the nest seldom being left unattended, even for a few minutes. Period at least 17, but less than 21 days (n=1)[48, 506]. **Nestling** Hatch naked, blind and have mouth spots. All members of group help brood, feed, guard and attend to nestlings. Contact *chuck* calls are often given by these members when feeding nestlings, who beg with chattering *tzzzereee-tzzzereee-* calls. Nestlings are seldom left alone, a member of the group brooding or guarding them most of the time. Fledge after 20 days (n=1). Fledglings remain huddled together, and are dependent for at least 3 months, attaining independence by *c.*7 months. Occasionally double-brooded when conditions favourable. However, although individual ♀♀ known to lay second clutches, some of these may be the result of the group dividing to produce 2 active ♀♀[506]. **Predation and longevity** Little known. Nestling mortality known to result from brood parasites and apparent starvation. Raptors are known to chase individuals[205]. **Brood parasite** Brood parasitism is thought to be an important cause of disturbance as the species is frequently parasitised by Thick-billed Cuckoo *Pachycoccyx audeberti*. In one study over 50% of nests affected. The cuckoo displaces the incubating bird from nest, removes an egg and flies off with it. Also seen pulling nestlings out and dropping them to the ground. Usually lays a single egg which is indistinguishable from those of host. Parasite nestling begging call similar to young helmet-shrike. Adult helmet-shrikes behave ambivalently towards cuckoo, feeding it when it begs and mobbing it when it flies[100, 205, 506].

MEASUREMENTS and WEIGHTS *P. r. retzii* ♂ (10) wing 130–137 (133.6), tail 94–99 (96.2); ♀ (10) wing 131.5–142 (134.8), tail 90–102 (96.7)[102]. ♂♀? (15) wing 115–130, tail 91–100, bill 23–27, tarsus 21–23[297]. **Weight** ♂ (19) 37.9–48 g (43.1), ♀ (19) 38.4–49.2 g (44.6); ♂♀? (41) 38–53.5 g (47.8) (southern Africa)[48]. For additional data see[102, 297, 299, 319, 588].

113 GABELA HELMET-SHRIKE (Angola or Rand's Helmet-Shrike)
Prionops gabela **Plate 41**

FIELD IDENTIFICATION Medium-sized (18–19 cm), greyish-brown, black and white helmet-shrike with red bill and small red wattle encircling a yellow eye. Head with frontal crest and breast black. Sexes similar except for indistinct white patch on ♀ primaries. White in tail, lower belly and undertail-coverts probably conspicuous in flight. Young similar to adult but browner. Little known; calls unreported. Occurs in groups of *c.*3–5 members, mainly in canopy of secondary forest and dry thickets. Uncommon resident in restricted area, mainly around Gabela in Angola. ***Flight characteristics***: Probably similar to other helmet-shrikes. Wings broad and rounded. Little white in wings of ♀, but white in tail, lower belly and undertail-coverts probably conspicuous in flight.

COMPARISONS Similar to larger Retz's Helmet-Shrike *Prionops retzii*, which has completely black (not greyish-brown) underparts, a much larger, conspicuous white band across primaries, larger fleshy serrated wattle and a small inconspicuous frontal crest. Juveniles are probably very similar, but note smaller size and much smaller amount of white in wing of Gabela Helmet-shrike.

DESCRIPTION **ADULT** Known from only 6 specimens; sexes apparently similar except for wing. ***Head*** Black with slight bluish gloss; bushy frontal forming a small crest curving forwards. Black extends over face and sides of neck to nape and upper mantle. ***Back*** Lower mantle, back and rump greyish-brown. ***Wings*** Tertials and secondary coverts like back; primary coverts black; flight feathers grey-brown without white patch in ♂, but with small white patch across centre of inner webs of P2–6 in ♀. In view of the small sample size, this may not be a reliable sexual character. ***Tail*** Black with all feathers except central pair having large white tips, decreasing inwards. ***Underparts*** Chin, throat and upper breast like head, this grading into greyish-brown lower breast and upper belly; lower belly and vent white; undertail-coverts white, unusually large. ***Bare parts*** Bill red with orange tip to lower mandible; palate unknown; legs orange to cherry-red; eye yellow with red outer ring; small serrated wattle red[79, 500, 602]. **JUVENILE** Unknown. **IMMATURE** Head and breast patchy black and brown. Imm ♀ has slightly less white in wings than adult ♀. Bare part colours similar to adult, but yellow eye lacks outer red ring and legs are bright orange-red[79].

GEOGRAPHICAL VARIATION None. Monotypic.

MOULT Unknown.

RANGE, HABITAT and STATUS **Breeding range** W Angola, confined to the Gabela area and S of Mumbondo including Amboim Forest. **Habitat** Occurs in canopy of secondary forest, forest underplanted with coffee and coffee plantations. Apparently not restricted to escarpment forest as collected (Sep) in dry thicket in an area of mixed thickets and cultivation 40 km S of Mumbondo on the road between Gabela and Muxima. There is also an unsubstantiated sight record from this area[7, 79, 423, 907, 910]. **Status** Unknown; formerly an uncommon resident[907]. **Conservation status** Not recorded since the mid-1970s. Known only from a small area of forest underplanted with coffee and thickets near Gabela. Habitat destruction appears to be its greatest threat. As much as 30% of the forest in the Gabela region has been cleared prior to 1992. Forest elsewhere on the escarpment is probably disappearing at a slower rate. Considered Endangered[343, 479, 586].

MOVEMENTS A record in Sep from dry thicket below the escarpment may be indicative of local movements.

GENERAL BEHAVIOUR and SOCIAL ORGANISATION Virtually unknown. Observed in the canopy feeding on insects and their larvae. Moves about in loose groups of 3–5 individuals[79, 343, 423].

SOUNDS Unknown.

SOCIAL ORGANISATION and BREEDING BEHAVIOUR Unknown; probably monogamous, cooperative and territorial like other known helmet-shrikes. **Season** Breeding condition of ♂ and ♀ Aug–Sep, immature Sep[79, 602, 910]. No further breeding information.

MEASUREMENTS and WEIGHTS *P. gabela* ♀ (2) wing 108.0–110.0, tail 76.0–78.0, bill (from skull) 23.0–24.0, tarsus 22.5–22.5[500]; wing 107–112[337]; ♂ (1) type specimen: wing 112, tail 80, bill (from skull) 22, tarsus 21, wattle 2–3 mm above eye (dried skin)[602]. **Weight** Unknown.

114 YELLOW-CRESTED HELMET-SHRIKE *Prionops alberti* **Plate 41**

FIELD IDENTIFICATION Large (20–24 cm) black helmet-shrike with large bushy yellow frontal crest, black bill, red legs and greenish-yellow eyes encircled by orange wattle. Sexes similar, wings sometimes show white or greyish patches on flight feathers. Young duller and browner with pale, sometimes greyish-white frontal and crown, and a brown bill. Little known; calls noisy, chorus with shrill clear double notes and rolling descending sounds. In groups up to about 20 members in mid levels and canopy of primary and montane forest above 1120 m. Resident in E Zaïre and S Uganda. ***Flight characteristics***: Generally short; wings broad and rounded, sometimes showing white to greyish patches in a band across inner primaries.

COMPARISONS Distinctive.

DESCRIPTION **ADULT** Sexes similar. ***Head*** Frontal to nape from top of eye deep yellow to lemon-yellow with bushy frontal feathers forming a large crest extending forwards, extending 14–18 mm from eye; sides of face black. ***Back*** Mantle and back with slight bluish-green gloss; rump black. ***Wings*** Above brownish-black with bluish gloss on outer web, below greyish-brown, paler at base; 5th primary the longest. Sometimes with whitish or greyish patches forming a band mainly on inner primaries. ***Tail*** Black with slight gloss above. ***Underparts*** Black; undertail-coverts unusually large. ***Bare parts*** Bill black; palate unknown; legs pale red; eye greenish-yellow; fleshy orange wattle encircles eye[290, 593, 688]. **JUVENILE** Little known; duller than adult, lacks gloss, more brownish-black. Head with pale frontal and crown; usually a few pale spots in primaries, with one specimen having an outer feather completely white. Feather-shafts are reported to be grey, but their location is not specified. Bare part colours unknown, bill and eye probably brown with wattle dark grey, and legs orange[306]. **IMMATURE** Similar to adult but browner, lacks gloss. Frontal and crown paler, sometimes appearing dirty white to greyish-white or yellowish-white on specimens; bill brown; leg and eye colour unknown[593].

GEOGRAPHICAL VARIATION None. Monotypic.

MOULT Unknown.

RANGE, HABITAT and STATUS **Breeding range** Known from four mountain ranges, W of Lake Edward, W of Lake Kivu, Itombwe (Volcanoes) and Mount Kabobo in Zaïre. An old record from the Impenetrable Forest in SW Uganda may indicate a more extensive former distribution. Possibly also in Ruwenzori Mts. Record from Rwanda rejected[313, 431, 479, 717, 766]. **Habitat** Primary forest in transition to montane forest from 1100–1700 m and locally up to 2600 m (Mount Kahuzi)[22, 688]. **Status** Unknown, formerly a rare resident. **Conservation status** Unknown. No longer occurs where originally discovered, but has been found in equatorial forest near Kamituga. Apparently very difficult to find, possibly due to habitat destruction, with few, if any recent records. Red Data Book species considered Vulnerable[479].

MOVEMENTS The type specimen was found dead on the summit of Mt Mikeno at 4400 m. This combined with the possible (but requiring confirmation) record from SW Uganda is suggestive of considerable wandering from its normal habitat. The former record may be indicative of altitudinal movements.

SOCIAL ORGANISATION and GENERAL BEHAVIOUR Little known; occurs in small groups of *c.*5 or 6 members (range 4–20, n=3), in Sepember a group of 12–15 recorded. Gregarious in all seasons. Group structure unknown, but probably similar to other helmet-shrikes (see White Helmet-shrike p.340). Forage in noisy groups in mid- to upper canopy. Behaviour resembles a flycatcher as it dives from a perch to catch insect prey on the wing. Flights are short, returning to same or nearby branch, where remains immobile for some time before sallying out again. Sometimes found in mixed foraging parties. As in other helmet-shrikes, an injured member of a group attracts the whole group. Captive birds tame within a day or two[22, 593, 688].

SOUNDS Little known. Calls loud; makes a shrill and clear *tlu-uk* or *Clu-uk* call repeated 2–6 times. Also *triii-tri-tri-trii-prii*, taken up in chorus by all members[22, 290, 688].

BREEDING BIOLOGY Little known. Probably monogamous, cooperative and territorial like other helmet-shrikes. **Season** Rainy season, Dec, Jan, Feb, Apr, Jun–Jul. Juveniles recorded in Feb, May and Aug–Oct, suggesting egg-laying Jun–Jul[22, 593, 688]. **Displays** Unknown. **Nest** Role of sexes and group members unknown. Built of twigs and lichens placed in a fork, halfway up a tree in montane forest (E Zaïre). This is very different to other known helmet-shrikes[22]. No further breeding information.

MEASUREMENTS and WEIGHTS *P. alberti* ♂ (8) wing 125–134 (130), tail 92–96 (94.1), bill (to skull) 23–26 (24.8), tarsus 22–24 (22.9); ♀ (5) wing 126–132 (128.6), tail 92–98 (93.8), bill (to skull) 23–25.5 (24.4), tarsus 22–24 (23.5)[500]; ♂♀? (5) wing 130–135 (132.2), tail 102–110 (105.2), bill 20–22 (21.2), tarsus 21–22 (21.8)[593, 688]; type specimen (unsexed) wing 131, tail 110, bill 20, tarsus 22[593]. **Weight** ♂ (1) 61.0 g, ♀ (2) 61–62 g, ♀ juvenile 58.0 g[593, 688].

REFERENCES

The short numbered references below are those used throughout the text. The full references follow and are listed alphabetically.

1. Stark 1901
2. Jackson 1938
3. White 1962
4. Williams 1995
5. Vincent 1935
6. Vincent 1949
7. Traylor 1963
8. Swynnerton 1908
9. Shelley 1912
10. Darwin 1859
11. Britton 1980
12. Brooke 1968
13. Brooke 1964
14. Milne-Edwards. 1871
15. Bannerman 1953
16. Wolters 1975–82
17. Benson 1941
18. White 1963
19. Priest 1948
20. Priest 1936
21. Louette 1981
22. Lippens and Wille 1976
23. Serle and Morel 1977
24. Benson and Irwin 1961
25. Friedmann and Loveridge 1937
26 Clancey 1971a
27. Markus 1972
28. Whitaker 1905
29. Deignan 1960
30. Irwin 1981
31. Cave and Macdonald 1955
32. Clancey 1964
33. Archer and Godman 1961
34. Bates 1930
35. Belcher 1930
36. Etchécopar and Hüe 1967
37. Elgood, Heigham, Moore, Nason, Sharland and Skinner 1994
38. Gore 1990
39. Jensen and Kirkeby 1980
40. Zedlitz 1915
41. Peirce 1984a
42. Swynnerton 1916
43. Sonnenschein and Reyer 1984
44. Tarboton 1971
45. Thomsen and Jacobsen 1979
46. van Someren 1956
47. Ledger 1980
48. Maclean 1996
49. De Vree 1969
50. Winterbottom 1962
51. Quickelberge 1967
52. Grimes 1976a
53. Winterbottom 1971
54. Steyn 1965
55. Plumb 1978
56. Clancey 1965
57. Nicol 1964
58. Clancey 1961a
59. Grimes 1980
60. Grimes 1979a
61. Tarboton 1984
62. Clancey 1970a
63. Andersson 1872
64. Hoesch and Niethammer 1940
65. Feduccia 1976
66. Clancey 1971b
67. Vernon 1984a
68. Fenn 1975
69. Chittenden 1977
70. Blencowe 1962
71. Brooke 1980
72. Clancey 1961b
73. Bennett, Whiteway and Woodworth-Lynas 1982
74. Dowsett-Lemaire and Dowsett 1984
75. Macleod and Hallack 1956
76. Rand 1953
77. Wilson 1975
78. Benson 1946
79. Hall 1960a
80. Irwin 1956a
81. Lawson 1963a
82. Stallcup 1961
83. Broekhuysen 1958
84. Vernon 1976
85. Clancey 1959a
86. Lawson 1964a
87. Ames 1975
88. Irwin 1961
89. Clancey 1970b
90. Brooke and Manson 1979
91. Scott 1984
92. Sharpe 1873
93. Hanmer 1979
94. Rowan 1983
95. Traylor 1970
96. Clancey 1976a
97. Greig-Smith 1976
98. Garcia 1975
99. Tarboton 1963
100. Vernon 1984b
101. Halleux 1994
102. Clancey 1960a
103. Vernon 1966
104. Britton and Britton 1977
105. Winter 1986
106. Hooker Hooker 1969
107. Slack 1975
108. Traylor 1962
109. Hall 1954
110. Field 1979
111. Kunkel 1974
112. Chapin 1947
113. Hall. Moreau and Galbraith 1966
114. Clancey 1959b
115. Moreau and Southern 1958
116. Traylor 1986
117. Arnott 1982
118. Clark 1981
119. Benson and Benson 1977
120. Benson 1945a
121. Grant and Mackworth-Praed 1942a
122. Harcus 1977
123. Macdonald 1957
124. Robinson 1953
125. Clancey 1960b
126. Irwin 1968
127. Wickler and Seibt 1982
128. Astley Maberly 1939
129. Clancey 1960c
130. Clancey 1982
131. Grobler 1979
132. Paterson 1984
133. Phillips 1979
134. Arman 1971
135. Mayr 1942
136. Payne 1971
137. Jensen and Clinning 1974
138. Quickelberge 1966
139. Britton 1968
140. Dowsett 1971
141. Moreau 1972
142. Brodkorb 1978
143. Oatley 1969
144. Brooke 1984
145. Dowsett and Dowsett-Lemaire 1980
146. Dowsett-Lemaire 1983
147. Clancey 1980a
148. Clancey 1973
149. Clancey 1969a
150. Took 1966
151. Cooper 1971a
152. Cooper 1971b
153. Wetherbee 1957
154. Ray-Chaudhuri and Chatterjee 1969
155. Banage 1969
156. Vincent 1946
157. Voous 1979
158. Dean 1982
159. Zumpt 1961
160. Haeselbarth, Segermann and Zumpt 1966
161. Cade 1962
162. Butticker 1960
163. Toschi 1950
164. Marshall and Cooper 1969
165. Olivier 1944
166. Walden 1867
167. James 1948
168. Clancey 1980b
169. Hargrove, Marshall and Mentz 1972
170. Hargrove, Marshall and Mentz 1973
171. Layard 1867
172. Macdonald 1980
173. Maclean and Maclean 1976
174. Clancey 1976b
175. Steyn 1976
176. Zack 1986a
177. Bulatova, Panov and Radjabli 1971
178. Bulatova 1981
179. van Ee 1955
180. Hall and Moreau 1970
181. Hantge 1957
182. Heim de Balsac and Mayaud 1962
183. Clancey 1948
184. Sibley and Ahlquist 1990
185. Voous 1960
186. Mees 1996
187. Oates 1883
188. Meyer de Schauensee 1984
189. Etchécopar and Hüe 1983
190. Cheng Tso-hsin 1987
191. Viney and Phillipps 1988
192. Clancey 1955
193. Brazil 1991
194. Deignan 1963
195. Gore and Pyong-Oh 1971
196. Bent 1950
197. Vaurie 1972
198. Lewington, Alstrom and Colston 1991
199. Tordoff 1954
200. Pearson 1981
201. Betts 1966
202. Sharpe 1877
203. Williams 1989
204. Howard and Moore 1980
205. Harris and Arnott 1988
206. Rand 1960
207. Sibley and Monroe 1990
208. Langrand 1990
209. Flint, Boehme, Kostin and Kuznetsov 1984
210. Vorobiev 1954
211. Vaurie 1955
212. Vaurie 1959
213. Stepanyan 1990
214. Dement'ev and Gladkov 1968
215. Gould 1986

216. Paz 1987
217. Gallagher and Woodcock 1980
218. Flint and Stewart 1992
219. Brown and Veltman 1987
220. Bundy, Connor and Harrison 1989
221. Inskipp and Inskipp 1991
222. Richardson 1990
223. Sclater and Mackworth-Praed 1918
224. Ali and Ripley 1987
225. Bergmann and Helb 1982
226. Rand 1936
227. Milon, Petter and Randrianasolo 1973
228. Macdonald 1940
229. Eck 1973
230. Rand 1957a
231. Goodman and Meininger 1989
232. Benson 1984
233. Houlihan and Goodman 1986
234. Grimes 1987
235. Olson 1989
236. Belcher 1922
237. Friedmann 1937
238. Gronvik 1934
239. Schmidl 1982
240. Benson and Irwin 1967
241. Komen 1987
242. Nikolaus 1987
243. Dorst 1960
244. Todd 1963
245. Broekhuysen 1971
246. Meinertzhagen 1954
247. Tufts 1987
248. van Marle and Voous 1988
249. White and Bruce 1986
250. Beehler, Pratt and Zimmerman 1986
251. Rand and Gilliard 1967
252. Medway and Wells 1976
253. Stresemann and Stresemann 1972
254. Roberts 1935
255. Miller 1931
256. Scott and Morrison 1990
257. Cramp and Perrins 1993
258. Deignan 1945
259. Colston and Curry-Lindahl 1986
260. Coates 1990
261. Smythies 1986
262. MacKinnon and Phillipps 1993
263. MacKinnon 1990
264. Harris 1990
265. Dickinson, Kennedy and Parkes 1991
266. Immelman 1968
267. McClure 1974
268. Durango 1956
269. LeFevre 1962
270. La Touche 1925
271. Kolthoff 1921–22
272. Cardwell and Cardwell 1931
273. Cheng Tso-hsin 1962
274. Paludan 1959
275. Ali 1962
276. Fleming, Fleming and Bangdel 1976
277. Ali 1977
278. Roberts 1992
279. Delacour 1947
280. Glenister 1955
281. Boonsong Lekagul and Round 1991
282. Editor. 1984
283. Yamagishi 1992
284. Panov 1983, 1996
285. Lefranc 1993
286. Lawson 1987
287. Lawson 1986
288. Appert 1970
289. Chapin 1953
290. Chapin 1954
291. Benson, Brooke, Dowsett and Irwin 1971
292. Urban and Brown 1971
293. Brown and Britton 1980
294. Brosset and Erard 1986
295. Rand, Friedmann and Traylor 1959
296. Fuggles-Couchman 1984
297. Pinto and Lamm 1955
298. Serle 1955
299. Sclater and Moreau 1933
300. Brooke 1992
301. Britton 1967
302. Wickler and Seibt 1979
303. Clancey 1959c
304. Harris 1984
305. Hollom, Porter, Christensen and Willis 1988
306. Schouteden 1938
307. Haas 1987
308. Miller 1928
309. Bowen 1931
310. Mundy and Woodruff 1998
311. Morrison, Kuehler, Scott, Lieberman, Everett, Phillips, Koehler, Aigner, Winchell and Burr 1995
312. Cuddy 1995
313. Schouteden 1966a
314. Schouteden 1966b
315. Atkinson 1995
316. Laporte Robert 1995
317. Olsson 1995
318. Lewis and Pomeroy 1989
319. Verheyen 1953
320. Tarboton, Kemp and Kemp 1987
321. Gadow 1883
322. Cyrus and Robson 1980
323. Stresemann and Stresemann 1971
324. King, Dickinson. and Woodcock 1978
325. Ash and Miskell 1983
326. van Someren 1939
327. Gee 1984
328. Serle 1940
329. Grant and Mackworth-Praed 1952
330. Rand 1951
331. Maclean and Vernon 1976
332. Uys 1989
333. Bennett, Pierce and Earlé 1990
334. Zimmer 1939
335. Grant and Mackworth-Praed 1942b
336. Mackworth-Praed and Grant 1955
337. Mackworth-Praed and Grant 1963
338. Mackworth-Praed and Grant 1973
339. Jourdain 1935
340. Theiler 1959
341. Serle 1952a
342. Serle 1952b
343. Collar and Stuart 1985
344. Bowden and Andrews 1994
345. Andrews 1994
346. Britton and Dowsett 1969
347. Serle 1950
348. Sessions 1966
349. Serle 1951
350. Bannerman 1938
351. Goodman 1984
352. Lack 1985
353. Payne and Payne 1967
354. Lorber 1984
355. Zack and Ligon 1985a
356. Zack and Ligon 1985b
357. Zack 1986b
358. Ogilvie-Grant 1902
359. Benson, Brooke and Vernon 1964
360. Benson 1950
361. Irwin, Niven and Winterbottom 1969
362. Chapin 1950
363. vander Wall
364. Pearson 1979
365. Nielsen 1981
366. Bruderer and Bruderer 1993
367. Yamashina 1951
368. Ray-Chaudhuri 1976
369. Harris 1998
370. Yamagishi 1982
371. Yamagishi, Nishiumi and Shimoda 1992
372. Yamagishi and Saito 1985
373. Ullrich 1971
374. LeFranc, Boet and Boet 1989
375. Curry-Lindahl 1981
376. Robertson 1992
377. Vatev, Simeonov, Michev and Ivanov 1980
378. Stuart, Adams and Jenkins 1990
379. Eck 1971
380. Ferguson-Lees 1960b
381. Dorka and Ullrich 1975
382. Toschi 1969
383. Cade and Swem 1995
384. Mayr and Short 1970
385. De Geus and Best 1991
386. Kridelbaugh 1983
387. Miller 1937
388. King 1981
389. Craig 1978
390. Shamsuddin and Mohammad 1980
391. Hahnke 1998
392. Olivier 1958
393. Meyer de Schauensee 1962
394. Hollom 1955
395. Cade 1967
396. Schön 1995a
397. Schön 1994a
398. Lorek 1995a
399. Schön 1995b
400. Temple 1993
401. Ferguson-Lees 1965
402. Hall 1960b
403. Peet and Atkinson 1994
404. Tyler 1992
405. Yosef 1992a
406. Smith 1973
407. Yosef and Grubb 1994
408. Yosef 1994a
409. Rand and Rabor 1958
410. Olivier 1947
411. Ripley 1949
412. Eisentraut 1973
413. Dittami. and Kramer 1986
414. Strange and Jeyarajasingam 1993
415. Thielcke 1956
416. Dorka. 1975
417. Gwinner 1961
418. Wemmer 1969
419. Wickler and Seibt 1980
420. Moreau and Moreau 1939
421. Zimmerman 1955
422. Balch 1979
423. Dean 1974a
424. Friedmann 1978
425. Friedmann and Williams 1969
426. Jakober and Stauber 1983
427. Atkinson, Dutton, Peet and Sequeira 1994
428. Jones, Burlison and Tye 1992
429. Jackson 1972
430. Dowsett & Forbes-Watson 1993
431. Dowsett and Dowsett-Lemaire 1993
432. Sargeant 1994
433. Chiba 1990
434. Erard and Etchécopar 1970
435. duPont 1971
436. Traylor 1967
437. Wildash 1968
438. Yamashina 1974
439. Collar 1997
440. Godfrey 1986
441. Peck and James 1987
442. Severinghaus and Blackshaw 1976
443. Jennings 1981
444. Round 1988
445. Willis 1983
446. Monroe and Sibley 1994
447. Collar and Stuart 1988
448. Dowsett-Lemaire 1989
449. Hüe and Etchécopar 1970
450. Bergier and Bergier 1990
451. Dutson and Branscombe 1990
452. Luder 1986
453. Eck 1992
454. Yosef 1992b
455. Elgood 1964
456. Erard 1987
457. Blake, Loiselle and Vande weghe 1990
458. Prigogine 1984
459. Stuart and Jensen 1985
460. Prigogine 1986

461. Safriel 1995
462. Isenmann and Lefranc 1994
463. Brosset 1976
464. Erard 1975
465. Ryall and Stoorvogel 1995
466. Atkinson, Peet and Alexander 1991
467. Lack 1994
468. Morioka and Sison 1987
469. Dohmann 1980
470. Parrott 1980
471. Prigogine 1969
472. Salomonsen 1953
473. Morioka and Sakane 1979
474. Devillers 1976
475. Raikow 1978
476. Bates and Lowther 1952
477. Dharmakumarsinhji and Lavkumar 1972
478. Dunning 1993
479. Collar, Crosby and Stattersfield 1994
480. Tucker and Heath 1994
481. Short, Horne and Gichuki 1990
482. Morel and Morel 1982
483. Wong 1986
484. Glutz von Blotzheim and Bauer 1993
485. Macleod and Parrott 1992
486. Keast 1992
487. Dowsett 1978
488. Poulsen 1995
489. Yosef 1993a
490. Harris 1986
491. Biswas 1962
492. Gyldenstolpe 1924
493. Pomeroy 1984
494. Fry 1970
495. Pantuwatana, Imlarp and Marshall 1969
496. Biswas 1950
497. Choudhurry 1976
498. England 1971
499. Clement and Worfolk 1995
500. Harris personal observations
501. Chappuis pers. comm
502. Aspinwall pers. comm
503. Carter pers. comm
504. Demey pers. comm
505. Johnson pers. comm
506. Vernon unpublished notes and pers. comm
507. Christy pers. comm
508. Andrews pers. comm
509. Pearson pers. comm
510. Herremans pers. comm
511. Scriven pers. comm
512. Chittenden pers. comm
513. Taylor pers. comm
514. Morel pers. comm
515. Dowsett-Lemaire pers. comm
516. Walters pers. comm
517. Brosset pers. comm
518. Jones pers. comm
519. Sonnenschein pers. comm
520. Lambert pers. comm
521. Lefranc 1995a
522. Lefranc 1995b
523. Rand 1958
524. Bennun 1985
525. Searcy and Brenowitz 1988
526. Webb 1936
527. Winterbottom 1936
528. Clancey 1987
529. Mundy and Cook 1972
530. Thorpe 1972
531. Sonnenschein and Reyer 1983
532. Wickler 1972
533. Rand 1957b
534. Dowsett 1980
535. Stuart and Jensen 1981
536. Schön 1994b
537. Schön 1994c
538. Irwin 1977
539. Pinto, Rosa 1963
540. Grimes 1966
541. Bannerman 1939
542. Smith, Arctander, Fjeldså and Amir 1991
543. LeCroy and Vuilleumier 1992
544. Pryce 1989
545. Benson 1948
546. Traylor 1965
547. Macleod, Macleod and Murray 1952
548. Irwin 1987
549. Langley 1982
550. Hunter 1988
551. Brosset 1989
552. Desai and Malhotra 1987
553. Ogilvie-Grant 1912
554. Britton 1970
555. Grimes 1976b
556. Stresemann 1947
557. Benson 1945b
558. Benson 1946
559. Winter 1987
560. Roseveare 1950
561. Hanmer and Manson 1988
562. Britton 1978
563. Rand and Flemming 1957
564. Grant and Mackworth-Praed 1947
565. Harwin 1970
566. Vernon 1980
567. Walsh 1968
568. Clancey 1953
569. Ripley and Heinrich 1966
570. Koford, Dunning, Ribic and Finch 1994
571. Blencowe and Allen 1960
572. Britton 1967
573. Rand 1959
574. Sinclair 1978
575. Benson and Benson 1947
576. van Someren 1916
577. Burnside 1987
578. Lawson 1989
579. Jourdain and Shuel 1935
580. Fraser 1983
581. Lawson 1984
582. Greig-Smith and Davidson 1977
583. Colston 1972
584. Field 1971
585. Short and Horne 1985
586. Hawkins 1993
587. Hart 1971
588. Irwin and Benson 1966
589. Dowsett-Lemaire in press
590. Roberts 1946
591. Lewis 1981
592. Lewis 1983
593. Prigogine 1949
594. Mariaux 1991
595. Hernandez 1995
596. Lawson 1964b
597. Yosef 1993b
598. Cram 1927
599. Lefranc 1995c
600. Panov 1995
601. Peters and Loveridge 1936
602. Rand 1957c
603. Lawson 1962
604. Vande weghe 1981
605. Hall and Moreau 1962
606. Gray 1972
607. Clancey 1967
608. Clancey 1974
609. Mayr and Amadon 1951
610. Sclater 1924–30
611. Haffer 1986
612. Mayr 1943
613. Burtt 1982
614. Swainson 1828
615. Donnelly 1978
616. Serle. 1965
617. Neumann 1972
618. van Someren 1932
619. Grimes 1979b
620. Blase 1960
621. Friedmann 1930
622. Clancey 1957
623. Grant and Mackworth-Praed 1950
624. Collister and Wicklum 1996
625. Owen 1967
626. Serle 1954
627. Lewis 1982
628. Chapman 1995
629. Atkinson 1996
630. Mundy, Winchell and Woodruff 1997
631. Zimmerman, Turner and Pearson 1996
632. Clancey 1975
633. Clancey 1986
634. Vernon 1985
635. Bowen St J. 1979
636. Fotso 1993
637. Gaugris 1976
638. McClure and Ratanaworabhan. Undated
639. Harrison, Allan, Underhill, Herremans, Tree, Parker and Brown 1997
640. Johnson 1984
641. Clancey 1969b
642. Berger 1969
643. Macleod 1986
644. Wilkinson 1978
645. Ullrich 1975
646. Bates 1911
647. Bates 1927
648. Marchant 1942
649. Vernon, Macdonald and Dean 1990
650. Herremans and Herremans-Tonnoeyr 1995
651. Eck 1990
652. Grimes 1978
653. Diamond 1983
654. Clancey 1952
655. *ISIS International Species Information System*
656. Herremans 1995
657. Hanmer 1981
658. van Someren 1922
659. Harrison 1969
660. Dowsett 1985
661. Payne 1970
662. Ndao 1989
663. Balchin 1988
664. Rodewald, Dejaifve and Green 1994
665. Yamashina 1939
666. de la Cruz Solis and de Lope Rebollo 1985
667. Isenmann and Bouchet 1993
668. Bonaccorsi and Isenmann 1994
669. Bates 1926
670. Prigogine 1953
671. Schiebel 1906
672. Bennun 1986
673. McClure, Poonswad, Greiner, and Laird 1978
674. Traylor 1960
675. Lefranc and Worfolk 1997
676. Urban, Fry and Keith 1997
677. Severinghaus 1996
678. Douglas 1992
679. Appert 1994
680. Prinzinger, Becker, Kleim, Schroth and Schierwater 1997
681. Takagi 1996a
682. Meise 1958
683. Chapin 1921
684. Schön 1996
685. Hartert 1894
686. Bates 1925
687. Austin and Kuroda 1953
688. Prigogine 1971
689. Isenmann and Fradet 1995
690. Serle 1957
691. Prys-Jones 1991
692. Stresemann 1923
693. Campbell and Lack 1985
694. Coates and Bishop 1997
695. Diamond 1972
696. Barlow, Wacher. and Dislet 1997
697. Cheke and Walsh 1996
698. Fanshawe 1994
699. Hunter, Carter, and Mlungu, 1996

700. Herremans 1992
701. Borello 1988
702. Herremans and Herremans-Tonnoeyr 1994
703. Herremans 1994
704. Tyler and Tyler 1996
705. Benson and Irwin 1972
706. Tarboton and Jones 1987
707. Harwin, Manson, Manson and Mwadziwana 1994
708. Pollard 1992
709. Caldwell-Bar 1996
710. Balchin 1990
711. Demey and Fishpool 1991
712. Demey and Fishpool 1994
713. Demey 1995
714. Scott 1985
715. Erard and Colston 1988
716. Prum 1990
717. Dowsett-Lemaire 1990
718. Ash, Dowsett and Dowsett-Lemaire 1989
719. Shirihai and Golan 1994
720. Mann and Diskin 1993
721. Ishizuka 1990
722. Ohata 1991
723. Friedmann and Bowen, 1933
724. Carpenter 1937
725. Wickler and Sonnenschein 1989
726. Schwabl and Sonnenschein 1992
727. Kryukov and Frisman 1980
728. Horvath 1959
729. England 1971
730. Naumann 1901
731. Cheng Kwang-mei and Wei Chao-sheng 1973
732. Emlen 1979
733. Lack and Quicke 1978
734. Fuggles-Couchman 1986
735. Ash, Dowsett and Dowsett-Lemaire 1991
736. Evans and Anderson 1993
737. Cordeiro 1994
738. Vande weghe 1992
739. Maclean and Prys-Jones 1988
740. Dowsett-Lemaire, Dowsett and Bulens 1993
741. Hawkins, Rabenandrasana, Virginie, Manese, Mulder, Ellis and Robert 1998
742. Sutton 1970
743. Dedekind 1991
744. Dedekind 1987
745. Meise 1968
746. Shirihai 1996
747. Porter, Christensen and Schiermacker-Hansen 1996
748. Ali 1996
749. Daniels 1997
750. Ali 1984
751. Vijayan 1989
752. Sundararaman 1989
753. Edington and Edington 1983
754. Young 1946
755. Lynes 1938
756. Wilson 1987
757. Stuart 1986
758. Desfayes 1975
759. Duckworth, Evans, Safford, Telfer, Timmins, and Zewdie 1992
760. Serle, 1943
761. Cheke 1978
762. Friedmann 1966
763. Chapin 1978
764. Friedmann and Williams 1970
765. Friedmann and Williams 1971
766. Keith, Twomey, Friedmann and Williams 1969
767. van Someren and van Someren 1949
768. Friedmann and Stager 1969
769. Tomlinson 1950
770. Yamagishi 1996
771. Croxall 1976
772. Hoogerwerf 1949
773. Chasen and Hoogerwerf 1941
774. Dean, Huntley, Huntley and Vernon. 1988
775. Jackson 1919
776. Grant and Macworth-Praed 1946
777. Moreau 1940
778. Vijayan 1992
779. Wenzel 1992
780. Colebrook-Robjent 1976
781. Aspinwall 1976
782. Quingwei and Xiaozhuang 1988
783. Takagi 1996b
784. Peirce, Backhurst and Backhurst 1977
785. Clancey 1989
786. Jenni and Winkler 1994
787. Hagemeijer and Blair 1997
788. Schön 1994d
789. Schön1994e
790. Schön 1994f
791. Schön 1994g
792. Martens and Eck 1995
793. Alexander 1900
794. Loye and Zuk 1991
795. Beesley 1995
796. Lamm, 1953a
797. Winterbottom 1963
798. Brain and Prozesky 1963
799. Bennett, Earlé, Du Toit and Huchzermeyer, 1992
800. Nöller 1975
801. Pocock, 1963
802. Uys and Macleod 1967
803. Bowen 1980
804. Smeek 1974
805. Moreau and Moreau 1940
806. Steyn 1982
807. Penry 1994
808. Britton 1977
809. Van der Willigen and Lovett 1981
810. Parker 1994
811. Gahr, Sonnenschein, and Wickler 1998
812. Kondo 1993
813. Rabor 1936
814. Svensson 1984
815. Hanmer 1978
816. Allport and Fanshawe 1994
817. Behrens and Behrens 1996
818. Martin 1996
819. Herremans 1997
820. Zheng Guang-mei and Wang Xiang-ting 1985
821. Ogawa 1977
822. Takagi and Ogawa 1995
823. Udagawa 1954
824. Haas and Ogawa 1995
825. Brooks, Lens, Barnes, Barnes, Kageche Kihuria and Wilder 1998
826. Jackson 1901
827. Yamagishi and Nishiumi 1994
828. Melville and Round 1984
829. Brosset and Erard 1977
830. Peirce 1984b
831. Benson and Irwin 1965
832. Lynes 1934
833. Sheppard 1910
834. Medland 1991
835. Nechayev 1976
836. Amadon 1953
837. Guichard 1950
838. Dowsett 1983
839. Butynski and Kalina 1993
840. Rookmaaker 1992
841. Nikolaus 1990
842. Moreau and Dolp 1970
843. Roos, Soderström and Pärt 1998
844. Fornasari and Massa 1998
845. Kikuchi, Ishii, Kansaku, Shimada and Imanishi 1998
846. Tryjanowski, Kuyniak and Kuczyñski 1998
847. Zimmerman 1972
848. Thiollay 1985
849. Walker 1939
850. Vernon 1989
851. Lawson 1963b
852. Germain and Cornet 1994
853. Warwick Tarboton. pers. comm
854. Jones 1996
855. Hanmer 1985
856. Carter 1978
857. Sonnenschein 1992
858. Gatter 1997
859. Ash and Miskell 1998
860. Zimmerman 1998
861. Wickler and Lunau 1996
862. Hustler 1996
863. Collar 1998
864. Williams 1998
865. Heinrich 1958
866. Clement 1995
867. Lamm 1953b
868. Ryan 1995
869. Irwin 1956b
870. Ash pers. comm
871. Sharp pers. comm
872. Skead pers. comm
873. Parker pers. comm
874. Won pers. comm
875. Manson pers. comm
876. Dowsett pers. comm
877. Cassidy pers. comm
878. Stjernstedt pers. comm
879. McVicker pers. comm
880. Dittami pers. comm
881. Skead 1975
882. Herremans 1993
883. Pearson and Lack 1992
884. Bruderer and Bruderer 1994
885. Underhill, Prys-Jones, Harrison and Martinez 1992
886. Sibley pers.comm
887. Bruderer pers. comm
888. Dunning pers. comm
889. Jarvis and Robertson 1997
890. Robertson, Simmons, Jarvis and Brown 1995
891. Vernon 1977
892. Dowsett-Lemaire and Dowsett 1990
893. Storr 1958
894. Sibley 1970
895. Dowsett 1990
896. Zack 1995
897. Beecher 1953
898. Jollie 1958
899. Pycraft 1907
900. Bock 1960
901. Pocock 1966
902. McFarlane 1963
903. Schulenberg 1993
904. Shimoda, Yamagishi, Tanimura and Miyazaki-Kishimoto 1996
905. van Bruggen 1960
906. Smithers and Paterson 1956
907. Dean (in prep.)
908. Dowsett-Lemaire and Dowsett 1991
909. Dean 1988
910. Pinto 1962
911. Dean 1974b
912. Pinto 1966
913. Sokolow and Vietinghoff-Scheel 1992
914. Gibbon 1995
915. Andrew 1961
916. Steyn 1998
917. Roberts 1934
918. Raikow, Polumbo and Borecky 1980
919. Ashley 1941
920. Bock 1962
921. Maclean 1990
922. Cracraft 1987
923. Herremans 1998
924. Grant and Grant 1992
925. Yosef and Deyrup 1998
926. Friedmann 1949
927. Bishop and Bennett 1992
928. Galushin and Polozov 1998
929. Harris 1995
930. Ogilvie-Grant 1910
931. Sinclair and Langrand 1998

932. Anonymous 1993
933. Clarke 1985
934. Serle 1938
935. Yom-Tov, Dunnett and Anderson 1974
936. Abuladze, Eligulashvili and Shergalin 1998
937. Holan 1998
938. Stastny, Hudec and Bejcek 1998
939. Yosef 1998
940. Neumann 1927
941. Rimmer and Darmstadt 1996
942. Yosef and Pinshow 1988a
943. Yosef and Pinshow 1988b
944. Yosef 1993c
945. Bonde 1993
946. Moore 1999
947. Schön 1998a
948. Kristin 1998
949. Kristin 1991
950. Kristin 1995
951. Kristjn and Zilinec 1998
952. Guerrieri, Pietrelli and Biondi 1995
953. Aldiss and Hunter 1985
954. Gwinner and Bieback 1977
955. Branch and Branch 1998
956. Atkinson 1997
957. Isenmann and Fradet 1998
958. Brooks and Temple 1990a
959. Cade and Woods 1994
960. Peterjohn and Sauer 1995
961. Everett and Koehler 1998
962. Schön 1998b
963. Flickinger 1995
964. Gorban and Bokotej 1995
965. Yosef 1994b
966. Anderson and Duzan 1978
967. Grubb and Yosef 1994
968. Atkinson 1993
969. Yosef, Layne and Lohrer 1993
970. Yosef and Lohrer 1995
971. Degen, Pinshow, Yosef, Kam and Nagy 1992
972. Speirs 1985
973. Gawlik and Bildstein 1990
974. Azua and Lieberman 1995
975. Yosef and Pinshow 1995
976. Scott and Morrison 1995
977. Rothhaupt 1995
978. Lorek 1995b
979. Elliott 1998
980. Gawlik, Papp and Bildstein 1991
981. Kiliaan 1996
982. Dunning 1984
983. Morrison 1979
984. Haas and Sloane 1996
985. Woods and Cade 1996
986. Bannerman 1923
987. Clancey 1960d
988. Johnson 1938
989. Reichenow 1894
990. Ryan 1992
991. Armstrong 1947
992. Weaving 1977
993. Schouteden 1963
994. Devereux 1998
995. Bruderer 1991
996. Maclean 1970
997. Tenovuo and Varrela 1998
998. Schwan and Hikes 1979
999. Roos and Roos 1988
1000. Winterbottom 1982
1001. Dowsett 1987
1002. Hanmer 1989
1003. Brown 1928
1004. Morrison 1980
1005. Moreau and Moreau 1941
1006. Dean and Macdonald. I.A.W 1981
1007. Bridgeford 1985
1008. White 1951
1009. Ionides 1954
1010. Woods 1995
1011. Fuggles-Couchman and Elliott 1946
1012. Clancey 1954
1013. Williamson 1973
1014. Busse 1995
1015. Lebedeva and Butiev 1995
1016. Peakall 1995
1017. Diehl 1995
1018. Massa, Bottoni, Fornasari and Sacchi 1995
1019. Esselink, Geertsma, Kuper, Hustings and van Berkel 1995
1020. Fuisz, Mosket and Young Park 1998
1021. Diehl 1998
1022. Favini, Fornasari, Bottoni and Massa 1998
1023. van Nieuwenhuyse 1996
1024. Hornman, Nijssen, Geertsma, Kuper and Esselink 1998
1025. van Nieuwenhuyse 1998
1026. Lefranc 1979
1027. Mann 1983
1028. Carlson 1985
1029. Cooper 1970
1030. Moskat pers. comm
1031. Parry pers. comm
1032. Ranger (unpublished notes)
1033. Horne pers. comm.
1034. Goodman pers. comm
1035. Rasa pers. comm
1036. Alamargot pers. comm
1037. du Toit pers. comm
1038. Steyn pers. comm
1039. Panov pers. comm
1040. Churn Law 1932
1041. Gartshore 1987
1042. Diehl and Myrcha 1973
1043. Pinshow, Degen, Yosef, Kam and Nagy 1995
1044. Shields 1982
1045. Owen 1917
1046. Christy 1916
1047. Wagner 1993
1048. Jakober and Stauber 1994
1049. Medway 1970
1050. Sharma 1989
1051. Rasmussen 1996
1052. Kryukov 1995
1053. Severinghaus and Liang 1995
1054. Yosef 1996
1055. Lohrer 1974
1056. Pounds 1972
1057. Pearson 1970
1058. Brooks and Temple 1990b
1059. Ericsson 1981
1060. Keith and Twomey 1968
1061. Friedmann and Williams. 1968
1062. Becker and Amir 1993
1063. Jörges 1972
1064. Praetorius 1988
1065. Porter 1932
1066. Hallett and Brown 1964
1067. Schmidt and Schmidt 1988
1068. de V. Little 1966
1069. Richmond 1899
1070. Eisentraut 1956
1071. Hurford, Lombard, Kemp and Benn 1996
1072. Sutherland 1998
1073. Cracraft 1983
1074. Snow 1997
1075. Greenwood 1997
1076. Raubenheimer and Crowe 1987
1077. Yosef, Carrel and Eisner 1996
1078. Zink 1997
1079. Wambuguh 1987
1080. Henley, Feduccia and Costello 1978
1081. Ames 1971
1082. Lack 1940
1083. Andrew 1956
1084. Simmons 1957
1085. Stephan 1965
1086. Theiler 1962

Abuladze, A., Eligulashvili, B. and Shergalin, J. 1998. Shrikes in Transcaucasia. In Yosef, R. and Lohrer, F.E. (eds.) Shrikes of the World: Conservation Implementation. *Int. Birdwatching Center in Eilat Tech. Publ.* 7: 14–15.
Alamargot, Jacques pers.comm.
Aldiss, D.T. and Hunter, N.D. 1985. A first record of the Southern Boubou in Botswana. *Babbler* 10: 34–35.
Alexander, B. 1900. An ornithological expedition to the Zambezi River. *Ibis* (7)6: 70–109.
Ali, S. 1962. *The Birds of Sikkim.* Oxford University Press, Oxford.
Ali, S. 1977. *Field Guide to the Birds of the Eastern Himalayas.* Oxford University Press, Delhi.
Ali, S. 1984. *Birds of Kerala.* Oxford University Press, Oxford.
Ali, S. 1996. *The Book of Indian Birds.* Bombay Natural History Society, Bombay.
Ali, S. and Ripley, S.D. 1987. *Handbook of the Birds of India and Pakistan.* Vol.5. Oxford University Press, Bombay.
Allport, G.A. and Fanshawe, J.H. 1994. Is the Thick-billed Cuckoo *Pachycoccyx audeberti* a forest dependent species in West Africa? *Malimbus* 16: 52–53.
Amadon, D. 1953. Avian systematics and evolution in the Gulf of Guinea. The J.G. Correia collection. *Bull. Amer. Mus. Nat Hist.* 100: 399–451.
Ames, P.L. 1971. The morphology of the syrinx in passerine birds. *Bull. Peabody Mus. Nat. Hist.* 37: 1–194.
Ames, P.L. 1975. The application of syringeal morphology to the classification of the Old World Insect Eaters (Muscicapidae). *Bonn. zool. Beitr.* 26: 107–134.
Anderson, W.C. and Duzan, R.E. 1978. DDE residues and eggshell thinning in Loggerhead Shrikes. *Wilson Bull.* 90: 215–220.
Andersson, C.J.1872. *The Birds of Damara Land.* John van Voorst, London.
Andrew, R.J. 1956. Intention movements of flight in certain passerines, and their use in systematics. *Behaviour* 10: 179–204.
Andrew, R.J. 1961. The displays given by passerines in courtship and reproductive fighting: a review. *Ibis* 103A: 315–348, 549–579.
Andrews, Mark pers. comm.
Andrews, S.M. 1994. Rediscovery of the Montiero's Bush-shrike *Malaconotus montieri* in Cameroon. *Bull. Afr. Bird Club* 1: 26–27.
Anonymous. 1993. Shrike me lucky. *Australian Nat. Hist.* 29: 12. (Colour photograph of *Laniarius liberatus*).

Appert, O. 1970. Zur biologie der Vangawürger (Vangidae) Sudwest-Madagaskars. *Orn. Beob.* 67: 101–133.
Appert, O. 1994. Is there a representative of the Oriolidae in Madagascar? a contribution to the systematics of the genus *Tylas. Orn. Beob.* 91: 255–267.
Archer, G. and Godman, E.M. 1961. *The Birds of British Somaliland and the Gulf of Aden.* Oliver and Boyd, Edinburgh and London.
Arman, P. 1971. Notes on the behaviour of the White-browed Robin-chat (*Cossypha heuglini*: Turdidae) and of the Black-headed Gonolek (*Laniarius erythrogaster*: Laniidae). *Uganda J.* 35: 75–78.
Armstrong, E.A. 1947. *Bird Display and Behaviour: an Introduction to the Study of Bird Psychology.* Lindsay Drummond Ltd., London.
Arnott, G. 1982. Observations: Olive Bush Shrike. *Diaz Diary* 102: 14.
Ash, J.S. and Miskell, J.E. 1983. Birds of Somalia, their habitat, status and distribution. *Scopus* (Special Suppl.) Number 1. East African Natural History Society.
Ash, J.S., and Miskell, J.E. 1998. *Birds of Somalia.* Pica Press.
Ash, J.S., Dowsett, R.J. and Dowsett-Lemaire, F. 1989. New ornithological distribution records from eastern Nigeria. *Tauraco Research Report* 1: 13–27.
Ash, J.S., Dowsett, R.J. and Dowsett-Lemaire, F. 1991. Additions to the East African avifauna. *Scopus* 14: 73–75.
Ash, John pers. comm.
Ashley, J.F. 1941. A study of the structure of the humerus in the Corvidae. *Condor* 43: 184–195.
Aspinwall, D.R. 1976. First record of Chestnut Wattle-eye (*Platysteira castanea*) in Zambia. *Bull. Zambian Orn. Soc.* 8: 65–66.
Aspinwall, Dylan, The late, pers. comm.
Astley Maberly, C.T. 1939. Some notes on the habits of the Four-coloured Bush-shrike. *Ostrich* 10: 43–46.
Atkinson, E.C. 1993. Winter territories and night roosts of Northern Shrikes in Idaho. *Condor* 95: 515–527.
Atkinson, E.C. 1995. Northern Shrikes (*Lanius excubitor*) wintering in North America a Christmas Bird Count analysis of trends, cycles, and interspecific interactions. In Yosef, R., and Lohrer, F.E. (eds.) Shrikes (Laniidae) of the World: Biology and Conservation. *Proc. Western Found. Vert. Zool.* 6: 39–44.
Atkinson, E.C. 1997. Singing for your supper: acoustical luring of avian prey by Northern Shrikes. *Condor* 99: 203–206.
Atkinson, P., Peet, N. and Alexander, J. 1991. The status and conservation of the endemic bird species of São Tomé and Príncipe, West Africa. *Bird Conserv. Internata.* 1: 255–282.
Atkinson, P.W. 1996. The journals of José G. Correia. *Gulf of Guinea Conservation Newsletter* 5: 3–5.
Atkinson, P.W., Dutton, J.S., Peet, N.B. and Sequeira, V.A.S. 1994. A study of the birds, small mammals, turtles and medicinal plants of Säo Tomé with notes on Príncipe. *BirdLife International Study Report* No. 56. Cambridge.
Austin, O.L. and Kuroda, N. 1953. Birds of Japan, their status and distribution. *Bull. Mus. Comp. Zool.* 109: 279–637.
Azua, J.V. and Lieberman, A. 1995. The captive propagation of three species of shrikes at the San Diego Zoo and Wild Animal Park. In Yosef, R., and Lohrer, F.E.(eds.) Shrikes (Laniidae) of the World: Biology and Conservation. *Proc. Western Found. Vert. Zool.* 6: 254–257.
Balch, L.G. 1979. Separation of Northern and Loggerhead Shrikes in the field. *Birding* 11: 9–12.
Balchin, C.S. 1988. Recent observations on the birds from the Ivory Coast. *Malimbus* 10: 201–206.
Balchin, C.S. 1990. Further observations of birds from the Ivory Coast. *Malimbus* 12: 52–53.
Banage, W.B. 1969. Territorial behaviour and population in the Grey-backed Fiscal Shrike. *Uganda J.* 33: 201–208.
Bannerman, D.A. 1923. Report on the birds collected during the British Museum Expedition to Ivory Coast (French West Africa). *Ibis* (11)5: 667–748.
Bannerman, D.A. 1938. A new genus of shrike. *Bull. Brit. Orn. Club* 59: 6–7.
Bannerman, D.A. 1939. A new bush-shrike from Angola. *Ibis* (14)3: 746–750.
Bannerman, D.A. 1953. *The Birds of West and Equatorial Africa.* Vol. 2. Oliver & Boyd, London.
Barlow, C., Wacher, T. and Dislet, T. 1997. *A Field Guide to Birds of The Gambia and Senegal.* Pica Press, Robertsbridge, UK.
Bates, G.L. 1911. Further notes on the birds of southern Cameroon. Part 1. With descriptions of the eggs by W.R. Ogilvie-Grant. *Ibis* (9)5: 479–545.
Bates, G.L. 1925. New subspecies of wattle-eye: *Diaphorophyia ansorgei harterti. Bull. Brit. Orn. Club* 65: 105–106.
Bates, G.L. 1926. New birds from the mountains of N.W. Cameroon. *Bull. Brit. Orn. Club* 46: 88–89.
Bates, G.L. 1927. Some birds of Cameroon and the Lake Chad Region. *Ibis* (12)3: 1–64.
Bates, G.L. 1930. *Handbook of The Birds of West Africa.* John Bale, Sons, and Danielsson, London.
Bates, R.S.P. and Lowther, E.H.N. 1952. *Breeding Birds of Kashmir.* Oxford University Press, Oxford.
Becker, P. and Amir, O.G. 1993. Effects on non-target birds through spraying operations on Quelea roosts and colonies in Somalia. *Lanioturdus* 27: 58–63.
Beecher, W.J. 1953. A phylogeny of the oscines. *Auk* 70: 270–333.
Beehler, B.M., Pratt, T.K. and Zimmerman, D.A. 1986. *Birds of New Guinea.* Princeton University Press, Princeton.
Beesley, A.J. 1995. The birds of the Chimanimani Mountains. *Honeyguide* Suppl. 1, 41: 1–57.
Behrens, B. and Behrens, G. 1996. Who is this fine feathered friend? *Bee-eater* 47: 27.
Belcher, C.F. 1922. Notes from Nyasaland, Part 3. *Oologists' Record* 2: 32–41.
Belcher, C.F. 1930. *The Birds of Nyasaland.* Crosby Lockwood & Son, London.
Bennett, G.F., Earlé, R.A., Du Toit, H. and Huchzermeyer, F.W. 1992. A host-parastite catalogue of the Haematozoa of the sub-saharan birds. *Onderstepoort J. Vet. Res.* 59: 1–73.
Bennett, G.F., Pierce, M.A. and Earlé, R.A. 1990. The haemoproteids of the shrikes of the avian family Laniidae (Passeriformes). *S. Afr. J. Zool.* 25: 194–198.
Bennett, G.F., Whiteway, M. and Woodworth-Lynas, C. 1982. A host-parasite catalogue of the avian Haematozoa. *Occas. Pap. Biol. Memorial Univ. Newfound.* No. 5: 1–243.
Bennun, L.A. 1985. Notes on behaviour and plumage dimorphism in Lagden's Bush Shrike *Malaconotus lagdeni. Scopus* 9: 111–114.
Bennun, L.A. 1986. Montane birds of the Bwindi Forest. *Scopus* 10: 87–91.
Benson, C.W. 1941. Further notes on Nyasaland Birds (with particular reference to those of the Northern Province). *Ibis* (14)5: 1–55.
Benson, C.W. 1945a. The races of the Rufous-breasted Bush-shrike *Chlorophoneus rubiginosus* (Sund.). *Ostrich* 16: 133–138.
Benson, C.W. 1945b. Notes on the birds of southern Abyssinia. *Ibis* 87: 366–400.
Benson, C.W. 1946. Notes on the birds of southern Abyssinia. *Ibis* 88: 180–205, 287–306, 444–461.
Benson, C.W. 1948. Geographical voice-variation in African birds. *Ibis* 90: 48–71.
Benson, C.W. 1950. The races of *Lanius souzae* Bocage. *Auk* 67: 394–395.
Benson, C.W. 1984. The birds of Madagascar. In Jolly, A., Oberle, P., and Albignac, R. (eds). *Key Environments-Madagascar.* Pergamon Press.
Benson, C.W. and Benson, F.M. 1947. On some breeding and other records from Nyasaland. *Ibis* 89: 279–290.
Benson, C.W. and Benson, F.M. 1977. *Birds of Malawi.* Montfort Press, Limbe.
Benson, C.W. and Irwin, M.P.S. 1961. The range of *Tchagra minuta reichenowi. Bull. Brit. Orn. Club* 81: 8–10.

Benson, C.W. and Irwin, M.P.S. 1965. The birds of *Cryptosepalum* forests, Zambia. *Arnoldia* 1: 1–12.
Benson, C.W. and Irwin, Z.M.P. 1967. A contribution to the ornithology of Zambia: notes on selected species in systematic order. *Zambia Museum Papers* No. 1: 1–139.
Benson, C.W. and Irwin, M.P.S. 1972. The Thick-billed Cuckoo *Pachycoccyx audeberti* (Schlegel) (Aves: Cuculidae). *Arnoldia* 5: 1–24.
Benson, C.W., Brooke, R.K. and Vernon, C.J. 1964. Bird breeding data for Rhodesias and Nyasaland. *Natn. Mus. Southern Rhodesia Occas. Pap.* 4. No. 27B: 30–127.
Benson, C.W., Brooke, R.K., Dowsett, R.J. and Irwin, M.P.S. 1971. *The Birds of Zambia.* Collins, London.
Benson, F.M. 1946. Field notes from Nyasaland. *Ostrich* 17: 300–320.
Bent, A.C. 1950. Life Histories of North American Wagtails, Shrikes, Vireos and their Allies. *Bull. U.S. Natn. Mus.* 197. Smithsonian Institution, Washington.
Berger, A.J. 1969. Appendicular myology of passerine birds. *Wilson Bull.* 81: 220–223.
Bergier, P. and Bergier, F. 1990. *A Birdwatchers Guide to Morocco.* Prion, Huntingdon, U.K.
Bergmann, H.-H. and Helb, H.-W. 1982. *Stimmen der Vögel Europas.* BLV Verlagsgesellschaft, München.
Betts, F.N. 1966. Resident breeding birds of SW Kenya. *Ibis* 108: 513–530.
Bishop, M.A. and Bennett, G.F. 1992. Host-parasite catalogue of the avian Haematozoa, and bibliography of the avian blood-inhabiting Haematozoa, Suppl. 1 and 2. *Mem. Univ. Newfoundland Occas Pap. Biol.* 15: 1–244.
Biswas, B. 1950. On the shrike *Lanius tephronotus* (Vigors), with remarks on the *erythronotus* and *tricolor* group of *Lanius schach* Linne, and their hybrids. *J. Bombay Nat. Hist. Soc.* 49: 444–455.
Biswas, B. 1962. Further notes on the shrikes *Lanius tephronotus* and *Lanius schach. Ibis* 104: 112–115.
Blake, J.G., Loiselle, B.A. and Vande weghe, J.P. 1990. Weights and measurements of some Central African Birds. *Gerfaut* 80: 3–11.
Blase, B. 1960. Die Lautäusserungen des Neuntöters *Lanius collurio.* Freilandbeobachtungen und Kaspar Hauser-Versuche. *Z. Tierpsychol.* 17: 293–344.
Blencowe, E.J. 1962. Pink-footed Puff-back breeding in Kakamega Forest. *J. E. Afr. Nat. Hist. Soc.* 24: 65.
Blencowe, E.J. and Allen, P.M. 1960. Notes on some birds seen on a trip to Kigezi District, S.W. Uganda, March 1960. *J. E Afr. Nat. Hist. Soc.* 23: 304–305.
Bock, W.J. 1960. The palatine process of the premaxilla in the Passeres. A study of variation, function, evolution, and taxonomic value of a single character throughout an avian Order. *Bull. Mus. Comp. Zool.* 122: 361–488.
Bock, W.J. 1962. The pneumatic fossa of the humerus in the passeres. *Auk* 79: 425–443.
Bonaccorsi, G. and Isenmann, P. 1994. Biologie de la reproduction et nourriture de la Pie-Grièche à Tête Rousse (*Lanius senator badius*) et de la Pie-Grièche Ecorcheur (*Lanius collurio*) en Corse (France). *Alauda* 62: 269–274.
Bonde, K. 1993. *Birds of Lesotho: a Guide to Distribution Past and Present.* University of Natal Press, Pietermaritzburg.
Boonsong Lekagul and Round, P.D. 1991. *A Guide to the Birds of Thailand.* Saha Karn Bhaet Co., Bangkok.
Borello, W. 1988. Alternative diet of Crimsonbreasted Shrike. *Babbler* 16: 20.
Bowden, C.G.R. and Andrews, S.M. 1994. Mount Kupe and its birds. *Bull. Afr. Bird Club* 1: 13–16.
Bowen, P. St J. 1979. Some notes on Margaret's Batis (*Batis margaritae*) in Zambia. *Bull. Zambian Orn. Soc.* 11: 1–10.
Bowen, P. St. J. 1980. A Redbacked Shrike (*Lanius collurio*) impaling prey on thorns in Zambia. *Bull. Zambian Orn. Soc.* 12: 36–37.
Bowen, W.W. 1931. East African birds collected during the Gray African Expidition, 1929. *Proc. Acad. Nat. Sci. Philadelphia* 83: 11–79.
Brain, C.K. and Prozesky, O.P.M. 1963. On the body temperature of birds collected on the Carp-Transvaal Museum Namib Desert Expedition. *Sci. Pap. Namib Res. Stat.* 16: 1–8.
Branch, W.R. and Branch, T.C. 1998. Birds of the Moebase region, Zambezia Province, northern Mozambique. *Bird Numbers* 7: 8–12.
Brazil, M.A. 1991. *The Birds of Japan.* Christopher Helm, London.
Bridgeford, P.A. 1985. Feeding associations between birds and mammals in the Skeleton Coast Park. *Madoqua* 14: 185–185.
Britton, J.A. 1967. The birds of Ilaro. Bull. *Nigerian Orn. Soc.* 4: 2–11.
Britton, P.L. 1967. Some records from Mozambique. *Ostrich* 38: 46–47.
Britton, P.L. 1968. Two African species pairs. *Bull. Brit. Orn. Club* 88: 164–166.
Britton, P.L. 1970. Two new shrikes for Kenya. *Bull. Brit. Orn. Club* 90: 133–134.
Britton, P.L. 1977. Weights of birds in western and coastal Kenya. *Scopus* 1: 70–73.
Britton, P.L. 1978. Seasonality, density and diversity of birds of papyrus swamp in West Kenya. *Ibis* 120: 450–466.
Britton, P.L. (ed.)1980. *Birds of East Africa.* East African Natural History Society, Nairobi.
Britton, P.L. and Britton, H.A. 1977. The nest and eggs of the Chestnut-fronted Helmet Shrike *Prionops scopifrons. Scopus* 1: 86.
Britton, P.L. and Dowsett, R.J. 1969. More bird weights from Zambia. *Ostrich* 40: 55–60.
Brodkorb, P. 1978. Catalogue of fossil birds, Part 5 (Passeriformes). *Bull. Florida State Mus. Biol. Sci.* 23: 139–228.
Broekhuysen, G.J. 1958. Notes on the breeding behaviour of the Cape Flycatcher *Batis capensis. Ostrich* 29: 143–152.
Broekhuysen, G.J. 1971. Third report on migration in southern Africa. *Ostrich* 42: 211–225.
Brooke, R.K. 1964. Avian observations on a journey across central Africa and additional information on some of the species seen. *Ostrich* 35: 277–292.
Brooke, R.K. 1968. More on Sheppard's bird work in the Portuguese Vumba. *Ostrich* 39: 185–190.
Brooke, R.K. 1980. The juvenile plumage of the Southern Puffback. *Honeyguide* 101: 22–23.
Brooke, R.K. 1984. South African Red Data Book:Birds. *SA Nat. Sci. Program Report.* No. 97, Pretoria.
Brooke, R.K. 1992. The bird community of *Tamarix*-clad drainages, northwestern Karoo, Cape Province. *Ostrich* 63: 42–43.
Brooke, R.K. and Manson, A.J. 1979. Towards a natural history of the Wattle-eyed Flycatcher, particularly in Rhodesia. *Honeyguide* 97: 15–17.
Brooks, B.L. and Temple, S.A. 1990a. Habitat availability and suitability for Loggerhead Shrikes in Upper Midwest. *Amer. Midl. Nat.* 123: 75–83.
Brooks, B.L. and Temple, S.A. 1990b. Dynamics of a Loggerhead Shrike population in Minnesota. *Wilson Bull.* 102: 441–450.
Brooks, T., Lens, L., Barnes, J., Barnes, R., Kageche Kihuria, J. and Wilder, C. 1998. The conservation status of the forest birds of the Taita Hills, Kenya. *Bird Conserv. Internatn.* 8: 119–139.
Brosset, A. 1976. Observations sur le parasitisme de la reproduction du Coucou Eméraude *Chrysococcyx cupreus* au Gabon. *Oiseau et R.F.O.* 46: 201–208.
Brosset, A. 1989. Un cas d'association à bénéfice mutuel, celui de la Pie grièche *Lanius cabanisi* avec les *Bubalornis Bubalornis* niger. *Rev. Ecol.* (*Terre Vie*) 44: 103–106.
Brosset, A. and Erard, C. 1977. New faunistic records from Gabon. *Bull. Brit. Orn. Club* 97: 125–132.
Brosset, A. and Erard, C. 1986. *Les Oiseaux des Régions Forestières du Nord-Est du Gabon.* Vol.1. Suppl. 3. Terre et Vie, Soc. Nat. Prot. Nature, Paris.
Brosset, André pers. comm.
Brown, C.E. 1928. Longevity of birds in captivity. *Auk* 65: 345–348.

Brown, E.D. and Veltman, C.J. 1987. Ethogram of the Australian Magpie (*Gymnorhina tibicen*) in comparison to other Cracticidae and Corvus species. *Ethology* 76: 309–333.
Brown, L.H. and Britton, P.L. 1980. *The Breeding Seasons of East African Birds.* East African Natural History Society, Nairobi.
Bruderer, B. 1991. Common Egg-eater *Dasypeltis scabra* killed at Fiscal Shrike *Lanius collaris* nest. *Ostrich* 62: 76–77.
Bruderer, B. and Bruderer, H. 1993. Distribution and habitat preference of Red-backed Shrikes (*Lanius collurio*) in southern Africa. *Ostrich* 64: 144–147.
Bruderer, B. and Bruderer, H. 1994. Numbers of Redbacked Shrikes *Lanius collurio* in southern Africa. *Bull. Brit. Orn. Club* 114: 192–201.
Bruderer, Bruno pers. comm.
Bulatova, N.S. 1981. A comparative karyological study of Passerine birds. *Act Sci. Nat. Acad. Sci. Bohemoslov. Brno* 15: 1–44.
Bulatova, N.S., Panov, E.N. and Radjabli, S.I. 1971. Description of karyotypes of some species of birds of the USSR fauna. *Proc. USSR Acad. Sci.* 199: 1420–1423.
Bundy, G., Connor, R.J. and Harrison, C.J.O. 1989. *Birds of the Eastern Province of Saudi Arabia.* H.F & G Witherby, London.
Burnside, F.L. 1987. Long-distance movements by Loggerhead Shrikes. *J. Field Orn.* 58: 62–65.
Burtt, E.H. 1982. Color convergence: is it only mimetic? *Amer. Nat.* 119: 738–740
Busse, P. 1995. Migration dynamics of Red-backed (*Lanius collurio*) and Great Grey Shrikes (*L. excubitor)* in the Baltic Region, 1961–1990. In Yosef, R., and Lohrer, F.E.(eds.) Shrikes (Laniidae) of the World: Biology and Conservation. *Proc. Western Found. Vert. Zool.* 6: 55–60.
Butticker, W. 1960. Artificial nesting devices in southern Africa. *Ostrich* 31: 44–45.
Butynski, T.M. and Kalina, J. 1993. Further additions to the known avifauna of the Impenetrable (Bwindi) Forest. *Scopus* 17: 1–7.
Cade, T.C. 1967. Ecological and behavioural aspects of predation by the Northern Shrike. *Living Bird* 6: 43–86.
Cade, T.J. 1962. Wing movements, hunting and displays of the Northern Shrike. *Wilson Bull.* 74: 386–408.
Cade, T.J. and Swem, T. 1995. Ecology of Northern Shrikes nesting in arctic Alaska. In Yosef, R. and Lohrer, F.E. (eds.) Shrikes (Laniidae) of the World: Biology and Conservation. *Proc. Western Found. Vert. Zool.* 6: 204–214.
Cade, T.J. and Woods, C.P. 1994. Changes in the distribution and abundance of Loggerhead Shrikes. *J. Orn.* 135: 288.
Caldwell-Bar, P.R. 1996. Vanga Flycatchers breeding in the Rusitu forest. *Honeyguide* 42: 166–167.
Campbell, B. and Lack, E. (eds.) 1985. *A Dictionary of Birds.* Poyser, Calton, UK.
Cardwell, H.R. and Cardwell, J.C. 1931. *South China Birds.* Hester May Vanderburgh, Shanghai.
Carlson, A. 1985. Prey detection in the Red-backed Shrike (*Lanius collurio*): an experimental study. *Anim. Behav.* 33: 1243–1249.
Carpenter, G.D.H. 1937. Observations by Mr R.E. Moreau on a nesting African shrike capturing butterflies. *Proc. R. Ent. Soc. Lond.* 12: 161–162.
Carter, C. 1978. Eastern Least Honeyguide (*Indicator meliphilus*) at Ndola. *Bull. Zambian Orn. Soc.* 10: 30–31.
Carter, Clyde pers. comm.
Cassidy, Rodney pers. comm.
Cave, F.O. and Macdonald, J.D. 1955. *The Birds of the Sudan.* Oliver and Boyd, London.
Chapin, J.P. 1921. Notes on birds of the Belgium Congo: The juvenile dress of *Sigmodus rufiventris mentalis. Amer. Mus. Novit.* 17: 11–13.
Chapin, J.P. 1947. Colour variation in shrikes of the genus *Chlorophoneus. Auk* 64: 53–64.
Chapin, J.P. 1950. Sousa's Shrike in Tanganyika Territory. *Auk* 67: 241–242.
Chapin, J.P. 1953. Birds of the Belgian Congo. Part 3. *Bull. Amer. Mus. Nat. Hist.* 75A: 653–685.
Chapin, J.P. 1954. Birds of the Belgian Congo. Part 4. *Bull. Amer. Mus. Nat. Hist.* 75B: 12–97.
Chapin, R.T. 1978. Brief accounts of some Central African birds based on the journals of James Chapin. *Rev. Zool. Bot. afr.* 92: 805–836.
Chapman, A. 1995. Breeding and moult of four bird species in tropical West Africa. *Tropical Zoology* 8: 227–238.
Chappuis, Claude pers. comm.
Chasen, F.N. and Hoogerwerf, A. 1941. The birds of the Netherlands Indian Mt Leuser expetition 1937 to north Sumatra. *Treubia* 18: 1–125 (Suppl.).
Cheke, R.A. 1978. Records of birds and their parasites from the Cherangani Mountains, Kenya. *E. Afr. Wildl. J.* 16: 61–64.
Cheke, R.A. and Walsh, J.F. 1996. *The Birds of Togo.* BOU Check-list No. 14. Tring, Herts.
Cheng Kwang-mei and Wei Chao-sheng 1973. On the breeding habits of the Red-tailed Shrike (*Lanius cristatus lucionensis* Linné). *Acta Zool. Sinica* 19: 182–189. (In Chinese.)
Cheng Tso-hsin (ed.) 1962. *China's Economic Fauna.* Science Publishing Soc. US Dept. Commerce, Joint Publications Research Service.
Cheng Tso-hsin, 1987. *A Synopsis of the Avifauna of China.* Paul Parey, Hamburg and Berlin, and Science Press, Peking.
Chiba, H. 1990. First breeding record of the Bull-headed Shrike from the Ogasawara Islands 1988–1989. *Japanese J. Orn.* 38: 151.
Chittenden, H. 1977. Puffback Shrike. *Bokmakierie* 29: 53–54.
Chittenden, Hugh pers. comm.
Choudhurry, A. M. 1976. New species of Trypanosome from *Lanius schach. Proc. zool. Soc.* (Calcutta) 29: 29–46.
Christy, M. 1916. Parasitic worms in Red-backed Shrike. *Brit. Birds* 10: 93–94.
Christy, Patrice pers. comm.
Churn Law, S. 1932. The status of the Indian Black-headed Shrike (*Lanius nigriceps*, Frank) in Lower Bengal. *J. Bombay Nat. Hist. Soc.* 36: 259–262.
Clancey, P.A. 1948. A new race of the Woodchat Shrike (*Lanius senator*) from the island of Sicily. *Bull. Br. Orn. Club* 68: 90–92.
Clancey, P.A. 1952. Clinal colour variation in *Laniarius atrococcineus. Ostrich* 23: 132.
Clancey, P.A. 1953. Four new races of birds from Eastern and South-eastern Africa. *Durban Mus. Novit.* 4: 57–64.
Clancey, P.A. 1954. Miscellaneous taxonomic notes on African birds IV. Three new geographical races of the African Fiscal Shrike *Lanius collaris* Linnaeus. *Durban Mus. Novit.* 4: 77–89.
Clancey, P.A. 1955. A new geographical race of the Fiscal Shrike *Lanius collaris* Linnaeus from the deserts of South-West Africa and Angola. *Bull. Brit Orn. Club* 75: 32–33.
Clancey, P.A. 1957. Geographical variation in the South African populations of *Malaconotus blanchoti* Stephens with the description of a new race. *Bull. Br. Orn. Club* 77: 99–102.
Clancey, P.A. 1959a. The South African Races of the Cape Batis *Batis capensis* (Linnaeus). *Bull. Br. Orn. Club* 79: 57–60.
Clancey, P.A. 1959b. Miscellaneous taxonomic notes on African birds: the South African races of the Orange-breasted Bush-shrike *Malaconotus sulfureopectus* (Lesson). *Durban Mus. Novit.* 5: 166–172.
Clancey, P.A. 1959c. Miscellaneous taxonomic notes on African birds 13: systematic and distributional observations on some South African bird forms. *Durban Mus. Novit.* 5: 197–218.
Clancey, P.A. 1960a. Miscellaneous taxonomic notes on African birds: the characters and ranges of the South African races of *Prionops retzii*, Wahlberg. *Durban Mus. Novit.* 6: 41–44.
Clancey, P.A. 1960b. The races of the Bokmakierie *Telophorus zeylonus* (Linnaeus), with the characters of a new form from South-West Africa. *Bull. Brit. Orn. Club* 80: 121–124.

Clancey, P.A. 1960c. Miscellaneous taxonomic notes on African birds: the South African races of the Gorgeous Bush Shrike *Telophorus quadricolor* (Cassin). *Durban Mus. Novit.* 6: 38–41.
Clancey, P.A. 1960d. Fourth Report of SAOS List Committee. *Ostrich* 31: 64–77.
Clancey, P.A. 1961a. Geographical variation in the South African populations of the Magpie-Shrike *Lanius melanoleucus* Jardine. *Bull. Brit. Orn. Club* 81: 52–54.
Clancey, P.A. 1961b. Miscellaneous taxonomic notes on African birds: the South African races of the Puffback *Dryoscopus cubla* (Shaw). *Durban Mus. Novit.* 6: 105–118.
Clancey, P.A. 1964. *The Birds of Natal and Zululand.* Oliver and Boyd, London
Clancey, P.A. 1965. Variation in the White-crowned Shrike *Eurocephalus anguitimens* Smith 1836. *Arnoldia* 1: 1–3.
Clancey, P.A. 1967. Miscellaneous notes on African birds 25: descriptions of four new races of African birds. *Durban Mus. Novit.* 8: 109–114.
Clancey, P.A. 1969a. The South African sub-region races of the Three-streaked *Tchagra tchagra australis* (Smith). *Arnoldia* 4: 1–12.
Clancey, P.A. 1969b. Miscellaneous taxonomic notes on African birds: *Batis fratrum sheppardi. Durban Mus. Novit.* 8: 264–265.
Clancey, P.A. 1970a. Miscellaneous taxonomic notes on African birds: two new subspecies of passerine birds from western Angola. *Durban Mus. Novit.* 9: 8–11.
Clancey, P.A. 1970b. A further subspecies of *Lanius souzae* Bocage. *Durban Mus. Novit.* 8: 340–344.
Clancey, P.A. 1971a. A Handlist of the Birds of Southern Mozambique. *Mem. Inst. Invest. cient. Mocamb.* 11. Sér. A. 1–167. Lourenço Marques.
Clancey, P.A. 1971b. Miscellaneous taxonomic notes on African birds: on the southern range limits of *Nilaus afer nigritemporalis* Reichenow, 1892. *Durban Mus. Novit.* 9: 122–129.
Clancey, P.A. 1973. The status and characters of the races of Red-backed Shrike wintering in the South African sub-region. *Bull. Brit. Orn. Club* 93: 92–96.
Clancey, P.A. 1974. Subspeciation studies in some Rhodesian birds. *Arnoldia* 6: 1–43.
Clancey, P.A. 1975. Endemic birds of the montane evergreen forest biome of the Transvaal. *Durban Mus. Novit.* 10: 151–180.
Clancey, P.A. 1976a. Miscellaneous taxonomic notes on African birds: on the validity of *Prionops talacoma* Smith, 1836. *Durban Mus. Novit.* 11: 135–138.
Clancey, P.A. 1976b. Intergradation between two subspecies of the Fiscal Shrike. *Ostrich* 47: 145.
Clancey, P.A. 1980a. On the Lesser Grey Shrike *Lanius minor* Gmelin in southern Africa. *Durban Mus. Novit.* 12: 161–165.
Clancey, P.A. (ed.) 1980b. *Checklist of Southern African Birds.* Southern African Ornithological Society, Johannesburg.
Clancey, P.A. 1982. Miscellaneus taxonomic notes on African birds: on *Malaconotus blanchoti* Stephens in South West Africa. *Durban Mus. Novit.* 13: 134–137.
Clancey, P.A. 1986. Endemicity in the southern African avifauna. *Durban Mus. Novit.* 13: 245–284.
Clancey, P.A. 1987. Morphological mimicry in some Afrotropical birds. *Albatross* (Newlsetter of the Natal Bird Club). 289: 17–20.
Clancey, P.A. 1989. Taxonomic and distributional findings on some birds from Namibia. *Cimbebasia* 11: 111–133.
Clark, G.A. 1981. Toe fusion in Oscines. *Wilson Bull.* 93: 67–76.
Clarke, G. 1985. Bird observations from northwest Somalia. *Scopus* 9: 24–42.
Clement, P. 1995. Identification pitfalls and assessment problems. 17 Woodchat Shrike *Lanius senator. Brit. Birds* 88: 291–295.
Clement, P. and Worfolk, T. 1995. Southern and eastern Great Grey Shrikes in northwest Europe. *Birding World* 8: 300–309.
Coates, B.J. 1990. *The Birds of Papua New Guinea.* Vol.2. Passerines. Dove Publications, Alderley.
Coates, B.J. and Bishop, K.D. 1997. *A Guide to the Birds of Wallacea: Sulawesi, the Moluccas and Lesser Sunda Islands, Indonesia.* Dove Publications, Alderly, Queensland.
Colebrook-Robjent, J.F.R. 1976. Undescribed nests and eggs of birds breeding in Zambia. *Bull. Zambian Orn. Soc.* 8: 45–56.
Collar, N.J. 1997. Taxonomy and conservation: chicken and egg. *Bull. Brit. Orn. Club* 117: 122–136.
Collar, N.J. 1998. Undiscovered country: the non-collection of the Somali shrike. *Bull. Afr. Bird Club* 5: 136–137.
Collar, N.J. and Stuart, S.N. 1985. *Threatened Birds of Africa and Related Islands.* The ICBP/IUCN Red Data Book. Part 1. Cambridge.
Collar, N.J., and Stuart, S.N. 1988. *Key Forests for Threatened Birds of Africa.* ICBP Monograph no. 3. Cambridge.
Collar, N.J., Crosby, M.J., and Stattersfield, A.J. 1994. *Birds to Watch 2: The World List of Threatened Birds.* BirdLife International, Cambridge.
Collister, D.M. and Wicklum, D. 1996. Intraspecific variation in Loggerhead Shrikes: sexual dimorphism and implication for subspecific classification. *Auk* 113: 221–223.
Colston, P.R. 1972. African bird weights. *Bull. Brit. Orn. Club* 92: 115–116.
Colston, P.R. and Curry-Lindahl, K. 1986. *The Birds of Mount Nimba, Liberia.* British Museum, (Natural History), London.
Cooper, J. 1970. A parasite of the Fiscal Shrike. *Honeyguide* 63: 27.
Cooper, J. 1971a. The breeding of the Fiscal Shrike in southern Africa. *Ostrich* 42: 166–174.
Cooper, J. 1971b. Post-nesting development in the Fiscal Shrike. *Ostrich* 42: 175–178.
Cordeiro, N.J. 1994. Forest birds on Mt Kilimanjaro, Tanzania. *Scopus* 17: 65–112.
Cracraft, J. 1983. Species concepts and speciation analysis. *Current Ornithology* 1: 159–187.
Cracraft, J. 1987. DNA hybridization and avian phylogenetics. In: Hecht, M.K., Wallace, B. and Prance, G.T., (eds.) *Evolutionary Biology.* Plenum Publishing Corporation, New York.
Craig, R.B. 1978. An analysis of the predatory behavior of the Loggerhead Shrike. *Auk* 95: 221–234.
Cram, E.B. 1927. Bird parasites of the nematode suborders Strongylata, Ascaridata and Spirurata. *U.S. Natn. Mus. Bull.* 140: 1–465.
Cramp, S. and Perrins, C.M. (eds) 1993. *Birds of the Western Palearctic.* Vol.7. Oxford University Press, Oxford.
Croxall, J.P. 1976. The composition and behaviour of some mixed-species bird flocks in Sarawak. *Ibis* 118: 333–346.
Cuddy, D. 1995. Protection and restoration of breeding habitat for the Loggerhead Shrike (*Lanius ludovicianus*) in Ontario, Canada. In Yosef, R., and F.E. Lohrer, (eds). Shrikes (Laniidae) of the World: Biology and Conservation. *Proc. Western Found. Vert. Zool.* 6: 283–286.
Curry-Lindahl, K. 1981. *Bird Migration in Africa.* Vol.1. Academic Press, London.
Cyrus, D. and Robson, N. 1980. *Bird Atlas of Natal.* University of Natal Press, Pietermaritzburg.
Daniels, R.J.R. 1997. *A Field Guide to the Birds of Southwestern India.* Oxford University Press, Delhi.
Darwin, C. 1859. *On the Origin of Species by Natural Selection.* John Murray, London.
De Geus, D.W. and Best, L.B. 1991. Brown-headed Cowbirds parasitize Loggerhead Shrikes. First record for family Laniidae. *Wilson Bull.* 103: 504–506.
de la Cruz Solis, C. and de Lope Rebollo, F. 1985. Reproduction de la Pie-grièche Méridionale (*Lanius excubitor meridionalis*) dans le sud-ouest de la penninsule Ibérique. *Gerfaut* 75: 199–209.
de V. Little, J. 1966. Bokmakierie attacks prinia. *Bokmakierie* 18: 75
De Vree, F. 1969. The pterylosis of the African Bushshrike *Tchagra m. minuta* (Hartlaub). *Gerfaut* 59: 157–191.
Dean, A.R. 1982. Field characters of Isabelline and Brown Shrikes. *Brit. Birds* 75: 395–406.
Dean, W.R.J. (in prep.). *The Birds of Angola.* BOU Check-list. Tring, Herts.
Dean, W.R.J. 1974a. Breeding and distributional notes on some Angolan birds. *Durban Mus. Novit.* 10: 109–127.

Dean, W.R.J. 1974b. Bird weights from Angola. *Bull. Brit. Orn. Club* 94: 170–172.
Dean, W.R.J. 1988. The avifauna of Angolan miombo woodlands. *Tauraco* 1: 99–104.
Dean, W.R.J. and Macdonald, I.A.W. 1981. A review of African birds feeding in association with mammals. *Ostrich* 52: 135–155.
Dean, W.R.J., Huntley, M.A., Huntley, B.J. and Vernon, C.J. 1988. Notes on some birds of Angola. *Durban Mus. Novit.* 14: 44–92.
Dedekind, H. 1987. Whitetailed Shrike nesting in the Naukluft Park. *Lanioturdus* 22: 82–83.
Dedekind, H. 1991. Notes on the nesting behaviour of the White-tailed Shrike. *Lanioturdus* 26: 31–34.
Degen, A.A., Pinshow, B., Yosef, R., Kam, M. and Nagy, K.A. 1992. Energetics and growth rate of Northern Shrike nestlings. *Ecology* 72: 2273–2283.
Deignan, H.G. 1945. The birds of northern Thailand. *U.S. Natn Mus. Bull.* 186.
Deignan, H.G. 1960. Campephagidae. In Mayr, E., and Greenway, J.C. (eds.) *Check-list of Birds of the World.* Vol. 9. Mus. Comp. Zool., Cambridge Massachusetts.
Deignan, H.G. 1963. Checklist of the Birds of Thailand. *U.S. Natn. Mus. Bull.* 226.
Delacour, J. 1947. *The Birds of Malaysia.* Macmillan, New York.
Dement'ev, G.P. and Gladkov, N.A. (eds.) 1968. *Birds of the Soviet Union.* Vol.6. Israel Program for Scientific Translation, Jerusalem.
Demey, R. 1995. *Birds of western Guinea. Malimbus* 17: 85–99.
Demey, R. and Fishpool, L.D.C. 1991. Additions and annotations to the avifauna of Cote d'Ivoire. *Malimbus* 12: 61–86.
Demey, R. and Fishpool, L.D.C. 1994. The birds of Yapo Forest, Ivory Coast. *Malimbus* 16: 100–122.
Demey, Ron pers. comm.
Desai, J.H. and Malhotra, A.K. 1987. Breeding biology of Baybacked Shrike (*Lanius vittatus*) at National Zoological Park, New Delhi. *J. Bombay Nat. Hist. Soc.* 83: 200–202.
Desfayes, M. 1975. Birds from Ethiopia. *Rev. Zool. Bot. Afr.* 89: 505–535.
Devereux, C. 1998. The Fiscal Shrike: Territorial imperative. *Africa: Birds and Birding* 3: 53–57.
Devillers, P. 1976. Observations ornithologiques de printemps au Garhwal, Himalaya indien. *Gerfaut* 66: 221–249.
Dharmakumarsinhji, R.S. and Lavkumar, K.S. 1972. *Sixty Indian Birds.* Publications Division, Ministry of Information and Broadcasting, Govt. of India.
Diamond, A.W. 1983. The Black and White Flycatcher *Bias musicus* in Kenya. *Scopus* 7: 22.
Diamond, J.M. 1972. Avifauna of the Eastern Highlands of New Guinea. *Publ. Nuttal Orn. Club* 12, Cambridge, Massachusetts
Dickinson, E.C., Kennedy, R.S.and Parkes, K.C. 1991. *The Birds of the Philippines.* BOU Check-list No. 12. Tring, Herts.
Diehl, B. 1995. A long-term population study of *Lanius collurio* in a heterogeneous and changing habitat. In Yosef, R., and Lohrer, F.E.(eds.) Shrikes (Laniidae) of the World: Biology and Conservation. *Proc. Western Found. Vert. Zool.* 6: 157–162.
Diehl, B. 1998. Reproduction in the Red-backed Shrike (*Lanius collurio*) – a long term study. In Yosef, R. and Lohrer, F.E (eds.) Shrikes of the World: Conservation Implementation. *Int. Birdwatching Center in Eilat Tech. Publ.* 7: 39–42.
Diehl, B. and Myrcha, A. 1973. Bioenergetics of nestling Red-backed Shrikes (*Lanius collurio*). *Condor* 75: 259–264.
Dittami, J.P. and Kramer, B. 1986. Seasonal organization of breeding and molting in the Fiscal Shrike (*Lanius collaris*). *J. Orn.* 127: 79–84.
Dittami, John pers. comm.
Dohmann, M. 1980. Geschlechtsdimorphes Schwanzzeichnungsmuster bei Raubwürgern *Lanius excubitor* ssp. Okol. *Vögel* 2: 151–175.
Donnelly, B.G. 1978. Albinistic Greyheaded Bush-shrike. *Ostrich* 49: 91.
Dorka, V. 1975. Zum 'Faust' Gebrauch beim Raubwürger (*Lanius excubitor*) (Laniinae) und Weibscheitelwürger (*Eurocephalus anguitimens*) (Prionopinae). *Anz. orn. Ges. Bayern* 14: 314–319.
Dorka, V. and Ullrich, B. 1975. Haben die Rassen des Raubwürgers *Lanius e. excubitor* und *Lanius e. meridionalis* unterschiedliche Paarbindungsmodi? *Anz. orn. Ges. Bayern* 14: 115–140.
Dorst, J. 1960. Les charactères de la scutellation du tarse chez les Vangides. *L'Oiseau et R.F.O.* 30: 32–44.
Douglas, R. 1992. Homing instinct in the Fiscal Shrike *Lanius collaris.* Mirafra 9: 31.
Dowsett, R.J. 1971. The Lesser Grey Shrike *Lanius minor* in Africa. *Ostrich* 42: 259–270.
Dowsett, R.J. 1978. Bird ringing in Zambia, 1977. *Bull. Zambian Orn. Soc.* 10: 57–61.
Dowsett, R.J. 1980. Bird ringing in Zambia 1979. *Bull. Zambian Orn. Soc.* 12: 65–69.
Dowsett, R.J. 1983. Sexual size dimorphism in some montane forest passerines from south-central Africa. *Bull. Brit. Orn. Club* 103: 59–64.
Dowsett, R.J. 1985. Site-fidelity and survival rates of some montane forest birds in Malawi, south-central Africa. *Biotropica* 17: 145–154.
Dowsett, R.J. 1987. Potential problems in aging and sexing southern African passerines. *Safring News* 16: 17–20.
Dowsett, R.J. 1990. The gender of the avian genus *Batis. Bull. Brit. Orn. Club* 110: 109–110.
Dowsett, R.J. and Dowsett-Lemaire, F. 1980. The systematics of some Zambian birds. *Gerfaut* 70: 151–199.
Dowsett, R.J. and Dowsett-Lemaire, F. (eds.) 1993. *A Contribution to the Distribution and Taxonomy of Afrotropical and Malagasy Birds.* Tauraco Research Report No.5. Tauraco Press, Belgium.
Dowsett, R.J. and Forbes-Watson, A.D. 1993. *Checklist of Birds of the Afrotropical and Malagasy Regions.* Vol.1: Species limits and distribution. Tauraco Press, Belgium.
Dowsett, Robert pers. comm.
Dowsett-Lemaire, F. 1983. Ecological and territorial requirements of montane forest birds on the Nyika Plateau, south-central Africa. *Gerfaut* 73: 364–365.
Dowsett-Lemaire, F. 1989. Ecology and biogeography of forest bird communities in Malawi. *Scopus* 13: 1–80.
Dowsett-Lemaire, F. 1990. Eco-ethology, distribution and status of Nyungwe Forest birds (Rwanda). *Tauraco Research Report* 3: 31–85.
Dowsett-Lemaire, F. and Dowsett, R.J. 1984. The effects of forest size on montane bird populations. *Proc. 5th Pan Afr. Orn. Congr.*: 237–248.
Dowsett-Lemaire, F. and Dowsett, R.J. 1990. Zoogeography and taxonomic relationships of the forest birds of the Albertine Rift Afromontane region. *Tauraco Res. Rep.* 3: 87–109.
Dowsett-Lemaire, F. and Dowsett, R.J. 1991. The avifauna of the Kouilou basin in Congo. In Dowsett, R.J., and Dowsett-Lemaire, F. (eds.) Flore et faune du bassin du Kouilou (Congo) et leur exploitation. *Tauraco Res. Rep.* 4: 189–239.
Dowsett-Lemaire, F. in press. First observations on the territorial song and display of the Kupé Bush Shrike *Malaconotus kupeensis. Malimbus.*
Dowsett-Lemaire, F., Dowsett, R.J. and Bulens, P. 1993. Additions and corrections to the avifauna of Congo. *Malimbus* 15: 68–80.
Dowsett-Lemaire, Françoise pers. comm.
Duckworth, J.W., Evans, M.I., Safford, R.J., Telfer, M.G., Timmins, R.J. and Zewdie, C. 1992. A survey of Nechisar National Park, Ethiopia. *ICBP Study Report* No. 50.
Dunning, J.B. 1984. Body weights of 686 species of North American birds. *Western Bird Banding Association Monograph* 1: 1–38.
Dunning, J.B. 1993. *CRC Handbook of Avian Body Masses.* CRC Press, Boca Raton, USA.

Dunning, John, The late, pers. comm.
duPont, J.E. 1971. *Philippine Birds.* Delaware Mus. Nat. Hist, Greenville, Delaware.
du Toit, pers. comm.
Durango, S. 1956. Territory in the Red-backed Shrike *Lanius collurio. Ibis* 98: 476–484.
Dutson, G., and Branscombe, J. 1990. Rainforest Birds in South West Ghana. *ICBP Study Report* No. 46, Cambridge.
Eck, S. 1971. Ein Würger-Bastard im Elbtal bei Pirna. *Zool. Abh. Ber. Mus. Tierk de Dresden* 32: 1–4.
Eck, S. 1973. Intraspezifische Ausformungen im Flügel- und Schwanzbau bei Würger-Formenkreisen der Gattung *Lanius* (Aves, Laniidae). *Zool. Abh. Staatl. Mus. Tierkde. Dresden* 32: 75–119.
Eck, S. 1990. Die systematische Stellung von *Lanius excubitor meridionalis* Temminck, 1820. *Zool. Abh. Mus. Tierkd. Dresden* 46: 57–62.
Eck, S. 1992. Der Handflugelindex südwestpalaearktischer Raubwürger (*Lanius excubitor*)-Kritik eines Klischees. *J. Orn.* 133: 349–364.
Edington, J.M. and Edington, M.A. 1983. Habitat partitioning and antagonistic behaviour amongst the birds of a West African scrub and plantation plot. *Ibis* 125: 74–89.
Editor. 1984. *Bull. Zambian Orn. Soc.* 20: 71.
Eisentraut, M. 1956. Notizen über einige *Vögel* des Kamerungebirges. *J. Orn.* 97: 291–300.
Eisentraut, M. 1973. Die Wirbeltierfauna von Fernando Poo und Westkamerun. *Bonn. Zool. Monog.* 3: 185–195.
Elgood, J.H. 1964. *Birds of the West African Town and Garden.* Longmans, London.
Elgood, J.H., Heigham, J.B., Moore, A.M., Nason, A.M., Sharland, R.E. and Skinner, N.J. 1994. *The Birds of Nigeria.* BOU Check-list No. 4 (second edition), Tring, Herts.
Elliott, B. 1998. Observations of a Loggerhead Shrike (*Lanius ludovicianus*) kleptoparasitizing Eurasian Starlings (*Sturnus vulgaris*). In Yosef, R., and Lohrer, F.E.(eds.) Shrikes of the World: Conservation Implementation. *Int. Birdwatching Center in Eilat Tech. Publ.* 7: 38.
Emlen, S.T. 1979. Fiscal attacks upon White-fronted Bee-eaters. *Scopus* 3: 101–102
England, D. 1971. Breeding the Great Grey Shrike. *Avicult. Mag.* 77: 1–9.
England, M.D. 1971. Breeding the Rufous-backed Shrike (*Lanius schach*). *Avicult. Mag.* 77: 219–223.
Erard, C. 1975. Affinities de *Batis minima* (J. et E. Verreaux) et de *B. ituriensis* Chapin. *Oiseau et R.F.O.* 45: 235–240.
Erard, C. 1987. *Ecologie et comportement des gobe-mouches (Aves: Muscicapinae, Platysteirinae, Monarchinae) du Nord-Est du Gabon.* Vol.1. Mémoires du Muséum National d'Histoire Naturelle. Serie A, Zoology 138: Editions du Muséum, Paris.
Erard, C. and Colston, P.R. 1988. *Batis minima* (Verreaux) new for Cameroon. *Bull. Brit. Orn. Club* 108: 182–184.
Erard, C. and Etchécopar, R.D. 1970. Contribution a l'étude des oiseaux d'Iran. *Mém. Mus. National d'Histoire Naturelle*, Ser. A: 77–79.
Ericsson, S. 1981. Loggerhead Shrike in Guatemala in December 1979. *Dutch Birding* 3: 27–28.
Esselink, H., Geertsma, M., Kuper, J., Hustings, F. and van Berkel, H. 1995. Can peat-moor regeneration rescue the Red-backed Shrike in the Netherlands? In Yosef, R., and Lohrer, (eds). Shrikes (Laniidae) of the World: Biology and Conservation. *Proc. Western Found. Vert. Zool.* 6: 287–292.
Etchécopar, R.D. and Hüe, F. 1967. *The Birds of North Africa.* Oliver & Boyd, London.
Etchécopar, R.D. and Hüe, F. 1983. *Les Oiseaux de Chine' de Mongolie et de Corée.* Passereaux. Boubée, Paris.
Evans, T.D. and Anderson, G.Q.A. 1993. Results of an ornithological survey in the Ukaguru and East Usambara mountains, Tanzania. *Scopus* 17: 40–47.
Everett, W.T. and Koehler, C.E. 1998. Breeding population parameters of wild San Clemente Loggerhead Shrikes (*Lanius ludovicianus mearnsi*): 1992–1995. In Yosef, R., and Lohrer, F.E.(eds.) Shrikes of the World: Conservation Implementation. *Int. Birdwatching Center in Eilat Tech. Publ.* 7: 43–44.
Fanshawe, J.H. 1994. Birding in Arabuko-Sokoke Forest and Kenya's northern coast. *Bull. Afr. Bird Club* 1: 79–89.
Favini, G., Fornasari, L., Bottoni, L. and Massa, R. 1998. A video-taping approach to study nestling diet and parental care of Red-backed Shrike (*Lanius collurio*). In Yosef, R., and Lohrer, F.E.(eds.) Shrikes of the World: Conservation Implementation. *Int. Birdwatching Center in Eilat Tech. Publ.* 7: 76–78.
Feduccia, A. 1976. A model for the evolution of perching birds. *Syst. Zool.* 26: 19–31.
Fenn, T. 1975. Observations on the nest-building of the Puff-back Shrike. *Honeyguide* 83: 41–42.
Ferguson-Lees, I.J. 1960. Studies of less familiar birds: Lesser Grey Shrike. *Brit. Birds* 53: 397–402.
Ferguson-Lees, I.J. 1965. Studies of less familiar birds: Woodchat Shrike. *Brit. Birds* 58: 461–464.
Field, G.D. 1971. Breeding behaviour of a pair of Black and White Flycatchers *Bias musicus. Bull. Nigerian. Orn. Soc.* 8: 1–6.
Field, G.D. 1979. The *Laniarius* bushshrikes in Sierra Leone. *Bull. Brit. Orn. Club* 99: 42–44.
Fleming, R.L., Fleming, R.L. and Bangdel, L.S. 1976. *The Birds of Nepal.* Avalok, Kathmandu.
Flickinger, E.L. 1995. Loggerhead Shrike fatalities on a highway in Texas. In Yosef, R., and Lohrer, F.E. (eds.) 1995. Shrikes (Laniidae) of the World: Biology and Conservation. *Proc. Western Found. Vert. Zool.* 6: 67–69.
Flint, P. and Stewart, P. 1992. *The Birds of Cyprus.* BOU Check-list No. 6 (2nd edition), Tring, Herts.
Flint, V.E., Boehme, R.L., Kostin, Y.V. and Kuznetsov, A.A.1984. *Field Guide to the Birds of the USSR.* Princeton University Press, Princeton.
Fornasari, I. and Massa, R. 1998. Extra pair copulation in the Red-backed Shrike *Lanius collurio.* In: Adams, N.J. & Slotow, R.H. (eds) Proc. 22 Int. Ornithol. Congr., Durban. *Ostrich* 69: 250.
Fotso, R.C. 1993. Breeding of Bannerman's Turaco *Tauraco bannermani* and Banded Wattle-eye *Platysteira laticincta* in Cameroon. *Proc. 8th Pan Afr. Orn. Congr.*: 438.
Fraser, W. 1983. Foraging patterns of some South African flycatchers. *Ostrich* 54: 150–155.
Friedmann, H. 1930. The forms of the Orange-breasted Bush-shrike, *Chlorophoneus sulfureopectus* (Lesson). *Occas. Pap. Boston Soc. Nat. Hist.* 5: 251–253.
Friedmann, H. 1937. Birds collected by the Childs Frick Expedition to Ethiopia and Kenya Colony. Part 2. Passeres. *Bull. U.S. Natn. Mus.* 153: 1–506.
Friedmann, H. 1949. Additional data on African parasitic cuckoos. *Ibis* 91: 514–516.
Friedmann, H. 1966. A contribution to the ornithology of Uganda. Bull. *Los Angeles County Mus. Nat. Hist. Sci.* 3: 1–55.
Friedmann, H. 1978. Results of the Lathrop Central African Republic Expedition 1976, Ornithology. *Los Angeles Co. Contrib. in Sci.* 287.
Friedmann, H. and Bowen, W.W. 1933. Geographic variation in the Yellow-billed Shrike *Corvinella corvina. Proc. Biol. Soc. Washington.* 46: 121–122.
Friedmann, H. and Loveridge, A. 1937. Notes on the ornithology of Tropical East Africa. *Bull. Mus. Comp. Zool.* 81: 1-413.
Friedmann, H. and Stager, K.E. 1969. Results of the 1968 Avil Expedition to Mt. Nyiru, Samburu District, Kenya. Ornithology. *Los Angeles Co Mus. Contrib. Sci.* 174.
Friedmann, H. and Williams, J.G. 1968. Notable records of rare or little-known birds from western Uganda. *Rev. Zool. Bot. Afr.* 77: 11–36.
Friedmann, H, and Williams, J.G. 1969. The birds of the Sango Bay Forests, Buddu Country, Masaka District, Uganda. *Los Angeles*

Co. Mus. Contrib. in Sci. 162: 1–48.
Friedmann, H. and Williams, J.G. 1970. The birds of the Kalinzu Forest, southwestern Ankole, Uganda. *Los Angeles Co. Mus. Contrib. Sci.* 195.
Friedmann, H. and Williams, J.G. 1971. The birds of the lowlands of Bwamba, Toro Province, Uganda. *Los Angeles Co. Mus. Contrib. Sci.* 211.
Fry, C.H. 1970. Migration, moult and weights of birds in northern Guinea savanna in Nigeria and Ghana. *Ostrich* Suppl. 8: 239–263.
Fuggles-Couchman, N.R. 1984. The distribution of, and other notes on, some birds of Tanzania. Part II. *Scopus* 8: 81–92.
Fuggles-Couchman, N.R. 1986. Breeding records of some Tanzanian birds. *Scopus* 10: 20–26.
Fuggles-Couchman, N.R. and Elliott, H.F.I. 1946. Some records and field-notes from North-Eastern Tanganyika Territory. *Ibis* 88: 327–347
Fuisz, T.I., Mosket, C. and Young Park, J. 1998. Nest site selection and habitat use in Red-backed Shrike (*Lanius collurio*) in Hungary. In Yosef, R., and Lohrer, F.E.(eds.) Shrikes of the World: Conservation Implementation. *Int. Birdwatching Center in Eilat Tech. Publ.* 7: 30–33.
Gadow, H. 1883. *Catalogue of the Passeriformes or Perching Birds in the collection of the British Museum.* British Museum, London.
Gahr, M., Sonnenschein, E. and Wickler, W. 1998. Sex difference in the size of the neural song control regions in a duetting songbird with similar song repertoire size of males and females. *J. Neuroscience* 18: 1124–1131.
Gallagher, M. and Woodcock, M.W. 1980. *The Birds of Oman.* Quartet Books, London.
Galushin, V.M. and Polozov, S.A. 1998. Population status and breeding ecology of the Long-tailed Shrike (*Lanius schach*) in Kabul, Afghanistan. In Yosef, R. and Lohrer, F.E. (eds.) Shrikes of the World: Conservation Implementation. *Int. Birdwatching Center in Eilat Tech. Publ.* 7: 9–13.
Garcia, E.F.J. 1975. Ornithological contributions at Chassa, Petauke District. *Bull. Zambian Orn. Soc.* 7: 85.
Gartshore, M.A. 1987. Rare bird sightings at the Prince Edward Islands, December 1983–May 1987. *Cormorant* 15: 48–58.
Gatter, W. 1997. *Birds of Liberia.* Pica Press, Robertsbridge, UK.
Gaugris, Y. 1976. Additions a l'inventaire des oiseaux du Burundi (Decembre 1971–Decembre 1975). *Oiseau et R.F.O.* 46: 273–289.
Gawlik, D.E. and Bildstein, K.L. 1990. Reproductive success and nesting habitat of Loggerhead Shrikes in north-central South Carolina. *Wilson Bull.* 102: 37–48.
Gawlik, D.E., Papp, J. and Bildstein, K.L. 1991. Nestling diet and prey-delivery rates of Loggerhead Shrikes (*Lanius ludovicianus*) in north-central South Carolina. *Chat* 55: 1–5.
Gee, J.P. 1984. The birds of Mauritania. *Malimbus* 6: 31–66.
Germain, M. and Cornet, J.P. 1994. Oiseaux nouveaux pour la République Centrafricaine ou dont les notifications de ce pays sont peu nombreuses. *Malimbus* 16: 30–51
Gibbon, N. 1995. (Photograph of suspected female Mount Kupe Bush-shrike). *Bull. Afr. Bird Club* 2: 31.
Glenister, A.G. 1955. *The Birds of the Malay Peninsula' Singapore and Penang.* Oxford University Press, London.
Glutz von Blotzheim, U.N. and Bauer, K.M. 1993. *Handbuch der Vögel Mitteleuropas.* Band 13/II, Passeriformes (4. Teil) Sittidae-Laniidae. Aula, Wiesbaden.
Godfrey, W.E. 1986. *The Birds of Canada.* National Museum of Natural Sciences, Ottawa.
Goodman, S.M. 1984. Report on two small bird collections from Gebel Elba region, southeastern Egypt. *Bonn. zool. Beitr.* 35: 39–54.
Goodman, S.M. and Meininger, P.L. 1989. *The Birds of Egypt.* Oxford University Press, Oxford.
Goodman, Steven pers. comm.
Gorban, I., and Bokotej, A. 1995. Distribution of Laniidae in western Ukrane, and the breeding biology of *Lanius collurio.* In Yosef, R., and Lohrer, F.E.(eds.) 1995. Shrikes (Laniidae) of the World: Biology and Conservation. *Proc. Western Found. Vert. Zool.* 6: 70–71.
Gore, M.E.J. 1990. *The Birds of Gambia.* BOU Check-list No. 3, Tring, Herts.
Gore, M.E.J. and Pyong-Oh, W. 1971. *The Birds of Korea.* Royal Asiatic Society, Seoul.
Gould, S.J. 1986. Evolution and the triumph of homology, or why history matters. *Amer. Scient.* 74: 60–69.
Grant, C.H.B. and Mackworth-Praed, C.W. 1942a. Notes on East African birds. *Bull. Brit. Orn. Club* 63: 19–28.
Grant, C.H.B. and Mackworth-Praed, C.W. 1942b. On the colour phases of *Chlorophoneus nigrifrons* (Reichenow) *Bull. Brit. Orn. Club* 63: 19–28.
Grant, C.H.B. and Macworth-Praed, C.W. 1946. Notes on eastern African birds: On status of *Chlorophoneus andaryae* Jackson. *Bull. Brit. Orn. Club* 67: 38–40.
Grant, C.H.B. and Mackworth-Praed, C.W. 1947. On the races of *Corvinella corvina corvina* (Shaw). *Bull. Brit. Orn. Club* 67: 62–63.
Grant, C.H.B. and Mackworth-Praed, C.W. 1950. A colour-phase of the Grey-headed Bush-shrike *Malaconotus blanchoti* Stephens. *Bull. Brit. Orn. Club* 70: 3–4.
Grant, C.H.B. and Mackworth-Praed, C.W. 1952. On the relationship of the European and African Great Grey Shrikes. *Bull. Brit. Orn. Club* 72: 94.
Grant, P.R. and Grant, B.R. 1992. Hybridization of bird species. *Science* 256: 193–197.
Gray, H.H. 1972. The nests of three forest birds. *Bull. Nigerian Orn. Soc.* 9: 24–25.
Greenwood, J.J.D. 1997. Introduction: the diversity of taxonomies. *Bull. Brit. Orn. Club* 117: 85–96.
Greig-Smith, P.W. 1976. Observations on the social behaviour of helmet shrikes. *Bull. Nigerian Orn. Soc.* 2: 25–30.
Greig-Smith, P.W, and Davidson, N.C. 1977. Weights of West African savanna birds. *Bull. Brit. Orn. Club* 97: 96–99.
Grimes, L.G. 1966. Antiphonal singing and call notes of *Laniarius barbarus barbarus. Ibis* 108: 122–126.
Grimes, L.G. 1976a. The occurrence of co-operative breeding behaviour in African birds. *Ostrich* 47: 1–15.
Grimes, L.G. 1976b. The duets of *Laniarius atroflavus, Cisticola discolor* and *Bradypterus barrattii. Bull. Brit. Orn. Club* 96: 113–120.
Grimes, L.G. 1978. Weights of Ghanaian birds. Bull. *Nigerian Orn. Soc.* 14: 85.
Grimes, L.G. 1979a. Sexual dimorphism in the Yellow-billed Shrike *Corvinella corvina* and other African shrikes (subfamily Laniinae). *Bull. Brit. Orn. Club* 99: 33–35.
Grimes, L.G. 1979b. The Yellow-billed Shrike *Corvinella corvina*: an abnormal host of the Yellow-billed Cuckoo *Cuculus gularis. Bull. Brit. Orn. Club* 99: 36–38.
Grimes, L.G. 1980. Observations of group behaviour and breeding biology of the Yellow-billed Shrike *Corninella corvina. Ibis* 122: 166–192.
Grimes, L.G. 1987. *The Birds of Ghana.* BOU Check-list No. 9. Tring, Herts.
Grobler, J.H. 1979. Observations on a breeding pair of Greyheaded Bush Shrikes. *Honeyguide* 98: 15.
Gronvik, H. 1934. The ornithology of N W Kenya Colony. *Revue. Zool. Bot. Afr.* 25. I: 116–123.
Grubb, T.C. and Yosef, R. 1994. Habitat-specific nutritional condition in Loggerhead Shrikes (*Lanius ludovicianus*): evidence from

ptilochronology. *Auk* 111: 756–759.
Guerrieri, G., Pietrelli, L. and Biondi, M. 1995. Status and reproductive habitat selection of three species of shrikes, *Lanius collurio, L. senator,* and *L. minor,* in a Mediterranean area. In Yosef, R., and Lohrer, F.E.(eds.) Shrikes (Laniidae) of the World: Biology and Conservation. *Proc. Western Found. Vert. Zool.* 6: 167–171.
Guichard, K.M. 1950. A summary of the birds of the Addis Abeba region, Ethiopia. *J. East. Afr. Nat. Hist. Soc.* 19: 154–188.
Gwinner, E. 1961. Uber die Entstachelungshandlung des Neuntoters (*Lanius collurio*). *Vogelwarte* 21: 36–48.
Gwinner, E. and Bieback, H. 1977. Endogene Kontrolle der Mauser und der Zugdisposition bei südfinnischen und südfranzösischen Neuntötern. *Vogelwarte* 29: 56–63.
Gyldenstolpe, N. 1924. Results of the Swedish Expedition 1921. *Kungl. Sv. Vet. Akademiens Handlingar.* 1: 1–230.
Haas, C.A. 1987. Eastern subspecies of the Loggerhead Shrike: the need for measurements of live birds. *North Amer. Bird Bander* 12: 99–102.
Haas, C.A. and Ogawa, I. 1995. Population trends of Bull-headed and Brown Shrikes in Hokkaido, Japan. In Yosef, R., and Lohrer, F.E. (eds.) Shrikes (Laniidae) of the World: Biology and Conservation. *Proc. Western Found. Vert. Zool.* 6: 72–75.
Haas, C.A. and Sloane, S. 1996. Low return rates of migratory Loggerhead Shrikes: winter mortality or low site fidelity. *Wilson Bull.* 101: 458–460.
Haeselbarth, E., Segermann, J. and Zumpt, F. (eds). 1966. *The Arthropod Parasites of vertebrates in Africa South of the Sahara.* Vol.3. South African Institute for Medical Research No. 13.
Haffer, J. 1986. Superspecies and species limits in vertebrates. *Z. zool. Syst. Evolut.-forsch.* 24: 169–190.
Hagemeijer, W.J.M. and Blair, M.J. (eds.) 1997. *The EBCC Atlas of European Breeding Birds.* T & A D Poyser, Calton, UK.
Hahnke, H. 1998. The Long-tailed Shrike (*Lanius schach*): a superspecies? In Yosef, R. and Lohrer, F.E. (eds.) Shrikes of the World: Conservation Implementation. *Int. Birdwatching Center in Eilat Tech. Publ.* 7: 113.
Hall, B.P. 1954. A review of the Boubou Shrike *Laniarius ferrugineus. Ibis* 96: 343–355.
Hall, B.P. 1960a. The ecology and taxonomy of some Angola birds. *Bull. Brit. Mus. Nat. Hist.* (*Zool.*) 6: 367–463.
Hall, B.P. 1960b. The faunistic importance of the scarp of Angola. *Ibis* 102: 420–442.
Hall, B.P. and Moreau, R.E. 1962. A study of the rare birds of Africa. *Bull. Brit. Mus. Nat. Hist.* (*Zool.*) 8: 315–375.
Hall, B.P. and Moreau, R.E. 1970. *An Atlas of Speciation in African Passerine Birds.* Trustees of British Museum (Natural History), London.
Hall, B.P., Moreau, R.E. and Galbraith, I.C.J. 1966. Polymorphism and parallelism in the African bush-shrikes of the genus *Malaconotus* (including *Chlorophoneus*). *Ibis* 108: 161–182.
Hallett, A.F. and Brown, A.R. 1964. A Bokmakierie (*Telophorus zeylonus*) with an unusually large clutch. *Ostrich* 35: 67–68.
Halleux, D. 1994. Annotates bird list of Macenta Prefecture, Guinea. *Malimbus* 16: 10-29.
Hanmer, D.B. 1978. The effects of latitude and altitude on bird weights. *Scopus* 2: 35–39.
Hanmer, D.B. 1979. Some data on the Wattle-eyed Flycatcher in Malawi. *Honeyguide* 100: 33–35.
Hanmer, D.B. 1981. Longevity from retraps. *Safring News* 10: 12–13.
Hanmer, D.B. 1985. Malawi longevity again. *Safring News* 14: 51–60.
Hanmer, D.B. 1989. The end of an era – final longevity figures for Nchalo. *Safring News* 18: 19–30.
Hanmer, D.B. and Manson, A.J. 1988. Weights of birds from different geographic areas. *Honeyguide* 34: 4–15.
Hantge, E. 1957. Zur Brutbiologie des Schwarzstirnwürgers (*Lanius minor*). Vogelwelt 78: 137–147.
Harcus, J.L. 1977. The functions of vocal duetting in some African birds. *Z. Tierpsychol.* 43: 23–45.
Hargrove, J.W., Marshall, B.E. & Mentz, D.L. 1972. Observations on the Fiscal Shrike. *Rhodesia Sci. News* 6: 349–351.
Hargrove, J.W., Marshall, B.E. & Mentz, D.L. 1973. A simple method of trapping the Fiscal Shrike. *Safring News* 2: 17.
Harris, T. 1984. The Marsh Tchagra revisited. *Bull. Transvaal Mus.* 20: 17–18.
Harris, T. 1986. Is the Whitetailed Shrike a terrestrial batis? *Lanioturdus* 22: 47–51.
Harris, T. 1990. Identifying bush shrikes. *Birding in South Africa.* 42: 47–49.
Harris, T. 1995. Species recognition in the southern African population of the Fiscal Shrike (*Lanius collaris*). In Yosef, R., and Lohrer, F.E. (eds.) Shrikes of the World: Biology and Conservation. *Proc. Western Found. Vert. Zool.* 6 : 11–21.
Harris, T. 1998. Conservation status of African true shrikes. In Yosef, R. and Lohrer, F.E. (eds.) Shrikes of the World: Conservation Implementation. *Int. Birdwatching Center in Eilat Tech. Publ.* 7: 102–111.
Harris, T. and Arnott, G. 1988. *Shrikes of Southern Africa.* Struik Winchester Press, Cape Town.
Harris, Tony personal observations, unpublished field notes, specimens, nest record cards etc.
Harrison, C.J.O. 1969. Additional information on the carpometacarpal process as a taxonomic character. *Bull. Brit. Orn. Club* 89: 27–29.
Harrison, J.A., Allan, D.G., Underhill, L.G., Herremans, M., Tree, A.J., Parker, V., and Brown, C.J. (eds.) 1997. *The Atlas of Southern African Birds.* vol.2. Passerines. BirdLife South Africa, Johannesburg.
Hart, J.A. 1971. The flocking and foraging behaviour of the West African red-billed Shrike. *Ostrich* 42: 294–295.
Hartert, E. 1894. List of the first collection of birds from Natuna Islands. *Novit. Zool.* 1: 469–483.
Harwin, R. 1970. The concept of sibling species. *Ostrich* Suppl. 8: 27–32.
Harwin, R.M., Manson, A.J., Manson, C. and Mwadziwana, P. 1994. The birds of the Bvumba Highlands. *Honeyguide* 40 Suppl. 1.: 1–51.
Hawkins, F. 1993. An integrated biodiversity conservation project under development: the ICBP Angola scarp project. *Proc. 8th Pan Afr. Orn. Congr.*: 279–284.
Hawkins, F., Rabenandrasana, M., Virginie, M.C., Manese, R.O., Mulder, R., Ellis, E.R. and Robert, R. 1998. Field observations of the Red-shouldered Vanga *Calicalicus rufocarpalis*: a newly described Malagasy endemic. *Bull. Afr. Bird Club* 5: 30–32.
Heim de Balsac, H. and Mayaud, N. 1962. *Les Oiseaux du Nord-Ouest de l'Afrique.* Lechevalier, Paris.
Heinrich, G.H. 1958. Zur Verbreitung und Lebensweise der *Vögel* von Angola. *J. Orn.* 99: 322–362, 399–421.
Henley, C., Feduccia, A. and Costello, D.P. 1978. Oscine spermatozoa: a light- and electron-microscopy study. *Condor* 80: 41–48.
Hernandez, A. 1995. Temporal-spatial patterns of food caching in two sympatric shrike species. *Condor* 97: 1002–1010.
Herremans, M. 1992. Interspecific song of Chinspot Batis *Batis molitor* to Pririt Batis *Batis pririt. Babbler* 23: 40–41.
Herremans, M. 1993. Seasonal dynamics in sub-Kalahari bird communities with emphasis on migrants. In: Birds and Environment: Wilson, R.T. (ed.). *Proc. 8th Pan Afr. Orn. Congr.*: 555–564.
Herremans, M. 1994. Fifteen years of migration phenology records in Botswana. A summary and prospects. *Babbler* 28: 47–68.
Herremans, M. 1995. The use of plumage features resulting from partial post-juvenile moult in age determination of southern African passerines. *Safring News* 24: 19–22.
Herremans, M. 1997. Habitat segregation of male and female Red-backed Shrikes *Lanius collurio* and Lesser Grey Shrikes *Lanius minor* in Kalahari basin, Botswana. *J. Avian Biol.* 28: 240–248.
Herremans, M. 1998. Monitoring the world population of the Lesser Grey Shrike (*Lanius minor*) on the non-breeding grounds in southern Africa. *J. Orn.* 139: 485–493.
Herremans, M. and Herremans-Tonnoeyr, D. 1994. Persistent foraging on the ground by Chinspot Batis *Batis molitor. Babbler* 26–27: 18–19.
Herremans, M. and Herremans-Tonnoeyr, D. 1995. Non-breeding site-fidelity of Red-backed Shrikes *Lanius collurio* in Botswana.

Ostrich 66: 145–147.
Herremans, Marc pers. comm.
Hoesch, W. and Niethammer, G. 1940. Vogelwelt Deutsch-Südwestafrikas. *J. Orn.* 88: 1–390.
Holan, V. 1998. Status of shrikes in the Czech Republic. In Yosef, R., and Lohrer, F.E. (eds.) Shrikes of the World: Conservation Implementation. *Int. Birdwatching Center in Eilat Tech. Publ.* 7: 16–17.
Hollom, P.A.D. 1955. Fortnight in South Turkey. *Ibis* 97: 1–17.
Hollom, P.A.D., Porter, R.F., Christensen, S. and Willis, I. 1988. *Birds of the Middle East and North Africa.* T & A.D. Poyser, Calton.
Hoogerwerf, A. 1949. Bijdrage tot de oologie van Java. *Limosa* 22: 1–277.
Hooker, T. and Hooker, B.I. 1969. Duetting. Pp 185–205 in Hinde, R.A. (ed.) *Bird Vocalizations.* Cambridge University Press, Cambridge.
Horne, Jennifer pers. comm.
Hornman, M., Nijssen, M., Geertsma, M., Kuper, J., and Esselink, H. 1998. Temporal effects on diet composition in nesting Red-backed Shrike (*Lanius collurio*) in Bargerveen, The Netherlands. In Yosef, R., and Lohrer, F.E. (eds.) Shrikes of the World: Conservation Implementation. *Int. Birdwatching Center in Eilat Tech. Publ.* 7: 83–87.
Horvath, L. 1959. The life history of the Lesser Grey Shrike (*Lanius minor*) in Hungary. *Acta Zool.* 4: 319–332.
Houlihan, P.F., and Goodman, S.M. 1986. *The Birds of Ancient Egypt.* Vol.1. Aris & Philips, Warminster, England.
Howard, R. and Moore, A. 1980. *A Complete Checklist of Birds of the World.* Oxford University Press, Oxford.
Hüe, F. and Etchécopar, R.D. 1970. *Les Oiseaux du Proche et du Moyen Orient.* Editions N. Boubée & Cie.
Hunter, N. 1988. Systematics of the Southern and Tropical Boubous in Botswana. *Babbler* 16: 7–10.
Hunter, N., Carter, C. and Mlungu, E. 1996. Recent observations in the Udzungwa and Uluguru Mountains, Central Tanzania. *Bull. Afr. Bird Club* 3: 96–98.
Hurford, J.L., Lombard, A.T., Kemp, A.C. and Benn, G.A. 1996. Geographical analysis of six rare bird species in the Kruger National Park, South Africa. *Bird Conserv. Internatn.* 6: 117–137.
Hustler, K. 1996. To collect or not to collect – that is the question. *Bull. Afr. Bird Club* 3: 53–54.
Immelman, K. 1968. *Lanius souzae* near Spitkopje, South West Africa. *Ostrich* 39: 41.
Inskipp, C. and Inskipp, T. 1991. *A Guide to the Birds of Nepal.* Christopher Helm, London.
Ionides, C.J.P. 1954. Passerines attacking snakes. *Ibis* 96: 310–311.
Irwin, M.P.S. 1956a. Field notes on a collection from Mozambique. *Ostrich* 27: 28–39.
Irwin, M.P.S. 1956b. Notes on the drinking habits of birds in semi– desertic Bechuanaland. *Bull. Br. Orn. Club* 76: 99–101.
Irwin, M.P.S. 1961. The specific status of *Batis soror* and its relationship to *Batis molitor. Ostrich* 33: 17–28.
Irwin, M.P.S. 1968. A new race of the Bokmakierie *Telophorus zeylonus* (Linnaeus) (Aves) from the Chimanimani Mountains, Rhodesia. *Arnoldia* 3: 1–5.
Irwin, M.P.S. 1977. Some little known and inadequately documented Rhodesian birds. *Honeyguide* 90: 9–15.
Irwin, M.P.S. 1981. *The Birds of Zimbabwe.* Quest, Salisbury (Zimbabwe).
Irwin, M.P.S. 1987. Systematics of the Southern and Tropical Boubous in the Transvaal, Zimbabwe and Southern Mozambique. *Honeyguide* 33: 151–153.
Irwin, M.P.S. and Benson, C.W. 1966. Notes on the birds of Zambia. *Arnoldia* 2: 1–19.
Irwin, M.P.S., Niven, P.N.F. and Winterbottom, J.M. 1969. Some birds of the lower Chobe river area, Botswana. *Arnoldia* 4: 1–40.
Isenmann, P. and Bouchet, M.-A. 1993. L'aire de distribution francaise et le statut taxonomique de la Pie-grièche Grise Méridionale *Lanius elegans meridionalis. Alauda* 61: 223–227.
Isenmann, P. and Fradet, G. 1995. Is the nesting association between the Orphean Warbler (*Sylvia hortensis*) and the Woodchat Shrike (*Lanius senator*) an anti-predator orientated behaviour? *J. Orn.* 136: 288–291.
Isenmann, P. and Fradet, G. 1998. Nest site, laying period, and breeding success of the Woodchat Shrike (*Lanius senator*) in Mediterranean France. *J. Orn.* 139: 49–54.
Isenmann, P. and Lefranc, N. 1994. Le statut taxonomique de la Pie-Grièche Meridionale *Lanius meridionalis* (Temminck 1820). *Alauda* 62: 138.
Ishizuka, T. 1990. A case of hybridization in Brown Shrike subspecies *Lanius cristatus lucionensis* and *L. c. superciliosus* in Kanazawa. *Strix* 9: 71–75.
ISIS International Species Information System. International Species Catalogue of captive-held animals. Dallas, Zoo.
Jackson, F.J. 1901. List of birds obtained in British East Africa with notes by R.B. Sharpe. *Ibis* (8)1: 33–97.
Jackson, F.J. 1919. *Chlorophoneus andaryae* new species. *Bull. Brit. Orn. Club* 39: 94.
Jackson, F.J. 1938. *The Birds of Kenya Colony and the Uganda Protectorate.* Vol. 3. Gurney and Jackson, London.
Jackson, H.D. 1972. Comment on *Telophorus zeylonus restrictus* Irwin, the Chimanimani Mountains race of the Bokmakierie (Aves: Laniidae). *Arnoldia* 6: 1–6.
Jakober, H. and Stauber, W. 1983. Zur Phänologie einer Population des Neuntöters *Lanius collurio. J. Orn.* 124: 29–46.
Jakober, H. and Stauber, W. 1994. Kopulationen und Partnerbewachung beim Neuntöter *Lanius collurio. J. Orn.* 135: 535–547.
James, G.K. 1948. Notes on a jacana, shrike and coly. *Ostrich* 19: 167–170.
Jarvis, A., and Robertson, T. 1997. *Endemic birds of Namibia: evaluating their status and mapping biodiversity hotspots.* Directorate of Environmental Affairs, Ministry of Environment and Tourism, Windhoek, Namibia.
Jenni, L. and Winkler, R. 1994. *Moult and Ageing of European Passerines.* Academic Press, London.
Jennings, M.C. 1981. *The Birds of Saudi Arabia: a Check-List.* Published privately, Cambridge.
Jensen, J.V. and Kirkeby, J. 1980. *The Birds of Gambia.* Aros Nature Guides, Orhus, Denmark.
Jensen, R.A.C. and Clinning, C.F. 1974. Breeding biology of two cuckoos and their hosts in South West Africa. *Living Bird* 13: 5–50.
Johnson, A. 1938. Nest building behaviour in the Loggerhead Shrike group. *Wilson Bull.* 50: 246–248.
Johnson, D.N. 1984. The coexistence of the Red-billed Paradise Flycatcher *Tchitrea rufiventer* and the Chestnut Wattle-eye *Dyaphorophyia castanea* (Muscicapidae) in Nigerian rain forest. *Proc. 5th Pan Afr. Orn. Congr.*: 263–274.
Johnson, David pers. comm.
Jollie, M. 1958. Comments on the phylogeny and skull of the passeriformes. *Auk* 75: 26–35.
Jones, J.M.B. 1996. Chestnut-fronted Helmet-Shrike and others from the Honde Valley. *Honeyguide* 42: 167–168.
Jones, John pers. comm.
Jones, P.J., Burlison, J.P. and Tye, A. 1992. The status of endemic birds and their habitats on São Tomé and Príncipe. *Proc. 8th Pan-Afr. Orn. Congr.*: 453–459.
Jourdain, F.C.R. 1935. The courtship of the Red-backed Shrike and the Woodchat. *Brit. Birds* 28: 95–97.
Jourdain, F.C.R. and Shuel, R. 1935. Eggs of Nigerian birds. *Ibis* (13)5: 623–663.
Jörges, B. 1972. Der Drosselwürger *Laniopturdus torquatus*: eine Verhaltensbeobachtung. *Mitt. Orn. Arbeitsgr. SWA Wiss. Ges.* 8: 6–8.
Keast, A. 1992. Utilisation of the 'flycatcher' adaptive zone in Africa, with comparisons from other continents. In Bennun, L. (ed.). *Proc. 7th Pan Afr. Orn. Congr.*: 381–389.
Keith, S. and Twomey, A. 1968. New distributional records of some East African birds. *Ibis* 110: 537–548.

Keith, S., Twomey, A., Friedmann, H. and Williams, J. 1969. The avifauna of the Impenetrable Forest, Uganda. *Amer. Mus. Novit.* 2389.
Kikuchi, M., Ishii, S., Kansaku, K., Shimada, K. and Imanishi, S. 1998. Changes in the plasma levels of prolactin and luteinizing hormone throughout the breeding season in the shrike *Lanius bucephalus.* In: Adams, N.J. & Slotow, R.H. (eds) Proc. 22 Int. Ornithol. Congr., Durban. *Ostrich* 69: 325.
Kiliaan, H.P.L. 1996. An unusual Loggerhead Shrike nest location. *Blue Jay* 54: 107–108.
King, B., Dickinson, E.C., and Woodcock, M. 1978. *A Field Guide to the Birds of South-East Asia.* Collins, London.
King, W. 1981. *Endangered Birds of the World: the ICBP Bird Red Data Book.* Smithsonian Institution Press, Washington, D.C.
Koford, R.R., Dunning, J.B., Ribic, C.A. and Finch, D.M. 1994. A glossary for avian conservation biology. *Wilson Bull.* 106: 121–137.
Kolthoff, K. 1921–22. Studies on birds in Chinese province of Kiangsum and Anhwei. *Meddelanden fran Goteborgs Musei Zoologiska Avdelning* 59 ser. B Bd. 3 no. 1: 1–190.
Komen, J. 1987. Batis meets batis in Namibia. *Lanioturdus* 22: 79–81.
Kondo, K. 1993. The first record of the Chinese Great Grey Shrike *Lanius sphenocercus* from Sado Island. *Strix* 12: 248–251.
Kridelbaugh, A. 1983. Nesting ecology of the Loggerhead Shrike in Central Missouri. *Wilson Bull.* 95: 303–308.
Kristin, A. 1991. Brutbestand und Brutbiologie des Schwarzstirnwürgers (*Lanius minor*) in der Mittelkslowakei (Tschechoslowakei). *Orn. Mitt.* 43: 131–133.
Kristin, A. 1995. Why the Lesser Grey Shrike (*Lanius minor*) survives in Slovakia: food and habitat preferences, breeding biology. *Folia Zool.* 44: 325–334.
Kristin, A. 1998 Breeding range trends of four shrike species in Slovakia. In Yosef, R. and Lohrer, F.E. (eds.) Shrikes of the World: Conservation Implementation. *Int. Birdwatching Center in Eilat Tech. Publ.* 7: 18–21.
Kristin, A. and Zilinec, M. 1998. Lesser Grey Shrike (*Lanius minor*) diet and foraging strategies during and after Cockchafer (*Melolontha melolontha* Insecta, Coleoptera) swarming. In Yosef, R., and Lohrer, F.E. (eds.) Shrikes of the World: Conservation Implementation. *Int. Birdwatching Center in Eilat Tech. Publ.* 7: 34–37.
Kryukov, A.P. 1995. Systematics of small Palearctic shrikes of the '*cristatus* group'. In Yosef, R., and Lohrer, F.E. (eds.) Shrikes (Laniidae) of the World: Biology and Conservation. *Proc. Western Found. Vert. Zool.* 6: 22–25.
Kryukov, A.P. and Frisman, E. 1980. Phenetic classification of small Palearctic shrikes. *Izv. Sib. Otd. Akad. Nauk. USSR Ser. Biol. Nauk* (2): 35–40. (In Russian.)
Kunkel, P. 1974. Mating systems of tropical birds: the effects of weakness or absence of external reproduction-timing factors with special reference to prolonged pair bonds. *Z. Tierpsychol.* 34: 265–307.
La Touche, J.D.D. 1925. *A Handbook of the Birds of Eastern China.* Vol.1. Taylor and Francis, London.
Lack, D. 1940. Courtship feeding in birds. *Auk* 57: 169–178.
Lack, P. 1985. Ecology of land birds in Tsavo East National Park, Kenya. *Scopus* 9: 57–96.
Lack, P.C. 1994. Three-streaked Tchagra *Tchagra jamesi*: a new record for Tanzania. *Scopus* 17: 140–141.
Lack, P.C. and Quicke, D.L.J. 1978. Dietary notes on some Kenyan birds. *Scopus* 2: 86–91.
Lambert, Frank pers. comm.
Lamm, D.W. 1953a. Taxonomic status of *Batis molitor soror. Ostrich* 24: 171–173.
Lamm, D.W. 1953b. Records from northern Sul do Save, Mozambique. *Ostrich* 24: 208.
Langley, C.H. 1982. Unusual diet of Boubou Shrike. *Ostrich* 53: 118.
Langrand, O. 1990. *Guide to the Birds of Madagascar.* Yale University Press.
Laporte, P. and Robert, M. 1995. The decline and current status of the Loggerhead Shrike in Quebec. In Yosef, R., and F.E. Lohrer (eds). Shrikes (Laniidae) of the World: Biology and Conservation. *Proc. Western Found. Vert. Zool.* 6: 85–87.
Lawson, W.J. 1962. Systematic notes on African birds: geographical variation in Woodward's Batis *Batis fratrum* (Shelley). *Durban Mus. Novit.* 6: 220–224.
Lawson, W.J. 1963a. Geographical variation in *Batis pririt* (Vieillot). *Bull. Br. Orn. Club* 83: 29–32.
Lawson, W.J. 1963b. On the geographical variation of the Wattle-eye Flycatcher *Platysteira peltata* (Sundevall). *Bull. Brit. Orn. Club* 83: 114–116.
Lawson, W.J. 1964a. Geographical variation in the Cape Batis *Batis capensis* (Linnaeus). *Durban Mus. Novit.* 7: 189–200.
Lawson, W.J. 1964b. Instability of feather pigmentation in the White Helmet Shrike *Prionops plumatus. Bull. Brit. Orn. Club* 84: 117–118.
Lawson, W.J. 1984. The West African mainland forest dwelling population of *Batis*: a new species. *Bull. Brit. Orn. Club* 104: 144–146.
Lawson, W.J. 1986. Speciation in the forest-dwelling populations of the avian genus *Batis. Durban Mus. Novit.* 13: 285–304.
Lawson, W.J. 1987. Systematics and evolution in the savanna species of the genus *Batis* (Aves) in Africa. *Bonn. zool. Beitr.* 38: 19–45.
Lawson, W.J. 1989. *The genus Batis: Systematics and evolution.* Ph.D. thesis, School of Australian Environmental Studies, Griffith University.
Layard, E.L. 1867. *Birds of South Africa.* Juta, Cape Town.
Lebedeva, E.A. and Butiev, V.T. 1995. Shrikes in southern Daghestan (western coast of Caspian Sea). In Yosef, R., and Lohrer, F.E. (eds.) Shrikes (Laniidae) of the World: Biology and Conservation. *Proc. Western Found. Vert. Zool.* 6: 88–92.
LeCroy, M. and Vuilleumier, F. 1992. Guidleines for the description of new species in ornithology. *Bull. Brit. Orn. Club* Centenary Suppl. 112A: 191–198.
Ledger, J.A. 1980. *The Arthropod parasites of vertebrates in Africa south of the Sahara* Vol.4. South African Institute for Medical Research No. 56: 1–327.
LeFevre, R.H. 1962. *The Birds of Northern Shantung Province of China.*
Lefranc, N. 1979. Contribution à l'écologie de la Pie-grièche ecorcheur *Lanius collurio* dans les Vosges moyennes. *l'Oiseau et R.F.O.* 49: 245–298.
Lefranc, N. 1993. *Les Pies-grièches d'Europe' d'Afrique du Nord et du Moyen-Orient.* Delachaux et Niestlé, Lausanne and Paris.
Lefranc, N. 1995a. Le complexe Pie-grièche grise/Pie-grièche méridionale *Lanius* (*e.*) *excubitor*/*L.* (*e.*) *meridionalis*: des 'groupes' aux espèces. *Ornithos* 2: 107–109.
Lefranc, N. 1995b. Identification des pies-grièches 'grises' de France et du Paléarctique occidental. *Ornithos* 2: 110–123.
Lefranc, N. 1995c. Decline and current status of the Lesser Grey Shrike (*Lanius minor*) in western Europe. In Yosef, R. and Lohrer, F.E. (eds.) Shrikes (Laniidae) of the World: Biology and Conservation. *Proc. Western Found. Vert. Zool.* 6: 93–97.
Lefranc, N. and Worfolk, T. 1997. *Shrikes: A Guide to the Shrikes of the World.* Pica Press, Robertbridge, U.S.A.
Lefranc, N., Boet, M. and Boet, M. 1989. Observations de couples mixtes *Lanius senator*/*Lanius collurio* en France. *Alauda* 57: 109–118.
Lewington, I., Alstrom, P. and Colston, P. 1991. *A Field Guide to the Rare Birds of Britain and Europe.* Collins, London.
Lewis, A. and Pomeroy, D. 1989. *A Bird Atlas of Kenya.* A.A.Balkema, Rotterdam.

Lewis, A.D. 1981. The past and present status and distribution of the Grey-crested Helmet Shrike *Prionops poliolopha. Scopus* 5: 66–70.
Lewis, A.D. 1982. Further records of the Grey-crested Helmet-shrike. *Scopus* 6: 47–48.
Lewis, A.D. 1983. A record of the Grey Helmet shrike near Naivasha, Kenya. *Scopus* 7: 26–27.
Lippens, L, and Wille, H. 1976. *Les Oiseaux du Zaïre.* Lannoo, Tielt.
Lohrer, F.E. 1974. Post-hatching growth and development of the Loggerhead Shrike in Florida. Master's Thesis, Univ. of South Florida, Tampa.
Lorber, P. 1984. Feeding methods, mate replacement and development of the call in the Tropical Boubou. *Honeyguide* 30: 78–79.
Lorek, G. 1995a. Copulation behaviour, mixed reproductive strategy, and mate guarding in the Great Grey Shrike. In Yosef, R. and Lohrer, F.E. (eds.) Shrikes (Laniidae) of the World: Biology and Conservation. *Proc. Western Found. Vert. Zool.* 6: 218–227.
Lorek, G. 1995b. Breeding status of the Great Grey Shrike in Poland. In Yosef, R., and Lohrer, F.E. (eds.) Shrikes (Laniidae) of the World: Biology and Conservation. *Proc. Western Found. Vert. Zool.* 6: 98–104.
Louette, M. 1981. *The Birds of Cameroon: an Annotated Checklist.* Paleis der Academmien, Brussels.
Loye, J.E. and Zuk, M. (eds) 1991. *Bird–Parasite Interactions: Ecology' Evolution and Behaviour.* Oxford University Press, Oxford.
Luder, R. 1986. Abnahme der Gelegegrosse beim Neuntoter. *Orn. Beob.* 83: 1–6.
Lynes, H. 1934. Contribution to the ornithology of southern Tanganyika Territory. Birds of the Ubene-Uhehe highlands and Iringa highlands. *J. Orn.* Suppl. 82: 1–147.
Lynes, H. 1938. Contribution to the ornithology of the southern Congo Basin. *Rev. Zool. Bot. Afr.* 31: 1–129.
Macdonald, J.D. 1940. Notes on African birds. *Bull. Brit. Orn. Club* 60: 71–74.
Macdonald, J.D. 1957. *Contribution to the ornithology of western South Africa.* Trustees of British Museum, London.
Macdonald, M.A. 1980. The ecology of the Fiscal Shrike in Ghana, and a comparison with studies from southern Africa. *Ostrich* 51: 65–74.
MacKinnon, J. 1990. *A Field Guide to the Birds of Java and Bali.* Oxford University Press, Oxford.
MacKinnon, J.and Phillipps, K. 1993. *The Birds of Borneo' Sumatra' Java and Bali: the Greater Sunda Islands.* Oxford University Press, Oxford.
Mackworth-Praed, C.W. and Grant, C.H.B. 1955. *Birds of Eastern and North Eastern Africa.* Vol.2, Series I. Longmans, London.
Mackworth-Praed, C.W. and Grant, C.H.B. 1963. *Birds of the Southern Third of Africa.* Vol.2, Series II. Longmans, London.
Mackworth-Praed, W. and Grant, C.H.B. 1973. *Birds of West central and Western Africa.* Vol. 2, Series III. Longmans.
Maclean, G.L. 1970. The breeding seasons of birds in the south-western Kalahari. In Maclean, G.L. (ed). Proc. 3rd Pan Afr. Orn. Congr. *Ostrich* Suppl. 8: 179–192.
Maclean, G.L. 1990. Evolution of the passerines in the southern hemisphere. Third Austin Roberts Commemorative lecture. *Transvaal Museum Bull.* Suppl. 22: 1–11.
Maclean, G.L. 1996. *Roberts' Birds of Southern Africa.* 6th edition. John Voelcker Bird Book Fund, Cape Town.
Maclean, G.L. and Maclean, C.M. 1976. Extent of overlap in two races of the Fiscal Shrike. *Ostrich* 47: 66.
Maclean, G.L. and Prys-Jones, R.P. 1988. Kleptoparasitism in three species of passerine birds. *Ostrich* 59: 45–46.
Maclean, G.L. and Vernon, C.J. 1976. Mouthspots of passerine nestlings. *Ostrich* 47: 95–98.
Macleod, H., and Parrott, J. 1992. Conservation of the Kilum (Oku) mountain forests in the Bamenda Highlands of Cameroon. *Proc. 8th Pan Afr. Orn. Congr.*: 447–451.
Macleod, H.L. 1986. Plans to save Cameroon Mountain forests. *WWF Monthly Report.*,October 1986: 261–267.
Macleod, J.G.R. and Hallack, M. 1956. Some notes on the breeding of Klaas's Cuckoo. *Ostrich* 27: 2–5.
Macleod, J.G.R., Macleod, E.M. and Murray, C. 1952. The birds of Hottentots Holland. *Ostrich* 23: 23.
Mann, C.F. and Diskin, D.A. 1993. Northern Shrike *Lanius excubitor*, a species new to Borneo and South-East Asia. *Forktail* 8: 153–154.
Mann, W. 1983. Zur Ernährung des Neuntöters (*Lanius collurio*) in Abhängigkeit vom Insektenangebot auf verschiedenen Dauergrunlandtypen. *Vogelkunde Hefte Edertal* 9: 5–41.
Manson, Alec, The late, pers. comm.
Marchant, S. 1942. Birds of the Owerri Province, S. Nigeria. *Ibis* (14)6: 137–196.
Mariaux, J. 1991. Cestodes of birds from the Ivory Coast: species of the genus *Anonchotaenia* Cohn 1990. *Syst. Parasitol.* 20: 109–120.
Markus, M.B. 1972. Notes on the natal plumage of South African passeriform birds. *Ostrich* 43: 17–22.
Marshall, B.E. and Cooper, J. 1969. Observations on the breeding biology of the Fiscal Shrike. *Ostrich* 40: 141–149.
Martens, J. and Eck, S. 1995. Towards an ornithology of the Himalayas: systematics, ecology and vocalisations of Nepal birds. *Bonn. Zool. Monog.* 38: 370–372.
Martin, P. 1996. More on aberrant Bokmakieries. *Bee-eater* 47: 41–42.
Massa, R., Bottoni, L., Fornasari, L. and Sacchi, N. 1995. Studies on the socio-sexual and territorial system of the Red-backed Shrike. In Yosef, R., and Lohrer, F.E. (eds.) Shrikes (Laniidae) of the World: Biology and Conservation. *Proc. Western Found. Vert. Zool.* 6: 172–175.
Mayr, E. 1942. *Systematics and the Origin of Species.* Columbia Univ. Press, New York.
Mayr, E. 1943. What genera belong to the family Prionopidae? *Ibis* 85: 216–218.
Mayr, E. and Amadon, D. 1951. A classification of recent birds. *Amer. Mus. Novit.* 1496.
Mayr, E. and Short, L.L. 1970. Species taxa of North America. *Publ. Nuttall Orn. Club* 9: 1–127.
McClure, H.E. 1974. *Migration and Survival of the Birds of Asia. United States Army Medical Component, Medical Project.* Applied Scientific Research Corporation, Bangkok, Thailand.
McClure, H.E., Poonswad, P. Greiner, E.C., and Laird, M. 1978. *Haematozoa in the birds of eastern and southern Asia.* 1–296. Memorial Univ. Newfoundland. Canada.
McClure, H.E. and Ratanaworabhan, N. Undated. *Some Ectoparasites of the Birds of Asia (1963–1971).* Jintana Printing Ltd., Bangkok.
McFarlane, R.W. 1963. The taxonomic significance of avian sperm. *Intern. Orn. Congr. (Ithaca, New York) Proc.* 13: 91–102.
McVicker, Rowland pers. comm.
Medland, R.D. 1991. Souza's Shrike attacking Violet-backed Sunbird. *Nyala* 15: 49.
Medway, Lord. 1970. A ringing study of the migratory Brown Shrike in West Malaysia. *Ibis* 112: 184–198.
Medway, Lord. and Wells, D.R. 1976. *The Birds of the Malay Peninsula.* Vol.5. H.F. & G Witherby, London.
Mees, G.F. 1996. Geographical Variation in Birds of Java. *Nuttall Orn. Club*, Cambridge, Massachusetts.
Meinertzhagen, R. 1954. *Birds of Arabia.* Oliver & Boyd, London.
Meise, W. 1958. Uber neue Huhner-, Specht- und Singvogelrassen von Angola. *Arb. Verh. Nat. Ver. Bd.* 2: 63–82.
Meise, W. 1968. Zur Speciation afrikanischer, besonders angolesischer Singvögel der Gattungen *Terpsiphone, Dicrurus* und *Malaconotus. Bonn. Zool. Beitr.* (Suppl.) 14: 1–60.
Melville, D.S. and Round, P.D. 1984. Weights and gonad condition of some Thai birds. *Bull. Brit. Orn. Club* 104: 127–138.

Meyer de Schauensee, R. 1962. Birds from the Philippine Islands. *Proc. Acad. Nat. Sci. Philadelphia* 114: 149–173.
Meyer de Schauensee, R. 1984. *The Birds of China.* Oxford University Press, Oxford.
Miller, A.H. 1928. The moult of the Loggerhead Shrike *Lanius ludovicianus* Linnaeus. *Univ. California Publ. Zool.* 30: 393–414.
Miller, A.H. 1931. Systematic revision and natural history of the American shrikes (*Lanius*). *Univ. California Publ. Zool.* 38: 11–242.
Miller, A.H. 1937. A comparison of behaviour of certain North American and European shrikes. *Condor* 39: 119–122.
Milne-Edwards, A. 1871. *Recherches anatomiques et paleonotologiques pour servir a l'histoire des oiseaux fossiles de la France.* Vol.2. Victor Masson, Paris.
Milon, P., Petter, J.J. and Randrianasolo, G. 1973. *Fauna de Madagascar, 35: Oiseaux.* ORSTOM, Paris.
Monroe, B.L., and Sibley, C.G. 1994. *A World Checklist of Birds.* Yale University Press.
Moore, P.D. 1999. A shrike for mobility. *Nature* 397: 21–22.
Moreau, R.E. 1940. Contributions to the ornithology of East African islands. *Ibis* (14)4: 48–91.
Moreau, R.E. 1972. *The Palaearctic-African Bird migration Systems.* Academic Press, London.
Moreau, R.E. and Dolp, P. 1970. Fat, water, weights and wing-lengths of autumn migrants in transit on the northwest coast of Egypt. *Ibis* 112: 209–228.
Moreau, R.E. and Moreau, W.M. 1939. Biology and other notes on some East African birds. *Ibis* (14)3: 313–325.
Moreau, R.E. and Moreau, W.M. 1940. Incubation and fledging periods of African birds. *Auk* 57: 313–325.
Moreau, R.E. and Moreau, W.M. 1941. Piracy by *Lanius collaris humeralis. Ibis* (14)5: 614–615.
Moreau, R.E. and Southern, H.N. 1958. Geographical variation and polymorphism in *Chlorophoneus* shrikes. *Proc. Zool. Soc. Lond.* 130: 301–329.
Morel, G.J. and Morel, M.Y. 1982. Dates de reproduction des oiseaux de Sénégambie. *Bonn. zool. Beitr.* 33: 249–267
Morel, Gérard pers. comm.
Morioka, H. and Sakane, T. 1979. Breeding avifaunas of Mt. Puguis, northern Luzon and Baracatan, Mindanao, Philippines (Part I). *Bull. Nat. Sci. Mus. Japan,* Ser. A (Zool.), 5: 65–74.
Morioka, H. and Sison, R.V. 1987. Birds of the highlands of Mt. Halcon, Mindoro, Philippines. Japanese. *J. Orn.* 35: 109–124.
Morrison, M.L. 1979. Loggerhead Shrike eggshell thickness in California and Florida. *Wilson Bull.* 91: 469–470.
Morrison, M.L. 1980. Seasonal aspects of the predatory behavior of Loggerhead Shrikes. *Condor* 82: 296–300.
Morrison, M.L., Kuehler, C.M., Scott, T.A., Lieberman, A.A., Everett, W.T., Phillips, R.B., Koehler, C.E., Aigner, P.A., Winchell, C. and Burr, T. 1995. San Clemente Loggerhead Shrike: Recovery Plan for endangered species. In Yosef, R. and Lohrer, F.E. (eds.) Shrikes (Laniidae) of the World: Biology and Conservation. *Proc. Western Found. Vert. Zool.* 6: 293–295
Moskat, Csaba pers. comm.
Mundy, N.I. and Woodruff, D.S. 1998. Comnservation genetics of the endangered San Clemente Loggerhead Shrike (*Lanius ludovicianus mearnsi*). In Yosef, R. and Lohrer, F.E (eds.) Shrikes of the World: Conservation Implementation. *Int. Birdwatching Center in Eilat Tech. Publ.* 7: 60–63.
Mundy, N.I., Winchell, C.S. and Woodruff, D.S. 1997. Genetic differences between the endangered San Clemente Island Loggerhead Shrike *Lanius ludovicianus mearnsi* and two neighbouring subspecies demonstrated by mtDNA control region and cytochrome b sequence variation. *Molecular Ecology* 6: 29–37.
Mundy, P.J. and Cook, A.W. 1972. The birds of Sokoto. *Bull. Nigerian Orn. Soc.* 9: 60–76.
Naumann, J.F. 1901. *Naturgeschichte der Vögel' Mitteleuropas.* (Hennicke, C.R., ed). Vol. 4., Gera-Untermhaus, E Kökler.
Ndao, B. 1989. Au Senegal, un Gonolek de Barbarie (*Laniarius barbarus*) à dessous jaune apparie à un sujet normal. *Malimbus* 11: 97–98.
Nechayev, V.A. 1976. Biology of the Chinese Great Grey Shrike. *Ornitologija* 12: 118–124. (Russian)
Neumann, N. 1972. Double brooding by the Long-tailed Shrike *Urolestes melanoleucus. Natal Bird Club News Sheet* 202: 1.
Neumann, O. 1927. Critical remarks on some Cameroon birds. *Ibis* (12)3: 502–508.
Nicol, W. 1964. Two males and one female of Long-tailed Shrike *Corvinella melanoleuca* attending to the same nest. *Ostrich* 35: 68–69.
Nielsen, B.P. 1981. Taxonomy of shrikes. *Brit. Birds* 74: 534–535.
Nikolaus, G. 1987. Distribution atlas of Sudan's birds with notes on habitat and status. *Bonn. Zool. Monog.* 25.
Nikolaus, G. 1990. Shrikes, Laniidae, feeding on Marsh Warblers *Acrocephalus palustris* during migration. *Scopus* 14: 26–29.
Nöller, R. 1975. Pririt Flycatcher fanning young. *Bokmakierie* 27: 16.
Oates, E.W. 1883. *A Handbook to the Birds of British Burmah.* Vol.1. R.H. Porter, London.
Oatley, T.B. 1969. Bird ecology in the evergreen forests north western Zambia. *Puku. Occas. Pap.* No. 5: 157–176.
Ogawa, I. 1977. Pellet analysis of the Bull-headed Shrike *Lanius bucephalus* and the seasonal change of food habits. *Tori* 26: 63–75.
Ogilvie-Grant, W.R. 1902. A review of the species of shrikes of the genus *Lanius. Novit. Zool.* 9: 449–486.
Ogilvie-Grant, W.R. 1910. Zoological results of the Ruwenzori expedition. *Trans. Zool. Soc. Lond.* 19: 253–453.
Ogilvie-Grant, W.R. 1912. Notes on *Laniarius mufumbiri. Ibis* (9)6: 332–334.
Ohata, K. 1991. Nesting and courtship feeding by Brown and Thickbilled Shrikes, *Lanius cristatus* and *L. tigrinus. Strix* 10: 280–281.
Olivier, G. 1944. *Monographie des Pies-grièches du genre Lanius.* Lecerf, Rouen.
Olivier, G. 1947. Note sur *Lanius validirostris* Grant 1894 des iles Philippines. *Oiseau et R.F.O.*17: 182–185.
Olivier, G. 1958. Observations sur le comportement d'une Pie-Grièche a longue queue (*Lanius cabanisi*) et d'une jeune Huppe africaine (*Upupa africana*). *Oiseau et R.F.O.* 28: 88–89.
Olson, S.L. 1989. Preliminary systematic notes on some old passerines. *Riv. Ital. Orn.* 59: 183–195.
Olsson, V. 1995. The effects of habitat changes on the distribution and population trends of the Great Grey Shrike and the Red-backed Shrike in Sweden. In Yosef, R. and Lohrer, F.E. (eds.) Shrikes (Laniidae) of the World: Biology and Conservation. *Proc. Western Found. Vert. Zool.* 6: 108–111.
Owen, J.H. 1917. Notes on the breeding habits of the Red-backed Shrike. *Brit. Birds* 10: 175–180.
Owen, D.F. 1967. Interpretation of polymorphism in the African bush-shrikes. *Ibis* 109: 278–279.
Paludan, K. 1959. *The Birds of Afghanistan.* C.A. Reitzel, Kobenhavn.
Panov, E.N. 1983, 1986. *Die Würger der Paläarktis.* Neue Brehm Bucherei. Ziemsen, Wittenburg Lutherstadt.
Panov, E.N. 1995. Superspecies of shrikes in the former USSR. In Yosef, R. and Lohrer, F.E. (eds.) Shrikes (Laniidae) of the World: Biology and Conservation. *Proc. Western Found. Vert. Zool.* 6: 26–33.
Panov, Eugene pers. comm.
Pantuwatana, S., Imlarp, S. and Marshall, J.T. 1969. Vertebrate ecology of Bang Phra. *Nat. Hist. Bull. Siam Soc.* 23: 161.
Parker, V. 1994. *Swaziland Bird Atlas 1985–1991.* Websters, Mbabane, Swaziland.
Parker, Vincent pers. comm.
Parrott, J. 1980. Frugivory by Great Grey Shrikes *Lanius excubitor. Ibis* 122: 532–533.
Parry, Don pers. comm.

Paterson, H.E.W. 1984. The recognition concept of species. In Species and Speciation (E. Verba, ed.). *Transvaal Mus. Monogr.* 4: 21–34.
Payne, R.B. 1970. Temporal pattern of duetting in the Barbary Shrike *Laniarius barbarus. Ibis* 112: 106–108.
Payne, R.B. 1971. Duetting and chorus singing in African birds. *Ostrich* Suppl. 9: 125–146.
Payne, R.B. and Payne, K. 1967. Cuckoo hosts in southern Africa. *Ostrich* 38: 135–143.
Paz, U. 1987. *The Birds of Israel.* Ministry of Defense Publication, Tel-Aviv.
Peakall, D.B. 1995. The decline and fall of the Red-backed Shrike in Britain. In Yosef, R., and Lohrer, F.E. (eds.) Shrikes (Laniidae) of the World: Biology and Conservation. *Proc. Western Found. Vert. Zool.* 6: 112–116.
Pearson, D.J. 1970. Weights of Red-backed Shrikes on autumn passage in Uganda. *Ibis* 112: 114–115.
Pearson, D.J. 1979. The races of the Red-tailed Shrike *Lanius isabellinus* occurring in East Africa. *Scopus* 3: 74–78.
Pearson, D.J. 1981. Field identification of Isabelline Shrike. *Dutch Birding* 3: 119–122.
Pearson, D.J. and Lack, P.C. 1992. Migration patterns and habitat use by passerines and near-passerine migrant birds in eastern Africa. *Ibis* 134 Suppl. 1: 89–98.
Pearson, David pers. comm.
Peck, G.K. and James, R.D. 1987. *Breeding Birds of Ontario: Nidiology and Distribution.* Vol.2. Passerines. Royal Ontario Museum, Ontario.
Peet, N.B. and Atkinson, P.W. 1994. The biodiversity and conservation of the birds of São Tomé and Príncipe. *Biodiversity. and Conservation.* 3: 851–867.
Peirce, M.A. 1984a. Haematozoa of Zambian birds. 1 General survey. *J. Nat. Hist.* 18: 105–122.
Peirce, M.A. 1984b. Weights of birds from Balmoral, Zambia. *Bull. Brit. Orn. Club* 104: 84–85.
Peirce, M.A., Backhurst, C.B. and Backhurst, D.E.G. 1977. Haematozoa of East African birds. *E. Afr. Wildl. J.* 15: 71–79.
Penry, H. 1994. *Bird Atlas of Botswana.* University of Natal, Pietermaritzburg.
Peterjohn, B.G. and Sauer, J.R. 1995. Population trends of the Loggerhead Shrike from the North American Breeding Bird Survey. In Yosef, R. and Lohrer, F.E. (eds.) Shrikes (Laniidae) of the World: Biology and Conservation. *Proc. Western Found. Vert. Zool.* 6: 117–121.
Peters, J.L. and Loveridge, A. 1936. Scientific results of an expedition to rain forest regions of East Africa. *Bull. Mus. Comp. Zool.* 79: 129–205.
Phillips, R.L. 1979. Observations on the nesting of the Grey-headed Bush Shrike *Malaconotus blanchoti. Honeyguide* 98: 31–33.
Pinshow, B., Degen, A.A., Yosef, R., Kam, M. and Nagy, K.A. 1995. Energy and water use by Great Grey Shrike nestlings in unpredictable desert environments. In Yosef, R., and Lohrer, F.E. (eds.) Shrikes (Laniidae) of the World: Biology and Conservation. *Proc. Western Found. Vert. Zool.* 6: 182–185.
Pinto, A.A. Rosa. 1962. As observações de maior destaque das expedições ornitólogicos do Instituto Investigação Científica de Angola. *Bol. Inst. Invest. cient. Angola.* 1: 21–38.
Pinto, A.A. Rosa. 1963. Notas sobre uma recente colecção de aves de Moçambique do Museu Dr Alvaro de Castro, com a descrição de duas novas subespecies. *Mem. Inst. Invest. cient. Moçamb.* (*Lourenço Marques*) 5: 31–49.
Pinto, A.A. Rosa. 1966. Notas sobre as colecoes ornitologicos recolhidas em Angola nas expedicoes efectuadas pelo Instituto de Investigacão Cientifica de Angola da 1959 a 1961. *Bol. Inst. Invest. cient. Angola* 3: 149–236.
Pinto, A.A. Rosa and Lamm, D.W. 1955. Contribution to the study of the ornithology of Sul do Save (Mozambique). *Mem. Mus. Dr. Alvaro de Castro,* Part 3: 88–159.
Plumb, W.J. 1978. Cooperative feeding of young by White Crowned Shrikes. *Bull. E. Afr. Nat. Hist. Soc.*: 89.
Pocock, T.N. 1963. Occurrence of Cape and Pririt Flycatcher *Batis capensis* and *B. pririt* respectively together in the Oudtshoorn District. *Ostrich* 34: 174–175.
Pocock, T.N. 1966. Contributions to the osteology of African birds. In Proc. 2nd Pan Afr Orn. Congr. *Ostrich* Suppl. 6: 83–94.
Pollard, C.J.W. 1992. Swamp Boubou at Kazungula. *Honeyguide* 38: 29–30.
Pomeroy, D. 1984. Secondary contacts in Central Africa. *Proc. 5th Pan Afr. Orn. Congr.*: 81–95.
Porter, O. 1932. Window panes attacked by a Sparrow and flower buds by a Bokmakierie and an unknown prancing bird. *Ostrich* 3: 64–65.
Porter, R.F., Christensen, S. and Schiermacker-Hansen, P. 1996. *Field Guide to the Birds of the Middle East.* T & A D Poyser, Calton, UK.
Poulsen, M.K. 1995. The threatened and near-threatened birds of Luzon, Philippines, and the role of the Sierra Madre mountains in their conservation. *Bird Conserv. Internatn.* 5: 79–115.
Pounds, H.E. 1972. Two Red-backed Shrikes laying in one nest. *Brit. Birds* 65: 357–358.
Praetorius, L. 1988. Whitetailed Shrike. *Newsletter State Mus. Windhoek* 16: 10–11.
Priest, C.D. 1936. *The Birds of Southern Rhodesia.* Vol. 4. William Clowes & Sons, London.
Priest, C.D. 1948. *Eggs of Birds Breeding in Southern Africa.* Robert Maclehose & Company Ltd, Glasgow.
Prigogine, A. 1949. Notes sur le *Prionops alberti* Schout. *Revue. Zool. Bot. Afr.* 42: 307–321.
Prigogine, A. 1953. Notes sur les Pies-grièches multicolores du Congo belge. *Revue. Zool. Bot. Afr.* 68: 313–324.
Prigogine, A. 1969. Polymorphism of the Chestnut-bellied Wattle-eye *Dyaphorophyia concreta. Ibis* 111: 95–97.
Prigogine, A. 1971. Les oiseaux de l'Itombwe et de son hinterland. *Tervuren Mus. Royal Afr. Cent. Annales Sci. Zool.* 185: 1–298.
Prigogine, A. 1984. Note sur deux gladiateurs (*Malaconotus*). *Le Gerfaut* 74: 75–81.
Prigogine, A. 1986. Le plumage immature du Gladiateur de Lagden (*Malaconotus lagdeni*), et du Gladiateur Ensanglante (*Malaconotus cruentus*). *Gerfaut* 76: 255–261.
Prinzinger, R., Becker, P., Kleim, J.-P., Schroth, W. and Schierwater, B. 1997. Der taxonomische Status von *Laniarius dubiosus* (Rchw. 1899) mit erganzenden Daten zur Typusbeschreibung von *Laniarius liberatus,* Bulo Burti Boubou (Smith, Arctander, Fjeldså & Amir 1991). *J. Orn.* 138: 283–290.
Prum, R.O. 1990. Phylogenetic analysis of the evolution of display behaviour in neotropical manakins (Aves: Pipridae). *Ethology* 84: 202–231.
Pryce, E. 1989. A Black Cuckoo raised by Swamp Boubous. *Babbler* 18: 38.
Prys-Jones, R.P. 1991. The occurrence of biannual primary moult in passerines. *Bull. Brit. Orn. Club* 111: 150–152.
Pycraft, W.P. 1907. Contributions to the osteology of birds, part 9. Tyranni, Hirundines, Muscicapae, Lanii and Gymnorhines. *Proc. Zool. Soc. Lond*: 352–379.
Quickelberge, C.D. 1966. A taxonomic study of the Boubou Shrike in southern Africa. *Ann. Cape Prov. Mus.* 5: 117–137.
Quickelberge, C.D. 1967. A systematic revision of the Tchagra Shrike. *Ann. Cape Prov. Mus.* (Nat. Hist.) 6: 47–54.
Quingwei, L. and Xiaozhuang, B. 1988. Studies on the karyotypes of birds. The 19 species of 12 families of Passerine birds. *Zoologica Research* 9: 326–333.
Rabor, D.S. 1936. Life histories of some common birds in the vicinity of Novaliches, Rizal Province, Luzon, I. *Philippine J. Sci.* 59: 337–353.
Raikow, R.J. 1978. Appendicular myology and relationships of the New World nine-primaried oscines. *Bull. Carnegie Mus. Nat. Hist.* 7: 1–43.

Raikow, R.J., Polumbo, P.J. and Borecky, S.R. 1980. Appendicular myology and relationships of the shrikes (Aves: Passeriformes: Laniidae). *Annals Carnegie Mus. Nat. Hist.* 49: 131–152.
Rand, A.L. 1936. The distribution and habits of Madagascar birds. *Bull. Amer. Mus. Nat. Hist.* 72: 143–499.
Rand, A.L. 1951. Birds of Liberia. *Fieldiana Zool.* 32: 561–653.
Rand, A.L. 1953. Notes on flycatchers of the genus *Batis. Fieldiana Zool.* 34: 133–149.
Rand, A.L. 1957a. *Lanius ludovicianus miamensis* Bishop, a valid race from southern Florida. *Auk* 74: 503–505.
Rand, A.L. 1957b. The subspecies of the bush shrike *Laniarius fuelleborni* (including *Laniarius poensis*). *Fieldiana Zool.* 39: 47–50.
Rand, A.L. 1957c. Two new species of birds from Angola. *Fieldiana Zool.* 39: 43–45.
Rand, A.L. 1958. The races of the bush shrike *Drypscopus cubla. Fieldiana Zool.* 39: 87–89.
Rand, A.L. 1959. Tarsal scutellation of song birds as a taxonomic character. *Wilson Bull.* 71: 274–277.
Rand, A.L. 1960. Laniidae and Vangidae. In Mayr, E., and Greenway, J.C. (eds.) *Check-list of Birds of the World.* Vol. 9. Mus. Comp. Zool., Cambridge.
Rand, A.L. and Flemming, R.L. 1957. Birds from Nepal: a systematic list of species collected. *Fieldiana Zool.* 41: 48–217.
Rand, A.L. and Gilliard, E.T. 1967. *Handbook of New Guinea Birds.* Weidenfeld and Nicolson, London.
Rand, A.L. and Rabor, D.S. 1958. The races of the shrike *Lanius validirostris. Fieldiana Zool.* 39: 85–86.
Rand, A.L., Friedmann, H. and Traylor, M.A. 1959. Birds from Gabon and Moyen Congo. *Fieldiana Zool.* 41: 1–400.
Rasa, Ann pers. comm.
Rasmussen, P.A.F. 1996. Rare birds in Denmark and Greenland in 1994. *Dansk Ornitologisk Forenings Tidsskrift* 90: 141–152.
Raubenheimer, D. and Crowe, T.M. 1987. The Recognition Species Concept: is it really an alternative? *South. Afr. J. Sci.* 83: 530–534.
Ray-Chaudhuri, C. and Chatterjee, I.B. 1969. L-Ascorbic Acid synthesis in birds. Phylogenetic Trends *Science* 164: 435–436.
Ray-Chaudhuri, R. 1976. Cyclotaxonomy and chromosome evolution in Passeriformes (Aves): a comparative karyotype study of seventeen species. *Z. zool. Syst. Evolut. Forsch.* 14: 299–320.
Reichenow, A. 1894. Zur Vogelfauna von Kamerun. *J. Orn.* 42: 29–43.
Richardson, C. 1990. *The Birds of the United Arab Emirates.* Hobby, Dubai and Washington.
Richmond, C.W. 1899. Four preoccupied names. *Auk* 16: 186–187.
Rimmer, C.C. and Darmstadt, C.H. 1996. Non-breeding site fidelity in Northern Shrikes. *J. Field Orn.* 67: 360–366.
Ripley, S.D. 1949. A new race of shrike from the Philippines. *Bull. Brit. Orn. Club* 69: 121–122.
Ripley, S.D. and Heinrich, G.H. 1966. Additions to the avifauna of Angola II. *Postilla Yale Peabody Museum.* 95: 1–29.
Roberts, A. 1935. Dr. H. Exton and his unpublished notes on South African birds. *Ostrich* 6: 1–33.
Roberts, A. 1946. Nest and eggs of the White-tailed Shrike. *Ostrich* 17: 364–365.
Roberts, T.J. 1992. *The Birds of Pakistan.* Vol. 2. Oxford University Press, Karachi.
Roberts, W.W. 1934. The Fiscal's larder. *Blythswood Review* 11: 88
Robertson, A., Simmons, R.E., Jarvis, A.M. and Brown, C.J. 1995. Can bird atlas data be used to estimate population size? A case study using Namibian endemics. *Biological Conservation* 71: 87–95.
Robertson, I. 1992. New information on birds in Cameroon. *Bull. Brit. Orn. Club* 112: 36–42.
Robinson, C.St.C. 1953. Notes on the breeding of the Bokmakiri (*Telophorus zeylonus*). *Ostrich* 24: 153–158.
Rodewald, P.G., Dejaifve, P.-A. and Green, A.A. 1994. The birds of Korup National Park, Cameroon. *Bird Conserv. Internatn.* 4: 1–68.
Rookmaaker, L.C. 1992 African birds in the Histoire Naturelle des Oiseaux d'Afrique (1796–1813) by Francois Levaillant. *Scopus* 16: 9–13.
Roos, L. and Roos, M. 1988. Do Fiscal Shrikes feed on their stored food? *Mirafra* 5: 28–29.
Roos, S., Soderström, B.H , and Pärt, T. 1998. Avian nest predators affect the spatial distribution of nesting Red-backed Shrikes *Lanius collurio.* In: Adams, N.J. & Slotow, R.H. (eds.) Proc. 22 Int. Ornithol. Congr., Durban. *Ostrich* 69: 225.
Roseveare, W.L. 1950. Notes on birds of the irrigated area of Minbu District, Burma. *J. Bombay Nat. Hist. Soc.* 49: 244–287.
Rothhaupt, G. 1995. Current status and habitat of the Great Grey Shrike in Germany. In Yosef, R., and Lohrer, F.E. (eds.) Shrikes (Laniidae) of the World: Biology and Conservation. *Proc. Western Found. Vert. Zool.* 6: 122–127.
Round, P.D. 1988. *Resident Forest Birds in Thailand: their Status and Conservation.* ICBP Monograph No. 2, Cambridge.
Rowan, M.K. 1983. *The Doves, Parrots, Louries and Cuckoos of Southern Africa.* David Philip, Cape Town.
Ryall, C. and Stoorvogel, J.J. 1995. Observations on nesting and associated behaviour of the Shrike-Flycatcher *Megabyas flammulatus* in Tai National Park, Ivory Coast. *Malimbus* 17: 19–24.
Ryan, P. 1995. Exploitation of tropical hardwood trees in Mozambique. *African Wildlife* 49: 18–19.
Ryan, P.G. 1992. Fiscal Shrike feeding by plunge-diving. *Ostrich* 63: 42.
Safriel, U.N. 1995. The evolution of Palearctic migration: the case for southern ancestry. *Isr. J. Zool.* 41: 417–431.
Salomonsen, F. 1953. Miscellaneous notes on Philippine birds. *Vidensk. Medd. fra Dansk. naturh. Foren.* 115:205-281.
Sargeant, D.E. 1994. Recent ornithological observations from São Tome' and Príncipe Islands. *Bull. Afr. Bird Club* 1: 96–102.
Schiebel, G. 1906. Die Phylogenese der *Lanius*-Arten. *J. Orn.* 54: 1–219.
Schmidl, D. 1982. *The Birds of the Serengeti National Park Tanzania.* BOU Check-list No. 5. Tring, Herts.
Schmidt, O. and Schmidt, R. 1988. Bokmakierie mimicing Redchested Cuckoo. *Promerops* 182: 13.
Schouteden, H. 1938. *Exploration du Parc National Albert, Mission G.F.F. de Witte.* Inst. des Parcs Nat. du Congo Belge: 1–197.
Schouteden, H. 1963. La faune ornithologique du district de l'Ituri. *Koninklijk Mus. mid. Afr. Tervuren, Belgie, Zool.* 5.
Schouteden, H. 1966a. La faune ornithologique du Rwanda. *Koninklijk Mus. Mid. Afr. Tervuren, Belgie, Zool.* 10: 1–30.
Schouteden, H. 1966b. La faune ornithologique du Burundi. *Koninklijk Mus. Mid. Afr. Tervuren, Belgie, Zool.* 11: 1–81.
Schön, M. 1994a. Characteristics of the habitats of the Great Grey Shrike *Lanius e. excubitor* in the region of the southwestern Schwäbische Alb, southwestern Germany: seasonal utilization and territory size, structural characteristics and their changes, micro-structures and cultivation. *Ecol. Birds* 16: 253–495.
Schön, M. 1994b. Sex-, age- and individual characteristics in the pattern of the Great Grey Shrike *Lanius excubitor* in comparison with other shrikes on the effectiveness of optical signals. *Okol. Vögel* 16: 11–80.
Schön, M. 1994c. Breeding biology of the Great Grey Shrike *Lanius excubitor*: clutch size, brood size, and breeding success in the region of the southwestern Schwabische Alb in comparison with other populations. *Okol Vögel* 6: 173–217
Schön, M. 1994d. Density and trends, sex, and age ratios, and group formation in a population of Great Grey Shrike *Lanius e. excubitor* in the region of southwestern Schwäbische Alb. *Okol. Vögel* 16: 219–252.
Schön, M. 1994e. Breeding behaviour of the Great Grey Shrike *Lanius excubitor* in the region of the southwestern Schwäbische Alb (southwestern Germany): on pair formation, pair dissolution, and pair-bond. *Okol. Vögel* 16: 81–172.
Schön, M. 1994f. Morphological basis of some raptor-features of the Great Grey Shrike (*Lanius excubitor*). *Okol. Vögel.* 16: 1–10.
Schön, M. 1994g. On the structure of the nest sites of the Great Grey Shrike *Lanius e. excubitor*: types of nests, their environment and defence, change and reuse of nests. *Okol. Vögel* 16: 497–566.
Schön, M. 1995a. Habitat structure, habitat changes, and causes of decline in the Great Grey Shrike (*Lanius excubitor*) in southwestern Germany. In Yosef, R. and Lohrer, F.E (eds.) Shrikes (Laniidae) of the World: Biology and Conservation. *Proc. Western*

Found. Vert. Zool. 6: 142–149.
Schön, M. 1995b. Breeding behaviour of the Great Grey Shrike in southwestern Germany. In Yosef, R. and Lohrer, F.E. (eds.) Shrikes (Laniidae) of the World: Biology and Conservation. *Proc. Western Found. Vert. Zool.* 6: 235–241.
Schön, M. 1996. Raptor-like passerines: some similarities and differences of shrikes (*Lanius*) and raptors. *Okol. Vögel* 18: 173–216.
Schön, M. 1998a. On the evolution of the northern and southern group of subspecies in the Great Grey Shrike superspecies (*Lanius excubitor*). In Yosef, R., and Lohrer, F.E. (eds.) Shrikes of the World: Conservation Implementation. *Int. Birdwatching Center in Eilat Tech. Publ.* 7: 9–13.
Schön, M. 1998b. Conservation measures and implementation for the Great Grey Shrike (*Lanius excubitor*) in southwestern Schwäbische Alb of southwestern Germany. In Yosef, R. and Lohrer, F.E. (eds.) Shrikes of the World: Conservation Implementation. *Int. Birdwatching Center in Eilat Tech. Publ.* 7: 68–73.
Schulenberg, T.S. 1993. Phylogeny of the Vangidae: inferences from mitochondrial DNA. *Proc. 8th Pan Afr. Orn. Congr.*: 23–28.
Schwabl, H. and Sonnenschein, E. 1992. Antiphonal duetting and sex hormones in the Tropical Bush-shrike *Laniarius funebris*. *Hormones and Behaviour* 26: 295–307.
Schwan, T.G. and Hikes, N. 1979. Fiscal Shrike predation on the bat *Pipistrellus kuhli* in Kenya. *Biotropica* 11: 21.
Sclater, M.A. and Moreau, R.E. 1933. Taxonomic and field notes on some birds of the North Eastern Tanganyika Territory. Part 4. *Ibis* (3)3: 199–201.
Sclater, W.L. 1924–30. *Systema Avium Aethiopicarum.* British Ornithologists' Union, London.
Sclater, W.L. and Mackworth-Praed, C. 1918. A list of the birds of the Anglo-Egyptian Sudan, based on the collections of Mr. A.L. Butler, Mr. A. Chapman and Capt. H. Lynes, R.N., and Major Cuthbert Christy, R.A.M.C. (T.F.). Part II. *Ibis* (10)6: 602–720.
Scott, J.A. 1984. Breeding behaviour of the Black-throated Wattle-eye. *Honeyguide* 30: 72–74.
Scott, J.A. 1985. Ringing recovery. *Bull. Zambian Orn. Soc.* 15: 50.
Scott, T.A. and Morrison, M.L. 1990. Natural history and management of the San Clemente Loggerhead Shrike. *Proc. Western Found. Vert. Zool.* 4: 23–57.
Scott, T.A. and Morrison, M.L. 1995. Opportunistic foraging behaviour of Loggerhead Shrikes. In Yosef, R., and Lohrer, F.E. (eds.) Shrikes (Laniidae) of the World: Biology and Conservation. *Proc. Western Found. Vert. Zool.* 6: 186–193.
Scriven, Ken pers. comm.
Searcy, W.A. and Brenowitz, E.A. 1988. Sexual differences in species recognition of avian song. *Nature* Vol. 332 March : 152–154.
Serle, W. 1938. Nesting notes on Nigerian birds. *Oologists' Record* 18: 10–18.
Serle, W. 1940. Field observations on some northern Nigerian birds. *Ibis* (14)4: 25–26.
Serle, W. 1943. Notes on East African birds. *Ibis* 85: 55–82.
Serle, W. 1950. A contribution to the ornithology of the British Cameroons. *Ibis* 92: 602–627.
Serle, W. 1951. A new species of shrike and a new race of *Apalis* from West Africa. *Bull. Br. Orn. Club* 71: 41–42.
Serle, W. 1952a. The polymorphic forms of *Chlorophoneus multicolor multicolor* (Gray), in British Cameroons. *Bull. Brit. Orn. Club* 72: 26–27.
Serle, W. 1952b. Colour variation in *Malaconotus cruentus* (Lesson). *Bull. Brit. Orn. Club* 72: 27–28.
Serle, W. 1954. A second contribution to the ornithology of the British Cameroons. *Ibis* 96: 47–80.
Serle, W. 1955. On the birds of the Eastern Highlands of Southern Rhodesia. *Ostrich* 26: 115–127.
Serle, W. 1957. A contribution to the ornithology of the eastern region of Nigeria. *Ibis* 99: 628–685.
Serle, W. 1965. A third contribution to the ornithology of the British Cameroons. *Ibis* 107: 230–235.
Serle, W. and Morel, G.J. 1977. *Field Guide to the Birds of West Africa.* Collins, London.
Sessions, P.H.B. 1966. Notes on the birds of Lengetia farm, Mau Narok. *J. E. Afr. Nat. Hist. Soc.* 26: 18–48.
Severinghaus, L.L. 1996. Territory strategy of the migratory Brown Shrike *Lanius cristatus*. *Ibis* 138: 460–465.
Severinghaus, S.R. and Blackshaw, K.T. 1976. *The Birds of Taiwan.* Mei Ya Publications, Taipei.
Severinghaus, L.L. and Liang, C.T. 1995. Food and foraging behaviour of the Brown Shrike (*Lanius cristatus*) in Taiwan. In Yosef, R. and Lohrer, F.E.(eds.) Shrikes (Laniidae) of the World: Biology and Conservation. *Proc. Western Found. Vert. Zool.* 6: 194–199.
Shamsuddin, M. and Mohammad, M.K. 1980. Haematozoa of some Iraqi birds with description of two new species, *Haemoproteus pteroclis* and *Leucocytozoon nycticoraxi*. *Bull. Nat. Hist. Res. Centre* 7: 111–154.
Sharma, V.L. 1989. Descriptions of karyotypes in four species of birds belonging to the family Laniidae. *Res. Bull. Panjab Univ. Sci.* 40: 193–206.
Sharp, Cathy pers. comm.
Sharpe, R.B. 1873. On the genus *Platystira* and its allies. *Ibis* (3)3: 156–160.
Sharpe, R.B. 1877. *Catalogue of Birds in the British Museum*, Vol.3. Trustees of the British Museum, London.
Shelley, G.E. 1912. *The Birds of Africa.* Vol.5. H. Sotheran & Co, London.
Sheppard, P.A. 1910. Field notes on little-known birds near Beira. *J. South. Afr. Orn. Un.* 6: 42–43.
Shields, G.F. 1982. Comparative avian cytogenetics: a review. *Condor* 84: 45–58.
Shimoda, C., Yamagishi, S., Tanimura, M. and Miyazaki-Kishimoto, M. 1996. Molecular phylogeny of Madagascar vangids: sequence analysis of the PCR-amplified mitochondrial cytochrome b region. In Yamagishi, S. (ed). *Social Evolution of Birds in Madagascar with Special Respect to Vangas.* 19–26. Osaka City University, Osaka.
Shirihai, H. 1996. *The Birds of Israel.* Academic Press, London.
Shirihai, H. and Golan, Y. F. 1994. First records of Long-tailed Shrike *Lanius schach* in Israel and Turkey. *Sandgrouse* 16: 36–40.
Short, L.L. and Horne, J.F.M. 1985. Notes on some birds of the Arabuko-Sokoke Forest. *Scopus* 9: 117–126.
Short, L.L., Horne, J.F.M., and Gichuki, C.M. 1990. *Annotated checklist of the birds of East Africa.* Western Found. Vert. Zool. 4: 155–162.
Sibley, C.G. 1970. A comparative study of the egg-white protiens of passerine birds. *Bull. Peabody Mus. Nat. Hist.* 32: 1–131.
Sibley, C.G. and Ahlquist, J.E. 1990. *Phylogeny and Classification of Birds: a Study in Molecular Evolution.* Yale University Press, New Haven.
Sibley, C.G. and Monroe, B.L. 1990. *Distribution and Taxonomy of Birds of the World.* Yale University Press, New Haven.
Sibley, Charles, The late, pers.comm.
Simmons, K.E.L. 1957. The taxonomic significance of the head-scratching methods of birds. *Ibis* 99: 178–181.
Sinclair, A.R.E. 1978. Factors affecting the food supply and breeding season of resident birds and movements of Palaearctic migrants in a tropical African savanna. *Ibis* 120: 480–496.
Sinclair, I. and Langrand, O. 1998. *Birds of Indian Ocean Islands.* Struik, Cape Town.
Skead, D.M. 1975. Drinking habits of birds in central Transvaal bushveld. *Ostrich* 46: 139–146.
Skead, Jack, The late, pers. comm, including notes held in Transvaal Museum.
Slack, R.S. 1975. Effects of prey size on Loggerhead Shrike predation. *Auk* 92: 812–814.
Smeek, C. 1974. Ecology of some raptors in East Africa. *Ardea* 62: 1–97.
Smith, E.F.G., Arctander, P., Fjeldså, J. and Amir, O.G. 1991. A new species of shrike (Laniidae: *Laniarius*) from Somalia, verified

by DNA sequence data from the only known individual. *Ibis* 133: 227–235.
Smith, S.M. 1973. An aggressive display and related behavior in the Loggerhead Shrike. *Auk* 90: 287–298.
Smithers, R.H.N. and Paterson, M. 1956. New geographical races of *Camaroptera fasciolata* and *Batis capensis* from Southern Rhodesia. *Bull. Brit. Orn. Club* 76: 119–120.
Smythies, B.E. 1986. *The Birds of Burma*. Third Edition: Nimrod Press, Liss, UK.
Snow, D.W. 1997. Should the biological be superseded by the phylogenetic species concept? *Bull. Br. Orn. Club* 117: 110–121.
Sokolow, E.P. and Vietinghoff-Scheel, E.V. 1992. *Lanius sphenocercus* Cabanis. In H. Dathe and W.M. Loskot (eds.) *Atlas der Verbreitung Palaearktischer Vögel*. Lief. 18. Akadkemie Verlag, Berlin.
Sonnenschein, E. 1992. Die Karriereder 'schiefen Würger. *Gefiederte Welt* 116: 197–199.
Sonnenschein, E. and Reyer, H.-U. 1984. Biology of the Slatecoloured Boubou and other Bush Shrikes. *Ostrich* 55: 86–96.
Sonnenschein, E. and Reyer, H.-U. 1983. Mate-guarding and other functions of antiphonal duets in the Slate-coloured Boubou (*Laniarius funebris*). *Z. Tierpsychol.* 63: 112–140.
Sonnenschein, Edith pers. comm.
Speirs, J.M. 1985. *Birds of Ontario*. Natural Heritage/Natural History Inc., Toronto.
Stallcup, W.B. 1961. Relationships of some families of the suborder Passeres (songbirds) as indicated by comparisons of tissue proteins. *J. Grad. Res. Center' Southern Methodist Univ.* 29: 43–65.
Stark, A.C. 1901. *The Birds of South Africa*. Vol. 2. R.H.Porter, London.
Stastny, K., Hudec, K. and Bejcek, V. 1998. Twentieth century breeding distribution changes of shrikes in the Czech Republic. In Yosef, R. and Lohrer, F.E. (eds.) Shrikes of the World: Conservation Implementation. *Int. Birdwatching Center in Eilat Tech. Publ.* 7: 22–27.
Stepanyan, L.S. 1990. *Conspectus of the Ornithological Faunal of the USSR*. Academy of Sciences of the USSR, Moscow. (English translation).
Stephan, B. 1965. Die Zahl der Armschwingen bei den Passeriformes. *J. Orn.* 106: 446–458.
Steyn, D. 1998. Blackcrowned Tchagra feeds on Boomslang. *Hornbill* 52: 21.
Steyn, P. 1965. Some observations on the Bateleur *Terathopius ecaudatus* (Daudin). *Ostrich* 36: 203–213.
Steyn, P. 1976. Protracted prelaying nest building by a Fiscal Shrike. *Ostrich* 47: 68.
Steyn, P. 1982. *Birds of Prey of Southern Africa*. David Philip, Cape Town.
Steyn, Peter pers. comm.
Stjernstedt, Bob pers. comm.
Storr, G.M. 1958. On the classification of the Old World Flycatchers. *Emu* 58: 277–283.
Strange, M. and Jeyarajasingam, A. 1993. *A Photographic Guide to the Birds of Peninsular Malaysia and Singapore*. Sun Tree Publishing, Singapore.
Stresemann, E. 1923. *Lanius fuscatus* Lesson: eine mutante von *Lanius schach schach L. Orn. Mber.* 31: 79–82.
Stresemann, E. 1947. *Laniarius nigerrimus* (Rchw.): a mutation of *Laniarius ferrugineus sublacteus* (Cassin). *Ibis* 89 : 518–519.
Stresemann, E. and Stresemann, V. 1971. Die Postnuptiale und die Praenuptiale Vollmauser der asiatischen Würger *Lanius tigrinus* und *L. cristatus*. *J. Orn.* 112: 373–395.
Stresemann, E. and Stresemann, V. 1972. Uber die Mauser in der Gruppe *Lanius isabellinus*. *J. Orn.* 113: 60–75.
Stuart, S.N. (ed.) 1986. *Conservation of Cameroon Montane Forests: Report of the ICBP Cameroon Montane Forest Survey' November 1983–April 1984*. ICBP, Cambridge.
Stuart, S.N. and Jensen, F.P. 1981. Further range extensions and other notable records of forest birds from Tanzania. *Scopus* 5: 106–115.
Stuart, S.N. and Jensen, F.P. 1985. The avifauna of the Uluguru Mountains. *Gerfaut* 75: 155–197.
Stuart, S.N., Adams, R.J. and Jenkins, M.D. 1990. Biodiversity in sub-Saharan Africa and its islands: conservation, management and sustainable use. *Occas. Pap. IUCN Species Survival Commission* No. 6: 1–242.
Sundararaman, V. 1989. On the parental care of Wood Shrike (*Tephrodornis pondicerianus*). *J. Bombay Nat. Hist. Soc.* 86: 95.
Sutherland, W.J. 1998. The importance of behavioural studies in observation biology. *Animal Behaviour* 56: 801–809.
Sutton, R.W.W. 1970. Bird records from Ghana in 1967 and 1968/69. *Bull. Nigerian Orn. Soc.* 7: 76–93.
Svensson, L. 1984. *Identification Guide to European Passerines*. (Self published), Stockholm.
Swainson, W. 1828. On several groups and forms in ornithology, not hitherto defined. *Zool. J.* 3: 158–163.
Swynnerton, C.F.M. 1908. Further notes on the birds of Gazaland. *Ibis* (9) 2: 1–107.
Swynnerton, C.F.M. 1916. On the colouration of the mouths and eggs of birds. I. The mouths of birds. *Ibis* (10)4: 264–294.
Takagi, M. 1996a. A sexual difference in plumage of Brown Shrike subspecies *Lanius cristatus superciliosus*. *J. Yamashina Inst. Orn.* 28: 103–105.
Takagi, M. 1996b. Sexual size dimorphism and sex determination of a Brown Shrike subspecies, *Lanius cristatus superciliosus*. *Japanese. J. Orn.* 45: 187–190.
Takagi, M. and Ogawa, I. 1995. Comparative studies on nest sites and diet of *Lanius bucephalus* and *L. cristatus* in northern Japan. In Yosef, R., and Lohrer, F.E. (eds.) Shrikes (Laniidae) of the World: Biology and Conservation. *Proc. Western Found. Vert. Zool.* 6: 200–203.
Tarboton, W.R. 1963. Breeding observations on the Red-billed Helmet Shrike. *Bokmakierie* 15: 1–3.
Tarboton, W.R. 1971. Breeding biology of the Crimson-breasted Shrike at Olifantsfontein, Transvaal. *Ostrich* 42: 271–290.
Tarboton, W.R. 1984. Breeding of the Brubru Shrike. *Ostrich* 55: 97–101.
Tarboton, W.R. and Jones, J.M.B. 1987. Breeding of the Vanga or Black and White Flycatcher. *Honeyguide* 33: 63–64.
Tarboton, W.R., Kemp, M.I. and Kemp, A.C. 1987. *Birds of the Transvaal*. Transvaal Museum, Pretoria.
Tarboton, Warwick, pers. comm.
Taylor, Barry pers. comm. (Kenyan Nest Record Cards)
Temple, S.A. 1993. When and where are shrike populations limited. In Yosef, R., and Lohrer, F.E. (eds.) Shrikes (Laniidae) of the World: Biology and Conservation. *Proc. Western Found. Vert. Zool.* 6: 6–10.
Tenovuo, J. and Varrela, J. 1998. Identification of Great Grey Shrike complex in Europe. *Alula* 1: 2–11.
Theiler, G. 1959. African ticks and birds. *Ostrich* Suppl. 3: 353–378.
Theiler, G. 1962. The Ixodoidea parasites of vertebrates in Africa south of the Sahara. Report to Director of Veterinary Services, Onderstepoort. Project S. 9958. Onderstepoort, Pretoria.
Thielcke, G. 1956. Zum Beuteverhalten des Raubwürgers (*Lanius excubitor*) und anderer Mausejäger. *Z. Tierpsychol.* 13: 272–277.
Thiollay, J.-M. 1985. The birds of Ivory Coast: status and distribution. *Malimbus* 7: 1–59.
Thomsen, P., and Jacobsen, P. 1979. *The Birds of Tunisia*. Copenhagen.
Thorpe, W.H. 1972. Duetting and antiphonal song in birds. *Behaviour* Suppl. 18: 1–193.
Todd, W.E.C. 1963. *Birds of the Labrador Peninsula and Adjacent Areas*. Carnegie Museum & University of Toronto Press, Toronto.
Tomlinson, W. 1950. Bird notes chiefly from the northern frontier district of Kenya. Part 2. *Jour. East Afr. Nat. Hist. Soc.* 19: 225–250.
Took, J.M.E. 1966. The nest of Souza's Shrike, *Lanius souzae*. *Ostrich* 37: 155–156.
Tordoff, H.B. 1954. Relationships of the New World nine-primaried oscines. *Auk* 71: 273–284.

Toschi, A. 1950. Sulla biologia del *Lanius collaris humeralis* Stanley. *Lab. Zool. Appl. Caccia* Suppl. 11. Univ. Bologna (English summary).
Toschi, A. 1969. *Introduzione alla ornitologia della Libia. Supplemento alle Ricerche di Zoologia applicata alla Caccia*, vol.6 : 345–350.
Traylor, M.A. 1960. Mutation in an African flycatcher *Dyaphorophyia concerta. Auk*: 77: 80–82.
Traylor, M.A. 1962. Notes on the birds of Angola-Passeres. *Publ. Cult. Co. Diam. Angola* 58: 53-142.
Traylor, M.A. 1963. Check-list of Angolan Birds. *Pub. Cult. Comp. Diam. Angola* 61: 1–250.
Traylor, M.A. 1965. Birds of Barotseland and Bechuanaland. *Ibis* 107: 357–384.
Traylor, M.A. 1967. A collection of birds from Szechwan. *Fieldiana Zool.* 53: 1–67.
Traylor, M.A. 1970. Notes on African Muscicapidae. *Ibis* 112: 395–399.
Traylor, M.A. 1986. Platysteiridae In Mayr, E., and Cottrell, G.W. (eds). 1986. *Check-list of Birds of the World.* Vol. 11.,1–636. Mus. Comp. Zool., Cambridge, Massachusetts.
Tryjanowski, P., Kuyniak S. and Kuczyński, L. 1998. Long-term changes of the Red-backed Shrike *Lanius collurio* eggs size. In: Adams, N.J. & Slotow, R.H. (eds.) Proc. 22 Int. Ornithol. Congr., Durban. *Ostrich* 69: 338.
Tucker, G.M. and Heath, M.F. 1994. *Birds in Europe: their Conservation Status.* BirdLife International, Cambridge.
Tufts, R.W. 1987. *Birds of Nova Scotia.* Nimbus Publishing, Nova Scotia Museum, Halifax.
Tyler, J.D. 1992. Nesting ecology of the Loggerhead Shrike in Southwestern Oklahoma. *Wilson Bull.* 104: 95–104.
Tyler, S.J. and Tyler, L. 1996. Feeding associations of the Crimsonbreasted Shrike *Laniarius atrococcineus. Babbler* 31: 24–25.
Udagawa, T. 1954. Karyogram studies in birds IV. The chromosomes of four Passers and two Columbine species. *Anno. Zool. Jap.* 27: 208–214.
Ullrich, B. 1971. Untersuchungen zur Ethologie und Okologie des Rotkopfwürgers (*Lanius senator*) in Sudwestdeutschland im Vergleich zu Raubwürger (*L. excubitor*), Schwarzstirnwürger (*L. minor*) und Neuntoter (*L. collurio*). *Vogelwarte* 26: 1–77.
Ullrich, B. 1975. Ueber die postnuptiale Mauser des Rotkopfwürgers (*Lanius senator*). *J. Orn.* 115: 79–85.
Underhill, L.G., Prys-Jones, R.P., Harrison, J.A. and Martinez, P. 1992. Seasonal patterns of occurrence of Palaearctic migrants in southern Africa using atlas data. *Ibis* 134: 99–108.
Urban, E.K. and Brown, L.H. 1971. *A Checklist of the Birds of Ethiopia.* Dept. Zool. Haile Sellassie University, Addis Ababa, Ethiopia.
Urban, E.K. Fry, C.H. and Keith, S. (eds.) 1997. *Birds of Africa: Thrushes to Puffback Flycatchers.* Vol.5. Academic Press, London.
Uys, C.J. 1989. The southern Tchagra in the Western Cape. *Promerops* 187: 9–10.
Uys, C.J. and Macleod, J.G.R. 1967. The birds of the de Hoop Vlei region, Bredasdorp, and the effect of the 1957 inundation over a 10–year period (1957–1966) on the distribution of species, bird numbers and breeding. *Ostrich* 38: 233–254.
van Bruggen, A.C. 1960. Notes and observations on birds in the Transvaal, Southern Rhodesia, and Portuguese East Africa. *Ostrich* 31: 30–31.

Vande weghe, J.P. 1981. L'avifaune des papyraies au Rwanda et au Burundi. *Gerfaut* 71: 489–536.
Vande weghe, J.P. 1992. New records for Uganda and Tanzania along the Rwandan and Burundian borders. *Scopus* 16: 59–60.
vander Wall, S.B. *Food Hoarding in Animals.* University of Chicago Press, Chicago.
van der Willigen, T.A. and Lovett, J. 1981. *Report of the Oxford Expedition to Tanzania, 1979.* Unpublished.
van Ee, C.A. 1955. Laksman-wyfie en mannetjie wat twee nessies bebroei. *Ostrich* 26: 135.
van Marle, J.G. and Voous, K.H. 1988. *The Birds of Sumatra.* BOU Check-list No. 10. Tring, Herts.
van Nieuwenhuyse, D. 1996. Propositions pour la conservation de la Pie-Grièche Ecorcheur (*Lanius collurio*). *Alauda* 64: 45–55.
van Nieuwenhuyse, D. 1998. Conservation opportunities for the Red-backed Shrike (*Lanius collurio*). In Yosef, R. and Lohrer, F.E. (eds.) Shrikes of the World: Biology and Conservation. *Proc. Western Found. Vert. Zool.* 6: 6–10.
van Someren, V.G.L. 1916. A list of birds collected in Uganda and British East Africa, with notes on their nesting and other habits. *Ibis* 4: 373–472.
van Someren, V.G.L 1922. Notes on the birds of East Africa. *Novit. Zool.* 29: 1–246.
van Someren, V.G.L. 1932. Birds of Kenya and Uganda, being addenda and corrigenda to my previous paper in Novitates Zoologicae 29, 1922. *Novit. Zool.* 37: 252–380.
van Someren, V.G.L. 1939. Coryndon Memorial Museum Expedition to the Chylu Hills, April–July 1938. *J. E. Afr. Nat. Hist. Soc.* 14: 1–129.
van Someren, V.G.L. 1956. Days with Birds, studies of habits of some East African species. *Fieldiana Zool.* 38: 1–520.
van Someren, V.G.L. and van Someren, G.R.C. 1949. The birds of Bwamba, Toro District, Uganda. Special Suppl. *Uganda J.* 13: 1–107.
Vatev, I.T., Simeonov, P.S., Michev, T.M. and Ivanov, B.E. 1980. The Masked Shrike (*Lanius nubicus*), a breeding species in Bulgaria. *Acta zool. Bulgarica* 15: 115–118.
Vaurie, C. 1955. Systematic notes on Palearctic birds. No. 17. Laniidae. *Amer. Mus. Novit.* 1752.
Vaurie, C. 1959. *The Birds of the Palearctic Fauna: a Systematic Reference. Order Passeriformes.* H.F. and G. Witherby, London.
Vaurie, C. 1972. *Tibet and its Birds.* H.F. and G. Witherby, London.
Verheyen, R. 1953. Exploration du Parc National de l'Upemba. Oiseaux Mission G.F. de Witte. *Inst. des Parcs Nat. du Congo belge.* 19: 1–687.
Vernon, C.J. 1966. Observations on the winter behaviour of the White Helmet Shrike, *Prionops plumata. Ostrich* 37: 3–5.
Vernon, C.J. 1976. Notes on parental care in Cape Batis. *Ostrich* 47: 144.
Vernon, C.J. 1977. Birds of Zimbabwe Ruins area, Rhodesia. *Southern Birds* 4: 1–49.
Vernon, C.J. 1980. Bird parties in central and South Africa. *Proc. 4th Pan Afr. Orn. Congr.*: 313–325.
Vernon, C.J. 1984a. Population dynamics of birds in Brachystegia woodland. *Proc. 5th Pan Afr. Orn. Congr.*. 201–216.
Vernon, C.J. 1984b. The breeding biology of the Thickbilled Cuckoo. *Proc. 5th Pan Afr. Orn. Congr.*: 825–840.
Vernon, C.J. 1985. The systematics of the southern African flycatchers, Muscicapidae. *Honeyguide* 31: 93–100.
Vernon, C.J. 1989. Observations on the forest birds around East London. *Ostrich* Suppl. 14: 75–84.
Vernon, C.J., Macdonald, I.A.W. and Dean, W.R.J. 1990. The birds of the Haroni-Lusitu. *Honeyguide* 36: 14–35.
Vernon, Carl unpublished notes and pers. comm.
Vijayan, L. 1989. Feeding behaviour of the Malabar Woodshrike *Tephrodornis virgatus sylvicola* Jerdon at Thekkady, Kerala. *J. Bombay Nat. Hist. Soc.* 86: 396–399.
Vijayan, L. 1992. Breeding biology of the Malabar Wood Shrike *Tephrodornis virgatus sylvicola*, Jerdon, at Thekkady, Kerala. *J. Bombay Nat. Hist. Soc.* 89: 125–126.
Vincent, A.W. 1946. On the breeding habits of some African birds. *Ibis* 88: 56–57.
Vincent, A.W. 1949. On the breeding habits of some African Birds. *Ibis* 91: 111–139.
Vincent, J. 1935. On the birds of Northern Portuguese East Africa. Parts 7 & 9. *Ibis* (13) 5: 355–397, 707–762.
Viney, C. and Phillipps, K. 1988. *Birds of Hong Kong.* 4th ed. Government Printer, Hong Kong.
Voous, K.H. 1960. *Atlas of European Birds.* Nelson, London.
Voous, K.H. 1979. Capricious taxonomic history of Isabelline Shrike. *Brit. Birds* 72: 573–578.

Vorobiev, K.A. 1954. *Birds of the Ussuri Region.* Academy of Sciences of the USSR, Moscow. (English translation).
Wagner, T. 1993. Saisonale Veränderungen in der Zusammensetzung der Nahrung beim Neuntöter. *J. Orn.* 134: 5–11.
Walden, Viscount 1867. On the Rufous-tailed Shrikes. *Ibis* (2)3: 211–226.
Walker, G.R. 1939. Notes on the birds of Sierra Leone. *Ibis* (14)3: 401–450.
Walsh, F. 1968. Emin's Bush Shrike in Borgu. *Bull. Nigerian Orn. Soc.* 5: 26–27.
Walters, Michael (The Natural History Museum) pers. comm.
Wambuguh, O. 1987. Black-shouldered Kite with a freshly killed Fiscal Shrike in Masai Mara Game Reserve. *J. East. Afr. Nat. Hist. Soc.* 17: 55.
Weaving, A. 1977. Unusual prey of Fiscal Shrikes. *Honeyguide* 89: 43.
Webb, S. 1936. The Gaboon Fiery-breasted Bush-shrike. *J. Avicultural Soc.* 1: 1–2.
Wemmer, C. 1969. Impaling behaviour of the Loggerhead Shrike, *Lanius ludovicianus* Linnaeus. *Z. Tierpsychol.* 26: 208–224.
Wenzel, J.W. 1992. Behavioural homology and phylogeny. *Annu. Rev. Ecol. Syst.* 23: 361–381.
Wetherbee, D.K. 1957. Natal plumages and downy pteryloses of passerine birds of North America. *Bull. Amer. Mus. Nat. Hist.* 113: 343–346.
Whitaker, J.I.S. 1905. *The Birds of Tunisia.* Vol.1. R.H.Porter, London.
White, C.M.N. 1951. Systematic notes on African birds. *Ibis* 93: 460–465.
White, C.M.N. 1962. *A Revised Check List of African Shrikes, Orioles, Drongos, Starlings, Crows, Waxbills, Cuckoo-shrikes, Bulbuls, Accentors, Thrushes and Babblers.* Govt. Printer, Lusaka.
White, C.M.N. 1963. *A Revised Check List of African Flycatchers, Tits, Tree-creepers, Sunbirds, White-eyes, Honey-eaters, Buntings, Finches, Weavers and Waxbills.* Govt Printer, Lusaka.
White, C.M.N. and Bruce, M.D. 1986. *The Birds of Wallacea.* BOU Check-list No.7. Tring, Herts.
Wickler, W. 1972. Structure and pair-specificity of duetting in the Slate-coloured Boubou (*Laniarius funebris*). *Z. Tierpsychol.* 30: 464–476.
Wickler, W. and Seibt, U. 1979. Duetting: a daily routine of *Laniarius funebris,* the Slate-coloured Boubou (Aves, Laniidae). *Z. Tierpsychol.* 51: 153–157.
Wickler, W. and Seibt, U. 1980. Einflüsse auf Paarpartner und Rivalen in 'Duett-Kämpfen' revierverteidigender Vögel. *J. Orn.* 121: 162–170.
Wickler, W. and Seibt, U. 1982. Song splitting in the evolution of dueting. *Z. Tierpsychol.* 59: 127–140.
Wickler, W. and Sonnenschein, E. 1989. Ontogeny of song in captive duet-singing Slate-coloured Boubous (*Laniarius funebris*). A study in birdsong epigenesis. *Behaviour* 111: 220–233.
Wickler, W., and Lunau, K. 1996. How do East African bush shrikes *Laniarius funebris* recognise male and female tutors during gender dialect development? *Naturwissenschaften* 83: 579–580.
Wildash, P. 1968. *Birds of South Vietnam.* Charles E Tuttle Co, Rutland, Vermont.
Wilkinson, R. 1978. Behaviour of Grey-headed Bush-shrikes at their nest. *Bull. Nigerian Orn. Soc.* 14: 87.
Williams, E. 1998. Green-breasted Bush-shrike (*Malaconotus gladiator*) and its relationship with Monteiro's Bush-shrike (*M. monteiri*). *Bull. Afr. Bird Club* 5: 101–104.
Williams, J. 1989. Icterine Warblers feeding White-crowned Shrike chicks. *Honeyguide* 35: 26.
Williams, J.G. 1995. *Birds of East Africa.* HarperCollins, London.
Williamson, K. 1973. The 'British' Red-backed Shrike. *Bird Study* 20: 142–143.
Willis, E.O. 1983. Wrens, Gnatwrens, Rockfowl, Babblers and shrikes (Troglodytidae, Polioptilidae, Picathartidae, Timaliidae and laniidae) as ant followers. *Le Gerfaut* 73: 393–404.
Wilson, E.O. 1975. *Sociobiology.* Harvard Univ. Press, Cambridge, Massachusettes.
Wilson, J.D. (ed.) 1987. *A report on the status and conservation of the montane forest avifauna of Mt Oku, Cameroon in 1985.* International Council for Bird Preservation, University of Oxford.
Winter, S.J. 1987. On food and feeding behaviour of the Chinese Grey Shrike *Lanius sphenocercus* in Middle Amurland. *Mitt. Zool. Mus. Berl.* 63 Suppl.: *Ann. Orn.* 11: 13–34.
Winter, S.N. 1986. Biology of the Chinese Great Grey Shrike in middle Amur region. *Ornitologija* 21: 59–69. (Russian)
Winterbottom, J.M. 1936. Distribution and other notes on some Northern Rhodesian birds. *Ibis* (13)6: 763–791.
Winterbottom, J.M. 1962. Range of *Tchagra tchagra. Ostrich* 33: 74.
Winterbottom, J.M. 1963. Notes from Namaqualand and Bushmanland. *Ostrich* 35: 156–159.
Winterbottom, J.M. 1971. The birds of the Deka Expedition. *Ostrich* Suppl. 9: 5–26.
Winterbottom, J.M. 1982. Karoo longevity. *Safring News* 11: 46–48.
Wolters, H.E. 1975–82. *Die Vogelarten der Erde.* Hamburg.
Won, Pyong-oh pers. comm.
Wong, M. 1986. Trophic organization of understory birds in a Malaysian dipterocarp forest. *Auk* 103: 100–116.
Woods, C.P. 1995. Food delivery and food holding during copulation in the Loggerhead Shrike. *Wilson Bull.* 107: 762–764.
Woods, C.P. and Cade, T.J. 1996. Nesting habits of the Loggerhead Shrike in Sagebrush. *Condor* 98: 75–81.
Yamagishi, S. 1982. Age determination in the Bull-headed Shrike (*Lanius bucephalus*) based on buff tips of greater primary coverts. *J. Yamashina Inst. Orn.* 14: 96–102.
Yamagishi, S. (ed.) 1992. *Social structure of Madagascar Higher Vertebrates in Relation to their Adaptive Radiation.* Osaka City University, Osaka.
Yamagishi, S. (ed.) 1996. *Social Evolution of Birds in Madagascar, with Special Respect to Vangas.* Osaka City University, Osaka.
Yamagishi, S. and Nishiumi, I. 1994. Extrapair fertilization in monogamous Bull-headed Shrike. *J. Orn.* 135: 289.
Yamagishi, S. and Saito, M. 1985. Function of courtship feeding in the Bull-headed Shrike (*Lanius bucephalus*). *J. Ethology* 3: 113–121.
Yamagishi, S., Nishiumi, I. and Shimoda, C. 1992. Extrapair fertilization in monogamous Bull-headed Shrikes revealed by DNA fingerprinting. *Auk* 109: 711–721.
Yamashina, M.Y. 1939. Notes on the specimens of Manchurian birds chiefly made by Mr Hyojiro Orii in 1935. *Tori* 10: 446–520.
Yamashina, Y. 1951. Studies on the chromosomes of 25 species of birds. *Pap. Coord. Commit. Res. Genet.* 2: 27–38.
Yamashina, Y. 1974. *A Field Guide to Birds in Japan.* Tokyo New Service, Tokyo.
Yom-Tov, Y., Dunnett, G.M. and Anderson, A. 1974. Intraspecific nest parasitism in the Starling *Sturnus vulgaris. Ibis* 116: 87–90.
Yosef, R. 1992a. Behavior of polygynous and monogamous Loggerhead Shrikes and a comparison with Northern Shrikes. *Wilson Bull.* 104: 747–749.
Yosef, R. 1992b. From nest building to fledging of young in Great Grey Shrikes (*Lanius excubitor*) at Sede Boqer. *Israel.Orn.* 133: 279–285.
Yosef, R. 1993a. Prey transport by Loggerhead Shrikes. *Condor* 95: 231–233.
Yosef, R. 1993b. Effects of Little Owl predation on Northern Shrike postfledging success. *Auk* 110: 396–398.
Yosef, R. 1993c. Influence of observation posts on territory size of Northern Shrikes. *Wilson Bull.* 105: 180–183.
Yosef, R. 1994a. Evaluation of the global decline in the true shrikes (family Laniidae). *Auk* : 228–233.
Yosef, R. 1994b. The effects of fencelines on the reproductive success of Loggerhead Shrikes. *Conservation Biology* 8: 281–285.

Yosef, R. 1996. Loggerhead Shrike *Lanius ludovicianus*. In Poole, A. and Gill, F. (eds.) *The Birds of North America*, No. 231: 1–27.
Yosef, R. 1998. Migration of Red-backed (*Lanius collurio*). Masked (*L. nubicus*), and Woodchat Shrikes (*L. senator*) at Eilat, Israel. In Yosef, R. and Lohrer, F.E. (eds.) Shrikes of the World: Conservation Implementation. *Int. Birdwatching Center in Eilat Tech. Publ.* 7: 5–8.
Yosef, R. and Deyrup, M.A. 1998. Effects of fertitizer-induced reduction of invertebrates on reproductive success of Loggerhead Shrikes (*Lanius ludovicianus*). *J. Orn.* 139: 307–312.
Yosef, R. and Grubb, T.C. 1994. Resource dependence and territory size in Loggerhead Shrikes (*Lanius ludovicianus*). *Auk* 111: 465–469.
Yosef, R., Carrel, J.E. and Eisner, T. 1996. Contrasting reactions of Loggerhead Shrikes to two types of chemically defended insect prey. *J. Chemical Ecol.* 22: 173–181.
Yosef, R., Layne, J.N. and Lohrer, F. 1993. Trends in numbers of Loggerhead Shrikes on roadside cencuses in peninsular Florida, 1974–1992. *Florida Scientist* 56: 92–96.
Yosef, R. and Lohrer, F.E. 1995. Loggerhead Shrikes, red fire ants and red herrings? *Condor* 97: 1053–1056.
Yosef, R. and Pinshow, B. 1988a. Nestling transfer in the Northern Shrike (*Lanius excubitor*). *Auk* 105: 580–581.
Yosef, R. and Pinshow, B. 1988b. Polygyny in the Northern Shrike (*Lanius excubitor*) in Israel. *Auk* 105: 581–582.
Yosef, R. and Pinshow, B. 1995. Parallel versus serial breeding strategies in the Great Grey Shrike at Sede Boqer, Israel. In Yosef, R., and Lohrer, F.E. (eds.) Shrikes (Laniidae) of the World: Biology and Conservation. *Proc. Western Found. Vert. Zool.* 6: 251–253.
Young, C.G. 1946. Notes on some birds of the Cameroon Mountain district. *Ibis* 88: 348–382.
Zack, S. 1986a. Breeding biology and inter-territory movements in a Fiscal Shrike population in Kenya. *Ostrich* 57: 65–74.
Zack, S. 1986b. Behaviour and breeding biology of the cooperatively breeding Grey-backed Fiscal Shrike *Lanius excubitorius* in Kenya. *Ibis* 128: 214–233.
Zack, S. 1995. Cooperative breeding in *Lanius* shrikes III: a reply in hindsight to Zack and Ligon I, II (1985). In Yosef, R., and Lohrer, F.E. (eds.) Shrikes (Laniidae) of the World: Biology and Conservation. *Proc. Western Found. Vert. Zool.* 6: 34–36
Zack, S. and Ligon, J.D. 1985a. Cooperative breeding in *Lanius* shrikes, I. Habitat and demography of two sympatric species. *Auk* 102: 754–765.
Zack, S. and Ligon, J.D. 1985b. Cooperative breeding in *Lanius* shrikes, II. Maintenance of group living in a nonsaturated habitat. *Auk* 102: 766–773.
Zedlitz, O. 1915. Das Sud-Somaliland als zoogeographisches Gebiet. *J. Orn.* 63: 1–69.
Zheng Guang-mei and Wang Xiang-ting 1985. On the intraspecific categories of Bull-headed Shrike (*Lanius bucephalus*) Temminck and Schlegel. *J. Beijing Norm. Univ.* (*Nat. Sci. Ed.*) 3: 75–79. (In Chinese.)
Zimmer, F. 1939. *Chlorophoneus nigrifrons nigrifrons* Rchw. = *Chlorophoneus rubiginosus munzneri* Rchw. *Orn. Mber.* 47: 46–48
Zimmerman, D.A. 1955. Notes on field identification and comparative behavior of shrikes in winter. *Wilson Bull.* 67: 200–208.
Zimmerman, D.A. 1972. The avaifauna of the Kakamega Forest, western Kenya, including a bird population study. *Bull. Amer. Mus. Nat. Hist.* 149: 259–339.
Zimmerman, D.A. 1998. Review of *Birds of Africa*, Vol. 5. *Auk* 115: 809–811.
Zimmerman, D.A., Turner, D.A. and Pearson, D.J. 1996. *Birds of Kenya and Northern Tanzania.* Christopher Helm, London.
Zink, R.M. 1997. Species concepts. *Bull. Brit. Orn. Club* 117: 97–107.
Zumpt, F. 1961 (ed). *The Arthropod Parasites of vertebrates in Africa South of the Sahara.* Vol.1. South African Institute for Medical Research No. 1.

APPENDIX A: PROBLEMS OF SPECIES LIMITS AND RELATIONSHIPS IN LANIIDAE and MALACONOTIDAE

(Refer to communication summaries, species text and Appendix B for comparative characters)

Eurocephalus

a) Confirm relationship within family and superfamily.
b) Confirm species limits of *anguitimens* and *rueppelli*.

Corvinella

a) Confirm relationship within family and superfamily.

Lanius

a) Confirm relationship within family and superfamily.
b) Confirm relationship of Lesser Grey Shrike *L. minor* within genus. Traditionally thought to form a superspecies with Long-tailed Shrike *L. schach* on plumage and broad tail feathers. Also related to Long-tailed Fiscal *L. cabanisi* and Grey-backed Fiscal *L. excubitoroides* on similar characters[180, 185, 185, 229, 481]. Known to hybridise with Red-backed Shrike *L. collurio*, with some calls being similar[373, 379]. Shares some communication characters with Woodchat *L. senator*, Long-tailed and Bay-back Shrike *L. vittatus*. Chattering alarm call is unlike other grey shrikes[600], except possibly Mackinnon's Fiscal *L. mackinnoni* . Vocal analysis confirms apparent relationship to Woodchat/Bay-backed/Long-tailed Shrike assemblage.
c) Confirm relationship of Woodchat Shrike within genus. Traditionally placed with Lesser Grey Shrike and Masked Shrike *L. nubicus*. Other suggestions include a relationship to Common Fiscal *L. collaris* or São Tomé Fiscal *L. newtoni* or Bull-headed Shrike *L. bucephalus*[165, 229, 257]. However, its courtship display is very different to Bull-headed Shrike and Common Fiscal[229, 284, 285, 929]. Known to hybridise with Red-backed Shrike[374]. DNA characters do not resolve its position[184]. Communication characters suggest a relationship with Lesser Grey Shrike[600]. Within *Lanius* it has a unique threat and courtship head-nodding display and head-back appeasement display. Vocal analysis suggests a relationship to Lesser Grey/Bay-backed/Long-tailed Shrike assemblage.
d) Confirm relationships within Long-tailed Shrike *L. schach* complex: Long-tailed *L. schach*, Grey-backed *L. tephronotus* and Philippine Shrike *L. validirostris*. Thought to form a superspecies, and have sometimes been considered conspecific[391, 496]. Hybridisation has not been reported between Grey-backed and Long-tailed, although *L. t. lahulensis* suggested as a hybrid *L. s. erythronotus* x *L. t. tephronotus*[284, 491, 496]. Grey-backed race *lahulensis* and Philippine Shrike have a different juvenile plumage to Long- tailed Shrike, as well as a shorter brown, not black, tail and heavier bill. Regional migratory habits and apparent lack of brood parasites of Grey-backed Shrike, compared to Long-tailed *L. s. erythronotus*[224], strengthens its specific status. This complex is thought to be closely related to the Isabelline Shrike *L. isabellinus* group[284, 600]. A close relationship with some long-tailed African shrikes and Lesser Grey Shrike has also been suggested (see b)[180, 229]. Vocal analysis confirms its apparent relationship to Lesser Grey and Bay-backed assemblage.
e) Confirm relationship of Bay-backed and Burmese Shrike *L. collurioides* complex. Thought to form a superspecies, but little is known of the apparently gregarious Burmese Shrike[284]. Bay-backed traditionally placed close to Red-backed Shrike on colouration, while one study suggests a closer relationship to Brown Shrike *L. cristatus*. Some aspects of courtship and flight displays show similarities to these species. However, mating displays, calls, nest display and nest are different. Bay-backed calls have a distinctive nasal quality. Its high-intensity territorial flight display resembles Lesser Grey Shrike, a species which is known to have approached Bay-backed Shrike, apparently in courtship[214, 284, 600, 675, 727]. Probably most closely related to the Long-tailed Shrike complex[284, 600], as suggested by vocal analysis.
f) Confirm relationships of Eurasian brown shrike complex: Red-backed, Isabelline, Brown, Thick-billed *L. tigrinus* and Bull-headed Shrike *L. bucephalus*. Relationships between Red-backed, Isabelline and Brown Shrike traditionally controversial, with little consensus on species limits[3, 16, 157, 180, 184, 185, 206, 211, 214, 229, 257, 484, 727]. Hybrids known between Red-backed and Isabelline, and between Brown and Isabelline. Brown also occasionally hybridises with Thick-billed Shrike. Red-backed known to hybridise with Lesser Grey[365, 374, 1052]. Behavioural characters, including different departure times and non-breeding areas, suggest they are distinct species. The group should probably include the Turkestan Red-backed Shrike *L. i. phoenicuroides*, traditionally a race of Isabelline Shrike, as some calls of *L. i. speculigerus* are not given by this shrike[284, 600]. The Brown Shrike shares a number of behavioural characters with the Thick-billed and Bull-headed Shrike[284, 323, 600, 691]. Brown Shrike males are known to courtship feed and nest build with female Thick-billed Shrikes. Vocal analysis confirms relationships of some brown shrikes, but suggests Red-backed and Isabelline Shrikes (and presumably *phoenicuroides*) are more similar vocally than either is to Emin's Shrike *L. gubernator*.
g) Confirm relationships of African brown shrike complex: Souza's *L. souzae* and Emin's Shrike. Both little known; Emin's virtually unknown. Some authors consider they form a superspecies with other brown shrikes or on their own[180, 481]. Based on plumage, Souza's has been suggested as related to Thick-billed Shrike[229]. This is not supported on communication or other behavioural characters. Both African brown shrikes are remarkably quiet species, and both appear to show low levels of gregariousness. In addition, Souza's incorporates an unusual amount of spider web and camouflage into its nest. Eggs and nest apparently resemble Mackinnon's Fiscal *L. mackinnoni*[236]. Vocal analysis suggests Souza's and Emin's are more similar than either is to Eurasian brown shrikes.
h) Confirm relationships of northern hemisphere grey shrike complex: Great Grey *L. excubitor*, Southern Grey *L. meridionalis*, Chinese Grey *L. sphenocercus* and Loggerhead Shrike *L. ludovicianus*. Believed to form a superspecies, and sometimes considered to include a number of African shrikes[165, 180, 229, 329, 384, 651]. Hybridisation unknown[257]. DNA confirms the close relationship of most species[184]. However, studies on base-sequencing in mitochondrial DNA suggest Loggerhead Shrike is closer to the Southern Grey Shrike than it is to the Great Grey Shrikes, as would be expected[675]. Surprisingly, communication behaviour of Loggerhead Shrike is relatively poorly known[255, 1054]. This aspect of the Chinese Grey Shrike is also poorly known, although its ecology, behaviour and calls are believed to be similar to

the Southern Grey Shrike, race *pallidirostris*[214, 284]. Recent separation of *meridionalis* from *excubitor*, mainly on the basis of ecological and morphological characters, provides an ideal case study for comparing mate recognition systems, particularly since the Great Grey Shrike is reasonably well known[257, 329, 381, 397, 462, 536, 666, 737, 789, 947]. Both species are thought to have been derived from a more tropical grey shrike[789]. Within the Southern Grey group, the race *pallidirostris*, or 'Steppe Grey Shrike,' deserves greater attention, as its communication system differs from the nominate species by apparently lacking a flight display, and having a harsh double-noted territorial call. The double call note is also absent in the race *lahtora*[284, 285, 462, 521, 600, 1039].

i) Confirm relationship of Masked Shrike *L. nubicus* within genus. Little known, and has been suggested that it may not even be a *Lanius* shrike[186]. However, it is usually thought to be related to some brown shrikes, including Red-backed, Isabelline and Brown[180]. DNA characters suggest a closer relationship to the Holarctic grey shrike complex (see h)[184]. Although communication behaviour is poorly known, communication characters suggest it may be related to some African fiscal shrikes, such as São Tomé Fiscal.
j) Confirm relationships within African fiscal shrike complex: Common *L. collaris*, Taita *L. dorsalis*, and Somali Fiscal *L. somalicus*, Mackinnon's Fiscal *L. mackinnoni*, Long-tailed *L. cabanisi* and Grey-backed Fiscal *L. excubitoroides*. Traditionally considered to form a superspecies made up of cooperative breeding Grey-backed and Long-tailed Fiscals, and a species group made up of the rest of the species, as well as the Holarctic grey shrikes[180, 481, 671]. Alternatively, Common, Taita and Somali Fiscals have been placed in a superspecies, from which Mackinnon's Fiscal is excluded[481]. The two cooperative species have similar displays which resemble those found in the genus *Corvinella*[155, 205, 357, 896]. It has been suggested that cooperative breeding is primitive character in *Lanius*[896]. However, these similarities may equally be due to convergence, thus masking their true relationships[500]. Both species have long tails with broad feathers, a character found in the Lesser Grey and Long-tailed Shrikes[180]. Taita and Somali Fiscals share morphological and communication characters, particularly a whistled phrase not found in other fiscals, with the possible exception of Mackinnon's Fiscal. This shrike also has long whistles apparently similar to those found in the East African Common Fiscal. It may also have a chattering alarm call. Communication behaviour of the Common Fiscal shows at least two distinct populations, *collaris* in southern Africa, and *humeralis* in East Africa. This is supported by some morphological characters[568]. Little is known about the West African population (*smithii*), which may prove to be allied to the East African population[205, 929]. The recent elevation of the race *marwitzi* to species status[675], is not supported. It shows widespread integration with the adjacent race *capelli* and lacks any distinctive behavioural or morphological characters. Vocal analysis suggests the assemblage forms two groups, comprising the mainly grey, black and white fiscals, and the mainly black and white fiscals. The relationships of Mackinnon's Fiscal, Masked Shrike and São Tomé Fiscal remain uncertain.
k) Confirm relationship of São Tomé Fiscal *L. newtoni* within genus. Little known, traditionally considered either a race of the Common Fiscal *L. collaris*[3, 16, 180, 431], or a distinct species[184, 206, 675]. Vocal analysis supports the view that it is a distinct species, which is here thought to be most similar in vocalisations to the Masked Shrike, both apparently being related to the Common Fiscal assemblage. Requires urgent study in view of its critical conservation status.

Malaconotus

a) Confirm relationship within family.
b) Grey-headed Bush-shrike *M. blanchoti*. Scientific name may require revision, as *Lanius major* (Wilkes 1812) predates current name[840].
c) Confirm relationship of Green-breasted Bush-shrike *M. gladiator* within genus. Virtually unknown. Vocalisations similar to Monteiro's *M. monteiri* and Grey-headed Bush-shrike.
d) Confirm species limits of separate populations and relationships of Lagden's Bush-shrike *M. lagdeni* within genus. Vocal differences suspected in separate populations[431, 501, 515]. Vocal analysis suggests close relationship to Fiery-breasted Bush-shrike.
e) Confirm species limits of Monteiro's Bush-shrike *M. monteiri* and relationship to Grey-headed and Green-breasted Bush-shrike *M. gladiator*. Nominate Angolan population virtually unknown. Cameroon population is thought to be *M. m. perspicillatus*[121, 431].
f) Confirm relationship of Uluguru Bush-shrike *M.? alius* within genus. Virtually unknown. Vocalisations do not support inclusion in this genus; possibly related to Madagascan vangas.

Chlorophoneus

a) Confirm relationship within family.
b) Confirm species limits of Black-fronted Bush-shrike *C. nigrifrons* and Many-coloured Bush-shrike *C. multicolor*.
c) Confirm species limits of Gorgeous Bush-shrike *C. quadricolor* and Perrin's Bush-shrike *C. viridis*. Calls of female *viridis* unknown and may prove decisive.
d) Confirm relationship of Mount Kupé Bush-shrike *C.? kupeensis* within genus and family. Note critical conservation status. Some calls reminiscent of flycatcher-shrikes, others of vangas[500].

Telophorus

a) Confirm relationship within family, particularly to *Chlorophoneus*, *Tchagra* and *Rhodophoneus*.

Rhodophoneus

a) Confirm relationship within family, particularly to *Telophorus*, *Chlorophoneus* and *Tchagra*.
b) Confirm species limits of race *cathemagmena*, particularly since both sexes have a black gorget, which is only present in ♀♀ of other races. Apparently it does not intergrade with *hilgerti*[237].

Tchagra

a) Confirm relationship to *Telophorus*, *Rhodophoneus* and *Antichromus*.

Antichromus

a) Confirm relationship to *Tchagra*, *Laniarius* and *Dryoscopus*.
b) Confirm species limits of *minuta* and *anchietae*[24, 180, 291, 431]. Recent elevation to species level, based on apparent lack of integration, is not supported[184]. Here retained as conspecific, based mainly on similar whistled calls.

Laniarius

a) Confirm relationship within family.
b) Confirm relationship of Tropical *L. aethiopicus*, Southern *L. ferrugineus* and Swamp Boubou *L. bicolor*. Their specific status has been questioned, with Tropical Boubou sometimes considered a sibling species of Swamp Boubou[145, 565]. Some authors continue to express doubt as to their status[207]. However, where they overlap they are ecologically segregated, and their communication behaviour is distinct[205]. Based on communication characters they are considered distinct, in spite of suspected hybridisation in overlap areas[48, 108, 109, 138, 205, 548, 550].
c) Confirm species limits of small *savensis* race of Southern Boubou[538], and dark *sublacteus* race of Tropical Boubou.
d) Confirm relationship of Slate-coloured Boubou *L. funebris* within genus. Originally placed in superspecies with other all-black boubous, but now recognised as being too divergent[180, 481]. Differs from them in adult plumage colour, presence of concealed white spots on rump, fewer or no bristles on the nape, barred juvenile plumage, smaller body size, finer bill, ecology and communication behaviour. Here thought to be more closely related to the black and white boubous.
e) Confirm relationship of Sooty Boubou *L. leucorhynchus* within genus. Traditionally thought to form a superspecies with other all-black boubous[180, 481, 493]. Unique in the genus in that immature has an ivory-coloured bill[180, 290]. Little known, but main duet calls are remarkably similar to some black and white boubous. Anatomical, behavioural and ecological characters suggest it is closely related to the black and white boubous. Note occurrence of an all-black form of the Tropical Boubou *L. aethiopicus* in East Africa.
f) Confirm species limits of Mountain Sooty Boubou *L. poensis* and Fülleborn's Black Boubou *L. fuelleborni*. They are either considered conspecific[3, 206, 431, 481, 533], or separate species[16, 180, 207, 336, 338, 610]. Situation complex as Mountain Sooty Boubou occurs in two widely separated populations which show variation in plumage colouration and vocalisations. Juvenile plumage suggested as different[180]. However, apparently much geographical variation in immature and adult plumages[533]. Here retained as separate species based on differences in calls. Note *poensis* shows marked geographical variation in calls, while *fuelleborni* is remarkably consistent[515, 892].
g) Confirm relationship of Yellow-breasted Boubou *L. atroflavus* within genus. Shares plumage and vocal characteristics with the crimson-breasted gonoleks and black boubous, particularly Mountain Sooty Boubou. Plumage and communication characters suggest a closer relationship to crimson gonolek group (see h).
h) Confirm species limits in crimson gonoleks: Crimson-breasted *L. atrococcineus*, Black-headed *L. erythrogaster*, Yellow-crowned *L. barbarus* and Papyrus Gonolek *L. mufumbiri*. Yellow-crowned has been considered conspecific with Black-headed, presumably because the latter may sometimes show a few yellow feathers on the crown. However, they do not integrate. Black-headed Gonolek has also been suggested as being conspecific with Crimson-breasted. This is not supported, in spite of field playback evidence, where Crimson-breasted responded positively to calls of Black-headed[431] (see Introduction – Shrike Communication). All three species share similar whip-lash whistled calls and duetting behaviour[3, 180, 289, 431, 530, 540]. They are here retained as separate species on the basis of different plumage and communication behaviour, particularly female vocalisations. The little known *helenae* race of Yellow-crowned Gonolek may prove to be specifically distinct[207].
i) Confirm relationship of Lühder's Bush-shrike within genus. Some consider the Papyrus Gonolek to be its closest relative, but Lühder's is vocally and morphologically distinct[481]. Traditionally throught to form part of a species group comprising the crimson gonoleks and Red-naped Bush-shrike *L. ruficeps*. However, its communication behaviour shows greater similarities with the black and white boubous[500, 529, 540]. The specimen named *Laniarius dubiosus* (Reichenow 1899) has recently been found to be a juvenile of the western race of Lühder's Bush-shrike[680].
j) Confirm species limits of races *brauni* and *amboimensis* of Lühder's Bush-shrike. They are sometimes considered incipient species, but have also recently been elevated to species status (Braun's and Amboim or Gabela Bush-shrike). This decision appears to have been made without new information[180, 184, 431]. Consequently, here retained as races of Lühder's Bush-shrike.
k) Confirm relationship of Red-naped Bush-shrike *L. ruficeps* within genus. Traditionally considered closely related to Lühder's Bush-shrike and a member of the species group comprising the crimson gonoleks[180], but not supported by some authors[481]. A DNA study suggests a closer relationship with the black and white boubou group[542]. Communication behaviour suggests it is closely related to Lühder's Bush-shrike.
l) Bulo Burti Boubou *L. liberatus*. as already indicated, the validity of this species is controversial[479, 543, 631, 862, 863]. Had the molecular study not been made, it would probably have been considered a hybrid, particularly in view of its similarity to the smaller Red-naped Bush-shrike in general coloration and bill shape. Its occurrence between two subspecies of *ruficeps* in central Somalia supports this view[859]. However, the DNA model rejects hybridisation because its DNA pair-base sequence is as distinct as other currently recognised species used in the comparison. However, Slate-coloured Boubou was not compared. The model suggests Bulo Burti Boubou is more closely related to the black and white boubou group[542]. It should be noted that a few Black-headed Gonoleks are also characterised by having the crown spotted yellow. The suggestion that the formerly named *Laniarius dubiosus* (Reichenow 1899) may have been a juvenile form of the Bulo Burti Boubou is not supported based on DNA analysis of cytochrome b[680]. Clearly, further evidence is required; it is included here because it is central to the wider unresolved issue of species limits and their definition.

Dryoscopus

a) Confirm relationship within family.
b) Confirm status of race *affinis* of Black-backed Puffback *D. cubla*. It is strikingly similar to Black-shouldered Puffback *D. senegalensis*. Possibly vocally distinct from Black-backed[631].

c) Confirm relationship of Pringle's Puffback *D. pringlii* within genus. Thought by some to form a superspecies with Black-backed, Northern *D. gambensis* and Black-shouldered[180]. However, others exclude it on the basis of its morphological differences and sympatry with both Northern and Black-backed Puffback[481]. Plumage similarity suggests a close relationship to Northern, but its communication behaviour appears more like Black-backed and Black-shouldered Puffback.

d) Confirm relationship of Pink-footed Puffback *D. angolensis* within genus, particularly since it exhibits a number of unique characters (brown eye and flesh-coloured legs). Communication behaviour suggests its closest relative is Sabine's Puffback *D. sabini*.

e) Confirm relationship of Sabine's Puffback within genus. Earlier placed in the genus *Chaunonotus* on account of its unusually large, conical bill, which lacks a distinct culmen[34, 202, 338, 610]. Recent authors tend to combine it with all other puffbacks in *Dryoscopus*[3, 16, 206, 207, 431]. Communication behaviour suggests its closest relative is the Pink-footed Puffback.

Nilaus

a) Confirm relationship within family.

b) Confirm species limits of races *nigritemporalis* and *affinis*. Both apparently restricted to *Brachystegia* belt separating northern and southern populations. Interbreeding known to occur[180]. The trilling call does not appear to show any obvious differences to the southern race *brubru*[500].

Lanioturdus

a) Confirm relationships within family[205, 490, 676].

Tephrodornis

a) Confirm relationship within family, particularly to *Prionops*[184].

Philentoma

a) Confirm relationship with family. Virtually unknown[184].

Bias

a) Confirm relationship to *Megabyas* and within family. Little known[634, 676].

Megabyas

a) Confirm relationship to *Bias* and within family. Little known[634, 676].

Batis

a) Confirm relationship within family[184, 205, 490, 634, 676].

b) Confirm relationship of Chinspot Batis *B. molitor* to Black-headed Batis *B. minor*. Vocal analysis suggest they are each other's closest relatives. Both have a short descending 3-note phrase and a longer constant-pitch series, as well as similar ♀ calls[500, 717]. Juvenile plumage appears similar, with breast-band chestnut in juvenile and immature dress. This differs from Senegal *B. senegalensis*, Grey-headed *B. orientalis* and Pririt *B. pririt*, which have a blackish breast-band in juvenile plumage followed by chestnut in immature dress. Juvenile plumage remains unknown for the other savanna species[676]. Vocal analysis suggests savanna woodland batises are more closely related to the mainly western forest batises than to the mainly eastern forest batises[180, 500].

c) Confirm relationship of Black-headed Batis to Grey-headed Batis. It is extremely difficult to separate these two species on plumage, even in the hand[631, 286]. Vocalisations of Grey-headed suggest it is intermediate between the groups formed by the Black-headed and Chinspot and by the Senegal, Grey-headed, Pygmy *B. perkeo*, Mozambique *B. soror* and Pririt Batis. Juvenile plumage suggests closer related to the latter group (see b).

d) Confirm relationship of Senegal Batis to other savanna woodland batises. A more distinct savanna species, with di- and trisyllabic notes, sometimes with a distinctive initial buzzy quality to phrases. Calls show some relationship to Grey-headed Batis and Bioko Batis *B. poensis*, with which it shares the initial buzzy quality. Distinctive vocalisations are supported by a mathematical analysis of plumage characters, which places it as independently distant from other savanna woodland batises[286]. Juvenile plumage characters are similar to the group formed by Grey-headed and Pririt Batis (see b). Plumage and vocal characters suggest it is most closely related to the group formed by Grey-headed, Mozambique, Pririt and Pygmy Batis.

f) Confirm relationship of Pririt Batis within genus. Vocal analysis suggests it is most closely related to Mozambique Batis, a finding supported by a mathematical analysis of plumage characters[286]. Note juvenile plumage (see b)[137, 676].

g) Confirm relationship of Mozambique Batis within genus. Vocal analysis suggests it is closely related to Pririt (see f). This is supported by a mathematical analysis of plumage characters[286]. Juvenile plumage unknown (see b).

h) Confirm relationship of Pygmy Batis within genus. Generally ecologically segregated from Black-headed, Grey-headed, Mozambique and Chinspot Batis. However, apparently shows some overlap with Grey-headed in Ethiopia[558]. On plumage, traditionally linked to Mozambique[18], presumably due to the buffy wash on sides of throat. However, a mathematical analysis of plumage characters suggests it is independently distant from other savanna woodland batises[286]. Vocally poorly known, although a preliminary analysis suggests it is closely related to either Black-headed or Mozambique Batis. Juvenile plumage unknown (see b).

i) Confirm relationship of Angola Batis *B. minulla* within genus. Range overlaps Black-headed and Chinspot. It has been placed either in a superspecies with Bioko, Gabon *B. minima*, Ituri *B. iturensis* and Black-headed[180], or as independently distant, with Bioko Batis likewise, and Gabon and Ituri forming a superspecies[676]. It has also been suggested that it may be more closely related to Bioko Batis[402]. Its whistle calls resemble a number of savanna woodland and western forest batises. However, it apparently lacks the buzzy introductory notes found in Gabon, Bioko and Senegal Batis, which may suggest a more distant relationship. This is supported by a mathematical analysis of plumage characters[287]. Here thought to be closely related to the western forest batises, but tentatively retained as independently distant from these, awaiting additional information.

j) Confirm relationship and species limits of Gabon Batis. Range overlaps Bioko Batis, with which it was originally considered conspecific[18]. Also sometimes considered conspecific with Ituri Batis[180, 715]. However since ♀ and immatures of Gabon and Ituri Batis are distinct[464], they have recently been retained as separate species (see i). Calls appear identical to Bioko Batis, and both species respond to the playback of each other's calls[515].

k) Confirm relationship of Bioko Batis to mainland race *occulta*. They are either split into two species; *B. poensis* and *B. occulta*)[207, 287, 581], or conspecific as *B. poensis*[180, 206, 259, 431, 676, 715]. Here tentatively retained as conspecific because Bioko population is virtually unknown, and problems with some plumage characters used originally to differentiate the two species[431, 715]. Note relationships to Gabon Batis (see j).

l) Confirm relationships of Ituri Batis. Virtually unknown. Thought to be conspecific with Gabon Batis before the ♀ of latter was described[180, 464]. Also considered conspecific, or as an allospecies with Bioko Batis[431, 715]. Calls are unknown but predicted to be similar to other western forest and northern savanna batises[500].

m) Confirm relationships of Cape Batis *B. capensis*, Forest Batis *B. mixta* and the races *dimorpha* and *reichenowi*. Forest Batis, although having a separate range, has been considered a race of *capensis*[3, 86, 119, 145, 459], or as a distinct species[180, 287, 431, 448, 481]. Similarly *dimorpha* has been considered a race of Forest Batis[116, 287], as an independent species[207], or as a race of *capensis*[3, 85, 119, 145, 287, 291, 448, 481, 676]. The relationship of the allopatric *reichenowi* is similarly unresolved, being sometimes considered a race of Forest Batis[3, 204, 206, 633], a race of Cape Batis[431, 676], or a separate species[204, 207, 287]. On vocal evidence Cape and Forest Batis are separate species. Forest Batis does not respond to Cape Batis calls[448]. Similarly, *dimorpha* is a race of Cape Batis, not of Forest Batis[448, 500]. However, in the absence of vocal evidence, *reichenowi* is retained as a race of Cape Batis for convenience. A statement, that it is closely related to Cape Batis on vocal grounds is erroneous[515, 676].

n) Confirm relationships of the mainly eastern forest species: Cape, Forest, Woodwards' *B. fratrum*, Margaret's Batis *B. margaritae* and Ruwenzori Batis *B. diops*. Traditionally united in a superspecies[180, 430, 481, 676], and evidently related on basis of ecology, plumage (particularly white underwing-coverts, rufous wing-stripe in all ♀♀ and some ♂♂ and reddish eye) and behaviour (especially low-pitched whistles and stone-rubbing or chuntering calls). Cape, Forest, Woodwards' and Margarets' Batis are closely related, with Ruwenzori Batis independently distant. Cape Batis appears most closely related to Forest and Woodwards' Batis. This is not supported by a mathematical analysis of only plumage characters, which also suggests that Ruwenzori and Margaret's are closely related[287]. In playback trials, Cape never responded to Forest Batis calls, or visa versa[448, 515], but Margaret's Batis does react to calls of northern Cape Batis[515]. Communication characters suggest Forest Batis is closer to Woodwards' Batis[448, 515]. Margaret's Batis is more closely related to Cape, Forest and Woodwards', particularly on ♀ calls. Communication characters, particularly ♀ calls, suggest Woodward's Batis is closely related to Forest Batis[448, 500], but mathematical analysis of plumage characters places it as independently distant from other eastern forest batises[287, 413].

o) Confirm relationships of Ruwenzori Batis within genus. Several characters suggest it is intermediate between eastern and western forest batises. Its whistle and chuntering calls are similar to the eastern forest batises, but its short sharp *wik* or *zik* calls appear more similar to those given by western forest and savanna woodland batises. Some plumage characteristics also suggest a link to these batises, particularly western forest species. In Ruwnzori Batis, only ♂ eye is yellow, ♀ is reddish like other eastern forest batises. Consequently, in spite of sharing characters common to both forest groups, it is placed in eastern group on the following characters: plaintive low-pitched whistle notes and stone-rubbing (chuntering) calls, white underwing-coverts, orange-red eye in ♀, and evergreen forest habitat.

Dyaphorophyia

a) Confirm relationships of genus within family[184, 634, 676].

b) Confirm species limits of Jameson's *D. jamesoni* and Red-cheeked Wattle-eye *D. blissetti* and their relationship to Black-necked Wattle-eye *D. chalybea*. First two species little known; sometimes considered conspecific with Black-necked[3, 16, 289], as distinct species[116, 431, 481, 610], or allospecies[207]. Here retained as separate species for convenience, requiring additional information.

Platysteira

a) Confirm relationship of genus within family[184, 205, 634, 676].

b) Confirm species limits of little known Banded Wattle-eye *P. laticincta*. Considered by some to be conspecific with Black-throated Wattle-eye *P. peltata*[3, 16, 180, 338, 431, 481, 676], while others retain it as a separate species[116, 610]. Here tentatively retained as a separate species awaiting additional information.

c) Confirm specific status of virtually unknown White-fronted Wattle-eye *P. albifrons*. Earlier believed to be conspecific with Brown-throated Wattle-eye *P. cyanea*[22, 289, 338].

Prionops

a) Confirm relationship within family.

b) Confirm relationships within *Prionops*, particularly with the red-billed species, which were formally placed in *Sigmodus*. Jaw musculature and nestling plumage suggest they are separate[683, 897]. In addition, begging calls appear more complex in White Helmet-shrikes *P. plumata* compared with Retz's or Chestnut Helmet-shrike *P. scopifrons*[500].

c) Confirm relationship of race *rufiventris* of Chestnut-bellied Helmet-shrike *P. caniceps*. Sometimes given specific status[207], others believe it is conspecific[3, 16, 206, 431]. Differences in plumage and distribution suggest allospecies status; also sometimes treated as incipient species[180]. Here retained as conspecific based on vocal analysis.

d) Confirm species limits and relationship of virtually unknown Gabela Helmet-shrike *P. gabela* to Retz's Helmet-shrike.

e) Confirm relationship of Grey-crested Helmet-shrike *P. poliolopha* to White Helmet-shrike.

f) Confirm relationship of Yellow-crested Helmet-shrike *P. alberti* within genus.

APPENDIX B: COMPARATIVE CHARACTERS

CHARACTER followed by GENUS/SPECIES

MORPHOLOGY — osteology

1. Maxillo-palatines[899] — *Lanius, Laniarius, Dryoscopus.* 2. Pterygoid[898, 899] —*Prionops, Laniinae, Malaconotinae.* 3. Palatine process of pre-maxilla fused[500, 898, 900] — *Lanius, Eurocephalus, Corvinella, Malaconotus, Chlorophoneus, Telophorus, Tchagra, Dryoscopus, Laniarius, Nilaus, Tephrodornis, Lanioturdus, Batis, Platysteira, Prionops.* 4. Humeral fossa[500, 894, 918, 919, 920] — a. single: *Lanius, Lanioturdus.* b. tends towards double: some *Prionops, Batis, Platysteira.* 5. Paired foramen on post-orbital wall present[500, 901] — *Eurocephalus, Lanius, Corvinella, Malaconotus, Chlorophoneus, Laniarius, Telophorus, Dryoscopus, Tchagra, Lanioturdus, Nilaus, Batis, Platysteira, Prionops.* 6. Process D of carpometacarpus absent[500, 659, 901] — *Lanius, Eurocephalus, Corvinella, Prionops, Malaconotus, Chlorophoneus, Telophorus, Laniarius, Lanioturdus, Tchagra, Dryoscopus, Nilaus, Batis, Platysteira, Dyaphorophyia, Tephrodornis.* 7. Ectethmoid foramen[500, 897, 899] — a. single: *Prionops Tephrodornis, Batis, Platysteira, Lanioturdus, Dyaphorophyia, Malaconotus, Chlorophoneus, Telophorus, Laniarius, Tchagra, Nilaus, Dryoscopus.* b. double: *Eurocephalus, Corvinella, Lanius.* 8. Ectethmoid plate with lachrymal[897, 898] — *Prionops* (including *Sigmodus*), *Tephrodornis, Batis, Platysteira, Lanioturdus, Dyaphorophyia.* 9. Post-orbital process[897] — *Laniidae, Malaconotidae.* 10. Nostril osteology[227] — *Eurocephalus, Prionops, Lanius.*

MORPHOLOGY — general

11. Wing and tail relationship[229, 536] — *Lanius.* 12. Lanceolate feathers[180] — *Corvinella.* 13. Pigment instability[289, 471, 596] — *Prionops plumatus, Dyaphorophyia chalybea, Lanius newtoni.* 14. Number of primaries[609, 1085] — *Eurocephalus, Prionops, Corvinella, Lanius, Malaconotus, Tchagra, Laniarius.* 15. Tarsal scutellation[573] — *Prionops, Eurocephalus, Nilaus* share similar pattern. 16. Sperm structure[902, 1080] — *Lanius.* 17. Toe fusion[118] — *Laniinae, Prionopinae, Chlorophoneus, Telophorus, Philentoma, Platysteirinae.* 18. Bill shape — a. shrike-like: all genera except those listed below. b. flycatcher-like: *Batis, Platysteira, Bias, Megabyas, Philentoma.* 19. Pterylosis[255, 302, 319] — *Lanius ludovicianus, Antichromus minuta, Tchagra senegala.* 20. Neossoptiles[27,153, 205, 255, 500] — a. present: *Lanius* (only abdominal, caudal and alar tracts represented), ?*Prionops*, occasional in *Tchagra, Telophorus.* b. absent: *Batis, Platysteira, Bias,* probably *Dyaphorophyia,* probably *Eurocephalus, Corvinella, Nilaus, Dryoscopus, Laniarius, ?Tchagra, Malaconotus, ?Prionops.* 21. Eggs (see species accounts)[19] 22. Mouth (tongue) spots[42, 205, 331, 500, 634] — a. present: *Chlorophoneus v. quadricolor, C. sulfureopectus, Dryoscopus, Laniarius, Rhodophoneus, Prionops* b. absent: *Lanius, Corvinella, Malaconotus blanchoti, Telophorus zeylonus, Tchagra, Lanioturdus, Batis, Platysteira,* predicted to be absent in *Bias.*

MORPHOLOGY— potential signal areas[205, 536]

23. Palate colour[205, 500] — a. black: *Tchagra, Dryoscopus, Laniarius, Batis, Malaconotus, Chlorophoneus Telophorus, Rhodophoneus, Antichromus, Nilaus, Lanioturdus.* b. flesh, orange or yellow: *Eurocephalus, Lanius, Corvinella, Chlorophoneus kupeensis, Prionops, Platysteira, ?Philentoma, ?Bias, ?Megabyas ?Dyaphorophyia.* 24. Wattle present — *Platysteira, Dyaphorophyia,* some *Prionops.* 25. Eye colour — a. purple ring: *Dryoscopus angolensis, Laniarius atrococcineus, Tchagra, Prionops caniceps, Platysteira peltata, Platysteira cyanea, Dyaphorophyia concreta, Batis diops.* b. yellow: some *Batis, Bias,* some *Malaconotus,* some *Prionops.* c. greenish: *Tephrodornis.* d. orange-red: some *Batis,* some *Dryoscopus, Megabyas,* some *Prionops.* e. red-brown: *Lanius collurioides, Chlorophoneus,* some *Laniarius,* some *Batis,* most *Dryoscopus, Antichromus, Philentoma, Nilaus,* some *Platysteira.* f. brown: *Eurocephalus, Corvinella,* some *Lanius, Dryoscopus angolensis, Malaconotus alius,* some *Tchagra, Telophorus,* some *Tephrodornis, Nilaus, Platysteira,* some *Dyaphorophyia.* g. grey-purple: some *Lanius,* some *Dyaphorophyia,* some *Laniarius,* some *Tchagra,* also *Telophorus,* some *Chlorophoneus,* some *Malaconotus.* 26. Eye colour sexual dimorphism — *Batis diops, B. margaritae.* 27. Leg colour — a. grey-black: all genera except the following. b. yellow: *Bias.* c. orange-red: *Prionops.* d. pink: *Dryoscopus angolensis.* 28. Bill colour — a. black to dark brown: all genera except some *Prionops.* b. reddish-orange: *Prionops scopifrons, P. retzii, P. gabela, P. caniceps.* 29. Flanks chestnut — *Lanius, Corvinella, Nilaus,* some *Batis.* 30. Plumage sexual dimorphism — a. present: some *Lanius*[469, 536], *Chlorophoneus, C. kupeensis, Rhodophoneus,* some *Laniarius, Dryoscopus, Antichromus, Telophorus, Bias, Megabyas, Philentoma, Nilaus,* most *Batis, Platysteira, Dyaphorophyia.* b. lacking: *Tchagra,* some *Laniarius,* some *Lanius, Lanioturdus,* a few *Batis, Malaconotus, Prionops, Eurocephalus.* 31. Underwing-coverts (black or white) — (see *Batis* plumage descriptions in species accounts.) 32. White patch in primaries — some *Corvinella,* some *Lanius,* some *Prionops, Bias, Lanioturdus.* 33. White wing-stripe — *Nilaus,* some *Laniarius,* some *Dryoscopus, Lanioturdus,* some *Prionops,* some *Platysteira,* most *Batis.* 34. White scapulars -most *Lanius,* some *Corvinella.* 35. Dark face mask — *Eurocephalus, Lanius, Tephrodornis, Batis, Chlorophoneus,* some *Laniarius, Tchagra, ?Nilaus, Lanioturdus.* 36. White throat patch — *Lanioturdus,* some *Batis,* some *Platysteira,* some *Dyaphorophyia,* some female *Rhodophoneus.* 37. Black breast-band — *Lanioturdus, Batis, Platysteira,* some *Dyaphorophyia, Telophorus,* some *Chlorophoneus, Rhodophoneus.* 38. White nuchal (nape) patch — *Batis, Nilaus, Lanioturdus, ?Eurocephalus.*

JUVENILE/IMMATURE — potential signal areas

Mouth (tongue) spots — see above. 39. Juv plumage, head spotted — *Tephrodornis, Batis, Platysteira, Bias.* 40. Juv breast-band, first black, then ♀-like — *Batis pririt, B. orientalis, B. senegalensis.* 41. Juv plumage, barred — *Eurocephalus, Lanius, Chlorophoneus, Telophorus, Laniarius, Dryoscopus, Tephrodornis, Nilaus, Dyaphorophyia, Prionops.* 42. Juv eye colour brown, different from adult — *Malaconotus, Chlorophoneus,* some *Laniarius, Dryoscopus, Tephrodornis, Prionops, Lanioturdus, Batis, Philentoma, Nilaus.* 43. Buff-tipped primary wing-coverts — most genera.

ANATOMY

44. Syrinx — generalised[87], see also[1081] — *Batis, Platysteira, Dyaphorophyia, Tephrodornis.* 45. Jaw muscles described[199, 897, 898, 899] — *Lanius, Corvinella, Tephrodornis, Prionops, Dyaphorophyia, Platysteira, Batis, Lanioturdus, Dryoscopus, Laniarius, Tchagra, Malaconotus.* 46. Moult[253, 323, 436, 656, 691, 786] — a. single annual: apparently all genera except some *Lanius.* b. double annual: *Lanius cristatus, L. tigrinus.* Hind limb muscles (see below)[475, 642, 918] — 47. M. iliotibialis lateralis*Prionops, Eurocephalus.* 48. M. iliofemoralis externus — a. present: *Telophorus zeylonus, Chlorophoneus dohertyi.* b. absent: *Chlorophoneus sulfureopectus, C.dohertyi, Telophorus zeylonus, Laniarius ferrugineus, Tchagra senegala, Dryoscopus cubla, D. sabini, Lanius vittatus, L. collurio, L. cristatus, Corvinella corvina, Eurocephalus anguitimens, E. rueppelli, Prionops plumatus, P. cristatus.* 49. M. obturatorius lateralis, Pars dorsalis — present in all species studied (see above). 50. M. gastrocnemis, Pars interna — Type I occurs in Laniinae, Malaconotinae, Type 3 in Prionopinae (*Prionops, Eurocephalus*). 51. M. tibialis cranialis — Prionopinae (*Prionops, Eurocephalus*). 52. M. peroneus longus — Prionopinae (*Prionops, Eurocephalus*). 53. Mm. flexor perforatus digiti III and flexor perforatus digiti IV — Laniidae. 54. M. flexor hallucis longus — Laniidae, *Eurocephalus, Prionops* and bush-shrikes. 55. M. flexor digitorium longus (femoral head) — *Lanius, Corvinella, Eurocephalus.* 56. Insertion pattern — a. ABB: *Nilaus, Dryoscopus sabini, D. cubla, Tchagra senegalensis, Laniarius ferrugineus, Telophorus sulfureopectus, T. zeylonus, T. dohertyi.* b. AAB: *Prionops plumata, Lanius collurio.* c. AAA: *Corvinella, Lanius cristatus, L. vittatus, Eurocephalus.* 57. M. extensor hallucis longus — Malaconotinae, *Lanius,* Prionopinae (*Prionops, Eurocephalus*), *Corvinella.* 58. M. flexor hallucis brevis — *Prionops, Eurocephalus*

BIOCHEMICAL

59. Incapable of L-ascorbic acid synthesis[154] — *Lanius schach, L. vittatus, L. excubitor* (probably *meridionalis*). 60. Serology studied[82, 894] — *Lanius.* 61. Egg-white protein[894] — *Chlorophoneus sulfureopectus, C. v. quadricolor, Lanius collaris, L. senator, L. collurio, Corvinella, Telophorus zeylonus, Nilaus, Laniarius atrococcineus, L. ferrugineus, Tchagra senegala, T. australis, Batis capensis.* 62. DNA-DNA hybridisation studied[184, 310] — *Eurocephalus rueppelli, E. anguitimens, Corvinella corvina, Lanius excubitor, L. ludovicianus, L. nubicus, L. collaris,*

L. collurio, L. minor, L. senator, L. tigrinus, Chlorophoneus olivaceus, C. sulfureopectus, C. v. quadricolor, Telophorus zeylonus, Nilaus, Laniarius barbarus, L. ferrugineus, Dryoscopus cubla, D. gambensis, Tchagra australis, T. senegala, Malaconotus cruentus, Platysteira cyanea, Dyaphorophyia castanea, Batis capensis, B. senegalensis, Philentoma velatum, P. pyrhopterum, Tephrodornis gularis, T. pondicerianus, Prionops plumatus, P. retzii. 63. Mitochondrial mtDNA cyt-b gene studied[542, 680, 903, 904] — *Malaconotus blanchoti, Chlorophoneus bocagei, Telophorus zeylonus, Laniarius barbarus, L. luehderi, L. ruficeps, L. liberatus, L. aethiopicus, L. turatii, L. atrococcineus, L. barbarus, Prionops plumatus, P. retzii.* 64. Karyotype described[177, 178, 284, 368, 782, 823, 1044, 1050, 1052] — *Lanius excubitor/meridionalis* (2n=62), *L. cristatus* (2n=72-76), *L. bucephalus* (2n=72), *L. minor* (2n=76), *L. collurio* (2n=76), *L. isabellinus* (*phoenicuroides*) (2n=76), *L. tigrinus* (2n=72-76), *L. vittatus* (2n=72), *L. schach* (*tricolor*) (2n=72), (*erythronotus*) (2n=76), *Tephrodornis pondicerianus* (2n=62).

BEHAVIOUR — general[284, 915, 1083]

65. Slow side-to-side swaying of head — *Lanius excubitor, L. senator, L. collurio, Tchagra, Malaconotus, Chlorophoneus kupeensis, Batis, Dyaphorophyia, Platysteira, Prionops, Bias.* 66. Body side-to-side swaying — *Lanius, Chlorophoneus, C. kupeensis, Batis.* 67. Body-bowing — *Corvinella, Lanius, Malaconotus, Chlorophoneus, C. kupeensis, Antichromus, Tchagra, Rhodophoneus, Nilaus, Prionops, Dryoscopus, Laniarius, Platysteira, Batis, Dyaphorophyia.* 68. Bill-raising *Lanius, Telophorus, ?Rhodophoneus, Malaconotus.* 69. Head-down display - *Lanius, Corvinella.* 70. Head bow *Lanius, Malaconotus, Chlorophoneus, Rhodophoneus.* 71.Head bobbing display — *Lanius senator.* 72. Crest-raising — *Lanius, Antichromus, Nilaus, Dyaphorophyia, Bias, Prionops.* 73. Tail-flicking — *Eurocephalus, Corvinella, Lanius excubitor, L. minor, L. collaris, L. isabellinus, L. collurio, Chlorophoneus, Laniarius, Antichromus, Tchagra.* 74. General tail side-to-side swinging — *Lanius, Nilaus, Batis, Platysteira.* 75. Unique tail side-to-side swinging — *Megabyas.* 76. Wings-up display[205, 500] — *Eurocephalus, Corvinella, ?Lanius excubitoroides, Batis.* 77. Wing-flicking — *Lanius, Chlorophoneus, C. kupeensis, Telophorus, Antichromus, Bias, Philentoma, Batis, Platysteira.* 77. Wing-shuffling — *Eurocephalus.* 79. Wing-drooping — most genera droop wings while begging; given in other contexts by *Eurocephalus, Corvinella, Chlorophoneus kupeensis, Rhodophoneus, Laniarius, Dryoscopus, Dyaphorophyia, Prionops.* 80. Outstretched wing-display — *Lanius, Rhodophoneus.* 81. Tail-fanning in display — *Lanius excubitoroides, L. excubitor, L. meridionalis, L. ludovicianus, L. minor, L. cabanisi, L. bucephalus, L. isabellinus, L. cristatus, L. collurio, Malaconotus blanchoti, Chlorophoneus olivaceus, C. kupeensis, Telophorus, Rhodophoneus, Laniarius, Dryoscopus cubla, Antichromus, Tchagra, Bias, Nilaus, Batis, Platysteira, Prionops, Eurocephalus.* 82. Body-bobbing while calling — *Chlorophoneus, Rhodophoneus, Telophorus, Laniarius.* 83. Non-breeding gatherings or 'parliaments' — *Lanius, Laniarius, Batis, Platysteira.* 84. Indirect head-scratching[205, 500, 1084] — apparently all genera. 85. Allopreening recorded — *Eurocephalus, Lanius, Laniarius, Prionops.* 86. Bathing by dipping into pond — *Philentoma, Bias.* 87. Roosting posture — a. head under scapulars: *Lanius.* b. head under wing: *Eurocephalus anguitimens, Prionops.*

BEHAVIOUR — courtship[915]

88. Tandem bouncing through vegetation — *Chlorophoneus, Laniarius, Dryoscopus.* 89. Display-flight *Eurocephalus, Lanius, Malaconotus, Tchagra, Laniarius, Dryoscopus, Batis, Antichromus, Lanioturdus, Bias, Nilaus, Platysteira, Dyaphorophyia, Prionops.* 90. Display-flight with wings in V — *Eurocephalus, Malaconotus.* 91. Bobbing and swooping display-flight — *Platysteira, Dyaphorophyia.* 92. Wing-up display — *Eurocephalus, Corvinella, Batis.* 93. Rump-fluffing — *Tchagra, Laniarius, Dryoscopus, ?Chlorophoneus, ?Malaconotus, Telophorus, Bias, Batis, Antichromus, Lanioturdus, Platysteira, Dyaphorophyia.* 94. Flicks tail up and down — *Batis, Antichromus.* 95. Head held up in display-flight — *Dryoscopus, Tchagra, Antichromus, Batis.* 96. ♂ high-pitched nest-building call — *Dryoscopus, Batis poensis, Dyaphorophyia.* 97. ♂ escorts ♀ during nest-building — *Dyaphorophyia, Dryoscopus, Bias.* 98. Courtship-feeding[1082] — a. present: *Corvinella, Lanius, Malaconotus, Dryoscopus, Batis, Platysteira, Dyaphorophyia,* probably in *Bias,* probably in *C. kupeensis,* probably in *Nilaus.* b. absent: *Chlorophoneus, Telophorus, Tchagra, Laniarius, ? Lanioturdus, ? Prionops.* c. unknown: *Eurocephalus, Antichromus, Tephrodornis, Megabyas.* 99. Crouched begging wing-fluttering posture — apparently all genera. 100. Beg with loose open-wing slow fluttering — *Malaconotus, Prionops.* 101. Pre-copulatory display recorded — *Lanius, Prionops, Laniarius, Nilaus, Lanioturdus* (no elaborate display), *Batis, Prionops.* 102. Nest-site display recorded — *Lanius, Malaconotus, Bias, Nilaus, Prionops.*

BEHAVIOUR — breeding

103. Monogamous — all genera, except for a few polygamous *Lanius.* 104. Cooperative — *Eurocephalus, Corvinella, Lanius excubitoroides, ?L. cabanisi, Prionops.* 105. Helpers recorded at nest — *Eurocephalus, Corvinella, Lanius excubitoroides, ?L. cabanisi,* occasional *L.collurio, ?Megabyas, ?Platysteira, Dyaphorophyia, Prionops.* 106. Nest-relief calling — *Chlorophoneus sulfureopectus, C. olivaceus, Telophorus, Laniarius* funebris, *L. atrococcineus, L. ferrugineus, L. aethiopicus, L. bicolor, Dryoscopus, ?Tchagra* australis, *?Lanioturdus, Bias, Nilaus.* 107. Extensive use of spider web in nest — *Lanius souzae, L. vittatus, Batis, Platysteira, Dyaphorophyia, Prionops, Tephrodornis, Eurocephalus, Dryoscopus, Nilaus, Philentoma, Megabyas, Bias.* 108. Nest camouflaged — *Lanius souzae, Dryoscopus, Antichromus, Tephrodornis, Nilaus, Batis, Bias, Megabyas, Philentoma, Platysteira, Dyaphorophyia, Prionops.* 109. Nest concealed — *Nilaus, Lanioturdus, Philentoma, Batis, Platysteira, Bias, Megabyas, Prionops.* 110. Use of bark in nest — *Eurocephalus, Lanius, Laniarius, Dryoscopus, Tchagra, Tephrodornis, Megabyas, Bias, Platysteira, Batis, Dyaphorophyia, Prionops.* 111. Nest moulded onto branch — *Eurocephalus, Nilaus, Lanioturdus, Batis, Platysteira, Dyaphorophyia, Prionops, Tephrodornis.* 112. Nest with roof structure — *Dyaphorophyia.* 113. Large untidy nest — *Corvinella,* many *Lanius.* 114. Flimsy nest structure — *Laniarius, Chlorophoneus,* some *Tchagra, Rhodophoneus.* 115. Nest constructed by both sexes — *Lanius, Chlorophoneus, Telophorus, Laniarius, Tchagra, Tephrodornis, Megabyas, Nilaus, Lanioturdus, Batis, Platysteira,* most *Dyaphorophyia.* 116. Nest constructed by ♀ only — *Dryoscopus, Bias, Dyaphorophyia concreta.* 117. Incubation mainly or only by ♀ — *Corvinella,* most *Lanius, Malaconotus blanchoti, Dryoscopus, Tchagra senegalensis, Lanioturdus, Batis, Platysteira, Dyaphorophyia, ?Laniarius leucorhynchus.* 118. Incubation by both sexes — *Lanius mackinnoni, Chlorophoneus, Telophorus,* most *Laniarius, Antichromus, Tchagra, Tephrodornis, Megabyas, Bias, Nilaus.* 119. Brood division recorded — *Lanius, Malaconotus lagdeni, Batis pririt.* 120. Nest parasitism — *Corvinella corvina, Lanius excubitor, L. ludovicianus, L. minor, L. collaris, L. bucephalus, L. cristatus, L. isabellinus, L. collurio, L. schach, Laniarius atrococcineus, L. ferrugineus, L. aethiopicus, L. bicolor, Dryoscopus cubla, Tchagra tchagra, Batis capensis, B. pririt, B. molitor, Platysteira peltata, Dyaphorophyia castanea, Prionops plumatus* (accidental), *P. retzii, ?P. caniceps.* 121. Intraspecific nest parasitism[935] — *Eurocephalus, Lanius, Prionops.*

BEHAVIOUR — vocals

Call structure — 122. ♂ whistle, ♀ harsh call — *Malaconotus, Chlorophoneus, Telophorus, Dryoscopus, Laniarius, Tchagra, Antichromus, Lanioturdus, Nilaus, ?Tephrodornis, ?Philentoma, Batis,* probably *Dyaphorophyia.* 123. Duets — *Eurocephalus, Corvinella, Lanius excubitoroides, L. cabanisi, Lanius excubitor, L. ludovicianus, L. collaris, L. senator, Malaconotus lagdeni, M. gladiator, M. blanchoti, Chlorophoneus sulfureopectus, C. bocagei, C. multicolor, C. nigrifrons, C. olivaceus, C. viridis, C. dohertyi, Telophorus, Rhodophoneus, Laniarius, Dryoscopus, Tchagra, Antichromus, Tchagra, ?Tephrodornis, ?Megabyas, ?Bias, Nilaus, Lanioturdus, Batis, Platysteira, Dyaphorophyia, Prionops.* 124. Chorus singing — *Eurocephalus, Corvinella, L. excubitoroides, L. cabanisi, Prionops, ?Tephrodornis.* 125. Territorial call — a. harsh sounds: *Lanius.* b. bleating sounds: *Eurocephalus.* c. whistles: all other genera. d. whistle and harsh sounds: some *Lanius* and *Corvinella.* 126. Mimicry — *Lanius.* 127. Whistling— all genera except *Eurocephalus.* 128. Alarm call — a. harsh: *Lanius, Corvinella, Chlorophoneus kupeensis.* b. harsh buzzing: *Batis, Platysteira, ?Dyaphorophyia, ?Bias, ?Megabyas.* c. short *Tok* or *Chuk*: *Tchagra, Laniarius, Antichromus, Telophorus.* d. tearing call: *Dryoscopus, Chlorophoneus, Malaconotus.* e. Rattling *K-K-K-K-K*: *Malaconotus, Tchagra, Antichromus, Laniarius, Dryoscopus, Bias, Platysteira.* 129. Bill snapping — a. slow: *Lanius, Malaconotus, Dryoscopus.* b. rapid: *Bias, ?Megabyas, Batis, Dyaphorophyia, Platysteira, Prionops.* 130. Bill clashing — *Chlorophoneus, C. kupeensis, Bias.* 131. Begging call — a. loud nasal: *Lanius.* b. high-pitched: *Chlorophoneus, Laniarius, Dryoscopus, Lanioturdus.* c. chattering: *Batis, Bias, Platysteira, Dyaphorophyia, ?Prionops.* d. nasal buzzing: *Tchagra, Telophorus, Malaconotus, ?Prionops.* 132. 'Wing-fripping' — *Lanius minor, Malaconotus lagdeni, M. blanchoti, M. cruentus, Chlorophoneus, C. kupeensis, Telophorus, Laniarius, Tchagra, Antichromus, Dryoscopus, ?Megabyas, Bias, Philentoma, Nilaus, Batis, Dyaphorophyia, Platysteira, Prionops caniceps.*

BEHAVIOUR — foraging

133. Main foraging method —a. sit and wait: *Eurocephalus, Corvinella, Lanius.* b. general gleaner: *Malaconotus, Chlorophoneus, Dryoscopus, Tephrodornis, Nilaus, Prionops.* c. aerial foliage gleaner: *Bias, Megabyas, Philentoma, Batis, Platysteira, Dyaphorophyia.* d. terrestrial: *Eurocephalus, Corvinella, Lanius, Telophorus, Tchagra, Rhodophoneus, Antichromus, Laniarius, Lanioturdus.* 134. Hangs upside-down sometimes: *Eurocephalus, Corvinella, Tephrodornis, Nilaus, Lanioturdus, Prionops plumatus, P. scopifrons, P. retzii, Batis molitor.* 135. Gait — a. hops: all genera except those listed below for 'run'. b. runs: *Telophorus, Rhodophoneus, Tchagra, ?Megabyas.* 136. Impales or wedges prey — *Lanius, Malaconotus, Laniarius, Tchagra, Batis senegalensis.* 137. Caches prey — *Lanius, ?Malaconotus.* 138. Holds prey with foot — *Lanius, Eurocephalus, Corvinella, Malaconotus cruentus, M. blanchoti, Laniarius, Dryoscopus, Nilaus, Batis pririt, B. molitor.* 139. Regularly eats wasps (Hymenoptera) — *Eurocephalus, Corvinella, Malaconotus, Chlorophoneus, Laniarius, Dryoscopus, Tchagra, Tephrodornis, Megabyas, Bias, Nilaus, Batis, Platysteira, Dyaphorophyia, Prionops.* 140. Regularly eats millipedes (Diplopoda) — *Lanius, Corvinella, Eurocephalus.*

141 PARASITES[794]

HOST	PARASITE
Eurocephalus rueppelli	
Blood parasites	negative sample[73]
Eurocephalus anguitimens	
Blood parasites	*Haemoproteus* sp.[73, 799]
Ectoparasites	*Hyalomma marginatum rufipes*[500]
Corvinella melanoleuca	
Blood parasites	*Trypanosoma* sp.[73, 799], also recently recorded as negative[927]
Ectoparasites	*Myrsidea seguyi*[47], *Ptilonyssus lanii, Sternostoma cuculorum*[159], *Amblyomma hebraeum*[1086]
Corvinella corvina	
Blood parasites	*Haemoproteus columbae, Haemoproteus* sp., *Leucocytozoon* sp.[73, 799]
Lanius excubitoroides	
Blood parasites	Negative sample[73]
Ectoparasites	*Ptilonyssus lanii, Sternostoma laniorum*[159]
Lanius excubitor and ***L. meridionalis*** combined	
Blood parasites	*Haemoproteus danilewskyi, H. lanii, H. lanii* var. *nucleophilus, Haemoproteus* sp., *Lankesterella* sp., *Leucocytozoon* sp., microfilaria, *Plasmodium relictum, Plasmodium* sp., *Trypanosoma avium, Trypanosoma* sp.[73, 333, 673, 927]
Ectoparasites	*Docophorus fuscicollis, Menacanthus camelinus, Brueelia imponderrabilica, Philopterus coarctatus, D. communis.*
Endoparasites	*Spirocerca sanguinolenta*[47, 255, 598, 730] *Ascaris laniorum, Spiroptera euryoptera, Paruterina parallelepideda, Filaria strigis*[730]
Lanius ludovicianus	
Blood parasites	*Plasmodium cathemerium, P. relictum, Trypanosoma avium, Trypanosoma* sp., *Hepatozoon lanis*, microfilaria[73, 927]
Ectoparasites	*Docophorus communis, Nirmus foldus, Ornithomyia fringillina, Ornithoica vicina, Menacanthus chrysophaeum, Philopterus subflavescens, Ixodes* sp.
Endoparasites	*Acuaria* sp., *Lemdana* sp., *Physocephalus sexalatus*[255, 598, 1054]
Lanius minor	
Blood parasites	*Haemoproteus danilewskyi, H. lanii, Haemoproteus* sp., *Lankesterella* sp., *Leucocytozoon* sp., microfilaria sp. *Plasmodium garnhami, P. praecox, P. relictum, Plasmodium* sp., *Trypanosoma* sp.[73, 927]
Ectoparasites	*Menacanthus brevidentatus, Philopterus coarctatus, Ptilonyssus lanii, Sternostoma laniorum, Hyalomma turanicum*[47, 159, 340]
Endoparasites	*Ascaris laniorum, Spirotera euryoptera, Physaloptera bilabiata, Filaria obtusocaudata, Trichina affinis, Distomum ovatum, Paruterina parallelopideda*[598, 730]
Lanius mackinnoni	
Ectoparasites	*Ptilonyssus lanii, Ornithoctona laticornis*[159, 160]
Lanius dorsalis	
Blood parasites	Negative sample[73, 799]
Lanius collaris	
Blood parasites	*Atoxoplasma* sp., *Haemoproteus lanii, Leucocytozoon fringillinarum, L. majoris* (re-identified as *L. balmorali*), *Plasmodium relictum, P. vaughani, Plasmodium* sp., *Hepatozoon lanis, Hepatozoon* sp.[73, 333, 779, 927]
Ectoparasites	*Menacanthus* sp., *Philopterus coarctatus, Ptilonyssus lanii, Sternostoma laniorum, Ornithoctona laticornis, Lynchia minor, Passeromyia heterochaeta*[47, 159, 160, 872, 1029]
Lanius nubicus	
Blood parasites	*Haemoproteus lanii, H. fringillae, Haemoproteus* sp., *Trypanosoma avium*, microfilaria[73, 390, 799, 927]
Lanius senator	
Blood parasites	*Haemoproteus lanii, H. fringillae, H. danilewskyi* and microfilaria[73, 333, 390, 927]
Ectoparasites	*Philopterus coarctatus*[47]

Endoparasites — Same as for Lesser Grey Shrike *Lanius minor*, including *Filaria obtusocaudata*, *F. nodulosa*, *F. coelebs*, *Bothriocephalus lanii* var. *pomerani*, *Paruterina parallelopideda*, *Harterteria zakhorowi*, *Viguiera euryoptera* and *Cheilospirura rotundata*[598, 730].

Lanius bucephalus
Blood parasites — *Haemoproteus lanii*, *Haemoproteus* sp., *Trypanosoma* sp.[73, 333, 673, 927].
Ectoparasites — *Proctophyllodes leptocaulus*, *Menacanthus* sp. ,*Myrsidea* sp., *Philopterus* sp., *P. coarctatus*[638].

Lanius cristatus
Blood parasites — *Aegyptianella* sp., *Haemoproteus lanii*, *Haemoproteus* sp., *Lankesterella garnhami*, *Lankesterella* sp., *Leucocytozoon* sp., microfilaria of *Cardiofilaria pavlovskyi* and *Splendidofilaria powlowskyi*, microfilaria, *Plasmodium cathemerium/relictum*, *P. praecox*, *P. polare*, *P. relictum*, *P. vaughani*, *Plasmodium* sp., *Trypanosoma* sp.[73, 333, 673, 927].
Ectoparasites — *Ornithonyssus sylviarum*, *Pellonyssus reedi*, *Proctophyllodes* sp., *Menacanthus* sp., *Myrsidea* sp., *Philopterus* sp., *Icosta holoptera omnisetosa*, *I. sensilis* [638].

Lanius isabellinus — see *Lanius collurio*

Lanius tigrinus
Blood parasites — *Haemoproteus lanii*, *Haemoproteus* sp., *Trypanosoma* sp.[73, 333, 673, 927].

Lanius collurio
Blood parasites — (Includes parasites from *Lanius isabellinus*), *Atoxoplasma* sp., *Haemoproteus danilewskyi*, *H. fringillae*, *H. lanii*, *Haemoproteus* sp., *Leucocytozoon fringillinarum*, *Leucocytozoon* sp., *L. balmorali*, microfilaria of *Splendidofilaria powlovskyi*, microfilaria, *Plasmodium praecox*, *P. relictum*, *P. vaughani*, *Plasmodium* sp., *Trypanosoma avium*, *Trypanosoma* sp.[73, 333, 390, 799, 927].
Ectoparasites — *Hyalomma m. turanicum*, *Ptilonyssus lanii*, *Sternostoma laniorum*, *Lynchia minor*[159, 160, 340, 1046], *Menacanthus inaequalis*, *M. camelinum*, *M. cinctus*, *Brueelia cruciata*, *Philopterus coarcatus*; *Docophorus communis*, *D. fuscicollis*.
Endoparasites — *Ascaris laniorum*, *Spiroptera euryoptera*, *Filaria nodulosa*, *F. tridens*, *Echinorhynchus contortus*, *Distomum macrourum*, *Holostomum sphaerula*, *Viguiera euryoptera*, *Acuaria cordata*[47, 730].

Lanius vittatus
Blood parasites — *Haemoproteus lanii*, *Haemoproteus* sp.[73, 333, 673, 927].
Ectoparasites — *Analges* sp., *Proctophyllodes* sp., *Menacanthus* sp.[638].

Lanius collurioides
Blood parasites — *Haemoproteus lanii*[333], *Haemoproteus* sp., *Plasmodium* sp.[73, 673].
Ectoparasites — *Icosta s. sensilis*[638].

Lanius schach
Blood parasites — *Haemoproteus danilewskyi*, *H. lanii*, *Haemoproteus* sp., *Leucocytozoon* sp., *Plasmodium cathemerium*, *P. relictum*, *P. praecox*, *Plasmodium* sp., *Trypanosoma lanii*, microfilaria[73, 497, 673, 927].
Ectoparasites (*nasutus*) — *Proctophyllodes* sp., *Trouessartia* sp., *Ornithonyssus bursa*, *Pellonyssus reedi*, *Myrsidea* sp., *Philopterus* sp., *Ornithoica bistativa*, *Hyalomma* sp.[638].

Lanius tephronotus
Blood parasites — *Haemoproteus* sp., *Haemoproteus lanii*[73, 333, 673, 927].
Ectoparasites — *Menacanthus* sp., *Myrsidea* sp.[638].

Lanius validirostris
Blood parasites — *Haemoproteus lanii*, *Haemoproteus* sp., *Plasmodium relictum*[73, 333, 673, 927].

Malaconotus cruentus
Blood parasites — *Haemoproteus* sp., *Trypanosoma* sp.[779].

Malaconotus blanchoti
Blood parasites — *Leucocytozoon balmorali*, *Leucocytozoon* sp., microfilaria[41, 73,799, 927].
Ectoparasites — *Philopterus coarctatus*[47].
Endoparasites — *Anoncotaenia malaconoti*[594].

Chlorophoneus sulfureopectus
Blood parasites — *Haemoproteus cublae*, *H. lanii*, *Haemoproteus* sp., *Plasmodium relictum*, *Leucocytozoon balmorali*, *Trypanosoma everetti*[73, 333, 927].
Ectoparasites — *Amblyomma hebraeum*[340, 1086].

Chlorophoneus bocagei
Blood parasites — Sampled, none detected[73, 799].

Chlorophoneus olivaceus
Blood parasites — *Haemoproteus cublae*, *Leucocytozoon balmorali*[927].

Chlorophoneus viridis
Ectoparasites (*viridis*) — *Leptotrombidium scutellare*, *Proterothrix* sp., *Myrsidea* sp.[638].

Chlorophoneus dohertyi

Ectoparasites — *Astridiella capitatus, Ornithoctona laticornis*[159, 160].

Telophorus zeylonus

Blood parasites — *Leucocytozoon balmorali, Leucocytozoon* sp., *Plasmodium* sp.[927].

Ectoparasites — *Pellonyssus viator, Astridiella capitatus*[159], *Ornithophila metallica, Lynchia minor*[160], *Hyalomma* sp., *Haemaphysalis l. leachii*[1086].

Rhodophoneus cruentus

Blood parasites — *Haemoproteus* sp., microfilaria, *Trypanosoma* sp.[73].

Laniarius poensis

Ectoparasites — *Xolalges diplospilus*[159].

Laniarius funebris

Blood parasites — *Haemoproteus* sp., *Leucocytozoon* sp., *Plasmodium* sp.[73, 799].

Laniarius atrococcineus

Blood parasites — *Hepatozoon malacotinus, Hepatozoon* sp., *Leucocytozoon* sp., *microfilaria*[73, 799, 927].

Ectoparasites — *Ornithonyssus bursa*; *Hyalomma m. rufipes, Hyalomma* sp., *Ornithophila metallica*[44, 160, 340, 1086].

Laniarius erythrogaster

Blood parasites — *Haemoproteus lanii, Haemoproteus* sp., *Leucocytozoon* sp.[73, 799].

Ectoparasites — *Haemaphysalis hoodi, Blankaartia laniarius, Ornithoica turdi*[159, 160, 340, 1086].

Laniarius barbarus

Blood parasites — *Haemoproteus cublae*[333], *Haemoproteus* sp., *Leucocytozoon* sp., microfilaria[73, 927].

Laniarius luehderi.

Ectoparasites (nominate race) — *Xolalges diplospilus*[159].

Laniarius ferrugineus

Blood parasites — *Haemoproteus cublae, Hepatozoon malacotinus, Leucocytozoon fringillinarum, L. majoris* (re-identified as *L. balmorali*), *Leucocytozoon* sp., microfilaria[73, 799].

Ectoparasites — *Ixodes* sp., *Hyalomma m. rufipes, Pteronyssus hoplophorus* (possibly referable to Tropical Boubou *L. aethiopicus* as previously conspecific), *Ornithoica turdi, Echidnophaga gallinacea* (possibly referable to *L. aethiopicus*), *Haemaphysalis hoodi, Hyalomma m. rufipes*[159, 160, 340, 500].

Laniarius aethiopicus

Blood parasites — *Haemoproteus* sp., *Leucocytozoon* sp., microfilaria, *Plasmodium circumflexum, P. relictum, P. vaughani*[73, 799, 927].

Ectoparasites — See Southern Boubou *L. ferrugineus*.

Laniarius turatii

Ectoparasites — *Haemaphysalis leachi*[340, 1086].

Dryoscopus cubla

Blood parasites — *Haemogregarina* sp. (probably *Hepatozoon* sp.), *Haemoproteus lanii, H. cublae, Leucocytozoon balmorali, Leucocytozoon* sp., *Plasmodium vaughani, Plasmodium* sp., *Trypanosoma everetti, Trypanosoma* sp., *Hepatozoon malacotinus*, microfilaria[73, 333, 799, 927].

Ectoparasites — *Philopterus* sp., *Haemaphysalis hoodi, Rhipicephalus simus*[41, 340, 1086], *Ptilonyssus dryoscopi*[159], *Ornithoctona laticornis*[160].

Dryoscopus pringlii

Blood parasites — Negative sample[799, 927].

Dryoscopus gambensis

Blood parasites — *Leucocytozoon* sp., microfilaria, *Plasmodium relictum, P. rouxi, Trypanosoma* sp.[73, 799].

Ectoparasites — *Xolalges ditrichus, Ornithoica turdi*[159, 160].

Antichromus minuta

Blood parasites — *Haemoproteus cublae, H. lanii, Haemoproteus* sp., *Leucocytozoon* sp., microfilaria, *Plasmodium vaughani, Trypanosoma* sp.[73, 333, 799, 927].

Ectoparasites — *Ornithoctona laticornis*[160].

Tchagra senegala

Blood parasites — *Leucocytozoon balmorali, Leucocytozoon* sp., microfilaria, *Plasmodium rouxi, P. vaughani*[799, 927].

Ectoparasites — *Sturnidoecus wittei, Haemaphysalis hoodi, H. leachi, Amblyomma hebraeum, A. variegatum, Ptilonyssus dryoscopi, Pterodectes andrei, Ornithoica turdi, Lynchia minor, Ornithonyssus bursa*[44,47, 159, 160, 340, 1086].

Tchagra australis

Blood parasites — *Leucocytozoon balmorali, Leucocytozoon* sp., *Plasmodium vaughani, Trypanosoma avium*, microfilaria[41, 73, 799, 927].

Ectoparasites — *Ornithoctona laticornis, Haemaphysalis leachi muhsami, Hyalomma rufipes, Rhipicephalus evertsi*[160, 340, 1086].

Tchagra tchagra
Ectoparasites — *Rhipicephalus pravus*[1086].

Tephrodornis gularis
Blood parasites — *Haemoproteus* sp., *Leucocytozoon* sp., *Plasmodium* sp., microfilaria[673, 927].

Tephrodornis pondicerianus
Blood parasites — *Haemoproteus* sp., *Leucocytozoon* sp.[673].
Ectoparasites — *Brueelia* sp., *Ornithonyssus sylviarum*[638].

Nilaus afer
Blood parasites — *Plasmodium relictum, Leucocytozoon balmorali*[73, 799, 927].

Batis capensis
Blood parasites — Negative sample[927].
Ectoparasites — ?*Ptilonyssus estrildicola*[159].

Batis mixta
Blood parasites — Negative sample[927].

Batis pririt
Blood parasites — Negative sample[799, 927].
Ectoparasites — Unidentified tick[205].

Batis molitor
Blood parasite — *Plasmodium relictum, Plasmodium* sp., *Hepatozoon* sp.[41, 73, 799, 927].
Ectoparasites — *Ricinus mugimaki*[47], *Sternostoma laniorum* var. *batis*[159], *Ornithoctona laticornis*[160].

Batis orientalis
Blood parasites — *Leucocytozoon* sp., *Plasmodium rouxi*[73, 799].

Batis minor
Blood parasites — Negative sample[799].

Batis diops
Ectoparasites — *Ornithoctona laticornis*[160].

Platysteira peltata
Blood parasites — Negative sample[799, 927].

Platysteira cyanea
Blood parasites — *Leucocytozoon* sp., *Plasmodium* sp., *Trypanosoma* sp.[73, 927].
Ectoparasites — *Dermoglyphus elongatus, Proctophyllodes rhynchocaulus, Pterodectes allocaulus*[159].

Dyaphorophyia castanea
Blood parasites — *Haemoproteus* sp.[73, 927].

Prionops plumatus
Blood parasites — *Leucocytozoon* sp., *Trypanosoma everetti, Hepatozoon* sp., microfilaria, *Haemoproteus* sp., *Trypanosoma* sp.[73, 799, 927].
Ectoparasites — *Hyalomma rufipes, Ornithoica turdi.*
Endoparasites — *Anoncotaenia prionopos*[160, 340, 594, 1086].

Prionops retzii
Blood parasite — *Hepatozoon* sp.[799, 927].

142 OUTGROUP COMPARISON

The following families are potential outgroups of Laniidae and Malaconotidae. The text after the long dash in each case is a list of potential comparative characters.

Campephagidae — *Philentoma* previously placed in this family, later in tribe Malaconotinae on DNA[207], with which it shares nest structure with some members. Differs in egg-white protein, natal plumage (has neossoptiles), process D absent on carpometacarpus[659, 894], maxillo-palatines[899]

Corvidae — egg-white protein similar to *Lanius*[894], sperm similar to *Lanius*[902], neossoptiles present, process D of carpometacarpus absent[659], single humeral fossa[919, 920], ectethmoid foramen double[899], free lachrymal[897, 899], L-ascorbic acid synthesis in kidney and liver[154], wing and hind limb muscles[642], intraspecific nest parasitism[935], indirect head scratching[1084], Karyotype (2n=76-80)[177], pterylosis studied[153], number of primaries documented[1085] and ethogram described[219].

Monarchinae[634] — post orbital process[897], egg-white protein[894], DNA[184], use of foot to hold down prey, nest structure, have neossoptiles[27, 153], tarsal scutellation studied[573], lack tongue spots, lack juv spotted plumage, usually courtship-feed, fan tail in display, have concealed nest[634], use of bark in nests[893] and eggs documented[893].

Vangidae[208, 226, 227, 232, 243, 283, 288, 679, 741, 770, 903, 904] — cranial osteology, pterygoid[898, 899], wing and hind limb muscles[642], jaw muscles[897], DNA-DNA hybridisation[184], nostril osteology[227], toe fusion[118], number of primaries[1085].

Gymnorhinae — pterygoid[898, 899], ethogram[219].

Artamidea — pterygoid[898, 899], single humeral fossa[920], number of primaries[1085].

Muscicapidae — maxillo-palatines[899], toe fusion[118].

Cracticidae — cranial osteology[898], process D of carpometacarpus absent[659], jaw muscles[897], single humeral fossa[920], number of primaries[1085] and ethogram described[219].

Dicruridae — process D of carpometacarpus absent[659].

Vireonidae — jaw muscles described[199, 897], cranial osteology[899], sperm morphology[902, 1080], toe fusion[118], number of primaries documented[199].

INDEX OF SPECIES